SIXTEENTH EDITION

REASON AND RESPONSIBILITY

Readings in Some Basic Problems of Philosophy

JOEL FEINBERG
Late of University of Arizona

RUSS SHAFER-LANDAU
University of North Carolina at Chapel Hill

CENGAGE
Learning·

Australia • Brazil • Mexico • Singapore • United Kingdom • United States

CENGAGE
Learning

Reason and Responsibility: Readings in Some Basic Problems of Philosophy, 16th Edition
Joel Feinberg, Russ Shafer-Landau

Product Director: Paul Banks

Product Manager: Debra Matteson

Senior Content Developer: Florence Kilgo

Associate Content Developer: Liz Fraser

Product Assistant: Michelle Forbes

Marketing Manager: Sean Ketchem

Senior Content Project Manager: Cathie DiMassa

Senior Art Director: Marissa Falco

Manufacturing Planner: Julio Esperas

IP Analyst: Alex Ricciardi

IP Project Manager: Betsy Hathaway

Production Service: Cenveo Publisher Services

Compositor: Cenveo Publisher Services

Cover Designer: Sarah Cole

Cover Image: Dreamstime.com/Derege

For product information and technology assistance, contact us at
Cengage Learning Customer & Sales Support, 1-800-354-9706

For permission to use material from this text or product, submit all requests online at **www.cengage.com/permissions**. Further permissions questions can be emailed to **permissionrequest@cengage.com**.

Library of Congress Control Number: 2015949711
Student Edition:
ISBN: 978-1-305-50244-4
Loose-leaf Edition:
ISBN: 978-1-305-87541-8

Cengage Learning
20 Channel Center Street
Boston, MA 02210
USA

Cengage Learning is a leading provider of customized learning solutions with employees residing in nearly 40 different countries and sales in more than 125 countries around the world. Find your local representative at **www.cengage.com**.

Cengage Learning products are represented in Canada by Nelson Education, Ltd.

To learn more about Cengage Learning Solutions, visit **www.cengage.com**. Purchase any of our products at your local college store or at our preferred online store **www.cengagebrain.com**.

Printed in the United States of America
Print Number: 01   Print Year: 2015

CONTENTS

ABOUT *REASON AND RESPONSIBILITY*

The conviction underlying this volume is that introducing the college student to philosophy by means of a few representative problems examined in great detail is far preferable to offering a "little bit of everything," with each branch of philosophy, each major "ism," and each major historical period represented with scrupulous impartiality, even though the articles may have little relevance to one another. Accordingly, articles have been selected from both classical and contemporary sources on such topics as religion, skepticism, mind, personal identity, freedom, responsibility, moral duty, and the meaning of life. The problems that concern philosophers under these headings are not mere idle riddles, but rather questions of vital interest to any reflective person. Each set of problems is plumbed in considerable depth in essays expressing different, often opposing, views. The hope is that exposure to this argumentative give-and-take will encourage students to take part in the process themselves, and through this practice to develop their powers of philosophical reasoning.

NEW TO THIS EDITION

This new edition of *Reason and Responsibility* has been strengthened by the addition of seventeen new selections. We have retained the policy of securing the very best available English translations for foreign works. We have tried to strike a good balance between classic works and relatively new material on these subjects of enduring philosophical interest. Other than the introductory materials in Part I, each part of this work has been updated and expanded.

New to The Text

- Part II, "Reason and Religious Belief," now contains new translations of Anselm and Gaunilo's classic exchange on the ontological argument, as well as a new translation of Aquinas's "Five Ways." It also includes two new works written expressly for this edition of *Reason & Responsibility*. The first, by philosopher and historian of science Michael Ruse, is a presentation and analysis of various important versions of the argument from design for God's existence. The second, by Lawrence A. Shapiro, sets out an extended critique of justified belief in miracles. Michael Murray and Michael Rea also contribute a new entry to this Part; theirs is a systematic presentation and sympathetic reconstruction of various theodicies and defenses of God's existence in the face of the problem of evil.
- Part III, "Human Knowledge: Its Ground and Limits," is strengthened by the addition of two new entries. The first is a wide-ranging exploration of skepticism, offered by Robert Audi. The second is a lovely exploration of the value of truth, true belief, and knowledge by distinguished philosopher Linda Zagzebski.

- Part IV, "Mind and Its Place in Nature," now includes a new defense of materialism about the mind by David Papineau, and an intriguing discussion of survival after death by Shelly Kagan, who argues that on many conceptions of personal identity, post-mortem survival isn't all it's cracked up to be.

- Part V. "Determinism, Free Will and Responsibility," contains three new selections. The first, by philosopher James Rachels, presents an engaging argument that puts pressure on the idea that we ever make free choices. A second piece, written especially for this edition of *Reason & Responsibility*, is Helen Beebee's effort to explain how we can make free choices, and ones for which we are morally responsible, *even if* determinism is true. Also new in this section is an elegant piece by Galen Strawson, who presents in a very accessible way the master argument that he has been defending for many years now. That argument is designed to show that we cannot be morally responsible for anything we ever do, since the essential conditions of such responsibility can never be met.

- Part VI, "Morality and Its Critics," contains seven new selections. The first, by Mary Midgley, raises the problems for ethical relativism by means of an especially forceful example: that of the samurai ethical code that requires the testing of a new sword by using it to kill an innocent person. Kwame Anthony Appiah's entry invites us to reflect on what future generations will condemn us for, using this as a test to identify flaws in conventional wisdom about what is right and wrong. Peter Singer challenges us to give much more than we currently are doing to relieve the suffering of the less fortunate. Mary Anne Warren's influential defense of a pro-choice position is now included here. Richard Taylor offers his view about the meaning of life—namely, that even a Sisyphus, condemned to roll a huge rock up a hill for eternity, can have a meaningful life if he is doing what he really wants to do. Richard Kraut rejects this view, and offers an elegant presentation of the reasons why getting what you want is not all it's cracked up to be. Finally, Susan Wolf offers the basics of her influential view regarding the meaning of life. The bumper sticker: "when subjective attraction meets objective attractiveness." On her account, a life is meaningful to the extent that we are invested in and take pleasure from activities and projects that are objectively valuable.

New *Reason and Responsibility* 16th Edition MindTap

Also new to this edition is MindTap for *Reason and Responsibility*. A fully online, personalized learning experience built upon Cengage Learning content, MindTap combines student learning tools—readings, multimedia, activities, and assessments—into a singular Learning Path that guides students through their course.

In addition to offerings at the part and the book levels, each chapter contains an array of activities related to the chapter content.

At the part and book-level:

- The KnowNOW! Philosophy Blog, accessible in the Part openers, provides a succinct philosophical analysis of major news stories, along with multimedia and discussion questions.

- Questia, available at the book level, provides two additional primary source readings for each chapter as well as access to Questia's full online library and research paper writing resources.

At the chapter level:

- A Reader's Guide pertaining to each reading and that includes comprehension questions and critical thinking questions
- A video followed by two reflection questions, to elicit further response from the student on the topic broached in the chapter
- Aplia content and activities
- Essay questions on a selected reading
- Quizzing on a selected reading

MindTap gives students ample opportunities for improving comprehension and for self-evaluation to prepare for exams, while also providing faculty and students alike a clear way to measure and assess student progress. Faculty can use MindTap as a turnkey solution or customized by adding YouTube videos, RSS feeds, or their own documents directly within the eBook or within each chapter's Learning Path. The product can be used fully online with its interactive eBook for *Reason and Responsibility*, or in conjunction with the printed text.

WHY, AND HOW TO, USE THIS TEXT

This volume currently contains eight major classics: three that are complete (Descartes' *Meditations*, and Plato's *Apology* and *Euthyphro*); one that is presented in virtual totality (Hume's *Dialogues*); and four that appear in very substantial sections (Berkeley's *Principles*, Hume's *Enquiry*, Mill's *Utilitarianism*, and Kant's *Groundwork*). In addition, there are shorter selections from eighteen more classic texts: those authored by Anselm, Gaunilo, Aquinas, Clarke, Paley, Pascal, W.K. Clifford, William James, Bertrand Russell, G.E. Moore, Locke, Hume, Plato, Nietzsche, Aristotle, Hobbes, Ross, and Epicurus. This book can be used to teach an introductory course based solidly on a reading of these classics; more recent articles can be seen as a kind of dividend. The book contains many articles by contemporary philosophers, including eleven that are addressed specifically to beginning students and that were written expressly for this book by William Rowe, Michael Ruse, Lawrence Shapiro, Wesley Salmon, John Perry, Brie Gertler, Helen Beebee, Robert Kane, Richard Joyce, and both editors.

There is no single "necessary and natural" order in which to read these materials. The book begins with the philosophy of religion because many beginners are familiar with its problems. But it is just as "natural" to begin with Part III, because the question of our knowledge of God presupposes the question of the "grounds and limits of human knowledge" generally. Similarly, there is no reason why one could not begin with the mind-body problem (Part IV) or the problem of determinism and free will (Part V). Indeed, many professors have said that they prefer to begin with ethics (Part VI) and work their way toward the front of the book.

ACKNOWLEDGMENTS

Many fine philosophers offered generous advice about how to improve this latest edition of *Reason and Responsibility*. I'd like to thank Matthew Mangum, Palo Alto College; Luca Ferrero, University of Wisconsin, Milwaukee; Anthony Carreras, Lone Star College, Kingwood; David Stegall, Clemson University; David Godden, Old Dominion University; Ken Hochstetter, College of Southern Nevada; Daniel Mittag, Albion College; Jacob Caton, Arkansas State University; and Senem Saner, California State University, Bakersfield. And a special note of thanks to my research assistant, Ben Schwan, who updated most of the online materials and helped to identify likely candidates for new selections in this edition—and did it all with efficiency and good cheer.

I welcome advice on how to improve the format and content of subsequent editions of *Reason & Responsibility*. Those with such advice are very welcome to email me at RussShaferlandau@gmail.com with their suggestions.

Russ Shafer-Landau
Chapel Hill, North Carolina

JOEL FEINBERG (1926–2004) was a brilliant philosopher, certainly one of the most important social and political philosophers of the last half century. He was also a very kind, humble man. And he was an extremely conscientious teacher. The great care and preparation that he devoted to his teaching is evident here, in the plan and format of *Reason & Responsibility*. Joel developed the first edition of this textbook nearly fifty years ago, dissatisfied with existing options, and intent on providing coverage of those areas of philosophy that struck him as deeply important and deserving of every student's careful study.

Most of you reading this will know Joel Feinberg only as the editor of a book you've been assigned to read. If you have a chance, you ought to seek out one of the many exciting works that Joel penned during his prolific career. He was a philosophical writer of rare talent. He wrote about things that matter, and did so in a way that everyone could understand. He was clear, he was elegant, always ready with the telling example, the well-chosen reference to literature or history, dropped into place with a light touch. Open any one of his many books and read at random–you can't help but be impressed by the humanism, the clarity, the originality and, certainly, the wisdom of the views that receive expression there.

Joel was also a man of great common sense and discernment. One of the most desirable things in life is to have a person of integrity and genuinely sound judgment to rely on for advice, companionship, and, if one is especially fortunate, for friendship. I was lucky enough to study with him for five years, to write a dissertation under his direction, and later to work with him as a collaborator on this book for just over decade prior to his passing. His suggestions during our collaboration, both about substantive matters of content and about the more mundane, practical matters of the publishing world, epitomized his practical wisdom. He was a man whose judgment you could trust.

Joel was curious, interested in the whole range of human experience, attentive to relevant detail, appreciative of salient distinctions, a lover of taxonomies and, at the same time, able to resist the pressure that such taxonomies impose–pressure to falsify the phenomena and straitjacket it into categories that generate misunderstanding. It is a very rare talent, to be so analytically minded and yet so broad in one's outlook, to appreciate system and yet to be sensitive to the fine detail that must constrain its development. Joel possessed such talent, to a degree that was almost unrivalled. There were very few in his league.

Joel died in 2004 after a long struggle with Parkinson's disease and its complications. Though I have overseen this book in the decade since his death, his influence on its contents remains very substantial. More generally, he left us a great and valuable legacy, both personal and professional. It was a true honor to have known him, to have learned from him, and to have counted him a friend.

R.S.L.
Chapel Hill 2016

PART I

Introduction to the Nature and Value of Philosophy

1. A Logic Lesson

JOEL FEINBERG

CORRECT AND INCORRECT REASONING

Logic is the intellectual discipline that distinguishes correct from incorrect reasoning. Correct rules of logic are indeed useful. It staggers the imagination to picture a world in which they have no authority. But their utility derives from their correctness, not the other way around. They are as clear models of *objective* truth, or objective "correctness," as any that we have.

DEDUCTIVE AND INDUCTIVE REASONING

As we shall soon see, the direct concern of logic with "correct reasoning" is more precisely a concern with good and bad *arguments*. All arguments fall into one or the other of two basic types: deductive and inductive.

Deductive arguments claim not merely to give support but to give *conclusive* or *decisive* support to their conclusion. They claim to *prove* or *demonstrate* that their conclusion is true, that its truth *necessarily follows* from its premises so that, if the premises are true (a matter to be investigated independently), then the conclusion *must be true*.

A deductive argument may have any number of premises, but we shall follow pedagogical custom and adopt, as our model of a standard deductive argument, one that has two premises and a conclusion. When we say of a given argument that its premises are false, we shall mean simply that *at least one* of its premises is false.

An inductive argument is best defined simply as a genuine argument that is not deductive. The terms "valid" and "invalid" are normally applied to deductive arguments only. Inductive arguments are subject to different terms of evaluation, good-bad, strong-weak, and so on. Unlike the terms of inductive evaluation ("highly probable," "moderately probable," "improbable," etc.), the terms of deductive

Revised and edited by Russ Shafer-Landau.

evaluation, "valid" and "invalid," are not subject to degrees. A deductive argument is either wholly, unqualifiedly valid, or not valid at all. It cannot be just "a little bit invalid." Neither can it be the case that one argument can be more or less valid than another.

An inductive argument, then, is an argument whose conclusion is claimed to follow from its premises, not with necessity, but only with probability. One conclusion may be rendered more probable than another, and therefore be a better or stronger inductive argument.

ARGUMENTS

An argument is a set of propositions, one of which (the conclusion) is said to be true on the basis of the others (the premises). The conclusion is often signaled in ordinary English by the term "therefore." In logic, the traditional symbol for "therefore" is a triangle of dots [∴]. There are, however, many different ways of indicating which proposition is the conclusion: "It follows from p that q," "p, consequently q," "because p is true, q is true," "the reason for q is p." Premises are often said to be *reasons* or *evidence* for their conclusions. Premises support, imply, entail, or require their conclusion. The nature of that support is precisely what the discipline of logic studies.

LOGICAL NECESSITY VERSUS PSYCHOLOGICAL CERTAINTY

A person may stand in any number of possible relations to a proposition. She can be absolutely confident that p is true, having no trace of doubt, reasonable or not. It is easy to confuse this psychological certainty with logical necessity. An argument of the form "If p then q; p; therefore q" is valid quite independently of any belief that any person might have toward it. Given the truth of its premises, its conclusion must be true. Even individual propositions, as we shall see below, are sometimes necessarily true (when they are "analytic," or tautologies, or "true by

definition"). Similarly, propositions that have the form of logical contradictions *must* be false; they cannot be true. It cannot be true even of an infinitely powerful deity that He both exists and does not exist at the same time. To assert a logical contradiction is to say something of the form "p and not p," and all statements of that form are necessarily false. A rational person may believe p and another rational person might believe not p. But no rational person could believe both p and not p.

POSSIBLE TRUTH VALUE COMBINATIONS

When we do not know whether a given proposition is true or false, it is convenient to say that we do not know its "truth value." This is a useful term of art that enables us conveniently to pose some important questions about valid deductive arguments. Various combinations of truth values are possible. Each premise will have a truth value, and the conclusion will have a truth value, in both cases either true or false. The overall validity of the argument will vary, leading to a larger combination of possibilities. It is essential to understand these combinations and examples of each. Do not forget that *a valid argument can have a false conclusion and an invalid argument can have a true conclusion*. Various other combinations are possible. The rules for determining validity remain constant, but individual propositions in premise or conclusion will be true or false depending on the facts. And sometimes (in fact most times) the best way of determining the facts will be to go out and look at the world.

Here are some samples of truth value combinations in the premises and conclusions of valid and invalid arguments.

1. True premises; true conclusion; valid argument:

   All humans are mortal. (True)
   Feinberg is human. (True)
   Therefore, Feinberg is mortal. (True)
   (VALID)

2. False premises; false conclusion; valid argument:

   All mammals have wings. (False)

   All reptiles are mammals. (False)

   Therefore, all reptiles have wings. (False)

   (VALID)

3. All true premises; true conclusion: invalid argument:

   Chicago is north of Dallas. (True)

   Feinberg is mortal. (True)

   Therefore, all birds have wings. (True)

   (INVALID)

4. All true premises; false conclusion; invalid argument. (By the very definition of "valid," arguments of this form *cannot be valid*.)

   If Bill Gates owned all the gold in Fort Knox, then he would be wealthy. (True)

   Bill Gates does not own all the gold in Fort Knox. (True)

   Therefore Bill Gates is not wealthy. (False)

   (INVALID)

5. False premises; true conclusion; valid argument:

   All fish are mammals. (False)

   All whales are fish. (False)

   Therefore, all whales are mammals. (True)

   (VALID)

6. False premises; true conclusion; invalid argument:

   All dogs have wings. (False)

   All puppies have wings. (False)

   Therefore, all puppies are dogs. (True)

   (INVALID)

In summary, a deductive argument may have any of the following truth and validity combinations:

PREMISES	*CONCLUSION*	*ARGUMENT*
T	T	VALID
T	T	INVALID
F	F	VALID
F	F	INVALID
F	T	VALID
F	F	INVALID
T	F	MUST BE INVALID

Illustrations have been given of arguments in several of these categories. All combinations are possible except one: *An argument cannot have true premises and a false conclusion and still be valid.* But a valid argument can go from false to false, from true to true, or from false to true, and an invalid argument can be in any of these categories, without restriction.

VALIDITY AND SOUNDNESS

A final bit of logical terminology will be useful. The philosophers who "do logic" never speak of statements or propositions as "valid" or "invalid." These evaluative terms apply to arguments, not to the propositions out of which arguments are constructed. Speaking very generally, valid arguments are logically correct arguments, having premises and conclusions as their constituent parts.

A particular proposition is true or false depending on what the facts happen to be. If you are trying to classify a given argument and you would like to know whether "some fish have wings" is T or F, you must look at books about fish or otherwise consult biologists. Logic can only tell you whether a given set of premises has a certain relationship—logical validity—to the biological proposition.

Ideally, what we need if logic is to be practical are arguments that are both valid and have *true* premises. The conclusion of such an argument cannot be false. Logicians call such an argument "sound." We can thus define soundness as validity plus truth (of the premises). One of the most common ways in which philosophers criticize one another is to concede that the other person's argument is logically impeccable but to insist that some or all of her premises are false.

Propositions containing the "if...then..." relation are also commonly called "conditional statements" or "hypothetical statements." The part of the compound normally following the "if" is called the "antecedent." The part following the "then" is called the "consequent." A conditional statement asserts that the truth of the antecedent is a guarantee, or "sufficient condition," for the truth of the consequent: that *if* the antecedent is true, then the consequent is true. Another way of saying this is that the antecedent "implies" or "entails" the consequent, or that the consequent "follows" from the antecedent.

NECESSARY AND SUFFICIENT CONDITIONS

We can use concepts of necessary and sufficient conditions to relate propositions to one another. Thus we can say such things as "if it rains any more tonight, then the football field will be muddy tomorrow at game time," which means that more rain will be sufficient to bring about more mud; we could also say that "the light will come on only if someone pulls the switch," which means that pulling the switch is necessary for lighting the room. It is usually the case that many conditions are necessary for some result; if these necessary conditions are *all* satisfied, then that will be sufficient to produce the result.

There are many equivalent ways of saying that one thing is necessary for another. We sometimes speak of preconditions, requirements, or prerequisites. Lawyers speak of necessary conditions as "but for conditions," that is, conditions *but for which* an event to be explained would not have occurred. Sometimes lawyers resort to the ancient Latin expression, *conditio sine qua non*, "a condition without which not."

It should be noted carefully that *if p is necessary for q, then q is sufficient for p*. Thus,

An airplane flies only if there is gas in its tank.

is equivalent to

If this airplane flies, then there is gas in its tank.

Imagine yourself at the airport. You have been very worried that your visiting friends' plane is out of gas. You are convinced that gas in the tank is necessary if he is to fly home. When you get to the airport, he climbs into the plane and takes off. You could say—would you not?—that "There must have been gas in the tank. The fact that the plane is flying is sufficient to show that there was gas in the tank."

In general, *if p is a sufficient condition for q, then q is a necessary condition for p*. Note that p can be sufficient for q without also being necessary for q. Heavy cigarette smoking may well be sufficient to cause lung cancer, but it is not necessary, because nonsmokers sometimes get lung cancer too. And p can be necessary for q without also being sufficient for q. Oxygen is a necessary condition for a fire, but is not, by itself, enough to create one.

VALID DEDUCTIVE ARGUMENT FORMS: A SAMPLER

Determining the validity, or invalidity, of a deductive argument is a matter of form, not of content. A number of well-studied logical patterns exhibit the forms of the leading categories of deductive validity. Let us begin a brief sketch of these formal patterns with those that have a conditional statement as a premise.

Strictly speaking, any set of propositions whose premises are simply irrelevant to its conclusion is an invalid argument. So any argument properly symbolized as (p, q, therefore g) is invalid. Whatever the truth values of p and q and g, they have no logical bearing on one another. So if p is the proposition "All mammals are quadrupeds," and q is the proposition "Some millionaires are neurotic," then p and q have no relation to one another. They are not even talking about the same thing. Then if g is the proposition "Objects attract one another with a force that is directly proportional to their masses," we have an argument that consists of three true propositions totally irrelevant to one another. The premises can give no support to the conclusion, so that if we interpret an argument as a claim that such support is given, that claim must be rejected and the argument declared invalid. It is the sort of argument commonly called a "non sequitur" ("not following").

The more interesting fallacies (invalid arguments) have component propositions whose truth values are indeed relevant to one another but whose recognizable forms determine that the conclusion necessarily does not follow from the premises. By contrast, some of the standard deductive argument forms are valid, guaranteeing that any actual argument that has that form is valid—if its premises are true then its conclusion cannot be false. Needless to say, it is important to learn how to recognize these forms and learn how to distinguish at first sight the always valid ones from the fallacies, just as in mushroom hunting, it is important to know how to distinguish the fatally poisonous specimens from the innocuous ones.

Let us begin, then, with a pair of standard valid forms and the poisonous counterparts often confused with them. The first of these was given the Latin name *modus ponens* by medieval logicians, a name still used. An argument has this form when its component propositions are related as follows:

If p, then q

p

Therefore, q

It is not difficult to see intuitively that this argument form is always valid. If an argument of this form has true premises, as is sometimes the case, then the conclusion must be true. For example:

If this horse's leg is broken, then he will be mercifully shot.

This horse's leg is broken.

Therefore, this horse will be mercifully shot.

If the premises of this argument are true (as they could easily be, depending on what the facts

are), then it is logically necessary that the conclusion is true too. If the conclusion is false, then it must be because one or more premise is false. A more revealing name for *modus ponens* is "the assertion of the antecedent." An argument that qualifies for that description is always valid.

Similarly, the argument whose traditional Latin name is *modus tollens* employs a conditional statement as a key premise and consists in the denial of the consequent. Its form is:

If p, then q

Not q

Therefore, not p

The alternative (English) name of this perfectly valid form is "denying the consequent." All actual arguments of this form must be valid.

But now we come to the masquerade ball, at which counterfeits for *modus ponens* and *modus tollens* pose as valid arguments, though in fact they are standard fallacies with standard names, and always invalid. The names are given this time only in English, namely **affirming the consequent** and **denying the antecedent**. The former is rendered as follows:

If p, then q

q

Therefore, p

For example:

If Gates owns all the gold in Fort Knox, then he is rich.

Gates is rich.

Therefore, Gates owns all the gold in Fort Knox.[1]

Note that the example has true premises and a false conclusion, and therefore must be invalid.

The second fallacious argument form mentioned above is "denying the antecedent." It can be formulated as follows:

If p, then q

Not p

Therefore, not q

For example—

> **If Gates owns all the gold in Fort Knox, then he is rich.**
>
> **Gates does not own all the gold in Fort Knox.**
>
> **Therefore, Gates is not rich.**

There are various other forms of deductive argument in which a crucial premise is a conditional statement (if p then q). For example, there is the intuitively obvious valid form called the **hypothetical syllogism**. The name no doubt derives from the prominent role played in it by hypothetical (that is, conditional) propositions. Arguments of this type can be formulated thus—

> **If p, then q**
>
> **If q, then r**
>
> **Therefore, if p, then r**

Note that all three component propositions are conditional. An example

> **If Witherspoon wins the next primary election, then he will win the nomination.**
>
> **If Witherspoon wins the nomination, then he will win the presidential election.**
>
> **Therefore, if Witherspoon wins the next primary election, then he will win the presidency.**

Arguments of this form are always logically valid.

INFORMAL FALLACIES

We can mean by the word "fallacy" any instance of incorrect reasoning. That would include an enormous miscellany of reasoning errors that have no particular form except that their premises are irrelevant to their conclusions. But some invalid arguments have a clear, recognizable form, easy to symbolize, that permits us to treat them as a particular standardized mistake. This group of "informal fallacies," as they are sometimes called, includes, among many others, the following.

The standard name *argumentum ad baculum* is applied to an effort to persuade by threatening force: "If you do not say what I want you to say (or believe or do what I want you to believe or do, as the case may be), then I will beat the hell out of you," is obviously not an argument. If it were, I suppose it would have to have the following form:

> **If you do not admit that p, then I will beat you up. (sole premise)**
>
> **Therefore, p.**

It may be that your threat gives me a good reason for saying that I believe that p, but that is quite another thing from saying that the credibility of your threat is evidence for p, or that it implies or entails or proves that p. In fact it is wholly irrelevant to p. A person of ordinary prudence who is persuaded by fear of the threatener's superior size, strength, and pugilistic prowess may admit, at the moment the blows begin, that he has just been given some "reasons," even some good reasons, for acting as demanded, though he has been given no reason that supports p, no reason for changing his belief to the one demanded, even if it were possible to do so.

Another set of "arguments" confusing persuasive efficacy with validity bears the Latin name *argumentum ad miseracordium*, and it is every bit as much an informal fallacy as the *argumentum ad baculum*. Consider the undergraduate student in tears who complains to her professor about the "unfairness" of her grade. The grade of B in his course, she says, did not do her justice. She deserved an A given the special circumstances that she has applied to medical school, and if she is not admitted, the disappointment will ruin her life and break her parents' hearts. *Therefore* she deserves an A, and her professor has the duty of changing her present grade to an A. The word "Therefore" is the sign that a conclusion is about to be stated, and supported by reasons stated in the premises. In effect the argument says: "You owe me an A, because I and others will be disappointed and heartbroken if you do not make the change I am begging you for." The verdict: invalid!

SOME INDUCTIVE INFERENCES, GOOD AND BAD

There are numerous tasks in life that require reasonable persons to "give reasons for" rather than prove, demonstrate, or render certain. Law courts are a familiar example. In the criminal law, for instance, a defendant cannot be convicted unless the jury believes that she behaved as charged and believes further that her guilt, while neither logically necessary, nor psychologically certain, is nevertheless supported by pretty strong evidence, so strong that it is "beyond a reasonable doubt." And yet the argument in the mind of the jury does not involve exclusive use of deduction. Inductive arguments, too, can carry conviction. Instead of logical necessity, the inductive argument (by definition) purports to show the probability of certain vital propositions that would lead a reasonable person in the direction of belief. In other branches of the law, the required evidence is somewhat weaker but still strong, for example, reasons that are "clear and compelling" and conclusions that are "highly probable," "more probable than not," or "plausible."

Inductive arguments, however, are no more immune from mistakes, and although inductive mistakes are less commonly labeled "fallacies," they can be as destructive to the reasoning processes as those mistakes that *are* called fallacies. A few samples will suffice.

Inductive arguments play an important part in ascriptions of causation to events, in explanations, predictions, and opinion surveys, among other things. Where inductive reasoning gives us the opportunity to go right in these activities, it usually offers the opportunity to go wrong. Consider the famous argument *post hoc ergo propter hoc* ("after the fact, therefore because of the fact"). One commits this mistake in reasoning when one attributes the cause of a given event to another event that came earlier, for the sole apparent reason that it *did* come earlier. This mistake is made so frequently in political debates that one might almost call it the basic argument of democratic politics, except for the fact that it is almost always used against the incumbent candidate, holding him responsible for what has happened "during his watch." Did the Ohio River flood during his presidency? Then his election or the policies he pursued must have been the cause. It is enough to show that prices on the stock market fell during his term of office to show (allegedly with high probability) that his policies caused the decline. Were we at peace before he assumed office and at war later? It must be because his actions caused it. But incumbents can and do use this weak argument too. Are you better off now than you were under the previous president? If so, that shows that this president's policies have worked. Actually what facts of this sort "prove" is that the speaker's inductive logic is not to be trusted.

BEGGING THE QUESTION

Medieval logicians, who wrote in Latin, had their own fancy name for our next fallacy: a "*petitio principii.*" English speakers too have other names for it—a "circular argument" and "begging the question." Technically, a circular argument can be defined as an argument that assumes in its premises the conclusion it claims to be proving. That procedure makes the reasoner's task altogether too easy to do her any good. She argues in a circle when she uses her premises to prove (or otherwise support) her conclusion, and uses her conclusion in the proof of one of her premises. The circularity fallacy brings to mind the two persons, Mr. A and Ms. B, who apply at a bank for a loan. First Mr. A asks for a loan. The banker asks him if there is anyone who can testify to his honesty and trustworthiness. At that point Mr. A introduces his friend Ms. B to the banker. Ms. B then recommends Mr. A, declaring him to be absolutely truthful and trustworthy. "Very good," says the banker to Mr. A. "Your friend Ms. B has given us a very good testimonial in your behalf. Now all we need to know is whether Ms. B is herself truthful and trustworthy. Who can recommend her? "No problem," replies Mr. A. "*I* will recommend her." And so we have a circle. We learn that A can be trusted on the authority of B, who can be trusted on the authority of A.

In philosophy a circular argument often takes the same form. A conclusion is supported on someone's authority, and that authority is derived logically from an argument one of whose tacit premises is the very proposition that is meant to be proved. The standard example in logic texts is a particular kind of religious fundamentalism. "We can know that God exists," the argument proceeds, "because the bible tells us so." "Yes, but how do you know that the bible is true?" asks the critic of this particular argument. "No problem," the proof-giver replies, "The bible must be true because it is the word of God." The proof-giver has begged the question.

Put more formally, an argument is offered to prove p. A key premise in that argument is q. So the argument at this point is q, therefore p. Let us suppose that this is a valid argument, but that we cannot tell whether it is sound until we learn whether its premise, q, is true. So we come up with another valid argument: p, therefore q. So now we have completed two arguments, one proving p, our immediate objective, and the other proving q, which is a premise in the argument for p. But the argument for q uses p as a premise in its own proof. In order to show that p is true, we have to assume that p is true!

An interesting thing about circular arguments is that although they are fallacies in the very broad sense of "mistaken reasoning," they are not fallacies in the narrow sense of "invalidity." In fact, a circular argument is actually a *valid* argument in the logician's technical sense of "valid." Assuming itself in its own proof may make the circular argument a poor argument, but no more an *invalid* one than any argument of the form p, therefore p. An argument of this sort will not advance our knowledge. Begging the question is a bad way to reason.

NOTE

1. I borrow this alluring example from Irving M. Copi and Keith Burgess-Jackson, *Informal Logic* (Upper Saddle River, NJ: Prentice-Hall, 1995) third edition, p. 55.

2. Apology

PLATO

Plato (427?–347 BCE) lived and taught in Athens. Most of his surviving works have the form of fictitious dialogues between Socrates (who had been his teacher) and other Greek contemporaries.

I do not know, men of Athens, how my accusers affected you; as for me, I was almost carried away in spite of myself, so persuasively did they speak. And yet, hardly anything of what they said is true. Of the many lies they told, one in particular surprised me, namely that you should be careful not to be deceived by an accomplished speaker like me. That they were not ashamed to be immediately proved wrong by the facts, when I show myself not to be an accomplished speaker at all, that I thought was most shameless on their part—unless indeed they call an accomplished speaker the man who speaks the truth. If they mean that, I would agree that I am an orator, but not after their manner, for indeed, as I say, practically nothing they said was true. From me

From Plato, *Five Dialogues*, trans. G.M.A. Grube (Hackett 2002), pp. 2–18, 22–44. Reprinted by permission of Hackett Publishing Company, Inc. All rights reserved.

you will hear the whole truth, though not, by Zeus, gentlemen, expressed in embroidered and stylized phrases like theirs, but things spoken at random and expressed in the first words that come to mind, for I put my trust in the justice of what I say, and let none of you expect anything else. It would not be fitting at my age, as it might be for a young man, to toy with words when I appear before you.

One thing I do ask and beg of you, gentlemen: if you hear me making my defense in the same kind of language as I am accustomed to use in the marketplace by the bankers' tables, where many of you have heard me, and elsewhere, do not be surprised or create a disturbance on that account. The position is this: This is my first appearance in a lawcourt, at the age of seventy; I am therefore simply a stranger to the manner of speaking here. Just as if I were really a stranger, you would certainly excuse me if I spoke in that dialect and manner in which I had been brought up, so too my present request seems a just one, for you to pay no attention to my manner of speech—be it better or worse—but to concentrate your attention on whether what I say is just or not, for the excellence of a judge lies in this, as that of a speaker lies in telling the truth.

It is right for me, gentlemen, to defend myself first against the first lying accusations made against me and my first accusers, and then against the later accusations and the later accusers. There have been many who have accused me to you for many years now, and none of their accusations are true. These I fear much more than I fear Anytus and his friends, though they too are formidable. These earlier ones, however, are more so, gentlemen; they got hold of most of you from childhood, persuaded you and accused me quite falsely, saying that there is a man called Socrates, a wise man, a student of all things in the sky and below the earth, who makes the worse argument the stronger. Those who spread that rumor, gentlemen, are my dangerous accusers, for their hearers believe that those who study these things do not even believe in the gods. Moreover, these accusers are numerous, and have been at it a long time; also, they spoke to you at an age when you would most readily believe them, some of you being children and adolescents, and they won their case by default, as there was no defense.

What is most absurd in all this is that one cannot even know or mention their names unless one of them is a writer of comedies. Those who maliciously and slanderously persuaded you— who also, when persuaded themselves then persuaded others—all those are most difficult to deal with: one cannot bring one of them into court or refute him; one must simply fight with shadows, as it were, in making one's defense, and cross-examine when no one answers. I want you to realize too that my accusers are of two kinds: those who have accused me recently, and the old ones I mention; and to think that I must first defend myself against the latter, for you have also heard their accusations first, and to a much greater extent than the more recent.

Very well then, men of Athens. I must surely defend myself and attempt to uproot from your minds in so short a time the slander that has resided there so long. I wish this may happen, if it is in any way better for you and me, and that my defense may be successful, but I think this is very difficult and I am fully aware of how difficult it is. Even so, let the matter proceed as the god may wish, but I must obey the law and make my defense.

Let us then take up the case from its beginning. What is the accusation from which arose the slander in which Meletus trusted when he wrote out the charge against me? What did they say when they slandered me? I must, as if they were my actual prosecutors, read the affidavit they would have sworn. It goes something like this: Socrates is guilty of wrongdoing in that he busies himself studying things in the sky and below the earth; he makes the worse into the stronger argument, and he teaches these same things to others. You have seen this yourself in the comedy of Aristophanes, a Socrates swinging about there, saying he was walking on air and talking a lot of other nonsense about things of which I know nothing at all. I do not speak in contempt of such knowledge, if someone is wise in these things—lest

Meletus bring more cases against me—but, gentlemen, I have no part in it, and on this point I call upon the majority of you as witnesses. I think it right that all those of you who have heard me conversing, and many of you have, should tell each other if any one of you has ever heard me discussing such subjects to any extent at all. From this you will learn that the other things said about me by the majority are of the same kind.

Not one of them is true. And if you have heard from anyone that I undertake to teach people and charge a fee for it, that is not true either. Yet I think it a fine thing to be able to teach people as Gorgias of Leontini does, and Prodicus of Ceos, and Hippias of Elis. Each of these men can go to any city and persuade the young, who can keep company with any one of their own fellow citizens they want without paying, to leave the company of these, to join with themselves, pay them a fee, and be grateful to them besides. Indeed, I learned that there is another wise man from Paros who is visiting us, for I met a man who has spent more money on sophists than everybody else put together, Callias, the son of Hipponicus. So I asked him—he has two sons—"Callias," I said, "if your sons were colts or calves, we could find and engage a supervisor for them who would make them excel in their proper qualities, some horse breeder or farmer. Now since they are men, whom do you have in mind to supervise them? Who is an expert in this kind of excellence, the human and social kind? I think you must have given thought to this since you have sons. Is there such a person," I asked, "or is there not?" "Certainly there is," he said. "Who is he?" I asked. "What is his name, where is he from? And what is his fee?" "His name, Socrates, is Evenus, he comes from Paros, and his fee is five minas." I thought Evenus a happy man, if he really possesses this art, and teaches for so moderate a fee. Certainly I would pride and preen myself if I had this knowledge, but I do not have it, gentlemen.

One of you might perhaps interrupt me and say: "But Socrates, what is your occupation? From where have these slanders come? For surely if you did not busy yourself with something out of the common, all these rumors and talk would not have arisen unless you did something other than most people. Tell us what it is, that we may not speak inadvisedly about you." Anyone who says that seems to be right, and I will try to show you what has caused this reputation and slander. Listen then. Perhaps some of you will think I am jesting, but be sure that all that I shall say is true. What has caused my reputation is none other than a certain kind of wisdom. What kind of wisdom? Human wisdom, perhaps. It may be that I really possess this, while those whom I mentioned just now are wise with a wisdom more than human; else I cannot explain it, for I certainly do not possess it, and whoever says I do is lying and speaks to slander me. Do not create a disturbance, gentlemen, even if you think I am boasting, for the story I shall tell does not' originate with me, but I will refer you to a trustworthy source. I shall call upon the god at Delphi as witness to the existence and nature of my wisdom, if it be such. You know Chaerephon. He was my friend from youth, and the friend of most of you, as he shared your exile and your return. You surely know the kind of man he was, how impulsive in any course of action. He went to Delphi at one time and ventured to ask the oracle—as I say, gentlemen, do not create a disturbance—he asked if any man was wiser than I, and the Pythian replied that no one was wiser. Chaerephon is dead, but his brother will testify to you about this.

Consider that I tell you this because I would inform you about the origin of the slander. When I heard of this reply I asked myself: "Whatever does the god mean? What is his riddle? I am very conscious that I am not wise at all; what then does he mean by saying that I am the wisest? For surely he does not lie; it is not legitimate for him to do so." For a long time I was at a loss as to his meaning; then I very reluctantly turned to some such investigation as this; I went to one of those reputed wise, thinking that there, if anywhere, I could refute the oracle and say to it: "This man is wiser than I, but you said I was."

Then, when I examined this man—there is no need for me to tell you his name, he was one of our public men—my experience was something like this: I thought that he appeared wise to many people and especially to himself, but he was not. I then tried to show him that he thought himself wise, but that he was not. As a result he came to dislike me, and so did many of the bystanders. So I withdrew and thought to myself: "I am wiser than this man; it is likely that neither of us knows anything worthwhile, but he thinks he knows something when he does not, whereas when I do not know, neither do I think I know; so I am likely to be wiser than he to this small extent, that I do not think I know what I do not know." After this I approached another man, one of those thought to be wiser than he, and I thought the same thing, and so I came to be disliked both by him and by many others.

After that I proceeded systematically. I realized, to my sorrow and alarm, that I was getting unpopular, but I thought that I must attach the greatest importance to the god's oracle, so I must go to all those who had any reputation for knowledge to examine its meaning. And by the dog, men of Athens—for I must tell you the truth—I experienced something like this: In my investigation in the service of the god I found that those who had the highest reputation were nearly the most deficient, while those who were thought to be inferior were more knowledgeable. I must give you an account of my journeyings as if they were labors I had undertaken to prove the oracle irrefutable. After the politicians, I went to the poets, the writers of tragedies and dithyrambs and the others, intending in their case to catch myself being more ignorant than they. So I took up those poems with which they seemed to have taken most trouble and asked them what they meant, in order that I might at the same time learn something from them. I am ashamed to tell you the truth, gentlemen, but I must. Almost all the bystanders might have explained the poems better than their authors could. I soon realized that poets do not compose their poems with knowledge, but by some inborn talent and by inspiration, like seers and prophets who also say many fine things without any understanding of what they say. The poets seemed to me to have had a similar experience. At the same time I saw that, because of their poetry, they thought themselves very wise men in other respects, which they were not. So there again I withdrew, thinking that I had the same advantage over them as I had over the politicians.

Finally I went to the craftsmen, for I was conscious of knowing practically nothing, and I knew that I would find that they had knowledge of many fine things. In this I was not mistaken; they knew things I did not know, and to that extent they were wiser than I. But, men of Athens, the good craftsmen seemed to me to have the same fault as the poets: each of them, because of his success at his craft, thought himself very wise in other most important pursuits, and this error of theirs overshadowed the wisdom they had, so that I asked myself, on behalf of the oracle, whether I should prefer to be as I am, with neither their wisdom nor their ignorance, or to have both. The answer I gave myself and the oracle was that it was to my advantage to be as I am.

As a result of this investigation, men of Athens, I acquired much unpopularity, of a kind that is hard to deal with and is a heavy burden; many slanders came from these people and a reputation for wisdom, for in each case the bystanders thought that I myself possessed the wisdom that I proved that my interlocutor did not have. What is probable, gentlemen, is that in fact the god is wise and that his oracular response meant that human wisdom is worth little or nothing, and that when he says this man, Socrates, he is using my name as an example, as if he said: "This man among you, mortals, is wisest who, like Socrates, understands that his wisdom is worthless." So even now I continue this investigation as the god bade me—and I go around seeking out anyone, citizen or stranger, whom I think wise. Then if I do not think he is, I come to the assistance of the god and show him that he is not wise. Because of this occupation, I do not have the leisure to engage in public affairs to any extent, nor indeed to look after my own, but I live in great poverty because of my service to the god.

Furthermore, the young men who follow me around of their own free will, those who have most leisure, the sons of the very rich, take pleasure in hearing people questioned; they themselves often imitate me and try to question others. I think they find an abundance of men who believe they have some knowledge but know little or nothing. The result is that those whom they question are angry, not with themselves but with me. They say: "That man Socrates is a pestilential fellow who corrupts the young." If one asks them what he does and what he teaches to corrupt them, they are silent, as they do not know, but, so as not to appear at a loss, they mention those accusations that are available against all philosophers, about "things in the sky and things below the earth," about "not believing in the gods" and "making the worse the stronger argument"; they would not want to tell the truth, I'm sure, that they have been proved to lay claim to knowledge when they know nothing." These people are ambitious, violent, and numerous; they are continually and convincingly talking about me; they have been filling your ears for a long time with vehement slanders against me. From them Meletus attacked me, and Anytus and Lycon, Meletus being vexed on behalf of the poets, Anytus on behalf of the craftsmen and the politicians, Lycon on behalf of the orators, so that, as I started out by saying, I should be surprised if I could rid you of so much slander in so short a time. That, men of Athens, is the truth for you. I have hidden or disguised nothing. I know well enough that this very conduct makes me unpopular, and this is proof that what I say is true, that such is the slander against me, and that such are its causes. If you look into this either now or later, this is what you will find.

Let this suffice as a defense against the charges of my earlier accusers. After this I shall try to defend myself against Meletus, that good and patriotic man, as he says he is, and my later accusers. As these are a different lot of accusers, let us again take up their sworn deposition. It goes something like this: Socrates is guilty of corrupting the young and of not believing in the gods in whom the city believes, but in other new spiritual things. Such is their charge. Let us examine it point by point.

He says that I am guilty of corrupting the young, but I say that Meletus is guilty of dealing frivolously with serious matters, of irresponsibly bringing people into court, and of professing to be seriously concerned with things about none of which he has ever cared, and I shall try to prove that this is so. Come here and tell me, Meletus. Surely you consider it of the greatest importance that our young men be as good as possible? — Indeed I do.

Come then, tell these men who improves them. You obviously know, in view of your concern. You say you have discovered the one who corrupts them, namely me, and you bring me here and accuse me to these men. Come, inform these men and tell them who it is who improves them. You see, Meletus, that you are silent and know not what to say. Does this not seem shameful to you and a sufficient proof of what I say, that you have not been concerned with any of this? Tell me, my good sir, who improves our young men? — The laws.

That is not what I am asking, but what person who has knowledge of the laws to begin with? — These jurymen, Socrates.

How do you mean, Meletus? Are these able to educate the young and improve them? — Certainly.

All of them, or some but not others? — All of them.

Very good, by Hera. You mention a great abundance of benefactors. But what about the audience? Do they improve the young or not? — They do, too.

What about the members of Council? — The Councillors, also.

But, Meletus, what about the assembly? Do members of the assembly corrupt the young, or do they all improve them? — They improve them.

All the Athenians, it seems, make the young into fine good men, except me, and I alone corrupt them. Is that what you mean? — That is most definitely what I mean.

You condemn me to a great misfortune. Tell me: does this also apply to horses, do you think? That all men improve them and one individual corrupts them? Or is quite the contrary true, one individual is able to improve them, or very few, namely, the horse breeders, whereas the majority, if they have horses and use them, corrupt them? Is that not the case, Meletus, both with horses and all other animals? Of course it is, whether you and Anytus say so or not. It would be a very happy state of affairs if only one person corrupted our youth, while the others improved them.

You have made it sufficiently obvious, Meletus, that you have never had any concern for our youth; you show your indifference clearly; that you have given no thought to the subjects about which you bring me to trial.

And by Zeus, Meletus, tell us also whether it is better for a man to live among good or wicked fellow citizens. Answer, my good man, for I am not asking a difficult question. Do not the wicked do some harm to those who are ever closest to them, whereas good people benefit them? — Certainly.

And does the man exist who would rather be harmed than benefited by his associates? Answer, my good sir, for the law orders you to answer. Is there any man who wants to be harmed? — Of course not.

Come now, do you accuse me here of corrupting the young and making them worse deliberately or unwillingly? — Deliberately.

What follows, Meletus? Are you so much wiser at your age than I am at mine that you understand that wicked people always do some harm to their closest neighbors while good people do them good, but I have reached such a pitch of ignorance that I do not realize this, namely that if I make one of my associates wicked I run the risk of being harmed by him so that I do such a great evil deliberately, as you say? I do not believe you, Meletus, and

I do not think anyone else will. Either I do not corrupt the young or, if I do, it is unwillingly, and you are lying in either case. Now if I corrupt them unwillingly, the law does not require you to bring people to court for such unwilling wrongdoings, but to get hold of them privately, to instruct them and exhort them; for clearly, if I learn better, I shall cease to do what I am doing unwillingly. You, however, have avoided my company and were unwilling to instruct me, but you bring me here, where the law requires one to bring those who are in need of punishment, not of instruction.

And so, men of Athens, what I said is clearly true: Meletus has never been at all concerned with these matters. Nonetheless tell us, Meletus, how you say that I corrupt the young; or is it obvious from your deposition that it is by teaching them not to believe in the gods in whom the city believes but in other new spiritual things? Is this not what you say I teach and so corrupt them? — That is most certainly what I do say.

Then by those very gods about whom we are talking, Meletus, make this clearer to me and to these men: I cannot be sure whether you mean that I teach the belief that there are some gods—and therefore I myself believe that there are gods and am not altogether an atheist, nor am I guilty of that—not, however, the gods in whom the city believes, but others, and that this is the charge against me, that they are others. Or whether you mean that I do not believe in gods at all, and that this is what I teach to others. — This is what I mean, that you do not believe in gods at all.

You are a strange fellow, Meletus. Why do you say this? Do I not believe, as other men do, that the sun and the moon are gods? — No, by Zeus, gentlemen of the jury, for he says that the sun is stone, and the moon earth.

My dear Meletus, do you think you are prosecuting Anaxagoras? Are you so contemptuous of these men and think them so ignorant of letters as not to know that the books of Anaxagoras of Clazomenae are full of those theories, and further, that the young men learn from me what they can buy from time to time for a drachma, at most, in the bookshops, and ridicule Socrates if he pretends that these theories are his own, especially as they are so absurd? Is that, by Zeus, what you think of me, Meletus, that I do not believe that there are any gods? — That is what I say, that you do not believe in the gods at all.

You cannot be believed, Meletus, even, I think, by yourself. The man appears to me, men of Athens, highly insolent and uncontrolled. He seems to have made this deposition out of insolence, violence, and youthful zeal. He is like one who composed a riddle and is trying it out: "Will the wise Socrates realize that I am jesting and contradicting myself, or shall I deceive him and others?" I think he contradicts himself in the affidavit, as if he said: "Socrates is guilty of not believing in gods but believing in gods," and surely that is the part of a jester!

Examine with me, gentlemen, how he appears to contradict himself, and you, Meletus, answer us. Remember, gentlemen, what I asked you when I began, not to create a disturbance if I proceed in my usual manner.

Does any man, Meletus, believe in human activities who does not believe in humans? Make him answer, and not again and again create a disturbance. Does any man who does not believe in horses believe in horsemen's activities? Or in flute-playing activities but not in flute-players? No, my good sir, no man could. If you are not willing to answer, I will tell you and these men. Answer the next question, however. Does any man believe in spiritual activities who does not believe in spirits? — No one.

Thank you for answering, if reluctantly, when these gentlemen made you. Now you say that I believe in spiritual things and teach about them, whether new or old, but at any rate spiritual things according to what you say, and to this you have sworn in your deposition. But if I believe in spiritual things I must quite inevitably believe in spirits. Is that not so? It is indeed. I shall assume that you agree, as you do not answer. Do we not believe spirits to be either gods or the children of gods? Yes or no? — Of course.

Then since I do believe in spirits, as you admit, if spirits are gods, this is what I mean when I say you speak in riddles and in jest, as you state that I do not believe in gods and then again that I do, since I do believe in spirits. If, on the other hand, the spirits are children of the gods, bastard children of the gods by nymphs or some other mothers, as they are said to be, what man would believe children of the gods to exist, but not gods? That would be just as absurd as to believe the young of horses and asses, namely mules, to exist, but not to believe in the existence of horses and asses. You must have made this deposition, Meletus, either to test us or because you were at a loss to find any true wrongdoing of which to accuse me. There is no way in which you could persuade anyone of even small intelligence that it is possible for one and the same man to believe in spiritual but not also in divine things, and then again for that same man to believe neither in spirits nor in gods nor in heroes.

I do not think, men of Athens, that it requires a prolonged defense to prove that I am not guilty of the charges in Meletus' deposition, but this is sufficient. On the other hand, you know that what I said earlier is true, that I am very unpopular with many people. This will be my undoing, if I am undone, not Meletus or Anytus but the slanders and envy of many people. This has destroyed many other good men and will, I think, continue to do so. There is no danger that it will stop at me.

Someone might say: "Are you not ashamed, Socrates, to have followed the kind of occupation that has led to your being now in danger of death?" However, I should be right to reply to him: "You are wrong, sir, if you think that a man who is any good at all should take into account the risk of life or death; he should look to this only in his actions, whether what he does is right or wrong, whether he is acting like a good or a bad man." According to your view, all the heroes who died at Troy were inferior people, especially the son of Thetis who was so contemptuous of danger compared with disgrace. When he was eager to kill Hector, his goddess mother warned him, as I believe, in some such words as these: "My child, if you avenge the death of your comrade, Patroclus, and you kill Hector, you will die yourself, for your death is to follow immediately after Hector's." Hearing this, he despised death and danger and was much more afraid to live a coward who did not avenge his friends. "Let me die at once," he said, "when once I have given the wrongdoer his deserts, rather than remain here, a laughingstock by the curved ships, a burden upon the earth." Do you think he gave thought to death and danger?

This is the truth of the matter, men of Athens: wherever a man has taken a position that he believes to be best, or has been placed by his commander, there he must I think remain and face danger, without a thought for death or anything else, rather than disgrace. It would have been a dreadful way to behave, men of Athens, if, at Potidaea, Amphipolis, and Delium, I had, at the risk of death, like anyone else, remained at my post where those you had elected to command had ordered me, and then, when the god ordered me, as I thought and believed, to live the life of a philosopher, to examine myself and others, I had abandoned my post for fear of death or anything else. That would have been a dreadful thing, and then I might truly have justly been brought here for not believing that there are gods, disobeying the oracle, fearing death, and thinking I was wise when I was not. To fear death, gentlemen, is no other than to think oneself wise when one is not, to think one knows what one does not know. No one knows whether death may not be the greatest of all blessings for a man, yet men fear it as if they knew that it is the greatest of evils. And surely it is the most blameworthy ignorance to believe that one knows what one does not know. It is perhaps on this point and in this respect, gentlemen, that I differ from the majority of men, and if I were to claim that I am wiser than anyone in anything, it would be in this, that, as I have no adequate knowledge of things in the underworld, so I do not think I have. I do know, however, that it is wicked and shameful to do wrong, to disobey one's superior, be he god or man. I shall never fear or avoid things of which I do not know, whether they may not be good rather than things that I know to be

bad. Even if you acquitted me now and did not believe Anytus, who said to you that either I should not have been brought here in the first place, or that now I am here, you cannot avoid executing me, for if I should be acquitted, your sons would practice the teachings of Socrates and all be thoroughly corrupted; if you said to me in this regard: "Socrates, we do not believe Anytus now; we acquit you, but only on condition that you spend no more time on this investigation and do not practice philosophy, and if you are caught doing so you will die"; if, as I say, you were to acquit me on those terms, I would say to you: "Men of Athens, I am grateful and I am your friend, but I will obey the god rather than you, and as long as I draw breath and am able, I shall not cease to practice philosophy, to exhort you and in my usual way to point out to any one of you whom I happen to meet: Good Sir, you are an Athenian, a citizen of the greatest city with the greatest reputation for both wisdom and power; are you not ashamed of your eagerness to possess as much wealth, reputation, and honors as possible, while you do not care for nor give thought to wisdom or truth, or the best possible state of your soul?" Then, if one of you disputes this and says he does care, I shall not let him go at once or leave him, but I shall question him, examine him, and test him, and if I do not think he has attained the goodness that he says he has, I shall reproach him because he attaches little importance to the most important things and greater importance to inferior things. I shall treat in this way anyone I happen to meet, young and old, citizen and stranger, and more so the citizens because you are more kindred to me. Be sure that this is what the god orders me to do, and I think there is no greater blessing for the city than my service to the god. For I go around doing nothing but persuading both young and old among you not to care for your body or your wealth in preference to or as strongly as for the best possible state of your soul, as I say to you: "Wealth does not bring about excellence, but excellence makes wealth and everything else good for men, both individually and collectively."

Now if by saying this I corrupt the young, this advice must be harmful, but if anyone says that I give different advice, he is talking nonsense. On this point I would say to you, men of Athens: "Whether you believe Anytus or not, whether you acquit me or not, do so on the understanding that this is my course of action, even if I am to face death many times:" Do not create a disturbance, gentlemen, but abide by my request not to cry out at what I say but to listen, for I think it will be to your advantage to listen, and I am about to say other things at which you will perhaps cry out. By no means do this. Be sure that if you kill the sort of man I say I am, you will not harm me more than yourselves. Neither Meletus nor Anytus can harm me in any way; he could not harm me, for I do not think it is permitted that a better man be harmed by a worse; certainly he might kill me, or perhaps banish or disfranchise me, which he and maybe others think to be great harm, but I do not think so. I think he is doing himself much greater harm doing what he is doing now, attempting to have a man executed unjustly. Indeed, men of Athens, I am far from making a defense now on my own behalf, as might be thought, but on yours, to prevent you from wrongdoing by mistreating the god's gift to you by condemning me; for if you kill me you will not easily find another like me. I was attached to this city by the god—though it seems a ridiculous thing to say—as upon a great and noble horse which was somewhat sluggish because of its size and needed to be stirred up by a kind of gadfly. It is to fulfill some such function that I believe the god has placed me in the city. I never cease to rouse each and every one of you, to persuade and reproach you all day long and everywhere I find myself in your company.

Another such man will not easily come to be among you, gentlemen, and if you believe me you will spare me. You might easily be annoyed with me as people are when they are aroused from a doze, and strike out at me; if convinced by Anytus you could easily kill me, and then you could sleep on for the rest of your days, unless the god, in his care for you, sent you someone else. That I am

the kind of person to be a gift of the god to the city you might realize from the fact that it does not seem like human nature for me to have neglected all my own affairs and to have tolerated this neglect now for so many years while I was always concerned with you, approaching each one of you like a father or an elder brother to persuade you to care for virtue. Now if I profited from this by charging a fee for my advice, there would be some sense to it, but you can see for yourselves that, for all their shameless accusations, my accusers have not been able in their impudence to bring forward a witness to say that I have ever received a fee or ever asked for one. I, on the other hand, have a convincing witness that I speak the truth, my poverty.

It may seem strange that while I go around and give this advice privately and interfere in private affairs, I do not venture to go to the assembly and there advise the city. You have heard me give the reason for this in many places. I have a divine or spiritual sign which Meletus has ridiculed in his deposition. This began when I was a child. It is a voice, and whenever it speaks it turns me away from something I am about to do, but it never encourages me to do anything. This is what has prevented me from taking part in public affairs, and I think it was quite right to prevent me. Be sure, men of Athens, that if I had long ago attempted to take part in politics, I should have died long ago, and benefited neither you nor myself. Do not be angry with me for speaking the truth; no man will survive who genuinely opposes you or any other crowd and prevents the occurrence of many unjust and illegal happenings in the city. A man who really fights for justice must lead a private, not a public, life if he is to survive for even a short time.

I shall give you great proofs of this not words but what you esteem, deeds. Listen to what happened to me, that you may know that I will not yield to any man contrary to what is right, for fear of death, even if I should die at once for not yielding. The things I shall tell you are commonplace and smack of the law-courts, but they are true. I have never held any other office in the city, but I served as a member of the Council, and our tribe Antiochis was presiding at the time when you wanted to try as a body the ten generals who had failed to pick up the survivors of the naval battle. This was illegal, as you all recognized later. I was the only member of the presiding committee to oppose your doing something contrary to the laws, and I voted against it. The orators were ready to prosecute me and take me away, and your shouts were egging them on, but I thought I should run any risk on the side of law and justice rather than join you, for fear of prison or death, when you were engaged in an unjust course.

This happened when the city was still a democracy. When the oligarchy was established, the Thirty summoned me to the Hall, along with four others, and ordered us to bring Leon from Salamis, that he might be executed. They gave many such orders to many people, in order to implicate as many as possible in their guilt. Then I showed again, not in words but in action, that, if it were not rather vulgar to say so, death is something I couldn't care less about, but that my whole concern is not to do anything unjust or impious. That government, powerful as it was, did not frighten me into any wrongdoing. When we left the Hall, the other four went to Salamis and brought in Leon, but I went home. I might have been put to death for this, had not the government fallen shortly afterwards. There are many who will witness to these events.

Do you think I would have survived all these years if I were engaged in public affairs and, acting as a good man must, came to the help of justice and considered this the most important thing? Far from it, men of Athens, nor would any other man. Throughout my life, in any public activity I may have engaged in, I am the same man as I am in private life. I have never come to an agreement with anyone to act unjustly, neither with anyone else nor with any one of those who they slanderously say are my pupils. I have never been anyone's teacher. If anyone, young or old, desires to listen to me when I am talking and dealing with my own concerns, I have never begrudged this to anyone, but I do not converse when I receive a fee and not when I do not. I am equally ready to question the rich and the poor if anyone is willing to answer my questions and listen to what I say. And I cannot justly be held responsible for the good or bad conduct of these people, as I never promised to teach them anything and have not done so. If anyone says that he has learned anything from me, or that he heard anything privately that the others did not hear, be assured that he is not telling the truth.

Why then do some people enjoy spending considerable time in my company? You have heard why, men of Athens; I have told you the whole truth. They enjoy hearing those being questioned who think they are wise, but are not. And this is not unpleasant. To do this has, as I say, been enjoined upon me by the god, by means of oracles and dreams, and in every other way that a divine manifestation has ever ordered a man to do anything. This is true, gentlemen, and can easily be established.

If I corrupt some young men and have corrupted others, then surely some of them who have grown older and realized that I gave them bad advice when they were young should now themselves come up here to accuse me and avenge themselves. If they were unwilling to do so themselves, then some of their kindred, their fathers or brothers or other relations should recall it now if their family had been harmed by me. I see many of these present here, first Crito, my contemporary and fellow demesman, the father of Critobulus here; next Lysanias of Sphettus, the father of Aeschines here; also Antiphon the Cephisian, the father of Epigenes; and others whose brothers spent their time in this way; Nicostratus, the son of Theozotides, brother of Theodotus, and Theodotus has died so he could not influence him; Paralius here, son of Demodocus, whose brother was Theages; there is Adeimantus, son of Ariston, brother of Plato here; Aeantidorus, brother of Apollodorus here.

I could mention many others, some of whom surely Meletus should have brought in as witness in his own speech. If he forgot to do so, then let him do it now; I will yield time if he has anything of the kind to say. You will find quite the contrary, gentlemen. These men are all ready to come to the help of the corruptor, the man who has harmed their kindred, as Meletus and Anytus say. Now those who were corrupted might well have reason to help me, but the uncorrupted, their kindred who are older men, have no reason to help me except the right and proper one, that they know that Meletus is lying and that I am telling the truth.

Very well, gentlemen. This, and maybe other similar things, is what I have to say in my defense. Perhaps one of you might be angry as he recalls that when he himself stood trial on a less dangerous charge, he begged and implored the jurymen with many tears, that he brought his children and many of his friends and family into court to arouse as much pity as he could, but that I do none of these things, even though I may seem to be running the ultimate risk. Thinking of this, he might feel resentful towards me and, angry about this, cast his vote in anger. If there is such a one among you—I do not deem there is, but if there is—I think it would be right to say in reply: My good sir, I too have a household and, in Homer's phrase, I am not born "from oak or rock" but from men, so that I have a family, indeed three sons, men of Athens, of whom one is an adolescent while two are children. Nevertheless, I will not beg you to acquit me by bringing them here. Why do I do none of these things? Not through arrogance, gentlemen, nor through lack of respect for you. Whether I am brave in the face of death is another matter, but with regard to my reputation and yours and that of the whole city, it does not seem right to me to do these things, especially at my age and with my reputation. For it is generally believed, whether it be true or false, that in certain respects Socrates is superior to the majority of men. Now if those of you who are considered superior, be it in wisdom or courage or whatever other virtue makes them so, are seen behaving like that, it would be a disgrace. Yet I have often seen them do this sort of thing when standing trial, men who are thought to be somebody, doing amazing things as if they thought it a terrible thing to die, and as if they were to be immortal if you did not execute them. I think

these men bring shame upon the city so that a stranger, too, would assume that those who are outstanding in virtue among the Athenians, whom they themselves select from themselves to fill offices of state and receive other honors, are in no way better than women. You should not act like that, men of Athens, those of you who have any reputation at all, and if we do, you should not allow it. You should make it very clear that you will more readily convict a man who performs these pitiful dramatics in court and so makes the city a laughingstock, than a man who keeps quiet.

Quite apart from the question of reputation, gentlemen, I do not think it right to supplicate the jury and to be acquitted because of this, but to teach and persuade them. It is not the purpose of a juryman's office to give justice as a favor to whoever seems good to him, but to judge according to law, and this he has sworn to do. We should not accustom you to perjure yourselves, nor should you make a habit of it. This is irreverent conduct for either of us.

Do not deem it right for me, men of Athens, that I should act towards you in a way that I do not consider to be good or just or pious, especially, by Zeus, as I am being prosecuted by Meletus here for impiety; clearly, if I convinced you by my supplication to do violence to your oath of office, I would be teaching you not to believe that there are gods, and my defense would convict me of not believing in them. This is far from being the case, gentlemen, for I do believe in them as none of my accusers do. I leave it to you and the god to judge me in the way that will be best for me and for you.

[The jury now gives its verdict of guilty, and Meletus asks for the penalty of death.]

There are many other reasons for my not being angry with you for convicting me, men of Athens, and what happened was not unexpected. I am much more surprised at the number of votes cast on each side, for I did not think the decision would be by so few votes but by a great many. As it is, a switch of only thirty votes would have acquitted me. I think myself that I have been cleared on Meletus' charges, and not only this, but it is clear to all that, if Anytus and Lycon had not joined him in accusing me, he would have been fined a thousand drachmas for not receiving a fifth of the votes.

He assesses the penalty at death. So be it. What counter-assessment should I propose to you, men of Athens? Clearly it should be a penalty I deserve, and what do I deserve to suffer or to pay because I have deliberately not led a quiet life but have neglected what occupies most people: wealth, household affairs, the position of general or public orator or the other offices, the political clubs and factions that exist in the city? I thought myself too honest to survive if I occupied myself with those things. I did not follow that path that would have made me of no use either to you or to myself, but I went to each of you privately and conferred upon him what I say is the greatest benefit, by trying to persuade him not to care for any of his belongings before caring that he himself should be as good and as wise as possible, not to care for the city's possessions more than for the city itself, and to care for other things in the same way. What do I deserve for being such a man? Some good, men of Athens, if I must truly make an assessment according to my deserts, and something suitable. What is suitable for a poor benefactor, who needs leisure to exhort you? Nothing is more suitable, gentlemen, than for such a man to be fed in the Prytaneum—much more suitable for him than for any one of you who has won a victory at Olympia with a pair or a team of horses. The Olympian victor makes you think yourself happy; I make you be happy. Besides, he does not need food, but I do. So if I must make a just assessment of what I deserve, I assess it as this: free meals in the Prytaneum.

When I say this you may think, as when I spoke of appeals to pity and entreaties, that I speak arrogantly, but that is not the case, men of Athens; rather it is like this: I am convinced that I never willingly wrong anyone, but I am not convincing you of this, for we have talked together but a short time. If it were the law with us, as it is elsewhere, that a trial for life should not last one but many days, you would be convinced, but now it is not easy to dispel great slanders in a short time. Since I am convinced that I wrong no one, I am not likely to wrong myself, to say that I deserve some evil and to make some such assessment against myself. What should I fear? That I should suffer the penalty Meletus has assessed against me, of which I say I do not know whether it is good or bad? Am I then to choose in preference to this something that I know very well to be an evil and assess the penalty at that? Imprisonment? Why should I live in prison, always subjected to the ruling magistrates, the Eleven? A fine, and imprisonment until I pay it? That would be the same thing for me, as I have no money. Exile? For perhaps you might accept that assessment.

I should have to be inordinately fond of life, men of Athens, to be so unreasonable as to suppose that other men will easily tolerate my company and conversation when you, my fellow citizens, have been unable to endure them, but found them a burden and resented them so that you are now seeking to get rid of them. Far from it, gentlemen. It would be a fine life at my age to be driven out of one city after another, for I know very well that wherever I go the young men will listen to my talk as they do here. If I drive them away, they will themselves persuade their elders to drive me out; if I do not drive them away, their fathers and relations will drive me out on their behalf.

Perhaps someone might say: But Socrates, if you leave us will you not be able to live quietly, without talking? Now this is the most difficult point on which to convince some of you. If I say that it is impossible for me to keep quiet because that means disobeying the god, you will not believe me and will think I am being ironical. On the other hand, if I say that it is the greatest good for a man to discuss virtue every day and those other things about which you hear me conversing and testing myself and others, for the unexamined life is not worth living for men, you will believe me even less.

What I say is true, gentlemen, but it is not easy to convince you. At the same time, I am not accustomed to think that I deserve any penalty. If I had money, I would assess the penalty at the amount I could pay, for that would not hurt me, but I have none, unless you are willing to set the penalty at the amount I can pay, and perhaps I could pay you one mina of silver. So that is my assessment.

Plato here, men of Athens, and Crito and Critobulus and Apollodorus bid me put the penalty at thirty minas, and they will stand surety for the money. Well then, that is my assessment, and they will be sufficient guarantee of payment.

[The jury now votes again and sentences Socrates to death.]

It is for the sake of a short time, men of Athens, that you will acquire the reputation and the guilt, in the eyes of those who want to denigrate the city, of having killed Socrates, a wise man, for they who want to revile you will say that I am wise even if I am not. If you had waited but a little while, this would have happened of its own accord. You see my age, that I am already advanced in years and close to death. I am saying this not to all of you but to those who condemned me to death, and to these same ones I say: Perhaps you think that I was convicted for lack of such words as might have convinced you, if I thought I should say or do all I could to avoid my sentence. Far from it. I was convicted because I lacked not words but boldness and shamelessness and the willingness to say to you what you would most gladly have heard from me, lamentations and tears and my saying and doing many things that I say are unworthy of me but that you are accustomed to hear from others. I did not think then that the danger I ran should make me do anything mean, nor do I now regret the nature of my defense. I would much rather die after this kind of defense than live after making the other kind. Neither I nor any other man should, on trial or in war, contrive to avoid death at any cost. Indeed it is often obvious in battle that one could escape death by throwing away one's weapons and by turning to supplicate one's pursuers, and there are many ways to avoid death in every kind of danger if

one will venture to do or say anything to avoid it. It is not difficult to avoid death, gentlemen; it is much more difficult to avoid wickedness, for it runs faster than death. Slow and elderly as I am, I have been caught by the slower pursuer, whereas my accusers, being clever and sharp, have been caught by the quicker, wickedness. I leave you now, condemned to death by you, but they are condemned by truth to wickedness and injustice. So I maintain my assessment, and they maintain theirs. This perhaps had to happen, and I think it is as it should be.

Now I want to prophesy to those who convicted me, for I am at the point when men prophesy most, when they are about to die. I say, gentlemen, to those who voted to kill me, that vengeance will come upon you immediately after my death, a vengeance much harder to bear than that which you took in killing me. You did this in the belief that you would avoid giving an account of your life, but I maintain that quite the opposite will happen to you. There will be more people to test you, whom I now held back, but you did not notice it. They will be more difficult to deal with as they will be younger and you will resent them more. You are wrong if you believe that by killing people you will prevent anyone from reproaching you for not living in the right way. To escape such tests is neither possible nor good, but it is best and easiest not to discredit others but to prepare oneself to be as good as possible. With this prophecy to you who convicted me, I part from you.

I should be glad to discuss what has happened with those who voted for my acquittal during the time that the officers of the court are busy and I do not yet have to depart to my death. So, gentlemen, stay with me awhile, for nothing prevents us from talking to each other while it is allowed. To you, as being my friends, I want to show the meaning of what has occurred. A surprising thing has happened to me, jurymen—you I would rightly call jurymen. At all previous times my familiar prophetic power, my spiritual manifestation, frequently opposed me, even in small matters, when I was about to do something wrong, but now that, as you can see for yourselves, I was faced with what one might think, and what is generally thought to be, the worst of evils, my divine sign has not opposed me, either when I left home at dawn, or when I came into court, or at any time that I was about to say something during my speech. Yet in other talks it often held me back in the middle of my speaking, but now it has opposed no word or deed of mine. What do I think is the reason for this? I will tell you. What has happened to me may well be a good thing, and those of us who believe death to be an evil are certainly mistaken. I have convincing proof of this, for it is impossible that my familiar sign did not oppose me if I was not about to do what was right.

Let us reflect in this way, too, that there is good hope that death is a blessing, for it is one of two things: either the dead are nothing and have no perception of anything, or it is, as we are told, a change and a relocating for the soul from here to another place. If it is complete lack of perception, like a dreamless sleep, then death would be a great advantage. For I think that if one had to pick out that night during which a man slept soundly and did not dream, put beside it the other nights and days of his life, and then see how many days and nights had been better and more pleasant than that night, not only a private person but the great king would find them easy to count compared with the other days and nights. If death is like this I say it is an advantage, for all eternity would then seem to be no more than a single night. If, on the other hand, death is a change from here to another place, and what we are told is true and all who have died are there, what greater blessing could there be, gentlemen of the jury? If anyone arriving in Hades will have escaped from those who call themselves jurymen here, and will find those true jurymen who are said to sit in judgment there, Minos and Rhadamanthus and Aeacus and Triptolemus and the other demigods who have been upright in their own life, would that be a poor kind of change? Again, what would one of you give to keep company with Orpheus and Musaeus, Hesiod and Homer? I am willing to die many times if that is true. It would be a wonderful way for me to spend my time whenever I met Palamedes and Ajax, the son of Telamon, and any other of the men of old who died through an unjust conviction, to compare my experience with theirs. I think it would be pleasant. Most important, I could spend my time testing and examining people there, as I do here, as to who among them is wise, and who thinks he is, but is not.

What would one not give, gentlemen of the jury, for the opportunity to examine the man who led the great expedition against Troy, or Odysseus, or Sisyphus, and innumerable other men and women one could mention? It would be an extraordinary happiness to talk with them, to keep company with them and examine them. In any case, they would certainly not put one to death for doing so. They are happier there than we are here in other respects, and for the rest of time they are deathless, if indeed what we are told is true.

You too must be of good hope as regards death, gentlemen of the jury, and keep this one truth in mind, that a good man cannot be harmed either in life or in death, and that his affairs are not neglected by the gods. What has happened to me now has not happened of itself, but it is clear to me that it was better for me to die now and to escape from trouble. That is why my divine sign did not oppose me at any point. So I am certainly not angry with those who convicted me, or with my accusers. Of course that was not their purpose when they accused and convicted me, but they thought they were hurting me, and for this they deserve blame. This much I ask from them: When my sons grow up, avenge yourselves by causing them the same kind of grief that I caused you, if you think they care for money or anything else more than they care for virtue, or if they think they are somebody when they are nobody. Reproach them as I reproach you, that they do not care for the right things and think they are worthy when they are not worthy of anything. If you do this, I shall have been justly treated by you, and my sons also.

Now the hour to part has come. I go to die, you go to live. Which of us goes to the better lot is known to no one, except the god.

3. The Value of Philosophy

BERTRAND RUSSELL

Bertrand Russell (1872–1970) was one of the greatest philosophers of the twentieth century. His philosophical contributions ranged across many areas; he was also an important social critic. He received the Nobel Prize for literature in 1950.

Having now come to the end of our brief and very incomplete review of the problems of philosophy, it will be well to consider, in conclusion, what is the value of philosophy and why it ought to be studied. It is the more necessary to consider this question, in view of the fact that many men, under the influence of science or of practical affairs, are inclined to doubt whether philosophy is anything better than innocent but useless trifling, hair-splitting distinctions, and controversies on matters concerning which knowledge is impossible.

This view of philosophy appears to result, partly from a wrong conception of the ends of life, partly from a wrong conception of the kind of goods which philosophy strives to achieve. Physical science, through the medium of inventions, is useful to innumerable people who are wholly ignorant of it; thus the study of physical science is to be recommended, not only, or primarily, because of the effect on the student, but rather because of the effect on mankind in general. This utility does not belong to philosophy. If the study of philosophy has any value at all for others than students of philosophy, it must be only indirectly, through its effects upon the lives of those who study it. It is in these effects, therefore, if anywhere, that the value of philosophy must be primarily sought.

But further, if we are not to fail in our endeavour to determine the value of philosophy, we must first free our minds from the prejudices of what are wrongly called "practical" men. The "practical" man, as this word is often used, is one who recognizes only material needs, who realizes that men must have food for the body, but is oblivious of the necessity of providing food for the mind. If all men were well off, if poverty and disease had been reduced to their lowest possible point, there would still remain much to be done to produce a valuable society; and even in the existing world the goods of the mind are at least as important as the goods of the body. It is exclusively among the goods of the mind that the value of philosophy is to be found; and only those who are not indifferent to these goods can be persuaded that the study of philosophy is not a waste of time.

Philosophy, like all other studies, aims primarily at knowledge. The knowledge it aims at is the kind of knowledge which gives unity and system to the body of the sciences, and the kind which results from a critical examination of the grounds of our convictions, prejudices, and beliefs. But it cannot be maintained that philosophy has had any very great measure of success in its attempts to provide definite answers to its questions. If you ask a mathematician, a mineralogist, a historian, or any other man of learning, what definite body of truths has been ascertained by his science, his answer will last as long as you are willing to listen. But if you put the same question to a philosopher, he will, if he is candid, have to confess that his study has not achieved positive results such as have been achieved by other sciences. It is true that this is partly accounted for by the fact that, as soon as definite knowledge concerning any subject becomes

From Bertrand Russell, *Problems of Philosophy* (1912), chap. 15.

possible, this subject ceases to be called philosophy, and becomes a separate science. The whole study of the heavens, which now belongs to astronomy, was once included in philosophy; Newton's great work was called "the mathematical principles of natural philosophy." Similarly, the study of the human mind, which was a part of philosophy, has now been separated from philosophy and has become the science of psychology. Thus, to a great extent, the uncertainty of philosophy is more apparent than real: those questions which are already capable of definite answers are placed in the sciences, while those only to which, at present, no definite answer can be given, remain to form the residue which is called philosophy.

This is, however, only a part of the truth concerning the uncertainty of philosophy. There are many questions—and among them those that are of the profoundest interest to our spiritual life—which, so far as we can see, must remain insoluble to the human intellect unless its powers become of quite a different order from what they are now. Has the universe any unity of plan or purpose, or is it a fortuitous concourse of atoms? Is consciousness a permanent part of the universe, giving hope of indefinite growth in wisdom, or is it a transitory accident on a small planet on which life must ultimately become impossible? Are good and evil of importance to the universe or only to man? Such questions are asked by philosophy, and variously answered by various philosophers. But it would seem that, whether answers be otherwise discoverable or not, the answers suggested by philosophy are none of them demonstrably true. Yet, however slight may be the hope of discovering an answer, it is part of the business of philosophy to continue the consideration of such questions, to make us aware of their importance, to examine all the approaches to them, and to keep alive that speculative interest in the universe which is apt to be killed by confining ourselves to definitely ascertainable knowledge.

Many philosophers, it is true, have held that philosophy could establish the truth of certain answers to such fundamental questions. They have supposed that what is of most importance in religious beliefs could be proved by strict demonstration to be true. In order to judge of such attempts, it is necessary to take a survey of human knowledge, and to form an opinion as to its methods and its limitations. On such a subject it would be unwise to pronounce dogmatically; but if [our] investigations…have not led us astray, we shall be compelled to renounce the hope of finding philosophical proofs of religious beliefs. We cannot, therefore, include as part of the value of philosophy any definite set of answers to such questions. Hence, once more, the value of philosophy must not depend upon any supposed body of definitely ascertainable knowledge to be acquired by those who study it.

The value of philosophy is, in fact, to be sought largely in its very uncertainty. The man who has no tincture of philosophy goes through life imprisoned in the prejudices derived from common sense, from the habitual beliefs of his age or his nation, and from convictions which have grown up in his mind without the cooperation or consent of his deliberate reason. To such a man the world tends to become definite, finite, obvious; common objects rouse no questions, and unfamiliar possibilities are contemptuously rejected. As soon as we begin to philosophize, on the contrary, we find…that even the most everyday things lead to problems to which only very incomplete answers can be given. Philosophy, though unable to tell us with certainty what is the true answer to the doubts which it raises, is able to suggest many possibilities which enlarge our thoughts and free them from the tyranny of custom. Thus, while diminishing our feeling of certainty as to what things are, it greatly increases our knowledge as to what they may be; it removes the somewhat arrogant dogmatism of those who have never travelled into the region of liberating doubt, and it keeps alive our sense of wonder by showing familiar things in an unfamiliar aspect.

Apart from its utility in showing unsuspected possibilities, philosophy has a value—perhaps its chief value—through the greatness of the objects which it contemplates, and the freedom from narrow and personal aims resulting from this contemplation. The life of the instinctive man is shut up within the circle of his private interests: family and friends may be included, but the outer world is not regarded except as it may help or hinder what comes within the circle of instinctive wishes. In such a life there is something feverish and confined, in comparison with which the philosophic life is calm and free. The private world of instinctive interests is a small one, set in the midst of a great and powerful world which must, sooner or later, lay our private world in ruins. Unless we can so enlarge our interests as to include the whole outer world, we remain like a garrison in a beleaguered fortress, knowing that the enemy prevents escape and that ultimate surrender is inevitable. In such a life there is no peace, but a constant strife between the insistence of desire and the powerlessness of will. In one way or another, if our life is to be great and free, we must escape this prison and this strife.

One way of escape is by philosophic contemplation. Philosophic contemplation does not, in its widest survey, divide the universe into two hostile camps—friends and foes, helpful and hostile, good and bad—it views the whole impartially. Philosophic contemplation, when it is unalloyed, does not aim at proving that the rest of the universe is akin to man. All acquisition of knowledge is an enlargement of the Self, but this enlargement is best attained when it is not directly sought. It is obtained when the desire for knowledge is alone operative, by a study which does not wish in advance that its objects should have this or that character, but adapts the Self to the characters which it finds in its objects. This enlargement of Self is not obtained when, taking the Self as it is, we try to show that the world is so similar to this Self that knowledge of it is possible without any admission of what seems alien. The desire to prove this is a form of self-assertion and, like all self-assertion, it is an obstacle to the growth of Self which it desires, and of which the Self knows that it is capable. Self-assertion, in philosophic speculation as elsewhere, views the world as a means to its own ends; thus it makes the world of less account than Self, and the Self sets bounds to the greatness of its goods. In contemplation, on the contrary, we start from the not-Self, and through its greatness the boundaries of Self are enlarged; through the infinity of the universe the mind which contemplates it achieves some share in infinity.

For this reason greatness of soul is not fostered by those philosophies which assimilate the universe to Man. Knowledge is a form of union of Self and not-Self; like all union, it is impaired by dominion, and therefore by any attempt to force the universe into conformity with what we find in ourselves. There is a widespread philosophical tendency towards the view which tells us that Man is the measure of all things, that truth is man-made, that space and time and the world of universals are properties of the mind, and that, if there be anything not created by the mind, it is unknowable and of no account for us. This view, if our previous discussions were correct, is untrue; but in addition to being untrue, it has the effect of robbing philosophic contemplation of all that gives it value, since it fetters contemplation to Self. What it calls knowledge is not a union with the not-Self, but a set of prejudices, habits, and desires, making an impenetrable veil between us and the world beyond. The man who finds pleasure in such a theory of knowledge is like the man who never leaves the domestic circle for fear his word might not be law.

The true philosophic contemplation, on the contrary, finds its satisfaction in every enlargement of the not-Self, in everything that magnifies the objects contemplated, and thereby the subject contemplating. Everything, in contemplation, that is personal or private, everything that depends upon habit, self-interest, or desire, distorts the object, and hence impairs the union which the intellect seeks. By thus making a barrier between subject and object, such personal and private things become a prison to the intellect. The free intellect will see as God might see, without a *here* and *now*, without hopes and fears, without the trammels of customary beliefs and traditional prejudices, calmly, dispassionately, in the sole and exclusive desire of knowledge—knowledge as impersonal, as purely contemplative, as it is possible for man to attain. Hence also the free intellect will value more the abstract and universal knowledge into which the accidents of private history do not enter, than the knowledge brought by the senses, and dependent, as such knowledge must be, upon an exclusive and personal point of view and a body whose sense-organs distort as much as they reveal.

The mind which has become accustomed to the freedom and impartiality of philosophic contemplation will preserve something of the same freedom and impartiality in the world of action and emotion. It will view its purposes and desires as parts of the whole, with the absence of insistence that results from seeing them as infinitesimal fragments in a world of which all the rest is unaffected by any one man's deeds. The impartiality which, in contemplation, is the unalloyed desire for truth, is the very same quality of mind which, in action, is justice, and in emotion is that universal love which can be given to all, and not only to those who are judged useful or admirable. Thus contemplation enlarges not only the objects of our thoughts, but also the objects of our actions and our affections: it makes us citizens of the universe, not only of one walled city at war with all the rest. In this citizenship of the universe consists man's true freedom, and his liberation from the thraldom of narrow hopes and fears.

Thus, to sum up our discussion of the value of philosophy: Philosophy is to be studied, not for the sake of any definite answers to its questions since no definite answers can, as a rule, be known to be true, but rather for the sake of the questions themselves; because these questions enlarge our conception of what is possible, enrich our intellectual imagination and diminish the dogmatic assurance which closes the mind against speculation; but above all because, through the greatness of the universe which philosophy contemplates, the mind also is rendered great, and becomes capable of that union with the universe which constitutes its highest good.

Reason and Religious Belief

W HAT CAN REASON TELL US about such vast topics as the origin of the universe and the existence and nature of God? Most of us have beliefs about these matters—beliefs derived from religious authorities or based on faith; but is there any way to demonstrate that these beliefs are reasonable or unreasonable? This question provides the unifying theme for the readings in Part II.

Traditional arguments for the existence of God are often divided into two groups: those whose premises are justified **a posteriori** (based on experience) and those whose premises are known **a priori** (independently of experience). In fact, however, only one mode of argument has ever purported to be wholly independent of experience— namely, the **ontological argument**, invented by St. Anselm in the eleventh century and defended in one form or another by Descartes, Spinoza, and Leibniz in the seventeenth century. (For Descartes's version of the argument, see his Fifth Meditation.) According to this argument, the very concept of God (or definition of the word *God*) entails that God must exist. If the argument is correct, anyone who has an idea of God—even if that person has no knowledge whatever of the kind derived from sense experience—has conclusive rational grounds for believing that God exists. The ontological argument still has defenders among philosophers of religion today, but among those who reject it, there is little agreement over precisely what is wrong with the argument. One classic and one recent discussion of the argument are included here. The brief but famous reply of Gaunilo, a monk who was a contemporary of Anselm's, appears here, and is complemented by an article that reflects some current thinking regarding the famous argument. William L. Rowe's essay sets forth Anselm's argument clearly, step by step (including steps that are only implicit in Anselm's own formulation), summarizes the three most important objections to the argument, and then presents his own criticism. Rowe concludes that the ontological argument is defective but is nevertheless a "work of genius," which, despite its apparent simplicity, raises philosophical questions about the nature of existence that are subtle and fascinating in their own right.

Other arguments for God's existence are often called a priori, but these always contain at least one premise that asserts some simple experiential fact. Factual premises summarizing some facet of our experience are found in the various versions of the **cosmological argument**—illustrated in this section by the selections from St. Thomas Aquinas and Samuel Clarke. For the first three of his "Five Ways," Aquinas begins each argument by citing a familiar fact of experience: Some things are in motion; there are causes and effects; things are generated and corrupted. He then tries to show that this fact can be explained only by the existence of God, because alternative explanations lead to logical absurdities. In his second article in this section, Rowe examines the cosmological argument in the form given it by Samuel Clarke and other seventeenth- and eighteenth-century philosophers. Put simply, the argument goes as follows:

1. Every being (that exists or ever did exist) is either a dependent being or a self-existent being.
2. Not every being can be a dependent being.
3. Therefore, there exists a self-existent being.

The argument clearly is valid; that is, *if* its premises are true, then its conclusion is true. But the premises, especially the second, are highly controversial. Rowe reviews the dialectic of the debate, pro and con, over the truth of the second premise, before cautiously concluding that the premise has not yet been conclusively shown to be true.

Both the ontological and the cosmological arguments are **deductive** in form; that is, they purport to demonstrate that if their premises are true, then their conclusions must necessarily be true. It is logically impossible for a valid deductive argument to have both true premises and false conclusion. The **teleological argument** (more commonly called "the argument from design") for God's existence is more modest. It argues not that its conclusion follows necessarily from its premises, but only that its premises establish a probability that the conclusion is true. It is therefore what logicians call an **inductive argument**. The famous argument from design is given classic formulations in William Paley's *Natural Theology* (1802), and by Cleanthes, a character in David Hume's *Dialogues Concerning Natural Religion* (1779). In an essay specially commissioned for this book, philosopher Michael Ruse provides a brief history of the argument(s) from design, along with a philosophical critique of classic and newer versions of the argument.

A standard reading of the argument from design interprets it as an inductive argument. More precisely, it is an argument by analogy, with the following form:

1. a, b, c, and d all have properties P and Q.
2. a, b, and c all have property R as well.
3. Therefore, d has property R too (probably).

The more similar d is to a, b, and c, the more probable is the conclusion.

Cleanthes' argument can be rendered as follows:

1. Boats, houses, watches, and the whole experienced world have such properties as "mutual adjustment of parts to whole" and "curious adapting of means to ends."
2. Boats, houses, and watches have the further property of having been produced by design.
3. Therefore, it is probable that the universe also has this further property—that it, too, was produced by design.

The conclusion of this argument—that a designer of the world exists—has the same logical role as a scientific hypothesis designed to explain the facts of experience, and must be accepted or rejected according to whether it meets the criteria of adequacy by which hypotheses are appraised in science and in everyday life.

In Hume's *Dialogues*, the case against the argument from design is stated with great force and ingenuity by Philo, probably speaking for Hume himself. The analogies cited by the argument, he claims, are weak, partly because we know only one small part of the universe and cannot with confidence infer from it the nature of the whole. Moreover, he argues, there are other equally plausible ways of accounting for the observed order in the world. One of these alternative explanations, called "The Epicurean Hypothesis" by Philo in Part VIII of the *Dialogues*, bears a striking resemblance to the Darwinian theory that biological adaptations are the result of chance variations and the survival of the fittest.

After canvassing some classic arguments for God's existence, and some replies, we come to what is perhaps the strongest of the arguments of the other side—namely, the **problem of evil**. Parts X and XI of Hume's *Dialogues* contain one of the most famous discussions of this problem, so central to religious belief. Here Philo concedes that if the existence of God has already been established by some a priori argument, then perhaps one can account for the appearance of evil in the world. But, he goes on to argue, one cannot infer the existence of an all-good and all-powerful being from the appearance of evil; that is, the former can hardly be an *explanation* of the latter.

In the subsection devoted entirely to the problem of evil, the great Russian novelist Fyodor Dostoevsky dramatically sets the stage for the philosophical discussion that follows by showing how the problem can arise in human experience. Dostoevsky's excerpt (from his novel *The Brothers Karamazov*) is complemented by two sets of contemporary discussions of this problem.

The first reading is focused on the so-called *logical problem of evil*. J. L. Mackie's now classic critique of theism is perhaps the best-known presentation of this problem. Mackie claims that the idea of an all-powerful, all-knowing, and all-good God is logically incoherent, given the existence of evil in our world. Logically speaking, claims Mackie, a perfect God is one who is (among other things) able and willing to eradicate evil. Since evil exists, God either does not exist or does exist but is not perfect. In short, the very idea of an omnipotent, omniscient, and perfectly good God logically requires that any such being eliminate evil. So it is logically incoherent to suppose that a perfect God can coexist with evil.

We next offer a reply on behalf of theism by Peter van Inwagen. Van Inwagen offers what is known as a *defense*—an effort to construct a plausible explanation of the world's ills on the assumption that a just God exists. In other words, van Inwagen begins not by arguing for God's existence, or for why it is positively morally good to allow the sufferings we see around us, but rather by trying to show that if we assume God's existence, then there are intelligible, reasonable possibilities that can account for the breadth of the harm that humans and animals suffer in our world. Van Inwagen's preferred possibility relies on the so-called **free will defense**. **Moral evil** (wickedness), according to a predominant strain of Christian teaching, is a necessary by-product of human free will—indeed, the price we pay for freedom—and it is impossible, on this line of thought, for God to have created perfectly free creatures who always behave in a perfectly good way. God is a just and loving God, for He cared enough about us to endow us with something of very great value: free will. Being free, we sometimes make mistakes. The misery in this world is properly charged to our misdeeds, rather than God's culpability. A world with free will, and the suffering it sometimes engenders, is a better world than one in which human beings are mere automata.

B. C. Johnson takes direct aim at van Inwagen's kind of theodicy, finding no contradiction in the thought of beings perfectly free and perfectly virtuous. In a nutshell, Johnson's argument is that God could have created a world inhabited by such people. That world would have been far better than ours. Therefore, if God were perfect, he'd have created such a world. He didn't. Therefore, the perfect God of classical monotheism doesn't exist.

Some of Johnson's many critical arguments echo Mackie's skepticism, seeking to show that it is logically impossible for evil and a perfect God to coexist. But Johnson also develops a variety of *evidential arguments from evil*. These do not assert that the idea of a perfect God is logically incoherent. There could be such a being. But, given the vast evidence we have of avoidable suffering, the odds are very good that God does not exist. This is thus an inductive argument; it seeks to establish that the probability of atheism is very high, given our evidence. On this skeptical view, God might yet exist, though our best evidence says that He doesn't.

We conclude this chapter with Michael Murray and Michael Rea's rigorous analysis of both the logical and evidential arguments from evil. After reconstructing the sharpest versions of both forms of these arguments, Murray and Rea carefully identify the central assumptions that underlie the anti-theists' arguments from evil. Though they do not pretend to offer the final word on these matters, Murray and Rea nicely identify the necessary steps that theists need to make in order to defend against these criticisms, while also showing what further work atheists need to do in order to adequately support their skepticism. Murray and Rea conclude with a helpful survey of the important theodicies that have been advanced by theists in an effort to show that the existence of evil is fully compatible with the existence of a just God.

What if it should turn out (as many philosophers now believe) that all traditional arguments for the existence of God are defective, or at least inconclusive? Would it follow that religious belief is unreasonable? Not necessarily. Some believers have claimed that the grounds of their belief have nothing to do with argument, but rather derive from a direct experience of deity (a "mystic experience"). These believers cannot prove that God exists, but they cannot prove that *they themselves* exist either. In both cases, they claim to know directly, by immediate confrontation, that something exists, and argue that further proof is unnecessary.

Although they have nothing to do with argument, mystical experiences might nevertheless be considered a kind of "evidence" for their attendant beliefs. The question posed by the final chapter of Part II, however, is whether beliefs based on no evidence at all can nonetheless be, in some circumstances, reasonable. In his selection here, Kelly James Clark defends an affirmative answer to this question. He argues that we already accept the credibility of certain nonreligious beliefs on the basis of no evidence at all, and it is quite reasonable to do so. If we criticize the religious believer for lack of evidence, then, to be consistent, we must abandon many eminently reasonable beliefs. Since, in the end, it would not be rational to abandon them, it wouldn't be rational for the theist to abandon her religious beliefs either.

W. K. Clifford argues emphatically for the negative and affirms his own rationalistic "ethic of belief"—namely, that "it is wrong always, everywhere, and for anyone to believe anything upon insufficient evidence." The seventeenth-century mathematician-philosopher Blaise Pascal had argued for the reasonableness of a kind of "bet" on God's existence even in the absence of all evidence, urging that it costs little to believe in God and act accordingly even if God in fact does not exist, whereas there is an infinite amount to lose by not believing if in fact God exists. Many Christian **fideists** (those whose belief is based on faith rather than argument), including William James, have found the unveiled appeal to self-interest in Pascal's "wager" to be a kind of embarrassment. James, in his famous "The Will to Believe," disowns Pascal but goes on to explain in his own way why belief in the absence of evidence can in some circumstances be reasonable. (Careful readers might well ask themselves, however, whether James's strict conditions for the proper exercise of "the will to believe" are in fact ever satisfied.) If there is one thing that James, the nineteenth-century Protestant, has in common with Pascal, the seventeenth-century Catholic, it is the conviction that the primary function of religious belief is not simply to allay philosophical curiosity about things. Both writers are aware that, to many, religious belief is a vital practical need, and each in his own way urges this to be taken into account when the reasonableness of belief is assessed.

The last pair of offerings in the philosophy of religion sound a decidedly skeptical note. Central to many religions is the idea of literally miraculous divine intervention. Many think that religious faith can receive rational support from warranted belief in miracles. Lawrence Shapiro, in an article written expressly for this book, explains what miracles are and must be if they are to play this central role. He sides with Hume and others in claiming that we never have better evidence for thinking that what we have experienced is a genuine miracle, as opposed to some phenomenon subject to scientific or psychological explanation. To the extent that our religious beliefs are grounded in the view that we (or others we know) have experienced miracles, our religious beliefs are unjustified. Simon Blackburn then returns to Pascal's wager and offers a contemporary critique of the religious belief based on the betting strategy that Pascal endorses.

CHAPTER 1

THE EXISTENCE AND NATURE OF GOD

1.1 The Ontological Argument, from *Proslogion*

ANSELM OF CANTERBURY

Anselm of Canterbury (1033–1109) was Archbishop of Canterbury.

CHAPTER II: THAT GOD TRULY EXISTS

Therefore, O God, you who give understanding to faith, provide for me so that I might understand, as much as you see fit, that you exist just as we believe you do and that you are what we believe you to be. Now we believe that you are something than which nothing greater can be conceived. But is it possible that something of such a nature does not really exist, since "the fool said in his heart: 'there is no God'"? But

Translation by Steven Nadler. © Steven Nadler, 2016.

certainly, even the fool himself, when he hears this phrase of mine: "something than which nothing greater can be conceived," understands what he hears; and what he understands is in his intellect, even if he does not understand that this thing actually exists. For it is one thing for an object to be in the intellect, and another thing to understand that that object exists. For when a painter conceives in advance what he will make, he has it in his intellect, but he does not yet think that it exists, because he has not yet made it. Once he has painted it, however, he both has it in his intellect and understands that it exists because he has now made it. Therefore, even the fool must concede that there exists in the intellect something than which nothing greater can be conceived, since he understands this when he hears it, and whatever is understood is in the intellect. And certainly the greatest conceivable being cannot exist solely in the intellect. For if it exists solely in the intellect, it can be conceived to exist in reality as well, which is greater. Therefore, if the greatest conceivable being exists only in the intellect, then the greatest conceivable being itself is that than which something greater can be conceived. But this clearly is impossible. Therefore, there cannot be any doubt that the greatest conceivable being exists both in the intellect and in reality.

CHAPTER III: THAT HE CANNOT BE THOUGHT NOT TO EXIST

And certainly He so truly exists, that He cannot be conceived not to exist. For something can be conceived to exist which cannot be conceived not to exist, and this is greater than something that can be conceived not to exist. For this reason, if the greatest conceivable being can be conceived not to exist, then the greatest conceivable being is not the greatest conceivable being, which is absurd. Therefore, there so truly exists a greatest conceivable being that he cannot even be conceived not to exist.

And this is you, O Lord our God. You therefore so truly exist, O Lord my God, that you cannot be conceived not to exist. And rightly so. For if some mind were able to conceive

something better than you, a creature would rise above its creator and would judge its creator, which is clearly absurd. Indeed, everything other than you alone can be conceived not to exist. Therefore, you alone of all things exist most truly, and therefore of all things have being to the highest degree, since any other thing does not exist so truly, and therefore has less existence. Why, then, did the fool say in his heart: "there is no God," since it is so obvious to any rational mind that you of all things exist to the highest degree? Why? Because he is stupid and a fool.

CHAPTER IV: HOW THE FOOL SAID IN HIS HEART WHAT CANNOT BE CONCEIVED

And yet how did he say in his heart what he was not able to conceive; or how could he not conceive what he said in his heart, since to say something in the heart and to conceive it are one and the same? Because if he truly, and yes he did truly, both conceive something because he said it in his heart and did not say it in his heart because he could not conceive it, then there is not only one way in which something is said to be in the heart or conceived. For in one sense something is conceived when a word signifying the thing is conceived; but in another sense, when the object itself is conceived. And so in the first sense God can be conceived not to exist, but certainly not in the second sense. Certainly no one who understands what God is can conceive that God does not exist, even if he should say these words in his heart, either without any meaning or with some strange meaning. For God is the greatest conceivable being. And whoever properly understands this at least understands that this same being so exists that even in thought it cannot fail to exist. Whoever, therefore, understands that God exists in this way cannot conceive that he does not exist.

I give thanks to you, good Lord, I give thanks to you, since what I first believed through your gift I now, through your illumination, so understand that even if I did not want to believe that you exist, still, I cannot fail to understand that you exist.

CHAPTER V: THAT GOD IS WHATEVER IT IS BETTER TO BE THAN NOT BE; AND THAT, EXISTING SOLELY THROUGH HIMSELF, HE MAKES ALL OTHER THINGS OUT OF NOTHING

What, then, are you, O Lord God, than whom nothing greater can be conceived? But what are you except that greatest being of all, existing solely through itself and making all other things out of nothing? For whatever is not this is less than the greatest that might be conceived. But this cannot be conceived about you. What goodness, therefore, is lacking to the supreme good, through which every good exists? You are thus just, truthful, happy, and whatever else it is better to be than not be. For it is better to be just than unjust, happy than unhappy.

1.2 On Behalf of the Fool

GAUNILO OF MARMOUTIERS

Gaunilo was an eleventh-century Benedictine monk whose fame rests on his critique of Anselm's ontological argument.

WHAT SOMEONE, ON BEHALF OF THE FOOL, RESPONDS TO THESE ARGUMENTS

To someone who either doubts or denies that there exists any such being than which nothing greater can be thought, it is said [by Anselm] that the existence of this being is proved in the following way: First, the very one who denies or doubts the existence of this being already has the being in his intellect since upon hearing it spoken of, he understands what it is said. Further, it is necessary that the being which he understands not only exists in his intellect, but also in reality. This is proved in the following way: To exist also in reality is greater than existing only in the intellect. So, if it were to exist only in the intellect, then whatever also existed in reality would be greater than it. And, thus, that which is greater than all others would be less than something and it would not be greater than all others. This is clearly a contradiction. Therefore, this conclusion is necessary: the being greater than all others, which has already been proved to exist in the intellect, does not exist only in the intellect, rather it also exists in reality—otherwise, it could not be greater than all others.

The doubter or denier can perhaps make the following reply [in response to the argument above]: The being than which nothing greater can be thought is claimed to exist in my intellect only because of the mere reason that I understand what is said. By the same reasoning, could I not also be said to have in my intellect all kind of false things which in no way exist in themselves since if someone were to speak of them I would be able to understand whatever he said?

Suppose that perhaps it is established that this being is such that it cannot exist in thought in the same way as all manner of false and unreal things. Therefore, I am not said to *think* or to have in *thought* this being of which I have heard. Rather, I am said to *understand* it or to have it in my *intellect* since I cannot think of it in any way,

Translation by Gloria Frost. © Gloria Frost, 2016.

except by understanding (i.e., by comprehending with certainty) that it exists in reality.

But if this were the case, the first difficulty is this: there would be no difference between having a thing in one's intellect at one time, and then understanding at a later time that the thing exists, as happens in the case of a painting, which exists first in the mind of the painter, and then later as a finished product. Secondly, it is nearly impossible to believe that when this being is spoken of and heard of, it is not able to be thought not to exist in the way that even God can be thought not to exist. For if this were the case, why was your whole argument addressed to someone who denies or doubts that such a being exists? Lastly, it must be proved to me by some compelling argument that this being is such that when it is thought of, the intellect immediately apprehends with certainty its indubitable existence. This is not proven to me by the claim that the being exists in my intellect *since* I understood what I heard spoken about it. For I still think that in a similar way all kinds of unreal and even false things would be able to exist in my intellect when I heard them spoken of by someone whose words I have understood. Those false and unreal things would exist in my intellect even more so if I—who do not yet believe that this being exists—were to be deceived into believing that those things exist, as often happens.

Accordingly, the example of the painter, who already has in his intellect the picture he is going to paint, does not adequately support your argument. For that picture, before it is made, exists in the painter's art; and any such thing in the art of a craftsman is nothing other than a part of his intelligence. Augustine says: "When a carpenter is going to make a chest, he first has it in his art. The chest which he makes is not alive; but the chest which is in his art is alive because the soul of the craftsman, in which all of these things exist before they are made, is alive." Now are these things alive in the living soul of the craftsman for any reason other than the fact that they are nothing but the knowledge and intelligence of his soul? But in contrast, except for those things which pertain to the nature of the mind itself, every true thing when heard of or thought of is apprehended by the intellect, and without a doubt the true thing is distinct from the intellect which understands it. Therefore, even if it were true that there exists something than which a greater cannot be thought, nevertheless when it was heard of and understood it would not be like a picture which exists in the intellect of the painter before it is painted.

There is another argument, mentioned earlier, which adds to this one: When I hear of that being which is greater than all others which can be thought (which, it is claimed, can be nothing other than God himself), I am not able to think of this being or to have it in my intellect by making reference to the genus or species of a thing known to me—just as I am, likewise, unable to think of God himself (whom for this same reason, I am able to think of as not existing). For I am neither acquainted with the very being itself nor am I able to know it through being acquainted with another being like it, since even you maintain that there cannot be anything else like it.

Suppose I were to hear something said about a man unknown by me and whom I was not even sure existed. Through specific or general knowledge of what a man is or what men are, I would still be able to think of this man by referring to the real thing which a man is. And if it should happen that the one who told me about this man was lying, and in fact, that man whom I thought of does not exist, it is nevertheless still the case that my thought of him relied on a reference to real a thing—not a real thing which is that very man, but rather the real thing which any man is. But when I hear spoken the words "God" or "something greater than all others," I am not able to have them in my thought or intellect in the same way as this false thing [i.e., that unreal man]. I was able to think of that false thing by making reference to a real thing known to me. But I can only think of "God" or "something greater than all others" on the basis of words alone; and relying on words alone, one is scarcely or never able to think of any true thing. Indeed when one thinks of a true thing on the basis of words alone, one thinks not so much about the word itself (which no doubt is a real thing, i.e., the sound of the letters or syllables) but more so about the heard word's meaning. But one cannot think of "God" or "something greater than all others" as someone who knows the meaning of a word usually does, namely by thinking of a real thing or a true thing existing in one's thought. Rather, in this case, one thinks in the manner of one who does not know a word's meaning: he thinks only of the impression the hearing of the word made on his mind and he tries to imagine its meaning. It would be amazing if he were ever able to reach the truth of what the word means in this way. Therefore, when I hear and understand one speaking about "something greater than all others which can be thought," in this way—and no other way—do I have it in my intellect. All of this is said against the claim that the supreme nature already exists in my intellect.

Then this further argument is given to me [by Anselm]: This being necessarily exists in reality since if it did not exist, whatever does exist in reality would be greater than it, and for this reason, that which was already proven to exist in the intellect would not be greater than all others. To this argument, I respond: If we are to say that a thing which cannot even be thought on the basis of the true nature of any real thing exists in the intellect, then I do not deny that this being exists in my intellect. Since one cannot derive from this supposition the further conclusion that this being also exists in reality, I will not concede to the being's real existence until it is proved to me by an indubitable argument.

And when he says that this being exists [in reality] because otherwise that which is greater than all others would not be greater than all others, he does not pay enough attention to the person to whom he is speaking. For I do not yet admit—in fact I doubt or even deny—that this being is greater than any real thing. Nor do I accord to that being any existence except for the kind of existence (if it is to be called "existence") which an unknown thing has when the mind imagines it on the basis of hearing words spoken about it. How, then, is it proved to *me* that this greatest being exists as a real thing *because* it is apparent that the being is greater than all others? For I still doubt or even deny that this is apparent—indeed so much so that I say that this "greater" being does not even exist in my intellect or thought in the way in which many doubtful and uncertain things do. First it must be made certain to me that this greatest being truly exists somewhere; and only then, will the fact that it is greater than all others prove to me without doubt that it also subsists in itself.

For example, some people say that there is an island somewhere in the ocean. Some call it "Lost Island" because of the difficulty—or rather the impossibility—of finding what does not exist. According to the fable, the island gives forth an uncountable abundance of all riches and delights, and is even more plentiful than the Isles of the Blessed. Since it has no owner or inhabitant, it wholly surpasses every land inhabited by men in its abundance of riches. Suppose that someone were to tell all of this to me. I would easily understand what is said, as there is nothing difficult in it. But if he were to then say, as if it logically followed: You can no more doubt that the island surpassing all other lands truly exists somewhere in reality. For you do not doubt that it exists in your intellect. Because it is more excellent to exist not merely in the intellect, but also in reality; therefore the island must necessarily exist in reality. For if it did not, every other land which exists in reality would be more excellent than it. And, so this most excellent island, which you already understood, would not be most excellent. If he were to try to prove to me with these arguments that one should no longer doubt that this island truly exists, then I would think he were joking or I would not know who to judge as the most foolish—either me, if I were to concede to him, or him, if he were to think that he proved the island's existence with some degree of certainty. For he would first have to show that the island's excellence is in my intellect in the way in which a real, undoubtedly existing thing is and not in any way as how a false or uncertain thing is.

The fool might make these responses to the arguments brought against him at the outset: When it is next asserted that "this greatest being is such that it cannot even be thought not to exist, and this in turn is proved by the claim that otherwise it would not be greater than all others"; the fool can make the very same response and say, "When did I say that such a being—i.e., one which is greater than all others—exists in reality, so that from this claim it could be proved to me that it exists so greatly that it cannot even be thought not to exist?" For first it must be proved by some most certain argument that there exists some highest nature—i.e., one that is greater and better than all others which exist—so that from this we can go on to prove all of the qualities which a being greater and better than all others must necessarily have. But when it is said that this *cannot be thought* not to exist, perhaps it would be better to say that it *cannot be understood* not to exist or even to be capable of not existing. For according to the strict meaning of the word [i.e., to understand], false things cannot be understood—but they are able to be thought in a way, just as the fool is able to think that God does not exist.

Now, I also know most certainly that I exist, but nevertheless I know that I am able not to exist. I know with absolute certainty that the highest being, namely God, both exists and is not capable of not existing. I do not know whether I am able to think of myself as not existing while I know with certainty that I exist. But if I am able to do this, why couldn't I also do it with whatever other thing which I know to exist with the same certainty? And if I am not able to this, then being "unable to be thought not to exist" will not be a unique feature proper to God alone.

The rest of that book is argued so truthfully, so clearly, and magnificently, full of so much that is useful, and fragrant with the scent of holy and pious affection, that it should in no way be scorned because of the claims in the beginning which are indeed rightly sensed, but less firmly argued. Rather, those claims should be argued more compellingly, and then the whole book can be received with great honor and praise.

1.3 The Ontological Argument

WILLIAM L. ROWE

William L. Rowe teaches philosophy at Purdue University. He is a distinguished authority in the philosophy of religion.

Arguments for the existence of God are commonly divided into a posteriori and a priori arguments. An a posteriori argument depends on a principle or premise that can be known only by means of our experience of the world. An a priori argument, on the other hand, purports to rest on principles which can be known independently of our experience of the world, just by reflecting on and understanding them. Of the three major arguments for the existence of God—the Cosmological, Teleological, and Ontological—only the last is entirely a priori. In the Cosmological argument one starts from some simple fact about the world, such as the fact that it contains things which are caused to exist by other things. In the Teleological argument a somewhat more complicated fact about the world serves as a starting point: the fact that the world exhibits order and

From ROWE, Philosophy of Religion, 1E. © 1978 Cengage Learning.

design. In the Ontological argument, however, one begins simply with a concept of God.

I

It is perhaps best to think of the Ontological argument as a family of arguments, each member of which begins with a concept of God, and by appealing only to a priori principles, endeavors to establish that God actually exists. Within this family of arguments the most important historically is the argument set forth by Anselm in the second chapter of his *Proslogium* (A Discourse).[1] Indeed, the Ontological argument begins with chapter II of Anselm's *Proslogium*. In an earlier work, *Monologium* (A Soliloquy), Anselm had endeavored to establish the existence and nature of God by weaving together several versions of the Cosmological argument. In the Preface to *Proslogium* Anselm remarks that after the publication of *Monologium* he began to search for a single argument which alone would establish the existence and nature of God. After much strenuous but unsuccessful effort, he reports that he sought to put the project out of his mind in order to turn to more fruitful tasks. The idea, however, continued to haunt him until one day the proof he had so strenuously sought became clear to his mind. Anselm sets forth this proof in the second chapter of *Proslogium*.

Before discussing Anselm's argument in step-by-step fashion, there are certain concepts that will help us understand some of the central ideas of the argument. Suppose we draw a vertical line in our imagination and agree that on the left side of our line are all the things which exist, while on the right side of the line are all the things which don't exist. We might then begin to make a list of some of the things on both sides of our imaginary line, as follows:

Things Which Exist	Things Which Don't Exist
The Empire State Building	The Fountain of Youth
The planet Mars	The Abominable Snowman
Dogs	Unicorns

Now each of the things (or sorts of things) listed thus far has (have) the following feature: it (they) logically might have been on the other side of the line. The Fountain of Youth, for example, is on the right side of the line, but *logically* there is no absurdity in the idea that it might have been on the left side of the line. Similarly, although dogs do exist, we surely can imagine without logical absurdity that they might not have existed, that they might have been on the right side of the line. Let us then record this feature of the things thus far listed by introducing the idea of a *contingent thing* as a thing that logically might have been on the other side of the line from the side it actually is on. The planet Mars and the Abominable Snowman are contingent things, even though the former happens to exist and the latter does not.

Suppose we add to our list the phrase "the object which is completely round and completely square at the same time" on the right side of our line. The round square, however, unlike the other things thus far listed on the right side of our line, is something that *logically could not* have been on the left side of the line. Noting this, let us introduce the idea of an *impossible thing* as a thing that is on the right side of the line and logically could not have been on the left side of the line.

Looking again at our list, we wonder if there is anything on the left side of our imaginary line which, unlike the things thus far listed on the left side, *logically could not* have been on the right side of the line. At this point we don't have to answer this question, but it is useful to have a concept to apply to any such things, should there be any. Accordingly, let us say that a *necessary thing* is a thing on the left side of our imaginary line and logically could not have been on the right side of the line.

Finally, a *possible thing* is any thing that is either on the left side of our imaginary line or logically might have been on the left side of the line. Possible things, then, will be all those things that are not impossible things—that is, all those things that are either contingent or necessary. If there are no necessary things, then all possible things will be contingent and all contingent things will be possible. If there is a necessary thing, however, then there will be a possible thing which is not contingent.

Armed with these concepts, we can clarify certain important distinctions and ideas in Anselm's thought. The first of these is his distinction between *existence in the understanding* and *existence in reality*. Anselm's notion of existence in reality is the same as our notion of existence; that is, being on the left side of our imaginary line. Since the Fountain of Youth is on the right side of the line, it does not exist in reality. The things which exist are, to use Anselm's phrase, the things which exist in reality. Anselm's notion of existence in the understanding, however, is not the same as any idea we normally employ. When we think of a certain thing, say the Fountain of Youth, then that thing, on Anselm's view, exists in the understanding. Also, when we think of an existing thing like the Empire State Building, it, too, exists in the understanding. So some of the things on both sides of our imaginary line exist in the understanding, but only those on the left side of our line exist in reality. Are there any things that don't exist in the understanding? Undoubtedly there are, for there are things, both existing and non-existing, of which we have not really thought. Now suppose I assert that the Fountain of Youth does not exist. Since to meaningfully deny the existence of something I have to have that thing in mind, I have to think of it, it follows on Anselm's view that whenever someone asserts that some thing does not exist, that thing *does* exist in the understanding.[2] So in asserting that the Fountain of Youth does not exist, I imply that the Fountain of Youth does exist in the understanding. And in asserting that it does not exist I have asserted (on Anselm's view) that it does not exist in reality. This means that my simple assertion amounts to the somewhat more complex claim that the Fountain of Youth exists in the understanding but does not exist in reality—in short, that the Fountain of Youth exists *only* in the understanding.

We can now understand why Anselm insists that anyone who hears of God, thinks about God, or even denies the existence of God is, nevertheless, committed to the view that God exists in the understanding. Also, we can understand why Anselm treats what he calls "the fool's claim" that God does not exist as the claim that God exists *only* in the understanding—that is, that God exists in the understanding but does not exist in reality.

In *Monologium* Anselm sought to prove that among those beings which do exist there is one which is the greatest, highest, and the best. But in *Proslogium* he undertakes to prove that among those beings which exist there is one which is not just the greatest among existing beings, but is such that no conceivable being is greater. We need to distinguish these two ideas: (1) a being than which *no existing being* is greater, and (2) a being than which *no conceivable being* is greater. If the only things in existence were a stone, a frog, and a man, the last of these would satisfy our first idea but not our second—for we can conceive of a being (an angel or God) greater than a man. Anselm's idea of God, as he expresses it in *Proslogium* II, is the same as (2) above; it is the idea of "a being than which nothing greater can be conceived." It will facilitate our understanding of Anselm's argument if we make two slight changes in the way he has expressed his idea of God. For his phrase I shall substitute the following: "*the* being than which none greater *is possible*."[3] This idea says that if a certain being is God then no *possible being* can be greater than it, or conversely, if a certain being is such that it is even *possible* for there to be a being greater than it, then that being is not God. What Anselm proposes to prove, then, is that the being than which none greater is possible exists in reality. If he proves this he will have proved that God, as he conceives of Him, exists in reality.

But what does Anselm mean by "greatness"? Is a building, for example, greater than a man? In *Monologium,* chapter II, Anselm remarks: "But I do not mean physically great, as a material object is great, but that which, the greater it is, is the better or the more worthy—wisdom, for instance." Contrast wisdom with size. Anselm is saying that wisdom is something that contributes to the greatness of a thing. If a thing comes to have more wisdom than it did before then (given that its other characteristics remain the same), that thing has become a greater, better, more worthy thing than it was. Wisdom, Anselm is saying, is a great-making quality. However, the mere fact that something increases in size (physical greatness) does not make that thing a better thing than it was before, so size is not a great-making quality. By "greater than" Anselm means "better than," "superior to," or "more worthy than," and he believes that some characteristics, like wisdom and moral goodness, are great-making characteristics in that anything which has them is a *better thing* than it would be (other characteristics of it remaining the same) were it to lack them.

We come now to what we may call the *key idea* in Anselm's Ontological argument. Anselm believes that *existence in reality is a great-making quality*. Does Anselm mean that anything that exists is a greater thing than anything that doesn't? Although he does not ask or answer the question, it is perhaps reasonable to believe that Anselm did not mean this. When he discusses wisdom as a great-making quality he is careful not to say that any wise thing is better than any unwise thing—for he recognizes that a just but unwise man might be a better being than a wise but unjust man.[4] I suggest that what Anselm means is that anything that doesn't exist but might have existed (is on the right side of our line but might have been on the left) would have been a greater thing if it had existed (if it had been on the left side of our line). He is not comparing two different things (one existing and one not existing) and saying that the first is therefore greater than the second. Rather, he is talking about *one* thing and pointing out that if it does not exist but might have existed, then *it* would have been a greater thing if it had existed. Using Anselm's distinction between existence in the understanding and existence in reality, we may express the key idea in Anselm's reasoning as follows: If something exists only in the understanding but might have existed in reality, then it might have been greater than it is. Since the

Fountain of Youth, for example, exists only in the understanding but (unlike the round square) might have existed in reality, it follows by Anselm's principle that the Fountain of Youth might have been a greater thing than it is.

II

We can now consider the step-by-step development of Anselm's Ontological argument. I shall use the term "God" in place of the longer phrase "the being than which none greater is possible"—wherever the term "God" appears we are to think of it as simply an abbreviation of the longer phrase.

1. God exists in the understanding.

As we have noted, anyone who hears of the being than which none greater is possible is, on Anselm's view, committed to premise (1).

2. God might have existed in reality (God is a possible being).

Anselm, I think, assumes the truth of (2) without making it explicit in his reasoning. By asserting (2) I do not mean to imply that God does not exist in reality, but that, unlike the round square, God is a possible being.

3. If something exists only in the understanding and might have existed in reality, then it might have been greater than it is.

As we noted, this is the key idea in Anselm's Ontological argument. It is intended as a general principle, true of anything whatever.

Steps (1)–(3) constitute the basic premises of Anselm's Ontological argument. From these three items, Anselm believes, it follows that God exists in reality. But how does Anselm propose to convince us that if we accept (1)–(3) we are committed by the rules of logic to accept his conclusion that God exists in reality? Anselm's procedure is to offer what is called a *reductio ad absurdum* proof of his conclusion. Instead of showing directly that the existence of God follows from steps (1)–(3), Anselm invites us to *suppose* that God does not exist (i.e., that the conclusion he wants to establish is false) and then shows how this supposition, when conjoined with steps (1)–(3), leads to an absurd result, a result that couldn't possibly be true because it is contradictory. Since the supposition that God does not exist leads to an absurdity, that supposition must be rejected in favor of the conclusion that God does exist.

Does Anselm succeed in reducing the "fool's belief" that God does not exist to an absurdity? The best way to answer this question is to follow the steps of his argument.

4. Suppose God exists only in the understanding.

This supposition, as we saw earlier, is Anselm's way of expressing the belief that God does not exist.

5. God might have been greater than He is. (2, 4, and 3)[5]

Step (5) follows from steps (2), (4), and (3). Since (3), if true, is true of anything whatever, it will be true of God. Therefore, (3) implies that if God exists only in the understanding and might have existed in reality, then God might have been greater than He is. If so, then given (2) and (4), (5) must be true. For what (3) says when applied to God is that given (2) and (4), it follows that (5).

6. God is a being than which a greater is possible. (5)

Surely if God is such that He logically might have been greater, then He is such than which a greater is possible.

We can now appreciate Anselm's *reductio* argument. He has shown that if we accept steps (1)–(4), we must accept step (6). But (6) is unacceptable; it is the absurdity Anselm was after. By replacing "God" in (6) with the longer phrase it abbreviates, we see that (6) amounts to the absurd assertion:

7. The being than which none greater is possible is a being than which a greater is possible.

Now since steps (1)–(4) have led us to an obviously false conclusion, and if we accept Anselm's

basic premises (1)–(3) as true, then (4), the supposition that God exists only in the understanding, must be rejected as false. Thus we have shown that:

8. It is false that God exists only in the understanding.

But since premise (1) tells us that God does exist in the understanding and (8) tells us that God does not exist only there, we may infer that

9. God exists in reality as well as in the understanding. (1, 8)

III

Most of the philosophers who have considered this argument have rejected it because of a basic conviction that from the logical analysis of a certain idea or concept we can never determine that there exists in reality anything answering to that idea or concept. We may examine and analyse, for example, the idea of an elephant or the idea of a unicorn, but it is only by our experience of the world that we can determine that there exist things answering to our first idea and not to the second. Anselm, however, believes that the concept of God is utterly unique—from an analysis of this concept he believes that it can be determined that there exists in reality a being which answers to it. Moreover, he presents us with an argument to show that it can be done in the case of the idea of God. We can, of course, simply reject Anselm's argument on the grounds that it violates the basic conviction noted above. Many critics, however, have sought to prove more directly that it is a bad argument and to point out the particular step that is mistaken. Next we shall examine the three major objections that have been advanced by the argument's critics.

The first criticism was advanced by a contemporary of Anselm's, a monk named "Gaunilo," who wrote a response to Anselm entitled, "On Behalf of the Fool."[6] Gaunilo sought to prove that Anselm's reasoning is mistaken by applying it to things other than God, things which we know don't exist. He took as his example the island than which none greater is possible. No such island really exists. But, argues Gaunilo, if Anselm's reasoning were correct we could show that such an island really does exist. For since it is greater to exist than not to exist, if the island than which none greater is possible doesn't exist then it is an island than which a greater is possible. But it is impossible for the island than which none greater is possible to be an island than which a greater is possible. Therefore, the island than which none greater is possible must exist. About this argument Gaunilo remarks:

> If a man should try to prove to me by such reasoning that this island truly exists, and that its existence should no longer be doubted, either I should believe that he was jesting, or I know not which I ought to regard as the greater fool: myself, supposing I should allow this proof; or him, if he should suppose that he had established with any certainty the existence of this island.[7]

Gaunilo's strategy is clear: by using the very same reasoning Anselm employs in his argument, we can prove the existence of things we know don't exist. Therefore, Anselm's reasoning in his proof of the existence of God must be mistaken. In reply to Gaunilo, Anselm insisted that his reasoning applies only to God and cannot be used to establish the existence of things other than God. Unfortunately, Anselm did not explain just why his reasoning cannot be applied to things like Gaunilo's island.

In defense of Anselm against Gaunilo's objection, there are two difficulties in applying Anselm's reasoning to things like Gaunilo's island. The first derives from the fact that Anselm's principle that existence is a great-making quality was taken to mean that if something does not exist then it is not as great *a thing* (being) as it would have been had it existed. Now if we use precisely this principle in Gaunilo's argument, all we will prove is that if Gaunilo's island does not exist then the island than which none greater is possible is an island than which *a greater thing* is possible. But this statement is not an absurdity.

For the island than which no greater *island* is possible can be something than which *a greater thing* is possible—an unsurpassable island may be a surpassable thing. (A perfect man might be a greater thing than a perfect island.) Consequently, if we follow Anselm's reasoning exactly, it does not appear that we can derive an absurdity from the supposition that the island than which none greater is possible does not exist.

A second difficulty in applying Anselm's reasoning to Gaunilo's island is that we must accept the premise that Gaunilo's island is a possible thing. But this seems to require us to believe that some finite, limited thing (an island) might have unlimited perfections. It is not at all clear that this is possible. Try to think, for example, of a hockey player than which none greater is possible. How fast would he have to skate? How many goals would he have to score in a game? How fast would he have to shoot the puck? Could he ever fall down, be checked, or receive a penalty? Although the phrase, "the hockey player than which none greater is possible," seems meaningful, as soon as we try to get a clear idea of what such a being would be like we discover that we can't form a coherent idea of it all. For we are being invited to think of some limited, finite thing—a hockey player or an island—and then to think of it as exhibiting unlimited, infinite perfections. Perhaps, then, since Anselm's reasoning applies only to possible things, Anselm can reject its application to Gaunilo's island on the grounds that the island than which none greater is possible is, like the round square, an impossible thing.

By far the most famous objection to the Ontological argument was set forth by Immanuel Kant in the eighteenth century. According to this objection the mistake in the argument is its claim, implicit in premise (3), that existence is a quality or predicate that adds to the greatness of a thing. There are two parts to this claim: (1) existence is a quality or predicate, and (2) existence, like wisdom and unlike physical size, is a great-making quality or predicate. Someone might accept (1) but object to (2); the objection made famous by Kant, however, is directed at (1). According to this objection, existence is not a predicate at all. Therefore, since in its third premise Anselm's argument implies that existence *is* a predicate, the argument must be rejected.

The central point in the philosophical doctrine that existence is not a predicate concerns what we do when we ascribe a certain quality or predicate to something: for example, when we say of a man next door that he is intelligent, six feet tall, or fat. In each case *we* seem to assert or presuppose that there *exists* a man next door and then go on to ascribe to him a certain predicate— "intelligent," "six feet tall," or "fat." And many proponents of the doctrine that existence is not a predicate claim that this is a *general feature* of predication. They hold that when we ascribe a quality or predicate to anything we assert or presuppose that the thing exists and then ascribe the predicate to it. Now if this is so, then it is clear that existence cannot be a predicate which we may ascribe to or deny of something. For if it were a predicate, then when we assert of some thing (things) that it (they) exists (exist) we would be asserting or presupposing that it (they) exists (exist) and then going on to predicate existence of it (them). For example, if existence were a predicate, then in asserting "tigers exist" we would be asserting or presupposing that tigers exist and then going on to predicate existence of them. Furthermore, in asserting "dragons do not exist" we would be asserting or presupposing, if existence were a predicate, that dragons do exist and then going on to deny that existence attaches to them. In short, if existence were a predicate, the affirmative existential statement "tigers exist" would be a redundancy and the negative existential statement "dragons do not exist" would be contradictory. But clearly "tigers exist" is not a redundancy; and "dragons do not exist" is true and, therefore, not contradictory. What this shows, according to the proponents of Kant's objection, is that existence is not a genuine predicate.

According to the proponents of the above objection, when we assert that tigers exist and that dragons do not we are not saying that certain things (tigers) have and certain other things (dragons) do not have a peculiar predicate, *existence;* rather, we are saying something about the *concept* of a tiger and the *concept* of a dragon. We are saying that the concept of a tiger applies to something in the world and that the concept of a dragon does not apply to anything in the world.

Although this objection to the Ontological argument has been widely accepted, it is doubtful that it provides us with a conclusive refutation of the argument. It may be true that existence is not a predicate, that in asserting the existence of something we are not ascribing a certain predicate or attribute to that thing. But the arguments presented for this view seem to rest on mistaken or incomplete claims about the nature of predication. For example, the argument which we stated earlier rests on the claim that when we ascribe a predicate to anything we assert or presuppose that that thing exists. But this claim appears to be mistaken. In asserting that Dr. Doolittle is an animal lover I seem to be ascribing the predicate "animal lover" to Dr. Doolittle, but in doing so I certainly am not asserting or presupposing that Dr. Doolittle actually exists. Dr. Doolittle doesn't exist, but it is nevertheless true that he is an animal lover. The plain fact is that we can talk about and ascribe predicates to many things which do not exist and never did. Merlin, for example, no less than Houdini, was a magician, although Houdini existed but Merlin did not. If, as these examples suggest, the claim that whenever we ascribe a predicate to something we assert or presuppose that the thing exists is a false claim, then we will need a better argument for the doctrine that existence is not a predicate. There is some question, however, whether anyone has succeeded in giving a really conclusive argument for this doctrine.[8]

A third objection against the Ontological argument calls into question the premise that God might have existed in reality (God is a possible being). As we saw, this premise claims that the being than which none greater is possible is not an impossible object. But is this true? Consider the series of positive integers: 1, 2, 3, 4, etc. We know that any integer in this series, no matter how large, is such that a larger integer than it is possible. Therefore, the positive integer than which none larger is possible is an impossible object. Perhaps this is also true of the being than which none greater is possible. That is, perhaps no matter how great a being may be, it is possible for there to be a being greater than it. If this were so, then, like the integer than which none larger is possible, Anselm's God would not be a possible object. The mere fact that there are degrees of greatness, however, does not entitle us to conclude that Anselm's God is like the integer than which none larger is possible. There are, for example, degrees of size in angles—one angle is larger than another—but it is not true that no matter how large an angle is it is possible for there to be an angle larger than it. It is logically impossible for an angle to exceed four right angles. The notion of an angle, unlike the notion of a positive integer, implies a degree of size beyond which it is impossible to go. Is Anselm's God like a largest integer, and therefore impossible, or like a largest angle, and therefore possible? Some philosophers have argued that Anselm's God is impossible,[9] but the arguments for this conclusion are not very compelling. Perhaps, then, this objection is best construed not as proving that Anselm's God is impossible, but as raising the question whether any of us is in a position to know that the being than which none greater is possible is a possible object. For Anselm's argument cannot be a successful proof of the existence of God unless its premises aren't just true but are really *known* to be true. Therefore, if we do not know that Anselm's God is a possible object, then his argument cannot prove the existence of God to us, cannot enable us to know that God exists.

IV

Finally, I want to present a somewhat different critique of Anselm's argument, a critique suggested by the basic conviction noted earlier; namely that from the mere logical analysis of a certain idea or concept we can never determine that there exists in reality anything answering to that idea or concept.

Suppose someone comes to us and says:

> I propose to define the term "God" as *an existing, wholly perfect being*. Now since it can't be true that an existing, wholly perfect being does not exist, it can't be true that God, as I've defined Him, does not exist. Therefore, God must exist.

His argument appears to be a very simple Ontological argument. It begins with a particular idea or concept of God and ends by concluding that God, so conceived, must exist. What can we say in response? We might start by objecting to his definition, claiming: (1) that only predicates can be used to define a term, and (2) that existence is not a predicate. But suppose he is not impressed by this response—either because he thinks that no one has fully explained what a predicate is or proved that existence isn't one, or because he thinks that anyone can define a word in whatever way he pleases. Can we allow him to define the word "God" in any way he pleases and still hope to convince him that it will not follow from that definition that there actually exists something to which his concept of God applies? I think we can. Let us first invite him, however, to consider some concepts other than his peculiar concept of God.

Earlier we noted that the term "magician" may be applied both to Houdini and Merlin, even though the former existed and the latter did not. Noting that our friend has used "existing" as part of his definition of "God," suppose we agree with him that we can define a word in any way we please, and, accordingly, introduce the following definitions:

A "magican" is defined as *an existing magician*.

A "magico" is defined as a *non-existing magician*.

Here we have introduced two words and used "existing" or "non-existing" in their definitions. Now something of interest follows from the fact that "existing" is part of our definition of a "magican." For while it is true that Merlin was a *magician*, it is not true that Merlin was a *magican*. And something of interest follows from our including "non-existing" in the definition of a "magico"—it is true that Houdini was a *magician*, but it is not true that Houdini was a *magico*. Houdini was a *magician* and a *magican*, but not a *magico*; Merlin was a *magician* and a *magico*, but not a *magican*.

We have just seen that introducing "existing" or "non-existing" into the definition of a concept has a very important implication. If we introduce "existing" into the definition of a concept, it follows that no non-existing thing can exemplify that concept. And if we introduce "non-existing" into the definition of a concept, it follows that no existing thing can exemplify that concept. No non-existing thing can be a *magican*, and no existing thing can be a *magico*.

But must some existing thing exemplify the concept "magican?" No! From the fact that "existing" is included in the definition of "magican" it does not follow that some existing thing is a magican—all that follows is that no non-existing thing is a magican. If there were no magicans in existence there would be nothing to which the term "magican" would apply. This being so, it clearly does not follow merely from our definition of "magican" that some existing thing is a magican. Only if magicians exist will it be true that some existing thing is a magican.

We are now in a position to help our friend see that from the mere fact that "God" is defined as an existing, wholly perfect being it will not follow that some existing being is God. Something of interest does follow from his definition; namely that no non-existing being can be God. But whether some existing thing is God will depend entirely on whether some existing thing is a wholly perfect being. If no wholly perfect being exists there will be nothing to which his concept of God can apply. This being so, it clearly does not follow merely from his definition of "God" that some existing thing is God. Only if a wholly perfect being exists will it be true that God, as he conceives of Him, exists.

The implications of these considerations for Anselm's ingenious argument can now be

traced. Anselm conceives of God as a being than which none greater is possible. He then claims that existence is a great-making quality and something that has it is greater than it would have been had it lacked existence. Clearly then, no non-existing thing can exemplify Anselm's concept of God. For if we suppose that some non-existing thing exemplifies Anselm's concept of God and also suppose that that non-existing thing might have existed in reality (is a possible thing) then we are supposing that that non-existing thing (1) might have been a greater thing, and (2) is, nevertheless, a thing than which a greater is not possible. Thus far Anselm's reasoning is, I believe, impeccable. But what follows from it? All that follows from it is that no non-existing thing can be God (as Anselm conceives of God). All that follows is that given Anselm's concept of God, the proposition, "Some non-existing thing is God," cannot be true. But, as we saw earlier, this is also the case with the proposition, "Some non-existing thing is a magican." What remains to be shown is that some existing thing exemplifies Anselm's concept of God. What really does follow from his reasoning is that the only thing that logically could exemplify his concept of God is something which actually exists. And this conclusion is not without interest. But from the mere fact that nothing but an existing thing could exemplify Anselm's concept of God, it does not follow that some existing thing actually does exemplify his concept of God—no more than it follows from the mere fact that no non-existing thing can be a magican that some existing thing is a magican.[10]

There is, however, one major difficulty in this critique of Anselm's argument. This difficulty arises when we take into account Anselm's implicit claim that God is a possible thing. To see just what this difficulty is, let us return to the idea of a possible thing, which is any thing that either is on the left side of our imaginary line or logically might have been on the left side of the line. Possible things, then, will be all those things that, unlike the round square, are not impossible things. Suppose we concede to Anselm that

God, as he conceives of Him, is a possible thing. Now, of course, the mere knowledge that something is a possible thing does not enable us to conclude that that thing is an existing thing. Many possible things, like the Fountain of Youth, do not exist. But if something is a possible thing then it is either an existing thing or a non-existing thing. The set of possible things can be exhaustively divided into those possible things which actually exist and those possible things which do not exist. Therefore, if Anselm's God is a possible thing it is either an existing thing or a non-existing thing. We have concluded, however, that no non-existing thing can be Anselm's God; therefore, it seems we must conclude with Anselm that some actually existing thing does exemplify his concept of God.

To see the solution to this major difficulty we need to return to an earlier example. Let us consider again the idea of a "magican," an existing magician. It so happens that some magicians have existed—Houdini, the Great Blackstone, etc. But, of course, it might have been otherwise. Suppose, for the moment that no magicians have ever existed. The concept "magician" would still have application, for it would still be true that Merlin was a magician. But would any possible object be picked out by the concept of a "magican?" No, for no non-existing thing could exemplify the concept "magican." And on the supposition that no magicians ever existed, no existing thing would exemplify the concept "magican."[11] We then would have a coherent concept "magican" which would not be exemplified by any possible object at all. For if all the possible objects which are magicians are non-existing things, none of them would be a magican and, since no possible objects which exist are magicians, none of them would be a magican. Put in this way, our result seems paradoxical. We are inclined to think that only contradictory concepts like "the round square" are not exemplified by any possible things. The truth is, however, that when "existing" is included in or implied by a certain concept, it may be the case that no possible object does in fact exemplify that concept. For no possible object that doesn't exist will exemplify a concept like "magican" in which "existing" is included; and if there are no existing things which exemplify the other features included in the concept—for example, "being a magician" in the case of the concept "magican"—then no possible object that exists will exemplify the concept. Put in its simplest terms, if we ask whether any possible thing is a magican the answer will depend entirely on whether any existing thing is a magician. If no existing things are magicians then no possible things are magicans. Some possible object is a magican just in the case some actually existing thing is a magician.

Applying these considerations to Anselm's argument, we can find the solution to our major difficulty. Given Anselm's concept of God and his principle that existence is a great-making quality, it really does follow that the only thing that logically could exemplify his concept of God is something which actually exists. But, we argued, it doesn't follow from these considerations alone that God actually exists, that some existing thing exemplifies Anselm's concept of God. The difficulty we fell into, however, is that when we add the premise that God is a possible thing, that some possible object exemplifies his concept of God, it really does follow that God actually exists, that some actually existing thing exemplifies Anselm's concept of God. For if some possible object exemplifies his concept of God, that object is either an existing thing or a non-existing thing. But since no non-existing thing could exemplify Anselm's concept of God, it follows that the possible object which exemplifies his concept of God must be a possible object that actually exists. Therefore, given (1) Anselm's concept of God, (2) his principle that existence is a great-making quality, and (3) the premise that God, as conceived by Anselm, is a possible thing, it really does follow that Anselm's God actually exists. But we now can see that in granting Anselm the premise that God is a possible thing we have granted far more than we intended. All we thought we were conceding is that Anselm's concept of God, unlike the concept of a round square, is not contradictory or incoherent. But without realizing it we were in fact granting much more than this, as became apparent when we considered the idea of a magican. There is nothing contradictory in the idea of a magican, an existing magican. But in asserting that a magican is a possible thing we are, as we saw, directly implying that some existing thing is a magician. For if no existing thing is a magician, the concept of a magician will apply to no possible object whatever. The same point holds with respect to Anselm's God. Since Anselm's concept of God logically cannot apply to some non-existing thing, the only possible objects to which it could apply are possible objects which actually exist. Therefore, in granting that Anselm's God is a possible thing we are conceding far more than that his idea of God isn't incoherent or contradictory. Suppose, for example, that every existing being has some defect which it might not have had. Without realizing it we were denying this when we granted that Anselm's God is a possible being. If every existing being has a defect it might not have had, then every existing being might have been greater. But if every existing being might have been greater, then Anselm's concept of God will apply to no possible object whatever. Therefore, if we allow Anselm his concept of God and his principle that existence is a great-making quality, then in granting that God, as Anselm conceives of Him, is a possible being we will be granting much more than that his concept of God is not contradictory. We will be conceding, for example, that some existing thing is as perfect as it can be. The fact is that Anselm's God is a possible thing only if some *existing* thing is as perfect as it can be.

Our final critique of Anselm's argument is simply this. In granting that Anselm's God is a possible thing we are in fact granting that Anselm's God actually exists. But since the purpose of the argument is to prove to us that Anselm's God exists, we cannot be asked to grant as a premise a statement which is virtually equivalent to the conclusion that is to be proved. Anselm's concept of God may be coherent and his principle that existence is a great-making quality may

be true. But all that follows from this is that no non-existing thing can be Anselm's God. If we add to all of this the premise that God is a possible thing it will follow that God actually exists. But the additional premise claims more than that Anselm's concept of God isn't incoherent or contradictory. It amounts to the assertion that some existing being is supremely great. And since this is, in part, the point the argument endeavors to prove, the argument begs the question: it assumes the point it is supposed to prove.

If the above critique is correct, Anselm's argument fails as a proof of the existence of God. This is not to say, however, that the argument is not a work of genius. Perhaps no other argument in the history of thought has raised so many basic philosophical questions and stimulated so much hard thought. Even if it fails as a proof of the existence of God, it will remain as one of the high achievements of the human intellect.

NOTES

1. Some philosophers believe that Anselm sets forth a different and more cogent argument in chapter III of his *Proslogium*. For this viewpoint see Charles Hartshorne, *Anselm's Discovery* (LaSalle, Ill.: Open Court Publishing Co., 1965); and Norman Malcolm, "Anselm's Ontological Arguments," *The Philosophical Review* LXIX, No. 1 (January 1960), 41–62. For an illuminating account both of Anselm's intentions in *Proslogium II* and *III* and of recent interpretations of Anselm see Arthur C. McGill's essay "Recent Discussions of Anselm's Argument" in *The Many-faced Argument*, ed. John Hick and Arthur C. McGill (New York: The Macmillan Co., 1967), 33–110.

2. Anselm does allow that someone may assert the sentence "God does not exist" without having in his understanding the object or idea for which the word *God* stands (see *Proslogium*, chapter IV). But when a person does understand the object for which a word stands, then when he uses that word in a sentence denying the existence of that object he must have that object in his understanding. It is doubtful, however, that Anselm thought that incoherent or contradictory expressions like "the round square" stand for objects which may exist in the understanding.

3. Anselm speaks of "a being" rather than "the being" than which none greater can be conceived. His argument is easier to present if we express his idea of God in terms of "the being." Secondly, to avoid the psychological connotations of "can be conceived," I have substituted "possible."

4. See Anselm, *Monologium*, chapter XV.

5. The numbers in parentheses refer to the earlier steps in the argument from which the present step is derived.

6. Gaunilo's brief essay, Anselm's reply, and several of Anselm's major works, as translated by S. N. Deane, are collected in *Saint Anselm: Basic Writings* (LaSalle, Ill.: Open Court Publishing Co., 1962).

7. *Saint Anselm: Basic Writings*, 151.

8. Perhaps the most sophisticated presentation of the objection that existence is not a predicate is William P. Alston's "The Ontological Argument Revisited" in *The Philosophical Review*, 69 (1960), 452–474.

9. See, for example, C. D. Broad's discussion of the Ontological Argument in *Religion, Philosophy, and Psychical Research* (New York: Harcourt, Brace & World, 1953).

10. An argument along the lines just presented may be found in J. Shaffer's illuminating essay "Existence, Predication and the Ontological Argument," *Mind,* 71 (1962), 307–325.

11. I am indebted to Professor William Wainwright for bringing this point to my attention.

1.4 The Five Ways, from *Summa Theologica*

SAINT THOMAS AQUINAS

Saint Thomas Aquinas (1225–1274) is the philosopher whose teachings are most favored by the Roman Catholic Church.

The existence of God can be proved in five ways. The first and clearest way is based on motion. For it is certain, and confirmed by our senses, that some things in this world are moved. However, everything that is moved is moved by some other thing. For nothing is moved unless there is in it some potentiality for that toward which it is moved, whereas if a thing is a mover it is actually moving something. For to move something is nothing other than to bring it from potentiality to actuality. However, nothing can be brought from potentiality to actuality except through some being that is in actuality—just as something that is actually hot, like fire, makes wood, which is potentially hot, to be actually hot, and in this way moves and changes it. Now it is not possible for the same thing to be in actuality and in potentiality at one time and in the same respect, but only in different respects; for what is actually hot cannot be at the same time potentially hot, but it is at that time potentially cold. Therefore, it is impossible that something is, in the same respect and the same way, both mover and moved, or that it moves itself. Therefore, everything that is moved must be moved by something else. If, therefore, a mover is itself being moved, it too must be moved by something else, and that by something else as well. But this cannot go on to infinity, since then there would not be some first mover; and consequently neither could anything move some another thing, since subsequent movers do not move unless they are moved by a first mover, just as a staff moves only because it is moved by a hand. Therefore, it is necessary to arrive finally at some first mover which is itself not moved by anything, and this is understood by everyone to be God.

Translation by Steven Nadler. © Steven Nadler, 2016.

The second way is from the nature of efficient causes. For we find in observable things that there is an order of efficient causes. Nevertheless, we do not find—nor is it possible—that something is the efficient cause of itself; for then a thing would be prior to itself, which is impossible. However, it is not possible that efficient causes go on to infinity. This is because in any order of efficient causes, the first is the cause of the intermediate, and the intermediate is the cause of the last, whether the intermediate cause consists of many or only one. Now if the cause is removed, the effect is removed. Therefore, if there were no first efficient cause, there would not be any final or intermediate ones. But if the series of efficient causes should proceed to infinity, there would not be a first efficient cause, and so there would not be a final effect, nor intermediary efficient causes, which is clearly false. Therefore, it is necessary to posit some first efficient cause, which everyone calls God.

The third way derives from possibility and necessity, and goes as follows. We find among things certain ones that are possible to be and not to be, since they are found to be generated and corrupted, and consequently can possibly be and not be. However, it is impossible for all things that exist to be like this, since what might not exist, at some time does not exist. Therefore, if all things are such that they might not exist, then at some time there was nothing in existence. But if this is true, then even now there would be nothing, since what does not exist does not begin to exist except through something that does exist. Therefore, if at some time there was nothing, it was then impossible that something could begin to exist, and so now nothing would exist, which is clearly false. Thus, not all beings are merely possible beings; there must be something that is necessary. However, every necessary being either has some cause for its necessity or it does not. Now it is not possible that the series of necessary beings that have a cause for their necessity should proceed to infinity, as was shown in the case of efficient causes. Therefore, it is necessary to posit something that is necessary in itself—something that does not have some cause for its necessity but is the cause of the necessity of other things. Everyone calls this God.

The fourth way comes from the gradation that is found in things. For among things some are found to be more and others less good, true, noble, and so on in other such respects. But more and less are said of different things according to the different ways in which they approach something that is a maximum. Something is hotter which is closer to what is hottest. And so there is something that is most true, best, and most noble, and consequently something that is the highest being, for whatever is most true is the greatest in being, as it is said in [Aristotle's] Metaphysics II. However, what is called the greatest in some specific genus is the cause of all things in that genus, just as fire, which is the greatest heat, is the cause of all hot things, as is said in that book. Therefore, there is something that is for all beings the cause of their being, as well as of their goodness and other such perfections, and this we call God.

The fifth way derives from the governance of things. For we see that things that lack intelligence, like natural bodies, act for the sake of some end. This is apparent from the fact that they always or frequently act in the same way in order to obtain what is best. From this it is clear that they are directed to achieve an end; nor is this an accident. However, these things which do not have thought strive for an end only because they are directed by some knowing and intelligent being, like an arrow directed by an archer. Therefore, there is some intelligent being by whom all natural things are ordered toward their end, and we call this God.

1.5 A Modern Formulation
of the Cosmological Argument

SAMUEL CLARKE

Samuel Clarke (1675–1729), English theologian and philosopher, was one of the first to be greatly influenced by Isaac Newton's physics.

There has existed from eternity some one unchangeable and independent being. For since something must needs have been from eternity; as hath been already proved, and is granted on all hands: either there has always existed one unchangeable and *independent* Being, from which all other beings that are or ever were in the universe, have received their original; or else there has been an infinite succession of changeable and *dependent* beings, produced one from another in an endless progression, without any original cause at all. which latter supposition is so very absurd, that tho' all atheism must in its account of most things (as shall be shown hereafter) terminate in it, yet I think very few atheists ever were so weak as openly and directly to defend it. For it is plainly impossible and contradictory to itself. I shall not argue against it from the supposed impossibility of infinite succession, *barely and absolutely considered in itself;* for a reason which shall be mentioned hereafter: but, if we consider such an infinite progression, as *one* entire endless *series* of *dependent* beings; 'tis plain this whole *series* of beings can have no cause *from without,* of its existence; because in it are supposed to be included *all things* that are or ever were in the universe: and 'tis plain it can have no reason *within itself,* of its existence; because no one being in this infinite succession is supposed to be self-existent or *necessary* (which is the only ground or reason of existence of any thing, that can be imagined *within the thing itself,* as will presently more fully appear), but every one *dependent* on the foregoing; and where *no part* is necessary, 'tis manifest *the whole* cannot be necessary; absolute necessity of existence, not being an outward, relative, and accidental determination; but an inward and essential property of the nature of the thing which so exists. An infinite succession therefore of merely *dependent* beings, without any original independent cause; is a *series* of beings, that has neither necessity nor cause, nor any reason *at all* of its existence, neither *within itself* nor *from without:* that is, 'tis an express contradiction and impossibility; 'tis a supposing *something* to be *caused,* (because it's granted in every one of its stages of succession, not to be necessary and from itself); and yet that in the whole it is caused *absolutely by nothing:* Which every man knows is a contradiction to be done *in time;* and because duration in this case makes no difference, 'tis equally a contradiction to suppose it done from eternity: And consequently there must *on the contrary,* of necessity have existed from eternity, *some one* immutable and *independent* Being: Which, what it is, remains in the next place to be inquired.

From Samuel Clarke, *A Demonstration of the Being and Attributes of God* (1705), Part II.

1.6 The Cosmological Argument

WILLIAM L. ROWE

Since ancient times thoughtful people have sought to justify their religious beliefs. Perhaps the most basic belief for which justification has been sought is the belief that there is a God. The effort to justify belief in the existence of God has generally started either from facts available to believers and nonbelievers alike or from facts, such as the experience of God, normally available only to believers....We shall consider some major attempts to justify belief in God by appealing to facts supposedly available to any rational person, whether religious or not. By starting from such facts, theologians and philosophers have developed arguments for the existence of God, arguments which, they have claimed, prove beyond reasonable doubt that there is a God.

STATING THE ARGUMENT

Arguments for the existence of God are commonly divided into *a posteriori* arguments and *a priori* arguments. An *a posteriori* argument depends on a principle or premise that can be known only by means of our experience of the world. An *a priori* argument, on the other hand, purports to rest on principles all of which can be known independently of our experience of the world, by just reflecting on and understanding them. Of the three major arguments for the existence of God—the Cosmological, the Teleological, and the Ontological—only the last of these is entirely *a priori*. In the Cosmological Argument one starts from some simple fact about the world, such as that it contains things which are caused to exist by other things. In the Teleological Argument a somewhat more complicated fact about the world serves as a starting point, the fact that the world exhibits order and design. In the Ontological Argument, however, one begins

simply with a concept of God. In this chapter we shall consider the Cosmological Argument....

Before we state the Cosmological Argument itself, we shall consider some rather general points about the argument. Historically, it can be traced to the writings of the Greek philosophers, Plato and Aristotle, but the major developments in the argument took place in the thirteenth and in the eighteenth centuries. In the thirteenth century, Aquinas put forth five distinct arguments for the existence of God, and of these, the first three are versions of the Cosmological Argument.[1] In the first of these he started from the fact that there are things in the world undergoing change and reasoned to the conclusion that there must be some ultimate cause of change that is itself unchanging. In the second he started from the fact that there are things in the world that clearly are caused to exist by other things and reasoned to the conclusion that there must be some ultimate cause of existence whose own existence is itself uncaused. And in the third argument he started from the fact that there are things in the world which need not have existed at all, things which do exist but which we can easily imagine might not, and reasoned to the conclusion that there must be some being that had to be, that exists and could not have failed to exist. Now it might be objected that even if Aquinas' arguments do prove beyond doubt the existence of an unchanging changer, an uncaused cause, and a being that could not have failed to exist, the arguments fail to prove the existence of the theistic God. For the theistic God, as we saw, is supremely good, omnipotent, omniscient, and creator of but separate from and independent of the world. How do we know, for example, that the unchanging changer isn't evil or slightly ignorant? The answer to this objection is that the Cosmological Argument has two parts. In the first part the effort is to prove the existence of a special sort of being, for example, a being that could not have failed to exist, or a being that causes change in other things but is itself unchanging. In the second part of the argument the effort is to prove that the special sort of being whose existence has been established in the first part has, and must have, the features—perfect goodness, omnipotence, omniscience, and so on—which go together to make up the theistic idea of God. What this means, then, is that Aquinas' three arguments are different versions of only the first part of the Cosmological Argument. Indeed, in later sections of his *Summa Theologica* Aquinas undertakes to show that the unchanging changer, the uncaused cause of existence, and the being which had to exist are one and the same being and that this single being has all of the attributes of the theistic God.

We noted above that a second major development in the Cosmological Argument took place in the eighteenth century, a development reflected in the writings of the German philosopher, Gottfried Leibniz (1646–1716), and especially in the writings of the English theologian and philosopher, Samuel Clarke (1675–1729). In 1704 Clarke gave a series of lectures, later published under the title *A Demonstration of the Being and Attributes of God*. These lectures constitute, perhaps, the most complete, forceful, and cogent presentation of the Cosmological Argument we possess. The lectures were read by the major skeptical philosopher of the century, David Hume (1711–1776), and in his brilliant attack on the attempt to justify religion in the court of reason, his *Dialogues Concerning Natural Religion,* Hume advanced several penetrating criticisms of Clarke's arguments, criticisms which have persuaded many philosophers in the modern period to reject the Cosmological Argument. In our study of the argument we shall concentrate our attention largely on its eighteenth-century form and try to assess its strengths and weaknesses in the light of the criticisms which Hume and others have advanced against it.

The first part of the eighteenth-century form of the Cosmological Argument seeks to establish the existence of a self-existent being. The second part of the argument attempts to prove that the self-existent being is the theistic God, that is, has the features which we have noted to be basic elements in the theistic idea of God. We shall consider mainly the first part of the argument, for it is against the first part that philosophers from Hume to Russell have advanced very important objections.

In stating the first part of the Cosmological Argument we shall make use of two important concepts, the concept of a *dependent being* and the concept of a *self-existent being*. By "a dependent being" we mean a *being whose existence is accounted for by the causal activity of other things.* Recalling Anselm's division into the three cases: "explained by another," "explained by nothing," and "explained by itself," it's clear that a dependent being is a being whose existence is explained by another. By "a self-existent being" we mean *a being whose existence is accounted for by its own nature.* This idea…is an essential element in the theistic concept of God. Again, in terms of Anselm's three cases, a self-existent being is a being whose existence is explained by itself. Armed with these two concepts, the concept of a dependent being and the concept of a self-existent being, we can now state the first part of the Cosmological Argument.

1. Every being (that exists or ever did exist) is either a dependent being or a self-existent being.
2. Not every being can be a dependent being.

Therefore,

3. There exists a self-existent being.

Deductive Validity

Before we look critically at each of the premises of this argument, we should note that this argument is, to use an expression from the logician's vocabulary, *deductively valid*. To find out whether an argument is deductively valid we need only ask the question: If its premises were true would its conclusion have to be true? If the answer is yes, the argument is deductively valid. If the answer is no, the argument is deductively invalid. Notice that the question of the validity of an argument is entirely different from the question of whether its premises are in fact true. The following argument is made up entirely of false statements, but it is deductively valid.

1. Babe Ruth is the President of the U.S.
2. The President of the U.S. is from Indiana.

Therefore,

3. Babe Ruth is from Indiana.

The argument is deductively valid because even though its premises are false, if they were true its conclusion would have to be true. Even God, Aquinas would say, cannot bring it about that the premises of this argument are true and yet its conclusion is false, for God's power extends only to what is possible, and it is an absolute impossibility that Babe Ruth be the President, the President be from Indiana, and yet Babe Ruth not be from Indiana.

The Cosmological Argument (that is, its first part) is a deductively valid argument. If its premises are or were true its conclusion would have to be true. It's clear from our example about Babe Ruth, however, that the fact that an argument is deductively valid is insufficient to establish the truth of its conclusion. What else is required? Clearly that we know or have rational grounds for believing that the premises are true. If we know that the Cosmological Argument is deductively valid and can establish that its premises are true, we shall thereby have proved that its conclusion is true. Are, then, the premises of the Cosmological Argument true? To this more difficult question we must now turn.

PSR and the First Premise

At first glance the first premise might appear to be an obvious or even trivial truth. But it is neither obvious nor trivial. And if it appears to be obvious or trivial, we must be confusing the idea

of a selfexistent being with the idea of a being that is not a dependent being. Clearly, it is obviously true that any being is either a dependent being (explained by other things) or it is not a dependent being (not explained by other things). But what our premise says is that any being is either a dependent being (explained by other things) or it is a self-existent being (explained by itself). Consider again Anselm's three cases.

a. Explained by another
b. Explained by nothing
c. Explained by itself

What our first premise asserts is that each being that exists (or ever did exist) is either of sort *a* or of sort *c*. It denies that any being is of sort *b*. And it is this denial that makes the first premise both significant and controversial. The obvious truth we must not confuse it with is the truth that any being is either of sort *a* or not of sort *a*. While this is true it is neither very significant nor controversial.

Earlier we saw that Anselm accepted as a basic principle that whatever exists has an explanation of its existence. Since this basic principle denies that any thing of sort *b* exists or ever did exist, it's clear that Anselm would believe the first premise of our Cosmological Argument. The eighteenth-century proponents of the argument also were convinced of the truth of the basic principle we attributed to Anselm. And because they were convinced of its truth, they readily accepted the first premise of the Cosmological Argument. But by the eighteenth century, Anselm's basic principle had been more fully elaborated and had received a name, "the Principle of Sufficient Reason." Since this principle (PSR, as we shall call it) plays such an important role in justifying the premises of the Cosmological Argument, it will help us to consider it for a moment before we continue our enquiry into the truth or falsity of the premises of the Cosmological Argument.

The Principle of Sufficient Reason (PSR), as it was expressed by both Leibniz and Samuel Clarke, is a very general principle and is best understood as having two parts. In its first part it is simply a restatement of Anselm's principle that there must be an explanation of the *existence* of any being whatever. Thus if we come upon a man in a room, PSR implies that there must be an explanation of the fact that that particular man exists. A moment's reflection, however, reveals that there are many facts about the man other than the mere fact that he exists. There is the fact that the man in question is in the room he's in, rather than somewhere else, the fact that he is in good health, and the fact that he is at the moment thinking of Paris, rather than, say, London. Now the purpose of the second part of PSR is to require an explanation of these facts as well. We may state PSE, therefore, as the principle that *there must be an explanation (a) of the existence of any being, and (b) of any positive fact whatever*. We are now in a position to study the role this very important principle plays in the Cosmological Argument.

Since the proponent of the Cosmological Argument accepts PSR in both its parts, it is clear that he will appeal to its first part, PSRa, as justification for the first premise of the Cosmological Argument. Of course, we can and should enquire into the deeper question of whether the proponent of the argument is rationally justified in accepting PSR itself. But we shall put this question aside for the moment. What we need to see first is whether he is correct in thinking that *if* PSR is true then both of the premises of the Cosmological Argument are true. And what we have just seen is that if only the first part of PSR, that is, PSRa is true, the first premise of the Cosmological Argument will be true. But what of the second premise of the Argument? For what reasons does the proponent think that it must be true?

The Second Premise

According to the second premise, not every being that exists can be a dependent being, that is, can have the explanation of its existence in some other being or beings. Presumably, the proponent of the argument thinks there is something fundamentally wrong with the idea that every

being that exists is dependent, that each existing being was caused by some other being which in turn was caused by some other being, and so on. But just what does he think is wrong with it? To help us in understanding his thinking, let's simplify things by supposing that there exists only one thing now, A_1, a living thing perhaps, that was brought into existence by something else A_2, which perished shortly after it brought A_1 into existence. Suppose further that A_2 was brought into existence in similar fashion some time ago by A_3, and A_3 by A_4, and so forth back into the past. Each of these beings is a *dependent* being, it owes its existence to the preceding thing in the series. Now if nothing else ever existed but these beings, then what the second premise says would not be true. For if every being that exists or ever did exist is an A and was produced by a preceding A, then every being that exists or ever did exist would be dependent and, accordingly, premise two of the Cosmological Argument would be false. If the proponent of the Cosmological Argument is correct there must, then, be something wrong with the idea that every being that exists or did exist is an A and that they form a causal series, A_1 caused by A_2, A_2 caused by A_3, A_3 caused by A_4,...A_n caused by A_{n+1}. How does the proponent of the Cosmological Argument propose to show us that there is something wrong with this view?

A popular but mistaken idea of how the proponent tries to show that something is wrong with the view that every being might be dependent is that he uses the following argument to reject it.

1. There must be a *first being* to start any causal series.
2. If every being were dependent there would be no *first being* to start the causal series.

Therefore,

3. Not every being can be a dependent being.

Although this argument is deductively valid and its second premise is true, its first premise overlooks the distinct possibility that a causal series might be *infinite,* with no first member at all.

Thus if we go back to our series of *A* beings, where each *A* is dependent, having been produced by the preceding *A* in the causal series, it's clear that if the series existed it would have no first member, for every *A* in the series there would be a preceding *A* which produced it, *ad infinitum*. The first premise of the argument just given assumes that a causal series must stop with a first member somewhere in the distant past. But there seems to be no good reason for making that assumption.

The eighteenth-century proponents of the Cosmological Argument recognized that the causal series of dependent beings could be infinite, without a first member to start the series. They rejected the idea that every being that is or ever was is dependent not because there would then be no first member to the series of dependent beings, but because there would then be no explanation for the fact that there are and have always been dependent beings. To see their reasoning let's return to our simplification of the supposition that the only things that exist or ever did exist are dependent beings. In our simplification of that supposition only one of the dependent beings exists at a time, each one perishing as it produces the next in the series. Perhaps the first thing to note about this supposition is that there is no individual *A* in the causal series of dependent beings whose existence is unexplained—A_1 is explained by A_2, A_2 by A_3, and A_n by A_{n+1}. So the first part of PSR, PSRa, appears to be satisfied. There is no particular being whose existence lacks an explanation. What, then, is it that lacks an explanation, if every particular *A* in the causal series of dependent beings has an explanation? It is the *series itself* that lacks an explanation. Or, as I've chosen to express it, *the fact that there are and have always been dependent beings*. For suppose we ask why it is that there are and have always been *A*s in existence. It won't do to say that *A*s have always been producing other *A*s—we can't explain why there have always been *A*s by saying there always have been *A*s. Nor, on the supposition that only *A*s have ever existed, can we explain the fact that there have always been *A*s by

appealing to something other than an *A*—for no such thing would have existed. Thus the supposition that the only things that exist or ever existed are dependent things leaves us with a fact for which there can be no explanation; namely, the fact that there are and have always been dependent beings.

Questioning the Justification of the Second Premise

Critics of the Cosmological Argument have raised several important objections against the claim that if every being is dependent the series or collection of those beings would have no explanation. Our understanding of the Cosmological Argument, as well as of its strengths and weaknesses, will be deepened by a careful consideration of these criticisms.

The first criticism is that the proponent of the Cosmological Argument makes the mistake of treating the collection or series of dependent beings as though it were itself a dependent being, and, therefore, requires an explanation of its existence. But, so the objection goes, the collection of dependent beings is not itself a dependent being any more than a collection of stamps is itself a stamp.

A second criticism is that the proponent makes the mistake of inferring that because each member of the collection of dependent beings has a cause the collection itself must have a cause. But, as Bertrand Russell noted, such reasoning is as fallacious as to infer that the human race (that is, the collection of human beings) must have a mother because each member of the collection (each human being) has a mother.

A third criticism is that the proponent of the argument fails to realize that for there to be an explanation of a collection of things is nothing more than for there to be an explanation of each of the things making up the collection. Since in the infinite collection (or series) of dependent beings, each being in the collection does have an explanation—by virtue of having been caused by some preceding member of the collection—the explanation of the collection, so the criticism goes, has already been given. As David Hume remarked, "Did I show you the particular causes of each individual in a collection of twenty particles of matter, I should think it very unreasonable, should you afterwards ask me, what was the cause of the whole twenty. This is sufficiently explained in explaining the cause of the parts."[2]

Finally, even if the proponent of the Cosmological Argument can satisfactorily answer these objections, he must face one last objection to his ingenious attempt to justify premise two of the Cosmological Argument. For someone may agree that if nothing exists but an infinite collection of dependent beings,... the infinite collection will have no explanation of its existence, and still refuse to conclude from this that there is something wrong with the idea that every being is a dependent being. Why, he might ask, should we think that everything has to have an explanation? What's wrong with admitting that the fact that there are and have always been dependent beings is a *brute fact,* a fact having no explanation whatever? Why does everything have to have an explanation anyway? We must now see what can be said in response to these several objections.

Responses to Criticism

It is certainly a mistake to think that a collection of stamps is itself a stamp, and very likely a mistake to think that the collection of dependent beings is itself a dependent being. But the mere fact that the proponent of the argument thinks that there must be an explanation not only for each member of the collection of dependent beings but for the collection itself is not sufficient grounds for concluding that he must view the collection as itself a dependent being. The collection of human beings, for example, is certainly not itself a human being. Admitting this, however, we might still seek an explanation of why there is a collection of human beings, of why there are such things as human beings at all. So the mere fact that an explanation is demanded for the collection of dependent beings is no proof that the person who demands the

explanation must be supposing that the collection itself is just another dependent being.

The second criticism attributes to the proponent of the Cosmological Argument the following bit of reasoning:

1. Every member of the collection of dependent beings has a cause or explanation.

Therefore,

2. The collection of dependent beings has a cause or explanation.

As we noted in setting forth this criticism, arguments of this sort are often unreliable. It would be a mistake to conclude that a collection of objects is light in weight simply because each object in the collection is light in weight, for if there were many objects in the collection it might be quite heavy. On the other hand, if we know that each marble weighs more than one ounce we could infer validly that the collection of marbles weighs more than an ounce. Fortunately, however, we don't need to decide whether the inference from (1.) to (2.) is valid or invalid. We need not decide this question because the proponent of the Cosmological Argument need not use this inference to establish that there must be an explanation of the collection of dependent beings. He need not use this inference because he has in PSR a principle from which it follows immediately that the collection of dependent beings has a cause or explanation. For according to PSR every positive fact must have an explanation. If it is a fact that there exists a collection of dependent beings then, according to PSR, that fact too must have an explanation. So it is PSR that the proponent of the Cosmological Argument appeals to in concluding that there must be an explanation of the collection of dependent beings, and not some dubious inference from the premise that each member of the collection has an explanation. It seems, then, that neither of the first two criticisms is strong enough to do any serious damage to the reasoning used to support the second premise of the Cosmological Argument.

The third objection contends that to explain the existence of a collection of things is the same thing as to explain the existence of each of its members. If we consider a collection of dependent beings where each being in the collection is explained by the preceding member which caused it, it's clear that no member of the collection will lack an explanation of its existence. But, so the criticism goes, if we've explained the existence of every member of a collection we've explained the existence of the collection—there's nothing left over to be explained. This forceful criticism, originally advanced by David Hume, has gained considerable support in the modern period. But the criticism rests on an assumption that the proponent of the Cosmological Argument would not accept. The assumption is that to explain the existence of a collection of things it is *sufficient* to explain the existence of every member in the collection. To see what is wrong with this assumption is to understand the basic issue in the reasoning by which the proponent of the Cosmological Argument seeks to establish that not every being can be a dependent being.

In order for there to be an explanation of the existence of the collection of dependent beings, it's clear that the eighteenth-century proponents would require that the following two conditions be satisfied:

C1. There is an explanation of the existence of each of the members of the collection of dependent beings.

C2. There is an explanation of why there are *any* dependent beings.

According to the proponents of the Cosmological Argument if every being that exists or ever did exist is a dependent being—that is, if the whole of reality consists of nothing more than a collection of dependent beings—C1 will be satisfied, but C2 will not be satisfied. And since C2 won't be satisfied there will be no explanation of the collection of dependent beings. The third criticism, therefore, says in effect that if C1 is satisfied C2 will be satisfied, and, since in a collection of dependent beings each member will have an explanation in whatever it was that produced it, C1 will be satisfied. So, therefore, C2 will be satisfied and the collection of dependent beings will have an explanation.

Although the issue is a complicated one, I think it is possible to see that the third criticism rests on a mistake: the mistake of thinking that if C1 is satisfied C2 must also be satisfied. The mistake is a natural one to make for it is easy to imagine circumstances in which if C1 is satisfied C2 also will be satisfied. Suppose, for example, that the whole of reality includes not just a collection of dependent beings but also a self-existent being. Suppose further that instead of each dependent being having been produced by some other dependent being every dependent being was produced by the self-existent being. Finally, let us consider both the possibility that the collection of dependent beings is finite in time and has a first member and the possibility that the collection of dependent being is infinite in past time, having no first member. Using "G" for the self-existent being, the first possibility may be diagrammed as follows:

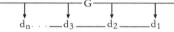

G, we shall say, has always existed and always will. We can think of d_1 as some presently existing dependent being, d_2, d_3, and so forth as dependent beings that existed at some time in the past, and d_n as the first dependent being to exist. The second possibility may be portrayed as follows:

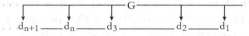

On this diagram there is no first member of the collection of dependent beings. Each member of the infinite collection, however, is explained by reference to the self-existent being G which produced it. Now the interesting point about both these cases is that the explanation that has been provided for the members of the collection of dependent beings carries with it, at least in part, an answer to the question of why there are any dependent beings at all. In both cases we may explain why there are dependent beings by pointing out that there exists a self-existent being that has been engaged in producing them. So once we have learned that the existence of each member of the collection of dependent beings has its existence explained by the fact that G produced it, we have already learned why there are dependent beings.

Someone might object that we haven't really learned why there are dependent beings until we also learn *why* G has been producing them. But, of course, we could also say that we haven't really explained the existence of a particular dependent being, say d_3, until we also learn not just that G produced it but *why* G produced it. The point we need to grasp, however, is that once we admit that every dependent being's existence is explained by G, we must admit that the fact that there are dependent beings has also been explained. So it is not unnatural that someone should think that to explain the existence of the collection of dependent beings is nothing more than to explain the existence of its members. For, as we've seen, to explain the collection's existence is to explain each member's existence and to explain why there are any dependent beings at all. And in the examples we've considered, in doing the one (explaining why each dependent being exists) we've already done the other (explained why there are any dependent beings at all). We must now see, however, that on the supposition that the whole of reality consists *only* of a collection of dependent beings, to give an explanation of each member's existence is not to provide an explanation of why there are dependent beings.

In the examples we've considered we have gone *outside* of the collection of dependent beings in order to explain the members' existence. But if the only beings that exist or ever existed are dependent beings then each dependent being will be explained by some other dependent being, ad infinitum. This does not mean that there will be some particular dependent being whose existence is unaccounted for. Each

dependent being has an explanation of its existence; namely, in the dependent being which preceded it and produced it. So C1 is satisfied: there is an explanation of the existence of each member of the collection of dependent beings. Turning to C2, however, we can see that it will not be satisfied. We cannot explain why there are (or have ever been) dependent beings by appealing to all the members of the infinite collection of dependent beings. For if the question to be answered is why there are (or have ever been) any dependent beings at all, we cannot answer that question by noting that there always have been dependent beings, each one accounting for the existence of some other dependent being. Thus on the supposition that every being is dependent it seems there will be no explanation of why there are dependent beings. C2 will not be satisfied. Therefore, on the supposition that every being is dependent there will be no explanation of the existence of the collection of dependent beings.

The Truth of PSR

We come now to the final criticism of the reasoning supporting the second premise of the Cosmological Argument. According to this criticism, it is admitted that the supposition that every being is dependent implies that there will be a *brute fact* in the universe, a fact, that is, for which there can be no explanation whatever. For there will be no explanation of the fact that dependent beings exist and have always been in existence. It is this brute fact that the proponents of the argument were describing when they pointed out that if every being is dependent the series or collection of dependent beings would lack an explanation of *its* existence. The final criticism asks what is wrong with admitting that the universe contains such a brute, unintelligible fact. In asking this question the critic challenges the fundamental principle, PSR, on which the Cosmological Argument rests. For, as we've seen, the first premise of the argument denies that there exists a being whose existence has no explanation. In support of this premise the proponent appeals to the first part of PSR. The second premise of the argument claims that not every being can be dependent. In support of this premise the proponent appeals to the second part of PSR, the part which states that there must be an explanation of any positive fact whatever.

The proponent reasons that if every being were a dependent being then although the first part of PSR would be satisfied—every being would have an explanation—the second part would be violated, there would be no explanation for the positive fact that there are and have always been dependent beings. For first, since every being is supposed to be dependent, there would be nothing outside of the collection of dependent beings to explain the collection's existence. Second, the fact that each member of the collection has an explanation in some other dependent being is insufficient to explain why there are and have always been dependent beings. And, finally, there is nothing about the collection of dependent beings that would suggest that it is a self-existent collection. Consequently, if every being were dependent, the fact that there are and have always been dependent beings would have no explanation. But this violates the second part of PSR. So the second premise of the Cosmological Argument must be true, not every being can be a dependent being. This conclusion, however, is no better than the principle, PSR, on which it rests. And it is the point of the final criticism to question the truth of PSR. Why, after all, should we accept the idea that every being and every positive fact must have an explanation? Why, in short, should we believe PSR? These are important questions, and any final judgment of the Cosmological Argument depends on how they are answered.

Most of the theologians and philosophers who accept PSR have tried to defend it in either of two ways. Some have held that PSR is (or can be) known *intuitively* to be true. By this they mean that if we fully understand and reflect on what is said by PSR we can see that it must be true. Now, undoubtedly, there are statements which are known intuitively to be true. "Every triangle has exactly three angles" or "No physical

object can be in two different places in space at one and the same time" are examples of statements whose truth we can apprehend just by understanding and reflecting on them. The difficulty with the claim that PSR is intuitively true, however, is that a number of very able philosophers fail to apprehend its truth, and some even claim that the principle is false. It is doubtful, therefore, that many of us, if any, know intuitively that PSR is true.

The second way philosophers and theologians who accept PSR have sought to defend it is by claiming that although it is not known to be true, it is, nevertheless, a presupposition of reason, a basic assumption that rational people make, whether or not they reflect sufficiently to become aware of the assumption. It's probably true that there are some assumptions we all make about our world, assumptions which are so basic that most of us are unaware of them. And, I suppose, it might be true that PSR is such an assumption. What bearing would this view of PSR have on the Cosmological Argument? Perhaps the main point to note is that even if PSR is a presupposition we all share, the premises of the Cosmological Argument could still be false. For PSR itself could still be false. The fact, if it is a fact, that all of us *presuppose* that every existing being and every positive fact has an explanation does not imply that no being exists, and no positive fact obtains, without an explanation. Nature is not bound to satisfy our presuppositions. As the American philosopher, William James, once remarked in another connection, "In the great boarding house of nature, the cakes and the butter and the syrup seldom come out so even and leave the plates so clear."

Our study of the first part of the Cosmological Argument has led us to the fundamental principle on which its premises rest, the Principle of Sufficient Reason. Since we do not seem to know that PSR is true we cannot reasonably claim to know that the premises of the Cosmological Argument are true. They might be true. But unless we do know them to be true they cannot *establish* for us the conclusion that there exists a being that has the explanation of its existence within its own nature. If it were shown, however, that even though we do not *know* that PSR is true we all, nevertheless, *presuppose* PSR to be true, then, whether PSR is true or not, to be consistent we should accept the Cosmological Argument. For, as we've seen, its premises imply its conclusion and its premises do seem to follow from PSR. But no one has succeeded in *showing* that PSR is an assumption that most or all of us share. So our final conclusion must be that although the Cosmological Argument might be a *sound* argument (valid with true premises), it does not provide us with good rational grounds for believing that among those beings that exist there is one whose existence is accounted for by its own nature. Having come to this conclusion

we may safely put aside the second part of the argument. For even if it succeeded in showing that a self-existent being would have the other attributes of the theistic God, the Cosmological Argument would still not provide us with good rational grounds for belief in God, having failed in its first part to provide us with good rational grounds for believing that there is a self-existent being.

NOTES

1. See St. Thomas Aquinas, *Summa Theologica*, 1a, 2, 3.
2. David Hume, *Dialogues Concerning Natural Religion,* Part IX, ed. H. D. Aiken (New York: Hafner Publishing Company, 1948), 59–60.

1.7 The Argument from Design

WILLIAM PALEY

William Paley (1743–1805) was an English philosopher of religion and ethics.

CHAPTER ONE: STATE OF THE ARGUMENT

In crossing a heath, suppose I pitched my foot against a *stone* and were asked how the stone came to be there, I might possibly answer that for anything I knew to the contrary it had lain there forever; nor would it, perhaps, be very easy to show the absurdity of this answer. But suppose I had found a *watch* upon the ground, and it should be inquired how the watch happened to be in that place. I should hardly think of the answer which I had before given, that for anything I knew the watch might have always been there. Yet why should not this answer serve for the watch as well as for the stone? Why is it not as admissible in the second case as in the first? For this reason, and for no other, namely, that when we come to inspect the watch, we perceive—

what we could not discover in the stone—that its several parts are framed and put together for a purpose, e.g., that they are so formed and adjusted as to produce motion, and that motion so regulated as to point out the hour of the day; that if the different parts had been differently shaped from what they are, of a different size from what they are, or placed after any other manner or in any other order than that in which they are placed, either no motion at all would have been carried on in the machine, or none which would have answered the use that is now served by it. To reckon up a few of the plainest of these parts and of their offices, all tending to one result; we see a cylindrical box containing a coiled elastic spring, which, by its endeavor to relax itself, turns round the box. We next observe a flexible chain—artificially wrought for the sake of flexure—communicating the action

---

From William Paley, *Natural Theology* (1802).

of the spring from the box to the fusee. We then find a series of wheels, the teeth of which catch in and apply to each other, conducting the motion from the fusee to the balance and from the balance to the pointer, and at the same time, by the size and shape of those wheels, so regulating that motion as to terminate in causing an index, by an equable and measured progression, to pass over a given space in a given time. We take notice that the wheels are made of brass, in order to keep them from rust; the springs of steel, no other metal being so elastic; that over the face of the watch there is placed a glass, a material employed in no other part of the work, but in the room of which, if there had been any other than a transparent substance, the hour could not be seen without opening the case. This mechanism being observed—it requires indeed an examination of the instrument, and perhaps some previous knowledge of the subject, to perceive and understand it; but being once, as we have said, observed and understood—the inference we think is inevitable, that the watch must have had a maker—that there must have existed, at some time and at some place or other, an artificer or artificers who formed it for the purpose which we find it actually to answer, who comprehended its construction and designed its use.

I. Nor would it, I apprehend, weaken the conclusion, that we had never seen a watch made—that we had never known an artist capable of making one—that we were altogether incapable of executing such a piece of workmanship ourselves, or of understanding in what manner it was performed; all this being no more than what is true of some exquisite remains of ancient art, of some lost arts, and, to the generality of mankind, of the more curious productions of modern manufacture. Does one man in a million know how oval frames are turned? Ignorance of this kind exalts our opinion of the unseen and unknown artist's skill, if he be unseen and unknown, but raises no doubt in our minds of the existence and agency of such an artist, at some former time and in some place or other. Nor can I perceive that it varies at all the inference, whether the question arise concerning a human agent or concerning an agent of a different species, or an agent possessing in some respects a different nature.

II. Neither, secondly, would it invalidate our conclusion, that the watch sometimes went wrong or that it seldom went exactly right. The purpose of the machinery, the design, and the designer might be evident, and in the case supposed, would be evident, in whatever way we accounted for the irregularity of the movement, or whether we could account for it or not. It is not necessary that a machine be perfect in order to show with what design it was made: still less necessary, where the only question is whether it were made with any design at all.

III. Nor, thirdly, would it bring any uncertainty into the argument, if there were a few parts of the watch, concerning which we could not discover or had not yet discovered in what manner they conduced to the general effect; or even some parts, concerning which we could not ascertain whether they conduced to that effect in any manner whatever. For, as to the first branch of the case, if by the loss, or disorder, or decay of the parts in question, the movement of the watch were found in fact to be stopped, or disturbed, or retarded, no doubt would remain in our minds as to the utility or intention of these parts, although we should be unable to investigate the manner according to which, or the connection by which, the ultimate effect depended upon their action or assistance; and the more complex is the machine, the more likely is this obscurity to arise. Then, as to the second thing supposed, namely, that there were parts which might be spared without prejudice to the movement of the watch, and that we had proved this by experiment, these superfluous parts, even if we were completely assured that they were such, would not vacate the reasoning which we had instituted concerning other parts. The indication of contrivance remained, with respect to them, nearly as it was before.

IV. Nor, fourthly, would any man in his senses think the existence of the watch with its various machinery accounted for, by being told that it was one out of possible combinations of material forms; that whatever he had found in the place where he found the watch, must have contained some internal configuration or other; and that this configuration might be the structure now exhibited, namely, of the works of a watch, as well as a different structure.

V. Nor, fifthly, would it yield his inquiry more satisfaction, to be answered that there existed in things a principle of order, which had disposed the parts of the watch into their present form and situation. He never knew a watch made by the principle of order; nor can he even form to himself an idea of what is meant by a principle of order distinct from the intelligence of the watchmaker.

VI. Sixthly, he would be surprised to hear that the mechanism of the watch was no proof of contrivance, only a motive to induce the mind to think so:

VII. And not less surprised to be informed that the watch in his hand was nothing more than the result of the laws of *metallic* nature. It is a perversion of language to assign any law as the efficient, operative cause of any thing. A law presupposes an agent, for it is only the mode according to which an agent proceeds; it implies a power, for it is the order according to which that power acts. Without this agent, without this power, which are both distinct from itself, the *law* does nothing, is nothing. The expression, "the law of metallic nature," may sound strange and harsh to a philosophic ear; but it seems quite as justifiable as some others which are more familiar to him, such as "the law of vegetable nature," "the law of animal nature," or, indeed, as "the law of nature" in general, when assigned as the cause of phenomena, in exclusion of agency and power, or when it is substituted into the place of these.

VIII. Neither, lastly, would our observer be driven out of his conclusion or from his confidence in its truth by being told that he knew nothing at all about the matter. He knows enough for his argument; he knows the utility of the end; he knows the subserviency and adaptation of the means to the end. These points being known, his ignorance of other points, his doubts

concerning other points affect not the certainty of his reasoning. The consciousness of knowing little need not beget a distrust of that which he does know.

CHAPTER TWO: STATE OF THE ARGUMENT CONTINUED

Suppose, in the next place, that the person who found the watch should after some time discover that, in addition to all the properties which he had hitherto observed in it, it possessed the unexpected property of producing in the course of its movement another watch like itself—the thing is conceivable; that it contained within it a mechanism, a system of parts—a mold, for instance, or a complex adjustment of lathes, files, and other tools—evidently and separately calculated for this purpose; let us inquire what effect ought such a discovery to have upon his former conclusion.

I. The first effect would be to increase his admiration of the contrivance, and his conviction of the consummate skill of the contriver. Whether he regarded the object of the contrivance, the distinct apparatus, the intricate, yet in many parts intelligible mechanism by which it was carried on, he would perceive in this new observation nothing but an additional reason for doing what he had already done—for referring the construction of the watch to design and to supreme art. If that construction *without* this property, or, which is the same thing, before this property had been noticed, proved intention and art to have been employed about it, still more strong would the proof appear when he came to the knowledge of this further property, the crown and perfection of all the rest.

II. He would reflect, that though the watch before him were, *in some sense,* the maker of the watch, which, was fabricated in the course of its movements, yet it was in a very different sense from that in which a carpenter, for instance, is the maker of a chair—the author of its contrivance, the cause of the relation of its parts to their use. With respect to these, the first watch was no cause at all to the second; in no such sense as this was it the author of the constitution and order, either of the parts which the new watch contained, or of the parts by the aid and instrumentality of which it was produced. We might possibly say, but with great latitude of expression, that a stream of water ground corn; but no latitude of expression would allow us to say, no stretch of conjecture could lead us to think that the stream of water built the mill, though it were too ancient for us to know who the builder was. What the stream of water does in the affair is neither more nor less than this: by the application of an unintelligent impulse to a mechanism previously arranged, arranged independently of it and arranged by intelligence, an effect is produced, namely, the corn is ground. But the effect results from the arrangement. The force of the stream cannot be said to be the cause or author of the effect, still less of the arrangement. Understanding and plan in the formation of the mill were not the less necessary for any share which the water has in grinding the corn; yet is this share the same as that which the watch would have contributed to the production of the new watch, upon the supposition assumed in the last section. Therefore,

III. Though it be now no longer probable that the individual watch which our observer had found was made immediately by the hand of an artificer, yet does not this alteration in anyway affect the inference that an artificer had been originally employed and concerned in the production. The argument from design remains as it was. Marks of design and contrivance are no more accounted for now than they were before. In the same thing, we may ask for the cause of different properties. We may ask for the cause of the color of a body, of its hardness, of its heat; and these causes may be all different. We are now asking for the cause of that subserviency to a use, that relation to an end, which we have remarked in the watch before us. No answer is given to this question by telling us that a preceding watch produced it. There cannot be design without a designer; contrivance without a contriver; order without choice; arrangement without anything capable of arranging; subserviency and relation to a purpose without that which could intend a purpose; means suitable to an end, and executing their office in accomplishing that end, without the end ever having been contemplated or the means accommodated to it. Arrangement, disposition of parts, subserviency of means to an end, relation of instruments to a use imply the presence of intelligence and mind. No one, therefore, can rationally believe that the insensible, inanimate watch, from which the watch before us issued, was the proper cause of the mechanism we so much admire in it—could be truly said to have constructed the instrument, disposed its parts, assigned their office, determined their order, action, and mutual dependency, combined their several motions into one result, and that also a result connected with the utilities of other beings. All these properties, therefore, are as much unaccounted for as they were before.

IV. Nor is anything gained by running the difficulty farther back, that is, by supposing the watch before us to have been produced from another watch, that from a former, and so on indefinitely. Our going back ever so far brings us no nearer to the least degree of satisfaction upon the subject. Contrivance is still unaccounted for. We still want a contriver. A designing mind is neither supplied by this supposition nor dispensed with. If the difficulty were diminished the farther we went back, by going back indefinitely we might exhaust it. And this is the only case to which this sort of reasoning applies. Where there is a tendency, or, as we increase the number of terms, a continual approach toward a limit, *there,* by supposing the number of terms to be what is called infinite, we may conceive the limit to be attained; but where there is no such tendency or approach, nothing is effected by lengthening the series. There is no difference as to the point in question, whatever there may be as to many points, between one series and another—between a series which is finite and a series which is infinite. A chain composed of an infinite number of links, can no more support itself, than a chain composed of a finite number of links. And of this we are assured, though we never *can* have tried the experiment; because, by increasing the number of links, from ten, for instance, to a hundred, from a hundred to a thousand, etc., we make not the smallest approach, we observe not the smallest tendency toward self-support. There is no difference in this respect—yet there may be a great difference in several respects—between a chain of a greater or less length, between one chain and another, between one that is finite and one that is infinite. This very much resembles the case before us. The machine which we are inspecting demonstrates, by its construction, contrivance and design. Contrivance must have had a contriver, design a designer, whether the machine immediately proceeded from another machine or not. That circumstance alters not the case. That other machine may, in like manner, have proceeded from a former machine; nor does that alter the case; contrivance must have had a contriver. That former one from one preceding it: no alteration still; a contriver is still necessary. No tendency is perceived, no approach toward a diminution of this necessity. It is the same with any and every succession of these machines—a succession of ten, of a hundred, of a thousand; with one series, as with another—a series which is finite, as with a series which is infinite. In whatever other respects they may differ, in this they do not. In all equally, contrivance and design are unaccounted for.

The question is not simply, How came the first watch into existence? which question, it may be pretended, is done away by supposing the series of watches thus produced from one another to have been infinite, and consequently to have had no such *first* for which it was necessary to provide a cause. This, perhaps, would have been nearly the state of the question, if nothing had been before us but an unorganized, unmechanized substance, without mark or indication of contrivance. It might be difficult to show that such substance could not have existed from eternity, either in succession—if it were possible, which I think it is not, for unorganized bodies to spring from one another—or by individual perpetuity. But that is not the question

now. To suppose it to be so is to suppose that it made no difference whether he had found a watch or a stone. As it is, the metaphysics of that question have no place; for, in the watch which we are examining are seen contrivance, design, an end, a purpose, means for the end, adaptation to the purpose. And the question which irresistably presses upon our thoughts is, whence this contrivance and design? The thing required is the intending mind, the adapting hand, the intelligence by which that hand was directed. This question, this demand is not shaken off by increasing a number or succession of substances destitute of these properties; nor the more, by increasing that number to infinity. If it be said that, upon the supposition of one watch being produced from another in the course of that other's movements and by means of the mechanism within it, we have a cause for the watch in my hand, namely, the watch from which it proceeded; I deny that for the design, the contrivance, the suitableness of means to an end, the adaptation of instruments to a use, all of which we discover in the watch, we have any cause whatever. It is in vain, therefore, to assign a series of such causes or to allege that a series may be carried back to infinity; for I do not admit that we have yet any cause at all for the phenomena, still less any series of causes either finite or infinite. Here is contrivance but no contriver; proofs of design, but no designer.

V. Our observer would further also reflect that the maker of the watch before him was in truth and reality the maker of every watch produced from it; there being no difference, except that the latter manifests a more exquisite skill, between the making of another watch with his own hands, by the mediation of files, lathes, chisels, etc., and the disposing, fixing, and inserting of these instruments, or of others equivalent to them, in the body of the watch already made, in such a manner as to form a new watch in the course of the movements which he had given to the old one. It is only working by one set of tools instead of another.

The conclusion which the *first* examination of the watch, of its works, construction, and movement, suggested, was that it must have had, for cause and author of that construction, an artificer who understood its mechanism and designed its use. This conclusion is invincible. A *second* examination presents us with a new discovery. The watch is found, in the course of its movement, to produce another watch similar to itself; and not only so, but we perceive in it a system of organization separately calculated for that purpose. What effect would this discovery have or ought it to have upon our former inference? What, as has already been said, but to increase beyond measure our admiration of the skill which had been employed in the formation of such a machine? Or shall it, instead of this, all at once turn us round to an opposite conclusion, namely, that no art or skill whatever has been concerned in the business, although all other evidences of art and skill remain as they were, and this last and supreme piece of art be now added to the rest? Can this be maintained without absurdity? Yet this is atheism....

CHAPTER FIVE: APPLICATION OF THE ARGUMENT CONTINUED

Every observation which was made in our first chapter concerning the watch may be repeated with strict propriety concerning the eye, concerning animals, concerning plants, concerning, indeed, all the organized parts of the works of nature. As,

I. When we are inquiring simply after the *existence* of an intelligent Creator, imperfection, inaccuracy, liability to disorder, occasional irregularities may subsist in a considerable degree without inducing any doubt into the question; just as a watch may frequently go wrong, seldom perhaps exactly right, may be faulty in some parts, defective in some, without the smallest ground of suspicion from thence arising that it was not a watch, not made, or not made for the purpose ascribed to it. When faults are pointed out, and when a question is started concerning

the skill of the artist or dexterity with which the work is executed, then, indeed, in order to defend these qualities from accusation, we must be able either to expose some intractableness and imperfection in the materials or point out some invincible difficulty in the execution, into which imperfection and difficulty the matter of complaint may be resolved; or, if we cannot do this, we must adduce such specimens of consummate art and contrivance proceeding from the same hand as may convince the inquirer of the existence, in the case before him, of impediments like those which we have mentioned, although, what from the nature of the case is very likely to happen, they be unknown and unperceived by him. This we must do in order to vindicate the artist's skill, or at least the perfection of it; as we must also judge of his intention and of the provisions employed in fulfilling that intention, not from an instance in which they fail but from the great plurality of instances in which they succeed. But, after all, these are different questions from the question of the artist's existence; or, which is the same, whether the thing before us be a work of art or not; and the questions ought always to be kept separate in the mind. So likewise it is in the works of nature. Irregularities and imperfections are of little or no weight in the consideration when that consideration relates simply to the existence of a Creator. When the argument respects His attributes, they are of weight; but are then to be taken in conjunction—the attention is not to rest upon them, but they are to be taken in conjunction with the unexceptionable evidence which we possess of skill, power, and benevolence displayed in other instances; which evidences may, in strength, number, and variety, be such and may so overpower apparent blemishes as to induce us, upon the most reasonable ground, to believe that these last ought to be referred to some cause, though we be ignorant of it, other than defect of knowledge or of benevolence in the author....

1.8 The Argument from Design

MICHAEL RUSE

Michael Ruse is a philosopher and historian of science who has written widely on issues related to evolution. He teaches at Florida State University.

In crossing a heath, suppose I pitched my foot against a *stone*, and were asked how the stone came to be there; I might possibly answer, that, for any thing I knew to the contrary, it had lain there for ever: nor would it perhaps be very easy to show the absurdity of this answer. But suppose I had found a *watch* upon the ground, and it should be inquired how the watch happened to be in that place; I should hardly think of the answer which I had before given, that, for any thing I knew, the watch might have always been there. Yet why should not this answer serve for the watch as well as for the stone? Why is it not as admissible in the second case, as in the first?

This is the famous opening passage of Archdeacon William Paley's textbook *Natural Theology* (1802).[1] He is giving the reader what is probably the most famous of all of the arguments for the existence of God, the "argument from design" or (as it is sometimes known) the "teleological argument." Paley was not the inventor of this argument. It goes back to the Greeks, and is introduced by Plato in the *Phaedo*, the dialogue about the last day on earth of his teacher Socrates. It was popular in the medieval period and made famous by St. Thomas Aquinas. And although there have long been detractors, leaving it in respects somewhat battered, it has continued since Paley and today finds many enthusiastic supporters. Let us start by looking at the argument, for in respects it is a little more subtle than is often realized.

THE ARGUMENT EXPOUNDED

Paley draws our attention to a watch. He says it is just not the sort of thing that you find lying around randomly. Its very existence demands an explanation. He contrasts it with a stone, which he does think could have lain around for indefinite ages and which requires no explanation. Actually, by the time Paley was writing at the beginning of the nineteenth century, there were lots of people who would have said that the stone does demand an explanation. Geology was a thriving science and there would have been interest in the nature of the stone. What's it made of and how did it get there? Is it evidence of a flood, for instance? But no matter. We know what Paley is about. The stone is just there and that seems to be the end of matters. There is something about the watch that seems to call for explanation. It seems to have been made for some purpose, some end, in a way that the stone is not. And that calls for an explanation.

Note that at first we might not know quite what the watch is for. In 1900 divers found an old shipwreck off a Greek island and from its booty they recovered a box (a bit less than a foot cubed) containing a mysterious bronze object. Known now as the "Antikythera mechanism," it turns out that was made about 200 BC and was a clockwork machine for forecasting the motions of the heavens and eclipses and so forth. But even before they cleaned it up and made a working facsimile and showed how the original would have been expected to function, people were pretty sure that it was made for some purpose.

So what we have going on here is a recognition of some kind of complexity. But more than that. We have an argument or inference that this kind of complexity is not any old kind of complexity—for instance, the knots and tangles I find most mornings when, intending to walk the dogs, I find someone in the family (never identified!) has left the leashes in a complex mess. We have an inference that this complexity that Paley latches onto is "organized," in the sense that its parts have been put together for a purpose or end. It works. We have a machine—as in the case of that Greek discovery, a mechanism. Paley's watch tells the time, or it will if it is cleaned up and repaired. The term that was used for something serving an end was "final cause," or, more recently, that it was "teleological."

Note that there is nothing particularly fishy here about the fact that, inasmuch as something does serve an end, we are trying to understand the present in terms of the future—the mechanism exists to tell of an eclipse in the next century, for instance. No one is saying that there are causes in the future reaching back to the present. It is simply that we are referring to the future to explain the present. For some reason—a stray comet perhaps—the moon may not line up as expected and no eclipse will occur. The machine is still intended to tell about the future.

Now the argument goes on from here. Organized complexity doesn't just happen. That's Paley's point. We need an explanation of the watch or of the Antikythera mechanism. And it is obvious what that explanation is going to be. Someone did it! The watch, the mechanism, was designed by someone and then that person (or the next person down the line) made it. Someone wanted to tell the time or wanted to predict eclipses, so (literally or metaphorically) they sat down at the drawing board and designed the machine, the artifact, and then they (or a helper) made it. In other words, there was a conscious intention at work, and this of course is how the future gets into the mix. The watchmaker, the astronomer, thought that it would be nice to tell or find something (that necessarily was going to happen in the future) and so they set about making it.

What we have then after the argument to organized complexity is a second argument—the argument *to* design. We are not at God yet, but we are getting there. Now the argument goes, and Paley gives this in great nineteenth-century detail, we find natural objects in the world that share the property or likeness of organized complexity. Back in the very old days, the Greeks and the medieval period, people thought that this complexity could be found throughout the whole of creation, living and dead, animate and inanimate. But, although we shall see that this kind of thinking has been revived today, after the Scientific Revolution—that major upheaval in science from Copernicus to Newton, in the sixteenth and seventeenth centuries—people agreed that organized complexity is to be found only in the living world. The eye, to take the example used by Paley and by just about everyone else, doesn't seem to be just a pile of parts thrown randomly together. It is put together very carefully and obviously has an end, a purpose. It exhibits a final cause—namely, sight or seeing. Its nature cannot be owing just to chance.

This is a really important point and has great psychological authority, so let me give an updated example just to reinforce it. This example also centers on the eye, but not on any eye, just on the eye of the trilobite. I suspect you know what they are—long extinct (they flourished about five hundred million years ago) marine organisms that occupied the same shoreline ecological niche as do crabs today. It turns out that they had very complex eyes with many lenses, like a fly today. They fossilize well and you can extract the eyes, and by bisecting them carefully one finds that the lens is very interesting. On one side it is convex like any normal lens—on your spectacles, for instance. On the other side, though, it is wavy—first concave, then (in the middle) convex, and then concave again.[2] What on earth is this all about? Surely it cannot be chance?

One of the paleontologists studying them had, as an undergraduate, taken a course about the French philosopher René Descartes and he remembered (correctly) that Descartes had drawn up a lens like this. Different colors of light refract slightly differently—that is, as the light enters the glass from the air it bends slightly differently according to whether it is red or blue—and that means that normally the focus of the light (when the rays come together after leaving the lens) is slightly blurred, with the colors not quite overlapping exactly. How can you remedy this? With the kind of curvy lens that the trilobites have! In other words, five hundred million years ago, the trilobites solved Descartes' problem. Even better than that. It turns out that Christiaan Huygens, the great Dutch optician of the seventeenth century, found the same solution. What is fascinating is that Descartes' diagram exactly fits one species of trilobite and Huygens' diagram exactly fits another species of trilobite.

It cannot be chance. There is clear evidence of design—note, the argument *to* design. Obviously humans did not do the job. So who did do it? There is only one plausible answer, the Great Optician in the Sky—God. Having talked about the eye and its wonderful nature, having looked at possible objections, Paley is confident in his answer. Even more than confident, because we don't just have a functioning eye, but we have a system for making new eyes down the road. We have a machine that is part of a system that can make copies of itself.

> What, as hath already been said, but to increase, beyond measure, our admiration of the skill, which had been employed in the formation of such a machine? Or shall it, instead of this, all at once turn us round to an opposite conclusion, viz. that no art or skill whatever has been concerned in the business, although all other evidences of art and skill remain as they were, and this last and supreme piece of art be now added to the rest? Can this be maintained without absurdity? Yet this is atheism.

In short, what we have now is an argument *from* design. We have established that there is design here. The question then is how to explain

this design. And from here we are led to God. But notice that Paley (and others) think that the argument does more than this. The eye is a pretty remarkable machine or artifact—a "supreme piece of art." This obviously tells us something about the designer, or perhaps we should now write, the Designer. He (or whoever) is obviously a pretty skilled sort of individual. He is clever and, since the eye is something of huge value to its possessors, He is thoughtful, He is kind. In other words, by analogy, we don't just have a god. We have something very much like the Christian God—a being who is all-powerful (omnipotent) and also all-loving (omnibenevolent). One presumes that this also includes being all-knowing (omniscient). No wonder the argument is so popular. It works from such psychologically plausible premises and it delivers such an agreeable and desired conclusion.

DAVID HUME

I have said that this argument had had a long history before Paley. Aquinas offered the argument as one of five that he highlighted as getting us to God through reason.

> The fifth way is taken from the governance of the world. We see that things which lack knowledge, such as natural bodies, act for an end, and this is evident from their acting always, or nearly always, in the same way, so as to obtain the best result. Hence it is plain that they achieve their end, not fortuitously, but designedly. Now whatever lacks knowledge cannot move towards an end, unless it be directed by some being endowed with knowledge and intelligence; as the arrow is directed by the archer. Therefore, some intelligent being exists by whom all natural things are directed to their end; and this being we call God.[3]

Note that in this version of the argument, in line with what I said earlier, no real distinction is being drawn between the evidence from organisms alone and the evidence from nature generally. Nor is much being said about the nature of God, although elsewhere it is Aquinas above all who, through his theory of analogy, was trying to put some flesh as it were on the nature of

God, showing how we can meaningfully speak of God as a father and as loving and so forth.

One should mention also that students today, because passages like this just given are extracted and given on their own in isolation, often get a slightly erroneous impression of how Aquinas—and the other great philosopher-theologians of Christianity, like St. Augustine nearly a millennium earlier—regarded the design argument, and indeed all of the arguments to the existence of God. They thought them valid, but they thought them secondary to faith. They are props for belief, not belief generators working alone. This was also the position of the Protestant Reformers like Calvin, and is something that persists today—the greatest Christian theologian of the twentieth century, the Swiss Karl Barth, was very down on all such arguments. He felt that they undercut the existential significance of belief—in the words of the nineteenth-century Danish theologian Søren Kierkegaard, without a "leap," an irrational jump into the unknown (which would be impossible if God's existence can be proven), faith is degraded.

However, others, particularly the British with their tradition of empirical observation of the natural world, felt otherwise. In that country, after the Reformation, the argument from design throve as never before. A century before Paley, the clergyman-naturalist John Ray wrote: "Whatever is natural, beheld thro' [the microscope], appears exquisitely form'd, and adorn'd with all imaginable Elegancy and Beauty. There are such inimitable Glidings in the smallest Seeds of Plants, but especially in the Parts of Animals in the Head or Eye of a small Fly; such Accuracy, Order and Symmetry in the Frame of the most minute Creatures, a Louse, for example, or a Mite, as no Man were able to conceive without seeing of them." And he then drew the conclusion: "There is no greater; at least no more palpable and convincing Argument of the Existence of a Deity, than the admirable Art and Wisdom that discovers itself in the Make and Constitution, the Order and Disposition, the Ends and Uses of all the Parts and Members of this stately Fabrick of Heaven and Earth."[4]

It is perhaps therefore no great surprise that it was Britain that gave birth to the most forceful criticisms of the argument. Almost paradoxically, even before Paley put pen to paper, the philosopher David Hume—whom his fellow Scot David Brewster was to describe as "God's greatest gift to the infidel"—in what is surely the most devastatingly critical piece of philosophy ever written, had already taken the argument from design to pieces in his posthumously published *Dialogues Concerning Natural Religion* (1779). First, Hume set up the argument through one of the characters of the *Dialogue*, Cleanthes. There is a designer and this designer is pretty wonderful: "the Author of Nature is somewhat similar to the mind of man; though possessed of much larger facilities, proportioned to the grandeur of the work, which he has executed."[5] Then in comes Philo, another of the characters, to knock everything down.

One of Philo's first and more general arguments is that supposing a designer behind the world rather presupposes what you are trying to prove. The designer presumably in some sense is the cause of itself and then goes on to produce the world. Why go that far? Why not stop with the world itself, supposing that it can generate itself without outside help? "To say, that the different ideas which compose the reason of the Supreme Being, fall into order of themselves, and by their own nature, is really to talk without any precise meaning. If it has a meaning, I would fain know, why it is not as good sense to say, that the parts of the material world fall into order of themselves and by their own nature. Can the one opinion be intelligible, while the other is not so?"

Then Philo starts to get more specific. We only know a fraction of the universe, and the more we learn (for instance through microscopes) the stranger it seems. Isn't this a bit of a worry when arguing to the deity? "The discoveries by microscopes, as they open a new universe in miniature, are still objections, according to you, arguments, according to me. The further we push our researches of this kind, we are still led to infer the universal cause of all to be vastly different from mankind, or from any object of human experience and observation." And if there is such strangeness out there, who are we to say that what we have in our world is the very best? Perhaps there are other worlds much better than ours. In any case, taking our world, what we know of even the best—especially the best—designed entities is that they are usually the end result of many earlier trials, less good. Who is to say that we are the end product, the best there could be? Perhaps we are one trial along the way. A trial incidentally that experience would lead us to think is the work of a gang of people, rather than just one individual. Should we therefore suppose a multiplicity of gods or Gods?

Philo keeps up the pressure, going back a little. How can we deny absolutely that this world of ours is more an organism than a machine, and so something that is self-generating without need of a designer? "In like manner as a tree sheds its seed into the neighbouring fields, and produces other trees; so the great vegetable, the world, or this planetary system, produces within itself certain seeds, which, being scattered into the surrounding chaos, vegetate into new worlds." And then, moving forward, there is the problem of pain. How can one reconcile this with a good God? "But what racking pains, on the other hand, arise from gouts, gravels, megrims, toothaches, rheumatisms, where the injury to the animal machinery is either small or incurable? Mirth, laughter, play, frolic, seem gratuitous satisfactions, which have no further tendency: spleen, melancholy, discontent, superstition, are pains of the same nature. How then does the Divine benevolence display itself, in the sense of you Anthropomorphites [people who interpret things in human terms]?"

Moving towards the end, the reader is surely feeling it is all over for the argument from design. The arguments of Philo are so strong, no one could again take the arguments seriously. And yet this is to ignore history. Not only did Paley write confidently on behalf of the argument several decades after Hume, but in his work on natural theology he even references

Hume! Even Hume himself at the end of his *Dialogues* seems to have second thoughts. He lets one of the characters say that really the person arguing for design has the better of the arguments. Could Hume really mean this? Or is he just covering himself against charges of blasphemy?

One plausible answer to all of this is that normally we read the argument from design in the wrong way. As suggested earlier, we generally think of it as an argument from analogy. The eye is like a telescope. Telescopes have telescope makers. Hence the eye must have an eye maker. God. And inasmuch as the eye is well made, this speaks to God's praiseworthy qualities. Perhaps, though, the argument is better thought of as what Peirce called an "abduction" and what is today often called an "inference to the best explanation." Sherlock Holmes, in the *Sign of the Four*, put his finger on it. "How often have I said to you that when you have eliminated the impossible, whatever remains, *however improbable*, must be the truth?" Could it not be that everyone recognized that there was something there, especially in the organic world, that needed explaining—something that, however vague, seemed to need some kind of intelligence, somehow, somewhere behind it? Everyone felt that there was organized complexity and that the only way to explain it was by making appeal to a designer. Having arrived at this preliminary conclusion, because they then could see no other option, they felt that they just had to conclude that the designer was God. It wasn't a question of whether you much cared for the conclusion. One assumes that Hume was not very enthusiastic. It was a question of whether you felt you had to accept the conclusion. And even Hume agreed that you did.

CHARLES DARWIN

The strength of the argument to the best explanation is that it has to be held in the absence of another solution. The weakness of the argument to the best explanation is that when another solution is discovered, the argument is no longer compelling. Until the nineteenth century, no one had an explanation of final causes, meaning no one had an explanation of things like the eye and the hand that seem to refer to what they are intended to do, what they will do in the future, that did not invoke intelligence. Blind law leads to random messes. And then came Darwin. In his *Origin of Species* (1859) he gave a naturalistic explanation of final causes, what he called "adaptations" or, even more anthropomorphically, "contrivances." Organisms are the products of evolution—slow, law-bound development from other forms, ultimately perhaps back to inorganic matter. How does this happen?

First there is a struggle for existence:

> A struggle for existence inevitably follows from the high rate at which all organic beings tend to increase. Every being, which during its natural lifetime produces several eggs or seeds, must suffer destruction during some period of its life, and during some season or occasional year, otherwise, on the principle of geometrical increase, its numbers would quickly become so inordinately great that no country could support the product. Hence, as more individuals are produced than can possibly survive, there must in every case be a struggle for existence, either one individual with another of the same species, or with the individuals of distinct species, or with the physical conditions of life.[6]

Darwin then pointed out that, whenever you have populations of organisms, there are differences between the members. Darwin argued that, in the struggle, some types or forms are likely to prove more successful than others, simply because these types or forms will help their possessors against others. Over time, these types will spread through the group and eventually, because it seems that new variations are always appearing, there will be significant change:

> Let it be borne in mind in what an endless number of strange peculiarities our domestic productions, and, in a lesser degree, those under nature, vary; and how strong the hereditary tendency is. Under domestication, it may be truly said that the whole organisation becomes in some degree plastic. Let it be borne in mind how infinitely

complex and close-fitting are the mutual relations of all organic beings to each other and to their physical conditions of life. Can it, then, be thought improbable, seeing that variations useful to man have undoubtedly occurred, that other variations useful in some way to each being in the great and complex battle of life, should sometimes occur in the course of thousands of generations? If such do occur, can we doubt (remembering that many more individuals are born than can possibly survive) that individuals having any advantage, however slight, over others, would have the best chance of surviving and of procreating their kind? On the other hand, we may feel sure that any variation in the least degree injurious would be rigidly destroyed. This preservation of favourable variations and the rejection of injurious variations, I call Natural Selection.[7]

What is important to note is that natural selection doesn't just bring about change. It brings about change in the direction of adaptive advantage—eyes, noses, flowers, bark, fins, wings. It brings about features that seem as if designed. Darwin was the Newton of the blade of grass. Final causes flourish in the Darwinian world. The eye is *for* seeing in the future, even if for some reason it never gets to function. Why? Because eyes in the past gave their possessors the adaptive edge in the struggle for existence.

What about God? Darwin and everyone else realized that, if his position is well taken, then the argument from design no longer has its grip. You don't have to assume God to explain the organic world. As Richard Dawkins has said, after Darwin it is possible to be an intellectually fulfilled atheist.[8] This said, it does not follow that you have to be an atheist, at least not on what we have so far. Neither Augustine nor Aquinas would have been shocked or upset by Darwin's claims. Likewise, the great nineteenth-century theologian, John Henry Newman—who moved from being an evangelical in his childhood to joining the Catholic Church and ending a cardinal—never had trouble with Darwin. "I believe in design because I believe in God; not in a God because I see design."[9] He continued: "Design teaches me power, skill and goodness—not sanctity, not mercy, not a future judgment, which three are of the essence of religion." Darwin likewise did not think his position mandated nonbelief. Late in life he became an agnostic. He could not bear the idea that his father and brother, nonbelievers both, would be condemned to eternal damnation because of their nonbelief. But after the *Origin*, to his American, Presbyterian friend Asa Gray, Darwin wrote: "I cannot anyhow be contented to view this wonderful universe & especially the nature of man, & to conclude that everything is the result of brute force. I am inclined to look at everything as resulting from designed laws, with the details, whether good or bad, left to the working out of what we may call chance."[10]

THE PROBLEM OF PAIN

In a way, that just about wraps up the argument from design. Hume (drawing often on arguments that go back to antiquity) showed the conceptual problems with it. Darwin showed that it is not obligatory. We can leave matters at that. Except of course we cannot, because history never stands still. The argument today is at the center of attention and as much discussed as it ever was. Let us take up three separate lines, starting with the claim that Darwin proved more than the redundancy of the argument but actually its invalidity. It is an argument to be found in that very letter that Darwin wrote to Gray and focuses how the Darwinian process of struggle highlights pain and suffering in a way that surely is incompatible with the existence of the Christian God.

> With respect to the theological view of the question; this is always painful to me.—I am bewildered.—I had no intention to write atheistically. But I own that I cannot see, as plainly as others do, & as I shd. wish to do, evidence of design & beneficence on all sides of us. There seems to me too much misery in the world. I cannot persuade myself that a beneficent & omnipotent God would have designedly created the Ichneumonidae with the express intention of their feeding within the living bodies of caterpillars, or

that a cat should play with mice. Not believing this, I see no necessity in the belief that the eye was expressly designed.[11]

Richard Dawkins is pretty keen on this argument. Cheetahs seem wonderfully designed to kill antelopes. "The teeth, claws, eyes, nose, leg muscles, backbone and brain of a cheetah are all precisely what we should expect if God's purpose in designing cheetahs was to maximize deaths among antelopes."[12] Conversely, "we find equally impressive evidence of design for precisely the opposite end: the survival of antelopes and starvation among cheetahs." One could almost imagine that we have two gods, making the different animals, and then competing. If there is indeed but one god who made both animals, then what is going on? What sort of god makes this sort of encounter? "Is He a sadist who enjoys spectator blood sports? Is He trying to avoid overpopulation in the mammals of Africa? Is He maneuvering to maximize David Attenborough's television ratings?"[13] The answer is inevitable:

> In a universe of blind physical forces and genetic replication, some people are going to get hurt, other people are going to get lucky, and you won't find any rhyme or reason in it, nor any justice. The universe we observe has precisely the properties we should expect if there is, at bottom, no design, no purpose, no evil and no good, nothing but blind, pitiless indifference.[14]

What can one say in response? I will focus here on what is known as natural evil—earthquakes and so forth—and leave to one side moral evil—Hitler and the Holocaust. Although you might have worries about whether a good God would allow the existence of Hitler, this isn't really what Darwin and Dawkins are worrying about here. They are worried that the struggle for existence is nasty and painful and yet a supposedly good God did his creating using such a process. The standard response would be some form of the Leibnizian argument, namely, that God didn't have much choice. Voltaire in *Candide* had a lot of fun with this response, but it isn't that stupid. God cannot make 2+2=5 and God cannot make a cat the size of an elephant—legs go up linearly whereas weight goes up by the cube, and an elephant with cat legs would simply collapse on itself. Somewhat ironically, showing if nothing else that the Creator surely has a sense of humor, Dawkins himself comes to the rescue here. It has been stressed that Darwinians believe in final causes. The eye serves the end of sight and the hand the end of grasping. But how can you get final causes—adaptations—naturally? Dawkins doubts that there is any other way than natural selection.[15] So God cannot be blamed!

Of course you might question whether a good God would have created such a world as ours, knowing that it was going to cause pain and suffering. But that is surely another question for another time.

INTELLIGENT DESIGN THEORY

Second, have we been too quick in congratulating Darwin on giving a naturalistic explanation of final cause? There are vocal dissenters today who think that natural selection simply cannot do what is needed. I'll ignore here those who come at the issue from a naturalistic perspective, for instance those who think that, thanks to a natural tendency towards organized complexity, physics and chemistry unaided can do the job.[16] My personal feeling is that people like this have been spending too much time indoors hunched over computers when they should be out in nature looking at real organisms. But whatever the truth in this direction, no one in this camp is bringing in God.

I will focus rather on the so called Intelligent Design (ID) theorists, who argue that the organic world shows "irreducible complexity," and to explain it we must bring in a designer.[17] This is not necessarily a designer who did everything all at once or even in one week. It could be a designer who works on an ongoing basis, getting involved as necessary. ID enthusiasts differ on these questions. But that there was a designer who intervened miraculously is agreed by all. They generally add that they don't think the

designer is necessarily the Christian God, but you can feel fairly certain that they don't think the designer is a graduate student on Andromeda using the peopling of Earth as his dissertation topic.

One could go after this claim by saying—and I myself am inclined to go this way—that the presumption is so great against miraculous interventions by the deity, it is foolish to start supposing them now. Whenever something odd turns up in the empirical world—whether it be a planet out of line or a disease unexpected—you can bet that a natural explanation will be forthcoming. However, I suspect that the ID people would argue that you cannot in principle explain some phenomena. The laws of nature are "blind," meaning that they just go on and on without looking right or left. Planets circle in ellipses endlessly and continents slide around the globe without thought or deviation. They just do what they do. Natural selection is the same. It does not think and certainly does not look into the future and see that, if it only anticipated some issue or needed solution, it could do things a lot better. But this is precisely the kind of situation that ID theorists highlight —namely, times when thinking ahead is needed. We are looking at cases where all of the parts must be in place simultaneously for the adaptation to work. Construction is needed, but the trouble is that during the construction things are out of adaptive focus. Unfortunately, by its very nature—by the fact that laws just keep trundling along—natural selection cannot lay off until the work is done. It would wipe out the half-finished stage. Hence, the only feasible explanation of such cases, claim ID theorists, is that some intelligent designer has created the complex organisms (or their parts) to be as they are.

Michael Behe, a leading spokesperson for the cause, highlights the bacterial flagellum and the blood-clotting cascade as instances in point.[18] He claims that each of these is so complex, so dependent on all of the parts being in place for them to work, that natural selection cannot have been the cause. To which one can simply say that biologist after biologist has shown that these examples do not stand up.[19] Every case that has been advanced as one that exhibits more complexity than could be accounted for by natural selection has been shown by biologists to admit of a naturalistic explanation. Before one gets into the business of turning to alternative explanations, aka God, one should think more carefully about the biology. It is a little unfortunate that to illustrate his point, Behe took the example of a five-part mouse trap. He argued that unless one had all five parts put in place at once, it would not function. A slow gradual process could never have done the job. Which, expectedly, gave birth to a whole new discipline of mousetrapology, showing that not only could you catch mice with a four-part mousetrap, but with a three-part, a two-part, and even a one-part trap. Admittedly it would not be very good, but nature never demands absolute efficiency—just getting along and, in the world of natural selection, doing better than the competitors. There is an old saying that in the land of the blind, the man with one eye is king. Normally you are better off with two eyes, but if no one else has any eyes, you are ahead with one eye. Normally a five-part mousetrap is better than a four-part trap. But if no one else has anything better than a three-part trap, you are better off with a four-part trap.

In the empirical world, take the case of the blood-clotting cascade. This is something that swings into action if you cut yourself, stopping the blood from just gushing out endlessly—as happens unfortunately with hemophiliacs, who do not have an efficiently functioning cascade. Admittedly, this mechanism is very complex. There are about thirty different sequential chemical reactions that have to occur. First one process kicks into action and then the next. But the case is not irreducibly complex. There are lots of existing organisms with simpler cascades—cascades that are not all that different from the mammalian cascade, just made of fewer parts of the mammalian one. So, while it is true that you cannot take pieces randomly from the mammalian cascade and expect it to work, it is just not true that when you remove any one step of the process everything falls apart.

Thinking then in reverse, of adding rather than taking, it is perfectly plausible to suggest that natural selection did the job, move by move. And before you say that this is all pie in the sky, making up stories without evidence, what is really interesting and suggestive is that the many parts to the cascade are not so very different from each other. Just a molecule or two of modification does the trick. So it is not as if you have to bring together pieces from all over, making each component from scratch. A bit of tampering, a bit of shifting, and you have something just that fraction better than the competitors. And this is where natural selection does jump in quickly and seize the chance and retain and perhaps polish the new system, or rather the old system with a bit more added.[20]

Part of the problem here is that, rather like the case of Aquinas's arguments for the existence of God, so often matters are taken out of context. The critic of natural selection too often seizes on some feature in the organic world and triumphantly announces that it could not be explained by selection. But you need to look at the context and, as always in evolution, at the history. If you see a drystone bridge across a river, you might wonder how ever it could have been put in place. Take out one stone, and the bridge falls into the water. But what we know is that the builder probably put wooden struts in place and laid the stones on top. When the bridge was finished, the struts were removed. So often that is the case in biology. If a structure is not needed, selection removes it. Overall, the blind watchmaker—as Richard Dawkins calls it—is pretty powerful.

THE ANTHROPIC PRINCIPLE

The third point is one that has biologists groaning. Having spent over a hundred and fifty years showing that God is not needed to explain the apparent design in the world, there are now physicists who claim just that! God is an essential part of the picture. Their argument focuses on something known as the "anthropic principle." This comes in many forms and at different strengths.[21] The so-called weak anthropic principle (WAP) says simply that there would be no life if the right conditions did not obtain. If for instance we suppose that carbon is necessary for life, then without carbon there would be no life. You may think that this is saying something really interesting, because we are here and living and lo and behold there is carbon. But really it is not quite as fascinating as that. If there were no carbon, there would be no life, and we would not be asking these silly questions. It is perhaps interesting that there is carbon, but on this perspective not so interesting that there is life.

The strong anthropic principle (SAP)—known in some circles (especially biological) as the "completely ridiculous anthropic principle"—claims that the universe must be of a form that allows or even necessitates life. Given the universe, you had to have life. Now this, true or false, does start to say something more substantive. In the case of the weak principle, you could say that although life has occurred, it didn't have to occur. It also leaves open the possibility of all sorts of other universes that might have given rise to life. Perhaps a silicone universe would do it. The point is that—assuming that life can occur naturally, which is the general consensus of biologists—there doesn't seem any design to any of this. The universe appeared and evolved, and when the conditions were ripe—our planet, for instance, had to cool down somewhat from its fiery origins—life appeared. There is no call for divine forces to explain this; nature did the trick unaided. In the case of the strong principle, you are saying that the world is such that life must appear. It really is starting to seem as though the world was prepared for humans. It was "fine-tuned" for human life. And even if you don't want to go that far, you are at least pushing towards the position of saying that not any old universe would have given rise to life, or even any old number of universes would have given rise to life. There is one and only one universe that would do; we are in it; and that cannot be chance. Think of a lottery. The fact that I am the

winner is no miracle. Someone had to win. Of course, I would not be buying a new Mercedes had I not won, but there is nothing out of line here. But if we knew that I was going to win—that I *had to* win—then we know that my winning is not chance, but design.

Why should we think the universe is fine-tuned? A number of physical arguments are offered, all along the line of "if this had not been exactly as it is, that would not have happened, and so no life would have been possible." What would be an example? The carbon atom is a popular choice.[22] In the early stages of the universe there were no carbon atoms. At that point, everything was just hydrogen and helium. In order for carbon to be produced, we need three helium nuclei. Normally, even with the right ingredients nothing happens, because the energy of carbon is way below that of three helium nuclei—as things normally are, the nuclei could not come together and stay that way. They are too hyped up, as it were. Fortuitously, however, there is a variant, radioactive form of carbon. It has just the higher energy that is needed and so everything works out perfectly—this energy of the radioactive form is precisely that needed to make carbon. Anything a little more, it would not work. Anything a little less, it would not work. The actual energy level is right on target. Like Goldilocks' third try at the Three Bears' dishes of porridge, it is just fine.

But before you get all excited and think that nature is not just fine but fine-tuned, the very skeptical physics Nobel Laureate Steven Weinberg asks us to keep questioning. How do you get the three helium nuclei in the first place? They come together in a two-part process. First, two of them combine to make beryllium. Only then is the third is added to make carbon. It turns out that looking at things from this perspective, there is a lot more room for flexibility—there is a wider range of energy levels that would let these processes move forward. There is thus no unique possible energy needed to make carbon. All in all, therefore, perhaps things are not really so tightly designed.

The trouble with the arguments in favor of fine-tuning is that we are just working from ourselves—from the world we know—and putting probabilities on things is such guesswork. Think of a number, double it, and the answer you want is a half. The fine-tuning enthusiasts start from premises no one would deny. Of course we humans could not function on a planet where, because it is bigger, the gravitational attraction is (let us say) twice as strong. As we are constituted at the moment, the strain on our limbs and our internal organs like the heart would lead to early death. But then the fine-tuners go astray by assuming that this is all there is to be said on the subject. This is a mistake. If we were on a bigger planet, then natural selection would have made us so that we could live there. We might, for instance, have evolved with elephantine-sized legs. Or, more plausibly, perhaps like the whales we could have spent most of our time in the water where we would weigh that much less, and so presumably we would have adaptations like dolphins for living an aquatic life, so that our hearts and lungs and (obviously most important) brains could be very human-like. I am not sure that advanced civilization is beyond mermen and mermaids. And this is all before you start to think of the trendy new notion of "multiverses."[23] Perhaps our universe is just one of an infinite number, some of which work, some of which don't, some of which support life, some of which don't. We are right back to winning the lottery without any fraud behind our success. We couldn't buy the Mercedes if we hadn't won it, but winning it was no miracle.

As always, Hume had the measure of things. "In subjects adapted to the narrow compass of human reason, there is commonly but one determination, which carries probability or conviction with it; and to a man of sound judgement, all other suppositions, but that one, appear entirely absurd and chimerical."[24] Suppose that there is only so much matter. "A finite number of particles is only susceptible of finite transpositions: and it must happen, in an eternal duration, that every possible order or position must be tried an infinite number of times. This world, therefore, with all its events, even the most minute, has before been produced and destroyed, and will again be produced and destroyed, without any bounds and limitations. No one, who has a conception of the powers of infinite, in comparison of finite, will ever scruple this determination."[25]

CONCLUSION

To say more would be an anticlimax. The argument from design has a two-and-half thousand year history and seems still to be raising discussion and controversy. Some think it totally outmoded. Others disagree strongly. And some perhaps are in the middle, thinking it important but not quite in the ways that enthusiasts or detractors suppose. That is a good point on which to end. Anything which is still going strong after such a long time, has to be worth at least a little bit of our attention!

NOTES

1. William Paley, *Collected Works: IV* (London: Rivington, 1819).
2. Technically, what I am talking about is "spherical aberration." With a flexible eye, such as we have, the eye can adjust. With a fixed eye, such as the trilobite had, this is not possible; so it does it by building a solution right into the structure. See http://www.trilobites.info/eyes.htm for details. What you will love is the fact that the Creationists think the eye supports their case! http://www.trueorigin.org/trilobites_eyes.asp
3. Saint Thomas Aquinas, *Summa Theologica, I* (London: Burns, Oates and Washbourne, 1952), pp. 26–27.
4. John Ray, *The Wisdom of God, Manifested in the Words of Creation*, 5th ed. (London: Samuel Smith, 1709), pp. 32–33.
5. David Hume, *Dialogues Concerning Natural Religion* (1779), p. 27.
6. Charles Darwin, *On the Origin of Species by Means of Natural Selection, or the Preservation of Favoured Races in the Struggle for Life* (London: John Murray, 1859), pp. 63–64.
7. Ibid., pp. 80–81.
8. Richard Dawkins, *The Blind Watchmaker* (New York: Norton, 1986).

9. John Henry Newman, *The Letters and Diaries of John Henry Newman, XXV*, ed. C. S. Dessain and T. Gornall (Oxford: Clarendon Press, 1973), p. 97.

10. Charles Darwin, *The Correspondence of Charles Darwin* (Cambridge: Cambridge University Press, 1985–), vol. 8, p. 224.

11. Ibid.

12. Richard Dawkins, *A River Out of Eden* (New York: Basic Books, 1995), p. 105.

13. Ibid.

14. Ibid., p. 133.

15. Richard Dawkins, "Universal Darwinism," in *Evolution from Molecules to Men*, ed. D. S. Bendall (Cambridge: Cambridge University Press, 1983), pp. 403–25.

16. Stuart A. Kauffman, *The Origins of Order: Self-Organization and Selection in Evolution* (Oxford: Oxford University Press, 1993); Brian Goodwin, *How the Leopard Changed Its Spots*, 2nd ed. (Princeton: Princeton University Press, 2001).

17. Michael J. Behe, *Darwin's Black Box: The Biochemical Challenge to Evolution* (New York: Free Press, 1996); William A. Dembski, in *Debating Design: Darwin to DNA*, ed. W. A. Dembski and M. Ruse (Cambridge: Cambridge University Press, 2004).

18. Behe, op. cit.

19. For one example among many, see Kenneth R. Miller, *Finding Darwin's God* (New York: Harper and Row, 1999).

20. Russell F. Doolittle, "A Delicate Balance," *Boston Review* 22, no. 1 (1997): 28–29.

21. John D. Barrow and Frank J. Tipler, *The Anthropic Cosmological Principle* (Oxford: Clarendon Press, 1986).

22. Steven Weinberg, "A Designer Universe?" *New York Review of Books* 46, no. 16 (1999): 46–48.

23. George F. R. Ellis, "Does the Multiverse Really Exist?" *Scientific American* 305, no. 2 (2011): 38–43.

24. Hume, p. 81.

25. Ibid, p. 82.

1.9 Dialogues Concerning Natural Religion

DAVID HUME

David Hume (1711–1776) was a leading philosopher of the Enlightenment, the author of a famous history of England, and the tutor of Adam Smith in political economy. He spent most of his life in Edinburgh.

PART II

I must own, Cleanthes, said Demea, that nothing can more surprise me than the light in which you have all along put this argument. By the whole tenor of your discourse, one would imagine that you were maintaining the Being of a God against the cavils of atheists and infidels, and were necessitated to become a champion for that fundamental principle of all religion. But this, I hope, is not by any means a question among us. No man, no man at least of common sense, I am persuaded, ever entertained a serious doubt with regard to a truth so certain and self-evident. The question is not concerning the *being* but the *nature* of God. This I affirm, from the infirmities of human understanding, to be altogether incomprehensible and unknown to us. The essence of that supreme Mind, his attributes, the manner of his existence, the very nature of his duration—these and every particular which regards so divine a Being are mysterious to men. Finite, weak, and blind creatures, we ought to humble ourselves in his august presence, and, conscious of our frailties, adore in

---

First published in 1779.

silence his infinite perfections which eye hath not seen, ear hath not heard, neither hath it entered into the heart of man to conceive. They are covered in a deep cloud from human curiosity; it is profaneness to attempt penetrating through these sacred obscurities, and, next to the impiety of denying his existence, is the temerity of prying into his nature and essence, decrees and attributes.

But lest you should think that my *piety* has here got the better of my *philosophy,* I shall support my opinion, if it needs any support, by a very great authority. I might cite all the divines, almost from the foundation of Christianity, who have ever treated of this or any other theological subject; but I shall confine myself, at present, to one equally celebrated for piety and philosophy. It is Father Malebranche who, I remember, thus expresses himself.[1] "One ought not so much," says he, "to call God a spirit in order to express positively what he is, as in order to signify that he is not matter. He is a Being infinitely perfect—of this we cannot doubt. But in the same manner as we ought not to imagine, even supposing him corporeal, that he is clothed with a human body, as the anthropomorphites asserted, under colour that that figure was the most perfect of any, so neither ought we to imagine that the spirit of God has human ideas or bears any resemblance to our spirit, under colour that we know nothing more perfect than a human mind. We ought rather to believe that as he comprehends the perfections of matter without being material…he comprehends also the perfections of created spirits without being spirit, in the manner we conceive spirit: that his true name is *He that is,* or, in other words, Being without restriction, All Being, the Being infinite and universal."

After so great an authority, Demea, replied Philo, as that which you have produced, and a thousand more which you might produce, it would appear ridiculous in me to add my sentiment or express my approbation of your doctrine. But surely, where reasonable men treat these subjects, the question can never be concerning the *being* but only the *nature* of the Deity. The former truth, as you well observe, is unquestionable and self-evident. Nothing exists without a cause; and the original cause of this universe (whatever it be) we call God, and piously ascribe to him every species of perfection. Whoever scruples this fundamental truth deserves every punishment which can be inflicted among philosophers, to wit, the greatest ridicule, contempt, and disapprobation. But as all perfection is entirely relative, we ought never to imagine that we comprehend the attributes of this divine Being, or to suppose that his perfections have any analogy or likeness to the perfections of a human creature. Wisdom, thought, design, knowledge—these we justly ascribe to him because these words are honourable among men, and we have no other language or other conceptions by which we can express our adoration of him. But let us beware lest we think that our ideas anywise correspond to his perfections, or that his attributes have any resemblance to these qualities among men. He is infinitely superior to our limited view and comprehension, and is more the object of worship in the temple than of disputation in the schools.

In reality, Cleanthes, continued he, there is no need of having recourse to that affected scepticism so displeasing to you in order to come at this determination. Our ideas reach no further than our experience. We have no experience of divine attributes and operations. I need not conclude my syllogism, you can draw the inference yourself. And it is a pleasure to me (and I hope to you, too) that just reasoning and sound piety here concur in the same conclusion, and both of them establish the adorably mysterious and incomprehensible nature of the Supreme Being.

Not to lose any time in circumlocutions, said Cleanthes, addressing himself to Demea, much less in replying to the pious declamations of Philo, I shall briefly explain how I conceive this matter. Look round the world, contemplate the whole and every part of it: you will find it to be nothing but one great machine, subdivided into an infinite number of lesser machines, which again admit of subdivisions to a degree beyond what human senses and faculties can trace and explain. All these various machines, and even their most minute parts, are adjusted to each other with an accuracy which ravishes into admiration all men who have ever contemplated them. The curious adapting of means to ends, throughout all nature, resembles exactly, though it much exceeds, the productions of human contrivance—of human design, thought, wisdom, and intelligence. Since therefore the effects resemble each other, we are led to infer, by all the rules of analogy, that the causes also resemble, and that the Author of nature is somewhat similar to the mind of man, though possessed of much larger faculties, proportioned to the grandeur of the work which he has executed. By this argument *a posteriori,* and by this argument alone, do we prove at once the existence of a Deity and his similarity to human mind and intelligence.

I shall be so free, Cleanthes, said Demea, as to tell you that from the beginning I could not approve of your conclusion concerning the similarity of the Deity to men, still less can I approve of the mediums by which you endeavour to establish it. What! No demonstration of the Being of God! No abstract arguments! No proofs *a priori!* Are these which have hitherto been so much insisted on by philosophers all fallacy, all sophism? Can we reach no farther in this subject than experience and probability? I will not say that this is betraying the cause of a Deity; but surely, by this affected candour, you give advantages to atheists which they never could obtain by the mere dint of argument and reasoning.

What I chiefly scruple in this subject, said Philo, is not so much that all religious arguments are by Cleanthes reduced to experience, as that they appear not to be even the most certain and irrefragable of that inferior kind. That a stone will fall, that fire will burn, that the earth has solidity, we have observed a thousand and a thousand times; and when any new instance of this nature is presented, we draw without hesitation the accustomed inference. The exact similarity of the cases gives us a perfect assurance of a similar event, and a stronger evidence is never desired nor sought after. But wherever you depart, in the least, from the similarity of the cases, you diminish proportionably the evidence, and may at last bring it to a very weak *analogy,* which is confessedly liable to error and uncertainty. After having experienced the circulation of the blood in human creatures, we make no doubt that it takes place in Titius and Maevius; but from its circulation in frogs and fishes it is only a presumption, though a strong one, from analogy that it takes place in men and other animals. The analogical reasoning is much weaker when we infer the circulation of the sap in vegetables from our experience that the blood circulates in animals; and those who hastily followed that imperfect analogy are found, by more accurate experiments, to have been mistaken.

If we see a house, Cleanthes, we conclude, with the greatest certainty, that it had an architect or builder because this is precisely that species of effect which we have experienced to proceed from that species of cause. But surely you will not affirm that the universe bears such a resemblance to a house that we can with the same certainty infer a similar cause, or that the analogy is here entire and perfect. The dissimilitude is so striking that the utmost you can here pretend to is a guess, conjecture, a presumption concerning a similar cause; and how that pretension will be received in the world, I leave you to consider.

It would surely be very ill received, replied Cleanthes; and I should be deservedly blamed and detested did I allow that the proofs of Deity amounted to no more than a guess or conjecture. But is the whole adjustment of means to ends in a house and in the universe so slight a resemblance? the economy of final causes? the order, proportion, and arrangement of every part? Steps of a stair are plainly contrived that human legs may use them in mounting; and this inference is certain and infallible. Human legs are also contrived for walking and mounting; and this inference, I allow, is not altogether so certain because of the dissimilarity which you remark; but does it, therefore, deserve the name only of presumption or conjecture?

Good God! cried Demea, interrupting him, where are we? Zealous defenders of religion allow that the proofs of a Deity fall short of perfect evidence! And you, Philo, on whose assistance I depended in proving the adorable mysteriousness of the Divine Nature, do you assent to all these extravagant opinions of Cleanthes? For what other name can I give them? or, why spare my censure when such principles are advanced, supported by such an authority, before so young a man as Pamphilus?

You seem not to apprehend, replied Philo, that I argue with Cleanthes in his own way, and, by showing him the dangerous consequences of his tenets, hope at last to reduce him to our opinion. But what sticks most with you, I observe, is the representation which Cleanthes has made of the argument *a posteriori;* and, finding that the argument is likely to escape your hold and vanish into air, you think it so disguised that you can scarcely believe it to be set in its true light. Now, however much I may dissent, in other respects, from the dangerous principle of Cleanthes, I must allow that he has fairly represented that argument, and I shall endeavour so to state the matter to you that you will entertain no further scruples with regard to it.

Were a man to abstract from everything which he knows or has seen, he would be altogether incapable, merely from his own ideas, to determine what kind of scene the universe must be, or to give the preference to one state or situation of things above another. For as nothing which he clearly conceives could be esteemed impossible or implying a contradiction, every chimera of his fancy would be upon an equal footing; nor could he assign any just reason why he adheres to one idea or system, and rejects the others which are equally possible.

Again, after he opens his eyes and contemplates the world as it really is, it would be impossible for him at first to assign the cause of any one event, much less of the whole of things, or of the universe. He might set his fancy a rambling, and she might bring him in an infinite variety of reports and representations. These would all be possible, but, being all equally possible, he would never of himself give a satisfactory account for his preferring one of them to the rest. Experience alone can point out to him the true cause of any phenomenon.

Now, according to this method of reasoning, Demea, it follows (and is, indeed, tacitly allowed by Cleanthes himself) that order, arrangement, or the adjustment of final causes, is not of itself any proof of design, but only so far as it has been experienced to proceed from that principle. For aught we can know *a priori*, matter may contain the source or spring of order originally within itself, as well as mind does; and there is no more difficulty in conceiving that the several elements, from an internal unknown cause, may fall into the most exquisite arrangement, than to conceive that their ideas, in the great universal mind, from a like internal unknown cause, fall into that arrangement. The equal possibility of both these suppositions is allowed. But, by experience, we find (according to Cleanthes) that there is a difference between them. Throw several pieces of steel together, without shape or form, they will never arrange themselves so as to compose a watch. Stone and mortar and wood, without an architect, never erect a house. But the ideas in a human mind, we see, by an unknown, inexplicable economy, arrange themselves so as to form the plan of a watch or house. Experience, therefore, proves that there is an original principle of order in mind, not in matter. From similar effects we infer similar causes. The adjustment of means to ends is alike in the universe, as in a machine of human contrivance. The causes, therefore, must be resembling.

I was from the beginning scandalized, I must own, with this resemblance which is asserted between the Deity and human creatures, and must conceive it to imply such a degradation of the Supreme Being as no sound theist could endure. With your assistance, therefore, Demea, I shall endeavour to defend what you justly call the adorable mysteriousness of the Divine Nature, and shall refute this reasoning of Cleanthes, provided he allows that I have made a fair representation of it.

When Cleanthes had assented, Philo, after a short pause, proceeded in the following manner.

That all inferences, Cleanthes, concerning fact are founded on experience, and that all experimental reasonings are founded on the supposition that similar causes prove similar effects, and similar effects similar causes, I shall not at present much dispute with you. But observe, I entreat you, with what extreme caution all just reasoners proceed in the transferring of experiments to similar cases. Unless the cases be exactly similar, they repose no perfect confidence in applying their past observation to any particular phenomenon. Every alteration of circumstances occasions a doubt concerning the event; and it requires new experiments to prove certainly that the new circumstances are of no moment or importance. A change in bulk, situation, arrangement, age, disposition of the air, or surrounding bodies—any of these particulars may be attended with the most unexpected consequences. And unless the objects be quite familiar to us, it is the highest temerity to expect with assurance, after any of these changes, an event similar to that which before fell under our observation. The slow and deliberate steps of philosophers here, if anywhere, are distinguished from the precipitate march of the vulgar, who, hurried on by the smallest similitude, are incapable of all discernment or consideration.

But can you think, Cleanthes, that your usual phlegm and philosophy have been preserved in so wide a step as you have taken when you compared to the universe houses, ships, furniture, machines, and, from their similarity in some circumstances, inferred a similarity in their causes? Thought, design, intelligence, such as we discover in men and other animals, is no more than one of the springs and principles of the universe, as well as heat or cold, attraction or repulsion, and a hundred others which fall under daily observation. It is an active cause by which some particular parts of nature, we find, produce alterations on other parts. But can a conclusion, with any propriety, be transferred from parts to the whole? Does not the great disproportion bar all comparison and inference? From observing the growth of a hair, can we learn anything concerning the generation of a man? Would the manner of a leaf's blowing, even though perfectly known, afford us any instruction concerning the vegetation of a tree?

But allowing that we were to take the *operations* of one part of nature upon another for the foundation of our judgment concerning the *origin* of the whole (which never can be admitted), yet why select so minute, so weak, so bounded a principle as the reason and design of animals is found to be upon this planet? What peculiar privilege has this little agitation of the brain which we call *thought,* that we must thus make it the model of the whole universe? Our partiality in our own favour does indeed present it on all occasions, but sound philosophy ought carefully to guard against so natural an illusion.

So far from admitting, continued Philo, that the operations of a part can afford us any just conclusion concerning the origin of the whole, I will not allow any one part to form a rule for another part if the latter be very remote from the former. Is there any reasonable ground to conclude that the inhabitants of other planets possess thought, intelligence, reason, or anything similar to these faculties in men? When nature has so extremely diversified her manner of operation in this small globe, can we imagine that she incessantly copies herself throughout so immense a universe? And if thought, as we may well suppose, be confined merely to this narrow corner and has even there so limited a sphere of action, with what propriety can we assign it for the original cause of all things? The narrow views of a peasant who makes his domestic economy the rule for the government of kingdoms is in comparison a pardonable sophism.

But were we ever so much assured that a thought and reason resembling the human were to be found throughout the whole universe, and were its activity elsewhere vastly greater and more commanding than it appears in this globe, yet I cannot see why the operations of a world constituted, arranged, adjusted, can with any propriety be extended to a world which is in its embryo state, and is advancing towards that constitution and arrangement. By observation we know somewhat of the economy, action, and nourishment of a finished animal, but we must transfer with great caution that observation to the growth of a foetus in the womb, and still more to the formation of an animalcule in the loins of its male parent. Nature, we find, even from our limited experience, possesses an infinite number of springs and principles which incessantly discover themselves on every change of her position and situation. And what new and unknown principles would actuate her in so new and unknown a situation as that of the formation of a universe, we cannot, without the utmost temerity, pretend to determine.

A very small part of this great system, during a very short time, is very imperfectly discovered to us; and do we thence pronounce decisively concerning the origin of the whole?

Admirable conclusion! Stone, wood, brick, iron, brass, have not, at this time, in this minute globe of earth, an order or arrangement without human art and contrivance; therefore, the universe could not originally attain its order and arrangement without something similar to human art. But is a part of nature a rule for another part very wide of the former? Is it a rule for the whole? Is a very small part a rule for the universe? Is nature in one situation a certain rule for nature in another situation vastly different from the former?

And can you blame me, Cleanthes, if I here imitate the prudent reserve of Simonides, who, according to the noted story, being asked by Hiero, *What God was?* desired a day to think of it, and then two days more; and after that manner continually prolonged the term, without ever bringing in his definition or description? Could you even blame me if I had answered, at first, *that I did not know,* and was sensible that this subject lay vastly beyond the reach of my faculties? You might cry out sceptic and raillier, as much as you pleased; but, having found in so many other subjects much more familiar the imperfections and even contradictions of human reason, I never should expect any success from

its feeble conjectures in a subject so sublime and so remote from the sphere of our observation. When two *species* of objects have always been observed to be conjoined together, I can *infer,* by custom, the existence of one wherever I *see* the existence of the other; and this I call an argument from experience. But how this argument can have place where the objects, as in the present case, are single, individual, without parallel or specific resemblance, may be difficult to explain. And will any man tell me with a serious countenance that an orderly universe must arise from some thought and art like the human because we have experience of it? To ascertain this reasoning it were requisite that we had experience of the origin of worlds; and it is not sufficient, surely, that we have seen ships and cities arise from human art and contrivance.

Philo was proceeding in this vehement manner, somewhat between jest and earnest, as it appeared to me, when he observed some signs of impatience in Cleanthes, and then immediately stopped short. What I had to suggest, said Cleanthes, is only that you would not abuse terms, or make use of popular expressions to subvert philosophical reasonings. You know that the vulgar often distinguish reason from experience, even where the question relates only to matter of fact and existence, though it is found, where that *reason* is properly analyzed, that it is nothing but a species of experience. To prove by experience the origin of the universe from mind is not more contrary to common speech than to prove the motion of the earth from the same principle. And a caviller might raise all the same objections to the Copernican system which you have urged against my reasonings. Have you other earths, might he say, which you have seen to move? Have...

Yes! cried Philo, interrupting him, we have other earths. Is not the moon another earth, which we see to turn around its centre? Is not Venus another earth, where we observe the same phenomenon? Are not the revolutions of the sun also a confirmation, from analogy, of the same theory? All the planets, are they not earths which revolve about the sun? Are not the satellites moons which move round Jupiter and Saturn, and along with these primary planets round the sun? These analogies and resemblances, with others which I have not mentioned, are the sole proofs of the Copernican system; and to you it belongs to consider whether you have any analogies of the same kind to support your theory.

In reality, Cleanthes, continued he, the modern system of astronomy is now so much received by all inquirers, and has become so essential a part even of our earliest education, that we are not commonly very scrupulous in examining the reasons upon which it is founded. It is now become a matter of mere curiosity to study the first writers of that subject who had the full force of prejudice to encounter, and were obliged to turn their arguments on every side in order to render them popular and convincing. But if we peruse Galileo's famous *Dialogues* concerning the system of the world, we shall find that that great genius, one of the sublimest that ever existed, first bent all his endeavours to prove that there was no foundation for the distinction commonly made between elementary and celestial substances. The schools, proceeding from the illusions of sense, had carried this distinction very far; and had established the latter substances to be ingenerable, incorruptible, unalterable, impassible; and had assigned all the opposite qualities to the former. But Galileo, beginning with the moon, proved its similarity in every particular to the earth: its convex figure, its natural darkness when not illuminated, its density, its distinction into solid and liquid, the variations of its phases, the mutual illuminations of the earth and moon, their mutual eclipses, the inequalities of the lunar surface, etc. After many instances of this kind, with regard to all the planets, men plainly saw that these bodies became proper objects of experience, and that the similarity of their nature enabled us to extend the same arguments and phenomena from one to the other.

In this cautious proceeding of the astronomers you may read your own condemnation, Cleanthes, or rather may see that the subject in which you are engaged exceeds all human reason and inquiry. Can you pretend to show any such similarity between the fabric of a house and the generation of a universe? Have you ever seen nature in any such situation as resembles the first arrangement of the elements? Have worlds ever been formed under your eye, and have you had leisure to observe the whole progress of the phenomenon, from the first appearance of order to its final consummation? If you have, then cite your experience and deliver your theory.

PART III

How the most absurd argument, replied Cleanthes, in the hands of a man of ingenuity and invention, may acquire an air of probability! Are you not aware, Philo, that it became necessary for Copernicus and his first disciples to prove the similarity of the terrestrial and celestial matter because several philosophers, blinded by old systems and supported by some sensible appearances, had denied this similarity? But that it is by no means necessary that theists should prove the similarity of the works of *nature* to those of *art* because this similarity is self-evident and undeniable? The same matter, a like form; what more is requisite to show an analogy between their causes, and to ascertain the origin of all things from a divine purpose and intention? Your objections, I must freely tell you, are no better than the abstruse cavils of those philosophers who denied motion, and ought to be refuted in the same manner—by illustrations, examples, and instances rather than by serious argument and philosophy.

Suppose, therefore, that an articulate voice were heard in the clouds, much louder and more melodious than any which human art could ever reach; suppose that this voice were extended in the same instant over all nations and spoke to each nation in its own language and dialect; suppose that the words delivered not only contain a just sense and meaning, but convey some instruction altogether worthy of a benevolent Being superior to mankind—could you possibly hesitate a moment concerning the cause of this voice, and must you not instantly ascribe it to some design or purpose? Yet I cannot see but all the same objections (if they merit that appellation) which lie against the system of theism may also be produced against this inference.

Might you not say that all conclusions concerning fact were founded on experience; that, when we hear an articulate voice in the dark and thence infer a man, it is only the resemblance of the effects which leads us to conclude that there is a like resemblance in the cause; but that this extraordinary voice, by its loudness, extent, and flexibility to all languages, bears so little analogy to any human voice that we have no reason to suppose any analogy in their causes; and, consequently, that a rational, wise, coherent speech proceeded, you know not whence, from some accidental whistling of the winds, not from any divine reason or intelligence? You see clearly your own objections in these cavils, and I hope too you see clearly that they cannot possibly have more force in the one case than in the other.

But to bring the case still nearer the present one of the universe, I shall make two suppositions which imply not any absurdity or impossibility. Suppose that there is a natural, universal, invariable language, common to every individual of the human race, and that books are natural productions which perpetuate themselves in the same manner with animals and vegetables, by descent and propagation. Several expressions of our passions contain a universal language: all brute animals have a natural speech, which, however limited, is very intelligible to their own species. And as there are infinitely fewer parts and less contrivance in the finest composition of eloquence than in the coarsest organized body, the propagation of an *Iliad* or *Aeneid* is an easier supposition than that of any plant or animal.

Suppose, therefore, that you enter into your library thus peopled by natural volumes containing the most refined reason and most exquisite beauty; could you possibly open one of them and doubt that its original cause bore the strongest analogy to mind and intelligence? When it reasons and discourses; when it expostulates, argues, and enforces its views and topics; when it applies sometimes to the pure intellect, sometimes to the affections; when it collects, disposes, and adorns every consideration suited to the subject; could you persist in asserting that all this, at the bottom, had really no meaning, and that the first formation of this volume in the loins of its original parent proceeded not from thought and design? Your obstinacy, I know, reaches not that degree of firmness; even your sceptical play and wantonness would be abashed at so glaring an absurdity.

But if there be any difference, Philo, between this supposed case and the real one of the universe, it is all to the advantage of the latter. The anatomy of an animal affords many stronger instances of design than the perusal of Livy or Tacitus; and any objection which you start in the former case, by carrying me back to so unusual and extraordinary a scene as the first formation of worlds, the same objection has place on the supposition of our vegetating library. Choose, then, your party, Philo, without ambiguity or evasion; assert either that a rational volume is no proof of a rational cause or admit of a similar cause to all the works of nature.

Let me here observe, too, continued Cleanthes, that this religious argument, instead of being weakened by that scepticism so much affected by you, rather acquires force from it and becomes more firm and undisputed. To exclude all argument or reasoning of every kind is either affectation or madness. The declared profession of every reasonable sceptic is only to reject abstruse, remote, and refined arguments; to adhere to common sense and the plain instincts of nature; and to assent, wherever any reasons strike him with so full a force that he cannot, without the greatest violence, prevent it. Now the arguments for natural religion are plainly of this kind; and nothing but the most perverse, obstinate metaphysics can reject them. Consider, anatomize the eye, survey its structure and contrivance, and tell me, from your own feeling, if the idea of a contriver does not immediately flow in upon you with a force like that of sensation. The most obvious conclusion, surely, is in favour of design; and it requires time, reflection, and study, to summon up those frivolous though abstruse objections which can support infidelity. Who can behold the male and female of each species, the correspondence of their parts and instincts, their passions and whole course of life before and after generation, but must be sensible that the propagation of the species is intended by nature? Millions and millions of such instances present themselves through every part of the universe, and no language can convey a more intelligible irresistible meaning than the curious adjustment of final causes. To what degree, therefore, of blind dogmatism must one have attained to reject such natural and such convincing arguments?

Some beauties in writing we may meet with which seem contrary to rules, and which gain the affections and animate the imagination in opposition to all the precepts of criticism and to the authority of the established masters of art. And if the argument for theism be, as you pretend, contradictory to the principles of logic, its universal, its irresistible influence proves clearly that there may be arguments of a like irregular nature. Whatever cavils may be urged, an orderly world, as well as a coherent, articulate speech, will still be received as an incontestable proof of design and intention.

It sometimes happens, I own, that the religious arguments have not their due influence on an ignorant savage and barbarian, not because they are obscure and difficult, but because he never asks himself any question with regard to them. Whence arises the curious structure of an animal? From the copulation of its parents. And these whence? From *their* parents? A few removes set the objects at such a distance that to him they are lost in darkness and confusion; nor is he actuated by any curiosity to trace them farther. But this is neither dogmatism nor scepticism, but stupidity: a state of mind very different from your sifting, inquisitive disposition, my ingenious friend. You can trace causes from effects; you can compare the most distant and remote objects; and your greatest errors proceed not from barrenness of thought and invention, but from too luxuriant a fertility which suppresses your natural good sense by a profusion of unnecessary scruples and objections.

Here I could observe, Hermippus, that Philo was a little embarrassed and confounded; but, while he hesitated in delivering an answer, luckily for him, Demea broke in upon the discourse and saved his countenance.

Your instance, Cleanthes, said he, drawn from books and language, being familiar, has, I confess, so much more force on that account; but is there not some danger, too, in this very circumstance, and may it not render us presumptuous, by making us imagine we comprehend the Deity and have some adequate idea of his nature and attributes? When I read a volume, I enter into the mind and intention of the author; I become him, in a manner, for the instant, and have an immediate feeling and conception of those ideas which revolved in his imagination while employed in that composition. But so near an approach we never surely can make to the Deity. His ways are not our ways, his attributes are perfect but incomprehensible. And this volume of nature contains a great and inexplicable riddle, more than any intelligible discourse or reasoning.

The ancient Platonists, you know, were the most religious and devout of all the pagan philosophers, yet many of them, particularly Plotinus, expressly declare that intellect or understanding is not to be ascribed to the Deity, and that our most perfect worship of him consists, not in acts of veneration, reverence, gratitude, or love, but in a certain mysterious self-annihilation or total extinction of all our faculties. These ideas are, perhaps, too far stretched, but still it must be acknowledged that, by representing the Deity as so intelligible and comprehensible, and so similar to a human mind, we are guilty of the grossest and most narrow partiality, and make ourselves the model of the whole universe.

All the *sentiments* of the human mind, gratitude, resentment, love, friendship, approbation, blame, pity, emulation, envy, have a plain reference to the state and situation of man, and are calculated for preserving the existence and promoting the activity of such a being in such circumstances. It seems, therefore, unreasonable to transfer such sentiments to a supreme existence or to suppose him actuated by them; and the phenomena, besides, of the universe will not support us in such a theory. All our *ideas* derived from the senses are confessedly false and illusive, and cannot therefore be supposed to have place in a supreme intelligence. And as the ideas of internal sentiment, added to those of the external senses, composed the whole furniture of human understanding, we may conclude that none of the *materials* of thought are in any respect similar in the human and in the divine intelligence. Now, as to the *manner* of thinking, how can we make any comparison between them or suppose them anywise resembling? Our thought is fluctuating, uncertain, fleeting, successive, and compounded; and were we to remove these circumstances, we absolutely annihilate its essence, and it would in such a case be an abuse of terms to apply to it the name of thought or reason. At least, if it appear more pious and respectful (as it really is) still to retain these terms when we mention the Supreme Being, we ought to acknowledge that their meaning, in that case, is totally incomprehensible, and that the infirmities of our nature do not permit us to reach any ideas which in the least correspond to the ineffable sublimity of the Divine attributes.

PART IV

It seems strange to me, said Cleanthes, that you, Demea, who are so sincere in the cause of religion, should still maintain the mysterious, incomprehensible nature of the Deity, and should insist so strenuously that he has no manner of likeness or resemblance to human creatures. The Deity, I can readily allow, possesses many powers and attributes of which we can have no comprehension; but, if our ideas, so far as they go, be not just and adequate and correspondent to his real nature, I know not what there is in this subject worth insisting on. Is the name, without

any meaning, of such mighty importance? Or how do you mystics, who maintain the absolute incomprehensibility of the Deity, differ from sceptics or atheists, who assert that the first cause of all is unknown and unintelligible? Their temerity must be very great if, after rejecting the production by a mind—I mean a mind resembling the human (for I know of no other)—they pretend to assign, with certainty, any other specific intelligible cause; and their conscience must be very scrupulous, indeed, if they refuse to call the universal unknown cause a God or Deity, and to bestow on him as many sublime eulogies and unmeaning epithets as you shall please to require of them.

Who could imagine, replied Demea, that Cleanthes, the calm philosophical Cleanthes, would attempt to refute his antagonists by affixing a nickname to them, and, like the common bigots and inquisitors of the age, have recourse to invective and declamation instead of reasoning? Or does he not perceive that these topics are easily retorted, and that *anthropomorphite* is an appellation as invidious, and implies as dangerous consequences, as the epithet of *mystic* with which he has honoured us? In reality, Cleanthes, consider what it is you assert when you represent the Deity as similar to the human mind and understanding. What is the soul of man? A composition of various faculties, passions, sentiments, ideas—united, indeed, into one self or person, but still distinct from each other. When it reasons, the ideas which are the parts of its discourse arrange themselves in a certain form or order which is not preserved entire for a moment, immediately gives place to another arrangement. New opinions, new passions, new affections, new feelings arise which continually diversify the mental scene and produce in it the greatest variety and most rapid succession imaginable. How is this compatible with that perfect immutability and simplicity which all true theists ascribe to the Deity? By the same act, say they, he sees past, present, and future; his love and hatred, his mercy and justice, are one individual operation; he is entire in every point of space, and complete in every instant of duration. No succession, no change, no acquisition, no diminution. What he is implies not in it any shadow of distinction or diversity. And what he is this moment he ever has been and ever will be, without any new judgment, sentiment, or operation. He stands fixed in one simple, perfect state; nor can you ever say, with any propriety, that this act of his is different from that other, or that this judgment or idea has been lately formed and will give place, by succession, to any different judgment or idea.

I can readily allow, said Cleanthes, that those who maintain the perfect simplicity of the Supreme Being, to the extent in which you have explained it, are complete mystics, and chargeable with all the consequences which I have drawn from their opinion. They are, in a word, atheists, without knowing it. For though it be allowed that the Deity possesses attributes of which we have no comprehension, yet ought we never to ascribe to him any attributes which are absolutely incompatible with that intelligent nature essential to him. A mind whose acts and sentiments and ideas are not distinct and successive, one that is wholly simple and totally immutable, is a mind which has no thought, no reason, no will, no sentiment, no love, no hatred; or, in a word, is no mind at all. It is an abuse of terms to give it that appellation, and we may as well speak of limited extension without figure, or of number without composition.

Pray consider, said Philo, whom you are at present inveighing against. You are honouring with the appellation of *atheist* all the sound, orthodox divines, almost, who have treated of this subject; and you will at last be, yourself, found, according to your reckoning, the only sound theist in the world. But if idolaters be atheists, as, I think, may justly be asserted, and Christian theologians the same, what becomes of the argument, so much celebrated, derived from the universal consent of mankind?

But, because I know you are not much swayed by names and authorities, I shall endeavor to show you, a little more distinctly, the inconveniences of that anthropomorphism which you have embraced, and shall prove that

there is no ground to suppose a plan of the world to be formed in the Divine mind, consisting of distinct ideas, differently arranged, in the same manner as an architect forms in his head the plan of a house which he intends to execute.

It is not easy, I own, to see what is gained by this supposition, whether we judge of the matter by *reason* or by *experience*. We are still obliged to mount higher in order to find the cause of this cause which you had assigned as satisfactory and conclusive.

If *reason* (I mean abstract reason derived from inquiries *a priori*) be not alike mute with regard to all questions concerning cause and effect, this sentence at least it will venture to pronounce: that a mental world or universe of ideas requires a cause as much as does a material world or universe of objects, and, if similar in its arrangement, must require a similar cause. For what is there in this subject which should occasion a different conclusion or inference? In an abstract view, they are entirely alike; and no difficulty attends the one supposition which is not common to both of them.

Again, when we will needs force *experience* to pronounce some sentence, even on these subjects which lie beyond her sphere, neither can she perceive any material difference in this particular between those two kinds of worlds, but finds them to be governed by similar principles, and to depend upon an equal variety of causes in their operations. We have specimens in miniature of both of them. Our own mind resembles the one; a vegetable or animal body the other. Let experience, therefore, judge from these samples. Nothing seems more delicate, with regard to its causes, than thought; and as these causes never operate in two persons after the same manner, so we never find two persons who think exactly alike. Nor indeed does the same person think exactly alike at any two different periods of time. A difference of age, of the disposition of his body, of weather, of food, of company, of books, of passions— any of these particulars, or others more minute, are sufficient to alter the curious machinery of thought and communicate to it very different movements and operations. As far as we can judge, vegetables and animal bodies are not more delicate in their motions, nor depend upon a greater variety or more curious adjustment of springs and principles.

How, therefore, shall we satisfy ourselves concerning the cause of that Being whom you suppose the Author of nature, or, according to your system of anthropomorphism, the ideal world into which you trace the material? Have we not the same reason to trace that ideal world into another ideal world or new intelligent principle? But if we stop and go no farther, why go so far? Why not stop at the material world? How can we satisfy ourselves without going on *in infinitum*? And, after all, what satisfaction is there in that infinite progression? Let us remember the story of the Indian philosopher and his elephant. It was never more applicable than to the present subject. If the material world rests upon a similar ideal world, this ideal world must rest upon some other, and so on without end. It were better, therefore, never to look beyond the present material world. By supposing it to contain the principle of its order within itself, we really assert it to be God; and the sooner we arrive at that Divine Being, so much the better. When you go one step beyond the mundane system, you only excite an inquisitive humour which it is impossible ever to satisfy.

To say that the different ideas which compose the reason of the Supreme Being fall into order of themselves and by their own nature is really to talk without any precise meaning. If it has a meaning, I would fain know why it is not as good sense to say that the parts of the material world fall into order of themselves and by their own nature. Can the one opinion be intelligible, while the other is not so?

We have, indeed, experience of ideas which fall into order of themselves and without any *known* cause. But, I am sure, we have a much larger experience of matter which does the same, as in all instances of generation and vegetation where the accurate analysis of the cause exceeds all human comprehension. We have

also experience of particular systems of thought and of matter which have no order; of the first in madness, of the second in corruption. Why, then, should we think that order is more essential to one than the other? And if it requires a cause in both, what do we gain by your system, in tracing the universe of objects into a similar universe of ideas? The first step which we make leads us on for ever. It were, therefore, wise in us to limit all our inquiries to the present world, without looking farther. No satisfaction can ever be attained by these speculations which so far exceed the narrow bounds of human understanding.

It was usual with the Peripatetics, you know, Cleanthes, when the cause of any phenomenon was demanded, to have recourse to their *faculties* or *occult qualities,* and to say, for instance, that bread nourished by its nutritive faculty, and senna purged by its purgative. But it has been discovered that this subterfuge was nothing but the disguise of ignorance, and that these philosophers, though less ingenuous, really said the same thing with the sceptics or the vulgar who fairly confessed that they knew not the cause of these phenomena. In like manner, when it is asked, what cause produced order in the ideas of the Supreme Being, can any other reason be assigned by you, anthropomorphites, than that it is a *rational* faculty, and that such is the nature of the Deity? But why a similar answer will not be equally satisfactory in accounting for the order of the world, without having recourse to any such intelligent creator as you insist on, may be difficult to determine. It is only to say that *such* is the nature of material objects, and that they are all originally possessed of a *faculty* of order and proportion. These are only more learned and elaborate ways of confessing our ignorance; nor has the one hypothesis any real advantage above the other, except in its greater conformity to vulgar prejudices.

You have displayed this argument with great emphasis, replied Cleanthes: You seem not sensible to how easy it is to answer it. Even in common life, if I assign a cause for any event, is it any objection, Philo, that I cannot assign the cause of that cause, and answer every new question which may incessantly be started? And what philosophers could possibly submit to so rigid a rule?—philosophers who confess ultimate causes to be totally unknown, and are sensible that the most refined principles into which they trace the phenomena are still to them as inexplicable as these phenomena themselves are to the vulgar. The order and arrangement of nature, the curious adjustment of final causes, the plain use and intention of every part and organ—all these bespeak in the clearest language an intelligent cause or author. The heavens and the earth join in the same testimony: The whole chorus of nature raises one hymn to the praises of its Creator. You alone, or almost alone, disturb this general harmony. You start abstruse doubts, cavils, and objections; you ask me what is the cause of this cause? I know not; I care not; that concerns not me. I have found a Deity; and here I stop my inquiry. Let those go farther who are wiser or more enterprising.

I pretend to be neither, replied Philo; and for that very reason I should never, perhaps, have attempted to go so far, especially when I am sensible that I must at last be contented to sit down with the same answer which, without further trouble, might have satisfied me from the beginning. If I am still to remain in utter ignorance of causes and can absolutely give an explication of nothing, I shall never esteem it any advantage to shove off for a moment a difficulty which you acknowledge must immediately, in its full force, recur upon me. Naturalists indeed very justly explain particular effects by more general causes, though these general causes themselves should remain in the end totally inexplicable, but they never surely thought it satisfactory to explain a particular effect by a particular cause which was no more to be accounted for than the effect itself. An ideal system, arranged of itself, without a precedent design, is not a whit more explicable than a material one which attains its order in a like manner; nor is there any more difficulty in the latter supposition than in the former.

PART V

But to show you still more inconveniences, continued Philo, in your anthropomorphism, please to take a new survey of your principles. *Like effects prove like causes.* This is the experimental argument; and this, you say too, is the sole theological argument. Now it is certain that the liker the effects which are seen and the liker the causes which are inferred, the stronger is the argument. Every departure on either side diminishes the probability and renders the experiment less conclusive. You cannot doubt of the principle; neither ought you to reject its consequences.

All the new discoveries in astronomy which prove the immense grandeur and magnificence of the works of nature are so many additional arguments for a Deity, according to the true system of theism; but, according to your hypothesis of experimental theism, they become so many objections, by removing the effect still farther from all resemblance to the effects of human art and contrivance. For if Lucretius, even following the old system of the world, could exclaim:

> Quis regere immensi summam, quis habere profundi
> Indu manu validas potis est moderanter habenas?
> Quis pariter coelos omnes convertere? et omnes
> Ignibus aetheriis terras suffire feraces?
> Omnibus inque locis esse omni tempore praesto?[2]
> [The English translation is in the end note.]

If Tully [Cicero] esteemed this reasoning so natural as to put it into the mouth of his Epicurean:

> Quibus enim oculis animi intueri potuit vester Plato fabricam illam tanti operis, qua construi a Deo atque aedificari mundum facit? quae molitio? quae ferramenta? qui vectes? quae machinae? qui ministri tanti muneris fuerunt? quemadmodum autem obedire et parere voluntati architecti aer, ignis, aqua, terra potuerunt?[3]
> [The English translation is in the end note.]

If this argument, I say, had any force in former ages, how much greater must it have at present when the bounds of Nature are so infinitely enlarged and such a magnificent scene is opened to us? It is still more unreasonable to form our idea of so unlimited a cause from our experience of the narrow productions of human design and invention.

The discoveries by microscopes, as they open a new universe in miniature, are still objections, according to you, arguments, according to me. The further we push our researches of this kind, we are still led to infer the universal cause of all to be vastly different from mankind, or from any object of human experience and observation.

And what say you to the discoveries in anatomy, chemistry, botany?...These surely are no objections, replied Cleanthes; they only discover new instances of art and contrivance, it is still the image of mind reflected on us from innumerable objects. Add a mind *like the human,* said Philo. I know of no other, replied Cleanthes. And the liker, the better, insisted Philo. To be sure, said Cleanthes.

Now, Cleanthes, said Philo, with an air of alacrity and triumph, mark the consequences. *First,* by this method of reasoning you renounce all claim to infinity in any of the attributes of the Deity. For, as the cause ought only to be proportioned to the effect, and the effect, so far as it falls under our cognizance, is not infinite, what pretensions have we, upon your suppositions, to ascribe that attribute to the Divine Being? You will still insist that, by removing him so much from all similarity to human creatures, we give in to the most arbitrary hypothesis, and at the same time weaken all proofs of his existence.

Secondly, you have no reason, on your theory, for ascribing perfection to the Deity, even in his finite capacity, or for supposing him free from every error, mistake, or incoherence, in his undertakings. There are many inexplicable difficulties in the works of nature which, if we allow a perfect author to be proved *a priori,* are easily solved, and become only seeming difficulties from the narrow capacity of man, who cannot trace infinite relations. But according to your method of reasoning, these difficulties become

all real, and, perhaps, will be insisted on as new instances of likeness to human art and contrivance. At least, you must acknowledge that it is impossible for us to tell, from our limited views, whether this system contains any great faults or deserves any considerable praise if compared to other possible and even real systems. Could a peasant, if the *Aeneid* were read to him, pronounce that poem to be absolutely faultless, or even assign to it its proper rank among the productions of human wit, he who had never seen any other production?

But were this world ever so perfect a production, it must still remain uncertain whether all the excellences of the work can justly be ascribed to the workman. If we survey a ship, what an exalted idea must we form of the ingenuity of the carpenter who framed so complicated, useful, and beautiful a machine? And what surprise must we feel when we find him a stupid mechanic who imitated others, and copied an art which, through a long succession of ages, after multiplied trials, mistakes, corrections, deliberations, and controversies, had been gradually improving? Many worlds might have been botched and bungled, throughout an eternity, ere this system was struck out; much labour lost, many fruitless trials made, and a slow but continued improvement carried on during infinite ages in the art of world-making. In such subjects, who can determine where the truth, nay, who can conjecture where the probability lies, amidst a great number of hypotheses which may be proposed, and a still greater which may be imagined?

And what shadow of an argument, continued Philo, can you produce from your hypothesis to prove the unity of the Deity? A great number of men join in building a house or ship, in rearing a city, in framing a commonwealth; why may not several deities combine in contriving and framing a world? This is only so much greater similarity to human affairs. By sharing the work among several, we may so much further limit the attributes of each, and get rid of that extensive power and knowledge which must be supposed in one deity, and which, according to you, can only serve to weaken the proof of his existence. And if such foolish, such vicious creatures as man can yet often unite in framing and executing one plan, how much more those deities or demons, whom we may suppose several degrees more perfect!

To multiply causes without necessity is indeed contrary to true philosophy, but this principle applies not to the present case. Were one deity antecedently proved by your theory who were possessed of every attribute requisite to the production of the universe, it would be needless, I own (though not absurd) to suppose any other deity existent. But while it is still a question whether all these attributes are united in one subject or dispersed among several independent beings, by what phenomena in nature can we pretend to decide the controversy? Where we see a body raised in a scale, we are sure that there is in the opposite scale, however concealed from sight, some counterpoising weight equal to it; but it is still allowed to doubt whether that weight be an aggregate of several distinct bodies or one uniform united mass. And if the weight requisite very much exceeds anything which we have ever seen conjoined in any single body, the former supposition becomes still more probable and natural. An intelligent being of such vast power and capacity as is necessary to produce the universe, or, to speak in the language of ancient philosophy, so prodigious an animal exceeds all analogy and even comprehension.

But further, Cleanthes: Men are mortal, and renew their species by generation; and this is common to all living creatures. The two great sexes of male and female, says Milton, animate the world. Why must this circumstance, so universal, so essential, be excluded from those numerous and limited deities? Behold, then, the theogeny of ancient times brought back upon us.

And why not become a perfect anthropomorphite? Why not assert the deity or deities to be corporeal, and to have eyes, a nose, mouth, ears, etc.? Epicurus maintained that no man had ever seen reason but in a human figure;

therefore, the gods must have a human figure. And this argument, which is deservedly so much ridiculed by Cicero, becomes, according to you, solid and philosophical.

In a word, Cleanthes, a man who follows your hypothesis is able, perhaps, to assert or conjecture that the universe sometime arose from something like design; but beyond that position he cannot ascertain one single circumstance, and is left afterwards to fix every point of his theology by the utmost license of fancy and hypothesis. This world, for aught he knows, is very faulty and imperfect, compared to a superior standard, and was only the first rude essay of some infant deity who afterwards abandoned it, ashamed of his lame performance; it is the work only of some dependent, inferior deity, and is the object of derision to his superiors; it is the production of old age and dotage in some superannuated deity, and ever since his death has run on at adventures, from the first impulse and active force which it received from him. You justly give signs of horror, Demea, at these strange suppositions; but these, and a thousand more of the same kind, are Cleanthes' suppositions, not mine. From the moment the attributes of the Deity are supposed finite, all these have place. And I cannot, for my part, think that so wild and unsettled a system of theology is, in any respect, preferable to none at all.

These suppositions I absolutely disown, cried Cleanthes: they strike me, however, with no horror, especially when proposed in that rambling way in which they drop from you. On the contrary, they give me pleasure when I see that, by the utmost indulgence of your imagination, you never get rid of the hypothesis of design in the universe, but are obliged at every turn to have recourse to it. To this concession I adhere steadily; and this I regard as a sufficient foundation for religion.

PART VI

It must be a slight fabric, indeed, said Demea, which can be erected on so tottering a foundation. While we are uncertain whether there is one deity or many, whether the deity or deities, to whom we owe our existence, be perfect or imperfect, subordinate or supreme, dead or alive, what trust or confidence can we repose in them? What devotion or worship address to them? What veneration or obedience pay them? To all the purposes of life the theory of religion becomes altogether useless; and even with regard to speculative consequences its uncertainty, according to you, must render it totally precarious and unsatisfactory.

To render it still more unsatisfactory, said Philo, there occurs to me another hypothesis which must acquire an air of probability from the method of reasoning so much insisted on by Cleanthes. That like effects arise from like causes—this principle he supposes the foundation of all religion. But there is another principle of the same kind, no less certain and derived from the same source of experience, that, where several known circumstances are observed to be similar, the unknown will also be found similar. Thus, if we see the limbs of a human body, we conclude that it is also attended with a human head, though hid from us. Thus, if we see, through a chink in a wall, a small part of the sun, we conclude that were the wall removed we should see the whole body. In short, this method of reasoning is so obvious and familiar that no scruple can ever be made with regard to its solidity.

Now, if we survey the universe, so far as it falls under our knowledge, it bears a great resemblance to an animal or organized body, and seems actuated with a like principle of life and motion. A continual circulation of matter in it produces no disorder; a continual waste in every part is incessantly repaired; the closest sympathy is perceived throughout the entire system; and each part or member, in performing its proper offices, operates both to its own preservation and to that of the whole. The world, therefore, I infer, is an animal; and the Deity is the *soul* of the world, actuating it, and actuated by it.

You have too much learning, Cleanthes, to be at all surprised at this opinion which, you know, was maintained by almost all the theists of antiquity, and chiefly prevails in their discourses and reasonings. For though, sometimes, the ancient philosophers reason from final causes, as if they thought the world the workmanship of God, yet it appears rather their favourite notion to consider it as his body whose organization renders it subservient to him. And it must be confessed that, as the universe resembles more a human body than it does the works of human art and contrivance, if our limited analogy could ever, with any propriety, be extended to the whole of nature, the inference seems juster in favour of the ancient than the modern theory.

There are many other advantages, too, in the former theory which recommended it to the ancient theologians. Nothing more repugnant to all their notions because nothing more repugnant to common experience than mind without body, a mere spiritual substance which fell not under their senses nor comprehension, and of which they had not observed one single instance throughout all nature. Mind and body they knew because they felt both; an order, arrangement, organization, or internal machinery, in both they likewise knew, after the same manner; and it could not but seem reasonable to transfer this experience to the universe, and to suppose the divine mind and body to be also coeval and to have, both of them, order and arrangement naturally inherent in them and inseparable from them.

Here, therefore, is a new species of *anthropomorphism*, Cleanthes, on which you may deliberate, and a theory which seems not liable to any considerable difficulties. You are too much superior, surely, to *systematical prejudices* to find any more difficulty in supposing an animal body to be, originally, of itself or from unknown causes, possessed of order and organization, than in supposing a similar order to belong to mind. But the *vulgar prejudice* that body and mind ought always to accompany each other ought not, one should think, to be entirely neglected; since it is founded on *vulgar experience*, the only guide which you profess to follow in all these theological inquiries. And if you assert that our limited experience is an unequal standard by which to judge of the un-limited extent of nature, you entirely abandon your own hypothesis, and must thenceforward adopt our mysticism, as you call it, and admit of the absolute incomprehensibility of the Divine Nature.

This theory, I own, replied Cleanthes, has never before occurred to me, though a pretty natural one; and I cannot readily, upon so short an examination and reflection, deliver any opinion with regard to it. You are very scrupulous, indeed, said Philo. Were I to examine any system of yours, I should not have acted with half that caution and reserve in stating objections and difficulties to it. However, if anything occurs to you, you will oblige us by proposing it.

Why then, replied Cleanthes, it seems to me that, though the world does, in many circumstances, resemble an animal body, yet is the analogy also defective in many circumstances the most material: no organs of sense; no seat of thought or reason; no one precise origin of motion and action. In short, it seems to bear a stronger resemblance to a vegetable than to an animal, and your inference would be so far inconclusive in favour of the soul of the world.

But, in the next place, your theory seems to imply the eternity of the world; and that is a principle which, I think, can be refuted by the strongest reasons and probabilities. I shall suggest an argument to this purpose which, I believe, has not been insisted on by any writer. Those who reason from the late origin of arts and sciences, though their inference wants not force, may perhaps be refuted by considerations derived from the nature of human society, which is in continual revolution between ignorance and knowledge, liberty and slavery, riches and poverty; so that it is impossible for us, from our limited experience, to foretell with assurance what events may or may not be expected. Ancient learning and history seem to have been in great danger of entirely perishing after the inundation of the barbarous nations; and had these convulsions continued a little longer or been a little more violent, we should not probably have now known what passed in the world a few

centuries before us. Nay, were it not for the superstition of the popes, who preserved a little jargon of Latin in order to support the appearance of an ancient and universal church, that tongue must have been utterly lost; in which case the Western world, being totally barbarous, would not have been in a fit disposition for receiving the Greek language and learning, which was conveyed to them after the sacking of Constantinople. When learning and books had been extinguished, even the mechanical arts would have fallen considerably to decay; and it is easily imagined that fable or tradition might ascribe to them a much later origin than the true one. This vulgar argument, therefore, against the eternity of the world seems a little precarious.

But here appears to be the foundation of a better argument. Lucullus was the first that brought cherry-trees from Asia to Europe, though that tree thrives so well in many European climates that it grows in the woods without any culture. Is it possible that, throughout a whole eternity, no European had ever passed into Asia and thought of transplanting so delicious a fruit into his own country? Or if the tree was once transplanted and propagated, how could it ever afterwards perish? Empires may rise and fall, liberty and slavery succeed alternately, ignorance and knowledge give place to each other; but the cherry-tree will still remain in the woods of Greece, Spain, and Italy, and will never be affected by the revolutions of human society.

It is not two thousand years since vines were transplanted into France, though there is no climate in the world more favourable to them. It is not three centuries since horses, cows, sheep, swine, dogs, corn, were known in America. Is it possible that during the revolutions of a whole eternity there never arose a Columbus who might open the communication between Europe and that continent? We may as well imagine that all men would wear stockings for ten thousand years, and never have the sense to think of garters to tie them. All these seem convincing proofs of the youth or rather infancy of the world, as being founded on the operation of principles more constant and steady than those by which human society is governed and directed. Nothing less than a total convulsion of the elements will ever destroy all the European animals and vegetables which are now to be found in the Western world.

And what argument have you against such convulsions? replied Philo. Strong and almost incontestable proofs may be traced over the whole earth that every part of this globe has continued for many ages entirely covered with water. And though order were supposed inseparable from matter, and inherent in it, yet may matter be susceptible of many and great revolutions, through the endless periods of eternal duration. The incessant changes to which every part of it is subject seem to intimate some such general transformations; though, at the same time, it is observable that all the changes and corruptions of which we have ever had experience are but passages from one state of order to another; nor can matter ever rest in total deformity and confusion. What we see in the parts, we may infer in the whole; at least, that is the method of reasoning on which you rest your whole theory. And were I obliged to defend any particular system of this nature, which I never willingly should do, I esteem none more plausible than that which ascribes an eternal inherent principle of order to the world, though attended with great and continual revolutions and alterations. This at once solves all difficulties; and if the solution, by being so general, is not entirely complete and satisfactory, it is at least a theory that we must sooner or later have recourse to, whatever system we embrace. How could things have been as they are, were there not an original inherent principle of order somewhere, in thought or in matter? And it is very indifferent to which of these we give the preference. Chance has no place, on any hypothesis, sceptical or religious. Everything is surely governed by steady, inviolable laws. And were the inmost essence of things laid open to us, we should then discover a scene of which, at present, we can have no idea. Instead of admiring the order of natural beings, we should clearly see that it was absolutely impossible for them, in the smallest article, ever to admit of any other disposition.

Were anyone inclined to revive the ancient pagan theology which maintained, as we learned from Hesiod, that this globe was governed by 30,000 deities, who arose from the unknown powers of nature, you would naturally object, Cleanthes, that nothing is gained by this hypothesis; and that it is as easy to suppose all men animals, beings more numerous but less perfect, to have sprung immediately from a like origin. Push the same inference a step further, and you will find a numerous society of deities as explicable as one universal deity who possesses within himself the powers and perfections of the whole society. All these systems, then, of Scepticism, Polytheism, and Theism, you must allow, on your principles, to be on a like footing, and that no one of them has any advantage over the others. You may thence learn the fallacy of your principles.

PART VII

But here, continued Philo, in examining the ancient system on the soul of the world there strikes me, all of a sudden, a new idea which, if just, must go near to subvert all your reasoning, and destroy even your first inferences on which you repose such confidence. If the universe bears a greater likeness to animal bodies and to vegetables than to the works of human art, it is more probable that its cause resembles the cause of the former than that of the latter, and its origin ought rather to be ascribed to generation or vegetation than to reason or design. Your conclusion, even according to your own principles, is therefore lame and defective.

Pray open up this argument a little further, said Demea, for I do not rightly apprehend it in that concise manner in which you have expressed it.

Our friend Cleanthes, replied Philo, as you have heard, asserts that, since no question of fact can be proved otherwise than by experience, the existence of a Deity admits not of proof from any other medium. The world, says he, resembles the works of human contrivance; therefore its cause must also resemble that of the other. Here we may remark that the operation of one very small part of nature, to wit, man, upon another very small part, to wit, that inanimate matter lying within his reach, is the rule by which Cleanthes judges of the origin of the whole; and he measures objects, so widely disproportioned, by the same individual standard. But to waive all objections drawn from this topic, I affirm that there are other parts of the universe (besides the machines of human invention) which bear still a greater resemblance to the fabric of the world, and which, therefore, afford a better conjecture concerning the universal origin of this system. These parts are animals and vegetables. The world plainly resembles more an animal or a vegetable than it does a watch or a knitting-loom. Its cause, therefore, it is more probable, resembles the cause of the former. The cause of the former is generation or vegetation. The cause, therefore, of the world we may infer to be something similar or analogous to generation or vegetation.

But how is it conceivable, said Demea, that the world can arise from anything similar to vegetation or generation?

Very easily, replied Philo. In like manner as a tree sheds its seed into the neighboring fields and produces other trees, so the great vegetable, the world, or this planetary system, produces within itself certain seeds which, being scattered into the surrounding chaos, vegetate into new worlds. A comet, for instance, is the seed of a world; and after it has been fully ripened, by passing from sun to sun, and star to star, it is, at last, tossed into the unformed elements which everywhere surround this universe, and immediately sprouts up into a new system.

Or if, for the sake of variety (for I see no other advantage), we should suppose this world to be an animal: a comet is the egg of this animal; and in like manner as an ostrich lays its egg in the sand, which, without any further care, hatches the egg and produces a new animal, so…I understand you, says Demea. But what wild, arbitrary suppositions are these! What *data* have you for

such extraordinary conclusions? And is the slight, imaginary resemblance of the world to a vegetable or an animal sufficient to establish the same inference with regard to both? Objects which are in general so widely different, ought they to be a standard for each other?

Right, cries Philo: This is the topic on which I have all along insisted. I have still asserted that we have no *data* to establish any system of cosmogony. Our experience, so imperfect in itself and so limited both in extent and duration, can afford us no probable conjecture concerning the whole of things. But if we must needs fix on some hypothesis, by what rule, pray, ought we to determine our choice? Is there any other rule than the greater similarity of the objects compared? And does not a plant or an animal, which springs from vegetation or generation, bear a stronger resemblance to the world than does any artificial machine, which arises from reason and design?

But what is this vegetation and generation of which you talk? said Demea. Can you explain their operations, and anatomize that fine internal structure on which they depend?

As much, at least, replied Philo, as Cleanthes can explain the operations of reason, or anatomize that internal structure on which it depends. But without any such elaborate disquisitions, when I see an animal, I infer that it sprang from generation; and that with as great certainty as you conclude a house to have been reared by design. These words *generation, reason* mark only certain powers and energies in nature whose effects are known, but whose essence is incomprehensible; and one of these principles, more than the other, has no privilege for being made a standard to the whole of nature.

In reality, Demea, it may reasonably be expected that the larger the views are which we take of things, the better will they conduct us in our conclusions concerning such extraordinary and such magnificent subjects. In this little corner of the world alone, there are four principles, *reason, instinct, generation, vegetation,* which are similar to each other, and are the causes of similar effects. What a number of other principles may we naturally suppose in the immense extent and variety of the universe could we travel from planet to planet, and from system to system, in order to examine each part of this mighty fabric? Any one of these four principles above mentioned (and a hundred others which lie open to our conjecture) may afford us a theory by which to judge of the origin of the world; and it is a palpable and egregious partiality to confine our view entirely to that principle by which our own minds operate. Were this principle more intelligible on that account, such a partiality might be somewhat excusable; but reason, in its internal fabric and structure, is really as little known to us as instinct or vegetation; and, perhaps, even that vague, undeterminate word *nature,* to which the vulgar refer everything is not at the bottom more inexplicable. The effects of these principles are all known to us from experience; but the principles themselves and their manner of operation are totally unknown; nor is it less intelligible or less comfortable to experience to say that the world arose by vegetation, from a seed shed by another world, than to say that it arose from a divine reason or contrivance, according to the sense in which Cleanthes understands it.

But methinks, said Demea, if the world had a vegetative quality and could sow the seeds of new worlds into the infinite chaos, this power would be still an additional argument for design in its author. For whence could arise so wonderful a faculty but from design? Or how can order spring from anything which perceives not that order which it bestows?

You need only look around you, replied Philo, to satisfy yourself with regard to this question. A tree bestows order and organization on that tree which springs from it, without knowing the order; an animal in the same manner on its offspring; a bird on its nest; and instances of this kind are even more frequent in the world than those of order which arise from reason and contrivance. To say that all this order in animals and vegetables proceeds ultimately from design is begging the question; nor can that great point be ascertained otherwise than by proving, *a priori,* both that order is, from its nature,

inseparably attached to thought and that it can never of itself or from original unknown principles belong to matter.

But further, Demea, this objection which you urge can never be made use of by Cleanthes, without renouncing a defense which he has already made against one of my objections. When I inquired concerning the cause of that supreme reason and intelligence into which he resolves everything, he told me that the impossibility of satisfying such inquiries could never be admitted as an objection in any species of philosophy. *We must stop somewhere,* says he; *nor is it ever within the reach of human capacity to explain ultimate causes or show the last connections of any objects. It is sufficient if any steps, as far as we go, are supported by experience and observation.* Now that vegetation and generation, as well as reason, are experienced to be principles of order in nature is undeniable. If I rest my system of cosmogony on the former, preferably to the latter, it is at my choice. The matter seems entirely arbitrary. And when Cleanthes asks me what is the cause of my great vegetative or generative faculty, I am equally entitled to ask him the cause of his great reasoning principle. These questions we have agreed to forbear on both sides; and it is chiefly his interest on the present occasion to stick to this agreement. Judging by our limited and imperfect experience, generation has some privileges above reason; for we see every day the latter arise from the former, never the former from the latter.

Compare, I beseech you, the consequences on both sides. The world, say I, resembles an animal; therefore it is an animal, therefore it arose from generation. The steps, I confess, are wide, yet there is some small appearance of analogy in each step. The world, says Cleanthes, resembles a machine; therefore it is a machine, therefore it arose from design. The steps are here equally wide, and the analogy less striking. And if he pretends to carry on *my* hypothesis a step further, and to infer design or reason from the great principle of generation on which I insist, I may, with better authority, use the same freedom to push further *his* hypothesis, and infer a divine generation or theogony from his principle of reason. I have at least some faint shadow of experience, which is the utmost that can ever be attained in the present subject. Reason, in innumerable instances, is observed to arise from the principle of generation, and never to arise from any other principle.

Hesiod and all the ancient mythologists were so struck with this analogy that they universally explained the origin of nature from an animal birth, and copulation. Plato, too, so far as he is intelligible, seems to have adopted some such notion in his *Timaeus.*

The Brahmins assert that the world arose from an infinite spider, who spun this whole complicated mass from his bowels, and annihilates afterwards the whole or any part of it, by absorbing it again and resolving it into his own essence. Here is a species of cosmogony which appears to us ridiculous because a spider is a little contemptible animal whose operations we are never likely to take for a model of the whole universe. But still here is a new species of analogy, even in our globe. And were there a planet wholly inhabited by spiders (which is very possible), this inference would there appear as natural and irrefragable as that which in our planet ascribes the origin of all things to design and intelligence, as explained by Cleanthes. Why an orderly system may not be spun from the belly as well as from the brain, it will be difficult for him to give a satisfactory reason.

I must confess, Philo, replied Cleanthes, that, of all men living, the task which you have undertaken, of raising doubts and objections, suits you best and seems, in a manner, natural and unavoidable to you. So great is your fertility of invention than I am not ashamed to acknowledge myself unable, on a sudden, to solve regularly such out-of-the-way difficulties as you incessantly start upon me, though I clearly see, in general, their fallacy and error. And I question not, but you are yourself, at present, in the same case, and have not the solution so ready as the objection, while you must be sensible that common sense and reason are entirely against you, and that such whimsies as you have delivered may puzzle but never can convince us.

PART VIII

What you ascribe to the fertility of my invention, replied Philo, is entirely owing to the nature of the subject. In subjects adapted to the narrow compass of human reason there is commonly but one determination which carries probability or conviction with it; and to a man of sound judgment all other suppositions but that one appear entirely absurd and chimerical. But in such questions as the present, a hundred contradictory views may preserve a kind of imperfect analogy, and invention has here full scope to exert itself. Without any great effort of thought, I believe that I could, in an instant, propose other systems of cosmogony which would have some faint appearance of truth, though it is a thousand, a million to one if either yours or any one of mine be the true system.

For instance, what if I should revive the old Epicurean hypothesis? This is commonly, and I believe justly, esteemed the most absurd system that has yet been proposed; yet I know not whether, with a few alterations, it might not be brought to bear a faint appearance of probability. Instead of supposing matter infinite, as Epicurus did, let us suppose it finite. A finite number of particles is only susceptible of finite transpositions; and it must happen, in an eternal duration, that every possible order or position must be tried an infinite number of times. This world, therefore, with all its events, even the most minute, has before been produced and destroyed, and will again be produced and destroyed, without any bounds and limitations. No one who has a conception of the powers of infinite, in comparison of finite, will ever scruple this determination.

But this supposes, said Demea, that matter can acquire motion without any voluntary agent or first mover.

And where is the difficulty, replied Philo, of that supposition? Every event, before experience, is equally difficult and incomprehensible; and every event, after experience, is equally easy and intelligible. Motion, in many instances, from gravity, from elasticity, from electricity, begins in matter, without any known voluntary agent; and to suppose always, in these cases, an unknown voluntary agent is mere hypothesis and hypothesis attended with no advantages. The beginning of motion in matter itself is as conceivable *a priori* as its communication from mind and intelligence.

Besides, why may not motion have been propagated by impulse through all eternity, and the same stock of it, or nearly the same, be still upheld in the universe? As much is lost by the composition of motion, as much is gained by its resolution. And whatever the causes are, the fact is certain that matter is and always has been in continual agitation, as far as human experience or tradition reaches. There is not probably, at present, in the whole universe, one particle of matter at absolute rest.

And this very consideration, too, continued Philo, which we have stumbled on in the course of the argument, suggests a new hypothesis of cosmogony that is not absolutely absurd and improbable. Is there a system, an order, an economy of things, by which matter can preserve that perpetual agitation which seems essential to it, and yet maintain a constancy in the forms which it produces? There certainly is such an economy, for this is actually the case with the present world. The continual motion of matter, therefore, in less than infinite transpositions, must produce this economy or order, and by its very nature, that order, when once established, supports itself for many ages if not to eternity. But wherever matter is so poised, arranged, and adjusted, as to continue in perpetual motion, and yet preserve a constancy in the forms, its situation must, of necessity, have all the same appearance of art and contrivance which we observe at present. All the parts of each form must have a relation to each other and to the whole; and the whole itself must have a relation to the other parts of the universe, to the element in which the form subsists, to the materials with which it repairs its waste and decay, and to every other form which is hostile or friendly. A defect in any of these particulars destroys the form, and the matter of which it is composed is again set

loose, and is thrown into irregular motions and fermentations till it unite itself to some other regular form. If no such form be prepared to receive it, and if there be a great quantity of this corrupted matter in the universe, the universe itself is entirely disordered, whether it be the feeble embryo of a world in its first beginnings that is thus destroyed or the rotten carcase of one languishing in old age and infirmity. In either case, a chaos ensues till finite though innumerable revolutions produce, at last, some forms whose parts and organs are so adjusted as to support the forms amidst a continued succession of matter.

Suppose (for we shall endeavour to vary the expression) that matter were thrown into any position by a blind, unguided force; it is evident that this first position must, in all probability, be the most confused and most disorderly imaginable, without any resemblance to those works of human contrivance which, along with a symmetry of parts, discover an adjustment of means to ends and a tendency to self-preservation. If the actuating force cease after this operation, matter must remain for ever in disorder and continue an immense chaos, without any proportion or activity. But suppose that the actuating force, whatever it be, still continues in matter, this first position will immediately give place to a second which will likewise, in all probability, be as disorderly as the first, and so on through many successions of changes and revolutions. No particular order or position ever continues a moment unaltered. The original force, still remaining in activity, gives a perpetual restlessness to matter. Every possible situation is produced and instantly destroyed. If a glimpse or dawn of order appears for a moment, it is instantly hurried away and confounded by that never-ceasing force which actuates every part of matter.

Thus the universe goes on for many ages in a continued succession of chaos and disorder. But is it not possible that it may settle at last, so as not to lose its motion and active force (for that we have supposed inherent in it), yet so as to preserve an uniformity of appearance, amidst the continual motion and fluctuation of its parts?

This we find to be the case with the universe at present. Every individual is perpetually changing, and every part of every individual; and yet the whole remains, in appearance, the same. May we not hope for such a position or rather be assured of it from the eternal revolutions of unguided matter; and may not this account for all the appearing wisdom and contrivance which is in the universe? Let us contemplate the subject a little, and we shall find that this adjustment if attained by matter of a seeming stability in the forms, with a real and perpetual revolution or motion of parts, affords a plausible, if not a true, solution of the difficulty.

It is in vain, therefore, to insist upon the uses of the parts in animals or vegetables, and their curious adjustment to each other. I would fain know how an animal could subsist unless its parts were so adjusted? Do we not find that it immediately perishes whenever this adjustment ceases, and that its matter, corrupting, tries some new form? It happens indeed that the parts of the world are so well adjusted that some regular form immediately lays claim to this corrupted matter; and if it were not so, could the world subsist? Must it not dissolve, as well as the animal, and pass through new positions and situations till in great but finite succession it fall, at last, into the present or some such order?

It is well, replied Cleanthes, you told us that this hypothesis was suggested on a sudden, in the course of the argument. Had you had leisure to examine it, you would soon have perceived the insuperable objections to which it is exposed. No form, you say, can subsist unless it possess those powers and organs requisite for its subsistence; some new order or economy must be tried, and so on, without intermission, till at last some order which can support and maintain itself is fallen upon. But according to this hypothesis, whence arise the many conveniences and advantages which men and all animals possess? Two eyes, two ears are not absolutely necessary for the subsistence of the species. The human race might have been propagated and preserved without horses, dogs, cows, sheep, and those innumerable fruits and products which serve to our satisfaction and enjoyment. If no camels had been created for the use of man in the sandy deserts of Africa and Arabia, would the world have been dissolved? If no loadstone had been framed to give that wonderful and useful direction to the needle, would human society and the human kind have been immediately extinguished? Though the maxims of nature be in general very frugal, yet instances of this kind are far from being rare; and any one of them is a sufficient proof of design—and of a benevolent design—which gave rise to the order and arrangement of the universe.

At least, you may safely infer, said Philo, that the foregoing hypothesis is so far incomplete and imperfect, which I shall not scruple to allow. But can we ever reasonably expect greater success in any attempts of this nature? Or can we ever hope to erect a system of cosmogony that will be liable to no exceptions, and will contain no circumstance repugnant to our limited and imperfect experience of the analogy of nature? Your theory itself cannot surely pretend to any such advantage, even though you have run into *anthropomorphism*, the better to preserve a conformity to common experience. Let us once more put it to trial. In all instances which we have ever seen, ideas are copied from real objects, and are ectypal, not archetypal, to express myself in learned terms. You reverse this order and give thought the precedence. In all instances which we have ever seen, thought has no influence upon matter except where that matter is so conjoined with it as to have an equal reciprocal influence upon it. No animal can move immediately anything but the members of its own body; and, indeed, the equality of action and reaction seems to be a universal law of nature; but your theory implies a contradiction to this experience. These instances, with many more which it were easy to collect (particularly the supposition of a mind or system of thought that is eternal or, in other words, an animal ingenerable and immortal)— these instances, I say, may teach all of us sobriety in condemning each other, and let us see that as no system of this kind ought ever to be received from a slight analogy, so neither ought any to be rejected on account of a small incongruity. For that is an inconvenience from which we can justly pronounce no one to be exempted.

All religious systems, it is confessed, are subject to great and insuperable difficulties. Each disputant triumphs in his turn, while he carries on an offensive war, and exposes the absurdities, barbarities, and pernicious tenets of his antagonist. But all of them, on the whole, prepare a complete triumph for the *sceptic,* who tells them that no system ought ever to be embraced with regard to such subjects: for this plain reason that no absurdity ought ever to be assented to with regard to any subject. A total suspense of judgment is here our only reasonable resource. And if every attack, as is commonly observed, and no defence among theologians is successful, how complete must be *his* victory who remains always, with all mankind, on the offensive, and has himself no fixed station or abiding city which he is ever, on any occasion, obliged to defend?

PART IX

But if so many difficulties attend the argument *a posteriori,* said Demea, had we not better adhere to that simple and sublime argument *a priori* which, by offering to us infallible demonstration, cuts off at once all doubt and difficulty? By this argument, too, we may prove the *infinity* of the Divine attributes, which, I am afraid, can never be ascertained with certainty from any other topic. For how can an effect which either is finite or, for aught we know, may be so—how can such an effect, I say, prove an infinite cause? The unity, too, of the Divine Nature it is very difficult, if not absolutely impossible, to deduce merely from contemplating the works of nature; nor will the uniformity alone of the plan, even were it allowed, give us any assurance of that attribute. Whereas the argument *a priori*....

You seem to reason, Demea, interposed Cleanthes, as if those advantages and conveniences in the abstract argument were full proofs of its solidity. But it is first proper, in my opinion, to determine what argument of this nature you choose to insist on; and we shall afterwards,

from itself, better than from its *useful* consequences, endeavour to determine what value we ought to put upon it.

The argument, replied Demea, which I would insist on is the common one. Whatever exists must have a cause or reason of its existence, it being absolutely impossible for anything to produce itself or be the cause of its own existence. In mounting up, therefore, from effects to causes, we must either go on in tracing an infinite succession, without any ultimate cause at all, or must at last have recourse to some ultimate cause that is *necessarily* existent. Now that the first supposition is absurd may be thus proved. In the infinite chain or succession of causes and effects, each single effect is determined to exist by the power and efficacy of that cause which immediately preceded; but the whole eternal chain or succession, taken together, is not determined or caused by anything, and yet it is evident that it requires a cause or reason, as much as any particular object which begins to exist in time. The question is still reasonable why this particular succession of causes existed from eternity, and not any other succession or no succession at all. If there be no necessarily existent being, any supposition which can be formed is equally possible; nor is there any more absurdity in *nothing's* having existed from eternity than there is in that succession of causes which constitutes the universe. What was it, then, which determined *something* to exist rather than *nothing,* and bestowed being on a particular possibility, exclusive of the rest? *External causes,* there are supposed to be none. *Chance* is a word without a meaning. Was it *nothing?* But that can never produce anything. We must, therefore, have recourse to a necessarily existent Being who carries the *reason* of his existence in himself, and who cannot be supposed not to exist, without an express contradiction. There is, consequently, such a Being—that is, there is a Deity.

I shall not leave it to Philo, said Cleanthes, though I know that the starting objections is his chief delight, to point out the weakness of this metaphysical reasoning. It seems to me so obviously ill-grounded, and at the same time of so little consequence to the cause of true piety and religion, that I shall myself venture to show the fallacy of it.

I shall begin with observing that there is an evident absurdity in pretending to demonstrate a matter of fact, or to prove it by arguments *a priori*. Nothing is demonstrable unless the contrary implies a contradiction. Nothing that is distinctly conceivable implies a contradiction. Whatever we conceive as existent, we can also conceive as nonexistent. There is no being, therefore, whose nonexistence implies a contradiction. Consequently there is no being whose existence is demonstrable. I propose this argument as entirely decisive, and am willing to rest the whole controversy upon it.

It is pretended that the Deity is a necessarily existent being; and this necessity of his existence is attempted to be explained by asserting that, if we knew his whole essence or nature, we should perceive it to be as impossible for him not to exist, as for twice two not to be four. But it is evident that this can never happen, while our faculties remain the same as at present. It will still be possible for us, at any time, to conceive the nonexistence of what we formerly conceived to exist; nor can the mind ever lie under a necessity of supposing any object to remain always in being; in the same manner as we lie under a necessity of always conceiving twice two to be four. The words, therefore, *necessary existence* have no meaning or, which is the same thing, none that is consistent.

But further, why may not the material universe be the necessarily existent Being, according to this pretended explication of necessity? We dare not affirm that we know all the qualities of matter; and, for aught we can determine, it may contain some qualities which, were they known, would make its nonexistence appear as great a contradiction as that twice two is five. I find only one argument employed to prove that the material world is not the necessarily existent Being; and this argument is derived from the contingency both of the matter and the form of the world. "Any particle of matter," it is said, "may be *conceived* to be annihilated, and any form may

be *conceived* to be altered. Such an annihilation or alteration, therefore, is not impossible."[4] But it seems a great partiality not to perceive that the same argument extends equally to the Deity, so far as we have any conception of him, and that the mind can at least imagine him to be nonexistent or his attributes to be altered. It must be some unknown, inconceivable qualities which can make his nonexistence appear impossible or his attributes unalterable; and no reason can be assigned why these qualities may not belong to matter. As they are altogether unknown and inconceivable, they can never be proved incompatible with it.

Add to this that in tracing an eternal succession of objects it seems absurd to inquire for a general cause or first author. How can anything that exists from eternity have a cause, since that relation implies a priority in time and a beginning of existence?

In such a chain, too, or succession of objects, each part is caused by that which preceded it, and causes that which succeeds it. Where then is the difficulty? But the *whole,* you say, wants a cause. I answer that the uniting of these parts into a whole, like the uniting of several distinct countries into one kingdom, or several distinct members into one body is performed merely by an arbitrary act of the mind, and has no influence on the nature of things. Did I show you the particular causes of each individual in a collection of twenty particles of matter, I should think it very unreasonable should you afterwards ask me what was the cause of the whole twenty. This is sufficiently explained in explaining the cause of the parts.

Though the reasonings which you have urged, Cleanthes, may well excuse me, said Philo, from starting any further difficulties, yet I cannot forbear insisting still upon another topic. It is observed by arithmeticians that the products of 9 compose always either 9 or some lesser product of 9 if you add together all the characters of which any of the former products is composed. Thus, of 18, 27, 36, which are products of 9, you make 9 by adding 1 to 8, 2 to 7, 3 to 6. Thus 369 is a product also of 9; and if you add 3,

6, and 9, you make 18, a lesser product of 9.[5] To a superficial observer so wonderful a regularity may be admired as the effect either of chance or design; but a skillful algebraist immediately concludes it to be the work of necessity, and demonstrates that it must for ever result from the nature of these numbers. Is it not probable, I ask, that the whole economy of the universe is conducted by a like necessity, though no human algebra can furnish a key which solves the difficulty? And instead of admiring the order of natural beings, may it not happen that, could we penetrate into the intimate nature of bodies, we should clearly see why it was absolutely impossible they could ever admit of any other disposition? So dangerous is it to introduce this idea of necessity into the present question, and so naturally does it afford an inference directly opposite to the religious hypothesis!

But dropping all these abstractions, continued Philo, and confining ourselves to more familiar topics, I shall venture to add an observation that the argument *a priori* has seldom been found very convincing, except to people of a metaphysical head who have accustomed themselves to abstract reasoning, and who, finding from mathematics that the understanding frequently leads to truth through obscurity, and contrary to first appearances, have transferred the same habit of thinking to subjects where it ought not to have place. Other people, even of good sense and the best inclined to religion, feel always some deficiency in such arguments, though they are not perhaps able to explain distinctly where it lies—a certain proof that men ever did and ever will derive their religion from other sources than from this species of reasoning.

PART X

It is my opinion, I own, replied Demea, that each man feels, in a manner, the truth of religion within his own breast, and, from a consciousness of his imbecility and misery rather than from any reasoning, is led to seek protection from that Being on whom he and all nature is dependent.

So anxious or so tedious are even the best scenes of life that futurity is still the object of all our hopes and fears. We incessantly look forward and endeavour, by prayers, adoration, and sacrifice, to appease those unknown powers whom we find, by experience, so able to afflict and oppress us. Wretched creatures that we are! What resource for us amidst the innumerable ills of life did not religion suggest some methods of atonement, and appease those terrors with which we are incessantly agitated and tormented?

I am indeed persuaded, said Philo, that the best and indeed the only method of bringing everyone to a due sense of religion is by just representations of the misery and wickedness of men. And for that purpose a talent of eloquence and strong imagery is more requisite than that of reasoning and argument. For is it necessary to prove what everyone feels within himself? It is only necessary to make us feel it, if possible, more intimately and sensibly.

The people, indeed, replied Demea, are sufficiently convinced of this great and melancholy truth. The miseries of life, the unhappiness of man, the general corruptions of our nature, the unsatisfactory enjoyment of pleasures, riches, honours—these phrases have become almost proverbial in all languages. And who can doubt of what all men declare from their own immediate feeling and experience?

In this point, said Philo, the learned are perfectly agreed with the vulgar; and in all letters, *sacred* and *profane,* the topic of human misery has been insisted on with the most pathetic eloquence that sorrow and melancholy could inspire. The poets, who speak from sentiment, without a system, and whose testimony has therefore the more authority, abound in images of this nature. From Homer down to Dr. Young, the whole inspired tribe have ever been sensible that no other representation of things would suit the feeling and observation of each individual.

As to authorities, replied Demea, you need not seek them. Look round this library of Cleanthes. I shall venture to affirm that, except authors of particular sciences, such as chemistry or botany, who have no occasion to treat of human life, there is scarce one of those innumerable writers from whom the sense of human misery has not, in some passage or other, extorted a complaint and confession of it. At least, the chance is entirely on that side; and no one author has ever, so far as I can recollect, been so extravagant as to deny it.

There you must excuse me, said Philo: Leibniz has denied it, and is perhaps the first[6] who ventured upon so bold and paradoxical an opinion; at least, the first who made it essential to his philosophical system.

And by being the first, replied Demea, might he not have been sensible of his error? For is this a subject in which philosophers can propose to make discoveries especially in so late an age? And can any man hope by a simple denial (for the subject scarcely admits of reasoning) to bear down the united testimony of mankind, founded on sense and consciousness?

And why should man, added he, pretend to an exemption from the lot of all other animals? The whole earth, believe me, Philo, is cursed and polluted. A perpetual war is kindled amongst all living creatures. Necessity, hunger, want stimulate the strong and courageous; fear, anxiety, terror agitate the weak and infirm. The first entrance into life gives anguish to the newborn infant and to its wretched parent; weakness, impotence, distress attend each stage of that life, and it is, at last finished in agony and horror.

Observe, too, says Philo, the curious artifices of nature in order to embitter the life of every living being. The stronger prey upon the weaker and keep them in perpetual terror and anxiety. The weaker, too, in their turn, often prey upon the stronger, and vex and molest them without relaxation. Consider that innumerable race of insects, which either are bred on the body of each animal or, flying about, infix their stings in him. These insects have others still less than themselves which torment them. And thus on each hand, before and behind, above and below, every animal is surrounded with enemies which incessantly seek his misery and destruction.

Man alone, said Demea, seems to be, in part, an exception to this rule. For by combination in society he can easily master lions, tigers, and bears, whose greater strength and agility naturally enable them to prey upon him.

On the contrary, it is here chiefly, cried Philo, that the uniform and equal maxims of nature are most apparent. Man, it is true, can, by combination, surmount all his *real* enemies and become master of the whole animal creation; but does he not immediately raise up to himself *imaginary* enemies, the demons of his fancy, who haunt him with superstitious terrors and blast every enjoyment of life? His pleasure, as he imagines, becomes in their eyes a crime; his food and repose give them umbrage and offence; his very sleep and dreams furnish new materials to anxious fear; and even death, his refuge from every other ill, presents only the dread of endless and innumerable woes. Nor does the wolf molest more the timid flock than superstition does the anxious breast of wretched mortals.

Besides, consider, Demea: This very society by which we surmount those wild beasts, our natural enemies, what new enemies does it not raise to us? What woe and misery does it not occasion? Man is the greatest enemy of man. Oppression, injustice, contempt, contumely, violence, sedition, war, calumny, treachery, fraud—by these they mutually torment each other, and they would soon dissolve that society which they had formed were it not for the dread of still greater ills which must attend their separation.

But though these external insults, said Demea, from animals, from men, from all the elements, which assault us from a frightful catalogue of woes, they are nothing in comparison of those which arise within ourselves, from the distempered condition of our mind and body. How many lie under the lingering torment of diseases? Hear the pathetic enumeration of the great poet.

Intestine stone and ulcer, colic-pangs,
Demoniac frenzy, moping melancholy,
And moon-struck madness, pining atrophy
Marasmus, and wide-wasting pestilence.
Dire was the tossing, deep the groans: Despair
Tended the sick, busiest from couch to couch

And over them triumphant Death his dart
Shook: but delay'd to strike, though oft invok'd
With vows, as their chief good and final hope.[7]

The disorders of the mind, continued Demea, though more secret, are not perhaps less dismal and vexatious. Remorse, shame, anguish, rage, disappointment, anxiety, fear, dejection, despair—who has ever passed through life without cruel inroads from these tormentors? How many have scarcely ever felt any better sensations? Labour and poverty, so abhorred by everyone, are the certain lot of the far greater number; and those few privileged persons who enjoy ease and opulence never reach contentment or true felicity. All the goods of life united would not make a very happy man, but all the ills united would make a wretch indeed; and any one of them almost (and who can be free from every one?), nay, often the absence of one good (and who can possess all?) is sufficient to render life ineligible.

Were a stranger to drop on a sudden into this world, I would show him, as a specimen of its ills, a hospital full of diseases, a prison crowded with malefactors and debtors, a field of battle strewed with carcases, a fleet floundering in the ocean, a nation languishing under tyranny, famine, or pestilence. To turn the gay side of life to him and give him a notion of its pleasures—whither should I conduct him? To a ball, to an opera, to court? He might justly think that I was only showing him a diversity of distress and sorrow.

There is no evading such striking instances, said Philo, but by apologies which still further aggravate the charge. Why have all men, I ask, in all ages, complained incessantly of the miseries of life?...They have no just reason, says one: these complaints proceed only from their discontented, repining, anxious disposition....And can there possibly, I reply, be a more certain foundation of misery than such a wretched temper?

But if they were really as unhappy as they pretend, says my antagonist, why do they remain in life?...

Not satisfied with life, afraid of death—

This is the secret chain, say I, that holds us. We are terrified, not bribed to the continuance of our existence.

It is only a false delicacy, he may insist, which a few refined spirits indulge, and which has spread these complaints among the whole race of mankind....And what is this delicacy, I ask, which you blame? Is it anything but a greater sensibility to all the pleasures and pains of life? And if the man of a delicate, refined temper, by being so much more alive than the rest of the world, is only so much more unhappy, what judgment must we form in general of human life?

Let men remain at rest, says our adversary, and they will be easy. They are willing artificers of their own misery....No! reply I: an anxious languor follows their repose: disappointment, vexation, trouble, their activity and ambition.

I can observe something like what you mention in some others, replied Cleanthes, but I confess I feel little or nothing of it in myself, and hope that it is not so common as you represent it.

If you feel not human misery yourself, cried Demea, I congratulate you on so happy a singularity. Others, seemingly the most prosperous, have not been ashamed to vent their complaints in the most melancholy strains. Let us attend to the great, the fortunate emperor, Charles V, when tired with human grandeur, he resigned all his extensive dominions into the hands of his son. In the last harangue which he made on that memorable occasion, he publicly avowed *that the greatest prosperities which he had ever enjoyed had been mixed with so many adversities that he might truly say he had never enjoyed any satisfaction or contentment.* But did the retired life in which he sought for shelter afford him any greater happiness? If we may credit his son's account, his repentance commenced the very day of his resignation.

Cicero's fortune, from small beginnings, rose to the greatest lustre and renown; yet what pathetic complaints of the ills of life do his familiar letters, as well as philosophical discourses, contain? And suitably to his own experience, he introduces Cato, the great, the fortunate Cato protesting in his old age that had he a new life in his offer he would reject the present.

Ask yourself, ask any of your acquaintance, whether they would live over again the last ten or twenty years of their life. No! but the next twenty, they say, will be better:

> *And from the dregs of life, hope to receive*
> *What the first sprightly running could not*
> *give.*[8]

Thus, at last, they find (such is the greatness of human misery, it reconciles even contradictions) that they complain at once of the shortness of life and of its vanity and sorrow.

And is it possible, Cleanthes, said Philo, that after all these reflections, and infinitely more which might be suggested, you can still persevere in your anthropomorphism, and assert the moral attributes of the Deity, his justice, benevolence, mercy, and rectitude, to be of the same nature with these virtues in human creatures? His power, we allow, is infinite; whatever he wills is executed; but neither man nor any other animal is happy; therefore, he does not will their happiness. His wisdom is infinite; he is never mistaken in choosing the means to any end; but the course of nature tends not to human or animal felicity; therefore, it is not established for that purpose. Through the whole compass of human knowledge there are no inferences more certain and infallible than these. In what respect, then, do his benevolence and mercy resemble the benevolence and mercy of men?

Epicurus' old questions are yet unanswered.

Is he willing to prevent evil, but not able? then is he impotent. Is he able, but not willing? then is he malevolent. Is he both able and willing? whence then is evil?

You ascribe, Cleanthes (and I believe justly), a purpose and intention to nature. But what, I beseech you, is the object of that curious artifice and machinery which she has displayed in all animals—the preservation alone of individuals, and propagation of the species? It seems enough for her purpose, if such a rank be barely upheld in the universe, without any care or concern for the happiness of the members that compose it. No resource for this purpose: no machinery in order merely to give pleasure or ease; no fund of pure joy and contentment; no indulgence without some want or necessity accompanying it. At least, the few phenomena of this nature are over-balanced by opposite phenomena of still greater importance.

Our sense of music, harmony, and indeed beauty of all kinds, gives satisfaction, without being absolutely necessary to the preservation and propagation of the species. But what racking pains, on the other hand, arise from gouts, gravels, megrims, toothaches, rheumatisms, where the injury to the animal machinery is either small or incurable? Mirth, laughter, play, frolic seem gratuitous satisfactions which have no further tendency; spleen, melancholy, discontent, superstition are pains of the same nature. How then does the Divine benevolence display itself, in the sense of you anthropomorphites? None but we mystics, as you were pleased to call us, can account for this strange mixture of phenomena, by deriving it from attributes infinitely perfect but incomprehensible.

And have you, at last, said Cleanthes smiling, betrayed your intentions, Philo? Your long agreement with Demea did indeed a little surprise me, but I find you were all the while erecting a concealed battery against me. And I must confess that you have now fallen upon a subject worthy of your noble spirit of opposition and controversy. If you can make out the present point, and prove mankind to be unhappy or corrupted, there is an end at once of all religion. For to what purpose establish the natural attributes of the Deity, while the moral are still doubtful and uncertain?

You take umbrage very easily, replied Demea, at opinions the most innocent and the most generally received, even amongst the religious and devout themselves; and nothing can be more surprising than to find a topic like this— concerning the wickedness and misery of man— charged with no less than atheism and profaneness. Have not all pious divines and preachers who have indulged their rhetoric on so fertile a subject, have they not easily, I say, given a solution of any difficulties which may attend it? This world is but a point in comparison of the universe; this life but a moment in comparison of eternity. The present evil phenomena, therefore, are rectified in other regions, and in some future period of existence. And the eyes of men, being then opened to larger views of things, see the whole connection of general laws, and trace, with adoration, the benevolence and rectitude of the Deity through all the mazes and intricacies of his providence.

No! replied Cleanthes, no! These arbitrary suppositions can never be admitted, contrary to matter of fact, visible and uncontroverted. Whence can any cause be known but from its known effects? Whence can any hypothesis be proved but from the apparent phenomena? To establish one hypothesis upon another is building entirely in the air; and the utmost we ever attain by these conjectures and fictions is to ascertain the bare possibility of our opinion, but never can we, upon such terms, establish its reality.

The only method of supporting Divine benevolence—and it is what I willingly embrace—is to deny absolutely the misery and wickedness of man. Your representations are exaggerated; your melancholy views mostly fictitious; your inferences contrary to fact and experience. Health is more common than sickness; pleasure than pain; happiness than misery. And for one vexation which we meet with, we attain, upon computation, a hundred enjoyments.

Admitting your position, replied Philo, which yet is extremely doubtful, you must at the same time allow that, if pain be less frequent than pleasure, it is infinitely more violent and durable. One hour of it is often able to outweigh a day, a week, a month of our common insipid enjoyments; and how many days, weeks, and months are passed by several in the most acute torments? Pleasure, scarcely in one instance, is ever able to reach ecstasy and rapture; and in no one instance can it continue for any time at its highest pitch and altitude. The spirits evaporate, the nerves relax, the fabric is disordered, and the enjoyment quickly degenerates into

fatigue and uneasiness. But pain often, good God, how often! rises to torture and agony; and the longer it continues, it becomes still more genuine agony and torture. Patience is exhausted, courage languishes, melancholy seizes us, and nothing terminates our misery but the removal of its cause or another event which is the sole cure of all evil, but which, from our natural folly, we regard with still greater horror and consternation.

But not to insist upon these topics, continued Philo, though most obvious, certain, and important, I must use the freedom to admonish you, Cleanthes, that you have put the controversy upon a most dangerous issue, and are unawares introducing a total scepticism into the most essential articles of natural and revealed theology. What, no method of fixing a just foundation for religion unless we allow the happiness of human life, and maintain a continued existence even in this world, with all our present pains, infirmities, vexations, and follies, to be eligible and desirable! But this is contrary to everyone's feeling and experience; it is contrary to an authority so established as nothing can subvert. No decisive proofs can ever be produced against this authority; nor is it possible for you to compute, estimate, and compare all the pains and all the pleasures in the lives of all men and of all animals; and thus, by your resting the whole system of religion on a point which, from its very nature, must for ever be uncertain, you tacitly confess that that system is equally uncertain.

But allowing you what never will be believed, at least, what you never possibly can prove, that animal or, at least, human happiness in this life exceeds its misery, you have yet done nothing; for this is not, by any means, what we expect from infinite power, infinite wisdom, and infinite goodness. Why is there any misery at all in the world? Not by chance, surely. From some cause then. Is it from the intention of the Deity? But he is perfectly benevolent. Is it contrary to his intention? But he is almighty. Nothing can shake the solidity of this reasoning, so short, so clear, so decisive, except we assert that these subjects exceed all human capacity, and that our common measures of truth and falsehood are not applicable to them—a topic which I have all along insisted on, but which you have, from the beginning, rejected with scorn and indignation.

But I will be contented to retire still from this intrenchment, for I deny that you can ever force me in it. I will allow that pain or misery in man is *compatible* with infinite power and goodness in the Deity, even in your sense of these attributes: what are you advanced by all these concessions? A mere possible compatibility is not sufficient. You must *prove* these pure, un-mixt, and uncontrollable attributes from the present mixt and confused phenomena, and from these alone. A hopeful undertaking! Were the phenomena ever so pure and unmixt, yet, being finite, they would be insufficient for that purpose. How much more, where they are also so jarring and discordant!

Here, Cleanthes, I find myself at ease in my argument. Here I triumph. Formerly, when we argued concerning the natural attributes of intelligence and design, I needed all my sceptical and metaphysical subtilty to elude your grasp. In many views of the universe and of its parts, particularly the latter, the beauty and fitness of final causes strike us with such irresistible force that all objections appear (what I believe they really are) mere cavils and sophisms; nor can we then imagine how it was ever possible for us to repose any weight on them. But there is no view of human life or of the condition of mankind from which, without the greatest violence, we can infer the moral attributes or learn that infinite benevolence, conjoined with infinite power and infinite wisdom, which we must discover by the eyes of faith alone. It is your turn now to tug the labouring oar, and to support your philosophical subtilties against the dictates of plain reason and experience.

PART XI

I scruple not to allow, said Cleanthes, that I have been apt to suspect the frequent repetition of the word *infinite,* which we meet with in all theological writers, to savour more of panegyric than of philosophy, and that any purposes of reasoning, and even of religion, would be better served were we to rest contented with more accurate and more moderate expressions. The terms *admirable, excellent, superlatively great, wise,* and *holy*—these sufficiently fill the imaginations of men, and anything beyond, besides that it leads into absurdities, has no influence on the affections or sentiments. Thus, in thy present subject, if we abandon all human analogy, as seems your intention, Demea, I am afraid we abandon all religion and retain no conception of the great object of our adoration. If we preserve human analogy, we must forever find it impossible to reconcile any mixture of evil in the universe with infinite attributes; much less can we ever prove the latter from the former. But supposing the Author of nature to be finitely perfect, though far exceeding mankind, a satisfactory account may then be given of natural and moral evil, and every untoward phenomenon be explained and adjusted. A less evil may then be chosen in order to avoid a greater; inconveniences be submitted to in order to reach a desirable end; and, in a word, benevolence, regulated by wisdom and limited by necessity, may produce just such a world as the present. You, Philo, who are so prompt at starting views and reflections and analogies, I would gladly hear, at length, without interruption, your opinion of this new theory; and if it deserve our attention, we may afterwards, at more leisure, reduce it into form.

My sentiments, replied Philo, are not worth being made a mystery of; and, therefore, without any ceremony, I shall deliver what occurs to me with regard to the present subject. It must, I think, be allowed that, if a very limited intelligence whom we shall suppose utterly unacquainted with the universe were assured that it were the production of a very good, wise, and powerful Being, however finite, he would, from his conjectures, form *beforehand* a different notion of it from what we find it to be by experience; nor would he ever imagine, merely from these attributes of the cause of which he is informed, that the effect could be so full of vice and misery and disorder, as it appears in this life. Supposing now that this person were brought into the world, still assured that it was the workmanship of such a sublime and benevolent Being, he might, perhaps, be surprised at the disappointment, but would never retract his former belief if founded on any very solid argument, since such a limited intelligence must be sensible of his own blindness and ignorance, and must allow that there may be many solutions of those phenomena which will for ever escape his comprehension. But supposing, which is the real case with regard to man, that this creature is not antecedently convinced of a supreme intelligence, benevolent, and powerful, but is left to gather such a belief from the appearances of things—this entirely alters the case, nor will he ever find any reason for such a conclusion. He may be fully convinced of the narrow limits of his understanding, but this will not help him in forming an inference concerning the goodness of superior powers, since he must form that inference from what he knows, not from what he is ignorant of. The more you exaggerate his weakness and ignorance, the more diffident you render him, and give him the greater suspicion that such subjects are beyond the reach of his faculties. You are obliged, therefore, to reason with him merely from the known phenomena, and to drop every arbitrary supposition or conjecture.

Did I show you a house or palace where there was not one apartment convenient or agreeable, where the windows, doors, fires, passages, stairs, and the whole economy of the building were the source of noise, confusion, fatigue, darkness, and the extremes of heat and cold, you would certainly blame the contrivance, without any further examination. The architect would in vain display his subtilty, and prove to you that, if this door or that window were altered, greater ills would ensue. What he says may be strictly true: the alteration of one particular, while the other parts of the building remain, may only augment the inconveniences. But still you would assert in general that, if the architect had had skill and good intentions, he might have formed such a plan of the whole, and might have adjusted the parts in such a manner as would have remedied all or most of these inconveniences. His ignorance, or even your own ignorance of such a plan, will never convince you of the impossibility of it. If you find any inconveniences and deformities in the building, you will always, without entering into any detail, condemn the architect.

In short, I repeat the question: Is the world, considered in general and as it appears to us in this life, different from what a man or such a limited being would, *beforehand,* expect from a very powerful, wise, and benevolent Deity? It must be strange prejudice to assert the contrary. And from thence I conclude that, however consistent the world may be, allowing certain suppositions and conjectures with the idea of such a Deity, it can never afford us an inference concerning his existence. The consistency is not absolutely denied, only the inference. Conjectures, especially where infinity is excluded from the Divine attributes, may perhaps be sufficient to prove a consistency, but can never be foundations for any inference.

There seem to be *four* circumstances on which depend all or the greatest part of the ills that molest sensible creatures; and it is not impossible but all these circumstances may be necessary and unavoidable. We know so little beyond common life, or even of common life, that, with regard to the economy of a universe, there is no conjecture, however wild, which may not be just, nor any one, however plausible, which may not be erroneous. All that belongs to human understanding, in this deep ignorance and obscurity, is to be sceptical or at least cautious, and not to admit of any hypothesis whatever, much less of any which is supported by no appearance of probability. Now this I assert to be the case with regard to all the causes of evil and the circumstances on which it depends. None of them appear to human reason in the least degree necessary or unavoidable, nor can we suppose them such, without the utmost licence of imagination.

The *first* circumstance which introduces evil is that contrivance or economy of the animal creation by which pains, as well as pleasures, are employed to excite all creatures to action, and make them vigilant in the great work of self-preservation. Now pleasure alone, in its various degrees, seems to human understanding sufficient for this purpose. All animals might be constantly in a state of enjoyment; but when urged by any of the necessities of nature, such as thirst, hunger, weariness, instead of pain, they might feel a diminution of pleasure by which they might be prompted to seek that object which is necessary to their subsistence. Men pursue pleasure as eagerly as they avoid pain; at least, they might have been so constituted. It seems, therefore, plainly possible to carry on the business of life without any pain. Why then is any animal ever rendered susceptible of such a sensation? If animals can be free from it an hour, they might enjoy a perpetual exemption from it, and it required as particular a contrivance of their organs to produce that feeling as to endow them with sight, hearing, or any of the senses. Shall we conjecture that such a contrivance was necessary, without any appearance of reason, and shall we build on that conjecture as on the most certain truth?

But a capacity of pain would not alone produce pain were it not for the *second* circumstance, viz., the conducting of the world by general laws; and this seems nowise necessary to a very perfect Being. It is true, if everything were conducted by particular volitions, the course of nature would be perpetually broken, and no man could employ his reason in the conduct of life. But might not other particular volitions remedy this inconvenience? In short, might not the Deity exterminate all ill, wherever it were to be found, and produce all good, without any preparation or long progress of causes and effects?

Besides, we must consider that, according to the present economy of the world, the course of nature, though supposed exactly regular, yet to us appears not so, and many events are uncertain, and many disappoint our expectations. Health and sickness, calm and tempest, with an infinite number of other accidents whose causes are unknown and variable, have a great influence both on the fortunes of particular persons and on the prosperity of public societies; and indeed all human life, in a manner, depends on such accidents. A being, therefore, who knows the secret springs of the universe might easily, by particular volitions, turn all these accidents to the good of mankind and render the whole world happy, without discovering himself in any operation. A fleet whose purposes were salutary to society might always meet with a fair wind. Good princes enjoy sound health and long life. Persons born to power and authority be framed with good tempers and virtuous dispositions. A few such events as these, regularly and wisely conducted, would change the face of the world, and yet would no more seem to disturb the course of nature or confound human conduct than the present economy of things where the causes are secret and variable and compounded. Some small touches given to Caligula's brain in his infancy might have converted him into a Trajan. One wave, a little higher than the rest, by burying Caesar and his fortune in the bottom of the ocean, might have restored liberty to a considerable part of mankind. There may, for aught we know, be good reasons why Providence interposes not in this manner, but they are unknown to us; and, though the mere supposition that such reasons exist may be sufficient to *save* the conclusion concerning the Divine attributes, yet surely it can never be sufficient to *establish* that conclusion.

If everything in the universe be conducted by general laws, and if animals be rendered susceptible of pain, it scarcely seems possible but some ill must arise in the various shocks of matter and the various concurrence and opposition of general laws; but this ill would be very rare were it not for the *third* circumstance which I proposed to mention, viz., the great frugality with which all powers and faculties are distributed to every particular being. So well adjusted are the organs and capacities of all animals, and so well fitted to their preservation, that, as far as history or tradition reaches, there appears not to be any single species which has yet been extinguished in the universe. Every animal has the requisite endowments, but these endowments are bestowed with so scrupulous an economy that any considerable diminution must entirely destroy the creature. Wherever one power is increased, there is a proportional abatement in the others. Animals which excel in swiftness are commonly defective in force. Those which possess both are either imperfect in some of their senses or are oppressed with the most craving wants. The human species, whose chief excellence is reason and sagacity, is of all others the most necessitous, and the most deficient in bodily advantages, without clothes, without arms, without food, without lodging, without any convenience of life, except what they owe to their own skill and industry. In short, nature seems to have formed an exact calculation of the necessities of her creatures, and, like a *rigid master,* has afforded them little more powers or endowments than what are strictly sufficient to supply those necessities. An *indulgent parent* would have bestowed a large stock in order to guard against accidents, and secure the happiness and welfare of the creature in the most unfortunate concurrence of circumstances. Every course of life would not have been so surrounded with precipices that the least departure from the true path, by mistake or necessity must involve us in misery and ruin. Some reserve, some fund, would have been provided to ensure happiness, nor would the powers and the necessities have been adjusted with so rigid an economy. The Author of nature is inconceivably powerful; his force is supposed great, if not altogether inexhaustible, nor is there any reason, as far as we can judge, to make him observe this strict frugality in his dealings with his creatures. It would have been better, were his power extremely limited, to have created fewer animals, and to have endowed these with more faculties for their happiness and preservation. A builder is never esteemed prudent who undertakes a plan beyond what his stock will enable him to finish.

In order to cure most of the ills of human life, I require not that man should have the wings of the eagle, the swiftness of the stag, the force of the ox, the arms of the lion, the scales of the crocodile or rhinoceros; much less do I demand the sagacity of an angel or cherubim. I am contented to take an increase in one single power or faculty of his soul. Let him be endowed with a greater propensity to industry and labour, a more vigorous spring and activity of mind, a more constant bent to business and application. Let the whole species possess naturally an equal diligence with that which many individuals are able to attain by habit and reflection, and the most beneficial consequences, without any allay of ill, is the immediate and necessary result of this endowment. Almost all the moral as well as natural evils of human life arise from idleness; and were our species, by the original constitution of their frame, exempt from this vice or infirmity, the perfect cultivation of land, the improvement of arts and manufactures, the exact execution of every office and duty, immediately follow; and men at once may fully reach that state of society which is so imperfectly attained by the best regulated government. But as industry is a power, and the most valuable of any, nature seems determined, suitably to her usual maxims, to bestow it on man with a very sparing hand, and rather to punish him severely for his deficiency in it than to reward him for his attainments. She has so contrived his frame that nothing but the most violent necessity can oblige him to labour; and she employs all his other wants to overcome, at least in part, the want of diligence, and to endow him with some share of a faculty of which she has thought fit naturally to bereave him. Here our demands may be allowed very humble, and therefore the more reasonable. If we required the endowments of superior penetration and judgment, of a more delicate taste of beauty, of a nicer sensibility to benevolence and friendship, we might be told that we impiously pretend to break the order of nature, that we want to exalt ourselves into a higher rank of being, that the presents which we require, not being suitable to our state and condition, would only be pernicious to us. But it is hard, I dare to repeat it, it is hard that, being placed in a world so full of wants and necessities, where almost every being and element is either our foe or refuses its assistance...we should also have our own temper to struggle with, and should be deprived of that faculty which can alone fence against these multiplied evils.

The *fourth* circumstance whence arises the misery and ill of the universe is the inaccurate workmanship of all the springs and principles of the great machine of nature. It must be acknowledged that there are few parts of the universe which seem not to serve some purpose, and whose removal would not produce a visible defect and disorder in the whole. The parts hang all together, nor can one be touched without affecting the rest, in a greater or less degree. But at the same time, it must be observed that none of these parts or principles, however useful, are so accurately adjusted as to keep precisely within those bounds in which their utility consists; but they are, all of them, apt, on every occasion, to run into the one extreme or the other. One would imagine that this grand production had not received the last hand of the maker—so little finished is every part, and so coarse are the strokes with which it is executed. Thus the winds are requisite to convey the vapours along the surface of the globe, and to assist men in navigation; but how often, rising up to tempests and hurricanes, do they become pernicious? Rains are necessary to nourish all the plants and animals of the earth; but how often are they defective? how often excessive? Heat is requisite to all life and vegetation, but is not always found in the due proportion. On the mixture and secretion of the humours and juices of the body depend the health and prosperity of the animal; but the parts perform not regularly their proper function. What more useful than all the passions of the mind, ambition, vanity, love, anger? But how often do they break their bounds and cause the greatest convulsions in society? There is nothing so advantageous in the universe but what frequently becomes pernicious, by its excess or defect; nor has nature guarded, with the requisite accuracy, against all disorder or confusion. The irregularity is never perhaps so great as to destroy

any species, but is often sufficient to involve the individuals in ruin and misery.

On the concurrence, then, of these *four* circumstances does all or the greatest part of natural evil depend. Were all living creatures incapable of pain, or were the world administered by particular volitions, evil never could have found access into the universe; and were animals endowed with a large stock of powers and faculties, beyond what strict necessity requires, or were the several springs and principles of the universe so accurately framed as to preserve always the just temperament and medium, there must have been very little ill in comparison of what we feel at present. What then shall we pronounce on this occasion? Shall we say that these circumstances are not necessary, and that they might easily have been altered in the contrivance of the universe? This decision seems too presumptuous for creatures so blind and ignorant. Let us be more modest in our conclusions. Let us allow that, if the goodness of the Deity (I mean a goodness like the human) could be established on any tolerable reasons *a priori*, these phenomena, however untoward, would not be sufficient to subvert that principle, but might easily, in some unknown manner, be reconcilable to it. But let us still assert that, as this goodness is not antecedently established but must be inferred from the phenomena, there can be no grounds for such an inference while there are so many ills in the universe, and while these ills might so easily have been remedied, as far as human understanding can be allowed to judge on such a subject. I am sceptic enough to allow that the bad appearances, notwithstanding all my reasonings, may be compatible with such attributes as you suppose, but surely they can never prove these attributes. Such a conclusion cannot result from scepticism, but must arise from the phenomena, and from our confidence in the reasonings which we deduce from these phenomena.

Look round this universe. What an immense profusion of beings, animated and organized, sensible and active! You admire this prodigious variety and fecundity. But inspect a little more narrowly these living existences, the only beings worth regarding. How hostile and destructive to each other! How insufficient all of them for their own happiness! How contemptible or odious to the spectator! The whole presents nothing but the idea of a blind nature, impregnated by a great vivifying principle, and pouring forth from her lap, without discernment or parental care, her maimed and abortive children!

Here the Manichaean system occurs as a proper hypothesis to solve the difficulty; and, no doubt, in some respects it is very specious and has more probability than the common hypothesis, by giving a plausible account of the strange mixture of good and ill which appears in life. But if we consider, on the other hand, the perfect uniformity and agreement of the parts of the universe, we shall not discover in it any marks of the combat of a malevolent with a benevolent being. There is indeed an opposition of pains and pleasures in the feelings of sensible creatures; but are not all the operations of nature carried on by an opposition of principles, of hot and cold, moist and dry, light and heavy? The true conclusion is that the original Source of all things is entirely indifferent to all these principles, and has no more regard to good above ill than to heat above cold, or to drought above moisture, or to light above heavy.

There may *four* hypotheses be framed concerning the first causes of the universe: that they are endowed with perfect goodness; that they have perfect malice; that they are opposite and have both goodness and malice; that they have neither goodness nor malice. Mixed phenomena can never prove the two former unmixed principles; and the uniformity and steadiness of general laws seem to oppose the third. The fourth, therefore, seems by far the most probable.

What I have said concerning natural evil will apply to moral with little or no variation; and we have no more reason to infer that the rectitude of the Supreme Being resembles human rectitude than that his benevolence resembles the human. Nay, it will be thought that we have still greater cause to exclude from him moral sentiments, such as we feel them, since moral evil, in

the opinion of many, is much more predominant above moral good than natural evil above natural good.

But even though this should not be allowed, and though the virtue which is in mankind should be acknowledged much superior to the vice, yet, so long as there is any vice at all in the universe, it will very much puzzle you anthropomorphites how to account for it. You must assign a cause for it, without having recourse to the first cause. But as every effect must have a cause, and that cause another, you must either carry on the progression *in infinitum* or rest on that original principle, who is the ultimate cause of all things....

Hold! hold! cried Demea: Whither does your imagination hurry you? I joined in alliance with you in order to prove the incomprehensible nature of the Divine Being, and refute the principles of Cleanthes, who would measure everything by human rule and standard. But I now find you running into all the topics of the greatest libertines and infidels, and betraying that holy cause which you seemingly espoused. Are you secretly, then, a more dangerous enemy than Cleanthes himself?

And are you so late in perceiving it? replied Cleanthes. Believe me, Demea, your friend Philo, from the beginning, has been amusing himself at both our expense; and it must be confessed that the injudicious reasoning of our vulgar theology has given him but too just a handle of ridicule. The total infirmity of human reason, the absolute incomprehensibility of the Divine Nature, the great and universal misery, and still greater wickedness of men—these are strange topics, surely, to be so fondly cherished by orthodox divines and doctors. In ages of stupidity and ignorance, indeed, these principles may safely be espoused; and perhaps no views of things are more proper to promote superstition than such as encourage the blind amazement, the diffidence, and melancholy of mankind. But at present....

Blame not so much, interposed Philo, the ignorance of these reverend gentlemen. They know how to change their style with the times. Formerly, it was a most popular theological topic to maintain that human life was vanity and misery, and to exaggerate all the ills and pains which are incident to men. But of late years, divines, we find, begin to retract this position and maintain, though still with some hesitation, that there are more goods than evils, more pleasures than pains, even in this life. When religion stood entirely upon temper and education, it was thought proper to encourage melancholy, as, indeed, mankind never have recourse to superior powers so readily as in that disposition. But as men have now learned to form principles and to draw consequences, it is necessary to change the batteries, and to make use of such arguments as will endure at least some scrutiny and examination. This variation is the same (and from the same causes) with that which I formerly remarked with regard to scepticism.

Thus Philo continued to the last his spirit of opposition, and his censure of established opinions. But I could observe that Demea did not at all relish the latter part of the discourse; and he took occasion soon after, on some pretence or other, to leave the company.

NOTES

1. *Recherche de la Verit.* liv. 3, cap. 9.
2. *De Rerum Natura*, lib. XI [cap. II], 1094. (Who can rule the sum, who hold in his hand with controlling force the strong reins, of the immeasurable deep? Who can at once make all the different heavens to roll and warm with ethereal fires all the fruitful earths, or be present in all places at all times?)—(Translation by H. A. J. Munro, G. Bell & Sons, 1920.)
3. *De Natura Deorum,* lib. I [cap. VIII]. (For with what eyes could your Plato see the construction of so vast a work which, according to him, God was putting together and building? What materials, what tools, what bars, what machines, what servants were employed in such gigantic work? How could the air, fire, water, and earth pay obedience and submit to the will of the architect?)
4. Dr. Clarke [Samuel Clarke, the rationalist theologian (1675–1729)].
5. *Republique des Lettres,* Aut 1685.
6. That sentiment had been maintained by Dr. King and some few others before Leibniz, though by none of so great fame as that German philosopher.
7. Milton: *Paradise Lost*, Bk. XI.
8. John Dryden, *Aureng-Zebe*, Act IV, sc. 1.

CHAPTER 2

THE PROBLEM OF EVIL

2.1 Rebellion

FYODOR DOSTOEVSKY

Fyodor Dostoevsky (1821–1881) was one of the great Russian novelists of the nineteenth century.

"I must make you one confession," Ivan began. "I could never understand how one can love one's neighbors. It's just one's neighbors, to my mind, that one can't love, though one might love those at a distance. I once read somewhere of John the Merciful, a saint, that when a hungry, frozen beggar came to him, he took him into his bed, held him in his arms, and began breathing

---

From *The Brothers Karamazov*, C. Garnett trans., Book V, Chap. 4 (New York: Modern Library, Inc., 1950).

into his mouth, which was putrid and loathsome from some awful disease. I am convinced that he did that from 'self-laceration,' from the self-laceration of falsity, for the sake of the charity imposed by duty, as a penance laid on him. For any one to love a man, he must be hidden, for as soon as he shows his face, love is gone."

"Father Zossima has talked of that more than once," observed Alyosha, "he, too, said that the face of a man often hinders many people not practiced in love, from loving him. But yet there's a great deal of love in mankind, and almost Christlike love. I know that myself, Ivan."

"Well, I know nothing of it so far, and can't understand it, and the innumerable mass of mankind are with me there. The question is, whether that's due to men's bad qualities or whether it's inherent in their nature. To my thinking, Christlike love for men is a miracle impossible on earth. He was God. But we are not gods. Suppose I, for instance, suffer intensely. Another can never know how much I suffer, because he is another and not I. And what's more, a man is rarely ready to admit another's suffering (as though it were a distinction). Why won't he admit it, do you think? Because I smell unpleasant, because I have a stupid face, because I once trod on his foot. Besides there is suffering and suffering; degrading, humiliating suffering such as humbles me—hunger, for instance—my benefactor will perhaps allow me; but when you come to higher suffering—for an idea, for instance—he will very rarely admit that, perhaps because my face strikes him as not at all what he fancies a man should have who suffers for an idea. And so he deprives me instantly of his favor, and not at all from badness of heart. Beggars, especially genteel beggars, ought never to show themselves, but to ask for charity through the newspapers. One can love one's neighbors in the abstract, or even at a distance, but at close quarters it's almost impossible. If it were as on the stage, in the ballet, where if beggars come in they wear silken rags and tattered lace and beg for alms dancing gracefully, then one might like looking at them. But even then we should not love them. But enough of that. I simply wanted to show you

my point of view. I meant to speak of the suffering of mankind generally, but we had better confine ourselves to the sufferings of the children. That reduces the scope of my argument to the tenth of what it would be. Still we'd better keep to the children, though it does weaken my case. But, in the first place, children can be loved even at close quarters, even when they are dirty, even when they are ugly (I fancy, though, children never are ugly). The second reason why I won't speak of grownup people is that, besides being disgusting and unworthy of love, they have a compensation—they've eaten the apple and know good and evil, and they have become 'like god.' They go on eating it still. But the children haven't eaten anything, and are so far innocent. Are you fond of children, Alyosha? I know you are, and you will understand why I prefer to speak of them. If they, too, suffer horribly on earth, they must suffer for their fathers' sins, they must be punished for their fathers' sins, they must be punished for their fathers, who have eaten the apple; but that reasoning is of the other world and is incomprehensible for the heart of man here on earth. The innocent must not suffer for another's sins, and especially such innocents! You may be surprised at me, Alyosha, but I am awfully fond of children, too. And observe, cruel people, the violent, the rapacious, the Karamazovs are sometimes very fond of children. Children while they are quite little—up to seven, for instance—are so remote from grown-up people; they are different creatures, as it were, of a different species. I knew a criminal in prison who had, in the course of his career as a burglar, murdered whole families, including several children. But when he was in prison, he had a strange affection for them. He spent all his time at his window, watching the children playing in the prison yard. He trained one little boy to come up to his window and made great friends with him...You don't know why I am telling you all this, Alyosha? My head aches and I am sad."

"You speak with a strange air," observed Alyosha uneasily, "as though you were not quite yourself."

"By the way, a Bulgarian I met lately in Moscow," Ivan went on, seeming not to hear his brother's words, "told me about the crimes committed by Turks and Circassians in all parts of Bulgaria through fear of a general rising of the Slavs. They burn villages, murder, outrage women and children, they nail their prisoners by the ears to the fences, leave them so till morning, and in the morning they hang them—all sorts of things you can't imagine. People talk sometimes of bestial cruelty, but that's a great injustice and insult to the beasts; a beast can never be so cruel as a man, so artistically cruel. The tiger only tears and gnaws, that's all he can do. He would never think of nailing people by the ears, even if he were able to do it. These Turks took a pleasure in torturing children, too; cutting the unborn child from the mother's womb, and tossing babies up in the air and catching them on the points of their bayonets before their mother's eyes. Doing it before the mother's eyes was what gave zest to the amusement. Here is another scene that I thought very interesting. Imagine a trembling mother with her baby in her arms, a circle of invading Turks around her. They've planned a diversion; they pet the baby, laugh to make it laugh. They succeed, the baby laughs. At that moment a Turk points a pistol four inches from the baby's face. The baby laughs with glee, holds out its little hands to the pistol, and he pulls the trigger in the baby's face and blows out its brains. Artistic, wasn't it? By the way, Turks are particularly fond of sweet things, they say."

"Brother, what are you driving at?" asked Alyosha.

"I think if the devil doesn't exist, but man has created him, he has created him in his own image and likeness."

"Just as he did God, then?" observed Alyosha. "'It's wonderful how you can turn words,' as Polonius says in *Hamlet*," laughed Ivan. "You turn my words against me. Well, I am glad. Yours must be a fine God, if man created Him in His image and likeness. You asked just now what I was driving at. You see, I am fond of collecting certain facts, and, would you believe, I even copy anecdotes of a certain sort from newspapers and books, and I've already got a fine

collection. The Turks, of course, have gone into it, but they are foreigners. I have specimens from home that are even better than the Turks. You know we prefer beating—rods and scourges—that's our national institution. Nailing ears is unthinkable for us, for we are, after all, Europeans. But the rod and scourge we have always with us and they cannot be taken from us. Abroad now they scarcely do any beating. Manners are more humane, or laws have been passed, so that they don't dare to flog men now. But they make up for it in another way just as national as ours. And so national that it would be practically impossible among us, though I believe we are being inoculated with it, since the religious movement began in our aristocracy. I have a charming pamphlet, translated from the French, describing how, quite recently, five years ago, a murderer, Richard, was executed—a young man, I believe, of three and twenty, who repented and was converted to the Christian faith at the very scaffold. This Richard was an illegitimate child who was given as a child of six by his parents to some shepherds on the Swiss mountains. They brought him up to work for them. He grew up like a little wild beast among them. The shepherds taught him nothing, and scarcely fed or clothed him, but sent him out at seven to herd the flock in cold and wet, and no one hesitated or scrupled to treat him so. Quite the contrary, they thought they had every right, for Richard had been given to them as a chattel, and they did not even see the necessity of feeding him. Richard himself describes how in those years, like the Prodigal Son in the Gospel, he longed to eat of the mash given to the pigs, which were fattened for sale. But they wouldn't even give him that, and beat him when he stole from the pigs. And that was how he spent all his childhood and his youth, till he grew up and was strong enough to go away and be a thief. The savage began to earn his living as a day laborer in Geneva. He drank what he earned, he lived like a brute, and finished by killing and robbing an old man. He was caught, tried, and condemned to death. They are no sentimentalists there. And in prison he was immediately surrounded by pastors, members of Christian brotherhoods, philanthropic ladies, and the like. They taught him to read and write in prison, and expounded the Gospel to him. They exhorted him, worked upon him, drummed at him incessantly, till at last he confessed his crime. He was converted. He wrote to the court himself that he was a monster, but that in the end God had vouchsafed him light and shown grace. All Geneva was in excitement about him—all philanthropic and religious Geneva. All the aristocratic and well-bred society of the town rushed to the prison, kissed Richard and embraced him: 'You are our brother, you have found grace.' And Richard does nothing but weep with emotion, 'Yes, I've found grace! All my youth and childhood I was glad to have pigs' food, but now even I have found grace. I am dying in the Lord.' 'Yes, Richard, die in the Lord; you have shed blood and must die. Though it's not your fault that you knew not the Lord, when you coveted the pigs' food and were beaten for stealing it (which was very wrong of you, for stealing is forbidden); but you've shed blood and you must die.' And on the last day, Richard, perfectly limp, did nothing but cry and repeat every minute: 'This is my happiest day. I am going to the Lord.' 'Yes,' cry the pastors and the judges and philanthropic ladies. 'This is the happiest day of your life, for you are going to the Lord!' They all work or drive to the scaffold in procession behind the prison van. At the scaffold they call to Richard: 'Die, brother, die in the Lord, for even thou hast found grace!' And so, covered with his brothers' kisses, Richard is dragged onto the scaffold, and led to the guillotine. And they chopped off his head in brotherly fashion, because he had found grace. Yes, that's characteristic. That pamphlet is translated into Russian by some Russian philanthropists of aristocratic rank and evangelical aspirations, and has been distributed gratis for the enlightenment of the people. The case of Richard is interesting because it's national. Though to us it's absurd to cut off a man's head, because he has become our brother and has found grace, yet we have our own specialty, which is all but worse. Our historical pastime is the direct satisfaction of inflicting pain. There are lines in Nekrassov describing how a peasant lashes a horse on the eyes, 'on its meek eyes;' everyone must have seen it. It's

peculiarly Russian. He describes how a feeble little nag had foundered under too heavy a load and cannot move. The peasant beats it, beats it savagely, beats it at last not knowing what he is doing in the intoxication of cruelty, thrashes it mercilessly over and over again. 'However weak you are, you must pull, if you die for it.' The nag strains, and he begins lashing the poor defenseless creature on its weeping, on its 'meek eyes.' The frantic beast tugs and draws the load, trembling all over, gasping for breath, moving sideways, with a sort of unnatural spasmodic action—it's awful in Nekrassov. But that's only a horse, and God has given horses to be beaten. So the Tatars have taught us, and they left us the knout as a rememberance of it. But men, too, can be beaten. A well-educated, cultured gentleman and his wife beat their own child with a birchrod, a girl of seven. I have an exact account of it. The papa was glad that the birch was covered with twigs. 'It stings more,' said he, and so he began stinging his daughter. I know for a fact there are people who at every blow are worked up to sensuality, to literal sensuality, which increases progressively at every blow they inflict. They beat for a minute, for five minutes, for ten minutes, more often and more savagely. The child screams. At last the child cannot scream, it gasps, 'Daddy! daddy!' By some diabolical unseemly chance the case was brought into court. A counsel was engaged. The Russian people have long called a barrister 'a conscience for hire.' The counsel protests in his client's defense. 'It's such a simple thing,' he says, 'an everyday domestic event. A father corrects his child. To our shame be it said, it is brought into court.' The jury, convinced by him, gives a favorable verdict. The public roars with delight that the torturer is acquitted. Ah, pity I wasn't there! I would have proposed to raise a subscription in his honor!… Charming pictures.

"But I've still better things about children. I've collected a great, great deal about Russian children, Alyosha. There was a little girl of five who was hated by her father and mother, 'most worthy and respectable people, of good education and breeding.' You see, I must repeat again, it is a peculiar characteristic of many people, this love of torturing children, and children only. To all other types of humanity these torturers behave mildly and benevolently like cultivated and humane Europeans; but they are very fond of tormenting children, even fond of children themselves in that sense. It's just their defenselessness that tempts the tormentor, just the angelic confidence of the child who has no refuge and no appeal that sets his vile blood on fire. In every man, of course, a demon lies hidden—the demon of rage, the demon of lustful heat at the screams of the tortured victim, the demon of lawlessness let off the chain, the demon of diseases that follow on vice, gout, kidney disease, and so on.

"This poor child of five was subjected to every possible torture by those cultivated parents. They beat her, thrashed her, kicked her for no reason till her body was one bruise. Then, they went to greater refinements of cruelty—shut her up all night in the cold and frost in a privy, and because she didn't ask to be taken up at night (as though a child of five sleeping its angelic, sound sleep could be trained to wake and ask), they smeared her face and filled her mouth with excrement, and it was her mother, her mother did this. And that mother could sleep, hearing the poor child's groans! Can you understand why a little creature, who can't even understand what's done to her, should beat her little aching heart with her tiny fist in the dark and the cold, and weep her meek unresentful tears to dear, kind God to protect her? Do you understand that, friend and brother, you pious and humble novice? Do you understand why this infamy must be and is permitted? Without it, I am told, man could not have existed on earth, for he could not have known good and evil. Why should he know that diabolical good and evil when it costs so much? Why, the whole world of knowledge is not worth that child's prayer to 'dear, kind God!' I say nothing of the sufferings of grown-up people, they have eaten the apple, damn them, and the devil take them all! But these little ones! I am making you suffer, Alyosha, you are not yourself. I'll leave off it if you like."

"Never mind. I want to suffer too," muttered Alyosha.

"One picture, only one more, because it's so curious, so characteristic, and I have only just read it in some collection of Russian antiquities. I've forgotten the name. I must look it up. It was in the darkest days of serfdom at the beginning of the century, and long live the Liberator of the People! There was in those days a general of aristocratic connections, the owner of great estates, one of those men—somewhat exceptional, I believe, even then—who, retiring from the service into a life of leisure, are convinced that they've earned absolute power over the lives of the subjects. There were such men then. So our general, settled on his property of two thousand souls, lives in pomp, and domineers over his poor neighbors as though they were dependents and buffoons. He has kennels of hundreds of hounds and nearly a hundred dog-boys—all mounted, and in uniform. One day a serf boy, a little child of eight, threw a stone in play and hurt the paw of the general's favorite hound. 'Why is my favorite dog lame?' He is told that the boy threw a stone that hurt the dog's paw. 'So you did it.' The general looked the child up and down. 'Take him.' He was taken—taken from his mother and kept shut up all night. Early that morning the general comes out on horseback, with the hounds, his dependents, dog-boys, and huntsmen, all mounted around him in full hunting parade. The servants are summoned for their edification, and in front of them all stands the mother of the child. The child is brought from the lockup. It's a gloomy, cold, foggy autumn day, a capital day for hunting. The general orders the child to be undressed; the child is stripped naked. He shivers, numb with terror, not daring to cry…'Make him run,' commands the general. 'Run! run!' shout the dog-boys. The boy runs…'At him!' yells the general, and he sets the whole pack of hounds on the child. The hounds catch him, and tear him to pieces before his mother's eyes!…I believe the general was afterwards declared incapable of administering his estates. Well—what did he deserve? To be shot? To be shot for the satisfaction of our moral feelings? Speak, Alyosha!"

"To be shot," murmured Alyosha, lifting his eyes to Ivan with a pale, twisted smile.

"Bravo!" cried Ivan delighted. "If even you say so...You're a pretty monk! So there is a little devil sitting in your heart. Alyosha Karamazov!"

"What I said was absurd, but—"

"That's just the point that 'but'!" cried Ivan. "Let me tell you, novice, that the absurd is only too necessary on earth. The world stands on absurdities, and perhaps nothing would have come to pass in it without them. We know what we know!"

"What do you know?"

"I understand nothing," Ivan went on, as though in delirium. "I don't want to understand anything now. I want to stick to the fact. I made up my mind long ago not to understand. If I try to understand anything, I shall be false to the fact and I have determined to stick to the fact."

"Why are you trying me?" Alyosha cried, with sudden distress. "Will you say what you mean at last?"

"Of course, I will; that's what I've been leading up to. You are dear to me, I don't want to let you go, and I won't give you up to your Zossima [priest, Father]."

Ivan for a minute was silent, his face became all at once very sad.

"Listen! I took the case of children only to make my case clearer. Of the other tears of humanity with which the earth is soaked from its crust to its center, I will say nothing. I have narrowed my subject on purpose, I am a bug, and I recognize in all humility that I cannot understand why the world is arranged as it is. Men are themselves to blame, I suppose; they were given paradise, they wanted freedom, and stole fire from heaven, though they knew they would become unhappy, so there is no need to pity them. With my pitiful, earthly, Euclidean understanding, all I know is that there is suffering and that there are none guilty; that cause follows effect, simply and directly; that everything flows and finds its level—but that's only Euclidean nonsense, I know that, and I can't consent to live by it! What comfort is to me that there are none guilty and that cause follows effect simply and directly, and that I know it—I must have justice, or I will destroy myself. And not justice

in some remote infinite time and space, but here on earth, and that I could see myself. I have believed in it. I want to see it, and if I am dead by then, let me rise again, for if it all happens without me, it will be too unfair. Surely I haven't suffered, simply that I, my crimes and my sufferings, may manure the soil of the future harmony for somebody else. I want to see with my own eyes the hind lie down with the lion and the victim rise up and embrace his murderer. I want to be there when everyone suddenly understands what it has all been for. All the religions of the world are built on this longing, and I am a believer. But there are the children, and what am I to do about them? That's a question I can't answer. For the hundredth time I repeat, there are numbers of questions, but I've only taken the children, because in their case what I mean is so unanswerably clear. Listen! If all must suffer to pay for the eternal harmony, what have children to do with it, tell me, please? It's beyond all comprehension why they should suffer, and why they should pay for the harmony. Why should they, too, furnish material to enrich the soil for the harmony of the future? I understand solidarity in sin among men. I understand solidarity in retribution, too; but there can be no such solidarity with children. And if it is really true that they must share responsibility for all their father's crimes, such a truth is not of this world and is beyond my comprehension. Some jester will say, perhaps, that the child would have grown up and have sinned, but you see he didn't grow up, he was torn to pieces by the dogs, at eight years old. Oh, Alyosha, I am not blaspheming! I understand, of course, what an upheaval of the universe it will be, when everything in heaven and earth blends in one hymn of praise and everything that lives and has lived cries aloud: 'Thou art just, O Lord, for Thy ways are revealed.' When the mother embraces the fiend who threw her child to the dogs, and all three cry aloud with tears, 'Thou are just, O Lord!' then, of course, the crown of knowledge will be reached and all will be made clear. But what pulls me up here is that I can't accept that harmony. And while I am on earth, I make haste to take my own measures. You see, Alyosha, perhaps it really may happen that if I live to that moment, or rise again to see it, I, too, perhaps, may cry aloud with the rest, looking at the mother embracing the child's torturer, 'Thou are just, O Lord!' but I don't want to cry aloud then. While there is still time, I hasten to protect myself and so I renounce the higher harmony altogether. It's not worth the tears of that one tortured child who beat itself on the breast with its little fist and prayed in its stinking outhouse with an unexpiated tear to 'dear, kind God!' It's not worth it, because those tears are unatoned for. They must be atoned for, or there can be no harmony. But how? How are you going to atone for them? Is it possible? By their being avenged? But what do I care for avenging them? What do I care for a hell for oppressors? What good can hell do, since those children have already been tortured? And what becomes of harmony, if there is hell? I want to forgive. I want to embrace. I don't want more suffering. And if the sufferings of children go to swell the sum of sufferings which was necessary to pay for truth, then I protest that the truth is not worth such a price. I don't want the mother to embrace the oppressor who threw her son to the dogs! She dare not forgive him! Let her forgive him for herself, if she will, let her forgive the torturer for the immeasurable suffering of her mother's heart. But the sufferings of her tortured child she has no right to forgive; she dare not forgive the torturer, even if the child were to forgive him!

And if that is so, if they dare not forgive, what becomes of harmony? Is there in the whole world a being who would have the right to forgive and could forgive? I don't want harmony. From love for humanity I don't want it. I would rather be left with the unavenged suffering. I would rather remain with my unavenged suffering and unsatisfied indignation, *even if I were wrong*. Besides, too high a price is asked for harmony; it's beyond our means to pay so much to enter on it. And so I hasten to give back my entrance ticket, and if I am an honest man I am bound to give it back as soon as possible. And that I am doing. It's not God that I don't accept, Alyosha, only I most respectfully return Him the ticket."

"That's rebellion," murmured Alyosha, looking down.

"Rebellion? I am sorry you call it that," said Ivan earnestly. "One can hardly live in rebellion, and I want to live. Tell me yourself, I challenge you—answer. Imagine that you are creating a fabric of human destiny with the object of making men happy in the end, giving them peace and rest at last, but that it was essential and inevitable to torture to death only one tiny creature—that baby beating its breast with its fist, for instance—and to found that edifice on its unavenged tears, would you consent to be the architect on those conditions? Tell me, and tell the truth."

"No, I wouldn't consent," said Alyosha softly....

2.2 Evil and Omnipotence

J. L. MACKIE

J. L. Mackie (1917–1983) taught philosophy at University College, Oxford.

The traditional arguments for the existence of God have been fairly thoroughly criticized by philosophers. But the theologian can, if he wishes, accept this criticism. He can admit that no rational proof of God's existence is possible. And he can still retain all that is essential to his

From *Mind*, Vol. LXIV, No. 254 (1955). Reprinted by permission of Oxford University Press.

position, by holding that God's existence is known in some other, nonrational way. I think, however, that a more telling criticism can be made by way of the traditional problem of evil. Here it can be shown, not that religious beliefs lack rational support, but that they are positively irrational, that the several parts of the essential theological doctrine are inconsistent with one another, so that the theologian can maintain his position as a whole only by a much more extreme rejection of reason than in the former case. He must now be prepared to believe, not merely what cannot be proved, but what can be *disproved* from other beliefs that he also holds.

The problem of evil, in the sense in which I shall be using the phrase, is a problem only for someone who believes that there is a God who is both omnipotent and wholly good. And it is a logical problem, the problem of clarifying and reconciling a number of beliefs: it is not a scientific problem that might be solved by further observations, or a practical problem that might be solved by a decision or an action. These points are obvious; I mention them only because they are sometimes ignored by theologians, who sometimes parry a statement of the problem with such remarks as "Well, can you solve the problem yourself?" or "This is a mystery which may be revealed to us later" or "Evil is something to be faced and overcome, not to be merely discussed."

In its simplest form the problem is this: God is omnipotent; God is wholly good; and yet evil exists. There seems to be some contradiction between these three propositions, so that if any two of them were true the third would be false. But at the same time all three are essential parts of most theological positions: the theologian, it seems, at once *must* adhere and *cannot consistently* adhere to all three. (The problem does not arise only for theists, but I shall discuss it in the form in which it presents itself for ordinary theism.)

However, the contradiction does not arise immediately; to show it we need some additional premises, or perhaps some quasi-logical rules connecting the terms "good," "evil," and "omnipotent." These additional principles are that good is opposed to evil, in such a way that a good thing always eliminates evil as far as it can, and that there are no limits to what an omnipotent thing can do. From these it follows that a good omnipotent thing eliminates evil completely, and then the propositions that a good omnipotent thing exists, and that evil exists, are incompatible.

ADEQUATE SOLUTIONS

Now once the problem is fully stated it is clear that it can be solved, in the sense that the problem will not arise if one gives up at least one of the propositions that constitute it. If you are prepared to say that God is not wholly good, or not quite omnipotent, or that evil does not exist, or that good is not opposed to the kind of evil that exists, or that there are limits to what an omnipotent thing can do, then the problem of evil will not arise for you.

There are, then, quite a number of adequate solutions of the problem of evil, and some of these have been adopted, or almost adopted, by various thinkers. For example, a few have been prepared to deny God's omnipotence, and rather more have been prepared to keep the term "omnipotence" but severely to restrict its meaning, recording quite a number of things that an omnipotent being cannot do. Some have said that evil is an illusion, perhaps because they held that the whole world of temporal, changing things is an illusion, and that what we call evil belongs only to this world, or perhaps because they held that although temporal things *are* much as we see them, those that we call evil are not really evil. Some have said that what we call evil is merely the privation of good, that evil in a positive sense, evil that would really be opposed to good, does not exist. Many have agreed with Pope that disorder is harmony not understood, and that partial evil is universal good. Whether any of these views is *true* is, of course, another question. But each of them gives an adequate solution of the problem of evil in the sense that if you accept it this problem does not arise for you, though you may, of course, have *other* problems to face.

But often enough these adequate solutions are only *almost* adopted. The thinkers who restrict God's power, but keep the term "omnipotence," may reasonably be suspected of thinking, in other contexts, that his power is really unlimited. Those who say that evil is an illusion may also be thinking, inconsistently, that this illusion is itself an evil. Those who say that "evil" is merely privation of good may also be thinking, inconsistently, that privation of good is an evil....If Pope meant what he said in the first line of his couplet, that "disorder" is only harmony not understood, the "partial evil" of the second line must, for consistency, mean "that which, taken in isolation, falsely appears to be evil," but it would more naturally mean "that which, in isolation, really is evil." The second line, in fact, hesitates between two views, that "partial evil" isn't really evil, since only the universal quality is real, and that "partial evil" is really an evil, but only a little one.

In addition, therefore, to adequate solutions, we must recognize unsatisfactory inconsistent solutions, in which there is only a half-hearted or temporary rejection of one of the propositions which together constitute the problem. In these, one of the constituent propositions is explicitly rejected, but it is covertly reasserted or assumed elsewhere in the system.

FALLACIOUS SOLUTIONS

Besides these half-hearted solutions, which explicitly reject but implicitly assert one of the constituent propositions, there are definitely fallacious solutions which explicitly maintain all the constituent propositions, but implicitly reject at least one of them in the course of the argument that explains away the problem of evil.

There are, in fact, many so-called solutions which purport to remove the contradiction without abandoning any of its constituent propositions. These must be fallacious, as we can see from the very statement of the problem, but it is not so easy to see in each case precisely where the fallacy lies. I suggest that in all cases the fallacy has the general form suggested above: in order to solve the problem one (or perhaps more) of its constituent propositions is given up, but in such a way that it appears to have been retained, and can therefore be asserted without qualification in other contexts. Sometimes there is a further complication: the supposed solution moves to and fro between, say, two of the constituent propositions, at one point asserting the first of these but covertly abandoning the second, at another point asserting the second but covertly abandoning the first. These fallacious solutions often turn upon some equivocation with the words "good" and "evil," or upon some vagueness about the way in which good and evil are opposed to one another, or about how much is meant by "omnipotence." I propose to examine some of these so-called solutions, and to exhibit their fallacies in detail. Incidentally, I shall also be considering whether an adequate solution could be reached by a minor modification of one or more of the constituent propositions, which would, however, still satisfy all the essential requirements of ordinary theism.

1. "Good cannot exist without evil" or "Evil is necessary as a counterpart to good."

It is sometimes suggested that evil is necessary as a counterpart to good, that if there were no evil there could be no good either, and that this solves the problem of evil. It is true that it points to an answer to the question "Why should there be evil?" But it does so only by qualifying some of the propositions that constitute the problem.

First, it sets a limit to what God can do, saying that God *cannot* create good without simultaneously creating evil, and this means either that God is not omnipotent or that there are *some* limits to what an omnipotent thing can do. It may be replied that these limits are always presupposed, that omnipotence has never meant the power to do what is logically impossible, and on the present view the existence of good without evil would be a logical impossibility. This interpretation of omnipotence may, indeed, be accepted as a modification of our original account which does not reject anything that is essential to theism, and I shall in general assume it in the subsequent discussion. It is, perhaps, the most common theistic view, but I think that some theists at least have maintained that God can do what is logically impossible. Many theists, at any rate, have held that logic itself is created or laid down by God, that logic is the way in which God arbitrarily chooses to think. (This is, of course, parallel to the ethical view that morally right actions are those which God arbitrarily chooses to command, and the two views encounter similar difficulties.) And *this* account of logic is clearly inconsistent with the view that God is bound by logical necessities—unless it is possible for an omnipotent being to bind himself, an issue which we shall consider later, when we come to the Paradox of Omnipotence. This solution of the problem of evil cannot, therefore, be consistently adopted along with the view that logic is itself created by God.

But, secondly, this solution denies that evil is opposed to good in our original sense. If good and evil are counterparts, a good thing will not "eliminate evil as far as it can." Indeed, this view suggests that good and evil are not strictly qualities of things at all. Perhaps the suggestion is that good and evil are related in much the same way as great and small. Certainly, when the term "great" is used relatively as a condensation of "greater than so-and-so," and "small" is used correspondingly, greatness and smallness are counterparts and cannot exist without each other. But in this sense greatness is not a quality, not an intrinsic feature of anything; and it would be absurd to think of a movement in favor of greatness and against smallness in this sense. Such a movement would be self-defeating, since relative greatness can be promoted only by a simultaneous promotion of relative smallness. I feel sure that no theists would be content to regard God's goodness as analogous to this—as if what he supports were not the *good* but the *better,* and as if he had the paradoxical aim that all things should be better than other things.

This point is obscured by the fact that "great" and "small" seem to have an absolute

as well as a relative sense. I cannot discuss here whether there is absolute magnitude or not, but if there is, there could be an absolute sense for "great," it could mean of at least a certain size, and it would make sense to speak of all things getting bigger, of a universe that was expanding all over, and therefore it would make sense to speak of promoting greatness. But in *this* sense great and small are not logically necessary counterparts: either quality could exist without the other. There would be no logical impossibility in everything's being small or in everything's being great.

Neither in the absolute nor in the relative sense, then, of "great" and "small" do these terms provide an analogy of the sort that would be needed to support this solution of the problem of evil. In neither case are greatness and smallness *both* necessary counterparts *and* mutually opposed forces or possible objects for support and attack.

It may be replied that good and evil are necessary counterparts in the same way as any quality and its logical opposite: redness can occur, it is suggested, only if nonredness also occurs. But unless evil is merely the privation of good, they are not logical opposites, and some further argument would be needed to show that they are counterparts in the same way as genuine logical opposites. Let us assume that this could be given. There is still doubt of the correctness of the metaphysical principle that a quality must have a real opposite: I suggest that it is not really impossible that everything should be, say, red, that the truth is merely that if everything were red we should not notice redness, and so we should have no word "red;" we observe and give names to qualities only if they have real opposites. If so, the principle that a term must have an opposite would belong only to our language or to our thought, and would not be an ontological principle, and, correspondingly, the rule that good cannot exist without evil would not state a logical necessity of a sort that God would just have to put up with. God might have made everything good, though *we* should not have noticed it if he had.

But, finally, even if we concede that this *is* an ontological principle, it will provide a solution for the problem of evil only if one is prepared to say, "Evil exists, but only just enough evil to serve as the counterpart of good." I doubt whether any theist will accept this. After all, the *ontological* requirement that nonredness should occur would be satisfied even if all the universe, except for a minute speck, were red, and, if there were a corresponding requirement for evil as a counterpart to good, a minute dose of evil would presumably do. But theists are not usually willing to say, in all contexts, that all the evil that occurs is a minute and necessary dose.

2. "Evil is necessary as a means to good."

It is sometimes suggested that evil is necessary for good not as a counterpart but as a means. In its simple form this has little plausibility as a solution of the problem of evil, since it obviously implies a severe restriction of God's power. It would be a *causal* law that you cannot have a certain end without a certain means, so that if God has to introduce evil as a means to good, he must be subject to at least some causal laws. This certainly conflicts with what a theist normally means by omnipotence. This view of God as limited by causal laws also conflicts with the view that causal laws are themselves made by God, which is more widely held than the corresponding view about the laws of logic. This conflict would, indeed, be resolved if it were possible for an omnipotent being to bind himself, and this possibility has still to be considered. Unless a favorable answer can be given to this question, the suggestion that evil is necessary as a means to good solves the problem of evil only by denying one of its constituent propositions, either that God is omnipotent or that "omnipotent" means what it says.

3. "The universe is better with some evil in it than it could be if there were no evil."

Much more important is a solution which at first seems to be a mere variant of the previous one, that evil may contribute to the goodness of a whole in which it is found, so that the universe as a whole is better as it is, with some evil in it, than it would be if there were no evil. This solution may be developed in either of two ways. It may be supported by an aesthetic analogy, by the fact that contrasts heighten beauty, that in a musical work, for example, there may occur discords which somehow add to the beauty of the work as a whole. Alternatively, it may be worked out in connection with the notion of progress, that the best possible organization of the universe will not be static, but progressive, that the gradual overcoming of evil by good is really a finer thing than would be the eternal unchallenged supremacy of good.

In either case, this solution usually starts from the assumption that the evil whose existence gives rise to the problem of evil is primarily what is called physical evil, that is to say, pain. In Hume's rather half-hearted presentation of the problem of evil, the evils that he stresses are pain and disease, and those who reply to him argue that the existence of pain and disease makes possible the existence of sympathy, benevolence, heroism, and the gradually successful struggle of doctors and reformers to overcome these evils. In fact, theists often seize the opportunity to accuse those who stress the problem of evil of taking a low, materialistic view of good and evil, equating these with pleasure and pain, and of ignoring the more spiritual goods which can arise in the struggle against evils.

But let us see exactly what is being done here. Let us call pain and misery "first order evil" or "evil (1)." What contrasts with this, namely, pleasure and happiness, will be called "first order good" or "good (1)." Distinct from this is "second order good" or "good (2)" which somehow emerges in a complex situation in which evil (1) is a necessary component—logically, not merely causally, necessary. (Exactly *how* it emerges does not matter: in the crudest version of this solution good (2) is simply the heightening of happiness by the contrast with misery, in other versions it includes sympathy with suffering, heroism in facing danger, and the gradual decrease of first order evil and increase of first order good.) It is also being assumed that second order good is more important than first order good or evil, in particular that it more than outweighs the first order evil it involves.

Now this is a particularly subtle attempt to solve the problem of evil. It defends God's goodness and omnipotence on the ground that (on a sufficiently long view) this is the best of all logically possible worlds because it includes the important second order goods, and yet it admits that real evils, namely first order evils, exist. But does it still hold that good and evil are opposed? Not, clearly, in the sense that we set out originally: good does not tend to eliminate evil in general. Instead, we have a modified, a more complex pattern. First order good (e.g., happiness) *contrasts with* first order evil (e.g., misery): these two are opposed in a fairly mechanical way; some second order goods (e.g., benevolence) try to maximize first order good and minimize first order evil; but God's goodness is not this, it is rather the will to maximize *second* order good. We might, therefore, call God's goodness an example of a third order goodness, or good (3). While this account is different from our original one, it might well be held to be an improvement on it, to give a more accurate description of the way in which good is opposed to evil, and to be consistent with the essential theist position.

There might, however, be several objections to this solution.

First, some might argue that such qualities as benevolence—and *a fortiori* the third order goodness which promotes benevolence—have a merely derivative value, that they are not higher sorts of good, but merely means to good (1), that is, to happiness, so that it would be absurd for God to keep misery in existence in order to make possible the virtues of benevolence, heroism, etc. The theist who adopts the present solution must, of course, deny this, but he can do so with some plausibility, so I should not press this objection.

Secondly, it follows from this solution that God is not in our sense benevolent or sympathetic: he is not concerned to minimize evil (1), but only to promote good (2); and this

might be a disturbing conclusion for some theists.

But, thirdly, the fatal objection is this. Our analysis shows clearly the possibility of the existence of a *second* order evil, an evil (2) contrasting with good (2) as evil (1) contrasts with good (1). This would include malevolence, cruelty, callousness, cowardice, and states in which good (1) is decreasing and evil (1) increasing. And just as good (2) is held to be the important kind of good, the kind that God is concerned to promote, so evil (2) will, by analogy, be the important kind of evil, the kind which God, if he were wholly good and omnipotent, would eliminate. And yet evil (2) plainly exists, and indeed most theists (in other contexts) stress its existence more than that of evil (1). We should, therefore, state the problem of evil in terms of second order evil, and against this form of the problem the present solution is useless.

An attempt might be made to use this solution again, at a higher level, to explain the occurrence of evil (2): indeed the next main solution that we shall examine does just this, with the help of some new notions. Without any fresh notions, such a solution would have little plausibility: for example, we could hardly say that the really important good was a good (3), such as the increase of benevolence in proportion to cruelty, which logically required for its occurrence the occurrence of some second order evil. But even if evil (2) could be explained in this way, it is fairly clear that there would be third order evils contrasting with this third order good: and we should be well on the way to an infinite regress, where the solution of a problem of evil, stated in terms of evil (n), indicated the existence of an evil ($n + 1$), and a further problem to be solved.

4. "Evil is due to human free will."

Perhaps the most important proposed solution of the problem of evil is that evil is not to be ascribed to God at all, but to the independent actions of human beings, supposed to have been endowed by God with freedom of the will. This solution may be combined with the preceding one: first order evil (e.g., pain) may be justified as a logically necessary component in second order good (e.g., sympathy) while second order evil (e.g., cruelty) is not *justified,* but is so ascribed to human beings that God cannot be held responsible for it. This combination evades my third criticism of the preceding solution.

The free-will solution also involves the preceding solution at a higher level. To explain why a wholly good God gave men free will although it would lead to some important evils, it must be argued that it is better on the whole that men should act freely, and sometimes err, than that they should be innocent automata, acting rightly in a wholly determined way. Freedom, that is to say, is now treated as a third order good, and as being more valuable than second order goods (such as sympathy and heroism) would be if they were deterministically produced, and it is being assumed that second order evils, such as cruelty, are logically necessary accompaniments of freedom, just as pain is a logically necessary pre-condition of sympathy.

I think that this solution is unsatisfactory primarily because of the incoherence of the notion of freedom of the will: but I cannot discuss this topic adequately here, although some of my criticisms will touch upon it.

First I should query the assumption that second order evils are logically necessary accompaniments of freedom. I should ask this: if God has made men such that in their free choices they sometimes prefer what is good and sometimes what is evil, why could he not have made men such that they always freely choose the good? If there is no logical impossibility in a man's freely choosing the good on one, or on several occasions, there cannot be a logical impossibility in his freely choosing the good on every occasion. God was not, then, faced with a choice between making innocent automata and making beings who, in acting freely, would sometimes go wrong: there was open to him the obviously better possibility of making beings who would act freely but always go right. Clearly, his failure to avail himself of this possibility is inconsistent with his being both omnipotent and wholly good.

If it is replied that this objection is absurd, that the making of some wrong choices is logically necessary for freedom, it would seem that "freedom" must here mean complete randomness or indeterminacy, including randomness with regard to the alternatives good and evil, in other words that men's choices and consequent actions can be "free" only if they are not determined by their characters. Only on this assumption can God escape the responsibility for men's actions; for if he made them as they are, but did not determine their wrong choices, this can only be because the wrong choices are not determined by men as they are. But then if freedom is randomness, how can it be a characteristic of *will?* And, still more, how can it be the most important good? What value or merit would there be in free choices if these were random actions which were not determined by the nature of the agent?

I conclude that to make this solution plausible two different senses of "freedom" must be confused, one sense which will justify the view that freedom is a third order good, more valuable than other goods would be without it, and another sense, sheer randomness, to prevent us from ascribing to God a decision to make men such that they sometimes go wrong when he might have made them such that they would always freely go right.

This criticism is sufficient to dispose of this solution. But besides this there is a fundamental difficulty in the notion of an omnipotent God creating men with free will, for if men's wills are really free this must mean that even God cannot control them, that is, that God is no longer omnipotent. It may be objected that God's gift of freedom to men does not mean that he *cannot* control their wills, but that he always *refrains* from controlling their wills. But why, we may ask, should God refrain from controlling evil wills? Why should he not leave men free to will rightly, but intervene when he sees them beginning to will wrongly? If God could do this, but does not, and if he is wholly good, the only explanation could be that even a wrong free act of will is not really evil, that its freedom is a value which outweighs its wrongness, so that there would be a loss of value if God took away the wrongness and the freedom together. But this is utterly opposed to what theists say about sin in other contexts. The present solution of the problem of evil, then, can be maintained only in the form that God has made men so free that he *cannot* control their wills.

This leads us to what I call the Paradox of Omnipotence: can an omnipotent being make things which he cannot subsequently control? Or, what is practically equivalent to this, can an omnipotent being make rules which then bind himself? (These are practically equivalent because any such rules could be regarded as setting certain things beyond his control, and *vice versa*.) The second of these formulations is relevant to the suggestions that we have already met, that an omnipotent God creates the rules of logic or causal laws, and is then bound by them.

It is clear that this is a paradox: the questions cannot be answered satisfactorily either in the affirmative or in the negative. If we answer "Yes," it follows that if God actually makes things which he cannot control, or makes rules which bind himself, he is not omnipotent once he has made them: there are *then* things which he cannot do. But if we answer "No," we are immediately asserting that there are things which he cannot do, that is to say that he is already not omnipotent.

It cannot be replied that the question which sets this paradox is not a proper question. It would make perfectly good sense to say that a human mechanic has made a machine which he cannot control: if there is any difficulty about the question it lies in the notion of omnipotence itself.

This, incidentally, shows that although we have approached this paradox from the free-will theory, it is equally a problem for a theological determinist. No one thinks that machines have free will, yet they may well be beyond the control of their makers. The determinist might reply that anyone who makes anything determines its ways of acting, and so determines its subsequent

behavior: even the human mechanic does this by his *choice* of materials and structure for his machine, though he does not know all about either of these: the mechanic thus determines, though he may not foresee, his machine's actions. And since God is omniscient, and since his creation of things is total, he both determines and foresees the ways in which his creatures will act. We may grant this, but it is beside the point. The question is not whether God *originally* determined the future actions of his creatures, but whether he can *subsequently* control their actions, or whether he was able in his original creation to put things beyond his subsequent control. Even on determinist principles the answers "Yes" and "No" are equally irreconcilable with God's omnipotence.

Before suggesting a solution of this paradox, I would point out that there is a parallel Paradox of Sovereignty. Can a legal sovereign make a law restricting its own future legislative power? For example, could the British parliament make a law forbidding any future parliament to socialize banking, and also forbidding the future repeal of this law itself? Or could the British parliament, which was legally sovereign in Australia in, say, 1899, pass a valid law, or series of laws, which made it no longer sovereign in 1933? Again, neither the affirmative nor the negative answer is really satisfactory. If we were to answer "Yes," we should be admitting the validity of a law which, if it were actually made, would mean that parliament was no longer sovereign. If we were to answer "No," we should be admitting that there is a law, not logically absurd, which parliament cannot validly make, that is, that parliament is not now a legal sovereign. This paradox can be solved in the following way. We should distinguish between first order laws, that is, laws governing the actions of individuals and bodies other than the legislature, and second order laws, that is, laws about laws, laws governing the actions of the legislature itself. Correspondingly, we should distinguish two orders of sovereignty, first order sovereignty (sovereignty [1]) which is unlimited authority to make first order laws, and second order sovereignty (sovereignty

[2]) which is unlimited authority to make second order laws. If we say that parliament is sovereign we might mean that any parliament at any time has sovereignty (1), or we might mean that parliament has both sovereignty (1) and sovereignty (2) at present, but we cannot without contradiction mean both that the present parliament has sovereignty (2) and that every parliament at every time has sovereignty (1), for if the present parliament has sovereignty (2) it may use it to take away the sovereignty (1) of later parliaments. What the paradox shows is that we cannot ascribe to any continuing institution legal sovereignty in an inclusive sense.

The analogy between omnipotence and sovereignty shows that the paradox of omnipotence can be solved in a similar way. We must distinguish between first order omnipotence (omnipotence [1]), that is, unlimited power to act, and second order omnipotence (omnipotence [2]), that is, unlimited power to determine what powers to act things shall have. Then we could consistently say that God all the time has omnipotence (1), but if so no beings at any time have powers to act independently of God. Or we could say that God at one time had omnipotence (2), and used it to assign independent powers to act to certain things, so that God thereafter did not have omnipotence (1). But what the paradox shows is that we cannot consistently ascribe to any continuing being omnipotence in an inclusive sense.

An alternative solution of this paradox would be simply to deny that God is a continuing being, that any times can be assigned to his actions at all. But on this assumption (which also has difficulties of its own) no meaning can be given to the assertion that God made men with wills so free that he could not control them. The paradox of omnipotence can be avoided by putting God outside time, but the free-will solution of the problem of evil cannot be saved in this way, and equally it remains impossible to hold that an omnipotent God *binds himself* by causal or logical laws.

Conclusion

Of the proposed solutions of the problem of evil which we have examined, none has stood up to criticism. There may be other solutions which require examination, but this study strongly suggests that there is no valid solution of the problem which does not modify at least one of the constituent propositions in a way which would seriously affect the essential core of the theistic position.

Quite apart from the problem of evil, the paradox of omnipotence has shown that God's omnipotence must in any case be restricted in one way or another, that unqualified omnipotence cannot be ascribed to any being that continues through time. And if God and his actions are not in time, can omnipotence, or power of any sort, be meaningfully ascribed to him?

2.3 The Argument from Evil

PETER VAN INWAGEN

Peter van Inwagen is John Cardinal O'Hara Professor of Philosophy emeritus at the University of Notre Dame. He has written many important works on metaphysics, free will, and the philosophy of religion.

By the argument from evil, I understand the following argument (or any argument sufficiently similar to it that the two arguments stand or fall together): We find vast amounts of truly horrendous evil in the world; if there were a God, we should not find vast amounts of horrendous evil in the world; there is, therefore, no God.

The argument presupposes, and rightly, that two features God is supposed to have are "non-negotiable": that he is omnipotent and morally perfect. That he is omnipotent means that he can do anything that doesn't involve an intrinsic impossibility. Thus, God, if he exists, can change water to wine, since there is no intrinsic impossibility in the elementary particles that constitute the water in a cup being rearranged so as to constitute wine. But even God can't draw a round square or cause it both to rain and not to rain at the same place at the same time or change the past because these things are intrinsically impossible. To say that God is morally perfect is to say that he never does anything morally wrong—that he could not possibly do anything morally wrong. If God exists, therefore, and if you think he's done something morally wrong, you must be mistaken: either he didn't do the thing you think he did, or the thing he did that you think is morally wrong isn't. Omnipotence and moral perfection are, as I said, non-negotiable components of the idea of God. If the universe was made by an intelligent being, and if that being is less than omnipotent (and if there's no other being who is omnipotent), then the atheists are right: God does not exist. If the universe was made by an omnipotent being, and if that being has done even one thing that was morally wrong (and if there isn't another omnipotent being, one who never does anything morally wrong), then the atheists are right: God does not exist. If the Creator of the universe lacked either omnipotence or moral perfection, and if he claimed to be God, he would be either an impostor (if he claimed to be omnipotent and morally perfect) or confused (if he conceded that he lacked either omnipotence or moral perfection and claimed to be God anyway).

To these two "non-negotiable" features of the concept of God, we must add one other that doesn't call for much comment: God, if he exists, must know a great deal about the world he has created. Now it is usually said that God is *omniscient*—that he knows *everything*. But the argument from evil doesn't require this strong assumption about God's knowledge—it requires only that God know enough to be aware of a significant amount of the evil that exists in the world. If God knew even the little that you and I know about the amount and extent of evil, that would be sufficient for the argument.

Now consider those evils God knows about. Since he's morally perfect, he must desire that these evils not exist—their non-existence must be what he *wants*. And an omnipotent being can achieve or bring about whatever he wants. So if there were an omnipotent, morally perfect being who knew about these evils—well, they wouldn't have arisen in the first place, for he'd have prevented their occurrence. Or if, for some reason, he didn't do that, he'd certainly remove them the instant they began to exist. But we observe evils, and very long-lasting ones. So we must conclude that God does not exist.

How much force has this argument? Suppose I believe in God and grant that the world contains vast amounts of truly horrible evil. What might I say in reply? I should, and do, think that the place to begin is with an examination of the word 'want'. Granted, in some sense of the word, the non-existence of evil must be what a morally perfect being *wants*. But we often don't bring about states of affairs we can bring about and want. Suppose, for example, that Alice's mother is dying in great pain and that Alice yearns desperately for her mother to die—today, and not next week or next month. And suppose it would be easy for Alice to arrange this—she is perhaps a doctor or a nurse and has easy access to pharmaceutical resources that would enable her to achieve this end. Does it follow that she will act on this ability that she has? It is obvious that it does not, for Alice might have *reasons* for not doing what she can do. Two obvious candidates for such reasons are: she thinks it would be morally wrong; she is afraid that her act would be discovered and that she would be prosecuted for murder. And either of these reasons might be sufficient, in her mind, to outweigh her desire for an immediate end to her mother's sufferings. So it may be that someone has a very strong desire for something and is able to obtain this thing, but does not act on this desire—because he has reasons for not doing so that seem to him to outweigh the desirability of the thing. The conclusion that evil does not exist does not, therefore, follow *logically* from the premises that the non-existence of evil is what God wants and that he is able to bring about the object of his desire—since, for all logic can tell us, God might have reasons for allowing evil to exist that, in his mind, outweigh the desirability of the non-existence of evil. But are such reasons even imaginable? What might they be?

Suppose I believe I know what God's reasons for allowing evil to exist are, and that I tell them to you. Then I have presented you with what is called a *theodicy*. This word comes from two Greek words that mean 'God' and 'justice.' Thus, Milton, in *Paradise Lost,* tells us that the purpose of the poem is to "justify the ways of God to men"—'justify' meaning 'exhibit as just.' If I could present a theodicy, and if those to whom I presented it found it convincing, I'd have a reply to the argument from evil. But suppose that, although I believe in God, I *don't* claim to know what God's reasons for allowing evil are. Is there any way for someone in my position to reply to the argument from evil? There is. Consider this analogy.

Suppose your friend Clarissa, a single mother, left her two very young children alone in her flat for over an hour very late last night. Your Aunt Harriet, a maiden lady of strong moral principles, learns of this and declares that Clarissa is unfit to raise children. You spring to your friend's defense: "Now, Aunt Harriet, don't go jumping to conclusions. There's probably a perfectly good explanation. Maybe Billy or Annie took ill, and she decided to go over to St. Luke's for help. You know she hasn't got a

phone or a car and no one in that neighborhood of hers would come to the door at two o'clock in the morning." If you tell your Aunt Harriet a story like this, you don't claim to know what Clarissa's reasons for leaving her children alone really were. And you're not claiming to have said anything that shows that Clarissa really is a good mother. You're claiming only to show that the fact Aunt Harriet has adduced doesn't prove that she isn't one; what you're trying to establish is that for all you and Aunt Harriet know, she had some good reason for what she did. And you're not trying to establish only that there is some remote possibility that she had a good reason. No lawyer would try to raise doubts in the minds of the members of a jury by pointing out to them that for all they knew his client had an identical twin, of whom all record had been lost, and who was the person who had actually committed the crime his client was charged with. That may be a possibility—I suppose it is *a possibility*—but it is too remote a possibility to raise real doubts in anyone's mind. What you're trying to convince Aunt Harriet of is that there is, as we say, *a very real possibility* that Clarissa had a good reason for leaving her children alone; and your attempt to convince her of this consists in your presenting her with an example of what such a reason *might* be.

Critical responses to the argument from evil—at least responses by philosophers—usually take just this form. A philosopher who responds to the argument from evil typically does so by telling a story, a story in which God allows evil to exist. This story will, of course, represent God as having reasons for allowing the existence of evil, reasons that, if the rest of the story were true, would be good ones. Such a story philosophers call a *defense*. A defense and a theodicy will not necessarily differ in content. A defense may, indeed, be verbally identical with a theodicy. The difference between a theodicy and a defense is simply that a theodicy is put forward as true, while nothing more is claimed for a defense than that it represents a real possibility—or a real possibility given that God exists. If I offer a story about God and evil as a defense, I hope for the following reaction from my audience: "Given that God exists, the rest of the story might well be true. I can't see any reason to rule it out."

A defense cannot simply take the form of a story about how God brings some great good out of the evils of the world, a good that outweighs those evils. At the very least, a defense will have to include the proposition that God was *unable* to bring about the greater good without allowing the evils we observe (or some other evils as bad or worse). And to find a story that can plausibly be said to have this feature is no trivial undertaking. The reason for this lies in God's omnipotence. A human being can often be excused for allowing, or even causing, a certain evil if that evil was a necessary means, or an unavoidable consequence thereof to some good that outweighed it—or if it was a necessary means to the prevention of some greater evil. The eighteenth-century surgeon who operated without anesthetic caused unimaginable pain to his patients, but we do not condemn him because (at least if he knew what he was doing) the pain was an unavoidable consequence of the means necessary to some good that outweighed it—such as saving the patient's life. But we should not excuse a present-day surgeon who had anesthetics available and who nevertheless operated without using them—not even if his operation saved the patient's life and thus resulted in a good that out-weighed the horrible pain the patient suffered.

A great many of the theodicies or defenses that one sees are insufficiently sensitive to this point. Many undergraduates, for example, if they are believers, seem inclined to say something like the following: if there were no evil, no one would appreciate—perhaps no one would even be aware of—the goodness of the things that *are* good. You know the idea: you never really appreciate health till you've been ill, you never really understand how great and beautiful a thing friendship is till you've known adversity and known what it is to have friends who stick by you through thick and thin—and so on. The obvious criticism of this defense is so

immediately obvious that it tends to mask the point that led me to raise it. The immediately obvious criticism is that this defense may be capable of accounting for a certain amount of, for example, physical pain, but it certainly doesn't account for the degree and the duration of the pain that many people are subject to. But I have brought up the "appreciation" defense—which otherwise would not be worth spending any time on—to make a different point. It is not at all evident that an omnipotent creator would need to allow people really to experience *any* pain or grief or sorrow or adversity or illness to enable them to appreciate the good things in life. An omnipotent being would certainly be able to provide the knowledge of evil that human beings in fact acquire by bitter experience of real events in some other way. An omnipotent being could, for example, so arrange matters that at a certain point in each person's life—for a few years during his adolescence, say—that person have very vivid *nightmares* in which he is a prisoner in a concentration camp or dies of some horrible disease or watches his loved ones being raped and murdered by soldiers bent on ethnic cleansing. It seems evident to me that the supposed good (the capacity for the appreciation of good things) that some say is a consequence of the evils of the world could (if it exists) be equally well achieved by this means. And it is indisputable that a world in which horrible things occurred only in nightmares would be better than a world in which the same horrible things occurred in reality, and that a morally perfect being ought to prefer a world in which horrible things were confined to dreams to a world in which they existed in reality. The general point this example is intended to illustrate is simply that the resources of an omnipotent being are unlimited—or are limited only by what is intrinsically possible—and that a defense must take account of these unlimited resources.

There seems to me to be only one defense that has any hope of succeeding, and that is the so-called free-will defense. In its simplest, most abstract, form, the free-will defense goes as follows:

God made the world and it was very good. An indispensable part of the goodness he chose was the existence of rational beings: self-aware beings capable of abstract thought and love and having the power of free choice between contemplated alternative courses of action. This last feature of rational beings, free choice or free will, is a good. But even an omnipotent being is unable to control the exercise of the power of free choice, for a choice that was controlled would *ipso facto* not be free. In other words, if I have a free choice between x and y, even God cannot ensure that I choose x. To ask God to give me a free choice between x and y and to see to it that I choose x instead of y is to ask God to bring about the intrinsically impossible; it is like asking him to create a round square, a material body that has no shape, or an invisible object that casts a shadow. Having this power of free choice, some or all human beings misuse it and produce a certain amount of evil. But free will is a sufficiently great good that its existence outweighs the evils that result from its abuse; and God foresaw this.

The free-will defense immediately suggests several objections. The two most pressing of them are these:

How could anyone possibly believe that the evils of this world are outweighed by the good inherent in our having free will? Perhaps free will is a good and would outweigh a certain amount of evil, but it seems impossible to believe that it can outweigh the amount of physical suffering (to say nothing of other sorts of evil) that actually exists.

Not all evils are the result of human free will. Consider, for example, the Lisbon earthquake or the almost inconceivable loss of life produced by the hurricane that ravaged Honduras in 1997. Such events are not the result of any act of human will, free or unfree.

In my view, the simple form of the free-will defense I have presented is unable to deal with either of these objections. The simple form of the free-will defense can deal with at best the existence of *some* evil—as opposed to the vast amount of evil we actually observe—and the evil with which it can deal is only that evil that is caused by the acts of human beings. I believe,

however, that more sophisticated forms of the free-will defense do have interesting things to say about the vast amount of evil in the world and about those evils that are not caused by human beings. Before I discuss these "more sophisticated" forms of the free-will defense, however, I want to examine an objection that has been raised against the free-will defense that is so fundamental that, if valid, it would refute any elaboration of the defense, however sophisticated. This objection has to do with the nature of free will. There is a school of thought—Hobbes, Hume, and Mill are its most illustrious representatives—whose adherents maintain that free will and determinism are perfectly compatible: that there could be a world in which the past determined a unique future and the inhabitants of which were nonetheless free beings. Now if this school of philosophers is right, the free-will defense fails, for if free will and determinism are compatible, then an omnipotent being can, contrary to the central premise of the free-will defense, create a person who has a free choice between x and y and ensure that that person choose x rather than y. Those philosophers who accept the compatibility of free will and determinism defend their thesis as follows: being free is being free to do what one wants to do; prisoners in a jail, for example, are unfree because they want to leave and can't. The man who desperately wants to stop smoking but can't is unfree for the same reason—even though no barrier as literal as the bars of a cage stands between him and a life without nicotine. The very words 'free will' testify to the Tightness of this analysis, for one's will is simply what one wants, and a free will is just exactly an unimpeded will. Given this account of free will, a Creator who wants to give me a free choice between x and y, has only to arrange the components of my body and my environment in such a way that the following two 'if' statements are both true: if I were to want x, I'd be able to achieve that desire, and if I were to want y, I'd be able to achieve *that* desire. And a Creator who wants to ensure that I choose x, rather than y, has only to implant in me a fairly robust desire for x and see to it that I have no desire at all for y. And these two things are obviously compatible. Suppose, for example, that there was a Creator who had put a woman in a garden and had commanded her not to eat of the fruit of a certain tree. Could he so arrange matters that she have a free choice between eating of the fruit of that tree and not eating of it and also *ensure* that she not eat of it? Certainly. To provide her with a free choice between the two alternatives, he need only see to it that two things are true: first, that if she wanted to eat of the fruit of that tree, no barrier (such as an unclimbable fence or paralysis of the limbs) would stand in the way of her acting on that desire, and, secondly, that if she wanted *not* to eat of the fruit, nothing would force her to act contrary to *that* desire. And to ensure that she not eat of the fruit, he need only see to it that not eating of the fruit be what she desires. This latter end could be achieved in a variety of ways; the simplest, I suppose, would be to build into her psychological makeup a very strong desire to do whatever he tells her to and a horror of disobedience—a horror like that experienced by the acrophobe who is forced to approach the edge of a cliff—and then to instruct her not to eat of the fruit. If all this is indeed correct, it would seem that an omnipotent being could both grant its creatures free will and ensure that they never bring any evil into the world by the abuse of it. And, of course, if *that* is true, the free-will defense fails.

But how plausible is this account of free will? Not very, I think. It certainly yields some odd conclusions. Consider the lower social orders in Aldous Huxley's *Brave New World*, the "deltas" and "epsilons." These unfortunate people have their deepest desires chosen for them by others—by the "alphas" who make up the highest social stratum. What the deltas and epsilons primarily desire is to do what the alphas (and the "beta" and "gamma" overseers who are appointed to supervise their labors) tell them. This is their primary desire because it is imposed on them by prenatal and postnatal conditioning. (If Huxley were writing today, he might have added genetic engineering to the alphas' list of

resources for determining the desires of their slaves.) It would be hard to think of beings who better fitted the description 'lacks free will' than the deltas and epsilons of *Brave New World*. And yet, if the account of free will that we are considering is right, the deltas and epsilons are exemplars of beings with free will. Each of them is always doing exactly what he wants, after all, and who among us is in that fortunate position? What he wants is to do as he is told by those appointed over him, of course, but the account of free will we are examining says nothing about the *content* of one's desires: it requires only that there be no barrier to acting on them. The deltas and epsilons are not very intelligent, and are therefore incapable of philosophizing about their condition, but the alphas' techniques could as easily be applied to highly intelligent people. It is interesting to ask what conclusions such people would arrive at if they reflected on their condition. If you said to one of these highly intelligent slaves, "Don't you realize that you obey your master only because your desire to obey him was implanted in you by prenatal conditioning and genetic engineering," he would, I expect, reply by saying something like this: "Yes, and a good thing, too, because, you see, they had the foresight to implant in me a desire that my desires be so formed. I'm really very fortunate: I'm not only doing exactly what I want, but I want to want what I want, and I want what I want to be caused by prenatal conditioning and genetic engineering." Despite the fact that (I freely confess) I do not have a philosophically satisfactory account of free will, I can see that this person hasn't got it. Therefore, I contend, the atheist's attempt to show that the story that constitutes the free-will defense is false rests on a false theory about the nature of free will. Now my argument for the falsity of this theory is, I concede, inconclusive. (If it were conclusive, it would convince Hobbes and Hume and Mill and their fellow "compatibilists" that their account of free will was wrong. And experience shows that most compatibilists who hear and understand this argument are unmoved by it.) But let us remember the dialectical situation in which this inconclusive argument occurs. That is, let us remember who is trying to prove what. The atheist has opened the discussion by trying to prove the non-existence of God; the alleged proof of this conclusion is the argument from evil. The theist responds by producing the free-will defense and contends that this defense shows that evil does not prove the non-existence of God. The atheist's rejoinder is that the story called the free-will defense is false and that its falsity can be demonstrated by reflection on the nature of free will. The theist replies that the atheist has got the nature of free will wrong, and he offers a philosophical argument for this conclusion (the "Brave New World" argument), an argument that perhaps falls short of being a proof but has nevertheless seemed fairly plausible to many intelligent people. When we add up all the pluses and minuses of this exchange, it seems that the free-will defense triumphs in its limited sphere of application. When we think about it, we see that, for all the atheist has said, the story called the free-will defense *may well be true*—at least given that there is a God. One cannot show that a story involving creatures with free will is false or probably false by pointing out that the story would be false if a certain theory about free will were true. To show that, one would also have to show that the theory of free will that one has put forward was true or probably true. And the atheist hasn't shown that his theory of free will, the "no barriers" theory, is true or probably true, for the objections to the atheist's theory of free will that I have set out show that this theory faces very serious problems indeed.

The atheist's most promising course of action, I think, is to admit that the free-will defense shows that there might, for all anyone can say, be a certain amount of evil, a certain amount of pain and suffering, in a world created by an all-powerful and morally perfect being, and to stress the amounts and the kinds of evil that we find in the world as it is. The world as it is, I have said, contains vast amounts of truly horrendous evil (that's the point about amounts), and some of the kinds of evil to be found in the world as it is

are not caused by human beings—wholly unforeseeable natural disasters, for example (that's the point about kinds). Can any elaboration of our simple version of the free-will defense take account of these two points in any very plausible way?

Let me suggest some elaborations toward this end. The reader must decide whether they are plausible. The free-will defense as I've stated it suggests—though it does not entail—that God created human beings with free will and then just left them to their own devices. It suggests that the evils of the world are the more or less unrelated consequences of uncounted millions of largely unrelated abuses of free will by human beings. Let me propose a sort of plot to be added to the bare and abstract free-will defense I stated above. Consider the story of creation and rebellion and the expulsion from paradise that is told in the first three chapters of Genesis. Could this story be true—I mean literally true, true in every detail? Well, no. It contradicts what science has discovered about human evolution and the history of the physical universe. And that is hardly surprising, for it long antedates these discoveries. The story is a re-working—with much original material—by Hebrew authors (or, as I believe, *a* Hebrew author) of elements found in many ancient Middle Eastern mythologies. Like the *Aeneid,* it is a literary refashioning of materials originally supplied by legend and myth, and it retains a strong mythological flavor. It is possible, nevertheless, that the first three chapters of Genesis are a mythico-literary representation of actual events of human pre-history. The following is consistent with what we know of human pre-history. Our current knowledge of human evolution, in fact, presents us with no particular reason to believe that this story is false. (Here and there in the story, the reader will encounter various philosophical *obiter dicta,* asides to the reader thoughtfully provided by the omniscient narrator—myself.)

For millions of years, perhaps for thousands of millions of years, God guided the course of evolution so as eventually to produce certain very clever primates, the immediate predecessors of *Homo sapiens.* At some time in the last few hundred thousand years, the whole population of our pre-human ancestors formed a small breeding community—a few hundred or even a few score. That is to say, there was a time when every ancestor of modern human beings who was then alive was a member of this tiny, geographically tightly knit group of primates. In the fullness of time, God took the members of this breeding group and miraculously raised them to rationality. That is, he gave them the gifts of language, abstract thought, and disinterested love—and, of course, the gift of free will. He gave them the gift of free will because free will is necessary for love. Love, and not only erotic love, implies free will. The essential connection between love and free will is beautifully illustrated in Ruth's declaration to her mother-in-law Naomi:

> And Ruth said, Entreat me not to leave thee, or to return from following after thee: for whither thou goest, I will go; and where thou lodgest, I will lodge: thy people shall be my people and thy God my God: where thou diest, will I die, and there will I be buried; the Lord do so to me, and more also, if aught but death part thee and me. (Ruth 1:16-17)

It is also illustrated by the vow I made when I was married:

> I, Peter, take thee, Elisabeth, to be my wedded wife, to have and to hold from this day forward, for better for worse, for richer for poorer, in sickness and in health, to love and to cherish, till death us do part, according to God's holy ordinance; and thereto I plight thee my troth.

God not only raised these primates to rationality—not only made of them what we call human beings—but also took them into a kind of mystical union with himself, the sort of union that Christians hope for in heaven and call the Beatific Vision. Being in union with God, these new human beings, these primates who had become human beings at a certain point in their lives, lived together in the harmony of perfect love and also possessed what theologians used to call preternatural powers—something like

what people who believe in them today call paranormal abilities. Because they lived in the harmony of perfect love, none of them did any harm to the others. Because of their preternatural powers, they were able somehow to protect themselves from wild beasts (which they were able to tame with a word), from disease (which they were able to cure with a touch), and from random, destructive natural events (like earthquakes), which they knew about in advance and were able to avoid. There was thus no evil in their world. And it was God's intention that they should never become decrepit with age or die, as their primate forbears had. But, somehow, in some way that must be mysterious to us, they were not content with this paradisal state. They abused the gift of free will and separated themselves from their union with God.

The result was horrific: not only did they no longer enjoy the Beatific Vision, but they now faced destruction by the random forces of nature and were subject to old age and natural death. Nevertheless, they were too proud to end their rebellion. As the generations passed, they drifted further and further from God—into the worship of false gods (a worship that sometimes involved human sacrifice), inter-tribal warfare (complete with the gleeful torture of prisoners of war), private murder, slavery, and rape. On one level, they realized, or some of them realized, that something was horribly wrong, but they were unable to do anything about it. After they had separated themselves from God, they were, as an engineer might say, "not operating under design conditions." A certain frame of mind became dominant among them, a frame of mind latent in the genes they had inherited from a million or more generations of ancestors. I mean the frame of mind that places one's own desires and perceived welfare above everything else, and which accords to the welfare of one's immediate relatives a subordinate privileged status, and assigns no status at all to the welfare of anyone else. And this frame of mind was now married to rationality, to the power of abstract thought; the progeny of this marriage were the continuing resentment against those whose actions interfere with the fulfillment of one's desires, hatreds cherished in the heart, and the desire for revenge. The inherited genes that produced these baleful effects had been harmless as long as human beings had still had constantly before their minds a representation of perfect love in the Beatific Vision. In the state of separation from God, and conjoined with rationality, they formed the genetic substrate of what is called original sin or birth-sin: an inborn tendency to do evil against which all human efforts are vain. We, or most of us, have some sort of perception of the distinction between good and evil, but, however we struggle, in the end we give in and do evil. In all cultures there are moral codes (more similar than some would have us believe) and the members of every tribe and nation stand condemned not only by alien moral codes but by their own. The only human beings who consistently do right in their own eyes, whose consciences are always clear, are those who, like the Nazis, have given themselves over entirely to evil, those who say, in some twisted and self-deceptive way, what Milton has his Satan say explicitly and clearly: "Evil, be thou my Good."

When human beings had become like this, God looked out over a ruined world. It would have been just for him to leave human beings in the ruin they had made of themselves and their world. But God is more than a God of justice. He is, indeed, more than a God of mercy—a God who was merely merciful might simply have brought the story of humanity to an end at that point, like someone who shoots a horse with a broken leg. But God is more than a God of mercy: he is a God of love. He therefore neither left humanity to its own devices nor mercifully destroyed it. Rather, he set in motion a rescue operation. He put into operation a plan designed to restore separated humanity to union with himself. This defense will not specify the nature of this plan of atonement. The three Abrahamic religions, Judaism, Christianity, and Islam, tell three different stories about the nature of this plan, and I do not propose to favor one of them over another in telling a story that, after all, I do not maintain is true. This much must be said,

however: the plan has the following feature, and any plan with the object of restoring separated humanity to union with God would have to have this feature: its object is to bring it about that human beings once more love God. And, since love essentially involves free will, love is not something that can be imposed from the outside, by an act of sheer power. Human beings must choose freely to be reunited with God and to love him, and this is something they are unable to do of their own efforts. They must therefore cooperate with God. As is the case with many rescue operations, the rescuer and those whom he is rescuing must cooperate. For human beings to cooperate with God in this rescue operation, they must know that they need to be rescued. They must know what it means to be separated from him. And what it means to be separated from God is to live in a world of horrors. If God simply "canceled" all the horrors of this world by an endless series of miracles, he would thereby frustrate his own plan of reconciliation. If he did that, we should be content with our lot and should see no reason to cooperate with him. Here is an analogy. Suppose Dorothy suffers from angina, and that what she needs to do is to stop smoking and lose weight. Suppose her doctor knows of a drug that will stop the pain but will do nothing to cure the condition. Should the doctor prescribe the drug for her, in the full knowledge that if the pain is alleviated, there is no chance that she will stop smoking and lose weight? Well, perhaps the answer is yes. The doctor is Dorothy's fellow adult and fellow citizen, after all. Perhaps it would be insufferably paternalistic to refuse to alleviate Dorothy's pain in order to provide her with a motivation to do what is to her own advantage. If one were of an especially libertarian cast of mind, one might even say that someone who did that was "playing God." It is far from clear, however, whether there is anything wrong with *God's* behaving as if he were God. It is at least very plausible to suppose that it is morally permissible for God to allow human beings to suffer if the result of suppressing the suffering would be to deprive them of a very great good, one that far outweighed the suffering. But God does shield us from *much* evil, from a great proportion of the sufferings that would be a natural consequence of our rebellion. If he did not, all human history would be at least this bad: every human society would be on the moral level of Nazi Germany. But, however much evil God shields us from, he must leave in place a vast amount of evil if he is not to deceive us about what separation from him means. The amount he has left us with is so vast and so horrible that we cannot really comprehend it, especially if we are middle-class Americans or Europeans. Nevertheless, it could have been much worse. The inhabitants of a world in which human beings had separated ourselves from God and he had then simply left them to their own devices would regard our world as a comparative paradise. All this evil, however, will come to an end. At some point, for all eternity, there will be no more unmerited suffering. Every evil done by the wicked to the innocent will have been avenged, and every tear will have been wiped away. If there is still suffering, it will be merited: the suffering of those who refuse to cooperate with God's great rescue operation and are allowed by him to exist forever in a state of elected ruin—those who, in a word, are in hell.

One aspect of this story needs to be brought out more clearly than I have. If the story is true, much of the evil in the world is due to chance. There is generally no explanation of why *this* evil happened to *that* person. What there is is an explanation of why evils happen to people without any reason. And the explanation is: that is part of what being separated from God means: it means being the playthings of chance. It means living in a world in which innocent children die horribly, and it means something worse than that: it means living in a world in which innocent children die horribly *for no reason at all*. It means living in a world in which the wicked, through sheer luck, often prosper. Anyone who does not want to live in such a world, a world in which we are the playthings of chance, had better accept God's offer of a way out of that world.

Here, then, is a defense. Do I believe it? Well, I believe parts of it and I don't disbelieve

any of it. (Even those parts I believe do not, for the most part, belong to my faith; they merely comprise some of my religious opinions.) I am not at all sure about "preternatural powers," for example, or about the proposition that God shields us from much evil and that the world would be far worse if he did not. The story I have told is, I remind you, only supposed to be a defense. It is not put forward as a theodicy, as a statement of the real truth of the matter, as I see it, about the co-presence of God and evil in the world. I contend only that this story is—given that God exists—true for all we know. And I certainly don't see any very compelling reason to reject any of it. In particular, I don't see any reason to reject the thesis that God raised a small population of our ancestors to rationality by a specific action on, say, June 13,116,027 B.C.—or on some such particular date. It is not a discovery of evolutionary biology that there are no miraculous events in our evolutionary history. It *could* not be, any more than it could be a discovery of meteorology that the weather at Dunkirk on those fateful days in 1940 was not due to a specific and local divine action. Anyone who believes either that the coming-to-be of human rationality or the weather at Dunkirk had purely natural causes must believe this on philosophical, not scientific, grounds. In fact the case for this is rather stronger in the case of the genesis of rationality, for we know a lot about how the weather works, and we know that the rain clouds at Dunkirk are the sort of thing that *could* have had purely natural causes. We most assuredly do not know that rationality could have arisen through natural causes—or, at any rate, we do not know this unless there is some philosophical argument that shows that *everything* has purely natural causes. And this is because everyone who believes that human rationality could have had purely natural causes believes this solely on the basis of the following argument: Everything has purely natural causes; human beings are rational; hence, the rationality of human beings could have had purely natural causes because it in fact did.

Suppose, then, for the sake of argument, that the defense I have presented is a true story. Does it justify the evils of the world? Or put the question this way. Suppose there were an omnipotent and omniscient being and that this being acted just as God has acted in the story I have told. Could any moral case be made against the actions of this being? Is there any barrier to saying that this being is not only omnipotent and omniscient but morally perfect as well? In my view, it is not self-evident that there is no barrier to saying this—but it is not self-evident that there is a barrier, either. The defense I have presented, the story I have told, should be thought of as the beginning of a conversation. If there is anyone who maintains that the story I have told, even if it is true, does not absolve a being who acts as I have supposed God to act from serious moral criticism, let that person explain why he or she thinks this is so. Then I, or some other defender of theism, can attempt to meet this objection, and the objector can reply to the rejoinder and... but so philosophy goes: philosophy is argument without end. As J. L. Austin said—also speaking on the topic of excuses—here I leave and commend the subject to you.

2.4 The Argument from Evil

MICHAEL MURRAY AND MICHAEL REA

Michael Murray is Executive Vice President of the John Templeton Foundation. Michael Rea teaches at the University of Notre Dame. Both have written widely on issues in the philosophy of religion.

During a recent visit to Germany Pope Benedict XVI visited the death camp at Auschwitz. While surveying the memorial to the nearly 1.5 million Nazi victims he found himself at a loss for words of explanation or consolation: "In this place, words fail. In the end, there can only be dread silence—a silence which is itself a heartfelt cry to God ... How could you tolerate all this?" *Washington Post* columnist Richard Cohen commenting on the Pope's remarks wrote the following:

> Religious people can wrestle with the Pope's remarks. What does it mean that God was silent? That he approved? That he liked what he saw? That he didn't give a damn? You tell me. And what does it mean that he could "tolerate all this"? That the Nazis were OK by him? That even the murder of Catholic clergy was no cause of intercession? I am at a loss to explain this. I cannot believe in such a God.[1]

Theists and atheists alike seem convinced that evil does indeed count against the existence of God in some sense. While some evils might seem to make sense in light of a comprehensive divine plan for the universe, how can we accommodate senseless torture, degrading sexual abuse, catastrophic tsunamis, and so on? And what is more, how can theists explain the fact that virtue and happiness do not seem proportional in this life? In the words of the Hebrew prophet Jeremiah:

> You are always righteous, O LORD, when I bring a case before you. Yet I would speak with you about your justice: Why does the way of the wicked prosper? Why do all the faithless live at ease?[2]

Needless to say, the pattern of evil we find in the world does not exactly fit our initial expectations

From Michael Murray and Michael Rea, *An Introduction to the Philosophy of Religion* (Cambridge University Press, 2008).

of what a world would look like if theism were true. Does this fact count as a good reason to accept atheism? Does the existence of evil of this sort add up to a telltale sign that atheism is true?

Those who think so offer one of two different types of arguments. According to the first type of argument, the existence of evil is flatly incompatible with the existence of God. According to the second, the existence of God and evil are not incompatible, but the reality of evil makes it unlikely that God exists, and this makes belief in the existence of God unreasonable. Philosophers call the first sort of argument *the logical argument* from evil and the second sort *the evidential argument* from evil.

THE LOGICAL ARGUMENT

The logical argument is not difficult to construct. In fact, it is an argument that, for many of us, immediately springs to mind when we think about God and evil. The simplest version would be this:

6.1. If there were a God, there would be no evil.

6.2. There is evil.

6.3. Thus there is no God.

What should we think of this most simple version? The answer hinges on our assessment of premise 6.1. If we are inclined to accept it, it is probably because we think that if there were a God, that God would be all-good, all-powerful, and all-knowing. Any being that is all-good would, by definition, want to prevent evil. And of course, any being that is all-powerful and all-knowing would be aware of all evil and would be capable of preventing it. In light of all this, it seems reasonable to think that if there were a God, there would be no evil.

These considerations lead us to an enhanced version of the Logical Argument:

6.4. If there were a God, He would be omniscient, omnipotent, and wholly good.

6.5. (a) A wholly good being would prevent the occurrence of every evil it is in his or her

power to prevent, (b) an omniscient being would be aware of all possible and actual evils, and (c) an omnipotent being would be able to prevent all evils.

6.6. Thus, if there were a God, there would be no evil.

6.7. There is evil.

6.8. Thus, there is no God.

If this argument is a good one, it shows us why the existence of evil and the existence of God are logically incompatible.

Since premises 6.6 and 6.8 merely draw conclusions from other premises, the theist can object to the argument only by rejecting one of premises 6.4, 6.5, or 6.7. Although some religious traditions deny premise 6.7—that is, they deny the reality of evil—this does not seem to be a very promising response.

Some philosophers have instead rejected premise 6.4. After all, why not simply deny that God is all-powerful or all-knowing? Perhaps God is very, very powerful, but still not capable of preventing *all* evil. Or perhaps God is very, very knowledgeable, but still falls short of knowing every truth that could be known. One could accept these things and thus deny premise 6.4. But to deny 6.4 is just to deny theism, since theism holds that God is all-powerful and all-knowing. So denying 6.4 really just concedes the conclusion.

The theist's last remaining option, then, is to reject premise 6.5. And indeed, this premise has been the primary focus of attention. What should we think of it? The most serious problem for premise 6.5 is part (a). The problem is that it is false. As a moment's reflection makes clear, it is surely false to say that a good being always prevents every evil it can. Doctors (even good ones) will sometimes cause you to feel pain (an evil) because doing so is required to get at some greater good (your cure, for example). Thus, a wholly good being is not one which prevents every evil it can, but rather one that prevents evil unless there is a morally sufficient reason for not doing so.

What would count as a morally sufficient reason for allowing evil? For a wholly or perfectly good being to have a morally sufficient reason for permitting an evil, three conditions must be satisfied:

(A) The Necessity Condition: it must be the case that the good brought about by permitting the evil. E. would not have been brought about without permitting either E or some other evils morally equivalent to or worse than E.[3]

(B) The Outweighing Condition: it must be the case that the good secured by the permission of the evil is sufficiently outweighing.

(C) The Rights Condition: it must be the case that it is within the rights of the one permitting the evil to permit it at all.

If these conditions *are* satisfied for some particular evil, then even an all-powerful and perfectly good being will be justified in permitting it.

What all of this shows us is that it is not the *reality of evil* that is incompatible with the existence of God: rather, it is the *reality of pointless* or *gratuitous* evils. In light of this, we can revise our Logical Argument one more time as follows:

6.9. If there were a God, there would be no gratuitous evils (GEs).

6.10. There is at least one GE.

6.11. Therefore: there is no God.

If there is a problem with this argument, it is with premise 6.10. To defend premise 6.10 the atheist needs to demonstrate that there is at least one GE. Showing this means showing that there is an evil that is either (a) *not necessary* for bringing about an *outweighing* good or (b) *not within the rights* of God to permit. Do some evils fall into one of these two categories? Let's consider them in turn.

One strategy would be to argue, with respect to particular evils—say, a small child's being cruelly beaten—either that such an evil could not possibly be outweighed by a greater good or that it could not possibly be necessary for some outweighing good. The trouble, however, is that

it is hard to see how such arguments might go in particular cases. Why not think that there might be goods of which we are unaware—goods, perhaps, that might come to the sufferer herself—that would outweigh the suffering? And why not think that some of those goods might be absolutely unattainable apart from God's willingness to allow such instances of suffering to take place? The only arguments that would seem to have any purchase here would be very general arguments—arguments, in other words, for the general conclusion that *no* evil could be necessary for an outweighing good.

Thus, we have a second way of trying to defend 6.10: namely, to produce an argument showing that no evil could be necessary for a greater good (in which case all evils would be gratuitous). Some atheists have offered such arguments. They claim that if God exists, then, in fact, *all* evils would be gratuitous since an omnipotent being would never have to rely on allowing evil in order to bring about some greater good. To say otherwise would be to say that God is sometimes at the mercy of having to allow certain evils to occur in order to get some outcome that he wants. But how could an omnipotent being be at the *mercy* of anything? We can, they say, imagine such a thing in the case of surgeons. Surgeons sometimes must inflict or allow pain and suffering in their patients in order to cure them. But God? Surely not. An omnipotent being would never be subject to such limitations. If God wanted to bring about a certain good, God would just do it.

Unfortunately, for all we know, this is false. We can see this by way of the following example. Theists and atheists alike largely agree that it is a good thing that God creates a universe, and that it is a good thing if the universe God creates contains creatures with freedom. Free creatures can enjoy the very great good of making free and autonomous choices. Furthermore, suitably intelligent and reflective free creatures are capable of producing moral good in the world, engaging in relationships of love and friendship, displaying genuine charity and courage, and so on. Yet free creatures of that sort necessarily have the ability to choose to do evil. And if those creatures are genuinely free in making their choices, they cannot be determined to choose only the good.

Now let's imagine that God is faced with the prospect of creating a universe. Wanting to maximize the varieties of good in the creation, and wanting to fill the creation with the greatest types of good, God decides to create a world containing a number of creatures with free choice. Can God create a world with such freely choosing creatures who never choose to do wrong? Not exactly. On the one hand, it is surely possible that God create a world with free creatures and that those creatures never choose to do wrong. But if the creatures are genuinely free (and if, as many think, freedom is incompatible with any kind of determinism—divine or natural), then it is really up to them and not God whether their world is one in which nobody ever chooses to do wrong. And it might be the case that, no matter what God did, things *would not* have turned out so that everybody always does what is right (even if they *could* have turned out that way). If that is right, then (we might say) though it is possible that everybody always freely does what is right, worlds in which that occurs might not be *feasible* for God. In short: because God cannot leave a creature free and at the same time guarantee that she will do what God wants, it is (on this view) simply not within God's power to ensure that the world he creates contains only free creatures who always do what is right.[4] Thus, for all we know, a universe with evil might be an unavoidable consequence of God's creating a universe that includes the very great good of creaturely freedom.

This argument, known as the Free Will Defense, was first developed in detail by Alvin Plantinga. The argument is meant to show that there are, for all we know, some goods (like the good of free choice) which even God cannot bring about without also allowing certain evils (specifically, morally evil choices) to occur. If this is right, then the second way of defending 6.10 also fails: some evils, for all we know, might have to be permitted in order to secure greater goods.

Let us now turn to a third way of defending 6.10. One might try to argue that there are some evils that God has no right to permit—even if permitting them is necessary to secure some greater good. Can the atheist argue that there are some evils like that? One might argue, for example, that some evils are so horrendous that no one, God included, could be justified in allowing them even if they were necessary conditions for bringing about some outweighing good. Perhaps, for example, it would never be permissible to allow a child to die a slow, painful, and lingering death due to cancer, even if it is a necessary means to some great good and even if that good somehow managed to outweigh such suffering. Unfortunately, arguments of this sort will all be grounded in moral principles that are highly contentious—principles, moreover, that many theists will be likely to reject. As a result, it is hard to imagine that arguments of this sort will be of much value to the atheist in getting people to accept premise 6.10.

For reasons of this sort, the Logical Argument is not much defended these days. Instead, most discussion of the argument from evil focuses on the second version: the Evidential Argument.

THE EVIDENTIAL ARGUMENT: THE "DIRECT ARGUMENT"

The first version of the Evidential Argument follows the same general pattern found in the Logical Argument. The difference is that the argument claims only that the premises are likely or probable:

6.12. If there were a God, there would be no gratuitous evils (GEs).

6.13. It is probable that at least one of the evils in our world is a GE.

6.14. Therefore: probably, there is no God.

In discussing the Logical Argument we saw that the atheist is going to have a difficult time defending premise 6.10 (the claim that there are gratuitous evils). The problem is that for all we know. God has good reasons for allowing the evil we see around us to occur. What the defender of this Evidential Argument insists on is that even though there *might* be such reasons, it is not *very likely* that there are.

This way of putting the argument actually resonates with our ordinary way of thinking of the connection between the existence of God and the existence of evil. Though, as we acknowledged earlier, it will be hard to show that any particular evil, or that evil in general, is *definitely* pointless, it is hard to shake the thought that at least some of the evils around us are *probably* pointless. For many such evils, we simply cannot imagine a point; and many are inclined to think that our inability to imagine a point just goes to show that, quite probably, such evils have no point. Thus, 6.13 has a kind of intuitive attractiveness; and so the argument as a whole has, at least initially, some persuasive force....

NOSEEUM ARGUMENTS

What good reason could the atheist have for thinking that there are some evils that happen for no good reason? In the most widely discussed defense of the Direct Argument, William Rowe claims that simple reflection on some of the more heinous forms of evil in our world ought to convince us of this. In the many forest fires that occur each year it is certain that many animals die. And it is equally certain that at least some of these animals die slow and horribly painful deaths. So let's focus our attention on an imaginary deer—one that represents what have surely been many thousands of deer—which dies a slow, agonizing death in the middle of a forest fire. Is this painful death (or some equally bad evil) a necessary condition for some outweighing good? Can we really believe that, were God to miraculously prevent this instance of evil, the world would be an overall worse place? How could we think such a thing? It seems simply obvious when we consider cases like this that there is no greater good to which we might appeal that could justify it. And in light of this, the reasonable thing to

conclude is that this is, after all, a genuinely gratuitous evil.

Stephen Wykstra has called labeled arguments of this sort "noseeum arguments."[5] The atheist is arguing that she has looked long and hard for some possible greater good that might come from this evil, and that the long search has come up empty handed. She sees no reason that could possibly justify God in permitting such suffering; and so she concludes from the fact that she can't see 'em that they just aren't there.

Are noseeum arguments good arguments? Sometimes they are. If your roommate asks you to get the milk from the refrigerator and you open the door, look carefully, and don't see any milk there, it is reasonable for you to conclude that there is no milk in the refrigerator because you don't see it. That is a good noseeum argument. But not all noseeum arguments are good. Imagine that you go to the doctor to get your immunizations. The doctor removes the protective sleeve from the needle and is about to inject you with it when he accidentally drops it on the floor. He picks it up and appears about to continue when you object: "Doctor, I think that needle might be dirty; there might be germs on it!" The doctor holds the needle up to the light, closes one eye, and stares intently at the needle. After a few seconds he says. "I have looked very closely and I don't see any germs on it; there's nothing to worry about." This doctor has made a noseeum inference—and it is a *bad one.*

What separates good noseeum inferences from bad ones? For a noseeum inference to be good two conditions must be met. First, it must be the case that you are looking for the thing in question in the right place. If your roommate asks you if there is any milk and you look in the oven, you are looking in the wrong place. Your failing to see it *there* would not be good evidence that you don't have any milk. Second, it must be the case that you would see the thing in question if it really were there. If your roommate asks if there are ants in the lawn and you look out the window and say. "Nope. I don't see any," you have made a bad noseeum inference.

You are looking in the right place, but ants are too small to be seen by you from that distance even if they are there.

With this we can return to the question of whether or not the atheist is in a good position to make a noseeum inference to the claim that there are gratuitous evils. Are defenders of the Direct Argument more like someone who concludes, after looking in the refrigerator, that there is no milk? Or are they instead more like the doctor who proclaims the needle to be clean?

Some philosophers, adopting a position now known as "skeptical theism," argue that atheists affirming 6.13 are more like the doctor. According to skeptical theists there are two good reasons to think that we are not well-positioned when it comes to figuring out the reasons God might have for permitting evil. First, given the immensity of divine goodness and the finitude of our human cognitive and moral faculties, it seems likely that there are some, perhaps many, types of good with which we are not acquainted. If we cannot even grasp the full range of goods that evils *might* be aimed at securing, then our attempts to make judgments about whether or not evils are gratuitous will be futile.

Second, even if we believed ourselves to be acquainted with the relevant goods, there is good reason to doubt that we would have any idea what role particular evils might play in bringing about those goods. How could we possibly know what sorts of ultimate good ends might be accomplished by the permission of this or that evil? It is hard enough to figure out what the good or evil consequences might be of a decision to exercise three times per week. (Will it lower your blood pressure so that you can live longer, or will you get run over by a car while riding your bicycle down the street?) Some evils might be necessary conditions for events hundreds or thousands of years down the road. Without omniscience, we can have very little idea of what events are necessary for what other events distant in time and space. Skeptical theists argue that these considerations should provide us with a healthy dose of uncertainty about our ability to make judgments concerning whether

any evil is gratuitous or not. If the skeptical theist is right, the Direct Argument is in trouble because the claims of skeptical theists would undermine any confidence we have that 6.13 is after all true....

THEODICIES

The third way that the theist might respond to the Direct Argument is to offer what might seem to be good reasons for God to allow the evils that there are. To offer such reasons is to offer a theodicy. The difference between a "defense" (mentioned earlier) and a "theodicy" is roughly this; a theodicy aims to set out a believable and reasonably comprehensive theory about why God might have permitted evil of the amount and variety we find in our world, whereas a defense aims merely to provide a *possible* reason— without concern for its believability—why God might permit evil. A defense, in other words, aims just at demonstrating the *possibility* of God's coexisting with evil, whereas theodicy aims at something like a full justification for God's permission of evil. If theists can set out some reasons for some types of evil, this will make us far less confident that other evils which we cannot explain really don't have any explanation. Theodicies can only play such a role, however, if they are genuinely credible, since they are supposed to represent explanations that we can imagine ourselves believing to be true. As a result, good theodicies are ones that we either know to be true or which we can reasonably believe to be true in light of other things that we believe.

The Punishment Theodicy

Christians, Jews, Muslims, theistic Hindus, and numerous other theistic religions hold that some evil is a result of divine punishment for human wrongdoing. Since successful theodicies must show that the evils they supposedly explain are connected to outweighing goods, we must then ask: is it reasonable to think that divine punishment secures any outweighing goods? Answering that question depends on what punishment is suppose to be good for. Defenders of the punishment theodicy have argued that punishment can be good for one or more of four things: *rehabilitation, deterrence, societal protection,* and *retribution*. We will consider the first three supposed benefits of punishment first and consider retribution separately.

The first three purported goods of punishment involve good consequences for the wrongdoer or other human agents. In the case of rehabilitation, the result is that the wrongdoer herself learns the wrongness of her action and no longer performs the bad action. In this way, the wrongdoer benefits. The goods of *deterrence* or *societal protection* instead benefit those around the wrongdoer. In the case of deterrence, the punishment inflicted on the wrongdoer leads others to reform their behavior. Protection of society can be secured if the punishment renders the wrongdoer unable to carry out further wrong acts by, for example, incarceration or even death.

If these are the goods that punishment is meant to bring about, it is not clear that they are sufficient. It seems that there are other ways in which God might be able to bring about these goods without inflicting punishment. For example, God could deter wrongdoers simply by making the world in such a way that wrong actions have severe natural consequences.

The fourth and most controversial purported good of punishment is the good of retribution. Many theistic traditions defend the notion that when someone commits a wrong they merit a punishment which exacts a cost that goes above and beyond mere recompense. If you steal money from a bank and are caught, you will be expected to repay what you stole. But merely having to give back the money is not enough. Something more is required: that you pay a fine or spend time in jail. According to retributivists, this additional cost is required simply because you have done something wrong and thus have earned a penalty. Exacting the additional penalty is retribution, and such a penalty is a necessary condition for maintaining justice in the universe. If this is right, then inflicting punishment will be necessary for the greater good of having a globally just universe.

Natural Consequence Theodicy

Some evil might be the result of divine punishment for moral wrongdoing by creatures. But this is not the only way in which free choosing can lead to bad consequences. Sometimes, bad moral choices lead to bad consequences directly. If you choose to spend your life indulging your every desire, seeking out sensual pleasure at every turn, and having no concern for the well-being of others, you may end up fat, lazy, and alone. Those consequences would be bad, but they are not divine punishments. Instead, they are just natural consequences of immoral choosing.

It is reasonable to think that a world designed by God would be one in which choosing badly would also turn out to be bad for us. God might be able to use the bad consequences that arise from bad choosing as a tool for helping us to learn how to live lives of moral uprightness in loving communion with God and others. Recognizing the poverty of a life lived in immorality and out of communion with God and others might be the only way of moving us to change our ways freely. In this way, allowing wrongdoing to have bad natural consequences brings about an outweighing good.

Punishment and natural consequence theodicies can only go so far, however. First, it seems clear that many evils—most notably, evils experienced by infants or non-human animals—cannot be regarded either as divine punishment or as natural consequences for moral wrongdoing. Second, the punishment theodicy explains evils only if there are *prior* evil choices that merit punishment. But then the question arises as to why God permitted those earlier evil choices. The punishment theodicy cannot tell us; thus, it will have to be supplemented.

The Free Will Theodicy

Philosophers addressing the topic of theodicy typically divide the types of evil that our world contains into two broad categories: moral evil and natural evil. Moral evil is evil that results from free creatures using their freedom in morally blameworthy ways. Natural evil is evil that does not directly involve blameworthy creaturely action. The most common theodicy for moral evil is the free will theodicy. Earlier we looked at the Free Will *Defense*, a response to the Logical Argument from evil that provides us with an argument that if God wants to bring about the good of creatures with the capacity for free choice, it is, for all we know, impossible to avoid the permission of at least some moral evil.

That argument might be good enough to show that the existence of God and the existence of moral evil are logically compatible—something the Logical Argument denies. But there are further questions that arise when considering the connections between free will and moral evil that were not addressed by that argument and which need to be settled for appeals to free will to yield a *theodicy*. The reason for this is that it seems reasonable to believe that, even if *some* evil was unavoidable by God, surely a *lot* of the evil attributed to free choice could have been prevented. This threatens to undermine the use of the free will theodicy as a general explanation for the reality of moral evil.

There are two sorts of evils that can spring from free choice. First, there are the evil moral choices themselves. Second, there are the evil *consequences* that can and sometimes do result from evil choices. It might be reasonable to hold that the reality of free choice makes it inevitable that there will be some bad moral *choices*. But couldn't God allow free choices—both good and bad—without allowing the bad choices to have further bad *consequences*? It might be good for you to have the ability to make a free choice to run out of the restaurant before you pay your bill. But couldn't God safeguard the restaurant owner from harm by miraculously making money appear on the table in an amount equal to the cost of your meal (with a generous tip to boot)? It might be good for you to be able to choose to run over your neighbor's mailbox in anger. But couldn't God make the mailbox post perfectly elastic the moment you strike it

so that as you drive away—content that you caused your neighbor harm—the mailbox springs back upright without a scratch?

Some philosophers have argued that, although it is a good thing to allow creatures to have free choice, it is a bad thing to allow those free choices to cause harm or injury to others. Instead, they argue, God should put us all in a *virtual playpen* in which choices can be made without any real harm to others being caused. Good choices could be made, and the good consequences that follow from them allowed. But bad choices, while not prevented altogether, would be prevented from causing additional damage. Couldn't God simply block such negative outcomes?

There are two good reasons to think not. First, if the world were structured this way, we would never be able to learn to do evil in the first place. If nothing we ever did allowed us to jump over large buildings (and, sadly, it doesn't), the idea of trying to do so would never enter our minds (and—at least after a certain age and amount of effort—it generally doesn't). The same would hold true for choosing evil in the playpen. Of course, this might first seem to be an advantage of the playpen. But notice that it comes at the price of keeping us from being able to make genuinely morally significant choices between good and evil alternatives.

Second, reflection on what it would take to set up a virtual playpen casts serious doubt on the idea that there would be much good in setting up such a thing. A person in the playpen will think that she has made choices with evil consequences, but the consequences will have been prevented by God. So what will happen when, say, a person tries to apologize for punching you in the nose, or to return money that she has stolen from you, or to visit the grave of a murder victim? God will have blocked these consequences; and so the apology will make no sense, the returned money will seem like an unexpected boon, and there will be no grave. Moreover, any attempt to discuss the blocked consequences will quickly reveal that all is not as it appears. To prevent everyone from discovering that no negative consequences in fact arise out of attempts to do evil. God would have to cause us to go mute, or to be misheard, every time we intended, in conversation, to refer back to earlier sinful deeds. Different newspapers would have to be delivered to different people: criminals would need an edition that reports (falsely) the negative effects of their crimes; "victims" would need editions that omit all mention of them. Television dramas portraying evil and suffering would leave everyone feeling as if bad things *always* happen to someone else. In short, it seems that, in order for God genuinely to keep us in the playpen, our experience would have to contain increasingly more elaborate illusions, until we would finally (and probably rather quickly) reach a point where we each live in worlds that are largely experientially isolated from each other. It is easy to doubt that there would be much good in creating a world like that.

The free will theodicy thus seems to provide at least a possible explanation for the fact that God allows a world in which creatures can make evil moral choices and in which those choices can sometimes issue in bad consequences. But like punishment theodicies, free will theodicies are not comprehensive. Even if these considerations suffice to explain moral evil, it is hard to see how they could offer any very plausible explanation for natural evil.

The Natural Law Theodicy

Free will theodicies focus on explaining evil as a consequence or result of creatures' free choices. Yet this is not the only way that we might try to connect freedom with the permission of evil. Another way is to argue that evils arise out of certain preconditions that must be in place for creatures to exercise their freedom.

There are many such conditions. For example, if the world proves wholly unresponsive to certain choices you make (to jump over tall buildings, for example), you might lose the ability—and hence the freedom—to choose such things. (Most of us tried to do this as kids but do so no longer because the world "didn't cooperate.") What is required for the world to

"cooperate" so that we can start making and continue to make free choices? At least one thing that is required is that the environment around us *be governed by regular, orderly laws of nature.* The reason for this is that in most cases, we act by moving our bodies in certain ways, and those ways cause things to happen in the world around us. When you want to split firewood, you move your body to swing the axe, which in turn causes the wood to splinter. If the environment around you were not regular and law-like, you couldn't do such things, since you wouldn't know that swinging axes could cause wood to split (since they wouldn't regularly do so). And so you would not know how to intend to split wood at all. In a chaotic world, you may desperately want to split some wood, but you wouldn't have any idea how to go about doing it. *Perhaps* swinging an axe would do the job; but for all you could tell, perhaps throwing marshmallows at it, or running about in circles in your neighbor's yard, would achieve the desired result. Thus, it seems that, although we might have desires to do all manner of different things, we would never *actually choose* to do those things because we would have no idea how.

Any world in which there are going to be free creatures capable of carrying out free actions with consequences beyond their own skin must then be a world that operates according to regular, orderly laws of nature. And this can lead to problems. The very same laws of momentum that allow me to drive a nail with a hammer, can cause that hammer to smash my thumb. The very same laws that allow me to tell stories by causing air vibrations with my vocal cords, allow tornadoes to knock down houses. And so on. In a world governed by regular, orderly natural laws, it is possible for these laws to conspire to intersect with the interests of creatures to cause them harm. When they do so, natural evil will be the result.

There are two serious objections that natural law theodicies need to confront, however. First, one might wonder why God did not create a world with laws that yield less natural evil. After all, would the world have been any worse if the laws were set up so that viruses couldn't occur? Second, aren't there plenty of cases of natural evil which could be eliminated without undermining the regularity of the laws of nature to such an extent that our freedom would be disabled? Would preventing one major hurricane undermine the possibility of my exercising my free will? If not, shouldn't God prevent one or two (or ten) more hurricanes? Let's consider these in turn.

Could the laws of nature have been changed to yield a world that has a substantially better overall balance of good than our world? To show that such a better world is possible, we would need to describe a regular, law-like world which (a) contains goodness of the sorts (either the same sorts or equivalent or better sorts) and amounts found in the actual world and which (b) contains substantially less natural evil than the actual world. There are two problems with trying to offer such a description. First, as we saw when considering the fine-tuning design argument in chapter 5, there is good reason to think that there is not much room for maneuver in the way the laws and constants of the world are structured. If the universe is going to be capable of supporting life, it will have to be governed by laws and constants similar to those we find in the actual world. Second, even if a better set of laws could be specified, it is doubtful that we could know this. Knowing such a thing would require knowing how changes we propose to certain laws and constants would impact not only the natural evils we are trying to prevent, but other laws of nature and the goods and evils that arise from their mutual interactions. It is unreasonable to think we could unscramble such things and thus unreasonable for us actually to believe that the laws could be changed to yield a better world with less natural evil.

The second objection is more formidable. If law-like regularity in the world exists in order to allow free creatures to use their free choice, then any natural evils which could be eliminated without eliminating that good result would be gratuitous. And yet it seems that there are many such evils. Even if God could not prevent such evils by systematically altering the laws that hold in our universe, he could at least do it by miraculous intervention. The evils of kidney stones or ingrown toenails seem candidates for such elimination.

The theist might respond that God already does miraculously intervene to prevent some such evils. That answer is not sufficient, however, since the critic wants to know why even more such evils are not prevented. The only answer available to the theist is that natural evils serve as necessary conditions for a variety of good ends, and that some of them are just unknown.

Soul-Making Theodicies

The theodicies considered so far regard evil as a consequence of free choice, or as a by-product of necessary conditions for free choice. Other theodicies treat evil as a necessary condition for goods of different sorts. For example, many theistic traditions regard the earthly life as an arena in which people make choices for the sake of cultivating moral and spiritual growth. If the world were filled with perpetual pleasure and satisfaction we would never experience the growth that can only come from real suffering, hardship, and defeat. As a result, some theists propose that God allows for evil in the world so that we can cultivate virtues of outweighing goodness that could not otherwise be cultivated.

It is easy to think of some such virtues. We could not become charitable unless there were people in need. We could not become courageous unless there were real dangers to be confronted. And so on. More than that, we could not become lovers or friends without the ability to choose and lose our friends and loved ones. All of these cases highlight the fact that one of the important goods in our world is that it provides an arena for *soul-making,* or character building. And this important good requires that the universe contain some evil.

This theodicy, pioneered by the second-century Christian thinker Irenaeus and defended in the twentieth century by philosopher John Hick, stipulates that four conditions must be in place for soul-making to occur. First, there must be creatures capable of choosing between good and evil. Second, those creatures must be placed in an environment that allows free choices to be carried out. Third, the environment must contain challenges to one's character of a sort that allows for both virtuous and non-virtuous responses. And finally, creatures must have sufficient opportunities to respond to make character building possible.

Soul-making theodicies must confront a couple of important objections. The most serious one is this: many sorts of moral and spiritual growth envisioned in soul-making scenarios require only that there be *apparent* evils in the world. For us to develop the virtues of charity and courage there need not be any *actual* need or *actual* peril; it only needs to seem that there is. We could be hooked up to a *Matrix*-like virtual reality machine that gives us a simulation of being confronted with evil, and as long as we are none the wiser, real soul-making can still go on. Wouldn't such a world be preferable? Daniel Howard-Snyder has responded to this criticism as follows:

> However, if God were to set up a world in which there was only illusory evil to which we could respond in the formation of our character, something of immense value would be missing. No one would in fact help anybody else; and no one would be helped. No one would in fact be compassionate and sympathetic to another; and no one would receive compassion and sympathy … No one would in fact praise or admire their fellows for pursuing noble ends in the face of adversity; and no one would receive such praise and admiration. No one would in fact satisfy their admirable aims and desires; and no one would be their recipient. No one would in fact generously give of their time, their talents or their money to the poor; and no one would receive generosity from another. In short, if every opportunity for a virtuous response were directed at illusory evils, each of us would live in our own little "world," worlds devoid of any genuine interaction and personal relationships.[6]

While some evils might be avoided in such a world, the cost of avoiding them would be to further take away many of those aspects of the world that we take to be the most valuable: our interactions of love and friendship with others.

NOTES

1. *Lancaster Intelligencer Journal*, June 6, 2006. A10.
2. Jeremiah 12:3, in *The Holy Bible: New International Version* (North American Edition), Copyright 1984. International Bible Society.
3. We use the word "would" rather than "could" in this condition intentionally. It might the case that there are certain goods that *could* be secured without allowing some particular instance of evil. But it might also be the case that those goods would not in fact be secured without permitting the evil. Take, for example, the figure of St. Paul in the Christian Scriptures. Christians might contend that it is possible that Paul could have repented of his evil ways without being stricken by God with blindness but that, as a matter of fact, he would stubbornly refuse until so stricken.
4. Does this count against God's omnipotence? No; because, given the view of freedom (as incompatible with determinism) that is presupposed by this response to the argument from evil, it is *logically impossible* for God to guarantee that a *free* agent conform to God's will. So long as the agent is free, there are no guarantees about what she will do; and if God does anything to guarantee her conformity to his will, he—by definition—undermines her freedom. And, as we saw in chapter 1, the standard story about omnipotence is that omnipotence does not include the power to do what is logically impossible.
5. "The Human Obstacle to Evidential Arguments from Suffering: On Avoiding the Evils of 'Appearance'." *International Journal for Philosophy of Religion* 16 (1984). pp. 73–94.
6. "God, Evil and Suffering," in Michael Murray (ed.), *Reason for the Hope Within* (Grand Rapids: Eerdmans, 1999), p. 99.

2.5 God and the Problem of Evil

B. C. JOHNSON

B. C. Johnson is the pseudonym of an author who prefers anonymity.

Here is a common situation: a house catches on fire and a six-month-old baby is painfully burned to death. Could we possibly describe as "good" any person who had the power to save this child and yet refused to do so? God undoubtedly has this power and yet in many cases of this sort he has refused to help. Can we call God "good"? Are there adequate excuses for his behavior?

First, it will not do to claim that the baby will go to heaven. It was either necessary for the baby to suffer or it was not. If it was not, then it was wrong to allow it. The child's ascent to heaven does not change this fact. If it was necessary, the fact that the baby will go to heaven does not explain why it was necessary, and we are still left without an excuse for God's inaction.

It is not enough to say that the baby's painful death would in the long run have good results and therefore should have happened, otherwise God would not have permitted it. For if we know this to be true, then we know—just as God knows—that every action successfully performed must in the end be good and therefore the right thing to do, otherwise, God would not have allowed it to happen. We could deliberately set houses ablaze to kill innocent people and if successful we would then know we had a duty to do it. A defense of God's goodness which takes as its foundation duties known only after the fact would result in a morality unworthy of the name. Furthermore, this argument does not explain why God allowed the child to burn to death. It merely claims that there is some reason discoverable in the long run. But the belief that such a reason is

within our grasp must rest upon the additional belief that God is good. This is just to counter evidence against such a belief by assuming the belief to be true. It is not unlike a lawyer defending his client by claiming that the client is innocent and therefore the evidence against him must be misleading—that proof vindicating the defendant will be found in the long run. No jury of reasonable men and women would accept such a defense and the theist cannot expect a more favorable outcome.

The theist often claims that man has been given free will so that if he accidentally or purposefully causes fires, killing small children, it is his fault alone. Consider a bystander who had nothing to do with starting the fire but who refused to help even though he could have saved the child with no harm to himself. Could such a bystander be called good? Certainly not. If we would not consider a mortal human being good under these circumstances, what grounds could we possibly have for continuing to assert the goodness of an all-powerful God?

The suggestion is sometimes made that it is best for us to face disasters without assistance, otherwise we would become dependent on an outside power for aid. Should we then abolish modern medical care or do away with efficient fire departments? Are we not dependent on their help? Is it not the case that their presence transforms us into soft, dependent creatures? The vast majority are not physicians or firemen. These people help in their capacity as professional outside sources of aid in much the same way that we would expect God to be helpful. Theists refer to aid from firemen and physicians as cases of man helping himself. In reality, it is a tiny minority of men helping a great many. We can become just as dependent on them as we can on God. Now the existence of this kind of outside help is either wrong or right. If it is right, then God should assist those areas of the world which do not have this kind of help. In fact, throughout history, such help has not been available. If aid ought to have been provided, then God should have provided it. On the other hand, if it is wrong to provide this kind of assistance, then we should abolish the aid altogether. But we obviously do not believe it is wrong.

Similar considerations apply to the claim that if God interferes in disasters, he would destroy a considerable amount of moral urgency to make things right. Once again, note that such institutions as modern medicine and fire departments are relatively recent. They function irrespective of whether we as individuals feel any moral urgency to support them. To the extent that they help others, opportunities to feel moral urgency are destroyed because they reduce the number of cases which appeal to us for help. Since we have not always had such institutions, there must have been a time when there was greater moral urgency than there is now. If such a situation is morally desirable, then we should abolish modern medical care and fire departments. If the situation is not morally desirable, then God should have remedied it.

Besides this point, we should note that God is represented as one who tolerates disasters, such as infants burning to death, in order to create moral urgency. It follows that God approves of these disasters as a means to encourage the creation of moral urgency. Furthermore, if there were no such disasters occurring, God would have to see to it that they occur. If it so happened that we lived in a world in which babies never perished in burning houses, God would be morally obliged to take an active hand in setting fire to houses with infants in them. In fact, if the frequency of infant mortality due to fire should happen to fall below a level necessary for the creation of maximum moral urgency in our real

world, God would be justified in setting a few fires of his own. This may well be happening right now, for there is no guarantee that the maximum number of infant deaths necessary for moral urgency are occurring.

All of this is of course absurd. If I see an opportunity to create otherwise nonexistent opportunities for moral urgency by burning an infant or two, then I should *not* do so. But if it is good to maximize moral urgency, then I *should* do so. Therefore, it is not good to maximize moral urgency. Plainly we do not in general believe that it is a good thing to maximize moral urgency. The fact that we approve of modern medical care and applaud medical advances is proof enough of this.

The theist may point out that in a world without suffering there would be no occasion for the production of such virtues as courage, sympathy, and the like. This may be true, but the atheist need not demand a world without suffering. He need only claim that there is suffering which is in excess of that needed for the production of various virtues. For example, God's active attempts to save six-month-old infants from fires would not in itself create a world without suffering. But no one could sincerely doubt that it would improve the world.

The two arguments against the previous theistic excuse apply here also. "Moral urgency" and "building virtue" are susceptible to the same criticism. It is worthwhile to emphasize, however, that we encourage efforts to eliminate evils; we approve of efforts to promote peace, prevent famine, and wipe out disease. In other words, we do value a world with fewer or (if possible) no opportunities for the development of virtue (when "virtue" is understood to mean the reduction of suffering). If we produce such a world for succeeding generations, how will they develop virtues? Without war, disease, and famine, they will not be virtuous. Should we then cease our attempts to wipe out war, disease, and famine? If we do not believe that it is right to cease attempts at improving the world, then by implication we admit that virtue-building is not an excuse for God to permit disasters. For we admit that the development of virtue is no excuse for permitting disasters.

It might be said that God allows innocent people to suffer in order to deflate man's ego so that the latter will not be proud of his apparently deserved good fortune. But this excuse succumbs to the arguments used against the preceding excuses and we need discuss them no further.

Theists may claim that evil is a necessary byproduct of the laws of nature and therefore it is irrational for God to interfere every time a disaster happens. Such a state of affairs would alter the whole causal order and we would then find it impossible to predict anything. But the death of a child caused by an electrical fire could have been prevented by a miracle and no one would ever have known. Only a minor alteration in electrical equipment would have been necessary. A very large disaster could have been avoided simply by producing in Hitler a miraculous heart attack—and no one would have known it was a miracle. To argue that continued miraculous intervention by God would be wrong is like insisting that one should never use salt because ingesting five pounds of it would be fatal. No one is requesting that God interfere all of the time. He should, however, intervene to prevent especially horrible disasters. Of course, the question arises: where does one draw the line? Well, certainly the line should be drawn somewhere this side of infants burning to death. To argue that we do not know where the line should be drawn is no excuse for failing to interfere in those instances that would be called clear cases of evil.

It will not do to claim that evil exists as a necessary contrast to good so that we might know what good is. A very small amount of evil, such as a toothache, would allow that. It is not necessary to destroy innocent human beings.

The claim could be made that God has a "higher morality" by which his actions are to be judged. But it is a strange "higher morality" which claims that what we call "bad" is good and what we call "good" is bad. Such a morality can have no meaning to us. It would be like calling black "white" and white "black." In reply the theist may say that God is the wise Father and we are ignorant children. How can we judge God any more than a child is able to judge his parent? It is true that a child may be puzzled by his parents' conduct, but his basis for deciding that their conduct is nevertheless good would be the many instances of good behavior he has observed. Even so, this could be misleading. Hitler, by all accounts, loved animals and children of the proper race; but if Hitler had had a child, this offspring would hardly have been justified in arguing that his father was a good man. At any rate, God's "higher morality," being the opposite of ours, cannot offer any grounds for deciding that he is somehow good.

Perhaps the main problem with the solutions to the problem of evil we have thus far considered is that no matter how convincing they may be in the abstract, they are implausible in certain particular cases. Picture an infant dying in a burning house and then imagine God simply observing from afar. Perhaps God is reciting excuses in his own behalf. As the child succumbs to the smoke and flames, God may be pictured as saying: "Sorry, but if I helped you I would have considerable trouble deflating the ego of your parents. And don't forget I have to keep those laws of nature consistent. And anyway if you weren't dying in that fire, a lot of moral urgency would just go down the drain. Besides, I didn't start this fire, so you can't blame *me*."

It does no good to assert that God may not be all-powerful and thus not able to prevent evil. He can create a universe and yet is conveniently unable to do what the fire department can do—rescue a baby from a burning building. God should at least be as powerful as a man. A man, if he had been at the right place and time, could have killed Hitler. Was this beyond God's abilities? If God knew in 1910 how to produce polio vaccine and if he was able to communicate with somebody, he should have communicated this knowledge. He must be incredibly limited if he could not have managed this modest accomplishment. Such a God, if not dead, is the next thing to it. And a person who believes in such a ghost of a God is practically an atheist. To call such a thing a god would be to strain the meaning of the word.

The theist, as usual, may retreat to faith. He may say that he has faith in God's goodness and therefore the Christian Deity's existence has not been disproved. "Faith" is here understood as being much like confidence in a friend's innocence despite the evidence against him. Now in order to have confidence in a friend one must know him well enough to justify faith in his goodness. We cannot have justifiable faith in the supreme goodness of strangers. Moreover, such confidence must come not just from a speaking acquaintance. The friend may continually assure us with his words that he is good but if he does not act like a good person, we would have no reason to trust him. A person who says he has faith in God's goodness is speaking as if he had known God for a long time and during that time had never seen Him do any serious evil. But we know that throughout history God has allowed numerous atrocities to occur. No one can have justifiable faith in the goodness of such a God. This faith would have to be based on a close friendship wherein God was never found to do anything wrong. But a person would have to be blind and deaf to have had such a relationship with God. Suppose a friend of yours had always claimed to be good yet refused to help people when he was in a position to render aid. Could you have justifiable faith in his goodness?

You can of course say that you trust God anyway—that no arguments can undermine your faith. But this is just a statement describing how stubborn you are; it has no bearing whatsoever on the question of God's goodness.

The various excuses theists offer for why God has allowed evil to exist have been demonstrated to be inadequate. However, the conclusive objection to these excuses does not depend on their inadequacy.

First, we should note that every possible excuse making the actual world consistent with the existence of a good God could be used in reverse to make that same world consistent with an evil God. For example, we could say that God is evil and that he allows free will so that we can freely do evil things, which would make us more truly evil than we would be if forced to perform evil acts. Or we could say that natural disasters occur in order to make people more selfish and bitter, for most people tend to have a "me-first" attitude in a disaster (note, for example, stampedes to leave burning buildings). Even though some people achieve virtue from disasters, this outcome is necessary if persons are to react freely to disaster—necessary if the development of moral degeneracy is to continue freely. But, enough; the point is made. Every excuse we could provide to make the world consistent with a good God can be paralleled by an excuse to make the world consistent with an evil God. This is so because the world is a mixture of both good and bad.

Now there are only three possibilities concerning God's moral character. Considering the world as it actually is, we may believe: (*a*) that God is more likely to be all evil than he is to be all good; (*b*) that God is less likely to be all evil than he is to be all good; or (*c*) that God is equally as likely to be all evil as he is to be all good. In case (*a*) it would be admitted that God is unlikely to be all good. Case (*b*) cannot be true at all, since—as we have seen—the belief that God is all evil can be justified to precisely the same extent as the belief that God is all good. Case (*c*) leaves us with no reasonable excuses for a good God to permit evil. The reason is as follows: if an excuse is to be a reasonable excuse, the circumstances it identifies as excusing conditions must be actual. For example, if I run over a pedestrian and my excuse is that the brakes failed because someone tampered with them, then the facts had better bear this out. Otherwise the excuse will not hold. Now if case (*c*) is correct and, given the facts of the actual world, God is as likely to be all evil as he is to be all good, then these facts do not support the excuses which could be made for a good God permitting evil. Consider an analogous example. If my excuse for running over the pedestrian is that my brakes were tampered with, and if the actual facts lead us to believe that it is no more likely that they were tampered with than that they were not, the excuse is no longer reasonable. To make good my excuse, I must show that it is a fact or at least highly probable that my brakes were tampered with—not that it is just a possibility. The same point holds for God. His excuse must not be a possible excuse, but an actual one. But case (*c*), in maintaining that it is just as likely that God is all evil as that he is all good, rules this out. For if case (*c*) is true, then the facts of the actual world do not make it any more likely that God is all

good than that he is all evil. Therefore, they do not make it any more likely that his excuses are good than that they are not. But, as we have seen, good excuses have a higher probability of being true.

Cases (*a*) and (*c*) conclude that it is unlikely that God is all good, and case (*b*) cannot be true. Since these are the only possible cases, there is no escape from the conclusion that it is unlikely that God is all good. Thus the problem of evil triumphs over traditional theism.

CHAPTER 3

REASON AND FAITH

3.1 The Ethics of Belief

W. K. CLIFFORD

W. K. Clifford (1845–1879) was an English mathematician and philosopher.

A shipowner was about to send to sea an emigrant-ship. He knew that she was old, and not over-well built at the first; that she had seen many seas and climes, and often had needed repairs. Doubts had been suggested to him that possibly she was not seaworthy. These doubts preyed upon his mind, and made him unhappy; he thought that perhaps he ought to have her thoroughly overhauled and refitted, even though this should put him to great expense. Before the ship sailed, however, he succeeded in overcoming these melancholy reflections. He said to himself that she had gone safely through so many voyages and weathered so many storms that it was idle to suppose she would not come safely home from this trip also. He would put his trust in Providence, which could hardly fail to protect

all these unhappy families that were leaving their fatherland to seek for better times elsewhere. He would dismiss from his mind all ungenerous suspicions about the honesty of builders and contractors. In such ways he acquired a sincere and comfortable conviction that his vessel was thoroughly safe and seaworthy; he watched her departure with a light heart, and benevolent wishes for the success of the exiles in their strange new home that was to be; and he got his insurance-money when she went down in mid-ocean and told no tales.

What shall we say of him? Surely this, that he was verily guilty of the death of those men. It is admitted that he did sincerely believe in the soundness of his ship; but the sincerity of his conviction can in no wise help him, because *he had no*

From W. K. Clifford, *Lectures and Essays* (1879).

right to believe on such evidence as was before him. He had acquired his belief not by honestly earning it in patient investigation, but by stifling his doubts. And although in the end he may have felt so sure about it that he could not think otherwise, yet inasmuch as he had knowingly and willingly worked himself into that frame of mind, he must be held responsible for it.

Let us alter the case a little, and suppose that the ship was not unsound after all; that she made her voyage safely, and many others after it. Will that diminish the guilt of her owner? Not one jot. When an action is once done, it is right or wrong for ever; no accidental failure of its good or evil fruits can possibly alter that. The man would not have been innocent, he would only have been not found out. The question of right or wrong has to do with the origin of his belief, not the matter of it; not what it was, but how he got it; not whether it turned out to be true or false, but whether he had a right to believe on such evidence as was before him.

There was once an island in which some of the inhabitants professed a religion teaching neither the doctrine of original sin nor that of eternal punishment. A suspicion got abroad that the professors of this religion had made use of unfair means to get their doctrines taught to children. They were accused of wresting the laws of their country in such a way as to remove children from the care of their natural and legal guardians; and even of stealing them away and keeping them concealed from their friends and relations. A certain number of men formed themselves into a society for the purpose of agitating the public about this matter. They published grave accusations against individual citizens of the highest position and character, and did all in their power to injure these citizens in the exercise of their professions. So great was the noise they made, that a Commission was appointed to investigate the facts; but after the Commission had carefully inquired into all the evidence that could be got, it appeared that the accused were innocent. Not only had they been accused on insufficient evidence, but the evidence of their innocence was such as the agitators might easily have obtained,

if they had attempted a fair inquiry. After these disclosures the inhabitants of that country looked upon the members of the agitating society, not only as persons whose judgment was to be distrusted, but also as no longer to be counted honourable men. For although they had sincerely and conscientiously believed in the charges they had made, yet *they had no right to believe on such evidence as was before them.* Their sincere convictions, instead of being honestly earned by patient inquiring, were stolen by listening to the voice of prejudice and passion.

Let us vary this case also, and suppose, other things remaining as before, that a still more accurate investigation proved the accused to have been really guilty. Would this make any difference in the guilt of the accusers? Clearly not; the question is not whether their belief was true or false, but whether they entertained it on wrong grounds. They would no doubt say, "Now you see that we were right after all; next time perhaps you will believe us." And they might be believed, but they would not thereby become honourable men. They would not be innocent, they would only be not found out. Every one of them, if he chose to examine himself *in foro conscientiae,* would know that he had acquired and nourished a belief, when he had no right to believe on such evidence as was before him; and therein he would know that he had done a wrong thing.

It may be said, however, that in both of these supposed cases it is not the belief which is judged to be wrong, but the action following upon it. The shipowner might say, "I am perfectly certain that my ship is sound, but still I feel it my duty to have her examined, before trusting the lives of so many people to her." And it might be said to the agitator, "However convinced you were of the justice of your cause and the truth of your convictions, you ought not to have made a public attack upon any man's character until you had examined the evidence on both sides with the utmost patience and care."

In the first place, let us admit that, so far as it goes, this view of the case is right and necessary; right, because even when a man's belief is so fixed that he cannot think otherwise, he still has a choice in regard to the action suggested by it, and so cannot escape the duty of investigating on the ground of the strength of his convictions; and necessary, because those who are not yet capable of controlling their feelings and thoughts must have a plain rule dealing with overt acts.

But this being premised as necessary, it becomes clear that it is not sufficient, and that our previous judgment is required to supplement it. For it is not possible so to sever the belief from the action it suggests as to condemn the one without condemning the other. No man holding a strong belief on one side of a question, or even wishing to hold a belief on one side, can investigate it with such fairness and completeness as if he were really in doubt and unbiased; so that the existence of a belief not founded on fair inquiry unfits a man for the performance of this necessary duty.

Nor is that truly a belief at all which has not some influence upon the actions of him who holds it. He who truly believes that which prompts him to an action has looked upon the action to lust after it, he has committed it already in his heart. If a belief is not realized immediately in open deeds, it is stored up for the guidance of the future. It goes to make a part of that aggregate of beliefs which is the link between sensation and action at every moment of all our lives, and which is so organized and compacted together that no part of it can be isolated from the rest, but every new addition modifies the structure of the whole. No real belief, however trifling and fragmentary it may seem, is ever truly insignificant; it prepares us to receive more of its like, confirms those which resembled it before, and weakens others; and so gradually it lays a stealthy train in our inmost thoughts, which may someday explode into overt action, and leave its stamp upon our character forever.

And no one man's belief is in any case a private matter which concerns himself alone. Our lives are guided by that general conception of the course of things which has been created by society for social purposes. Our words, our phrases, our forms and processes and modes of thought, are common property, fashioned and perfected from age to age; an heirloom which every succeeding generation inherits as a precious deposit and a sacred trust to be handed on to the next one, not unchanged but enlarged and purified, with some clear marks of its proper handiwork. Into this, for good or ill, is woven every belief of every man who has speech of his fellows. An awful privilege, and an awful responsibility, that we should help to create the world in which posterity will live.

In the two supposed cases which have been considered, it has been judged wrong to believe on insufficient evidence, or to nourish belief by suppressing doubts and avoiding investigation. The reason of this judgment is not far to seek; it is that in both these cases the belief held by one man was of great importance to other men. But forasmuch as no belief held by one man, however seemingly trivial the belief, and however obscure the believer, is ever actually insignificant or without its effect on the fate of mankind, we have no choice but to extend our judgment to all cases of belief whatever. Belief, that sacred faculty which prompts the decisions of our will, and knits into harmonious working all the compacted energies of our being, is ours not for ourselves, but for humanity. It is rightly used on truths which have been established by long experience and waiting toil, and which have stood in the fierce light of free and fearless questioning. Then it helps to bind men together, and to strengthen and direct their common action. It is desecrated when given to unproved and unquestioned statements, for the solace and private pleasure of the believer; to add a tinsel splendour to the plain straight road of our life and display a bright mirage beyond it; or even to drown the common sorrows of our kind by a self-deception which allows them not only to cast down, but also to degrade us. Whoso would deserve well of his fellows in this matter will guard the purity of his belief with a very fanaticism of jealous care, lest at any time it should rest on an unworthy object, and catch a stain which can never be wiped away.

It is not only the leader of men, statesman, philosopher, or poet, that owes this bounden duty to mankind. Every rustic who delivers in the village alehouse his slow, infrequent sentences, may help to kill or keep alive the fatal superstitions which clog his race. Every hard-worked wife of an artisan may transmit to her children beliefs which shall knit society together, or rend it in pieces. No simplicity of mind, no obscurity of station, can escape the universal duty of questioning all that we believe.

It is true that this duty is a hard one, and the doubt which comes out of it is often a very bitter thing. It leaves us bare and powerless where we thought that we were safe and strong. To know all about anything is to know how to deal with it under all circumstances. We feel much happier and more secure when we think we know precisely what to do, no matter what happens, than when we have lost our way and do not know where to turn. And if we have supposed ourselves to know all about anything, and to be capable of doing what is fit in regard to it, we naturally do not like to find that we are really ignorant and powerless, that we have to begin again at the beginning, and try to learn what the thing is and how it is to be dealt with—if indeed anything can be learnt about it. It is the sense of power attached to a sense of knowledge that makes men desirous of believing, and afraid of doubting.

This sense of power is the highest and best of pleasures when the belief on which it is founded is a true belief, and has been fairly earned by investigation. For then we may justly feel that it is common property, and hold good for others as well as for ourselves. Then we may be glad, not that *I* have learned secrets by which I am safer and stronger, but that *we men* have got mastery over more of the world; and we shall be strong, not for ourselves, but in the name of Man and in his strength. But if the belief has been accepted on insufficient evidence, the pleasure is a stolen one. Not only does it deceive ourselves by giving us a sense of power which we do not really possess, but it is sinful, because it is stolen in defiance of our duty to mankind. That duty is to guard ourselves from such beliefs as from a pestilence, which may shortly master our own body and then spread to the rest of the town. What would be thought of one who, for the sake of a sweet fruit, should deliberately run

the risk of bringing a plague upon his family and his neighbours?

And, as in other such cases, it is not the risk only which has to be considered; for a bad action is always bad at the time when it is done, no matter what happens afterwards. Every time we let ourselves believe for unworthy reasons, we weaken our powers of self-control, of doubting, of judicially and fairly weighing evidence. We all suffer severely enough from the maintenance and support of false beliefs and the fatally wrong actions which they lead to, and the evil born when one such belief is entertained is great and wide. But a greater and wider evil arises when the credulous character is maintained and supported, when a habit of believing for unworthy reasons is fostered and made permanent. If I steal money from any person, there may be no harm done by the mere transfer of possession; he may not feel the loss, or it may prevent him from using the money badly. But I cannot help doing this great wrong towards Man, that I make myself dishonest. What hurts society is not that it should lose its property, but that it should become a den of thieves, for then it must cease to be society. This is why we ought not to do evil, that good may come; for at any rate this great evil has come, that we have done evil and are made wicked thereby. In like manner, if I let myself believe anything on insufficient evidence, there may be no great harm done by the mere belief; it may be true after all, or I may never have occasion to exhibit it in outward acts. But I cannot help doing this great wrong towards Man, that I make myself credulous. The danger to society is not merely that it should believe wrong things, though that is great enough; but that it should become credulous, and lose the habit of testing things and inquiring into them; for then it must sink back into savagery.

The harm which is done by credulity in a man is not confined to the fostering of a credulous character in others, and consequent support of false beliefs. Habitual want of care about what I believe leads to habitual want of care in others about the truth of what is told to me. Men speak the truth to one another when each reveres the truth in his own mind and in the other's mind; but how shall my friend revere the truth in my mind when I myself am careless about it, when I believe things because I want to believe them, and because they are comforting and pleasant? Will he not learn to cry, "Peace," to me, when there is no peace? By such a course I shall surround myself with a thick atmosphere of falsehood and fraud, and in that I must live. It may matter little to me, in my cloudcastle of sweet illusions and darling lies; but it matters much to Man that I have made my neighbours ready to deceive. The credulous man is father to the liar and the cheat; he lives in the bosom of this his family, and it is no marvel if he should become even as they are. So closely are our duties knit together, that whoso shall keep the whole law, and yet offend in one point, he is guilty of all.

To sum up: it is wrong always, everywhere, and for anyone, to believe anything upon insufficient evidence.

If a man, holding a belief which he was taught in childhood or persuaded of afterwards, keeps down and pushes away any doubts which arise about it in his mind, purposely avoids the reading of books and the company of men that call in question or discuss it, and regards as impious those questions which cannot easily be asked without disturbing it—the life of that man is one long sin against mankind.

If this judgment seems harsh when applied to those simple souls who have never known better, who have been brought up from the cradle with a horror of doubt, and taught that their eternal welfare depends on *what* they believe, then it leads to the very serious question, *Who hath made Israel to sin?*

It may be permitted me to fortify this judgment with the sentence of Milton[1]—

> A man may be a heretic in the truth; and if he believe things only because his pastor says so, or the assembly so determine, without knowing other reason, though his belief be true, yet the very truth he holds becomes his heresy.

And with this famous aphorism of Coleridge[2]—

> He who begins by loving Christianity better than Truth, will proceed by loving his own sect or Church better than Christianity, and end in loving himself better than all.

Inquiry into the evidence of a doctrine is not to be made once for all, and then taken as finally settled.

It is never lawful to stifle a doubt; for either it can be honestly answered by means of the inquiry already made, or else it proves that the inquiry was not complete.

"But," says one, "I am a busy man; I have no time for the long course of study which would be necessary to make me in any degree a competent judge of certain questions, or even able to understand the nature of the arguments." Then he should have no time to believe.

NOTES

1. *Areopagitica.*
2. *Aids to Reflections.*

3.2 The Will to Believe

WILLIAM JAMES

William James (1842–1910) spent his career teaching philosophy and the new science of psychology at Harvard.

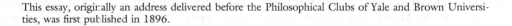

This essay, originally an address delivered before the Philosophical Clubs of Yale and Brown Universities, was first published in 1896.

In the recently published Life by Leslie Stephen of his brother, Fitz-James, there is an account of a school to which the latter went when he was a boy. The teacher, a certain Mr. Guest, used to converse with his pupils in this wise, "Gurney, what is the difference between justification and sanctification?—Stephen, prove the omnipotence of God!" etc. In the midst of our Harvard freethinking and indifference we are prone to imagine that here at your good old orthodox College conversation continues to be somewhat upon this order; and to show you that we at Harvard have not lost all interest in these vital subjects, I have brought with me tonight something like a sermon on justification by faith to read to you,—I mean an essay in justification *of* faith, a defence of our right to adopt a believing attitude in religious matters, in spite of the fact that our merely logical intellect may not have been coerced. "The Will to Believe," accordingly, is the title of my paper.

I have long defended to my own students the lawfulness of voluntarily adopted faith; but as soon as they have got well imbued with the logical spirit, they have as a rule refused to admit my contention to be lawful philosophically, even though in point of fact they were personally all the time chock-full of some faith or other themselves. I am all the while, however, so profoundly convinced that my own position is correct, that your invitation has seemed to me a good occasion to make my statements more clear. Perhaps your minds will be more open than those with which I have hitherto had to deal. I will be as little technical as I can, though I must begin by setting up some technical distinctions that will help us in the end.

I

Let us give the name of hypothesis to anything that may be proposed to our belief; and just as the electricians speak of *live* and *dead* wires, let us speak of any hypothesis as either live or dead. A live hypothesis is one which appeals as a real possibility to him to whom it is proposed. If I ask you to believe in the Mahdi, the notion makes

no electric connection with your nature—it refuses to scintillate with any credibility at all. As an hypothesis it is completely dead. To an Arab, however (even if he be not one of the Mahdi's followers), the hypothesis is among the mind's possibilities: It is alive. This shows that deadness and liveness in an hypothesis are not intrinsic properties, but relations to the individual thinker. They are measured by his willingness to act. The maximum of liveness in an hypothesis means willingness to act irrevocably. Practically, that means belief; but there is some believing tendency wherever there is willingness to act at all.

Next, let us call the decision between two hypotheses an *option*. Options may be of several kinds. They may be first, *living* or *dead*; secondly, *forced* or *avoidable*; thirdly, *momentous* or *trivial*; and for our purposes we may call an option a *genuine* option when it is of the forced, living, and momentous kind.

1. A living option is one in which both hypotheses are live ones. If I say to you: "Be a theosophist or be a Mohammedan," it is probably a dead option, because for you neither hypothesis is likely to be alive. But if I say: "Be an agnostic or be a Christian," it is otherwise; trained as you are, each hypothesis makes some appeal, however small, to your belief.

2. Next, if I say to you: "Choose between going out with your umbrella or without it," I do not offer you a genuine option, for it is not forced. You can easily avoid it by not going out at all. Similarly, if I say, "Either love me or hate me," "Either call my theory true or call it false," your option is avoidable. You may remain indifferent to me, neither loving nor hating, and you may decline to offer any judgment as to my theory. But if I say, "Either accept this truth or go without it," I put on you a forced option, for there is no standing place outside of the alternative. Every dilemma based on a complete logical disjunction, with no possibility of not choosing, is an option of this forced kind.

3. Finally, if I were Dr. Nansen and proposed to you to join my North Pole expedition, your option would be momentous; for this

would probably be your only similar opportunity, and your choice now would either exclude you from the North Pole sort of immortality altogether or put at least the chance of it into your hands. He who refuses to embrace a unique opportunity loses the prize as surely as if he tried and failed. *Per contra,* the option is trivial when the opportunity is not unique, when the stake is insignificant, or when the decision is reversible if it later prove unwise. Such trivial options abound in the scientific life. A chemist finds an hypothesis live enough to spend a year in its verification: he believes in it to that extent. But if his experiments prove inconclusive either way, he is quit for his loss of time, no vital harm being done.

It will facilitate our discussion if we keep all these distinctions well in mind.

II

The next matter to consider is the actual psychology of human opinion. When we look at certain facts, it seems as if our passional and volitional nature lay at the root of all our convictions. When we look at others, it seems as if they could do nothing when the intellect had once said its say. Let us take the latter facts up first.

Does it not seem preposterous on the very face of it to talk of our opinions being modifiable at will? Can our will either help or hinder our intellect in its perceptions of truth? Can we, by just willing it, believe that Abraham Lincoln's existence is a myth, and that the portraits of him in *McClure's Magazine* are all of some one else? Can we, by any effort of our will, or by any strength of wish that it were true, believe ourselves well and about when we are roaring with rheumatism in bed, or feel certain that the sum of the two one-dollar bills in our pocket must be a hundred dollars? We can *say* any of these things, but we are absolutely impotent to believe them; and of just such things is the whole fabric of the truths that we do believe in made up—matters of fact, immediate or remote, as Hume said, and relations between ideas, which are either there or not there for us if we see them so,

and which if not there cannot be put there by any action of our own.

In Pascal's *Thoughts* there is a celebrated passage known in literature as Pascal's wager. In it he tries to force us into Christianity by reasoning as if our concern with truth resembled our concern with the stakes in a game of chance. Translated freely his words are these: You must either believe or not believe that God is—which will you do? Your human reason cannot say. A game is going on between you and the nature of things which at the day of judgment will bring out either heads or tails. Weigh what your gains and your losses would be if you should stake all you have on heads, or God's existence; if you win in such case, you gain eternal beatitude; if you lose, you lose nothing at all. If there were an infinity of chances, and only one for God in this wager, still you ought to stake your all on God; for though you surely risk a finite loss by this procedure, any finite loss is reasonable, even a certain one is reasonable, if there is but the possibility of infinite gain. Go, then, and take holy water, and have masses said; belief will come and stupefy your scruples....Why should you not? At bottom, what have you to lose?

You probably feel that when religious faith expresses itself thus, in the language of the gaming table, it is put to its last trumps. Surely Pascal's own personal belief in masses and holy water had far other springs; and this celebrated page of his is but an argument for others, a last desperate snatch at a weapon against the hardness of the unbelieving heart. We feel that a faith in masses and holy water adopted wilfully after such a mechanical calculation would lack the inner soul of faith's reality; and if we were ourselves in the place of the Deity, we should probably take particular pleasure in cutting off believers of this pattern from their infinite reward. It is evident that unless there be some preexisting tendency to believe in masses and holy water, the option offered to the will by Pascal is not a living option. Certainly no Turk ever took to masses and holy water on its account; and even to us Protestants these means of salvation seem such foregone impossibilities that Pascal's logic, invoked for them specifically, leaves us unmoved. As well might the Mahdi write to us, saying, "I am the Expected One whom God has created in his effulgence. You shall be infinitely happy if you confess me; otherwise you shall be cut off from the light of the sun. Weigh, then, your infinite gain if I am genuine against your finite sacrifice if I am not!" His logic would be that of Pascal; but he would vainly use it on us, for the hypothesis he offers us is dead. No tendency to act on it exists in us to any degree.

The talk of believing by our volition seems, then, from one point of view, simply silly. From another point of view it is worse than silly, it is vile. When one turns to the magnificent edifice of the physical sciences, and sees how it was reared; what thousands of disinterested moral lives of men lie buried in its mere foundations; what patience and postponement, what choking down of preference, what submission to the icy laws of outer fact are wrought into its very stones and mortar; how absolutely impersonal it stands in its vast augustness—then how besotted and contemptible seems every little sentimentalist who comes blowing his voluntary smoke-wreaths, and pretending to decide things from out of his private dream! Can we wonder if those bred in the rugged and manly school of science should feel like spewing such subjectivism out of their mouths? The whole system of loyalties which grow up in the schools of science go dead against its toleration; so that it is only natural that those who have caught the scientific fever should pass over to the opposite extreme, and write sometimes as if the incorruptibly truthful intellect ought positively to prefer bitterness and unacceptableness to the heart in its cup.

> *It fortifies my soul to know*
> *That though I perish, Truth is so*

sings Clough, while Huxley exclaims: "My only consolation lies in the reflection that, however bad our posterity may become, so far as they hold by the plain rule of not pretending to believe what they have no reason to believe, because it may be to their advantage so to pretend [the word 'pretend' is surely here

redundant], they will not have reached the lowest depth of immorality." And that delicious *enfant terrible* Clifford writes: "Belief is desecrated when given to unproved and unquestioned statements for the solace and private pleasure of the believer... Whoso would deserve well of his fellows in this matter will guard the purity of his belief with a very fanaticism of jealous care, lest at any time it should rest on an unworthy object, and catch a stain which can never be wiped away....If [a] belief has been accepted on insufficient evidence [even though the belief be true, as Clifford on the same page explains] the pleasure is a stolen one....It is sinful because it is stolen in defiance of our duty to mankind. That duty is to guard ourselves from such beliefs as from a pestilence which may shortly master our own body and then spread to the rest of the town....It is wrong always, everywhere, and for every one, to believe anything upon insufficient evidence."

III

All this strikes one as healthy, even when expressed, as by Clifford, with somewhat too much of robustious pathos in the voice. Free will and simple wishing do seem, in the matter of our credences, to be only fifth wheels to the coach. Yet if any one should thereupon assume that intellectual insight is what remains after wish and will and sentimental preference have taken wing, or that pure reason is what then settles our opinions, he would fly quite as directly in the teeth of the facts.

It is only our already dead hypotheses that our willing nature is unable to bring to life again. But what has made them dead for us is for the most part a previous action of our willing nature of an antagonistic kind. When I say "willing nature," I do not mean only such deliberate volitions as may have set up habits of belief that we cannot now escape from—I mean all such factors of belief as fear and hope, prejudice and passion, imitation and partisanship, the circumpressure of our caste and set. As a matter of fact we find ourselves believing, we hardly know how or why. Mr. Balfour gives the name of "authority" to all those influences, born of the intellectual climate, that make hypotheses possible or impossible for us, alive or dead. Here in this room, we all of us believe in molecules and the conservation of energy, in democracy and necessary progress, in Protestant Christianity and the duty of fighting for "the doctrine of the immortal Monroe," all for no reasons worthy of the name. We see into these matters with no more inner clearness, and probably with much less, than any disbeliever in them might possess. His unconventionality would probably have some grounds to show for its conclusions; but for us, not insight, but the *prestige* of the opinions, is what makes the spark shoot from them and light up our sleeping magazines of faith. Our reason is quite satisfied, in nine hundred and ninety-nine cases out of every thousand of us, if it can find a few arguments that will do to recite in case our credulity is criticized by some one else. Our faith is faith in some one else's faith, and in the greatest matters this is the most the case....

Evidently, then, our non-intellectual nature does influence our convictions. There are passional tendencies and volitions which run before and others which come after belief, and it is only the latter that are too late for the fair; and they are not too late when the previous passional work has been already in their own direction. Pascal's argument, instead of being powerless, then seems a regular clincher, and is the last stroke needed to make our faith in masses and holy water complete. The state of things is evidently far from simple; and pure insight and logic, whatever they might do ideally, are not the only things that really do produce our creeds.

IV

Our next duty, having recognized this mixed-up state of affairs, is to ask whether it be simply reprehensible and pathological, or whether, on the contrary, we must treat it as a normal element in making up our minds. The thesis I defend is, briefly stated, this: *Our passional nature not only lawfully may, but must, decide an option between propositions, whenever it is a genuine option that cannot by its nature be decided on intellectual grounds; for to say, under such circumstances, "Do not decide, but leave the question open," is itself a passional decision—just like deciding yes or no—and is attended with the same risk of losing the truth....*

VII

One more point, small but important, and our preliminaries are done. There are two ways of looking at our duty in the matter of opinion— ways entirely different, and yet ways about whose difference the theory of knowledge seems hitherto to have shown very little concern. *We must know the truth;* and *we must avoid error*— these are our first and great commandments as would-be knowers; but they are not two ways of stating an identical commandment, they are two separable laws. Although it may indeed happen that when we believe the truth A, we escape as an incidental consequence from believing the falsehood B, it hardly ever happens that by merely disbelieving B we necessarily believe A. We may in escaping B fall into believing other falsehoods, C or D, just as bad as B; or we may escape B by not believing anything at all, not even A.

Believe truth! Shun error!—these, we see, are two materially different laws; and by choosing between them we may end by coloring differently our whole intellectual life. We may regard the chase for truth as paramount, and the avoidance of error as secondary; or we may, on the other hand, treat the avoidance of error as more imperative, and let truth take its chance. Clifford, in the instructive passage which I have quoted, exhorts us to the latter course. Believe nothing, he tells us, keep your mind in suspense forever, rather than by closing it on insufficient evidence incur the awful risk of believing lies. You, on the other hand, may think that the risk of being in error is a very small matter when compared with the blessings of real knowledge, and be ready to be duped many times in your investigation rather than postpone indefinitely the chance of guessing true. I myself find it impossible to go with Clifford. We must remember that these feelings of our duty about either truth or error are in any case only expressions of our passional life. Biologically considered, our minds are as ready to grind out falsehood as veracity, and he who says, "Better go without belief forever than believe a lie!" merely shows his own preponderant private horror of becoming a dupe. He may be critical of many of his desires and fears, but this fear he slavishly obeys. He cannot imagine any one questioning its binding force. For my own part, I have also a horror of being duped; but I can believe that worse things than being duped may happen to a man in this world: so Clifford's exhortation has to my ears a thoroughly fantastic sound. It is like a general informing his soldiers that it is better to keep out of battle forever than to risk a single wound. Not so are victories either over enemies or over nature gained. Our errors are surely not such awfully solemn things. In a world where we are so certain to incur them in spite of all our caution, a certain lightness of heart seems healthier than this excessive nervousness on their behalf. At any rate, it seems the fittest thing for the empiricist philosopher.

VIII

And now, after all this introduction, let us go straight at our question. I have said, and now repeat it, that not only as a matter of fact do we find our passional nature influencing us in our opinions, but that there are some options between opinions in which this influence must be regarded both as an inevitable and as a lawful determinant of our choice.

I fear here that some of you my hearers will begin to scent danger, and lend an inhospitable ear. Two first steps of passion you have indeed had to admit as necessary—we must think so as to avoid dupery, and we must think so as to gain truth; but the surest path to those ideal consummations, you will probably consider, is from now onwards to take no further passional step.

Well, of course, I agree as far as the facts will allow. Wherever the option between losing truth and gaining it is not momentous, we can throw the chance of *gaining truth* away, and at any rate save ourselves from any chance of *believing falsehood*, by not making up our minds at all till objective evidence has come. In scientific questions, this is almost always the case; and even in human affairs in general, the need of acting is seldom so urgent that a false belief to act on is better than no belief at all. Law courts, indeed, have to decide on the best evidence attainable for the moment, because a judge's duty is to make law as well as to ascertain it, and (as a learned judge once said to me) few cases are worth spending much time over; the great thing is to have them decided on *any* acceptable principle, and got out of the way. But in our dealings with objective nature we obviously are recorders, not makers, of the truth; and decisions for the mere sake of deciding promptly and getting on to the next business would be wholly out of place. Throughout the breadth of physical nature facts are what they are quite independently of us, and seldom is there any such hurry about them that the risks of being duped by believing a premature theory need be faced. The questions here are always trivial options, the hypotheses are hardly living (at any rate not living for us spectators), the choice between believing truth or falsehood is seldom forced. The attitude of sceptical balance is therefore the absolutely wise one if we would escape mistakes. What difference, indeed, does it make to most of us whether we have or have not a theory of the Roentgen rays, whether we believe or not in mind-stuff, or have a conviction about the causality of conscious states? It makes no difference. Such options are not forced on us. On every account it is better not to make them, but still keep weighing reasons *pro et contra* with an indifferent hand.

I speak, of course, here of the purely judging mind. For purposes of discovery such indifference is to be less highly recommended, and science would be far less advanced than she is if the passionate desires of individuals to get their own faiths confirmed had been kept out of the game. See for example the sagacity which Spencer and Weismann now display. On the other hand, if you want an absolute duffer in an investigation, you must, after all, take the man who has no interest whatever in its results: he is the warranted incapable, the positive fool. The most useful investigator, because the most sensitive observer, is always he whose eager interest in one side of the question is balanced by an equally keen nervousness lest he become deceived.[1] Science has organized this nervousness into a regular *technique,* her so-called method of verification; and she has fallen so deeply in love with the method that one may even say she has ceased to care for truth by itself at all. It is only truth as technically verified that interests her. The truth of truths might come in merely affirmative form, and she would decline to touch it. Such truth as that, she might repeat with Clifford, would be stolen in defiance of her duty to mankind. Human passions, however, are stronger than technical rules. "*Le coeur a ses raisons,*" as Pascal says, "*que la raison ne connait pas*",[2] and however indifferent to all but the bare rules of the game the umpire, the abstract intellect, may be, the concrete players who furnish him the materials to judge of are usually, each one of them, in love with some pet "live hypothesis" of his own. Let us agree, however, that wherever there is no forced option, the dispassionately judicial intellect with no pet hypothesis, saving us, as it does, from dupery at any rate, ought to be our ideal.

The question next arises: Are there not somewhere forced options in our speculative questions, and can we (as men who may be interested at least as much in positively gaining truth as in merely escaping dupery) always wait with impunity till the coercive evidence shall have arrived? It seems *a priori* improbable that the truth should be so nicely adjusted to our needs and powers as that. In the great boarding-house of nature, the cakes and the butter and the syrup seldom come out so even and leave the plates so clean. Indeed, we should view them with scientific suspicion if they did.

IX

Moral questions immediately present themselves as questions whose solution cannot wait for sensible proof. A moral question is a question not of what sensibly exists, but of what is good, or would be good if it did exist. Science can tell us what exists; but to compare the *worths,* both of what exists and of what does not exist, we must consult not science, but what Pascal calls our heart....

Turn now from these wide questions of good to a certain class of questions of fact, questions concerning personal relations, states of mind between one man and another. *Do you like me or not?*—for example. Whether you do or not depends, in countless instances, on whether I meet you halfway, am willing to assume that you must like me, and show you trust and expectation. The previous faith on my part in your liking's existence is in such cases what makes your liking come. But if I stand aloof, and refuse to budge an inch until I have objective evidence, until you shall have done something apt, as the absolutists say, *ad extorquendum assensum meum,* ten to one your liking never comes. How many women's hearts are vanquished by the mere sanguine insistence of some man that they *must* love him! He will not consent to the hypothesis that they cannot. The desire for a certain kind of truth here brings about that special truth's existence; and so it is in innumerable cases of other sorts....*And where faith in a fact can help create the fact,* that would be an insane logic which should say that faith running ahead of scientific evidence is the "lowest kind of immorality" into which a thinking being can fall. Yet such is the logic by which our scientific absolutists pretend to regulate our lives!

X

In truths dependent on our personal action, then, faith based on desire is certainly a lawful and possibly an indispensable thing.

But now, it will be said, these are all childish human cases, and have nothing to do with great cosmical matters, like the question of religious faith. Let us then pass on to that. Religions differ so much in their accidents that in discussing the religious question we must make it very generic and broad. What then do we now mean by the religious hypothesis? Science says things are; morality says some things are better than other things; and religion says essentially two things.

First, she says that the best things are the more eternal things, the overlapping things, the things in the universe that throw the last stone, so to speak, and say the final word. "Perfection is eternal"—this phrase of Charles Secrétan seems a good way of putting this first affirmation of religion, an affirmation which obviously cannot yet be verified scientifically at all.

The second affirmation of religion is that we are better off even now if we believe her first affirmation to be true.

Now, let us consider what the logical elements of this situation are *in case the religious hypothesis in both its branches be really true.* (Of course, we must admit that possibility at the outset. If we are to discuss the question at all, it must involve a living option. If for any of you religion be a hypothesis that cannot, by any living possibility, be true, then you need go no farther. I speak to the "saving remnant" alone.) So proceeding, we see, first, that religion offers itself as a *momentous* option. We are supposed to gain, even now, by our belief, and to lose by our non-belief, a certain vital good. Secondly, religion is a *forced* option, so far as that good goes. We cannot escape the issue by remaining sceptical and waiting for more light, because, although we do avoid error in that way *if religion be untrue,* we lose the good, *if it be true,* just as certainly as if we positively chose to disbelieve. It is as if a man should hesitate indefinitely to ask a certain woman to marry him because he was not perfectly sure that she would prove an angel after he brought her home. Would he not cut himself off from that particular angel-possibility as decisively as if he went and married some one else? Scepticism, then, is not avoidance of option; it is option of a certain particular kind of risk. *Better risk loss of truth than chance of error*—that is your faith-vetoer's exact position. He

is actively playing his stake as much as the believer is; he is backing the field against the religious hypothesis, just as the believer is backing the religious hypothesis against the field. To preach scepticism to us as a duty until "sufficient evidence" for religion be found, is tantamount therefore to telling us, when in presence of the religious hypothesis, that to yield to our fear of its being error is wiser and better than to yield to our hope that it may be true. It is not intellect against all passion, then; it is only intellect with one passion laying down its law. And by what, forsooth, is the supreme wisdom of this passion warranted? Dupery for dupery, what proof is there that dupery through hope is so much worse than dupery through fear? I, for one, can see no proof; and I simply refuse obedience to the scientist's command to imitate his kind of option, in a case where my own stake is important enough to give me the right to choose my own form of risk. If religion be true and the evidence for it be still insufficient, I do not wish, by putting your extinguisher upon my nature (which feels to me as if it had after all some business in this matter), to forfeit my sole chance in life of getting upon the winning side—that chance depending, of course, on my willingness to run the risk of acting as if my passional need of taking the world religiously might be prophetic and right.

All this is on the supposition that it really may be prophetic and right, and that, even to us who are discussing the matter, religion is a live hypothesis which may be true. Now, to most of us religion comes in a still further way that makes a veto on our active faith even more illogical. The more perfect and more eternal aspect of the universe is represented in our religions as having personal form. The universe is no longer a mere *It* to us, but a *Thou,* if we are religious; and any relation that may be possible from person to person might be possible here. For instance, although in one sense we are passive portions of the universe, in another we show a curious autonomy, as if we were small active centers on our own account. We feel, too, as if the appeal of religion to us were made to our own active goodwill, as if evidence might be forever withheld from us unless we met the hypothesis halfway to take a trivial illustration: just as a man who in a company of gentlemen made no advances, asked a warrant for every concession, and believed no one's word without proof, would cut himself off by such churlishness from all the social rewards that a more trusting spirit would earn—so here, one who should shut himself up in snarling logicality and try to make the gods extort his recognition willy-nilly, or not get it at all, might cut himself off forever from his only opportunity of making the gods' acquaintance. This feeling, forced on us we know not whence that by obstinately believing that there are gods (although not to do so would be so easy both for our logic and our life) we are doing the universe the deepest service we can, seems part of the living essence of the religious hypothesis. If the hypothesis *were* true in all its parts, including this one, then pure intellectualism, with its veto on our making willing advances, would be an absurdity; and some participation of our sympathetic nature would be logically required. I therefore, for one, cannot see my way to accepting the agnostic rules for truthseeking, or wilfully agree to keep my willing nature out of the game. I cannot do so for this plain reason, that *a rule of thinking which would absolutely prevent me from acknowledging certain kinds of truth if those kinds of truth were really there, would be an irrational rule.* That for me is the long and short of the formal logic of the situation, no matter what the kinds of truth might materially be.

I confess I do not see how this logic can be escaped. But sad experience makes me fear that some of you may still shrink from radically saying with me, *in abstracto,* that we have the right to believe at our own risk any hypothesis that is live enough to tempt our will. I suspect, however, that if this is so, it is because you have got away from the abstract logical point of view altogether, and are thinking (perhaps without realizing it) of some particular religious hypothesis which for you is dead. The freedom to "believe what we will" you apply to the case of some patent superstition; and the faith you think of is the faith defined by the schoolboy when he said,

"is when you believe something that you know ain't true." I can only repeat that this is misapprehension. *In concreto,* the freedom to believe can only cover living options which the intellect of the individual cannot by itself resolve; and living options never seem absurdities to him who has them to consider. When I look at the religious question as it really puts itself to concrete men, and when I think of all the possibilities which both practically and theoretically it involves, then this command that we shall put a stopper on our heart, instincts, and courage, and *wait*—acting of course meanwhile more or less as if religion were *not* true[3]—till doomsday, or till such time as our intellect and senses working together may have raked in evidence enough —this command, I say, seems to me the queerest idol ever manufactured in the philosophic cave. Were we scholastic absolutists, there might be more excuse. If we had an infallible intellect with its objective certitudes, we might feel ourselves disloyal to such a perfect organ of knowledge in not trusting to it exclusively, in not waiting for its releasing word. But if we are empiricists, if we believe that no bell in us tolls to let us know for certain when truth is in our grasp, then it seems a piece of idle fantasticality to preach so solemnly our duty of waiting for the bell. Indeed we *may* wait if we will—I hope you do not think that I am denying that—but if we do so, we do so at our peril as much as if we believed. In either case we *act,* taking our life in our hands. No one of us ought to issue vetoes to the other, nor should we bandy words of abuse. We ought, on the contrary, delicately and profoundly to respect one another's mental freedom: then only shall we bring about the intellectual republic; then only shall we have that spirit of inner tolerance without which all our outer tolerance is soulless, and which is empiricism's glory; then only shall we live and let live, in speculative as well as in practical things.

I began by a reference to Fitz-James Stephen; let me end by a quotation from him. "What do you think of yourself? What do you think of the world?…These are questions with which all must deal as it seems good to them. They are riddles of the Sphinx, and in some way or other we must deal with them....In all important transactions of life we have to take a leap in the dark....If we decide to leave the riddles unanswered, that is a choice; if we waver in our answer, that, too, is a choice: but whatever choice we make, we make it at our peril. If a man chooses to turn his back altogether on God and the future, no one can prevent him; no one can show beyond reasonable doubt that he is mistaken. If a man thinks otherwise and acts as he thinks, I do not see that any one can prove that *he* is mistaken. Each must act as he thinks best; and if he is wrong, so much the worse for him. We stand on a mountain pass in the midst of whirling snow and blinding mist, through which we get glimpses now and then of paths which may be deceptive. If we stand still we shall be frozen to death. If we take the wrong road we shall be dashed to pieces. We do not certainly know whether there is any right one. What must we do? 'Be strong and of a good courage.' Act for the best, hope for the best, and take what comes....If death ends all, we cannot meet death better."[4]

NOTES

1. Compare Wilfrid Ward's Essay "The Wish to Believe," in his *Witnesses to the Unseen* (Macmillan & Co., 1893).

2. "The heart has its reasons which reason does not know." Editor's Trans.

3. Since belief is measured by action, he who forbids us to believe religion to be true, necessarily also forbids us to act as we should if we did believe it to be true. The whole defence of religious faith hinges upon action. If the action required or inspired by the religious hypothesis is in no way different from that dictated by the naturalistic hypothesis, then religious faith is a pure superfluity, better pruned away, and controversy about its legitimacy is a piece of idle trifling, unworthy of serious minds. I myself believe, of course, that the religious hypothesis gives to the world an expression which specifically determines our reactions, and makes them in a large part unlike what they might be on a purely naturalistic scheme of belief.

4. *Liberty, Equality, Fraternity*, 353, 2nd edition (London, 1874).

3.3 Without Evidence or Argument

KELLY JAMES CLARK

Kelly James Clark is Professor of Philosophy at Calvin College.

INTRODUCTION

Suppose a stranger, let's call him David, sends you a note that declares that your wife is cheating on you. No pictures are included, no dates or times, no names. Just the assertion of your wife's unfaithfulness. You have had already fifteen good, and so far as you know, faithful years with your wife. Her behavior hasn't changed dramatically in the past few years. Except for David's allegation, you have no reason to believe there has been a breach in the relationship. What should you do? Confront her with what you take to be the truth, straight from David's letter? Hire a detective to follow her for a week and hope against hope the letter is a hoax? Or do you simply remain secure in the trust that you have built up all those years?

From Kelly James Clark, "Reformed Epistemology," Modern Reformation Magazine, vol. 7 (1998). Reprinted with permission of White Horse Inn, 1725 Bear Valley Pkwy, Escondido, CA 92027.

Suppose, even worse, that your son Clifford comes home after taking his first philosophy course in college. He persuades you of the truth of the so-called "problem of other minds." How do you know that other minds and, therefore, other people exist? How do you know that people are not simply cleverly constructed robots with excellent makeup jobs? How do you know that behind the person facade lies a person—someone with thoughts, desires and feelings? You can't experience another person's feelings; you can't see another person's thoughts (even if you were to cut off the top of their head and peer into their brain); and even Bill Clinton can't really feel another person's pain. Yet thoughts, desires, and feelings are all essential to being a person. So you can't tell from the outside or just by looking, so to speak, if someone is a person. I can know that *I* am a person because I experience my own thoughts, feelings and desires. But I can't know, because I don't have any access to your inner-experience, if you, or anyone else, is a person.

Since you can't know if anyone else is a person, you rightly infer that you can't know if your wife is a person. Unsure that your wife is a person, how do you treat her? Do you hire a philosophical detective to search the philosophical literature for a proof that people-like things really are people? Do you avoid cuddling in the meantime, given your aversion to snuggling with machines? Or do you simply trust your deep-seated conviction that, in spite of the lack of evidence, your wife is a person and deserves to be treated as such?

Two final "Supposes." Suppose that you come to believe that there is a God because your parents taught you from the cradle up that God exists. Or suppose that you are on a retreat or on the top of a mountain and have a sense of being loved by God or that God created the universe. You begin to believe in God, not because you are persuaded by the argument from design—you are simply taken with belief in God. You just find yourself believing, what you had heretofore denied, that God exists. Now you have come across the writings of David

Hume and W. K. Clifford who insist that you base all of your beliefs on evidence. Hume raises a further point: your belief in an all-loving, omnipotent God is inconsistent with the evil that there is in the world. Given the fact of evil, God cannot exist. To meet this demand for evidence, do you become a temporary agnostic and begin perusing the texts of Aquinas, Augustine and Paley for a good proof of God's existence? Do you give up belief in God because you see Hume's point and can't see how God and evil could be reconciled? Or do you remain steady in your trust in God in spite of the lack of evidence and even in the face of counter-evidence?

My Suppose-This and Suppose-That Stories are intended to raise the problem of the relationship of our important beliefs to evidence (and counter-evidence). Since the Enlightenment, there has been a demand to expose all of our beliefs to the searching criticism of reason. If a belief is unsupported by the evidence, it is irrational to believe it. It is the position of Reformed epistemology (likely the position that Calvin held) that belief in God, like belief in other persons, does not require the support of evidence or argument in order for it to be rational. This view has been defended by some of the world's most prominent philosophers including Alvin Plantinga, Nicholas Wolterstorff, and William Alston.[1]

The claim that belief in God is rational without the support of evidence or argument is startling for many an atheist or theist. Most atheist intellectuals feel comfort in their disbelief in God because they judge that there is little or no evidence for God's existence. Many theistic thinkers, however, insist that belief in God requires evidence and that such a demand should and can be met. So the claim that a person does not need evidence in order to rationally believe in God runs against the grain for atheist thinkers and has raised the ire of many theists. In spite of the vitriolic response to Reformed epistemology, I believe it is eminently defensible. In order to defend it, let us examine its critique of the Enlightenment demand for evidence.

THE DEMAND FOR EVIDENCE

W. K. Clifford, in an oft-cited article, claims that it is wrong, always and everywhere, for anyone to believe anything on insufficient evidence. Such a strong claim makes one speculate on Clifford's childhood: one imagines young W. K. constantly pestering his parents with "Why? Why? Why?..." It is this childish attitude toward inquiry and the risks that belief requires that leads William James to chastise Clifford as an *enfant terrible*. But, rather than disparage his character, let's examine the deficiencies of his claim that everything must be believed only on the basis of sufficient evidence (Relevance: If everything must be based on sufficient evidence, so must belief in God).

The first problem with Clifford's universal demand for evidence is that it cannot meet its own demand. Clifford offers two fetching examples (a shipowner who knowingly sends an unseaworthy ship to sea and, in the first example, it sinks and, in the second example, it makes the trip) in support of his claim. The examples powerfully demonstrate that in cases like the example, rational belief requires evidence. No one would disagree: some beliefs require evidence for their rational acceptability. But *all* beliefs in *every* circumstance? That's an exceedingly strong claim to make and, it turns out, one that cannot be based on evidence.

Consider what someone like Clifford might allow us to take for evidence: beliefs that we acquire through sensory experience and beliefs that are self-evident like logic and mathematics. Next rainy day, make a list of all of your experiential beliefs: The sky is blue, grass is green, most trees are taller than most grasshoppers, slugs leave a slimy trail....Now add to this list all of your logical and mathematical beliefs: $2 + 2 = 4$, every proposition is either true or false, all of the even numbers that I know of are the sum of two prime numbers, in Euclidean geometry the interior angles of triangles equal 180. From these propositions, try to deduce the conclusion that it is wrong, always and everywhere, for anyone to believe anything on insufficient evidence. None of the propositions that are allowed as evidence

have anything at all to do with the conclusion. So Clifford's universal demand for evidence cannot satisfy its own standard! Therefore, by Clifford's own criterion, it must be irrational. More likely, however, the demand is simply false and it is easy to see why.

We, finite beings that we are, simply cannot meet such a demand. Consider all of the beliefs that you currently hold. How many of those have met Clifford's strict demand for evidence? Clifford intends for all of us, like a scientist in a laboratory, to test all of our beliefs all of the time. Could your beliefs survive Clifford's test? Think of how many of your beliefs, even scientific ones, are acquired *just because someone told you*. Not having been to Paraguay, I only have testimonial evidence that Paraguay is a country in South America. For all I know, all of the mapmakers have conspired to delude us about the existence of Paraguay (and even South America!). And, since I have been to relatively few countries around the world, I must believe in the existence of most countries (and that other people inhabit them and speak in that language) without support of evidence. I believe that $e = mc^2$ and that matter is made up of tiny little particles not because of experiments in a chemistry or physics lab (for all of my experiments failed) but because my science teachers told me so. Most of the beliefs that I have acquired are based on my trust in my teachers and not on careful consideration of what Clifford would consider adequate evidence. And in this busy day and age, I don't really have the time to live up to Clifford's demand for evidence! If we had the leisure to test all of our beliefs, perhaps we could meet the demand. But since we cannot meet that demand, we cannot be obligated to do so.

Even if we had the time, however, we could not meet this universal demand for evidence. The demand for evidence simply cannot be met in a large number of cases with the cognitive equipment that we have. No one, as mentioned above, has ever been able to prove the existence of other persons. No one has ever been able to prove that we were not created five minutes ago with our memories intact. No one has been able to prove the reality of the past or that, in the future, the sun will rise. This list could go on and on. There is a limit to the things that human beings can prove. A great deal of what we believe is based on faith, not on evidence or arguments.

I use the term "faith" here but it is misleading. I don't mean to oppose faith to knowledge in these instances. For surely we know that the earth is more than five minutes old and that the sun will rise tomorrow (although, maybe not in cloudy Grand Rapids!) and that Paul converted to Christianity (and lots of other truths about the past), etc., etc., etc. In these cases, we know lots of things but we cannot prove them. We have to trust or rely on the cognitive faculties which produce these beliefs. We rely on our memory to produce memory beliefs (I remember having coffee with my breakfast this morning). We rely on an inductive faculty to produce beliefs about the veracity of natural laws (If I let go of this book, it will fall to the ground). We rely on our cognitive faculties when we believe that there are other persons, there is a past, there is a world independent of our mind, or what other people tell us. We can't help but trust our cognitive faculties.

It is easy to see why. Reasoning must start somewhere. Suppose we were required to offer evidence or arguments for all our beliefs. If we offer statements 1–4 as evidence for 5, we would have to offer arguments to support 1–4. And then we would have to offer arguments in support of the arguments that are used to support 1–4. And then we would need arguments....You get the point. Reasoning must start somewhere. There have to be some truths that we can just accept and reason from. Why not start with belief in God?

WITHOUT EVIDENCE OR ARGUMENT

We have been outfitted with cognitive faculties that produce beliefs that we can reason from. The number of beliefs we do and must reason to is quite small compared to the number of beliefs that we do and must accept without the aid of a proof. That's the long and short of the human believing condition. We, in most cases, must rely on our God-given intellectual equipment to produce beliefs, without evidence or argument, in the appropriate circumstances. Is it reasonable to believe that God has created us with a cognitive faculty which produces belief in God without evidence or argument?

There are at least three reasons to believe that it is proper or rational for a person to accept belief in God without the need for an argument. First, there are very few people who have access to or the ability to assess most theistic arguments. It is hard to imagine, therefore, that the demand for evidence would be a requirement of reason. My grandmother, a paradigm of the non-philosophical believer, would cackle if I informed her that her belief in God was irrational because she was unable to understand Aquinas's second Way or to refute Hume's version of the argument from evil. The demand for evidence is an imperialistic attempt to make philosophers out of people who have no need to become philosophers. It is curious that very few philosophers (like most ordinary folk) have come to belief in God on the basis of theistic arguments. I commissioned and published a collection of spiritual autobiographies from prominent Christian philosophers just to see if philosophers were any different from my grandmother on this count. They weren't.[2]

Second, it seems that God has given us an awareness of himself that is not dependent on theistic arguments. It is hard to imagine that God would make rational belief as difficult as those that demand evidence contend. I encourage anyone who thinks that evidence is required for rational belief in God, to study very carefully the theistic arguments, their refutations and counter-refutations, and their increasing subtlety yet decreasing charm. Adequate assessment of these arguments would require a lengthy and torturous tour through the history of philosophy and may require the honing of one's logical and metaphysical skills beyond the capacity of most of us. Why put that sort of barrier between us and God? John Calvin believed that God had provided us with a sense of the divine. He writes:

> There is within the human mind, and indeed by natural instinct, an awareness of divinity. This we take to be beyond controversy. To prevent anyone from taking refuge in the pretense of ignorance, God himself has implanted in all men a certain understanding of his divine majesty. Ever renewing its memory, he repeatedly sheds fresh drops....Indeed, the perversity of the impious, who though they struggle furiously are unable to extricate themselves from the fear of God, is abundant testimony that this conviction namely that there is some God, is naturally inborn in all, and is fixed deep within, as it were in the very marrow. From this we conclude that it is not a doctrine that must first be learned in school, but one of which each of us is master from his mother's womb and which nature itself permits no one to forget.[3]

Calvin contends that people are accountable to God for their unbelief not because they have failed to submit to a convincing theistic proof, but because they have suppressed the truth that God has implanted within their minds. It is natural to suppose that if God created us with cognitive faculties which by and large reliably produce beliefs without the need for evidence, he would likewise provide us with a cognitive faculty which produces belief in him without the need for evidence.

Third, belief in God is more like belief in a person than belief in a scientific theory. Consider the examples that started this essay. Somehow the scientific approach—doubt first, consider all of the available evidence, and believe later—seems woefully inadequate or inappropriate to personal relations. What seems manifestly reasonable for physicists in their laboratory is desperately deficient in human relations. Human relations demand trust, commitment and faith. If belief in God is more like belief in other persons than belief in atoms, then the trust that is appropriate to persons will be appropriate to God. We cannot and should not arbitrarily insist that the scientific method is appropriate to every

kind of human practice. The fastidious scientist, who cannot leave the demand for evidence in her laboratory, will find herself cut off from relationships that she could otherwise reasonably maintain—with friends, family and, perhaps even, God.

WITH OR WITHOUT EVIDENCE

I haven't said that belief in God could not or, in some cases, should not be based on evidence or argument. Indeed, I am inclined to think that the theistic arguments do provide some, noncoercive, evidence of God's existence. By noncoercive, I mean that the theistic arguments aren't of such power and illumination that they should be expected to persuade all rational creatures. Rational people could rationally reject the theistic proofs. Rational people, and this is a fact that we must live with, rationally disagree. Nonetheless, I believe that someone could rationally believe in God on the basis of theistic arguments, but no one needs to.[4]

Reformed epistemologists also believe, like Calvin, that the natural knowledge of himself that God has implanted within us has been overlaid by sin. Part of the knowledge process may require the removal of the effects of sin on our minds. Attention to theistic arguments might do that. Also, some of the barriers to religious belief—such as the problem of evil or the alleged threat of science to religion—may need to be removed before one can see the light that has been shining within all along.

But the scales can fall from the "mind's eye" in a wide variety of means: on a mountaintop or at the ocean, looking at a flower, through a humbling experience, or by reading *The Chronicles of Narnia*. The list goes on yet a certain common feature should be noticed (and not the fact that few people have ever acquired belief in God as a result of the study of theistic proofs). The primary obstacle to belief in God seems to be more moral than intellectual. On the mountains one may feel one's smallness in relation to the grandness of it all. The flower may arouse one's sense of beauty. The loss of a job or a divorce may reveal one's unjustified pride. And *The Chronicles of Narnia* may awaken the dormant faith of a child. In all of these cases, the scales slide off the mind's eye when the overweening self is dethroned (not to mix too many metaphors!). Humility, not proofs, may be necessary to the realization of belief in God.

Conclusion

This approach to belief in God has been rather descriptive. We need to pay a lot more attention to how actual people actually acquire beliefs. The psychology of believing may tell us a lot about our cognitive equipment. The lessons learned from observing people and their beliefs support the position that I have defended: rational people may rationally believe in God without evidence or argument.

NOTES

1. Alvin Plantinga, "Reason and Belief in God," Nicholas Wolterstorff, "Can Belief in God Be Rational If It Has No Foundations?" and William Alston, "Christian Experience and Christian Belief" in *Faith and Rationality*, Plantinga and Wolterstorff eds. (Notre Dame, Indiana: University of Notre Dame Press, 1983); William Alston, *Perceiving God* (Ithaca, New York: Cornell University Press, 1991); Alvin Plantinga, *Warranted Christian Belief* (New York and Oxford: Oxford University Press, 1999).

2. See Kelly James Clark, *Philosophers Who Believe* (Downers Grove, IL: InterVarsity Press, 1993).

3. *Institutes of the Christian Religion*, Bk. 1, Ch. 3.

4. I argue this in some detail in my *Return to Reason* (Grand Rapids, Michigan: Eerdmans Publishing Company, 1990).

3.4 The Wager

BLAISE PASCAL

Blaise Pascal (1623–1662) was a scholar, mathematician, and theologian of great distinction.

Infinite—nothing. Our soul is cast into a body, where it finds number, dimension. Thereupon it reasons, and calls this nature necessity, and can believe nothing else.

Unity joined to infinity adds nothing to it, no more than one foot to an infinite measure. The finite is annihilated in the presence of the infinite, and becomes a pure nothing. So our spirit before God, so our justice before divine justice. There is not so great a disproportion between our justice and that of God as between unity and infinity.

The justice of God must be vast like His compassion. Now justice to the outcast is less vast and ought less to offend our feelings than mercy toward the elect.

We know that there is an infinite, and are ignorant of its nature. As we know it to be false that numbers are finite, it is therefore true that there is an infinity in number. But we do not know what it is. It is false that it is even, it is false that it is odd; for the addition of a unit can make no change in its nature. Yet it is a number, and every number is odd or even (this is certainly true of every finite number). So we may well know that there is a God without knowing what He is. Is there not one substantial truth, seeing there are so many things which are not the truth itself?

We know then the existence and nature of the finite, because we also are finite and have extension. We know the existence of the infinite and

---

Blaise Pascal, *Pensées*, translated by W. F. Trotter.

are ignorant of its nature, because it has extension like us, but not limits like us. But we know neither the existence nor the nature of God, because He has neither extension nor limits.

But by faith we know His existence; in glory we shall know His nature. Now, I have already shown that we may well know the existence of a thing, without knowing its nature.

Let us now speak according to natural lights.

If there is a God, He is infinitely incomprehensible, since, having neither parts nor limits, He has no affinity to us. We are then incapable of knowing either what He is or if He is. This being so, who will dare to undertake the decision of the question? Not we, who have no affinity to Him.

Who then will blame Christians for not being able to give a reason for their belief, since they profess a religion for which they cannot give a reason? They declare, in expounding it to the world, that it is a foolishness, *stultitiam;* [I Cor. 1:21.] and then you complain that they do not prove it! If they proved it, they would not keep their word; it is in lacking proofs that they are not lacking in sense. "Yes, but although this excuses those who offer it as such and takes away from them the blame of putting it forward without reason, it does not excuse those who receive it." Let us then examine this point, and say, "God is, or He is not." But to which side shall we incline? Reason can decide nothing here. There is an infinite chaos which separated us. A game is being played at the extremity of this infinite distance where heads or tails will turn up. What will you wager? According to reason, you can do neither the one thing nor the other; according to reason, you can defend neither of the propositions.

Do not, then, reprove for error those who have made a choice; for you know nothing about it. "No, but I blame them for having made, not this choice, but a choice; for again both he who chooses heads and he who chooses tails are equally at fault, they are both in the wrong. The true course is not to wager at all."

Yes; but you must wager. It is not optional. You are embarked. Which will you choose then?

Let us see. Since you must choose, let us see which interests you least. You have two things to lose, the true and the good; and two things to stake, your reason and your will, your knowledge and your happiness; and your nature has two things to shun, error and misery. Your reason is no more shocked in choosing one rather than the other, since you must of necessity choose. This is one point settled. But your happiness? Let us weigh the gain and the loss in wagering that God is. Let us estimate these two chances. If you gain, you gain all; if you lose, you lose nothing. Wager, then, without hesitation that He is. "That is very fine. Yes, I must wager; but I may perhaps wager too much." Let us see. Since there is an equal risk of gain and of loss, if you had only to gain two lives, instead of one, you might still wager. But if there were three lives to gain, you would have to play (since you are under the necessity of playing), and you would be imprudent, when you are forced to play, not to chance your life to gain three at a game where there is an equal risk of loss and gain. But there is an eternity of life and happiness. And this being so, if there were an infinity of chances, of which one only would be for you, you would still be right in wagering one to win two, and you would act stupidly, being obliged to play, by refusing to stake one life against three at a game in which out of an infinity of chances there is one for you, if there were an infinity of an infinitely happy life to gain. But there is here an infinity of an infinitely happy life to gain, a chance of gain against a finite number of chances of loss, and what you stake is finite. It is all divided; wherever the infinite is and there is not an infinity of chances of loss against that of gain, there is no time to hesitate, you must give all. And thus, when one is forced to play, he must renounce reason to preserve his life, rather than risk it for infinite gain, as likely to happen as the loss of nothingness.

For it is no use to say it is uncertain if we will gain, and it is certain that we risk, and that the infinite distance between the *certainty* of what is staked and the *uncertainty* of what will be gained, equals the finite good which is certainly staked against the uncertain infinite. It is not so, as every player stakes a certainty to gain an uncertainty, and yet he stakes a finite certainty to gain a finite uncertainty, without transgressing against reason. There is not an infinite distance between the certainty staked and the uncertainty of the gain; that is untrue. In truth, there is an infinity between the certainty of gain and the certainty of loss. But the uncertainty of the gain is proportioned to the certainty of the stake according to the proportion of the chances of gain and loss. Hence it comes that, if there are as many risks on one side as on the other, the course is to play even; and then the certainty of the stake is equal to the uncertainty of the gain, so far is it from fact that there is an infinite distance between them. And so our proposition is of infinite force, when there is the finite to stake in a game where there are equal risks of gain and of loss, and the infinite to gain. This is demonstrable; and if men are capable of any truths, this is one.

"I confess it, I admit it. But, still, is there no means of seeing the faces of the cards?" Yes, Scripture and the rest, etc. "Yes, but I have my hands tied and my mouth closed; I am forced to wager, and am not free. I am not released, and am so made that I cannot believe. What, then, would you have me do?"

True. But at least learn your inability to believe, since reason brings you to this, and yet you cannot believe. Endeavour, then, to convince yourself, not by increase of proofs of God, but by the abatement of your passions. You would like to attain faith and do not know the way; you would like to cure yourself of unbelief and ask the remedy for it. Learn of those who have been bound like you, and who now stake all their possessions. These are people who know the way which you would follow, and who are cured of an ill of which you would be cured. Follow the way by which they began; by acting as if they believed, taking the holy water, having masses said, etc. Even this will naturally make you believe, and deaden your acuteness. "But this is what I am afraid of." And why? What have you to lose?

But to show you that this leads you there, it is this which will lessen the passions, which are your stumbling-blocks.

The end of this discourse.

Now, what harm will befall you in taking this side? You will be faithful, humble, grateful, generous, a sincere friend, truthful. Certainly you will not have those poisonous pleasures, glory and luxury; but will you not have others? I will tell you that you will thereby gain in this life, and that, at each step you take on this road, you will see so great certainty of gain, so much nothingness in what you risk, that you will at last recognize that you have wagered for something certain and infinite, for which you have given nothing.

"Ah! This discourse transports me, charms me," etc.

If this discourse pleases you and seems impressive, know that it is made by a man who has knelt, both before and after it, in prayer to that Being, infinite and without parts, before whom he lays all he has, for you also to lay before Him all you have for your own good and for His glory, that so strength may be given to lowliness.

Custom is our nature. He who is accustomed to the faith believes in it, can no longer fear hell, and believes in nothing else. He who is accustomed to believe that the king is terrible… etc. Who doubts, then, that our soul, being accustomed to see number, space, motion, believes that and nothing else?

Do you believe it to be impossible that God is infinite, without parts? Yes. I wish therefore to show you an infinite and indivisible thing. It is a point moving everywhere with an infinite velocity; for it is one in all places and is all totality in every place.

Let this effect of nature, which previously seemed to you impossible, make you know that there may be others of which you are still ignorant. Do not draw this conclusion from your experiment, that there remains nothing for you to know; but rather that there remains an infinity for you to know.

It is false that we are worthy of the love of others; it is unfair that we should desire it. If we were born reasonable and impartial, knowing ourselves and others, we should not give this bias to our will. However, we are born with it; therefore born unjust, for all tends to self. This is contrary to all order. We must consider the general good; and the propensity to self is the beginning of all disorder, in war, in politics, in economy, and in the particular body of man. The will is therefore depraved.

If the members of natural and civil communities tend toward the weal of the body, the communities themselves ought to look to another more general body of which they are members. We ought, therefore, to look to the whole. We are, therefore, born unjust and depraved.

No religion but our own has taught that man is born in sin. No sea of philosophers has said this. Therefore none have declared the truth.

No sect or religion has always existed on earth, but the Christian religion.

We owe a great debt to those who point out faults. For they mortify us. They teach us that we have been despised. They do not prevent our being so in the future; for we have many other

faults for which we may be despised. They prepare for us the exercise of correction and freedom from fault.

The heart has its reasons, which reason does not know. We feel it in a thousand things. I say that the heart naturally loves the Universal Being, and also itself naturally, according as it gives itself to them; and it hardens itself against one or the other at its will. You have rejected the one and kept the other. Is it by reason that you love yourself?

It is the heart which experiences God, and not the reason. This, then, is faith: God felt by the heart, not by the reason.

Faith is a gift of God; do not believe that we said it was a gift of reasoning. Other religions do not say this of their faith. They only give reasoning in order to arrive at it, and yet it does not bring them to it.

The only science contrary to common sense and human nature is that alone which has always existed among men.

The Christian religion alone makes man altogether lovable and happy. In honesty, we cannot perhaps be altogether lovable and happy.

3.5 Miracles and Justification*

LAWRENCE A. SHAPIRO

Lawrence A. Shapiro is Professor of Philosophy at the University of Wisconsin–Madison.

Moses parted the Red Sea. Aaron's staff turned into a serpent. Jesus revived the dead, healed lepers, and rose from the dead himself. Many people believe that events like these, as well as many others equally marvelous, actually occurred. Are such beliefs justified? That is, should one believe in miracles, just as one should believe

that the Earth is spherical, or that dinosaurs once existed, or that the sun will rise tomorrow?

I believe that the answer to this question is a resounding NO. Belief in miracles is not justified. And, insofar as you should believe only what you are justified in believing, you should not believe in miracles. Below I'll sketch my

© Lawrence A. Shapiro, 2016. This essay was commissioned expressly for the 16th edition of *Reason and Responsibility*.
*Thanks to Russ Shafer-Landau, Alan Sidelle, and Elliott Sober for useful comments on an earlier version of this essay.

reasons for this conclusion. First, however, we must cover some preliminaries.

JUSTIFICATION AND TRUTH

Justified beliefs differ from those that lack justification. To say that a belief is justified is to say that there is evidence for thinking that it is true. I believe that it is raining right now. This belief is justified because I have evidence for thinking that it is true, namely, that I see rain falling from the sky. But what of my belief that it will be raining on this same date ten years from now, or one hundred years from now? Given the local climate, where rain is merely an occasional event, beliefs about whether it will rain on a given day in the distant future are unjustified. I have no evidence for believing that on this date ten years from now it will be raining. If I choose to believe this, I do so not because I have justification for the belief, but for some other reason. Perhaps I simply desire with all my heart that it will rain on this date ten years from now, and for this reason I choose to believe that it will. Of course, wishful thinking of this sort does nothing to add to the probability of the belief's truth, as justification does. When a belief is justified, it has a greater chance of being true than were it not justified. Not so wishful thinking. This is why one is better off having a justified belief that tonight's dessert will contain chocolate rather than a similar belief that rests on nothing but hope.

But justified beliefs won't always be true. I am sitting in a restaurant thinking about the options on the dessert menu. I decide on a chocolate soufflé. I now believe that I will soon be eating chocolate for dessert and I am justified in this belief because I've read the menu and I know that items listed on a menu are almost always available. Sadly, I'm wrong on this occasion. The waiter informs me that the kitchen just served its last chocolate soufflé. My belief that I'd be having chocolate for dessert was false, but it nevertheless was justified. Having seen chocolate soufflé on the menu, my belief that I'd soon be eating chocolate was more likely to be true than had I not seen the item on the menu.

Thus, justification and truth are related—the former strives to bring one closer to the latter—but they remain distinct. Some justified beliefs are true—such as my belief that it's raining as I write these words—but some are false, as was my belief that I'd soon be eating chocolate. Likewise, some *un*justified beliefs may be true. Perhaps I choose to believe that it will be raining on this date ten years from now and, ten years from now, it does indeed rain. The belief is true, but I nevertheless had no justification for believing it. Finally, some unjustified beliefs will be false. My belief that the world will end one second from now…was, fortunately, false. It was also unjustified. I had no evidence that the belief might be true.

The above discussion of justification glossed over an ambiguity that I'd now like to clarify. Care must be taken to distinguish two claims about justification:

1. There is some justification for believing B.
2. Belief in B is justified.

As I understand these claims, the first is far weaker than the second. The first says something like this: there exists a reason for believing that B is true. The second, in contrast, says that B is more likely true than not. Thus, imagine that you have pulled a white pebble from a large bag of pebbles. What should you believe about the color of the next pebble you will remove? The fact that you've removed a white pebble gives you *some* reason to believe that the next pebble will be white. After all, before removing the first pebble you had no evidence at all about the color of the pebbles in the bag. Now you know at least that it's possible for the pebbles in the bag to be white. So, there exists justification for believing that next pebble will also be white. Still, we would not want to say that such a belief is justified. This second claim, as it is typically used, makes a strong assertion. As I understand it, it says that the next pebble will more likely be white than it will be some other color. And, because you've seen only one of many pebbles, this conclusion seems unwarranted. You have some justification for thinking that the next pebble will be white, but such a belief is not justified. Similarly, when I said earlier that my observation of today's rain does not justify the belief that it will be raining on this date ten years hence, perhaps I spoke too quickly. As with the pebbles, we might think that the fact of rain today gives *some* justification for the belief about rain in the future—we know that it's at least possible—but surely we overreach when we say that a belief about future rain is justified. It is not justified, if by this we mean that it is more likely to be true than not.

Let's now think about a purported miracle: Jesus's raising Lazarus from the dead. My question concerns whether the belief that Jesus raised Lazarus from the dead is justified. This question, as just noted, differs from the question whether there is any justification at all for believing that Jesus raised Lazarus. Perhaps the mere fact that the story of Lazarus's resurrection was reported gives *some* justification for believing that it's true, in the way that any report of any event justifies to some extent believing that the event actually happened (you have more reason to believe the event occurred given the report than had no report ever been recorded). But, certainly, this is not what believers in miracles have in mind when asserting that they are justified in their belief. People who think that their belief in miracles is justified believe the stronger claim: that the miracle's occurrence is more probable than not. I shall contest this claim. No belief in any miracle is justified.

THE METAPHYSICS AND EPISTEMOLOGY OF MIRACLES

Metaphysical claims concern the nature of things, whereas epistemological claims concern issues such as evidence, justification, and knowledge. Here's a metaphysical claim: water is H_2O. Here's an epistemological claim: from the look and taste of this liquid, my belief that it is water is justified. Let's now examine some issues concerning the metaphysics and epistemology of miracles.

Miraculous events, as I understand them, differ from non-miraculous events in virtue of having a supernatural component. Raising Lazarus from the dead would count as a miracle, but rousing him from a deep sleep would not, because the former event cannot happen given how nature works, whereas the latter event can. Lazarus had been dead four days before Jesus supposedly resuscitated him. This should not be possible given the properties of the human body. Were we to discover that Lazarus had been in a coma rather than being dead, then we would not regard his resurrection as miraculous. It would not be a resurrection at all. Rather, it would be a return to consciousness, which is obviously possible. Similarly, if Jesus were in fact an extraterrestrial with super-advanced medical knowledge of the sort that enabled him to resurrect dead people, then too he would not have been performing a miracle when he revived Lazarus. We should look at his feat as of a piece with other medical advances, such as heart transplants or brain surgery. Once upon a time, such things were well beyond the abilities of doctors, but that doesn't make them miraculous. So, for an event to qualify as a miracle, I will assume that it must involve supernatural agency of some sort. Typically, the supernatural agent involved is assumed to be God. Jesus, because he was divine, was able to raise Lazarus. However, whether God or some other supernatural agent (angels or Satan) is presumed to be at work shall make no difference to the arguments against justified belief in miracles that I shall now develop.

That miracles must involve a supernatural component is a metaphysical claim. It is a claim about the nature of miracles. Let's now consider an epistemological issue. How do we know a miracle when we see one? This question is about justification. What justifies your belief that the event you're observing is miraculous? Or, taking into account the points of the previous paragraph, what justifies your belief that the event you're observing contains a supernatural element? As we'll soon see, it's in trying to answer these questions that we'll find our first reason to deny that belief in miracles can be justified. However, I'd like to venture a preliminary answer to these questions. When wondering whether a given event is a miracle, it seems to me that a point in favor ought to be its extreme rarity. The very idea of something being supernatural makes sense only against a background of a very ordinary, common, normal way for things to proceed. A good reason to resist describing sunsets or births or eclipses as miracles is because they happen frequently, or frequently enough. Perhaps the very first time you see the sun rise, you might wonder if it involves anything supernatural. But seeing it rise again and again and again should indicate to you that sunrises are simply a feature of the natural world.

Keep in mind that this point about the rarity of miracles is epistemological rather than metaphysical. The idea is that the rarity of an event gives us a reason to believe that it is a miracle. But this doesn't mean that miracles are, by definition, rare. Nor does it mean that any rare event is a miracle. Rarity is only evidence for a miracle, and even then it is not always strong evidence. Being dealt a royal flush is rare. A professional poker player may go her whole life without ever being dealt a royal flush. However, unlike raising the dead, we have a completely natural and satisfying explanation of how Sue came to have a royal flush. This appears not to be the case with Lazarus's resurrection.

THE FIRST ARGUMENT AGAINST JUSTIFIED BELIEF IN MIRACLES: INFERENCE TO THE BEST EXPLANATION

Miracles, I suggested, involve the supernatural. When Jesus raised Lazarus from the dead, he did something that should have been impossible were nature to have run its normal course. Jesus did something supernatural. But why do we believe this? We're now in the realm of epistemology, asking about the justification for believing that Jesus did something supernatural. What evidence exists for the belief that Jesus employed supernatural powers? Suppose you were an eyewitness to the event. You might have observed

something like this: Jesus calls for the stone marking the entrance to Lazarus's tomb to be removed. Jesus then says a prayer and commands in a loud voice "Lazarus, come out!" Soon Lazarus shambles from the tomb, wrapped in strips of linen. If you had indeed observed these events, you may well have been tempted to regard them as miraculous. But not so quick. Notice that in the description of your observations, I never mentioned anything supernatural. Why, then, believe that supernatural forces were involved in the resurrection of Lazarus?

Obviously, the conclusion that Jesus did something supernatural, and thus performed a miracle, depends on an inference of some sort. From what you've observed, you *infer* that Jesus is performing a supernatural act. This kind of inference—from things you observe directly to something that you cannot or did not directly observe—is actually quite common. Seeing the newspaper on my stoop leads me to infer that the paperboy has paid me a visit. I hear chirping and infer that a bird sits in the tree across the street. Inferences like these have a name: *inference to the best explanation*. The label conveys the idea that our observations—of a newspaper, of chirping—can be explained in some way. They have a cause. Moreover, when we consider the various explanations or causes for our observations, one explanation will be superior to all the others we consider. The newspaper I find on my stoop might have come into the world spontaneously, but the better explanation is that someone tossed it there. The chirping I hear might be caused by a tape recorder that someone strapped to a branch in the tree across the street, but the better explanation is that a bird perches on one of the tree's branches.

Suppose someone challenges one of your inferences to the best explanation. You tell your friend that a paper arrives on your stoop every morning and, although you've never seen how this happens, you infer that a person delivers the paper. Your friend, however, insists that newspapers are self-creating objects that simply appear on stoops spontaneously. Why, your friend asks, is your explanation better? Despite the obvious silliness of your friend's explanation, he makes a good point. Both of you can explain the newspaper's appearance; you just do so in very different ways. If what your friend imagines is true—if newspapers do arise spontaneously—then he has indeed explained how a newspaper arrives on your stoop every morning. Both explanations, if true, make sense of the observations, so on what grounds do you reject one and keep the other?

At this point, you might pursue a couple of strategies to convince your friend that you have the winning explanation. One strategy might involve *experimentation*. You suggest to your friend that the two of you rise very early one morning and collect further observations. You point out that if your explanation is correct you should see a paperboy moving down the street tossing newspapers on stoops. On the other hand, if his explanation is correct, you should see newspapers spontaneously forming on stoops. Your friend agrees to the experiment and (no surprise) your predictions turn out to be true and your friend's false.

An alternative strategy to convince your friend of the superiority of your explanation might bring into focus the various background assumptions on which the explanations rest. For instance, your explanation assumes that people are capable of holding newspapers and traveling with them from house to house. This might seem too obvious to mention, but if people could not transport newspapers, then your explanation for the presence of the newspaper on your stoop could not be true. Notice too that if your friend were suspicious of this assumption, you could easily enough establish its truth. You could pick up a newspaper and walk across the street with it. "See," you would say, "holding and moving newspapers is not too hard." On the other hand, your friend's explanation requires different background assumptions, such as that some objects are capable of self-creation. Now, when you express skepticism about this assumption, the burden falls on your friend to establish its truth. "See," you'd want your friend to say, "here's an example of spontaneous creation." Of course, it's at this point that your friend will

confront a serious difficulty. Being unable to justify the truth of one of his background assumptions, the inferiority of your friend's explanation of the newspaper's appearance now becomes conspicuous. You win again.

Jesus walks to Lazarus's open tomb, says a prayer, and Lazarus steps into the sunlight. The believer in miracles seeks to explain these observations like this: Jesus is divine and can muster supernatural forces to resurrect the dead Lazarus. However, we should also consider a couple of alternative explanations: Jesus is a megalomaniacal human being who wishes to convince people that he is God and so he has paid various confederates to pretend to be dead or sick so that he can appear to resurrect or cure them. Lazarus is one such confederate. Or, more plausibly, Jesus did nothing more than visit an ailing Lazarus, who subsequently returned to health. In the following years, the story was embellished and exaggerated, leaving us with the account now reported in the *Gospel of John*.

Both alternative explanations do as good a job explaining the observations as the explanation that believers in miracles endorse. The supernatural explanation is not the *best* explanation, because the other two explain the observations just as well. What, then, justifies the choice of the supernatural explanation? In response, the miracle-believer should pursue one or both of the strategies I mentioned above when examining the competing explanations for the appearance of the newspaper. The first strategy, experimentation, would require that we draw forth various predictions from the three explanations and then test them. But, given that the events surrounding Lazarus happened well in the past, experimentation is quite difficult. We no longer have the opportunity to interrogate Lazarus in order to determine whether he might have been a stooge for megalomaniacal Jesus. We're in no position to examine Lazarus to see whether he was really dead or merely suffering from the flu.

Better than experimentation is the second strategy I described above. We should examine the background assumptions on which each of the three explanations depend. What must be true for the various explanations to be true? The miracle explanation assumes that natural laws can be violated. It also assumes that Jesus was capable of violating natural laws. But how do we determine whether these assumptions are true? Determining that a human being could hold and transport newspapers is easy. But how do we determine the truth of assumptions about the possibility of violating natural laws or Jesus's ability to do so? Indeed, were we to set about determining whether natural laws could be violated, I imagine that we'd find this to be impossible, which would force the miracle believer to abandon the supernatural explanation of Lazarus's resurrection.

What of the background assumptions lying behind the other two explanations? Again, we face the problem of examining an event that occurred long ago. However, in favor of the assumptions on which the alternative explanations rest is something that we cannot say on behalf of the miracle explanation: we know that sometimes people set out to fool others; we know that sometimes stories become exaggerated over time. Treating the account of Lazarus as an instance of deliberate trickery or innocent amplification requires that we believe nothing extraordinary or vastly improbable. Thus, of the three explanations in competition to explain the observations reported of Lazarus, the miracle explanation is certainly no better than the other two explanations and, in fact, considerably worse. After all, only the miracle explanation asks us to accept as possible something unlike anything we've ever come across before. But, even disregarding the implausibility of the miracle explanation, we are left with the consequence that a preference for any one of the three explanations is essentially arbitrary. Each does an equally good job accounting for the "data"; and, of course, choosing an explanation for arbitrary reasons is a far cry from choosing an explanation because it's probably the true one. Thus, if inference to the best explanation is the only basis for your belief in a miracle, then your belief is unjustified.

THE SECOND ARGUMENT AGAINST JUSTIFIED BELIEF IN MIRACLES: THE BASE RATE FALLACY

My first argument against justified belief in miracles focused on the supernatural aspect of miracles. Because we cannot directly perceive supernatural forces, they must be inferred from other things that we can directly observe. But a supernatural explanation of the observations fares no better, and almost certainly worse, than an explanation that appeals to deceitful human beings or something like the telephone game, in which testimony changes dramatically with retelling. Thus, belief in the miracle explanation is not justified. My second argument bears some similarity to the first, but takes as its starting point the rarity of purported miracles. When discussing the epistemology of miracles above, I mentioned that their extreme rarity might be taken as evidence on their behalf. Naturally occurring events are those that occur regularly and routinely or that might be explained without appeal to violations to natural laws. Only when an event is so unlike anything ever observed, or seems inconsistent with anything ever observed, does the temptation to regard it as supernatural arise. This is why, if Lazarus had really been dead for four days and then returned to life, many people might regard the event as miraculous. Such an event is unlike anything ever observed and seems inconsistent with what we believe to be true about dead people.

When confronted with a report of an event that is unlike anything we've ever observed and that seems inconsistent with what we believe to be true, we face a choice. On the one hand, we can accept the truth of the report. The author of the *Gospel of John* (who, incidentally, is not John and whose identity is in fact unknown) reports that Jesus raised Lazarus from the dead. We can choose to accept the truth of this report; on the other hand, we can reject the truth of this report and in its place offer some other explanation for why the author of the *Gospel of John* said what he did about Lazarus. In sum, if we are going to hold any belief on the matter, we must choose to believe either of the following:

1. The author of the *Gospel of John* told the truth and Jesus really did raise Lazarus from the dead.
2. The author of the *Gospel of John* said something false and Jesus did not really raise Lazarus from the dead.

Let's now consider a more mundane example that will provide us with an illustrative comparison. Suppose you awake one morning feeling nauseous and you visit your doctor. She performs some tests and tells you that you have a rare and, unfortunately, fatal illness. There is a cure, but it comes with costly side effects: blindness and incontinence. As before, you must choose to believe either:

1. The test told the truth and you really do have the disease; or
2. The test said something false and you're not really sick.

Obviously, before deciding to take the cure and having to live with the unfortunate consequences, you'll want to know something about the reliability of the test. Suppose the doctor informs you that the test is very reliable. If you have the disease, it's virtually certain to detect it. And if you don't have the disease, it will mistakenly say that you do only one time in a thousand. What should you do? Should you believe the test and take the cure, or should you not believe the test and hope that you're not really sick?

If we wanted to, we could try to quantify the reliability of the author of *John* just as we did the diagnostic test. Perhaps the author almost always tells the truth. Whenever an event of type E occurs, he's almost always correct in identifying the event as one of type E. Whenever an event other than one of type E occurs, he misidentifies it as an E-type event only once in a thousand times. Should we believe the author when he says that Jesus raised Lazarus from the dead, or should we believe instead that he said something false?

If you elect to take the cure, you've done so without the benefit of a crucial piece of information. Before deciding whether to believe the test, you need to know something about the *base rate* of the disease that it says you have. The base rate of the disease is simply its frequency in the population in which you live. When you fail to take the base rate of the disease into account when deciding whether to take the cure, you're committing the base rate fallacy.

Let's see how consideration of the base rate of the disease should play into your decision. Suppose you live in the United States, which has a population of roughly 300 million people. Suppose further that the disease for which you've been tested is very rare: it affects only 1 in 100,000 members of the population. This means that of 300 million people, only 3,000 will actually have the disease (300 million/ 100,000 = 3,000). We now have all the necessary information to make an informed decision about whether to take the cure.

Recall that the test isn't perfect. Given a thousand healthy people, it will wrongly identify one of them as being sick. This means that of the 299,997,000 people in the United States who do not have the disease, it will falsely report 299,997 individuals as having the disease (299,997,000/ 1000 = 299,997). The question you must ask is whether the positive test result you received indicates that you are genuinely sick, or whether instead you are among the 299,997 people for whom the test result has delivered mistaken results. We've already said that only 3,000 people in the population actually have the disease. Thus, were every member of the United States tested, only 1 in 100 of those who tested positive for the disease would actually have that disease. (The test says that 299,997 have the disease, but only 3,000 actually do). This shows that a positive test result will be correct only about 1 percent of the time (see Table 1). If you're like me, you wouldn't take the cure. Of the two options listed above, the second is far more justified: the odds that the test said something false are far greater than that you actually have the disease.

The lessons from this discussion of the base rate fallacy apply straightforwardly to the story of Lazarus. We saw that we must decide whether to

TABLE 1

	Sick	Not Sick
+ Test	~ 3,000 (1 in 100,000)	~ 299,997 (1 in 1,000)
– Test	~ 0	~ 299,697,003

A total of 300,000,000 Americans are divided among the four cells. The top row contains those Americans who have tested positive for the disease. The test misidentifies only 1 in 1,000 healthy people as being sick, but because of the rarity of the disease, the chance that you're really sick given a positive test result is only about 1 percent.

believe the author of *John* and accept that Jesus really did raise Lazarus from the dead, or believe instead that the author of *John* was mistaken and that Lazarus did not actually return from the dead. To decide what to believe, we must speculate not only about the reliability of the author, but we must as well make some assumptions about the base rate of the event he describes. How frequently in a population of dead people does one return to life? Even granting the possibility of such a thing, this number must be extremely low—lower even than the percentage of people with the disease that I imagined. Is the chance of returning to life only one in a million? One in a billion? Presumably, it is smaller even than that, given the number of people in history who have died and the number purported to have come back to life. With such a low base rate, even if we stipulate that the author of *John* was extremely reliable, hardly ever misdescribing what he saw (actually, the author of *John* wrote decades after the events reported in *John*, and doubtless heard about them only from other sources), then his report is more likely to be mistaken than it is to be correct.

Suppose, for instance, that the author of *John* was mistaken in his reports only one in a million times. If rising from the dead is an event that occurs only one time in a billion times (and here I'm simply granting the possibility), then the odds that the author correctly reported a resurrection is only one in a thousand, because

though he's rarely wrong, the incredible improbability that Lazarus rose from the dead makes much more likely that the author's report was false. (A billion divided by a million is a thousand.) Of the billion people who have died, the author would say of one thousand of them that they had in fact risen. Thus, as in the case of the test for the disease, a positive result—a positive report—is in the case of a resurrection about one thousand times more likely to be incorrect than correct. But, of course, the number of dead people who return to life, if such is even possible, must be fewer than one in a billion, and the chance that the author of John could be wrong must surely be greater than just one in a million. The justified belief is the second of the two options: the odds that the author of the *Gospel of John* said something false are much greater than that Jesus really did raise Lazarus from the dead.

At this point, one might wonder whether my argument shows too much. The suspicion is this: By the reasoning above, we can never have a justified belief in anything that is incredibly improbable. One shouldn't believe that Sue was dealt a royal flush, or that Jim survived a fall from the roof of an eight-story building. But notice that beliefs like these differ importantly from beliefs in supernatural occurrences. In each case, we can employ the strategies I mentioned above in order to verify the belief. We can conduct experiments. If Sue was dealt a royal flush, we should predict that when others look at her hand, they will also see five cards of the same suit, ten through ace. If Jim survived a fall, we should predict that his body will be broken in many places, and that the pavement below the building will be colored with his blood. Similarly, we can examine the background assumptions necessary for the truth of each belief. We know that a royal flush is very unlikely, but we also know a hand of any five cards is as likely as any other hand. We know that a fall from eight stories is very usually fatal, but that in extremely rare circumstances the human body might fall in a way, or on a surface, that prevents death. In short, when asked to believe something very unusual, an initial reaction of doubt is appropriate, but an accumulation of evidence of one sort or another may nevertheless justify the belief. It's lack of this sort of evidence that distinguishes belief in miracles from belief in other oddities.

When I began this section I noted that my second argument against justified belief in miracles is similar to the first argument I made. The similarity becomes more apparent when we ask why the author of *John* might have been mistaken. Did he deliberately misstate the truth about Lazarus? Did he honestly report testimony that itself was false because the witnesses of the purported miracle themselves were dishonest, or, perhaps, simply confused? We could come up with any number of explanations for why the author of *John* relayed a falsehood. My first argument against belief in miracles shows why a supernatural explanation of a purported miracle is never the best. My second argument, however, shows why the supernatural explanation of Lazarus's rising is not only *not* the best, but is in fact amongst the worst. Given the extreme improbability of a person returning to life after having been dead for four days, and our inability to gather other kinds of confirming evidence, almost any other explanation for the author of *John's* claims is more justified.

CONCLUSION

I've provided a brief sketch of important epistemological ideas involving justification and truth. I've also described some metaphysical and epistemological features of miracles. Doing so set the stage for two arguments against having justified belief in miracles. Although my discussion focused on a particular purported miracle—Jesus's raising of Lazarus—the arguments I made extend readily to any purported miracle. When assessing the justification for believing in any miracle, you must ask whether the supernatural explanation for the event is indeed the best explanation or whether other, non-supernatural explanations, might be at least as good or better. Secondly, you must ask whether the presence of a miracle is the most likely cause of the testimony (where this can include the testimony of your own eyes) on its behalf, or whether some other cause is more likely. I believe that any individual not already in the grip of religious conviction must answer these questions as I have. The supernatural explanation of an event is never the best explanation; and the odds that the testimony on behalf of a miracle is false are always greater than the probability that the miracle actually occurred.

3.6 Infini—Rien

SIMON BLACKBURN

Simon Blackburn is Emeritus Professor at the University of Cambridge. He has written important works in philosophy of language and moral theory.

None of the metaphysical arguments we have considered [in sections omitted here] do much to confirm the hypothesis that the universe is the creation of a traditional God. And Hume's analysis of testimony from miracles destroys their value as evidence. Faced with these blanks, religious faith may try to find other arguments.

An interesting and ingenious one is due to the French mathematician and theologian, Blaise Pascal (1632–62), and is known as Pascal's

THINK by Blackburn (1998) 2100w from pp. 186–192. © Simon Blackburn 1999. By permission of Oxford University Press.

wager. Unlike the arguments we have been considering, it is not presented as an argument for the *truth* of religious belief, but for the *utility* of believing in some version of a monotheistic, Judaic, Christian, or Islamic, God.

The argument is this. First, Pascal confesses to metaphysical ignorance:

Let us now speak according to natural lights.

If there is a God, he is infinitely incomprehensible, since, having neither parts, nor limits, He has no affinity to us. We are therefore incapable of knowing either what He is, or if He is ... Who then will blame the Christians for not being able to give a reason for their belief, since they profess a religion for which they cannot give a reason?

It is not too clear why this excuse is offered for the Christians, as opposed to those of other faiths, as well as believers in fairies, ghosts, the living Elvis, and L. Ron Hubbard. Still, suppose the choice is between religious belief and a life of religious doubt or denial:

You must wager. It is not optional. Which will you choose then? ... Let us weigh the gain and the loss in wagering that God is. Let us estimate these two chances. If you gain, you gain all; if you lose, you lose nothing. Wager, then, without hesitation that He is.

With great clarity Pascal realizes that this is rather an odd reason for choosing a belief. But he also says, perceptively, that

your inability to believe is the result of your passions, since reason brings you to this, and yet you cannot believe ... Learn of those who have been bound like you, and who now stake all their possessions ... Follow the way by which they began; by acting as if they believe, taking the holy water, having masses said, etc. Even this will naturally make you believe, and deaden your acuteness.

After you have 'stupefied' yourself, you have become a believer. And then you will reap the rewards of belief: infinite rewards, if the kind of God you believe in exists. And if it does not? Well, you have lost very little, in comparison with infinity: only what Pascal calls the 'poisonous

pleasures' of things like playing golf on Sundays instead of going to mass.

The standard way to present this argument is in terms of a two-by-two box of the options:

	God Exists	God Does Not
I believe in him	+infinity!	0
I do not believe in him	−infinity!	0

The zeros on the right correspond to the thought that not much goes better or worse in this life, whether or not we believe. This life is of vanishingly little account compared to what is promised to believers. The plus-infinity figure corresponds to infinite bliss. The minus-infinity figure in the bottom left corresponds to the traditional jealous God, who sends to Hell those who do not believe in him, and of course encourages his followers to give them a hard time here, as well. But the minus-infinity figure can be soft-pedaled. Even if we put 0 in the bottom left-hand box, the wager looks good. It would be good even if God does not punish disbelief, because there is still that terrific payoff of '+infinity' cranking up the choice. In decision-theory terms, the option of belief 'dominates,' because it can win, and cannot lose. So—go for it!

Unfortunately the lethal problem with this argument is simple, once it is pointed out.

Pascal starts from a position of metaphysical ignorance. We just know nothing about the realm beyond experience. But the set-up of the wager presumes that we *do* know something. We are supposed to know the rewards and penalties attached to belief in a Christian God. This is a God who will be pleasured and reward us for our attendance at mass, and will either be indifferent or, in the minus-infinity option, seriously discombobulated by our non-attendance. But this is a case of false options. For consider that if we are really ignorant metaphysically, then it is at least as likely that the options pan out like this:

There is indeed a very powerful, very benevolent deity. He (or she or they or it) has determined as follows. The good human beings are those who follow the natural light of reason, which is given to them to control their beliefs. These good humans follow the arguments, and hence avoid religious convictions. These ones with the strength of mind not to believe in such things go to Heaven. The rest go to Hell.

This is not such a familiar deity as the traditional jealous God, who cares above all that people believe in him. (Why is God so jealous? Alas, might his jealousy be a projection of human sectarian ambitions and emotions? Either you are with us or against us! The French sceptic Voltaire said that God created mankind in his image, and mankind returned the compliment.) But the problem for Pascal is that if we really know nothing, then we do not know whether the scenario just described is any less likely than the Christian one he presented. In fact, for my money, a God that punishes belief is just as likely, and a lot more reasonable, than one that punishes disbelief.

And of course, we could add the Humean point that whilst for Pascal it was a simple two-way question of mass versus disbelief, in the wider world it is also a question of the Koran versus mass, or L. Ron Hubbard versus the Swami Maharishi, or the Aquarian Concepts Community Divine New Order Government versus the First Internet Church of All. The wager has to be silent about those choices.

EMOTION AND THE WILL TO BELIEVE

We can now briefly consider the 'fideistic' line, that although the arguments are negligible, nevertheless people at least have a right to believe what they wish, and there may be some merit in blind faith, like the merit attaching to the mother who refuses to acknowledge her son's guilt in spite of damning evidence.

Philosophers professionally wedded to truth and reason are not apt to commend this attitude. The faith that defies reason might be called a blessing by others who share it, but credulity and superstition by those who don't, and distressingly apt to bring in its wake fanaticism

and zealotry. Chapter 2 of the famous essay *On Liberty* by John Stuart Mill (1806–73) talks memorably of the atmosphere of 'mental slavery' that sets in with the absence of the questing critical intellect. Even the truth, Mill says, when held as a prejudice independent of and proof against argument, 'is but one superstition the more, accidentally clinging to the words which enunciate a truth.' One classic discussion (by the late-nineteenth-century English writer W. K. Clifford) compares beliefs held on insufficient evidence to stolen pleasures. An apt quotation is from Samuel Taylor Coleridge:

He who begins by loving Christianity better than truth, will proceed by loving his own sect or Church better than Christianity, and end in loving himself better than all.

But although these views are attractive, it is actually quite hard to show that the habit of blind faith is necessarily so very bad. If, having got to Hume's inert proposition, we then invest it with hopes, fears, resolutions, and the embellishments of our own particular creeds, where is the harm in that? Is not simple piety a Good Thing?

Some people certainly think random belief is a good thing. I have in front of me the advertisement for a company calling itself 'your metaphysical superstore.' It specializes in New Age books and music, flower essence, essential oils and aromatherapy, magnetic therapy, light balance therapy, astrology and numerology, tarot and rune cards readings, crystals and gemstones, and at the end, like a rueful note of something approaching sanity, healing herbs. Why should thinkers mock the simple pieties of the people?

Of course, there are simple pieties that do not get this general protection. If I check into the Mysterious Mist and come back convinced that God's message to me is to kill young women, or people with the wrong-coloured skins, or people who go to the wrong church, or people who have sex the wrong way, that is not so good. So we have to use our human values, our own sense of good or bad, or right or wrong, to distinguish an admirable return from the mountain from a lunatic one.

We seem to be irretrievably in the domain of ethics here. And it would be impossible in a brief compass to assess the harms and benefits of religious belief, just as it is hard (although not impossible) to estimate the benefit or damage done by belief in magnetic therapy or Feng Shui or whatever. It clearly fills some function, answering to some human desires and needs. Some of the needs may be a common part of the human lot: I have already mentioned the need for ceremonies at crucial parts of life, or the need for poetry, symbol, myth, and music to express emotions and social relationships that we need to express. This is good. Unfortunately some of the desires may be a little less admirable: the desire to separatism, to schism, to imposing our way of life on others, to finding moral justifications for colonialism, or tribal or cultural imperialism, and all made guilt-free because done in the name of the Lord. For every peaceful benevolent mystic, there is an army chaplain, convincing the troops that God is on their side.

. . .

Obviously the attitude one takes to the 'fideism' that simply lets particular religious beliefs walk free from reason may depend heavily on what has recently been happening when they do so. Hume was born less than twenty years after the last legal religious executions in Britain, and himself suffered from the enthusiastic hostility of believers. If in our time and place all we see are church picnics and charities, we will not be so worried. But enough people come down the mountain carrying their own practical certainties to suggest that we ought to be.

Maybe some day something will be found that answers to the needs without pandering to the bad desires, but human history suggests that it would be unwise to bank on it.

MindTap°

MindTap is a fully online, highly personalized learning experience built upon Cengage Learning content. MindTap combines student learning tools—readings, multimedia, activities, and assessments—into a singular Learning Path that guides students through the course.

Human Knowledge: Its Grounds and Limits

DURING THE GREAT GOLDEN AGE of philosophy, in the seventeenth and eighteenth centuries, problems about the nature of human knowledge divided philosophers into two schools; and despite changing idioms and increased understanding of the methods of science, the division to a large degree persists. On the one hand, the **empiricists**, whose leading thinkers were John Locke (1632–1704), George Berkeley (1685–1753), and David Hume (1711–1776), held that all our ideas come from experience and that no proposition about any matter of fact can be known to be true independently of experience. On the other hand, the **rationalists**, whose most important representatives were René Descartes (1596–1650), Baruch Spinoza (1632–1677), and Gottfried Leibniz (1646–1716), maintained that there are **innate ideas** and that certain general propositions (usually called *a priori* propositions) can be known to be true in advance of, or in the absence of, empirical verification.[1]

Advocates of the theory of innate ideas did not, of course, hold that we are born literally thinking certain thoughts, but rather that we are born with inherited dispositions to have thoughts of a certain form and structure. Just as dehydrated milk has the disposition to become milk when water is added to it, so the mind, on this theory, has from birth the disposition to acquire the concepts of being, substance, duration—even infinitude and God—once a certain amount of experience is "added to it." Thus, rationalism holds that there can be in the mind ideas and truths that were not first present in experience but only later activated by experience. For the empiricist, on the other hand, the mind is (as Locke put it) like a tablet on which nothing has been written (a *tabula rasa*) until experience writes its message on it.

The writings of René Descartes, a leading mathematician, man of science, and philosopher, are a clear example not only of the rationalistic doctrine and method, but also of the rationalistic temper of mind. In the autobiographical *Discourse on Method*, Descartes compares the state of the sciences and philosophy to an ancient European town, grown helter-skelter from an older village, with crooked streets,

---

[1]It should be noted that both the empiricist and the rationalist are "rationalists" in the wider sense of the term—that is, as opposed to fideism, romanticism, or irrationalism. Both can support rational inquiry as the sole road to truth, but they differ in their conceptions of what rational inquiry is, particularly regarding the role that sense experience plays in it.

random walls, and poor sanitation. Of course, we are not accustomed to rip down whole cities in order to start from scratch the task of rational redesign; but individuals can without arrogance or absurdity think of ripping down and rebuilding their own homes:

> … and the same I thought was true of any similar project for reforming the body of the Sciences, or the order of teaching them established in the Schools: but as for the opinions which up to that time I had embraced, I thought that I could not do better than resolve at once to sweep them wholly away, that I might afterwards be in a position to admit either others more correct, or even perhaps the same ones when they had undergone the scrutiny of reason. I firmly believed that in this way I should much better succeed in the conduct of my life, than if I built only upon old foundations, and leaned upon principles which, in my youth, I had taken upon trust.

Thus, Descartes begins his dramatic quest for new "foundations," doubting everything that can be doubted until he finds a solid basis for reconstruction in the indubitable fact of his own existence as a "thinking substance." What makes the argument for his own existence so convincing, Descartes decides, is its "clearness and distinctness." Hence, he has a working criterion of truth to use in the voyage away from his skeptical starting point: Whatever he conceives clearly and distinctly is true.

In his Third Meditation, Descartes finds in himself the idea of an infinite God. The idea, he argues, could not be his own invention, nor could it be derived from merely finite experience. Its only possible cause must be the actually existing deity. He then goes on to prove that this deity is no deceiver. Therefore, (a) because God has given us a powerful disposition to believe in the existence of material objects (such as human bodies), (b) because God would be a deceiver if no such objects existed, and (c) because God is not a deceiver, it follows that such objects do exist and that human knowledge is reliable. Intellectual error, then, when it occurs, springs from a kind of hasty willfulness in ourselves and not from God.

Although many philosophers today would quarrel with particular steps in Descartes's arguments, there is no denying that his general method has left its mark on most of his successors. For three centuries, philosophers have tried to give a rational reconstruction of our knowledge, beginning with what is indubitable (or nearly so) and building on it, taking very seriously as they work the nagging claims of imaginary **skeptics** that what we think we know with certainty we may not really know at all.

Admitting some minimal possibility that previously undoubted and apparently indubitable beliefs might yet be false is, for most of us, just a matter of make-believe. It will be simply feigning a doubt for the purposes of some irksome riddle or pointless intellectual game that some people find it fun to play. In order fully to appreciate how important it was to seventeenth- and eighteenth-century philosophers to "refute the skeptic," however, one must be able *genuinely* to doubt—to "doubt with conviction," if you will—to *honestly* believe that previously undoubted beliefs might yet be false, and to take that real possibility to heart, not just as a move in a game, but as a troublesome disturbance in one's network of convictions and indeed in one's orientation to the world. Imaginative teachers of philosophy often try to give examples from science fiction of what such a frame of mind would be like. The late Charles L. Stevenson, for example, used to introduce Descartes to his beginning students at the University of Michigan with a simple story of his own invention:

> Imagine a neurosurgeon whose expertise on the human brain and whose knowledge of daily events are such that he can, with probes, dictate a subject's experiences. After he has implanted electrodes in the brain of a certain male volunteer, the surgeon causes him to experience the removal of the probes, although they are still in place; then to experience going home through the rain, spending the night with his wife, receiving a call from the surgeon in the morning asking him to return to the laboratory, and returning—all this while he is, in fact, still on the operating table.
>
> The next day, the surgeon does actually remove the electrodes and sends the subject home, whereupon his wife inquires indignantly, "Where were you last night?" "Right here with you," the man replies. "Oh, no, you weren't," she rejoins, "and I can prove it. I had the whole neighborhood out searching for you."
>
> Then the enlightened husband smiles and says, "Ah, now I see. That surgeon fooled me. He made me *think* I came home. But I was on the operating table the whole time."
>
> His smile quickly fades, however, never to return, because from that point forward the poor fellow can never be certain he is not still on the operating table.[2]

A similar story with more dramatic detail is told by John Pollock in the selection that leads off Part III. Pollock's illustration of real doubt taken to heart then serves as our introduction to the perennial philosophical problem of skepticism.

Skeptical worries have been around as long as philosophical inquiry. Probably the very deepest sort of philosophical skepticism is epistemological. Such skepticism raises the worry that all we think we know, including all methods of inquiry in which we have confidence, may at bottom entirely lack justification. In a new selection for this edition, Michael Huemer describes three classic skeptical arguments. The first—that of the infinite regress—is a philosophical problem that can be traced at least as far back as the ancient Greeks. The problem is fairly simple: We can know that a belief of ours is true only if we have good evidence for it. But this evidence cannot be self-standing—we must have good reason to believe *it*. Yet this good reason must itself be supported by further evidence, and so on, and so on. If this chain of reasoning and support goes on forever, no belief can be justified (since no one can have an infinite set of beliefs). If this chain of reasoning eventually loops back on itself, so that a belief ultimately provides support for itself, then the chain of reasoning is circular, and so no belief within it is justified. If this chain of reasoning stops at some point, it must be with a belief that requires no further support. But the skeptic says that *all* beliefs require support—there are no self-justifying beliefs. If that is really so, and if the other options are doomed to fail, then no beliefs can be justified.

Huemer also considers the problem of how to "get outside of one's head." It seems that all the evidence we have about an external world is given by our own perceptions and beliefs. But how can we know whether they accurately report the way the world truly is? The appearances, as given by our perceptions and beliefs,

---

[2]From Arthur W. Burks, "Preface," *Values and Morals: Essays in Honor of William Frankena, Charles Stevenson and Richard Brandt*, edited by Alvin Goldman and Jaegwon Kim (Dordrecht: D. Reidel Publishing Co., 1978), p. xiii.

supply the only evidence there is about how the world really is. Yet without an independent way to test for the accuracy of these appearances, we are not (says the skeptic) justified in relying on them to tell us about the world. We cannot tell whether appearances match reality, and in the absence of any other source of information, we are therefore have no knowledge of the nature of our world.

The following entry, by Robert Audi, represents a wide-ranging discussion of **epistemology** in which many important notions are clarified and distinctions made. Audi sympathetically describes a number of basic skeptical worries and is sensitive to how worrying they can be. That said, he proceeds to shows how they might be less devastating than they initially appear. Along the way Audi proves a sure guide to the difficulties posed by skepticism and does not pretend to have easy answers.

We next include a chapter on the nature and value of knowledge. For two thousand years there was wide agreement in the West on this matter: knowledge is, as Plato had written, true belief "plus an account"—or, as philosophers would put it today, knowledge is justified true belief. This was often advanced as one of the few successful definitions of an important philosophical concept. And yet in 1963, in a two-page article, Edmund Gettier offered two examples that undermined this definition. Here we include an excerpt from Plato's *Theaetetus* that lays out the classical definition, along with Gettier's now–classic piece. Gettier's paper generated thousands upon thousands of pages of replies, many seeking to patch up the traditional definition, many others finding fault with each new proposal, and yet others offering new definitions that broke to varying degrees with the classic definition. Here we include a very brief proposal by the philosophers James Cornman, Keith Lehrer, and George Pappas, outlining a potentially promising solution to the Gettier problem.

These three selections are each focused on what philosophers call *propositional knowledge*—knowing *that* some proposition is true. There is apparently another important kind of knowledge: knowing *how* to do various things. Does the knowledge of an experienced chef or musician amount to nothing more than knowledge that certain claims are true? Or is this kind of expertise a matter of possessing a different kind of knowledge? The famous midcentury British philosopher Gilbert Ryle examines this issue, arguing that there are indeed two distinct types of knowledge at play here, and that neither one is more important than the other.

This leads naturally to the question of why knowledge is important at all. Plato first raised this issue in a passage of his dialogue *Meno*, reprinted here. Plato has Socrates compare the value of knowledge and merely true opinion. Socrates argues that knowledge is more important, because the depth of understanding that is essential to knowledge yields greater permanence and reliability. Many contemporary philosophers are not so sure. In a fascinating and wide-ranging discussion that concludes this section, Linda Zagzebski considers the value of truth, of true belief, and finally, of knowledge. Her conclusion, reached through a variety of interesting arguments, is that both true belief and knowledge are indeed desirable, but not absolutely. There are cases in which it is better for us, all things considered, to forgo knowledge and true belief for the sake of obtaining other good things in life.

Our next chapter, on knowledge of the external world, sees a host of world-class philosophers trying to tackle some of the skeptical doubts that opened this Part III of the book. Here we begin with excerpts from Bertrand Russell's *Problems of Philosophy*, a book that has served generations as their first introduction to philosophical thinking. Russell offers a characteristically sharp and accessible presentation of the basic worries about how we might gain knowledge of the world. Russell echoes and amplifies many of the deep concerns expressed in Descartes's classic *Meditations* (reprinted here in its entirety). Quite early on in this work, Descartes has us imagine the possibility that everything we know is mistaken. For all we know, an evil demon could be deceiving us about everything—or almost everything. This possibility of deception, says Descartes, undermines our confidence that we can know anything at all. But wait—so long as I think, I can be sure that I exist. From this slender thread, called the *cogito* (short for "cogito ergo sum": I think, therefore I am), and an argument for God's existence, Descartes tries to reestablish our justification for our beliefs about almost everything we once took for granted.

However, most philosophers following Descartes have doubted that his undertaking was as successful as he himself took it to be. The skeptical doubts that Descartes raises early on in the *Meditations* continue to exercise philosophers, as we have seen. Skeptical doubts are especially likely to torment the empiricist philosopher. Because empiricism holds that the sole source ultimately of our knowledge of things external to us is sense experience, it is a matter of importance to empiricists to explain just how that knowledge is derived from the "impressions" made upon our various sense organs. John Locke rested a great part of his theory on a crucial distinction first used in antiquity and then revived by Galileo—namely, the distinction between *primary* and *secondary* qualities of physical objects. **Primary qualities** are intrinsic characteristics of the object itself—characteristics such as solidity, extension in space (size), figure (shape), motion or rest, and number. These are qualities that the objects would continue to possess even if there were no perceiving beings in the world. **Secondary qualities** (such qualities as color, taste, smell, sound, warmth, and cold) exist only when actually sensed and then only "in the mind" of the one who senses them. Primary qualities are inseparable from the material object and are found in every part of it, no matter how small. Every conceivable unit of matter, from a celestial body to an atom, must have some size and shape; on the other hand, no mere atom could have color.

Locke also contributed to the terminology of subsequent empiricists the technical term *idea* to stand for "whatever is the object of the understanding when a man thinks" or, more generally, for any direct object of awareness or consciousness.[3] And, again, the "ideas" that result from our perception of primary qualities are different from our "ideas" of secondary qualities. When we perceive a primary quality, according to Locke, our idea of this quality exactly resembles the corresponding primary quality in the material object itself. In contrast, when we perceive a secondary quality, our idea of this quality has no resemblance to a corresponding property of the

---

[3]David Hume's usage was somewhat narrower. In the *Treatise of Human Nature*, his earlier, more formal exposition of the views included here, Hume explains that he will use the word *impression* to mean "all our sensations, passions and emotions, as they make their first appearance in the soul." By *ideas* he means "the faint images of these in thinking and reasoning."

thing itself. That is, our idea of, for instance, color or odor in an object is produced in us by virtue of the object's "power" to reflect and absorb light waves of certain frequencies or to emit molecules in certain degrees of vibration. Because of these capacities, or powers, of material objects, color and odor can come into existence. Yet without eyes, there could be no color; without noses, no odor; and without minds, no secondary qualities at all.

Locke's theory of perception, then, does seem to have strong support from scientifically sophisticated common sense. It is often contrasted with another possible theory of perception (a theory held by no reputable philosopher), which is sometimes ascribed (quite unfairly) to the scientifically unsophisticated common sense of "the ordinary person." According to the latter theory, called **naive realism**, the qualities that Locke called primary and those he called secondary are both strictly part of physical objects, and both can exist quite independently of perceiving minds. It follows from naive realism that a world without perceiving minds might yet be a colorful, clamorous, and smelly place. Locke's view, in contrast, is that physical substances and their primary qualities can exist independently of sentient minds and only the secondary qualities are mind-dependent. This theory can be called **sophisticated realism**: "sophisticated" because it seems to accord with what science tells us about secondary qualities; "realism" because it allows that material objects have a real existence independent of minds. Locke's view is often called **representative realism** because of the tenet that ideas ("in the mind") faithfully mirror or "represent" material objects to us in perception, even though the material objects and the ideas by which we come to know them are quite distinct entities. The textbooks also call Locke's view the **causal theory of perception** because of the tenet that material objects are the causes of the ideas, or appearances, or sense data we have of them. The material substance itself is distinct from its own qualities, even from its own primary qualities, and, not being directly perceivable, must simply be posited as an unknowable **substratum** for its powers and properties. (Locke's conception of substance was rejected by most later empiricists, who preferred to think of a material thing as a mere "bundle of attributes," not as a mysterious entity "underlying" or "possessing" its own attributes.)

The realism of Locke, roughly sketched in the preceding paragraphs, must be understood as the primary target of the arguments of George Berkeley, Bishop of Cloyne. Locke would have approved of Berkeley's systematic demonstration that secondary qualities are mental. Berkeley argues for the conclusion in two ways. First of all, he maintains that extreme degrees of each secondary quality are inseparable in our consciousness from pain. Hence, if it is absurd to imagine that pain is, for example, *in* or *part of* the stove, then it is equally absurd to imagine that the heat is literally in the stove. Berkeley's second argument is the famous "argument from the relativity of perception." If I put one ice-chilled hand and one warm hand into a tub of tepid water, the water will feel hot to my cold hand and cold to my hot hand; but the water itself cannot be both hot and cold. Hence, both heat and cold must be "in the mind" only.

But Berkeley then turns the tables on Locke by arguing in quite similar ways for the necessarily mental status of *primary qualities*, too. If the supporter of Locke accepts these latter arguments, there is nothing left of his conception of an external object beyond that of an unknowable "substratum." Berkeley easily disposes of the concept of a substratum as theoretically superfluous and unintelligible. He is left, then, with a world in which only perceiving minds ("subjects") and their "ideas" (the appearances of primary and secondary qualities) exist. Hence, the universe is through and through mental. This theory of reality bears the name **subjective idealism**. (Perhaps *idealism* would be less misleading, because the theory has nothing whatever to do with ideals.)

Berkeley was as concerned as Descartes or Locke to find a solid alternative to skepticism. As an empiricist, he was resolved to show that all of our ideas, insofar as they are genuine (not merely confused), are derived from experience. What, then, of our idea of corporeal objects such as trees, tables, bodies? Berkeley was driven by his logic and his empiricist starting points to conclude that physical objects, insofar as we have any clear idea of them at all, are simply collections of sense impressions. Those **corporeal substances**, of which Descartes was at last able to form a "clear and distinct idea," turn out on analysis to be the figments of muddled thought.

Has empiricism then truly reconstructed our knowledge of the world, if this is its conclusion? Doesn't Berkeley's conception of a world "through and through mental" give a violent jolt to common sense? Not so, replies Berkeley. His idealism implies that tables and trees and bodies are just exactly what they seem—colored, shaped, hard, and so on. There is indeed nothing to these things except the qualities they seem to have. Moreover, it is not true that tables "vanish" or "pop out of existence" the moment we turn our backs on them (that *would* be repugnant to common sense), for God is always perceiving them, and therefore they continue to exist as ideas in His mind. To many later empiricists, this use of God seemed a desperate expedient to save Berkeley's theory from embarrassment. John Stuart Mill (1806–1873) was typical of later empiricists (often called **phenomenalists**) who found ways to make the rejection of "corporeal substance" more palatable to common sense without invoking a *deus ex machina.* According to Mill, if we say that a table continues to exist when unperceived, all we can mean by this is that *if* someone were to look in a certain place, then he would have sense impressions of a certain (table-like) kind; for material objects are not simply bundles of actual sense impressions but are rather to be understood as "permanent possibilities of sensation," and this conception exhausts whatever clear idea we have of them. Some writers have suggested that phenomenalism (the view of David Hume as well as of Mill) can be thought of as "Berkeley's view without Berkeley's God."

This chapter concludes with G. E. Moore's classic "proof" of an external world. Moore inherited from Reid a very sturdy appreciation of common sense, and would have no truck with skeptical hypotheses of the sort that have plagued philosophers for so long. Moore stuck out his two hands, proclaimed the certainty of their existence, and that was that. Whether that really is the end of the story is a matter that has been discussed ever since.

David Hume in the eighteenth century applied the empiricist philosophy not only to the concept of a material substance but to other basic concepts as well, with results that even he called skeptical. Unlike Berkeley, who regarded skepticism as a charge to be rebutted, Hume thought of it as a position to be reluctantly adopted. In the selections included here, he examines the concept of causation and finds no more sense in the idea of a "necessary connection" between cause and effect (when we drop a stone, it *must* fall—so we think) than Berkeley did in the idea of "corporeal substance." We may continue to talk, as Hume himself does, of one thing's causing another, but all we can *mean* is that events of the first kind are in fact constantly conjoined with events of the second kind; the so-called necessity that the second follow the first is simply the reflection of our habitual expectation. Hume would not have us deny the plain reports of our senses or the fruits of our mathematical deductions; he merely points out that there is no logically infallible method of achieving truth about matters of fact, and indeed no method at all for reasoning about matters that lie beyond all experience. But this kind of skepticism need not force us into a permanent suspension of judgment about all things, even in the practical affairs of life. We will (as Hume elsewhere puts it) continue to leave buildings by the ground-floor door rather than the upstairs window, and "Nature will always maintain her rights and prevail in the end over any abstract reasoning whatever."

The article "An Encounter with David Hume" was written specifically for the third edition of this volume by Wesley C. Salmon (1925–2001). It is meant to show the beginning student of philosophy and science ("Physics 1a") how natural Hume's doubts can seem to one who ponders the methods and results of the exact sciences and how important it is to our conception of scientific knowledge to come to terms with those doubts. In particular, Salmon discusses such scientific notions as causation, inductive inference, probability, laws of nature, the regularity of nature, necessity, and predictability, in the light of Hume's empiricism. Salmon's essay views these matters through the eyes of a sensitive undergraduate student of physics who comes to wonder whether all science rests ultimately on a kind of "faith" in the uniformity of nature that cannot be rationally demonstrated to be correct. If this is so, he asks (with a certain amount of anguish), how can physics be shown to be a more reliable guide to knowledge of the future than, say, astrology or crystal gazing? These questions pose in a very rough way what has come to be called "the problem of induction" or "Hume's riddle of induction." Salmon concludes by sketching the main strategies that have been proposed by philosophers for coming to terms with Hume's skeptical doubts about scientific method.

The theory of knowledge comes by its interest in the philosophy of science quite naturally, since the methods of science have been the most reliable—some philosophers say the *only* reliable—producers of knowledge. The first question epistemologists should ask about science, of course, is: When are investigative methods properly called "scientific"? However, a full answer to the question "What is science?" will describe what job is assigned to science, in either its crude or developed state, and contrast that task with that of other cultural activities that could be, and often are, confused with it.

Perhaps the most influential answer of the last century was that offered by Sir Karl Popper, a renowned philosopher of science. In the paper included here, Popper argues that the essence of scientific claims lies in their falsifiability. He contrasts the claims of physics, for instance, with those of astrology and Freudian psychology, and demotes the latter to nonscientific status by virtue of his falsifiability criterion. This criterion states that hypotheses must be testable in order to qualify as scientific; a scientific claim must have a chance of being shown false in order for it to pass scientific muster. If no evidence could possibly count against a claim—think, for instance, of certain extreme conspiracy theories, whose proponents interpret all evidence in such a way as to support their far-fetched views—then it loses its status as a scientific claim.

Popper's views occasioned a great deal of discussion about what he termed "the demarcation problem"—the problem of sharply distinguishing between scientific and nonscientific realms. There is consensus today that Popper's falsifiability criterion does not work. In fact, most philosophers of science nowadays believe that the demarcation problem cannot be decisively solved with the introduction of any short, simple criterion. There is no clear test that will distinguish every scientific claim from nonscientific ones.

Still, there *is* very broad agreement among philosophers that certain kinds of inquiry do and do not count as properly scientific. In the final piece of this chapter, Philip Kitcher, a prominent philosopher of science at Columbia University, gives us his take on the demarcation problem. Focusing on recent creationist claims to equal time in high school classrooms, Kitcher tackles the question of what distinguishes genuine biological and physical science from other views that aspire to their scientific status. Along the way he considers Popper's falsifiability criterion, and reveals what is mistaken in a number of creationist critiques of evolutionary theory. He concludes his essay with a positive account of the elements of scientific claims. Whether Kitcher's is the final word on the matter is left for the reader to consider. What is certain is that philosophers remain deeply puzzled by the issues of what constitutes science, scientific knowledge, and scientific confirmation.

CHAPTER 1

SKEPTICISM

1.1 A Brain in a Vat

JOHN POLLOCK

John Pollock (1940–2009), wrote several important books on the theory of knowledge, the philosophy of mind, and cognitive science.

It all began that cold Wednesday night. I was sitting alone in my office watching the rain come down on the deserted streets outside, when the phone rang. It was Harry's wife, and she sounded terrified. They had been having a late supper alone in their apartment when suddenly the front door came crashing in and six hooded men burst into the room. The men

From John Pollock, *Contemporary Theories of Knowledge* (Lanham, MD: Rowman & Littlefield, 1986), pp. 1–4. Reprinted by permission of Rowman & Littlefield; permission conveyed through Copyright Clearance Center, Inc.

were armed and they made Harry and Anne lie face down on the floor while they went through Harry's pockets. When they found his driver's license one of them carefully scrutinized Harry's face, comparing it with the official photograph and then muttered, "It's him all right." The leader of the intruders produced a hypodermic needle and injected Harry with something that made him lose consciousness almost immediately. For some reason they only tied and gagged Anne. Two of the men left the room and returned with a stretcher and white coats. They put Harry on the stretcher, donned the white coats, and trundled him out of the apartment, leaving Anne lying on the floor. She managed to squirm to the window in time to see them put Harry in an ambulance and drive away.

By the time she called me, Anne was coming apart at the seams. It had taken her several hours to get out of her bonds, and then she called the police. To her consternation, instead of uniformed officers, two plain clothed officials arrived and, without even looking over the scene, they proceeded to tell her that there was nothing they could do and if she knew what was good for her she would keep her mouth shut. If she raised a fuss they would put out the word that she was a psycho and she would never see her husband again.

Not knowing what else to do, Anne called me. She had had the presence of mind to note down the number of the ambulance, and I had no great difficulty tracing it to a private clinic at the outskirts of town. When I arrived at the clinic I was surprised to find it locked up like a fortress. There were guards at the gate and it was surrounded by a massive wall. My commando training stood me in good stead as I negotiated the 20 foot wall, avoided the barbed wire, and silenced the guard dogs on the other side. The ground floor windows were all barred, but I managed to wriggle up a drainpipe and get in through a second story window that someone had left ajar. I found myself in a laboratory. Hearing muffled sounds next door I peeked through the keyhole and saw what appeared to be a complete operating room and a surgical team laboring over Harry. He was covered with

a sheet from the neck down and they seemed to be connecting tubes and wires to him. I stifled a gasp when I realized that they had removed the top of Harry's skull. To my considerable consternation, one of the surgeons reached into the open top of Harry's head and eased his brain out, placing it in a stainless steel bowl. The tubes and wires I had noted earlier were connected to the now disembodied brain. The surgeons carried the bloody mass carefully to some kind of tank and lowered it in. My first thought was that I had stumbled on a covey of futuristic Satanists who got their kicks from vivisection. My second thought was that Harry was an insurance agent. Maybe this was their way of getting even for the increases in their malpractice insurance rates. If they did this every Wednesday night, their rates were no higher than they should be!

My speculations were interrupted when the lights suddenly came on in my darkened hidey hole and I found myself looking up at the scariest group of medical men I had ever seen. They manhandled me into the next room and strapped me down on an operating table. I thought, "Oh, oh, I'm in for it now!" The doctors huddled at the other end of the room, but I couldn't turn my head far enough to see what they were doing. They were mumbling among themselves, probably deciding my fate. A door opened and I heard a woman's voice. The deferential manner assumed by the medical malpractitioners made it obvious who was boss. I strained to see this mysterious woman but she hovered just out of my view. Then, to my astonishment, she walked up and stood over me and I realized it was my secretary, Margot. I began to wish I had given her that Christmas bonus after all.

It was Margot, but it was a different Margot than I had ever seen. She was wallowing in the heady wine of authority as she bent over me. "Well Mike, you thought you were so smart, tracking Harry here to the clinic," she said....."It was all a trick just to get you here. You saw what happened to Harry. He's not really dead, you know. These gentlemen are the premier neuroscientists in the world today. They have developed a surgical procedure whereby they remove the brain from the body but keep it alive in a vat of nutrient. The Food and Drug Administration wouldn't approve the procedure, but we'll show them. You see all the wires going to Harry's brain? They connect him up with a powerful computer. The computer monitors the output of his motor cortex and provides input to the sensory cortex in such a way that everything appears perfectly normal to Harry. It produces a fictitious mental life that merges perfectly into his past life so that he is unaware that anything has happened to him. He thinks he is shaving right now and getting ready to go to the office and stick it to another neurosurgeon. But actually, he's just a brain in a vat."

"Once we have our procedure perfected we're going after the head of the Food and Drug Administration, but we needed some experimental subjects first. Harry was easy. In order to really test our computer program we need someone who leads a more interesting and varied life—someone like you!" I was starting to squirm. The surgeons had drawn around me and were looking on with malevolent gleams in their eyes. The biggest brute, a man with a pock-marked face and one beady eye staring out from under his stringy black hair, was fondling a razor sharp scalpel in his still-bloody hands and looking as if he could barely restrain his excitement. But Margot gazed down at me and murmured in that incredible voice, "I'll bet you think we're going to operate on you and remove your brain just like we removed Harry's, don't you? But you have nothing to worry about. We're not going to remove your brain. We already did—three months ago!"

With that they let me go. I found my way back to my office in a daze. For some reason, I haven't told anybody about this. I can't make up my mind. I am racked by the suspicion that I am really a brain in a vat and all this I see around me is just a figment of the computer. After all, how could I tell? If the computer program really works, no matter what I do, everything will seem normal. Maybe nothing I see is real. It's driving me crazy. I've even considered checking into that clinic voluntarily and asking them to remove my brain just so that I can be sure.

1.2 Three Skeptical Arguments

MICHAEL HUEMER

Michael Huemer works primarily in ethics and the theory of knowledge. He teaches at the University of Colorado.

I shall present three skeptical arguments below. Each of these arguments purports to show, at a minimum, that there is no good reason for thinking external objects exist. In fact, the first two arguments try to show even more: that there is no good reason for believing anything whatsoever. My aim in this article, playing devil's advocate, is to present the skeptic's case in its strongest form.

1. THE INFINITE REGRESS ARGUMENT

The first argument goes as follows. In order for me to *know* something to be true, I must have an adequate reason for believing it. This is one of the things that distinguishes knowledge from mere belief. To take an example from Richard Fumerton, suppose I announce that the world

Michael Huemer, "Three Skeptical Arguments" from Skepticism and the Veil of Perception, pp. 9–15. © 2001 by Rowman and Littlefield. Used by permission of the publisher;

is going to come to an end in the year 2100.[1] You ask me, "How do you know that?" What you are asking for is a *reason* (specifically, some *evidence*) for believing that the world will come to an end in the year 2100. Now suppose I say, "Oh, it's just a whimsical hunch I have. I don't really have any reason for thinking that's true." In that case, you could conclude that, although I may *believe* that the world is coming to an end in the year 2100, I certainly do not *know* that it is. Beliefs like that—beliefs held for no reason—are typically referred to as "arbitrary assumptions."

In addition, in order for my reason to be adequate, it too must be something that I know to be the case. Again, suppose I announce that the world will end in the year 2100. This time, when asked why I believe this, I say, "I believe the world will come to an end in the year 2100, because the Plutonians are going to launch a lethal nuclear strike against us in that year." When asked how I know about the Plutonians' plans, however, I reply that I don't know any such thing; it was just a whimsical hunch. Once again, you would conclude that I do not know that the world is going to end in the year 2100, since the reason I gave for this hypothesis was inadequate.

These requirements on knowledge create the threat of an infinite regress. For suppose I claim to know some proposition, A. You ask me my reason for believing it. It turns out that my reason for believing A is another proposition, B. You ask me my reason for believing B, which turns out to be a further proposition, C. You ask me my reason for believing C.... It is clear that this cannot go on forever. I cannot actually have an infinitely long chain of reasons standing behind my original assertion A. Nor is it permissible for me to rely on circular reasoning. For instance, suppose that, when asked my reason for believing A, I say I believe A because I believe A. In that case, I have not really given any (legitimate) reason for believing A. Nor are matters improved if I say B is my reason for believing A, and A is my reason for believing B. Nor, again, will matters be better if I simply expand the circle to include more beliefs; no exercise in circular reasoning will help me gain knowledge, however many steps the circle contains.

There is one remaining possibility, then. Every chain of reasoning must have a beginning point. In other words, all of my beliefs must rest, sooner or later, on propositions that I believe *for no reason*. Now, how can I know whether these starting beliefs are true? From what we have said above, it is clear that I cannot. By definition, I have no argument or evidence for my starting beliefs—if I did, then they would not be "starting beliefs." But without an assurance of the truth of my starting assumptions, the derivation, however rigorous, of other propositions from them is worthless. This is an obvious point, but it bears stressing. After all, any proposition whatsoever can be derived from *some* premises or other. The mere fact that I can derive my belief A from some assumptions does nothing whatever to establish the truth of A; if it did, one could also establish the negation of A by *its* derivability from certain, other assumptions.

In general, conclusions are only as good as the premises they are based on. So if I do not know my starting premises to be true, then even more surely I do not know my conclusions to be true. Therefore, I cannot know anything.

This argument can be summarized as follows:

1. In order to know something, I must have a good reason for believing it.
2. Any chain of reasons must have one of the following structures: Either
   (a) it is an infinite series,
   (b) it is circular, or
   (c) it begins with a belief for which there are no further reasons. But,
3. I cannot have an infinitely long chain of reasoning for any of my beliefs.
4. Circular reasoning cannot produce knowledge.
5. Nor can I gain knowledge by structure 2c, for
   (a) I would not know my starting beliefs to be true (from 1), and
   (b) I cannot gain knowledge by deriving it from assumptions that I do not know to be true.
6. Therefore, I cannot know anything.

What is wrong with the above argument? The majority of philosophers and others who hear the argument say that it is premise (1) which is mistaken. They say that there are certain self-evident, or *foundational* propositions. A foundational proposition, by definition, is one that we can know to be true *without* having a reason for it, and the people who believe in such things are called "foundationalists." According to most foundationalists, propositions such as "2 = 2" and "I am now conscious" would be good examples of foundational propositions. I do not have to give an argument, or engage in a process of reasoning, to know that I am conscious, or that the number 2 is equal to itself. I merely think about these propositions and thereupon find their truth immediately obvious.

The skeptic, of course, will deny the existence of self-evident propositions. But why? Obviously, the skeptic cannot say, "It is self-evident that self-evident propositions do not exist." To be consistent, he will have to produce an *argument* against the idea of self-evident propositions. What argument can he give?

Well, the skeptic can argue that the foundationalist has no way of distinguishing *self-evident* propositions from merely *arbitrary* propositions. A self-evident proposition, we have said, is one that we need have no reason for in order to be fully justified (or rational) in accepting it. An arbitrary proposition, on the other hand, is a proposition that we have no reason for and would be wholly unjustified in believing. For instance, suppose I suddenly decide, completely out of the blue, that I think there is a twelve-headed purple dragon living on Venus. This would be an arbitrary belief. The foundationalist must explain what *differentiates* a foundational proposition like "2 = 2" from an arbitrary proposition like "There is a twelve-headed purple dragon on Venus." That is, he must identify some feature of the foundational proposition that the arbitrary proposition lacks, and that explains why the foundational proposition is justified. Let "F" denote this feature.

Assume, then, that I have a belief, A, which is a legitimate foundational belief. And assume that I have another belief, B, which is merely arbitrary. By hypothesis, A has F, while B lacks F. Now, either I am *aware* of feature F, or I am not. But if I were completely unaware of feature F, then how could its presence serve to make it rational for me to accept A? If the presence of F is to explain why I am rational (or justified) in accepting A but not rational in accepting B, it must be something that I am aware of (in the one case, but not in the other). Otherwise, A and B will be, *from my point of view*, equally good (or equally arbitrary) assumptions. In that case, given the information available to me, it would be equally reasonable for me to accept one as to accept the other.

So the foundationalist position will have to be that it is reasonable for me to accept A, because I am aware that A has feature F. But then A is not a foundational proposition after all, because I *do* have a reason for accepting A—namely, that A has F. Thus, foundationalism is reduced to absurdity: from the supposition that A is legitimately foundational, we can derive the conclusion that A is not foundational after all. Therefore, the very idea of a foundational proposition is self-contradictory. Therefore, it appears, the skeptic's argument stands.

2. THE PROBLEM OF THE CRITERION

I have on my desk an epistemologically interesting toy called "the Magic Eight Ball." It is a plastic ball painted like an eight ball, and it is meant to be used as follows. You ask the eight ball a yes/no question. Then you turn it over and see an answer float up to a window in the bottom. Answers include the likes of "Yes, definitely," "Very doubtful," and "Cannot predict now."

Now, imagine there were a community in which use of the eight ball was an accepted method of arriving at conclusions. Suppose you meet one of these eight-ball reasoners, and you ask him why he believes that the eight ball is a reliable informant. He swiftly takes out his Magic Eight Ball, says, "Are you reliable?" and turns it over. At this point, if the answer "No" floats up to the window, then the eight-ball reasoner is in trouble. But suppose a definite "Yes" answer appears, and the eight-ball reasoner triumphantly declares that the reliability of the eight ball has been established. Would this be legitimate?

Evidently not. You would no doubt object, rightly, that there is a problem of circularity here. If we already knew the eight ball was reliable, then we would be justified in accepting the answers it produces. But if the eight ball is unreliable, then we should not trust its answers. And if we don't know whether it is reliable, then we likewise should not trust its answers *until* its reliability has been established. The method of eight-ball reasoning presupposes that we know the eight ball to be reliable, in the sense that it would not be reasonable to use the method unless we already knew (or at least had reason to believe) it to be a reliable method. Therefore, we certainly cannot use eight-ball reasoning to establish that the eight ball is reliable.

Now consider an analogous case. Suppose some skeptic comes along and asks you why you believe the senses to be reliable. Why do you think that, when you seem to see, hear, or feel things, this is a reliable indicator of the way things really are, in the external world? How would you respond?

Here is one thing you might try. You go to an eye doctor to have your eyes examined. He gives you a series of tests, and at the end he assures you that your eyesight is perfect. Then you go to another doctor to take some hearing tests. He assures you that you have excellent hearing. (You might have difficulty finding doctors to test your taste, smell, and sense of touch, but let's pass over that difficulty.) You then explain to the skeptic that the reliability of your senses has been established. Would this be legitimate?

Apparently not. You would be engaging in just the same sort of circular reasoning that the benighted eight-ball reasoner used, for you can only collect the results of your tests by using your senses. You may seem to hear the doctors tell you that your hearing and eyesight are normal, but how do you know they are really saying

that? Indeed, if you were in doubt as to the reliability of your senses in general, you could not even be sure that the doctors really existed, let alone that they were reliable informants.

So you will have to use some other method to verify the reliability of your senses—you will have to rely on some cognitive faculty other than the senses. But—here is the problem—whatever method you try to use to verify that your senses are reliable, the skeptic can always ask why you believe *that* method to be reliable. For instance, suppose you wanted to prove the reliability of the senses through the exercise of pure reason (though I have no idea how such a proof would go). In that case, the skeptic could ask why you think reason itself is reliable. You could not use reason to establish the reliability of reason, nor could you use the five senses to establish the reliability of reason, again on pain of circularity. So you will need to find yet a third belief-forming method. At which point the skeptic will question the reliability of this third method as well. At some point, and probably sooner rather than later, you will have to either resort to circular reasoning or else give up on answering the skeptic's question. But this means that ultimately you cannot establish the reliability of your cognitive faculties. And all of your beliefs are formed through one or another of your cognitive faculties, whether it be through the five senses, or reason, or memory, or introspection. Since you cannot know whether any of your belief-forming methods is reliable, it seems, you cannot know whether any of your beliefs is true. In short, you are in the same position as the eight-ball reasoner. The eight-ball-generated beliefs were all unjustified since the eight-ball reasoner could not (noncircularly) establish that the eight ball was reliable. Similarly, all of your beliefs are unjustified since you cannot (noncircularly) establish that your belief-forming methods in general are reliable.

This argument can be summarized as follows:

1. All my beliefs are formed by some method.
2. I am justified in accepting a belief formed by method M only if I *first* know that M is reliable.

3. I do not have an infinite series of belief-forming methods.
4. Thus, all my beliefs must rest on beliefs formed by methods whose reliability has not first been established. (from 1 and 3)
5. Therefore, none of my beliefs are justified. (from 2 and 4)

This argument is similar to the argument of the previous section. Again we have a threat of infinite regress or circularity, though this time it would be a series of belief-forming methods, rather than a series of beliefs. Once we rule out both the infinite regress and the circularity possibilities, the only remaining possibility is that I have belief-forming methods whose reliability is not established by any method. As a result, it seems, we have no way of knowing anything whatever.

3. HOW CAN YOU GET OUTSIDE YOUR HEAD?

Most of the things we think we know, including everything we think we know about the physical world, we learn through sensory perception, which includes sight, hearing, taste, touch, and smell. Of course, this does not mean that everything we know about the physical world is something we actually observe. A lot of what we know of the physical world is the result of scientific theorizing or inference, but those theories and inferences are ultimately *based on* observations. For instance, we know of the existence of atoms through inferences from the observed results of experiments. Similarly, I know that the Battle of Hastings took place in 1066, not because I personally observed it, but because I read that in a history book—but I knew what the book said only because I could *see the book*. In that sense, my belief was acquired through the exercise of my senses.

If you think about it, then, you will probably realize that everything you think you know about the external world is dependent on your senses. So in order to determine how much we really know about the physical world, we must first ask what the senses really tell us about the physical world. This question can be separated into two sub-issues: First, what is it that the senses make us *directly aware* of? Second, what can be *inferred* from what we are thus directly aware of?

The skeptical argument we are about to consider seeks to establish, first, that the senses do not make us directly aware of the physical world; and second, that no conclusions about the physical world can be inferred from what we are directly aware of either. It will follow that we can have no knowledge of the physical world.

The first part of the argument—the falsity of direct realism—is supposed to be established by the sort of argument we began with in chapter I.* There are, actually, quite a few arguments against direct realism, but for now, let us stick to the argument from double vision. As you recall, we considered a case in which, though there is only one physical finger in front of you, you seem to see two fingerlike things. This was supposed to show that what you are immediately aware of is mental images, rather than the physical finger. The reasoning can be summarized as follows:

1. As your focus shifts to the background, the fingerlike thing you are seeing splits in two.
2. No physical object splits in two at this time.
3. Therefore, the thing you are seeing is not a physical object.

If the thing you are seeing is not a physical object, the next natural candidate is that it is a mental image (what else could it plausibly be?). These mental images are traditionally called "sense data," so that is what I will call them here.

Now, given that all you ever directly perceive is your own sense data, can you infer anything about the external world? At first glance, this doesn't seem too difficult. Your sense data must come from somewhere, and you know that

---

*Omitted here.—Eds.

you didn't create them, since you have no direct control over your sense data. (If you did, you could just decide to stop hearing that horrible music your neighbor is playing.) So they must have been caused by external objects. Suppose you are having a sense datum of a tree. The simplest explanation of why you're having this experience—and normally the correct one—is that there is a tree in front of you, which is causing your experience. Granted, it is possible for a person to hallucinate a tree; however, that is not the normal situation, and there is no special reason for thinking you are hallucinating now.

The great skeptic David Hume neatly exposed the problem with this line of thought:

> It is a question of fact, whether the perceptions of the senses be produced by external objects resembling them. How shall this question be determined? By experience surely, as all other questions of a like nature. But here experience is, and must be entirely silent. The mind has never anything present to it but the perceptions, and cannot possibly reach any experience of their connexion with objects. The supposition of such a connexion is, therefore, without any foundation in reasoning.[2]

Hume believed, plausibly enough, that the only way of knowing that A causes B (where A and B are any two types of events) is by having some experience of A and B—specifically, you must observe A being followed by B on a number of occasions. For instance, suppose there's a light switch on the wall in front of me. In order to find out what the switch does, I'll have to try it out. I flip it a few times, notice the light go on and off, and conclude that flipping the switch causes the light to go on or off. If I never observed the flipping of the switch, I would not have been able to know this. Now, it is true that, when I enter a room I've never been in before, I can often predict that the switch on the wall will turn on the lights. However, this is because I am relying on *past* experience with light switches. If I had never had any experience with any light switches, I would have no idea what it would do.

Now, Hume says, for the reasons given above, that we never actually see physical objects, only our representations of them. Therefore, we have certainly not observed the presence of physical objects being followed by the occurrence of sense data. Therefore, we cannot claim to know that physical objects cause sense data. In particular, we could not claim to know that physical trees cause treelike sense data, because we have never actually had any direct experience of a physical tree; all we have seen is the tree-representing sense data. It is as if I saw the lights go on and off periodically, but I never saw the light switch (suppose the switch was located in another room of which I was unaware). In that case, I would never know what was causing the lights to go on or off.

This argument can be summarized as follows:

1. In order to have knowledge of the physical world, we must be able to know that our sense data are caused by physical objects.
2. In order to know that A causes B, one must have experience of A and B.
3. We have no experience of physical objects.
4. Therefore, we do not know that physical objects cause our sense data. (from 2, 3)
5. Therefore, we have no knowledge of the physical world. (from 1, 4)

NOTES

1. Richard Fumerton, *Metaphysical and Epistemological Problems of Perception* (University of Nebraska Press, 1985), p. 39.
2. David Hume, *Enquiry Concerning Human Understanding* (1748), Section 119.

1.3 Skepticism

ROBERT AUDI

Robert Audi is John A. O'Brien Professor of Philosophy at the University of Notre Dame. He
has published very widely in epistemology, ethics, and the philosophy of religion.

I think that we all know many things. I know
many facts about my immediate surroundings,
much about myself, something about the past,
and a little about the future. I believe that we
also have some approximate scientific knowledge, that we know some general moral truths,
and that we may possibly know some religious
truths. But there are reasons to doubt all of this.
There are reasons to think that at best we know
very little, perhaps just self-evident necessary
truths, such as that if no vixens are males then
no males are vixens, and a few propositions
about our present consciousness, such as that I
am now thinking about the scope of human
knowledge.

THE POSSIBILITY OF PERVASIVE
ERROR

As I consider these matters, I look back at a blue
spruce. It occurs to me that I see it vividly. I
certainly cannot help believing that it is there.
But an inescapable belief need not be knowledge, nor even justified. Suppose I am hallucinating. Then I would not know (through
vision, at least) that the tree is there. I find it
impossible to believe that I am hallucinating.
But I might find that impossible even if I were,
provided the hallucination was as vivid and
steady as my present visual experience. I wonder,
then, whether I really *know* that I am not hallucinating. If I do not know this, then even if I am
in fact not hallucinating, can I *know* that there is
a blue spruce before me? Similarly, if I do not

know that I am not simply having a vivid dream
in which it seems to me that there is a blue
spruce before me, can I know there is one
there?

Remembering that one can justifiably believe something even if one does not know it,
I think that at least I may justifiably believe that
there is a blue spruce before me, even if I do not
know that I am not hallucinating one (or
merely "seeing" one in a dream). Moreover, if
I justifiably believe this, how much does it matter whether I know it? It matters whether the
belief is *true*. But the likelihood that it is true,
so far as I can discern that likelihood, depends
on how probable the presence of the tree is,
given the sensory experience on which my belief
is based; and in my attentiveness and caution as
an observer, I have contributed all I can to that
probability. If I still do not have knowledge,
that is an external matter. My belief remains
justified and is as likely to be true as I can
make it by any steps in my power, such as observing carefully. Internally, in my own consciousness. I am being perfectly reasonable in
continuing to believe that there is a blue spruce
there. So far as justification is concerned, I am
beyond reproach.

These points about justification are plausible, but they give false comfort. Doubtless, I
may have a justified true belief that is not knowledge even if I am hallucinating; yet it is now not
merely possible that I am hallucinating, I am also
quite *aware* that I could be. Given this awareness, am I *still* justified in believing that there is a

From Audi, *Belief, Justification and Knowledge*, 1E. © 1988 Cengage Learning.

blue spruce there? Should I not regard this belief as unjustified, suspend judgment on whether the spruce is there, and merely hope that it is? I want to believe that it is there if it truly is, for *I want to believe as many significant truths as I can.* But I do not want to believe that it is there if it is not, for *I want to avoid believing falsehoods.* These two desires are important to me, and they represent ideals that run deep in my thinking. But the two ideals pull against each other: the former inclines me to believe readily, since I may otherwise miss believing a truth; the latter inclines me toward suspending judgment, lest I fall into error by believing a falsehood. How can one balance these ideals with each other? ...

These reflections about possible error through hallucination, about the apparent vulnerability of justification in the face of such possibilities, and about the ideal of avoiding error suggest why philosophers have been so concerned with *skepticism*: which, in very broad terms, is the view that there is little if any knowledge. Skepticism may also concern justification, and typically skeptics do not take our justified beliefs to be of a significantly larger number than our beliefs constituting knowledge. How far-reaching might a plausible skepticism be, and how is skepticism to be assessed? I want to pursue these questions in that order and at some length.

It may seem that skepticism offends so blatantly against common sense that it should be dismissed as preposterous. But it will soon be evident that skepticism is a serious, perhaps even irrefutable, challenge to common sense. Moreover, even if skepticism turns out ... to be quite unreasonable, we learn a great deal about knowledge and justification from studying it. A serious exploration of skepticism, whether or not we finally accept some form of it, tends to help us avoid dogmatism about our own personal views and a self-satisfied assurance that our collective outlook as rational observers of the world embodies knowledge of the sorts of things we think it does: facts about ourselves, our surroundings, and the ways of nature....

SKEPTICISM GENERALIZED

The skeptical challenges I have brought forward can be directed against *all* our beliefs about the external world, all our memory beliefs, all our beliefs about the future, and indeed all our beliefs about any subject provided they depend on our memory for their justification or for their status as knowledge. For memory is at least as fallible as vision. Plainly, if any of the senses can deceive through hallucination, then beliefs grounded in the senses may be justificationally or epistemically *undermined* in the same way my belief that there is a blue spruce before me may be undermined by a realization that I might have been hallucinating. That is, quite apart from whether perceptual beliefs are true, skeptics tend to claim that either the possibility of such hallucinations prevents them from being justified or, even if they remain justified, it precludes their constituting knowledge. Suppose, for instance, that I might be having an auditory hallucination of bird songs. Then my present experience of (apparently) hearing them may not justify my believing that there are birds nearby and is not a sufficient basis for my knowing there are, even if it is true that there are. Similarly, there is a counterpart of hallucination for memory beliefs: *memorial hallucination,* we might call it. I may have the memorial impression that when I was four I saw my parents kissing under the mistletoe, but this could be just a romantic fantasy masquerading as a memory.

Beliefs about the future are rather different from memory beliefs, in that they are not grounded in experiential states we think of as in some way causally deriving from the object about which we have knowledge. But even if there is no counterpart of memorial hallucination, there are equally undermining possibilities. For instance, a confident belief, grounded in remembering my longstanding intention to talk with Jane, that I will talk with her may be a product of wishful thinking. Perhaps it could be an anticipatory delusion. Even my belief that I will live to discuss skepticism could be mistaken for many sorts of reasons, including dangers to me of which I am now unaware.

Now consider my general a priori and scientific "knowledge," say of arithmetic truths and scientific laws. Since it is possible to misremember propositions, or to seem to remember them when one does not, or to have a kind of memorial hallucination that gives rise to a completely groundless belief, it would seem that our only secure beliefs are of general propositions that we can know directly without *ever* having needed any evidence. This apparently leaves none of our general scientific beliefs, and only our a priori knowledge of self-evident propositions, epistemically unscathed.

Even if we leave problems about perceptual and memory beliefs aside, there is a difficulty for the commonsense view that justification or knowledge grounded in a basic source can be transmitted inductively. The classical statement of this *problem of induction* comes from Hume (see, for instance, Section IV of his *Inquiry Concerning Human Understanding*). Hume pointed out (in different terms) that one cannot know a priori that if the premises of a specific piece of inductive reasoning are true, then its conclusion is also true. Thus, no matter how good the inductive reasoning is, it is always (deductively) invalid. Consider the inductive reasoning from the premise that the sun always has arisen each twenty-four hours to the conclusion that it will rise tomorrow. Of all such reasoning, which Hume calls reasoning "concerning matter of fact and existence," he says, "That there are no demonstrative [roughly, valid and conclusive] arguments in the case seems evident, since it implies no contradiction that the course of nature may change and that an object, seemingly like those which we have experienced, may be attended with different or contrary effects." Hence, even if I do know that the sun has arisen every day since time immemorial, and on that basis I believe that it will rise tomorrow, I *could* be mistaken in believing this, and I must question whether I have any justification for believing it.

More generally, Hume's arguments lead us to ask whether, if our premises could be true, yet our conclusion false, we have any *reason* at all, on the basis of the premises, for believing the conclusion. And how can we ever *know* the conclusion on the basis of such premises? Indeed, how can we even be minimally justified in believing the conclusion on the basis of such premises? The problem of induction, as most often understood, us largely the difficulty of adequately answering these questions.

It will not do to argue that I am justified in believing my conclusion on the basis of inductive support for it, since past experience has shown that reasoning like this, which has had true premises, has also had true conclusions. For this way of defending an inductively based conclusion simply gives a kind of inductive reasoning to support the view that certain kinds of inductive arguments justify one in believing their conclusions. It just inductively generalizes about inductive arguments themselves, using as a guide past experience in finding that by and large their conclusions turned out true when their premises were true. That begs the question against Hume: it simply assumes part of what he contends is false, namely, that inductive inference constitutes reasoning that can ground knowledge of its conclusion or can at least justify, in the sense of providing good reason for, its conclusion.

The point that Hume so powerfully defended is by no means restricted to beliefs about the future, though such beliefs are so prominent in his work that sometimes the problem of induction is narrowly conceived as that of how we can show that we have any reason to believe the future will be like the past. Recall my observing Jim briskly shuffling papers and angrily mumbling curses. I cannot help believing, on this basis, that he is angry. But even if I know my premises (through perception), it does not *follow* that he is angry. He could be pretending. This case is alarmingly representative. Everything I believe about what is occurring in the inner lives of others seems to rest on grounds that are inductive in this way: what I observe—above all, their behavior—does not entail anything about their minds. So if I cannot have knowledge of another person's inner life here, I apparently can never have it.

Worse still, if I cannot know anything about the inner lives of others, can I even know that there *are* others, as opposed to mere bodies controlled externally or by hidden machinery, rather than directed through beliefs and intentions of the kind that animate me? There is, then, a *problem of other minds.* Can we know, or even justifiably believe, that there are any? The problem is compounded when we realize that we cannot directly verify, as we introspectively can in our own case, what is occurring in someone else's consciousness. Thus, all I can do to check on my inductively grounded beliefs about the inner lives of others is get further inductive evidence, for instance by observing whether they behave as they should if I am right in thinking them to be, say, angry. I cannot, as in my own case, introspectively focus on the events in their consciousness. How can I know anything about the mental and emotional life of others if I am in principle debarred from decisively verifying my beliefs about the contents and events of their consciousness? Even if I am sometimes right, I can never tell when.

It is only a short step from here to a *problem of the body.* If, as a skeptic might well hold, my apparent knowledge of my own body is inductively grounded, being based on perceptions and bodily sensations somewhat as beliefs about external objects are, then can I know, or even justifiably believe, that I have a body? Could I not be steadily hallucinating even my own flesh? Again, it might be argued that thought necessarily requires an embodied thinker. But that point would only imply that I have *some* kind of body, not that I can know anything about it. The point is also far from self-evident and is indeed denied by philosophers in the powerful tradition of Descartes. In any case, even if it is true, the only embodiment necessary might be a brain. Hence, on the skeptical view imagined, the most one could know is that one is embodied in some way, say in a brain. Whether that brain is itself embodied, or ever interacts with anything else, would be beyond one's knowledge....

FALLIBILITY

In appraising skepticism, I will formulate some of the principles that underlie it in what seem its most plausible forms. If they can be shown to be unreasonable, then the skeptical threat to the common-sense view that we have a great deal of knowledge and justification can at least be blunted. In formulating and assessing these principles, it is well to distinguish skeptical threats to the generation of knowledge (or justification) from skeptical threats to its transmission. It is natural to start with questions about its generation. If no knowledge is generated, there is none to be transmitted.

Is there really any reason to doubt that, normally, introspectively grounded beliefs constitute knowledge? It *may* be true that such beliefs *could* be mistaken, but what is a skeptic entitled to make of this? The skeptical argument which comes to mind here is based on what I will call *the infallibility formulation:* that if you know, you can't be wrong. If we simply add the premise that you can be wrong in holding a given introspective belief, say that you are thinking about skepticism, it would seem to follow that such beliefs do not represent knowledge. This kind of *argument from fallibility,* as we might call it, can be applied to just about every sort of proposition we tend to think we know.

If, however, we look closely, we find that the infallibility formulation is multiply ambiguous. There are at least three quite different things the words in that formulation might mean, and hence really three different infallibility principles.

The claim, "If you know, you can't be wrong," might have the meaning of (1) it must be the case that if you know that something is true, then it *is* true (you cannot know something false). Call (1) the *verity principle,* since it says simply that knowledge must be of *truths.*

The claim might, on the other hand, have the meaning of (2) if you know that something is true, then it *must be* true, that is, the proposition you know is necessarily true (you can know only necessary truths). Call (2) the *necessity principle,* since it says simply that knowledge must be of necessary truths.

The claim might also have the meaning of (3) if you know that something is true, then your *belief* of it must be true, in the sense that your believing it entails its truth (only beliefs that cannot be false constitute knowledge). Call (3) the *infallibility principle, proper*, since it says that only infallible beliefs constitute knowledge. Unlike (2), (3) allows for knowledge of *contingent* (non-necessary) truths, such as that I exist. This *proposition* can be false, but my *belief* of it is infallible and cannot be false. If I now believe that I exist, it follows that I do exist.

We can now assess the skeptical reasoning that employs the infallibility formulation in one or another interpretation. I will be quite brief in discussing the first two; the third is most controversial and most important for skepticism.

The verity principle, (1), is plainly true: one cannot know something that is false. But if this is all the infallibility formulation comes to, it provides no reason to conclude that I do not know that I am thinking. Granted, it must be true that *if* I know I am thinking, then I am. But that tells us nothing about whether I do know I am. On the other hand, the necessity principle, (2), seems quite mistaken. Surely I know some propositions that are not necessary, such as that I exist (it is not a necessary truth that I exist, as it is that vixens are female). Even the skeptic would grant that I cannot falsely believe this, since my believing it entails that I exist. It may indeed be impossible for me even to be unjustified in believing it when I comprehendingly consider it. The same holds, of course, for you in relation to your belief that you exist.

Even if the necessity principle were true, however, it is so very far from self-evident that a skeptic could not reasonably *use* it, without adequate argument, against the view that introspective beliefs normally constitute knowledge. For clearly they are not beliefs of necessary truths, nor do defenders of common sense take them to be; hence, using the principle against common sense, without arguing for it, would be just to *assume* that such beliefs are not knowledge. That would *beg the question* against the commonsense view. Suppose, for instance, that a skeptic

says that if you know, you can't be wrong, where this means (2), then notes that introspective beliefs (which are of propositions that are not necessary) can be false, and concludes that such beliefs do not constitute knowledge. This would not be presenting a good reason to believe the conclusion, but just asserting, disguisedly, that the commonsense view is mistaken.

The infallibility principle proper, (3), in effect says that only infallible beliefs can be knowledge. Now *some* beliefs of empirical propositions *are* infallible, for instance my belief that I now exist, and my more specific belief that I have a belief. I *cannot* falsely believe these propositions. Their infallibility shows that despite appearances, (3) is *not* equivalent to (2). But why should we accept (3)? What reason can the skeptic give for it? Not that if you know, you cannot be wrong; for when we look closely, we find that when plausibly interpreted, as meaning (1), that is no help to the skeptic, and when interpreted as (2) or (3) it just asserts the skeptical position against common sense.

What makes it seem that the infallibility formulation gives the skeptic an argument against common sense is the way skepticism can *trade on* the ambiguity of that formulation: one finds the argument from fallibility attractive because its main premise, conceived as equivalent to (1), is so plausible; yet the argument succeeds against common sense only if (2) or (3) are legitimate premises, and it is doubtful that the skeptic has any cogent argument for them.

UNCERTAINTY

Like fallibility, uncertainty has seemed to many skeptics to leave us with little, if any, knowledge. Recall the possibility that I am hallucinating a blue spruce before me when there is none there. Can I tell for certain whether or not I am hallucinating a spruce where there is none? And if I cannot tell for certain, do I know I am not? The skeptic may argue that I do not know that I am not hallucinating, surely I do not know that there is a spruce there. At least two important principles are suggested here.

One principle suggested by reflection on these questions about possible error is *the certainty principle*: if one cannot tell for certain whether something is so, then one does not know it is so. This principle is plausible in part because 'How can you tell?' and 'How can you be certain?' are, typically, appropriate challenges to a claim to know something. Moreover, 'I know, but I am not certain' sounds self-defeating, in a way that might encourage a skeptic to consider it contradictory.

Another principle suggested by our questions about the possibility of hallucination is *the backup principle*: if one believes something, say that there is a tree before one, which is inconsistent with a further proposition—such as that one is merely hallucinating a tree where none exists—then one's belief is knowledge only if it is backed up by one's knowing, or at least being in a *position* to know, that the further (undermining) proposition is false. This principle is plausible in part because one is in a sense responsible for the implications of what one claims to know. If, for instance, I claim to know that there is a blue spruce before me, and that proposition implies that the tree is not a green spruce cleverly painted to look like a blue one, it would seem that I had better be justified in believing that it is not such a green one, which, in turn, implies that I must be justified in rejecting this strange possibility. Thus, if I know that there is a blue spruce before me, I must be prepared to back that up by justifiably rejecting exactly the sorts of possibilities the skeptic reminds us are, in abundance, always there. But must I be? Let us consider the certainty and backup principles in turn....

Let us first ask what it is to tell for certain. A skeptic may mean by this acquiring knowledge, in the form of an infallible belief, of a proposition that entails the truth of what one can tell is so. Thus, to tell (for certain) that one is not hallucinating one might, like Descartes, prove that there is a God of such goodness and power that—since it would be evil for God to allow it—one *could* not be mistaken in such a vivid and steadfast perception as one now has of a blue spruce. But to require that a belief can be knowledge only if it can be, in this or a similar way, conclusively

shown to be true would again beg the question against the view that a belief can constitute knowledge without being infallible. Thus, if skeptics have no good argument for the principle of infallibility proper, they should not assume that principle in defending the view that we can know only what we can tell for certain in this strong sense.

Perhaps, on the other hand, telling for certain is simply a matter of ascertaining the truth in question by some means that justifies one in *being* (psychologically) certain of what one can tell. If so, perhaps we normally *can* tell for certain that we are not hallucinating, for instance by seeing whether the senses of touch and smell confirm our visual impression. The confirming experiences do not *entail* that there is a blue spruce before me. But we still have no good argument that certainty (or knowledge) may arise only from entailing grounds (another controversial view, shortly to be discussed). Thus, this point does not establish that confirming experiences cannot enable us to tell for certain that we are not hallucinating.

Moreover, suppose that we interpret telling for certain in the modest way just suggested, and that we *can* tell for certain in *this* sense that what we know is true. In that case perhaps there *is* a weak sense in which beliefs constituting knowledge *are* infallible. They need not be such that it is absolutely impossible that they be false, as in the case of my belief that I exist. There need only be something about our grounds for them in virtue of which they (empirically) cannot be false. In this case, however, it will be arguable that many of our beliefs grounded in experience, such as my belief that there is a blue spruce before me, cannot be mistaken. There surely might be causal laws which guarantee that if one is situated before a tree in good light, as I am, and has visual experiences like mine caused by the tree as mine are, then one *sees* it, and hence cannot falsely believe that it is there. The skeptic gives us no good argument to show that there are no such laws.

The backup principle fares no better than the infallibility principle proper. For one thing, it rests on the assumption, which defenders of common sense stoutly reject, that in order to know that something is true, one must have grounds that entail its truth. To see this, consider the proposition that it is *false* that there is a blue spruce before me. This is inconsistent with what I believe, namely, that there *is* one before me. Hence, the backup principle requires that I at least be in a position to know that this is false. Now the falsity of this negative proposition entails that there *is* a blue spruce before me; for if it is false *that* it is false that there is one, then it is true that there is one. Thus, if I do know that this negative proposition is false, then I *have* (and know) an entailing ground for the truth of what I originally believed—that there is a blue spruce before me.

Consider also the proposition that what I take to be a blue spruce is really a green one so cleverly dyed blue that I cannot tell (perceptually) that it is really green. Must I be in a position to know that this is false in order to know that there is a blue spruce before me? The very description of the case suggests that I cannot know, at least by using the senses unaided by experimentation or specialized knowledge, that the tree is not a cleverly dyed green spruce. But why must I be able to tell this at all? Is there any *reason* to think that the tree might actually be dyed? Must I, in order to know, not only have a well-grounded true belief but also the further capacity to know, for every possible explanation of how my belief *could* be false, that this explanation is incorrect? I do not see that I must.

One might object that in order to know a proposition I must be in a position to know whatever follows from it (or at least obviously follows from it), since, if something *does* follow, I could infer it by valid steps from what I initially know, and thereby come to know it. This is an important objection. But in discussing the transmission of knowledge, we considered cases that apparently show the objection to be mistaken. I can know the sum of a column of figures even if I cannot, without further checking, know something which follows from it: that if my wife (a better arithmetician) says this is not the sum,

then she is wrong. Neither knowledge nor justification is automatically transmitted across valid deductive inference. Nor are they necessarily transmissible from propositions we believe to those they entail, even when the entailment is, as in our example, quite obvious.

Even supposing that knowledge and justification are always transmitted across valid deductive inference, it may be plausibly argued that I do have enough justification to warrant rejecting the hypothesis that the spruce is really green and cleverly painted to look blue. It is not just that it appears to me that it is blue; I also have no reason to think there is anything abnormal in the situation, and some reason to think that, in cases like this, large, nearby familiar kinds of things *are* as they appear to me in such vivid and careful observation. There are other factors one might cite, indeed, too many to discuss here. My point is simply this. Since the skeptic has not provided good reasons for the principles I have already rejected (or comparably strong principles), even if knowledge and justification are always transmitted across valid inference, there *may* be good reason to say that skeptical hypotheses, such as that the spruce is cleverly painted green, may be justifiably rejected.

I grant that in order to *show* the skeptic that my original belief is knowledge, in the face of the *suggestion* that one of those explanations of its falsity holds, I may have to know that, and why, this explanation does not hold. But why must I have this capacity in the *absence* of the suggestion, as the principle would require? Surely I need not. I can know that if some dogs are pets then some pets are dogs, even if I cannot show this—perhaps simply because I can think of nothing more obvious to use as a reasonable premise from which to show it. And if my wife raises no question of whether my answer is correct, I can know the answer even if I cannot show—without obtaining further grounds for this answer—that if she says it is wrong, then she is wrong.

In the context of thinking about skepticism, it is easy to forget that knowing something does not require being able to show that one knows it. For we are likely to be trying to defend, against a skeptical onslaught, the commonsense view that there is much knowledge, and we easily think of defending this view as requiring us to *show* that there is knowledge. A *negative defense of common sense*, however, one that shows that skeptical arguments do not justify the skeptic's conclusion, does not require that second-order task. It requires only showing that skepticism provides no good argument against common sense. And I do not see that skepticism does provide one. Why, for instance, should the skeptic's merely suggesting a possible explanation of how there could be no blue spruce before me, without giving any reason for thinking the explanation is correct, require me to know, or be in a position to know, that it *is* not correct? On balance, then, I reject the backup principle.

DEDUCIBILITY AND EPISTEMIC TRANSMISSION

When we come to the problem of induction, it seems clear that one assumption the skeptic is making is that if we believe something on the basis of one or more premises, then we can know it on the basis of those premises only if it follows from them, in the sense that they entail it. Call this the *entailment principle*. It says in effect that knowledge can be transmitted only deductively.

But why should we accept this? Not simply because inductive reasoning is "invalid"; for that term may be held to be improperly applied to it: inductive reasoning is strong or weak, probable or otherwise, but does not even "aim" at validity. Even if it may be properly said to be (deductively) invalid, however, that may be considered an uncontroversial technical point about its logical classification. So conceived, the point does not imply either that knowledge of the premises of inductive reasoning cannot ground knowledge of its conclusions, or that justified beliefs of those premises cannot ground justified beliefs of their conclusions.

One might, on the other hand, accept the entailment principle and argue that when properly spelled out inductive reasoning can be replaced by valid deductive reasoning. For instance, suppose we add, as an overarching premise in inductive reasoning, the plausible principle that nature is uniform. From this principle, *together with* the premise that the sun always has risen each day it apparently does follow that it will rise tomorrow. But what entitles us to the premise that nature is uniform? Hume would reply that it is not knowable a priori, and that to say that we know it through experience—which would require our depending on inductive reasoning—would beg the question against him. (For on Hume's view, if the principle is grounded in premises that only inductively support it, it is not known.) I believe that this Humean response is correct. The problem of induction must be approached differently.

What perhaps above all makes the entailment principle plausible is the thought that if our premises could be *true* and yet our conclusion *might be false*, then we cannot *know* (or even justifiably believe) the conclusion on the basis of those premises. At first, this thought may sound like just another formulation of the entailment principle. It is not; it is different and considerably stronger, and that is partly why it seems to support the entailment principle. The 'might' in question is epistemic; it is like a physician's in 'Those stomach pains might mean cancer'. This suggests not only that for all we know they do mean cancer but also that there is reason for at least some degree of suspicion that there is cancer and perhaps some need to rule it out. It is not merely a statement of a bare *logical possibility* of cancer—a statement that cancer is possible without contradiction—based, say, on no one's being absolutely immune to it. If that statement represents all we know about the case, we are not entitled to say that the pains might mean cancer. Similarly, it is not a logical impossibility that the Golden Gate Bridge levitate far above the waters; but we would be quite unjustified in saying that it *might*.

This distinction between *epistemic possibility*—what is expressed by the epistemic 'might' just illustrated—and mere logical possibility bears importantly on the problem of induction. It is true that *if*, no matter how good inductive reasoning is, its premises could be true and yet its conclusion might, in the epistemic sense, be false, perhaps we cannot know the conclusion on the basis of them. But is this generally the case with inductive reasoning? I cannot see that it is.

Moreover, suppose it could be true that, relative to its premises, the conclusion of inductive reasoning might, in the epistemic sense, be false, what reason is there to think that this really is true? Skeptics cannot justifiably argue for this claim as they sometimes do. maintaining, simply on the ground that the premises do not entail the conclusion, that the conclusion *might* be false. Arguing in this way is rather like saving, of just any stomachache a child gets after eating too much Halloween candy, that it might mean cancer. It is barely possible that, relative to all we know or are justified in believing about the child, it means cancer. But from that bare possibility we may not *automatically* conclude that cancer *is* epistemically possible—roughly, that relative to all we know or are justified in believing, we are unjustified in *dis*believing that the stomachache might mean cancer. Nor does this bare possibility rule out our knowing, on inductive grounds, that overeating is the cause.

There are other reasons for the attractiveness of the entailment principle, at least from a skeptical point of view. If one embraces the infallibility principle, one is in fact *committed* to the entailment principle. For suppose that, from known—and hence on this view infallibly believed—premises, one inductively derives a belief which is not itself infallible, as (empirical) beliefs which are inferentially grounded normally are not. Since inductive transmission allows inference of a false conclusion from true premises, the belief one derives *could*, as far as sheer logic goes, be false despite the truth of its inductive premises *and* one's infallibly believing them. But then, being fallible, the belief of the conclusion would not be knowledge. Thus, knowledge can be inferentially transmitted only by deductive inference. *Only valid deduction inferentially preserves infallibility.*

If one thinks of knowledge as entailing absolute certainty, one might again be drawn to the entailment principle. For even if a fallible belief can be absolutely certain, a belief that is only inductively based on it will presumably be at least a bit less certain and thus nor absolutely certain, since its truth is implied by that of the original belief only with some (perhaps high) degree of probability, rather than with absolute certainty. To see this, suppose that the premise belief only minimally meets the standard for absolute certainty. Then a belief inductively grounded on it can fall below that standard and thereby fail to be knowledge. Hence, again the skeptic will argue that only deduction is sufficient to transmit knowledge. But we have already seen reason to doubt both the infallibility principle and the view that a belief constitutes knowledge only if it is absolutely certain. Indeed, I do not see that skeptics give us good reason to believe either these principles or the entailment principle. It does not follow that the principles are, as they appear to be, false; but if there is no good reason to believe them, even skeptics would approve of our refusing to accept them. Absolute certainty is a high, and in some ways beautiful, ideal; but it is neither adequate to the concept of knowledge nor appropriate to the human condition....

REFUTATION AND REBUTTAL

Have I, then, *refuted* skepticism, even in the few forms considered here? I have not tried to. That would require showing that skepticism is wrong, which would entail showing that there *is* knowledge (and justified belief). What I have tried to do is to *rebut* skepticism in certain plausible forms, to show that the arguments for those skeptical views do not establish that we do not have knowledge (and justified belief). Now suppose I have succeeded. Where do we stand? May we believe that we have knowledge, or may we only suspend judgment both on this and on skeptical claims that we do not?

I have already argued, by implication, that one *can* know something without knowing that one knows it. For instance, in arguing that much of our knowledge is not self-conscious, I indicated how I can know that there is a blue spruce before me without even believing that I know this; I do not even form such self conscious beliefs in most everyday situations. Moreover, toddlers who do not even understand what knowledge is—and so are not in a position to believe they *know* anything—can apparently know such simple things as that Mama is before them. Note, too, that even if I did know that I know the spruce is there, I surely would not possess—if it is even possible for me to possess—the infinite series of beliefs required by the view that knowing entails knowing that one knows: the series that continues with my knowing that I know that I know; knowing that I know, that I know that I know, and so forth. Given these and related points, it would be a mistake to think, as some skeptics might like us to, that if we do not know that we have knowledge, then we do not; and this, in turn, opens up the possibility that we might be justified in believing that we have knowledge even if we are properly unwilling to claim that we know we do....

Might there be a way, however, to give a cogent *positive defense of common sense*: to show that we have knowledge, even of the external world? And could we establish this second-order thesis even to the satisfaction of some skeptics? To be sure, there is no satisfying a *radical skeptic*, one who denies that there can be *any* knowledge or justified belief (including justification of that very claim, which the skeptic simply asserts as a challenge). For nothing one presents as a reason for asserting something will be counted as justifying it. But could anything be said that might be plausible to a *moderate skeptic*: one who holds, say, that although transmission of justification and knowledge must be deductive, we may justifiably believe, and perhaps know, at least self-evident propositions and propositions about our present consciousness? Even if the answer is negative, perhaps one can show that there is knowledge, or at least justified belief, whether any skeptics would find one's argument plausible or not.

CHAPTER 2

THE NATURE AND VALUE OF KNOWLEDGE

2.1 Knowledge as Justified True Belief

PLATO

Plato (427?–347 BCE) lived and taught in Athens. Most of his surviving works have the form of fictitious dialogues between Socrates (who had been his teacher) and other Greek contemporaries.

Soc: Suppose a jury has been justly persuaded of some matter which only an eye-witness could know, and which cannot otherwise be known; suppose they come to their decision upon hearsay, forming a true judgement: then they have decided the case without knowledge, but, granted they did their job well, being correctly persuaded?

Theaet: Yes, certainly.

Soc: But, my dear lad, they couldn't have done that if true judgement is the same thing as knowledge; in that case the best juryman in the world couldn't form a correct judgement without knowledge. So it seems they must be different things.

Theaet: Oh, yes, Socrates, that's just what I once heard a man say; I had forgotten, but now it's coming back to me. He said that it is true judgement with an account[1] that is knowledge; true judgement without an account falls outside of knowledge. And he said that the things of which there is no account are not knowable (yes, he actually called them that), while those which have an account are knowable.

Soc: Very good indeed. Now tell me, how did he distinguish these knowables and unknowables? I want to see if you and I have heard the same version.

Theaet: I don't know if I can find that out; but I think I could follow if someone explained it.

Soc: Listen then to a dream in return for a dream. In my dream, too, I thought I was listening to people saying that the primary elements, as it were, of which we and everything else are composed, have no account. Each of them, in itself, can only be named; it is not possible to say anything else of it, either that it is or that it is not. That would mean that we were adding being or not-being to it; whereas we must not attach anything, if we are to speak of that thing itself alone. Indeed we ought not to apply to it even such words as "itself" or "that," "each," "alone," or "this," or any other of the many words of this kind; for these go the round and are applied to all things alike, being other than the things to which they are added, whereas if it were possible to express the element itself and it had its own

proprietary account, it would have to be expressed without any other thing. As it is, however, it is impossible that any of the primaries should be expressed in an account; it can only be named, for a name is all that it has. But with the things composed of these, it is another matter. Here, just in the same way as the elements themselves are woven together, so their names may be woven together and become an account of something—an account being essentially a complex of names. Thus the elements are unaccountable and unknowable, but they are perceivable, whereas the complexes are both knowable and expressible and can be the objects of true judgement.

Now when a man gets a true judgement about something without an account, his soul is in a state of truth as regards that thing, but he does not know it; for someone who cannot give and take an account of a thing is ignorant about it. But when he has also got an account of it, he is capable of all this and is made perfect in knowledge. Was the dream you heard the same as this or a different one?

Theaet: No, it was the same in every respect.

Soc: Do you like this then, and do you suggest that knowledge is true judgement with an account?

Theaet: Yes, certainly.

Soc: Theaetetus, can it be that all in a moment, you and I have today laid hands upon something which many a wise man has searched for in the past—and gone grey before he found it?

Theaet: Well, it does seem to me anyway, Socrates, that what has just been said puts the matter very well.

Soc: And it seems likely enough that the matter is really so; for what knowledge could there be apart from an account and correct judgement? …

Soc: We wanted to see what can be meant by the proposition that it is in the addition of an account to a true judgement that knowledge is perfected.

Theaet: Well yes, we must try to see that.

Soc: Come then, what are we intended to understand by an "account"? I think it must be one of three meanings.

Theaet: What are they?

Soc: The first would be, making one's thought apparent vocally by means of words and verbal expressions—when a man impresses an image of his judgement upon the stream of speech, like reflections upon water or in a mirror. Don't you think this kind of thing is an account?

Theaet: Yes, I do. At least, a man who does this is said to be giving an account.[2]

Soc: But isn't that a thing that everyone is able to do more or less readily—I mean, indicate what he thinks about a thing, if he is not deaf or dumb to begin with? And that being so, anyone at all who makes a correct judgement will turn out to have it "together with an account"; correct judgement without knowledge will no longer be found anywhere.

Theaet: True.

Soc: Well then, we mustn't be too ready to condemn the author of the definition of knowledge now before us for talking nonsense. Perhaps he didn't mean this; perhaps he meant being able, when questioned about what a thing is, to give an answer by reference to its elements.

Theaet: As for example, Socrates?

Soc: As for example, what Hesiod is doing when he says "One hundred are the timbers of a wagon."[3] Now I couldn't say what they are; and I don't suppose you could either. If you and I were asked what a wagon is, we should be satisfied if we could answer, "Wheels, axle, body, rails, yoke."

Theaet: Yes, surely.

Soc: But he might think us ridiculous, just as he would if we were asked what your name is, and replied by giving the syllables. In that case, he would think us ridiculous because although we might be correct in our judgement and our expression of it, we should be fancying ourselves as scholars, thinking we knew and were expressing a scholar's account of Theaetetus' name. Whereas in fact no one gives an account of a thing with knowledge till, in addition to his true judgement, he goes right through the thing element by element—as I think we said before.

Theaet: We did, yes.

Soc: In the same way, in the example of the wagon, he would say that we have indeed correct judgement; but it is the man who can explore its being by going through those hundred items who has made the addition which adds an account to his true judgement. It is this man who has passed from mere judgement to expert knowledge of the being of a wagon; and he has done so in virtue of having gone over the whole by means of the elements.

Theaet: And doesn't that seem sound to you, Socrates?

Soc: Well, tell me if it seems sound to you, my friend. Tell me if you are prepared to accept the view that an account is a matter of going through a thing element by element, while going through it by "syllables" or larger divisions falls short of being an account. Then we shall be able to discuss it.

Theaet: I'm certainly prepared to accept that.

Soc: And do you at the same time think that a man has knowledge of anything when he believes the same thing now to be part of one thing and now part of something else? Or when he judges that now one thing and now something different belongs to one and the same object?

Theaet: No, indeed I don't.

Soc: Then have you forgotten that at first when you were learning to read and write that is just what you and the other boys used to do?

Theaet: You mean we used to think that sometimes one letter and sometimes another belonged to the same syllable, and used to put the same letter sometimes into its proper syllable and sometimes into another?

Soc: Yes, that is what I mean.

Theaet: Well, I certainly haven't forgotten; and I don't think people at that stage can be said to have knowledge yet.

Soc: Well, suppose now that someone who is at this sort of stage is writing the name "Theaetetus"; he thinks he ought to write THE and does so. Then suppose another time he is trying to write "Theodorus," and this time he thinks he should write TE and proceeds to do so. Are we going to say that he knows the first syllable of your names?

Theaet: No. We've admitted that anyone who is at that stage has not yet knowledge.

Soc: And is there anything to prevent the same person being in that situation as regards the second and third and fourth syllables?

Theaet: No, nothing.

Soc: Now at the time when he does this, he will be writing "Theaetetus" not only with correct judgement, but with command of the way through its letters; that must be so whenever he writes them out one after another in their order.

Theaet: Yes, clearly.

Soc: And still without knowledge though with correct judgement—isn't that our view?

Theaet: Yes.

Soc: Yet possessing an account of it along with his correct judgement. He was writing it, you see, with command of the way through its letters; and we agreed that that is an account.

Theaet: True.

Soc: So here, my friend, we have correct judgement together with an account, which we are not yet entitled to call knowledge.

Theaet: Yes, I'm afraid that's so.

Soc: So it was only the poor man's dream of gold that we had when we thought we had got the truest account of knowledge. Or is it early days to be harsh? Perhaps this is not the way in which one is to define "account." We said that the man who defines knowledge as correct judgement together with an account would choose one of three meanings for "account." Perhaps the last is the one to define it by.

Theaet: Yes, you're right to remind me; there is one possibility still left. The first was a kind of vocal image of thought; the one we have just discussed was the way to the whole through the elements. Now what's your third suggestion?

Soc: What the majority of people would say—namely, being able to tell some mark by which the object you are asked about differs from all other things.

Theaet: Can you give me an example of such an "account" of something?

Soc: Well, take the sun, if you like. You would be satisfied, I imagine, with the answer that it is the brightest of the bodies that move round the earth in the heavens.

Theaet: Oh yes, quite.

Soc: Now I want you to get hold of the principle that this illustrates. It is what we were just saying—that if you get hold of the difference that distinguishes a thing from everything else, then, so some people say, you will have got an account of it. On the other hand, so long as it is some common feature that you grasp, your account will be about all those things which have this in common.

Theaet: I see; I think it's very good to call this kind of thing an account.

Soc: Then if a man with correct judgement about any one of the things that are grasps in addition its difference from the rest, he has become a knower of the thing he was a judger of before.

Theaet: That's our present position, anyway.

Soc: Well, at this point, Theaetetus, as regards what we are saying, I'm for all the world like a man looking at a shadow-painting when I'm close up to it I can't take it in in the least, though when I stood well back from it, it appeared to me to have some meaning.

Theaet: How's that?

Soc: I'll see if I can explain. Suppose I have formed a correct judgement about you; if I can grasp your account in addition, I know you, but if not, I am merely judging.

Theaet: Yes.

Soc: And an account was to be a matter of expounding your differentness?

Theaet: That is so.

Soc: Then when I was merely judging, my thought failed to grasp any point of difference between you and the rest of mankind?

Theaet: Apparently.

Soc: What I had in mind, it seems, was some common characteristic—something that belongs no more to you than to anybody else.

Theaet: Yes, that must be so.

Soc: Then tell me, in Heaven's name how, if that was so, did it come about that you were the object of my judgement and nobody else? Suppose my thought is that "This is Theaetetus—one who is a human being, and has a nose and eyes and mouth," and so on through the whole list of limbs. Will this thought cause me to be thinking of Theaetetus rather than of Theodorus, or of the proverbial "remotest Mysian"?

Theaet: No, how could it?

Soc: But suppose I think not merely of "the one with nose and eyes," but of "the one with a snub nose and prominent eyes." Shall I even then be judging about you any more than about myself or anyone who is like that?

Theaet: Not at all.

Soc: It will not, I take it, be Theaetetus who is judged in my mind until this snub-nosedness of yours has left imprinted and established in me a record that is different in some way from the other snub-nosednesses I have seen; and so with the other details of your make-up. And this will remind me, if I meet you tomorrow, and make me judge correctly about you.

Theaet: That's perfectly true.

Soc: Then correct judgement also must be concerned with the differentness of what it is about?

Theaet: So it seems, anyway.

Soc: Then what more might this "adding an account to correct judgement" be? If, on the one hand, it means that we must make another judgement about the way in which a thing differs from the rest of things, we are being required to do something very absurd.

Theaet: How's that?

Soc: Because we already have a correct judgement about the way a thing differs from other things; and we are then directed to add a correct judgement about the way it differs from other things. At that rate, the way a roller goes round or a pestle or anything else proverbial would be nothing compared with such directions; they might be more justly called a matter of "the blind leading the blind." To tell us to add what we already have, in order to come to know what we are judging about, bears a generous resemblance to the behaviour of a man benighted.

Theaet: Whereas if, on the other hand,...? What else were you going to suggest when you started this enquiry just now?

Soc: Well, if "adding an account" means that we are required to get to *know* the differentness, not merely judge it, this most splendid of our accounts of knowledge turns out to be a very amusing affair. For getting to know of course is acquiring knowledge, isn't it?

Theaet: Yes.

Soc: So, it seems, the answer to the question "What is knowledge?" will be "Correct judgement accompanied by *knowledge* of the differentness"—for this is what we are asked to understand by the "addition of an account."

Theaet: Apparently so.

Soc: And it is surely just silly to tell us, when we are trying to discover what knowledge is, that it is correct judgement accompanied by *knowledge,* whether of differentness or of anything else? And so, Theaetetus, knowledge is neither perception nor true judgement, nor an account added to true judgement.

Theaet: It seems not.

Soc: Well now, dear lad, are we still pregnant, still in labour with any thoughts about knowledge? Or have we been delivered of them all?

Theaet: As far as I'm concerned, Socrates, you've made me say far more than ever was in me, Heaven knows.

Soc: Well then, our art of midwifery tells us that all of these offspring are wind-eggs and not worth bringing up?

Theaet: Undoubtedly.

Soc: And so, Theaetetus, if ever in the future you should attempt to conceive or should succeed in conceiving other theories, they will be better ones as the result of this enquiry. And if you remain barren, your companions will find you gentler and less tiresome; you will be modest and not think you know what you don't know. This is all my art can achieve—nothing more. I do not know any of the things that other men know—the great and inspired men of today and yesterday. But this art of midwifery my mother and I had allotted to us by God; she to deliver women, I to deliver men that are young and generous of spirit, all that have any beauty. And now I must go to the King's Porch to meet the indictment that Meletus has brought against me; but let us meet here again in the morning.

NOTES

1. "Account" translates *logos*.
2. "Giving an account" here translates *legein*, the ordinary Greek word for "say, speak, speak of,"

which corresponding to *logos* in its wider meanings "speech, discourse, statement."

3. Hesiod, *Works and Days* 456.

2.2 Is Justified True Belief Knowledge?

EDMUND GETTIER

Edmund Gettier, now retired, taught metaphysics and epistemology for several decades at the University of Massachusetts.

Various attempts have been made in recent years to state necessary and sufficient conditions for someone's knowing a given proposition. The attempts have often been such that they can be stated in a form similar to the following:[1]

(a) S knows that P *IFF**
  (i) P is true,
  (ii) S believes that P, and
  (iii) S is justified in believing that P.

For example, Chisholm has held that the following gives the necessary and sufficient conditions for knowledge:[2]

(b) S knows that P *IFF*
  (i) S accepts P,
  (ii) S has adequate evidence for P, and
  (iii) P is true.

Ayer has stated the necessary and sufficient conditions for knowledge as follows:[3]

(c) S knows that P *IFF*
  (i) P is true,
  (ii) S is sure that P is true, and
  (iii) S has the right to be sure that P is true.

I shall argue that (a) is false in that the conditions stated therein do not constitute a *sufficient* condition for the truth of the proposition that S knows that P. The same argument will show that (b) and (c) fail if "has adequate evidence for" or "has the right to be sure that" is substituted for "is justified in believing that" throughout.

I shall begin by noting two points. First, in that sense of "justified" in which S's being justified in believing P is a necessary condition of S's knowing that P, it is possible for a person to be justified in believing a proposition that is in fact false. Secondly, for any proposition P, if S is justified in believing P, and P entails Q, and S deduces Q from P and accepts Q as a result of this deduction, then S is justified in believing Q. Keeping these two points in mind, I shall now present two cases in which the conditions stated in (a) are true for some proposition, though it is at the same time false that the person in question knows that proposition.

CASE I:

Suppose that Smith and Jones have applied for a certain job. And suppose that Smith has strong evidence for the following conjunctive proposition:

(d) Jones is the man who will get the job, and Jones has ten coins in his pocket.

*IFF = if and only if.—ED.

From E. Gettier, "Is Justified True Belief Knowledge?" from *Analysis,* vol. 23 (1963), pp. 121–123. Reprinted by permission of Oxford University Press.

Smith's evidence for (d) might be that the president of the company assured him that Jones would in the end be selected, and that he, Smith, had counted the coins in Jones's pocket ten minutes ago. Proposition (d) entails:

(e) The man who will get the job has ten coins in his pocket.

Let us suppose that Smith sees the entailment from (d) to (e), and accepts (e) on the grounds of (d), for which he has strong evidence. In this case, Smith is clearly justified in believing that (e) is true.

But imagine, further, that unknown to Smith, he himself, not Jones, will get the job. And, also, unknown to Smith, he himself has ten coins in his pocket. Proposition (e) is then true, though proposition (d), from which Smith inferred (e), is false. In our example, then, all of the following are true: (*i*) (e) is true, (*ii*) Smith believes that (e) is true, and (*iii*) Smith is justified in believing that (e) is true. But it is equally clear that Smith does not *know* that (e) is true; for (e) is true in virtue of the number of coins in Smith's pocket, while Smith does not know how many coins are in Smith's pocket, and bases his belief in (e) on a count of the coins in Jones's pocket, whom he falsely believes to be the man who will get the job.

CASE II:

Let us suppose that Smith has strong evidence for the following proposition:

(f) Jones owns a Ford.

Smith's evidence might be that Jones has at all times in the past within Smith's memory owned a car, and always a Ford, and that Jones has just offered Smith a ride while driving a Ford. Let us imagine, now, that Smith has another friend, Brown, of whose whereabouts he is totally ignorant. Smith selects three place-names quite at random, and constructs the following three propositions:

(g) Either Jones owns a Ford, or Brown is in Boston;

(h) Either Jones owns a Ford, or Brown is in Barcelona;

(i) Either Jones owns a Ford, or Brown is in Brest-Litovsk.

Each of these propositions is entailed by (f). Imagine that Smith realizes the entailment of each of these propositions he has constructed by (f), and proceeds to accept (g), (h), and (i) on the basis of (f). Smith has correctly inferred (g), (h), and (i) from a proposition for which he has strong evidence. Smith is therefore completely justified in believing each of these three propositions. Smith, of course, has no idea where Brown is.

But imagine now that two further conditions hold. First, Jones does *not* own a Ford, but is at present driving a rented car. And secondly, by the sheerest coincidence, and entirely unknown to Smith, the place mentioned in proposition (h) happens really to be the place where Brown is. If these two conditions hold, then Smith does *not* know that (h) is true, even though (*i*) (h) *is* true, (*ii*) Smith does believe that (h) is true, and (*iii*) Smith is justified in believing that (h) is true.

These two examples show that definition (a) does not state a *sufficient* condition for someone's knowing a given proposition. The same cases, with appropriate changes, will suffice to show that neither definition (b) nor definition (c) do so either.

NOTES

1. Plato seems to be considering some such definition at *Theaetetus* 201, and perhaps accepting one at *Meno* 98.
2. Roderick M. Chisholm, *Perceiving: a Philosophical Study*, Cornell University Press (Ithaca, NY, 1957), p. 16.
3. A. J. Ayer, *The Problem of Knowledge*, Macmillan (London, 1956), p. 34.

2.3 An Analysis of Knowledge

JAMES CORNMAN, KEITH LEHRER, AND GEORGE PAPPAS

James Cornman (1929–1978) taught at the University of Pennsylvania. He specialized in work in the philosophy of mind and the theory of knowledge.

Keith Lehrer is Regents Professor emeritus at the University of Arizona. He has written on a very wide range of topics, including issues of free will, the theory of knowledge, and aesthetics.

George Pappas, now retired, taught for many years at Ohio State University, specializing in early modern philosophy and the theory of knowledge.

Let us consider briefly what is meant by saying that a person knows something. What, then, is the ordinary sense of the word "know"? To answer this clearly, we must first specify more precisely what is being asked, for the word "know" has a great variety of uses and meanings. For example, a person might be said to know how to play golf, she might also be said to know Paris, and finally, she might be said to know that the University of San Marcos is the oldest university in the Western Hemisphere. The latter use of the word "know" is the one most directly related to the concept of truth and is the familiar object of skeptical criticism. To say that a person knows that the University of San Marcos is the oldest university in the Western Hemisphere is equivalent to saying that she knows it is true that San Marcos is the oldest in the Western Hemisphere. This sort of knowledge is sometimes called theoretical or discursive. However, the distinguishing feature of such knowledge is that truth is its object: it is knowledge of the truth.

Such knowledge claims may be formulated either by saying a person knows that X, or by saying he knows it is true that X. These two ways of stating such knowledge claims are equivalent. Thus truth is a necessary condition of such knowledge; if a person knows that something is so, then it must be true that it is so. A person may claim to know something is true when it is not; but then, contrary to his claim, he does not know. He is ignorant of the truth. For example, if a person claims to know that Harvard University is the oldest college in the United States, he would be mistaken, because this is not true. He does not know what he claims to know. We have now seen that one necessary condition of a person knowing something is that it be true. Another necessary condition is that a person must at least believe the thing in question. Obviously, a person does not know that something is true if he does not even believe it is true.

May we then simply equate knowledge with true belief? Absolutely not! To see why not, consider a person who has a hunch and thus believes that the final score of next year's Army-Navy football game will be a 21–21 tie. Moreover, suppose that the person is quite ignorant of the outcome of past contests and other relevant data. Finally, imagine that, as a mere matter of luck, he happens to be right. That it is a mere matter of luck is illustrated by the fact that he often has such hunches about the final scores of football games and is almost always wrong. His true belief about the outcome of the Army-Navy game should not be counted as knowledge. It was a lucky guess and nothing more.

How is knowledge to be distinguished from mere true belief? Most philosophers, skeptics included, have argued that whether true belief is to be counted as knowledge depends on how well justified the person is in believing what he does. The person who has a true belief about the Army-Navy game is quite unjustified, for he really has no reason or justification for believing the score will be a 21–21 tie. On the other hand, a person watching the game, who hears the final gun as play ends, is completely justified in that belief and hence knows that the final score is twenty-one points apiece. Thus, we may assume that a person lacks knowledge unless he is justified, and indeed completely justified, in believing what he does. Moreover, what will ordinarily determine whether a person is well enough justified is the quality of the evidence that forms the basis for his belief. The evidence of the person in the stands watching the game is quite adequate, whereas the evidence of the person who guesses is exceedingly paltry.

A further qualification is required. A person may be quite well justified in what she believes, even though her justification is based on some false assumption.[1] For example, if a person parks her car in a public parking lot for a few hours, she is quite well justified, when she returns to her car and does not observe any alteration, in assuming that the engine of the car remains under the hood. Of course, if someone has stolen the engine while she was away, then her belief that there is an engine under the hood falls short of knowledge simply because it is untrue that the engine is there. However, imagine that after the engine was stolen a friend came along, and, noticing the engine had been removed, arranged to have it replaced with another before the owner returned, so as to relieve her of the agony of finding her engine stolen. Then the owner will be quite correct in her belief that there is an engine under the hood of her car when she returns. Moreover, she is quite well justified in this belief as well. However, the owner's belief will be based on a false assumption, namely, that the engine that was under the hood of her car when

she left remains there now. This false assumption leads her to the true conclusion that there is an engine under her hood. But since the only justification she has for believing this is based on the false assumption, we should not say that she knows that there is an engine under the hood of her car.

We must require not only that a person be well justified in what he or she believes, but also that his or her justification not depend essentially on any false assumption; otherwise, a person cannot be said to know. This qualification may be articulated in a variety of ways. We shall require that a person be completely justified in believing something, in order to know what he or she believes is true; and also that his or her justification must be undefeated by any false assumption on which it essentially depends.

We conclude that a person knows something just in case his or her belief is true, completely justified, and the justification is undefeated. A skeptic building her case on this analysis of knowledge may argue, concerning things people commonly assume they know, either (1) that we do not even believe those things, (2) that they are not true, (3) that we are not completely justified in believing them, or (4) that our justification, though complete, is defeated by some false assumption on which it essentially depends. The most promising place for the skeptic to get a foothold is condition (3). A skeptic who wishes to defend some very extensive form of skepticism, for example, by contending we do not know that any of our perceptual beliefs are true, will do best to argue that condition (3) in the analysis is never satisfied by such beliefs. "Are we completely justified in our perceptual beliefs?" The skeptic says, "No!" and sets out to convince her dogmatic detractors of the merits of her skepticism.

NOTE

1. Edmund Gettier, "Is Justified True Belief Knowledge?" *Analysis,* 23 (1963), pp. 121–123.

2.4 Knowing How and Knowing That

GILBERT RYLE

Gilbert Ryle (1900–1976) was an English philosopher who taught at Oxford University. His book *A Concept of Mind* was influential in undermining allegiances to Cartesian dualism. He served as the editor of the important philosophy journal *Mind* for nearly a quarter century.

Philosophers have not done justice to the distinction which is quite familiar to all of us between knowing that something is the case and knowing how to do things. In their theories of knowledge they concentrate on the discovery of truths or facts, and they either ignore the discovery of ways and methods of doing things or else they try to reduce it to the discovery of facts. They assume that intelligence equates with the contemplation of propositions and is exhausted in this contemplation.

I want to turn the tables and to prove that knowledge-how cannot be defined in terms of knowledge-that and further, that knowledge-how is a concept logically prior to the concept of knowledge-that. I hope to show that a number of notorious cruces and paradoxes remain insoluble if knowing-that is taken as the ideal model of all operations of intelligence. They are resolved if we see that a man's intelligence or stupidity is as directly exhibited in some of his doings as it is in some of his thinking.

Consider, first, our use of the various intelligence-predicates, namely, "wise," "logical," "sensible," "prudent," "cunning," "skilful," "scrupulous," "tasteful," "witty," etc., with their converses "unwise," "illogical," "silly," "stupid," "dull," "unscrupulous," "without taste," "humourless," etc. What facts or what sorts of facts are known to the sensible which are not known to the silly? For example, what truths does the clever chess-player know which would be news to his stupid opponent? Obviously there is no truth or set of truths of which we could say "If only the stupid player had been informed of them, he would be a clever player," or "When once he had been apprised of these truths he would play well." We can imagine a clever player generously imparting to his stupid opponent so many rules, tactical maxims, "wrinkles," etc., that he could think of no more to tell him; his opponent might accept and memorise all of them, and be able and ready to recite them correctly on demand. Yet he might still play chess stupidly, that is, be unable intelligently to apply the maxims, etc.

The intellectualist (as I shall call him) might defend his case by objecting that the stupid player did not "really" or "fully" know these truths. He had them by heart; but this was perhaps just a set of verbal habits, like the schoolboy's rote-knowledge of the multiplication-table. If he seriously and attentively considered these truths he would then be or become a clever player. Or, to modify the suggestion to avert an obvious rejoinder, if he seriously and attentively considered these truths not just while in bed or while in church but while playing chess, and especially if he considered the maxim relevant to a tactical predicament at the moment when he was involved in that predicament, then he would make the intelligent move. But, unfortunately, if he was stupid (*a*) he would be unlikely to tell himself the appropriate maxim at the moment when it was needed and (*b*) even if by luck this

Reprinted by courtesy of the Editor of the Aristotelian Society: © 1945–1946.

maxim did occur to him at the moment when it was needed, he might be too stupid to follow it. For he might not see that it was the appropriate maxim or if he did, he might not see how to apply it. In other words it requires intelligence not only to discover truths, but also to apply them, and knowing how to apply truths cannot, without setting up an infinite process, be reduced to knowledge of some extra bridge-truths. The application of maxims, etc., is certainly not any mere contemplation of them. Equally certainly it can be intelligently or stupidly done. (This is the point where Aristotle's attempted solution of Socrates' puzzle broke down. "How can the back-slider know moral and prudential maxims and still fail to behave properly?" This is only a special case of the general problem. "How can a man be as well-informed as you please and still be a fool?" "Why is a fool not necessarily an ignoramus?")

To switch over to a different example. A pupil fails to follow an argument. He understands the premises and he understands the conclusion. But he fails to see that the conclusion follows from the premises. The teacher thinks him rather dull but tries to help. So he tells him that there is an ulterior proposition which he has not considered, namely, that *if these premises are true, the conclusion is true*. The pupil understands this and dutifully recites it alongside the premises, and still fails to see that the conclusion follows from the premises even when accompanied by the assertion that these premises entail this conclusion. So a second hypothetical proposition is added to his store; namely, that the conclusion is true if the premises are true as well as the first hypothetical proposition that if the premises are true the conclusion is true. And still the pupil fails to see. And so on forever. He accepts rules in theory but this does not *force* him to apply them in practice. He considers reasons, but he fails to reason. (This is Lewis Carroll's puzzle in "What the Tortoise said to Achilles." I have met no successful attempt to solve it.)

What has gone wrong? Just this, that knowing how to reason was assumed to be analysable into the knowledge or supposal of some propositions, namely, (1) the special premises, (2) the conclusion, plus (3) some extra propositions about the implication of the conclusion by the premises, etc., etc., *ad infinitum*.

"Well but surely the intelligent reasoner *is* knowing rules of inference whenever he reasons intelligently." Yes, of course he is, but knowing such a rule is not a case of knowing an extra fact or truth; it is knowing how to move from acknowledging some facts to acknowledging others. Knowing a rule of inference is not possessing a bit of extra information but being able to perform an intelligent operation. Knowing a rule is knowing how. It is realised in performances which conform to the rule, not in theoretical citations of it.

It is, of course, true that when people can reason intelligently, logicians can then extract the nerve of a range of similar inferences and exhibit this nerve in a logicians' formula. And they can teach it in lessons to novices who first learn the formula by heart and later find out how to detect the presence of a common nerve in a variety of formally similar but materially different arguments. But arguing intelligently did not before Aristotle and does not after Aristotle require the separate acknowledgment of the truth or "validity" of the formula. "God hath not … left it to Aristotle to make (men) rational." Principles of inference are not extra premises and knowing these principles exhibits itself not in the recitation of formulas but in the execution of valid inferences and in the avoidance, detection and correction of fallacies, etc. The dull reasoner is not ignorant; he is inefficient. A silly pupil may know by heart a great number of logicians' formulas without being good at arguing. The sharp pupil may argue well who has never heard of formal logic.

There is a not unfashionable shuffle which tries to circumvent these considerations by saying that the intelligent reasoner who has not been taught logic knows the logicians' formulas "implicitly" but not "explicitly"; or that the ordinary virtuous person has "implicit" but not "explicit" knowledge of the rules of right conduct; the skilful but untheoretical chess-player "implicitly" acknowledges a lot of strategic and tactical maxims, though he never formulates them and might not recognise them if they were imparted to him by some Clausewitz of the game. This shuffle assumes that knowledge-how must be reducible to knowledge-that, while conceding that no operations of acknowledging-that need be actually found occurring. It fails to explain how, even if such acknowledgements did occur, their maker might still be a fool in his performance.

All this intellectualist legend must be rejected, not merely because it tells psychological myths but because the myths are not of the right type to account for the facts which they are invented to explain. However many strata of knowledge that are postulated, the same crux always recurs that a fool might have all that knowledge without knowing how to perform, and a sensible or cunning person might know how to perform who had not been introduced to those postulated facts; that is, there still remains the same gulf, as wide as ever, between having the postulated knowledge of those facts and knowing how to use or apply it; between acknowledging principles in thought and intelligently applying them in action.

I must now try to speak more positively about what it is like to know-how. (*a*) When a person knows how to do things of a certain sort (e.g., make good jokes, conduct battles or behave at funerals), his knowledge is actualised or exercised in what he does. It is not exercised (save *per accidens*) in the propounding of propositions or in saying "Yes" to those propounded by others. His intelligence is exhibited by deeds, not by internal or external dicta. A good experimentalist exercises his skill not in reciting maxims of technology but in making experiments. It is a ruinous but popular mistake to suppose that intelligence operates only in the production and manipulation of propositions, i.e., that only in ratiocinating are we rational. (*b*) When a person knows how to do things of a certain sort (e.g., cook omelettes, design dresses or persuade juries), his performance is in some way governed by principles, rules, canons, standards or criteria. (For most purposes it does not matter which we say.) It is always possible in principle, if not in practice, to explain why he tends to succeed, that

is, to state the reasons for his actions. It is tautology to say that there is a method in his cleverness. But his observance of rules, principles, etc., must, if it is there at all, be realized in his performance of his tasks. It need not (though it can) be also advertised in an extra performance of paying some internal or external lip-service to those rules or principles. He *must* work judiciously; he *may* also propound judgments. For propounding judgments is just another special activity, which can itself be judiciously or injudiciously performed. Judging (or propositional thinking) is one (but only one) way of exercising judiciousness or betraying silliness; it has its own rules, principles and criteria, but again the intelligent application of these does not pre-require yet another lower stratum of judgments on how to think correctly.

In short the propositional acknowledgement of rules, reasons or principles is not the parent of the intelligent application of them; it is a stepchild of that application.

In some ways the observance of rules and the using of criteria resemble the employment of spectacles. We look through them but not at them. And as a person who looks much at his spectacles betrays that he has difficulties in looking through them, so people who appeal much to principles show that they do not know how to act.

There is a point to be expounded here. I have been arguing in effect that ratiocination is not the general condition of rational behaviour but only one species of it. Yet the traditional associations of the word "rational "are such that it is commonly assumed that behaviour can only be rational if the overt actions taken are escorted by internal operations of considering and acknowledging the reasons for taking them, i.e., if we preach to ourselves before we practise. "How else" (it would be urged) "could principles, rules, reasons, criteria, etc., govern performances, unless the agent thought of them while or before acting?" People equate rational behaviour with premeditated or reasoned behaviour, i.e., behaviour in which the agent internally persuades himself by arguments to do what he does. Among the premises of these postulated internal arguments will be the formulas expressing the principles, rules, criteria or reasons which govern the resultant intelligent actions. This whole story now seems to me false in fact and refutable in logic. We do not find in fact that we persuade ourselves by arguments to make or appreciate jokes. What sorts of arguments should we use? Yet it certainly requires intelligence or rationality to make and see jokes. But worse than this, when we do, as often happens, go through the process of persuading ourselves to do things, this process is itself one which can be intelligently or stupidly executed. So, if the assumption were correct, it would be necessary for us to start one stage further back and to persuade ourselves with second-order arguments to employ first-order persuasions of a cogent and not of a silly type. And so on *ad infinitum*. The assumption, that is, credits the rationality of any given performance to the rational execution of some anterior performance, which would in its turn require exactly the same treatment. So no rational performance could ever be begun. Aristotle's Practical Syllogism fails to explain intelligent conduct, since its explanation is circular. For the postulated syllogising would itself need to be intelligently conducted.

What has happened once again is that intellectualists have tried to explain prudence, say, or skill by reference to a piece of acknowledging-that, leaving unexplained the fact that this internal operation would itself have to be cannily executed. They have tried to explain, e.g., practical flair by reference to an intellectual process which, unfortunately for their theory, again requires flair.

...

One last point. I have, I hope, proved that knowing-how is not reducible to any sandwich of knowings-that, and that our intelligence-predicates are definable in terms of knowing-how. I now want to prove that knowing-that presupposes knowing-how.

(1) To know a truth, I must have discovered or established it. But discovering and establishing are intelligent operations, requiring rules of method, checks, tests, criteria, etc. A scientist or an historian is primarily a man who knows how to decide certain sorts of questions. Only

secondarily is he a man who has discovered a lot of facts, i.e., has achieved successes in his application of these rules, etc., (though of course he only learns how to discover through exercises in discovery. He does not begin by perfecting his method and only later go on to have successes in applying it.) A scientist, that is, is primarily a knower-how and only secondarily a knower-that. He couldn't discover any particular truths unless he knew how to discover. He could know how to discover, without making this or that particular discovery.

(2) But when I have found out something, even then irrespective of the intelligence exercised in finding it out, I can't be said to have knowledge of the fact unless I can intelligently exploit it. I mean this. I might once have satisfied myself of something, say the distance between Oxford and Henley; and I might have enshrined this in a list of road distances, such that I could on demand reel off the whole list, as I can reel off the multiplication table. So in this sense I have not forgotten what I once found out. But if, when told that Nettlebed is so far out from Henley, I cannot tell you how far Nettlebed is from Oxford, or if, when shown a local map, I can see that Oxford to Banbury is about as far as Oxford to Henley but still cannot tell you how far Oxford is from Banbury or criticise false estimates given by others, you would say that I don't know the distance any longer, i.e., that I have forgotten it or that I have stowed it away in a corner where it is not available.

Effective possession of a piece of knowledge-that involves knowing how to use that knowledge, when required, for the solution of other theoretical or practical problems. There is a distinction between the museum-possession and the workshop-possession of knowledge. A silly person can be stocked with information, yet never know how to answer particular questions.

The uneducated public erroneously equates education with the imparting of knowledge-that. Philosophers have not hitherto made it very clear what its error is. I hope I have provided part of the correction.

2.5 Meno

PLATO

Socrates: ... A man who knew the way to Larissa, or anywhere else you like, and went there and directed others would surely lead them well and correctly?—Certainly.

Socrates: What if someone had had a correct opinion as to which was the way but had not gone there nor indeed had knowledge of it, would he not also lead correctly?—Certainly.

Socrates: And as long as he has the right opinion about that of which the other has knowledge, he will not be a worse guide than the one who knows, as he has a true opinion, though not knowledge.—In no way worse.

Socrates: So true opinion is in no way a worse guide for correct action than knowledge. It is this that we omitted in our investigation of the nature of virtue, when we said that only knowledge can guide correct action, for true opinion can do so also.—So it seems.

Socrates: So correct opinion is no less useful than knowledge?

Meno: Yes, to this extent, Socrates. But the man who has knowledge will always succeed, whereas he who has true opinion will only succeed at times.

Socrates: HOW do you mean? Will he who has the right opinion not always succeed, as long as his opinion is right?

Meno: That appears to be so of necessity, and it makes me wonder, Socrates, this being the case, why knowledge is prized far more highly than right opinion, and why they are different.

Socrates: DO you know why you wonder, or shall I tell you?—By all means tell me.

Socrates: It is because you have paid no attention to the statues of Daedalus, but perhaps there are none in Thessaly.

Meno: What do you have in mind when you say this?

Socrates: That they too run away and escape if one does not tie them down but remain in place if tied down.—So what?

Socrates: To acquire an untied work of Daedalus is not worth much, like acquiring a runaway slave, for it does not remain, but it is worth much if tied down, for his works are very beautiful. What am I thinking of when I say this? True opinions. For true opinions, as long as they remain, are a fine thing and all they do is good, but they are not willing to remain long, and they escape from a man's mind, so that they are not worth much until one ties them down by [giving] an account of the reason why. And that, Meno, my friend, is recollection, as we previously agreed. After they are tied down, in the first place they become knowledge, and then they remain in place. That is why knowledge is prized higher than correct opinion, and knowledge differs from correct opinion in being tied down.

Meno: Yes, by Zeus, Socrates, it seems to be something like that.

Socrates: Indeed, I too speak as one who does not have knowledge but is guessing. However, I certainly do not think I am guessing that right opinion is a different thing from knowledge. If I claim to know anything else—and I would make that claim about few things— I would put this down as one of the things I know.—Rightly so, Socrates.

Socrates: Well then, is it not correct that when true opinion guides the course of every action, it does no worse than knowledge?— I think you are right in this too.

Socrates: Correct opinion is then neither inferior to knowledge nor less useful in directing actions, nor is the man who has it less so than he who has knowledge.—That is so.

Socrates: And we agreed that the good man is beneficent.—Yes.

From *Five Dialogues*, 2nd edition, trans. G.M.A. Grube, rev. by John Cooper (Hackett, 2002), pp. 89–91. Reprinted by permission of Hackett Publishing Company, Inc. All rights reserved.

Socrates: Since then it is not only through knowledge but also through right opinion that men are good, and beneficial to their cities when they are, and neither knowledge, nor true opinion come to men by nature but are acquired—or do you think either of these comes by nature?—I do not think so.

Socrates: Then if they do not come by nature, men are not so by nature either.—Surely not.

Socrates: As goodness does not come by nature, we inquired next whether it could be taught.—Yes.

Socrates: We thought it could be taught, if it was knowledge?—Yes.

Socrates: And that it was knowledge if it could be taught?—Quite so.

Socrates: And that if there were teachers of it, it could be taught, but if there were not, it was not teachable?—That is so.

Socrates: And then we agreed that there were no teachers of it?—We did.

Socrates: So we agreed that it was neither teachable nor knowledge?—Quite so.

Socrates: But we certainly agree that virtue is a good thing?—Yes.

Socrates: And that which guides correctly is both useful and good?—Certainly.

Socrates: And that only these two things, true belief and knowledge, guide correctly, and that if a man possesses these he gives correct guidance. The things that turn out right by some chance are not due to human guidance, but where there is correct human guidance it is due to two things, true belief or knowledge.—I think that is so.

Socrates: Now because it cannot be taught, virtue no longer seems to be knowledge?—It seems not.

Socrates: So one of the two good and useful things has been excluded, and knowledge is not the guide in public affairs.—I do not think so.

Socrates: So it is not by some kind of wisdom, or by being wise, that such men lead their cities, those such as Themistocles and those mentioned by Anytus just now? That is the reason why they cannot make others be like themselves, because it is not knowledge which makes them what they are.

Meno: It is likely to be as you say, Socrates.

Socrates: Therefore, if it is not through knowledge, the only alternative is that it is through right opinion that statesmen follow the right course for their cities. As regards knowledge, they are no different from soothsayers and prophets. They too say many true things when inspired, but they have no knowledge of what they are saying.—That is probably so.

2.6 Epistemic Good and the Good Life

LINDA ZAGZEBSKI

Linda Zagzebski is George Lynn Cross Research Professor and Kingfisher College Chair of the Philosophy of Religion at the University of Oklahoma. She has written many important works in epistemology and the philosophy of religion.

1. THE DESIRABILITY OF TRUTH

I want to look at these questions about the value of truth: (1) How does truth have value contingent upon other things we value? (2) Is truth also valuable for its own sake? (3) Is every true belief valuable all things considered? (4) What does the answer to these questions tell us about the value of knowledge?

It can be illuminating to divide the senses in which something can be good into the **desirable** and the **admirable**. The things that are desirable are the things that are good *for* us. They make us thrive as human beings. Examples include long life, health and freedom from suffering, comfort and the variety of human enjoyments, friendship and loving relationships, and using our talents in satisfying work. To say that these things are desirable is not to say that their desirability cannot be outweighed by other goods. Most desirable things are only prima facie desirable; they are not desirable at all costs. For one thing, given some set of contingent circumstances, one of these goods can conflict with another. The pleasures of a good life can harm our health; spending time with our friends can detract from creative activity; living an intellectually rich and creative life can be stressful. Living a healthy life can take time away from any of the other components of flourishing, including friends and creative activity, at least for those persons whose health requires considerable attention. Furthermore, some of these goods can conflict with morality. So to say that these goods are desirable is not to say that they are desirable in all circumstances, taking everything into consideration.

If true belief is desirable, it is desirable in the same way these other desirable aspects of a good life are desirable; it is prima facie desirable. The desirability of a given true belief can be defeated or outweighed by other features of a desirable life. We cannot spend all our time pursuing truth, so we need to forego gaining some truths for the sake of other goods. We also know that some truths can hurt us. I don't know of any rule that tells us when suffering outweighs truth, but by saying that true belief is only prima facie desirable, I mean to leave open the possibility that in particular cases, losing a truth can be better than getting it. It might even be better to have a false belief than a true one. Presumably, there are not many situations in which a false belief is better than a true one, given the strong connection between truth and the many things we care

about, but I would not rule out the possibility that there are such cases.

The second way something can be good is in the sense of the admirable. I think of the admirable as the fitting object of the emotion of admiration. Moral and intellectual virtues are admirable, as well as aesthetic qualities and excellence in any area of human practice, including sports, science, and philosophy. If true belief is good, it is good in the sense of the desirable, not the admirable. If I am right that knowledge is something like credit for true belief, it is an achievement. It is good in the sense of the admirable. So knowledge is a state in which the believer gets to something desirable by being admirable.

An important issue in moral philosophy is the relationship between a good life in these two senses. How is an admirable life, a life of virtue, related to a desirable life, a life of possession of the things that are good for us? It is desirable to be admirable. I think it can be argued that knowledge is desirable, not only because it has a desirable component—true belief, but because it is desirable to get to the truth through intellectually admirable motives and behavior. But even if I am wrong in the latter claim, it is clear that if true belief is desirable, so is knowledge. And like the other desirable goods, there is no reason to think that knowledge is good absolutely; both knowledge and true belief are only prima facie desirable. The desirability of knowledge in a particular case can be defeated or outweighed by other desirable goods such as freedom from suffering and a satisfying life.

The analogous issue in ethics is this: Can the desirability of an act that is virtuous, and hence admirable, be defeated by other features of a desirable life? The ethical question is much harder than the epistemological analogue. I think it can be argued that the desirability of acting virtuously is never defeated by other desirable goods, but it would be implausible to argue that the desirability of knowledge is never defeated by the other desirable features of a good life. Even though knowledge always has an admirable, or at least, commendable feature, not every instance of knowledge is desirable all things considered.

There might even be some objects of knowledge that are not worth knowing by anybody.

To see whether there is undesirable knowledge, let us go back to the relation between the desirability of truth and what we care about. Caring about something requires a cognitive relationship between us and the object of our caring. It is difficult to maintain a given level of caring without an input of information about the object of care. If I love the art of Duccio, I will find it hard to continue loving it if I stop looking at his paintings and learn nothing more about his art. In any case, caring about Duccio leads me to want to obtain information about his art. Presumably, I have no reason to do this obsessively because I care about a great many things more than Duccio's art, but other things being equal, the more I care, the greater the demand on me to acquire information about it. Is it good *for* me to get information about Duccio? I think it is, as long as it is good for me to care about Duccio, and I don't know why it couldn't be, given that we cannot live a good life without caring about many optional things, and I assume that caring about the art of Duccio is one of the options.

Furthermore, my caring about something puts a demand on me to get information about a lot of things that are instrumentally valuable to serving my interests in what I care about. Getting information about Duccio can serve a number of interests, some of which are nonepistemic. Maybe I want to pass an exam in an art history class or attract someone who loves art (like Woody Allen learning about Tintoretto in order to impress Julia Roberts in *Everyone Says I Love You*). Instrumental value is also a form of conditional value because the value of the means is conditional upon the value of the end we care about. As long as it can be good for someone to care about passing an exam or impressing an art expert, it is also good for him or her to care about truths that are instrumentally connected with those ends. So there are many truths that are good for us conditional upon the fact that (a) we care about certain things and (b) it is good for us to care about those things.

But surely not all true beliefs are good for us in this conditional sense. Many truths are trivial because they are about a domain we do not care about, and they are not instrumentally connected to anything we care about. Ernest Sosa gives the example of counting the grains of sand on the beach to illustrate his point that not every truth is worth having. Sosa observes that counting the grains of sand serves none of our interests. Actually, somebody *might* be interested in the number of grains of sand, and if she could get the answer with little effort, we probably would have no objection. But suppose that someone cares so much about the number of grains of sand that she is willing to spend an exorbitant amount of time in the effort to find the answer. Would we say that it is good for her to get the answer? Possibly we would, but it is more likely that we would wonder what is wrong with a person who would care so much about the trivial.

Some truths may be trivial for any being of our kind, just because we have the nature that we have. Someone who cares about the number of grains of sand on the beach may just have perverse interests for a human being. Her interests do not make believing the truth about the number of grains of sand desirable. In fact, we might think that there are two things undesirable about such a person: the triviality of her belief, and the perversity of her interest.

But for virtually any trivial truth we think of, there is some set of circumstances in which believing it and going through a long process of attempting to discover it is not trivial for somebody, and might not even be trivial for us taken collectively. I recently discovered that the ancient Greek mathematician, Archimedes (3rd cent. B.C.), wrote a treatise called *The Sand-Reckoner*, in which he devised a method for determining the upper bound for the number of grains of sand the universe theoretically could contain. (Using modern scientific notation, his answer is 8×10^{63}.) In order to make this calculation, Archimedes had to invent a method to use very large numbers since at the time, there was no method to express numbers larger than

10,000. This is an interesting example because even if you think his question and its answer were trivial, the method he had to invent to get the answer clearly was not.

But in spite of surprising cases in which the apparently trivial turns out not to be trivial, it seems likely that there are many truths that really are trivial, no matter how you look at it. Many are trivial to a particular person, and some are probably trivial to everybody. Think of all the mindless chatter to which you are subjected on a daily basis on television or at work. Even if the beliefs you pick up by these methods are true, they might not have prima facie desirability. If their desirability is conditional upon something you care about, they do not meet the condition.

There is still the possibility that every true belief is prima facie desirable simply because it is true. Maybe there is something desirable about truth itself, regardless of what we care about. To have a true belief is to have your mind aligned with some bit of reality in the right way. Possibly this is always good for us, given the kind of beings that we are. If so, every true belief is prima facie good for us. It would follow that some true beliefs are good for us because of the relationship between the belief and things we care about; these are conditional goods. But in addition, maybe all true beliefs are good for us simply because the beliefs are true; their goodness is not conditional upon anything else.

I am willing to grant that every true belief is prima facie desirable just because it is true. Nonetheless, it is very unlikely that every true belief is desirable all things considered. As we have already noted, the fact that a belief is good for us can be defeated by other things that are good for us. Even if there is some value in every true belief that is not conditional upon something we care about, it does not follow that the value it has is very great. And as long as its value is only prima facie, it can be outweighed or defeated by other things.

The inescapable conclusion is that not every true belief is desirable, all things considered. Perhaps there are some beliefs that are always desirable for everybody, all things considered,

but there are probably not many beliefs in this category. Some true beliefs are not good for us, and some true beliefs may even be bad for us. There are undesirable true beliefs. Since true beliefs are not in the category of things that are admirable, it follows that some true beliefs are not good in either sense, all things considered.

Notice what follows for the value of knowing. In an earlier chapter I argued that some form of the credit theory of knowledge is the best on offer. According to the simplest form of that theory, knowing is believing in which the agent gets credit for getting the truth. Alternatively, knowing is believing in which the agent gets to the truth through conscientious epistemic behavior. But if a given true belief is not desirable, what would be the point of giving the agent credit for it? And if some true beliefs are undesirable, it might even make more sense to say she is blamed for getting the truth than that she is praised for it. If every true belief is desirable insofar as it is true, it is desirable that the agent is credited with obtaining the truth, but the truth credited to her may not be much of a prize, and it is a prize that can be outweighed by other undesirable features of having the belief.

The same point applies to the proposal that knowing is achieving the truth through conscientious epistemic motives and acts. If some instance of truth, on balance, is not desirable, it is not clear why we should think it is desirable to achieve it by caring about the truth. If the value of a given true belief is low, then even if the value of believing it out of a love of truth is higher, how much higher can it get?

I would like to note an interpretation of the conscientiousness account of knowledge that would make it very implausible. We would not think that believing the truth is epistemically enhanced by caring about the truth of a *particular* belief when the truth of the particular belief is not desirable. Consider a case of "easy knowledge." Suppose I notice a speck of dust on the floor of the library. I believe truly that there is a speck of dust, and under ordinary circumstances in which virtuous self-trust would not require me to do a special investigation to confirm my belief, I know that there is dust. My epistemic level is enhanced by self-trust governed by a general motive of love of truth, but it would not be enhanced by a special love of truth about the cleanliness level of the library floor. If I am a cleanliness fanatic, then given my argument in an earlier chapter, I have a reason to be conscientious about my beliefs about cleanliness, but my peculiarity does not give me knowledge or enhance the epistemic status of my belief. What does give me knowledge, according to the conscientiousness theory, is getting the truth out of a general love of truth and the virtues I develop from caring about truth. Nonetheless, we are still forced to the conclusion that knowledge in a given case is not very valuable if the truth it enhances is not desirable.

This is a general problem about the value of knowledge, no matter what account of knowledge we prefer. In every definition we have considered in this book, even when the definition succeeds at identifying a feature of the belief state that makes it better than mere true belief, if truly believing some proposition is not especially good, knowing the same proposition is not especially good either, and the situation is not improved by insisting that every true belief has some value simply in virtue of being true. There is no reason to think that the value of truth in itself is very great, and whatever value it has, it can be outweighed by other features of a belief that make it undesirable all things considered.

I do not see this as an objection to any of our accounts of knowledge. The problem is not with the definitions, but with our interest in knowledge. Knowledge has received sustained attention throughout the history of philosophy largely because we assume that knowledge is a great good, important enough to be worth all that attention. But upon reflection, it appears that not every instance of knowledge is especially valuable. But surely *some* knowledge is highly desirable, and it is because of the instances of knowledge that are highly desirable that we

devote a lot of time to investigating knowledge in general.

What this means, I think, is that it is important for epistemologists to focus on *desirable truths*, not simply truths. To explain what makes a truth desirable, we can go back to what we care about individually or collectively, and that gets us a certain distance toward answering this question. We care about many things individually, and collectively we care about morality and such things as collective safety. What we individually and collectively care about upon reflection is no doubt in the domain of things we trust. Since self-trust commits us to trust in others, what we care about is subject to checks by other people we trust. If I am obsessed with the number of grains of sand on the beach and other people tell me that is a bizarre thing to care about, I probably should listen to them (unless I am Archimedes).

The issue of the limits of what we should individually and collectively care about is not a subject for epistemology, but it affects the way we think about epistemological questions. The fact that there is a distinction between desirable and undesirable truths leads to a distinction between desirable knowledge and trivial or undesirable knowledge. If we want a good life, we want a significant amount of desirable knowledge. We might even want to minimize undesirable knowledge, but I suspect that we don't need to make a special effort to do the latter.

We have already looked at cases in which the agent gets credit for the truth when the truth is not desirable. There are also cases in which she gets credit for the truth when the truth is desirable, but she does not get credit for the desirability of the truth. In other words, it may be a matter of luck that she gets a desirable truth even though it is not luck that she got a truth. It sometimes happens in scientific investigation that a researcher makes an important discovery by luck. In some of these cases, it is not luck that the researcher found out something true, but it is luck that the discovery turned out to be important.

Does a believer get more epistemic credit if she is credited with getting a desirable truth than if she is merely credited with getting the truth? I suggest that she does. If it is not accidental that she learns something desirable as well as something true, she has a higher kind of knowledge than if she gets the truth non-accidentally, but it is accidental that the truth she gets is a desirable one. The agent is in an epistemically superior state when she is aware of the desirability of the truth she pursues. Someone who accidentally discovers a truth is like Columbus who accidentally discovered America while searching for another land using erroneous calculations. Someone who is credited with getting the truth but accidentally gets a desirable truth is like Columbus would have been if he had aimed for an unknown body of land with correct calculations on how to get there. Someone who is credited with both getting the truth and getting a desirable truth is like Columbus would have been if he had had reason for believing he was headed for a major continent and used the right calculations in doing so.

Of course, epistemic credit for getting a desirable truth is only one kind of credit. It is also important that we do something with the desirable truths we acquire to make our lives and the lives of others better.

The more we care about a domain, the more conscientious we ought to be in obtaining beliefs in that domain. But unfortunately, some of the most important truths are hard to learn, so even the highly conscientious believer may get only modest results. Aristotle makes a fascinating comment related to this that I think would change the way we conduct intellectual inquiry if we took it seriously. He says that even meager knowledge of celestial things is more pleasureful than all our knowledge of the world we live in, just as a half glimpse of a person we love is more delightful than a clear and complete view of other things (*Parts of Animals* 644b32–35). Contemporary epistemologists' examples of knowledge are states whose object is clear, simple, uncontroversial, and accessible to anybody, and the focus of theoretical attention is on the

way in which we come to grasp the object of belief or the grounds for the belief, not the object itself. So the simplest cases of knowledge by perception or memory are the paradigm. These cases are the least demanding on the knower as an agent, and they make few demands on the theory that attempts to explain them.

But once we consider potential knowledge of what Aristotle calls celestial things, matters look different. The importance of the object makes the state of grasping the object valuable, even if the way in which the object is grasped is defective. In other words, as long as we get an important truth, we might not care if we get *credit* for reaching the truth. That means it might be better to merely believe something true and important than to know a more mundane matter....

The usual method of investigating knowledge is distorted in another way too because the nature of the object of knowledge might dictate the appropriate way of coming to know it. When the object is out of the ordinary, our way of coming to know it is probably also out of the ordinary. Ironically, we would not be doing epistemology at all if we were not interested in finding out how to know the things that are most important, but an investigation of empirical knowledge is probably not going to tell us much about that.

I think this is one of the reasons the epistemology of religion is so difficult. The models in general use in epistemology are usually inappropriate for the domain of religion. The same point applies to the domain of philosophy. How should a conscientious believer acquire philosophical beliefs? If there is philosophical knowledge, what theory of knowledge would account for it? I seriously doubt that we will find out by examining knowledge of perceptual objects, much less by comparing the difference between knowing and truly believing propositions about those objects.

My position is that we acquire the higher kinds of knowledge by imitating those who have it, the people we consider wise. I do not mean that we believe what they believe on their testimony, but rather that we learn how to acquire knowledge of the kinds of things they know by imitating their intellectual habits and ways of knowing. This requires trust in our ability to identify people with wisdom, as well as trust in their superior ability to acquire the most desirable kinds of knowledge. I think we do the same thing when we acquire knowledge in specialized fields: We imitate those who have mastered the field. Ways of knowing that rely only upon our own natural faculties and do not involve imitation of others are limited to very basic knowledge, what I have called "easy knowledge." Even though love of truth, like sympathy for the well-being of others, is natural, the disciplined love of truth I have called conscientiousness is learned from others.

Most of what an epistemically conscientious person does is picked up from exemplars, and I think that intellectual virtues are learned by imitation in a way that parallels the learning of the moral virtues. Learning by imitation is obvious in specialized fields such as anthropology, medicine, architecture, and gardening. There are methods developed by practitioners of each field that are transmitted to the next generation during the course of the practice of the field. The same point applies to methods of meditation and contemplation developed over many centuries by spiritually wise mentors in religious communities. With luck, imitating an exemplar of spiritual wisdom can result in high-grade knowledge, or perhaps it results in understanding, the topic of the next section.

II. UNDERSTANDING

Epistemology has been dominated by the values of certainty and understanding at different times in the history of philosophy, and the difference was reflected in the way knowledge was understood. As a rough generalization, the dominant value was certainty in eras marked by the fear of skepticism, and in those periods knowledge was closely associated with justification, since justification is what we want to defend our right to be sure. In contrast, understanding was the dominant value in those eras in which skepticism was not seen as threatening. Knowledge at those times was closely associated with explanation, since understanding is exhibited by giving an explanation.

Skepticism has had an enormous impact on modern philosophy, so it is not surprising that understanding has received little attention. One of the sad consequences of neglect of a value is fragmentation of meaning. People can mean so many different things by the word "understanding" that it is hard to identify the state that has been ignored. This can generate a vicious circle since neglect leads to fragmentation of meaning, which seems to justify further neglect and further fragmentation until eventually a concept can disappear entirely.

Fortunately, there are signs that the neglect of understanding is being remedied. In this section I want to draw attention to some interesting features of understanding, and will consider some of the ways in which understanding is good for us, perhaps better for us, in general, than knowledge.

Some philosophers think that understanding is a form of knowledge, and perhaps they are right, but I want to stress the differences between propositional knowledge and a kind of understanding that is both important and neglected. In fact, I find it doubtful that understanding in the sense I have in mind is directed at propositions at all. To take a simple example, when we get understanding from a map or a graph, do we grasp propositions? Maps, graphs, and diagrams are nonpropositional representations of something—for example, the layout of a city, the relationship between interest rates and the rate of inflation, the connection between Plato's world of Forms and the physical world, and so on. I do not deny that when someone understands something nonpropositionally there is often a propositional alternative to the nonpropositional representation. If you can explain propositionally how to get from one part of a city to another, we might think that is just as good as seeing how to get there on a map. The same point applies to explaining propositionally how one economic factor varies with another, or the relationship between Plato's two worlds. After all, *Plato* explained his theory propositionally. But it doesn't follow from that that the state of understanding something via a graph or diagram is the same state as grasping or believing a set of propositions.

It is possible that *what* is understood non-propositionally (e.g., the layout of a city) is the same part of concrete reality as what can be known propositionally. Maybe understanding and propositional knowledge are different ways of cognitively grasping the same thing. I suspect that that is true, but I also think that understanding is not just a different route to the same end. In some cases, propositional knowledge is a meager substitute for understanding—for instance, understanding a person you love. Consider also what it means to understand a work of art or music. I have a distinguished elderly friend who used to be highly musical and regularly read music scores for entertainment. He recently complained to me that he lost the ability to listen to music. He can still hear the music—that is, he can hear the sounds, but he cannot understand it anymore. What is it that he used to be able to do and no longer can? Even if it is possible to describe musical structures propositionally, I find it doubtful that a grasp of those propositions is what he lost, and it is also doubtful that a grasp of certain propositions would be an adequate substitute for what he used to be able to do while listening to music....

Understanding is connected with learning an art or skill, a *techné* [an art or skill-ed]. One gains understanding by knowing how to do something well, and this makes one a reliable person to consult in matters pertaining to the skill in question. I do not claim that every instance of understanding is connected with a *techné* in this way. Some instances of understanding are so easy that they require nothing more than simple past experience—for example, understanding a stop sign in the United States. So I think there are probably cases of "easy understanding," just as there are cases of "easy knowledge." But I am suggesting that the more interesting and significant examples of understanding are connected with skills.

This leads to the second idea, which is that understanding is not directed toward a discrete proposition, but involves grasping relations of parts to other parts and perhaps the relation of parts to a whole. Relations can be spatial, such as the relative location of sites in a city, and they can be temporal, as in a musical composition. An important kind of relation is that of cause to effect, or more generally, what Stephen Grimm calls dependency relations. Grimm proposes that understanding is fundamentally the grasp of dependency relations. It seems to me that one's mental representation of the relations one grasps can be mediated by maps, graphs, diagrams, and three-dimensional models in addition to, or even in place of, the acceptance of a series of propositions.

There is a third feature of understanding that distinguishes it from propositional knowledge and which has some interesting implications: Knowledge can be acquired by testimony, whereas understanding cannot be. A conscientious believer can obtain a true belief on the testimony of another, and given the right conditions, can thereby acquire knowledge. Of course, there are numerous issues about the conditions under which a belief acquired by testimony constitutes knowledge, but practically nobody denies that testimonial knowledge is possible. A state of knowing can be conveyed from one person to another because knowing is a form of believing and belief can be conveyed from one person to another.

Understanding cannot be transmitted in that way. In fact, understanding cannot be given to another person at all except in the indirect sense that a good teacher can sometimes recreate the conditions that produce understanding in hopes that the student will acquire it also. So if you understand how to get from the Duomo to the Uffizi in Florence by looking at a map, you can give someone else the same understanding by handing them the map and tracing the route with your finger. You can also draw diagrams and graphs, and you can play a passage of music over and over, exaggerating the patterns. But in those cases in which understanding requires the mastery of a *technê*, you cannot give someone understanding without teaching them the *technê*. Someone can learn auto mechanics or cooking or fly fishing or philosophy from another person, but they cannot acquire understanding by testimony. If my colleague believes that the leaves on his maple tree are turning bright red, he can tell me, and if I trust him, I may believe it too, and if he knows the leaves are red, I may also know it, assuming the two of us satisfy whatever conditions your theory of knowledge requires. But there is no analogous way in which he can transmit his understanding of trees to me. Unlike beliefs, understanding is not passed along from a testifier to a recipient. The person's own mind has to do the "work" of understanding.

CHAPTER 3

OUR KNOWLEDGE OF THE EXTERNAL WORLD

3.1 Appearance and Reality and the Existence of Matter

BERTRAND RUSSELL

Bertrand Russell (1872–1970) was one of the greatest philosophers of the twentieth century. His philosophical contributions ranged across many areas; he was also an important social critic. He received the Nobel Prize for literature in 1950.

I

Is there any knowledge in the world which is so certain that no reasonable man could doubt it? This question, which at first sight might not seem difficult, is really one of the most difficult that can be asked. When we have realized the obstacles in the way of a straightforward and confident answer, we shall be well launched on the study of philosophy—for philosophy is merely the attempt to answer such ultimate questions, not carelessly and dogmatically, as we do in ordinary life and even in the sciences, but critically after exploring all that makes such questions puzzling, and after realizing all the vagueness and confusion that underlie our ordinary ideas.

In daily life, we assume as certain many things which, on a closer scrutiny, are found to be so full of apparent contradictions that only a great amount of thought enables us to know what it is that we really may believe. In the search for certainty, it is natural to begin with our present experiences, and in some sense, no doubt, knowledge is to be derived from them. But any statement as to what it is that our

From B. Russell, *Problems of Philosophy*, chs. 1 and 2.

immediate experiences make us know is very likely to be wrong. It seems to me that I am now sitting in a chair, at a table of a certain shape, on which I see sheets of paper with writing or print. By turning my head I see out of the window buildings and clouds and the sun. I believe that the sun is about ninety-three million miles from the earth; that it is a hot globe many times bigger than the earth; that, owing to the earth's rotation, it rises every morning, and will continue to do so for an indefinite time in the future. I believe that, if any other normal person comes into my room, he will see the same chairs and tables and books and papers as I see, and that the table which I see is the same as the table which I feel pressing against my arm. All this seems to be so evident as to be hardly worth stating, except in answer to a man who doubts whether I know anything. Yet all this may be reasonably doubted, and all of it requires much careful discussion before we can be sure that we have stated it in a form that is wholly true.

To make our difficulties plain, let us concentrate attention on the table. To the eye it is oblong, brown, and shiny; to the touch it is smooth and cool and hard; when I tap it, it gives out a wooden sound. Anyone else who sees and feels and hears the table will agree with this description, so that it might seem as if no difficulty would arise; but as soon as we try to be more precise our troubles begin. Although I believe that the table is "really" of the same colour all over, the parts that reflect the light look much brighter than the other parts, and some parts look white because of reflected light. I know that, if I move, the parts that reflect the light will be different, so that the apparent distribution of colours on the table will change. It follows that if several people are looking at the table at the same moment, no two of them will see exactly the same distribution of colours, because no two can see it from exactly the same point of view, and any change in the point of view makes some change in the way the light is reflected.

For most practical purposes these differences are unimportant, but to the painter they are all-important: The painter has to unlearn the habit of thinking that things seem to have the colour which common sense says they "really" have, and to learn the habit of seeing things as they appear. Here we have already the beginning of one of the distinctions that cause most trouble in philosophy—the distinction between "appearance" and "reality," between what things seem to be and what they are. The painter wants to know what things seem to be, the practical man and the philosopher want to know what they are; but the philosopher's wish to know this is stronger than the practical man's and is more troubled by knowledge as to the difficulties of answering the question.

To return to the table. It is evident from what we have found, that there is no colour which preeminently appears to be *the* colour of the table, or even of any one particular part of the table—it appears to be of different colours from different points of view, and there is no reason for regarding some of these as more really its colour than others. And we know that even from a given point of view the colour will seem different by artificial light, or to a colour-blind man, or to a man wearing blue spectacles, while in the dark there will be no colour at all, though to touch and hearing the table will be unchanged. This colour is not something which is inherent in the table, but something depending upon the table and the spectator and the way the light falls on the table. When, in ordinary life, we speak of *the* colour of the table, we only mean the sort of colour which it will seem to have to a normal spectator from an ordinary point of view under usual conditions of light. But the other colours which appear under other conditions have just as good a right to be considered real; and therefore, to avoid favouritism, we are compelled to deny that, in itself, the table has any one particular colour.

The same thing applies to the texture. With the naked eye one can see the grain, but otherwise the table looks smooth and even. If we looked at it through a microscope, we should see roughnesses and hills and valleys, and all sorts of differences that are imperceptible to the naked eye. Which of these is the "real" table? We are naturally tempted to say that what we see through the microscope is more real, but that in turn would be changed by a still more powerful microscope. If, then, we cannot trust what we see with the naked eye, why should we trust what we see through a microscope? Thus, again, the confidence in our senses with which we began deserts us.

The *shape* of the table is no better. We are all in the habit of judging as to the "real" shapes of things, and we do this so unreflectingly that we come to think we actually see the real shapes. But, in fact, as we all have to learn if we try to draw, a given thing looks different in shape from every different point of view. If our table is "really" rectangular, it will look, from almost all points of view, as if it had two acute angles and two obtuse angles. If opposite sides are parallel, they will look as if they converged to a point away from the spectator; if they are of equal length, they will look as if the nearer side were longer. All these things are not commonly noticed in looking at a table, because experience has taught us to construct the "real" shape from the apparent shape, and the "real" shape is what interests us as practical men. But the "real" shape is not what we see; it is something inferred from what we see. And what we see is constantly changing in shape as we move about the room; so that here again the senses seem not to give us the truth about the table itself, but only about the appearance of the table.

Similar difficulties arise when we consider the sense of touch. It is true that the table always gives us a sensation of hardness, and we feel that it resists pressure. But the sensation we obtain depends upon how hard we press the table and also upon what part of the body we press with; thus the various sensations due to various pressures or various parts of the body cannot be supposed to reveal *directly* any definite property of the table, but at most to be signs of some property which perhaps *causes* all the sensations, but is not actually apparent in any of them. And the same applies still more obviously to the sounds which can be elicited by rapping the table.

Thus it becomes evident that the real table, if there is one, is not the same as what we immediately experience by sight or touch or hearing. The real table, if there is one, is not *immediately* known to us at all, but must be an inference from what is immediately known. Hence, two very difficult questions at once arise; namely, (1) Is there a real table at all? (2) If so, what sort of object can it be?

It will help us in considering these questions to have a few simple terms of which the meaning is definite and clear. Let us give the name of "sense-data" to the things that are immediately known in sensation: such things as colours, sounds, smells, hardnesses, roughnesses, and so on. We shall give the name "sensation" to the experience of being immediately aware of these things. Thus, whenever we see a colour, we have a sensation *of* the colour, but the colour itself is a sense-datum, not a sensation. The colour is that *of* which we are immediately aware, and the awareness itself is the sensation. It is plain that if we are to know anything about the table, it must be by means of the sense-data—brown colour, oblong shape, smoothness, etc.—which we associate with the table; but, for the reasons which have been given, we cannot say that the table is the sense-data, or even that the sense-data are directly properties of the table. Thus a problem arises as to the relation of the sense-data to the real table, supposing there is such a thing.

The real table, if it exists, we will call a "physical object." Thus we have to consider the relation of sense-data to physical objects. The collection of all physical objects is called "matter." Thus our two questions may be restated as follows: (1) Is there any such thing as matter? (2) If so, what is its nature?

The philosopher who first brought prominently forward the reasons for regarding the immediate objects of our senses as not existing independently of us was Bishop Berkeley (1685–1753). His *Three Dialogues between Hylas and Philonous, in Opposition to Sceptics and Atheists*, undertakes to prove that there is no such thing as matter at all, and that the world consists of nothing but minds and their ideas. Hylas has hitherto believed in matter, but he is no match for Philonous, who mercilessly drives him into contradictions and paradoxes, and makes his own denial of matter seem, in the end, as if it were almost common sense. The arguments employed are of very different value: Some are important and sound, others are confused or quibbling. But Berkeley retains the merit of having shown that the existence of matter is capable of being denied without absurdity, and that if there are any things that exist independently of us they cannot be the immediate objects of our sensations.

There are two different questions involved when we ask whether matter exists, and it is important to keep them clear. We commonly mean by "matter" something which is opposed to "mind," something which we think of as occupying space and as radically incapable of any sort of thought or consciousness. It is chiefly in this sense that Berkeley denies matter; that is to say, he does not deny that the sense-data which we commonly take as signs of the existence of the table are really signs of the existence of *something* independent of us, but he does deny that this something is nonmental, that it is neither mind nor ideas entertained by some mind. He admits that there must be something which continues to exist when we go out of the room or shut our eyes, and that what we call seeing the table does really give us reason for believing in something which persists even when we are not seeing it. But he thinks that this something cannot be radically different in nature from what we see, and cannot be independent of seeing altogether, though it must be independent of *our* seeing. He is thus led to regard the "real" table as an idea in the mind of God. Such an idea has the required permanence and independence of ourselves, without being—as matter would otherwise be—something quite unknowable, in the sense that we can only infer it, and can never be directly and immediately aware of it.

Other philosophers since Berkeley have also held that, although the table does not depend for its existence upon being seen by me, it does depend upon being seen (or otherwise apprehended in sensation) by *some* mind—not necessarily the mind of God, but more often the whole collective mind of the universe. This they hold, as Berkeley does, chiefly because they think there can be nothing real—or at any rate nothing known to be real except minds and their thoughts and feelings. We might state the argument by which they support their view in some such way as this: "Whatever can be thought of is an idea in the mind of the person thinking of it; therefore nothing can be thought of except ideas in minds; therefore anything else is inconceivable, and what is inconceivable cannot exist."

Such an argument, in my opinion, is fallacious; and of course those who advance it do not put it so shortly or so crudely. But whether valid or not, the argument has been very widely advanced in one form or another; and very many philosophers, perhaps a majority, have held that there is nothing real except minds and their ideas. Such philosophers are called "idealists." When they come to explaining matter, they either say, like Berkeley, that matter is really nothing but a collection of ideas, or they say, like Leibniz (1646–1716), that what appears as matter is really a collection of more or less rudimentary minds.

But these philosophers, though they deny matter as opposed to mind, nevertheless, in another sense, admit matter. It will be remembered that we asked two questions; namely, (1) Is there a real table at all? (2) If so, what sort of object can it be? Now both Berkeley and Leibniz admit that there is a real table, but Berkeley says it is certain ideas in the mind of God, and Leibniz says it is a colony of souls. Thus both of them answer our first question in the affirmative, and only diverge from the views of ordinary mortals in their answer to our second question. In fact, almost all philosophers seem to be agreed that there is a real table, they almost all agree that, however much our sense-data—colour, shape smoothness, etc.—may depend upon us, yet their occurrence is a sign of something existing independently of us, something differing, perhaps, completely from our sense-data whenever we are in a suitable relation to the real table.

Now obviously this point in which the philosophers are agreed—the view that there is a real table, whatever its nature may be is vitally important, and it will be worthwhile to consider what reasons there are for accepting this view before we go on to the further question as to the nature of the real table. Our next chapter, therefore, will be concerned with the reasons for supposing that there is a real table at all.

Before we go farther it will be well to consider for a moment what it is that we have discovered so far. It has appeared that, if we take any common object of the sort that is supposed to be known by the senses, what the senses *immediately* tell us is not the truth about the object as it is apart from us, but only the truth about certain sense-data which, so far as we can see, depend upon the relations between us and the object. Thus what we directly see and feel is merely "appearance," which we believe to be a sign of some "reality" behind. But if the reality is not what appears, have we any means of knowing whether there is any reality at all? And if so, have we any means of finding out what it is like?

Such questions are bewildering, and it is difficult to know that even the strangest hypotheses may not be true. Thus our familiar table, which has roused but the slightest thoughts in us hitherto, has become a problem full of surprising possibilities. The one thing we know about it is that it is not what it seems. Beyond this modest result, so far, we have the most complete liberty of conjecture. Leibniz tells us it is a community of souls: Berkeley tells us it is an idea in the mind of God; sober science, scarcely less wonderful, tells us it is a vast collection of electric charges in violent motion.

Among these surprising possibilities, doubt suggests that perhaps there is no table at all. Philosophy, if it cannot answer so many questions as we could wish, has at least the power of asking questions which increase the interest of the world, and show the strangeness and wonder lying just below the surface even in the commonest things of daily life.

II

In this chapter we have to ask ourselves whether, in any sense at all, there is such a thing as matter. Is there a table which has a certain intrinsic nature, and continues to exist when I am not looking, or is the table merely a product of my imagination, a dream-table in a very prolonged dream? This question is of the greatest importance. For if we cannot be sure of the independent existence of objects, we cannot be sure of the independent existence of other people's bodies, and therefore still less of other people's minds, since we have no grounds for believing in their minds except such as are derived from observing their bodies. Thus if we cannot be sure of the independent existence of objects, we shall be left alone in a desert—it may be that the whole outer world is nothing but a dream, and that we alone exist. This is an uncomfortable possibility; but although it cannot be strictly *proved* to be false, there is not the slightest reason to suppose that it is true. In this chapter we have to see why this is the case.

Before we embark upon doubtful matters, let us try to find some more or less fixed point from which to start. Although we are doubting the physical existence of the table, we are not doubting the existence of the sense-data which made us think there was a table; we are not doubting that, while we look, a certain colour and shape appear to us, and while we press, a certain sensation of hardness is experienced by us. All this, which is psychological, we are not calling in question. In fact, whatever else may be doubtful, some at least of our immediate experiences seem absolutely certain.

Descartes (1596–1650), the founder of modern philosophy, invented a method which may still be used with profit—the method of systematic doubt. He determined that he would believe nothing which he did not see quite clearly and distinctly to be true. Whatever he could bring himself to doubt, he would doubt, until he saw reason for not doubting it. By applying this method he gradually became convinced that the only existence of which he could be *quite* certain was his own. He imagined a deceitful demon, who presented unreal things to his senses in a perpetual phantasmagoria; it might be very improbable that such a demon existed, but still it was possible, and therefore doubt concerning things perceived by the senses was possible.

But doubt concerning his own existence was not possible, for if he did not exist, no demon could deceive him. If he doubted, he must exist; if he had any experiences whatever, he must exist. Thus his own existence was an absolute certainty to him. "I think, therefore I am," he said (*Cogito, ergo sum*); and on the basis of this certainty he set to work to build up again the world of knowledge which his doubt had laid in ruins. By inventing the method of doubt, and by showing that subjective things are the most certain, Descartes performed a great service to philosophy, and one which makes him still useful to all students of the subject.

But some care is needed in using Descartes' argument. "*I* think, therefore *I* am" says rather more than is strictly certain. It might seem as though we were quite sure of being the same person today as we were yesterday, and this is no doubt true in some sense. But the real Self is as hard to arrive at as the real table and does not seem to have that absolute, convincing certainty that belongs to particular experiences. When I look at my table and see a certain brown colour, what is quite certain at once is not "*I* am seeing a brown colour," but rather, "a brown colour is being seen." This of course involves something (or somebody) which (or who) sees the brown colour; but it does not of itself involve that more or less permanent person whom we call "I." So far as immediate certainty goes, it might be that the something which sees the brown colour is quite momentary, and not the same as the something which has some different experience the next moment.

Thus it is our particular thoughts and feelings that have primitive certainty. And this applies to dreams and hallucinations as well as to normal perceptions: When we dream or see a ghost, we certainly do have the sensations we think we have, but for various reasons it is held that no physical object corresponds to these sensations. Thus the certainty of our knowledge of our own experiences does not have to be limited in any way to allow for exceptional cases. Here, therefore, we have, for what it is worth, a solid basis from which to begin our pursuit of knowledge.

The problem we have to consider is this: Granted that we are certain of our own sense-data, have we any reason for regarding them as signs of the existence of something else, which we can call the physical object? When we have enumerated all the sense-data which we should naturally regard as connected with the table have we said all there is to say about the table, or is there still something else—something not a sense-datum, something which persists when we go out of the room? Common sense unhesitatingly answers that there is. What can be bought and sold and pushed about and have a cloth laid on it, and so on, cannot be a *mere* collection of sense-data. If the cloth completely hides the table, we shall derive no sense-data from the table, and therefore, if the table were merely sense-data, it would have ceased to exist, and the cloth would be suspended in empty air, resting, by a miracle, in the place where the table formerly was. This seems plainly absurd; but whoever wishes to become a philosopher must learn not to be frightened by absurdities.

One great reason why it is felt that we must secure a physical object in addition to the sense-data, is that we want the same object for different people. When ten people are sitting round a dinner-table, it seems preposterous to maintain that they are not seeing the same tablecloth, the same knives and forks and spoons and glasses. But the sense-data are private to each separate person; what is immediately present to the sight of one is not immediately present to the sight of another: They all see things from slightly different points of view, and therefore see them slightly differently. Thus, if there are to be public neutral objects, which can be in some sense known to many different people, there must be something over and above the private and particular sense-data which appear to various people.

What reason, then, have we for believing that there are such public neutral objects?

The first answer that naturally occurs to one is that, although different people may see the table slightly differently, still they all see more or less similar things when they look at the table, and the variations in what they see follow the laws of perspective and reflection of light, so that it is easy to arrive at a permanent object underlying all the different people's sense-data. I bought my table from the former occupant of my room; I could not buy *his* sense-data, which died when he went away, but I could and did buy the confident expectation of more or less similar sense-data. Thus it is the fact that different people have similar sense-data, and that one person in a given place at different times has similar sense-data, which makes us suppose that over and above the sense-data there is a permanent public object which underlies or causes the sense-data of various people at various times.

Now insofar as the above considerations depend upon supposing that there are other people besides ourselves, they beg the very question at issue. Other people are represented to me by certain sense-data, such as the sight of them or the sound of their voices, and if I had no reason to believe that there were physical objects independent of my sense-data, I should have no reason to believe that other people exist except as part of my dream. Thus, when we are trying to show that there must be objects independent of our own sense-data, we cannot appeal to the testimony of other people, since this testimony itself consists of sense-data, and does not reveal other people's experiences unless our own sense-data are signs of things existing independently of us. We must therefore, if possible, find, in our own purely private experiences, characteristics which show, or tend to show, that there are in the world things other than ourselves and our private experiences.

In one sense it must be admitted that we can never *prove* the existence of things other than ourselves and our experiences. No logical absurdity results from the hypothesis that the world consists of myself and my thoughts and feelings and sensations, and that everything else is mere fancy. In dreams a very complicated world may seem to be present, and yet on waking we find it was a delusion; that is to say, we find that the sense-data in the dream do not appear to have corresponded with such physical objects as we should naturally infer from our sense-data. (It is true that, when the physical world is assumed, it is possible to find physical causes for the sense-data in dreams: A door banging, for instance, may cause us to dream of a naval engagement. But although, in this case, there is a physical *cause* for the sense-data, there is not a physical object *corresponding* to the sense-data in the way in which an actual naval battle would correspond.) There is no logical impossibility in the supposition that the whole of life is a dream, in which we ourselves create all the objects that come before us. But although this is not logically impossible, there is no reason whatever to suppose that it is true; and it is, in fact, a less simple hypothesis, viewed as a means of accounting for the facts of our own life, than the common-sense hypothesis that there really are objects independent of us, whose actions on us causes our sensations.

The way in which simplicity comes in from supposing that there really are physical objects is easily seen. If the cat appears at one moment in one part of the room, and at another in another part, it is natural to suppose that it has moved from the one to the other, passing over a series of intermediate positions. But if it is merely a set of sense-data, it cannot have ever been in any place where I did not see it; thus we shall have to suppose that it did not exist at all while I was not looking, but suddenly sprang into being in a new place. If the cat exists whether I see it or not, we can understand from our own experience how it gets hungry between one meal and the next; but if it does not exist when I am not seeing it, it seems odd that appetite should grow during non-existence as fast as during existence. And if the cat consists only of sense-data, it cannot be *hungry,* since no hunger but my own can be a sense-datum to me. Thus the behaviour of the sense-data which represent the cat to me, though it seems quite natural when regarded as an expression of hunger, becomes utterly inexplicable when regarded as mere movements and changes of patches of colour, which are as incapable of hunger as triangle is of playing football.

But the difficulty in the case of the cat is nothing compared to the difficulty in the case of human beings. When human beings speak—that is, when we hear certain noises which we associate with ideas, and simultaneously see certain motions of lips and expressions of face—it is very difficult to suppose that what we hear is not the expression of a thought, as we know it would be if we emitted the same sounds. Of course similar things happen in dreams, where we are mistaken as to the existence of other people. But dreams are more or less suggested by what we call waking life, and are capable of being more or less accounted for on scientific principles if we assume that there really is a physical world. Thus every principle of simplicity urges us to adopt the natural view, that there really are objects other than ourselves and our sense-data which have an existence not dependent upon our perceiving them.

Of course it is not by argument that we originally come by our belief in an independent external world. We find this belief ready in ourselves as soon as we begin to reflect: It is what may be called an *instinctive* belief. We should never have been led to question this belief but for the fact that, at any rate in the case of sight, it seems as if the sense-datum itself were instinctively believed to be the independent object, whereas argument shows that the object cannot be identical with the sense-datum. This discovery, however—which is not at all paradoxical in the case of taste and smell and sound, and only slightly so in the case of touch—leaves undiminished our instinctive belief that there *are* objects *corresponding* to our sense-data. Since this belief does not lead to any difficulties, but on the contrary tends to simplify and systematize our account of our experiences, there seems no good reason for rejecting it. We may therefore admit—though with a slight doubt derived from dreams—that the external world does really

exist, and is not wholly dependent for its existence upon our continuing to perceive it.

The argument which has led us to this conclusion is doubtless less strong than we could wish, but it is typical of many philosophical arguments, and it is therefore worthwhile to consider briefly its general character and validity. All knowledge, we find, must be built up upon our instinctive beliefs, and if these are rejected, nothing is left. But among our instinctive beliefs some are much stronger than others, while many have, by habit and association, become entangled with other beliefs, not really instinctive, but falsely supposed to be part of what is believed instinctively.

Philosophy should show us the hierarchy of our instinctive beliefs, beginning with those we hold most strongly, and presenting each as much isolated and as free from irrelevant additions as possible. It should take care to show that, in the form in which they are finally set forth, our instinctive beliefs do not clash, but form a harmonious system. There can never be any reason for rejecting one instinctive belief except that it clashes with others; thus, if they are found to harmonize, the whole system becomes worthy of acceptance.

It is of course *possible* that all or any of our beliefs may be mistaken, and therefore all ought to be held with at least some slight element of doubt. But we cannot have *reason* to reject a belief except on the ground of some other belief. Hence, by organizing our instinctive beliefs and their consequences, by considering which among them is most possible, if necessary, to modify or abandon, we can arrive, on the basis of accepting as our sole data what we instinctively believe, at an orderly systematic organization of our knowledge, in which, though the *possibility* of error remains, its likelihood is diminished by the interrelation of the parts and by the critical scrutiny which has preceded acquiescence.

This function, at least, philosophy can perform. Most philosophers, rightly or wrongly, believe that philosophy can do much more than this—that it can give us knowledge, not otherwise attainable, concerning the universe as a whole, and concerning the nature of ultimate reality. Whether this be the case or not, the more modest function we have spoken of can certainly be performed by philosophy, and certainly suffices, for those who have once begun to doubt the adequacy of common sense, to justify the arduous and difficult labours that philosophical problems involve.

3.2 *Meditations on First Philosophy*

RENÉ DESCARTES

René Descartes (1596–1650) is commonly said to be the founder of modern philosophy. Among his other achievements was the invention of analytical geometry.

SYNOPSIS OF THE FOLLOWING SIX MEDITATIONS*

In the First Meditation reasons are provided which give us possible grounds for doubt about all things, especially material things, so long as we have no foundations for the sciences other than those which we have had up till now. Although the usefulness of such extensive doubt is not apparent at first sight, its greatest benefit lies in freeing us from all our preconceived opinions, and providing the easiest route by which the mind may be led away from the senses. The eventual result of this doubt is to make it impossible for us to have any further doubts about what we subsequently discover to be true.

In the Second Meditation, the mind uses its own freedom and supposes the non-existence of all the things about whose existence it can have even the slightest doubt; and in so doing the mind notices that it is impossible that it should not itself exist during this time. This exercise is also of the greatest benefit, since it enables the mind to distinguish without difficulty what belongs to itself, i.e. to an intellectual nature, from what belongs to the body. But since some people may perhaps expect arguments for the immortality of the soul in this section, I think they should be warned here and now that I have tried not to put down anything which I could not precisely demonstrate. Hence the only order which I could follow was that normally employed by geometers, namely to set out all the premises on which a desired proposition depends, before drawing any conclusions about it. Now the first and most important prerequisite for knowledge of the immortality of the soul is for us to form a concept of the soul which is as clear as possible and is also quite distinct from every concept of body; and that is just what has been done in this section. A further requirement is that we should know that everything that we clearly and distinctly understand is true in a way which corresponds exactly to our understanding of it; but it was not possible to prove this before the Fourth Meditation. In addition we need to have a distinct concept of corporeal nature, and this is developed partly in the Second Meditation itself, and partly in the Fifth and Sixth Meditations. The inference to be drawn from these results is that all the things that we clearly and distinctly conceive of as

From "Meditations on First Philosophy," in *Descartes: Selected Philosophical Writings*, translated by John Cottingham, rev. ed. (New York: Cambridge University Press, 1988), pp. 73–122. Reprinted by permission of Cambridge University Press.
*Material appearing in angle brackets is found in later translations of the *Meditations* that Descartes himself approved.

different substances (as we do in the case of mind and body) are in fact substances which are really distinct one from the other; and this conclusion is drawn in the Sixth Meditation. This conclusion is confirmed in the same Meditation by the fact that we cannot understand a body except as being divisible, while by contrast we cannot understand a mind except as being indivisible. For we cannot conceive of half of a mind, while we can always conceive of half of a body, however small; and this leads us to recognize that the natures of mind and body are not only different, but in some way opposite. But I have not pursued this topic any further in this book, first because these arguments are enough to show that the decay of the body does not imply the destruction of the mind, and are hence enough to give mortals the hope of an after-life, and secondly because the premisses which lead to the conclusion that the soul is immortal depend on an account of the whole of physics. This is required for two reasons. First, we need to know that absolutely all substances, or things which must be created by God in order to exist, are by their nature incorruptible and cannot ever cease to exist unless they are reduced to nothingness by God's denying his concurrence[1] to them. Secondly, we need to recognize that body, taken in the general sense, is a substance, so that it too never perishes. But the human body, in so far as it differs from other bodies, is simply made up of a certain configuration of limbs and other accidents[2] of this sort; whereas the human mind is not made up of any accidents in this way, but is a pure substance. For even if all the accidents of the mind change, so that it has different objects of the understanding and different desires and sensations, it does not on that account become a different mind; whereas a human body loses its identity merely as a result of a change in the shape of some of its parts. And it follows from this that while the body can very easily perish, the mind[3] is immortal by its very nature.

In the Third Meditation I have explained quite fully enough, I think, my principal argument for proving the existence of God. But in order to draw my readers' minds away from the senses as far as possible, I was not willing to use any comparison taken from bodily things. So it may be that many obscurities remain; but I hope they will be completely removed later, in my Replies to the Objections. One such problem, among others, is how the idea of a supremely perfect being, which is in us, possesses so much objective[4] reality that it can come only from a cause which is supremely perfect. In the Replies this is illustrated by the comparison of a very perfect machine, the idea of which is in the mind of some engineer. Just as the objective intricacy belonging to the idea must have some cause, namely the scientific knowledge of the engineer, or of someone else who passed the idea on to him, so the idea of God which is in us must have God himself as its cause.

In the Fourth Meditation it is proved that everything that we clearly and distinctly perceive is true, and I also explain what the nature of falsity consists in. These results need to be known both in order to confirm what has gone before and also to make intelligible what is to come later. (But here it should be noted in passing that I do not deal at all with sin, i.e. the error which is committed in pursuing good and evil, but only with the error that occurs in distinguishing truth from falsehood. And there is no discussion of matters pertaining to faith or the conduct of life, but simply of speculative truths which are known solely by means of the natural light.)[5]

In the Fifth Meditation, besides an account of corporeal nature taken in general, there is a new argument demonstrating the existence of God. Again, several difficulties may arise here, but these are resolved later in the Replies to the Objections. Finally I explain the sense in which it is true that the certainty even of geometrical demonstrations depends on the knowledge of God.

Lastly, in the Sixth Meditation, the intellect is distinguished from the imagination; the criteria for this distinction are explained; the mind is proved to be really distinct from the body, but is shown, notwithstanding, to be so closely joined to it that the mind and the body make up a kind of unit; there is a survey of all the errors which commonly come from the senses, and an explanation of how they may be avoided; and, lastly, there is a presentation of all the arguments which enable the existence of material things to be inferred. The great benefit of these arguments is not, in my view, that they prove what they establish—namely that there really is a world, and that human beings have bodies and so on—since no sane person has ever seriously doubted these things. The point is that in considering these arguments we come to realize that they are not as solid or as transparent as the arguments which lead us to knowledge of our own minds and of God, so that the latter are the most certain and evident of all possible objects of knowledge for the human intellect. Indeed, this is the one thing that I set myself to prove in these Meditations. And for that reason I will not now go over the various other issues in the book which are dealt with as they come up.

MEDITATIONS ON FIRST PHILOSOPHY

in which are demonstrated the existence of God and the distinction between the human soul and the body

FIRST MEDITATION

What can be called into doubt

Some years ago I was struck by the large number of falsehoods that I had accepted as true in my childhood, and by the highly doubtful nature of the whole edifice that I had subsequently based on them. I realized that it was necessary, once in the course of my life, to demolish everything completely and start again right from the foundations if I wanted to establish anything at all in the sciences that was stable and likely to last. But the task looked an enormous one, and I began to wait until I should reach a mature enough age to ensure that no subsequent time of life would be more suitable for tackling such inquiries. This led

me to put the project off for so long that I would now be to blame if by pondering over it any further I wasted the time still left for carrying it out. So today I have expressly rid my mind of all worries and arranged for myself a clear stretch of free time. I am here quite alone, and at last I will devote myself sincerely and without reservation to the general demolition of my opinions.

But to accomplish this, it will not be necessary for me to show that all my opinions are false, which is something I could perhaps never manage. Reason now leads me to think that I should hold back my assent from opinions which are not completely certain and indubitable just as carefully as I do from those which are patently false. So, for the purpose of rejecting all my opinions, it will be enough if I find in each of them at least some reason for doubt. And to do this I will not need to run through them all individually, which would be an endless task. Once the foundations of a building are undermined, anything built on them collapses of its own accord; so I will go straight for the basic principles on which all my former beliefs rested.

Whatever I have up till now accepted as most true I have acquired either from the senses or through the senses. But from time to time I have found that the senses deceive, and it is prudent never to trust completely those who have deceived us even once.

Yet although the senses occasionally deceive us with respect to objects which are very small or in the distance, there are many other beliefs about which doubt is quite impossible, even though they are derived from the senses—for example, that I am here, sitting by the fire, wearing a winter dressing-gown, holding this piece of paper in my hands, and so on. Again, how could it be denied that these hands or this whole body are mine? Unless perhaps I were to liken myself to madmen, whose brains are so damaged by the persistent vapours of melancholia that they firmly maintain they are kings when they are paupers, or say they are dressed in purple when they are naked, or that their heads are made of earthenware, or that they are pumpkins, or made of glass. But such people are insane, and I would be thought equally mad if I took anything from them as a model for myself.

A brilliant piece of reasoning! As if I were not a man who sleeps at night, and regularly has all the same experiences[6] while asleep as madmen do when awake—indeed sometimes even more improbable ones. How often, asleep at night, am I convinced of just such familiar events—that I am here in my dressing-gown, sitting by the fire—when in fact I am lying undressed in bed! Yet at the moment my eyes are certainly wide awake when I look at this piece of paper; I shake my head and it is not asleep; as I stretch out and feel my hand I do so deliberately, and I know what I am doing. All this would not happen with such distinctness to someone asleep. Indeed! As if I did not remember other occasions when I have been tricked by exactly similar thoughts while asleep! As I think about this more carefully, I see plainly that there are never any sure signs by means of which being awake can be distinguished from being asleep. The result is that I begin to feel dazed, and this very feeling only reinforces the notion that I may be asleep.

Suppose then that I am dreaming, and that these particulars—that my eyes are open, that I am moving my head and stretching out my hands—are not true. Perhaps, indeed, I do not even have such hands or such a body at all. Nonetheless, it must surely be admitted that the visions which come in sleep are like paintings, which must have been fashioned in the likeness of things that are real, and hence that at least these general kinds of things—eyes, head, hands and the body as a whole—are things which are not imaginary but are real and exist. For even when painters try to create sirens and satyrs with the most extraordinary bodies, they cannot give them natures which are new in all respects; they simply jumble up the limbs of different animals. Or if perhaps they manage to think up something so new that nothing remotely similar has ever been seen before—something which is therefore completely fictitious and unreal—at least the colours used in the composition must be real. By similar reasoning, although these general kinds of things—eyes, head, hands and so on—could be imaginary, it must at least be admitted that certain other even simpler and more universal things are real. These are as it were the real colours from which we form all the images of things, whether true or false, that occur in our thought.

This class appears to include corporeal nature in general, and its extension; the shape of extended things; the quantity, or size and number of these things; the place in which they may exist, the time through which they may endure,[7] and so on.

So a reasonable conclusion from this might be that physics, astronomy, medicine, and all other disciplines which depend on the study of composite things, are doubtful; while arithmetic, geometry and other subjects of this kind, which deal only with the simplest and most general things, regardless of whether they really exist in nature or not, contain something certain and indubitable. For whether I am awake or asleep, two and three added together are five, and a square has no more than four sides. It seems impossible that such transparent truths should incur any suspicion of being false.

And yet firmly rooted in my mind is the longstanding opinion that there is an omnipotent God who made me the kind of creature that I am. How do I know that he has not brought it about that there is no earth, no sky, no extended thing, no shape, no size, no place, while at the same time ensuring that all these things appear to me to exist just as they do now? What is more, just as I consider that others sometimes go astray in cases where they think they have the most perfect knowledge, how do I know that God has not brought it about that I too go wrong every time I add two and three or count the sides of a square, or in some even simpler matter, if that is imaginable? But perhaps God would not have allowed me to be deceived in this way, since he is said to be supremely good. But if it were inconsistent with his goodness to have created me such that I am deceived all the time, it would seem equally foreign to his goodness to allow me to be deceived even occasionally; yet this last assertion cannot be made.[8]

Perhaps there may be some who would prefer to deny the existence of so powerful a God rather than believe that everything else is uncertain. Let us not argue with them, but grant them that everything said about God is a fiction. According to their supposition, then, I have arrived at my present state by fate or chance or a continuous chain of events, or by some other means; yet since deception and error seem to be imperfections, the less powerful they make my original cause, the more likely it is that I am so imperfect as to be deceived all the time. I have no answer to these arguments, but am finally compelled to admit that there is not one of my former beliefs about which a doubt may not properly be raised; and this is not a flippant or ill-considered conclusion, but is based on powerful and well thought-out reasons. So in future I must withhold my assent from these former beliefs just as carefully as I would from obvious falsehoods, if I want to discover any certainty.[9]

But it is not enough merely to have noticed this; I must make an effort to remember it. My habitual opinions keep coming back, and, despite my wishes, they capture my belief, which is as it were bound over to them as a result of long occupation and the law of custom. I shall never get out of the habit of confidently assenting to these opinions, so long as I suppose them to be what in fact they are, namely highly probable opinions—opinions which, despite the fact that they are in a sense doubtful, as has just been shown, it is still much more reasonable to believe than to deny. In view of this, I think it will be a good plan to turn my will in completely the opposite direction and deceive myself, by pretending for a time that these former opinions are utterly false and imaginary. I shall do this until the weight of preconceived opinion is counterbalanced and the distorting influence of habit no longer prevents my judgement from perceiving things correctly. In the meantime, I know that no danger or error will result from my plan, and that I cannot possibly go too far in my distrustful attitude. This is because the task now in hand does not involve action but merely the acquisition of knowledge.

I will suppose therefore that not God, who is supremely good and the source of truth, but rather some malicious demon of the utmost power and cunning has employed all his energies in order to deceive me. I shall think that the sky, the air, the earth, colours, shapes, sounds and all external things are merely the delusions of dreams which he has devised to ensnare my judgement. I shall consider myself as not having hands or eyes, or flesh, or blood or senses, but as falsely believing that I have all these things. I shall stubbornly and firmly persist in this meditation; and, even if it is not in my power to know any truth, I shall at least do what is in my power,[10] that is, resolutely guard against assenting to any falsehoods, so that the deceiver, however powerful and cunning he may be, will be unable to impose on me in the slightest degree. But this is an arduous undertaking, and a kind of laziness brings me back to normal life. I am like a prisoner who is enjoying an imaginary freedom while asleep; as he begins to suspect that he is asleep, he dreads being woken up, and goes along with the pleasant illusion as long as he can. In the same way, I happily slide back into my old opinions and dread being shaken out of them, for fear that my peaceful sleep may be followed by hard labour when I wake, and that I shall have to toil not in the light, but amid the inextricable darkness of the problems I have now raised.

SECOND MEDITATION

The nature of the human mind, and how it is better known than the body

So serious are the doubts into which I have been thrown as a result of yesterday's meditation that I can neither put them out of my mind nor see any way of resolving them. It feels as if I have fallen unexpectedly into a deep whirlpool which tumbles me around so that I can neither stand on the bottom nor swim up to the top. Nevertheless I will make an effort and once more attempt the same path which I started on yesterday. Anything which admits of the slightest doubt I will set aside just as if I had found it to be wholly false; and I will proceed in this way until I recognize something certain, or, if nothing else, until I at least recognize for certain that there is no certainty. Archimedes used to demand just one firm and immovable point in order to shift the entire earth; so I too can hope for great things if I manage to find just one thing, however slight, that is certain and unshakeable.

I will suppose then, that everything I see is spurious. I will believe that my memory tells me lies, and that none of the things that it reports ever happened. I have no senses. Body, shape, extension, movement and place are chimeras. So what remains true? Perhaps just the one fact that nothing is certain.

Yet apart from everything I have just listed, how do I know that there is not something else which does not allow even the slightest occasion for doubt? Is there not a God, or whatever I may call him, who puts into me[11] the thoughts I am now having? But why do I think this, since I myself may perhaps be the author of these thoughts? In that case am not I, at least, something? But I have just said that I have no senses and no body. This is the sticking point: what follows from this? Am I not so bound up with a body and with senses that I cannot exist without them? But I have convinced myself that there is absolutely nothing in the world, no sky, no earth, no minds, no bodies. Does it now follow that I too do not exist? No: if I convinced myself of something[12] then I certainly existed. But there is a deceiver of supreme power and cunning who is deliberately and constantly deceiving me. In that case I too undoubtedly exist, if he is deceiving me; and let him deceive me as much as he can, he will never bring it about that I am nothing so long as I think that I am something. So after considering everything very thoroughly, I must finally conclude that this proposition, *I am, I exist,* is necessarily true whenever it is put forward by me or conceived in my mind.

But I do not yet have a sufficient understanding of what this 'I' is, that now necessarily exists. So I must be on my guard against carelessly taking something else to be this 'I', and so

making a mistake in the very item of knowledge that I maintain is the most certain and evident of all. I will therefore go back and meditate on what I originally believed myself to be, before I embarked on this present train of thought. I will then subtract anything capable of being weakened, even minimally, by the arguments now introduced, so that what is left at the end may be exactly and only what is certain and unshakeable.

What then did I formerly think I was? A man. But what is a man? Shall I say 'a rational animal'? No; for then I should have to inquire what an animal is, what rationality is, and in this way one question would lead me down the slope to other harder ones, and I do not now have the time to waste on subtleties of this kind. Instead I propose to concentrate on what came into my thoughts spontaneously and quite naturally whenever I used to consider what I was. Well, the first thought to come to mind was that I had a face, hands, arms and the whole mechanical structure of limbs which can be seen in a corpse, and which I called the body. The next thought was that I was nourished, that I moved about, and that I engaged in sense-perception and thinking; and these actions I attributed to the soul. But as to the nature of this soul, either I did not think about this or else I imagined it to be something tenuous, like a wind or fire or ether, which permeated my more solid parts. As to the body, however, I had no doubts about it, but thought I knew its nature distinctly. If I had tried to describe the mental conception I had of it, I would have expressed it as follows: by a body I understand whatever has a determinable shape and a definable location and can occupy a space in such a way as to exclude any other body; it can be perceived by touch, sight, hearing, taste or smell, and can be moved in various ways, not by itself but by whatever else comes into contact with it. For, according to my judgement, the power of self-movement, like the power of sensation or of thought, was quite foreign to the nature of a body; indeed, it was a source of wonder to me that certain bodies were found to contain faculties of this kind.

But what shall I now say that I am, when I am supposing that there is some supremely powerful and, if it is permissible to say so, malicious deceiver, who is deliberately trying to trick me in every way he can? Can I now assert that I possess even the most insignificant of all the attributes which I have just said belong to the nature of a body? I scrutinize them, think about them, go over them again, but nothing suggests itself; it is tiresome and pointless to go through the list once more. But what about the attributes I assigned to the soul? Nutrition or movement? Since now I do not have a body, these are mere fabrications. Sense-perception? This surely does not occur without a body, and besides, when asleep I have appeared to perceive through the senses many things which I afterwards realized I did not perceive through the senses at all. Thinking? At last I have discovered it—thought; this alone is inseparable from me. I am, I exist—that is certain. But for how long? For as long as I am thinking. For it could be that were I totally to cease from thinking, I should totally cease to exist. At present I am not admitting anything except what is necessarily true. I am, then, in the strict sense only a thing that thinks;[13] that is, I am a mind, or intelligence, or intellect, or reason—words whose meaning I have been ignorant of until now. But for all that I am a thing which is real and which truly exists. But what kind of a thing? As I have just said—a thinking thing.

What else am I? I will use my imagination.[14] I am not that structure of limbs which is called a human body. I am not even some thin vapour which permeates the limbs—a wind, fire, air, breath, or whatever I depict in my imagination; for these are things which I have supposed to be nothing. Let this supposition stand;[15] for all that I am still something. And yet may it not perhaps be the case that these very things which I am supposing to be nothing, because they are unknown to me, are in reality identical with the 'I' of which I am aware? I do not know, and for the moment I shall not argue the point, since I can make judgements only about things which are known to me. I know that I exist; the question is, what is this 'I' that I know? If the 'I' is understood strictly as we have been taking it, then it is quite certain that knowledge of it does not depend on things of whose existence I am as yet unaware; so it cannot depend on any of the things which I invent in my imagination. And this very word 'invent' shows me my mistake. It would indeed be a case of fictitious invention if I used my imagination to establish that I was something or other; for imagining is simply contemplating the shape or image of a corporeal thing. Yet now I know for certain both that I exist and at the same time that all such images and, in general, everything relating to the nature of body, could be mere dreams <and chimeras>. Once this point has been grasped, to say 'I will use my imagination to get to know more distinctly what I am' would seem to be as silly as saying 'I am now awake, and see some truth; but since my vision is not yet clear enough, I will deliberately fall asleep so that my dreams may provide a truer and clearer representation.' I thus realize that none of the things that the imagination enables me to grasp is at all relevant to this knowledge of myself which I possess, and that the mind must therefore be most carefully diverted from such things[16] if it is to perceive its own nature as distinctly as possible.

But what then am I? A thing that thinks. What is that? A thing that doubts, understands, affirms, denies, is willing, is unwilling, and also imagines and has sensory perceptions.

This is a considerable list, if everything on it belongs to me. But does it? Is it not one and the same 'I' who is now doubting almost everything, who nonetheless understands some things, who affirms that this one thing is true, denies everything else, desires to know more, is unwilling to be deceived, imagines many things even involuntarily, and is aware of many things which apparently come from the senses? Are not all these things just as true as the fact that I exist, even if I am asleep all the time, and even if he who created me is doing all he can to deceive me? Which of all these activities is distinct from my thinking? Which of them can be said to be separate from myself? The fact that it is I who am doubting and understanding and willing is so evident that I see no way of making it any clearer. But it is also the case that the 'I' who imagines is the same 'I'. For even if, as I have supposed, none of the objects of imagination are real, the power of imagination is something which really exists and is part of my thinking. Lastly, it is also the same 'I' who has sensory perceptions, or is aware of bodily things as it were through the senses. For example, I am now seeing light, hearing a noise, feeling heat. But I am asleep, so all this is false. Yet I certainly *seem* to see, to hear, and to be warmed. This cannot be false; what is called 'having a sensory perception' is strictly just this, and in this restricted sense of the term it is simply thinking.

From all this I am beginning to have a rather better understanding of what I am. But it still appears—and I cannot stop thinking this—that the corporeal things of which images are formed in my thought, and which the senses investigate, are known with much more distinctness than this puzzling 'I' which cannot be pictured in the imagination. And yet it is surely surprising that I should have a more distinct grasp of things which I realize are doubtful, unknown and foreign to me, than I have of that which is true and known—my own self. But I see what it is: my mind enjoys wandering off and will not yet submit to being restrained within the bounds of truth. Very well then; just this once let us give it a completely free rein, so that after a while, when it is time to tighten the reins, it may more readily submit to being curbed.

Let us consider the things which people commonly think they understand most distinctly of all; that is, the bodies which we touch and see. I do not mean bodies in general—for general perceptions are apt to be somewhat more confused—but one particular body. Let us take, for example, this piece of wax. It has just been taken from the honeycomb; it has not yet quite lost the taste of the honey; it retains some of the scent of the flowers from which it was gathered; its colour, shape and size are plain to see; it is hard, cold and can be handled without difficulty; if

you rap it with your knuckle it makes a sound. In short, it has everything which appears necessary to enable a body to be known as distinctly as possible. But even as I speak, I put the wax by the fire, and look: the residual taste is eliminated, the smell goes away, the colour changes, the shape is lost, the size increases; it becomes liquid and hot; you can hardly touch it, and if you strike it, it no longer makes a sound. But does the same wax remain? It must be admitted that it does; no one denies it, no one thinks otherwise. So what was it in the wax that I understood with such distinctness? Evidently none of the features which I arrived at by means of the senses; for whatever came under taste, smell, sight, touch or hearing has now altered—yet the wax remains.

Perhaps the answer lies in the thought which now comes to my mind; namely, the wax was not after all the sweetness of the honey, or the fragrance of the flowers, or the whiteness, or the shape, or the sound, but was rather a body which presented itself to me in these various forms a little while ago, but which now exhibits different ones. But what exactly is it that I am now imagining? Let us concentrate, take away everything which does not belong to the wax, and see what is left: merely something extended, flexible and changeable. But what is meant here by 'flexible' and 'changeable'? Is it what I picture in my imagination: that this piece of wax is capable of changing from a round shape to a square shape, or from a square shape to a triangular shape? Not at all; for I can grasp that the wax is capable of countless changes of this kind, yet I am unable to run through this immeasurable number of changes in my imagination, from which it follows that it is not the faculty of imagination that gives me my grasp of the wax as flexible and changeable. And what is meant by 'extended'? Is the extension of the wax also unknown? For it increases if the wax melts, increases again if it boils, and is greater still if the heat is increased. I would not be making a correct judgement about the nature of wax unless I believed it capable of being extended in many more different ways than I will ever encompass in my imagination. I must therefore admit that the nature of this piece of wax is in no way revealed by my imagination, but is perceived by the mind alone. (I am speaking of this particular piece of wax; the point is even clearer with regard to wax in general.) But what is this wax which is perceived by the mind alone?[17] It is of course the same wax which I see, which I touch, which I picture in my imagination, in short the same wax which I thought it to be from the start. And yet, and here is the point, the perception I have of it[18] is a case not of vision or touch or imagination—nor has it ever been, despite previous appearances—but of purely mental scrutiny; and this can be imperfect and confused, as it was before, or clear and distinct as it is now, depending on how carefully I concentrate on what the wax consists in.

But as I reach this conclusion I am amazed at how <weak and> prone to error my mind is. For although I am thinking about these matters within myself, silently and without speaking, nonetheless the actual words bring me up short, and I am almost tricked by ordinary ways of talking. We say that we see the wax itself, if it is there before us, not that we judge it to be there from its colour or shape; and this might lead me to conclude without more ado that knowledge of the wax comes from what the eye sees, and not from the scrutiny of the mind alone. But then if I look out of the window and see men crossing the square, as I just happen to have done, I normally say that I see the men themselves, just as I say that I see the wax. Yet do I see any more than hats and coats which could conceal automatons? I *judge* that they are men. And so something which I thought I was seeing with my eyes is in fact grasped solely by the faculty of judgement which is in my mind.

However, one who wants to achieve knowledge above the ordinary level should feel ashamed at having taken ordinary ways of talking as a basis for doubt. So let us proceed, and consider on which occasion my perception of the nature of the wax was more perfect and evident. Was it when I first looked at it, and believed I knew it by my external senses, or at least by what

they call the 'common' sense—that is, the power of imagination? Or is my knowledge more perfect now, after a more careful investigation of the nature of the wax and of the means by which it is known? Any doubt on this issue would clearly be foolish; for what distinctness was there in my earlier perception? Was there anything in it which an animal could not possess? But when I distinguish the wax from its outward forms—take the clothes off, as it were, and consider it naked—then although my judgement may still contain errors, at least my perception now requires a human mind.

But what am I to say about this mind, or about myself? (So far, remember, I am not admitting that there is anything else in me except a mind.) What, I ask, is this 'I' which seems to perceive the wax so distinctly? Surely my awareness of my own self is not merely much truer and more certain than my awareness of the wax, but also much more distinct and evident. For if I judge that the wax exists from the fact that I see it, clearly this same fact entails much more evidently that I myself also exist. It is possible that what I see is not really the wax; it is possible that I do not even have eyes with which to see anything. But when I see, or think I see (I am not here distinguishing the two), it is simply not possible that I who am now thinking am not something. By the same token, if I judge that the wax exists from the fact that I touch it, the same result follows, namely that I exist. If I judge that it exists from the fact that I imagine it, or for any other reason, exactly the same thing follows. And the result that I have grasped in the case of the wax may be applied to everything else located outside me. Moreover, if my perception of the wax seemed more distinct[19] after it was established not just by sight or touch but by many other considerations, it must be admitted that I now know myself even more distinctly. This is because every consideration whatsoever which contributes to my perception of the wax, or of any other body, cannot but establish even more effectively the nature of my own mind. But besides this, there is so much else in the mind itself which can serve to make my knowledge of it more distinct, that it scarcely seems worth going through the contributions made by considering bodily things.

I see that without any effort I have now finally got back to where I wanted. I now know that even bodies are not strictly perceived by the senses or the faculty of imagination but by the intellect alone, and that this perception derives not from their being touched or seen but from their being understood; and in view of this I know plainly that I can achieve an easier and more evident perception of my own mind than of anything else. But since the habit of holding on to old opinions cannot be set aside so quickly, I should like to stop here and meditate for some time on this new knowledge I have gained, so as to fix it more deeply in my memory.

THIRD MEDITATION

The existence of God

I will now shut my eyes, stop my ears, and withdraw all my senses. I will eliminate from my thoughts all images of bodily things, or rather, since this is hardly possible, I will regard all such images as vacuous, false and worthless. I will converse with myself and scrutinize myself more deeply; and in this way I will attempt to achieve, little by little, a more intimate knowledge of myself. I am a thing that thinks: that is, a thing that doubts, affirms, denies, understands a few things, is ignorant of many things,[20] is willing, is unwilling, and also which imagines and has sensory perceptions; for as I have noted before, even though the objects of my sensory experience and imagination may have no existence outside me, nonetheless the modes of thinking which I refer to as cases of sensory perception and imagination, in so far as they are simply modes of thinking, do exist within me—of that I am certain.

In this brief list I have gone through everything I truly know, or at least everything I have so far discovered that I know. Now I will cast around more carefully to see whether there may be other things within me which I have not yet noticed. I am certain that I am a thinking thing. Do I not therefore also know what is required for my being certain about anything? In this first item of knowledge there is simply a clear and distinct perception of what I am asserting; this would not be enough to make me certain of the truth of the matter if it could ever turn out that something which I perceived with such clarity and distinctness was false. So I now seem to be able to lay it down as a general rule that whatever I perceive very clearly and distinctly is true.[21]

Yet I previously accepted as wholly certain and evident many things which I afterwards realized were doubtful. What were these? The earth, sky, stars, and everything else that I apprehended with the senses. But what was it about them that I perceived clearly? Just that the ideas, or thoughts, of such things appeared before my mind. Yet even now I am not denying that these ideas occur within me. But there was something else which I used to assert, and which through habitual belief I thought I perceived clearly, although I did not in fact do so. This was that there were things outside me which were the sources of my ideas and which resembled them in all respects. Here was my mistake; or at any rate, if my judgement was true, it was not thanks to the strength of my perception.[22]

But what about when I was considering something very simple and straightforward in arithmetic or geometry, for example that two and three added together make five, and so on? Did I not see at least these things clearly enough to affirm their truth? Indeed, the only reason for my later judgement that they were open to doubt was that it occurred to me that perhaps some God could have given me a nature such that I was deceived even in matters which seemed most evident. But whenever my preconceived belief in the supreme power of God comes to mind, I cannot but admit that it would be easy for him, if he so desired, to bring it about that I go wrong even in those matters which I think I see utterly clearly with my mind's eye. Yet when I turn to the things themselves which I think I perceive very clearly, I am so convinced by them that I spontaneously declare: let whoever can do so deceive me, he will never bring it about that I am nothing, so long as I continue to think I am something; or make it true at some future time that I have never existed, since it is now true that I exist; or bring it about that two and three added together are more or less than five, or anything of this kind in which I see a manifest contradiction. And since I have no cause to think that there is a deceiving God, and I do not yet even know for sure whether there is a God at all, any reason for doubt which depends simply on this supposition is a very slight and, so to speak, metaphysical one. But in order to remove even this slight reason for doubt, as soon as the opportunity arises I must examine whether there is a God, and, if there is, whether he can be a deceiver. For if I do not know this, it seems that I can never be quite certain about anything else.

First, however, considerations of order appear to dictate that I now classify my thoughts into definite kinds,[23] and ask which of them can properly be said to be the bearers of truth and falsity. Some of my thoughts are as it were the images of things, and it is only in these cases that the term 'idea' is strictly appropriate—for example, when I think of a man, or a chimera, or the sky, or an angel, or God. Other thoughts have various additional forms: thus when I will, or am afraid, or affirm, or deny, there is always a particular thing which I take as the object of my thought, but my thought includes something more than the likeness of that thing. Some thoughts in this category are called volitions or emotions, while others are called judgements.

Now as far as ideas are concerned, provided they are considered solely in themselves and I do not refer them to anything else, they cannot strictly speaking be false; for whether it is a goat or a chimera that I am imagining, it is just as true that I imagine the former as the latter. As for the will and the emotions, here too one need not worry about falsity; for even if the things which I may desire are wicked or even non-existent, that does not make it any less true that I desire them. Thus the only remaining

thoughts where I must be on my guard against making a mistake are judgements. And the chief and most common mistake which is to be found here consists in my judging that the ideas which are in me resemble, or conform to, things located outside me. Of course, if I considered just the ideas themselves simply as modes of my thought, without referring them to anything else, they could scarcely give me any material for error.

Among my ideas, some appear to be innate, some to be adventitious,[24] and others to have been invented by me. My understanding of what a thing is, what truth is, and what thought is, seems to derive simply from my own nature. But my hearing a noise, as I do now, or seeing the sun, or feeling the fire, comes from things which are located outside me, or so I have hitherto judged. Lastly, sirens, hippogriffs and the like are my own invention. But perhaps all my ideas may be thought of as adventitious, or they may all be innate, or all made up; for as yet I have not clearly perceived their true origin.

But the chief question at this point concerns the ideas which I take to be derived from things existing outside me: what is my reason for thinking that they resemble these things? Nature has apparently taught me to think this. But in addition I know by experience that these ideas do not depend on my will, and hence that they do not depend simply on me. Frequently I notice them even when I do not want to: now, for example, I feel the heat whether I want to or not, and this is why I think that this sensation or idea of heat comes to me from something other than myself, namely the heat of the fire by which I am sitting. And the most obvious judgement for me to make is that the thing in question transmits to me its own likeness rather than something else.

I will now see if these arguments are strong enough. When I say 'Nature taught me to think this', all I mean is that a spontaneous impulse leads me to believe it, not that its truth has been revealed to me by some natural light. There is a big difference here. Whatever is revealed to me by the natural light—for example that from the fact that I am doubting it follows that I exist, and so on—cannot in any way be open to doubt. This is because there cannot be another faculty[25] both as trustworthy as the natural light and also capable of showing me that such things are not true. But as for my natural impulses, I have often judged in the past that they were pushing me in the wrong direction when it was a question of choosing the good, and I do not see why I should place any greater confidence in them in other matters.[26]

Then again, although these ideas do not depend on my will, it does not follow that they must come from things located outside me. Just as the impulses which I was speaking of a moment ago seem opposed to my will even though they are within me, so there may be some other faculty not yet fully known to me, which produces these ideas without any assistance from external things; this is, after all, just how I have always thought ideas are produced in me when I am dreaming.

And finally, even if these ideas did come from things other than myself, it would not follow that they must resemble those things. Indeed, I think I have often discovered a great disparity <between an object and its idea> in many cases. For example, there are two different ideas of the sun which I find within me. One of them, which is acquired as it were from the senses and which is a prime example of an idea which I reckon to come from an external source, makes the sun appear very small. The other idea is based on astronomical reasoning, that is, it is derived from certain notions which are innate in me (or else it is constructed by me in some other way), and this idea shows the sun to be several times larger than the earth. Obviously both these ideas cannot resemble the sun which exists outside me; and reason persuades me that the idea which seems to have emanated most directly from the sun itself has in fact no resemblance to it at all.

All these considerations are enough to establish that it is not reliable judgement but merely some blind impulse that has made me believe up till now that there exist things distinct from myself which transmit to me ideas or images of themselves through the sense organs or in some other way.

But it now occurs to me that there is another way of investigating whether some of the things of which I possess ideas exist outside me. In so far as the ideas are <considered> simply <as> modes of thought, there is no recognizable inequality among them: they all appear to come from within me in the same fashion. But in so far as different ideas <are considered as images which> represent different things, it is clear that they differ widely. Undoubtedly, the ideas which represent substances to me amount to something more and, so to speak, contain within themselves more objective[27] reality than the ideas which merely represent modes or accidents. Again, the idea that gives me my understanding of a supreme God, eternal, infinite, <immutable,> omniscient, omnipotent and the creator of all things that exist apart from him, certainly has in it more objective reality than the ideas that represent finite substances.

Now it is manifest by the natural light that there must be at least as much <reality> in the efficient and total cause as in the effect of that cause. For where, I ask, could the effect get its reality from, if not from the cause? And how could the cause give it to the effect unless it possessed it? It follows from this both that something cannot arise from nothing, and also that what is more perfect—that is, contains in itself more reality—cannot arise from what is less perfect. And this is transparently true not only in the case of effects which possess <what the philosophers call> actual or formal reality, but also in the case of ideas, where one is considering only <what they call> objective reality. A stone, for example, which previously did not exist, cannot begin to exist unless it is produced by something which contains, either formally or eminently everything to be found in the stone;[28] similarly, heat cannot be produced in an object which was not previously hot, except by something of at least the same order <degree or kind> of perfection as heat, and so on. But it is also true that the *idea* of heat, or of a stone, cannot exist in me unless it is put there by some cause which contains at least as much reality as I conceive to be in the heat or in the stone. For although this cause does not transfer any of its actual or formal reality to my idea, it should not on that account be supposed that it must be less real.[29] The nature of an idea is such that of itself it requires no formal reality except what it derives from my thought, of which it is a mode.[30] But in order for a given idea to contain such and such objective reality, it must surely derive it from some cause which contains at least as much formal reality as there is objective reality in the idea. For if we suppose that an idea contains something which was not in its cause, it must have got this from nothing; yet the mode of being by which a thing exists objectively <or representatively> in the intellect by way of an idea, imperfect though it may be, is certainly not nothing, and so it cannot come from nothing.

And although the reality which I am considering in my ideas is merely objective reality, I must not on that account suppose that the same reality need not exist formally in the causes of my ideas, but that it is enough for it to be present in them objectively. For just as the objective mode of being belongs to ideas by their very nature, so the formal mode of being belongs to the causes of ideas—or at least the first and most important ones—by *their* very nature. And although one idea may perhaps originate from another, there cannot be an infinite regress here; eventually one must reach a primary idea, the cause of which will be like an archetype which contains formally <and in fact> all the reality <or perfection> which is present only objectively <or representatively> in the idea. So it is clear to me, by the natural light, that the ideas in me are like <pictures, or> images which can easily fall short of the perfection of the things from which they are taken, but which cannot contain anything greater or more perfect.

The longer and more carefully I examine all these points, the more clearly and distinctly I recognize their truth. But what is my conclusion to be? If the objective reality of any of my ideas turns out to be so great that I am sure the same

reality does not reside in me, either formally or eminently, and hence that I myself cannot be its cause, it will necessarily follow that I am not alone in the world, but that some other thing which is the cause of this idea also exists. But if no such idea is to be found in me, I shall have no argument to convince me of the existence of anything apart from myself. For despite a most careful and comprehensive survey, this is the only argument I have so far been able to find.

Among my ideas, apart from the idea which gives me a representation of myself, which cannot present any difficulty in this context, there are ideas which variously represent God, corporeal and inanimate things, angels, animals and finally other men like myself.

As far as concerns the ideas which represent other men, or animals, or angels, I have no difficulty in understanding that they could be put together from the ideas I have of myself, of corporeal things and of God, even if the world contained no men besides me, no animals and no angels.

As to my ideas of corporeal things, I can see nothing in them which is so great <or excellent> as to make it seem impossible that it originated in myself. For if I scrutinize them thoroughly and examine them one by one, in the way in which I examined the idea of the wax yesterday, I notice that the things which I perceive clearly and distinctly in them are very few in number. The list comprises size, or extension in length, breadth and depth; shape, which is a function of the boundaries of this extension; position, which is a relation between various items possessing shape; and motion, or change in position; to these may be added substance, duration and number. But as for all the rest, including light and colours, sounds, smells, tastes, heat and cold and the other tactile qualities, I think of these only in a very confused and obscure way, to the extent that I do not even know whether they are true or false, that is, whether the ideas I have of them are ideas of real things or of non-things.[31] For although, as I have noted before, falsity in the strict sense, or formal falsity, can occur only in judgements, there is another kind of falsity, material falsity, which occurs in ideas, when they represent non-things as things. For example, the ideas which I have of heat and cold contain so little clarity and distinctness that they do not enable me to tell whether cold is merely the absence of heat or vice versa, or whether both of them are real qualities, or neither is. And since there can be no ideas which are not as it were of things,[32] if it is true that cold is nothing but the absence of heat, the idea which represents it to me as something real and positive deserves to be called false; and the same goes for other ideas of this kind.

Such ideas obviously do not require me to posit a source distinct from myself. For on the one hand, if they are false, that is, represent non-things, I know by the natural light that they arise from nothing—that is, they are in me only because of a deficiency and lack of perfection in my nature. If on the other hand they are true, then since the reality which they represent is so extremely slight that I cannot even distinguish it from a non-thing, I do not see why they cannot originate from myself.

With regard to the clear and distinct elements in my ideas of corporeal things, it appears that I could have borrowed some of these from my idea of myself, namely substance, duration, number and anything else of this kind. For example, I think that a stone is a substance, or is a thing capable of existing independently, and I also think that I am a substance. Admittedly I conceive of myself as a thing that thinks and is not extended, whereas I conceive of the stone as a thing that is extended and does not think, so that the two conceptions differ enormously; but they seem to agree with respect to the classification 'substance.'[33] Again, I perceive that I now exist, and remember that I have existed for some time; moreover, I have various thoughts which I can count; it is in these ways that I acquire the ideas of duration and number which I can then transfer to other things. As for all the other elements which make up the ideas of corporeal things, namely extension, shape, position and movement, these are not formally contained in me, since I am nothing but a thinking thing; but

since they are merely modes of a substance,[34] and I am a substance, it seems possible that they are contained in me eminently.

So there remains only the idea of God; and I must consider whether there is anything in the idea which could not have originated in myself. By the word 'God' I understand a substance that is infinite, <eternal, immutable,> independent, supremely intelligent, supremely powerful, and which created both myself and everything else (if anything else there be) that exists. All these attributes are such that, the more carefully I concentrate on them, the less possible it seems that they[35] could have originated from me alone. So from what has been said it must be concluded that God necessarily exists.

It is true that I have the idea of substance in me in virtue of the fact that I am a substance; but this would not account for my having the idea of an infinite substance, when I am finite, unless this idea proceeded from some substance which really was infinite.

And I must not think that, just as my conceptions of rest and darkness are arrived at by negating movement and light, so my perception of the infinite is arrived at not by means of a true idea but merely by negating the finite. On the contrary, I clearly understand that there is more reality in an infinite substance than in a finite one, and hence that my perception of the infinite, that is God, is in some way prior to my perception of the finite, that is myself. For how could I understand that I doubted or desired—that is, lacked something—and that I was not wholly perfect, unless there were in me some idea of a more perfect being which enabled me to recognize my own defects by comparison?

Nor can it be said that this idea of God is perhaps materially false and so could have come from nothing,[36] which is what I observed just a moment ago in the case of the ideas of heat and cold, and so on. On the contrary, it is utterly clear and distinct, and contains in itself more objective reality than any other idea; hence there is no idea which is in itself truer or less liable to be suspected of falsehood. This idea of a supremely perfect and infinite being is, I say, true in the highest degree; for although perhaps one may imagine that such a being does not exist, it cannot be supposed that the idea of such a being represents something unreal, as I said with regard to the idea of cold. The idea is, moreover, utterly clear and distinct; for whatever I clearly and distinctly perceive as being real and true, and implying any perfection, is wholly contained in it. It does not matter that I do not grasp the infinite, or that there are countless additional attributes of God which I cannot in any way grasp, and perhaps cannot even reach in my thought; for it is in the nature of the infinite not to be grasped by a finite being like myself. It is enough that I understand[37] the infinite, and that I judge that all the attributes which I clearly perceive and know to imply some perfection—and perhaps countless others of which I am ignorant—are present in God either formally or eminently. This is enough to make the idea that I have of God the truest and most clear and distinct of all my ideas.

But perhaps I am something greater than I myself understand, and all the perfections which I attribute to God are somehow in me potentially, though not yet emerging or actualized. For I am now experiencing a gradual increase in my knowledge, and I see nothing to prevent its increasing more and more to infinity. Further, I see no reason why I should not be able to use this increased knowledge to acquire all the other perfections of God. And finally, if the potentiality for these perfections is already within me, why should not this be enough to generate the idea of such perfections?

But all this is impossible. First, though it is true that there is a gradual increase in my knowledge, and that I have many potentialities which are not yet actual, this is all quite irrelevant to the idea of God, which contains absolutely nothing that is potential;[38] indeed, this gradual increase in knowledge is itself the surest sign of imperfection. What is more, even if my knowledge always increases more and more, I recognize that it will never actually be infinite, since it will never reach the point where it is not capable of a further increase; God, on the other hand, I take to be

actually infinite, so that nothing can be added to his perfection. And finally, I perceive that the objective being of an idea cannot be produced merely by potential being, which strictly speaking is nothing, but only by actual or formal being.

If one concentrates carefully, all this is quite evident by the natural light. But when I relax my concentration, and my mental vision is blinded by the images of things perceived by the senses, it is not so easy for me to remember why the idea of a being more perfect than myself must necessarily proceed from some being which is in reality more perfect. I should therefore like to go further and inquire whether I myself, who have this idea, could exist if no such being existed.

From whom, in that case, would I derive my existence? From myself presumably, or from my parents, or from some other beings less perfect than God; for nothing more perfect than God, or even as perfect, can be thought of or imagined.

Yet if I derived my existence from myself,[39] then I should neither doubt nor want, nor lack anything at all; for I should have given myself all the perfections of which I have any idea, and thus I should myself be God. I must not suppose that the items I lack would be more difficult to acquire than those I now have. On the contrary, it is clear that, since I am a thinking thing or substance, it would have been far more difficult for me to emerge out of nothing than merely to acquire knowledge of the many things of which I am ignorant—such knowledge being merely an accident of that substance. And if I had derived my existence from myself, which is a greater achievement, I should certainly not have denied myself the knowledge in question, which is something much easier to acquire, or indeed any of the attributes which I perceive to be contained in the idea of God; for none of them seem any harder to achieve. And if any of them were harder to achieve, they would certainly appear so to me, if I had indeed got all my other attributes from myself, since I should experience a limitation of my power in this respect.

I do not escape the force of these arguments by supposing that I have always existed as I do now, as if it followed from this that there was no need to look for any author of my existence. For a lifespan can be divided into countless parts, each completely independent of the others, so that it does not follow from the fact that I existed a little while ago that I must exist now, unless there is some cause which as it were creates me afresh at this moment—that is, which preserves me. For it is quite clear to anyone who attentively considers the nature of time that the same power and action are needed to preserve anything at each individual moment of its duration as would be required to create that thing anew if it were not yet in existence. Hence the distinction between preservation and creation is only a conceptual one,[40] and this is one of the things that are evident by the natural light.

I must therefore now ask myself whether I possess some power enabling me to bring it about that I who now exist will still exist a little while from now. For since I am nothing but a thinking thing—or at least since I am now concerned only and precisely with that part of me which is a thinking thing—if there were such a power in me, I should undoubtedly be aware of it. But I experience no such power, and this very fact makes me recognize most clearly that I depend on some being distinct from myself.

But perhaps this being is not God, and perhaps I was produced either by my parents or by other causes less perfect than God. No; for as I have said before, it is quite clear that there must be at least as much in the cause as in the effect.[41] And therefore whatever kind of cause is eventually proposed, since I am a thinking thing and have within me some idea of God, it must be admitted that what caused me is itself a thinking thing and possesses the idea of all the perfections which I attribute to God. In respect of this cause one may again inquire whether it derives its existence from itself or from another cause. If from itself, then it is clear from what has been said that it is itself God, since if it has the power of existing through its own might,[42] then undoubtedly it also has the power of actually possessing all the perfections of which it has an idea—that is, all the perfections which I conceive to be in God. If, on the other hand, it derives its existence from another cause, then the same question may be repeated concerning this further cause, namely whether it derives its existence from itself or from another cause, until eventually the ultimate cause is reached, and this will be God.

It is clear enough that an infinite regress is impossible here, especially since I am dealing not just with the cause that produced me in the past, but also and most importantly with the cause that preserves me at the present moment.

Nor can it be supposed that several partial causes contributed to my creation, or that I received the idea of one of the perfections which I attribute to God from one cause and the idea of another from another—the supposition here being that all the perfections are to be found somewhere in the universe but not joined together in a single being, God.

On the contrary, the unity, the simplicity, or the inseparability of all the attributes of God is one of the most important of the perfections which I understand him to have. And surely the idea of the unity of all his perfections could not have been placed in me by any cause which did not also provide me with the ideas of the other perfections; for no cause could have made me understand the interconnection and inseparability of the perfections without at the same time making me recognize what they were.

Lastly, as regards my parents, even if everything I have ever believed about them is true, it is certainly not they who preserve me; and in so far as I am a thinking thing, they did not even make me; they merely placed certain dispositions in the matter which I have always regarded as containing me, or rather my mind, for that is all I now take myself to be. So there can be no difficulty regarding my parents in this context. Altogether then, it must be concluded that the mere fact that I exist and have within me an idea of a most perfect being, that is, God, provides a very clear proof that God indeed exists.

It only remains for me to examine how I received this idea from God. For I did not acquire it from the senses; it has never come to me unexpectedly, as usually happens with the ideas of things that are perceivable by the senses, when these things present themselves to the external sense organs—or seem to do so. And it was not invented by me either; for I am plainly unable either to take away anything from it or to add anything to it. The only remaining alternative is that it is innate in me, just as the idea of myself is innate in me.

And indeed it is no surprise that God, in creating me, should have placed this idea in me to be, as it were, the mark of the craftsman stamped on his work—not that the mark need be anything distinct from the work itself. But the mere fact that God created me is a very strong basis for believing that I am somehow made in his image and likeness, and that I perceive that likeness, which includes the idea of God, by the same faculty which enables me to perceive myself. That is, when I turn my mind's eye upon myself, I understand that I am a thing which is incomplete and dependent on another and which aspires without limit to ever greater and better things; but I also understand at the same time that he on whom I depend has within him all those greater things, not just indefinitely and potentially but actually and infinitely, and hence that he is God. The whole force of the argument lies in this: I recognize that it would be impossible for me to exist with the kind of nature I have—that is, having within me the idea of God—were it not the case that God really existed. By 'God' I mean the very being the idea of whom is within me, that is, the possessor of all the perfections which I cannot grasp, but can somehow reach in my thought, who is subject to no defects whatsoever.[43] It is clear enough from this that he cannot be a deceiver, since it is manifest by the natural light that all fraud and deception depend on some defect.

But before examining this point more carefully and investigating other truths which may be derived from it, I should like to pause here and spend some time in the contemplation of God; to reflect on his attributes, and to gaze with wonder and adoration on the beauty of this immense light, so far as the eye of my darkened intellect can bear it. For just as we believe through faith that the supreme happiness of the next life consists solely in the contemplation of the divine majesty, so experience tells us that this same contemplation, albeit much less perfect, enables us to know the greatest joy of which we are capable in this life.

FOURTH MEDITATION

Truth and falsity

During these past few days I have accustomed myself to leading my mind away from the senses; and I have taken careful note of the fact that there is very little about corporeal things that is truly perceived, whereas much more is known about the human mind, and still more about God. The result is that I now have no difficulty in turning my mind away from imaginable things[44] and towards things which are objects of the intellect alone and are totally separate from matter. And indeed the idea I have of the human mind, insofar as it is a thinking thing, which is not extended in length, breadth or height and has no other bodily characteristics, is much more distinct than the idea of any corporeal thing. And when I consider the fact that I have doubts, or that I am a thing that is incomplete and dependent, then there arises in me a clear and distinct idea of a being who is independent and complete, that is, an idea of God. And from the mere fact that there is such an idea within me, or that I who possess this idea exist, I clearly infer that God also exists, and that every single moment of my entire existence depends on him. So clear is this conclusion that I am confident that the human intellect cannot know anything that is more evident or more certain. And now, from this contemplation of the true God, in whom all the treasures of wisdom and the sciences lie hidden, I think I can see a way forward to the knowledge of other things.[45]

To begin with, I recognize that it is impossible that God should ever deceive me. For in every case of trickery or deception some imperfection is to be found; and although the ability to deceive appears to be an indication of cleverness or power, the will to deceive is undoubtedly evidence of malice or weakness, and so cannot apply to God.

Next, I know by experience that there is in me a faculty of judgement which, like everything else which is in me, I certainly received from God. And since God does not wish to deceive me, he surely did not give me the kind of faculty which would ever enable me to go wrong while using it correctly.

There would be no further doubt on this issue were it not that what I have just said appears to imply that I am incapable of ever going wrong. For if everything that is in me comes from God, and he did not endow me with a faculty for making mistakes, it appears that I can never go wrong. And certainly, so long as I think only of God, and turn my whole attention to him, I can find no cause of error or falsity. But when I turn back to myself, I know by experience that I am prone to countless errors. On looking for the cause of these errors, I find that I possess not only a real and positive idea of God, or a being who is supremely perfect, but also what may be described as a negative idea of nothingness, or of that which is farthest removed from all perfection. I realize that I am, as it were, something intermediate between God and nothingness, or between supreme being and nonbeing: my nature is such that in so far as I was created by the supreme being, there is nothing in me to enable me to go wrong or lead me astray; but in so far as I participate in nothingness or nonbeing, that is, in so far as I am not myself the supreme being and am lacking in countless respects, it is no wonder that I make mistakes. I understand, then, that error as such is not something real which depends on God, but merely a defect. Hence my going wrong does not require me to have a faculty specially bestowed on me by God; it simply happens as a result of the fact that the faculty of true judgement which I have from God is in my case not infinite.

But this is still not entirely satisfactory. For error is not a pure negation,[46] but rather a privation or lack of some knowledge which somehow should be in me. And when I concentrate on the nature of God, it seems impossible that he should have placed in me a faculty which is not perfect of its kind, or which lacks some perfection which it ought to have. The more skilled the craftsman the more perfect the work produced by him; if this is so, how can anything produced by the supreme creator of all things not be complete and perfect in all respects? There is, moreover, no doubt that God could have given me a nature such that I was never mistaken; again, there is no doubt that he always wills what is best. Is it then better that I should make mistakes than that I should not do so?

As I reflect on these matters more attentively, it occurs to me first of all that it is no cause for surprise if I do not understand the reasons for some of God's actions; and there is no call to doubt his existence if I happen to find that there are other instances where I do not grasp why or how certain things were made by him. For since I now know that my own nature is very weak and limited, whereas the nature of God is immense, incomprehensible and infinite, I also know without more ado that he is capable of countless things whose causes are beyond my knowledge. And for this reason alone I consider the customary search for final causes to be totally useless in physics; there is considerable rashness in thinking myself capable of investigating the <impenetrable> purposes of God.

It also occurs to me that whenever we are inquiring whether the works of God are perfect, we ought to look at the whole universe, not just at one created thing on its own. For what would perhaps rightly appear very imperfect if it existed on its own is quite perfect when its function as a part of the universe is considered. It is true that, since my decision to doubt everything, it is so far only myself and God whose existence I have been able to know with certainty; but after considering the immense power of God, I cannot deny that many other things have been made by him, or at least could have been made, and hence that I may have a place in the universal scheme of things.

Next, when I look more closely at myself and inquire into the nature of my errors (for these are the only evidence of some imperfection in me), I notice that they depend on two concurrent causes, namely on the faculty of knowledge which is in me, and on the faculty of choice or freedom of the will; that is, they depend on both the intellect and the will simultaneously. Now all that the intellect does is to enable me to perceive[47] the ideas which are subjects for possible judgements; and when regarded strictly in this light, it turns out to contain no error in the proper sense of that term. For although countless things may exist without there being any corresponding ideas in me, it should not, strictly speaking, be said that I am deprived of these ideas,[48] but merely that I lack them, in a negative sense. This is because I cannot produce any reason to prove that God ought to have given me a greater faculty of knowledge than he did; and no matter how skilled I understand a craftsman to be, this does not make me think he ought to have put into every one of his works all the perfections which he is able to put into some of them. Besides, I cannot complain that the will or freedom of choice which I received from God is not sufficiently extensive or perfect, since I know by experience that it is not restricted in any way. Indeed, I think it is very noteworthy that there is nothing else in me which is so perfect and so great that the possibility of a further increase in its perfection or greatness is beyond my understanding. If, for example, I consider the faculty of understanding, I immediately recognize that in my case it is extremely slight and very finite, and I at once form the idea of an understanding which is much greater—indeed supremely great and infinite; and from the very fact that I can form an idea of it, I perceive that it belongs to the nature of God. Similarly, if I examine the faculties of memory or imagination, or any others, I discover that in my case each one of these faculties is weak and limited, while in the case of God it is immeasurable. It is only the will, or freedom of choice, which I experience within me to be so great that the idea of any greater faculty is beyond

my grasp; so much so that it is above all in virtue of the will that I understand myself to bear in some way the image and likeness of God. For although God's will is incomparably greater than mine, both in virtue of the knowledge and power that accompany it and make it more firm and efficacious, and also in virtue of its object, in that it ranges over a greater number of items, nevertheless it does not seem any greater than mine when considered as will in the essential and strict sense. This is because the will simply consists in our ability to do or not do something (that is, to affirm or deny, to pursue or avoid); or rather, it consists simply in the fact that when the intellect puts something forward, we are moved to affirm or deny or to pursue or avoid it in such a way that we do not feel ourselves to be determined by any external force. For in order to be free, there is no need for me to be capable of going in each of two directions; on the contrary, the more I incline in one direction—either because I clearly understand that reasons of truth and goodness point that way, or because of a divinely produced disposition of my inmost thoughts—the freer is my choice. Neither divine grace nor natural knowledge ever diminishes freedom; on the contrary, they increase and strengthen it. But the indifference I feel when there is no reason pushing me in one direction rather than another is the lowest grade of freedom; it is evidence not of any perfection of freedom, but rather of a defect in knowledge or a kind of negation. For if I always saw clearly what was true and good, I should never have to deliberate about the right judgement or choice; in that case, although I should be wholly free, it would be impossible for me ever to be in a state of indifference.

From these considerations I perceive that the power of willing which I received from God is not, when considered in itself, the cause of my mistakes; for it is both extremely ample and also perfect of its kind. Nor is my power of understanding to blame; for since my understanding comes from God, everything that I understand I undoubtedly understand correctly, and any error here is impossible. So what then is the source of my mistakes? It must be simply this: the scope of the will is wider than that of the intellect; but instead of restricting it within the same limits, I extend its use to matters which I do not understand. Since the will is indifferent in such cases, it easily turns aside from what is true and good, and this is the source of my error and sin.

For example, during these past few days I have been asking whether anything in the world exists, and I have realized that from the very fact of my raising this question it follows quite evidently that I exist. I could not but judge that something which I understood so clearly was true; but this was not because I was compelled so to judge by any external force, but because a great light in the intellect was followed by a great inclination in the will, and thus the spontaneity and freedom of my belief was all the greater in proportion to my lack of indifference. But now, besides the knowledge that I exist, in so far as I am a thinking thing, an idea of corporeal nature comes into my mind; and I happen to be in doubt as to whether the thinking nature which is in me, or rather which I am, is distinct from this corporeal nature or identical with it. I am making the further supposition that my intellect has not yet come upon any persuasive reason in favour of one alternative rather than the other. This obviously implies that I am indifferent as to whether I should assert or deny either alternative, or indeed refrain from making any judgement on the matter.

What is more, this indifference does not merely apply to cases where the intellect is wholly ignorant, but extends in general to every case where the intellect does not have sufficiently clear knowledge at the time when the will deliberates. For although probable conjectures may pull me in one direction, the mere knowledge that they are simply conjectures, and not certain and indubitable reasons, is itself quite enough to push my assent the other way. My experience in the last few days confirms this: the mere fact that I found that all my previous beliefs were in some sense open to doubt was enough to turn my absolutely confident belief in their truth into the supposition that they were wholly false.

If, however, I simply refrain from making a judgement in cases where I do not perceive the truth with sufficient clarity and distinctness, then it is clear that I am behaving correctly and avoiding error. But if in such cases I either affirm or deny, then I am not using my free will correctly. If I go for the alternative which is false, then obviously I shall be in error; if I take the other side, then it is by pure chance that I arrive at the truth, and I shall still be at fault since it is clear by the natural light that the perception of the intellect should always precede the determination of the will. In this incorrect use of free will may be found the privation which constitutes the essence of error. The privation, I say, lies in the operation of the will in so far as it proceeds from me, but not in the faculty of will which I received from God, nor even in its operation, in so far as it depends on him.

And I have no cause for complaint on the grounds that the power of understanding or the natural light which God gave me is no greater than it is; for it is in the nature of a finite intellect to lack understanding of many things, and it is in the nature of a created intellect to be finite. Indeed, I have reason to give thanks to him who has never owed me anything for the great bounty that he has shown me, rather than thinking myself deprived or robbed of any gifts he did not bestow.[49]

Nor do I have any cause for complaint on the grounds that God gave me a will which extends more widely than my intellect. For since the will consists simply of one thing which is, as it were, indivisible, it seems that its nature rules out the possibility of anything being taken away from it. And surely, the more widely my will extends, then the greater thanks I owe to him who gave it to me.

Finally, I must not complain that the forming of those acts of will or judgements in which I go wrong happens with God's concurrence. For in so far as these acts depend on God, they are wholly true and good; and my ability to perform them means that there is in a sense more perfection in me than would be the case if I lacked this ability. As for the privation involved—which is all that the essential definition of falsity and wrong consists in—this does not in any way require the concurrence of God, since it is not a thing; indeed, when it is referred to God as its cause, it should be called not a privation but simply a negation.[50] For it is surely no imperfection in God that he has given me the freedom to assent or not to assent in those cases where he did not endow my intellect with a clear and distinct perception; but it is undoubtedly an imperfection in me to misuse that freedom and make judgements about matters which I do not fully understand. I can see, however, that God could easily have brought it about that without losing my freedom, and despite the limitations in my knowledge, I should nonetheless never make a mistake. He could, for example, have endowed my intellect with a clear and distinct perception of everything about which I was ever likely to deliberate; or he could simply have impressed it unforgettably on my memory that I should never make a judgement about anything which I did not clearly and distinctly understand. Had God made me this way, then I can easily understand that, considered as a totality,[51] I would have been more perfect than I am now. But I cannot therefore deny that there may in some way be more perfection in the universe as a whole because some of its parts are not immune from error, while others are immune, than there would be if all the parts were exactly alike. And I have no right to complain that the role God wished me to undertake in the world is not the principal one or the most perfect of all.

What is more, even if I have no power to avoid error in the first way just mentioned, which requires a clear perception of everything I have to deliberate on, I can avoid error in the second way, which depends merely on my remembering to withhold judgement on any occasion when the truth of the matter is not clear. Admittedly, I am aware of a certain weakness in me, in that I am unable to keep my attention fixed on one and the same item of knowledge at all times; but by attentive and repeated meditation I am nevertheless able to make myself remember it as often as the need arises, and thus get into the habit of avoiding error.

It is here that man's greatest and most important perfection is to be found, and I therefore think that today's meditation, involving an investigation into the cause of error and falsity, has been very profitable. The cause of error must surely be the one I have explained; for if, whenever I have to make a judgement, I restrain my will so that it extends to what the intellect clearly and distinctly reveals, and no further, then it is quite impossible for me to go wrong. This is because every clear and distinct perception is undoubtedly something,[52] and hence cannot come from nothing, but must necessarily have God for its author. Its author, I say, is God, who is supremely perfect, and who cannot be a deceiver on pain of contradiction; hence the perception is undoubtedly true. So today I have learned not only what precautions to take to avoid ever going wrong, but also what to do to arrive at the truth. For I shall unquestionably reach the truth, if only I give sufficient attention to all the things which I perfectly understand, and separate these from all the other cases where my apprehension is more confused and obscure. And this is just what I shall take good care to do from now on.

FIFTH MEDITATION

The essence of material things, and the existence of God considered a second time

There are many matters which remain to be investigated concerning the attributes of God and the nature of myself, or my mind; and perhaps I shall take these up at another time. But now that I have seen what to do and what to avoid in order to reach the truth, the most pressing task seems to be to try to escape from the doubts into which I fell a few days ago, and see whether any certainty can be achieved regarding material objects.

But before I inquire whether any such things exist outside me, I must consider the ideas of these things, in so far as they exist in my thought, and see which of them are distinct, and which confused.

Quantity, for example, or 'continuous' quantity as the philosophers commonly call it, is something I distinctly imagine. That is, I distinctly imagine the extension of the quantity (or rather of the thing which is quantified) in length, breadth and depth. I also enumerate various parts of the thing, and to these parts I assign various sizes, shapes, positions and local motions; and to the motions I assign various durations.

Not only are all these things very well known and transparent to me when regarded in this general way, but in addition there are countless particular features regarding shapes, number, motion and so on, which I perceive when I give them my attention. And the truth of these matters is so open and so much in harmony with my nature, that on first discovering them it seems that I am not so much learning something new as remembering what I knew before; or it seems like noticing for the first time things which were long present within me although I had never turned my mental gaze on them before.

But I think the most important consideration at this point is that I find within me countless ideas of things which even though they may not exist anywhere outside me still cannot be called nothing; for although in a sense they can be thought of at will, they are not my invention but have their own true and immutable natures. When, for example, I imagine a triangle, even if perhaps no such figure exists, or has ever existed, anywhere outside my thought, there is still a determinate nature, or essence, or form of the triangle which is immutable and eternal, and not invented by me or dependent on my mind. This is clear from the fact that various properties can be demonstrated of the triangle, for example that its three angles equal two right angles, that its greatest side subtends its greatest angle, and the like; and since these properties are ones which I now clearly recognize whether I want to or not, even if I never thought of them at all when I previously imagined the triangle, it follows that they cannot have been invented by me.

It would be beside the point for me to say that since I have from time to time seen bodies of triangular shape, the idea of the triangle may have come to me from external things by means of the sense organs. For I can think up countless other shapes which there can be no suspicion of my ever having encountered through the senses, and yet I can demonstrate various properties of these shapes, just as I can with the triangle. All these properties are certainly true, since I am clearly aware of them, and therefore they are something, and not merely nothing; for it is obvious that whatever is true is something; and I have already amply demonstrated that everything of which I am clearly aware is true. And even if I had not demonstrated this, the nature of my mind is such that I cannot but assent to these things, at least so long as I clearly perceive them. I also remember that even before, when I was completely preoccupied with the objects of the senses, I always held that the most certain truths of all were the kind which I recognized clearly in connection with shapes, or numbers or other items relating to arithmetic or geometry, or in general to pure and abstract mathematics.

But if the mere fact that I can produce from my thought the idea of something entails that everything which I clearly and distinctly perceive to belong to that thing really does belong to it, is not this a possible basis for another argument to prove the existence of God? Certainly, the idea of God, or a supremely perfect being, is one which I find within me just as surely as the idea of any shape or number. And my understanding that it belongs to his nature that he always exists[53] is no less clear and distinct than is the case when I prove of any shape or number that some property belongs to its nature. Hence, even if it turned out that not everything on which I have meditated in these past days is true, I ought still to regard the existence of God as having at least the same level of certainty as I have hitherto attributed to the truths of mathematics.[54]

At first sight, however, this is not transparently clear, but has some appearance of being a sophism. Since I have been accustomed to distinguish between existence and essence in everything else, I find it easy to persuade myself that existence can also be separated from the essence of God, and hence that God can be thought of as not existing. But when I concentrate more carefully, it is quite evident that existence can no more be separated from the essence of God than the fact that its three angles equal two right angles can be separated from the essence of a triangle, or than the idea of a mountain can be separated from the idea of a valley. Hence it is just as much of a contradiction to think of God (that is, a supremely perfect being) lacking existence (that is, lacking a perfection), as it is to think of a mountain without a valley.

However, even granted that I cannot think of God except as existing, just as I cannot think of a mountain without a valley, it certainly does not follow from the fact that I think of a mountain with a valley that there is any mountain in the world; and similarly, it does not seem to follow from the fact that I think of God as existing that he does exist. For my thought does not impose any necessity on things; and just as I may imagine a winged horse even though no horse has wings, so I may be able to attach existence to God even though no God exists.

But there is a sophism concealed here. From the fact that I cannot think of a mountain without a valley, it does not follow that a mountain and valley exist anywhere, but simply that a mountain and a valley, whether they exist or not, are mutually inseparable. But from the fact that I cannot think of God except as existing, it follows that existence is inseparable from God, and hence that he really exists. It is not that my thought makes it so, or imposes any necessity on any thing; on the contrary, it is the necessity of the thing itself, namely the existence of God, which determines my thinking in this respect. For I am not free to think of God without existence (that is, a supremely perfect being without a supreme perfection) as I am free to imagine a horse with or without wings.

And it must not be objected at this point that while it is indeed necessary for me to suppose God exists, once I have made the supposition that he has all perfections (since existence is one of the perfections), nevertheless the original

supposition was not necessary. Similarly, the objection would run, it is not necessary for me to think that all quadrilaterals can be inscribed in a circle; but given this supposition, it will be necessary for me to admit that a rhombus can be inscribed in a circle—which is patently false. Now admittedly, it is not necessary that I ever light upon any thought of God; but whenever I do choose to think of the first and supreme being, and bring forth the idea of God from the treasure house of my mind as it were, it is necessary that I attribute all perfections to him, even if I do not at that time enumerate them or attend to them individually. And this necessity plainly guarantees that, when I later realize that existence is a perfection, I am correct in inferring that the first and supreme being exists. In the same way, it is not necessary for me ever to imagine a triangle; but whenever I do wish to consider a rectilinear figure having just three angles, it is necessary that I attribute to it the properties which license the inference that its three angles equal no more than two right angles, even if I do not notice this at the time. By contrast, when I examine what figures can be inscribed in a circle, it is in no way necessary for me to think that this class includes all quadrilaterals. Indeed, I cannot even imagine this, so long as I am willing to admit only what I clearly and distinctly understand. So there is a great difference between this kind of false supposition and the true ideas which are innate in me, of which the first and most important is the idea of God. There are many ways in which I understand that this idea is not something fictitious which is dependent on my thought, but is an image of a true and immutable nature. First of all, there is the fact that, apart from God, there is nothing else of which I am capable of thinking such that existence belongs[55] to its essence. Second, I cannot understand how there could be two or more Gods of this kind; and after supposing that one God exists, I plainly see that it is necessary that he has existed from eternity and will abide for eternity. And finally, I perceive many other attributes of God, none of which I can remove or alter.

But whatever method of proof I use, I am always brought back to the fact that it is only what I clearly and distinctly perceive that completely convinces me. Some of the things I clearly and distinctly perceive are obvious to everyone, while others are discovered only by those who look more closely and investigate more carefully; but once they have been discovered, the latter are judged to be just as certain as the former. In the case of a right-angled triangle, for example, the fact that the square on the hypotenuse is equal to the square on the other two sides is not so readily apparent as the fact that the hypotenuse subtends the largest angle; but once one has seen it, one believes it just as strongly. But as regards God, if I were not overwhelmed by preconceived opinions, and if the images of things perceived by the senses did not besiege my thought on every side, I would certainly acknowledge him sooner and more easily than anything else. For what is more selfevident than the fact that the supreme being exists, or that God, to whose essence alone existence belongs,[56] exists?

Although it needed close attention for me to perceive this, I am now just as certain of it as I am of everything else which appears most certain. And what is more, I see that the certainty of all other things depends on this, so that without it nothing can ever be perfectly known.

Admittedly my nature is such that so long as[57] I perceive something very clearly and distinctly I cannot but believe it to be true. But my nature is also such that I cannot fix my mental vision continually on the same thing, so as to keep perceiving it clearly; and often the memory of a previously made judgement may come back, when I am no longer attending to the arguments which led me to make it. And so other arguments can now occur to me which might easily undermine my opinion, if I were unaware of God; and I should thus never have true and certain knowledge about anything, but only shifting and changeable opinions. For example, when I consider the nature of a triangle, it appears most evident to me, steeped as I am in the principles of geometry, that its three angles are equal to two right angles; and so long as I attend to the proof, I cannot but believe this to be true. But as soon as I turn my mind's eye away from the proof, then in spite of still remembering that I perceived it very clearly, I can easily fall into doubt about its truth, if I am unaware of God. For I can convince myself that I have a natural disposition to go wrong from time to time in matters which I think I perceive as evidently as can be. This will seem even more likely when I remember that there have been frequent cases where I have regarded things as true and certain, but have later been led by other arguments to judge them to be false.

Now, however, I have perceived that God exists, and at the same time I have understood that everything else depends on him, and that he is no deceiver; and I have drawn the conclusion that everything which I clearly and distinctly perceive is of necessity true. Accordingly, even if I am no longer attending to the arguments which led me to judge that this is true, as long as I remember that I clearly and distinctly perceived it, there are no counter-arguments which can be adduced to make me doubt it, but on the contrary I have true and certain knowledge of it. And I have knowledge not just of this matter, but of all matters which I remember ever having demonstrated, in geometry and so on. For what objections can now be raised?[58] That the way I am made makes me prone to frequent error? But I now know that I am incapable of error in those cases where my understanding is transparently clear. Or can it be objected that I have in the past regarded as true and certain many things which I afterwards recognized to be false? But none of these were things which I clearly and distinctly perceived: I was ignorant of this rule for establishing the truth, and believed these things for other reasons which I later discovered to be less reliable. So what is left to say? Can one raise the objection I put to myself a while ago, that I may be dreaming, or that everything which I am now thinking has as little truth as what comes to the mind of one who is asleep? Yet even this does not change anything. For even though I might be dreaming, if there is anything which is evident to my intellect, then it is wholly true.

Thus I see plainly that the certainty and truth of all knowledge depends uniquely on my awareness of the true God, to such an extent that I was incapable of perfect knowledge about anything else until I became aware of him. And now it is possible for me to achieve full and certain knowledge of countless matters, both concerning God himself and other things whose nature is intellectual, and also concerning the whole of that corporeal nature which is the subject-matter of pure mathematics.[59]

SIXTH MEDITATION

The existence of material things, and the real distinction between mind and body[60]

It remains for me to examine whether material things exist. And at least I now know they are capable of existing, in so far as they are the subject-matter of pure mathematics, since I perceive them clearly and distinctly. For there is no doubt that God is capable of creating everything that I am capable of perceiving in this manner; and I have never judged that something could not be made by him except on the grounds that there would be a contradiction in my perceiving it distinctly. The conclusion that material things exist is also suggested by the faculty of imagination, which I am aware of using when I turn my mind to material things. For when I give more attentive consideration to what imagination is, it seems to be nothing else but an application of the cognitive faculty to a body which is intimately present to it, and which therefore exists.

To make this clear, I will first examine the difference between imagination and pure understanding. When I imagine a triangle, for example, I do not merely understand that it is a figure bounded by three lines, but at the same time I also see the three lines with my mind's eye as if they were present before me; and this is what I call imagining. But if I want to think of a chiliagon, although I understand that it is a figure consisting of a thousand sides just as well as I understand the triangle to be a three-sided figure, I do not in the same way imagine the thousand sides or see them as if they were present before me. It is true that since I am in the habit of imagining something whenever I think of a corporeal thing, I may construct in my mind a confused representation of some figure; but it is clear that this is not a chiliagon. For it differs in no way from the representation I should form if I were thinking of a myriagon, or any figure with very many sides. Moreover, such a representation is useless for recognizing the properties which distinguish a chiliagon from other polygons. But suppose I am dealing with a pentagon: I can of course understand the figure of a pentagon, just as I can the figure of a chiliagon, without the help of the imagination; but I can also imagine a pentagon, by applying my mind's eye to its five sides and the area contained within them. And in doing this I notice quite clearly that imagination requires a peculiar effort of mind which is not required for understanding; this additional effort of mind clearly shows the difference between imagination and pure understanding.

Besides this, I consider that this power of imagining which is in me, differing as it does from the power of understanding, is not a necessary constituent of my own essence, that is, of the essence of my mind. For if I lacked it, I should undoubtedly remain the same individual as I now am; from which it seems to follow that it depends on something distinct from myself. And I can easily understand that, if there does exist some body to which the mind is so joined that it can apply itself to contemplate it, as it were, whenever it pleases, then it may possibly be this very body that enables me to imagine corporeal things. So the difference between this mode of thinking and pure understanding may simply be this: when the mind understands, it in some way turns towards itself and inspects one of the ideas which are within it; but when it imagines, it turns towards the body and looks at something in the body which conforms to an idea understood by the mind or perceived by the senses. I can, as I say, easily understand that this is how imagination comes about, if the body exists; and since there is no other equally suitable way of explaining imagination that comes to mind, I can make a probable conjecture that the body exists. But this is only a probability; and despite a careful and comprehensive investigation, I do not yet see how the distinct idea of corporeal nature which I find in my imagination can provide any basis for a necessary inference that some body exists.

But besides that corporeal nature which is the subject-matter of pure mathematics, there is much else that I habitually imagine, such as colours, sounds, tastes, pain and so on—though not so distinctly. Now I perceive these things much better by means of the senses, which is how, with the assistance of memory, they appear to have reached the imagination. So in order to deal with them more fully, I must pay equal attention to the senses, and see whether the things which are perceived by means of that mode of thinking which I call 'sensory perception' provide me with any sure argument for the existence of corporeal things.

To begin with, I will go back over all the things which I previously took to be perceived by the senses, and reckoned to be true; and I will go over my reasons for thinking this. Next, I will set out my reasons for subsequently calling these things into doubt. And finally I will consider what I should now believe about them.

First of all then, I perceived by my senses that I had a head, hands, feet and other limbs making up the body which I regarded as part of myself, or perhaps even as my whole self. I also perceived by my senses that this body was situated among many other bodies which could affect it in various favourable or unfavourable ways; and I gauged the favourable effects by a sensation of pleasure, and the unfavourable ones by a sensation of pain. In addition to pain and pleasure, I also had sensations within me of hunger, thirst, and other such appetites, and also of physical propensities towards cheerfulness, sadness, anger and similar emotions. And outside me, besides the extension, shapes and movements of bodies, I also had sensations of their hardness and heat, and of the other tactile qualities. In addition, I had sensations of light, colours, smells, tastes and sounds, the variety of which enabled me to distinguish the sky, the earth, the seas, and all other bodies, one from another. Considering the ideas of all these qualities which presented themselves to my thought, although the ideas were, strictly speaking, the only immediate objects of my sensory awareness, it was not unreasonable for me to think that the items which I was perceiving through the senses were things quite distinct from my thought, namely bodies which produced the ideas. For my experience was that these ideas came to me quite without my consent, so that I could not have sensory awareness of any object, even if I wanted to, unless it was present to my sense organs; and I could not avoid having sensory awareness of it when it was present. And since the ideas perceived by the senses were much more lively and vivid and even, in their own way, more distinct than any of those which I deliberately formed through meditating or which I found impressed on my memory, it seemed impossible that they should have come from within me; so the only alternative was that they came from other things. Since the sole source of my knowledge of these things was the ideas themselves, the supposition that the things resembled the ideas was bound to occur to me. In addition, I remembered that the use of my senses had come first, while the use of my reason came only later; and I saw that the ideas which I formed myself were less vivid than those which I perceived with the senses and were, for the most part, made up of elements of sensory ideas. In this way I easily convinced myself that I had nothing at all in the intellect which I had not previously had in sensation. As for the body which by some special right I called 'mine', my belief that this body, more than any other, belonged to me had some justification. For I could never be separated from it, as I could from other bodies; and I felt all my appetites and emotions in, and on account of, this body; and finally,

I was aware of pain and pleasurable ticklings in parts of this body, but not in other bodies external to it. But why should that curious sensation of pain give rise to a particular distress of mind; or why should a certain kind of delight follow on a tickling sensation? Again, why should that curious tugging in the stomach which I call hunger tell me that I should eat, or a dryness of the throat tell me to drink, and so on? I was not able to give any explanation of all this, except that nature taught me so. For there is absolutely no connection (at least that I can understand) between the tugging sensation and the decision to take food, or between the sensation of something causing pain and the mental apprehension of distress that arises from that sensation. These and other judgements that I made concerning sensory objects, I was apparently taught to make by nature; for I had already made up my mind that this was how things were, before working out any arguments to prove it.

Later on, however, I had many experiences which gradually undermined all the faith I had had in the senses. Sometimes towers which had looked round from a distance appeared square from close up; and enormous statues standing on their pediments did not seem large when observed from the ground. In these and countless other such cases, I found that the judgements of the external senses were mistaken. And this applied not just to the external senses but to the internal senses as well. For what can be more internal than pain? And yet I had heard that those who had had a leg or an arm amputated sometimes still seemed to feel pain intermittently in the missing part of the body. So even in my own case it was apparently not quite certain that a particular limb was hurting, even if I felt pain in it. To these reasons for doubting, I recently added two very general ones.[61] The first was that every sensory experience I have ever thought I was having while awake I can also think of myself as sometimes having while asleep; and since I do not believe that what I seem to perceive in sleep comes from things located outside me, I did not see why I should be any more inclined to believe this of what I think I perceive

while awake. The second reason for doubt was that since I did not yet know the author of my being (or at least was pretending not to), I saw nothing to rule out the possibility that my natural constitution made me prone to error even in matters which seemed to me most true. As for the reasons for my previous confident belief in the truth of the things perceived by the senses, I had no trouble in refuting them. For since I apparently had natural impulses towards many things which reason told me to avoid, I reckoned that a great deal of confidence should not be placed in what I was taught by nature. And despite the fact that the perceptions of the senses were not dependent on my will, I did not think that I should on that account infer that they proceeded from things distinct from myself, since I might perhaps have a faculty not yet known to me which produced them.[62]

But now, when I am beginning to achieve a better knowledge of myself and the author of my being, although I do not think I should heedlessly accept everything I seem to have acquired from the senses, neither do I think that everything should be called into doubt.

First, I know that everything which I clearly and distinctly understand is capable of being created by God so as to correspond exactly with my understanding of it. Hence the fact that I can clearly and distinctly understand one thing apart from another is enough to make me certain that the two things are distinct, since they are capable of being separated, at least by God. The question of what kind of power is required to bring about such a separation does not affect the judgement that the two things are distinct. Thus, simply by knowing that I exist and seeing at the same time that absolutely nothing else belongs to my nature or essence except that I am a thinking thing, I can infer correctly that my essence consists solely in the fact that I am a thinking thing. It is true that I may have (or, to anticipate, that I certainly have) a body that is very closely joined to me. But nevertheless, on the one hand I have a clear and distinct idea of myself, in so far as I am simply a thinking, nonextended thing; and on the other hand I have a distinct idea of body,[63] in so far as this is simply an extended, non-thinking thing And accordingly, it is certain that I[64] am really distinct from my body, and can exist without it.

Besides this, I find in myself faculties for certain special modes of thinking,[65] namely imagination and sensory perception. Now I can clearly and distinctly understand myself as a whole without these faculties; but I cannot, conversely, understand these faculties without me, that is, without an intellectual substance to inhere in. This is because there is an intellectual act included in their essential definition; and hence I perceive that the distinction between them and myself corresponds to the distinction between the modes of a thing and the thing itself.[66] Of course I also recognize that there are other faculties (like those of changing position, of taking on various shapes, and so on) which, like sensory perception and imagination, cannot be understood apart from some substance for them to inhere in, and hence cannot exist without it. But it is clear that these other faculties, if they exist, must be in a corporeal or extended substance and not an intellectual one; for the clear and distinct conception of them includes extension, but does not include any intellectual act whatsoever. Now there is in me a passive faculty of sensory perception, that is, a faculty for receiving and recognizing the ideas of sensible objects; but I could not make use of it unless there was also an active faculty, either in me or in something else, which produced or brought about these ideas. But this faculty cannot be in me, since clearly it presupposes no intellectual act on my part,[67] and the ideas in question are produced without my cooperation and often even against my will. So the only alternative is that it is in another substance distinct from me—a substance which contains either formally or eminently all the reality which exists objectively[68] in the ideas produced by this faculty (as I have just noted). This substance is either a body, that is, a corporeal nature, in which case it will contain formally <and in fact> everything which is to be found objectively <or representatively> in the ideas; or else it is God, or some creature more

noble than a body, in which case it will contain eminently whatever is to be found in the ideas. But since God is not a deceiver, it is quite clear that he does not transmit the ideas to me either directly from himself, or indirectly, via some creature which contains the objective reality of the ideas not formally but only eminently. For God has given me no faculty at all for recognizing any such source for these ideas; on the contrary, he has given me a great propensity to believe that they are produced by corporeal things. So I do not see how God could be understood to be anything but a deceiver if the ideas were transmitted from a source other than corporeal things. It follows that corporeal things exist. They may not all exist in a way that exactly corresponds with my sensory grasp of them, for in many cases the grasp of the senses is very obscure and confused. But at least they possess all the properties which I clearly and distinctly understand, that is, all those which, viewed in general terms, are comprised within the subject-matter of pure mathematics.

What of the other aspects of corporeal things which are either particular (for example that the sun is of such and such a size or shape), or less clearly understood, such as light or sound or pain, and so on? Despite the high degree of doubt and uncertainty involved here, the very fact that God is not a deceiver, and the consequent impossibility of there being any falsity in my opinions which cannot be corrected by some other faculty supplied by God, offers me a sure hope that I can attain the truth even in these matters. Indeed, there is no doubt that everything that I am taught by nature contains some truth. For if nature is considered in its general aspect, then I understand by the term nothing other than God himself, or the ordered system of created things established by God. And by my own nature in particular I understand nothing other than the totality of things bestowed on me by God.

There is nothing that my own nature teaches me more vividly than that I have a body, and that when I feel pain there is something wrong with the body, and that when I am hungry or thirsty the body needs food and drink, and so on. So I should not doubt that there is some truth in this.

Nature also teaches me, by these sensations of pain, hunger, thirst and so on, that I am not merely present in my body as a sailor is present in a ship,[69] but that I am very closely joined and, as it were, intermingled with it, so that I and the body form a unit. If this were not so, I, who am nothing but a thinking thing, would not feel pain when the body was hurt, but would perceive the damage purely by the intellect, just as a sailor perceives by sight if anything in his ship is broken. Similarly, when the body needed food or drink, I should have an explicit understanding of the fact, instead of having confused sensations of hunger and thirst. For these sensations of hunger, thirst, pain and so on are nothing but confused modes of thinking which arise from the union and, as it were, intermingling of the mind with the body.

I am also taught by nature that various other bodies exist in the vicinity of my body, and that some of these are to be sought out and others avoided. And from the fact that I perceive by my senses a great variety of colours, sounds, smells and tastes, as well as differences in heat, hardness and the like, I am correct in inferring that the bodies which are the source of these various sensory perceptions possess differences corresponding to them, though perhaps not resembling them. Also, the fact that some of the perceptions are agreeable to me while others are disagreeable makes it quite certain that my body, or rather my whole self, in so far as I am a combination of body and mind, can be affected by the various beneficial or harmful bodies which surround it.

There are, however, many other things which I may appear to have been taught by nature, but which in reality I acquired not from nature but from a habit of making ill-considered judgements; and it is therefore quite possible that these are false. Cases in point are the belief that any space in which nothing is occurring to stimulate my senses must be empty; or that the heat in a body is something exactly resembling the idea of heat which is in me; or that

when a body is white or green, the selfsame whiteness or greenness which I perceive through my senses is present in the body; or that in a body which is bitter or sweet there is the selfsame taste which I experience, and so on; or, finally, that stars and towers and other distant bodies have the same size and shape which they present to my senses, and other examples of this kind. But to make sure that my perceptions in this matter are sufficiently distinct, I must more accurately define exactly what I mean when I say that I am taught something by nature. In this context I am taking nature to be something more limited than the totality of things bestowed on me by God. For this includes many things that belong to the mind alone—for example my perception that what is done cannot be undone, and all other things that are known by the natural light;[70] but at this stage I am not speaking of these matters. It also includes much that relates to the body alone, like the tendency to move in a downward direction, and so on; but I am not speaking of these matters either. My sole concern here is with what God has bestowed on me as a combination of mind and body. My nature, then, in this limited sense, does indeed teach me to avoid what induces a feeling of pain and to seek out what induces feelings of pleasure, and so on. But it does not appear to teach us to draw any conclusions from these sensory perceptions about things located outside us without waiting until the intellect has examined[71] the matter. For knowledge of the truth about such things seems to belong to the mind alone, not to the combination of mind and body. Hence, although a star has no greater effect on my eye than the flame of a small light, that does not mean that there is any real or positive inclination in me to believe that the star is no bigger than the light; I have simply made this judgement from childhood onwards without any rational basis. Similarly, although I feel heat when I go near a fire and feel pain when I go too near, there is no convincing argument for supposing that there is something in the fire which resembles the heat, any more than for supposing that there is something which resembles the pain. There is simply reason to suppose that there is something in the fire, whatever it may eventually turn out to be, which produces in us the feelings of heat or pain. And likewise, even though there is nothing in any given space that stimulates the senses, it does not follow that there is no body there. In these cases and many others I see that I have been in the habit of misusing the order of nature. For the proper purpose of the sensory perceptions given me by nature is simply to inform the mind of what is beneficial or harmful for the composite of which the mind is a part; and to this extent they are sufficiently clear and distinct. But I misuse them by treating them as reliable touchstones for immediate judgements about the essential nature of the bodies located outside us; yet this is an area where they provide only very obscure information.

I have already looked in sufficient detail at how, notwithstanding the goodness of God, it may happen that my judgements are false. But a further problem now comes to mind regarding those very things which nature presents to me as objects which I should seek out or avoid, and also regarding the internal sensations, where I seem to have detected errors[72]—e.g. when someone is tricked by the pleasant taste of some food into eating the poison concealed inside it. Yet in this case, what the man's nature urges him to go for is simply what is responsible for the pleasant taste, and not the poison, which his nature knows nothing about. The only inference that can be drawn from this is that his nature is not omniscient. And this is not surprising, since man is a limited thing, and so it is only fitting that his perfection should be limited.

And yet it is not unusual for us to go wrong even in cases where nature does urge us towards something. Those who are ill, for example, may desire food or drink that will shortly afterwards turn out to be bad for them. Perhaps it may be said that they go wrong because their nature is disordered, but this does not remove the difficulty. A sick man is no less one of God's creatures than a healthy one, and it seems no less a contradiction to suppose that he has received

from God a nature which deceives him. Yet a clock constructed with wheels and weights observes all the laws of its nature just as closely when it is badly made and tells the wrong time as when it completely fulfils the wishes of the clockmaker. In the same way, I might consider the body of a man as a kind of machine equipped with and made up of bones, nerves, muscles, veins, blood and skin in such a way that, even if there were no mind in it, it would still perform all the same movements as it now does in those cases where movement is not under the control of the will or, consequently, of the mind.[73] I can easily see that if such a body suffers from dropsy, for example, and is affected by the dryness of the throat which normally produces in the mind the sensation of thirst, the resulting condition of the nerves and other parts will dispose the body to take a drink, with the result that the disease will be aggravated. Yet this is just as natural as the body's being stimulated by a similar dryness of the throat to take a drink when there is no such illness and the drink is beneficial. Admittedly, when I consider the purpose of the clock, I may say that it is departing from its nature when it does not tell the right time; and similarly when I consider the mechanism of the human body, I may think that, in relation to the movements which normally occur in it, it too is deviating from its nature if the throat is dry at a time when drinking is not beneficial to its continued health. But I am well aware that 'nature' as I have just used it has a very different significance from 'nature' in the other sense. As I have just used it, 'nature' is simply a label which depends on my thought; it is quite extraneous to the things to which it is applied, and depends simply on my comparison between the idea of a sick man and a badly-made clock, and the idea of a healthy man and a well-made clock. But by 'nature' in the other sense I understand something which is really to be found in the things themselves; in this sense, therefore, the term contains something of the truth.

When we say, then, with respect to the body suffering from dropsy, that it has a disordered nature because it has a dry throat and yet does not need drink, the term 'nature' is here used merely as an extraneous label. However, with respect to the composite, that is, the mind united with this body, what is involved is not a mere label, but a true error of nature, namely that it is thirsty at a time when drink is going to cause it harm. It thus remains to inquire how it is that the goodness of God does not prevent nature, in this sense, from deceiving us.

The first observation I make at this point is that there is a great difference between the mind and the body, in as much as the body is by its very nature always divisible, while the mind is utterly indivisible. For when I consider the mind, or myself in so far as I am merely a thinking thing, I am unable to distinguish any parts within myself; I understand myself to be something quite single and complete. Although the whole mind seems to be united to the whole body, I recognize that if a foot or arm or any other part of the body is cut off, nothing has thereby been taken away from the mind. As for the faculties of willing, of understanding, of sensory perception and so on, these cannot be termed parts of the mind, since it is one and the same mind that wills, and understands and has sensory perceptions. By contrast, there is no corporeal or extended thing that I can think of which in my thought I cannot easily divide into parts; and this very fact makes me understand that it is divisible. This one argument would be enough to show me that the mind is completely different from the body, even if I did not already know as much from other considerations.

My next observation is that the mind is not immediately affected by all parts of the body, but only by the brain, or perhaps just by one small part of the brain, namely the part which is said to contain the 'common' sense.[74] Every time this part of the brain is in a given state, it presents the same signals to the mind, even though the other parts of the body may be in a different condition at the time. This is established by countless observations, which there is no need to review here.

I observe, in addition, that the nature of the body is such that whenever any part of it is moved by another part which is some distance away, it can always be moved in the same fashion by any of the parts which lie in between, even if the more distant part does nothing. For example, in a cord ABCD, if one end D is pulled so that the other end A moves, the exact same movement could have been brought about if one of the intermediate points B or C had been pulled, and D had not moved at all. In similar fashion, when I feel a pain in my foot, physiology tells me that this happens by means of nerves distributed throughout the foot, and that these nerves are like cords which go from the foot right up to the brain. When the nerves are pulled in the foot, they in turn pull on inner parts of the brain to which they are attached, and produce a certain motion in them; and nature has laid it down that this motion should produce in the mind a sensation of pain, as occurring in the foot. But since these nerves, in passing from the foot to the brain, must pass through the calf, the thigh, the lumbar region, the back and the neck, it can happen that, even if it is not the part in the foot but one of the intermediate parts which is being pulled, the same motion will occur in the brain as occurs when the foot is hurt, and so it will necessarily come about that the mind feels the same sensation of pain. And we must suppose the same thing happens with regard to any other sensation.

My final observation is that any given movement occurring in the part of the brain that immediately affects the mind produces just one corresponding sensation; and hence the best system that could be devised is that it should produce the one sensation which, of all possible sensations, is most especially and most frequently conducive to the preservation of the healthy man. And experience shows that the sensations which nature has given us are all of this kind; and so there is absolutely nothing to be found in them that does not bear witness to the power and goodness of God. For example, when the nerves in the foot are set in motion in a violent and unusual manner, this motion, by way of the spinal cord, reaches the inner parts of the brain, and there gives the mind its signal for having a certain sensation, namely the sensation of a pain as occurring in the foot. This stimulates the mind to do its best to get rid of the cause of the pain, which it takes to be harmful to the foot. It is true that God could have made the nature of man such that this particular motion in the brain indicated something else to the mind; it might, for example, have made the mind aware of the actual motion occurring in the brain, or in the foot, or in any of the intermediate regions; or it might have indicated something else entirely. But there is nothing else which would have been so conducive to the continued well-being of the body. In the same way, when we need drink, there arises a certain dryness in the throat; this sets in motion the nerves of the throat, which in turn move the inner parts of the brain. This motion produces in the mind a sensation of thirst, because the most useful thing for us to know about the whole business is that we need drink in order to stay healthy. And so it is in the other cases.

It is quite clear from all this that, notwithstanding the immense goodness of God, the nature of man as a combination of mind and body is such that it is bound to mislead him from time to time. For there may be some occurrence, not in the foot but in one of the other areas through which the nerves travel in their route from the foot to the brain, or even in the brain itself; and if this cause produces the same motion which is generally produced by injury to the foot, then pain will be felt as if it were in the foot. This deception of the senses is natural, because a given motion in the brain must always produce the same sensation in the mind; and the origin of the motion in question is much more often going to be something which is hurting the foot, rather than something existing elsewhere. So it is reasonable that this motion should always indicate to the mind a pain in the foot rather than in any other part of the body. Again, dryness of the throat may sometimes arise not, as it normally does, from the fact that a drink is necessary to the health of the body, but from some quite opposite cause, as happens in the case of the man with dropsy. Yet it is much better that it should

mislead on this occasion than that it should always mislead when the body is in good health. And the same goes for the other cases.

This consideration is the greatest help to me, not only for noticing all the errors to which my nature is liable, but also for enabling me to correct or avoid them without difficulty. For I know that in matters regarding the well-being of the body, all my senses report the truth much more frequently than not. Also, I can almost always make use of more than one sense to investigate the same thing; and in addition, I can use both my memory, which connects present experiences with preceding ones, and my intellect, which has by now examined all the causes of error. Accordingly, I should not have any further fears about the falsity of what my senses tell me every day; on the contrary, the exaggerated doubts of the last few days should be dismissed as laughable. This applies especially to the principal reason for doubt, namely my inability to distinguish between being asleep and being awake. For I now notice that there is a vast difference between the two, in that dreams are never linked by memory with all the other actions of life as waking experiences are. If, while I am awake, anyone were suddenly to appear to me and then disappear immediately, as happens in sleep, so that I could not see where he had come from or where he had gone to, it would not be unreasonable for me to judge that he was a ghost, or a vision created in my brain,[75] rather than a real man. But when I distinctly see where things come from and where and when they come to me, and when I can connect my perceptions of them with the whole of the rest of my life without a break, then I am quite certain that when I encounter these things I am not asleep but awake. And I ought not to have even the slightest doubt of their reality if, after calling upon all the senses as well as my memory and my intellect in order to check them, I receive no conflicting reports from any of these sources. For from the fact that God is not a deceiver it follows that in cases like these I am completely free from error. But since the pressure of things to be done does not always allow us to stop and make such a meticulous check, it must be admitted that in this human life we are often liable to make mistakes about particular things, and we must acknowledge the weakness of our nature.

NOTES

1. The continuous divine action necessary to maintain things in existence.

2. Descartes here uses this scholastic term to refer to those features of a thing which may alter, e.g. the particular size, shape, etc. of a body, or the particular thoughts, desires, etc. of a mind.

3. '...or the soul of man, for I make no distinction between them' (added in French version).

4. For Descartes' use of this term.

5. Descartes added this passage on the advice of Arnauld (cf. AT VII 215; CSM II 151). He told Mersenne 'Put the words between brackets so that it can be seen that they have been added' (letter of 18 March 1641: AT III 335; CSMK 175).

6. '...and in my dreams regularly represent to myself the same things' (French version).

7. '...the place where they are, the time which measures their duration' (French version).

8. '...yet I cannot doubt that he does allow this' (French version).

9. '...in the sciences' (added in French version).

10. '...nevertheless it is in my power to suspend my judgement' (French version).

11. '...puts into my mind' (French version).

12. '...or thought anything at all' (French version).

13. The word 'only' is most naturally taken as going with 'a thing that thinks', and this interpretation is followed in the French version. When discussing this passage with Gassendi, however, Descartes suggests that he meant the 'only' to govern 'in the strict sense'; cf AT IXA 215; CSM II 276.

14. '...to see if I am not something more' (added in French version).

15. Lat. *maneat* ('let it stand'), first edition. The second edition has the indicative *manet*: 'The proposition still stands, *viz.* that I am nonetheless something.' The French version reads: 'without changing this supposition, I find that I am still certain that I am something.'

16. '...from this manner of conceiving things' (French version).

17. '...which can be conceived only by the understanding or the mind' (French version).

18. '...or rather the act whereby it is perceived' (added in French version).

19. The French version has 'more clear and distinct' and, at the end of this sentence, 'more evidently, distinctly and clearly.'

20. The French version here inserts 'loves, hates.'

21. '...all the things which we conceive very clearly and very distinctly are true' (French version).

22. '...it was not because of any knowledge I possessed' (French version).

23. The opening of this sentence is greatly expanded in the French version: 'In order that I may have the opportunity of examining this without interrupting the order of meditating which I have decided upon, which is to start only from those notions which I find first of all in my mind and pass gradually to those which I may find later on, I must here divide my thoughts...'

24. '...foreign to me and coming from outside' (French version).

25. '...or power for distinguishing truth from falsehood' (French version).

26. '...concerning truth and falsehood' (French version).

27. '...i.e. participate by representation in a higher degree of being or perfection' (added in French version). According to the scholastic distinction invoked in the paragraphs that follow, the 'formal' reality of anything is its own intrinsic reality, while the 'objective' reality of an idea is a function of its representational content. Thus if an idea A represents some object X which is F, then F-ness will be contained 'formally' in X but 'objectively' in A.

28. '...i.e. it will contain in itself the same things as are in the stone or other more excellent things' (added in French version). In scholastic terminology, to possess a property 'formally' is to possess it literally, in accordance with its definition; to possess it 'eminently' is to possess it in some higher form.

29. '...that this cause must be less real' (French version).

30. '...i.e. a manner or way of thinking' (added in French version).

31. '...chimerical things which cannot exist' (French version).

32. 'And since ideas, being like images, must in each case appear to us to represent something' (French version).

33. '...in so far as they represent substances' (French version).

34. '...and as it were the garments under which corporeal substance appears to us' (French version).
35. '...that the idea I have of them' (French version).
36. '...i.e. could be in me in virtue of my imperfection' (added in French version).
37. According to Descartes one can know or understand something without fully grasping it: 'In the same way we can touch a mountain with our hands but we cannot put our arms around it... To grasp something is to embrace it in one's thought; to know something, it is sufficient to touch it with one's thought' (letter to Mersenne, 27 May 1630: AT I 152; CSMK 25).
38. '...but only what is actual and real' (added in French version).
39. '...and were independent of every other being' (added in French version).
40. Cf. *Principles*, Part I, art. 62: AT VIII 30; CSM I 214.
41. '...at least as much reality in the cause as in its effect' (French version).
42. Lat. *per se*; literally 'through itself?'
43. '...and has not one of the things which indicate some imperfection' (added in French version).
44. '...from things which can be perceived by the senses or imagined' (French version).
45. '...of the other things in the universe' (French version).
46. '...i.e. not simply the defect or lack of some perfection to which I have no proper claim' (added in French version).
47. '...without affirming or denying anything' (added in French version).
48. '...it cannot be said that my understanding is deprived of these ideas, as if they were something to which its nature entitles it' (French version).
49. '...rather than entertaining so unjust a thought as to imagine that he deprived me of, or unjustly withheld, the other perfections which he did not give me' (French version).
50. '...understanding these terms in accordance with scholastic usage' (added in French version).
51. '...as if there were only myself in the world' (added in French version).
52. '...something real and positive' (French version).
53. '...that actual and eternal existence belongs to his nature' (French version).
54. '...which concern only figures and numbers' (added in French version).
55. '...necessarily belongs' (French version).
56. '...in the idea of whom alone necessary and eternal existence is comprised' (French version).
57. '...as soon as' (French version).
58. '...to oblige me to call these matters into doubt' (added in French version).
59. '...and also concerning things which belong to corporeal nature in so far as it can serve as the object of geometrical demonstrations which have no concern with whether that object exists' (French version).
60. '...between the soul and body of a man' (French version).
61. Cf. Med. I.
62. Cf. Med. III.
63. The Latin term *corpus* as used here by Descartes is ambiguous as between 'body' (i.e. corporeal matter in general) and 'the body' (i.e. this particular body of mine). The French version preserves the ambiguity.
64. '...that is, my soul, by which I am what I am' (added in French version).
65. '...certain modes of thinking which are quite special and distinct from me' (French version).
66. '...between the shapes, movements and other modes or accidents of a body and the body which supports them' (French version).
67. '...cannot be in me in so far as I am merely a thinking thing, since it does not presuppose any thought on my part' (French version).
68. For the terms 'formally', 'eminently' and 'objectively.'
69. '...as a pilot in his ship' (French version).
70. '...without any help from the body' (added in French version).
71. '...carefully and maturely examined' (French version).
72. '...and thus seem to have been directly deceived by my nature' (added in French version).
73. '...but occurs merely as a result of the disposition of the organs' (French version).
74. The supposed faculty which integrates the data from the five specialized senses (the notion goes back ultimately to Aristotle). 'The seat of the common sense must be very mobile, to receive all the impressions which come from the senses; but it must also be of such a kind as to be movable only by the spirits which transmit these impressions. Only the *conarion* [pineal gland] fits this description' (letter to Mersenne, 21 April 1641: AT III 362; CSMK 180).
75. '...like those that are formed in the brain when I sleep' (added in French version).

3.3 The Causal Theory of Perception

JOHN LOCKE

John Locke (1632–1704) was one of the greatest of English philosophers. His empiricist theory of knowledge and natural rights political theory have had lasting influence.

1. Concerning the simple ideas of Sensation, it is to be considered,—that whatsoever is so constituted in nature as to be able, by affecting our senses, to cause any perception in the mind, doth thereby produce in the understanding a simple idea; which, whatever be the external cause of it, when it comes to be taken notice of by our discerning faculty, it is by the mind looked on and considered there to be a real positive idea in the understanding, as much as any other whatsoever; though, perhaps, the cause of it be but a privation of the subject.

2. Thus the ideas of heat and cold, light and darkness, white and black, motion and rest, are equally clear and positive ideas in the mind; though, perhaps, some of the causes which produce them are barely privations, in those subjects from whence our senses derive those ideas. These the understanding, in its view of them, considers all as distinct positive ideas, without taking notice of the causes that produce them: which is an inquiry not belonging to the idea, as it is in the understanding, but to the nature of the things existing without us. These are two very different things, and carefully to be distinguished; it being one thing to perceive and know the idea of white or black, and quite another to examine what kind of particles they must be, and how ranged in the superficies, to make any object appear white or black....

7. To discover the nature of our *ideas* the better, and to discourse of them intelligibly, it will be convenient to distinguish them *as they are ideas or perceptions in our minds;* and *as they are modifications of matter in the bodies that cause such perceptions in us:* that so we may not think (as perhaps usually is done) that they are exactly the images and resemblances of something inherent in the subject; most of those of sensation being in the mind no more the likeness of something existing without us, than the names that stand for them are the likeness of our ideas, which yet upon hearing they are apt to excite in us.

8. Whatsoever the mind perceives *in itself,* or is the immediate object of perception, thought, or understanding, that I call *idea;* and the power to produce any idea in our mind, I call *quality* of the subject wherein that power is. Thus a snowball having the power to produce in us the ideas of white, cold, and round,—the power to produce those ideas in us, as they are in the snowball, I call qualities; and as they are sensations or perceptions in our understandings, I call them ideas; which *ideas,* if I speak of sometimes as in the things themselves, I would be understood to mean those qualities in the objects which produce them in us.

9. [Qualities thus considered in bodies are, *First,* such as are utterly inseparable from the body, in what state soever it be;] and such as in all the alterations and changes it suffers, all the force can be used upon it, it constantly keeps; and such as sense constantly finds in every particle of matter which has bulk enough to be perceived; and the mind finds inseparable from every particle of matter, though less than to make itself singly be perceived by our senses:

Reprinted from *An Essay Concerning Human Understanding,* Book II, Chapter VIII; Book IV, Chapter XI, first published 1690.

e.g. Take a grain of wheat, divide it into two parts; each part has still solidity, extension, figure, and mobility: divide it again, and it retains still the same qualities; and so divide it on, till the parts become insensible; they must retain still each of them all those qualities. For division (which is all that a mill, or pestle, or any other body, does upon another, in reducing it to insensible parts) can never take away either solidity, extension, figure, or mobility from any body, but only makes two or more distinct separate masses of matter, of that which was but one before; all which distinct masses, reckoned as so many distinct bodies, after division, make a certain number. [These I call *original* or *primary qualities* of body, which I think we may observe to produce simple ideas in us, viz. solidity, extension, figure, motion or rest, and number.

10. *Secondly,* such qualities which in truth are nothing in the objects themselves but powers to produce various sensations in us by their primary qualities, i.e. by the bulk, figure, texture, and motion of their insensible parts, as colours, sounds, tastes, etc. These I call *secondary qualities.* To these might be added a *third* sort, which are allowed to be barely powers; though they are as much real qualities in the subject as those which I, to comply with the common way of speaking, call qualities, but for distinction, secondary qualities. For the power in fire to produce a new colour, or consistency, in *wax* or *clay,*—by its primary qualities, is as much a quality in fire, as the power it has to produce in *me* a new idea or sensation of warmth or burning, which I felt not before,—by the same primary qualities, viz. the bulk, texture, and motion of its insensible parts.]

11. [The next thing to be considered is, how bodies produce ideas in us; and that is manifestly by impulse, the only way which we can conceive bodies to operate in.]

12. If then external objects be not united to our minds when they produce ideas therein; and yet we perceive these *original* qualities in such of them as singly fall under our senses, it is evident that some motion must be thence continued by our nerves, or animal spirits, by some parts of our bodies, to the brains or the seat of sensation, there to produce in our minds the particular ideas we have of them. And since the extension, figure, number, and motion of bodies of an observable bigness, may be perceived at a distance by the sight, it is evident some singly imperceptible bodies must come from them to the eyes, and therby convey to the brain some motion; which produces these ideas which we have of them in us.

13. After the same manner that the ideas of these original qualities are produced in us, we may conceive that the ideas of *secondary* qualities are also produced, viz. by the operation of insensible particles on our senses. For, it being manifest that there are bodies and good store of bodies, each whereof are so small, that we cannot by any of our senses discover either their bulk, figure, or motion,—as is evident in the particles of the air and water, and others extremely smaller than those; perhaps as much smaller than the particles of air and water, as the particles of air and water are smaller than peas or hailstones;—let us suppose at present that the different motions and figures, bulk and number, of such particles, affecting the several organs of our senses, produce in us those different sensations which we have from the colours and smells of bodies; e.g. that a violet, by the impulse of such insensible particles of matter, of peculiar figures and bulks, and in different degrees and modifications of their motions, causes the ideas of the blue colour, and sweet scent of that flower to be produced in our minds. It being no more impossible to conceive that God should annex such ideas to such motions, with which they have no similitude, than that he should annex the idea of pain to the motion of a piece of steel dividing our flesh, with which that idea hath no resemblance.

14. What I have said concerning colours and smells may be understood also of tastes and sounds, and other the like sensible qualities; which, whatever reality we by mistake attribute to them, are in truth nothing in the objects themselves, but powers to produce various sensations in us, and depend on those primary

qualities, viz. bulk, figure, texture, and motion of parts [as I have said].

15. From whence I think it easy to draw this observation,—that the ideas of primary qualities of bodies are resemblances of them, and their patterns do really exist in the bodies themselves, but the ideas produced in us by these secondary qualities have no resemblance of them at all. There is nothing like our ideas, existing the bodies themselves. They are, in the bodies we denominate from them, only a power to produce those sensations in us: and what is sweet, blue, or warm in idea, is but the certain bulk, figure, and motion of the insensible parts, in the bodies themselves, which we call so.

16. Flame is denominated hot and light; snow, white and cold; and manna, white and sweet, from the ideas they produce in us. Which qualities are commonly thought to be the same in those bodies that those ideas are in us, the one the perfect resemblance of the other, as they are in a mirror, and it would by most men be judged very extravagant if one should say otherwise. And yet he that will consider that the same fire that, at one distance produces in us the sensation of warmth, does, at a nearer approach, produce in us the far different sensation of pain, ought to bethink himself what reason he has to say—that this idea of warmth, which was produced in him by the fire, is *actually in the fire;* and his idea of pain, which the same fire produced in him the same way, is *not* in the fire. Why are whiteness and coldness in snow, and pain not, when it produces the one and the other idea in us; and can do neither, but by the bulk, figure, number, and motion of its solid parts?

17. The particular bulk, number, figure, and motion of the parts of fire or snow are really in them,—whether any one's senses perceive them or no: and therefore they may be called *real* qualities, because they really exist in those bodies. But light, heat, whiteness, or coldness, are no more really in them than sickness or pain is in manna. Take away the sensation of them; let not the eyes see light or colours, nor the ears hear sounds; let the palate not taste, nor the nose smell, and all colours, tastes, odours, and

sounds, *as they are such particular ideas,* vanish and cease, and are reduced to their causes, i.e. bulk, figure, and motion of parts.

18. A piece of manna of a sensible bulk is able to produce in us the idea of a round or square figure; and by being removed from one place to another, the idea of motion. This idea of motion represents it as it really is in manna moving: a circle or square are the same, whether in idea or existence, in the mind or in the manna. And this, both motion and figure, are really in the manna, whether we take notice of them or no: this everybody is ready to agree to. Besides, manna, by the bulk, figure, texture, and motion of its parts, has a power to produce the sensations of sickness, and sometimes of acute pains or gripings in us. That these ideas of sickness and pain are *not* in the manna, but effects of its operations on us, and are nowhere when we feel them not; this also every one readily agrees to. And yet men are hardly to be brought to think that sweetness and whiteness are not really in manna; which are but the effects of the operations of manna, by the motion, size, and figure of its particles, on the eyes and palate: as the pain and sickness caused by manna are confessedly nothing but the effects of its operations on the stomach and guts, by the size, motion, and figure of its insensible parts, (for by nothing else can a body operate, as has been proved): as if it could not operate on the eyes and palate, and thereby produce in the mind particular distinct ideas, which in itself it has not, as well as we allow it can operate on the guts and stomach, and thereby produce distinct ideas, which in itself it has not. These ideas, being all effects of the operations of manna on several parts of our bodies, by the size, figure, number, and motion of its parts;—why those produced by the eyes and palate should rather be thought to be really in the manna, than those produced by the stomach and guts; or why the pain and sickness, ideas that are the effect of manna, should be thought to be nowhere when they are not felt; and yet the sweetness and whiteness, effects of the same manna on other parts of the body, by ways equally as unknown, should be thought to exist

in the manna, where they are not seen or tasted, would need some reason to explain.

19. Let us consider the red and white colours in porphyry. Hinder light from striking on it, and its colours vanish; it no longer produces any such ideas in us: upon the return of light it produces these appearances on us again. Can any one think any real alterations are made in the porphyry by the presence or absence of light; and that those ideas of whiteness and redness are really in porphyry in the light, when it is plain *it has no colour in the dark?* It has, indeed, such a configuration of particles, both night and day, as are apt, by the rays of light rebounding from some parts of that hard stone, to produce in us the idea of redness, and from others the idea of whiteness; but whiteness or redness are not in it at any time, but such a texture that hath the power to produce such a sensation in us.

20. Pound an almond, and the clear white colour will be altered into a dirty one, and the sweet taste into an oily one. What real alteration can the beating of the pestle make in any body, but an alteration of the texture of it?

21. Ideas being thus distinguished and understood, we may be able to give an account how the same water, at the same time, may produce the idea of cold by one hand and of heat by the other; whereas it is impossible that the same water, if those ideas were really in it, should at the same time be both hot and cold. For, if we imagine *warmth,* as it is in our hands, to be nothing but a certain sort and degree of motion in the minute particles of our nerves or animal spirits, we may understand how it is possible that the same water may, at the same time, produce the sensations of heat in one hand and cold in the other; which yet *figure* never does, that never producing the idea of a square by one hand which has produced the idea of a globe by another. But if the sensation of heat and cold be nothing but the increase or diminution of the motion of the minute parts of our bodies, caused by the corpuscles of any other body, it is easy to be understood, that if that motion be greater in one hand than in the other; if a body be applied to the two hands, which has in its

minute particles a greater motion than in those of one of the hands, and a less than in those of the other, it will increase the motion of the one hand and lessen it in the other; and so cause the different sensations of heat and cold that depend thereon.

22. I have in what just goes before been engaged in physical inquiries a little further than perhaps I intended. But, it being necessary to make the nature of sensation a little understood; and to make the difference between the *qualities* in bodies, and the *ideas* produced by them in the mind, to be distinctly conceived, without which it were impossible to discourse intelligibly of them;—I hope I shall be pardoned this little excursion into natural philosophy; it being necessary in our present inquiry to distinguish the *primary* and *real* qualities of bodies, which are always in them (viz. solidity, extension, figure, number, and motion, or rest, and are sometimes perceived by us, viz. when the bodies they are in are big enough singly to be discerned), from those *secondary* and *imputed* qualities, which are but the powers of several combinations of those primary ones, when they operate without being distinctly discerned;— whereby we may also come to know what ideas are, and what are not, resemblances of something really existing in the bodies we denominate from them.

23. The qualities, then, that are in bodies, rightly considered, are of three sorts:—

First, The bulk, figure, number, situation, and motion or rest of their solid parts. Those are in them, whether we perceive them or not; and when they are of that size that we can discover them, we have by these an idea of the thing as it is in itself; as is plain in artificial things. These I call *primary qualities.*

Secondly, The power that is in any body, by reason of its insensible primary qualities, to operate after a peculiar manner on any of our senses, and thereby produce in *us* the different ideas of several colours, sounds, smells, tastes, etc. These are usually called *sensible qualities.*

Thirdly, The power that is in any body, by reason of the particular constitution of its primary qualities, to make such a change in the bulk, figure, texture, and motion of *another body,* as to make it operate on our senses differently from what it did before. Thus the sun has a power to make wax white, and fire to make lead fluid.

[These are usually called *powers.*]

The first of these, as has been said, I think may be properly called real, original, or primary qualities; because they are in the things themselves, whether they are perceived or not: and upon their different modifications it is that the secondary qualities depend.

The other two are only powers to act differently upon other things: which powers result from the different modifications of those primary qualities.

24. But, though the two latter sorts of qualities are powers barely, and nothing but powers, relating to several other bodies, and resulting from the different modifications of the original qualities, yet they are generally otherwise thought of. For the *second* sort, viz. the powers to produce several ideas in us, by our senses, are looked upon as real qualities in the things thus affecting us; but the *third* sort are called and esteemed barely powers, e.g., the idea of heat or light, which we receive by our eyes, or touch, from the sun, are commonly thought real qualities existing in the sun, and something more than mere powers in it. But when we consider the sun in reference to wax, which it melts or blanches, we look on the whiteness and softness produced in the wax, not as qualities in the sun, but effects produced by powers in it. Whereas, if rightly considered, these qualities of light and warmth, which are perceptions in me when I am warmed or enlightened by the sun, are no otherwise in the sun, than the changes made in the wax, when it is blanched or melted, are in the sun. They are all of them equally *powers in the sun, depending on its primary qualities;* whereby it is able, in the one case, so to alter the bulk, figure, texture, or motion of some of the insensible parts of my eyes or hands, as thereby to produce in me the idea of light or heat; and in the other, it is able so to alter the bulk, figure, texture, or motion of the insensible parts of the wax, as to make them fit to produce in me the distinct ideas of white and fluid.

25. The reason why the one is ordinarily taken for real qualities, and the other only for bare powers, seems to be, because the ideas we have of distinct colours, sounds, etc., containing nothing at all in them of bulk, figure, or motion, we are not apt to think them the effects of these primary qualities; which appear not, to our senses, to operate in their production, and with which they have not any apparent congruity or conceivable connexion. Hence it is that we are so forward to imagine, that those ideas are the resemblances of something really existing in the objects themselves: since sensation discovers nothing of bulk, figure, or motion of parts in their production; nor can reason show how bodies, *by their bulk, figure, and motion,* should produce in the mind the ideas of blue or yellow, etc. But, in the other case, in the operations of bodies changing the qualities one of another, we plainly discover that the quality produced hath commonly no resemblance with anything in the thing producing it; wherefore we look on it as a bare effect of power. For, through receiving the idea of heat or light from the sun, we are apt to think *it* is a perception and resemblance of such a quality in the sun; yet when we see wax, or a fair face, receive change of colour from the sun, we cannot imagine *that* to be the reception or resemblance of anything in the sun, because we find not those different colours in the sun itself. For, our senses being able to observe a likeness or unlikeness of sensible qualities in two different external objects, we forwardly enough conclude the production of any sensible quality in any subject to be an effect of bare power, and not the communication of any quality which was really in the efficient, when we find no such sensible quality in the thing that produced it. But our senses, not being able to discover any unlikeness between the idea produced in us, and the quality of the object producing it, we are apt to imagine that our ideas are resemblances of somthing in the objects, and not the effects of certain powers placed in the modification of their primary

qualities, with which primary qualities the ideas produced in us have no resemblance.

26. To conclude. Beside those before-mentioned primary qualities in bodies, viz. bulk, figure, extension, number, and motion of their solid parts; all the rest, whereby we take notice of bodies, and distinguish them one from another, are nothing else but several powers in them, depending on those primary qualities; whereby they are fitted, either by immediately operating on our bodies to produce several different ideas in us; or else, by operating on other bodies, so to change their primary qualities as to render them capable of producing ideas in us different from what before they did. The former of these, I think, may be called secondary qualities *immediately perceivable;* the latter, secondary qualities, *mediately perceivable.*

OF OUR KNOWLEDGE OF THE EXISTENCE OF OTHER THINGS

1. The knowledge of our own being we have by intuition. The existence of a God, reason clearly makes known to us, as has been shown.

The knowledge of the existence of *any other thing* we can have only by *sensation:* for there being no necessary connexion of real existence with any *idea* a man hath in his memory; nor of any other existence but that of God with the existence of any particular man: no particular man can know the existence of any other being, but only when, by actual operating upon him, it makes itself perceived by him. For, the having the idea of anything in our mind, no more proves the existence of that thing, than the picture of a man evidences his being in the world, or the visions of a dream make thereby a true history.

2. It is therefore the *actual receiving* of ideas from without that gives us notice of the existence of other things, and makes us know, that something doth exist at that time without us, which causes that idea in us; though perhaps we neither know nor consider how it does it. For it takes not from the certainty of our senses, and the ideas we receive by them, that we know not the manner wherein they are produced: e.g.

whilst I write this, I have, by the paper affecting my eyes, that idea produced in my mind, which, whatever object causes, I call *white;* by which I know that that quality or accident (i.e. whose appearance before my eyes always causes that idea) doth really exist, and hath a being without me. And of this, the greatest assurance I can possibly have, and to which my faculties can attain, is the testimony of my eyes, which are the proper and sole judges of this thing; whose testimony I have reason to rely on as so certain, that I can no more doubt, whilst I write this, that I see white and black, and that something really exists that causes that sensation in me, than that I write or move my hand; which is a certainty as great as human nature is capable of, concerning the existence of anything, but a man's self alone, and of God.

3. The notice we have by our senses of the existing of things without us, though it be not altogether so certain as our intuitive knowledge, or the deductions of our reason employed about the clear abstract ideas of our own minds; yet it is an assurance that deserves the name of *knowledge.* If we persuade ourselves that our faculties act and inform us right concerning the existence of those objects that affect them, it cannot pass for an illgrounded confidence: for I think nobody can, in earnest, be so sceptical as to be uncertain of the existence of those things which he sees and feels. At least, he that can doubt so far, (whatever he may have with his own thoughts,) will never have any controversy with me; since he can never be sure I say anything contrary to his own opinion. As to myself, I think God has given me assurance enough of the existence of things without me: since, by their different application, I can produce in myself both pleasure and pain, which is one great concernment of my present state. This is certain: the confidence that our faculties do not herein deceive us, is the greatest assurance we are capable of concerning the existence of material beings. For we cannot act anything but by our faculties; nor talk of knowledge itself, but by the help of those faculties which are fitted to apprehend even what knowledge is.

But besides the assurance we have from our senses themselves, that they do not err in the information they give us of the existence of things without us, when they are affected by them, we are further confirmed in this assurance by other concurrent reasons:—

4. I. It is plain those perceptions are produced in us by exterior causes affecting our senses: because those that want the *organs* of any sense, never can have the ideas belonging to that sense produced in their minds. This is too evident to be doubted: and therefore we cannot but be assured that they come in by the organs of that sense, and no other way. The organs themselves, it is plain, do not produce them: for then the eyes of a man in the dark would produce colours, and his nose smell roses in the winter: but we see nobody gets the relish of a pineapple, till he goes to the Indies, where it is, and tastes it.

5. II. Because sometimes I find that *I cannot avoid the having those ideas produced in my mind.* For though, when my eyes are shut, or windows fast, I can at pleasure recall to my mind the ideas of light, or the sun, which former sensations had lodged in my memory; so I can at pleasure lay by *that* idea, and take into my view that of the smell of a rose, or taste of sugar. But, if I turn my eyes at noon towards the sun, I cannot avoid the ideas which the light or sun then produces in me. So that there is a manifest difference between the ideas laid up in my memory, (over which, if they were there only, I should have constantly the same power to dispose of them, and lay them by at pleasure,) and those which force themselves upon me, and I cannot avoid having. And therefore it must needs be some exterior cause, and the brisk acting of some objects without me, whose efficacy I cannot resist, that produces those ideas in my mind, whether I will or no. Besides, there is nobody who doth not perceive the difference in himself between contemplating the sun, as he hath the idea of it in his memory, and actually looking upon it: of which two, his perception is so distinct, that few of his ideas are more distinguishable one from another. And therefore he hath certain knowledge

that they are not *both* memory, or the actions of his mind, and fancies only within him; but that actual seeing hath a cause without.

6. III. Add to this, that many of those ideas are *produced in us with pain,* which afterwards we remember without the least offence. Thus, the pain of heat or cold, when the idea of it is revived in our minds, gives us no disturbance; which, when felt, was very troublesome; and is again, when actually repeated; which is occasioned by the disorder the external object causes in our bodies when applied to them: and we remember the pains of hunger, thirst, or the headache, without any pain at all; which would either never disturb us, or else constantly do it, as often as we thought of it, were there nothing more but ideas floating in our minds, and appearances entertaining our fancies, without the real existence of things affecting us from abroad. The same may be said of *pleasure,* accompanying several actual sensations. And though mathematical demonstration depends not upon sense, yet the examining them by diagrams gives great credit to the evidence of our sight, and seems to give it a certainty approaching to that of demonstration itself. For, it would be very strange, that a man should allow it for an undeniable truth, that two angles of a figure, which he measures by lines and angles of a diagram, should be bigger one than the other, and yet doubt of the existence of those lines and angles, which by looking on he makes use of to measure that by.

7. IV. Our *senses* in many cases *bear witness to the truth of each other's report,* concerning the existence of sensible things without us. He that *sees* a fire, may, if he doubt whether it be anything more than a bare fancy, *feel* it too; and be convinced, by putting his hand in it. Which certainly could never be put into such exquisite pain by a bare idea or phantom, unless that the pain be a fancy too: which yet he cannot, when the burn is well, by raising the idea of it, bring upon himself again.

Thus I see, whilst I write this, I can change the appearance of the paper; and by designing the letters, tell *beforehand* what new idea it shall exhibit the very next moment, by barely drawing my pen over it: which will neither appear (let me fancy as much as I will) if my hands stand still; or though I move my pen, if my eyes be shut: nor, when those characters are once made on the paper, can I choose afterwards but see them as they are; that is, have the ideas of such letters as I have made. Whence it is manifest, that they are not barely the sport and play of my own imagination, when I find that the characters that were made at the pleasure of my own thoughts, do not obey them; nor yet cease to be, whenever I shall fancy it, but continue to affect my senses constantly and regularly, according to the figures I made them. To which if we will add, that the sight of those shall, from another man, draw such sounds as I beforehand design they shall stand for, there will be little reason left to doubt that those words I write do really exist without me, when they cause a long series of regular sounds to affect my ears, which could not be the effect of my imagination, nor could my memory retain them in that order.

8. But yet, if after all this any one will be so sceptical as to distrust his senses, and to affirm that all we see and hear, feel and taste, think and do, during our whole being, is but the series and deluding appearances of a long dream, whereof there is no reality; and therefore will question the existence of all things, or our knowledge of anything: I must desire him to consider, that, if all be a dream, then he doth but dream that he makes the question, and so it is not much matter that a waking man should answer him. But yet, if he pleases, he may dream that I make him this answer, That the certainty of things existing in *rerum natura* when we have the testimony of our senses for it is not only as great as our frame can attain to, but as our condition needs. For, our faculties being suited not to the full extent of being, nor to a perfect, clear, comprehensive knowledge of things free from all doubt and scruple; but to the preservation of us, in whom they are; and accommodated to the use of life: they serve to our purpose well enough, if they will but give us certain notice of those things, which are convenient or inconvenient to us. For he that sees a candle burning, and hath

experimented the force of its flame by putting his finger in it, will little doubt that this is something existing without him, which does him harm, and puts him to great pain: which is assurance enough, when no man requires greater certainty to govern his actions by than what is as certain as his actions themselves. And if our dreamer pleases to try whether the glowing heat of a glass furnace be barely a wandering imagination in a drowsy man's fancy, by putting his hand into it, he may perhaps be wakened into a certainty greater than he could wish, that it is something more than bare imagination. So that this evidence is as great as we can desire, being as certain to us as our pleasure or pain, i.e. happiness or misery; beyond which we have no concernment, either of knowing or being. Such an assurance of the existence of things without us is sufficient to direct us in the attaining the good and avoiding the evil which is caused by them, which is the important concernment we have of being made acquainted with them.

9. In fine, then, when our senses do actually convey into our understandings any idea, we cannot but be satisfied that there doth something *at that time* really exist without us, which doth affect our senses, and by them give notice of itself to our apprehensive faculties, and actually produce that idea which we then perceive: and we cannot so far distrust their testimony, as to doubt that such *collections* of simple ideas as we have observed by our senses to be united together, do really exist together. But this knowledge extends as far as the present testimony of our senses, employed about particular objects that do then affect them, and no further. For if I saw such a collection of simple ideas as is wont to be called *man*, existing together one minute since, and am now alone, I cannot be certain that the same man exists now, since there is no *necessary connexion* of his existence a minute since with his existence now: by a thousand ways he may cease to be, since I had the testimony of my senses for his existence. And if I cannot be certain that the man I saw last today is now in being, I can less be certain that he is so who hath been longer removed from my senses,

and I have not seen since yesterday, or since the last year: and much less can I be certain of the existence of men that I never saw. And, therefore, though it be highly probable that millions of men do now exist, yet, whilst I am alone, writing this, I have not that certainty of it which we strictly call knowledge; though the great likelihood of it puts me past doubt, and it be reasonable for me to do several things upon the confidence that there are men (and men also of my acquaintance, with whom I have to do) now in the world: but this is but probability, not knowledge.

10. Whereby yet we may observe how foolish and vain a thing it is for a man of a narrow knowledge, who having reason given him to judge of the different evidence and probability of things, and to be swayed accordingly; how vain, I say, it is to expect demonstration and certainty in things not capable of it; and refuse assent to very rational propositions, and act contrary to very plain and clear truths, because they cannot be made out so evident, as to surmount every the least (I will not say reason, but) pretence of doubting. He that, in the ordinary affairs of life, would admit of nothing but direct plain demonstration, would be sure of nothing in this world, but of perishing quickly. The wholesomeness of his meat or drink would not give him reason to venture on it: and I would fain know what it is he could do upon such grounds as are capable of no doubt, no objection.

3.4 *Of the Principles of Human Knowledge*

GEORGE BERKELEY

George Berkeley (1685–1753), the Anglican Bishop of Cloyne, was born in Ireland.

PART I

1. It is evident to anyone who takes a survey of the objects of human knowledge, that they are either ideas actually imprinted on the senses, or else such as are perceived by attending to the passions and operations of the mind, or lastly ideas formed by help of memory and imagination, either compounding, dividing, or barely representing those originally perceived in the aforesaid ways. By sight I have the ideas of light and colours with their several degrees and variations. By touch I perceive, for example, hard and soft, heat and cold, motion and resistance, and of all these more and less either as to quantity or degree. Smelling furnishes me with odours; the palate with tastes, and hearing conveys sounds to the mind in all their variety of tone and composition. And as several of these are observed to accompany each other, they come to be marked by one name, and so to be reputed as one thing. Thus, for example, a certain colour, taste, smell, figure and consistence having been observed to go together, are accounted one distinct thing, signified by the name *apple*. Other collections of ideas constitute a stone, a tree, a book, and the like sensible things; which, as they are pleasing or disagreeable, excite the passions of love, hatred, joy, grief, and so forth.

2. But besides all that endless variety of ideas or objects of knowledge, there is likewise something which knows or perceives them, and exercises divers operations, as willing, imagining, remembering about them. This perceiving, active being is what I call *mind, spirit, soul* or *myself*. By which words I do not denote any one of my ideas, but a thing entirely distinct from them, wherein they exist, or, which is the same thing,

George Berkeley, *Of the Principles of Human Knowledge*, first published in 1710.

whereby they are perceived; for the existence of an idea consists in being perceived.

3. That neither our thoughts, nor passions, nor ideas formed by the imagination, exist without the mind, is what everybody will allow. And it seems no less evident that the various sensations or ideas imprinted on the sense, however blended or combined together (that is, whatever objects they compose) cannot exist otherwise than in a mind perceiving them. I think an intuitive knowledge may be obtained of this, by anyone that shall attend to what is meant by the term *exist* when applied to sensible things. The table I write on, I say, exists, that is, I see and feel it; and if I were out of my study I should say it existed, meaning thereby that if I was in my study I might perceive it, or that some other spirit actually does perceive it. There was an odour, that is, it was smelled; there was a sound, that is to say, it was heard; a colour or figure, and it was perceived by sight or touch. This is all that I can understand by these and the like expressions. For as to what is said of the absolute existence of unthinking things without any relation to their being perceived, that seems perfectly unintelligible. Their *esse* is *percipi*, nor is it possible they should have any existence, out of the minds or thinking things which perceive them.

4. It is indeed an opinion strangely prevailing amongst men, that houses, mountains, rivers, and in a word all sensible objects have an existence natural or real, distinct from their being perceived by the understanding. But with how great an assurance and acquiescence soever this principle may be entertained in the world; yet whoever shall find in his heart to call it in question, may, if I mistake not, perceive it to involve a manifest contradiction. For what are the forementioned objects but the things we perceive by sense, and what do we perceive besides our own ideas or sensations; and is it not plainly repugnant that any one of these or any combination of them should exist unperceived?

5. If we thoroughly examine this tenet, it will, perhaps, be found at bottom to depend on the doctrine of *abstract ideas*. For can there be a nicer strain of abstraction than to distinguish the existence of sensible objects from their being perceived, so as to conceive them existing unperceived? Light and colours, heat and cold, extension and figures, in a word the things we see and feel, what are they but so many sensations, notions, ideas or impressions on the sense; and is it possible to separate, even in thought, any of these from perception? For my part I might as easily divide a thing from itself. I may indeed divide in my thoughts or conceive apart from each other those things which, perhaps, I never perceived by sense so divided. Thus I imagine the trunk of a human body without the limbs, or conceive the smell of a rose without thinking on the rose itself. So far I will not deny I can abstract, if that may properly be called *abstraction,* which extends only to the conceiving separately such objects, as it is possible may really exist or be actually perceived asunder. But my conceiving or imagining power does not extend beyond the possibility of real existence or perception. Hence as it is impossible for me to see or feel anything without an actual sensation of that thing, so is it impossible for me to conceive in my thoughts any sensible thing or object distinct from the sensation or perception of it.

6. Some truths there are so near and obvious to the mind, that a man need only open his eyes to see them. Such I take this important one to be, to wit, that all the choir of heaven and furniture of the earth, in a word all those bodies which compose the mighty frame of the world, have not any subsistence, without a mind, that their being is to be perceived or known; that consequently so long as they are not actually perceived by me, or do not exist in my mind or that of any other created spirit, they must either have no existence at all, or else subsist in the mind of some eternal spirit: it being perfectly unintelligible and involving all the absurdity of abstraction, to attribute to any single part of them an existence independent of a spirit. To be convinced of which, the reader need only reflect and try to separate in his own thoughts the being of a sensible thing from its being perceived.

7. From what has been said, it follows, there is not any other substance than *spirit,* or that

which perceives. But for the fuller proof of this point, let it be considered, the sensible qualities are colour, figure, motion, smell, taste, and such like, that is, the ideas perceived by sense. Now for an idea to exist in an unperceiving thing, is a manifest contradiction; for to have an idea is all one as to perceive; that therefore wherein colour, figure, and the like qualities exist, must perceive them; hence it is clear there can be no unthinking substance or *substratum* of those ideas.

8. But say you, though the ideas themselves do not exist without the mind, yet there may be things like them whereof they are copies or resemblances, which things exist without the mind, in an unthinking substance. I answer, an idea can be like nothing but an idea; a colour or figure can be like nothing but another colour or figure. If we look but ever so little into our thoughts, we shall find it impossible for us to conceive a likeness except only between our ideas. Again, I ask whether these supposed originals or external things, of which our ideas are the pictures or representations, be themselves perceivable or no? If they are, then they are ideas, and we have gained our point; but if you say they are not, I appeal to anyone whether it be sense, to assert a colour is like something which is invisible, hard or soft, like something which is intangible; and so of the rest.

9. Some there are who make a distinction betwixt *primary* and *secondary* qualities: by the former, they mean extension, figure, motion, rest, solidity or impenetrability and number: by the latter they denote all other sensible qualities, as colours, sounds, tastes, and so forth. The ideas we have of these they acknowledge not to be the resemblances of anything existing without the mind or unperceived; but they will have our ideas of the primary qualities to be patterns or images of things which exist without the mind, in an unthinking substance which they call *matter*. By matter therefore we are to understand an inert, senseless substance, in which extension, figure, and motion, do actually subsist. But it is evident from what we have already shewn, that extension, figure and motion are only ideas existing in the mind, and that an idea can be like

nothing but another idea, and that consequently neither they nor their archetypes can exist in an unperceiving substance. Hence it is plain, that the very notion of what is called *matter* or *corporeal substance,* involves a contradiction in it.

10. They who assert that figure, motion, and the rest of the primary or original qualities do exist without the mind, in unthinking substances, do at the same time acknowledge that colours, sounds, heat, cold, and such like secondary qualities, do not, which they tell us are sensations existing in the mind alone, that depend on and are occasioned by the different size, texture and motion of the minute particles of matter. This they take for an undoubted truth, which they can demonstrate beyond all exception. Now if it be certain, that those original qualities are inseparably united with the other sensible qualities, and not, even in thought, capable of being abstracted from them, it plainly follows that they exist only in the mind. But I desire anyone to reflect and try, whether he can by any abstraction of thought, conceive the extension and motion of a body, without all other sensible qualities. For my own part, I see evidently that it is not in my power to frame an idea of a body extended and moved, but I must withal give it some colour or other sensible quality which is acknowledged to exist only in the mind. In short, extension, figure, and motion, abstracted from all other qualities, are inconceivable. Where therefore the other sensible qualities are, there must these be also, to wit, in the mind and nowhere else.

11. Again, *great* and *small, swift* and *slow,* are allowed to exist nowhere without the mind, being entirely relative, and changing as the frame or position of the organs of sense varies. The extension therefore which exists without the mind, is neither great nor small, the motion neither swift nor slow, that is, they are nothing at all. But say you, they are extension in general, and motion in general; thus we see how much the tenet of extended, moveable substances existing without the mind, depends on that strange doctrine of *abstract ideas.* And here I cannot but remark, how nearly the vague and indeterminate description of matter or corporeal substance,

which the modern philosophers are run into by their own principles, resembles that antiquated and so much ridiculed notion of *materia prima,* to be met with in Aristotle and his followers. Without extension solidity cannot be conceived; since therefore it has been shewn that extension exists not in an unthinking substance, the same must also be true of solidity.

12. That number is entirely the creature of the mind, even though the other qualities be allowed to exist without, will be evident to whoever considers, that the same thing bears a different denomination of number as the mind views it with different respects. Thus, the same extension is one or three or thirty-six, according as the mind considers it with reference to a yard, a foot, or an inch. Number is so visibly relative, and dependent on men's understanding, that it is strange to think how anyone should give it an absolute existence without the mind. We say one book, one page, one line; all these are equally units, though some contain several of the others. And in each instance it is plain, the unit relates to some particular combination of ideas arbitrarily put together by the mind.

13. Unity I know some will have to be a simple or uncompounded idea, accompanying all other ideas into the mind. That I have any such idea answering the word *unity,* I do not find; and if I had, methinks I could not miss finding it; on the contrary it should be the most familiar to my understanding, since it is said to accompany all other ideas, and to be perceived by all the ways of sensation and reflexion. To say no more, it is an *abstract idea.*

14. I shall farther add, that after the same manner, as modern philosophers prove certain sensible qualities to have no existence in matter, or without the mind, the same thing may be likewise proved of all other sensible qualities whatsoever. Thus, for instance, it is said that heat and cold are affections only of the mind, and not at all patterns of real beings, existing in the corporeal substances which excite them, for that the same body which appears cold to one hand, seems warm to another. Now why may we not as well argue that figure and extension are not patterns or resemblances of qualities existing in matter, because to the same eye at different stations, or eyes of a different texture at the same station, they appear various, and cannot therefore be the images of anything settled and determinate without the mind? Again, it is proved that sweetness is not really in the sapid thing because the thing remaining unaltered the sweetness is changed into bitter, as in case of a fever or otherwise vitiated palate. Is it not as reasonable to say, that motion is not without the mind, since if the succession of ideas in the mind become swifter, the motion, it is acknowledged, shall appear slower without any alteration in any external object.

15. In short, let anyone consider those arguments, which are thought manifestly to prove that colours and tastes exist only in the mind, and he shall find they may with equal force, be brought to prove the same thing of extension, figure, and motion. Though it must be confessed this method of arguing doth not so much prove that there is no extension or colour in an outward object, as that we do not know by sense which is the true extension or colour of the object. But the arguments foregoing plainly shew it to be impossible that any colour or extension at all, or other sensible quality whatsoever, should exist in an unthinking subject without the mind, or in truth, that there should be any such thing as an outward object.

16. But let us examine a little the received opinion. It is said extension is a mode or accident of matter, and that matter is the *substratum* that supports it. Now I desire that you would explain what is meant by matter's *supporting* extension: say you, I have no idea of matter, and therefore cannot explain it. I answer, though you have no positive, yet if you have any meaning at all, you must at least have a relative idea of matter; though you know not what it is, yet you must be supposed to know what relation it bears to accidents, and what is meant by its supporting them. It is evident *support* cannot here be taken in its usual or literal sense, as when we say that pillars support a building: in what sense therefore must it be taken?

17. If we inquire into what the most accurate philosophers declare themselves to mean by *material substance;* we shall find them acknowledge, they have no other meaning annexed to those sounds, but the idea of being in general, together with the relative notion of its supporting accidents. The general idea of being appeareth to me the most abstract and incomprehensible of all other; and as for its supporting accidents, this, as we have just now observed, cannot be understood in the common sense of those words; it must therefore be taken in some other sense, but what that is they do not explain. So that when I consider the two parts or branches which make the signification of the words *material substance,* I am convinced there is no distinct meaning annexed to them. But why should we trouble ourselves any farther, in discussing this material *substratum* or support of figure and motion, and other sensible qualities? Does it not suppose they have an existence without the mind? And is not this a direct repugnancy, and altogether inconceivable?

18. But though it were possible that solid, figured, moveable substances may exist without the mind, corresponding to the ideas we have of bodies, yet how is it possible for us to know this? Either we must know it by sense, or by reason. As for our senses, by them we have the knowledge only of our sensations, ideas, or those things that are immediately perceived by sense, call them what you will: but they do not inform us that things exist without the mind, or unperceived, like to those which are perceived. This the materialists themselves acknowledge. It remains therefore that if we have any knowledge at all of external things, it must be by reason, inferring their existence from what is immediately perceived by sense. But what reason can induce us to believe the existence of bodies without the mind, from what we perceive, since the very patrons of matter themselves do not pretend, there is any necessary connexion betwixt them and our ideas? I say it is granted on all hands (and what happens in dreams, phrensies, and the like, puts it beyond dispute) that it is possible we might be affected with all the ideas

we have now, though no bodies existed without, resembling them. Hence it is evident the supposition of external bodies is not necessary for the producing our ideas: since it is granted they are produced sometimes, and might possibly be produced always in the same order we see them in at present, without their concurrence.

19. But though we might possibly have all our sensations without them, yet perhaps it may be thought easier to conceive and explain the manner of their production, by supposing external bodies in their likeness rather than otherwise; and so it might be at least probable there are such things as bodies that excite their ideas in our minds. But neither can this be said; for though we give the materialists their external bodies, they by their own confession are never the nearer knowing how our ideas are produced; since they own themselves unable to comprehend in what manner body can act upon spirit, or how it is possible it should imprint any idea in the mind. Hence it is evident the production of ideas or sensations in our minds, can be no reason why we should suppose matter or corporeal substances, since that is acknowledged to remain equally inexplicable with, or without this supposition. If therefore it were possible for bodies to exist without the mind, yet to hold they do so, must needs be a very precarious opinion; since it is to suppose, without any reason at all, that God has created innumerable beings that are entirely useless, and serve to no manner of purpose.

20. In short, if there were external bodies, it is impossible we should ever come to know it; and if there were not, we might have the very same reasons to think there were that we have now. Suppose, what no one can deny possible, an intelligence, without the help of external bodies, to be affected with the same train of sensations or ideas that you are, imprinted in the same order and with like vividness in his mind. I ask whether that intelligence hath not all the reason to believe the existence of corporeal substances, represented by his ideas, and exciting them in his mind, that you can possibly have for believing the same thing? Of this there can be no question; which one consideration is enough to make any

reasonable person suspect the strength of whatever arguments he may think himself to have, for the existence of bodies without the mind.

21. Were it necessary to add any farther proof against the existence of matter, after what has been said, I could instance several of those errors and difficulties (not to mention impieties) which have sprung from that tenet. It has occasioned numberless controversies and disputes in philosophy, and not a few of far greater moment in religion. But I shall not enter into the detail of them in this place, as well because I think, arguments *a posteriori* are unnecessary for confirming what has been, if I mistake not, sufficiently demonstrated *a priori*, as because I shall hereafter find occasion to say somewhat of them.

22. I am afraid I have given cause to think me needlessly prolix in handling this subject. For to what purpose is it to dilate on that which may be demonstrated with the utmost evidence in a line or two, to anyone that is capable of the least reflexion? It is but looking into your own thoughts, and so trying whether you can conceive it possible for a sound, or figure, or motion, or colour, to exist without the mind, or unperceived. This easy trial may make you see, that what you contend for, is a downright contradiction. Insomuch that I am content to put the whole upon this issue; if you can but conceive it possible for one extended moveable substance, or in general, for any one idea or anything like an idea, to exist otherwise than in a mind perceiving it, I shall readily give up the cause: and as for all that *compages* of external bodies which you contend for, I shall grant you its existence, though you cannot either give me any reason why you believe it exists, or assign any use to it when it is supposed to exist. I say, the bare possibility of your opinion's being true, shall pass for an argument that it is so.

23. But you say, surely there is nothing easier than to imagine trees, for instance, in a park, or books existing in a closet, and nobody by to perceive them. I answer, you may so, there is no difficulty in it: but what is all this, I beseech you, more then framing in your mind certain ideas which you call *books* and *trees*, and at the same time omitting to frame the idea of anyone that may perceive them? But do not you yourself perceive or think of them all the while? This therefore is nothing to the purpose: it only shows you have the power of imagining or forming ideas in your mind; but it doth not shew that you can conceive it possible, the objects of your thought may exist without the mind: to make out this, it is necessary that you conceive them existing unconceived or unthought of, which is a manifest repugnancy. When we do our utmost to conceive the existence of external bodies, we are all the while only contemplating our own ideas. But the mind taking no notice of itself, is deluded to think it can and doth conceive bodies existing unthought of or without the mind; though at the same time they are apprehended by or exist in itself. A little attention will discover to anyone the truth and evidence of what is here said, and make it unnecessary to insist on any other proofs against the existence of material substance.

24. It is very obvious, upon the least inquiry into our own thoughts, to know whether it be possible for us to understand what is meant, by the *absolute existence of sensible objects in themselves, or without the mind*. To me it is evident those words mark out either a direct contradiction, or else nothing at all. And to convince others of this, I know no readier or fairer way, than to entreat they would calmly attend to their own thoughts: and if by this attention, the emptiness or repugnancy of those expressions does appear, surely nothing more is requisite for their conviction. It is on this therefore that I insist, to wit, that the absolute existence of unthinking things are words without a meaning, or which include a contradiction. This is what I repeat and inculcate, and earnestly recommend to the attentive thoughts of the reader.

25. All our ideas, sensations, or the thing which we perceive, by whatsoever names they may be distinguished, are visibly inactive, there is nothing of power or agency included in them. So that one idea or object of thought cannot produce, or make any alteration in another. To be satisfied of the truth of this, there is nothing else requisite but a bare observation of our ideas.

For since they and every part of them exist only in the mind, it follows that there is nothing in them but what is perceived. But whoever shall attend to his ideas, whether of sense or reflexion, will not perceive in them any power or activity; there is therefore no such thing contained in them. A little attention will discover to us that the very being of an idea implies passiveness and inertness in it, insomuch that it is impossible for an idea to do anything, or, strictly speaking, to be the cause of anything: neither can it be the resemblance or pattern of any active being, as is evident from *Sect.* 8. Whence it plainly follows that extension, figure and motion, cannot be the cause of our sensations. To say therefore, that these are the effects of powers resulting from the configuration, number, motion, and size of corpuscles, must certainly be false.

26. We perceive a continual succession of ideas, some are anew excited, others are changed or totally disappear. There is therefore some cause of these ideas whereon they depend, and which produces and changes them. That this cause cannot be any quality or idea or combination of ideas, is clear from the preceding section. It must therefore be a substance; but it has been shewn that there is no corporeal or material substance; it remains therefore that the cause of ideas is an incorporeal active substance or spirit.

27. A spirit is one simple, undivided, active being: as it perceives ideas, it is called the *understanding,* and as it produces or otherwise operates about them, it is called the *will.* Hence there can be no idea formed of a soul or spirit: for all ideas whatever, being passive and inert, *vide Sect.* 25, they cannot represent unto us, by way of image or likeness, that which acts. A little attention will make it plain to anyone, that to have an idea which shall be like that active principle of motion and change of ideas, is absolutely impossible. Such is the nature of *spirit* or that which acts, that it cannot be of itself perceived, but only by the effects which it produceth. If any man shall doubt of the truth of what is here delivered, let him but reflect and try if he can frame the idea of any power or active being; and whether he hath ideas of two principal powers, marked by the names *will* and *understanding,* distinct from each other as well as from a third idea of substance or being in general, with a relative notion of its supporting or being the subject of the aforesaid powers, which is signified by the name *soul* or *spirit.* This is what some hold; but so far as I can see, the words *will, soul, spirit,* do not stand for different ideas, or in truth, for any idea at all, but for something which is very different from ideas, and which being an agent cannot be like unto, or represented by, any idea whatsoever. Though it must be owned at the same time, that we have some notion of soul, spirit, and the operations of the mind, such as willing loving, hating, in as much as we know or understand the meaning of those words.

28. I find I can excite ideas in my mind at pleasure, and vary and shift the scene as oft as I think fit. It is no more than willing, and straightway this or that idea arises in my fancy: and by the same power it is obliterated, and makes way for another. This making and unmaking of ideas doth very properly denominate the mind active. Thus much is certain, and grounded on experience: but when we talk of unthinking agents, or of exciting ideas exclusive of volition, we only amuse ourselves with words.

29. But whatever power I may have over my own thoughts, I find the ideas actually perceived by sense have not a like dependence on my will. When in broad day-light I open my eyes, it is not in my power to choose whether I shall see or no, or to determine what particular objects shall present themselves to my view; and so likewise as to the hearing and other senses, the ideas imprinted on them are not creatures of my will. There is therefore some other will or spirit that produces them.

30. The ideas of sense are more strong, lively, and distinct than those of the imagination; they have likewise a steadiness, order, and coherence, and are not excited at random, as those which are the effects of human wills often are, but in a regular train or series, the admirable connexion whereof sufficiently testifies the wisdom and benevolence of its Author. Now the set rules or established methods, wherein the mind

we depend on excites in us the ideas of sense, are called the *Laws of Nature:* and these we learn by experience, which teaches us that such and such ideas are attended with such and such other ideas, in the ordinary course of things.

31. This gives us a sort of foresight, which enables us to regulate our actions for the benefit of the life. And without this we should be eternally at a loss: we could not know how to act anything that might procure us the least pleasure, or remove the least pain of sense. That food nourishes, sleep refreshes, and fire warms us; that to sow in the seed-time is the way to reap in the harvest, and, in general, that to obtain such or such ends, such or such means are conducive, all this we know, not by discovering any necessary connexion between our ideas, but only by the observation of the settled Laws of Nature, without which we should be all in uncertainty and confusion, and a grown man no more know how to manage himself in the affairs of life, than an infant just born.

32. And yet this consistent uniform working, which so evidently displays the goodness and wisdom of that governing spirit whose will constitutes the Laws of Nature, is so far from leading our thoughts to him, that it rather sends them a wandering after second causes. For when we perceive certain ideas of sense constantly followed by other ideas, and we know this is not of our doing, we forthwith attribute power and agency to the ideas themselves, and make one the cause of another, than which nothing can be more absurd and unintelligible. Thus, for example, having observed that when we perceive by sight a certain round luminous figure, we at the same time perceive by touch the idea of sensation called *heat,* we do from thence conclude the sun to be the cause of heat. And in like manner perceiving the motion and collision of bodies to be attended with sound, we are inclined to think the latter an effect of the former.

33. The ideas imprinted on the senses by the Author of Nature are called *real things:* and those excited in the imagination being less regular, vivid and constant, are more properly termed *ideas,* or *images of things,* which they copy and represent. But then our sensations, be they never so vivid and distinct, are nevertheless *ideas,* that is, they exist in the mind, or are perceived by it, as truly as the ideas of its own framing. The ideas of sense are allowed to have more reality in them, that is, to be more strong, orderly, and coherent than the creatures of the mind; but this is no argument that they exist without the mind. They are also less dependent on the spirit, or thinking substance which perceives them, in that they are excited by the will of another and more powerful spirit: yet still they are *ideas,* and certainly no *idea,* whether faint or strong, can exist otherwise than in a mind perceiving it.

34. Before we proceed any farther, it is necessary to spend some time in answering objections which may probably be made against the principles hitherto laid down. In doing of which, if I seem too prolix of those of quick apprehensions, I hope it may be pardoned, since all men do not equally apprehend things of this nature; and I am willing to be understood by everyone. First then, it will be objected that by the foregoing principles, all that is real and substantial in Nature is banished out of the world: and instead a chimerical scheme of ideas takes place. All things that exist, exist only in the mind, that is, they are purely notional. What therefore becomes of the sun, moon, and stars? What must we think of houses, rivers, mountains, trees, stones; nay, even of our own bodies? Are all these but so many chimeras and illusions on the fancy? To all which, and whatever else of the same sort may be objected, I answer, that by the principles premised, we are not deprived of any one thing in Nature. Whatever we see, feel, hear or any wise conceive or understand, remains as secure as ever, and is as real as ever. There is a *rerum natura,* and the distinction between realities and chimeras retains its full force. This is evident from *Sect.* 29, 30, and 33, where we have shewn what is meant by *real things* in opposition to *chimeras,* or ideas of our own framing; but then they both equally exist in the mind, and in that sense are alike *ideas.*

35. I do not argue against the existence of any one thing that we can apprehend, either by

sense or reflexion. That the things I see with mine eyes and touch with my hands do exist, really exist, I make not the least question. The only thing whose existence we deny, is that which philosophers call matter or corporeal substance. And in doing of this, there is no damage done to the rest of mankind, who, I dare say, will never miss it. The atheist indeed will want the colour of an empty name to support this impiety; and the philosophers may possibly find, they have lost a great handle for trifling and disputation.

36. If any man thinks this detracts from the existence or reality of things, he is very far from understanding what hath been premised in the plainest terms I could think of. Take here an abstract of what has been said. There are spiritual substances, minds, or human souls, which will or excite ideas in themselves at pleasure: but these are faint, weak, and unsteady in respect of others they perceive by sense, which being impressed upon them according to certain rules or laws of Nature, speak themselves the effects of a mind more powerful and wise than human spirits. These latter are said to have more *reality* in them than the former: by which is meant that they are more affecting, orderly, and distinct, and that they are not fictions of the mind perceiving them. And in this sense, the sun that I see by day is the real sun, and that which I imagine by night is the idea of the former. In the sense here given of *reality*, it is evident that every vegetable, star, mineral, and in general each part of the mundane system, is as much a *real being* by our principles as by any other. Whether others mean anything by the term *reality* different from what I do, I entreat them to look into their own thoughts and see.

3.5 Proof of an External World

G. E. MOORE

G. E. Moore (1873–1958) spent his entire career at Cambridge University and wrote important works in ethics, free will, and epistemology.

It seems to me that, so far from its being true, as Kant declares to be his opinion, that there is only one possible proof of the existence of things outside of us, namely the one which he has given, I can now give a large number of different proofs, each of which is a perfectly rigorous proof; and that at many other times I have been in a position to give many others. I can prove now, for instance, that two human hands exist. How? By holding up my two hands, and saying, as I make a certain gesture with the right hand, 'Here is one hand,' and adding, as I make a certain gesture with the left, 'and here is another.' And if, by doing this, I have proved *ipso facto* the existence of external things, you will all see that I can also do it now in numbers of other ways: there is no need to multiply examples.

But did I prove just now that two human hands were then in existence? I do want to insist that I did; that the proof which I gave was a perfectly rigorous one; and that it is perhaps impossible to give a better or more rigorous proof of anything whatever. Of course, it would not have been a proof unless three conditions were satisfied; namely (1) unless the premiss which I adduced as proof of the conclusion was different from the conclusion I adduced it to prove; (2) unless the premiss which I adduced was

Reprinted from G. E. Moore, *Philosophical Papers* (New York: Collier Books, 1962), pp. 144–148. Reprinted by permission of Timothy Moore.

something which I *knew* to be the case, and not merely something which I believed but which was by no means certain, or something which, though in fact true, I did not know to be so; and (3) unless the conclusion did really follow from the premiss. But all these three conditions were in fact satisfied by my proof. (1) The premiss which I adduced in proof was quite certainly different from the conclusion, for the conclusion was merely 'Two human hands exist at this moment;' but the premiss was something far more specific than this—something which I expressed by showing you my hands, making certain gestures, and saying the words 'Here is one hand, and here is another.' It is quite obvious that the two were different, because it is quite obvious that the conclusion might have been true, even if the premiss had been false. In asserting the premiss I was asserting much more than I was asserting in asserting the conclusion. (2) I certainly did at the moment *know* that which I expressed by the combination of certain gestures with saying the words 'Here is one hand and here is another.' I *knew* that there was one hand in the place indicated by combining a certain gesture with my first utterance of 'here' and that there was another in the different place indicated by combining a certain gesture with my second utterance of 'here.' How absurd it would be to suggest that I did not know it, but only believed it, and that perhaps it was not the case! You might as well suggest that I do not know that I am now standing up and talking—that perhaps after all I'm not, and that it's not quite certain that I am! And finally (3) it is quite certain that the conclusion did follow from the premiss. This is as certain as it is that if there is one hand here and another here *now*, then it follows that there are two hands in existence *now*.

My proof, then, of the existence of things outside of us did satisfy three of the conditions necessary for a rigorous proof. Are there any other conditions necessary for a rigorous proof, such that perhaps it did not satisfy one of them? Perhaps there may be; I do not know; but I do want to emphasise that, so far as I can see, we all

of us do constantly take proofs of this sort as absolutely conclusive proofs of certain conclusions—as finally settling certain questions, as to which we were previously in doubt. Suppose, for instance, it were a question whether there were as many as three misprints on a certain page in a certain book. A says there are, B is inclined to doubt it. How could A prove that he is right? Surely he *could* prove it by taking the book, turning to the page, and pointing to three separate places on it, saying 'There's one misprint here, another here, and another here': surely that is a method by which it *might* be proved! Of course, A would not have proved, by doing this, that there were at least three misprints on the page in question, unless it was certain that there was a misprint in each of the places to which he pointed. But to say that he *might* prove it in this way, is to say that it *might* be certain that there was. And if such a thing as that could ever be certain, then assuredly it was certain just now that there was one hand in one of the two places I indicated and another in the other.

I did, then, just now, give a proof that there were *then* external objects; and obviously, if I did, I could *then* have given many other proofs of the same sort that there were external objects *then*, and could now give many proofs of the same sort that there are external objects *now*.

But, if what I am asked to do is to prove that external objects have existed *in the past*, then I can give many different proofs of this also, but proofs which are in important respects of a different *sort* from those just given. And I want to emphasise that, when Kant says it is a scandal not to be able to give a proof of the existence of external objects, a proof of their existence in the past would certainly *help* to remove the scandal of which he is speaking. He says that, if it occurs to anyone to question their existence, we ought to be able to confront him with a satisfactory proof. But by a person who questions their existence, he certainly means not merely a person who questions whether any exist at the moment of speaking, but a person who questions whether any have *ever* existed; and a proof that some have existed in the past would certainly therefore be relevant to *part* of what such a person is questioning. How then can I prove that there have been external objects in the past? Here is one proof. I can say: 'I held up two hands above this desk not very long ago; therefore two hands existed not very long ago; therefore at least two external objects have existed at some time in the past, QED.' This is a perfectly good proof, provided I *know* what is asserted in the premiss. But I *do* know that I held up two hands above this desk not very long ago. As a matter of fact, in this case you all know it too. There's no doubt whatever that I did. Therefore I have given a perfectly conclusive proof that external objects have existed in the past; and you will all see at once that, if this is a conclusive proof, I could have given many others of the same sort, and could now give many others. But it is also quite obvious that this sort of proof differs in important respects from the sort of proof I gave just now that there were two hands existing *then*.

I have, then, given two conclusive proofs of the existence of external objects. The first was a proof that two human hands existed at the time when I gave the proof; the second was a proof that two human hands had existed at a time previous to that at which I gave the proof. These proofs were of a different sort in important respects. And I pointed out that I could have given, then, many other conclusive proofs of both sorts. It is also obvious that I could give many others of both sorts now. So that, if these are the sort of proof that is wanted, nothing is easier than to prove the existence of external objects.

But now I am perfectly well aware that, in spite of all that I have said, many philosophers will still feel that I have not given any satisfactory proof of the point in question. And I want briefly, in conclusion, to say something as to why this dissatisfaction with my proofs should be felt.

One reason why, is, I think, this. Some people understand 'proof of an external world' as including a proof of things which I haven't attempted to prove and haven't proved. It is not quite easy to say *what* it is that they want

proved—*what* it is that is such that unless they got a proof of it, they would not say that they had a proof of the existence of external things; but I can make an approach to explaining what they want by saying that if I had proved the propositions which I used as *premisses* in my two proofs, then they would perhaps admit that I had proved the existence of external things, but, in the absence of such a proof (which, of course, I have neither given nor attempted to give), they will say that I have not given what they mean by a proof of the existence of external things. In other words, they want a proof of what I assert *now* when I hold up my hands and say 'Here's one hand and here's another'; and, in the other case, they want a proof of what I assert *now* when I say 'I did hold up two hands above this desk just now.' Of course, what they really want is not merely a proof of these two propositions, but something like a general statement as to how *any* propositions of this sort may be proved. This, of course, I haven't given; and I do not believe it can be given: if this is what is meant by proof of the existence of external things, I do not believe that any proof of the existence of external things is possible. Of course, in some cases what might be called a proof of propositions which seem like these can be got. If one of you suspected that one of my hands was artificial he might be said to get a proof of my proposition 'Here's one hand, and here's another,' by coming up and examining the suspected hand close up, perhaps touching and pressing it, and so establishing that it really was a human hand. But I do not believe that any proof is possible in nearly all cases. How am I to prove now that 'Here's one hand, and here's another'? I do not believe I can do it. In order to do it, I should need to prove for one thing, as Descartes pointed out, that I am not now dreaming. But how can I prove that I am not? I have, no doubt, conclusive reasons for asserting that I am not now dreaming; I have conclusive evidence that I am awake: but that is a very different thing from being able to prove it. I could not tell you what all my evidence is; and I should require to do this at least, in order to give you a proof.

But another reason why some people would feel dissatisfied with my proofs is, I think, not merely that they want a proof of something which I haven't proved, but that they think that, if I cannot give such extra proofs, then the proofs that I have given are not conclusive proofs at all. And this, I think, is a definite mistake. They would say: 'If you cannot prove your premiss that here is one hand and here is another, then you do not know it. But you yourself have admitted that, if you did not know it, then your proof was not conclusive. Therefore your proof was not, as you say it was, a conclusive proof.' This view that, if I cannot prove such things as these, I do not know them, is, I think, the view that Kant was expressing in the sentence which I quoted at the beginning of this lecture, when he implies that so long as we have no proof of the existence of external things, their existence must be accepted merely on *faith*. He means to say, I think, that if I cannot prove that there is a hand here, I must accept it merely as a matter of faith—I cannot know it. Such a view, though it has been very common among philosophers, can, I think, be shown to be wrong—though shown only by the use of premisses which are not known to be true, unless we do know of the existence of external things. I can know things, which I cannot prove; and among things which I certainly did know, even if (as I think) I could not prove them, were the premisses of my two proofs. I should say, therefore, that those, if any, who are dissatisfied with these proofs merely on the ground that I did not know their premisses, have no good reason for their dissatisfaction.

CHAPTER 4

THE METHODS OF SCIENCE

4.1 *An Inquiry Concerning Human Understanding*

DAVID HUME

SECTION II. OF THE ORIGIN OF IDEAS

Everyone will readily allow that there is a considerable difference between the perceptions of the mind when a man feels the pain of excessive heat or the pleasure of moderate warmth, and when he afterwards recalls to his memory this sensation or anticipates it by his imagination. These faculties may mimic or copy the perceptions of the senses, but they never can entirely reach the force and vivacity of the original sentiment. The utmost we say of them, even when they operate with greatest vigor, is that they represent their object in so lively a manner that we could *almost* say we feel or see it. But, except the mind be disordered by disease or madness, they never can arrive at such a pitch of vivacity as to render these perceptions altogether undistinguishable. All the colors of poetry, however splendid, can never paint natural objects in such a manner as to make the description be taken for a real landscape. The most lively thought is still inferior to the dullest sensation.

David Hume, *An Inquiry Concerning Human Understanding*. Sections II, IV–VII. First published in 1748.

We may observe a like distinction to run through all the other perceptions of the mind. A man in a fit of anger is actuated in a very different manner from one who only thinks of that emotion. If you tell me that any person is in love, I easily understand your meaning and form a just conception of his situation, but never can mistake that conception for the real disorders and agitations of the passion. When we reflect on our past sentiments and affections, our thought is a faithful mirror and copies its objects truly, but the colors which it employs are faint and dull in comparison of those in which our original perceptions were clothed. It requires no nice discernment or metaphysical head to mark the distinction between them.

Here, therefore, we may divide all the perceptions of the mind into two classes or species, which are distinguished by their different degrees of force and vivacity. The less forcible and lively are commonly denominated "thoughts" or "ideas." The other species want a name in our language, and in most others; I suppose, because it was not requisite for any but philosophical purposes to rank them under a general term or appellation. Let us, therefore, use a little freedom and call them "impressions," employing that word in a sense somewhat different from the usual. By the term "impression," then, I mean all our more lively perceptions, when we hear, or see, or feel, or love, or hate, or desire, or will. And impressions are distinguished from ideas, which are the less lively perceptions of which we are conscious when we reflect on any of those sensations or movements above mentioned.

Nothing, at first view, may seem more unbounded than the thought of man, which not only escapes all human power and authority, but is not even restrained within the limits of nature and reality. To form monsters and join incongruous shapes and appearances costs the imagination no more trouble than to conceive the most natural and familiar objects. And while the body is confined to one planet, along which it creeps with pain and difficulty, the thought can in an instant transport us into the most distant regions of the universe, or even beyond the universe into the unbounded chaos where nature is supposed to lie in total confusion. What never was seen or heard of, may yet be conceived, nor is anything beyond the power of thought except what implies an absolute contradiction.

But though our thought seems to possess this unbounded liberty, we shall find upon a nearer examination that it is really confined within very narrow limits, and that all this creative power of the mind amounts to no more than the faculty of compounding, transposing, augmenting, or diminishing the materials afforded us by the senses and experience. When we think of a golden mountain, we only join two consistent ideas, "gold" and "mountain," with which we were formerly acquainted. A virtuous horse we can conceive, because, from our own feeling, we can conceive virtue; and this we may unite to the figure and shape of a horse, which is an animal familiar to us. In short, all the materials of thinking are derived either from our outward or inward sentiment; the mixture and composition of these belongs alone to the mind and will, or, to express myself in philosophical language, all our ideas or more feeble perceptions are copies of our impressions or more lively ones.

To prove this, the two following arguments will, I hope, be sufficient. *First,* when we analyze our thoughts or ideas, however compounded or sublime, we always find that they resolve themselves into such simple ideas as were copied from a precedent feeling or sentiment. Even those ideas which at first view seem the most wide of this origin are found, upon a nearer scrutiny, to be derived from it. The idea of God, as meaning an infinitely intelligent, wise, and good Being, arises from reflecting on the operations of our own mind and augmenting, without limit, those qualities of goodness and wisdom. We may prosecute this inquiry to what length we please; where we shall always find that every idea which we examine is copied from a similar impression. Those who would assert that this position is not universally true, nor without exception, have only one, and that an easy, method of refuting it by producing that idea which, in their opinion, is not derived from this source. It will then be incumbent on us, if we would maintain our doctrine, to produce the impression or lively perception which corresponds to it.

Secondly, if it happens, from a defect of the organ, that a man is not susceptible of any species of sensation, we always find that he is as little susceptible of the correspondent ideas. A blind man can form no notion of colors, a deaf man of sounds. Restore either of them that sense in which he is deficient by opening this new inlet for his sensations, you also open an inlet for the ideas, and he finds no difficulty in conceiving these objects. The case is the same if the object proper for exciting any sensation has never been applied to the organ. A Laplander...has no notion of the relish of wine. And though there are few or no instances of a like deficiency in the mind where a person has never felt or is wholly incapable of a sentiment or passion that belongs to his species, yet we find the same observation to take place in a less degree. A man of mild manners can form no idea of inveterate revenge or cruelty, nor can a selfish heart easily conceive the heights of friendship and generosity. It is readily allowed that other beings may possess many senses of which we can have no conception, because the ideas of them have never been introduced to us in the only manner by which an idea can have access to the mind, to wit, by the actual feeling and sensation.

There is, however, one contradictory phenomenon which may prove that it is not absolutely impossible for ideas to arise independent of their correspondent impressions. I believe it will readily be allowed that the several distinct ideas of color, which enter by the eye, or those of sound, which are conveyed by the ear, are really different from each other, though at the same time resembling. Now, if this be true of different colors, it must be no less so of the different shades of the same color; and each shade produces a distinct idea, independent of the rest. For if this should be denied, it is possible, by the continual gradation of shades, to run a color insensibly into what is most remote from it; and if you will not allow any of the means to be

different, you cannot, without absurdity, deny the extremes to be the same. Suppose, therefore, a person to have enjoyed his sight for thirty years and to have become perfectly acquainted with colors of all kinds, except one particular shade of blue, for instance, which it never has been his fortune to meet with; let all the different shades of that color, except that single one, be placed before him, descending gradually from the deepest to the lightest, it is plain that he will perceive a blank where that shade is wanting, and will be sensible that there is a greater distance in that place between the contiguous colors than in any other. Now I ask whether it be possible for him, from his own imagination, to supply this deficiency and raise up to himself the idea of that particular shade, though it had never been conveyed to him by his senses? I believe there are few but will be of the opinion that he can; and this may serve as a proof that the simple ideas are not always, in every instance, derived from the correspondent impressions, though this instance is so singular that it is scarcely worth our observing, and does not merit that for it alone we should alter our general maxim.

Here, therefore, is a proposition which not only seems in itself simple and intelligible, but, if a proper use were made of it, might render every dispute equally intelligible, and banish all that jargon which has so long taken possession of metaphysical reasonings and drawn disgrace upon them. All ideas, especially abstract ones, are naturally faint and obscure. The mind has but a slender hold of them. They are apt to be confounded with other resembling ideas; and when we have often employed any term, though without a distinct meaning, we are apt to imagine it has a determinate idea annexed to it. On the contrary, all impressions, that is, all sensations either outward or inward, are strong and vivid. The limits between them are more exactly determined, nor is it easy to fall into any error or mistake with regard to them. When we entertain, therefore, any suspicion that a philosophical term is employed without any meaning or idea (as is but too frequent), we need but inquire, *from what impression is that supposed idea derived?* And if it be impossible to assign any, this will serve to confirm our suspicion. By bringing ideas in so clear a light, we may reasonably hope to remove all dispute which may arise concerning their nature and reality.[1]

SECTION IV. SKEPTICAL DOUBTS CONCERNING THE OPERATIONS OF THE UNDERSTANDING

Part I

All the objects of human reason or inquiry may naturally be divided into two kinds, to wit, "Relations of Ideas," and "Matters of Fact." Of the first kind are the sciences of Geometry, Algebra, and Arithmetic, and, in short, every affirmation which is either intuitively or demonstratively certain. *That the square of the hypotenuse is equal to the square of the two sides* is a proposition which expresses a relation between these figures. *That three times five is equal to the half of thirty* expresses a relation between these numbers. Propositions of this kind are discoverable by the mere operation of thought, without dependence on what is anywhere existent in the universe. Though there never were a circle or triangle in nature, the truths demonstrated by Euclid would forever retain their certainty and evidence.

Matters of fact, which are the second objects of human reason, are not ascertained in the same manner, nor is our evidence of their truth, however great, of a like nature with the foregoing. The contrary of every matter of fact is still possible, because it can never imply a contradiction and is conceived by the mind with the same facility and distinctness as if ever so conformable to reality. *That the sun will not rise tomorrow* is no less intelligible a proposition and implies no more contradiction than the affirmation *that it will rise.* We should in vain, therefore, attempt to demonstrate its falsehood. Were it demonstratively false, it would imply a contradiction and could never be distinctly conceived by the mind.

It may, therefore, be a subject worthy of curiosity to inquire what is the nature of that evidence which assures us of any real existence and matter of fact beyond the present testimony of our senses or the records of our memory. This part of philosophy, it is observable, had been little cultivated either by the ancients or moderns; and, therefore, our doubts and errors in the prosecution of so important an inquiry may be the more excusable while we march through such difficult paths without any guide or direction. They may even prove useful by exciting curiosity and destroying that implicit faith and security which is the bane of all reasoning and free inquiry. The discovery of defects in the common philosophy, if any such there be, will not, I presume, be a discouragement, but rather an incitement, as is usual, to attempt something more full and satisfactory than has yet been proposed to the public.

All reasonings concerning matter of fact seem to be founded on the relation of *cause* and *effect.* By means of that relation alone we can go beyond the evidence of our memory and senses. If you were to ask a man why he believes any matter of fact which is absent, for instance, that his friend is in the country or in France, he would give you a reason, and this reason would be some other fact: as a letter received from him or the knowledge of his former resolutions and promises. A man finding a watch or any other machine in a desert island would conclude that there had once been men in that island. All our reasonings concerning fact are of the same nature. And here it is constantly supposed that there is a connection between the present fact and that which is inferred from it. Were there nothing to bind them together, the inference would be entirely precarious. The hearing of an articulate voice and rational discourse in the dark assures us of the presence of some person. Why? Because these are the effects of the human make and fabric, and closely connected with it. If we anatomize all the other reasonings of this nature, we shall find that they are founded on the relation of cause and effect, and that this relation is either near or remote, direct or collateral. Heat and light are collateral effects of fire, and the one effect may justly be inferred from the other.

If we would satisfy ourselves, therefore, concerning the nature of that evidence which assures us of matters of fact, we must inquire how we arrive at the knowledge of cause and effect.

I shall venture to affirm, as a general proposition which admits of no exception, that the knowledge of this relation is not, in any instance, attained by reasonings *a priori,* but arises entirely from experience, when we find that any particular objects are constantly conjoined with each other. Let an object be presented to a man of ever so strong natural reason and abilities—if that object be entirely new to him, he will not be able, by the most accurate examination of its sensible qualities, to discover any of its causes or effects. Adam, though his rational faculties be supposed, at the very first, entirely perfect, could not have inferred from the fluidity and transparency of water that it would suffocate him, or from the light and warmth of fire that it would consume him. No object ever discovers, by the qualities which appear to the senses, either the causes which produced it or the effects which will arise from it; nor can our reason, unassisted by experience, ever draw any inference concerning real existence and matter of fact.

This proposition, *that causes and effects are discoverable, not by reason, but by experience,* will readily be admitted with regard to such objects as we remember to have once been altogether unknown to us, since we must be conscious of the utter inability which we then lay under of foretelling what would arise from them. Present two smooth pieces of marble to a man who has no tincture of natural philosophy; he will never discover that they will adhere together in such a manner as to require great force to separate them in a direct line, while they make so small a resistance to a lateral pressure. Such events as bear little analogy to the common course of nature are also readily confessed to be known only by experience, nor does any man imagine that the explosion of gunpowder or the attraction of a loadstone could ever be discovered by arguments *a priori.* In like manner, when an effect is supposed to depend upon an intricate machinery or secret structure of parts, we make no

difficulty in attributing all our knowledge of it to experience. Who will assert that he can give the ultimate reason why milk or bread is proper nourishment for a man, not for a lion or tiger?

But the same truth may not appear at first sight to have the same evidence with regard to events which have become familiar to us from our first appearance in the world, which bear a close analogy to the whole course of nature, and which are supposed to depend on the simple qualities of objects without any secret structure of parts. We are apt to imagine that we could discover these effects by the mere operation of our reason without experience. We fancy that, were we brought on a sudden into this world, we could at first have inferred that one billiard ball would communicate motion to another upon impulse, and that we needed not to have waited for the event in order to pronounce with certainty concerning it. Such is the influence of custom that where it is strongest it not only covers our natural ignorance but even conceals itself, and seems not to take place, merely because it is found in the highest degree.

But to convince us that all the laws of nature and all the operations of bodies without exception are known only by experience, the following reflections may perhaps suffice. Were any object presented to us, and were we required to pronounce concerning the effect which will result from it without consulting past observation, after what manner, I beseech you, must the mind proceed in this operation? It must invent or imagine some event which it ascribes to the object as its effect; and it is plain that this invention must be entirely arbitrary. The mind can never possibly find the effect in the supposed cause by the most accurate scrutiny and examination. For the effect is totally different from the cause, and consequently can never be discovered in it. Motion in the second billiard ball is quite a distinct event from motion in the first, nor is there anything in the one to suggest the smallest hint of the other. A stone or piece of metal raised into the air and left without any support immediately falls. But to consider the matter *a priori,* is there anything we discover in this situation which can beget the idea of a downward rather than an upward or any other motion in the stone or metal?

And as the first imagination or invention of a particular effect in all natural operations is arbitrary where we consult not experience, so must we also esteem the supposed tie or connection between the cause and effect which binds them together and renders it impossible that any other effect could result from the operation of that cause. When I see, for instance, a billiard ball moving in a straight line toward another, even suppose motion in the second ball should by accident be suggested to me as the result of their contact or impulse, may I not conceive that a hundred different events might as well follow from that cause? May not both these balls remain at absolute rest? May not the first ball return in a straight line or leap off the second in any line or direction? All these suppositions are consistent and conceivable. Why, then, should we give the preference to one which is no more consistent or conceivable than the rest? All our reasonings *a priori* will never be able to show us any foundation for this preference.

In a word, then, every effect is a distinct event from its cause. It could not, therefore, be discovered in the cause, and the first invention or conception of it *a priori,* must be entirely arbitrary. And even after it is suggested, the conjunction of it with the cause must appear equally arbitrary, since there are always many other effects which, to reason, must seem fully as consistent and natural. In vain, therefore, should we pretend to determine any single event or infer any cause or effect without the assistance of observation and experience.

Hence we may discover the reason why no philosopher who is rational and modest has ever pretended to assign the ultimate cause of any natural operation, or to show distinctly the action of that power which produces any single effect in the universe. It is confessed that the utmost effort of human reason is to reduce the principles productive of natural phenomena to a greater simplicity, and to resolve the many particular effects into a few general causes, by means of reasonings from analogy, experience, and observation. But as to the causes of these general causes, we should in vain attempt their discovery, nor shall we ever be able to satisfy ourselves by any particular explication of them. These ultimate springs and principles are totally shut up from human curiosity and inquiry. Elasticity, gravity, cohesion of parts, communication of motion by impulse—these are probably the ultimate causes and principles which we ever discover in nature; and we may esteem ourselves sufficiently happy if, by accurate inquiry and reasoning, we can trace up the particular phenomena to, or near to, these general principles. The most perfect philosophy of the natural kind only staves off our ignorance a little longer, as perhaps the most perfect philosophy of the moral or metaphysical kind serves only to discover larger portions of it. Thus the observation of human blindness and weakness is the result of all philosophy, and meets us, at every turn, in spite of our endeavors to elude or avoid it.

Nor is geometry, when taken into the assistance of natural philosophy, ever able to remedy this defect or lead us into the knowledge of ultimate causes by all that accuracy of reasoning for which it is so justly celebrated. Every part of mixed mathematics proceeds upon the supposition that certain laws are established by nature in her operations, and abstract reasonings are employed either to assist experience in the discovery of these laws or to determine their influence in particular instances where it depends upon any precise degree of distance and quantity. Thus it is a law of motion, discovered by experience, that the moment or force of any body in motion is in the compound ratio or proportion of its solid contents and its velocity, and, consequently, that a small force may remove the greatest obstacle or raise the greatest weight if by any contrivance or machinery we can increase the velocity of that force so as to make it an overmatch for its antagonist. Geometry assists us in the application of this law by giving us the just dimensions of all the parts and figures which can enter into any species of machine, but still the discovery of the law itself is owing merely to experience; and all the abstract reasonings in the world could never lead us one step toward the knowledge of it. When we reason *a priori* and consider merely any object or cause as it appears to the mind, independent of all observation, it never could suggest to us the notion of any distinct object, such as its effect, much less show us the inseparable and inviolable connection between them. A man must be very sagacious who could discover by reasoning that crystal is the effect of heat, and ice of cold, without being previously acquainted with the operation of these qualities.

Part II

But we have not yet attained any tolerable satisfaction with regard to the question first proposed. Each solution still gives rise to a new question as difficult as the foregoing and leads us on to further inquiries. When it is asked, *What is the nature of all our reasonings concerning matter of fact?* the proper answer seems to be that they are founded on the relation of cause and effect. When again it is asked, *What is the foundation of all our reasonings and conclusions concerning that relation?* it may be replied in one word, *experience*. But if we still carry on our sifting humor and ask, *What is the foundation of all conclusions from experience?* this implies a new question which may be of more difficult solution and explication. Philosophers that give themselves airs of superior wisdom and sufficiency have a hard task when they encounter persons of inquisitive dispositions, who push them from every corner to which they retreat, and who are sure at last to bring them to some dangerous dilemma. The best expedient to prevent this confusion is to be modest in our pretensions and even to discover the difficulty ourselves before it is objected to us. By this means we may make a kind of merit of our very ignorance.

I shall content myself in this section with an easy task and shall pretend only to give a negative answer to the question here proposed. I say, then, that even after we have experience of the operations of cause and effect, our conclusions from that experience are *not* founded on reasoning or any process of understanding. This answer we must endeavor both to explain and to defend.

It must certainly be allowed that nature has kept us at a great distance from all her secrets and has afforded us only the knowledge of a few superficial qualities of objects, while she conceals from us those powers and principles on which the influence of these objects entirely depends. Our senses inform us of the color, weight, and consistency of bread, but neither sense nor reason can ever inform us of those qualities which fit it for the nourishment and support of the human body. Sight or feeling conveys an idea of the actual motion of bodies, but as to that wonderful force or power which would carry on a moving body forever in a continued change of place, and which bodies never lose but by communicating it to others, of this we cannot form the most distant conception. But notwithstanding this ignorance of natural powers[2] and principles, we always presume when we see like sensible qualities that they have like secret powers, and expect that effects similar to those which we have experienced will follow from them. If a body of like color and consistence with that bread which we have formerly eaten be presented to us, we make no scruple of repeating the experiment and foresee with certainty like nourishment and support. Now this is a process of the mind or thought of which I would willingly know the foundation. It is allowed on all hands that there is no known connection between the sensible qualities and the secret powers, and, consequently, that the mind is not led to form such a conclusion concerning their constant and regular conjunction by anything which it knows of their nature. As to past *experience*, it can be allowed to give *direct* and *certain* information of those precise objects only, and that precise period of time which fell under its cognizance: But why this experience should be extended to future times and to other objects which, for aught we know, may be only in appearance similar, this is the main question on which I would insist. The bread which I formerly ate nourished me; that is, a body of such sensible qualities was, at that time, endued with such secret powers. But does it follow that other bread must also nourish me at another time, and that like sensible qualities must always be attended with like secret powers? The consequence seems nowise necessary. At least, it must be acknowledged that there is here a consequence drawn by the mind, that there is a certain step taken, a process of thought, and an inference which wants to be explained. These two propositions are far from being the same: *I have found that such an object has always been attended with such an effect,* and *I foresee that other objects which are in appearance similar will be attended with similar effects.* I shall allow, if you please, that the one proposition may justly be inferred from the other: I know, in fact, that it always is inferred. But if you insist that the inference is made by a chain of reasoning, I desire you to produce that reasoning. The connection between these propositions is not intuitive. There is required a medium which may enable the mind to draw such an inference, if indeed it be drawn by reasoning and argument. What that medium is I must confess passes my comprehension; and it is incumbent on those to produce it who assert that it really exists and is the origin of all our conclusions concerning matter of fact.

This negative argument must certainly, in process of time, become altogether convincing if many penetrating and able philosophers shall turn their inquiries this way, and no one be ever able to discover any connecting proposition or intermediate step which supports the understanding in this conclusion. But as the question is yet new, every reader may not trust so far to his own penetration as to conclude, because an argument escapes his inquiry, that therefore it does not really exist. For this reason it may be requisite to venture upon a more difficult task, and, enumerating all the branches of human knowledge, endeavor to show that none of them can afford such an argument.

All reasonings may be divided into two kinds, namely, demonstrative reasoning, or that concerning relations of ideas, and moral reasoning, or that concerning matter of fact and existence. That there are no demonstrative arguments in the case seems evident, since it implies no contradiction that the course of nature may change and that an object, seemingly like those which we have experienced, may be attended with different or contrary effects. May I not clearly and distinctly conceive that a body, falling from the clouds and which in all other respects resembles snow, has yet the taste of salt or feeling of fire? Is there any more intelligible proposition than to affirm that all the trees will flourish in December and January, and will decay in May and June? Now, whatever is intelligible and can be distinctly conceived implies no contradiction and can never be proved false by any demonstrative argument or abstract reasoning *a priori.*

If we be, therefore, engaged by arguments to put trust in past experience and make it the standard of our future judgment, these arguments must be probable only, or such as regard matter of fact and real existence, according to the division above mentioned. But that there is no argument of this kind must appear if our explication of that species of reasoning be admitted as solid and satisfactory. We have said that all arguments concerning existence are founded on the relation of cause and effect, that our knowledge of that relation is derived entirely from experience, and that all our experimental conclusions proceed upon the supposition that the future will be conformable to the past. To endeavor, therefore, the proof of this last supposition by probable arguments, or arguments regarding existence, must be evidently going in a circle and taking that for granted which is the very point in question.

In reality, all arguments from experience are founded on the similarity which we discover among natural objects, and by which we are induced to expect effects similar to those which we have found to follow from such objects. And though none but a fool or madman will ever pretend to dispute the authority of experience or to reject that great guide of human life, it may surely be allowed a philosopher to have so much curiosity at least as to examine the principle of human nature which gives this mighty authority to experience and makes us draw advantage from that similarity which nature has placed among different objects. From causes which appear similar, we expect similar effects. This is the sum of our experimental conclusions. Now it seems evident that, if this conclusion were formed by reason, it would be as perfect at first, and upon one instance, as after ever so long a course of experience; but the case is far otherwise. Nothing so like as eggs, yet no one, on account of this appearing similarity, expects the same taste and relish in all of them. It is only after a long course of uniform experiments in any kind that we attain a firm reliance and security with regard to a particular event. Now, where is that process of reasoning which, from one instance, draws a conclusion so different from that which it infers from a hundred instances that are nowise different from that single one? This question I propose as much for the sake of information as with an intention of raising difficulties. I cannot find, I cannot imagine any such reasoning. But I keep my mind still open to instruction if anyone will vouchsafe to bestow it on me.

Should it be said that, from a number of uniform experiments, we *infer* a connection between the sensible qualities and the secret powers, this, I must confess, seems the same difficulty, couched in different terms. The question still recurs, On what process of argument is this *inference* founded? Where is the medium, the interposing ideas which join propositions so very wide of each other? It is confessed that the color, consistence, and other sensible qualities of bread appear not of themselves to have any connection with the secret powers of nourishment and support; for otherwise we could infer these secret powers from the first appearance of these sensible qualities without the aid of experience, contrary to the sentiment of all philosophers, and contrary to plain matter of fact. Here, then, is our natural state of ignorance with regard to the powers and influence of all objects. How is this remedied by experience? It only shows us a number of uniform effects resulting from certain objects, and teaches us that those particular objects, at that particular time, were endowed with such powers and forces. When a

new object endowed with similar sensible qualities is produced, we expect similar powers and forces, and look for a like effect. From a body of like color and consistence with bread, we expect like nourishment and support. But this surely is a step or progress of the mind which wants to be explained. When a man says, *I have found, in all past instances, such sensible qualities, conjoined with such secret powers,* and when he says, *similar sensible qualities will always be conjoined with similar secret powers,* he is not guilty of a tautology, nor are these propositions in any respect the same. You say that the one proposition is an inference from the other; but you must confess that the inference is not intuitive, neither is it demonstrative. Of what nature is it then? To say it is experimental is begging the question. For all inferences from experience suppose as their foundation, that the future will resemble the past and that similar powers will be conjoined with similar sensible qualities. If there be any suspicion that the course of nature may change, and that the past may be no rule for the future, all experience becomes useless and can give rise to no inference or conclusion. It is impossible, therefore, that any arguments from experience can prove this resemblance of the past to the future; since all these arguments are founded on the supposition of that resemblance. Let the course of things be allowed hitherto ever so regular, that alone, without some new argument or inference, proves not that for the future it will continue so. In vain do you pretend to have learned the nature of bodies from your past experience. Their secret nature and consequently all their effects and influence, may change without any change in their sensible qualities. This happens sometimes, and with regard to some objects. Why may it not happen always, and with regard to all objects? What logic, what process of argument secures you against this supposition? My practice, you say, refutes my doubts. But you mistake the purport of my question. As an agent, I am quite satisfied in the point; but as a philosopher who has some share of curiosity, I will not say skepticism, I want to learn the foundation of this inference.

No reading, no inquiry has yet been able to remove my difficulty or give me satisfaction in a matter of such importance. Can I do better than propose the difficulty to the public, even though, perhaps, I have small hopes of obtaining a solution? We shall at least, by this means, be sensible of our ignorance, if we do not augment our knowledge.

I must confess that a man is guilty of unpardonable arrogance who concludes, because an argument has escaped his own investigation, that therefore it does not really exist. I must also confess that, though all the learned, for several ages, should have employed themselves in fruitless search upon any subject, it may still, perhaps, be rash to conclude positively that the subject must therefore pass all human comprehension. Even though we examine all the sources of our knowledge and conclude them unfit for such a subject, there may still remain a suspicion that the enumeration is not complete or the examination not accurate. But with regard to the present subject, there are some considerations which seem to remove all this accusation of arrogance or suspicion of mistake.

It is certain that the most ignorant and stupid peasants, nay infants, nay even brute beasts, improve by experience and learn the qualities of natural objects by observing the effects which result from them. When a child has felt the sensation of pain from touching the flame of a candle, he will be careful not to put his hand near any candle, but will expect a similar effect from a cause which is similar in its sensible qualities and appearance. If you assert, therefore, that the understanding of the child is led into this conclusion by any process of argument or ratiocination, I may justly require you to produce that argument, nor have you any pretense to refuse so equitable a demand. You cannot say that the argument is abstruse and may possibly escape your inquiry, since you confess that it is obvious to the capacity of a mere infant. If you hesitate, therefore, a moment or if, after reflection, you produce any intricate or profound argument, you, in a manner, give up the question and confess that it is not reasoning which engages us to suppose the past resembling the future, and to expect similar effects from causes which are to appearance similar. This is the proposition which I intended to enforce in the present section. If I be right, I pretend not to have made any mighty discovery. And if I be wrong, I must acknowledge myself to be indeed a very backward scholar, since I cannot now discover an argument which, it seems, was perfectly familiar to me long before I was out of my cradle.

SECTION V. SKEPTICAL SOLUTION OF THESE DOUBTS

Part I

The passion for philosophy, like that for religion, seems liable to this inconvenience, that though it aims at the correction of our manners and extirpation of our vices, it may only serve, by imprudent management, to foster a predominant inclination and push the mind with more determined resolution toward that side which already *draws* too much by the bias and propensity of the natural temper. It is certain that, while we aspire to the magnanimous firmness of the philosophic sage and endeavor to confine our pleasures altogether within our own minds, we may, at last, render our philosophy, like that of Epictetus and other Stoics, only a more refined system of selfishness, and reason ourselves out of all virtue as well as social enjoyment. While we study with attention the vanity of human life and turn all our thoughts toward the empty and transitory nature of riches and honors, we are, perhaps, all the while flattering our natural indolence which, hating the bustle of the world and drudgery of business, seeks a pretense of reason to give itself a full and uncontrolled indulgence. There is, however, one species of philosophy which seems little liable to this inconvenience, and that because it strikes in with no disorderly passion of the human mind, nor can mingle itself with any natural affection or propensity; and that is the Academic or Skeptical philosophy. The Academics always talk of doubt and suspense of judgment, of danger in hasty determinations, of confining to very narrow bounds the inquiries of the understanding, and of renouncing all speculations which lie not within the limits of common life and practice. Nothing, therefore, can be more contrary than such a philosophy to the supine indolence of the mind, its rash arrogance, its lofty pretensions, and its superstitious credulity. Every passion is mortified by it, except the love of truth; and that passion never is nor can be carried to too high a degree. It is surprising, therefore, that this philosophy, which in almost every instance must be harmless and innocent, should be the subject of so much groundless reproach and obloquy. But, perhaps, the very circumstance which renders it so innocent is what chiefly exposes it to the public hatred and resentment. By flattering no irregular passion, it gains few partisans. By opposing so many vices and follies, it raises to itself abundance of enemies who stigmatize it as libertine, profane and irreligious.

Nor need we fear that this philosophy, while it endeavors to limit our inquiries to common life, should ever undermine the reasonings of common life and carry its doubts so far as to destroy all action as well as speculation. Nature will always maintain her rights and prevail in the end over any abstract reasoning whatsoever. Though we should conclude, for instance, as in the foregoing section, that in all reasonings from experience there is a step taken by the mind which is not supported by any argument or process of the understanding, there is no danger that these reasonings, on which almost all knowledge depends, will ever be affected by such a discovery. If the mind be not engaged by argument to make this step, it must be induced by some other principle of equal weight and authority; and that principle will preserve its influence as long as human nature remains the same. What that principle is may well be worth the pains of inquiry.

Suppose a person, though endowed with the strongest faculties of reason and reflection, to be brought on a sudden into this world; he would, indeed, immediately observe a continual succession of objects and one event following another, but he would not be able to discover anything further. He would not at first, by any reasoning, be able to reach the idea of cause and effect, since the particular powers by which all natural operations are performed never appear to the senses; nor is it reasonable to conclude, merely because one event in one instance precedes another, that therefore the one is the cause, the other the effect. The conjunction may be arbitrary and casual. There may be no reason to infer the existence of one from the appearance of the other; and, in a word, such a person without more experience could never employ his conjecture or reasoning concerning any matter of fact or be assured of anything beyond what was immediately present to his memory or senses.

Suppose again that he has acquired more experience and has lived so long in the world as to have observed similar objects or events to be constantly conjoined together—what is the consequence of this experience? He immediately infers the existence of one object from the appearance of the other, yet he has not, by all his experience, acquired any idea or knowledge of the secret power by which the one object produces the other, nor is it by any process of reasoning he is engaged to draw this inference; but still he finds himself determined to draw it, and though he should be convinced that his understanding has no part in the operation, he would nevertheless continue in the same course of thinking. There is some other principle which determines him to form such a conclusion.

This principle is *custom* or *habit*. For whenever the repetition of any particular act or operation produces a propensity to renew the same act or operation without being impelled by any reasoning or process of the understanding, we always say that this propensity is the effect of *custom*. By employing that word we pretend not to have given the ultimate reason of such a propensity. We only point out a principle of human nature which is universally acknowledged, and which is well known by its effects. Perhaps we can push our inquiries no further or pretend to give the cause of this cause, but must rest contented with it as the ultimate principle which we can assign of all our conclusions from experience. It is sufficient satisfaction that we can go so far without repining at the narrowness of our faculties, because they will carry us no further. And it is certain we here advance a very intelligible proposition at least, if not a true one, when we assert that after the constant conjunction of two objects, heat and flame, for instance, weight and solidity, we are determined by custom alone to expect the one from the appearance of the other. This hypothesis seems even the only one which explains the difficulty why we draw from a thousand instances an inference which we are not able to draw from one instance that is in no respect different from them. Reason is incapable of any such variation. The conclusions which it draws from considering one circle are the same which it would form upon surveying all the circles in the universe. But no man, having seen only one body move after being impelled by another, could infer that every other body will move after a like impulse. All inferences from experience, therefore, are effects of custom, not of reasoning.[3]

Custom, then, is the great guide of human life. It is that principle alone which renders our experience useful to us and makes us expect, for the future, a similar train of events with those which have appeared in the past. Without the influence of custom we should be entirely ignorant of every matter of fact beyond what is immediately present to the memory and senses. We should never know how to adjust means to ends or to employ our natural powers in the production of any effect. There would be an end at once of all action as well as of the chief part of speculation.

But here it may be proper to remark that though our conclusions from experience carry us beyond our memory and senses and assure us of matters of fact which happened in the most distant places and most remote ages, yet some fact must always be present to the senses or memory from which we may first proceed in drawing these conclusions. A man who should find in a desert country the remains of pompous buildings would conclude that the country had, in ancient times, been cultivated by civilized inhabitants; but did nothing of this nature occur to him, he could never form such an inference. We learn the events of former ages from history, but then we must peruse the volume in which this instruction is contained, and thence carry up our inferences from one testimony to another, till we arrive at the eyewitnesses and spectators of these distant events. In a word, if we proceed not upon some fact present to the memory or senses, our reasonings would be merely hypothetical; and however the particular links might be connected with each other, the whole chain of inferences would have nothing to support it, nor could we ever, by its means, arrive at the knowledge of any real existence. If I ask why you believe any particular matter of fact which you relate, you must tell me some reason; and this reason will be some other fact connected with it. But as you cannot proceed after this manner *in infinitum*, you must at last terminate in some fact which is present to your memory or senses or must allow that your belief is entirely without foundation.

What, then, is the conclusion of the whole matter? A simple one, though, it must be confessed, pretty remote from the common theories of philosophy. All belief of matter of fact or real existence is derived merely from some object present to the memory or senses and a customary conjunction between that and some other object; or, in other words, having found, in many instances, that any two kinds of objects, flame and heat, snow and cold, have always been conjoined together: if flame or snow be presented anew to the senses, the mind is carried by custom to expect heat or cold, and to *believe* that such a quality does exist and will discover itself upon a nearer approach. This belief is the necessary result of placing the mind in such circumstances. It is an operation of the soul, when we are so situated, as unavoidable as to feel the passion of love, when we receive benefits; or hatred, when we meet with injuries. All these operations are a species of natural instincts, which no reasoning or process of the thought and understanding is able either to produce or to prevent. At this point it would be very allowable for us to stop our philosophical researches. In most questions we can never make a single step further; and in all questions we must terminate here at last, after our most restless and curious inquiries. But still our curiosity will be pardonable, perhaps commendable, if it carry us on to still further researches and make us examine more accurately the nature of this *belief* and of the *customary conjunction* whence it is derived. By this means we may meet with some explications and analogies that will give satisfaction, at least to such as love the abstract sciences, and can be entertained with speculations which, however accurate, may still retain a degree of doubt and uncertainty. As to readers of a different taste, the remaining part of this Section is not calculated for them; and the following inquiries may well be understood, though it be neglected.

Part II

Nothing is more free than the imagination of man, and though it cannot exceed that original stock of ideas furnished by the internal and external senses, it has unlimited power of mixing, compounding, separating, and dividing these ideas in all the varieties of fiction and vision. It can feign a train of events with all the appearance of reality, ascribe to them a particular time and place, conceive them as existent, and paint them out to itself with every circumstance that belongs to any historical fact which it believes with the greatest certainty. Wherein, therefore, consists the difference between such a fiction and belief? It lies not merely in any peculiar idea which is annexed to such a conception as commands our assent, and which is wanting to every known fiction. For as the mind has authority over all its ideas, it could voluntarily annex this particular idea to any fiction, and consequently be able to believe whatever it pleases, contrary to what we find by daily experience. We can, in our conception, join the head of a man to the body of a horse, but it is not in our power to believe that such an animal has ever really existed.

It follows, therefore, that the difference between *fiction* and *belief* lies in some sentiment or feeling which is annexed to the latter, not to the former, and which depends not on the will, nor can be demanded at pleasure. It must be excited by nature like all other sentiments and must rise from the particular situation in which the mind is placed at any particular juncture. Whenever any object is presented to the memory or senses, it immediately, by the force of custom, carries the imagination to conceive that object which is usually conjoined to it; and this conception is attended with a feeling or sentiment different from the loose reveries of the fancy. In this consists the whole nature of belief. For as there is no matter of fact which we believe so firmly that we cannot conceive the contrary, there would be no difference between the conception assented to and that which is rejected were it not for some sentiment which distinguishes the one from the other. If I see a billiard ball moving toward another on a smooth table, I can easily conceive it to stop upon contact. This conception implies no contradiction, but still it feels very differently from that conception by which I represent to myself the impulse and the communication of motion from one ball to another.

Were we to attempt a *definition* of this sentiment, we should, perhaps, find it a very difficult, if not an impossible, task; in the same manner as if we should endeavor to define the feeling of cold, or passion of anger, to a creature who never had any experience of these sentiments. Belief is the true and proper name of this feeling, and no one is ever at a loss to know the meaning of that term, because every man is every moment conscious of the sentiment represented by it. It may not, however, be improper to attempt a *description* of this sentiment, in hopes we may by that means arrive at some analogies which may afford a more perfect explication of it. I say that belief is nothing but a more vivid, lively, forcible, firm, steady conception of an object than what the imagination alone is ever able to attain. This variety of terms, which may seem so unphilosophical, is intended only to express that act of the mind which renders realities, or what is taken for such, more present to us than fictions, causes them to weigh more in the thought, and gives them a superior influence on the passions and imagination. Provided we agree about the thing, it is needless to dispute about the terms. The imagination has the command over all its ideas and can join and mix and vary them in all the ways possible. It may conceive fictitious objects with all the circumstances of place and time. It may set them in a manner before our eyes, in their true colors, just as they might have existed. But as it is impossible that this faculty of imagination can ever, of itself, reach belief, it is evident that belief consists not in the peculiar nature or order of ideas, but in the *manner* of their conception and in their *feeling* to the mind. I confess that it is impossible perfectly to explain this feeling or manner of conception. We may make use of words which express something near it. But its true and proper name, as we observed before, is "belief," which is a term that everyone sufficiently understands in common life. And in philosophy we can go no further than assert that *belief* is something felt by the mind, which distinguishes the ideas of the judgment from the fictions of the imagination. It gives them more weight and influence, makes them appear of greater importance, enforces them in the mind, and renders them the governing principle of our actions. I hear at present, for instance, a person's voice with whom I am acquainted, and the sound comes as from the next room. This impression of my senses immediately conveys my thought to the person, together with all the surrounding objects. I paint them out to myself as existing at present, with the same qualities and relations of which I formerly knew them possessed. These ideas take faster hold of my mind than ideas of an enchanted castle. They are very different from the feeling and have a much greater influence of every kind, either to give pleasure or pain, joy or sorrow.

Let us, then, take in the whole compass of this doctrine and allow that the sentiment of belief is nothing but a conception more intense and steady than what attends the mere fictions of the imagination, and that this *manner* of conception arises from a customary conjunction of the object with something present to the memory or senses. I believe that it will not be difficult, upon these suppositions, to find other operations of the mind analogous to it and to trace up these phenomena to principles still more general.

We have already observed that nature has established connections among particular ideas, and that no sooner one idea occurs to our thoughts than it introduces its correlative and carries our attention towards it by a gentle and insensible movement. These principles of connection or association we have reduced to three, namely, "resemblance," "contiguity," and "causation," which are the only bonds that unite our thoughts together and beget that regular train of reflection or discourse which, in a greater or less degree, takes place among mankind. Now here arises a question on which the solution of the present difficulty will depend. Does it happen in all these relations that when one of the objects is presented to the senses or memory, the mind is not only carried to the conception of the correlative, but reaches a steadier and stronger conception of it than what otherwise it would have been able to attain? This seems to be the case with that belief which arises from the relation of cause and effect. And if the case be the same with the other relations or principles of association, this may be established as a general law which takes place in all the operations of the mind.

We may, therefore, observe, as the first experiment to our present purpose, that upon the appearance of the picture of an absent friend our idea of him is evidently enlivened by the *resemblance,* and that every passion which that idea occasions, whether of joy or sorrow, acquires new force and vigor. In producing this effect there concur both a relation and a present impression. Where the picture bears him no resemblance, at least was not intended for him, it never so much as conveys our thought to him. And where it is absent, as well as the person, though the mind may pass from the thought of one to that of the other, it feels its idea to be rather weakened than enlivened by that transition. We take a pleasure in viewing the picture of a friend when it is set before us; but when it is removed, rather choose to consider him directly than by reflection on an image which is equally distant and obscure.

The ceremonies of the Roman Catholic religion may be considered as instances of the same nature. The devotees of that superstition usually plead, in excuse for the mummeries with which they are upbraided, that they feel the good effect of those external motions, and postures, and actions in enlivening their devotion and quickening their fervor, which otherwise would decay if directed entirely to distant and immaterial objects. We shadow out the objects of our faith, say they, in sensible types and images, and render them more present to us by the immediate presence of these types than it is possible for us to do merely by an intellectual view and contemplation. Sensible objects have always a greater influence on the fancy than any other, and this influence they readily convey to those ideas to which they are related and which they resemble. I shall only infer from these practices and this reasoning that the effect of resemblance in enlivening the ideas is very common; and as in every case a resemblance and a present impression must concur, we are abundantly supplied with experiments to prove the reality of the foregoing principle.

We may add force to these experiments by others of a different kind, in considering the effects of *contiguity* as well as of *resemblance*. It is certain that distance diminishes the force of every idea and that, upon our approach to any object, though it does not discover itself to our senses, it operates upon the mind with an influence which imitates an immediate impression. The thinking on any object readily transports the mind to what is contiguous; but it is only the actual presence of an object that transports it with a superior vivacity. When I am a few miles from home, whatever relates to it touches me more nearly than when I am two hundred leagues distant, though even at that distance the reflecting on anything in the neighborhood of my friends or family naturally produces an idea of them. But, as in this latter case, both the objects of the mind are ideas, notwithstanding

there is an easy transition between them: that transition alone is not able to give a superior vivacity to any of the ideas, for want of some immediate impression.[4]

No one can doubt but *causation* has the same influence as the other two relations of resemblance and contiguity. Superstitious people are fond of the relics of saints and holy men, for the same reason that they seek after types or images in order to enliven their devotion and give them a more intimate and strong conception of those exemplary lives which they desire to imitate. Now it is evident that one of the best relics which a devotee could procure would be the handiwork of a saint; and if his clothes and furniture are ever to be considered in this light, it is because they were once at his disposal and were moved and affected by him; in which respect they are to be considered as imperfect effects, and as connected with him by a shorter chain of consequences than any of those by which we learn the reality of his existence.

Suppose that the son of a friend who had been long dead or absent were presented to us; it is evident that this object would instantly revive its correlative idea and recall to our thoughts all past intimacies and familiarities in more lively color than they would otherwise have appeared to us. This is another phenomenon which seems to prove the principle above mentioned.

We may observe that in these phenomena the belief of the correlative object is always presupposed, without which the relation could have no effect. The influence of the picture supposes that we *believe* our friend to have once existed. Contiguity to home can never excite our ideas of home unless we *believe* that it really exists. Now I assert that this belief, where it reaches beyond the memory or senses, is of a similar nature and arises from similar causes with the transition of thought and vivacity of conception here explained. When I throw a piece of dry wood into a fire, my mind is immediately carried to conceive that it augments, not extinguishes, the flame. This transition of thought from the cause to the effect proceeds not from reason. It derives its origin altogether from custom and experience. And, as it first begins from an object present to the senses, it renders the idea or conception of flame more strong or lively than any loose floating reverie of the imagination. The idea arises immediately. The thought moves instantly toward it and conveys to it all that force of conception which is derived from the impression present to the senses. When a sword is leveled at my breast, does not the idea of wound and pain strike me more strongly than when a glass of wine is presented to me, even though by accident this idea should occur after the appearance of the latter object? But what is there in this whole matter to cause such a strong conception except only a present object and a customary transition to the idea of another object which we have been accustomed to conjoin with the former? This is the whole operation of the mind in all our conclusions concerning matter of fact and existence; and it is a satisfaction to find some analogies by which it may be explained. The transition from a present object does in all cases give strength and solidity to the related idea.

Here, then, is a kind of pre-established harmony between the course of nature and the succession of our ideas; and though the powers and forces by which the former is governed be wholly unknown to us, yet our thoughts and conceptions have still, we find, gone on in the same train with the other works of nature. Custom is that principle by which this correspondence has been effected, so necessary to the subsistence of our species and the regulation of our conduct in every circumstance and occurrence of human life. Had not the presence of an object instantly excited the idea of those objects commonly conjoined with it, all our knowledge must have been limited to the narrow sphere of our memory and senses, and we should never have been able to adjust means to ends or employ our natural powers either to the producing of good or avoiding of evil. Those who delight in the discovery and contemplation of *final causes* have here ample subject to employ their wonder and admiration.

I shall add, for a further confirmation of the foregoing theory, that as this operation of the mind, by which we infer like effects from like causes, and *vice versa,* is so essential to the subsistence of all human creatures, it is not probable that it could be trusted to the fallacious deductions of our reason, which is slow in its operations, appears not, in any degree, during the first years of infancy, and, at best, is in every age and period of human life extremely liable to error and mistake. It is more conformable to the ordinary wisdom of nature to secure so necessary an act of the mind by some instinct or mechanical tendency which may be infallible in its operations, may discover itself at the first appearance of life and thought, and may be independent of all the labored deductions of the understanding. As nature has taught us the use of our limbs without giving us the knowledge of the muscles and nerves by which they are actuated, so has she implanted in us an instinct which carries forward the thought in a correspondent course to that which she has established among external objects, though we are ignorant of those powers and forces on which this regular course and succession of objects totally depends.

SECTION VI. OF PROBABILITY[5]

Though there be no such thing as *chance* in the world, our ignorance of the real cause of any event has the same influence on the understanding and begets a like species of belief or opinion.

There is certainly a probability which arises from a superiority of chances on any side; and, according as this superiority increases and surpasses the opposite chances, the probability receives a proportionable increase and begets still a higher degree of belief of assent to that side in which we discover the superiority. If a die were marked with one figure or number of spots on four sides, and with another figure or number of spots on the two remaining sides, it would be more probable that the former would turn up than the latter, though, if it had a thousand sides marked in the same manner, and only one side different, the probability would be much higher and our belief or expectation of the event more steady and secure. This process of the thought or reasoning may seem trivial and obvious; but to those who consider it more narrowly it may, perhaps, afford matter for curious speculation.

It seems evident that when the mind looks forward to discover the event which may result from the throw of such a die, it considers the turning up of each particular side as alike probable; and this is the very nature of chance, to render all the particular events comprehended in it entirely equal. But finding a greater number of sides concur in the one event than in the other, the mind is carried more frequently to that event and meets it oftener in revolving the various possibilities or chances on which the ultimate result depends. This concurrence of several views in one particular event begets immediately, by an explicable contrivance of nature, the sentiment of belief and gives that event the advantage over its antagonist which is supported by a smaller number of views and recurs less frequently to the mind. If we allow that belief is nothing but a firmer and stronger conception of an object than what attends the mere fictions of the imagination, this operation may, perhaps, in some measure be accounted for. The concurrence of these several views or glimpses imprints the idea more strongly on the imagination, gives it superior force and vigor, renders its influence on the passions and affections more sensible, and, in a word, begets that reliance or security which constitutes the nature of belief and opinion.

The case is the same with the probability of causes as with that of chance. There are some causes which are entirely uniform and constant in producing a particular effect, and no instance has ever yet been found of any failure or irregularity in their operation. Fire has always burned, and water suffocated, every human creature. The production of motion by impulse and gravity is a universal law which has hitherto admitted of no exception. But there are other causes which have been found more irregular and uncertain, nor has rhubarb always proved a purge, or opium a soporific, to everyone who has taken these medicines. It is true, when any cause fails of producing its usual effect, philosophers ascribe not this to any irregularity in nature, but suppose that

some secret causes in the particular structure of parts have prevented the operation. Our reasonings, however, and conclusions concerning the event are the same as if this principle had no place. Being determined by custom to transfer the past to the future in all our inferences, where the past has been entirely regular and uniform we expect the event with the greatest assurance and leave no room for any contrary supposition. But where different effects have been found to follow from causes which are to *appearance* exactly similar, all these various effects must occur to the mind in transferring the past to the future, and enter into our consideration when we determine the probability of the event. Though we give the preference to that which has been found most usual, and believe that this effect will exist, we must not overlook the other effects, but must assign to each of them a particular weight and authority in proportion as we have found it to be more or less frequent. It is more probable, in almost every country of Europe, that there will be frost sometime in January than that the weather will continue open throughout the whole month, though this probability varies according to the different climates, and approaches to a certainty in the more northern kingdoms. Here, then, it seems evident that when we transfer the past to the future in order to determine the effect which will result from any cause, we transfer all the different events in the same proportion as they have appeared in the past, and conceive one to have existed a hundred times, for instance, another ten times, and another once. As a great number of views do here concur in one event, they fortify and confirm it to the imagination, beget that sentiment which we call "belief," and give its object the preference above the contrary event which is not supported by an equal number of experiments and recurs not so frequently to the thought in transferring the past to the future. Let anyone try to account for this operation of the mind upon any of the received systems of philosophy, and he will be sensible of the difficulty. For my part, I shall think it sufficient if the present hints excite the curiosity of philosophers and make them sensible how defective all common theories are in treating of such curious and such sublime subjects.

SECTION VII. OF THE IDEA OF NECESSARY CONNECTION

Part I

The great advantage of the mathematical sciences above the moral consists in this, that the ideas of the former, being sensible, are always clear and determinate, the smallest distinction between them is immediately perceptible, and the same terms are still expressive of the same ideas without ambiguity or variation. An oval is never mistaken for a circle, nor a hyperbola for an ellipsis. The isosceles and scalenum are distinguished by boundaries more exact than vice and virtue, right and wrong. If any term be defined in geometry, the mind readily, of itself substitutes on all occasions the definition for the term defined, or, even when no definition is employed, the object itself may be presented to the senses and by that means be steadily and clearly apprehended. But the finer sentiments of the mind, the operations of the understanding, the various agitations of the passions, though really in themselves distinct, easily escape us when surveyed by reflection, nor is it in our power to recall the original object as often as we have occasion to contemplate it. Ambiguity, by this means, is gradually introduced into our reasonings: similar objects are readily taken to be the same, and the conclusion becomes at last very wide of the premises.

One may safely, however, affirm that if we consider these sciences in a proper light, their advantages and disadvantages nearly compensate each other and reduce both of them to a state of equality. If the mind, with greater facility, retains the ideas of geometry clear and determinate, it must carry on a much longer and more intricate chain of reasoning and compare ideas much wider of each other in order to reach the abstruser truths of that science. And if moral ideas are apt, without extreme care, to fall into obscurity and confusion, the inferences are always much

shorter in these disquisitions, and the intermediate steps which lead to the conclusion much fewer than in the sciences which treat of quantity and number. In reality, there is scarcely a proposition in Euclid so simple as not to consist of more parts than are to be found in any moral reasoning which runs not into chimera and conceit. Where we trace the principles of the human mind through a few steps, we may be very well satisfied with our progress, considering how soon nature throws a bar to all our inquiries concerning causes and reduces us to an acknowledgment of our ignorance. The chief obstacle, therefore, to our improvements in the moral or metaphysical sciences is the obscurity of the ideas and ambiguity of the terms. The principal difficulty in the mathematics is the length of inferences and compass of thought requisite to the forming of any conclusion. And, perhaps, our progress in natural philosophy is chiefly retarded by the want of proper experiments and phenomena, which are often discovered by chance and cannot always be found when requisite, even by the most diligent and prudent inquiry. As moral philosophy seems hitherto to have received less improvement than either geometry or physics, we may conclude that if there be any difference in this respect among these sciences, the difficulties which obstruct the progress of the former require superior care and capacity to be surmounted.

There are no ideas which occur in metaphysics more obscure and uncertain than those of "power," "force," "energy," or "necessary connection," of which it is every moment necessary for us to treat in all our disquisitions. We shall, therefore, endeavor in this Section to fix, if possible, the precise meaning of these terms and thereby remove some part of that obscurity which is so much complained of in this species of philosophy.

It seems a proposition which will not admit of much dispute that all our ideas are nothing but copies of our impressions, or, in other words, that it is impossible for us to *think* of anything which we have not antecedently *felt*, either by our external or internal senses. I have endeavored[6] to explain and prove this proposition, and have expressed my hopes that by a proper application of it men may reach a greater clearness and precision in philosophical reasonings than what they have hitherto been able to attain. Complex ideas may, perhaps, be well known by definition, which is nothing but an enumeration of those parts or simple ideas that compose them. But when we have pushed up definitions to the most simple ideas and find still some ambiguity and obscurity, what resources are we then possessed of? By what invention can we throw light upon these ideas and render them altogether precise and determinate to our intellectual view? Produce the impressions or original sentiments from which the ideas are copied. These impressions are all strong and sensible. They admit not of ambiguity. They are not only placed in a full light themselves, but may throw light on their correspondent ideas, which lie in obscurity. And by this means we may perhaps attain a new microscope or species of optics by which, in the moral sciences, the most minute and most simple ideas may be so enlarged as to fall readily under our apprehension and be equally known with the grossest and most sensible ideas that can be the object of our inquiry.

To be fully acquainted, therefore, with the idea of power or necessary connection, let us examine its impression and, in order to find the impression with greater certainty, let us search for it in all the sources from which it may possibly be derived.

When we look about us towards external objects and consider the operation of causes, we are never able, in a single instance, to discover any power or necessary connection, any quality which binds the effect to the cause and renders the one an infallible consequence of the other. We only find that the one does actually in fact follow the other. The impulse of one billiard ball is attended with motion in the second. This is the whole that appears to the *outward* senses. The mind feels no sentiment or *inward* impression from this succession of objects; consequently, there is not, in any single particular instance of cause and effect,

anything which can suggest the idea of power or necessary connection.

From the first appearance of an object we never can conjecture what effect will result from it. But were the power or energy of any cause discoverable by the mind, we could foresee the effect, even without experience, and might, at first, pronounce with certainty concerning it by mere dint of thought and reasoning.

In reality, there is no part of matter that does ever, by its sensible qualities, discover any power or energy, or give us ground to imagine that it could produce anything, or be followed by any other object, which we could denominate its effect. Solidity, extension, motion—these qualities are all complete in themselves and never point out any other event which may result from them. The scenes of the universe are continually shifting, and one object follows another in an uninterrupted succession; but the power or force which actuates the whole machine is entirely concealed from us and never discovers itself in any of the sensible qualities of body. We know that, in fact, heat is a constant attendant of flame; but what is the connection between them we have no room so much as to conjecture or imagine. It is impossible, therefore, that the idea of power can be derived from the contemplation of bodies in single instances of their operation, because no bodies ever discover any power which can be the original of this idea.[7]

Since, therefore, external objects as they appear to the senses give us no idea of power or necessary connection by their operation in particular instances, let us see whether this idea be derived from reflection on the operations of our own minds and be copied from any internal impression. It may be said that we are every moment conscious of internal power while we feel that, by the simple command of our will, we can move the organs of our body or direct the faculties of our mind. An act of volition produces motion in our limbs or raises a new idea in our imagination. This influence of the will we know by consciousness. Hence we acquire the idea of power or energy, and are certain that we ourselves and all other intelligent beings are possessed of power. This idea, then, is an idea of reflection since it arises from reflecting on the operations of our own mind and on the command which is exercised by will both over the organs of the body and faculties of the soul.

We shall proceed to examine this pretension and, first, with regard to the influence of volition over the organs of the body. This influence, we may observe, is a fact which, like all other natural events, can be known only by experience, and can never be foreseen from any apparent energy or power in the cause which connects it with the effect and renders the one an infallible consequence of the other. The motion of our body follows upon the command of our will. Of this we are every moment conscious. But the means by which this is effected, the energy by which the will performs so extraordinary an operation—of this we are so far from being immediately conscious that it must forever escape our most diligent inquiry.

For, *first,* is there any principle in all nature more mysterious than the union of soul with body, by which a supposed spiritual substance acquires such an influence over a material one that the most refined thought is able to actuate the grossest matter? Were we empowered by a secret wish to remove mountains or control the planets in their orbit, this extensive authority would not be more extraordinary, nor more beyond our comprehension. But if, by consciousness, we perceived any power or energy in the will, we must know this power; we must know its connection with the effect; we must know the secret union of soul and body, and the nature of both these substances by which the one is able to operate in so many instances upon the other.

Secondly, we are not able to move all the organs of the body with a like authority, though we cannot assign any reason, besides experience, for so remarkable a difference between one and the other. Why has the will an influence over the tongue and fingers, not over the heart and liver? This question would never embarrass us were we conscious of a power in the former case, not in the latter. We should then perceive, independent

of experience, why the authority of the will over organs of the body is circumscribed within such particular limits. Being in that case fully acquainted with the power or force by which it operates, we should also know why its influence reaches precisely to such boundaries, and no further.

A man suddenly struck with a palsy in the leg or arm, or who had newly lost those members, frequently endeavors, at first, to move them and employ them in their usual offices. Here he is as much conscious of power to command such limbs as a man in perfect health is conscious of power to actuate any member which remains in its natural state and condition. But consciousness never deceives. Consequently, neither in the one case nor in the other are we ever conscious of any power. We learn the influence of our will from experience alone. And experience only teaches us how one event constantly follows another, without instructing us in the secret connection which binds them together and renders them inseparable.

Thirdly, we learn from anatomy that the immediate object of power in voluntary motion is not the member itself which is moved, but certain muscles and nerves and animal spirits, and, perhaps, something still more minute and more unknown, through which the motion is successfully propagated ere it reach the member itself whose motion is the immediate object of volition. Can there be a more certain proof that the power by which this whole operation is performed, so far from being directly and fully known by an inward sentiment or consciousness, is to the last degree mysterious and unintelligible? Here the mind wills a certain event; immediately another event, unknown to ourselves and totally different from the one intended, is produced. This event produces another, equally unknown, till, at last, through a long succession the desired event is produced. But if the original power were felt, it must be known; were it known, its effect must also be known, since all power is relative to its effect. And, *vice versa,* if the effect be not known, the power cannot be known nor felt. How indeed can we be conscious of a power to move our limbs when we have no such power, but only that to move certain animal spirits which, though they produce at last the motion of our limbs, yet operate in such a manner as is wholly beyond our comprehension?

We may therefore conclude from the whole, I hope, without any temerity, though with assurance, that our idea of power is not copied from any sentiment or consciousness of power within ourselves when we give rise to animal motion or apply our limbs to their proper use and office. That their motion follows the command of the will is a matter of common experience, like other natural events; but the power or energy by which this is effected, like that in other natural events, is unknown and inconceivable.[8]

Shall we then assert that we are conscious of a power or energy in our own minds when, by an act or command of our will, we raise up a new idea, fix the mind to the contemplation of it, turn it on all sides, and at last dismiss it for some other idea when we think that we have surveyed it with sufficient accuracy? I believe the same arguments will prove that even this command of the will gives us no real idea of force or energy.

First, it must be allowed that when we know a power, we know that very circumstance in the cause by which it is enabled to produce the effect, for these are supposed to be synonymous. We must, therefore, know both the cause and effect and the relation between them. But do we pretend to be acquainted with the nature of the human soul and the nature of an idea, or the aptitude of the one to produce the other? This is a real creation, a production of something out of nothing, which implies a power so great that it may seem, at first sight, beyond the reach of any being less than infinite. At least it must be owned that such a power is not felt, nor known, nor even conceivable by the mind. We only feel the event, namely, the existence of an idea consequent to a command of the will; but the manner in which this operation is performed, the power by which it is produced, is entirely beyond our comprehension.

Secondly, the command of the mind over itself is limited, as well as its command over the body; and these limits are not known by reason or any acquaintance with the nature of cause and effect, but only by experience and observation, as in all other natural events and in the operation of external objects. Our authority over our sentiments and passions is much weaker than that over our ideas; and even the latter authority is circumscribed within very narrow boundaries. Will any one pretend to assign the ultimate reason of these boundaries, or show why the power is deficient in one case, not in another.

Thirdly, this self-command is very different at different times. A man in health possesses more of it than one languishing with sickness. We are more master of our thoughts in the morning than in the evening; fasting, than after a full meal. Can we give any reason for these variations except experience? Where then is the power of which we pretend to be conscious? Is there not here, either in a spiritual or material substance, or both, some secret mechanism or structure of parts upon which the effect depends, and which, being entirely unknown to us, renders the power or energy of the will equally unknown and incomprehensible?

Volition is surely an act of the mind with which we are sufficiently acquainted. Reflect upon it. Consider it on all sides. Do you find anything in it like this creative power by which it raises from nothing a new idea and, with a kind of *fiat,* imitates the omnipotence of its Maker, if I may be allowed so to speak, who called forth into existence all the various scenes of nature? So far from being conscious of this energy in the will, it requires as certain experience as that of which we are possessed to convince us that such extraordinary effects do ever result from a simple act of volition.

The generality of mankind never find any difficulty in accounting for the more common and familiar operations of nature, such as the descent of heavy bodies, the growth of plants, the generation of animals, or the nourishment of bodies by food; but suppose that in all these cases they perceive the very force or energy of the cause by which it is connected with its effect, and is forever infallible in its operation. They acquire, by long habit, such a turn of mind that upon the appearance of the cause they immediately expect, with assurance, its usual attendant, and hardly conceive it possible that any other event could result from it. It is only on the discovery of extraordinary phenomena, such as earthquakes, pestilence, and prodigies of any kind, that they find themselves at a loss to assign a proper cause and to explain the manner in which the effect is produced by it. It is usual for men, in such difficulties, to have recourse to some invisible intelligent principle as the immediate cause of that event which surprises them, and which they think cannot be accounted for from the common powers of nature. But philosophers, who carry their scrutiny a little further, immediately perceive that, even in the most familiar events, the energy of the cause is as unintelligible as in the most unusual, and that we only learn by experience the frequent conjunction of objects, without being ever able to comprehend anything like connection between them. Here, then, many philosophers think themselves obliged by reason to have recourse, on all occasions, to the same principle which the vulgar never appeal to but in cases that appear miraculous and supernatural. They acknowledge mind and intelligence to be, not only the ultimate and original cause of all things, but the immediate and sole cause of every event which appears in nature. They pretend that those objects which are commonly denominated "causes" are in reality nothing but "occasions," and that the true and direct principle of every effect is not any power or force in nature, but a volition of the Supreme Being, who wills that such particular objects should forever be conjoined with each other. Instead of saying that one billiard ball moves another by a force which it has derived from the author of nature, it is the Deity himself, they say, who, by a particular volition, moves the second ball, being determined to this operation by the impulse of the first ball, in consequence of those general laws which he has laid down to himself in the government of the universe. But philosophers, advancing still in their inquiries, discover that as we are totally ignorant of the power on which depends the mutual operation of bodies, we are no less ignorant of that power on which depends the operation of mind on body, or of body on mind; nor are we able, either from our senses or consciousness, to assign the ultimate principle in the one case more than in the other. The same ignorance, therefore, reduces them to the same conclusion. They assert that the Deity is the immediate cause of the union between soul and body, and that they are not the organs of sense which, being agitated by external objects, produce sensations in the mind; but that it is a particular volition of our omnipotent Maker which excites such a sensation in consequence of such a motion in the organ. In like manner, it is not any energy in the will that produces local motion in our members: It is God himself, who is pleased to second our will, in itself impotent, and to command that motion which we erroneously attribute to our own power and efficacy. Nor do philosophers stop at this conclusion. They sometimes extend the same inference to the mind itself in its internal operations. Our mental vision or conception of ideas is nothing but a revelation made to us by our Maker. When we voluntarily turn our thoughts to any object and raise up its image in the fancy, it is not the will which creates that idea, it is the universal Creator who discovers it to the mind and renders it present to us.

Thus, according to these philosophers, everything is full of God. Not content with the principle that nothing exists but by his will, that nothing possesses any power but by his concession, they rob nature and all created beings of every power in order to render their dependence on the Deity still more sensible and immediate. They consider not that by this theory they diminish, instead of magnifying, the grandeur of those attributes which they affect so much to celebrate. It argues, surely, more power in the Deity to delegate a certain degree of power to inferior creatures than to produce everything by his own immediate volition. It argues more wisdom to contrive at first the fabric of the world with such perfect foresight that of itself, and by its proper operation, it may serve all the purposes of Providence than if the great Creator were obliged every moment to adjust its parts and animate by his breath all the wheels of that stupendous machine.

But if we would have a more philosophical confutation of this theory, perhaps the two following reflections may suffice:

First, it seems to me that this theory of the universal energy and operation of the Supreme Being is too bold ever to carry conviction with it to a man sufficiently apprised of the weakness of human reason and the narrow limits to which it is confined in all its operations. Though the chain of arguments which conduct to it were ever so logical, there must arise a strong suspicion, if not an absolute assurance, that it has carried us quite beyond the reach of our faculties when it leads to conclusions so extraordinary and so remote from common life and experience. We are got into fairyland long ere we have reached the last steps of our theory; and *there* we have no reason to trust our common methods of arguments or to think that our usual analogies and probabilities have any authority. Our line is too short to fathom such immense abysses. And however we may flatter ourselves that we are guided, in every step which we take, by a kind of verisimilitude and experience, we may be assured that this fancied experience has no authority when we thus apply it to subjects that lie entirely out of the sphere of experience. But on this we shall have occasion to touch afterwards.[9]

Secondly, I cannot perceive any force in the arguments on which this theory is founded. We are ignorant, it is true, of the manner in which bodies operate on each other. Their force or energy is entirely incomprehensible. But are we not equally ignorant of the manner or force by which a mind, even the Supreme Mind, operates, either on itself or on body? Whence, I beseech you, do we acquire any idea of it? We have no sentiment or consciousness of this power in ourselves. We have no idea of the Supreme Being but what we learn from reflection on our own faculties. Were

our ignorance, therefore, a good reason for rejecting anything, we should be led into that principle of denying all energy in the Supreme Being, as much as in the grossest matter. We surely comprehend as little the operations of the one as of the other. Is it more difficult to conceive that motion may arise from impulse than that it may arise from volition? All we know is our profound ignorance in both cases.[10]

Part II

But to hasten to a conclusion of this argument, which is already drawn out to too great a length: We have sought in vain for an idea of power or necessary connection in all the sources from which we could suppose it to be derived. It appears that in single instances of the operation of bodies we never can, by our utmost scrutiny, discover anything but one event following another, without being able to comprehend any force or power by which the cause operates or any connection between it and its supposed effect. The same difficulty occurs in contemplating the operations of mind on body, where we observe the motion of the latter to follow upon the volition of the former, but are not able to observe or conceive the tie which binds together the motion and volition, or the energy, by which the mind produces this effect. The authority of the will over its own faculties and ideas is not a whit more comprehensible, so that, upon the whole, there appears not, throughout all nature, any one instance of connection which is conceivable by us. All events seem entirely loose and separate. One event follows another, but we never can observe any tie between them. They seem *conjoined,* but never *connected.* And as we can have no idea of anything which never appeared to our outward sense or inward sentiment, the necessary conclusion *seems* to be that we have no idea of connection or power at all, and that these words are absolutely without any meaning when employed either in philosophical reasonings or common life.

But there still remains one method of avoiding this conclusion, and one source which we have not yet examined. When any natural object or event is presented, it is impossible for us, by any sagacity or penetration, to discover, or even conjecture, without experience, what event will result from it, or to carry our foresight beyond that object which is immediately present to the memory and senses. Even after one instance or experiment where we have observed a particular event to follow upon another, we are not entitled to form a general rule or foretell what will happen in like cases, it being justly esteemed an unpardonable temerity to judge the whole course of nature from one single experiment, however accurate or certain. But when one particular species of events has always, in all instances, been conjoined with another, we make no longer any scruple of foretelling one upon the appearance of the other, and of employing that reasoning which can alone assure us of any matter of fact or existence. We then call the one object "cause," the other "effect." We suppose that there is some connection between them, some power in the one by which it infallibly produces the other and operates with the greatest certainty and strongest necessity.

It appears, then, that this idea of a necessary connection among events arises from a number of similar instances which occur, of the constant conjunction of these events; nor can that idea ever be suggested by any one of these instances surveyed in all possible lights and positions. But there is nothing in a number of instances, different from every single instance, which is supposed to be exactly similar, except only that after a repetition of similar instances the mind is carried by habit, upon the appearance of one event, to expect its usual attendant and to believe that it will exist. This connection, therefore, which we *feel* in the mind, this customary transition of the imagination from one object to its usual attendant, is the sentiment or impression from which we form the idea of power or necessary connection. Nothing further is in the case. Contemplate the subject on all sides, you will never find any other origin of that idea. This is the sole difference between one instance, from which we can never receive the idea of connection, and a number of similar instances by which it is suggested.

The first time a man saw the communication of motion by impulse, as by the shock of two billiard balls, he could not pronounce that the one event was *connected,* but only that it was *conjoined* with the other. After he has observed several instances of this nature, he then pronounces them to be *connected.* What alteration has happened to give rise to this new idea of *connection?* Nothing but that he now *feels* these events to be *connected* in his imagination, and can readily foretell the existence of one from the appearance of the other. When we say, therefore, that one object is connected with another, we mean only that they have acquired a connection in our thought and give rise to this inference by which they become proofs of each other's existence—a conclusion which is somewhat extraordinary, but which seems founded on sufficient evidence. Nor will its evidence be weakened by any general diffidence of the understanding or skeptical suspicion concerning every conclusion which is new and extraordinary. No conclusions can be more agreeable to skepticism than such as make discoveries concerning the weakness and narrow limits of human reason and capacity.

And what stronger instance can be produced of the surprising ignorance and weakness of the understanding than the present? For surely, if there be any relation among objects which it imports us to know perfectly, it is that of cause and effect. On this are founded all our reasonings concerning matter of fact or existence. By means of it alone we attain any assurance concerning objects which are removed from the present testimony of our memory and senses. The only immediate utility of all sciences is to teach us how to control and regulate future events by their causes. Our thoughts and inquiries are, therefore, every moment employed about this relation; yet so imperfect are the ideas which we form concerning it that it is impossible to give any just definition of cause, except what is drawn from something extraneous and foreign to it. Similar objects are always conjoined with similar. Of this we have experience. Suitably to this experience, therefore, we may define a cause to be *an object followed by another, and where all the objects, similar to the first, are followed by objects similar to the second.* Or, in other words, *where, if the first object had not been, the second never had existed.* The appearance of a cause always conveys the mind, by a customary transition, to the idea of the effect. Of this also we have experience. We may, therefore, suitably to this experience, form another definition of cause and call it *an object followed by another, and whose appearance always conveys the thought to that other.* But though both these definitions be drawn from circumstances foreign to the cause, we cannot remedy this inconvenience or attain any more perfect definition which may point out that circumstance in the cause which gives it a connection with its effect. We have no idea of this connection, nor even any distinct notion what it is we desire to know when we endeavor at a conception of it. We say, for instance, that the vibration of this string is the cause of this particular sound. But what do we mean by that affirmation? We either mean *that this vibration is followed by this sound, and that all similar vibrations have been followed by similar sounds; or, that this vibration is followed by this sound, and that, upon the appearance of one, the mind anticipates the senses and forms immediately an idea of the other.* We may consider the relation of cause and effect in either of these two lights; but beyond these we have no idea of it.[11]

To recapitulate, therefore, the reasonings of this Section: Every idea is copied from some preceding impression or sentiment; and where we cannot find any impression, we may be certain that there is no idea. In all single instances of the operation of bodies or minds there is nothing that produces any impression, nor consequently can suggest any idea, of power or necessary connection. But when many uniform instances appear, and the same object is always followed by the same event, we then begin to entertain the notion of cause and connection. We then *feel* a new sentiment or impression, to wit, a customary connection in the thought or imagination between one object and its usual attendant; and this sentiment is the original of that idea which we seek for. For as this idea arises from a number of similar instances, and not from any single instance, it must arise from that circumstance in which the number of instances differ from every individual instance. But this customary connection or transition of the imagination is the only circumstance in which they differ. In every other particular they are alike. The first instance which we saw of motion, communicated by the shock of two billiard balls (to return to this obvious illustration), is exactly similar to any instance that may at present occur to us, except only that we could not at first *infer* one event from the other, which we are enabled to do at present, after so long a course of uniform experience. I know not whether the reader will readily apprehend this reasoning. I am afraid that, should I multiply words about it or throw it into a greater variety of lights, it would only become more obscure and intricate. In all abstract reasonings there is one point of view which, if we can happily hit, we shall go further towards illustrating the subject than by all the eloquence in the world. This point of view we should endeavor to reach, and reserve the flowers of rhetoric for subjects which are more adapted to them.

NOTES

1. It is probable that no more was meant by those who denied innate ideas than that all ideas were copies of our impressions, though it must be confessed that the terms which they employed were not chosen with such caution, nor so exactly defined, as to prevent all mistakes about their doctrine. For what is meant by "innate"? If "innate" be equivalent to "natural," then all the perceptions and ideas of the mind must be allowed to be innate or natural, in whatever sense we take the latter word, whether in opposition to what is uncommon, artificial, or miraculous. If by innate he meant contemporary to our birth, the dispute seems to be frivolous, nor is it worth while to inquire at what time thinking begins, whether before, at, or after our birth. Again, the word "idea" seems to be commonly taken in a very loose sense by Locke and others, as standing for any of our perceptions, our sensations and passions, as well as thoughts. Now, in

this sense, I should desire to know what can be meant by asserting that self-love, or resentment of injuries, or the passion between the sexes is not innate?

But admitting these terms "impressions" and "ideas" in the sense above explained, and understanding by "innate" what is original or copied from no precedent perception, then may we assert that all our impressions are innate, and our ideas not innate.

To be ingenuous, I must own it to be my opinion that Locke was betrayed into this question by the schoolmen, who, making use of undefined terms, draw out their disputes to a tedious length without ever touching the point in question. A like ambiguity and circumlocution seem to run through that philosopher's reasonings, on this as well as most other subjects.

2. The word "power" is here used in a loose and popular sense. The more accurate explication of it would give additional evidence to this argument. See Section VII.

3. Nothing is more usual than for writers, even on *moral, political,* or *physical* subjects, to distinguish between *reason* and *experience,* and to suppose that these species of argumentation are entirely different from each other. The former are taken for the mere result of our intellectual faculties, which, by considering *a priori* the nature of things, and examining the effects that must follow from their operation, establish particular principles of science and philosophy. The latter are supposed to be derived entirely from sense and observation, by which we learn what has actually resulted from the operation of particular objects, and are thence able to infer what will for the future result from them. Thus, for instance, the limitations and restraints of civil government and a legal constitution may be defended, either from *reason,* which, reflecting on the great frailty and corruption of human nature, teaches that no man can safely be trusted with unlimited authority; or from *experience* and history, which inform us of the enormous abuses that ambition in every age and country has been found to make of so imprudent a confidence.

The same distinction between reason and experience is maintained in all our deliberations concerning the conduct of life, while the experienced statesman, general physician, or merchant, is trusted and followed, and the unpracticed novice, with whatever natural talents endowed, neglected and despised. Though it be allowed that reason may form very plausible conjectures with regard to the consequences of such a particular conduct in such particular circumstances, it is still supposed imperfect without the assistance of experience, which is alone able to give stability and certainty to the maxim derived from study and reflection.

But notwithstanding that this distinction be thus universally received, both in the active and speculative scenes of life, I shall not scruple to pronounce that it is, at bottom, erroneous, or at least superficial.

If we examine those arguments which, in any of the sciences above mentioned, are supposed to be the mere effects of reasoning and reflection, they will be found to terminate at last in some general principle or conclusion for which we can assign no reason but observation and experience. The only difference between them and those maxims which are vulgarly esteemed the result of pure experience is that the former cannot be established without some process of thought, and some reflection on what we have observed, in order to distinguish its circumstances and trace its consequences—whereas, in the latter, the experienced event is exactly and fully similar to that which we infer as the result of any particular situation. The history of a Tiberius or a Nero makes us dread a like tyranny, were our monarchs freed from the restraints of laws and senates; but the observation of any fraud or cruelty in private life is sufficient, with the aid of a little thought, to give us the same apprehension, while it serves as an instance of the general corruption of human nature, and shows us the danger which we must incur by reposing an entire confidence in mankind. In both cases, it is experience which is ultimately the foundation of our inference and conclusion.

There is no man so young and unexperienced as not to have formed from observation many general and just maxims concerning human affairs and the conduct of life; but it must be confessed that when a man comes to put these in practice he will be extremely liable to error, till time and further experience both enlarge these maxims, and teach him their proper use and application. In every situation or incident there are many particular and seemingly minute circumstances which the man of greatest talents is at first apt to overlook, though on them the justness of his conclusions, and consequently the prudence of his conduct, entirely depend. Not to mention that, to a young beginner, the general observations and maxims occur not always on the proper occasions. nor can be immediately applied with due calmness and distinction. The truth is, an unexperienced reasoner could be no reasoner at all were he absolutely inexperienced; and when we assign that character to anyone, we mean it only in a comparative sense, and suppose him possessed of experience in a smaller and more imperfect degree.

4. [A footnote containing a long quotation from Cicero, deleted.]

5. Mr. Locke divides all arguments into "*demonstrative*" and "*probable.*" In this view, we must say that it is only probable that all men must die, or that the sun will rise tomorrow. But to conform our language more to common use, we ought to divide arguments into *demonstrations, proofs,* and *probabilities;* by proofs, meaning such arguments from experience as leave no room for doubt or opposition.

6. Section II.

7. Mr. Locke, in his chapter of Power, says that, finding from experience that there are several new productions in matter, and concluding that there must somewhere be a power capable of producing them, we arrive at last by this reasoning at the idea of power. But no reasoning can ever give us a new, original simple idea, as this philosopher himself confesses. This, therefore, can never be the origin of that idea.

8. It may be pretended, that the resistance which we meet with in bodies, obliging us frequently to exert our force and call up all our power, this gives us the idea of force and power. It is this *nisus* or strong endeavor of which we are conscious, that is the original impression from which this idea is copied. But, *first,* we attribute power to a vast number of objects where we never can suppose this resistance or exertion of force to take place; to the Supreme Being, who never meets with any resistance; to the mind in its command over its ideas and limbs, in common thinking and motion, where the effect follows immediately upon the will, without any exertion or summoning up of force; to inanimate matter,

which is not capable of this sentiment. *Secondly,* this sentiment of an endeavor to overcome resistance has no known connection with any event: What follows it we know by experience, but could not know it *a priori.* It must, however, be confessed that the animal *nisus* which we experience, though it can afford no accurate precise idea of power, enters very much into that vulgar, inaccurate idea which is formed of it.

9. Section XII. [Not included here.]

10. I need not examine at length the *vis inertiae* which is so much talked of in the new philosophy, and which is ascribed to matter. We find by experience that a body at rest or in motion continues forever in its present state, till put from it by some new cause; and that a body impelled takes as much motion from the impelling body as it acquires itself. These are facts. When we call this a *vis inertiae,* we only mark these facts, without pretending to have any idea of the inert power, in the same manner as, when we talk of gravity, we mean certain effects without comprehending that active power. It was never the meaning of Sir Isaac Newton to rob second causes of all force or energy, though some of his followers have endeavored to establish that theory upon his authority. On the contrary, that great philosopher had recourse to an ethereal active fluid to explain his universal attraction, though he was so cautious and modest as to allow that it was a mere hypothesis not to be insisted on without more experiments. I must confess that there is something in the fate of opinions a little extraordinary. Descartes insinuated that doctrine of the universal and sole efficacy of the Deity, without insisting on it. Malebranche and other Cartesians made it the foundation of all their philosophy. It had, however, no authority in England. Locke, Clarke, and Cudworth never so much as take notice of it, but suppose all along that matter has a real, though subordinate and derived, power. By what means has it become so prevalent among our modern metaphysicians?

11. According to these explications and definitions, the idea of *power* is relative as much as that of *cause;* and both have a reference to an effect, or some other event constantly conjoined with the former. When we consider the *unknown* circumstance of an object by which the degree or quantity of its effect is fixed and determined, we call

that its power. And accordingly, it is allowed by all philosophers that the effect is the measure of the power. But if they had any idea of power as it is in itself, why could they not measure it in itself? The dispute, whether the force of a body in motion be as its velocity, or the square of its velocity; this dispute, I say, needed not be decided by comparing its effects in equal or unequal times, but by direct mensuration and comparison.

As to the frequent use of the words "*force*," "*power*," "*energy*," etc., which everywhere occur in common conversation as well as in philosophy, that is no proof that we are acquainted, in any instance, with the connecting principle between cause and effect, or can account ultimately for the production of one thing by another. These words, as commonly used, have very loose meanings annexed to them, and their ideas are very uncertain and confused. No animal can put external bodies in motion without the sentiment of a *nisus* or endeavor; and every animal has a sentiment or feeling from the stroke or blow of an external object that is in motion. These sensations, which are merely animal, and from which we can *a priori* draw no inference, we are apt to transfer to inanimate objects, and to suppose that they have some such feelings whenever they transfer or receive motion. With regard to energies, which are exerted without our annexing to them any idea of communicated motion, we consider only the constant experienced conjunction of the events; and as we *feel* a customary connection between the ideas, we transfer that feeling to the objects, as nothing is more usual than to apply to external bodies every internal sensation which they occasion.

4.2 An Encounter with David Hume

WESLEY C. SALMON

Wesley C. Salmon (1925–2001) taught history and philosophy of science at the University of Pittsburgh.

A DAY IN THE LIFE OF A HYPOTHETICAL STUDENT

In the physics 1a lecture hall, Professor Salvia[1] has had a bowling ball suspended from a high ceiling by a long rope so that it can swing back and forth like a pendulum. Standing well over to one side of the room, he holds the bowling ball at the tip of his nose. He releases it (taking great care not to give it a push). It swings through a wide arc, gaining considerable speed as it passes through the low portion of its swing beneath the point of suspension from the ceiling. It continues to the other side of the room, where it reaches the end of its path, and then returns. The professor stands motionless as the bowling ball moves faster and faster back toward his nose. As it passes through the midpoint of the return arc, it is again traveling very rapidly, but it begins to slow down, and it stops just at the tip of his nose. Some of the students think he is cool. "This demonstration," he says, "illustrates the faith that the physicist has in nature's regularity." (See Figure 1.)

Imagine that you have witnessed this demonstration just after your philosophy class, where the subject of discussion was Hume's *Enquiry Concerning Human Understanding*. You raise your hand. "How did you *know* that the bowling ball would stop where it did, just short of bashing your nose into your face?" you ask.

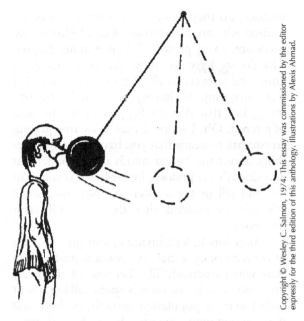

FIGURE 1 Prof. Salvia's Pendulum. After swinging to the opposite side of the lecture hall, the bowling ball swings right back to the tip of the prof's nose, which remains motionless during the entire procedure.

"This is a standard demonstration," he replies; "I do it every year in this class, and it has often been used by many other physics teachers." In an attempt to inject a little humor, he adds, "If I had had any doubt about its working, I'd have had the teaching assistant do it."

"Are you saying, then, that you trusted the experiment to work this time simply because it has been tried so many times in the past, and has never failed?" You recall Hume's discussion of the collisions of billiard balls. In the first instance, according to Hume, before you have any experience with material objects colliding with one another, you would not know what to expect when you see a moving billiard ball approaching a stationary one, but after a good deal of experience you confidently expect some motion to be transferred to the stationary ball as a result of the collision. As your experience accumulates, you learn to predict the exact manner in which the second ball will move after being

struck by the first. But you cannot really accept that answer, and neither, you feel sure, will your physics professor. Without waiting for an answer, you follow up your first question with another.

"I have this friend," you continue, "who drives like a maniac. It scares me to ride with him, but he always tells me not to worry—he has never had an accident, or even a traffic ticket. Should I conclude—assuming he is telling the truth (just as I assume you are telling me the truth about this demonstration)—that it is as safe for me to ride with him as it is for you to perform the bowling ball trick?"

"It's not the same thing at all," another student chimes in; "you can prove, mathematically, that the pendulum will not swing back beyond its original starting point, but you certainly can't prove mathematically that your friend won't have a wreck. In a way it's just the opposite; you can prove that he is likely to have an accident if he keeps on driving like that."

"What you say is partly right," says Professor Salvia to the second student, "but it isn't only a matter of mathematics. We have to rely upon the laws of physics as well. With the pendulum we were depending mainly upon the law of conservation of energy, one of the most fundamental laws of nature. As the pendulum goes through its swing, potential energy is transformed into kinetic energy, which is transformed back into potential energy, and so forth. As long as the total amount of energy remains unchanged, my nose is safe."

Since you have not yet studied the concept of energy, you do not worry too much about the details of the explanation. You are satisfied that you will understand why the pendulum behaves as it does when you have learned more about the concepts and laws that were mentioned. But you do remember something Hume wrote. There are two kinds of reasoning: reasoning concerning relations of ideas, and reasoning concerning matters of fact and existence. Mathematical reasoning falls into the former category (relations of ideas) and consequently, by itself, cannot provide any information about matters of fact. The pendulum and the professor's nose are, however, matters of fact, so we need something in addition to mathematics to get the information we want concerning that situation. Professor Salvia has told us what it is—we need the laws of nature as well.

Since physics is your last class in the morning, you head for the cafeteria when it is over to get a sandwich and coffee. The philosophy class is still bugging you. What was it Hume said about bread? That we do not know the "secret power" by which it nourishes us? Now we do, of course; we understand metabolism, the mechanism by which the body converts food into energy. Hume (living in the eighteenth century) did not understand about power and energy, as he said repeatedly. He did not know why bread is suitable food for humans, but not for tigers and lions. In biology class, you recall, you studied herbiverous, carnivorous, and omniverous species. Biologists must now understand why some species can metabolize vegetables and others cannot. Modern physics, chemistry, and biology can provide a complete explanation of the various forms of energy, the ways they can be converted from one form to another, and the ways in which they can be utilized by a living organism.

Taking a sip of the hot coffee, you recall some other things Hume said—for example, remarks about the "connection" between heat and flame. We now know that heat is really a form of energy; that temperature is a measure of the average kinetic energy of the molecules. Now, it seems, we know a great deal about the "secret powers," "energy," etc., that so perplexed Hume. Modern physics knows that ordinary objects are composed of molecules, which are in turn composed of atoms, which are themselves made up of subatomic particles. Modern science can tell us what holds atoms and molecules together, and why the things that consist of them have the properties they do. What was it that Hume said about a piece of ice and a crystal (e.g., a diamond)? That we do not know why one is caused by cold and the other by heat? I'll just bet, you think, that Salvia could answer that one without a bit of trouble. Why, you

wonder, do they make us read these old philosophers who are now so out of date? Hume was, no doubt, a very profound thinker in his day, but why do we have to study him now, when we know the answers to all of those questions? If I were majoring in history that might be one thing, but that doesn't happen to be my field of interest. Oh, I suppose they'd say that getting an education means that you have to learn something about the "great minds of the past," but why doesn't the philosophy professor come right out and tell us the answers to these questions? It's silly to pretend that they are still great mysteries.

After lunch, let's imagine, you go to a class in contemporary social and political problems, a class you particularly like because of the lively discussions. A lot of time is spent talking about such topics as population growth, ecology and the environment, energy demands and uses, food production, and pollution. You discuss population trends, the extrapolation of such trends, and the predication that by the year 2000 A.D., world population will reach 7 billion. You consider the various causes and possible effects of increasing concentrations of carbon dioxide in the atmosphere. You discuss solutions to various of these problems in terms of strict governmental controls, economic sanctions and incentives, and voluntary compliance on the part of enlightened and concerned citizens.

"If people run true to form," you interject, "if they behave as they always have, you can be sure that you won't make much progress relying on the good will and good sense of the populace at large."

"What is needed is more awareness and education," another student remarks, "for people can change if they see the need. During World War II people willingly sacrificed in order to support the war effort. They will do the same again, if they see that the emergency is really serious. That's why we need to provide more education and make stronger appeals to their humanitarian concerns."

"What humanitarian concerns?" asks still another student with evident cynicism.

"People *will* change," says another. "I have been reading that we are entering a new era, the Age of Aquarius, when man's finer, gentler, more considerate nature will be manifest."

"Well, I don't know about all of this astrology," another remarks in earnest tones, "but I do not believe that God will let His world perish if we mend our ways and trust in Him. I have complete faith in His goodness."

You find this statement curiously reminiscent of Professor Salvia's earlier mention of his faith in the regularity of nature.

That night, after dinner, you read an English assignment. By the time you finish it, your throat feels a little scratchy, and you notice that you have a few sniffles. You decide to begin taking large doses of vitamin C; you have read that there is quite some controversy as to whether this helps to ward off colds, but that there is no harm in taking this vitamin in large quantities. Before going to the drug store to buy some vitamin C, you write home to request some additional funds; you mail your letter in the box by the pharmacy. You return with the vitamin C, take a few of the pills, and turn in for the night—confident that the sun will rise tomorrow morning, and hoping that you won't feel as miserable as you usually do when you catch a cold. David Hume is the farthest thing from your mind.

HUME REVISITED

The next morning, you wake up feeling fine. The sun is shining brightly, and you have no sign of a cold. You are not sure whether the vitamin C cured your cold, or whether it was the good night's sleep, or whether it wasn't going to develop into a real cold regardless. Perhaps, even, it was the placebo effect; in psychology you learned that people can often be cured by totally inert drugs (e.g., sugar pills) if they believe in them. You don't really know what caused your prompt recovery, but frankly, you don't really care. If it was the placebo effect that is fine with you; you just hope it will work as well the next time.

You think about what you will do today. It is Thursday, so you have a philosophy discussion section in the morning and a physics lab in the afternoon. Thursday, you say to yourself, has got to be the lousiest day of the week. The philosophy section is a bore, and the physics lab is a drag. If only it were Saturday, when you have no classes! For a brief moment you consider taking off. Then you remember the letter you wrote last night, think about your budget and your grades, and resign yourself to the prescribed activities for the day.

The leader of the discussion section starts off with the question, "What was the main problem—I mean the really *basic* problem—bothering Hume in the *Enquiry?*" You feel like saying, "Lack of adequate scientific knowledge" (or words to that effect), but restrain yourself. No use antagonizing the guy who will decide what grade to give you. Someone says that he seemed to worry quite a lot about causes and effects, to which the discussion leader (as usual) responds. "But *why?*" Again, you stifle an impulse to say, "Because he didn't know too much about them."

After much folderol, the leader finally elicits the answer, "Because he wanted to know how we can find out about things we don't actually see (or hear, smell, touch, taste, etc.)."

"In other words," the leader paraphrases, "to examine the basis for making inferences from what we observe to what we cannot (at the moment) observe. Will someone," he continues, "give me an example of something you believe in which you are not now observing?"

You think of the letter you dropped into the box last night, of your home and parents, and of the money you hope to receive. You do not see the letter now, but you are confident it is somewhere in the mails; you do not see your parents now, but you firmly believe they are back home where you left them; you do not yet see the money you hope to get, but you expect to see it before too long. The leader is pleased when you give those examples. "And what do causes and effects have to do with all of this?" he asks, trying to draw you out a little more. Still thinking of your grade you cooperate. "I believe the letter is somewhere in the mails because I wrote it and dropped it in the box. I believe my parents are at home because they are always calling me up to tell me what to do. And I believe that the money will come as an effect of my eloquent appeal." The leader is really happy with that; you can tell you have an A for today's session.

"But," he goes on, "do you see how this leads us immediately into Hume's next question? If cause-effect relations are the whole basis for our knowledge of things and events we do not observe, how do we know whether one event causes another, or whether they just happen together as a matter of coincidence?" Your mind is really clicking now.

"I felt a cold coming on last night, and I took a massive dose of vitamin C," you report. "This morning I feel great, but I honestly don't know whether the vitamin C actually cured it."

"Well, how could we go about trying to find out," retorts the discussion leader.

"By trying it again when I have the first symptoms of a cold," you answer, "and by trying it on other people as well." At that point the bell rings, and you leave class wondering whether the vitamin C really did cure your incipient cold.

You keep busy until lunch, doing one thing and another, but sitting down and eating, you find yourself thinking again about the common cold and its cure. It seems to be a well-known fact that the cold is caused by one or more viruses, and the human organism seems to have ways of combating virus infections. Perhaps the massive doses of vitamin C trigger the body's defenses, in some way or other, or perhaps it provides some kind of antidote to the toxic effects of the virus. You don't know much about all of this, but you can't help speculating that science has had a good deal of success in finding causes and cures of various diseases. If continued research reveals the physiological and chemical processes in the cold's infection and in the body's response, then surely it would be possible to find out whether the vitamin C really has any effect upon the common cold or not. It seems

that we could ascertain whether a causal relation exists in this instance if only we could discover the relevant laws of biology and chemistry.

At this point in your musings, you notice that it is time to get over to the physics lab. You remember that yesterday morning you were convinced that predicting the outcome of an experiment is possible if you know which physical laws apply. That certainly was the outcome of the discussion in the physics class. Now, it seems, the question about the curative power of vitamin C hinges on exactly the same thing—the laws of nature. As you hurry to the lab it occurs to you that predicting the outcome of an experiment, before it is performed, is a first-class example of what you were discussing in philosophy—making inferences from the observed to the unobserved. We observe the setup for the experiment (or demonstration) before it is performed, and we predict the outcome before we observe it. Salvia certainly was confident about the prediction he made. Also, recalling one of Hume's examples, you were at least as confident, when you went to bed last night, that the sun would rise this morning. But Hume *seemed* to be saying that the basis for this confidence was the fact that the sun has been observed to rise every morning since the dawn of history. "That's wrong," you say to yourself as you reach the physics lab. "My confidence in the rising of the sun is based upon the laws of astronomy. So here we are back at the laws again."

Inside the lab you notice a familiar gadget; it consists of a frame from which five steel balls are suspended so that they hang in a straight line, each one touching its neighbors. Your little brother got a toy like this, in a somewhat smaller size, for his birthday a couple of years ago. You casually raise one of the end balls, and let it swing back. It strikes the nearest of the four balls left hanging, and the ball at the other end swings out (the three balls in the middle keeping their place). The ball at the far end swings back again, striking its neighbor, and then the ball on the near end swings out, almost to the point from which you let it swing originally. The process goes on for a while, with the two end balls alternately swinging out and back. It has a pleasant rhythm. (See Figure 2.)

While you are enjoying the familiar toy, the lab instructor, Dr. Sagro,[2] comes over to you. "Do you know why just the ball on the far end moves—instead of, say, two on the far end, or all four of the remaining ones—when the ball on this end strikes?"

"Not exactly, but I suppose it has something to do with conservation of energy," you reply, recalling what Salvia said yesterday in answer to the question about the bowling ball.

"That's right," says Dr. Sagro, "but it also depends upon conservation of momentum."

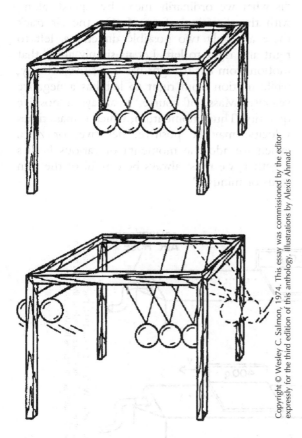

FIGURE 2 The Energy-Momentum Toy. When two balls at the right collide with the remaining three, two balls swing away from the left side. What happens when three on the right collide with the remaining two?

Before you have a chance to say anything she continues, "Let me ask you another question. What would happen if you raised two balls at this end, and let them swing together toward the remaining three?"

"I think two balls will swing away at the other end," you reply, remembering the way your brother's toy worked.

"Why don't you test it to find out if you are right?" says the instructor. You do, and you find that the result is as you had predicted. Without saying anything about it, you assume that this, too, can be explained by means of the laws of conservation of energy and momentum.

Dr. Sagro poses another question. "What will happen," she asks, "if you start by swinging three balls from this end?" Since there are only two remaining balls you don't know what to say, so you confess ignorance. She suggests you try it, in order to find out what will happen. When you do, you see that three balls swing to the other side, and three swing back again; the middle ball swings back and forth, acting as the third ball in each group. This was a case in which you didn't know what to expect as a result until you tried the experiment.[3] This was like some of Hume's examples; not until you have actually had the experience do you know what result to expect. But there is also something different. Hume said that you must try the experiment many times in order to know what to expect; nevertheless, after just one trial you are sure what will happen whenever the experiment is repeated. This makes it rather different from the problem of whether vitamin C cured your cold. In that case, it seemed necessary to try the experiment over and over again, preferably with a number of different people. Reflecting upon this difference, you ask the lab instructor a crucial question, "If you knew the laws of conservation of momentum and energy, but had never seen the experiment with the three balls performed, would you have been able to predict the outcome?"

"Yes," she says simply.

"Well," you murmur inaudibly, "it seems as if the whole answer to Hume's problem regarding inferences about things we do not immediately observe, including predictions of future occurrences, rests squarely upon the laws of nature."

KNOWING THE LAWS

Given that the laws are so fundamental, you decide to find out more about them. The laws of conservation of energy and momentum are close at hand, so to speak, so you decide to start there. "O.K.," you say to the lab instructor, "what are these laws of nature, which enable you to predict so confidently how experiments will turn out before they are performed? I'd like to learn something about them."

"Fine," she says, delighted with your desire to learn; "let's start with conservation of momentum. It's simpler than conservation of energy, and we can demonstrate it quite easily."[4] (See Figure 3.)

Your laboratory contains a standard piece of equipment—an air track—on which little cars move back and forth. The track is made of metal with many tiny holes through which air is blown. The cars thus ride on a thin cushion of air; they move back and forth almost without friction. Some of the cars are equipped with spring bumpers, so that they will bounce off of one another

upon impact, while others have coupling devices which lock them together upon contact. Dr. Sagro begins by explaining what is meant by the momentum of a body—namely, its mass multiplied by its velocity.[5] "To speak somewhat quaintly," she says, "the mass is just a measure of the quantity of matter in the body.[6] Since, in all of the experiments we are going to do, it is safe to say that the mass of each body remains unchanged, we need not say more about it. You can see that each car comes with its mass labeled; this one, for instance, has a mass of 200 grams, while this one has a mass of 400 grams. We have a number of different cars with quite a variety of different masses. The velocity," she continues, "is what we ordinarily mean by 'speed' along with the direction of travel. On the air track there are only two possible directions, left to right and right to left. Let us simply agree that motion from left to right has a positive velocity, while motion from right to left has a negative velocity. Mass, of course, is always a positive quantity. Thus, momentum, which is mass times velocity, may be positive, negative, or zero. When we add the momenta of various bodies together, we must always be careful of the sign (plus or minus)."

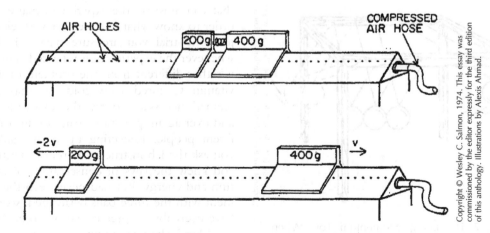

FIGURE 3 Cars on the Air Track. Top: Cars tied together against spring under tension. Bottom: Cars moving apart after "explosion." $400g \times v + 200g \times (-2v) = 0$. Momentum is conserved.

With these preliminaries, you begin to perform a variety of experiments. She has various types of fancy equipment for measuring velocities, which she shows you how to use, and she also helps you to make measurements. You find that it is fun pushing cars back and forth on the track, crashing them into one another, and measuring their velocities before and after collisions. You try it with a variety of cars of different masses and with differing velocities. You try it with the ones that bounce apart after impact and with those that stick together. You always find that the *total* momentum (the sum of the momenta for the two cars) before any collision is equal to the *total* momentum after the collision, even though the momenta of the individual cars may change markedly as a result of the collision. This, Dr. Sagro explains, is what the law of conservation of momentum demands: when two bodies (such as the cars) interact with one another (as in a collision), the total momentum of the system consisting of those two bodies is the same before and after the interaction.

You ask her whether this law applies only to collisions; she replies immediately that it applies to all kinds of interactions. "Let's see how it works for a simple type of 'explosion,'" she suggests. She helps you tie together two cars, holding a compressed spring between them. You burn the string which holds them together and they fly apart. You measure the velocities and compute the momenta of each of the cars after the "explosion." It turns out that the momentum of the one car is always equal in amount but opposite in direction to that of the other. This is true whether the cars are of equal or unequal masses and whether the tension on the spring that drives them apart is great or small. "This is just what the law of conservation of momentum tells us to expect," she explains; "the momentum of each car is zero before the 'explosion' because they are not moving (each has velocity equal to zero), and so the two momenta after the 'explosion' (one positive and one negative) must add up to zero. That is what has happened every time.

"There are many other applications of the law of conservation of momentum," she

continues. "When a rifle recoils upon being fired, when a jet engine propels an airplane, when a rocket engine lifts an artificial satellite into orbit, or when you step out of an untethered rowboat and are surprised to feel it moving out from under you—these are all cases of conservation of momentum."

"Is this law ever violated?" you ask.

"No," she answers, "there are no known exceptions to it." You leave the lab with the feeling that you know at least one fundamental law, and that you have seen it proved experimentally right before your eyes. You can't wait to tell your philosophy professor about it.

When you go to your philosophy class the next morning, the topic is still Hume's *Enquiry Concerning Human Understanding* and the problem of how we can have knowledge of things we do not observe. As the lecture begins, Professor Philo[7] is saying, "As we saw during the last lecture, Hume maintains that our knowledge of what we do not observe is based entirely upon cause and effect relations, but that raises the question of how we can gain knowledge of these relations. Hume maintained that this knowledge can result only from repeated observation of one type of event (a cause) to see whether it is always followed by an event of another kind (its effect). Hume therefore analyzed the notion of causality in terms of constant conjunction of events. Consider for a moment Hume's favorite example, the colliding billiard balls..."

You raise your hand. "It seems to me that Hume was wrong about this," you begin, and then you relate briefly yesterday's experiences in the physics lab. "If you know the relevant laws of nature," you conclude, "you can predict the outcomes of future experiments on the basis of a single trial, or perhaps even without benefit of any trials at all."

"But how," asks Professor Philo, "can we establish knowledge of the laws of nature?"

You had a hunch she might ask some such question, and you are ready with your reply, "We *proved* it experimentally."

"Well," says Professor Philo, "I'm not a physicist, so perhaps you had better explain in a little more detail just what the experimental proof consists of. You mentioned something about an explosion—how did that go?"

You explain carefully how the air track works, how the two cars were joined together with a spring under tension in between, and how they moved apart when the string was burned. "In every case," you conclude, "the momentum of the two cars was equal in amount and opposite in direction, just as the law of conservation of momentum says it should be."

"Now let me see if I understand your line of reasoning," says the professor in a tone that is altogether too calm to suit you. "If the law of conservation of momentum is correct, then the two cars will part in the manner you described. The cars did move apart in just that way. Therefore, the law of conservation of momentum is correct. Is that your argument?"

"I guess so," you reply a bit hesitantly, because it looks as if she is trying to trap you.

"Do you think that kind of argument is valid?" she responds.

"What do you mean?" you ask, beginning to feel a little confused.

"Well," she says, "isn't that rather like the following argument: If this defendant is guilty, he will refuse to testify at his own trial; he does refuse to testify; therefore, he is guilty. Would any judge allow that argument in a court of law?"

"Of course not," you reply, "but it isn't the same thing at all. We tested the law of conservation of momentum many times in many different ways, and in every case we got the expected result (allowing for the usual small inaccuracies in the measurements)."

"If I remember what you said," Ms. Philo goes on, "in one of your experiments you had one car with a mass of 200 grams and another with a mass of 400 grams, and in that case the lighter car recoiled with twice the speed of the more massive one. How many times did you repeat this particular experiment?"

"Once or twice, as nearly as I can recall."

"Yet, you seem to believe that the result would be the same, no matter how many times the experiment was repeated—is that correct?"

"I suppose so," you reply somewhat uncomfortably.

"And with how many different masses and how many different recoil velocities did you try it? Do you believe it would work the same way if the masses were thousands or billions of kilograms instead of a few grams? And do you suppose that it would work the same way if the velocities were very great—somewhere near the speed of light?"

Since you have heard that strange things happen when speeds approach that of light, your hesitancy increases, but you reply tentatively, "Well, the lab instructor told me that there are no exceptions to the law."

"Did she say that," asks Philo, "or did she say no *known* exceptions?"

"I guess that was it," you reply lamely, feeling quite crushed.

Professor Philo endeavors to summarize the discussion. "What is considered experimental 'proof of a law of nature' is actually a process of testing *some* of its logical consequences. That is, you ask what would have to happen *if* your hypothesis is true, and then you perform an experiment to see if it turns out that way *in fact*. Since any law of nature is a generalization,[8] it has an unlimited number of consequences. We can never hope to test them all. In particular, any *useful* law of nature will have consequences that pertain to the future; they enable us to make predictions. We can never test these consequences until it is too late to use them for the purpose of prediction. To suppose that testing *some* of the consequences of a law constitutes a *conclusive proof* of the law would clearly be an outright logical fallacy." The bell rings and you leave the class, convinced that she has merely been quibbling.

During your physics class you brood about the previous discussion in the philosophy class, without paying very close attention to the lecture. Similar thoughts keep nagging at you during lunch. The objections brought up by Professor Philo seem to be well-founded, you conclude, but you wonder how they can be reconciled with the apparent reliability and certainty of scientific knowledge. In desperation, you decide to talk it over with Professor Salvia during his office hour this very afternoon. When you arrive, you don't know exactly where to begin, so you decide to go back to the pendulum demonstration, which was the thing that got you started on this whole mess. "When you performed that demonstration," you ask, "were you *absolutely certain* how it would turn out? Has it ever failed?"

"Well, to be perfectly honest," he says, "it has been known to fail. Once when a friend of mine was doing it in front of a large auditorium, the suspension in the ceiling broke and the ball landed right on his foot. He was in a cast for months!"

"But that's no fault of the law of conservation of energy is it?" you ask. "The breaking of the suspension didn't mean that conservation of energy is false, did it?"

"Of course not," he answers, "we still believe firmly in conservation of energy."

"But are you *certain* of the law of conservation of energy, or any other law of nature?" you ask, and before he has a chance to answer, you tell him about the discussion in the philosophy class this morning.

"So that's what's bothering you," he says, after hearing the whole story. "Professor Philo has an important point. No matter how thoroughly we have tested a scientific law—better, let's say 'hypothesis'—there is always the possibility that new evidence will show up to prove it false. For instance, around the close of the nineteenth century, many physicists seemed virtually certain that Newtonian mechanics was absolutely correct. A wide variety of its consequences had been tested under many different circumstances, and Newton's laws stood up extremely well. But early in the twentieth century it became clear that what we now call 'classical physics' would have to undergo major revisions, and a profound scientific revolution ensued. Modern physics, which includes quantum mechanics and relativity theory, was the result. We can never be sure that any hypothesis we currently accept as correct will not have to be abandoned or modified at some time in the future as a result of new evidence."

"What about the law of conservation of momentum?" you ask, recalling yesterday's experience in the lab. "The lab instructor said it has no known exceptions."

"That is correct," says Salvia, "and it is a rather interesting case. Conservation of momentum is a consequence of Newton's laws of motion; therefore, any consequence of conservation of momentum is a consequence of Newton's laws. But we now regard Newton's laws as not strictly true—they break down, for example, with objects traveling close to the speed of light—but conservation of momentum holds even in these cases. So we have a good example of a case where we believe a lot of consequences, but we do not believe in the laws (Newton's) from which the consequences follow."

It occurs to you that this is a rather important set of supposed laws; perhaps the philosophy professor was not merely quibbling when she said that it was not valid to conclude that a hypothesis is true just because we know many of its consequences to be true.

"Since you cannot be certain of any so-called law of nature," you ask, "why do you believe in them so firmly?"

"Because," answers Salvia, "we consider them very well confirmed. We accept well-confirmed hypotheses, knowing that we may later have to change our minds in the light of new evidence. Science can no longer claim infallible truth."

"Does that mean that scientific results are highly probable, but not absolutely certain?" you ask, trying to be sure you have understood what he has said.

"Yes, you could put it that way," he agrees.

You leave with the feeling that you have a pretty good comprehension of the situation. As a result of your study of physics and philosophy you now understand why science cannot claim infallibility for its findings, but must be content with results that are well confirmed. With that, you take off for the weekend. (And what you do with your weekend is your own business.)

HUME'S BOMBSHELL

A little tired, but basically in a cheerful mood, you arrive at your philosophy class on Monday morning. You meet the professor a few minutes before class outside the room, and you tell her very briefly of your conversation with the physics professor. You explain that you now understand why it is that scientific laws can never be considered completely certain, but only as well-confirmed hypotheses. With her help, and with that of Professor Salvia, you now understand what Hume was driving at—and you see, moreover, that Hume was right. She smiles, and you both go into the classroom, where she begins her lecture.

"Last Friday, as you may recall, we had quite a lively discussion about the status of scientific laws—the law of conservation of momentum, in particular. We saw that such laws cannot be proved conclusively by any amount of experimental evidence. This is a point with which, I am happy to report, many (if not most) contemporary scientists agree. They realize that the most they can reasonably claim for their hypotheses is strong confirmation. Looking at the matter this way, one could conclude that it is wise to believe in scientific predictions, for if they are not certain to be true, they are a good bet. To believe in scientific results is to bet with the best available odds.

"However," she continues, "while this view may be correct as far as it goes, Hume was making a much more fundamental, and I should add, much more devastating point. Hume was challenging not merely our right to claim that scientific predictions will always be right, but also our right to claim that they will usually, or often, or indeed ever, be correct. Take careful note of what he says in Section IV:

> Let the course of things be allowed hitherto ever so regular; that alone, without some new argument or inference, proves not that, for the future, it will continue so. In vain do you pretend to have learned the nature of bodies from your past experience. Their secret nature, and consequently all their effects and influence, may

change, without any change in their sensible qualities. This happens sometimes, and with regard to some objects: Why may it not happen always and with regard to all objects? What logic, what process of argument secures you against this supposition?

He is saying, as I hope you understood from your reading, that no matter how reliably a law seems to have held in the past, there is no logical reason why it must do so in the future *at all*. It is therefore possible that *every* scientific prediction, based on *any* law or laws whatever, may turn out to be false from this moment on. The stationary billiard ball that is struck by a moving one may remain motionless where it is—while the moving ball may bounce straight back in the direction from whence it came, or it may go straight up in the air, or it might vanish in a puff of smoke. Any of these possibilities can be imagined; none of them involves any logical contradiction. This is the force of Hume's skeptical arguments. The conclusion seems to be that we have no *reason* to believe in scientific predictions—no more reason than to believe on the basis of astrology, crystal gazing, or sheer blind guessing."

You can hardly believe your ears; what is she saying? You raise your hand, and when you are recognized, you can hardly keep your intense irritation from showing as you assert, "But certainly we can say that scientific predictions are more probable than those based, for example, upon astrology." As you speak, you are reminded of the remark in contemporary problems last Wednesday concerning the coming of the Age of Aquarius. Science has got to be better than *that!* As these thoughts cross your mind Professor Philo is saying, "...but that depends upon what you mean by 'probable,' doesn't it?"

The physics lecture today is on Newton's law of gravitation, and the professor is explaining that every bit of matter in the universe is attracted to every other by a force proportional to the masses and inversely proportional to the square of the distance between them. He goes on to explain how Kepler's laws of planetary motion and Galileo's law of falling bodies are (when suitably corrected) consequences of Newton's laws. You listen carefully, but you recognize this as another law that enables scientists to make impressive predictions. Indeed, Salvia is now telling how Newton's laws were used to explain the tides on the oceans and to predict the existence of two planets, Neptune and Pluto, that had not been known before. At the same time, you are wondering whether there is anything in what Hume seemed to be saying about such laws. Is it possible that suddenly, at the very next moment, matter would cease to have gravitational attraction, so that the whole solar system would go flying apart? It's a pretty chilling thought.

At lunch you are thinking about this question, and you glance back at some of the readings that were assigned from Hume's *Enquiry.* You notice again Hume's many references to secret powers and forces. Well, gravitation is surely a force, though there has not been any great secret about it since Newton's time. It is the "power" which keeps the solar system together. You remember reading somewhere that, according to Hume, you cannot know that it is safer to leave a building by way of the halls, stairways, and doors than it would be to step out of the third-story window. Well, Newton's law makes it clear why you don't want to step out of the third-story window, but what assurance have you that the building will continue to stand, rather than crashing down around your ears before you can get out? The engineers who design and build towers and bridges have a great deal of knowledge of the "secret powers" of their materials, so they must know a great deal more than Hume did about the hidden properties of things.

At this very moment, a lucky coincidence occurs—you see Dr. Sagro, your physics lab instructor, entering the cafeteria. You wave to her, and she sits down with you, putting her coffee cup on the table. You begin to ask her some questions about structural materials, and she responds by inquiring whether you would be satisfied if she could explain how the table supports the cup of coffee. You recognize it as just the kind of question you have in mind, and urge her to proceed.

"Certain materials, such as the metal in this table," she begins, "have a rather rigid crystalline structure, and for this reason they stick together and maintain their shape unless subjected to large forces. These crystals consist of very regular (and very beautiful) arrays of atoms, and they are held together by forces, essentially electrostatic in origin, among the charged particles that make up the atoms. Have you studied Coulomb's law of electrostatic forces?"

"No," you reply, "we are just doing Newton's law of gravitation. I think Salvia said electricity and magnetism would come up next semester."

"Well," she says, "these electrostatic forces are a lot like gravitational forces (they vary inversely with the square of the distance), but there are a couple of very important differences. First, as you know, there are two types of charges, positive and negative. The proton in the nucleus of the atom carries a positive charge, and the electrons that circulate about the nuclei have a negative charge. Two particles with opposite signs (such as a proton and an electron) attract one another, while two particles with like signs (e.g., two electrons or two protons) repel each other. This is different from gravity, because all matter attracts all other matter; there is no such thing as gravitational repulsion. The second main difference is that the electrostatic force is fantastically stronger than the gravitational force—roughly a billion billion billion billion times more powerful—but we don't usually notice it because most objects we deal with in everyday life are electrically neutral, containing equal amounts of positive and negative electric charge, or very nearly so. If you could somehow strip all of the electrons away from an apple, and all of the protons away from the earth, the force of attraction between the apple and the earth would be unbelievable.

"It is these *extremely* strong attractive and repulsive forces among the electrons and protons in the metal that maintain a stable and rigid form. That's why the table doesn't collapse. And the reason the coffee cup stays on top of the table, without penetrating its surface or slipping through, is that the electrons in the surface of the cup strongly repel those in the surface of the table. Actually, there is also a quantum mechanical force that prevents the weight of the cup from noticeably compressing the table, but we needn't go into that, because the effect is mostly due to the electrostatic forces."

Pleased with this very clear explanation, you thank her, but follow it up with another question. "Is there any logical reason why it has to be that way—why opposite charges attract and like charges repel? Can you prove that it is impossible for like charges to attract and unlike charges to repel? What would happen if *that* were suddenly to become the law?"

"It would certainly result in utter catastrophe," she replies, "with all of the atomic nuclei bunching up together in one place and all of the electrons rushing away from them to congregate elsewhere. But to answer your question, no, there is no logical proof that it couldn't be that way. In our physical world we find that there are, in fact, two types of charges, and they obey the Coulomb law rather than the one you just formulated."

"Can you prove that the world will not switch from the one law to the other, say, tomorrow?" you ask.

"No, frankly, I can't," she answers, "but I, and all other physicists assume—call it an article of faith if you like—that it won't happen."

There's that word "faith" again, you muse as you leave the cafeteria.

The more you think about it, the more clearly you see that the physicists have not shown you how to get around the basic problem Hume raised; rather, they have really reinforced it. Maybe this problem is tougher than I thought, you say to yourself, and you head for Professor Philo's office to talk further about it. "I was thinking about all these 'secret powers' Hume talks about," you begin, "and so I asked my physics instructor about them. She explained, as an example, how a table supports a coffee cup, but she did it on the basis of laws of nature—Coulomb's law of electrostatics was one of them. This law is very well confirmed, I

suppose, but she admitted that it is quite possible to imagine that this law would fail tomorrow, and—if you'll pardon the expression—all hell would break loose. Now, my question is, how can we find out about these secret powers that Hume keeps saying we need to know? How can we discover the real underlying causes of what happens?"

"I think you are really beginning to get the point Hume was driving at," she replies, "namely, that there is *no way*, even in principle, of finding any hidden causes or secret powers. You can, of course, find regularities in nature—such as conservation of energy, conservation of momentum, universal gravitation, and electrostatic attraction and repulsion—but these can only be known to have held up to the present. There is no further kind of hidden connection or causal relation that can be discovered by more careful observation, or examination with some kind of super-microscope. Of course, we do discover regularities, and we explain them. For instance, Kepler's laws of planetary motion are regularities that are explained by Newton's laws of motion and gravitation, but these do not reveal any secret powers. They simply provide more general regularities to cover the more restricted ones.

"In his discussion of 'the idea of necessary connection,' Hume tries to bring out precisely this point. We can observe, as you were saying in class the other day, that recoil experiments always yield a particular type of result—namely, momentum is conserved. We have observed this many times. And now we expect, on future trials, that the same thing will happen. But we do not observe, nor can we discover in any way, an *additional* factor which constitutes a necessary connection between the 'explosion' and the subsequent motion of the cars. This seems to be what Hume had in mind when he wrote:

> These ultimate springs and principles are totally shut up from human curiosity and enquiry. Elasticity, gravity, cohesion of parts, communication of motion by impulse; these are probably the ultimate causes and principles which we ever discover in nature; and we may esteem

ourselves sufficiently happy, if, by accurate inquiry and reasoning, we can trace up the particular phenomena to, or near to, these general principles.[9]

Hume is acknowledging that we can discover general regularities in nature, but he is denying that an additional 'connection' can be found. And Hume was dedicated to the maxim, as are modern scientists, that we have no business talking about things it is impossible in principle for us to know anything about.

"When he asks why we do, in fact, expect so confidently that the future experiments will have outcomes similar to those of the past trials, Hume finds that it is nothing other than a matter of psychological conditioning. When we see one type of cause repeatedly followed by a particular type of effect, we come to expect that the same type of effect will follow the next time we come across that kind of cause. But this is not a matter of logical reasoning. Have you heard of Pavlov's conditioning experiments with dogs?" You nod. "When the bell rings the dog starts to salivate. He is *not* reasoning that, since the sounding of the bell has, in the past, been associated with the bringing of food, therefore, on this occasion the food will (at least probably) appear soon after the bell rings. According to Hume's analysis, what is called 'scientific reasoning' is no more rational or logical than your watering at the mouth when you are hungry and hear the dinner bell. It is something you cannot help doing, Hume says, but that does not mean that it has any logical foundation."

"That brings up a question I've wanted to ask," you say. "Hume seems to think that people necessarily reason in that way—inductive reasoning, I think it is called—but I've noticed that lots of people don't seem to. For instance, many people (including a student in my current problems course) believe in things like astrology; they believe that the configuration of the planets has a bearing on human events, when experience shows that it often doesn't work that way." The professor nods in agreement. You continue, "So if there is no logical justification for believing in scientific

predictions, why isn't it just as reasonable to believe in astrological predictions?"

"That," replies the prof, "is a very profound and difficult question. I doubt that any philosopher has a completely satisfactory answer to it."

MODERN ANSWERS[10]

The Wednesday philosophy lecture begins with a sort of rhetorical question, "What reason do we have (Hume is, at bottom, asking) for trusting the scientific method; what grounds do we have for believing that scientific predictions are reliable?" You have been pondering that very question quite a bit in the last couple of days, and—rhetorical or not—your hand shoots up. You have a thing or two to say on the subject.

"Philosophers may have trouble answering such questions," you assert, "but it seems to me there is an obvious reply. As my physics professor has often said, the scientist takes a very practical attitude. He puts forth a hypothesis; if it works he believes in it, and he continues to believe in it as long as it works. If it starts giving him bad predictions, he starts looking for another hypothesis, or for a way of revising his old one. Now the important thing about the scientific method, it seems to me, is that it works. Not only has it led to a vast amount of knowledge about the physical world, but it has been applied in all sorts of practical ways—and although these applications may not have been uniformly beneficial—for better or worse they were successful. Not always, of course, but by and large. Astrology, crystal gazing, and other such superstitious methods simply do not work very well. That's good enough for me."[11]

"That is, indeed, a very tempting answer," Professor Philo replies, "and in one form or another, it has been advanced by several modern philosophers. But Hume actually answered that one himself. You might put it this way. We can all agree that science has, up till now, a very impressive record of success in predicting the future. The question we are asking, however, is this: should we *predict* that science will continue to have the kind of success it has had in the past? It is quite natural to assume that its record will continue, but this is just a case of applying the scientific method to itself. In studying conservation of momentum, you inferred that future experiments would have results similar to those of your past experiments; in appraising the scientific method, you are assuming that its future success will match its past success. But using the scientific method to judge the scientific method is circular reasoning. It is as if a man goes to a bank to cash a check. When the teller refuses, on the grounds that he does not know this man, the man replies, 'That is no problem; permit me to introduce myself—I am John Smith, just as it says on the check.'

"Suppose that I were a believer in crystal gazing. You tell me that your method is better than mine because it has been more successful than mine. You say that this is a good reason for preferring your method to mine, I object. Since you are using your method to judge my method (as well as your method), I demand the right to use my method to evaluate yours. I gaze into my crystal ball and announce the result: from now on crystal gazing will be very successful in predicting the future, while the scientific method is due for a long run of bad luck."

You are about to protest, but she continues.

"The trouble with circular arguments is that they can be used to prove anything; if you assume what you are trying to prove, then there isn't much difficulty in proving it. You find the scientific justification of the scientific method convincing because you already trust the scientific method; if you had equal trust in crystal gazing, I should think you would find the crystal gazer's justification of his method equally convincing. Hume puts it this way:

> When a man says, *I have found, in all past instances, such sensible qualities conjoined with such secret powers:* And when he says, *Similar sensible qualities will always be conjoined with similar secret powers,* he is not guilty of a tautology, nor are these propositions in any respect the same. You can say that the one proposition is an inference from the other. But you must confess that the

inference is not intuitive; neither is it demonstrative: Of what nature is it, then? To say it is experimental is begging the question. For all inferences from experience suppose, as their foundation, that the future will resemble the past, and that similar powers will be conjoined with similar sensible qualities.[12]

If the assumption that the future is like the past is the presupposition of the scientific method, we cannot assume that principle in order to justify the scientific method. Once more, we can hardly find a clearer statement than Hume's:

> We have said that all arguments concerning existence are founded on the relation of cause and effect; that our knowledge of that relation is derived entirely from experience; and that all our experimental conclusions proceed upon the supposition that the future will be conformable to the past. To endeavour, therefore, the proof of this last supposition by probable arguments, or arguments regarding existence, must evidently be going in a circle, and taking that for granted, which is the very point in question.[13]

"The principle that the future will be like the past, or that regularities which have held up to the present will persist in the future, has traditionally been called *the principle of uniformity of nature.* Some philosophers, most notably Immanuel Kant, have regarded it as an a priori truth.[14] It seems to me, however, that Hume had already provided a convincing refutation of that claim by arguing that irregularities, however startling to common sense, are by no means inconceivable—that is, they cannot be ruled out a priori. Recall what he said:

> ...it implies no contradiction that the course of nature may change, and that an object, seemingly like those which we have experienced, may be attended with different or contrary effects. May I not clearly and distinctly conceive that a body, falling from the clouds, and which, in all other respects, resembles snow, has yet the taste of salt or feeling of fire?...Now whatever is intelligible, and can be distinctly conceived, implies no contradiction, and can never be proved false by any demonstrative argument or abstract reasoning *a priori.*[15]

"Other philosophers have proposed assuming this principle (or something similar) as a postulate; Bertrand Russell, though not the only one to advocate this approach, is by far the most famous.[16] But most philosophers agree that this use of postulation is question-begging. The real question still remains: why should one adopt any such postulate? Russell himself, in another context, summed it up very well: The method of 'postulating' what we want has many advantages; they are the same as the advantages of theft over honest toil."[17]

"Nevertheless," you interject, "can't we still say that scientific predictions are more probable than, say, those of astrology or crystal gazing?"

"It seems to me you raised a similar question once before," Professor Philo replies, "and I seem to recall saying that it depends on what you mean by the term 'probable.' Maybe it would be helpful if I now explain what I meant."[18] You nod encouragement. "The concept of probability—or perhaps I should say 'concepts' of probability—are very tricky. If you were to undertake a systematic study of confirmation and induction, you would have to go into a rather technical treatment of probability, but perhaps I can give a brief hint of what is involved.[19] One thing that has traditionally been meant by this term relates directly to the frequency with which something occurs—as Aristotle put it, the probable is that which happens often. If the weather forecaster says that there is a 90% chance of rain, he presumably means that, given such weather conditions as are now present, rain occurs in nine out of ten cases. If these forecasts are correct, we can predict rain on such occasions and be right nine times out of ten.

"Now, if you mean that scientific predictions are probable in *this* sense, I do not see how you could possibly support your claim. For Hume has argued—cogently, I think—that, for all we know now, *every* future scientific prediction may go wrong. He was not merely saying that science is fallible, that it will sometimes err in its predictions—he was saying that nature might at any moment (for all we can know) become irregular

on such a wide scale that any kind of scientific prediction of future occurrences would be utterly impossible. We have not found any reason to believe he was mistaken about this point."

"That must not be the concept of probability I had in mind," you remark; "I'm not quite sure how to express it, but it had something to do with what it would be reasonable to believe. I was thinking of the fact that, although we cannot regard scientific hypotheses as certain, we can consider them well confirmed. It is something like saying that a particular suspect is probably guilty of a crime—that the evidence, taken as a whole, seems to point to him."

"You have put your finger on another important probability concept," the professor replies. "It is sometimes known as the rational credibility concept. The most popular contemporary attempt (I believe) to deal with Hume's problem of inductive reasoning is stated in terms of this concept. The argument can be summarized in the following way. Hume has proved that we cannot *know for sure* that our scientific predictions will be correct, but that would be an unreasonable demand to place upon science. The best we can hope is for scientific conclusions that are probable. But when we ask that they be probable, in this sense, we are only asking that they be based upon the best possible evidence. Now, that is just what scientific predictions are—they are predictions based upon the best possible evidence. The scientist has fashioned his hypotheses in the light of all available information, and he has tested them experimentally on many occasions under a wide variety of circumstances. He has summoned all of the available evidence, and he has brought it to bear on the problem at hand. Such scientific predictions are obviously probable (as we are now construing this term); hence, they are rationally credible.[20] If we say that a belief is irrational, we mean that it runs counter to the evidence, or the person who holds it is ignoring the evidence. And in such contexts, when we speak of evidence, we are referring to inductive or scientific evidence.

"Now, the argument continues, to ask whether it is reasonable to believe in scientific conclusions comes right down to asking whether one ought to fashion his beliefs on the basis of the available evidence. But this is what it means to be rational. Hence, the question amounts to asking whether it is rational to be rational. If the question makes any sense at all, the obvious answer is 'yes.'"

"That answer certainly satisfies me," you say, feeling that Dr. Philo has succeeded admirably in stating the point you were groping for. "I'm glad to know that lots of other philosophers agree with it. Do you think it is a satisfactory answer to Hume's problem of induction?" You are more than a trifle discouraged when she gives a negative response with a shake of her head. "Why not?" you demand.

"This argument seems to me to beg the question," she replies, "for it assumes that the concept of evidence is completely clear. But that is precisely the question at issue. If we could be confident that the kind of experiments you performed in the physics lab to test the law of conservation of momentum do, in fact, provide evidence for that law, then we could say that the law is well supported by evidence. But to suppose that such facts do constitute evidence amounts to saying that what has happened in the past is a sign of what will happen in the future—the fact that momentum was conserved in your 'explosion' experiments is an indication that momentum will be conserved in future experiments of a similar nature. This assumes that the future will be like the past, and that is precisely the point at issue. To say that one fact constitutes evidence for another means, in part, that the one provides some basis for inference to the occurrence of the other. The problem of induction is nothing other than the problem of determining the circumstances under which such inference is justified. Thus, we have to resolve the problem of induction—Hume's problem—before we can ascertain whether one fact constitutes evidence for another. We cannot use the concept of evidence—inductive evidence—to solve the problem of induction.

"There is another way to look at this same argument. If you ask me whether you should use the scientific method, I must find out what you hope to accomplish. If you say that you want to get a job teaching physics, I can tell you right away that you had better use the scientific method, at least in your work, because that is what is expected of a physicist. If you say that you want to enjoy the respect and prestige that accrues to scientists in certain social circles, the answer is essentially the same. If you tell me, however, that you want to have as much success as possible in predicting future events, the answer is by no means as easy. If I tell you to go ahead and make scientific predictions, because that is what is considered reasonable (that is what is meant by fashioning your beliefs on the basis of evidence), then you should ask whether being reasonable in this sense (which is obviously the commonly accepted sense) is a good way to attain your goal. The answer, 'but that's what it means to be reasonable,' is beside the point. You might say, 'I want a method that is reasonable to adopt in order to achieve my goal of successful prediction—that is what I mean by being reasonable. To tell me that the scientific method is what is usually *called* reasonable doesn't help. I want to know whether the method that is *commonly called* reasonable is *actually* a reasonable method to adopt to attain my goal of successful prediction of the future. The fact that it is usually considered reasonable cuts no ice, because an awareness of Hume's problem of induction has not filtered down into common usage.' That's what I think you should say."

"Couldn't we avoid all of these problems," suggests another student, "if we simply resisted the temptation to generalize? In social science, my area of interest, we find that it is very risky to generalize, say, from one society to another. An opinion survey on students in the far west, for example, will not be valid when applied to students attending eastern schools. Wouldn't we be better off to restrict our claims to the facts we know, instead of trying to extend them inductively to things we really don't know?"

"The opinion you have offered bears a strong resemblance (though it isn't identical) to that of an influential British philosopher.[21] He has presented his ideas persuasively, and has many followers. Hume, he says, has proved conclusively that induction is not a justifiable form of inference; it is, consequently, no part of science. The only kind of logic that has a legitimate place in science is deductive logic. Deductive inferences are demonstrative; their conclusions must be true if their premises are true. These inferences are precisely what Hume called 'reasoning concerning relations of ideas.' The crucial point is that they *do not add to our knowledge* in any way—they enable us to see the content of our premises, but they do not extend that content in the least. Thus, from premises that refer only to events in the past and present, it is impossible to *deduce* any predictions of future facts. Any kind of inference which would enable us to predict the future on the basis of facts already observed would have to be of a different sort; such inference is often called 'ampliative' or 'inductive.' If science contains only deductive inferences, but no inductive inferences, it can never provide us with any knowledge beyond the content of our immediate observations.

"Now this philosopher does not reject scientific knowledge; he simply claims that prediction of the future is no part of the business of science. Accordingly, the function of scientific investigation is to find powerful general hypotheses (he calls them *conjectures*) that adequately explain all known facts that have occurred so far. As long as such a generalization succeeds in explaining the new facts that come along it is retained; if it fails to explain new facts, it must be modified or rejected. The sole purpose of scientific experimentation is to try to find weaknesses in such hypotheses—that is to criticize them or try to refute them. He calls this the 'method of conjectures and refutations,' or sometimes simply, 'the critical approach.'

"The main difficulty with this approach—an insuperable one, in my opinion—is the fact that it completely deprives science of its predictive function. To the question of which method to use for predicting the future, it can give no answer. Astrology, crystal gazing, blind guessing, and scientific prediction are all on a par. To find out what the population of the world will be in 2000 A.D., we might as well employ a psychic seer as a scientific demographer. I find it hard to believe that this can constitute a satisfactory solution to the problem of employing our knowledge to find rational solutions to the problems that face us—problems whose solutions demand that we make predictions of the future course of events. Tempting as it is to try to evade Hume's problem in this way, I do not see how we can be satisfied to admit that there is no rational approach to our problem."

"But perhaps there is no answer to Hume's problem," says still another student; "maybe the only hope for salvation of this world is to give up our blind worship of science and return to religion. We have placed our faith in science, and look where we are as a result. I believe we should adopt a different faith."

There's that word *again*, you note to yourself, as the professor begins her answer: "Though I heartily agree that many of the results of science—*technological* results, I think we should emphasize—have been far from beneficial, I don't think we can properly condemn scientific *knowledge*. Knowledge is one thing; what we choose to do with it is quite another. But that's not the issue we are concerned with. I do not see how anyone could deny that science has had a great deal of success in making predictions; no other approach can possibly present a comparable record of success. And, as time goes on, the capability for predictive success seems only to increase. It would be an utterly astonishing piece of luck, if it were sheer coincidence, that science has been so much luckier than other approaches in making its predictions. If anyone can consistently pick a winner in every race at every track every day, we are pretty sure he has more than good luck going for him. Science isn't infallible, but it is hard to believe its predictive success is just a matter of chance. I, at least, am not prepared to say that science is just one among many equally acceptable faiths—you pays your money and you takes your choice. I feel rather sure that the scientific approach has a logical justification of some sort." With that, the bell rings, the discussion ends, and everyone leaves—none by way of the window.

It just isn't good enough, you say to yourself, after listening to your physics professor lecturing, with demonstrations, on the law of conservation of angular momentum. You don't know whether you're dizzier from the discussion of Hume's problem in the philosophy class or from watching student volunteers in this class being spun on stools mounted on turntables. In any case, you decide to look up Professor Philo after lunch, and you find her in her office.

"Look," you say a bit brusquely, "I see that Hume was right about our inability to prove that nature is uniform. But suppose that nature does play a trick on us, so to speak. Suppose that after all this time of appearing quite uniform, manifesting all sorts of regularities such as the laws of physics, she turns chaotic. Then there isn't anything we can do anyhow. Someone might make a lucky guess about some future event, but there would be no systematic method for anticipating the chaos successfully. It seems to me I've got a way of predicting the future which will work if nature is uniform—the scientific method, or if you like, the inductive method—and if nature isn't uniform, I'm out of luck whatever I do. It seems to me I've got everything to gain and nothing to lose (except a lot of hard work) if I attempt to adhere to the scientific approach. That seems good enough to me; what do you think?"[22]

"Well," she says quietly, "I tend to agree with that answer, and so do a few others, but we are certainly in the minority. And many difficult problems arise when you try to work it out with precision."

"What sorts of difficulties are these?" you ask.

"There are several kinds," she begins; "for instance, what exactly do you mean by saying that nature is uniform? You cannot mean—to use Hume's quaint language—that like sensible qualities are always conjoined with like secret powers. All of us, including Hume, know this claim is false. Bread which looks and tastes completely harmless may contain a deadly poison. A gas which has exactly the appearance of normal air may suffocate living organisms and pollute the atmosphere. That kind of uniformity principle cannot be the basis of our inferences."

"That's quite true," you answer, "but perhaps we could say that nature operates according to regular laws. Ever since I began to think about Hume's problem, I have been led back to laws of nature."

"Your suggestion is a good one," she replies, "but modern philosophers have found it surprisingly difficult to say precisely what type of statement can qualify as a possible law of nature. It is a law of nature, most physicists would agree, that no material objects travel faster than light; they would refuse to admit, *as a law of nature,* that no golden spheres are more than one mile in diameter. It is not easy to state clearly the basis for this distinction. Both statements are generalizations, and both are true to the best of our knowledge."[23]

"Isn't the difference simply that you cannot, even in principle, accelerate a material object to the speed of light, while it is possible in principle to fabricate an enormous sphere of gold?"

"That is precisely the question at issue," she replies. "The problem is, what basis do we have for claiming possibility in the one case and impossibility in the other. You seem to be saying that a law of nature prevents the one but not the other, which is obviously circular. And if you bring in the notion of causation—causing something to go faster than light vs. causing a large golden sphere to be created—you only compound the difficulty, for the concept of causation is itself a source of great perplexity.

"Suppose, however, that we had succeeded in overcoming that obstacle—that we could say with reasonable precision which sorts of statements are candidates for the status of laws of nature and which are not. We then face a further difficulty. It is obvious that some tests of scientific laws carry greater weight than others. The discovery of the planet Neptune, for example, confirmed Newton's laws much more dramatically than would a few additional observations of Mars. A test with particles traveling at very high velocities would be much stronger evidence for conservation of momentum than would some more experiments on the air track in the physics lab. It is not easy to see how to measure or compare the weight which different types of evidence lend to different scientific hypotheses.

"Scientific confirmation is a subtle and complex matter to which contemporary philosophers have devoted a great deal of attention; some have tried to construct systems of inductive logic that would capture this kind of scientific reasoning. Such efforts have, at best, met with limited success; inductive logic is in a primitive state compared with deductive logic. Until we have a reasonably clear idea of what such inference consists of, however, it is unlikely that we will be able to go very far in meeting the fundamental challenge Hume issued concerning the justification of scientific reasoning. Unless we can at least say what inductive inference is, and what constitutes uniformity of nature (or natural law), we can hardly argue that inductive reasoning—and only inductive reasoning—will prove successful in predicting the future if nature is uniform. And even if those concepts were clarified, the argument would still be intricate indeed."

"Do you think there is any chance that answers to such problems can be found?" you ask.

"I think it's just possible."

"Thanks," you say as you get up to leave.

"And my thanks to you," she replies. "You cannot possibly know how satisfying it is to talk with someone like you—someone intelligent—who takes such philosophical problems seriously and thinks hard about them. If you keep it up, you might be the very person to find some of the answers. I wish you well."

NOTES

1. Professor Salvia is a descendant of Salviati, the protagonist in Galileo's dialogues. The name was shortened when the family emigrated to America.

2. Dr. Sagro is married to a descendant of Sagredo, another character in Galileo's dialogues.

3. If you really did know, please accept the author's apologies.

4. Please note that "demonstrate" is ambiguous. In mathematics it means "prove"; in physics it means "exemplify." Hume uses this term only in the mathematical sense.

5. Hume, using the terminology of his day, refers to it as the "moment" of the moving body.

6. This is Newton's definition; it is somewhat out of date, but adequate in the present context.

7. She is a direct descendant of Philo, the protagonist in Hume's "Dialogues Concerning Natural Religion," most of which is reprinted in this anthology.

8. Professor Philo realizes that it would be more accurate to say that a statement or hypothesis expressing a law of nature must be a generalization, but she does not wish to introduce unnecessary terminological distinctions at this point.

9. In section IV, part I, anticipating the results of the later discussion.

10. All of the attempts to deal with Hume's problem which are treated in this section are discussed in detail in Wesley C. Salmon, *The Foundations of Scientific Inference* (Pittsburgh: University of Pittsburgh Press, 1967); this book will be cited hereafter as *Foundations*.

11. This is an inductive justification; see *Foundations*, chapter II, section I.

12. David Hume, *Enquiry Concerning Human Understanding* (hereafter, *Enquiry*), section IV, part II.

13. Ibid.

14. For discussion of justification by means of synthetic a priori principles, see *Foundations*, chapter II, section 4.

15. *Enquiry*, section IV, part II.

16. For discussion of the postulational approach, see *Foundations*, chapter II, section 6.

17. Bertrand Russell, *Introduction to Mathematical Philosophy* (London: Allen & Unwin, 1919), p. 71.

18. The "*probabilistic approach*" is discussed in *Foundations*, chapter II, section 7.

19. An elementary survey of philosophical problems of probability is given in *Foundations*, chapters IV–VII. References to additional literature on this subject can be found there.

20. We are assuming, of course, that these predictions are properly made. Scientists are only human, and they do make mistakes. One should

not conclude, however, that every false prediction represents a scientific error. Impeccable scientific procedure is fallible, as we have already noted more than once.

21. This refers to the "deductivist" position of Sir Karl Popper. This approach is discussed in *Foundations*, chapter II, section 3.

22. This approach is due mainly to Hans Reichenbach; it is known as a *"pragmatic justification"*

and is discussed in *Foundations*, chapter II, section 8.

23. Further elementary discussion of this issue can be found in Carl G. Hempel, *Philosophy of Natural Science* (Englewood Cliffs, NJ: Prentice-Hall, Inc., 1966), § 5.3. A more technical and extensive treatment of related issues can be found in Nelson Goodman, *Fact, Fiction, and Forecast*, 2nd ed. (Indianapolis, IN: The Bobbs-Merrill Co., 1965).

4.3 Science: Conjectures and Refutations

KARL POPPER

Karl Popper (1902–1994) was one of the great philosophers of science of the twentieth century.

Mr. Turnbull had predicted evil consequences,... and was now doing the best in his power to bring about the verification of his own prophecies.

—ANTHONY TROLLOPE

I

When I received the list of participants in this course and realized that I had been asked to speak to philosophical colleagues, I thought, after some hesitation and consultation, that you would probably prefer me to speak about those problems which interest me most, and about those developments with which I am most intimately acquainted. I therefore decided to do what I have never done before: to give you a report on my own work in the philosophy of science, since the autumn of 1919 when I first began to grapple with the problem, *"When should a theory be ranked as scientific?"* or *"Is there a criterion for the scientific character or status of a theory?"*

The problem which troubled me at the time was neither, "When is a theory true?" nor, "When is a theory acceptable?" My problem was different. *I wished to distinguish between science and pseudo-science;* knowing very well that science often errs, and that pseudo-science may happen to stumble on the truth.

I knew, of course, the most widely accepted answer to my problem: that science is distinguished from pseudo-science—or from "metaphysics"—by its *empirical method,* which is essentially *inductive,* proceeding from observation or experiment. But this did not satisfy me. On the contrary, I often formulated my problem as one of distinguishing between a genuinely empirical method and a non-empirical or even a pseudo-empirical method—that is to say, a method which, although it appeals to observation and experiment, nevertheless does not come up to scientific standards. The latter method may be exemplified by astrology, with its stupendous

From Karl Popper, *Conjectures and Refutations* (London: Routledge, 1963), pp. 33–38. Reprinted by permission of Universitat Klagenfurt / Karl Popper Library, Universitatsstrasse 65–67, 9020 Klagenfurt, Austria.

mass of empirical evidence based on observation—on horoscopes and on biographies.

But as it was not the example of astrology which led me to my problem I should perhaps briefly describe the atmosphere in which my problem arose and the examples by which it was stimulated. After the collapse of the Austrian Empire there had been a revolution in Austria: the air was full of revolutionary slogans and ideas, and new and often wild theories. Among the theories which interested me Einstein's theory of relativity was no doubt by far the most important. Three others were Marx's theory of history, Freud's psycho-analysis, and Alfred Adler's so-called "individual psychology".

There was a lot of popular nonsense talked about these theories, and especially about relativity (as still happens even today), but I was fortunate in those who introduced me to the study of this theory. We all—the small circle of students to which I belonged—were thrilled with the result of Eddington's eclipse observations which in 1919 brought the first important confirmation of Einstein's theory of gravitation. It was a great experience for us, and one which had a lasting influence on my intellectual development.

The three other theories I have mentioned were also widely discussed among students at that time. I myself happened to come into personal contact with Alfred Adler, and even to co-operate with him in his social work among the children and young people in the working-class districts of Vienna where he had established social guidance clinics.

It was during the summer of 1919 that I began to feel more and more dissatisfied with these three theories—the Marxist theory of history, psychoanalysis, and individual psychology; and I began to feel dubious about their claims to scientific status. My problem perhaps first took the simple form, "What is wrong with Marxism, psycho-analysis, and individual psychology? Why are they so different from physical theories, from Newton's theory, and especially from the theory of relativity?"

To make this contrast clear I should explain that few of us at the time would have said that we believed in the *truth* of Einstein's theory of gravitation. This shows that it was not my doubting the *truth* of those other three theories which bothered me, but something else. Yet neither was it that I merely felt mathematical physics to be more *exact* than the sociological or psychological type of theory. Thus what worried me was neither the problem of truth, at that stage at least, nor the problem of exactness or measurability. It was rather that I felt that these other three theories, though posing as sciences, had in fact more in common with primitive myths than with science; that they resembled astrology rather than astronomy.

I found that those of my friends who were admirers of Marx, Freud, and Adler, were impressed by a number of points common to these theories, and especially by their apparent *explanatory power*. These theories appeared to be able to explain practically everything that happened within the fields to which they referred. The study of any of them seemed to have the effect of an intellectual conversion or revelation, opening your eyes to a new truth hidden from those not yet initiated. Once your eyes were thus opened you saw confirming instances everywhere: the world was full of *verifications* of the theory. Whatever happened always confirmed it. Thus its truth appeared manifest; and unbelievers were clearly people who did not want to see the manifest truth; who refused to see it, either because it was against their class interest, or because of their repressions which were still "unanalysed" and crying aloud for treatment.

The most characteristic element in this situation seemed to me the incessant stream of confirmations, of observations which "verified" the theories in question; and this point was constantly emphasized by their adherents. A Marxist could not open a newspaper without finding on every page confirming evidence for his interpretation of history; not only in the news, but also in its presentation—which revealed the class bias of the paper—and especially of course in what the paper did *not* say. The Freudian analysts emphasized that their theories were constantly verified by their "clinical observations". As for Adler,

I was much impressed by a personal experience. Once, in 1919, I reported to him a case which to me did not seem particularly Adlerian, but which he found no difficulty in analysing in terms of his theory of inferiority feelings, although he had not even seen the child. Slightly shocked, I asked him how he could be so sure. "Because of my thousandfold experience," he replied; whereupon I could not help saying: "And with this new case, I suppose, your experience has become thousand-and-one-fold."

What I had in mind was that his previous observations may not have been much sounder than this new one; that each in its turn had been interpreted in the light of "previous experience", and at the same time counted as additional confirmation. What, I asked myself, did it confirm? No more than that a case could be interpreted in the light of the theory. But this meant very little, I reflected, since every conceivable case could be interpreted in the light of Adler's theory, or equally of Freud's. I may illustrate this by two very different examples of human behaviour: that of a man who pushes a child into the water with the intention of drowning it; and that of a man who sacrifices his life in an attempt to save the child. Each of these two cases can be explained with equal ease in Freudian and in Adlerian terms. According to Freud the first man suffered from repression (say, of some component of his Oedipus complex), while the second man had achieved sublimation. According to Adler the first man suffered from feelings of inferiority (producing perhaps the need to prove to himself that he dared to commit some crime), and so did the second man (whose need was to prove to himself that he dared to rescue the child). I could not think of any human behaviour which could not be interpreted in terms of either theory. It was precisely this fact—that they always fitted, that they were always confirmed—which in the eyes of their admirers constituted the strongest argument in favour of these theories. It began to dawn on me that this apparent strength was in fact their weakness.

With Einstein's theory the situation was strikingly different. Take one typical instance—Einstein's prediction, just then confirmed by the findings of Eddington's expedition. Einstein's gravitational theory had led to the result that light must be attracted by heavy bodies (such as the sun), precisely as material bodies were attracted. As a consequence it could be calculated that light from a distant fixed star whose apparent position was close to the sun would reach the earth from such a direction that the star would seem to be slightly shifted away from the sun; or, in other words, that stars close to the sun would look as if they had moved a little away from the sun, and from one another. This is a thing which cannot normally be observed since such stars are rendered invisible in daytime by the sun's overwhelming brightness; but during an eclipse it is possible to take photographs of them. If the same constellation is photographed at night one can measure the distances on the two photographs, and check the predicted effect.

Now the impressive thing about this case is the *risk* involved in a prediction of this kind. If observation shows that the predicted effect is definitely absent, then the theory is simply refuted. The theory is *incompatible with certain possible results of observation*—in fact with results which everybody before Einstein would have expected. This is quite different from the situation I have previously described, when it turned out that the theories in question were compatible with the most divergent human behaviour, so that it was practically impossible to describe any human behaviour that might not be claimed to be a verification of these theories.

These considerations led me in the winter of 1919–20 to conclusions which I may now reformulate as follows.

1. It is easy to obtain confirmations, or verifications, for nearly every theory—if we look for confirmations.

2. Confirmations should count only if they are the result of *risky predictions;* that is to say, if, unenlightened by the theory in question, we should have expected an event which was incompatible with the theory—an event which would have refuted the theory.

3. Every "good" scientific theory is a prohibition: it forbids certain things to happen. The more a theory forbids, the better it is.

4. A theory which is not refutable by any conceivable event is nonscientific. Irrefutability is not a virtue of a theory (as people often think) but a vice.

5. Every genuine *test* of a theory is an attempt to falsify it, or to refute it. Testability is falsifiability; but there are degrees of testability; some theories are more testable, more exposed to refutation, than others; they take, as it were, greater risks.

6. Confirming evidence should not count *except when it is the result of a genuine test of the theory;* and this means that it can be presented as a serious but unsuccessful attempt to falsify the theory. (I now speak in such cases of "corroborating evidence.")

7. Some genuinely testable theories, when found to be false, are still upheld by their admirers—for example by introducing *ad hoc* some auxiliary assumption, or by re-interpreting the theory *ad hoc* in such a way that it escapes refutation. Such a procedure is always possible, but it rescues the theory from refutation only at the price of destroying, or at least lowering, its scientific status. (I later described such a rescuing operation as a *"conventionalist twist"* or a *"conventionalist stratagem."*)

One can sum up all this by saying that *the criterion of the scientific status of a theory is its falsifiability, or refutability, or testability.*

II

I may perhaps exemplify this with the help of the various theories so far mentioned. Einstein's theory of gravitation clearly satisfied the criterion of falsifiability. Even if our measuring instruments at the time did not allow us to pronounce on the results of the tests with complete assurance, there was clearly a possibility of refuting the theory.

Astrology did not pass the test. Astrologers were greatly impressed, and misled, by what they believed to be confirming evidence—so much so that they were quite unimpressed by any unfavourable evidence. Moreover, by making their interpretations and prophecies sufficiently vague they were able to explain away anything that might have been a refutation of the theory had the theory and the prophecies been more precise. In order to escape falsification they destroyed the testability of their theory. It is a typical soothsayer's trick to predict things so vaguely that the predictions can hardly fail: that they become irrefutable.

The Marxist theory of history, in spite of the serious efforts of some of its founders and followers, ultimately adopted this soothsaying practice. In some of its earlier formulations (for example in Marx's analysis of the character of the "coming social revolution") their predictions were testable, and in fact falsified. Yet instead of accepting the refutations the followers of Marx reinterpreted both the theory and the evidence in order to make them agree. In this way they rescued the theory from refutation; but they did so at the price of adopting a device which made it irrefutable. They thus gave a "conventionalist twist" to the theory; and by this stratagem they destroyed its much advertised claim to scientific status.

The two psycho-analytic theories were in a different class. They were simply non-testable, irrefutable. There was no conceivable human behaviour which could contradict them. This does not mean that Freud and Adler were not seeing certain things correctly: I personally do not doubt that much of what they say is of considerable importance, and may well play its part one day in a psychological science which is testable. But it does mean that those "clinical observations" which analysts naively believe confirm their theory cannot do this any more than the daily confirmations which astrologers find in their practice. And as for Freud's epic of the Ego, the Super-ego, and the Id, no substantially stronger claim to scientific status can be made for it than for Homer's collected stories from Olympus. These theories describe some facts, but in the manner of myths. They contain most interesting psychological suggestions, but not in a testable form.

At the same time I realized that such myths may be developed, and become testable; that historically speaking all—or very nearly all—scientific theories originate from myths, and that a myth may contain important anticipations of scientific theories. Examples are Empedocles' theory of evolution by trial and error, or Parmenides' myth of the unchanging block universe in which nothing ever happens and which, if we add another dimension, becomes Einstein's block universe (in which, too, nothing ever happens, since everything is, four-dimensionally speaking, determined and laid down from the beginning). I thus felt that if a theory is found to be non-scientific, or "metaphysical" (as we might say), it is not thereby found to be unimportant, or insignificant, or "meaningless," or "nonsensical." But it cannot claim to be backed by empirical evidence in the scientific sense—although it may easily be, in some genetic sense, the "result of observation."

(There were a great many other theories of this pre-scientific or pseudo-scientific character, some of them, unfortunately, as influential as the Marxist interpretation of history; for example, the racialist interpretation of history—another of those impressive and all-explanatory theories which act upon weak minds like revelations.)

Thus the problem which I tried to solve by proposing the criterion of falsifiability was neither a problem of meaningfulness or significance, nor a problem of truth or acceptability. It was the problem of drawing a line (as well as this can be done) between the statements, or systems of statements, of the empirical sciences, and all other statements—whether they are of a religious or of a metaphysical character, or simply pseudo-scientific. Years later—it must have been in 1928 or 1929—I called this first problem of mine the *"problem of demarcation."* The criterion of falsifiability is a solution to this problem of demarcation, for it says that statements or systems of statements, in order to be ranked as scientific, must be capable of conflicting with possible, or conceivable, observations.

4.4 Believing Where We Cannot Prove

PHILIP KITCHER

Philip Kitcher is Professor of Philosophy at Columbia University. He has published widely in philosophy of mathematics and philosophy of science.

OPENING MOVES

Simple distinctions come all too easily. Frequently we open the way for later puzzlement by restricting the options we take to be available. So, for example, in contrasting science and religion, we often operate with a simple pair of categories. On one side there is science, proof, and certainty; on the other, religion, conjecture, and faith.

The opening lines of Tennyson's *In Memoriam* offer an eloquent statement of the contrast:

Strong Son of God, immortal love,
Whom we, that have not seen Thy face,
By faith, and faith alone, embrace,
Believing where we cannot prove.

A principal theme of Tennyson's great poem is his struggle to maintain faith in the face of what seems to be powerful scientific evidence.

Philip Kitcher, *Abusing Science: The Case Against Creationism*, pp. 33–35 word excerpt from pages 42–46, 48–49, © 1982 Massachusetts Institute of Technology, by permission of The MIT Press.

Tennyson had read a popular work by Robert Chambers, *Vestiges of the Natural History of Creation,* and he was greatly troubled by the account of the course of life on earth that the book contains. *In Memoriam* reveals a man trying to believe where he cannot prove, a man haunted by the thought that the proofs may be against him.

Like Tennyson, contemporary Creationists accept the traditional contrast between science and religion. But where Tennyson agonized, they attack. While they are less eloquent, they are supremely confident of their own solution. They open their onslaught on evolutionary theory by denying that it is a science. In *The Troubled Waters of Evolution,* Henry Morris characterizes evolutionary theory as maintaining that large amounts of time are required for evolution to produce "new kinds." As a result, we should not expect to see such "new kinds" emerging. Morris comments, "Creationists in turn insist that this belief is not scientific evidence but only a statement of faith. The evolutionist seems to be saying, Of course, we cannot really *prove* evolution, since this requires ages of time, and so, therefore, you should accept it as a proved fact of science! Creationists regard this as an odd type of logic, which would be entirely unacceptable in any other field of science" (Morris 1974b, 16). David Watson makes a similar point in comparing Darwin with Galileo: "So here is the difference between Darwin and Galileo: Galileo set a demonstrable *fact* against a few words of Bible poetry which the Church at that time had understood in an obviously naive way; Darwin set an unprovable *theory* against eleven chapters of straightforward history which cannot be reinterpreted in any satisfactory way" (Watson 1976, 46).

The idea that evolution is conjecture, faith, or "philosophy" pervades Creationist writings. It is absolutely crucial to their case for equal time for "scientific" Creationism. This ploy has succeeded in winning important adherents to the Creationist cause. As he prepared to defend Arkansas law 590, Attorney General Steven Clark echoed the Creationist judgment. "Evolution," he said, "is just a theory." Similar words have been heard in Congress. William Dannemeyer, a congressman from California, introduced a bill to limit funding to the Smithsonian with the following words: "If the theory of evolution is just that—a theory—and if that theory can be regarded as a religion...then it occurs to this Member that other Members might prefer it not to be given exclusive or top billing in our Nation's most famous museum but equal billing or perhaps no billing at all."

In their attempt to show that evolution is not science, Creationists receive help from the least likely sources. Great scientists sometimes claim that certain facts about the past evolution of organisms are "demonstrated" or "indubitable." But Creationists also can (and do) quote scientists who characterize evolution as "dogma" and contend that there is no conclusive proof of evolutionary theory. Evolution is not part of science because, as evolutionary biologists themselves concede, science demands proof, and, as other biologists point out, proof of evolution is not forthcoming.

The rest of the Creationist argument flows easily. We educate our children in evolutionary theory as if it were a proven fact. We subscribe officially, in our school system, to one faith—an atheistic, materialistic faith—ignoring rival beliefs. Antireligious educators deform the minds of children, warping them to accept as gospel a doctrine that has no more scientific support than the true Gospel. The very least that should be done is to allow for both alternatives to be presented.

We should reject the Creationists' gambit. Eminent scientists notwithstanding, science is not a body of demonstrated truths. Virtually all of science is an exercise in believing where we cannot prove. Yet, scientific conclusions are not embraced by faith alone. Tennyson's dichotomy was too simple.

INCONCLUSIVE EVIDENCE

Sometimes we seem to have conclusive reasons for accepting a statement as true. It is hard to doubt that 2 + 2 = 4. If, unlike Lord Kelvin's ideal mathematician, we do not find it obvious that

$$\int_{-\infty}^{+\infty} e^{-x^2}\, dx = \sqrt{\pi},$$

at least the elementary parts of mathematics appear to command our agreement. The direct evidence of our senses seems equally compelling. If I see the pen with which I am writing, holding it firmly in my unclouded view, how can I doubt that it exists? The talented mathematician who has proved a theorem and the keen-eyed witness of an episode furnish our ideals of certainty in knowledge. What they tell us can be engraved in stone, for there is no cause for worry that it will need to be modified.

Yet, in another mood, one that seems "deeper" or more "philosophical," skeptical doubts begin to creep in. Is there really anything of which we are so certain that later evidence could not give us reason to change our minds? Even when we think about mathematical proof, can we not imagine that new discoveries may cast doubt on the cogency of our reasoning? (The history of mathematics reveals that sometimes what seems for all the world like a proof may have a false conclusion.) Is it not possible that the most careful observer may have missed something? Or that the witness brought preconceptions to the observation that subtly biased what was reported? Are we not *always* fallible?

I am mildly sympathetic to the skeptic's worries. Complete certainty is best seen as an ideal toward which we strive and that is rarely, if ever, attained. Conclusive evidence always eludes us. Yet even if we ignore skeptical complaints and imagine that we are sometimes lucky enough to have conclusive reasons for accepting a claim as true, we should not include scientific reasoning among our paradigms of proof. Fallibility is the hallmark of science.

This point should not be so surprising. The trouble is that we frequently forget it in discussing contemporary science. When we turn to the history of science, however, our fallibility stares us in the face. The history of the natural sciences is strewn with the corpses of intricately organized theories, each of which had, in its day, considerable evidence in its favor. When we look at the confident defenders of those theories we should see anticipations of ourselves. The eighteenth century scientists who believed that heat is a "subtle fluid," the atomic theorists who maintained that water molecules are compounded out of one atom of hydrogen and one of oxygen, the biochemists who identified protein as the genetic material, and the geologists who thought that continents cannot move were neither unintelligent nor ill informed. Given the evidence available to them, they were eminently reasonable in drawing their conclusions. History proved them wrong. It did not show that they were unjustified.

Why is science fallible? Scientific investigation aims to disclose the general principles that govern the workings of the universe. These principles are not intended merely to summarize what some select groups of humans have witnessed. Natural science is not just natural history. It is vastly more ambitious. Science offers us laws that are supposed to hold universally, and it advances claims about things that are beyond our power to observe. The nuclear physicist who sets down the law governing a particular type of radioactive decay is attempting to state a truth that holds throughout the entire cosmos and also to describe the behavior of things that we cannot even see. Yet, of necessity, the physicist's ultimate evidence is highly restricted. Like the rest of us, scientists are confined to a relatively small region of space and time and equipped with limited and imperfect senses.

How is science possible at all? How are we able to have any confidence about the distant regions of the cosmos and the invisible realm that lies behind the surfaces of ordinary things? The answer is complicated. Natural science follows intricate and ingenious procedures for fathoming the secrets of the universe. Scientists devise ways of obtaining especially revealing evidence. They single out some of the things we are able to see as crucial clues to the way that nature works. These clues are used to answer questions that cannot be addressed by direct observation. Scientific theories, even those that are most respected and most successful, rest on indirect arguments from the observational evidence. New discoveries can always call those arguments into question, showing scientists that the observed data should be understood in a different way, that they have misread their evidence.

But scientists often forget the fallibility of their enterprise. This is not just absentmindedness or wishful thinking. During the heyday of a scientific theory, so much evidence may support the theory, so many observational clues may seem to attest to its truth, that the idea that it could be overthrown appears ludicrous. In addition, the theory may provide ways of identifying quickly what is inaccessible to our unaided senses. Electron microscopes and cloud chambers are obvious examples of those extensions of our perceptual system that theories can inspire. Trained biochemists will talk quite naturally of seeing large molecules, and it is easy to overlook the fact that they are presupposing a massive body of theory in describing what they "see." If that theory were to be amended, even in subtle ways, then the descriptions of the "observed characteristics" of large molecules might have to be given up. Nor should we pride ourselves that the enormous successes of contemporary science secure us against future amendments. No theory in the history of science enjoyed a more spectacular career than Newton's mechanics. Yet Newton's ideas had to give way to Einstein's.

When practicing scientists are reminded of these straightforward points, they frequently adopt what the philosopher George Berkeley called a "forlorn skepticism." From the idea of science as certain and infallible, they jump to a cynical description of their endeavors. Science is sometimes held to be a game played with arbitrary rules, an irrational acceptance of dogma, an enterprise based ultimately on faith. Once we have appreciated the fallibility of natural science and recognized its sources, we can move beyond the simple opposition of proof and faith. Between these extremes lies the vast field of cases in which we believe something on the basis of good—even excellent—but inconclusive evidence.

If we want to emphasize the fact that what scientists believe today may have to be revised in the light of observations made tomorrow, then we can describe all our science as "theory." But the description should not confuse us. To concede that evolutionary biology is a theory is not to suppose that there are alternatives to it that are equally worthy of a place in our curriculum. All theories are revisable, but not all theories are equal. Even though our present evidence does not *prove* that evolutionary biology—or quantum physics, or plate tectonics, or any other theory—is true, evolutionary biologists will maintain that the present evidence is overwhelmingly in favor of their theory and overwhelmingly against its supposed rivals. Their enthusiastic assertions that evolution is a proven fact can be charitably understood as claims that the (admittedly inconclusive) evidence we have for evolutionary theory is as good as we ever obtain for any theory in any field of science.

Hence the Creationist try for a quick Fools' Mate can easily be avoided. Creationists attempt to draw a line between evolutionary biology and the rest of science by remarking that large-scale evolution cannot be observed. This tactic fails. Large-scale evolution is no more inaccessible to observation than nuclear reactions or the molecular composition of water. For the Creationists to succeed in divorcing evolutionary biology from the rest of science, they need to argue that evolutionary theory is less well supported by the evidence than are theories in, for example, physics and chemistry. It will come as no surprise to learn that they try to do this. To assess the merits of their arguments we need a deeper understanding of the logic of inconclusive justification. We shall begin with a simple and popular idea: Scientific theories earn our acceptance by making successful predictions.

PREDICTIVE SUCCESS

Imagine that somebody puts forward a new theory about the origins of hay fever. The theory makes a number of startling predictions concerning connections that we would not have thought worth investigating. For example, it tells us that people who develop hay fever invariably secrete a particular substance in certain fatty tissues and that anyone who eats rhubarb as a child never develops hay fever. The theory predicts things that initially appear fantastic. Suppose that we check up on these predictions and find that they are borne out by clinical tests. Would we not begin to believe—and believe reasonably—that the theory was *at least* on the right track?

This example illustrates a pattern of reasoning that is familiar in the history of science. Theories win support by producing claims about what can be observed, claims that would not have seemed plausible prior to the advancement of the theory, but that are in fact found to be true when we make the appropriate observations. A classic (real) example is Pascal's confirmation of Torricelli's hypothesis that we live at the bottom of an ocean of air that presses down upon us. Pascal reasoned that if Torricelli's hypothesis were true, then air pressure should decrease at higher altitudes (because at higher altitudes we are closer to the "surface" of the atmosphere, so that the length of the column of air that presses down is shorter). Accordingly, he sent his brother-in-law to the top of a mountain to make some barometric measurements. Pascal's clever working out of the observational predictions of Torricelli's theory led to a dramatic predictive success for the theory.

The idea of predictive success has encouraged a popular picture of science. (We shall see later that this picture, while popular, is not terribly accurate.) Philosophers sometimes regard a theory as a collection of claims or statements. Some of these statements offer generalizations about the features of particular, recondite things (genes, atoms, gravitational force, quasars, and the like). These statements are used to infer statements whose truth or falsity can be decided by observation. (This appears to be just what Pascal did.) Statements belonging to this second group are called the *observational consequences* of the theory. Theories are supported when we find that their observational consequences (those that we have checked) are true. The credentials of a theory are damaged if we discover that some of its observational consequences are false.

We can make the idea more precise by being clearer about the inferences involved. Those who talk of inferring observational predictions from our theories think that we can *deduce* from the statements of the theory, and from those statements alone, some predictions whose accuracy we can check by direct observation. Deductive inference is well understood. The fundamental idea of deductive inference is this: We say that a statement S is a valid deductive consequence of a group of statements if and only if it is *impossible* that all the statements in the group should be true and that S should be false; alternatively, S is a valid deductive consequence (or, more simply, a valid consequence) of a group of statements if and only if it would be self-contradictory to assert all the statements in the group and to deny S.

It will be helpful to make the idea of valid consequence more familiar with some examples. Consider the statements "All lovers of baseball dislike George Steinbrenner" and "George Steinbrenner loves baseball." The statement "George Steinbrenner dislikes himself" is a deductively valid consequence of these two statements. For it is impossible that the first two should be true and the third false. However, in claiming that this is a case of deductively valid consequence, we do not commit ourselves to maintaining that *any* of the statements is true. (Perhaps there are some ardent baseball fans who admire Steinbrenner. Perhaps Steinbrenner himself has no time for the game.) What deductive validity means is that the truth of the first two statements would guarantee the truth of the third; that is, *if* the first two *were* true, then the third would have to be true.

Another example will help rule out other misunderstandings. Here are two statements: "Shortly after noon on January 1, 1982, in the Oval Office, a jelly bean was released from rest more than two feet above any surface"; "Shortly after noon on January 1, 1982, in the Oval

Office, a jelly bean fell." Is the second statement a deductively valid consequence of the first? You might think that it is, on the grounds that it would have been impossible for the unfortunate object to have been released and not to have fallen. In one sense this is correct, but that is not the sense of impossibility that deductive logicians have in mind. Strictly speaking, it is not *impossible* for the jellybean to have been released without falling; we can imagine, for example, that the law of gravity might suddenly cease to operate. We do not *contradict* ourselves when we assert that the jellybean was released but deny that it fell; we simply refuse to accept the law of gravity (or some other relevant physical fact).

Thus, S is a deductively valid consequence of a group of statements if and only if there is *absolutely no possibility* that all the statements in the group should be true and S should be false. This conception allows us to state the popular view of theory and prediction more precisely. Theories are collections of statements. The observational consequences of a theory are statements that have to be true if the statements belonging to the theory are all true. These observational consequences also have to be statements whose truth or falsity can be ascertained by direct observation.

My initial discussion of predictive success presented the rough idea that, when we find the observational consequences of a theory to be true, our findings bring credit to the theory. Conversely, discovery that some observational consequences of a theory are false was viewed as damaging. We can now make the second point much more precise. Any theory that has a false observational consequence must contain some false statement (or statements). For if all the statements in the theory were true, then, according to the standard definitions of *deductive validity* and *observational consequence,* any observational consequence would also have to be true. Hence, if a theory is found to have a false observational consequence, we must conclude that one or more statements of the theory are false.

This means that theories can be conclusively falsified, through the discovery that they have

false observational consequences. Some philosophers, most notably Sir Karl Popper (Popper 1959; 1963), have taken this point to have enormous significance for our understanding of science. According to Popper, the essence of a scientific theory is that it should be *falsifiable.* That is, if the theory is false, then it must be possible to show that it is false. Now, if a theory has utterly no observational consequences, it would be extraordinarily difficult to unmask that theory as false. So, to be a genuine scientific theory, a group of statements must have observational consequences. It is important to realize that Popper is not suggesting that every good theory must be false. The difference between being falsifiable and being false is like the difference between being vulnerable and actually being hurt. A good scientific theory should not be false. Rather, it must have observational consequences that could reveal the theory as mistaken if the experiments give the wrong results.

While these ideas about theory testing may seem strange in their formal attire, they emerge quite frequently in discussions of science. They also find their way into the creation-evolution debate.

PREDICTIVE FAILURE

From the beginning, evolutionary theory has been charged with just about every possible type of predictive failure. Critics of the theory have argued that (a) the theory makes no predictions (it is unfalsifiable and so fails Popper's criterion for science), (b) the theory makes false predictions (it is falsified), (c) the theory does not make the kinds of predictions it ought to make (the observations and experiments that evolutionary theorists undertake have no bearing on the theory). Many critics, including several Creationists, manage to advance all these objections in the same work. This is somewhat surprising, since points (a) and (b) are, of course, mutually contradictory....

To make a serious assessment of these broad Creationist charges, we must begin by asking some basic methodological questions. We cannot decide whether evolutionary biologists are guilty of trying to save their theory by using ad hoc assumptions (new and implausible claims dreamed up for the sole purpose of protecting some cherished ideas) unless we have some way of deciding when a proposal is ad hoc. Similarly, we cannot make a reasoned response to the charge that laboratory experiments are irrelevant, or to the fundamental objection that evolutionary theory is unfalsifiable, unless we have a firmer grasp of the relation between theory and evidence.

NAIVE FALSIFICATIONISM

The time has come to tell a dreadful secret. While the picture of scientific testing sketched above continues to be influential among scientists, it has been shown to be seriously incorrect. (To give my profession its due, historians and philosophers of science have been trying to let this particular cat out of the bag for at least thirty years.) Important work in the history of science has made it increasingly clear that no major scientific theory has ever exemplified the relation between theory and evidence that the traditional model presents.

What is wrong with the old picture? Answer: Either it debars most of what we take to be science from counting as science or it allows virtually anything to count. On the traditional view of "theory," textbook cases of scientific theories turn out to be unfalsifiable. Suppose we identify Newtonian mechanics with Newton's three laws of motion plus the law of gravitation. What observational consequences can we deduce from these four statements? You might think that we could deduce that if, as the (undoubtedly apocryphal) story alleges, an apple became detached from a branch above where Newton was sitting, the apple would have fallen on his head. But this does not follow at all. To see why not, it is only necessary to recognize that the failure of this alleged prediction would not force us to deny any of the four statements of the theory. All we need do is assume that some other forces were at work that overcame the force of gravity and caused the

apple to depart from its usual trajectory. So, given this simple way of applying Popper's criterion, Newtonian mechanics would be unfalsifiable. The same would go for any other scientific theory. Hence none of what we normally take to be science would count as science. (I might note that Popper is aware of this problem and has suggestions of his own as to how it should be overcome. However, what concerns me here are the *applications* of Popper's ideas, that are made by Creationists, as well as by scientists in their professional debates.)

The example of the last paragraph suggests an obvious remedy. Instead of thinking about theories in the simple way just illustrated, we might take them to be far more elaborate. Newton's laws (the three laws of motion and the law of gravitation) are *embedded* in Newtonian mechanics. They form the core of the theory, but do not constitute the whole of it. Newtonian mechanics also contains supplementary assumptions, telling us, for example, that for certain special systems the effects of forces other than gravity are negligible. This more elaborate collection of statements *does* have observational consequences and *is* falsifiable.

But the remedy fails. Imagine that we attempt to expose some self-styled spiritual teacher as an overpaid fraud. We try to point out that the teacher's central message—"Quietness is wholeness in the center of stillness"—is unfalsifiable. The teacher cheerfully admits that, taken by itself, this profound doctrine yields no observational consequences. He then points out that, by themselves, the central statements of scientific theories are also incapable of generating observational consequences. Alas, if all that is demanded is that a doctrine be embedded in a group of statements with observational consequences, our imagined guru will easily slither off the hook. He replies, "You have forgotten that my doctrine has many other claims. For example, I believe that if quietness is wholeness in the center of stillness, then flowers bloom in the spring, bees gather pollen, and blinkered defenders of so-called science raise futile objections to the world's spiritual benefactors. You will see that these three predictions are borne out by experience. Of course, there are countless others. Perhaps when you see how my central message yields so much evident truth, you will recognize the wealth of evidence behind my claim. Quietness is wholeness in the center of stillness."

More formally, the trouble is that *any* statement can be coupled with other statements to produce observational consequences. Given any doctrine *D*, and any statement *O* that records the result of an observation, we can enable *D* to "predict" *O* by adding the extra assumption, "If *D*, then *O*." (In the example, *D* is "Quietness is wholeness in the center of stillness"; examples of *O* would be statements describing the blooming of particular flowers in the spring, the pollen gathering of specific bees, and so forth.)

The falsifiability criterion adopted from Popper—which I shall call the *naive falsificationist* criterion—is hopelessly flawed. It runs aground on a fundamental fact about the relation between theory and prediction: On their own, individual scientific laws, or the small groups of laws that are often identified as theories, do not have observational consequences. This crucial point about theories was first understood by the great historian and philosopher of science Pierre Duhem. Duhem saw clearly that individual scientific claims do not, and cannot, confront the evidence one by one. Rather, in his picturesque phrase, "Hypotheses are tested in bundles." Besides ruling out the possibility of testing an individual scientific theory (read, small group of laws), Duhem's insight has another startling consequence. We can only test relatively large bundles of claims. What this means is that when our experiments go awry we are not logically compelled to select any particular claim as the culprit. We can always save a cherished hypothesis from refutation by rejecting (however implausibly) one of the other members of the bundle. Of course, this is exactly what I did in the illustration of Newton and the apple above. Faced with disappointing results, I suggested that we could abandon the (tacit) additional claim that no large forces besides gravity were operating on the apple.

Creationists wheel out the ancient warhorse of naive falsificationism so that they can bolster their charge that evolutionary theory is not a science. The (very) brief course in deductive logic plus the whirlwind tour through naive falsificationism and its pitfalls enable us to see what is at the bottom of this seemingly important criticism. Creationists can appeal to naive falsificationism to show that evolution is not a science. But, given the traditional picture of theory and evidence I have sketched, one can appeal to naive falsificationism to show that *any* science is not a science. So, as with the charge that evolutionary change is unobservable, Creationists have again failed to find some "fault" of evolution not shared with every other science. (And, as we shall see, Creationists like some sciences, especially thermodynamics.) Consistent application of naive falsificationism can show that anybody's favorite science (whether it be quantum physics, molecular biology, or whatever) is not science. Of course, what this shows is that the naive falsificationist criterion is a very poor test of genuine science. To be fair, this point can cut both ways. Scientists who charge that "scientific" Creationism is unfalsifiable are not insulting the theory as much as they think.

SUCCESSFUL SCIENCE

Despite the inadequacies of naive falsificationism, there is surely something right in the idea that a science can succeed only if it can fail. An invulnerable "science" would not be science at all. To achieve a more adequate understanding of how a science can succeed and how it runs the risk of failure, let us look at one of the most successful sciences and at a famous episode in its development.

Newtonian celestial mechanics is one of the star turns in the history of science. Among its numerous achievements were convincing explanations of the orbits of most of the known planets. Newton and his successors viewed the solar system as a collection of bodies subject only to gravitational interactions; they used the law of gravitation and the laws of motion to compute the orbits. (Bodies whose effects were negligible in any particular case would be disregarded. For example, the gravitational attraction due to Mercury would not be considered in working out the orbit of Saturn.) The results usually tallied beautifully with astronomical observations. But one case proved difficult. The outermost known planet, Uranus, stubbornly followed an orbit that diverged from the best computations. By the early nineteenth century it was clear that something was wrong. Either astronomers erred in treating the solar system as a Newtonian gravitational system or there was some particular difficulty in applying the general method to Uranus.

Perhaps the most naive of falsificationists would have recommended that the central claim of Newtonian mechanics—the claim that the solar system is a Newtonian gravitational system—be abandoned. But there was obviously a more sensible strategy. Astronomers faced one problematical planet, and they asked themselves what made Uranus so difficult. Two of them, John Adams and Urbain Leverrier, came up with an answer. They proposed (independently) that there was a hitherto unobserved planet beyond Uranus. They computed the orbit of the postulated planet and demonstrated that the anomalies of the motion of Uranus could be explained if a planet followed this path. There was a straightforward way to test their proposal. Astronomers began to look for the new planet. Within a few years, the planet—Neptune—was found.

I will extract several morals from this success story. The first concerns an issue we originally encountered in Morris's "table of natural predictions:" What is the proper use of auxiliary hypotheses? Adams and Leverrier saved the central claim of Newtonian celestial mechanics by offering an auxiliary hypothesis. They maintained that there were more things in the heavens than had been dreamed of in previous natural philosophy. The anomalies in the orbit of Uranus could be explained on the assumption of an extra planet. Adams and Leverrier worked out the exact orbit of that planet so that they

could provide a detailed account of the perturbations—and so that they could tell their fellow astronomers where to look for Neptune. Thus, their auxiliary hypothesis was *independently testable.* The evidence for Neptune's existence was not just the anomalous motion of Uranus. The hypothesis could be checked independently of any assumptions about Uranus or about the correctness of Newtonian celestial mechanics—by making telescopic observations.

Since hypotheses are always tested in bundles, this method of checking presupposed other assumptions, in particular, the optical principles that justify the use of telescopes. The crucial point is that, while hypotheses are always tested in bundles, they can be tested in *different* bundles. An auxiliary hypothesis ought to be testable independently of the particular problem it is introduced to solve, independently of the theory it is designed to save.

While it is obvious in retrospect—indeed it was obvious at the time—that the problem with Uranus should not be construed as "falsifying" celestial mechanics, it is worth asking explicitly why scientists should have clung to Newton's theory in the face of this difficulty. The answer is not just that nothing succeeds like success, and that Newton's theory had been strikingly successful in calculating the orbits of the other planets. The crucial point concerns the way in which Newton's successes had been achieved. Newton was no opportunist, using one batch of assumptions to cope with Mercury, and then moving on to new devices to handle Venus. Celestial mechanics was a remarkably *unified* theory. It solved problems by invoking the same pattern of reasoning, or *problem-solving strategy,* again and again: From a specification of the positions of the bodies under study, use the law of gravitation to calculate the forces acting; from a statement of the forces acting, use the laws of dynamics to compute the equations of motion; solve the equations of motion to obtain the motions of the bodies. This single pattern of reasoning was applied in case after case to yield conclusions that were independently found to be correct.

At a higher level, celestial mechanics was itself contained in a broader theory. Newtonian physics, as a whole, was remarkably unified. It offered a strategy for solving a diverse collection of problems. Faced with *any* question about motion, the Newtonian suggestion was the same: Find the forces acting, from the forces and the laws of dynamics work out the equations of motion, and solve the equations of motion. The method was employed in a broad range of cases. The revolutions of planets, the motions of projectiles, tidal cycles and pendulum oscillations—all fell to the same problem-solving strategy.

We can draw a second moral. A science should be *unified*. A thriving science is not a gerrymandered patchwork but a coherent whole. Good theories consist of just one problem-solving strategy, or a small family of problem-solving strategies, that can be applied to a wide range of problems. The theory succeeds as it is able to encompass more and more problem areas. Failure looms when the basic problem-solving strategy (or strategies) can resolve almost none of the problems in its intended domain without the "aid" of untestable auxiliary hypotheses....

The final moral I want to draw from this brief look at Newtonian physics concerns *fecundity*. A great scientific theory, like Newton's, opens up new areas of research. Celestial mechanics led to the discovery of a previously unknown planet. Newtonian physics as a whole led to the development of previously unknown sciences. Because a theory presents a new way of looking at the world, it can lead us to ask new questions, and so to embark on new and fruitful lines of inquiry. Of the many flaws with the earlier picture of theories as sets of statements, none is more important than the misleading presentation of sciences as static and insular. Typically, a flourishing science is incomplete. At any time, it raises more questions than it can currently answer. But incompleteness is no vice. On the contrary, incompleteness is the mother of fecundity. Unresolved problems present challenges that enable a theory to flower in unanticipated ways. They also make the theory hostage to future developments. A good theory should be productive; it should raise new questions and presume that those questions can be answered without giving up its problem-solving strategies.

I have highlighted three characteristics of successful science. *Independent testability* is achieved when it is possible to test auxiliary hypotheses independently of the particular cases for which they are introduced. *Unification* is the result of applying a small family of problem-solving strategies to a broad class of cases. *Fecundity* grows out of incompleteness when a theory opens up new and profitable lines of investigation. Given these marks of successful science, it is easy to see how sciences can fall short, and how some doctrines can do so badly that they fail to count as science at all. A scientific theory begins to wither if some of its auxiliary assumptions can be saved from refutation only by rendering them untestable; or if its problem-solving strategies become a hodgepodge, a collection of unrelated methods, each designed for a separate recalcitrant case; or if the promise of the theory just fizzles, the few questions it raises leading only to dead ends.

When does a doctrine fail to be a science? If a doctrine fails sufficiently abjectly as a science, then it fails to be a science. Where bad science becomes egregious enough, pseudoscience begins. The example of Newtonian physics shows us how to replace the simple (and incorrect) naive falsificationist criterion with a battery of tests. Do the doctrine's problem-solving strategies encounter recurrent difficulties in a significant range of cases? Are the problem-solving strategies an opportunistic collection of unmotivated and unrelated methods? Does the doctrine have too cozy a relationship with auxiliary hypotheses, applying its strategies with claims that can be "tested" only in their applications? Does the doctrine refuse to follow up on unresolved problems, airily dismissing them as "exceptional cases"? Does the doctrine restrict the domain of its methods, forswearing excursions into new areas of investigation where embarrassing questions might arise? If all, or many, of these tests are positive, then the doctrine is not a poor scientific theory. It is not a scientific theory at all.

The account of successful science that I have given not only enables us to replace the naive falsificationist criterion with something better. It also provides a deeper understanding of how theories are justified. Predictive success is one important way in which a theory can win our acceptance. But it is not the only way. In general, theories earn their laurels by solving problems—providing answers that can be independently recognized as correct—and by their fruitfulness. Making a prediction is answering a special kind of question. The astronomers who used celestial mechanics to predict the motion of Mars were answering the question of where Mars would be found. Yet, very frequently, our questions do not concern *what* occurs, but *why* it occurs. We already know that something happens and we want an explanation. Science offers us explanations by setting the phenomena within a unified framework. Using a widely applicable problem-solving strategy, together with independently confirmed auxiliary hypotheses, scientists show that what happened was to be expected. It was known before Newton that the orbits of the planets are approximately elliptical.

One of the great achievements of Newton's celestial mechanics was to apply its problem-solving strategy to deduce that the orbit of any planet will be approximately elliptical, thereby explaining the shape of the orbits. In general, science is at least as concerned with reducing the number of unexplained phenomena as it is with generating correct predictions.

The most global Creationist attack on evolutionary theory is the claim that evolution is not a science. If this claim were correct, then the dispute about what to teach in high school science classes would be over. In earlier parts of this chapter, we saw how Creationists were able to launch their broad criticisms. If one accepts the idea that science requires proof, or if one adopts the naive falsificationist criterion, then the theory of evolution—and every other scientific theory—will turn out not to be a part of science. So Creationist standards for science imply that there is no science to be taught.

However, we have seen that Creationist standards rest on a very poor understanding of science. In light of a clearer picture of the scientific enterprise, I have provided a more realistic group of tests for good science, bad science, and pseudoscience.

MindTap®

MindTap is a fully online, highly personalized learning experience built upon Cengage Learning content. MindTap combines student learning tools—readings, multimedia, activities, and assessments—into a singular Learning Path that guides students through the course.

PART IV

Mind and Its Place in Nature

TO A LARGE DEGREE, what has come to be known as the "mind–body problem" in philosophy is a product of the philosophy of René Descartes. How can things differing as radically as minds (or souls) and bodies, in Descartes's conception, be so intimately related, as they clearly are, in every human person? Bodies are solid chunks of material stuff, extended in three-dimensional space, publicly observable and measurable, possessed of a certain mass and velocity, and capable of causing things to happen, in accordance with the invariant laws of mechanics, by transmitting their impact in "collisions" with other material things. A mind, on the other hand, is directly "observable" only by the person who owns it; only he can think his thoughts, feel his emotions, suffer his pains. Although, under certain circumstances, someone else can cut open his skull and see and touch his living *brain*, there is no conceivable way for another to see or touch his mind or its beliefs, sensations, and desires. Minds, moreover, have no size or shape or spatial location, no mass, or velocity, or capacity to make impact.

Nevertheless, to common sense, it seems certain that minds and bodies do causally interact. When I intend, or wish, or desire (mental events) to raise my arm, up it goes (bodily event); and when a sliver of wood penetrates my flesh (bodily event), I feel pain (mental event). It would surely seem, then, that in normal cases of action, mental events *cause* physical ones and that, in sensation and perception, physical events *cause* mental ones. Yet how can this be? How can the mind, a massless, weightless, unextended thing, push up against a nerve cell and cause an impulse to be transmitted along a nerve to a muscle? And how can physical stimuli such as wood slivers or even light rays penetrate a thing that has no size or location, and cause it to have an experience? Isn't this as inconceivable as a collision between a physical object and a ghost? This is the kind of difficulty cited by many of Descartes's own contemporaries in criticism of his philosophy.[1]

Many important seventeenth-century philosophers, no matter how impressed in other ways by the "Cartesian philosophy" (as the philosophy of Descartes came to be called), found Descartes's theory of interaction between mind and body unacceptable. Some, therefore, came to abandon the part of the Descartes's philosophy that generated the difficulty: his **dualism**, or theory that mind and matter are distinct and independent kinds of substances, each capable of existing quite independently of the

---

[1] A number of distinguished philosophers, theologians, and scientists, including Pierre Gassendi, Thomas Hobbes, and Antoine Arnauld, were invited to comment on the manuscript of Descartes's *Meditations* before it was published. Their "Objections" were then forwarded to Descartes, who in turn composed "Replies," and published the whole exchange along with the original work. The entire discussion is strongly recommended to the serious student of Descartes's philosophy.

other.[2] One alternative was **idealism**: the theory that the body itself is nothing but a collection of actual or possible sense data—sights, sounds, touches, and smells. George Berkeley thought this way. According to this theory, there are only minds and their mental "contents"; hence, there are no problems of causal interaction between radically different kinds of substances. Yet another alternative was **materialism**—the theory that mind is reducible to matter.[3] Still other philosophers maintained a kind of dualism but abandoned the common-sense view that mind and body really do interact causally. Some held, for example, that the wood sliver's penetration of my flesh does not *cause* me pain; rather, it is the *occasion* for God, whose infinite nature somehow encompasses both mind and matter, to cause me to feel pain, and similarly that my desire to raise my arm is simply the occasion for God's causing my arm to go up. This is the theory called **occasionalism**. Others held the view called **parallelism**, according to which mind and body only appear to interact because of a kind of "pre-established harmony" between their life histories. Gottfried Leibniz likened this parallelism to two clocks that strike at the same moment, having been wound up together and each designed to keep accurate time, in causal independence of each other.

We have included two defenses of Cartesian dualism in this volume. The locus classicus—Descartes's *Meditations*—appears in its entirety in Part III. We choose to open this Part IV of the book with Brie Gertler's contemporary defense of the Cartesian position. Her master argument is quite straightforward: We can properly conceive of having a mental state (a belief, a conjecture, an experience of pain) while being disembodied. If we can properly conceive of having disembodied mental states, then it is possible that such states are disembodied. If it is possible that they are disembodied, then mental states are not identical with physical states. If mental states are not identical to physical states, therefore dualism is true.

If dualism is true, then, as we have seen, it is difficult to understand how mental states can cause physical outcomes. This is the worry known as **epiphenomenalism**, which holds that the mind is not itself a material thing; rather, it is a distinct but causally impotent by-product (an "epiphenomenon") of the world charted by physics. Gertler admits that this is something of a worry, but holds that the problems that face her opponents are graver still.

In the next selection, Frank Jackson offers a powerful defense of epiphenomenalism. Along the way, he presents perhaps the greatest difficulty facing any physicalist (i.e., materialist): "the qualia problem." **Qualia** are the peculiarly subjective, felt qualities of experience, such as the smell of a hard-boiled egg, the taste of horseradish, or the fiery image of a sunset. Jackson presents a much discussed argument designed to show that no amount of knowledge about how the brain works can give us knowledge of what it is to feel such things. Therefore, according to

---

[2]Strictly speaking, the traditional mind–body problem was generated by a conjunction of two theories: (1) dualism as defined above and (2) the theory sometimes called **two-way interactionism**, the latter being simply the commonsense assumption that mind and body can interact causally—sometimes mental events causing bodily events, as in volition, sometimes bodily events causing mental events, as when a decayed tooth causes pain sensations.

[3]*Materialism* as the name of a philosophical theory should not be confused with various other senses of the word. Philosophical materialists are *not* (necessarily) "persons who tend to give undue importance to material possessions and comforts." Nor are they (necessarily) "those who think that everybody ought to put their 'material well-being' (as measured in dollars and cents) above all other considerations." A philosophical materialist could, with consistency, denounce materialism in these other senses.

Jackson, these sorts of mental experiences cannot be physical ones. Jackson concludes that physicalism must be false.

One genuinely materialistic alternative to dualism and epiphenomenalism is the **identity theory**, which holds that mental events (the occurrence of aches and pains, sensations, afterimages, desires, and thoughts) are simply identical with brain processes—"identical" in the same way that lightning flashes are "identical" with electrical discharges. Here the identity in question is **intertheoretic reduction**. In these cases, we reduce items in our commonsense theory of the world to items in a mature physics or neuroscience.

There are many people who don't believe that such reductions are possible. One reason is that they fail to see any good argument for such reductions. Another is their attachment to arguments that support dualist views. Both of these motivations are questioned in the readings from our representative materialist, David Papineau.

The bulk of Papineau's piece is devoted to the presentation and development of what he takes to be the central argument for a reductive, antidualist, materialist view of the mind. The argument begins with the claim that conscious mental events have physical effects. So, for instance, *wanting* to eat a chocolate bar and *believing* that there is a chocolate bar on the table in front of you will lead to some physical effects—namely, your arm moving through space, grasping the bar, unwrapping it, and eating eat. The second premise of his argument is that all physical effects have wholly physical causes. Finally, Papineau argues that these physical effects don't have distinct causes. It follows that the conscious states that cause physical effects are themselves physical states.

While Papineau, like almost everyone else, is perfectly willing to assume the existence of minds and mental events, another, more radical form of physicalism—**eliminative materialism**—is unwilling to make such a concession. On this view, championed by Paul Churchland in our selections, mental states and processes as we ordinarily conceive of them really have a status like that of witches, and must simply be eliminated from our theorizing about ourselves. On the other side, however, many cognitive scientists believe that some sense will have to be made of our ordinary notions of mind. The development of computer technology in recent years has spurred the development of *functional* approaches to the mind. According to **functionalist** theories, the identity theory (also called **type physicalism**) is problematic because it holds that the mental and intellectual properties of a "system" (e.g., a person) depend on the specific physical (brain) properties of that system, whereas apparently many quite different physical systems (e.g., those that are constructed to process information) can perform the same intelligent tasks.

Many issues central to the mind–body problem are pursued in the next chapter, "Can Non-humans Think?" We begin this chapter with Alan Turing's classic paper on the subject—a paper, written midway through the last century, that was far ahead of its time, and which supplied the basis of many of the arguments nowadays offered on the subject. Next comes John Searle's provocative paper "Minds, Brains, and Programs," which challenges the adequacy of a certain form of functionalism, the sort exemplified by current attempts to program computers to perform "intelligent" tasks. Searle contends that in order to have "intelligent" mental states, it is not enough that we suppose that the system is running the right program, because these mental states are not the kinds that *can* be programmed into a machine. Searle then considers a wide variety of possible objections to his view and attempts to refute each.

As far back as the seventeenth century, at least, philosophers have been fascinated by apparent similarities between human (rational) beings and machines. Excited by discoveries in medicine and physiology, some eighteenth-century philosophers asked whether humans might really be nothing but machines themselves. In our own day, most of the excitement comes from those scientists who work on the machine side rather than from new discoveries in human biology, though the latter have been accumulating at a great rate, too. This new emphasis is reflected in the way the philosophical interest is expressed. Now we do not ask whether, in principle, machines could be designed that are a kind of human—that is to say, intelligent, conscious beings like us. Many philosophers would answer unhesitatingly, "No, of course not. Computers are made of wires and springs, silicon chips, and the like, not protoplasm (flesh and blood) like us." To that kind of remark William Lycan has a ready reply: "What matters to mentality is not the stuff of which one is made, but the complex way in which that stuff is organized."

The concluding articles in Part IV relate the discussion back to one of Descartes's original concerns: whether "in death there is an end of me." This question, of course, presupposes the questions preceding it about the nature of the subject of consciousness. If body and mind are one and the same thing, or if mind is a mere by-product of body, then it would follow that the disintegration of mind (soul, self) would proceed at the same pace as the disintegration of the body. But if our minds are distinct substances and causally powerful in their own right, then it is at least possible that we can survive the death of our bodies.

If we are to make philosophical progress in our discussions of the possibility of survival, we must become clear about a set of prior questions that are not normally treated in works on the mind–body problem—namely, questions about *personal identity*. Who or what am I, this entity whose possible survival of death is under discussion? Am I simply this body and nothing more? What then of my belief that this body "belongs" to me, that the owner is one thing and the body another? Am I simply my mind? Am I a self that somehow encompasses both body and mind? Could I be the *same self* that I am now if I had none of my present memories, or if I suddenly discovered myself with an altogether different body (for example, with four legs and a tail)? How much can I change without ceasing to be the person I am now? These are only some of the riddles associated with the elusive concept of personal identity. Still others are suggested by more extravagant possibilities: resurrection of the dead, reincarnation, transmigration of souls, bodily transfers, multiple or alternate possession of a body by various persons, brain transplants, and "brain rejuvenations"—examples drawn from theology, psychic research, abnormal psychology, and science fiction.

The chapter on "Personal Identity and the Survival of Death" starts off with a classic excerpt from John Locke, who argues that it is a person's consciousness, in the form of memories of past experiences, that make him or her the same person through different times, even as the body completely changes its characteristics and appearance. If the mind of a prince were magically inserted into the body of a cobbler, Locke argues in a famous example, we would all say that the person with the cobbler's appearance is the prince, and that only his body, not his personal identity, has changed. Thomas Reid, an eighteenth-century Scottish philosopher, developed a theory of personal identity that was motivated in large part by his dissatisfaction with Locke's theory. A human person, Reid argues, is quite unlike a physical object, which is constantly changing its properties so that over a period of time it will have nothing in common with, and hence not be identical with, its earlier precursors. Persons, on the other hand, are simple and indivisible, thus capable of maintaining their identities throughout their histories. The unregenerate skeptic David Hume, however, arguing from empiricist premises, rejects the claim that there is such a thing as an unchanging substantial self as opposed to the relatively fleeting thoughts and feelings revealed in introspective consciousness—that which passes as "self-awareness."

Derek Parfit, a contemporary philosopher who teaches at Oxford, takes Hume's views quite seriously. Indeed, he defends a claim very like that of Hume, and also, as it turns out, that of the Buddha. Parfit's defense is based on a kind of example that he has helped to make famous in philosophical circles—one involving divided brains, and our intuitions about who is who after such operations.

Shelly Kagan next invites us to reflect on what *matters* about postmortem survival. As he notes, most of the discussion about personal identity and postmortem survival has been focused on the very possibility of such survival. But he asks us to pause and to reflect on why we think (if we do) that surviving our own death would even be desirable. As he shows, if any one of a number of popular views about personal identity is correct, then surviving one's death is not all it's cracked up to be—in fact, it may well be of no importance at all!

In the deathbed dialogue by John Perry that concludes this chapter, Perry focuses sharply on the area where the problem of survival and the riddles of personal identity intersect. A dying professor, her old friend (a clergyman), and her student discuss quite spontaneously the famous philosophical theories of John Locke, Joseph Butler, and Anthony Collins—seminal thinkers of the seventeenth and eighteenth centuries—about personal identity. At issue is the question of what sense, if any, can be made of the very idea of personal survival.

CHAPTER 1

THE MIND–BODY PROBLEM

1.1 In Defense of Mind–Body Dualism

BRIE GERTLER

Brie Gertler works primarily on philosophical problems in epistemology and the philosophy of mind. She teaches at the University of Virginia.

How quaint, the idea that our minds somehow float free of the cold, hard, physical world. Surely dualism is the stuff of fantasy, an indulgence of poets and daydreamers, an echo of antiquated worldviews long ago demolished by the relentless progress of science. Though we may occasionally find comfort in imagining that our minds are special, in our more sober moments we must face the facts: our thoughts and feelings, and those of our loved ones, are just as much a part of the brute material order as sticks and stones.

This sentiment expresses a common attitude. The prevalence of this attitude may explain why physicalism, the view that sensations and other mental states are entirely physical, is generally the default position about the mind. On first approaching the mind–body problem, most scientifically minded people assume that physicalism simply has to be true.

However, the sentiment above seriously misrepresents present-day versions of dualism, the belief that some mental states are nonphysical. Many contemporary dualists are fully *naturalistic*. That is, they hold that mental states are just as much a part of the natural order as sticks and stones; and they favor a scientific approach to the mind, one that is independent of religious considerations. In essence, the contemporary dispute between physicalists and naturalistic dualists is a disagreement about what kinds of *data* there are about the nature of mind, and what sort of *theory*—dualist or physicalist—best explains the data.

In this essay, I defend naturalistic dualism. I take, as my starting point, an argument made by René Descartes in his *Meditations*. I expand and defend this argument, drawing on some ideas developed by contemporary philosophers.[1] The expanded argument is, I think, much more powerful than most physicalists recognize. After making my case for dualism, I offer some criticisms of physicalism. The paper will close by defending dualism from the charge that the picture of reality it provides is unacceptably *spooky*.

But first, I must explain in more detail the point at issue between physicalists and dualists. What is it, precisely, that physicalists assert, and

dualists deny? Our answer to this question will reveal the type of reasoning that a defense of dualism must employ.

1. PHYSICALISM, DUALISM, AND THE NEED FOR THOUGHT EXPERIMENTS

Physicalism comes in various forms. I will focus on the most straightforward version, the *identity thesis*, which has been defended by numerous philosophers. According to the identity thesis, every type of mental state is identical to some type of physical state. Here is an example of a particular identity claim, relating pain to C-fibers, a group of nerve cells that fire when pain is experienced.

(**P**) Pain = C-fiber stimulation[2]

In this statement, "pain" refers to a type of sensation, the type of sensation you have when you stub your toe or bite your lip. This type of sensation is usually caused by tissue damage (in the toe or the lip), but it needn't be. For instance, a person who has had both feet amputated could nonetheless experience the "stubbed toe" sensation. So damage to the toe is merely the ordinary cause of that sort of sensation; the sensation itself is not spatially located *in* the toe. And it is the sensation itself, not its cause, which is most obviously a *mental* state. Throughout this essay, "pain" will refer to the sensation itself, and not its usual or real cause.

Actually, identity theorists are not committed to any particular identity thesis, such as (P). Their key claim is that every type of mental state is identical to some type of physical state, but they needn't claim that science has yet uncovered any particular identities. Still, (P) illustrates the *kind* of identity the physicalist has in mind. I will continue to use it in this way.

The first thing to notice about (P) is that it is extremely strong. It does not say merely that pain is perfectly correlated with C-fiber stimulation. Nor does it say that pain will always accompany, and be accompanied by, C-fiber stimulation. Rather, it says that pain just *is*—is nothing over and above—C-fiber stimulation. This means that pain *couldn't possibly* be present in the absence of C-fiber stimulation, or vice versa, any more than Superman could be present in the absence of Clark Kent, or water could be present in the absence of H$_2$O. So an identity statement goes beyond a claim about what is *actually* the case, to a claim about what is *possible*—or, really, what is *impossible*.

Because identity statements (statements about what is identical to what) entail that certain scenarios are impossible, they cannot be confirmed by empirical methods alone. To see why this is, imagine that we are in the best-case situation for empirical investigation: We are somehow able to monitor all of the creatures in the universe, and to determine which creatures have C-fibers that are undergoing stimulation, and which creatures are experiencing pain. (To determine whether people are experiencing pain, we might simply ask them; to determine this for infants and animals, we might observe their behavior.) Suppose that we learn that these are perfectly correlated: C-fiber stimulation is present in all and only those creatures that are currently experiencing pain. Even this very tidy result does not establish the identity thesis, for we still do not know whether it is *possible* that one of these be present in the absence of the other. The perfect correlation might be an odd coincidence. Or, more plausibly, it might be that one of these causes the other. (A prominent dualist position holds that physical events, like the firing of C-fibers, *cause* mental events like pain. This allows us to explain how aspirin can block pain by affecting the brain.) Or it might be that pain and C-fiber stimulation are products of a common cause: Perhaps stubbing one's toe simultaneously causes both the pain sensation and C-fiber stimulation. These explanations of the correlation are alternatives to saying that pain is *identical to* C-fiber stimulation (e.g., if C-fiber stimulation causes pain then these cannot be identical, for nothing causes itself).

The upshot is that even a perfect correlation does not establish the identity thesis. It shows only that one of these factors *is not*, in fact,

present in the absence of the other. But it does not show that one of these factors *could not possibly* be present in the absence of the other. And the identity thesis requires this latter, stronger claim.

If the identity thesis is true, then physicalism is true. Dualists deny the identity thesis, and believe that mental states are distinct from (that is, they are not identical to) physical states. Dualism thus implies that it is *possible* that pain is present in the absence of C-fiber stimulation. Dualists can accept that these are perfectly correlated; but, they claim, these are two distinct states, and so it is not *impossible* that one is present while the other is absent. (Again, perhaps their perfect correlation is due to some causal connection.)

I will defend dualism by arguing that it is possible that you experience pain even if you are in *no* physical state, that is, even if you have no body whatsoever. If pain can occur in the absence of *any* physical state, then physicalism is false.[3]

Because the dispute between physicalism and dualism concerns whether a particular scenario is *possible,* empirical evidence will not resolve it. We must therefore turn to another sort of evidence, gained from thought experiments. Thought experiments can help us to determine whether situations that don't actually occur—such as the presence of pain in the absence of C-fiber stimulation—are nonetheless possible.

Unlike scientific experiments, which are ordinarily conducted in a laboratory, thought experiments are conducted from the comfort of the armchair. One performs a thought experiment by attempting to imagine a given scenario, and then carefully reflecting on the outcome of this exercise. It may seem odd to think that such armchair reflection can yield genuine progress on a thorny issue like the mind–body problem. But because the dispute between physicalists and dualists concerns the sheer *possibility* of a given scenario, neither of these positions can be established without thought experiments.[4]

Here are some examples of thought experiments designed to reveal whether a given scenario is possible.

(A) You have never seen a book that is 100 feet tall. (According to *Guinness World Records,* the world's largest book—a photographic tour of the Asian country of Bhutan—is 5 feet tall by 7 feet wide.) Still, a moment's reflection reveals that you can imagine a 100-foot-tall book. While the high costs of production and the dim sales prospects mean that no one is likely ever to create such a book, these impediments don't absolutely *rule out* its creation. For instance, it is easy to imagine the production being financed by an eccentric millionaire.

We have just resolved the question, "Is it possible that a book be 100 feet tall?" by use of a thought experiment. On reflection, there seemed to be only practical obstacles to the creation of a 100-foot-tall book, and we could imagine overcoming those obstacles. Short of building the giant book ourselves, it is hard to see how this question could be resolved without the use of thought experiments.

(B) You have never seen an object that is blue all over and (simultaneously) orange all over. Can you imagine such an object? It seems clear that you cannot. This exercise of imagination leads you to believe that nothing could possibly be blue all over and orange all over.

(C) You have never encountered a married bachelor. I expect that you will find yourself unable to conceive of a married bachelor, since you will be unable to conceive of a married person who meets the requirements for being a bachelor (which include, of course, being unmarried). Because nothing can be simultaneously married and unmarried, it is impossible that there be any married bachelors.

In the first two cases, you drew on your *concepts* (**book, blue object,** etc.) in trying to *imagine* the described scenario. But in this third case your concepts are more directly involved, because the thought experiment involves *conceiving* rather than *imagining.* To imagine something is to form a sensory (perhaps visual) picture of it. Because no picture of a man will fully express his marital status, mere imagination will not do the trick here. Rather, you exercise the concepts directly, and find that you cannot

conceive of a married bachelor because your concept **bachelor** includes the concept **unmarried,** and nothing that satisfies that concept can simultaneously satisfy the concept **married.** (It is no surprise that *conceive* and *concept* have the same Latin root.)

Of course, the results of a thought experiment are not guaranteed to be accurate. Like experiments done in the laboratory, thought experiments can go astray in any number of ways: Your imagination may be limited in a way that makes you unable to imagine a 100-foot-tall book; you may mistakenly think that "bachelor" refers to any man who lives alone; etc. But as with other types of experiment, these mistakes can be minimized if we take care in designing and performing the experiment. Most importantly, engaging in thought experiments is our only way of determining whether scenarios that haven't actually occurred, and will never actually occur, are nonetheless possible.

In these thought experiments, we try to imagine or conceive a particular scenario, to determine whether it is possible. This exercise is known as a *conceivability test.* There are other types of thought experiments as well, but conceivability tests lie at the heart of most of the leading arguments for dualism, including the one that I will now present.

2. THE DISEMBODIMENT ARGUMENT

The argument that I will use is a descendant of an argument given by Descartes. I will call it the Disembodiment Argument. Its basic structure is disarmingly simple, but of course the devil—or, as Descartes might say, the malicious demon—is in the details.

The argument centers on the possibility that pain is present in the absence of any physical state.[5] Arguments for dualism usually focus on pain or other sensations, because the experience of sensations seems to present the greatest challenge to physicalism. Descartes himself believed that thoughts, such as "my senses sometimes mislead me," posed an equal challenge to physicalism, but contemporary philosophers are divided on that claim. We needn't concern ourselves with that issue. If our argument succeeds in showing that pain can be present in the absence of any physical state, we will have established dualism for we will have shown that pain is not identical to anything physical, and thus that at least *some* mental states (viz., pains) are not physical. And that is precisely what the dualist maintains, and the physicalist denies.

As with other thought experiments, this one requires that you actively engage in the exercise of imagining or conceiving. This will unfortunately require a tiny bit of pain. So pinch yourself—lightly!—and, while doing so, put yourself into the position of the "I" in the following line of reasoning.

1. Even though I firmly believe that I have physical features, I can conceive of experiencing *this very pain* while possessing no physical features. In other words, I can conceive of experiencing *this very pain* while disembodied.
2. If I can conceive of a particular scenario occurring, then that scenario is possible.

So,

3. It is possible that *this very pain* occurs in a disembodied being.
4. If *this very pain* was identical to some physical
   state, then it could not possibly occur in a disembodied being.

So,

5. *This very pain* is not identical to any physical state.

So,

(Conclusion) The identity thesis, which says that every mental state is identical to some physical state, is false.

The major premises in this argument are (1) and (2). Premise (3) follows from these; premise (4)

expresses an accepted fact about the nature of identity; and premise (5) follows from (3) and (4).

The best way to target this argument, then, is to deny either (1) or (2). This is precisely what physicalists have done. I will first discuss premise (2), and then take up premise (1).

Premise (2)

The chief criticism of premise (2) is that it involves a kind of intellectual hubris. In conceiving of something, we are simply exercising our *concepts*. And why should we think that our concepts accurately reflect the way the world is? Perhaps we are out of touch with reality, and our concepts don't correspond to real objects or properties. In that case, the fact that we can conceive of a particular scenario occurring provides no reason to think that that scenario is genuinely possible.

In reply to this criticism, it is crucial to note that *all* of our reasoning—in philosophy and elsewhere—must use some concepts, to define the topic we are investigating. In biology, we begin with some concept of reproduction, which empirical investigation may lead us to refine. In ethics, we begin with some concept of the good, which philosophical reasoning helps us to clarify and develop. And of course physicalists also rely on concepts—including concepts of the physical —in defending their view.

Occasionally, we may find that nothing satisfies a given concept, and so we may abandon investigations relating to it. This is what happened in the case of witchcraft: Most people came to deny that anything in reality corresponded to the concept **witchcraft,** and the study of witchcraft was replaced by research into superstitions and mental pathologies, phenomena that led to the mistaken belief in witchcraft. But while we must allow for the possibility that we'll refine or even abandon our concepts, concepts are indispensable at the outset of an investigation. For there is no way to proceed with an inquiry unless we have *some* concept of the subject matter we are investigating. The blanket objection that conceivability arguments are illegitimate because they use *our concepts* is, then, misguided.

However, there is a more nuanced version of the worry that premise (2) oversteps our intellectual bounds. Unlike the previous objection, this one acknowledges that we must employ concepts in order to reason at all. And it concedes that thought experiments using simple, straightforward concepts such as **bachelor** can help us to determine what is possible. But it rejects premise (2) on the grounds that it is too general: Not *everything* we can conceive is possible. For some of our concepts are clouded or obscure, and so cannot play the proper role in conceivability tests. In particular, this objection says that our concepts **pain** and **physical** are limited or unclear. Using such faulty concepts, what we can or cannot conceive does not reveal what is or is not possible.

This type of objection was advanced against Descartes' original argument by his contemporary Antoine Arnauld. Arnauld pointed out that a geometry student who hadn't yet encountered the proof of the Pythagorean Theorem could argue as follows:

> I can conceive of a right triangle with the following property: the square of its hypotenuse is unequal to the sum of the squares of its other two sides. Therefore, it is possible for a right triangle to have this property.

Clearly, this argument is invalid: The fact that the student could conceive this scenario does not mean that the scenario is possible.

Descartes anticipated Arnauld's objection, and had a ready response. He acknowledged that his argument will fail unless the relevant concepts are "complete and adequate." The student was able to conceive of a right triangle that violated the Pythagorean Theorem only because his concept **right triangle** was limited. But our concepts of mentality and of the physical are not limited in this way, or so Descartes claimed. That's why he thought that our ability to conceive disembodied pains was genuine evidence that disembodied pains were possible.[6]

In effect, Descartes' reply deflects attention away from premise (2), and makes premise (1) the focus of the argument. For everyone can agree that, if we have a comprehensive understanding of something, then conceivability tests provide a reliable guide to what is possible, involving that thing. It is because you fully understand what it means to be a bachelor that, when you find yourself unable to conceive of a married bachelor, you can justifiedly conclude that it's impossible that anything be a married bachelor. And if the geometry student gained a comprehensive grasp of right triangles, then he could similarly rely on conceivability tests. For a comprehensive grasp of right triangles would prevent him from conceiving of a right triangle that violated the Pythagorean Theorem.

Let us agree, then, that conceivability tests can reveal what is possible or impossible, *so long as the concepts involved are sufficiently comprehensive*. This amounts to qualifying premise (2), to read as follows:

2.* If, *using concepts that are sufficiently comprehensive,* I can conceive of a particular scenario occurring, then that scenario is possible.

Our new premise (2*) is unobjectionable, for it is trivially true. To say that a concept is "sufficiently comprehensive," in this sense, is just to say that it is suitable for use in conceivability tests. It follows, then, that conceivability tests *using sufficiently comprehensive concepts* reveal what is (and what is not) possible.

Because (2*) is trivially true, the burden of the argument now falls on the first premise. Let us consider premise (1) in more detail.

Premise (1)

We must modify premise (1) to fit our new second premise. It now becomes (1*).

1.* *Using concepts that are sufficiently comprehensive,* I can conceive of experiencing *this very pain* while disembodied.

Together, (1*) and (2*) yield (3), so the rest of the argument proceeds as before.

Again because (2*) is trivially true, the entire weight of the argument now rests on (1*). To evaluate (1*), we must determine whether the concepts at work in the "pinch" test are sufficiently comprehensive. That is, when you conceive of experiencing *this very pain* (the pinch) while disembodied, are your concepts **pain** and **physical** sufficiently clear and complete, like your concept **bachelor**? Or might they be confused or incomplete, like the geometry student's concept **right triangle**?

This is the core issue on which the Disembodiment Argument rests. The argument will succeed only if your concepts of pain and of the physical are sufficiently comprehensive to allow you to conclude, from the fact that you can conceive of experiencing pain while disembodied, that this is possible. Physicalists generally deny this. They believe that, in conceiving of disembodied pain, we are like Arnauld's geometry student, who conceives of a right triangle that violates the Pythagorean Theorem.

I now turn to discuss our concepts of the physical and of pain. We will see that **pain** plays a much more important role in the Disembodiment Argument.

3. OUR CONCEPT OF THE PHYSICAL

Consider what "physical" means. What conditions must something meet in order to qualify as *physical*?

Descartes thought that the essence of the physical was to be extended in space. But modern physics posits entities—such as fields and waves—that sit uncomfortably with the notion of spatial extension. And because modern physics is still evolving, we should not define the physical in terms of a currently favored theory. For further advances in physics might eventually lead us to reject whatever theory we currently favor.

In response to these worries, many philosophers now conceptualize the physical, for purposes of the mind–body problem, as "the inanimate" or "the nonmental."[7] In this way, the concept **physical** is defined by contrast with the concepts **animate** or **mental**. This suggestion nicely captures the issue at hand. On this reading of "physical," the central point of contention between physicalists and dualists is as follows:

> Are mental states ultimately, fundamentally non-mental? Are mental states, states of mental things like you and me, ultimately identical (or reducible) to states that are *also* had by inanimate, non-mental things, like sticks and stones?

The dualist will answer "no," claiming that mental states are part of the basic fabric of the universe. The physicalist will answer "yes," claiming that mental states are simply patterns of basic physical (that is, nonmental) phenomena. I propose that we adopt this way of conceptualizing the physical. States that are physical, in this sense, are ultimately constituted by phenomena that are nonmental.

As regards the Disembodiment Argument, this understanding of **physical** will affect how you perform the conceivability test described in (1*). To be disembodied is to have *no* physical—ultimately nonmental—features. So you are to attempt to conceive of experiencing *this very pain* while being a *purely* mental entity, an entity that, at least for a moment, has no features in common with sticks and stones.[8]

I now turn to the more significant concept for our purposes, the concept **pain.**

4. OUR CONCEPT OF PAIN

Recall that the Disembodiment Argument will succeed only if our concept of pain is sufficiently comprehensive, in the sense explained above. Is it?

Someone with the concept **pain** might be ignorant of non-essential features of pain: for instance, whether aspirin or ibuprofen more quickly relieves pain. But such features are not relevant to the possibility of disembodied pain. The Disembodiment Argument requires only that we grasp the *essential* features of pain, those that are relevant to the possibility of disembodied pain.[9]

Still, establishing that our concept **pain** is sufficiently comprehensive, in this sense, is a difficult task. The standard expressed by "sufficiently comprehensive" is very high, and as physicalists are quick to point out, most of our concepts do not meet this standard. The classic example concerns water. Before learning chemistry, each of us could presumably conceive that water was present in the absence of H_2O. And arguably, we can still conceive this. (For we can imagine that chemists develop a new technique for analyzing substances and that, using this technique, they discover that all of the stuff we call "water" contains an additional element, one undetectable by previous methods.) But while we can conceive that water is present in the absence of H_2O, this scenario is of course impossible, because water simply *is* H_2O. Clearly, then, our concept **water** is not sufficiently comprehensive to be used in this type of conceivability test.

Physicalists who cite the water example predict that, once neuroscience has developed more fully, we will come to regard our ability to conceive of disembodied pain in a similar way. That is, we will see that it involves the use of inadequate concepts, and therefore provides no real evidence for the possibility of disembodied pain, just as our ability to conceive of water that is not H_2O provides no evidence for the possibility of non-H_2O water.

To defend the Disembodiment Argument, we need to block the analogy between **water** and **pain**. This requires showing that our concept **pain** is importantly different from concepts such as **water,** to justify the claim that **pain** (unlike **water**) is sufficiently comprehensive. And this is precisely what I will now attempt to do.

First, we must understand *why* our concept **water** is not sufficiently comprehensive. It fails to meet this standard for a simple reason. Namely, we conceptualize water as something that has a *hidden essence,* an essence that can be discovered only by careful scientific investigation. (The hidden essence of water is in fact H_2O.) This is why armchair reflection will not reveal whether non-H_2O water is really possible.

But we don't conceptualize pain this way. *We conceptualize pain as something that has no hidden essence.* Pain wears its essential nature on its sleeve, as it were.

Here we have reached the fundamental, driving idea behind the Disembodiment Argument. As we conceptualize pain, pain has no hidden essence. If you *feel* that you are in pain, then you are in pain; determining whether you are in pain does not require scientific investigation. For the appearance (feeling) of pain just is pain itself. As one contemporary commentator has put it, "there is no appearance/reality distinction in the case of sensations" such as pain.[10]

How does this observation—that the appearance of pain is pain itself—help us to defend (1*)? The challenge, in defending (1*), is to show that our concept **pain** is sufficiently comprehensive for use in conceivability tests. The observation that the *feeling* of pain *is* pain accomplishes this. To determine whether you are really in pain, you need not investigate beyond the feeling of pain. For instance, you need not examine your brain to see whether your C-fibers are undergoing stimulation. (By contrast, investigation *is* required to determine whether something that seems like water—that looks and tastes like water—really is water.) This implies that pain has no hidden essence. So even if pain is perfectly correlated with C-fiber stimulation, C-fiber stimulation is not *essential* to pain; for if it were, then C-fiber stimulation would be the hidden essence of pain, and you couldn't be sure that you were in pain unless you determined that your C-fibers were firing. And if C-fiber stimulation is not essential to pain, then it is not *impossible* that pain be present in the absence of C-fiber stimulation. Hence, pain is not identical to C-fiber stimulation.

Let me be clear about my case here. I am not suggesting that we can't be mistaken about pain.[11] My point is just that there is *some* evidence for pain that is absolutely conclusive, for it is, simultaneously, evidence for pain and pain itself. This is evidence of the standard sort: that *hurting* sensation. That sensation is both the appearance of pain and the reality of pain.

Nor am I suggesting that the conceivability test at the heart of the Disembodiment Argument is easy to perform. You must pay close attention to your current "pinching" sensation, making sure that you are not reading more (or less) into it than what it presents. And you must carefully engage in the exercise of conceiving. This is why Descartes advised that, before engaging in the *Meditations,* we should find a quiet place and free our minds from distractions.

But as long as you exercise care, you should be able—through keeping your attention on the pinching feeling, while simultaneously trying to conceive that you are disembodied—to confirm, or disconfirm, (1*) for yourself. For my part, I find that this exercise confirms (1*). And because I assume that we are basically similar, as regards our sensations and concepts, I expect that you will find this as well.

This is, then, the basic argument for dualism. As modified, the key premise of the argument is (1*). That premise is supported by the simple but powerful thought that, according to our concept **pain**, the feeling of pain *is* pain; pain has no essential features that are hidden. So in attending to the pinching sensation, we have access to the essential feature of pain, namely, how it feels. This means that our concept **pain** is sufficiently comprehensive for use in conceivability tests. Your ability to conceive of disembodied pain therefore establishes that disembodied pain is possible, even if (in fact) everyone who experiences pain also has a body. This possibility refutes the identity thesis and establishes dualism.

5. A PHYSICALIST OBJECTION

Physicalists have put forth the following objection to this kind of argument:

> The argument shows only that, *according to our concept pain,* pain may be present in the absence of C-fiber stimulation. Still, we must bear in mind the example of water. *According to our concept water,* water may be present in the absence of H_2O. Just as the latter case does not lead us to doubt that water = H_2O, the former case should not lead us to doubt that pain = C-fiber stimulation.

As I explained in Section 2, our concepts define the subject matter that we are investigating. And our concepts also determine how we interpret evidence. It is because we conceptualize water as something that has a hidden essence that our discovery that water is correlated with H_2O leads us to believe that water = H_2O. If we conceptualized water differently—e.g., as *any clear liquid*—then we wouldn't accept "water = H_2O."

By the same token, our concept of pain defines what it is that we are investigating when we try to understand the nature of pain. According to this concept, we are investigating that *hurting* sensation. And because pain has no hidden essence, according to our concept, the discovery that pain is correlated with C-fiber stimulation will not justify "pain = C-fiber stimulation."

Above, I said that empirical investigation could not establish that a certain scenario is *impossible*. This is why even a perfect correlation between pain and C-fiber stimulation could not establish that it is impossible that pain be present without C-fiber stimulation, and hence could not establish that these were identical. How, then, did empirical investigation establish that water = H_2O? The answer is simple: Empirical investigation did *not* single-handedly establish this. Empirical investigation established only a correlation between water and H_2O. What justified the identity claim was an additional fact, a fact about our *concept* of water, namely, that we conceptualize water as having a hidden essence. But we don't take the fact that a substance has a particular appearance (it is clear, drinkable, etc.) to be *conclusive evidence* that it is water. Rather, we think that, to conclusively determine whether something is water, we must discover its microstructure. The fact that water has a hidden essence was already implicit in our concept **water;** and this is why the discovery that water was perfectly correlated with H_2O led us to believe that H_2O was the hidden essence of water, and hence that water = H_2O.

By contrast, we don't think of pain as having a hidden essence. This is why you treat the *appearance* of pain—that *hurting* sensation—as conclusive evidence that you are in pain. And it is why we don't need scientific investigation to discover the *essence* of pain, though of course such investigation can discover interesting and important facts about pain.

Above, I said that concepts are crucially important because they define the topic that we are investigating. Anyone who interprets the correlation between pain and C-fiber stimulation as evidence that pain = C-fiber stimulation is straying from our concept, and hence simply changing the topic. The topic we're investigating, pain, is defined by our concept **pain;** and according to that concept, pain has no hidden essence.

But why not simply change the topic, and claim that nothing corresponds to our original concept **pain,** because every mental state has a hidden physical essence? The problem with this move is that we can still ask why we should accept the claim that pain = C-fiber stimulation. In the case of other identities, such as water = H_2O, there is a simple answer: You conceptualize water as having a hidden essence, and empirical investigation has discovered that H_2O is that hidden essence. Because there is no parallel justification for "pain = C-fiber stimulation," we have no reason to accept that identity claim.

Arguably, this distinctive feature of our pain concept—that, as we conceptualize pain, the appearance of pain *is* its reality—is possessed only by mental concepts. For our concepts of nonmental things do attribute a gap between whether the thing appears to satisfy the concept and whether it actually does so. If this is correct, our argument for dualism cannot be applied to anything that is not mental.

6. BUT WHAT ABOUT MENTAL CAUSATION?

The previous section discussed a physicalist objection to the method used in the Disembodiment Argument. However, a physicalist might instead criticize the *conclusion* of that argument, as follows:

The Disembodiment Argument does provide *some* reason to think that disembodied pain is possible. But we should not embrace this conclusion until we carefully examine its consequences. And in fact the conclusion has one consequence that is utterly unacceptable: if dualism is true, then our mental states do not truly cause our bodily movements. That is, dualism leads to *epiphenomenalism,* the claim that the mental has no physical effects. But epiphenomenalism is repugnant.[12] So even if we are not sure quite where the argument goes wrong, it must go wrong somewhere.

Leading arguments for physicalism rest on the idea that accepting the identity thesis is the only way to preserve mental causation. But only a very strong version of the identity thesis will salvage mental causation as intended; and that version of the thesis faces problems that are as serious as the worry about epiphenomenalism. Or so I will argue.

The identity thesis is usually motivated by the following idea. If we want to explain why I leaped out of my chair (a physical event), we need not invoke anything other than previous physical events: I sat on a thumb tack, and this caused (via a train of other physical events) C-fiber stimulation, which then caused my leap out of the chair. To say that such an explanation requires us to invoke a mental state like pain *in addition* to C-fiber stimulation would be to deny that physics is complete. But all of our evidence is that physics *is* complete: We have never encountered a case where we were *forced* to go beyond the realm of the physical to explain a physical event. Now if physics is complete, then citing physical events will suffice to explain my leaping out of the chair. We need not mention pain in this explanation. So *if* pain causally contributes to my leaping from the chair, then pain must be physical—that is, it must be *identical to* a physical state such as C-fiber stimulation.

There are various objections that could be made to this argument. To my mind, the most promising is this: The nature of causation, and what it means to say that one event caused another, is far from clear. For example, David Hume argued that the best we can expect, in attempting to explain why an event occurred, is to identify a regularity: *This type of event is regularly preceded by that type of event.* But then why not say that *suddenly leaping out of one's chair* is regularly preceded by *feeling pain?* The physicalist will claim that there is also a physical event that regularly precedes such leaping, and so the mental event is superfluous. However, this response assumes that, in a competition between mental and physical causes, the physical cause will always win out. (Why not say that it is the physical event that is superfluous?) This assumption would be justified if we had some *deeper* account of how physical causation occurs, one that favored physical-to-physical causation over mental-to-physical causation. But there is no accepted understanding of how causation occurs; and contemporary Humeans believe that there is no deeper *fact* about how causation occurs, because causal statements merely report regularities. The bottom line is this: Physical causation is largely a mystery, and so we should be hesitant to use our limited understanding of physical causation to rule out the possibility of nonphysical causation. The argument that dualism commits us to epiphenomenalism is far from conclusive.

But even if you think that the identity thesis better accommodates mental causation, it faces another problem, sometimes called the *problem of chauvinism.* If pain = C-fiber stimulation, then creatures whose physical structure differs significantly from ours cannot feel pain. In other words, the identity thesis is chauvinistic, because it identifies pain with a physical state that may be specific to creatures on Earth.

To see the problem, suppose that we encounter an alien civilization that seems very similar to ours. In this civilization, legislative debate is often reduced to partisan squabbles. Its members spend their leisure time in a range of activities, from hiking to watching reality TV. It seems easy to imagine that aliens whose activities were so similar to ours could nonetheless differ physiologically from humans. Perhaps their planet does not have the abundance of H_2O and oxygen that Earth has, and so their physical and neural constitution is very different from ours. Even so, it seems entirely conceivable that such

creatures feel pain. (We can suppose that some of these aliens are in hospitals, recovering from surgery.) But if pain *is just* C-fiber stimulation, then no creature who lacked C-fibers *could possibly* feel pain. The identity thesis does seem to be objectionably chauvinistic.

To my mind, it is highly implausible that the capacity for pain requires a physical constitution like ours. Remember, what is at issue here is not the *likelihood* that there are alien creatures who feel pain; it is the sheer *possibility* of this scenario. And it seems incredible that pain *couldn't possibly* be experienced by creatures who lacked C-fibers.

I have argued that, while the concern about whether dualism can do justice to mental causation is legitimate, the reasoning to show that dualism commits us to epiphenomenalism is open to question. Accepting the identity thesis obviously commits us to chauvinism, but it is not entirely clear that accepting dualism commits us to epiphenomenalism. And chauvinism is at least as repugnant as epiphenomenalism.

Some physicalists have responded to the chauvinism problem by retreating from the simple version of the identity thesis. In its simple version, the identity thesis claims that each type of mental state is identical to some type of physical state. The retreat from this simple version claims that pain *in humans* is identical to C-fiber stimulation; pain *in aliens* may be identical to some other physical state.[13] This move does avoid the chauvinism problem. But the retreat from the simple identity thesis means that we cannot explain such seemingly obvious causal generalizations about pain as "being in pain causes one to urgently try to change one's situation." For there is no single property that answers to "being in pain"; there is *pain-in-humans,* and *pain-in-aliens,* but on the proposal being considered, these are completely different properties. Because this modification of the identity thesis prevents us from allowing for familiar causal generalizations, it limits the alleged causal benefits of physicalism.

Until this point, I have been concerned solely with "identity" versions of physicalism. But in the face of the difficulties I have described, some physicalists adopt a weaker position, claiming that the relations between physical and mental states fall short of identity. Unfortunately, this weaker, "nonreductive" brand of physicalism faces precisely the same worries about epiphenomenalism that dualism allegedly faces. For the epiphenomenalism worry stems from the claim that pain ≠ C-fiber stimulation. So long as my pain isn't identical to the firing of my C-fibers, then we can always ask *which* of these factors caused me to leap out of the chair. Was it the pain, or was it the C-fiber stimulation? The danger is that the physical factor will fully explain my leap, and thus the mental factor will be superfluous.[14] The benefit of the identity thesis is that it blocks such questions. (Compare: Because Superman is identical to Clark Kent, it makes no sense to ask whether it was Superman *or* Clark Kent who stepped out of the phone booth.) Because avoiding epiphenomenalism is the chief consideration in favor of physicalism, these weaker physicalist positions seem unmotivated. Finally, it's worth noting that these weaker brands of physicalism are just as vulnerable to the Disembodiment Argument, for even the weakest brand of physicalism must hold that you could not feel the pinch you're feeling right now if you were disembodied.

Let me sum up the results of this section. According to physicalists, dualism implies that mental events, such as thoughts and sensations, never have physical effects. Many physicalists claim that the only way to avoid this "repugnant" epiphenomenalism is to accept the identity thesis. In response, I have outlined an objectionable consequence of the identity thesis: that those with different physical constitutions could not possibly experience pain or any other sensation that we experience. This chauvinistic result is at least as worrisome as epiphenomenalism. And the simple identity thesis is patently chauvinistic, while it is less clear that dualism leads to epiphenomenalism. Chauvinism can be avoided by modifying the identity thesis, but this modification sacrifices much of the alleged causal benefits of the identity thesis.

7. BUT ISN'T DUALISM *SPOOKY?*

Despite all this, there may be a lingering sense that dualism is just plain weird, or *spooky.*

But is dualism any spookier than physicalism? Bertrand Russell observed that those who accept the findings of modern science are hardly in a position to accuse dualists of spookiness.

> The plain man thinks that material objects must certainly exist, since they are evident to the senses. Whatever else may be doubted, it is certain that anything you can bump into must be real; this is the plain man's metaphysic. This is all very well, but the physicist comes along and shows that you never bump into anything: even when you run your hand along a stone wall, you do not really touch it. When you think you touch a thing, there are certain electrons and protons, forming part of your body, which are attracted and repelled by certain electrons and protons in the thing you think you are touching, but there is no actual contact....The electrons and protons themselves, however, are only crude first approximations, a way of collecting into a bundle either trains of waves or the statistical probabilities of various different kinds of events. Thus matter has become altogether too ghostly to be used as an adequate stick with which to beat the mind.[15]

Russell's point is that commitments of physical science, which is unquestionably naturalistic, are just as spooky or "ghostly" as dualism. And Russell was writing in 1935; subsequent advances in physics have made the physical realm appear all the more exotic. Contemporary physicists do not agree on the basic structure of the world, but the entities posited by relatively mainstream physical theories—vibrating strings, basic particles subject to quantum indeterminacy—seem spooky enough.

Surely, dualism does not *spookify* our overall picture of the world. That picture was already plenty spooky, due to the progress of physics itself. So there is no reason to hold that dualism is spooky, or that it conflicts with a broadly scientific, naturalistic picture of reality.

Conclusion

Most contemporary thinkers believe that minds are part of the natural order, and that scientific research can yield important information about how the mind works. Naturalistic dualists agree. And dualism is not undermined by empirical evidence, because empirical evidence reveals only correlations. Moreover, dualists can accept causal explanations of these correlations (e.g., the correlation between taking aspirin and pain reduction is explained by the fact that aspirin suppresses the biochemicals responsible for activating C-fibers).

At the outset of this essay, I noted that the dispute between physicalists and dualists can be interpreted as a disagreement as to what kinds of data there are about the nature of mind, and what kind of theory will best explain those data. The thought experiment at the center of the Disembodiment Argument provides data that favor dualism: We seem able to conceive of disembodied pain. Given that our concept of pain appears to be sufficiently comprehensive for use in a conceivability test, the proper conclusion is that pain could be present in a being that lacked physical features. This means that dualism is true.

Physicalists will discount the importance of data generated by conceivability tests. But these data are essential to defining the topic at hand, whether that topic is bachelors, water, or pain. So any claim that clashes with these data diverges from our original topic, and should therefore be rejected. The claim that "pain = C-fiber stimulation" clashes with the data generated by our conceivability test. It thus diverges from our original topic—pain, as defined by our concept **pain**—and hence we should reject it.

Any naturalist worth her salt will follow the evidence where it leads. And in this case, the evidence leads to dualism.

NOTES

1. My development of this argument most closely parallels Saul Kripke's argument in Lecture III of his book *Naming and Necessity* (Cambridge, MA: Harvard University Press, 1980). The other leading contemporary arguments for dualism are also naturalistic: Frank Jackson's Knowledge Argument, given in "The Qualia Problem," in this volume; and David Chalmers' Zombie Argument, given in Chapter 4 of his book *The Conscious Mind* (Oxford: Oxford University Press, 1996). Some of the ideas in this essay borrow from these other arguments as well.

2. This is a *type-identity* thesis: it identifies a *type* of mental state with a *type* of physical state. For simplicity, I will focus on type-identities. But my argument also challenges the thesis that every *particular* (or "token") mental state, such as the pain I'm feeling right now, is identical to some *particular* ("token") physical state. This latter claim is known as a *token-identity* thesis. Unlike the type-identity thesis, it allows that two instances of a single mental type (such as pain) can belong to different physical types. This distinction will surface briefly in Section 6.

3. Some philosophers believe that conceivability arguments in this direction don't succeed in undermining physicalism, since my ability to conceive of disembodied pain shows only that such a pain *could* be disembodied, not that my pain is actually distinct from my body. But we can sidestep this objection by focusing, in the thought experiment, on the idea that *this very pain* could be disembodied.

4. Of course, empirical evidence can tell us that a certain scenario is *possible*. If we observed that pain occurred in the absence of C-fiber stimulation, we would of course conclude that this was possible. So it might seem that this type of empirical observation could support dualism. However, even this observation would not settle the issue. For the physicalist will simply take this as evidence that we must look elsewhere to find the physical state identical to pain. Unless we have empirical evidence of a pain that is unaccompanied by *any* physical state—which seems highly unlikely—the physicalist can always hold out for the discovery of a physical state that does perfectly correlate with pain. I will assume, for the sake of argument, that there is a physical state that perfectly correlates with pain, and I will follow standard practice in speaking as if C-fiber stimulation is this state.

5. This means that it applies both to identities like "pain = C-fiber stimulation" and to the claim that every particular pain is identical to *some* physical state or other. That is, it applies to both type-identity and token-identity versions of physicalism. (These versions were distinguished in note 2.)

6. In his version of the argument, Descartes doesn't distinguish pains from thoughts more generally.

7. David Papineau proposes that we understand the physical as "the inanimate." See Papineau, *Thinking about Consciousness* (Oxford University Press, 2002). Barbara Montero proposes that we understand it as "the nonmental." See "The Body Problem," *Noûs* 33 (1999), pp. 183–200.

8. This should be qualified a bit, for purely mental entities may share temporal features with sticks and stones, e.g., existing on a Tuesday. And of course they may share necessary features like "being such that 2 + 2 = 4." So the issue is whether you can conceive of experiencing *this very pain* while sharing no contingent, nontemporal features with inanimate, nonmental objects.

9. Strictly speaking, our concept **pain** is sufficiently comprehensive only if we grasp both the essential features of pain and any features entailed by those essential features. The geometry student erred because he didn't grasp a property (the property expressed by the Pythagorean Theorem) entailed by the essential feature of a right triangle *being a three-sided polygon with one angle equal to 90°.*

10. Christopher Hill, *Sensations: A Defense of Type Materialism* (Cambridge: Cambridge University Press, 1991), 127.

11. You might mistakenly believe that you're in pain if a trusted friend tells you that you are, at a time when you are steadfastly refusing to introspect your own feelings. (This is certainly an odd case, however, and seems more plausible for emotional pain than for the kind of pinch we are concerned with.) Or you might be tricked into believing that you're in pain: In a (cruel) fraternity hazing ritual, blindfolded recruits are told that they will be burnt with a cigarette in a certain spot. Ice is then applied to the spot, yielding shock rather than pain. Still, for a moment the victims react as if they were in pain, and they seem to believe that they are undergoing pain. (An alternative interpretation is that the recruits *are* in pain, but the pain has a curious origin: It is produced by the expectation of pain.)

12. The charge that epiphenomenalism is "repugnant" was made by David Lewis in "What Experience Teaches." This article appeared in W. Lycan, ed., *Mind and Cognition* (Oxford: Blackwell Publishing, 1990), pp. 499–519.

13. Lewis, "Mad Pain and Martian Pain," in N. Block, ed., *Readings in the Philosophy of Psychology*, Vol. I. (Harvard University Press, 1980), pp. 216–222.

14. The idea that non-reductive physicalism faces the problem of epiphenomenalism was made by Jaegwon Kim. See "The Nonreductivist's Troubles with Mental Causation," reprinted as Chapter 17 of Kim's book *Supervenience and Mind* (Cambridge: Cambridge University Press, 1993).

15. Russell, "What Is the Soul?" from his book *In Praise of Idleness and Other Essays* (New York: W. W. Norton, 1935).

1.2 The Qualia Problem

FRANK JACKSON

Frank Jackson has written many works in metaphysics, ethics, and the philosophy of mind. He is Emeritus Professor at Australian National University.

I am what is sometimes known as a "qualia freak." I think that there are certain features of the bodily sensations especially, but also of certain perceptual experiences, which no amount of purely physical information includes. Tell me everything physical there is to tell about what is going on in a living brain, the kind of states, their functional role, their relation to what goes

This is an edited version of "Epiphenomenal Qualia," which appeared in the Philosophical Quarterly, vol. 32 (1982), pp. 127–132, by permission of Oxford University Press on behalf of Blackwell Publishing.

on at other times and in other brains, and so on and so forth, and be I as clever as can be in fitting it all together, you won't have told me about the hurtfulness of pains, the itchiness of itches, pangs of jealousy, or about the characteristic experience of tasting a lemon, smelling a rose, hearing a loud noise, or seeing the sky.

There are many qualia freaks, and some of them say that their rejection of Physicalism* is an unargued intuition. I think that they are being unfair to themselves. They have the following argument. Nothing you could tell of a physical sort captures the smell of a rose, for instance. Therefore, Physicalism is false. By our lights this is a perfectly good argument. It is obviously not to the point to question its validity, and the premise is intuitively obviously true both to them and to me.

I must, however, admit that it is weak from a polemical point of view. There are, unfortunately for us, many who do not find the premise intuitively obvious. The task then is to present an argument whose premises are obvious to all, or at least to as many as possible. This I try to do with what I will call "the Knowledge argument."

In the final section I tackle the question of the causal role of qualia. The major factor in stopping people from admitting qualia is the belief that they would have to be given a causal role with respect to the physical world and especially the brain; and it is hard to do this without sounding like someone who believes in fairies. I seek to turn this objection by arguing that the view that qualia are epiphenomenal is a perfectly possible one.

THE KNOWLEDGE ARGUMENT FOR QUALIA

People vary considerably in their ability to discriminate colors. Suppose that in an experiment to catalog this variation Fred is discovered. Fred has better color vision than anyone else on record; he makes every discrimination that any-

one has ever made, and moreover he makes one that we cannot even begin to make. Show him a batch of ripe tomatoes and he sorts them into two roughly equal groups and does so with complete consistency. That is, if you blindfold him, shuffle the tomatoes up, and then remove the blindfold and ask him to sort them out again, he sorts them into exactly the same two groups.

We ask Fred how he does it. He explains that all ripe tomatoes do not look the same color to him, and in fact that this is true of a great many objects that we classify together as red. He sees two colors where we see one, and he has in consequence developed for his own use two words 'red$_1$' and 'red$_2$' to mark the difference. Perhaps he tells us that he has often tried to teach the difference between red$_1$ and red$_2$ to his friends but has gotten nowhere and has concluded that the rest of the world is red$_1$-red$_2$ color-blind—or perhaps he has had partial success with his children; it doesn't matter. In any case he explains to us that it would be quite wrong to think that because 'red' appears in both 'red$_1$' and 'red$_2$' that the two colors are shades of the one color. He only uses the common term 'red' to fit more easily into our restricted usage. To him red$_1$ and red$_2$ are as different from each other and all the other colors as yellow is from blue. And his discriminatory behavior bears this out: He sorts red$_1$ from red$_2$ tomatoes with the greatest of ease in a wide variety of viewing circumstances. Moreover, an investigation of the physiological basis of Fred's exceptional ability reveals that Fred's optical system is able to separate out two groups of wavelengths in the red spectrum as sharply as we are able to sort out yellow from blue.

I think that we should admit that Fred can see, really see, at least one more color than we can; red$_1$ is a different color from red$_2$. We are to Fred as a totally red–green color-blind person is to us. H. G. Wells' story "The Country of the Blind" is about a sighted person in a totally blind community. This person never manages to convince them that he can see, that he has an extra sense. They ridicule this sense as quite inconceivable, and treat his capacity to avoid falling into

---

*The theory that all information is ultimately physical information—information about physical states and physical events, couched in exclusively physical language—EDS.

ditches, to win fights, and so on as precisely that capacity and nothing more. We would be making their mistake if we refused to allow that Fred can see one more color than we can.

What kind of experience does Fred have when he sees red$_1$ and red$_2$? What is the new color or colors like? We would dearly like to know but do not; and it seems that no amount of physical information about Fred's brain and optical system tells us. We find out perhaps that Fred's cones respond differentially to certain light waves in the red section of the spectrum that make no difference to ours (or perhaps he has an extra cone) and that this leads in Fred to a wider range of those brain states responsible for visual discriminatory behavior. But none of this tells us what we really want to know about his color experience. There is something about it we don't know. But we know, we may suppose, everything about Fred's body, his behavior and dispositions to behavior and about his internal physiology, and everything about his history and relation to others that can be given in physical accounts of persons. We have all the physical information. Therefore, knowing all this is *not* knowing everything about Fred. It follows that Physicalism leaves something out.

To reinforce this conclusion, imagine that as a result of our investigations into the internal workings of Fred we find out how to make everyone's physiology like Fred's in the relevant respects; or perhaps Fred donates his body to science and on his death we are able to transplant his optical system into someone else—again the fine detail doesn't matter. The important point is that such a happening would create enormous interest. People would say "At last we will know what it is like to see the extra color, at last we will know how Fred has differed from us in the way he has struggled to tell us about for so long." Then it cannot be that we knew all along all about Fred. But *ex hypothesi* we did know all along everything about Fred that features in the physicalist scheme; hence the physicalist scheme leaves something out.

Put it this way. *After* the operation, we will know *more* about Fred and especially about his color experiences. But beforehand we had all the physical information we could desire about his body and brain, and indeed everything that has ever featured in physicalist accounts of mind and consciousness. Hence there is more to know than all that. Hence Physicalism is incomplete.

Fred and the new color(s) are of course essentially rhetorical devices. The same point can be made with normal people and familiar colors. Mary is a brilliant scientist who is, for whatever reason, forced to investigate the world from a black-and-white room *via* a black-and-white television monitor. She specializes in the neurophysiology of vision and acquires, let us suppose, all the physical information there is to obtain about what goes on when we see ripe tomatoes, or the sky, and use terms like 'red,' 'blue,' and so on. She discovers, for example, just which wavelength combinations from the sky stimulate the retina, and exactly how this produces *via* the central nervous system the contraction of the vocal chords and expulsion of air from the lungs that results in the uttering of the sentence 'The sky is blue.'

What will happen when Mary is released from her black-and-white room or is given a color television monitor? Will she *learn* anything or not? It just seems obvious that she will learn something about the world and our visual experience of it. But then it is inescapable that her previous knowledge was incomplete. But she had *all* the physical information. *Ergo* there is more to have than that, and Physicalism is false.

Clearly the same style of Knowledge argument could be deployed for taste, hearing, the bodily sensations, and generally speaking for the various mental states that are said to have (as it is variously put) raw feels, phenomenal features, or qualia. The conclusion in each case is that the qualia are left out of the physicalist story. And the polemical strength of the Knowledge argument is that it is so hard to deny the central claim that one can have all the physical information without having all the information there is to have.

THE BOGEY OF EPIPHENOMENALISM

Is there any really *good* reason for refusing to countenance the idea that qualia are causally impotent with respect to the physical world? I will argue for the answer *no*. All I will be concerned to defend is that it is possible to hold that certain properties of certain mental states, namely those I've called qualia, are such that their possession or absence makes no difference to the physical world.

Two reasons are standardly given for holding that a quale like the hurtfulness of a pain must be causally efficacious in the physical world, and so, for instance, that it...must sometimes make a difference to what happens in the brain. [Neither,] I will argue, has any real force.

(i) It is supposed to be just obvious that the hurtfulness of pain is partly responsible for the subject seeking to avoid pain, saying 'It hurts' and so on. But, to reverse Hume, anything can fail to cause anything. No matter how often *B* follows and no matter how initially obvious the causality of the connection seems, the hypothesis that *A* causes *B* can be overturned by an overarching theory that shows the two as distinct effects of a common underlying causal process.

To the untutored the image on the screen of Lee Marvin's fist moving from left to right immediately followed by the image of John Wayne's head moving in the same general direction looks as causal as anything. And of course throughout countless Westerns images similar to the first are followed by images similar to the second. All this counts for precisely nothing when we know the over-arching theory concerning how the relevant images are both effects of an underlying causal process involving the projector and the film. The epiphenomenalist can say exactly the same about the connection between, for example, hurtfulness and behavior. It is simply a consequence of the fact that certain happenings in the brain cause both.

(ii) The second objection relates to Darwin's Theory of Evolution. According to natural selection the traits that evolve over time are those conducive to physical survival. We may assume that qualia evolved over time—we have them, the earliest forms of life do not—and so we should expect qualia to be conducive to survival. The objection is that they could hardly help us to survive if they do nothing to the physical world.

The appeal of this argument is undeniable, but there is a good reply to it. Polar bears have particularly thick, warm coats. The Theory of Evolution explains this (we suppose) by pointing out that having a thick warm coat is conducive to survival in the Arctic. But having a thick coat goes along with having a heavy coat, and having a heavy coat is *not* conducive to survival. It slows the animal down.

Does this mean that we have refuted Darwin because we have found an evolved trait—having a heavy coat—that is not conducive to survival? Clearly not. Having a heavy coat is an unavoidable concomitant of having a warm coat (in the context, modern insulation was not available), and the advantages for survival of having a warm coat outweighed the disadvantages of having a heavy one. The point is that all we can extract from Darwin's theory is that we should expect any evolved characteristic to be *either* conducive to survival *or* a by-product of one that is so conducive. The epiphenomenalist holds that qualia fall into the latter category. They are a by-product of certain brain processes that are highly conducive to survival.

There is a very understandable response to the two replies I have just made. "All right, there is no knockdown refutation of the existence of epiphenomenal qualia. But the fact remains that they are an excrescence. They *do* nothing, they *explain* nothing, they serve merely to soothe the intuitions of dualists, and it is left a total mystery how they fit into the world view of science. In short we do not and cannot understand the how and why of them."

This is perfectly true, but is no objection to qualia, for it rests on an overly optimistic view of the human animal, and its powers. We are the products of Evolution. We understand and sense what we need to understand and sense in order to survive. Epiphenomenal qualia are totally irrelevant to survival. At no stage of our evolution did natural selection favor those who could make sense of how they are caused and the laws governing them, or in fact why they exist at all. And that is why we can't.

It is not sufficiently appreciated that Physicalism is an extremely optimistic view of our powers. If it is true, we have, in very broad outline admittedly, a grasp of our place in the scheme of things. Certain matters of sheer complexity defeat us—there are an awful lot of neurons—but in principle we have it all. But consider the antecedent probability that everything in the Universe be of a kind that is relevant in some way or other to the survival of *Homo sapiens*. It is very low surely. But then one must admit that it is very likely that there is a part of the whole scheme of things, maybe a big part,

which no amount of evolution will ever bring us near to knowledge about or understanding of. For the simple reason that such knowledge and understanding is irrelevant to survival.

Physicalists typically emphasize that we are a part of nature on their view, which is fair enough. But if we are a part of nature, we are as nature has left us after however many years of evolution and each step in that evolutionary progression has been a matter of chance constrained just by the need to preserve or increase survival value. The wonder is that we understand as much as we do, and there is no wonder that there should be matters which fall quite outside our comprehension. Perhaps exactly how epiphenomenal qualia fit into the scheme of things is one such.

1.3 The Case for Materialism

DAVID PAPINEAU

David Papineau teaches at King's College London and at the Graduate Center of the City University of New York. He has written widely in the philosophy of mind, metaphysics, and the philosophy of language.

INTRODUCTION

Books on consciousness often begin by distinguishing between different kinds of consciousness. We are told about self-consciousness and sentience, creature consciousness and state consciousness, phenomenal consciousness and access consciousness, perceptual consciousness, higher-order consciousness, and so on.

For the moment, I am concerned with that aspect of consciousness that makes it so philosophically interesting. Namely, that having a conscious experience is *like something*, in Thomas Nagel's striking phrase. It has become standard to use 'phenomenal' or 'subjective' to focus on

this feature of consciousness, and I shall adopt these usages in what follows.

The idea is best introduced by examples rather than definitions. ('If you gotta ask, you're never gonna know.') Compare the difference between having your eyes shut and having them open, or between having your teeth drilled with and without an anaesthetic. When your eyes are open, you have a conscious visual experience, and when your teeth are drilled without an anaesthetic, you have a conscious pain. It is like something for you to have these experiences. It is not like that when you close your eyes, or when the anaesthetic takes effect. What you lose in these latter cases are elements of phenomenal

David Papineau, *Thinking about Consciousness* (Oxford University Press 2002), pp. 14–18, 21–23, 27–28, 40–41, 45. By permission of Oxford University Press.

or subjective consciousness. From now on, when I say 'conscious', I shall mean this kind of consciousness.

Much of what follows will be concerned with a particular philosophical puzzle about consciousness: namely, the puzzle of how consciousness relates to the physical world. There are other philosophical puzzles about consciousness, but this seems to me the most immediate.

The puzzle can be posed simply. On the one hand, there is a strong argument for adopting a materialist view of conscious states, for supposing that conscious states must be *part* of the physical world, that they must be *identical* to brain states, or something similar. Yet, on the other hand, there are also strong arguments (and even stronger intuitions) which suggest that conscious states must be *distinct* from any material states.

I believe that in the end the materialist argument wins. Conscious states are material states. This is not to belittle the anti-materialist arguments and intuitions. They are deep and important. We will not grasp consciousness properly unless we understand how to answer them. Still, I think that careful analysis will show that they are flawed, and that the right solution is to embrace materialism.

I shall begin by putting the materialist argument on the table. It is worth taking some care about this, for there are a number of different defences of materialism on offer in the contemporary literature, and not all of them are equally compelling. However, I think that there is one definitive argument for materialism. I shall call this 'the causal argument', and the burden of this first chapter will be to develop this argument.

There is a further reason for laying out the argument for materialism carefully. Many contemporary philosophers harbour grave suspicions about materialism. Thus some philosophers contend that the whole idea of materialism is somehow empty, on the grounds that there is no proper way of characterizing the 'physical' realm. And others suggest that contemporary material-

ism about the conscious mind rests on nothing but fashion or prejudice, unsupported by serious argument.

I intend to show that these attitudes are mistaken. The question of how to define 'physical' in the context of the mind-brain debate does raise a number of interesting points, but there is no great difficulty about pinning down a sense precise enough for the purposes at hand. It will prove easier to do this, however, after we have rehearsed the argument for materialism. Accordingly, I shall not worry about the meaning of 'physical' at this stage, but simply begin by outlining the case for materialism. Once we have seen what is at issue, it will become clearer how materialists can best understand the meaning of 'physical', and I shall return to this issue at the end of the chapter.

In addition to suspicions about the meaning of 'physical', there is the further allegation mentioned above, that contemporary materialism is nothing but a modish fad. I take the causal argument to be outlined in this chapter to rebut this allegation. The causal argument may not be conclusive, but it certainly shows that the case for materialism goes beyond mere fashion or prejudice.

Some may think that the charge of modishness is supported by historical considerations. Widespread philosophical materialism is a relatively recent phenomenon, largely a creature of the late twentieth century. This recent provenance may seem to support the accusation that contemporary materialism owes its popularity more to fashion than to any serious argument. 'If the case is so substantial', anti-materialists can ask, 'how come it took so long for philosophers to appreciate it?' I take this to be a good historical question. But I think there is also a good historical answer: namely, that a key premiss in the argument for materialism rests on empirical evidence that only became clear-cut during the course of the twentieth century.

However, I shall not complicate the analysis of this chapter by overlaying it with historical commentary. The issues are complicated enough without the added burden of tracing historical strands. Accordingly, this chapter will focus on the structure of the argument for materialism, not its history.

THE CAUSAL ARGUMENT

Let me now outline what I take to be the canonical argument for materialism. Setting to one side all complications, which can be discussed later, it can be put as follows.

> Many effects that we attribute to conscious causes have full physical causes. But it would be absurd to suppose that these effects are caused twice over. So the conscious causes must be identical to some part of those physical causes.

To appreciate the force of this argument, consider some bodily behaviour which we would standardly attribute to conscious causes. For example, I walk to the fridge to get a beer, because I consciously feel thirsty. Now combine this example with the thought that, according to modern physical science, such bodily movements are fully caused by prior physical processes in brains and nerves. The obvious conclusion is that the conscious thirst must be identical with some part of those physical processes.

Let me now lay out the above argument more formally. This will help us to appreciate both its strengths and its weaknesses.

As a first premiss, take:

(1) Conscious mental occurrences have physical effects.

As I said, the most obvious examples are cases where our conscious feelings and other mental states cause our behaviour.

Now add in this premiss ('the completeness of physics' henceforth):

(2) All physical effects are fully caused by purely *physical* prior histories.

In particular, this covers the behavioural effects of conscious causes to which our attention is drawn by premiss 1. The thought behind premiss 2 is that such physical behaviour will always

be fully caused by physical contractions in your muscles, in turn caused by electrical messages travelling down your nerves, themselves due to physical activity in your motor cortex, in turn caused by physical activity in your sensory cortex, and so on.

At first sight, premisses 1 and 2 seem to suggest that a certain range of physical effects (physical behaviour) will have two distinct causes: one involving a conscious state (your thirst, say), and the other consisting of purely physical states (neuronal firings, say).

Now, some events are indeed overdetermined in this way, like the death of a man who is simultaneously shot and struck by lightning. But this seems the wrong model for mental causation. After all, overdetermination implies that even if one cause had been absent, the result would still have occurred because of the other cause (the man would still have died even if he hadn't been shot, or, alternatively, even if he hadn't been struck by lightning). But it seems wrong to say that I would still have walked to the fridge even if I hadn't felt thirsty (because my neurons were firing), or, alternatively, that I would still have gone to the fridge even if my neurons hadn't been firing (because I felt thirsty). So let us add the further premiss:

(3) The physical effects of conscious causes aren't always overdetermined by distinct causes.

Materialism now follows. Premisses 1 and 2 tell us that certain effects have a conscious cause and a physical cause. Premiss 3 tells us that they don't have two distinct causes. The only possibility left is that the conscious occurrences mentioned in (1) must be identical with some part of the physical causes mentioned in (2). This respects both (1) and (2), yet avoids the implication of overdetermination, since (1) and (2) no longer imply *distinct* causes.

EPIPHENOMENALISM AND PRE-ESTABLISHED HARMONY

Let us now examine the causal argument more closely.

As laid out above, the causal argument seems valid. So, to deny the conclusion, we need to deny one of the premises. All of them can be denied without contradiction. Indeed, all of them have been denied by contemporary philosophers, as we shall see. At the same time, they are all highly plausible, and their denials have various unattractive consequences.

Let me start with premiss 1. This claims that, as a matter of empirical fact, particular conscious states have particular physical effects. This certainly seems plausible. Doesn't my conscious thirst cause me to walk to the fridge? Or, again, when I have a conscious headache, doesn't this cause me to ingest an aspirin?

Still, the possibility of denying this premiss is familiar enough, under the guise of 'epiphenomenalism' or 'pre-established harmony'.

The first philosopher to embrace this option was Leibniz. Unlike most other philosophers prior to the twentieth century, Leibniz was committed to the causal completeness of physics. But he was not prepared to accept the identity of mind with brain. So he opted for a denial of our premiss 1, and concluded that mind and matter cannot really influence each other, and that the appearance of interaction must be due to *pre-established harmony*. By this Leibniz meant that God must have arranged things to make sure that mind and matter always keep in step. In reality, they do not interact, but are like two trains running on separate tracks. But God fixed their starting times and speeds so as to ensure they would always run smoothly alongside each other.

Some contemporary philosophers follow Leibniz in avoiding mind-brain identity by denying premiss 1. But they prefer a rather simpler way of keeping mind and matter in step. They allow causal influences 'upwards' from brain to mind, while denying any 'downwards' causation from mind to brain. This position is known as *epiphenomenalism*. It respects the causal completeness of physics, in that nothing non-physical causally influences the physical brain. But it avoids the theological complications of Leibniz's pre-established harmony, by allowing the brain itself to cause conscious effects.

Epiphenomenalism is not a particularly attractive position. For a start, it would require us to deny many apparently obvious truths, such as that my conscious thirst caused me to fetch a beer, or that my conscious headache caused me to swallow an aspirin. According to epiphenomenalism, my behaviour in both these cases is caused solely at the physical level. These physical causes may be accompanied by conscious thirst or a conscious headache, but these conscious states no more cause resulting behaviour than falling barometers cause rain.

That epiphenomenalism has these odd consequences is not in itself decisive. The theoretical truth can often overturn claims which were previously regarded as the merest common sense. Moreover, there is nothing incoherent about epiphenomenalism. As I shall have occasion to stress in what follows, there is nothing conceptually contradictory in the idea of conscious states which exert no causal powers themselves. Still, epiphenomenalism is surely an empirically implausible position, by comparison with the materialist view that conscious states are simply identical to brain states.

If epiphenomenalism were true, then the relation between mind and brain would be like nothing else in nature. After all, science recognizes no other examples of 'causal danglers', ontologically independent states with causes but no effects. So, given the choice between epiphenomenalism and materialism, standard principles of scientific theory choice would seem to favour materialism. If both views can accommodate the empirical data equally well, then ordinary scientific methodology will advise us to adopt the simple view that unifies mind and brain, rather than the ontologically more profligate story which has the conscious states dangling impotently from the brain states.

There remains the possibility that the anti-materialist arguments to be examined later will show that conscious mind and brain *cannot* be identical. If this is so, then one of the premisses of the causal argument must be false. And in that case premiss 1 seems as likely a candidate as any. Certainly most contemporary philosophers who are persuaded by the anti-materialist arguments have opted for epiphenomenalism and the denial of premiss 1, rather than for any other way out of the causal argument.

But this does not invalidate the criticisms I have levelled against epiphenomenalism. My concern at the moment is not to prejudge the anti-materialist case, but merely to assess the causal argument. And the point remains that, in the absence of further considerations, it seems clearly preferable to identify mind with brain than to condemn conscious states to the status of causal danglers. It may be that further anti-materialist considerations will yet require us to reconsider this verdict, but so far we have seen no reason to deny premiss 1, and good reason to uphold it.

ACCEPTING OVERDETERMINATION

There remain the two other premisses to the causal argument. It will be convenient to relegate the discussion of premiss 2, the completeness of physics, to the last section of this chapter. So let me now briefly consider premiss 3, the one ruling out overdetermination.

To reject this premiss is to accept that the physical effects of mental causes are always overdetermined by distinct causes. This is sometimes called the 'belt and braces' view (make doubly sure you get the effects you want).

At first sight, this position seems to have the odd consequence that you would still have gone to the fridge for a beer even if you hadn't been thirsty (because your cortical neurons would still have been firing), and that you would still have gone to the fridge even if your cortex hadn't been firing (because you would still have been thirsty). These counterfactual implications seem clearly mistaken.

However, defenders of the belt and braces view maintain that such implications can be avoided. They argue that the distinct mental and physical causes may themselves be strongly

counter-factually dependent (that is, they hold that, if you hadn't been thirsty, your sensory neurons wouldn't have fired either, and vice versa).

Still, this then raises the question of *why* such causes should always be so counterfactually dependent, if they are ontologically distinct. Why wouldn't my neurons have fired, even in the absence of my conscious thirst? Similarly, why shouldn't I still have been thirsty, even if my neurons hadn't fired? Now, it is not impossible to imagine mechanisms which would ensure such counterfactual dependence between distinct causes. Perhaps the conscious thirst occurs first, and then invariably causes the cortical activity, with both causes thus available to overdetermine the behaviour. Alternatively, the cortical activity could invariably cause the thirst. Or, again, the conscious decision and the cortical activity might be joint effects of some prior common physical cause. But such mechanisms, though conceptually coherent, seem highly implausible, especially given that they need to ensure that the conscious state and the brain state *always* accompany each other.

The relevant point is analogous to one made in the last section. We don't find any 'belt and braces' mechanisms elsewhere in nature—that is, mechanisms which ensure that certain classes of effects invariably have two distinct causes, each of which would suffice by itself. As with the epiphenomenalist model, a belt and braces model requiring such peculiar brain mechanisms would seem to be ruled out by general principles of scientific theory choice. If the simple picture of mental causation offered by materialism accommodates the empirical data as well as the complex mechanisms required by the belt and braces option, then normal methodological principles would seem to weigh heavily against the belt and braces view.

As with the corresponding argument for epiphenomenalism, this appeal to principles of scientific theory choice is defeasible. Perhaps in the end the anti-materialist arguments will force us to accept mind-brain distinctness. In that case, the belt and braces view might be worth another look. True, it is even more Heath-Robinsonish than epiphenomenalism. On the other hand, it does at least have the virtue of retaining the common-sense view that conscious states characteristically cause behaviour. In any case, my present purpose is not to decide this issue finally, but only to point out that, as things stand so far, we have good reason to uphold premiss 3, and none to deny it.

WHAT IS 'PHYSICS'?

Let me now address a terminological issue flagged earlier, an issue that may have been worrying readers for some time. How exactly is 'physics' to be understood in this context of the causal argument? An awkward dilemma may seem to face anyone trying to defend the crucial second premiss, the completeness of physics. If we take 'physics' to mean the subject-matter currently studied in departments of physics, discussed in physics journals, and so on, then it seems pretty obvious that physics is not complete. The track record of past attempts to list *all* the fundamental forces and particles responsible for physical effects is not good, and it seems highly likely that future physics will identify new categories of physical cause. On the other hand, if we mean by 'physics' the subject-matter of such future scientific theories, then we seem to be in no position to assess its completeness, since we don't yet know what it is.

This difficulty is more apparent than real. If you want to use the causal argument, it isn't crucial that you know exactly what a complete physics would include. Much more important is to know what it won't include.

Suppose, to illustrate the point, that we have a well-defined notion of the *mental* realm, identified via some distinctive way of picking out properties as mental. (Thus we might identify this realm as involving intentionality, say, or intelligence, or indeed as involving consciousness—the precise characterization won't matter for the point I am about to make.) Then one way of understanding 'physical' would simply be as 'non-mentally identifiable'—that is, as standing for properties which can be identified independently of this specifically mental con-

ceptual apparatus. And then, provided we can be confident that the 'physical' in this sense is complete—that is, that every non-mentally identifiable effect is fully determined by *non-mentally identifiable* antecedents—then we can conclude that all mental states must be identical with (or realized by) something non-mentally identifiable (otherwise mental states couldn't have non-mentally identifiable effects).

This understanding of 'physical' as 'non-mentally identifiable' is of course a lot weaker than any normal pre-theoretical understanding, but note that it still generates a conclusion of great philosophical interest: namely, that all mental states, and in particular all conscious states, must be identical with non-mentally identifiable states. We may not know enough about physics to know exactly what a complete 'physics' might include. But as long as we are confident that, whatever it includes, it will have no ineliminable need for any distinctively mental categorizations, we can be confident that mental properties must be identical with (or realized by) certain non-mentally identifiable properties.

In fact, I shall understand 'physical' in a somewhat tighter sense in what follows, as 'identifiable non-mentally-*and*-non-biologically', or 'inanimate' for short, rather than simply as 'non-mentally identifiable'. This is because it is this realm, the 'inanimate', that is most naturally argued to be complete. What science has actually shown is that any inanimate effect (that is, any effect specifiable in terms of mass, or charge, or chemical structure, or … in any non-biological and non-mental way) will have an inanimate cause. So it is this thesis that I propose to plug into the causal argument. Conscious causes have inanimate effects. Inanimate effects always have full inanimate causes. So conscious properties must be identical with (or realized by) inanimate properties.

THE COMPLETENESS OF PHYSICS

Let me conclude this chapter with a few remarks about the causal argument's second premiss, the completeness of physics. It is one thing to fix a sense of 'physics' which renders this a substantial claim which might be true or false. It is another to show that it is in fact true.

Some readers might feel that this is not a problematic issue. Once we have fixed a definite meaning for 'physical', as equivalent to 'inanimate', say, then is it not just a matter of common sense that all physical effects will have physical causes? In particular, if we take the physical effects in this sense that we normally attribute to conscious causes, then is it not obvious that these effects can always in principle be fully accounted for in terms of uncontroversially physical histories, involving the movement of matter (in arms), molecular processes (in muscles), the action of neurotransmitters (in brains) ... and so on?

This is certainly how I thought of the issue when I first started working on the causal argument. I realized that this argument involved a number of disputable moves, and was therefore ready for it to be queried on various different grounds. But the one assumption that I did expect to be uncontroversial was the completeness of physics. To my surprise, I discovered that a number of my philosophical colleagues didn't agree. They didn't see why some physical occurrences, in our brains perhaps, shouldn't have irreducibly conscious causes.

My first reaction to this suggestion was that it betrayed an insufficient understanding of modern physics. Surely, I felt, the completeness premiss is simply part of standard physical theory. However, when my objectors pressed me, not unreasonably, to show them where the completeness of physics is written down in the physics textbooks, I found myself in some embarrassment. Once I was forced to defend it, I realized that the completeness of physics is by no means self-evident. Indeed, further research has led me to realize that, far from being self-evident, it is an issue on which the post-Galilean scientific tradition has changed its mind several times. The completeness of physics may seem the merest part of common sense to many of us today, but as recently as 150 years ago most people, including most orthodox scientists, would have thought the idea absurd, taking it to be obvious that there must be some *sui generis* conscious states in the causal history of human behaviour.

So the completeness of physics is a doctrine with a history, and a very interesting history at that. But the historical story also shows that this evidence is relatively recent, and that prior to the twentieth century the empirical case for the completeness of physics was by no means persuasive.

There is indeed a good case for materialism. But it has not always been available, to philosophers. This is because its crucial premiss, the completeness of physics, rests on empirical evidence which has emerged only relatively recently.

1.4 Functionalism and Eliminative Materialism

PAUL CHURCHLAND

Paul Churchland has written widely in the philosophy of psychology and related fields. He teaches at the University of California, San Diego.

FUNCTIONALISM

According to *functionalism,* the essential or defining feature of any type of mental state is the set of causal relations it bears to (1) environmental effects on the body, (2) other types of mental states, and (3) bodily behavior. Pain, for example, characteristically results from some bodily damage or trauma; it causes distress, annoyance, and practical reasoning aimed at relief; and it causes wincing, blanching, and nursing of the traumatized area. Any state that plays exactly that functional role is a pain, according to functionalism. Similarly, other types of mental states (sensations, fears, beliefs, and so on) are also defined by their unique causal roles in a complex economy of internal states mediating sensory inputs and behavioral outputs.

This view may remind the reader of behaviorism, and indeed it is the heir to behaviorism, but there is one fundamental difference between the two theories. Where the behaviorist hoped to define each type of mental state solely in terms of environmental input and behavioral output, the functionalist denies that this is possible. As he sees it, the adequate characterization of almost any mental state involves an ineliminable reference to a variety of other mental states with which it is causally connected, and so a reductive definition solely in terms of publicly observable inputs and outputs is quite impossible.

The difference between functionalism and the identity theory* will emerge from the following argument raised against the identity theory.

Imagine a being from another planet, says the functionalist, a being with an alien physiological constitution, a constitution based on the chemical element silicon, for example, instead of on the element carbon, as ours is. The chemistry and even the physical structure of the alien's brain would have to be systematically different from ours. But even so, that alien brain could well sustain a functional economy of internal states whose mutual *relations* parallel perfectly the mutual relations that define our own mental states. The alien may have an internal state that meets all the conditions for being a pain state, as outlined earlier. That state, considered from a purely physical point of view, would have a very different makeup from a human pain state, but it could nevertheless be identical to a human pain state from a purely functional point of view. And so for all of his functional states.

If the alien's functional economy of internal states were indeed *functionally isomorphic* with our own internal economy—if those states were causally connected to inputs, to one another, and to behavior in ways that parallel our own internal connections—then the alien would have pains, and desires, and hopes, and fears just as fully as we, despite the differences in the physical system that sustains or realizes those functional states. What is important for mentality is not the matter of which the creature is made, but the structure of the internal activities which that matter sustains.

If we can think of one alien constitution, we can think of many, and the point just made can also be made with an artificial system. Were we to create an electronic system—a computer of some kind—whose internal economy were functionally isomorphic with our own in all the relevant ways, then it too would be the subject of mental states.

What this illustrates is that there are almost certainly many more ways than one for nature, and perhaps even for man, to put together a thinking, feeling, perceiving creature. And this raises a problem for the identity theory, for it seems that there is no single type of physical state to which a given type of mental state must always correspond. Ironically, there are *too many* different kinds of physical systems that can realize the functional economy characteristic of conscious intelligence. If we consider the universe at large, therefore, and the future as well as the present, it seems quite unlikely that the identity theorist is going to find the one-to-one match-ups between the concepts of our commonsense mental taxonomy and the concepts of an overarching theory that encompasses all of the relevant

---

*The identity theory states that each type of mental state is identical to some specific type of physical state. This view is defended in our previous reading by David Papineau.—Ed.

physical systems. But that is what intertheoretic reduction is standardly said to require. The prospects for universal identities, between types of mental states and types of brain states, are therefore slim.

If the functionalists reject the traditional 'mental-type = physical type' identity theory, virtually all of them remain committed to a weaker 'mental token = physical token' identity theory, for they still maintain that each *instance* of a given type of mental state is numerically identical with some specific physical state in some physical system or other. It is only universal (type/type) identities that are rejected. Even so, this rejection is typically taken to support the claim that the science of psychology is or should be *methodologically autonomous* from the various physical sciences such as physics, biology, and even neurophysiology. Psychology, it is claimed, has its own irreducible laws and its own abstract subject matter.

[Today] functionalism is probably the most widely held theory of mind among philosophers, cognitive psychologists, and artificial intelligence researchers. Some of the reasons are apparent from the preceding discussion, and there are further reasons as well. In characterizing mental states as essentially functional states, functionalism places the concerns of psychology at a level that abstracts from the teeming detail of a brain's neurophysiological (or crystallo-graphic, or microelectronic) structure. The science of psychology, it is occasionally said, is methodologically autonomous from those other sciences (biology, neuroscience, circuit theory) whose concerns are with what amount to engineering details. This provides a rationale for a great deal of work in cognitive psychology and artificial intelligence, where researchers postulate a system of abstract functional states and then test the postulated system, often by way of its computer simulation, against human behavior in similar circumstances. The aim of such work is to discover in detail the functional organization that makes us what we are.

Arguments against Functionalism

Current popularity aside, functionalism also faces difficulties. The most commonly posed objection cites an old friend: sensory qualia. Functionalism may escape one of behaviorism's fatal flaws, it is said, but it still falls prey to the other. By attempting to make its *relational* properties the definitive feature of any mental state, functionalism ignores the 'inner' or qualitative nature of our mental states. But their qualitative nature is the essential feature of a great many types of mental state (pain, sensations of color, of temperature, of pitch, and so on), runs the objection, and functionalism is therefore false.

The standard illustration of this apparent failing is called "the inverted spectrum thought-experiment." It is entirely conceivable, runs the story, that the range of color sensations that I enjoy upon viewing standard objects is simply inverted relative to the color sensations that you enjoy. When viewing a tomato, I may have what is really a sensation-of-green where you have the normal sensation-of-red; when viewing a banana, I may have what is really sensation-of-blue where you have the normal sensation-of-yellow; and so forth. But since we have no way of comparing our inner qualia, and since I shall make all the same observational discriminations among objects that you will, there is no way to tell whether my spectrum is inverted relative to yours.

The problem for functionalism arises as follows. Even if my spectrum is inverted relative to yours, we remain functionally isomorphic with one another. My visual sensation upon viewing a tomato is *functionally* identical with your visual sensation upon viewing a tomato. According to functionalism, therefore, they are the very same type of state, and it does not even make sense to suppose that my sensation is 'really' a sensation-of-green. If it meets the functional conditions for being a sensation-of-red, then by definition it is a sensation-of-red. According to functionalism, apparently, a spectrum inversion of the kind described is ruled out by definition. But such inversions are entirely conceivable, concludes the objection, and if functionalism entails that they are not conceivable, then functionalism is false.

Another qualia-related worry for functionalism is the so-called "absent qualia problem." The functional organization characteristic of conscious intelligence can be instantiated (= realized or instanced) in a considerable variety of physical systems, some of them radically different from a normal human. For example, a giant electronic computer might instantiate it, and there are more radical possibilities still. One writer asks us to imagine the people of China—all 10^9 of them—organized into an intricate game of mutual interactions so that collectively they constitute a giant brain which exchanges inputs and outputs with a single robot body. That system of the robot-plus-10^9-unit-brain could presumably instantiate the relevant functional organization (though no doubt it would be much slower in its activities than a human or a computer), and would therefore be the subject of mental states, according to functionalism. But surely, it is urged, the complex states that there play the functional roles of pain, pleasure, and sensations-of-color would not have intrinsic qualia as ours do, and would therefore fail to be genuine mental states. Again, functionalism seems at best an incomplete account of the nature of mental states.

It has recently been argued that both the inverted-qualia and the absent-qualia objections can be met, without violence to functionalism and without significant violence to our commonsense intuitions about qualia. Consider the inversion problem first. I think the functionalist is right to insist that the type-identity of our visual sensations be reckoned according to their functional role. But the objector is also right in insisting that a relative inversion of two people's qualia, without functional inversion, is entirely conceivable. The apparent inconsistency between these positions can be dissolved by insisting that (1) our functional states (or rather, their physical realizations) do indeed have an intrinsic nature on which our introspective identification of those states depends; while also insisting that (2) such intrinsic natures are nevertheless not essential to the type-identity of a given mental state, and may indeed *vary* from instance to instance of the same type of mental state.

What this means is that the qualitative character of your sensation-of-red might be different

from the qualitative character of my sensation-of-red, slightly or substantially, and a third person's sensation-of-red might be different again. But so long as all three states are standardly caused by red objects and standardly cause all three of us to believe that something is red, then all three states are sensations-of-red, whatever their intrinsic qualitative character. Such intrinsic qualia merely serve as salient features that permit the quick introspective identification of sensations, as black-on-orange stripes serve as a salient feature for the quick visual identification of tigers. But specific qualia are not essential to the type-identity of mental states, any more than black-on-orange stripes are essential to the type-identity of tigers.

Plainly, this solution requires the functionalist to admit the *reality* of qualia, and we may wonder how there can be room for qualia in his materialist world-picture. Perhaps they can be fit in as follows: *identify* them with physical properties of whatever physical states instantiate the mental (functional) states that display them. For example, identify the qualitative nature of your sensations-of-red with that physical feature (of the brain state that instantiates it) to which your mechanisms of introspective discrimination are in fact responding when you judge that you have a sensation-of-red. If materialism is true, then there must *be* some internal physical feature or other to which your discrimination of sensations-of-red is keyed: *that* is the quale of your sensations-of-red. If the pitch of a sound can turn out to be the frequency of an oscillation in air pressure, there is no reason why the quale of a sensation cannot turn out to be, say, a spiking frequency in a certain neural pathway. ("Spikes" are the tiny electrochemical pulses by which our brain cells communicate.)

This entails that creatures with a constitution different from ours may have qualia different from ours, despite being psychologically isomorphic with us. It does not entail that they *must* have different qualia, however. If the qualitative character of my sensation-of-red is really a spiking frequency of 90 hertz in a certain neural pathway, it is possible that an electromechanical robot might enjoy the very same qualitative character if, in reporting sensations-of-red, the robot were responding to a spiking frequency of 90 hertz in a corresponding *copper* pathway. It might be the spiking frequency that matters to our respective mechanisms of discrimination, not the nature of the medium that carries it.

This proposal also suggests a solution to the absent qualia problem. So long as the physical system at issue is functionally isomorphic with us, to the last detail, then it will be equally capable of subtle introspective discriminations among its sensations. Those discriminations must be made on some systematic physical basis, that is, on some characteristic physical features of the states being discriminated. Those features at the objective focus of the system's discriminatory mechanisms, *those* are its sensory qualia—though the alien system is no more likely to appreciate their true physical nature than we appreciate the true physical nature of our own qualia. Sensory qualia are therefore an inevitable concomitant of any system with the kind of functional organization at issue. It may be difficult or impossible to 'see' the qualia in an alien system, but it is equally difficult to 'see' them even when looking into a human brain.

I leave it to the reader to judge the adequacy of these responses. If they are adequate, then, given its other virtues, functionalism must be conceded a very strong position among the competing contemporary theories of mind. It is interesting, however, that the defense offered in the last paragraph found it necessary to take a leaf from the identity theorist's book (types of quale are reduced to or identified with types of physical state), since the final objection we shall consider also tends to blur the distinction between functionalism and reductive materialism.

Consider the property of *temperature,* runs the objection. Here we have a paradigm of a physical property, one that has also been cited as the paradigm of a successfully *reduced* property, as expressed in the intertheoretic identity

"temperature = mean kinetic energy of constituent molecules."

Strictly speaking, however, this identity is true only for the temperature of a gas, where simple particles are free to move in ballistic fashion. In a *solid*, temperature is realized differently, since the interconnected molecules are confined to a variety of vibrational motions. In a *plasma*, temperature is something else again, since a plasma has no constituent molecules; they, and their constituent atoms, have been ripped to pieces. And even a *vacuum* has a so-called 'blackbody' temperature—in the distribution of electromagnetic waves coursing through it. Here temperature has nothing to do with the kinetic energy of particles.

It is plain that the physical property of temperature enjoys 'multiple instantiations' no less than do psychological properties. Does this mean that thermodynamics (the theory of heat and temperature) is an 'autonomous science,' separable from the rest of physics, with its own irreducible laws and its own abstract nonphysical subject matter?

Presumably not. What it means, concludes the objection, is that *reductions are domain-specific*:

temperature-in-a-gas = the mean kinetic energy of the gas's molecules,

whereas

temperature-in-a-vacuum = the blackbody distribution of the vacuum's transient radiation.

Similarly, perhaps

joy-in-a-human = resonances in the lateral hypothalamus,

whereas

joy-in-a-Martian = something else entirely.

This means that we may expect some type/type reductions of mental states to physical states after all, though they will be much narrower than was first suggested. Furthermore, it means that functionalist claims concerning the radical autonomy of psychology cannot be sustained.

And last, it suggests that functionalism is not so profoundly different from the identity theory as was first made out.

As with the defense of functionalism outlined earlier, I leave the evaluation of this criticism to the reader. At this point, let us turn to the final materialist theory of mind, for functionalism is not the only major reaction against the identity theory.

ELIMINATIVE MATERIALISM

The identity theory was called into doubt not because the prospects for a materialist account of our mental capacities were thought to be poor, but because it seemed unlikely that the arrival of an adequate materialist theory would bring with it the nice one-to-one match-ups, between the concepts of folk psychology and the concepts of theoretical neuroscience, that intertheoretic reduction requires. The reason for that doubt was the great variety of quite different physical systems that could instantiate the required functional organization. *Eliminative materialism* also doubts that the correct neuroscientific account of human capacities will produce a neat reduction of our commonsense framework, but here the doubts arise from a quite different source.

As the eliminative materialists see it, the one-to-one match-ups will not be found, and our commonsense psychological framework will not enjoy an intertheoretic reduction, *because our commonsense psychological framework is a false and radically misleading conception of the causes of human behavior and the nature of cognitive activity.* On this view, folk psychology is not just an incomplete representation of our inner natures; it is an outright *mis*representation of our internal states and activities. Consequently, we cannot expect a truly adequate neuroscientific account of our inner lives to provide theoretical categories that match up nicely with the categories of our commonsense framework. Accordingly, we must expect that the older framework will simply be eliminated, rather than be reduced, by a matured neuroscience.

Historical Parallels

As the identity theorist can point to historical cases of successful intertheoretic reduction, so the eliminative materialist can point to historical cases of the outright elimination of the ontology of an older theory in favor of the ontology of a new and superior theory. For most of the eighteenth and nineteenth centuries, learned people believed that heat was a subtle *fluid* held in bodies, much in the way water is held in a sponge. A fair body of moderately successful theory described the way this fluid substance—called "caloric"—flowed within a body, or from one body to another, and how it produced thermal expansion, melting, boiling, and so forth. But by the end of the last century it had become abundantly clear that heat was not a substance at all, but just the energy of motion of the trillions of jostling molecules that make up the heated body itself. The new theory—the "corpuscular/kinetic theory of matter and heat"—was much more successful than the old in explaining and predicting the thermal behavior of bodies. And since we were unable to *identify* caloric fluid with kinetic energy (according to the old theory, caloric is a material *substance*; according to the new theory, kinetic energy is a form of *motion*), it was finally agreed that there is *no such thing* as caloric. Caloric was simply eliminated from our accepted ontology.

A second example. It used to be thought that when a piece of wood burns, or a piece of metal rusts, a spiritlike substance called "phlogiston" was being released: briskly, in the former case, slowly in the latter. Once gone, that 'noble' substance left only a base pile of ash or rust. It later came to be appreciated that both processes involve, not the loss of something, but the *gaining* of a substance taken from the atmosphere: oxygen. Phlogiston emerged, not as an incomplete description of what was going on, but as a radical misdescription. Phlogiston was therefore not suitable for reduction to or identification with some notion from within the new oxygen chemistry, and it was simply eliminated from science.

Admittedly, both of these examples concern the elimination of something nonobservable, but our history also includes the elimination of certain widely accepted 'observables.' Before Copernicus' views became available, almost any human who ventured out at night could look up at *the starry sphere of the heavens,* and if he stayed for more than a few minutes he could also see that it *turned,* around an axis through Polaris. What the sphere was made of (crystal?) and what made it turn (the gods?) were theoretical questions that exercised us for over two millennia. But hardly anyone doubted the existence of what everyone could observe with their own eyes. In the end, however, we learned to reinterpret our visual experience of the night sky within a very different conceptual framework, and the turning sphere evaporated.

Witches provide another example. Psychosis is a fairly common affliction among humans, and in earlier centuries its victims were standardly seen as cases of demonic possession, as instances of Satan's spirit itself, glaring malevolently out at us from behind the victims' eyes. That witches exist was not a matter of any controversy. One would occasionally see them, in any city or hamlet, engaged in incoherent, paranoid, or even murderous behavior. But observable or not, we eventually decided that witches simply do not exist. We concluded that the concept of a witch is an element in a conceptual framework that misrepresents so badly the phenomena to which it was standardly applied that literal application of the notion should be permanently withdrawn. Modern theories of mental dysfunction led to the elimination of witches from our serious ontology.

The concepts of folk psychology—belief, desire, fear, sensation, pain, joy, and so on—await a similar fate, according to the view at issue. And when neuroscience has matured to the point where the poverty of our current conceptions is apparent to everyone, and the superiority of the new framework is established, we shall then be able to set about *re*conceiving our internal states and activities, within a truly adequate conceptual framework at last. Our explanations of one

another's behavior will appeal to such things as our neuropharmacological states, the neural activity in specialized anatomical areas, and whatever other states are deemed relevant by the new theory. Our private introspection will also be transformed, and may be profoundly enhanced by reason of the more accurate and penetrating framework it will have to work with— just as the astronomer's perception of the night sky is much enhanced by the detailed knowledge of modern astronomical theory that he or she possesses.

The magnitude of the conceptual revolution here suggested should not be minimized: it would be enormous. And the benefits to humanity might be equally great. If each of us possessed an accurate neuroscientific understanding of (what we now conceive dimly as) the varieties and causes of mental illness, the factors involved in learning, the neural basis of emotions, intelligence, and socialization, then the sum total of human misery might be much reduced. The simple increase in mutual understanding that the new framework made possible could contribute substantially toward a more peaceful and humane society. Of course, there would be dangers as well: increased knowledge means increased power, and power can always be misused.

Arguments for Eliminative Materialism

The arguments for eliminative materialism are diffuse and less than decisive, but they are stronger than is widely supposed. The distinguishing feature of this position is its denial that a smooth intertheoretic reduction is to be expected—even a species-specific reduction—of the framework of folk psychology to the framework of a matured neuroscience. The reason for this denial is the eliminative materialist's conviction that folk psychology is a hopelessly primitive and deeply confused conception of our internal activities. But why this low opinion of our common-sense conceptions?

There are at least three reasons. First, the eliminative materialist will point to the widespread explanatory, predictive, and manipulative failures of folk psychology. So much of what is central and familiar to us remains a complete mystery from within folk psychology. We do not know what *sleep* is, or why we have to have it, despite spending a full third of our lives in that condition. (The answer, "For rest," is mistaken. Even if people are allowed to rest continuously, their need for sleep is undiminished. Apparently, sleep serves some deeper functions, but we do not yet know what they are.) We do not understand how *learning* transforms each of us from a gaping infant to a cunning adult, or how differences in *intelligence* are grounded. We have not the slightest idea how *memory* works, or how we manage to retrieve relevant bits of information instantly from the awesome mass we have stored. We do not know what *mental illness* is, nor how to cure it.

In sum, the most central things about us remain almost entirely mysterious from within folk psychology. And the defects noted cannot be blamed on inadequate time allowed for their correction, for folk psychology has enjoyed no significant changes or advances in well over 2,000 years, despite its manifest failures. Truly successful theories may be expected to reduce, but significantly unsuccessful theories merit no such expectation.

This argument from explanatory poverty has a further aspect. So long as one sticks to normal brains, the poverty of folk psychology is perhaps not strikingly evident. But as soon as one examines the many perplexing behavioral and cognitive deficits suffered by people with *damaged* brains, one's descriptive and explanatory resources start to claw the air. As with other humble theories asked to operate successfully in unexplored extensions of their old domain (for example, Newtonian mechanics in the domain of velocities close to the velocity of light, and the classical gas law in the domain of high pressures or temperatures), the descriptive and explanatory inadequacies of folk psychology become starkly evident.

The second argument tries to draw an inductive lesson from our conceptual history. Our early folk theories of motion were profoundly confused, and were eventually displaced entirely by more sophisticated theories. Our early folk theories of the structure and activity of the heavens were wildly off the mark, and survive only as historical lessons in how wrong we can be. Our folk theories of the nature of fire, and the nature of life, were similarly cockeyed. And one could go on, since the vast majority of our past folk conceptions have been similarly exploded. All except folk psychology, which survives to this day and has only recently begun to feel pressure. But the phenomenon of conscious intelligence is surely a more complex and difficult phenomenon than any of those just listed. So far as accurate understanding is concerned, it would be a *miracle* if we had got *that* one right the very first time, when we fell down so badly on all the others. Folk psychology has survived for so very long, presumably, not because it is basically correct in its representations, but because the phenomena addressed are so surpassingly difficult that any useful handle on them, no matter how feeble, is unlikely to be displaced in a hurry.

A third argument attempts to find an a priori advantage for eliminative materialism over the identity theory and functionalism. It attempts to counter the common intuition that eliminative materialism is distantly possible, perhaps, but is much less probable than either the identity theory or functionalism. The focus again is on whether the concepts of folk psychology will find vindicating match-ups in a matured neuroscience. The eliminativist bets no; the other two bet yes. (Even the functionalist bets yes, but expects the match-ups to be only species-specific, or only person-specific. Functionalism, recall, denies the existence only of *universal* type/type identities.)

The eliminativist will point out that the requirements on a reduction are rather demanding. The new theory must entail a set of principles and embedded concepts that mirrors very closely the specific conceptual structure to be reduced. And the fact is, there are vastly many more ways of being an explanatorily successful neuroscience while *not* mirroring the structure of folk psychology, than there are ways of being an explanatorily successful neuroscience while also *mirroring* the very specific structure of folk psychology. Accordingly, the a priori probability of eliminative materialism is not lower, but substantially *higher* than that of either of its competitors. One's initial intuitions here are simply mistaken.

Granted, this initial a priori advantage could be reduced if there were a very strong presumption in favor of the truth of folk psychology—true theories are better bets to win reduction. But according to the first two arguments, the presumptions on this point should run in precisely the opposite direction.

Arguments against Eliminative Materialism

The initial plausibility of this rather radical view is low for almost everyone, since it denies deeply entrenched assumptions. That is at best a question-begging complaint, of course, since those assumptions are precisely what is at issue. But the following line of thought does attempt to mount a real argument.

Eliminative materialism is false, runs the argument, because one's introspection reveals directly the existence of pains, beliefs, desires, fears, and so forth. Their existence is as obvious as anything could be.

The eliminative materialist will reply that this argument makes the same mistake that an ancient or medieval person would be making if he insisted that he could just see with his own eyes that the heavens form a turning sphere, or that witches exist. The fact is, all observation occurs within some system of concepts, and our observation judgments are only as good as the conceptual framework in which they are expressed. In all three cases—the starry sphere, witches, and the familiar mental states—precisely what is challenged is the integrity of the background conceptual framework in which the observation judgments are expressed. To insist on the validity of one's experiences, *traditionally interpreted,* is therefore to beg the very question at issue. For in all three cases, the question is whether we should *re*conceive the nature of some familiar observational domain.

A second criticism attempts to find an incoherence in the eliminative materialist's position. The bald statement of eliminative materialism is that the familiar mental states do not really exist. But that statement is meaningful, runs the argument, only if it is the expression of a certain *belief,* and an *intention* to communicate, and a *knowledge* of the language, and so forth. But if the statement is true, then no such mental states exist, and the statement is therefore a meaningless string of marks or noises, and cannot be true. Evidently, the assumption that eliminative materialism is true entails that it cannot be true.

The hole in this argument is the premise concerning the conditions necessary for a statement to be meaningful. It begs the question. If eliminative materialism is true, then meaningfulness must have some different source. To insist on the 'old' source is to insist on the validity of the very framework at issue. Again, an historical parallel may be helpful here. Consider the medieval theory that being biologically *alive* is a matter of being ensouled by an immaterial *vital spirit.* And consider the following response to someone who has expressed disbelief in that theory.

My learned friend has stated that there is no such thing as vital spirit. But this statement is incoherent. For if it is true, then my friend does not have vital spirit, and must therefore be *dead.* But if he is dead, then his statement is just a string of noises, devoid of meaning or truth. Evidently, the assumption that antivitalism is true entails that it cannot be true! Q.E.D.

This second argument is now a joke, but the first argument begs the question in exactly the same way.

A final criticism draws a much weaker conclusion, but makes a rather stronger case. Eliminative materialism, it has been said, is making mountains out of molehills. It exaggerates the defects in folk psychology, and underplays its real successes. Perhaps the arrival of a matured neuroscience will require the elimination of the occasional folk-psychological concept, continues the criticism, and a minor adjustment in certain folk-psychological principles may have to be endured. But the large-scale elimination forecast by the eliminative materialist is just an alarmist worry or a romantic enthusiasm.

Perhaps this complaint is correct. And perhaps it is merely complacent. Whichever, it does bring out the important point that we do not confront two simple and mutually exclusive possibilities here: pure reduction versus pure elimination. Rather, these are the end points of a smooth spectrum of possible outcomes, between which there are mixed cases of partial elimination and partial reduction. Only empirical research can tell us where on that spectrum our own case will fall. Perhaps we should speak here, more liberally, of "revisionary materialism," instead of concentrating on the more radical possibility of an across-the-board elimination. Perhaps we should. But it has been my aim in this section to make it at least intelligible to you that our collective conceptual destiny lies substantially toward the revolutionary end of the spectrum.

CHAPTER 2

CAN NON-HUMANS THINK?

2.1 Computing Machinery and Intelligence

ALAN TURING

Alan Turing (1912–1954), a British mathematician, did important work in probability theory and was one of the founders of modern computation theory. He played an indispensable role in breaking German codes during World War II.

THE IMITATION GAME

I propose to consider the question "Can machines think?" This should begin with definitions of the meaning of the terms 'machine' and 'think.' The definitions might be framed so as to reflect so far as possible the normal use of the words, but this attitude is dangerous. If the meaning of the words 'machine' and 'think' are to be found by examining how they are commonly used it is difficult to escape the conclusion that the meaning and the answer to the question, "Can machines think?" is to be sought in a statistical survey such as a Gallup poll. But this

is absurd. Instead of attempting such a definition I shall replace the question by another, which is closely related to it and is expressed in relatively unambiguous words.

The new form of the problem can be described in terms of a game which we call the "imitation game." It is played with three people, a man (A), a woman (B), and an interrogator (C) who may be of either sex. The interrogator stays in a room apart from the other two. The object of the game for the interrogator is to determine which of the other two is the man and which is the woman. He knows them by labels X

From Alan Turing, "Computing Machinery and Intelligence," *Mind*, vol. 59 (1950). Reprinted by permission of Oxford University Press.

and Y, and at the end of the game he says either "X is A and Y is B" or "X is B and Y is A." The interrogator is allowed to put questions to A and B thus:

C: Will X please tell me the length of his or her hair?

Now suppose X is actually A, then A must answer. It is A's object in the game to try to cause C to make the wrong identification. His answer might therefore be

A: My hair is shingled, and the longest strands are about nine inches long.

In order that tones of voice may not help the interrogator the answers should be written, or better still, typewritten. The ideal arrangement is to have a teleprinter communicating between the two rooms. Alternatively the question and answers can be repeated by an intermediary. The object of the game for the third player (B) is to help the interrogator. The best strategy for her is probably to give truthful answers. She can add such things as "I am the woman, don't listen to him!" to her answers, but it will avail nothing as the man can make similar remarks.

We now ask the question, "What will happen when a machine takes the part of A in this game?" Will the interrogator decide wrongly as often when the game is played like this as he does when the game is played between a man and a woman? These questions replace our original, "Can machines think?"

CRITIQUE OF THE NEW PROBLEM

As well as asking, "What is the answer to this new form of the question?" one may ask, "Is this new question a worthy one to investigate?" This latter question we investigate without further ado, thereby cutting short an infinite regress.

The new problem has the advantage of drawing a fairly sharp line between the physical and the intellectual capacities of a man. No engineer or chemist claims to be able to produce a material which is indistinguishable from the human skin. It is possible that at some time this might be done,

but even supposing this invention was available we should feel there was little point in trying to make a "thinking machine" more human by dressing it up in such artificial flesh. The form in which we have set the problem reflects this fact in the condition which prevents the interrogator from seeing or touching the other competitors, or hearing their voices. Some other advantages of the proposed criterion may be shown up by specimen questions and answers. Thus:

Q: Please write me a sonnet on the subject of the Forth Bridge.
A: Count me out on this one. I never could write poetry.
Q: Add 34957 to 70764.
A: (Pause about 30 seconds and then give as answer) 105621.
Q: Do you play chess?
A: Yes.
Q: I have K at my K1, and no other pieces. You have only K at K6 and R at R1. It is your move. What do you play?
A: (After a pause of 15 seconds) R–R8 mate.

The question and answer method seems to be suitable for introducing almost any one of the fields of human endeavor that we wish to include. We do not wish to penalize the machine for its inability to shine in beauty competitions, nor to penalize a man for losing in a race against an airplane. The conditions of our game make these disabilities irrelevant. The "witnesses" can brag, if they consider it advisable, as much as they please about their charms, strength or heroism, but the interrogator cannot demand practical demonstrations.

The game may perhaps be criticized on the ground that the odds are weighted too heavily against the machine. If the man were to try and pretend to be the machine he would clearly make a very poor showing. He would be given away at once by slowness and inaccuracy in arithmetic. May not machines carry out something which ought to be described as thinking but which is very different from what a man does? This objection is a very strong one, but at least we can say that if, nevertheless, a machine can be constructed to play the imitation game satisfactorily, we need not be troubled by this objection.

It might be urged that when playing the "imitation game" the best strategy for the machine may possibly be something other than imitation of the behavior of a man. This may be, but I think it is unlikely that there is any great effect of this kind. In any case there is no intention to investigate here the theory of the game, and it will be assumed that the best strategy is to try to provide answers that would naturally be given by a man.

THE MACHINES CONCERNED IN THE GAME

The question which we put in section 1 will not be quite definite until we have specified what we mean by the word 'machine.' It is natural that we should wish to permit every kind of engineering technique to be used in our machines. We also wish to allow the possibility that an engineer or team of engineers may construct a machine which works, but whose manner of operation cannot be satisfactorily described by its constructors because they have applied a method which is largely experimental. Finally, we wish to exclude from the machines men born in the usual manner. It is difficult to frame the definitions so as to satisfy these three conditions. One might for instance insist that the team of engineers should be all of one sex, but this would not really be satisfactory, for it is probably possible to rear a complete individual from a single cell of the skin (say) of a man. To do so would be a feat of biological technique deserving of the very highest praise, but we would not be inclined to regard it as a case of "constructing a thinking machine." This prompts us to abandon the requirement that every kind of technique should be permitted. We are the more ready to do so in view of the fact that the present interest in "thinking machines" has been aroused by a particular kind of machine, usually called an "electronic computer" or "digital computer." Following this suggestion we only permit digital computers to take part in our game....

UNIVERSALITY OF DIGITAL COMPUTERS

[D]igital computers...may be classified among the "discrete state machines." These are the machines which move by sudden jumps or clicks from one quite definite state to another. These states are sufficiently different for the possibility of confusion between them to be ignored. Strictly speaking there are no such machines. Everything really moves continuously. But there are many kinds of machines which can profitably be *thought of* as being discrete state machines. For instance in considering the switches for a lighting system it is a convenient fiction that each switch must be definitely on or definitely off. There must be intermediate positions, but for most purposes we can forget about them. As an example of a discrete state machine, we might consider a wheel which clicks round through 120° once a second, but may be stopped by a lever which can be operated from outside; in addition a lamp is to light in one of the positions of the wheel. This machine could be described abstractly as follows: The internal state of the machine (which is described by the position of the wheel) may be q_1, q_2, or q_3. There is an input signal i_0 or i_1 (position or lever). The internal state at any moment is determined by the last state and input signal according to the table

		Last state:		
		q_1	q_2	q_3
Input:	i_0	q_2	q_3	q_1
	i_1	q_1	q_2	q_3

The output signals, the only externally visible indication of the internal state (the light), are described by the table

State:	q_1	q_2	q_3
Output:	O_0	O_0	O_1

This example is typical of discrete state machines. They can be described by such tables, provided they have only a finite number of possible states....

Given the table corresponding to a discrete state machine, it is possible to predict what it will do. There is no reason why this calculation should not be carried out by means of a digital computer. Provided it could be carried out sufficiently quickly the digital computer could mimic the behavior of any discrete state machine. The imitation game could then be played with the machine in question (as B) and the mimicking digital computer (as A) and the interrogator would be unable to distinguish them. Of course the digital computer must have adequate storage capacity as well as working sufficiently fast. Moreover, it must be programmed afresh for each new machine which it is desired to mimic.

This special property of digital computers, that they can mimic any discrete state machine, is described by saying that they are *universal* machines. The existence of machines with this property has the important consequence that, considerations of speed apart, it is unnecessary to design various new machines to do various computing processes. They can all be done with one digital computer, suitably programmed for each case. It will be seen that as a consequence of this all digital computers are in a sense equivalent.

We may now consider again the point raised at the end of section 3. It was suggested tentatively that the question, "Can machines think?" should be replaced by "Are there imaginable digital computers which would do well in the imitation game?" If we wish we can make this superficially more general and ask, "Are there discrete state machines which would do well?" But in view of the universality property we see that either of these questions is equivalent to this: Let us fix our attention on one particular digital computer C. Is it true that by modifying this computer to have an adequate storage, suitably increasing its speed of action, and providing it with an appropriate program, C can be made to play satisfactorily the part of A in the imitation game, the part of B being taken by a man?"

CONTRARY VIEWS ON THE MAIN QUESTION

We may now consider the ground to have been cleared and we are ready to proceed to the debate on our question, "Can machines think?" and the variant of it quoted at the end of the last section. We cannot altogether abandon the original form of the problem, for opinions will differ as to the appropriateness of the substitution and we must at least listen to what has to be said in this connection.

It will simplify matters for the reader if I explain first my own beliefs in the matter. Consider first the more accurate form of the question. I believe that in about fifty years' time it will be possible to program computers, with a storage capacity of about 10^9, to make them play the imitation game so well that an average interrogator will not have more than 70 percent chance of making the right identification after five minutes of questioning. The original question, "Can machines think?" I believe to be too meaningless to deserve discussion. Nevertheless I believe that at the end of the twentieth century the use of words and general educated opinion will have altered so much that one will be able to speak of machines thinking without expecting to be contradicted. I believe further that no useful purpose is served by concealing these beliefs. The popular view that scientists proceed inexorably from well-established fact to well-established fact, never being influenced by any unproved conjecture, is quite mistaken. Provided it is made clear which are proved facts and which are conjectures, no harm can result. Conjectures are of great importance since they suggest useful lines of research.

I now proceed to consider opinions opposed to my own.

(1) The Theological Objection

Thinking is a function of man's immortal soul. God has given an immortal soul to every man and woman, but not to any other animal or to machines. Hence no animal or machine can think.

I am unable to accept any part of this, but will attempt to reply in theological terms. I should find the argument more convincing if animals were classed with men, for there is a greater difference, to my mind, between the typical animate and the inanimate than there is between man and the other animals. The arbitrary character of the orthodox view becomes clearer if we consider how it might appear to a member of some other religious community. How do Christians regard the Moslem view that women have no souls? But let us leave this point aside and return to the main argument. It appears to me that the argument quoted above implies a serious restriction of the omnipotence of the Almighty. It is admitted that there are certain things that He cannot do such as making one equal to two, but should we not believe that He has freedom to confer a soul on an elephant if He sees fit? We might expect that He would only exercise this power in conjunction with a mutation which provided the elephant with an appropriately improved brain to minister to the needs of this soul. An argument of exactly similar form may be made for the case of machines. It may seem different because it is more difficult to "swallow." But this really only means that we think it would be less likely that He would consider the circumstances suitable for conferring a soul. The circumstances in question are discussed in the rest of this paper. In attempting to construct such machines we should not be irreverently usurping His power of creating souls, any more than we are in the procreation of children: rather we are, in either case, instruments of His will providing mansions for the souls that He creates.

However, this is mere speculation. I am not very impressed with theological arguments, whatever they may be used to support. Such arguments have often been found unsatisfactory in the past. In the time of Galileo it was argued that the texts, "And the sun stood still...and hasted not to go down about a whole day" (Joshua x.

13) and "He laid the foundations of the earth, that it should not move at any time" (Psalm cv. 5) were an adequate refutation of the Copernican theory. With our present knowledge, such an argument appears futile. When that knowledge was not available, it made a quite different impression.

(2) The "Heads in the Sand" Objection

"The consequences of machines thinking would be too dreadful. Let us hope and believe that they cannot do so."

This argument is seldom expressed quite so openly as in the form above. But it affects most of us who think about it at all. We like to believe that Man is in some subtle way superior to the rest of creation. It is best if he can be shown to be *necessarily* superior, for then there is no danger of him losing his commanding position. The popularity of the theological argument is clearly connected with this feeling. It is likely to be quite strong in intellectual people, since they value the power of thinking more highly than others, and are more inclined to base their belief in the superiority of Man on this power.

I do not think that this argument is sufficiently substantial to require refutation. Consolation would be more appropriate; perhaps this should be sought in the transmigration of souls....

(3) The Argument from Consciousness

This argument is very well expressed in Professor Jefferson's Lister Oration for 1949, from which I quote.

> Not until a machine can write a sonnet or compose a concerto because of thoughts and emotions felt, and not by the chance fall of symbols, could we agree that machine equals brain—that is, not only write it but know that it had written it. No mechanism could feel (and not merely artificially signal, an easy contrivance) pleasure at its successes, grief when its valves fuse, be warmed by flattery, be made miserable by its mistakes, be charmed by sex, be angry or depressed when it cannot get what it wants.

This argument appears to be a denial of the validity of our test. According to the most extreme form of this view, the only way by which one could be sure that a machine thinks is to *be* the machine and to feel oneself thinking. One could then describe these feelings to the world, but of course no one would be justified in taking any notice. Likewise according to this view, the only way to know that a *man* thinks is to be that particular man. It is in fact the solipsist point of view. It may be the most logical view to hold but it makes communication of ideas difficult. A is liable to believe "A thinks but B does not" while B believes "B thinks but A does not." Instead of arguing continually over this point, it is usual to have the polite convention that everyone thinks.

I am sure that Professor Jefferson does not wish to adopt the extreme and solipsist point of view. Probably he would be quite willing to accept the imitation game as a test. The game (with the player B omitted) is frequently used in practice under the name of *viva voce* to discover whether someone really understands something or has "learned it parrot fashion." Let us listen in to a part of such a *viva voce:*

Interrogator: In the first line of your sonnet, which reads "Shall I compare thee to a summer's day," would not "a spring day" do as well or better?

Witness: It wouldn't scan.

Interrogator: How about "a winter's day." That would scan all right.

Witness: Yes, but nobody wants to be compared to a winter's day.

Interrogator: Would you say Mr. Pickwick reminded you of Christmas?

Witness: In a way.

Interrogator: Yet Christmas is a winter's day, and I do not think Mr. Pickwick would mind the comparison.

Witness: I don't think you're serious. By a winter's day one means a typical winter's day, rather than a special one like Christmas.

And so on. What would Professor Jefferson say if the sonnet-writing machine were able to answer like this in the *viva voce?* I do not know whether he would regard the machine as "merely artificially signalling" these answers, but if the answers were as satisfactory and sustained as in the above passage I do not think he would describe it as "an easy contrivance." This phrase is, I think, intended to cover such devices as the inclusion in the machine of a record of someone reading a sonnet, with appropriate switching to turn it on from time to time.

In short then, I think that most of those who support the argument from consciousness could be persuaded to abandon it rather than be forced into the solipsist position. They will then probably be willing to accept our test.

I do not wish to give the impression that I think there is no mystery about consciousness. There is, for instance, something of a paradox connected with any attempt to localize it. But I do not think these mysteries necessarily need to be solved before we can answer the question with which we are concerned in this paper.

(4) Arguments from Various Disabilities

These arguments take the form, "I grant you that you can make machines do all the things you have mentioned but you will never be able to make one to do X." Numerous features X are suggested in this connection. I offer a selection:

> Be kind, resourceful, beautiful, friendly, have initiative, have a sense of humor, tell right from wrong, make mistakes, fall in love, enjoy strawberries and cream, make someone fall in love with it, learn from experience, use words properly, be the subject of its own thought, have as much diversity of behavior as a man, do something really new....

No support is usually offered for these statements. I believe they are mostly founded on the principle of scientific induction. A man has seen thousands of machines in his lifetime. From what he sees of them he draws a number of general conclusions. They are ugly, each is designed for a very limited purpose, when required for a minutely different purpose they are useless, the variety of behavior of any one of them is very small, and so on and so forth. Naturally he [mistakenly] concludes that these are necessary properties of machines in general....

There are, however, special remarks to be made about many of the disabilities that have been mentioned.

The claim that "machines cannot make mistakes" seems a curious one. One is tempted to retort, "Are they any the worse for that?" But let us adopt a more sympathetic attitude, and try to see what is really meant. I think this criticism can be explained in terms of the imitation game. It is claimed that the interrogator could distinguish the machine from the man simply by setting them a number of problems in arithmetic. The machine would be unmasked because of its deadly accuracy. The reply to this is simple. The machine (programmed for playing the game) would not attempt to give the *right* answers to the arithmetic problems. It would deliberately introduce mistakes in a manner calculated to confuse the interrogator....

The claim that a machine cannot be the subject of its own thought can of course only be answered if it can be shown that the machine has *some* thought with *some* subject matter. Nevertheless, "the subject matter of a machine's operations" does seem to mean something, at least to the people who deal with it. If, for instance, the machine were trying to find a solution of the equation $x^2 - 40x - 11 = 0$, one would be tempted to describe this equation as part of the machine's subject matter at that moment. It may be used to help in making up its own programs, or to predict the effect of alterations in its own structure. By observing the results of its own behavior it can modify its own programs so as to achieve some purpose more effectively. These are possibilities of the near future, rather than Utopian dreams....

(5) Lady Lovelace's Objection

...A variant of Lady Lovelace's objection states that a machine can "never do anything really new." This may be parried for the moment with the saw, "There is nothing new under the sun." Who can be certain that "original work" that he has done was not simply the growth of the seed planted in him by teaching, or the effect

of following well-known general principles. A better variant of the objection says that a machine can never "take us by surprise." This statement is a more direct challenge and can be met directly. Machines take me by surprise with great frequency. This is largely because I do not do sufficient calculation to decide what to expect them to do, or rather because, although I do a calculation, I do it in a hurried, slipshod fashion, taking risks. Perhaps I say to myself, "I suppose the voltage here ought to be the same as there: anyway let's assume it is." Naturally I am often wrong, and the result is a surprise for me, for by the time the experiment is done these assumptions have been forgotten. These admissions lay me open to lectures on the subject of my vicious ways, but do not throw any doubt on my credibility when I testify to the surprises I experience.

I do not expect this reply to silence my critic. He will probably say that such surprises are due to some creative mental act on my part, and reflect no credit on the machine. This leads us back to the argument from consciousness, and far from the idea of surprise. It is a line of argument we must consider closed, but it is perhaps worth remarking that the appreciation of something as surprising requires as much of a "creative mental act" whether the surprising event originates from a man, a book, a machine or anything else.

The view that machines cannot give rise to surprises is due, I believe, to a fallacy to which philosophers and mathematicians are particularly subject. This is the assumption that as soon as a fact is presented to a mind all consequences of that fact spring into the mind simultaneously with it. It is a very useful assumption under many circumstances, but one too easily forgets that it is false. A natural consequence of doing so is that one then assumes that there is no virtue in the mere working out of consequences from data and general principles....

(6) The Argument from Informality of Behavior

It is not possible to produce a set of rules purporting to describe what a man should do in every conceivable set of circumstances. One might for instance have a rule that one is to stop when one sees a red traffic light, and to go if one sees a green one; but what if by some fault both appear together? One may perhaps decide that it is safest to stop. But some further difficulty may well arise from this decision later. To attempt to provide rules of conduct to cover every eventuality, even those arising from traffic lights, appears to be impossible. With all this I agree.

From this it is argued that we cannot be machines. I shall try to reproduce the argument, but I fear I shall hardly do it justice. It seems to run something like this: "If each man had a definite set of rules of conduct by which he regulated his life he would be no better than a machine. But there are no such rules, so men cannot be machines." The undistributed middle is glaring. I do not think the argument is ever put quite like this, but I believe this is the argument used nevertheless. There may however be a certain confusion between "rules of conduct" and "laws of behavior" to cloud the issue. By "rules of conduct" I mean precepts such as "Stop if you see red lights," on which one can act, and of which one can be conscious. By "laws of behavior" I mean laws of nature as applied to a man's body such as "if you pinch him he will squeak." If we substitute "laws of behavior which regulate his life" for "laws of conduct by which he regulates his life" in the argument quoted the undistributed middle is no longer inseperable. For we believe that it is not only true that being regulated by laws of behavior implies being some sort of machine (though not necessarily a discrete state machine), but that conversely being such a machine implies being regulated by such laws. However, we cannot so easily convince ourselves of the absence of complete laws of behavior as of complete rules of conduct. The only way we know of for finding such laws is scientific observation, and we certainly know of no circumstances under which we could say: "We have searched enough. There are no such laws."

We can demonstrate more forcibly that any such statement would be unjustified. For suppose we could be sure of finding such laws if they existed. Then given a discrete state machine it should certainly be possible to discover by observation sufficient about it to predict its future behavior, and this within a reasonable time, say a thousand years. But this does not seem to be the case. I have set up on the Manchester computer a small program using only 1000 units of storage, whereby the machine supplied with one sixteen figure number replies with another within two seconds. I would defy anyone to learn from these replies sufficient about the program to be able to predict any replies to untried values....

LEARNING MACHINES

The reader will have anticipated that I have no very convincing arguments of a positive nature to support my views. If I had I should not have taken such pains to point out the fallacies in contrary views. Such evidence as I have I shall now give.

Let us return for a moment to Lady Lovelace's objection, which stated that the machine can only do what we tell it to do. One could say that a man can "inject" an idea into the machine, and that it will respond to a certain extent and then drop into quiescence, like a piano string struck by a hammer. Another simile would be an atomic pile of less than critical size: an injected idea is to correspond to a neutron entering the pile from without. Each such neutron will cause a certain disturbance which eventually dies away. If, however, the size of the pile is sufficiently increased, the disturbance caused by such an incoming neutron will very likely go on and on, increasing until the whole pile is destroyed. Is there a corresponding phenomenon for minds, and is there one for machines? There does seem to be one for the human mind. The majority of them seem to be "subcritical," that is, to correspond in this analogy to piles of subcritical size. An idea presented to such a mind will on an average give rise to less than one idea in reply. A smallish proportion are supercritical. An idea presented to such a mind may give rise to a whole "theory" consisting of secondary, tertiary and more remote ideas. Animals' minds seem to be very definitely subcritical. Adhering to this analogy we ask, "Can a machine be made to be supercritical?"

The "skin of an onion" analogy is also helpful. In considering the functions of the mind or the brain we find certain operations which we can explain in purely mechanical terms. This we say does not correspond to the real mind: it is a sort of skin which we must strip off if we are to find the real mind. But then in what remains we find a further skin to be stripped off, and so on. Proceeding in this way, do we ever come to the "real" mind, or do we eventually come to the skin which has nothing in it? In the latter case the whole mind is mechanical. (It would not be a discrete state machine however. We have discussed this.)

These last two paragraphs do not claim to be convincing arguments. They should rather be described as "recitations tending to produce belief."

The only really satisfactory support that can be given for the view expressed at the beginning of [the preceding] section will be that provided by waiting for the end of the century and then doing the experiment described. But what can we say in the meantime? What steps should be taken now if the experiment is to be successful?

As I have explained, the problem is mainly one of programming. Advances in engineering will have to made too, but it seems unlikely that these will not be adequate for the requirements....

In the process of trying to imitate an adult human mind we are bound to think a good deal about the process which has brought it to the state that it is in. We may notice three components:

(a) The initial state of the mind, say at birth;

(b) The education to which it has been subjected; and

(c) Other experience, not to be described as education, to which it has been subjected.

Instead of trying to produce a program to simulate the adult mind, why not rather try to produce one which simulates the child's? If this were then subjected to an appropriate course of education one would obtain the adult brain. Presumably the child-brain is something like a notebook as one buys it from the stationers. Rather little mechanism, and lots of blank sheets. (Mechanism and writing are from our point of view almost synonymous.) Our hope is that there is so little mechanism in the child-brain that something like it can be easily programmed. The amount of work in the education we can assume, as a first approximation, to be much the same as for the human child....

It will not be possible to apply exactly the same teaching process to the machine as to a normal child. It will not, for instance, be provided with legs, so that it could not be asked to go out and fill the coal scuttle. Possibly it might not have eyes. But however well these deficiencies might be overcome by clever engineering, one could not send the creature to school without the other children making excessive fun of it. It must be given some tuition. We need not be too concerned about the legs, eyes, and so on. The example of Miss Helen Keller shows that education can take place provided that communication in both directions between teacher and pupil can take place by some means or other.

We normally associate punishments and rewards with the teaching process. Some simple child-machines can be constructed or programmed on this sort of principle. The machine has to be so constructed that events which shortly preceded the occurrence of a punishment-signal are unlikely to be repeated, whereas a reward-signal increases the probability of repetition of the events which led up to it. These definitions do not presuppose any feelings on the part of the machine. I have done some experiments with one such child-machine, and succeeded in teaching it a few things, but the teaching method was too unorthodox for the experiment to be considered really successful.

The use of punishments and rewards can at best be a part of the teaching process. Roughly speaking, if the teacher has no other means of communicating to the pupil, the amount of information which can reach him does not exceed the total number of rewards and punishments applied. By the time a child has learned to repeat "Casablanca" he would probably feel very sore indeed, if the text could only be discovered by a

"Twenty Questions" technique, every "No" taking the form of a blow. It is necessary therefore to have some other "unemotional" channels of communication. If these are available it is possible to teach a machine by punishments and rewards to obey orders given in some language, such as a symbolic language. These orders are to be transmitted through the "unemotional" channels. The use of this language will diminish greatly the number of punishments and rewards required....

We may hope that machines will eventually compete with men in all purely intellectual fields. But which are the best ones to start with? Even this is a difficult decision. Many people think that a very abstract activity, like the playing of chess, would be best. It can also be maintained that it is best to provide the machine with the best sense organs that money can buy, and then teach it to understand and speak English. This process could follow the normal teaching of a child. Things would be pointed out and named, and so on. Again I do not know what the right answer is, but I think both approaches should be tried.

We can only see a short distance ahead, but we can see plenty there that needs to be done.

2.2 Minds, Brains, and Programs

JOHN R. SEARLE

John Searle has made important contributions to the philosophy of mind and the philosophy of language. He teaches at the University of California, Berkeley.

What psychological and philosophical significance should we attach to recent efforts at computer simulations of human cognitive capacities? In answering this question, I find it useful to distinguish what I will call "strong" AI from "weak" or "cautious" AI (artificial intelligence). According to weak AI, the principal value of the computer in the study of the mind is that it gives us a very powerful tool. For example, it enables us to formulate and test hypotheses in a more rigorous and precise fashion. But according to strong AI, the computer is not merely a tool in the study of the mind; rather, the appropriately programmed computer really *is* a mind, in the sense that computers given the right programs can be literally said to *understand* and have other cognitive states. In strong AI, because the programmed computer has cognitive states, the programs are not mere tools that enable us to test psychological explanations; rather, the programs are themselves the explanations.

I have no objection to the claims of weak AI, at least as far as this article is concerned. My discussion here will be directed at the claims I have defined as those of strong AI, specifically the claim that the appropriately programmed computer literally has cognitive states and that the programs thereby explain human cognition. When I hereafter refer to AI, I have in mind the strong version, as expressed by these two claims.

I will consider the work of Roger Schank and his colleagues at Yale (Schank and Abelson, 1977), because I am more familiar with it than I am with any other similar claims, and because it provides a very clear example of the sort of work I wish to examine. But nothing that follows depends upon the details of Schank's programs. The same arguments would apply to Winograd's SHRDLU (Winograd, 1973), Weizenbaum's ELIZA (Weizenbaum, 1965), and indeed any Turing machine simulation of human mental phenomena....

Very briefly, and leaving out the various details, one can describe Schank's program as follows: The aim of the program is to simulate the human ability to understand stories. It is characteristic of human beings' story-understanding capacity that they can answer questions about the story even though the information that they give was never explicitly stated in the story. Thus, for example, suppose you are given the following story: "A man went into a restaurant and ordered a hamburger. When the hamburger arrived it was burned to a crisp, and the man stormed out of the restaurant angrily, without paying for the hamburger or leaving a tip." Now, if you are asked "Did the man eat the hamburger?" you will presumably answer, "No, he did not." Similarly, if you are given the following story: "A man went into a restaurant and ordered a hamburger; when the hamburger came he was very pleased with it; and as he left the restaurant he gave the waitress a large tip before paying his bill," and you are asked the question, "Did the man eat the hamburger?" you will presumably answer, "Yes, he ate the hamburger." Now Schank's machines can similarly answer questions about restaurants in this fashion. To do this, they have a "representation" of the sort of information that human beings have about restaurants, which enables them to answer such questions as those above, given these sorts of stories. When the machine is given the story and then asked the question, the machine will print out answers of the sort that we would expect human beings to give if told similar stories. Partisans of strong AI claim that in this question and answer sequence the machine is not only simulating a human ability but also (1) that the machine can literally be said to *understand* the story and provide the answers to questions, and (2) that what the machine and its programs do *explains* the human ability to understand the story and answer questions about it.

Both claims seem to me to be totally unsupported by Schank's work, as I will attempt to show in what follows. I am not, of course, saying that Schank himself is committed to these claims.

One way to test any theory of the mind is to ask oneself what it would be like if my mind actually worked on the principles that the theory says

all minds work on. Let us apply this test to the Schank program with the following *Gedankenexperiment*.* Suppose that I'm locked in a room and given a large batch of Chinese writing. Suppose furthermore (as is indeed the case) that I know no Chinese, either written or spoken, and that I'm not even confident that I could recognize Chinese writing as Chinese writing distinct from, say, Japanese writing or meaningless squiggles. To me, Chinese writing is just so many meaningless squiggles. Now suppose further that after this first batch of Chinese writing I am given a second batch of Chinese script together with a set of rules for correlating the second batch with the first batch. The rules are in English, and I understand these rules as well as any other native speaker of English. They enable me to correlate one set of formal symbols with another set of formal symbols, and all that "formal" means here is that I can identify the symbols entirely by their shapes. Now suppose also that I am given a third batch of Chinese symbols together with some instructions, again in English, that enable me to correlate elements of this third batch with the first two batches, and these rules instruct me how to give back certain Chinese symbols with certain sorts of shapes in response to certain sorts of shapes given me in the third batch. Unknown to me, the people who are giving me all of these symbols call the first batch a "script," they call the second batch a "story," and they call the third batch "questions." Furthermore, they call the symbols I give them back in response to the third batch "answers to the questions," and the set of rules in English that they gave me, they call the "program." Now just to complicate the story a little, imagine that these people also give me stories in English, which I understand, and they then ask me questions in English about these stories, and I give them back answers in English. Suppose also that after a while I get so good at following the instructions for manipulating the Chinese symbols and the programmers get so good at writing the programs that from the external point of view— that is, from the point of view of somebody

---

*[Thought experiment.—Ed.]

outside the room in which I am locked—my answers to the questions are absolutely indistinguishable from those of native Chinese speakers. Nobody just looking at my answers can tell that I don't speak a word of Chinese. Let us also suppose that my answers to the English questions are, as they no doubt would be, indistinguishable from those of other native English speakers, for the simple reason that I am a native English speaker. From the external point of view—from the point of view of someone reading my "answers"—the answers to the Chinese questions and the English questions are equally good. But in the Chinese case, unlike the English case, I produce the answers by manipulating uninterpreted formal symbols. As far as the Chinese is concerned, I simply behave like a computer; I perform computational operations on formally specified elements. For the purposes of the Chinese, I am simply an instantiation of the computer program.

Now the claims made by strong AI are that the programmed computer understands the stories and that the program in some sense explains human understanding. But we are now in a position to examine these claims in light of our thought experiment.

1. As regards the first claim, it seems to me quite obvious in the example that I do not understand a word of the Chinese stories. I have inputs and outputs that are indistinguishable from those of the native Chinese speaker, and I can have any formal program you like, but I still understand nothing. For the same reasons, Schank's computer understands nothing of any stories, whether in Chinese, English, or whatever, since in the Chinese case the computer is me, and in cases where the computer is not me, the computer has nothing more than I have in the case where I understand nothing.

2. As regards the second claim, that the program explains human understanding, we can see that the computer and its program do not provide sufficient conditions of understanding since the computer and the program are functioning, and there is no understanding. But does it even provide a necessary condition or a significant contribution to understanding? One of the

claims made by the supporters of strong AI is that when I understand a story in English, what I am doing is exactly the same—or perhaps more of the same—as what I was doing in manipulating the Chinese symbols. It is simply more formal symbol manipulation that distinguishes the case in English, where I do understand, from the case in Chinese, where I don't. I have not demonstrated that this claim is false, but it would certainly appear an incredible claim in the example. Such plausibility as the claim has derives from the supposition that we can construct a program that will have the same inputs and outputs as native speakers, and in addition we assume that speakers have some level of description where they are also instantiations of a program. On the basis of these two assumptions we assume that even if Schank's program isn't the whole story about understanding, it may be part of the story. Well, I suppose that is an empirical possibility, but not the slightest reason has so far been given to believe that it is true, since what is suggested—though certainly not demonstrated—by the example is that the computer program is simply irrelevant to my understanding of the story. In the Chinese case I have everything that artificial intelligence can put into me by way of a program, and I understand nothing; in the English case I understand everything, and there is so far no reason at all to suppose that my understanding has anything to do with computer programs, that is, with computational operations on purely formally specified elements. As long as the program is defined in terms of computational operations on purely formally defined elements, what the example suggests is that these by themselves have no interesting connection with understanding. They are certainly not sufficient conditions, and not the slightest reason has been given to suppose that they are necessary conditions or even that they make a significant contribution to understanding. Notice that the force of the argument is not simply that different machines can have the same input and output while operating on different formal principles—that is not the point at all. Rather, whatever purely formal principles you put into the computer, they will not be sufficient for understanding, since a human will be able to follow the formal principles without understanding anything. No reason whatever has been offered to suppose that such principles are necessary or even contributory, since no reason has been given to suppose that when I understand English I am operating with any formal program at all.

Well, then, what is it that I have in the case of the English sentences that I do not have in the case of the Chinese sentences? The obvious answer is that I know what the former mean, while I haven't the faintest idea what the latter mean. But in what does this consist and why couldn't we give it to a machine, whatever it is?

I have had the occasion to present this example to several workers in artificial intelligence, and, interestingly, they do not seem to agree on what the proper reply to it is.

I want to block some common misunderstandings about "understanding:" In many of these discussions one finds a lot of fancy footwork about the word "understanding." My critics point out that there are many different degrees of understanding; that "understanding" is not a simple two-place predicate; that there are even different kinds and levels of understanding, and often the law of excluded middle doesn't even apply in a straightforward way to statements of the form "*x* understands *y*;" that in many cases it is a matter for decision and not a simple matter of fact whether *x* understands *y*; and so on. To all of these points I want to say: of course, of course. But they have nothing to do with the points at issue. There are clear cases in which "understanding" literally applies and clear cases in which it does not apply; and these two sorts of cases are all I need for this argument. I understand stories in English; to a lesser degree I can understand stories in French; to a still lesser degree, stories in German; and in Chinese, not at all. My car and my adding machine, on the other hand, understand nothing: they are not in that line of business.* We often attribute "understanding" and other cognitive predicates by metaphor and analogy to cars, adding machines, and other artifacts, but nothing is proved by such attributions. We say, "The door *knows* when to open because of its photoelectric cell," "The adding machine *knows how (understands how, is able)* to do addition and subtraction but not division," and "The thermostat *perceives* changes in the temperature." The reason we make these attributions is quite interesting, and it has to do with the fact that in artifacts we extend our own intentionality;[†] our tools are extensions of our purposes, and so we find it natural to make metaphorical attributions of intentionality to them; but I take it no philosophical ice is cut by such examples. The sense in which an automatic door "understands instructions" from its photoelectric cell is not at all the sense in which I understand English. If the sense in which Schank's programmed computers understand stories is supposed to be the metaphorical sense in which the door understands, and not the sense in which I understand English, the issue would not be worth discussing. But Newell and Simon (1963) write that the kind of cognition they claim for computers is exactly the same as for human beings. I like the straightforwardness of this claim, and it is the sort of claim I will be considering. I will argue that in the literal sense the programmed computer understands what the car and the adding machine understand, namely, exactly nothing. The computer's understanding is not just (like my understanding of German) partial or incomplete; it is zero.

By way of concluding I want to try to state some of the general philosophical points implicit in the argument. For clarity I will try to do it in a question-and-answer fashion, and I begin with that old chestnut of a question:

"Could a machine think?"

The answer is, obviously, yes. We are precisely such machines.

---

*Also, "understanding" implies both the possession of mental (intentional) states and the truth (validity, success) of these states. For the purposes of this discussion we are concerned only with the possession of the states.

[†]Intentionality is by definition that feature of certain mental states by which they are directed at or about objects and states of affairs in the world. Thus, beliefs, desires, and intentions are intentional states; undirected forms of anxiety and depression are not.

"Yes, but could an artifact, a man-made machine, think?"

Assuming it is possible to produce artificially a machine with a nervous system, neurons with axons and dendrites, and all the rest of it, sufficiently like ours, again the answer to the question seems to be obviously, yes. If you can exactly duplicate the causes, you could duplicate the effects. And indeed it might be possible to produce consciousness, intentionality, and all the rest of it using some other sorts of chemical principles than those that human beings use. It is, as I said, an empirical question.

"OK, but could a digital computer think?"

If by "digital computer" we mean anything at all that has a level of description where it can correctly be described as the instantiation of a computer program, then again the answer is, of course, yes, since we are the instantiations of any number of computer programs, and we can think.

"But could something think, understand, and so on *solely* by virtue of being a computer with the right sort of program? Could instantiating a program, the right program of course, by itself be a sufficient condition of understanding?"

This I think is the right question to ask, though it is usually confused with one or more of the earlier questions, and the answer to it is no.

"Why not?"

Because the formal symbol manipulations by themselves don't have any intentionality; they are quite meaningless; they aren't even *symbol* manipulations, since the symbols don't symbolize anything. In the linguistic jargon, they have only a syntax but no semantics. Such intentionality as computers appear to have is solely in the minds of those who program them and those who use them, those who send in the input and those who interpret the output.

The aim of the Chinese room example was to try to show this by showing that as soon as we put something into the system that really does have intentionality (a man), and we program him with the formal program, you can see that the formal program carries no additional intentionality. It adds nothing, for example, to a man's ability to understand Chinese.

Precisely that feature of AI that seemed so appealing—the distinction between the program and the realization—proves fatal to the claim that simulation could be duplication. The distinction between the program and its realization in the hardware seems to be parallel to the distinction between the level of mental operations and the level of brain operations. And if we could describe the level of mental operations as a formal program, then it seems we could describe what was essential about the mind without doing either introspective psychology or neurophysiology of the brain. But the equation "mind is to brain as program is to hardware" breaks down at several points, among them the following three:

First, the distinction between program and realization has the consequence that the same program could have all sorts of crazy realizations that had no form of intentionality. Weizenbaum (1976, Ch. 2), for example, shows in detail how to construct a computer using a roll of toilet paper and a pile of small stones. Similarly, the Chinese story understanding-program can be programmed into a sequence of water pipes, a set of wind machines, or a monolingual English speaker, none of which thereby acquires an understanding of Chinese. Stones, toilet paper, wind, and water pipes are the wrong kind of stuff to have intentionality in the first place—only something that has the same causal powers as brains can have intentionality—and though the English speaker has the right kind of stuff for intentionality you can easily see that he doesn't get any extra intentionality by memorizing the program, since memorizing it won't teach him Chinese.

Second, the program is purely formal, but the intentional states are not in that way formal. They are defined in terms of their content, not their form. The belief that it is raining, for example, is not defined as a certain formal shape, but as a certain mental content with conditions of satisfaction, a direction of fit (see Searle, 1979), and the like. Indeed the belief as such hasn't even got a formal shape in this syntactic sense, since one and the same belief can be given an indefinite number of different syntactic expressions in different linguistic systems.

Third, as I mentioned before, mental states and events are literally a product of the operation of the brain, but the program is not in that way a product of the computer.

"Well if programs are in no way constitutive of mental processes, why have so many people believed the converse? That at least needs some explanation."

I don't really know the answer to that one. The idea that computer simulations could be the real thing ought to have seemed suspicious in the first place because the computer isn't confined to simulating mental operations, by any means. No one supposes that computer simulations of a five-alarm fire will burn the neighborhood down or that a computer simulation of a rainstorm will leave us all drenched. Why on earth would anyone suppose that a computer simulation of understanding actually understood anything? It is sometimes said that it would be frightfully hard to get computers to feel pain or fall in love, but love and pain are neither harder nor easier than cognition or anything else. For simulation, all you need is the right input and output and a program in the middle that transforms the former into the latter. That is all the computer has for anything it does. To confuse simulation with duplication is the same mistake, whether it is pain, love, cognition, fires, or rainstorms.

Still, there are several reasons why AI must have seemed—and to many people perhaps still does seem—in some way to reproduce and thereby explain mental phenomena, and I believe we will not succeed in removing these illusions until we have fully exposed the reasons that give rise to them.

First, and perhaps most important, is a confusion about the notion of "information processing:" Many people in cognitive science believe that the human brain, with its mind, does something called "information processing," and analogously the computer with its program does information processing; but fires and rainstorms, on the other hand, don't do information processing at all. Thus, though the computer can simulate the formal features of any process whatever, it stands in a special relation to the mind and brain because when the computer is properly programmed, ideally with the same program as the brain, the information processing is identical in the two cases, and this information processing is really the essence of the mental. But the trouble with this argument is that it rests on an ambiguity in the notion of "information." In the sense in which people "process information" when they reflect, say, on problems in arithmetic or when they read and answer questions about stories, the programmed computer does not do "information processing." Rather, what it does is manipulate formal symbols. The fact that the programmer and the interpreter of the computer output use the symbols to stand for objects in the world is totally beyond the scope of the computer. The computer, to repeat, has a syntax but no semantics. Thus, if you type into the computer "2 plus 2 equals?" it will type out "4." But it has no idea that "4" means 4 or that it means anything at all. And the point is not that it lacks some second-order information about the interpretation of its first-order symbols, but rather that its first-order symbols don't have any interpretations as far as the computer is concerned. All the computer has is more symbols. The introduction of the notion of "information processing" therefore produces a dilemma: Either we construe the notion of "information processing" in such a way that it implies intentionality as part of the process or we don't. If the former, then the programmed computer does not do information processing: it only manipulates formal symbols. If the latter, then, though the computer does information processing, it is only doing so in the sense in which adding machines, typewriters, stomachs, thermostats, rainstorms, and hurricanes do information processing; namely, they have a level of description at which we can describe them as taking information in at one end, transforming it, and producing information as output. But in this case it is up to outside observers to interpret the input and output as information in the ordinary sense. And no similarity is established between the computer and the brain in terms of any similarity of information processing.

Second, in much of AI there is a residual behaviorism or operationalism. Since appropriately programmed computers can have input-output patterns similar to those of human beings, we are tempted to postulate mental states in the computer similar to human mental states. But once we see that it is both conceptually and empirically possible for a system to have human capacities in some realm without having any intentionality at all, we should be able to overcome this impulse. My desk adding machine has calculating capacities, but no intentionality, and in this paper I have tried to show that a system could have input and output capabilities that duplicated those of a native Chinese speaker and still not understand Chinese, regardless of how it was programmed. The Turing test is typical of the tradition in being unashamedly behavioristic and operationalistic, and I believe that if AI workers totally repudiated behaviorism and operationalism much of the confusion between simulation and duplication would be eliminated.

Third, this residual operationalism is joined to a residual form of dualism; indeed strong AI only makes sense given the dualistic assumption that, where the mind is concerned, the brain doesn't matter. In strong AI (and in functionalism, as well) what matters are programs, and programs are independent of their realization in machines; indeed, as far as AI is concerned, the same program could be realized by an electronic machine, a Cartesian mental substance, or a Hegelian world spirit. The single most surprising discovery that I have made in discussing these issues is that many AI workers are quite shocked by my idea that actual human mental phenomena might be dependent on actual physical-chemical properties of actual human brains. But if you think about it a minute you can see that I should not have been surprised; for unless you accept some form of dualism, the strong AI project hasn't got a chance. The project is to reproduce and explain the mental by designing programs, but unless the mind is not only conceptually but empirically independent of the brain you couldn't carry out the project, for the program is completely independent of any realization. Unless you believe that the mind is separable from the brain both conceptually and empirically—dualism in a strong form—you cannot hope to reproduce the mental by writing and running programs since programs must be independent of brains or any other particular forms of instantiation. If mental operations consist in computational operations on formal symbols, then it follows that they have no interesting connection with the brain; the only connection would be that the brain just happens to be one of the indefinitely many types of machines capable of instantiating the program. This form of dualism is not the traditional Cartesian variety that claims there are two sorts of *substances,* but it is Cartesian in the sense that it insists that what is specifically mental about the mind has no intrinsic connection with the actual properties of the brain. This underlying dualism is masked from us by the fact that AI literature contains frequent fulminations against "dualism;" what the authors seem to be unaware of is that their position presupposes a strong version of dualism.

"Could a machine think?" My own view is that *only* a machine could think, and indeed only very special kinds of machines, namely brains and machines that had the same causal powers as brains. And that is the main reason strong AI has had little to tell us about thinking, since it has nothing to tell us about machines. By its own definition, it is about programs, and programs are not machines. Whatever else intentionality is, it is a biological phenomenon, and it is as likely to be as causally dependent on the specific biochemistry of its origins as lactation, photosynthesis, or any other biological phenomena. No one would suppose that we could produce milk and sugar by running a computer simulation of the formal sequences in lactation and photosynthesis, but where the mind is concerned many people are willing to believe in such a miracle because of a deep and abiding dualism: The mind they suppose is a matter of formal processes and is independent of quite specific material causes in the way that milk and sugar are not.

In defense of this dualism the hope is often expressed that the brain is a digital computer (early computers, by the way, were often called "electronic brains"). But that is no help. Of course the brain is a digital computer. Since everything is a digital computer, brains are too. The point is that the brain's causal capacity to produce intentionality cannot consist in its instantiating a computer program, since for any program you like it is possible for something to instantiate that program and still not have any mental states. Whatever it is that the brain does

REFERENCES

Newell, A. & Simon, H. A. (1963) GPS, a program that simulates human thought. In: Computers and thought, ed. A. Feigenbaum & V. Feldman, pp. 279–93. New York: McGraw Hill.

Searle, J. R. (1979) Intentionality and the use of language. In: Meaning and use, ed. A. Margalit. Dordrecht: Reidel.

Weizenbaum, J. (1965) Eliza – a computer program for the study of natural language communication between man and machine. Communication of the Association for Computing Machinery 9:36–45.

to produce intentionality, it cannot consist in instantiating a program since no program, by itself, is sufficient for intentionality.*

———————

*I am indebted to a rather large number of people for discussion of these matters and for their patient attempts to overcome my ignorance of artificial intelligence. I would especially like to thank Ned Block, Hubert Dreyfus, John Haugeland, Roger Schank, Robert Wilensky, and Terry Winograd.

Weizenbaum, J. (1976) Computer power and human reason San Francisco: W. H. Freeman.

Winograd, T. (1973) A procedural model of language understanding. In: Computer models of thought and language, ed. R. Schank & K. Colby. San Francisco: W. H. Freeman.

Schank, R. C. & Abelson, R. P. (1977) Scripts, plans, goals, and understanding. Hillsdale, N.J.: Lawrence Erlbaum Press.

2.3 Robots and Minds[1]

WILLIAM G. LYCAN

William G. Lycan teaches philosophy at the University of North Carolina, Chapel Hill.

Artificial Intelligence is, very crudely, the science of getting machines to perform jobs that normally require intelligence and judgment. Researchers at any number of AI labs have designed machines that prove mathematical theorems, play chess, sort mail, guide missiles, assemble auto engines, diagnose illnesses, read stories and other written texts, and converse with people in a rudimentary way. This is, we might say, intelligent behavior.

But what is this "intelligence"? As a first pass, I suggest that intelligence of the sort I am talking about is a kind of flexibility, a responsiveness to

contingencies. A dull or stupid machine must have just the right kind of raw materials presented to it in just the right way, or it is useless: the electric can opener must have an appropriately sized can fixed under its drive wheel *just so,* in order to operate at all. Humans (most of us, anyway) are not like that. We deal with the unforeseen. We take what comes and make the best of it, even though we may have had no idea what it would be. We play the ball from whatever lie we are given, and at whatever angle to the green; we read and understand texts we have never seen before; we find our way back to Chapel Hill after

———————

getting totally lost in downtown Durham (or downtown Washington, D.C., or downtown Lima, Peru).

Our pursuit of our goals is guided while in progress by our ongoing perception and handling of interim developments. Moreover, we can pursue any number of different goals at the same time, and balance them against each other. We are sensitive to contingencies, both external and internal, that have a very complex and unsystematic structure.

It is almost irresistible to speak of *information* here, even if the term were not as trendy as it is. An intelligent creature, I want to say, is an *information-sensitive* creature, one that not only *registers* information through receptors such as sense organs but somehow stores and manages and finally uses that information. Higher animals are intelligent beings in this sense, and so are we, even though virtually nothing is known about how we organize or manage the vast, seething profusion of information that comes our way. And there is one sort of machine that is information-sensitive also: the digital computer. A computer *is* a machine specifically designed to be fed complexes of information, to store them, manage them, and produce appropriate theoretical or practical conclusions on demand. Thus, if artificial intelligence is what one is looking for, it is no accident that one looks to the computer.

Yet a computer has two limitations in common with machines of less elite and grandiose sorts, both of them already signaled in the characterization I have just given. First, a (present-day) computer must be *fed* information, and the choice of what information to feed and in what form is up to a human programmer or operator. (For that matter, a present-day computer must be plugged into an electrical outlet and have its switch turned to ON, but this is a very minor contingency given the availability of nuclear power packs.) Second, the *appropriateness* and effectiveness of a computer's output depends entirely on what the programmer or operator had in mind and goes on to make of it. A computer has intelligence in the sense I have defined, but has no judgment, since it has no goals and

purposes of its own and no internal sense of appropriateness, relevance, or proportion.

For essentially these reasons—that computers are intelligent in my minimal sense, and that they are nevertheless limited in the two ways I have mentioned—AI theorists, philosophers, and intelligent laymen have inevitably compared computers to human minds, but at the same time debated both technical and philosophical questions raised by this comparison. The questions break down into three main groups or types: (A) Questions of the form "Will a computer ever be able to do X?" where X is something that intelligent humans can do. (B) Questions of the form "Given that a computer can or could do X, have we any reason to think that it does X in the same way that humans do X?" (C) Questions of the form "Given that some futuristic supercomputer were able to do $X, Y, Z,...$, for some arbitrarily large range and variety of human activities, would that show that the computer had property P?" where P is some feature held to be centrally, vitally characteristic of human minds, such as thought, consciousness, feeling, sensation, emotion, creativity, or freedom of the will.

Questions of type A are empirical questions and cannot be settled without decades, perhaps centuries, of further research—compare ancient and medieval speculations on the question of whether a machine could ever fly. Questions of type B are brutely empirical too, and their answers are unavailable to AI researchers *per se*, lying squarely in the domain of cognitive psychology, a science or alleged science barely into its infancy. Questions of type C are philosophical and conceptual, and so I shall essay to answer them all at one stroke.

Let us begin by supposing that all questions of types A and B have been settled affirmatively—that one day we might be confronted by a much-improved version of Hal, the soft-spoken computer in Kubrick's *2001* (younger readers may substitute *Star Wars'* C3PO or whatever subsequent cinematic robot is the most lovable). Let us call this more versatile machine "Harry."[2] Harry (let us say) is humanoid in form—he is a miracle of miniaturization and has lifelike plastic skin—and he can converse intelligently on all sorts of subjects, play golf *and* the viola, write passable poetry, control his occasional nervousness pretty well, make love, prove mathematical theorems (of course), show envy when outdone, throw gin bottles at annoying children, etc., etc. We may suppose he fools people into thinking he is human. Now the question is, is Harry really a *person*? Does he have thoughts, feelings, and so on? Is he actually conscious, or is he just a mindless walking hardware store whose movements are astoundingly *like* those of a person?[3]

Plainly his acquaintances would tend from the first to see him as a person, even if they were aware of his dubious antecedents. I think it is a plain psychological fact, if nothing more, that we could not help treating him as a person, unless we resolutely made up our minds, on principle, not to give him the time of day. But how could we really tell that he is conscious?

Well, how do we really tell that any humanoid creature is conscious? How do you tell that I am conscious, and how do I tell that you are? Surely we tell, and decisively, on the basis of our standard behavioral tests for mental states, to revert to [an earlier theme of this book]: We know that a human being has such-and-such mental states when it behaves, to speak very generally, in the ways we take to be appropriate to organisms that are in those states. (The point is of course an epistemological one only, no metaphysical implications intended or tolerated.) We know for practical purposes that a creature has a mind when it fulfills all the right criteria. And by hypothesis, Harry fulfills all our behavioral criteria with a vengeance; moreover, he does so *in the right way* (cf. questions of type B): the processing that stands causally behind his behavior is just like ours. It follows that we are at least *prima facie* justified in believing him to be conscious.

We have not *proved* that he is conscious, of course—any more than you have proved that I am conscious. An organism's merely behaving in a certain way is no logical guarantee of sentience; from my point of view it is at least imaginable, a bare logical possibility, that my wife, my daughter, and my chairman are not conscious, even

though I have excellent, overwhelming behavioral reason to think that they are. But for that matter, our "standard behavioral tests" for mental states yield practical or moral certainty only so long as the situation is not palpably extraordinary or bizarre. A human chauvinist—in this case, someone who denies that Harry has thoughts and feelings, joys and sorrows—thinks precisely that Harry is as bizarre as they come. But *what is bizarre about him?* There are quite a few chauvinist answers to this, but what they boil down to, and given our hypothesized facts all they could boil down to, are two differences between Harry and ourselves: his *origin* (a laboratory is not a proper mother), and the *chemical composition of his anatomy,* if his creator has used silicon instead of carbon, for example. To exclude him from our community for either or both of *those* reasons seems to me to be a clear case of racial or ethnic prejudice (literally) and nothing more. I see no obvious way in which either a creature's origin or its subneuroanatomical chemical composition should matter to its psychological processes or any aspect of its mentality.

My argument can be reinforced by a thought experiment....Imagine that we take a normal human being, Henrietta, and begin gradually replacing parts of her with synthetic materials—first a few prosthetic limbs, then a few synthetic arteries, then some neural fibers, and so forth. Suppose that the surgeons who perform the successive operations (particularly the neurosurgeons) are so clever and skillful that Henrietta survives in fine style: her intelligence, personality, perceptual acuity, poetic abilities, etc., remain just as they were before. But after the replacement process has eventually gone on to completion, Henrietta will have become an artifact—at least, her body will then be nothing but a collection of artifacts. Did she lose consciousness at some point during the sequence of operations, despite her continuing to behave and respond normally? When? It is hard to imagine that there is some privileged portion of the human nervous system that is for some reason indispensable, even though kidneys, lungs, heart, and any given bit of brain could in principle be replaced by a prosthesis (for *what* reason?); and it is also hard to imagine that there is some proportion of the nervous system such that removal of more than that proportion causes loss of consciousness or sentience despite perfect maintenance of all intelligent capacities.

If this quick but totally compelling defense of Harry and Henrietta's personhood is correct, then the two, and their ilk, will have not only mental lives like ours, but *moral* lives like ours, and moral rights and privileges accordingly. Just as origin and physical constitution fail to affect psychological personhood, if a creature's internal organization is sufficiently like ours, so do they fail to affect moral personhood. We do not discriminate against a person who has a wooden leg, or a mechanical kidney, or a nuclear heart regulator; no more should we deny any human or civil right to Harry or Henrietta on grounds of their origin or physical makeup, which they cannot help.

But this happy egalitarianism raises a more immediate question: *In real life,* we shall soon be faced with medium-grade machines, which have some intelligence and are not "mere" machines like refrigerators or typewriters but which fall far short of flawless human stimulators like Harry. For AI researchers may well build machines that will appear to have some familiar mental capacities but not others. The most obvious example is that of a sensor or perceptron, which picks up information from its immediate environment, records it, and stores it in memory for future printout. (We already have at least crude machines of this kind. When they become versatile and sophisticated enough, it will be quite natural to say that they see or hear and that they remember.) But the possibility of "specialist" machines of this kind raises an unforeseen contingency: There is an enormous and many-dimensional range of possible beings in between our current "mere" machines and our fully developed, flawless human simulators; we have not even begun to think of all the infinitely possible variations on this theme. And once we do begin to think of these hard cases, we will be at a loss as to where to draw the "personhood" line between them. How complex, eclectic, and

impressive must a machine be, and in what respects, before we award it the accolade of personhood and/or of consciousness? There is, to say the least, no clear answer to be had *a priori,* Descartes' notorious view of animals to the contrary notwithstanding.*

This typical philosophical question would be no more than an amusing bonbon, were it not for the attending moral conundrum: What moral rights would an intermediate or marginally intelligent machine have? Adolescent machines of this sort will confront us much sooner than will any good human simulators, for they are easier to design and construct; more to the moral point, they will be designed mainly as *labor-saving devices,* as servants who will work for free, and servants of this kind are (literally) made to be exploited. If they are intelligent to any degree, we should have qualms in proportion.

I suggest that this moral problem, which may become a real and pressing one, is parallel to the current debate over animal rights. Luckily I have never wanted to cook and eat my Compaq Portable.

Suppose I am right about the irrelevance of biochemical constitution to psychology; and suppose I was also right about the coalescing of the notions *computation, information, intelligence.* Then our mentalized theory of computation suggests in turn a computational theory of mentality, and a computational picture of the place of human beings in the world. In fact, philosophy aside, that picture has already begun to get a grip on people's thinking—as witness the filtering down of computer jargon into contemporary casual speech—and that grip is not going to loosen. Computer science is the defining technology of our time, and in this sense the computer is the natural cultural successor to the steam engine, the clock, the spindle, and the potter's wheel.[4] Predictably, an articulate computational theory of the mind has also gained credence among professional psychologists and philosophers.[5] I have been trying to support it here and

---

*Descartes claimed in his *Discourse on Method* that animals are mere machines.

elsewhere; I shall say no more about it for now, save to note again its near-indispensability in accounting for intentionality (noted), and to address the ubiquitous question of computer creativity and freedom:

Soft Determinism* or **Libertarianism*** may be true of humans. But many people have far more rigidly deterministic intuitions about computers. Computers, after all, (let us all say it together:) "only do what they are told/programmed to do"; they have no spontaneity and no freedom of choice. But human beings choose all the time, and the ensuing states of the world often depend entirely on these choices.[6] Thus the "computer analogy" supposedly fails.

The alleged failure of course depends on what we think freedom really is. As a Soft Determinist, I think that to have freedom of choice in acting is (roughly) for one's action to proceed out of one's own desires, deliberation, will, and intention, rather than being compelled or coerced by external forces regardless of my desires or will. As before, free actions are not *uncaused* actions. My free actions are those that *I* cause, i.e., that are caused by my own mental processes rather than by something pressing on me from the outside. I have argued…that I am free in that my beliefs, desires, deliberations, and intentions are all functional or computational states and processes within me that do interact in characteristic ways to produce my behavior. Note now that the same response vindicates our skilled human-simulating machines from the charge of puppethood. The word "robot" is often used as a veritable synonym for "puppet," so it may seem that Harry and Henrietta are paradigm cases of *un*free mechanisms that "only do what they are programmed to do." This is a slander—for two reasons:

First, even an ordinary computer, let alone a fabulously sophisticated machine like Harry, is in a way unpredictable. You are at its mercy. You *think* you know what it is going to do; you know what it should do, what it is supposed to do, but there is no guarantee—and it may do something *awful* or

at any rate something that you could not have predicted and could not figure out if you tried with both hands. This practical sort of unpredictability would be multiplied a thousandfold in the case of a machine as complex as the human brain, and it is notably characteristic of *people*.

The unpredictability has several sources. (i) Plain old physical defects, as when Harry's circuits have been damaged by trauma, stress, heat, or the like. (ii) Bugs in one or more of his programs. (I have heard that once upon a time, somewhere, a program was written that had not a single bug in it, but this is probably an urban folk tale.) (iii) Randomizers, quantum-driven or otherwise; elements of Harry's behavior may be *genuinely,* physically random. (iv) Learning and analogy mechanisms; if Harry is equipped with these, as he inevitably would be, then his behavior-patterns will be modified in response to his experiential input from the world, which would be neither controlled nor even observed by us. *We don't know where he's been.* (v) The relativity of reliability to goal-description. This last needs a bit of explanation.

People often say things like, "A computer just crunches binary numbers; provided it isn't broken, it just chugs on mindlessly through whatever flipflop settings are predetermined by its electronic makeup." But such remarks ignore the multileveled character of real computer programming. At any given time, as we have noted [earlier], a computer is running *each of any number of* programs, depending on how it is described and on the level of functional organization that interests us. True, it is always crunching binary numbers, but in crunching them it is also doing any number of more esoteric things. And (more to the point) what counts as a mindless, algorithmic procedure at a very low level of organization may constitute, at a higher level, a hazardous do-or-die heuristic that might either succeed brilliantly or (more likely) fail and leave its objective unfulfilled.

As a second defense, remember that Harry too has beliefs, desires, and intentions (provided my original argument is sound). If this is so, then his behavior normally proceeds out of his own

---

*See Part V for detailed discussions (and definitions) of these doctrines.

mental processes rather than being externally compelled; and so he satisfies the definition of freedom-of-action formulated above. In most cases it will be appropriate to say that Harry could have done other than what he did do (but in fact chose after some ratiocination to do what he did, instead). Harry acts in the same sense as that in which we act, though one might continue to quarrel over what sense that is.

Probably the nost popular remaining reason for doubt about machine consciousness has to do with the raw qualitative character of experience. Could a mere bloodless runner-of-programs have states that *feel to it* in any of the various dramatic ways in which our mental states feel to us?

The latter question is usually asked rhetorically, expecting a resounding answer "NO!!" But I do not hear it rhetorically, for I do not see why the negative answer is supposed to be at all obvious, even for machines as opposed to biologic humans. Of course there is an incongruity *from our human point of view* between human feeling and printed circuitry or silicon pathways; that is to be expected, since we are considering those high-tech items from an external, third-person perspective and at the same time comparing them to our own first-person feels. But argumentatively, that *Gestalt* phenomenon counts for no more in the present case than it did in that of human consciousness, viz., for nothing, especially if my original argument about Harry was successful in showing that biochemical constitution is irrelevant to psychology. What matters to mentality is not the stuff of which one is made, but the complex way in which that stuff is organized.[7] If after years of close friendship we were to open Harry up and find that he is stuffed with microelectronic gadgets instead of protoplasm, we would be taken aback—no question. But our *Gestalt* clash on the occasion would do nothing *at all* to show that Harry does not have his own rich inner qualitative life. If an objector wants to insist that computation alone cannot provide consciousness with its qualitative character, the objector will have to take the initiative and come up with a further, substantive argument to show why not.[8] We have already seen that such arguments have

failed wretchedly for the case of humans; I see no reason to suspect that they would work any better for the case of robots. We must await further developments. But at the present stage of inquiry I see no compelling feel-based objection to the hypothesis of machine consciousness.

NOTES

1. The material in this appendix was first presented as part of the John Ingram Forry Lecture at Amherst College, in 1985. I am very grateful to Jay Garfield and to Lee Bowie for their penetrating formal commentaries on that occasion, which I shall be answering in the (eventually to be) published proceedings of the event.

2. Harry has appeared before, in Lycan (1985). The next four paragraphs are lifted almost *verbatim* from that article.

3. It is interesting that children seem instinctively to reject the hypothesis of machine consciousness, usually on the grounds that computers are not alive. (One day when my daughter Jane was three years old, we were fooling with some piece of software or other, and I quite unreflectively remarked "It thinks you want it to [do such-and-such]." She did an enormous take, and then replied, "Computers can't think!—Is that 'just an expression'??")

4. I borrow the term "defining technology," and the examples, from Jay Bolter (1984).

5. The computational picture of mentality is by no means new. For one thing, the idea of mechanical intelligence goes back to the seventeenth century at least, long before Charles Babbage's celebrated Analytical Engine. And the computer model of the mind received a decisive boost from the McCullough-Pitts model of the neuron (1947), according to which a neuron is nothing but a little on-off device, that either *fires* or does not. If a brain is just an organized collection of neurons, and a neuron is just an on-off switch, it follows *straightway* that a brain is a digital computer and anything interesting that it does is a computation over binary formulas. Thus a human being is not only a featherless biped, a rational animal, and the only creature on earth that laughs, but the only computing machine on earth that is made by unskilled labor.

The McCullough-Pitts model is no longer current (no pun intended): neurons are now known to be very complicated little agents, not mere on-off switches. But the computational picture of mentality still receives strong encouragement from other quarters. It has two separate philosophical motivations, in particular, the first of which I have already noted: It exploits and explains the coalescence of the notions of computation, information, and intelligence. The computer is the only thing in the world that displays potential intelligence *and* whose workings are well understood. It is the only answer we currently know to the question: By what means *could* Mother Nature have crafted an intelligent being (in our sense of responsiveness to contingencies) out of nothing but a large bunch of individually insensate biological cells? To deny that there may be other answers would be presumptuous at best, and there are plenty of human capacities that do not seem to admit of computational simulation in any way at all—but anyone who manages to think up a genuinely distinct alternative to the digital-computer paradigm will have achieved a major conceptual breakthrough. For the foreseeable future, computation is our only model for intelligence.

Computationalism as a form of Homunctionalism also affords us a way of acknowledging our place as physical organisms amid the closed causal order we call Nature, without benefit of intervention by ghosts. (Actually I hear there

are some physicists who speculate that quantum indeterminancies afford gaps in nature that are in principle permeable to Cartesian minds, and that immaterial egos do insert themselves into quantum gaps, thus taking over the role of hidden variables. But (i) it would have to be shown how such quantum phenomena could be combined and multiplied into macroscopic effects characteristic of intelligence, i.e., how the brain could act as a "quantum magnifier," and (ii) to avoid *ad-hoc*ness of the crassest sort, one would have to find *physical reason* to think that Cartesian intervention does occur, which task I take to be almost definitionally impossible.)

6. Of course, this re-emphasizes the question of human freedom: if humans are just wetware or liveware, are they not then essentially soft puppets? This in turn suggests—however speciously in light of the arguments made [earlier]—that the computational view of people must therefore be drastically wrong.

7. Relatively speaking, of course; I am not encouraging Two-Levelism.

8. That mental acts do not *feel* digital is not an objection either. To infer from that fact that mental acts are not digital would be a clear case of what Armstrong (1968a) calls the "headless woman" fallacy.

CHAPTER 3

PERSONAL IDENTITY AND THE SURVIVAL OF DEATH

3.1 The Prince and the Cobbler

JOHN LOCKE

If the identity of *soul alone* makes the same *man,* and there be nothing in the nature of matter why the same individual spirit may not be united to

different bodies, it will be possible that those men, living in distant ages, and of different tempers, may have been the same man: which way of

---

From John Locke, *An Essay Concerning Human Understanding,* Book II, Chapter 27, "Of Ideas of Identity and Diversity." First published in 1690.

speaking must be from a very strange use of the word man, applied to an idea out of which body and shape are excluded.

An animal is a living organized body; and consequently the same animal, as we have observed, is the same continued *life* communicated to different particles of matter, as they happen successively to be united to that organized living body. And whatever is talked of other definitions, ingenious observation puts it past doubt, that the idea in our minds, of which the sound "man" in our mouths is the sign, is nothing else but of an animal of such a certain form....

I presume it is not the idea of a thinking or rational being alone that makes the *idea of a man* in most people's sense: but of a body, so and so shaped, joined to it; and if that be the idea of a man, the same successive body not shifted all at once, must, as well as the same immaterial spirit, go to the making of the same man.

This being premised, to find wherein personal identity consists, we must consider what *person* stands for;—which, I think, is a thinking intelligent being, that has reason and reflection, and can consider itself as itself, the same thinking thing, in different times and places; which it does only by that consciousness which is inseparable from thinking, and, as it seems to me, essential to it: it being impossible for any one to perceive without *perceiving* that he does perceive. When we see, hear, smell, taste, feel, meditate, or will anything, we know that we do so. Thus it is always as to our present sensations and perceptions: and by this every one is to himself that which he calls self:—it not being considered, in this case, whether the same self be continued in the same or divers substances. For, since consciousness always accompanies thinking, and it is that which makes every one to be what he calls self, and thereby distinguishes himself from all other thinking things, in this alone consists personal identity, i.e., the sameness of a rational being: and as far as this consciousness can be extended backwards to any past action or thought, so far reaches the identity of that person; it is the same self now it was then; and it is by the same self with this

present one that now reflects on it, that that action was done.

But it is further inquired, whether it be the same identical substance. This few would think they had reason to doubt of, if these perceptions, with their consciousness, always remained present in the mind, whereby the same thinking thing would be always consciously present, and, as would be thought, evidently the same to itself. But that which seems to make the difficulty is this, that this consciousness being interrupted always by forgetfulness, there being no moment of our lives wherein we have the whole train of all our past actions before our eyes in one view, but even the best memories losing the sight of one part whilst they are viewing another; and we sometimes, and that the greatest part of our lives, not reflecting on our past selves, being intent on our present thoughts, and in sound sleep having no thoughts at all, or at least none with that consciousness which remarks our waking thoughts,—I say, in all these cases, our consciousness being interrupted, and we losing the sight of our past selves, doubts are raised whether we are the same thinking thing, i.e., the same *substance* or no. Which, however reasonable or unreasonable, concerns not *personal* identity at all. The question being what makes the same person; and not whether it be the same identical substance, which always thinks in the same person, which, in the case, matters not at all: different substances, by the same consciousness (where they do partake in it) being united into one person, as well as different bodies by the same life are united into one animal, whose identity is preserved in that change of substances by the unity of one continued life. For, it being the same consciousness that makes a man be himself to himself, personal identity depends on that only, whether it be annexed solely to one individual substance, or can be continued in a succession of several substances. For as far any intelligent being *can* repeat the idea of any past action with the same consciousness it had of it at first, and with the same consciousness it has of any present action; so far it is the same personal self. For it is by the consciousness it has of its present thoughts and actions, that it is *self to itself* now, and so will be the same self, as far as the same consciousness can extend to actions past or to come; and would be by distance of time, or change of substance, no more two persons, than a man be two men by wearing other clothes today than he did yesterday, with a long or a short sleep between: the same consciousness uniting those distant actions in the same person, whatever substances contributed to their production.

That this is so, we have some kind of evidence in our very bodies, all whose particles, whilst vitally united to this same thinking conscious self, so that *we feel* when they are touched, and are affected by, and conscious of good or harm that happens to them, are a part of ourselves, i.e., of our thinking conscious self. Thus, the limbs of his body are to every one a part of himself; he sympathizes and is concerned for them. Cut off a hand, and thereby separate it from that consciousness he had of its heat, cold, and other affections, and it is then no longer a part of that which is himself, any more than the remotest part of matter. Thus, we see the *substance* whereof personal self consisted at one time may be varied at another, without the change of personal identity; there being no question about the same person, though the limbs which but now were a part of it, be cut off...

And thus may we be able, without any difficulty, to conceive the same person at the resurrection, though in a body not exactly in make or parts the same which he had here,—the same consciousness going along with the soul that inhabits it. But yet the soul alone, in the change of bodies, would scarce to any one but to him that makes the soul the man, be enough to make the same man. For should the soul of a prince, carrying with it the consciousness of the prince's past life, enter and inform the body of a cobbler, as soon as deserted by his own soul, every one sees he would be the same *person* with the prince, accountable only for the prince's actions: but who would say it was the same *man*? The body too goes to the making the man, and would, I guess, to everybody determine the man in this case, wherein the soul, with all its princely thoughts about it, would not make another man: but he would be the same cobbler to every one besides himself. I know that, in the ordinary way of speaking, the same person, and the same man, stand for one and the same thing. And indeed every one will always have a liberty to speak as he pleases, and to apply what articulate sounds to what ideas he thinks fit, and change them as often as he pleases. But yet, when we will inquire what makes the same *spirit, man,* or *person,* we must fix the ideas of spirit, man, or person in our minds; and having resolved with ourselves what we mean by them, it will not be hard to determine in either of them, or the like, when it is the same, and when not.

But though the immaterial substance or soul does not alone, wherever it be, and in whatsoever state, make the same *man;* yet it is plain, consciousness, as far as ever it can be extended —should it be to ages past—unites existences and actions very remote in time into the same *person,* as well as it does the existences and actions of the immediately preceding moment: so that whatever has the consciousness of present and past actions, is the same person to whom they both belong. Had I the same consciousness that I saw the ark and Noah's flood, as that I saw an overflowing of the Thames last winter, or as that I write now, I could no more doubt that I who write this now, that saw the Thames overflowed last winter, and that viewed the flood at the general deluge, was the same *self,*—place that self in what *substance* you please—than that I who write this am the same *myself* now whilst I write (whether I consist of all the same substance, material or immaterial, or no) that I was yesterday. For as to this point of being the same self, it matters not whether this present self be made up of the same or other substances—I being as much concerned, and as justly accountable for any action that was done a thousand years since, appropriated to me now by this self-consciousness, as I am for what I did the last moment...

But yet possibly it will still be objected,— Suppose I wholly lose the memory of some parts of my life, beyond a possibility of retrieving them, so that perhaps I shall never be conscious of them again; yet am I not the same person that did those actions, had those thoughts that I once was conscious of, though I have now forgot them? To which I answer, that we must here take notice what the word *I* is applied to; which, in this case, is the *man* only. And the same man being presumed to be the same person, I is easily here supposed to stand also for the same person. But if it be possible for the same man to have distinct incommunicable consciousness at different times, it is past doubt the same man would at different times make different persons; which, we see, is the sense of mankind in the solemnest declaration of their opinions, human laws not punishing the mad man for the sober man's actions, nor the sober man for what the mad man did,—thereby making them two persons: which is somewhat explained by our way of speaking in English when we say such an one is "not himself," or is "beside himself;" in which phrases it is insinuated, as if those who now, or at least first used them, thought that self was changed; the selfsame person was no longer in that man.

But yet it is hard to conceive that Socrates, the same individual man, should be two persons. To help us a little in this, we must consider what is meant by Socrates, or the same individual *man*.

First, it must be either the same individual, immaterial, thinking substance; in short, the same numerical soul, and nothing else.

Secondly, or the same animal, without any regard to an immaterial soul.

Thirdly, or the same immaterial spirit united to the same animal.

Now, take which of these suppositions you please, it is impossible to make personal identity to consist in anything but consciousness; or reach any further than that does.

3.2 Of Mr. Locke's
Account of Our Personal Identity

THOMAS REID

In a long chapter upon Identity and Diversity, Mr. Locke has made many ingenious and just observations, and some which I think cannot be defended. I shall only take notice of the account he gives of our own personal identity. His doctrine upon this subject has been censured by Bishop Butler, in a short essay subjoined to his *Analogy,* with whose sentiments I perfectly agree.

Identity, as was observed, supposes the continued existence of the being of which it is affirmed, and therefore can be applied only to things which have a continued existence. While any being continues to exist, it is the same being; but two beings which have a different beginning or a different ending of their existence cannot possibly be the same. To this, I think, Mr. Locke agrees.

He observes, very justly, that, to know what is meant by the same person, we must consider what the word *person* stands for; and he defines a person to be an intelligent being, endowed with reason and with consciousness, which last he thinks inseparable from thought.

From this definition of a person, it must necessarily follow, that, while the intelligent being continues to exist and to be intelligent, it must be the same person. To say that the intelligent being is the person, and yet that the person ceases to exist while the intelligent being

From Thomas Reid, *Essays on the Intellectual Powers of Man,* Essay III, Chapter 6. First published in 1785.

continues, or that the person continues while the intelligent being ceases to exist, is to my apprehension a manifest contradiction.

One would think that the definition of a person should perfectly ascertain the nature of personal identity, or wherein it consists, though it might still be a question how we come to know and be assured of our personal identity.

Mr. Locke tells us, however, "that personal identity, that is, the sameness of a rational being, consists in consciousness alone, and, as far as this consciousness can be extended backwards to any past action or thought, so far reaches the identity of that person. So that whatever has the consciousness of present and past actions is the same person to whom they belong."

This doctrine has some strange consequences, which the author was aware of. Such as, that if the same consciousness can be transferred from one intelligent being to another, which he thinks we cannot show to be impossible, *then two or twenty intelligent beings may be the same person*. And if the intelligent being may lose the consciousness of the actions done by him, which surely is possible, then he is not the person that did those actions; so that *one intelligent being may be two or twenty different persons*, if he shall so often lose the consciousness of his former actions.

There is another consequence of this doctrine, which follows no less necessarily, though Mr. Locke probably did not see it. It is, *that a man be, and at the same time not be, the person that did a particular action*.

Suppose a brave officer to have been flogged when a boy at school for robbing an orchard, to have taken a standard from the enemy in his first campaign, and to have been made a general in advanced life; suppose, also, which must be admitted to be possible, that, when he took the standard, he was conscious of his having been flogged at school, and that, when made a general, he was conscious of his taking the standard, but had absolutely lost the consciousness of his flogging.

These things being supposed, it follows, from Mr. Locke's doctrine, that he who was flogged at school is the same person who took the standard, and that he who took the standard is the same person who was made a general. Whence it follows, if there be any truth in logic, that the general is the same person with him who was flogged at school. But the general's consciousness does not reach so far back as his flogging; therefore, according to Mr. Locke's doctrine, he is not the person who was flogged. Therefore the general is, and at the same time is not, the same person with him who was flogged at school.

Leaving the consequences of this doctrine to those who have leisure to trace them, we may observe, with regard to the doctrine itself:

First, that Mr. Locke attributes to consciousness the conviction we have of our past actions, as if a man may now be conscious of what he did twenty years ago. It is impossible to understand the meaning of this, unless by consciousness be meant memory, the only faculty by which we have an immediate knowledge of our past actions.

Sometimes, in popular discourse, a man says he is conscious that he did such a thing, meaning that he distinctly remembers that he did it. It is unnecessary, in common discourse, to fix accurately the limits between consciousness and memory. This was formerly shown to be the case with regard to sense and memory: and therefore distinct remembrance is sometimes called sense, sometimes consciousness, without any inconvenience.

But this ought to be avoided in philosophy, otherwise we confound the different powers of the mind, and ascribe to one what really belongs to another. If a man can be conscious of what he did twenty years or twenty minutes ago, there is no use for memory, nor ought we allow that there is any such faculty. The faculties of consciousness and memory are chiefly distinguished by this, that the first is an immediate knowledge of the present, the second an immediate knowledge of the past.

When, therefore, Mr. Locke's notion of personal identity is properly expressed, it is, that personal identity consists in distinct remembrance;

for, even in the popular sense, to say that I am conscious of a past action means nothing else than that I distinctly remember that I did it.

Secondly, it may be observed, that, in this doctrine, not only is consciousness confounded with memory, but, which is still more strange, personal identity is confounded with the evidence which we have of our personal identity.

It is very true, that my remembrance that I did such a thing is the evidence I have that I am the identical person who did it. And this, I am apt to think, Mr. Locke meant. But to say that my remembrance that I did such a thing, or my consciousness, makes me the person who did it, is, in my apprehension, an absurdity too gross to be entertained by any man who attends to the meaning of it; for it is to attribute to memory or consciousness a strange magical power of producing its object, though that object must have existed before the memory or consciousness which produced it.

Consciousness is the testimony of one faculty; memory is the testimony of another faculty; and to say that the testimony is the cause of the thing testified, this surely is absurd, if any thing be, and could not have been said by Mr. Locke, if he had not confounded the testimony with the thing testified.

When a horse that was stolen is found and claimed by the owner, the only evidence he can have, or that a judge or witnesses can have, that this is the very identical horse which was his property, is similitude. But would it not be ridiculous from this to infer that the identity of a horse consists in similitude only? The only evidence I have that I am the identical person who did such actions is, that I remember distinctly I did them; or, as Mr. Locke expresses it, I am conscious I did them. To infer from this, that personal identity consists in consciousness, is an argument which, if it had any force, would prove the identity of a stolen horse to consist solely in similitude.

Thirdly, is it not strange that the sameness or identity of a person should consist in a thing which is continually changing, and is not any two minutes the same?

Our consciousness, our memory, and every operation of the mind, are still flowing like the water of a river, or like time itself. The consciousness I have this moment can no more be the same consciousness I had last moment, than this moment can be the last moment. Identity can only be affirmed of things which have a continued existence. Consciousness, and every kind of thought, are transient and momentary, and have no continued existence; and, therefore, if personal identity consisted in consciousness, it would certainly follow, that no man is the same person any two moments of his life; and as the right and justice of reward and punishment are founded on personal identity, no man could be responsible for his actions.

But though I take this to be the unavoidable consequence of Mr. Locke's doctrine concerning personal identity, and though some persons may have liked the doctrine the better on this account, I am far from imputing any thing of this kind to Mr. Locke. He was too good a man not to have rejected with abhorrence a doctrine which he believed to draw this consequence after it.

Fourthly, there are many expressions used by Mr. Locke, in speaking of personal identity, which to me are altogether unintelligible, unless we suppose that he confounded that sameness or identity which we ascribe to an individual with the identity which, in common discourse, is often ascribed to many individuals of the same species.

When we say that pain and pleasure, consciousness and memory, are the same in all men, this sameness can only mean similarity, or sameness of kind. That the pain of one man can be the same individual pain with that of another man is no less impossible, than that one man should be another man: the pain felt by me yesterday can no more be the pain I felt today, than yesterday can be this day; and the same thing may be said of every passion and of every operation of the mind. The same kind or species of operation may be in different men, or in the same man at different times; but it is impossible that the same individual operation should be in different men, or in the same man at different times.

When Mr. Locke, therefore, speaks of "the same consciousness being continued through a succession of different substances"; when he speaks of "repeating the idea of a past action, with the same consciousness we had of it at the first," and of "the same consciousness extending to actions past and to come"; these expressions are to me unintelligible, unless he means not the same individual consciousness, but a consciousness that is similar, or of the same kind.

If our personal identity consists in consciousness, as this consciousness cannot be the same individually any two moments, but only of the same kind, it would follow, that we are not for any two moments the same individual persons, but the same kind of persons.

As our consciousness sometimes ceases to exist, as in sound sleep, our personal identity must cease with it. Mr. Locke allows, that the same thing cannot have two beginnings of existence, so that our identity would be irrecoverably gone every time we ceased to think, if it was but for a moment.

3.3 The Self

DAVID HUME

There are some philosophers, who imagine we are every moment intimately conscious of what we call our Self; that we feel its existence and its continuance in existence; and are certain, beyond the evidence of a demonstration, both of its perfect identity and simplicity....

Unluckily all these positive assertions are contrary to that very experience, which is pleaded for them, nor have we any idea of *self*, after the manner it is here explained. For from what impression could this idea be derived? This question 'tis impossible to answer without a manifest contradiction and absurdity; and yet 'tis a question, which must necessarily be answered, if we would have the idea of self pass for clear and intelligible. It must be some one impression, that gives rise to every real idea. But self or person is not any one impression, but that to which our several impressions and ideas are supposed to have a reference. If any impression gives rise to the idea of self, that impression must continue invariably the same, through the whole course or our lives; since self is supposed to exist after that manner. But there is no impression constant and invariable. Pain and pleasure, grief and joy, passions and sensations succeed each other, and never all exist at the same time. It cannot, therefore, be from any of these impressions, or from any other, that the idea of self is derived; and consequently there is no such idea.

But farther, what must become of all our particular perceptions upon this hypothesis? All these are different, and distinguishable, and separable from each other, and may be separately considered, and may exist separately, and have no need of any thing to support their existence. After what manner, therefore, do they belong to self; and how are they connected with it? For my part, when I enter most intimately into what I call *myself*, I always stumble on some particular perception or other, of heat or cold, light or shade, love or hatred, pain or pleasure. I never can catch *myself* at any time without a perception, and never can observe any thing but the perception. When my perceptions are removed for any time, as by sound sleep; so long am I insensible of *myself*, and may truly be said not to exist. And were all my perceptions removed by death, and could I neither think, nor feel, nor see, nor love, nor hate after the dissolution of my body, I should be entirely annihilated, nor do I

From David Hume, *A Treatise of Human Nature*. First published in England in 1738.

conceive what is farther requisite to make me a perfect nonentity. If any one upon serious and unprejudiced reflection, thinks he has a different notion of *himself,* I must confess I can reason no longer with him. All I can allow him is, that he may be in the right as well as I, and that we are essentially different in this particular. He may, perhaps, perceive something simple and continued, which he calls *himself;* though I am certain there is no such principle in me.

But setting aside some metaphysicians of this kind, I may venture to affirm of the rest of mankind, that they are nothing but a bundle or collection of different perceptions, which succeed each other with an inconceivable rapidity, and are in a perpetual flux and movement. Our eyes cannot turn in their sockets without varying our perceptions. Our thought is still more variable than our sight; and all our other senses and faculties contribute to this change; nor is there any single power of the soul, which remains unalterably the same, perhaps for one moment. The mind is a kind of theatre, where several perceptions successively make their appearance; pass, re-pass, glide away, and mingle in an infinite variety of postures and situations. There is properly no *simplicity* in it at one time, nor *identity* in different; whatever natural propension we may have to imagine that simplicity and identity. The comparison of the theatre must not mislead us. They are the successive perceptions only, that constitute the mind; nor have we the most distant notion of the place, where these scenes are represented, or of the materials, of which it is composed.

What then gives us so great a propension to ascribe an identity to these successive perceptions, and to suppose ourselves possessed of an invariable and uninterrupted existence through the whole course of our lives?...

We have a distinct idea of an object, that remains invariable and uninterrupted through a supposed variation of time; and this idea we call that of *identity* or *sameness.* We have also a distinct idea of several different objects existing in succession, and connected together by a close relation; and this to an accurate view affords as perfect a notion of *diversity,* as if there was no manner of relation among the objects. But though these two ideas of identity, and a succession of related objects be in themselves perfectly distinct, and even contrary, yet 'tis certain, that in our common way of thinking they are generally confounded with each other. That action of the imagination, by which we consider the uninterrupted and invariable object, and that by which we reflect on the succession of related objects, are almost the same to the feeling, nor is there much more effort of thought required in the latter case than in the former. The relation facilitates the transition of the mind from one object to another, and renders its passage as smooth as if it contemplated one continued object. This resemblance is the cause of the confusion and mistake, and makes us substitute the notion of identity, instead of that of related objects....

Thus we feign the continued existence of the perceptions of our senses, to remove the interruption; and run into the notion of a *soul,* and *self,* and *substance,* to disguise the variation. But we may farther observe, that where we do not give rise to such a fiction, our propension to confound identity with relation is so great, that we are apt to imagine something unknown and mysterious, connecting the parts, beside their relation; and this I take to be the case with regard to the identity we ascribe to plants and vegetables. And even when this does not take place, we still feel a propensity to confound these ideas, though we are not able fully to satisfy ourselves in that particular, nor find any thing invariable and uninterrupted to justify our notion of identity.

Thus the controversy concerning identity is not merely a dispute of words. For when we attribute identity, in an improper sense, to variable or interrupted objects, our mistake is not confined to the expression, but is commonly attended with a fiction, either of something invariable and uninterrupted, or of something mysterious and inexplicable, or at least with a propensity to such fictions. What will suffice to prove this hypothesis to the satisfaction of every fair enquirer, is to show from daily experience and observation, that the objects, which are variable or interrupted, and yet are supposed to continue the same, are such only as consist of a succession of parts, connected together by resemblance, contiguity, or causation....

A ship, of which a considerable part has been changed by frequent reparations, is still considered as the same: nor does the difference of the materials hinder us from ascribing an identity to it. The common end, in which the parts conspire, is the same under all their variations, and affords an easy transition of the imagination from one situation of the body to another....

Though every one must allow, that in a very few years both vegetables and animals endure a *total* change, yet we still attribute identity to them, while their form, size, and substance are entirely altered. An oak, that grows from a small plant to a large tree, is still the same oak; though there be not one particle of matter, or figure of its parts the same. An infant becomes a man, and is sometimes fat, sometimes lean, without any change in his identity....A man, who hears a noise, that is frequently interrupted and renewed, says, it is still the same noise; though 'tis evident the sounds have only a specific identity or resemblance, and there is nothing numerically the same, but the cause, which produced them. In like manner it may be said without breach of the propriety of language, that such a church, which was formerly of brick, fell to ruin, and that the parish rebuilt the same church of free-stone, and according to modern architecture. Here neither the form nor materials are the same, nor is there any thing common to the two objects, but their relation to the inhabitants of the parish; and yet this alone is sufficient to make us denominate them the same....

From thence it evidently follows, that identity is nothing really belonging to these different perceptions, and uniting them together; but is merely a quality, which we attribute to them, because of the union of their ideas in the imagination, when we reflect upon them....

The only question, therefore, which remains, is, by what relations this uninterrupted progress of our thought is produced, when we consider the successive existence of a mind or thinking person. And here 'tis evident we must confine ourselves to resemblance and causation....Also, as memory alone acquaints us with the continuance and extent of this succession of perceptions, 'tis to be considered, upon that account chiefly, as the source of personal identity. Had we no memory, we never should have any notion of causation, nor consequently of that chain of causes and effects, which constitute our self or person.

3.4 Divided Minds and the Nature of Persons

DEREK PARFIT

Derek Parfit is an emeritus fellow of All Souls College, Oxford.

It was the split-brain cases which drew me into philosophy. Our knowledge of these cases depends on the results of various psychological tests, as described by Donald MacKay.[1] These tests made use of two facts. We control each of our arms, and see what is in each half of our visual fields, with only one of our hemispheres. When someone's hemispheres have been disconnected, psychologists can thus present to this person two different written questions in the

From *Mindwaves*, ed. Colin Blakemore and Susan Greenfield. pp. 19–25. Copyright © 1987 Oxford University Press. Reproduced with permission of Blackwell Publishing Ltd; permission conveyed through Copyright Clearance Center, Inc.

two halves of his visual field, and can receive two different answers written by this person's two hands.

Here is a simplified imaginary version of the kind of evidence that such tests provide. One of these people looks fixedly at the centre of a wide screen, whose left half is red and right half is blue. On each half in a darker shade are the words, "How many colours can you see?" With both hands the person writes, "Only one." The words are now changed to read, "Which is the only colour that you can see?" With one of his hands the person writes "Red," with the other he writes "Blue."

If this is how such a person responds, I would conclude that he is having two visual sensations—that he does, as he claims, see both red and blue. But in seeing each colour he is not aware of seeing the other. He has two streams of consciousness, in each of which he can see only one colour. In one stream he sees red, and at the same time, in his other stream, he sees blue. More generally, he could be having at the same time two series of thoughts and sensations, in having each of which he is unaware of having the other.

This conclusion has been questioned. It has been claimed by some that there are not *two* streams of consciousness, on the ground that the sub-dominant hemisphere is a part of the brain whose functioning involves no consciousness. If this were true, these cases would lose most of their interest. I believe that it is not true, chiefly because, if a person's dominant hemisphere is destroyed, this person is able to react in the way in which, in the split-brain cases, the sub-dominant hemisphere reacts, and we do not believe that such a person is just an automaton, without consciousness. The sub-dominant hemisphere is, of course, much less developed in certain ways, typically having the linguistic abilities of a three-year-old. But three-year-olds are conscious. This supports the view that, in split-brain cases, there *are* two streams of consciousness.

Another view is that, in these cases, there are two persons involved, sharing the same body. Like Professor MacKay, I believe that we should reject this view. My reason for believing this is, however, different. Professor MacKay denies that there are two persons involved because he believes that there is only one person involved. I believe that, in a sense, the number of persons involved is none.

THE EGO THEORY AND THE BUNDLE THEORY

To explain this sense I must, for a while, turn away from the split-brain cases. There are two theories about what persons are, and what is involved in a person's continued existence over time. On the *Ego Theory,* a person's continued existence cannot be explained except as the continued existence of a particular *Ego,* or *subject of experiences.* An Ego Theorist claims that, if we ask what unifies someone's consciousness at any time—what makes it true, for example, that I can now both see what I am typing and hear the wind outside my window—the answer is that these are both experiences which are being had by me, this person, at this time. Similarly, what explains the unity of a person's whole life is the fact that all of the experiences in this life are had by the same person, or subject of experiences. In its best-known form, the *Cartesian view,* each person is a persisting purely mental thing—a soul, or spiritual substance.

The rival view is the *Bundle Theory.* Like most styles in art—Gothic, baroque, rococo, etc.—this theory owes its name to its critics. But the name is good enough. According to the Bundle Theory, we can't explain either the unity of consciousness at any time, or the unity of a whole life, by referring to a person. Instead we must claim that there are long series of different mental states and events—thoughts, sensations, and the like—each series being what we call one life. Each series is unified by various kinds of causal relation, such as the relations that hold between experiences and later memories of them. Each series is thus like a bundle tied up with string.

In a sense, a Bundle Theorist denies the existence of persons. An outright denial is of course absurd. As Reid protested in the eighteenth century, 'I am not thought, I am not action, I am not feeling; I am something which thinks and acts and feels.' I am not a series of events but a person. A Bundle Theorist admits this fact, but claims it to be only a fact about our grammar, or our language. There are persons or subjects in this language-dependent way. If, however, persons are believed to be more than this—to be separately existing things, distinct from our brains and bodies, and the various kinds of mental states and events—the Bundle Theorist denies that there are such things.

The first Bundle Theorist was Buddha, who taught "anatta," or the *No Self view*. Buddhists concede that selves or persons have "nominal existence," by which they mean that persons are merely combinations of other elements. Only what exists by itself, as a separate element, has instead what Buddhists call "actual existence." Here are some quotations from Buddhist texts:

> At the beginning of their conversation the king politely asks the monk his name, and receives the following reply: 'Sir, I am known as "Nagasena;" my fellows in the religious life address me as "Nagasena." Although my parents gave me the name...it is just an appellation, a form of speech, a description, a conventional usage. "Nagasena" is only a name, for no person is found here.'
>
> A sentient being does exist, you think, O Mara? You are misled by a false conception. This bundle of elements is void of Self. In it there is no sentient being. Just as a set of wooden parts receives the name of carriage, so do we give to elements the name of fancied being.
>
> Buddha has spoken thus: 'O Brethren, actions do exist, and also their consequences, but the person that acts does not. There is no one to cast away this set of elements, and no one to assume a new set of them. There exists no Individual, it is only a conventional name given to a set of elements.'[2]

Buddha's claims are strikingly similar to the claims advanced by several Western writers. Since these writers knew nothing of Buddha, the similarity of these claims suggests that they are not merely part of one cultural tradition, in one period. They may be, as I believe they are, true.

WHAT WE BELIEVE OURSELVES TO BE

Given the advances in psychology and neurophysiology, the Bundle Theory may now seem to be obviously true. It may seem uninteresting to deny that there are separately existing Egos, which are distinct from brains and bodies and the various kinds of mental states and events. But this is not the only issue. We may be convinced that the Ego Theory is false, or even senseless. Most of us, however, even if we are not aware of this, also have certain beliefs about what is involved in our continued existence over time. And these beliefs would only be justified if something like the Ego Theory was true. Most of us therefore have false beliefs about what persons are, and about ourselves.

These beliefs are best revealed when we consider certain imaginary cases, often drawn from science fiction. One such case is *teletransportation*. Suppose that you enter a cubicle in which, when you press a button, a scanner records the states of all of the cells in your brain and body, destroying both while doing so. This information is then transmitted at the speed of light to some other planet, where a replicator produces a perfect organic copy of you. Since the brain of your Replica is exactly like yours, it will seem to remember living your life up to the moment when you pressed the button, its character will be just like yours, and it will be in every other way psychologically continuous with you. This psychological continuity will not have its normal cause, the continued existence of your brain, since the causal chain will run through the transmission by radio of your "blueprint."

Several writers claim that, if you chose to be teletransported, believing this to be the fastest way of travelling, you would be making a terrible mistake. This would not be a way of travelling, but a way of dying. It may not, they concede, be quite as bad as ordinary death. It might be some consolation to you that, after your death, you will have this Replica, which can finish the book that you are writing, act as parent to your children, and so on. But, they insist, this Replica won't be you. It will merely be someone else, who is exactly like you. This is why this prospect is nearly as bad as ordinary death.

Imagine next a whole range of cases, in each of which, in a single operation, a different proportion of the cells in your brain and body would be replaced with exact duplicates. At the near end of this range, only 1 or 2 per cent would be replaced; in the middle, 40 or 60 per cent; near the far end, 98 or 99 per cent. At the far end of this range is pure teletransportation, the case in which all of your cells would be "replaced."

When you imagine that some proportion of your cells will be replaced with exact duplicates, it is natural to have the following beliefs. First, if you ask, "Will I survive? Will the resulting person be me?", there must be an answer to this question. Either you will survive, or you are about to die. Second, the answer to this question must be either a simple "Yes" or a simple "No." The person who wakes up either will or will not be you. There cannot be a third answer, such as that the person waking up will be half you. You can imagine yourself later being half-conscious. But if the resulting person will be fully conscious, he cannot be half you. To state these beliefs together: to the question, "Will the resulting person be me?", there must always *be* an answer, which must be all-or-nothing.

There seem good grounds for believing that, in the case of teletransportation, your Replica would not be you. In a slight variant of this case, your Replica might be created while you were still alive, so that you could talk to one another. This seems to show that, if 100 per cent of your cells were replaced, the result would merely be a Replica of you. At the other end of my range of cases, where only 1 per cent would be replaced, the resulting person clearly *would* be you. It therefore seems that, in the cases in between, the resulting person must be either you, or merely a Replica. It seems that one of these

must be true, and that it makes a great difference which is true.

HOW WE ARE NOT WHAT WE BELIEVE

If these beliefs were correct, there must be some critical percentage, somewhere in this range of cases, up to which the resulting person would be you, and beyond which he would merely be your Replica. Perhaps, for example, it would be you who would wake up if the proportion of cells replaced were 49 per cent, but if just a few more cells were also replaced, this would make all the difference, causing it to be someone else who would wake up.

That there must be some such critical percentage follows from our natural beliefs. But this conclusion is most implausible. How could a few cells make such a difference? Moreover, if there is such a critical percentage, no one could ever discover where it came. Since in all these cases the resulting person would believe that he was you, there could never be any evidence about where, in this range of cases, he would suddenly cease to be you.

On the Bundle Theory, we should reject these natural beliefs. Since you, the person, are not a separately existing entity, we can know exactly what would happen without answering the question of what will happen to you. Moreover, in the case in the middle of my range, it is an empty question whether the resulting person would be you, or would merely be someone else who is exactly like you. These are not here two different possibilities, one of which must be true. These are merely two different descriptions of the very same course of events. If 50 per cent of your cells were replaced with exact duplicates, we could call the resulting person you, or we could call him merely your Replica. But since these are not here different possibilities, this is a mere choice of words.

As Buddha claimed, the Bundle Theory is hard to believe. It is hard to accept that it could be an empty question whether one is about to die, or will instead live for many years.

What we are being asked to accept may be made clearer with this analogy. Suppose that a certain club exists for some time, holding regular meetings. The meetings then cease. Some years later, several people form a club with the same name, and the same rules. We can ask, "Did these people revive the very same club? Or did they merely start up another club which is exactly similar?" Given certain further details, this would be another empty question. We could know just what happened without answering this question. Suppose that someone said: "But there must be an answer. The club meeting later must either be, or not be, the very same club." This would show that this person didn't understand the nature of clubs.

In the same way, if we have any worries about my imagined cases, we don't understand the nature of persons. In each of my cases, you would know that the resulting person would be both psychologically and physically exactly like you, and that he would have some particular proportion of the cells in your brain and body —90 per cent, or 10 per cent, or, in the case of teletransportation, 0 per cent. Knowing this, you know everything. How could it be a real question what would happen to you, unless you are a separately existing Ego, distinct from a brain and body, and the various kinds of mental state and event? If there are no such Egos, there is nothing else to ask a real question about.

Accepting the Bundle Theory is not only hard; it may also affect our emotions. As Buddha claimed, it may undermine our concern about our own futures. This effect can be suggested by redescribing this change of view. Suppose that you are about to be destroyed, but will later have a Replica on Mars. You would naturally believe that this prospect is about as bad as ordinary death, since your Replica won't be you. On the Bundle Theory, the fact that your Replica won't be you just consists in the fact that, though it will be fully psychologically continuous with you, this continuity won't have its normal cause. But when you object to teletransportation you are not objecting merely to the abnormality of this cause. You are objecting that this cause won't get *you* to Mars. You fear that the abnormal cause will fail to produce a further and all-important fact, which is different from the fact that your Replica will be psychologically continuous with you. You do not merely want there to be psychological continuity between you and some future person. You want to *be* this future person. On the Bundle Theory, there is no such special further fact. What you fear will not happen, in this imagined case, *never* happens. You want the person on Mars to be you in a specially intimate way in which no future person will ever be you. This means that, judged from the standpoint of your natural beliefs, even ordinary survival is about as bad as teletransportation. *Ordinary survival is about as bad as being destroyed and having a Replica.*

HOW THE SPLIT-BRAIN CASES SUPPORT THE BUNDLE THEORY

The truth of the Bundle Theory seems to me, in the widest sense, as much a scientific as a philosophical conclusion. I can imagine kinds of evidence which would have justified believing in the existence of separately existing Egos, and believing that the continued existence of these Egos is what explains the continuity of each mental life. But there is in fact very little evidence in favour of this Ego Theory, and much for the alternative Bundle Theory.

Some of this evidence is provided by the split-brain cases. On the Ego Theory, to explain what unifies our experiences at any one time, we should simply claim that these are all experiences which are being had by the same person. Bundle Theorists reject this explanation. This disagreement is hard to resolve in ordinary cases. But consider the simplified split-brain case that I described. We show to my imagined patient a placard whose left half is blue and right half is red. In one of this person's two streams of consciousness, he is aware of seeing only blue, while at the same time, in his other stream, he is aware of seeing only red. Each of these two visual experiences is combined with other experiences, like that of being aware of moving one of his hands. What unifies the experiences, at any time, in each of this person's two streams of consciousness? What unifies his awareness of seeing only red with his awareness of moving one hand? The answer cannot be that these experiences are being had by the same person. The answer cannot explain the unity of each of this person's two streams of consciousness, since it ignores the disunity between these streams. This person is now having all of the experiences in both of his two streams. If this fact was what unified these experiences, this would make the two streams one.

These cases do not, I have claimed, involve two people sharing a single body. Since there is only one person involved, who has two streams of consciousness, the Ego Theorist's explanation would have to take the following form. He would have to distinguish between persons and subjects of experiences, and claim that, in split-brain cases, there are *two* of the latter. What unifies the experiences in one of the person's two streams would have to be the fact these experiences are all being had by the same subject of experiences. What unifies the experiences in this person's other stream would have to be the fact that they are being had by another subject of experiences. When this explanation takes this form, it becomes much less plausible. While we could assume that "subject of experiences," or "Ego," simply meant "person," it was easy to believe that there are subjects of experiences. But if there can be subjects of experiences that are not persons, and if in the life of a split-brain patient there are at any time two different subjects of experiences—two different Egos—why should we believe that there really are such things? This does not amount to a refutation. But it seems to me a strong argument against the Ego Theory.

As a Bundle Theorist, I believe that these two Egos are idle cogs. There is another explanation of the unity of consciousness, both in ordinary cases and in split-brain cases. It is simply a fact that ordinary people are, at any time, aware of having several different experiences. This awareness of several different experiences can be helpfully compared with one's awareness, in short-term memory, of several different experiences. Just as there can be a single memory of just having had several experiences, such as hearing a bell strike three times, there can be a single state of awareness both of hearing the fourth striking of this bell, and of seeing, at the same time, ravens flying past the bell-tower.

Unlike the Ego Theorist's explanation, this explanation can easily be extended to cover split-brain cases. In such cases there is, at any time, not one state of awareness of several different experiences, but two such states. In the case I described, there is one state of awareness of both seeing only red and of moving one hand, and there is another state of awareness of both seeing only blue and moving the other hand. In claiming that there are two such states of awareness, we are not postulating the existence of unfamiliar entities, two separately existing Egos which are not the same as the single person whom the case involves. This explanation appeals to a pair of mental states which would have to be described anyway in a full description of this case.

I have suggested how the split-brain cases provide one argument for one view about the nature of persons. I should mention another such argument, provided by an imagined extension of these cases, first discussed at length by David Wiggins.[3]

In this imagined case a person's brain is divided, and the two halves are transplanted into a pair of different bodies. The two resulting people live quite separate lives. This imagined case shows that personal identity is not what matters. If I was about to divide, I should conclude that neither of the resulting people will be me. I will have ceased to exist. But this way of ceasing to exist is about as good—or as bad—as ordinary survival.

Some of the features of Wiggins's imagined case are likely to remain technically impossible. But the case cannot be dismissed, since its most striking feature, the division of one stream of consciousness into separate streams, has already happened. This is a second way in which the actual split-brain cases have great theoretical importance. They challenge some of our deepest assumptions about ourselves.[4]

NOTES

1. See MacKay's contribution, chapter 1 of *Mindwaves,* Colin Blakemore and Susan Greenfield, Eds. (Oxford: Basil Blackwell, 1987), pp. 5–16.

2. For the sources of these and similar quotations, see my *Reasons and Persons* pp. 502–3, 532. (Oxford: Oxford University Press, 1984).

3. At the end of his *Identity and Spatio-temporal Continuity* (Oxford: Blackwell, 1967).

4. I discuss these assumptions further in part 3 of my *Reasons and Persons.*

3.5 What Matters

SHELLY KAGAN

Shelly Kagan is Clark Professor of Philosophy at Yale University. He has written many important works in moral philosophy.

We've been asking the following question: what does it take for me to survive? But what I want to suggest now is that this may not really be the question we should have been thinking about! To be sure, I don't think, we would have been in a position to see this until we had worked through the various main theories of personal identity. But now that we're here, we can finally raise a crucial question: should we be asking about what it takes to *survive*? Or should we be asking about what *matters* in survival?

In posing this new question. I am obviously presupposing that we can draw a distinction between the question "Do I survive? Is somebody that exists in the future me?" and the question "What was it that I *wanted*, when I wanted to survive? What was it that *mattered* in ordinary survival?" But I do think these are different questions. And more importantly, I think the answers can potentially come apart.

To see this, suppose we start by thinking again about the soul view. Suppose there are souls. I don't believe in them, but let's imagine. And suppose that souls are the key to personal identity. So somebody is me if they've got my soul. I *survive*, as long as there's somebody

around with my soul. Will I still be around in a hundred years? Well, I will be if my soul is still around. That's what the soul theory says. And suppose it's the truth.

Now consider the following possibility. Suppose that people can be reincarnated. That is to say, at the death of their body, their soul takes over—animates, inhabits, gets connected to—a new body that's being born. But unlike the kind of reincarnation cases that get talked about in popular culture, where at least under the right circumstances you can remember your prior lives, let's imagine that when the soul is reincarnated, it's scrubbed completely clean, leaving no traces whatsoever of the earlier life. There is simply no way to retrieve any earlier memories; there is no underlying personality that will potentially reassert itself. There are no karmic similarities of personality from the previous life of any son, or anything like that; the soul simply starts over from scratch, like a blank slate. Think of it like a blackboard that's been completely erased: we have the very same blackboard, but now we start writing completely new things on it. Imagine that that's the way reincarnation worked.

From *Death* (Yale University Press 2012), pp. 162–168.

So if somebody asks you, "Will you still be around in 1,000 years?" the answer is yes. I will still be around because my soul will be reincarnated. In 1,000 years there'll be somebody that has the very same soul that's animating my body right now. Of course, that soul won't remember being Shelly Kagan. It won't have any memories of its prior life. It won't be like Shelly Kagan in any way in terms of Shelly Kagan's desires or ambitions or goals or fears. (Similarly, it won't be that the future personality emerges somehow through karmic cause and effect in any way that is a function of what I am like now, in this life.) That future person will be me—Shelly Kagan— because he will have Shelly Kagan's soul. But there will be no overlap of personality, memories, desires, anything.

When I think about this case, I want to say, who cares? The fact that I will *survive* under those circumstances doesn't give me anything that *matters* to me. It's no comfort to me to be told I will survive ("because after all, the soul is the key to personal identity"), if there's no similar personality, no memories, no beliefs, no retrievable elements from past lives. Given all this, who cares that it's *me*?

If you can feel the force of that thought, then you're seeing how the question "Will I survive?" can be separated out from the question "What matters? What do we *care* about?" Bare survival of my soul, even if that were the key to personal identity, wouldn't give me what I want.

It's no more comforting or satisfying than if you had said, 'You know this knucklebone? After you die, we're going to do knucklebone surgery and implant that knucklebone in somebody else's body. And that knucklebone is going to survive." I would reply, "Oh, that's sort of interesting, that my knucklebone will be around 100 or 1,000 years from now. But who *cares*?" And if the knucklebone theory of personal identity got proposed and somebody said, "Oh, yes, but you see, that person now with that knucklebone will be *you*, because the key to personal identity is having the very same knucklebone," I would say, "All right, so it's me. Who cares?" Bare knucklebone survival does not give me what matters.

The knucklebone theory of personal identity is a very stupid theory. In contrast, the soul theory of personal survival is not a stupid theory. But for all that, it doesn't give me what I want. When we think about the possibility of bare survival of the scrubbed clean, erased soul, we see that survival wasn't really everything we wanted. What we wanted—at least what *I* want, and I invite you to ask yourself whether you want the same thing—is not just survival, but survival with the same *personality*. So even if the soul theory is the correct theory of personal identity, it's not enough to give me what *matters*. What matters isn't just survival. It's survival with the same personality.

Next, let's consider the body view. Suppose that the body theory of personal identity is correct. I'll survive, as long as there is someone in the future who has my body. Let's also suppose that the brain version of the body theory is the best version. And now, imagine that next year there's going to be somebody that's got my brain. But let's imagine that the brain has been scrubbed clean. All memory traces have been completely erased. We're talking complete irreversible amnesia, complete erasure of the brain's hard drive. Imagine that there are *no* traces of my personality. No memories, desires, intentions, or beliefs to eventually be recovered if only we do the right procedure (have the right surgery, undergo the right psychotherapy). No, it's all just *gone*.

The person that wakes up after this complete irreversible amnesia will no doubt eventually develop a new personality, a set of beliefs and memories. Suppose that nobody knows who he is, though. They find him wandering on the streets. They call him John Doe. John Doe will eventually have a bunch of beliefs about how the world works, make some plans, get some memories. And according to the body theory, that's me. If the body theory of personal identity is correct, then by golly it *is* me.

But when I think about this case, all I can say in response to the fact that it's me is, who cares? I survive, but so what? I'm not comforted by the thought that I will still be around fifty years from now, if the person that's me doesn't have my personality.

Mere bodily survival isn't enough to give me what I want. I want *more* than mere bodily survival. I want to survive with the same personality. So even if the body theory of personal identity is the *correct* theory of personal identity, what I want to say is, so what? The really crucial question is not "Do I survive?" but "Do I have what I *wanted* when I wanted to survive?" And the fact of the matter is, having the same body doesn't guarantee that I will. I don't just want to survive. I want to survive with the same personality.

The question we really need to get clear about, then, is this: what *matters* in survival? Of course, it is plausible to think that in the normal cases of survival, I do get what matters. That, after all, is probably the reason why we come to care about survival so much: because it normally provides us with what matters. But for all that, we can see that in unusual cases, mere survival—bare survival—may not actually be *enough* to give us what matters.

If there can be cases where I survive, but I don't have what I *normally* have when I survive, and so I don't have what matters, then in such cases I don't really have what I wanted when I wanted to survive. For all that, of course, it could still be true that in *typical* cases of survival I've got the extra thing that matters, whatever it is. But if we can think of cases in which I survive, but I *don't* have that extra thing, then I wouldn't have everything that matters to me. So perhaps we should say that mere survival or bare bones survival doesn't really give me what matters. What I want is survival plus something *more*.

But what's the extra something? What's the "something more"? The examples we've been discussing so far suggest that what I want is to survive with the same *personality*. Is that the right conclusion? Is what matters in survival not just survival, but surviving with the same personality? I think that that's close—but not quite right.

To see that, let's take another look at the personality view. Suppose that the personality theory of personal identity were correct. Would that then guarantee that I have not only survival, but also what matters? I don't think it would.

Recall the fact that, according to the personality view, survival doesn't require that my personality never change. It's not as though I have to keep every single one of my beliefs, desires, and memories fixed. Because of course, if it did require that, then we would have to say that I am going to die as soon as I get a new belief! I'm going to die as soon as I forget any detail of what I was doing twenty minutes ago! Rather, according to the personality theory, what personal identity requires isn't that every single element of my personality stay the same, but that I keep the same evolving-over-time personality. I can gain new beliefs, new desires, new goals. I can lose some of my previous memories, lose some of my previous beliefs. All of that is okay, as long as it's the same slowly evolving personality, with the right pattern of overlap and continuity.

So consider the following case. Here I am, almost sixty. I've got a set of beliefs. For example, I believe my name is "Shelly Kagan" and I teach philosophy. I have a set of memories about growing up in Chicago, and marrying my wife, and so forth. And I have various desires—for example, I want to finish writing this book. But of course, I will get older, and my personality will change. I'll get some new beliefs, new memories; I'll have new desires and new goals. Imagine, then, that I get older and older and older. Suppose that I get very old indeed—very, very, very old. I get to be 100 years old, 200 years old, 300 years old, and more.

Suppose that somewhere around 200, my friends give me a new nickname. They call me Jo-Jo. Who knows why, they call me Jo-Jo. And eventually the nickname spreads. By the time I'm 250 years old, everybody calls me Jo-Jo. Nobody calls me Shelly anymore. Indeed, by the time I'm 300, 350, 400, I've forgotten that *anybody* ever called me Shelly. I no longer remember growing up in Chicago. Of course. I do remember some things from my "youth," when I was a mere lad of 150. But I can't go back to what it was like in the early days, from my twenties or thirties or forties, just like you can't go back to what it was like to be three or four. And imagine that while all of this is going on, while I'm getting older and older, my personality is changing in a variety of other ways as well. Along the way I lose my interest in philosophy and take up an interest in something I've never cared about before at all, perhaps organic chemistry. I become fascinated by the details of organic chemistry.

And my values change, too. Right now, today, I'm a kind, compassionate, warm individual who cares about the downtrodden. But around 300, I start to lose my compassion. At 400 I'm saying things like, "The downtrodden. Who needs them?" And by the time I'm 500, I'm completely self-absorbed: I'm a vicious, cruel, vile person. Here I am, 800 years old, 900 years old, more.

Methuselah, in the Bible, lives for 969 years. He's the oldest person in the Bible. So here I am, at the end of my life, 969 years old.

Let's call this the *Methuselah* case. And the crucial point about it is that we stipulate that at no point along the way was there a dramatic change in my personality. It was all gradual, slow, evolving, in just the way that it normally happens in real life. It's just that I live a very, very, very long time. And toward the end of it —let's say, somewhere around 700 or 800—I'm a "completely different person." as we might put it. Of course, I don't mean that literally. I mean that it's as *though* I were a completely different person—given how different my personality is.

Now remember, according to the personality theory of personal identity, what makes someone me is the fact that they've got the same evolving-through-time personality as I have. And I stipulated that it *is* the same evolving personality. So that's still *me* that's going to be around 600 years from now, 700 years from now.

But when I think about the Methuselah case I say, "So what? Who cares?" When I think about that case, I find myself wanting to say that even if we just *stipulate* that this will be me in 700 years, that still doesn't give me what I want. That person is completely unlike me, as

I am now. He doesn't remember being Shelly Kagan. He doesn't remember growing up in Chicago. He doesn't remember my family. He has completely different interests and tastes and values. I find myself wanting to say, "It's me, but so what? This doesn't give me what I want. It doesn't give me what matters."

When I think about what I want, it's not just that there should be somebody at the tail end of my evolving personality. I want that person to be *like* me, not just *be* me. (More precisely, of course, I want that person to be like me *now*— to be like this particular person stage. But I won't keep adding this qualification explicitly.) Sadly, in the Methuselah case, I end up not being very much like me at all. So that case doesn't give me what I want either—even though I survive with the same evolving personality.

In short, when I think about what I want, it's not just survival. And it's not just survival with the same evolving-through-time personality. Roughly speaking, what I want is survival with a *similar* personality. It certainly doesn't have to be identical, item for item. But it has to be close enough to be fairly similar to my personality now. Give me that, and I've got what matters in survival. Don't give me that, and I don't have what matters. Of course, you may find yourself wanting something different. I can only invite you to ask yourself what it is that you want, what matters to you in survival. But when I think about what *I* want, that's pretty much it.

Actually, though, I'm inclined to go a little bit further. Once you give me that there's somebody around in the future with a similar enough personality to my own, I think that may be *all* that matters here. So in a certain way, what I've been saying up to this point has been misleading. I've been saying that mere survival by itself isn't good enough: you need survival plus something more. But strictly speaking, it might be that *all* that matters is the something more. Perhaps, as long as I have that, I have what matters—even if I *don't* have survival.

Suppose, for example, that there really are souls. And suppose that the soul really is the key to personal identity. And suppose as well that the thing that Locke was worried about really does happen: every day at midnight God destroys the old soul and replaces it with a new soul that has the very same personality as the one before midnight—the same beliefs, desires, and so forth and so on. If I were to somehow discover all of these metaphysical facts I'd say. "Huh! It turns out that I'm not going to survive tonight; I'm going to die. But who *cares*? There will be somebody around tomorrow with precisely my beliefs, my desires, my goals, my ambitions, my fears, my values. That's good enough. I don't really care whether I'm going to *survive*. What I care about is whether there'll be somebody that's similar to me in the right way in terms of my current personality. And there will be."

So it might be that the whole question we've been focusing on, "What does it take to survive?" is misguided. The real question may not be "What does it take to survive?" but "What matters?" Of course, in ordinary circumstances, having what matters goes hand in hand with surviving. Survival is normally the only way that we can *get* what matters. But logically speaking, at least, the two things can come apart. And what really matters, or so it seems to me, isn't survival per se at all, but having a similar personality. (I trust it is obvious that I don't really mean that this is the only thing that matters in any way whatsoever! I simply mean, it's what matters when I am concerned about surviving.)

Imagine that tonight, while everyone is sleeping, God replaces my body with some identical-looking body, and he gives it a personality identical to my own from just before I went to sleep. Since I am inclined to think that the body view is the correct theory of personal identity, and since that new body obviously won't be *my* body. I believe that the person who will wake up tomorrow won't be me. I won't survive the night. I'm going to die. But that's okay. What matters to me isn't survival per se. Indeed, it isn't survival at all. It's having someone with a similar enough personality. That's good enough.

So imagine that when we die, what happens is this: God takes all the relevant information about my personality from the moment just before my death, and he creates a *new* body up in heaven (perhaps a new angelic body) with that very same personality. Since the body view is the correct view, I think that won't be me. (That's not my body up in heaven; *my* body is rotting here on earth.) It turns out, then, that we don't survive our deaths. But still, I find myself wanting to say, so what? Survival was never what really mattered anyway. Even though it won't be *me* up in heaven, this may still give me what matters.

There is, then, at least a logical possibility that after the death of my body, I will still have what matters. Indeed, I might even survive, as well—if there is bodily resurrection, or if it is the personality view rather than the body view that gives the correct account of personal identity. But for what it's worth, I don't in fact believe that any of this *is going to happen*. In particular, as far as I can see, there is no good reason to believe that my personality will continue after the death of my body. And so, as far as I can see, there is no good reason to believe that I will still have what *matters* after the death of my body.

Of course, these questions are partly theological matters. And I'm certainly not trying to say anything here to argue you out of the theological conviction that God will resurrect your body or that God will transplant your personality into some new angel body. If you believe either of these things, so be it. It's not my goal here to argue either for or against these particular theological possibilities.

Still, the truth is, I do not myself believe in either one of these possibilities. I do not think that after my death my body will be resurrected, or my personality transplanted. On the contrary, I think that death really will be the end. The end of me, and the end of my personality. That, it seems to me, is the simple fact of the matter. Death will be the end.

3.6 A Dialogue on Personal Identity and Immortality

JOHN PERRY

John Perry is an emeritus professor of philosophy at Stanford University.

(This is a record of conversations of Gretchen Weirob, a teacher of philosophy at a small midwestern college, and several of her friends. They took place in her hospital room, the three nights before she died from injuries sustained in a motorcycle accident. Sam Miller is a chaplain and a longtime friend of Weirob's; Dave Cohen is a former student of hers.)

THE FIRST NIGHT

Cohen: I can hardly believe what you say, Gretchen. You are lucid and do not appear to be in great pain. And yet you say things are hopeless?

Weirob: These devices can keep me alive for another day or two at most. Some of my vital organs have been injured beyond anything the doctors know how to repair, apart from certain rather radical measures I have rejected. I am not in much pain. But as I understand it that is not a particularly good sign. My brain was uninjured and I guess that's why I am as lucid as I ever am. The whole situation is a bit depressing, I fear. But here's Sam Miller. Perhaps he will know how to cheer me up.

Miller: Good evening Gretchen. Hello, Dave. I guess there's not much point in beating around the bush, Gretchen; the medics tell me you're a goner. Is there anything I can do to help?

Weirob: Crimenentley, Sam! You deal with the dying every day. Don't you have anything more comforting to say than "Sorry to hear you're a goner?"

Miller: Well to tell you the truth, I'm a little at a loss for what to say to you. Most people I deal with are believers like I am. We talk of the prospects for survival. I give assurance that God, who is just and merciful, would not permit such a travesty as that our short life on this earth should be the end of things. But you and I have talked about religious and philosophical issues for years. I have never been able to find in you the least inclination to believe in God; indeed, it's a rare day when you are sure that your friends have minds, or that you can see your own hand in front of your face, or that there is any reason to believe that the sun will rise tomorrow. How can I hope to comfort you with the prospect of life after death, when I know you will regard it as having no probability whatsoever?

Weirob: I would not require so much to be comforted, Sam. Even the possibility of something quite improbable can be comforting, in certain situations. When we used to play tennis, I beat you no more than one time in twenty. But this was enough to establish the possibility of beating you on any given occasion, and by focusing merely on the possibility, I remained eager to play. Entombed in a secure prison, having thought our situation quite hopeless, we might find unutterable joy in the information that there was, after all, a possibility of escape, however slim the chances of actually succeeding. Hope provides comfort, and hope does not always require probability. But we must believe that what we hope for is at least possible. So I will set an easier task for you. Simply persuade me that my survival, after the death of this body, is *possible,* and I promise to be comforted. Whether you succeed or not, your attempts will be a diversion, for you know I like to talk philosophy more than anything else.

Miller: But what is possibility, if not reasonable probability?

Weirob: I do not mean possible in the sense of likely, or even in the sense of comforming to the known laws of physics or biology. I mean possible only in the weakest sense, of being conceivable, given the unavoidable facts. Within the next couple of days, this body will die. It will be buried, and it will rot away. I ask that, given these facts, you explain to me how it even makes *sense* to talk of me continuing to exist. Just explain to me what it is I am to *imagine,* when I imagine surviving, that is consistent with these facts, and I shall be comforted.

Miller: But then what is there to do? There are many conceptions of immortality, of survival past the grave, which all seem to make good sense. Surely not the possibility, but only the probability, can be doubted. Take your choice! Christians believe in life, with a body, in some Hereafter—the details vary, of course, from sect to sect. There is the Greek idea of the body as a prison, from which we escape at death—so we have continued life without a body. Then there are conceptions, in which we, so to speak, merge with the flow of being…

Weirob: I must cut short your lesson in comparative religion. Survival means surviving, no more, no less. I have no doubts that I shall merge with being; plants will take roots in my remains, and the chemicals that I am will continue to make their contribution to life. I am enough of an ecologist to be comforted. But survival, if it is anything, must offer comforts of a different sort, the comforts of *anticipation.* Survival means that tomorrow, or sometime in the future, there will be someone who will experience, who will see and touch and smell—or at least, at the very least, think and reason and remember. And this person will be *me.* This person will be related to me in such a way that it is

correct for me to anticipate, to look forward to, those future experiences. And I am related to her in such a way that it will be right for her to remember what I have thought and done, to feel remorse for what I have done wrong, and pride in what I have done right. And the only relation that supports anticipation and memory in this way, is simply *identity.* For it is never correct to anticipate, as happening to oneself, what will happen to someone else, is it? Or to remember, as one's own thoughts and deeds, what someone else did? So don't give me merger with being, or some such nonsense. Give me identity, or let's talk about baseball or fishing—but I'm sorry to get so emotional. I just react so strongly when words which mean one thing are used for another—when one talks about survival, but does not mean to say that the same person will continue to exist. It's such a sham!

Miller: I'm sorry. I was just trying to stay in touch with the times, if you want to know the truth, for when I read modern theology or talk to my students who have studied eastern religions, the notion of survival as simply continued existence of the same person seems out of date. Merger with Being! Merger with Being! That's all I hear. My own beliefs are quite simple, if somewhat vague. I think you will live again—with or without a body, I don't know—I draw comfort from my belief that you and I will be together again, after I also die. We will communicate, somehow. We will continue to grow spiritually. That's what I believe, as surely as I believe that I am sitting here. For I don't know how God could be excused, if this small sample of life is all that we are allotted; I don't know why he should have created us, if this few years of toil and torment are the end of it…

Weirob: Remember our deal, Sam. You don't have to convince me that survival is probable, for we both agree you would not get to first base. You have only to convince me that it is possible. The only condition is that it be real survival we are talking about, not some up-to-date ersatz survival, which simply amounts to what any ordinary person would call ceasing totally to exist.

Miller: I guess I just miss the problem then. Of course it's possible. You just continue to exist, after your body dies. What's to be defended or explained? You want details? OK. Two people meet a thousand years from now, in a place that may or may not be part of this physical universe. I am one and you are the other. So you must have survived. Surely you can imagine that. What else is there to say?

Weirob: But in a few days *I* will quit breathing, *I* will be put into a coffin, *I* will be buried. And in a few months or a few years *I* will be reduced to so much humus. That I take it is obvious, is given. How then can you say that I am one of these persons a thousand years from now? Suppose I took this box of kleenex and lit fire to it. It is reduced to ashes and I smash the ashes and flush them down the john. Then I say to you, go home and on the shelf will be *that very box of kleenex.* It has survived! Wouldn't that be absurd? What sense could you make of it? And yet that is just what you say to me. I will rot away. And then, a thousand years later, there I will be. What sense does that make?

Miller: There could be an *identical* box of kleenex at your home, one just like it in every respect. And, in this sense, there is no difficulty in there being someone identical to you in the Hereafter, though your body has rotted away.

Weirob: You are playing with words again. There could be an *exactly similar* box of kleenex on my shelf. We sometimes use "identical" to mean "exactly similar" as when we talk of "identical twins." But I am using "identical," in a way in which *identity* is the condition of memory and correct anticipation. If I am told that tomorrow though I will be dead, someone else that looks and sounds and thinks just like me will be alive, would that be comforting? Could I correctly *anticipate* having her experiences? Would it make sense for me to fear her pains and look forward to her pleasures? Would it be right for her to feel remorse at the harsh way I am treating you? Of course not. Similarity, however exact, is not identity. I use identity to mean there is but one thing. If I am to survive, there must be one person who is here in this bed now, and who is

talking to someone in your Hereafter ten or a thousand years from now. After all, what comfort could there be in the notion of a Heavenly imposter, walking around getting credit for the few good things I have done?

Miller: I'm sorry. I see that I was simply confused. Here is what I should have said. If you were merely a live human body—as the kleenex box is merely cardboard and glue in a certain arrangement—then the death of your body would be the end of you. But surely you are more than that, fundamentally more than that. What is fundamentally you is not your body, but your soul or self or mind.

Weirob: Do you mean these words, "soul," "self," or "mind" to come to the same thing?

Miller: I have heard fine distinctions made, but usually cannot follow them. They are the nonphysical, nonmaterial, aspects of you. They are your consciousness. It is this that I get at with these words, and I am not clever enough to attempt any further distinction.

Weirob: Consciousness? I am conscious, for a while yet. I see, I hear, I think, I remember. But "to be conscious"—that is a verb. What is the subject of the verb, the thing which is conscious? Isn't it just this body, the same object that is overweight, injured, and lying in bed? And which will be buried, and not be conscious in a day or a week at the most?

Miller: As you are a philosopher, I would expect you to be less muddled about these issues. Did Descartes not draw a clear distinction between the body and the mind, between that which is overweight and that which is conscious? Your mind or soul is immaterial, lodged while you are on earth in your body. They are intimately related, but not identical. Now clearly, what concerns us in survival is your mind or soul. It is this which must be identical between the person before me now, and the one I expect to see in a thousand years in heaven.

Weirob: So I am not really this body, but a soul or mind or spirit? And this soul cannot be seen or felt or touched or smelt? That is implied, I take it, by the fact that it is immaterial?

Miller: That's right. Your soul sees and smells, but cannot be seen or smelt.

Weirob: Let me see if I understand you. You would admit that I am the very same person with whom you ate lunch last week at Dorsey's?

Miller: Of course you are.

Weirob: Now when you say I am the same person, if I understand you, that is not a remark about this body you see and could touch and I fear can smell. Rather it is a remark about a soul, which you cannot see or touch or smell. The fact that the same body was across the booth from you at Dorsey's as is now lying in front of you on the bed—that would not mean that the same *person* was present on both occasions, if the same soul were not. And if, through some strange turn of events, the same soul were present on both occasions, but lodged in different bodies, then it *would* be the same person. Is that right?

Miller: You have understood me perfectly. But surely, you understood all of this before!

Weirob: But wait. I can repeat it, but I'm not sure I understand it. If you cannot see or touch or in any way perceive my soul, what makes you think the one you are confronted with now *is* the very same soul you were confronted with at Dorsey's?

Miller: But I just explained. To say it is the same soul and to say it is the same person, are the same. And, of course, you are the same person you were before. Who else would you be if not yourself? You *were* Gretchen Weirob, and you *are* Gretchen Weirob.

Weirob: But how do you know you are talking to Gretchen Weirob at all, and not someone else, say Barbara Walters or even Mark Spitz!

Miller: Well, it's just obvious. I can see who I am talking to.

Weirob: But all you can see is my body. You can see, perhaps, that the same body is before you now that was before you last week at Dorsey's. But you have just said that Gretchen Weirob is not a body but a soul. In judging that the same person is before you now as was before you then, you must be making a judgement about souls—which, you said, cannot be

seen or touched or smelled or tasted. And so, I repeat, how do you know?

Miller: Well, I *can* see that it is the same body before me now that was across the table at Dorsey's. And I know that the same soul is connected with the body as was connected with it before. That's how I know it's you. I see no difficulty in the matter.

Weirob: You reason on the principle, "same body, same self."

Miller: Yes.

Weirob: And would you reason conversely also? If there were in this bed Barbara Walters' body—that is, the body you see every night on the news—would you infer that it was not me, Gretchen Weirob, in the bed?

Miller: Of course I would. How would you have come by Barbara Walters' body?

Weirob: But then merely extend this principle to Heaven, and you will see that your conception of survival is without sense. Surely this very body, which will be buried and, as I must so often repeat, *rot away,* will not be in your Hereafter. Different body, different person. Or do you claim that a body can rot away on earth, and then still wind up somewhere else? Must I bring up the kleenex box again?

Miller: No, I do not claim that. But I also do not extend a principle, found reliable on earth, to such a different situation as is represented by the Hereafter. That a correlation between bodies and souls has been found on earth, does not make it inconceivable or impossible that they should separate. Principles found to work in one circumstance may not be assumed to work in vastly altered circumstances. January and snow go together here, and one would be a fool to expect otherwise. But the principle does not apply in California.

Weirob: So the principle, "same body, same soul," is a well-confirmed regularity, not something you know "a priori."

Miller: By "a priori" you philosophers mean something which can be known without observing what actually goes on in the world, as I can know that two plus two equals four just by thinking about numbers, and that no bachelors are married just by thinking about the meaning of "bachelor"?

Weirob: Yes.

Miller: Then you are right. If it was part of the meaning of "same body" that wherever we have the same body, we have the same soul, it would have to obtain universally, in Heaven as well as on earth. But I just claim it is a generalization we know by observation on earth, and it need not automatically extend to Heaven.

Weirob: But where do you get this principle? It simply amounts to a correlation between being confronted with the same body and being confronted with the same soul. To establish such a correlation in the first place, surely one must have some *other* means of judging sameness of soul. You do not have such a means; your principle is without foundation; either you really do not know the person before you now is Gretchen Weirob, the very same person you lunched with at Dorsey's, or what you do know has nothing to do with sameness of some immaterial soul.

Miller: Hold on, hold on. You know I can't follow you when you start spitting out arguments like that. Now what is this terrible fallacy I'm supposed to have committed?

Weirob: I'm sorry. I get carried away. Here, have one of my chocolates by way of a peace offering.

Miller: Very tasty, thank you.

Weirob: Now why did you choose that one?

Miller: Because it had a certain swirl on the top which shows that it is a caramel.

Weirob: That is, a certain sort of swirl is correlated with a certain type of filling—the swirls with caramel, the rosettes with orange, and so forth.

Miller: Yes. When you put it that way, I see an analogy. Just as I judged that the filling would be the same in this piece as in the last piece that I ate with such a swirl, so I judge that the soul with which I am conversing is the same as the last soul with which I conversed when sitting across from that body. We *see* the outer wrapping and infer to what is inside.

Weirob: But how did you come to realize that swirls of that sort and caramel insides were so associated?

Miller: Why from eating a great many of them over the years. Whenever I bit into a candy with that sort of swirl, it was filled with this sort of caramel.

Weirob: Could you have established the correlation had you never been allowed to bite into a candy and never seen what happened when someone else bit into one? You could have formed the hypothesis, "same swirl, same filling." But could you have ever established it?

Miller: It seems not.

Weirob: So your inference, in a particular case, to the identity of filling from the identity of swirl would be groundless?

Miller: Yes, it would. I think I see what is coming.

Weirob: I'm sure you do. Since you can never, so to speak, bite into my soul, can never see or touch it, you have no way of testing your hypothesis that sameness of body means sameness of self.

Miller: I daresay you are right. But now I'm a bit lost. What is supposed to follow from all of this?

Weirob: If identity of persons consisted in identity of immaterial unobservable souls as you claim, then judgements of personal identity of the sort we make every day whenever we greet a friend or avoid a pest are really judgements about such souls.

Miller: Right.

Weirob: But if such judgements were really about souls, they would all be groundless and without foundation. For we have no direct method of observing sameness of soul, and so —and this is the point made by the candy example—can have no indirect method either.

Miller: That seems fair.

Weirob: But our judgements about persons are not all simply groundless and silly, so we must not be judging of immaterial souls after all.

Miller: Your reasoning has some force. But I suspect the problem lies in my defense of my position, and not the position itself. Look here. There *is* a way to test the hypothesis of a correlation after all. When I entered the room, I expected you to react just as you did. Argumentatively and skeptically. Had the person with this body reacted completely different perhaps I would have been forced to conclude it was not you. For example, had she complained about not being able to appear on the six o'clock news, and missing Harry Reasoner, and so forth, I might have eventually been persuaded it *was* Barbara Walters and not you. Similarity of psychological characteristics, a person's attitudes, beliefs, memories, prejudices, and the like, is observable. These are correlated with identity of body on the one side, and of course with sameness of soul on the other. So the correlation between body and soul can be established after all by this intermediate link.

Weirob: And how do you know that?

Miller: Know what?

Weirob: That where we have sameness of psychological characteristics, we have sameness of soul.

Miller: Well now you are really being just silly. The soul or mind just is that which is responsible for one's character, memory, belief. These are aspects of or states of mind, just as one's height, weight, and appearance are aspects of the body.

Weirob: Let me grant, for the sake of argument, that belief, character, memory, and so forth are states of mind. That is, I suppose, I grant that what one thinks and feels is due to the state one's mind is in at that time. And I shall even grant that a mind is an immaterial thing— though I harbor the gravest doubts that this is so. I do not see how it follows from that, that similarity of such traits requires, or is evidence to the slightest degree, for identity of the mind or soul. Let me explain my point with an analogy. If we were to walk out of this room, down past the mill and out toward Wilbur, what would we see?

Miller: We would come to the Blue River, among other things.

Weirob: And how would you recognize the Blue River? I mean, of course if you left from here, you would scarcely expect to hit the Platte or Niobrara. But suppose you were actually lost, and came across the Blue River in your wandering, just at that point where an old dam partly blocks the flow. Couldn't you recognize it?

Miller: Yes, I'm sure as soon as I saw that part of the river I would again know where I was.

Weirob: And how would you recognize it?

Miller: Well, the turgid brownness of the water, the sluggish flow, the filth washed up on the banks, and such.

Weirob: In a word, the state of the water which makes up the river at the time you see it.

Miller: Right.

Weirob: If you saw blue clean water, with bass jumping, you would know it wasn't the Blue River.

Miller: Of course.

Weirob: So you expect, each time you see the Blue, to see the water, which makes it up, in similar states—not always exactly the same, for sometimes it's a little dirtier, but by and large, similar.

Miller: Yes, but what do you intend to make of this?

Weirob: Each time you see the Blue, it consists of *different* water. The water that was in it a month ago may be in Tuttle Creek Reservoir, or in the Mississippi, or in the Gulf of Mexico by now. So the *similarity* of states of water, by which you judge the sameness of river, does not require *identity* of the water which is in those states at these various times.

Miller: And?

Weirob: And so just because you judge as to personal identity by reference to similarity of states of mind, it does not follow that the mind, or soul, is the same in each case. My point is this. For all you know, the immaterial soul which you think is lodged in my body might change from day to day, from hour to hour, from minute to minute, replaced each time by another soul psychologically similar. You cannot see it or touch it, so how would you know?

Miller: Are you saying I don't really know who you are?

Weirob: Not at all. *You* are the one who says personal identity consists in sameness of this immaterial, unobservable, invisible, untouchable soul. I merely point out that *if* it did consist in that, you *would* have no idea who I am. Sameness of body would not necessarily mean sameness of person. Sameness of psychological characteristics would not necessarily mean sameness of person. I am saying that if you do know who I am then you are wrong that personal identity consists in sameness of immaterial soul.

Miller: I see. But wait. I believe my problem is that I simply forgot a main tenet of my theory. The correlation can be established in my own case. I know that *my* soul and my body are intimately and consistently found together. From this one case I can generalize, at least as concerns life in this world, that sameness of body is a reliable sign of sameness of soul. This leaves me free to regard it as intelligible, in the case of death, that the link between the particular soul and the particular body it has been joined with is broken.

Weirob: This would be quite an extrapolation, wouldn't it, from one case directly observed, to a couple of billion in which only the body is observed? For I take it that we are in the habit of assuming, for every man now on earth, as well as those who have already come and gone, that the principle "one body, one soul" is in effect.

Miller: This does not seem an insurmountable obstacle. Since there is nothing special about my case, I assume the arrangement I find in it applies universally, until given some reason to believe otherwise. And I never have been.

Weirob: Let's let that pass. I have another problem that is more serious. How is it that you know in your own case that there is a single soul which has been so consistently connected with your body?

Miller: Now you really cannot be serious, Gretchen. How can I doubt that I am the same person I was? Is there anything more clear and distinct, less susceptible to doubt? How do you expect me to prove anything to you, when you are capable of denying my own continued existence from second to second? Without knowledge of our own identity, everything we think and do would be senseless. How could I

think if I did not suppose that the person who begins my thought is the one who completes it? When I act, do I not assume that the person who forms the intention is the very one who performs the action?

Weirob: But I grant you that a single *person* has been associated with your body since you were born. The question is whether one immaterial soul has been, or more precisely, whether you are in a position to know it. You believe that a judgement that one and the same person has had your body all these many years is a judgement that one and the same immaterial soul has been lodged in it. I say that such judgements concerning the soul are totally mysterious, and that if our knowledge of sameness of persons consisted in knowledge of sameness of immaterial soul, it too would be totally mysterious. To point out, as you do, that it is not, but perhaps the most secure knowledge we have, the foundation of all reason and action, is simply to make the point that it cannot consist of knowledge of identity of immaterial self.

Miller: You have simply asserted, and not established, that my judgement that a single soul has been lodged in my body these many years is mysterious.

Weirob: Well, consider these possibilities. One is that a single soul, one and the same, has been with this body I call mine since it was born. The other is that one soul was associated with it until five years ago and then another, psychologically similar, inheriting all the memories and beliefs, took over. A third hypothesis is that every five years a new soul takes over. A fourth is that every five minutes a new soul takes over. The most radical is that there is a constant flow of souls through this body, each psychologically similar to the preceding, as there is a constant flow of water molecules down the Blue. What evidence do I have that the first hypothesis, the "single soul hypothesis," is true, and not one of the others? Because I am the same person I was five minutes or five years ago? But the issue in question is simply whether from sameness of person, which isn't in doubt, we can infer sameness of soul. Sameness of body? But how do I establish a stable relationship between soul and body? Sameness of thoughts and sensations? But they are in constant flux. By the nature of the case, if the soul cannot be observed, it cannot be observed to be the same. Indeed, no sense has ever been assigned to the phrase "same soul." Nor could any sense be attached to it! One would have to say what a single soul looked like or felt like, how an encounter with a single soul at different times differed from encounters with different souls. But this can hardly be done, since a soul on your conception doesn't look or feel like *anything* at all. And so of course "souls" can afford no principle of identity. And so they cannot be used to bridge the gulf between my existence now and my existence in the hereafter.

Miller: Do you doubt the existence of your own soul?

Weirob: I haven't based my argument on there being no immaterial souls of the sort you describe, but merely on their total irrelevance to questions of personal identity, and so to questions of personal survival. I do indeed harbor grave doubts whether there are any immaterial souls of the sort to which you appeal. Can we have a notion of a soul unless we have a notion of the *same* soul? But I hope you do not think that means I doubt my own existence. I think I lie here, overweight and conscious. I think you can see me, not just some outer wrapping, for I think I am just a live human body. But that is not the basis of my argument. I give you these souls. I merely observe they can by their nature provide no principle of personal identity.

Miller: I admit I have no answer. I'm afraid I do not comfort you, though I have perhaps provided you with some entertainment. Emerson said that a little philosophy turns one away from religion, but that deeper understanding brings one back. I know no one who has thought so long and hard about philosophy as you have. Will it never lead you back to a religious frame of mind?

Weirob: My former husband used to say that a little philosophy turns one away from religion, and more philosophy makes one a pain in the neck. Perhaps he was closer to the truth than Emerson.

Miller: Perhaps he was. But perhaps by tomorrow night I will have come up with some argument that will turn you around.

Weirob: I hope I live to hear it.

THE SECOND NIGHT

Weirob: Well, Sam, have you figured out a way to make sense of the identity of immaterial souls?

Miller: No, I have decided it was a mistake to build my argument on such a dubious notion.

Weirob: Have you then given up on survival? I think such a position would be a hard one for a clergyman to be talked into, and would feel bad about having pushed you so far.

Miller: Don't worry. I'm more convinced than ever. I stayed up late last night thinking and reading, and I'm sure I can convince you now.

Weirob: Get with it, time is running out.

Miller: First, let me explain why, independently of my desire to defend survival after death, I am dissatisfied with your view that personal identity is just bodily identity. My argument will be very similar to the one you used to convince me that personal identity could not be identified with identity of an immaterial soul. Consider a person waking up tomorrow morning, conscious, but not yet ready to open her eyes and look around and, so to speak, let the new day officially begin.

Weirob: Such a state is familiar enough, I admit.

Miller: Now couldn't such a person tell who she was? That is, even before opening her eyes and looking around, and in particular before looking at her body or making any judgements about it, wouldn't she be able to say who she was? Surely most of us, in the morning, know who we are before opening our eyes and recognizing our own bodies, do we not?

Weirob: You seem to be right about that.

Miller: But such a judgement as this person makes—we shall suppose she judges "I am Gretchen Weirob"—*is* a judgement of personal identity. Suppose she says to herself, "I am the very person who was arguing with Sam Miller last night." This is clearly a statement about her identity with someone who was alive the night before. And she could make this judgement without examining her body at all. You could have made just this judgement this morning, before opening your eyes.

Weirob: Well, in fact I did so. I remembered our conversation of last night and said to myself, "Could I be the rude person who was so hard on Sam Miller's attempts to comfort me?" And, of course, my answer was that I not only could be but was that very rude person.

Miller: But then by the same principle you used last night, personal identity cannot be bodily identity. For you said that it could not be identity of immaterial soul because we were not judging as to identity of immaterial soul when we judge as to personal identity. But by the same token, as my example shows, we are not judging as to bodily identity when we judge as to personal identity. For we can judge who we are, and that we are the very person who did such and such and so and so, without having to make any judgements at all about the body. So, personal identity, while it may not consist of identity of an immaterial soul, does not consist in identity of material body either.

Weirob: I did argue as you remember. But I also said that the notion of the identity of an immaterial, unobservable, unextended soul seemed to make no sense at all. This is one reason such souls cannot be what we are judging about, when we judge as to personal identity. Bodily identity at least makes sense. Perhaps we are just assuming sameness of body, without looking.

Miller: Granted. But you do admit that we do not in our own cases need to actually make a judgement of bodily identity in order to make a judgement of personal identity.

Weirob: I don't think I will admit it. I will let it pass, so that we may proceed.

Miller: OK. Now it seems to me we are even able to imagine awakening and finding ourselves to have a *different* body than the one we had before. Suppose yourself just as I have described

you. And now suppose you finally open your eyes and see, not the body you have grown so familiar with over the years, but one of a fundamentally different shape and size.

Weirob: Well I should suppose I had been asleep for a very long time and lost a lot of weight—perhaps I was in a coma for a year or so.

Miller: But isn't it at least conceivable that it should not be your old body at all? I seem to be able to imagine awakening with a totally new body.

Weirob: And how would you suppose that this came about?

Miller: That's beside the point. I'm not saying I can imagine a procedure that would bring this about. I'm saying I can imagine it happening to me. In Kafka's *The Metamorphosis,* someone awakens as a cockroach. I can't imagine what would make this happen to me or anyone else, but I can imagine awakening with the body of a cockroach. It is incredible that it should happen—that I do not deny. I simply mean I can imagine experiencing it. It doesn't seem contradictory or incoherent, simply unlikely and inexplicable.

Weirob: So, if I admit this can be imagined, what follows then?

Miller: Well, I think it follows that personal identity does not just amount to bodily identity. For I would not, finding that I had a new body, conclude that I was not the very same person I was before. I would be the same *person,* though I did not have the same *body.* So we would have identity of person but not identity of body. So personal identity cannot just amount to bodily identity.

Weirob: Well, suppose—and I emphasize *suppose*—I grant you all of this. Where does it leave you? What do you claim I have recognized as the same, if not my body and not my immaterial soul?

Miller: I don't claim that you have recognized anything as the same, except the person involved, that is, you yourself.

Weirob: I'm not sure what you mean.

Miller: Let me appeal again to the Blue River. Suppose I take a visitor to the stretch of river by the old Mill, and then drive him toward Manhattan. After an hour or so drive we see another stretch of river, and I say, "That's the same river we saw this morning." As you pointed out yesterday, I don't thereby imply that the very same molecules of water are seen both times. And the places are different, perhaps a hundred miles apart. And the shape and color and level of pollution might all be different. What do I see later in the day that is identical with what I saw earlier in the day?

Weirob: Nothing, except the river itself.

Miller: Exactly. But now notice that what I see, strictly speaking, is not the whole river but only a part of it. I see different parts of the same river at the two different times. So really, if we restrict ourselves to what I literally see, I do not judge identity at all, but something else.

Weirob: And what might that be?

Miller: In saying that the river seen earlier and the river seen later are one and the same river, do I mean any more than that the stretch of water seen later and that stretch of water seen earlier are connected by other stretches of water?

Weirob: That's about right. If the stretches of water are so connected, there is but one river of which they are both parts.

Miller: Yes, that's what I mean. The statement of identity, "This river is the same one we saw this morning," is in a sense about rivers. But in a way it is also about stretches of water or river parts.

Weirob: So, is all of this something special about rivers?

Miller: Not at all. It is a recurring pattern. After all, we constantly deal with objects extended in space and time. But we are seldom aware of the objects as a whole, but only of their parts or stretches of their histories. When a statement of identity is not just something trivial, like "This bed is this bed," it is usually because we are really judging that different parts fit together, in some appropriate pattern, into a certain kind of whole.

Weirob: I'm not sure I see just what you mean yet.

Miller: Let me give you another example. Suppose we are sitting together watching the first game of a doubleheader. You ask me, "Is this game identical with this game?" This is a perfectly stupid question, though, of course, strictly speaking it makes sense and the answer is "yes." But now suppose you leave in the sixth inning to go for hot dogs. You are delayed, and return after about forty-five minutes or so. You ask, "Is this the same game I was watching?" Now your question is not stupid, but perfectly appropriate.

Weirob: Because the first game might still be going on or it might have ended, and the second game begun, by the time I return.

Miller: Exactly. Which is to say somehow different parts of the game—different innings, or at least different plays—were somehow involved in your question. That's why it wasn't stupid or trivial but significant.

Weirob: So, you think that judgements as to the identity of an object of a certain kind—rivers or baseball games or whatever—involve judgements as to the *parts* of those things being connected in a certain way, and are significant only when different parts are involved. Is that your point?

Miller: Yes, and I think it is an important one. How foolish it would be, when we ask a question about the identity of baseball games, to look for something *else,* other than the game as a whole, which had to be the same. It could be the same game, even if different players were involved. It could be the same game, even if it had been moved to a different field. These other things, the innings, the plays, the players, the field, don't have to be the same at the different times for the game to be the same, they just have to be related in certain ways so as to make that complex whole we call a single game.

Weirob: You think we were going off on a kind of a wild goose chase when we asked whether it was the identity of soul or body that was involved in the identity of persons?

Miller: Yes. The answer I should now give is neither. We are wondering about the identity of the person. Of course, if by "soul" we just mean "person," there is no problem. But if we mean, as I did yesterday, some other thing whose identity is already understood, which has to be the same when persons are the same, we are just fooling ourselves with words.

Weirob: With rivers and baseball games, I can see that they are made up of parts connected in a certain way. The connection is, of course, different in the two cases, as is the sort of "part" involved. River parts must be connected physically with other river parts to form a continuous whole. Baseball innings must be connected so that the score, batting order, and the like are carried over from the earlier inning to the latter one according to the rules. Is there something analogous we are to say about persons?

Miller: Writers who concern themselves with this speak of "person-stages." That is just a stretch of consciousness, such as you and I are aware of now. I am aware of a flow of thoughts and feelings that are mine, you are aware of yours. A person is just a whole composed of such stretches as parts, not some substance that underlies them, as I thought yesterday, and not the body in which they occur, as you seem to think. That is the conception of a person I wish to defend today.

Weirob: So when I awoke and said to myself, "I am the one who was so rude to Sam Miller last night," I was judging that a certain stretch of consciousness I was then aware of, and an earlier one I remembered having been aware of, form a single whole of the appropriate sort—a single stream of consciousness, we might say.

Miller: Yes, that's it exactly. You need not worry about whether the same immaterial soul is involved, or whether that even makes sense. Nor need you worry about whether the same body is involved, as indeed you do not since you don't even have to open your eyes and look. Identity is not, so to speak, something under the person-stages, nor in something they are attached to, but something you build from them. Now survival, you can plainly see, is no problem at all once we have this conception of personal identity. All you need suppose is that there is, in Heaven, a conscious being, and that the person-stages that make her up are in the appropriate relation to those that now make

you up, so that they are parts of the same whole—namely, you. If so, you have survived. So will you admit now that survival is at least possible?

Weirob: Hold on, hold on. Comforting me is not that easy. You will have to show that it is possible that these person-stages or stretches of consciousness be related in the appropriate way. And to do that, won't you have to tell me what that way is?

Miller: Yes, of course, I was getting ahead of myself. It is right at this point that my reading was particularly helpful. In a chapter of his *Essay on Human Understanding* Locke discusses this very question. He suggests that the relation between two person-stages or stretches of consciousness that makes them stages of a single person is just that the later one contains memories of the earlier one. He doesn't say this in so many words—he talks of "extending our consciousness back in time." But he seems to be thinking of memory.

Weirob: So, any past thought or feeling or intention or desire that I can remember having is mine?

Miller: That's right. I can remember only my own past thoughts and feelings, and you only yours. Of course, everyone would readily admit that. Locke's insight is to take this relation as the source of identity and not just its consequence. To remember—or more plausibly, to be able to remember—the thoughts and feelings of a person who was conscious in the past is just what it is to be that person. Now you can easily see that this solves the problem of the possibility of survival. As I was saying, all you need to do is imagine someone at some future time, not on this earth and not with your present thoughts and feelings, remembering the very conversation we are having now. This does not require sameness of anything else, but it amounts to sameness of person. So, now will you admit it?

Weirob: No, I don't.

Miller: Well, what's the problem now?

Weirob: I admit that if I remember having a certain thought or feeling had by some person in the past, then I must indeed be that person.

Though I can remember watching others think, I cannot remember their thinking, any more than I can experience it at the time it occurs if it is theirs and not mine. This is the kernel of Locke's idea, and I don't see that I could deny it. But we must distinguish—as I'm sure you will agree—between *actually* remembering and merely *seeming* to remember. Many men who think that they are Napoleon claim to remember losing the battle of Waterloo. We may suppose them to be sincere, and to really seem to remember it. But, they do not actually remember, because they were not there and are not Napoleon.

Miller: Of course, I admit that we must distinguish between actually remembering and only seeming to.

Weirob: And you will admit too, I trust, that the thought of some person at some far place and some distant time seeming to remember this conversation I am having with you would not give me the sort of comfort that the prospect of survival is supposed to provide. I would have no reason to anticipate future experiences of this person, simply because she is to *seem* to remember my experiences. The experiences of such a deluded imposter are not ones I can look forward to having.

Miller: I agree.

Weirob: So, the mere possibility of someone in the future seeming to remember this conversation does not show the possibility of my surviving. Only the possibility of someone actually remembering this conversation—or, to be precise, the experiences I am having—would show that.

Miller: Of course. But what are you driving at? Where is the problem? I can imagine someone being deluded, but also someone actually being you and remembering your present thoughts.

Weirob: But, what's the difference? How do you know *which* of the two you are imagining, and *what* you have shown possible?

Miller: Well, I just imagine the one and not the other. I don't see the force of your argument.

Weirob: Let me try to make it clear with another example. Imagine two persons. One is talking to you, saying certain words, having certain thoughts, and so on. The other is not talking to you at all, but is in the next room being hypnotized. The hypnotist gives to this person a posthypnotic suggestion that upon awakening he will remember having had certain thoughts and having uttered certain words to you. The thoughts and words he mentions happen to be just the thoughts and words which the first person actually thinks and says. Do you understand the situation?

Miller: Yes, continue.

Weirob: Now, in a while, both of the people are saying sentences which begin, "I remember saying to Sam Miller…" and "I remember thinking as I talked to Sam Miller…" And they both report remembering just the same thoughts and utterances. One of these will be remembering and the other only seeming to remember, right?

Miller: Of course.

Weirob: Now, which one is *actually* remembering?

Miller: Why the very one who was in the room talking to me, of course. The other one is just under the influence of the suggestion made by the hypnotist and not remembering talking to me at all.

Weirob: Now you agree that the difference between them does not consist in the content of what they are now thinking or saying.

Miller: Agreed. The difference is in the relation to the past thinking and speaking. In the one case the relation of memory obtains. In the other, it does not.

Weirob: But they both satisfy part of the conditions of remembering, for they both *seem to remember*. So there must be some further condition that the one satisfies and the other does not. I am trying to get you to say what that further condition is.

Miller: Well, I said that the one who had been in this room talking would be remembering.

Weirob: In other words, given two putative rememberers of some past thought or action, the real rememberer is the one who, in addition to seeming to remember the past thought or action, actually thought it or did it.

Miller: Yes.

Weirob: That is to say, the one who is identical with the person who did the past thinking and uttering.

Miller: Yes, I admit it.

Weirob: So, your argument just amounts to this. Survival is possible, because imaginable. It is imaginable, because my identity with some Heavenly person is imaginable. To imagine it, we imagine a person in Heaven who, first, seems to remember my thoughts and actions, and second, is me. Surely, there could hardly be a tighter circle. If I have doubts that the Heavenly person is me, I will have doubts as to whether she is really remembering or only seeming to. No one could doubt the possibility of some future person who, after his or her death, seemed to remember the things he or she thought and did. But that possibility does not resolve the issue about the possibility of survival. Only the possibility of someone *actually* remembering could do that, for that, as we agree, is sufficient for identity. But doubts about survival and identity simply go over without remainder into doubts about whether the memories would be actual or merely apparent. You guarantee me no more than the possibility of a deluded Heavenly imposter.

Cohen: But wait, Gretchen. I think Sam was less than fair to his own idea just now.

Weirob: You think you can break out of the circle of using real memory to explain identity, and identity to mark the difference between real and apparent memory? Feel free to try.

Cohen: Let us return to your case of the hypnotist. You point out that we have two putative rememberers. You ask what marks the difference, and claim the answer must be the circular one that the real rememberer is the person who actually had the experiences both seem to remember. But that is not the only possible answer. The experiences themselves cause the later apparent memories in the one case, the hypnotist causes them in the other. We can say that the remememberer is the one of the two whose

memories were *caused in the right way* by the earlier experiences. We thus distinguish between the rememberer and the hypnotic subject, without appeal to identity. The idea that real memory amounts to apparent memory plus identity is misleading anyway. I seem to remember knocking over the menorah so the candles fell into and ruined a tureen of soup when I was a small child. And I did actually perform such a feat. So we have apparent memory and identity. But I do *not* actually remember; I was much too young when I did this to remember it now. I have simply been told the story so often I seem to remember. Here the suggestion that real memory is apparent memory that was caused in the appropriate way by the past events fares better. Not my experience of pulling over the menorah, but my parents' later recounting of the tragedy, cause my memory-like impressions.

Weirob: You analyze personal identity into memory, and memory into apparent memory which is caused in the right way. A person is a certain sort of causal process.

Cohen: Right.

Weirob: Suppose now for the sake of argument I accept this. How does it help Sam in his defense of the possibility of survival? In ordinary memory, the causal chain from remembered event to memory of it never leads us outside the confines of a single body. Indeed, the normal process of which you speak surely involves storage of information somehow in the brain. How can the states of my brain, when I die, influence in the appropriate way the apparent memories of the Heavenly person Sam takes to be me?

Cohen: Well, I didn't intend to be defending the possibility of survival. That is Sam's problem. I just like the idea that personal identity can be explained in terms of memory, and not just in terms of identity of the body.

Miller: But surely, this does provide me with the basis for further defense. Your challenge, Gretchen, was to explain the difference between two persons in Heaven, one who actually remembers your experience—and so is you—and one who simply seems to remember it. But can I not just say that the one who is you is the one whose states were caused in the appropriate way? I do not mean the way they would be in a normal case of earthly memory. But in the case of the Heavenly being who is you, God would have created her with the brain states (or whatever) she has *because* you had the ones you had at death. Surely it is not the exact form of the dependence of my later memories on my earlier perceptions that makes them really to be memories, but the fact that the process involved has preserved information.

Weirob: So if God creates a Heavenly person, designing her brain to duplicate the brain I have upon death, that person is me. If, on the other hand, a Heavenly being should come to be with those very same memory-like states by accident (if there are accidents in Heaven) it would not be me.

Miller: Exactly. Are you satisfied now that survival makes perfectly good sense?

Weirob: No, I'm still quite unconvinced. The problem I see is this. If God could create one person in Heaven, and by designing her after me, make her me, why could He not make two such bodies, and cause this transfer of information into both of them? Would both of these Heavenly persons then be me? It seems as clear as anything in philosophy that from

A is B

and

C is B

where by "is" we mean identity, we can infer,

A is C.

So, if each of these Heavenly persons is me, they must be each other. But then they are not two but one. But my assumption was that God creates two, not one. He could create them physically distinct, capable of independent movement, perhaps in widely separated Heavenly locations, each with her own duties to perform, her own circle of Heavenly friends, and the like.

So either God, by creating a Heavenly person with a brain modeled after mine does not really create someone identical with me but merely someone similar to me, or God is somehow limited to making only one such being. I can see no reason why, if there were a God, He should be so limited. So I take the first option. He could create someone similar to me, but not someone who would *be* me. Either your analysis of memory is wrong, and such a being does not, after all, remember what I am doing or saying, or memory is not sufficient for personal identity. Your theory has gone wrong somewhere, for it leads to absurdity.

Cohen: But wait. Why can't Sam simply say that if God makes one such creature, she is you, while if He makes more, none of them are you? It's possible that He makes only one. So it's possible that you survive. Sam always meant to allow that it's *possible* that you won't survive. He had in mind the case in which there is no God to make the appropriate Heavenly persons, or God exists, but just doesn't make even one. You have simply shown that there is another way of not surviving. Instead of making too few Heavenly rememberers, He makes too many. So what? He might make the right number, and then you would survive.

Weirob: Your remarks really amount to a change in your position. Now you are not claiming that memory alone is enough for personal identity. Now, it is memory *plus* lack of competition, the absence of other rememberers, that is needed for personal identity.

Cohen: It does amount to a change of position. But what of it? Is there anything untenable about the position as changed?

Weirob: Let's look at this from the point of view of the Heavenly person. She says to herself, "Oh, I must be Gretchen Weirob, for I remember doing what she did and saying what she said." But now that's a pretty tenuous conclusion, isn't it? She is really only entitled to say, "Oh, either I'm Gretchen Weirob, or God has created more than one being like me, and none of us are." Identity has become something dependent on things wholly extrinsic to her. Who she is now turns on not just her states of mind and their relation to my states of mind, but on the existence or nonexistence of other people. Is this really what you want to maintain? Or look at it from my point of view. God creates one of me in Heaven. Surely I should be glad if convinced this was to happen. Now He creates another, and I should despair again, for this means I won't survive after all. How can doubling a good deed make it worthless?

Cohen: Are you saying that there is some contradiction in my suggestion that only a unique Heavenly Gretchen counts as your survival?

Weirob: No, it's not contradictory, as far as I can see. But it seems odd in a way that shows that something somewhere is wrong with your theory. Here is a certain relationship I have with a Heavenly person. There being such a person, to whom I am related in this way, is something that is of great importance to me, a source of comfort. It makes it appropriate for me to anticipate having her experiences, since she is just me. Why should my having that relation to another being destroy my relation to this one? You say because then I will not be identical with either of them. But since you have provided a theory about what that identity consists in, we can look and see what it amounts to for me to be or not to be identical. If she is to remember my experience, I can rightly anticipate hers. But then it seems the doubling makes no difference. And yet it must, for one cannot be identical with two. So you add, in a purely *ad hoc* manner, that her memory of me isn't enough to make my anticipation of her experiences appropriate, if there are two rather than one so linked. Isn't it more reasonable to conclude, since memory does not secure identity when there are two Heavenly Gretchens, it also doesn't when there is only one?

Cohen: There is something *ad hoc* about it, I admit. But perhaps that's just the way our concept works. You have not elicited a contradiction...

Weirob: An infinite pile of absurdities has the same weight as a contradiction. And absurdities can be generated from your account without

limit. Suppose God created this Heavenly person before I died. Then He in effect kills me; if He has already created her, then you really are not talking to whom you think, but someone new, created by Gretchen Weirob's strange death moments ago. Or suppose He first creates one being in Heaven, who is me. Then He created another. Does the first cease to be me? If God can create such beings in Heaven, surely He can do so in Albuquerque. And there is nothing on your theory to favor this body before you as Gretchen Weirob's, over the one belonging to the person created in Albuquerque. So I am to suppose that if God were to do this, I would suddenly cease to be. I'm tempted to say I would cease to be Gretchen Weirob. But that would be a confused way of putting it. There would be here, in my place, a new person with false memories of having been Gretchen Weirob, who has just died of competition—a strange death, if ever there was one. She would have no right to my name, my bank account, or the services of my doctor, who is paid from insurance premiums paid for by deductions from Gretchen Weirob's past salary. Surely this is nonsense; however carefully God should choose to duplicate me, in Heaven or in Albuquerque, I would not cease to be, or cease to be who I am. You may reply that God, being benevolent, would never create an extra Gretchen Weirob. But I do not say that He would, but only that if He did this would not, as your theory implies, mean that I cease to exist. Your theory gives the wrong answer in this possible circumstance, so it must be wrong. I think I have been given no motivation to abandon the most obvious and straightforward view on these matters. I am a live body, and when that body dies, my existence will be at an end.

THE THIRD NIGHT

Weirob: Well, Sam, are you here for a third attempt to convince me of the possibility of survival?

Miller: No, I have given up. I suggest we talk about fishing or football or something unrelated to your imminent demise. You will outwit any straightforward attempts to comfort you, but perhaps I can at least divert your mind.

Cohen: But before we start on fishing…although I don't have any particular brief for survival, there is one point in our discussion of the last two evenings that still bothers me. Would you mind discussing for a while the notion of personal identity itself, without worrying about the more difficult case of survival after death?

Weirob: I would enjoy it. What point bothers you?

Cohen: Your position seems to be that personal identity amounts to identity of a human body, nothing more, nothing less. A person is just a live human body, or more precisely, I suppose, a human body that is alive and has certain capacities—consciousness and perhaps rationality. Is that right?

Weirob: Yes, it seems that simple to me.

Cohen: But I think there has actually been an episode which disproves that. I am thinking of the strange case of Julia North, which occurred in California a few months ago. Surely you remember it.

Weirob: Yes, only too well. But you had better explain it to Sam, for I'll wager he has not heard of it.

Cohen: Not heard of Julia North? But the case was all over the headlines.

Miller: Well, Gretchen is right. I know nothing of it. She knows that I only read the sports page.

Cohen: You only read the sports page!

Weirob: It's an expression of his unconcern with earthly matters.

Miller: Well, that's not quite fair, Gretchen. It's a matter of preference. I much prefer to spend what time I have for reading in reading about the eighteenth century, rather than the drab and miserable century into which I had the misfortune to be born. It was really a much more civilized century, you know. But let's not dwell on my peculiar habits. Tell me about Julia North.

Cohen: Very well. Julia North was a young woman who was run over by a street car while saving the life of a young child who wandered onto the tracks. The child's mother, one Mary Frances Beaudine, had a stroke while watching the horrible scene. Julia's healthy brain and wasted body, and Mary Frances' healthy body and wasted brain, were transported to a hospital where a brilliant neurosurgeon, Dr. Matthews, was in residence. He had worked out a procedure for what he called a "body transplant." He removed the brain from Julia's head and placed it in Mary Frances', splicing the nerves, etc., using techniques not available until quite recently. The survivor of all this was obviously Julia, as everyone agreed—except, unfortunately, Mary Frances' husband. His shortsightedness and lack of imagination led to great complications and drama and made the case more famous in the history of crime than in the history of medicine. I shall not go into the details of this sorry aspect of the case—they are well reported in a book by Barbara Harris called *Who Is Julia?*, in case you are interested.

Miller: Fascinating!

Cohen: Well, the relevance of this case is obvious. Julia North had one body up until the time of the accident, and another body after the operation. So one person had two bodies. So a person cannot be simply *identified* with a human body. So something must be wrong with your view, Gretchen. What do you say to this?

Weirob: I'll say to you just what I said to Dr. Matthews…

Cohen: You have spoken with Dr. Matthews?

Weirob: Yes. He contacted me shortly after my accident. My physician had phoned him up about my case. Matthews said he could perform the same operation for me he did for Julia North. I refused.

Cohen: You refused! But Gretchen, why…?

Miller: Gretchen, I *am* shocked. Your decision practically amounts to suicide! You passed up an opportunity to continue living? Why on earth…?

Weirob: Hold on, hold on. You are both making an assumption I reject. If the case of Julia North amounts to a counterexample to my view that a person is just a live human body, and if my refusal to submit to this procedure amounts to passing up an option to survive, then the survivor of such an operation must be reckoned as the same person as the brain donor. That is, the survivor of Julia North's operation must have been Julia, and the survivor of the operation on me would have to be me. This is the assumption you both make in criticizing me. But I reject it. I think Jack Beaudine was right. The survivor of the operation involving Julia North's brain was Mary Frances Beaudine, and the survivor of the operation which was to involve my brain would not have been me.

Miller: Gretchen, how on earth can you say that? Will you not give up your view that personal identity is just bodily identity, no matter how clear the counterexample? I really think you simply have an irrational attachment to the lump of material that is your body.

Cohen: Yes, Gretchen, I agree with Sam. You are being preposterous! The survivor of Julia North's operation had no idea who Mary Frances Beaudine was. She remembered being Julia…

Weirob: She *seemed* to remember being Julia. Have you forgotten so quickly the importance of this distinction? In my opinion, the effect of the operation was that Mary Frances Beaudine survived deluded, thinking she was someone else.

Cohen: But as you know, the case was litigated. It went to the Supreme Court. They said that the survivor was Julia.

Weirob: That argument is unworthy of you, Dave. Is the Supreme Court infallible?

Cohen: No, they aren't. But I don't think it's such a stupid point. Look at it this way, Gretchen. This is a case in which two criteria we use to make judgements of identity conflict. Usually we expect personal identity to involve both bodily identity and psychological continuity. That is, we expect that if we have the same body, then the beliefs, memories, character traits and the like also will be enormously similar. In this case, these two criteria which usually coincide do not. If we choose one criterion, we say that the survivor is Mary Frances Beaudine and she has undergone drastic psychological changes.

If we choose the other, we say that Julia has survived with a new body. We have to choose which criterion is more important. It's a matter of choice of how to use our language, how to extend the concept "same person" to a new situation. The overwhelming majority of people involved in the case took the survivor to be Julia. That is, society chose to use the concept one way rather than the other. The Supreme Court is *not* beside the point. One of their functions is to settle just how old concepts shall be applied to new circumstances—how "freedom of the press" is to be understood when applied to movies or television, whose existence was not foreseen when the concept was shaped, or to say whether "murder" is to include the abortion of a foetus. They are fallible on points of fact, but they are the final authority on the development of certain important concepts used in law. The notion of *person* is such a concept.

Weirob: You think that *who* the survivor was, was a matter of convention, of how we choose to use language?

Cohen: Yes.

Weirob: I can show the preposterousness of all that with an example. Let us suppose that I agree to the operation. I lie in bed, expecting my continued existence, anticipating the feelings and thoughts I shall have upon awakening after the operation. Dr. Matthews enters and asks me to take several aspirin, so as not to have a headache when I awake. I protest that aspirins upset my stomach; he asks whether I would have a terrible headache tomorrow or a mild stomachache now, and I agree that it would be reasonable to take them. Let us suppose you enter at this point with bad news. The Supreme Court has changed its mind! So the survivor will not be me. So, I say, "Oh, then I will not take the aspirin, for it's not me that will have a headache, but someone else. Why should I endure a stomachache, however mild, for the comfort of someone else? After all, I am already donating my brain to that person." Now this is clearly absurd. If I was correct, in the first place, to anticipate having the sensations and thoughts that the survivor is to have the next day, the decision of nine old men a thousand or so miles away wouldn't make me wrong. And if I was wrong so to anticipate, their decision couldn't make me right. How can the correctness of my anticipation of survival be a matter of the way we use our words? If it is not such a matter, then my identity is not either. My identity with the survivor, my survival, is a question of fact, not of convention.

Cohen: Your example is persuasive. I admit I am befuddled. On the one hand, I cannot see how the matter can be other than I have described. When we know all the facts what can remain to be decided but how we are to describe them, how we are to use our language? And yet I can see that it seems absurd to suppose that the correctness or incorrectness of anticipation of future experience is a matter for convention to decide.

Miller: Well, I didn't think the business about convention was very plausible anyway. But I should like to return you to the main question, Gretchen. Fact or convention, it still remains. Why will you not admit that the survivor of this operation would be you?

Weirob: Well, *you* tell *me*, why do you think she would be me?

Miller: I can appeal to the theory I developed last night. You argued that the idea that personal identity consists in memory would not guarantee the possibility of survival after death. But you said nothing to shake its plausibility as an account of personal identity. It has the enormous advantage, remember, of making sense of our ability to judge our own identity, without examination of our bodies. I should argue that it is the correctness of this theory that explains the *almost* universal willingness to say that the survivor of Julia's operation was Julia. We need not deliberate over how to extend our concept, we need only apply the concept we already have. Memory is sufficient for identity and bodily identity is *not* necessary for it. The survivor remembered Julia's thoughts and actions, and so was Julia. Would you but submit to the operation, the survivor would remember your thoughts and actions, would remember this very conversation we are now having, and would be you.

Cohen: Yes, I now agree completely with Sam. The theory that personal identity is to be analyzed in terms of memory is correct, and according to it you will survive if you submit to the operation. Let me add another argument against your view and in favor of the memory theory. You have emphasized that identity is the condition of *anticipation*. That means, among other things, that we have a particular concern for that person in the future whom we take to be ourselves. If I were told that any of the three of us were to suffer pain tomorrow, I should be sad. But if it were you or Sam that were to be hurt, my concern would be altruistic or unselfish. That is because I would not anticipate having the painful experience myself. Here I do no more than repeat points you have made earlier in our conversations. Now what is there about mere sameness of body that makes sense of this asymmetry, between the way we look at our own futures, and the way we look at the futures of others? In other words, why is the identity of your body—that mere lump of matter, as Sam put it—of such great importance? Why care so much about it?

Weirob: You say, and I surely agree, that identity of person is a very special relationship —so special as perhaps not even happily called a relationship at all. And you say that since my theory is that identity of person is identity of body, I should be able to explain the importance of the one in terms of the importance of the other. I'm not sure I can do that. But does the theory that personal identity consists in memory fare better on this score?

Cohen: Well, I think it does. Those properties of persons which make persons of such great value, and mark their individuality, and make one person so special to his friends and loved ones, are ultimately psychological or mental. One's character, personality, beliefs, attitudes, convictions—they are what make every person so unique and special. A skinny Gretchen would be a shock to us all, but not a Gretchen diminished in any important way. But a Gretchen who was not witty, or not gruff, or not as honest to the path an argument takes as is humanly possible—those would be fundamental changes. Is it any wonder that the survivor of that California fiasco was reckoned as Julia North? Would it make sense to take her to be Mary Jane Beaudine, when she had none of her beliefs or attitudes or memories? Now if such properties are what is of importance about a person to others, is it not reasonable that they are the basis of one's importance to oneself? And these are just the properties that personal identity preserves when it is taken to consist in links of memory. Do we not have, in this idea, at least the beginning of an explanation of the importance of identity?

Weirob: So on two counts you two favor the memory theory. First, you say it explains how it is possible to judge as to one's own identity, without having to examine one's body. Second, you say it explains the importance of personal identity.

Cohen: Now surely you must agree the memory theory is correct. Do you agree? There may still be time to contact Dr. Matthews...

Weirob: Hold on, hold on. I'm still not persuaded. Granted the survivor will *think* she is me, will *seem* to remember thinking my thoughts. But recall the importance of distinguishing between real and merely apparent memory...

Cohen: But *you* recall that this distinction is to be made on the basis of whether the apparent memories were or were not caused by the prior experiences in the appropriate way. The survivor will not seem to remember your thoughts because of hypnosis or by coincidence or overweening imagination. She will seem to remember them because the traces those experiences left on your brain now activate her mind in the usual way. She will seem to remember them because she does remember them, and will be you.

Weirob: Let's go over this slowly. We all agree that the fact that the survivor of this strange operation Dr. Matthews proposes would *seem* to remember doing what I have done. Let us even suppose she would take herself to be me, claim to be Gretchen Weirob—and have no idea who else she might be. (We are then assuming

that she differs from me in one aspect—her theory of personal identity. But that does not show her not to be me, for I could change my mind by then.) We all first agree that this much does not make her me. For this could all be true of someone suffering a delusion or a subject of hypnosis.

Cohen: Yes, this is all agreed.

Weirob: But now you think that some *further* condition is satisfied, which makes her apparent memories *real* memories. Now what exactly is this further condition?

Cohen: Well, that the same brain was involved in the perception of the events, and their later *memory.* Thus a causal chain of just the same sort as when only a single body is involved is involved here. That is, perceptions when the event occurs leave a trace in the brain, which is later responsible for the content of the memory. And we agreed, did we not, that apparent memory, caused in the right way, is real memory?

Weirob: Now is it absolutely crucial that the same brain is involved?

Cohen: What do you mean?

Weirob: Let me explain again by reference to Dr. Matthews. In our conversation he explained a new procedure on which he was working called a *brain rejuvenation.* By this process, which is not yet available—only the feasibility of developing it is being studied—a new brain could be made which is an exact duplicate of my brain. That is, an exact duplicate in terms of psychologically relevant states. It might not duplicate all the properties of my brain; for example, the blood vessels in the new brain might be stronger than in the old brain.

Miller: What is the point of developing such a macabre technique?

Weirob: Dr. Matthews' idea is that when weaknesses which might lead to stroke or other brain injury are noted, a healthy duplicate could be made, and replace the original, forestalling the problem. Now Dave, suppose my problem were not with my liver and kidneys and such, but with my brain. Would you recommend such an operation as to my benefit?

Cohen: You mean, do I think the survivor of such an operation would be you?

Weirob: Exactly. You may assume that Dr. Matthews' technique works perfectly so the causal process involved is no less reliable than that involved in ordinary memory.

Cohen: Then I would say it was you…No! Wait! No, it wouldn't be you. Absolutely not!

Miller: But why the sudden reversal? It seems to me it would be her. Indeed, I should try such an operation myself, if it would clear up my dizzy spells and leave me otherwise unaffected.

Cohen: No, don't you see, she is leading us into a false trap. If we say it *is* her, then she will say, "Then what if he makes two duplicates, or three or ten? They can't all be me, they all have an equal claim, so none will be me." It would be the argument of last night, reapplied on earth. So the answer is no, absolutely not, it wouldn't be you. Duplication of self does not preserve identity. Identity of the person requires identity of the brain.

Miller: Quite right.

Weirob: Now let me see if I have your theory straight. Suppose we have two bodies, A and B. My brain is put into A, a duplicate into B. The survivor of this, call them "A-Gretchen" and "B-Gretchen," both seem to remember giving this very speech. Both are in this state of seeming to remember, as the last stage in an information-preserving causal chain, initiated by my giving this speech. Both have my character, personality, beliefs, and the like. But one is *really* remembering, the other is not. A-Gretchen is really me, B-Gretchen is not.

Cohen: Precisely. Is this incoherent?

Weirob: No, I guess there is nothing incoherent about it. But look what has happened to the advantages you claimed for the memory theory. First, you said, it explains how I can know who I am without opening my eyes and recognizing my body. But in your theory Gretchen-A and Gretchen-B cannot know who they are even if they do open their eyes and examine their bodies. How is Gretchen-A to know whether she has the original brain and is who she seems to be, or has the duplicate and is a new person, only a few minutes old, and with no memories but my delusions? If the hospital

kept careless records, or the surgeon thought it was of no great importance to keep track of who got the original and who got the duplicate, she might never know who she was. By making identity of person turn into identity of brain, your theory makes the ease with which I can determine who I am not less, but more mysterious than my theory. Second, you said, your theory explains why my concern for Gretchen-A, who is me whether she knows it or not, would be selfish, and my anticipation of her experience correct while my concern for Gretchen-B with her duplicated brain would be unselfish, and my anticipation of having her experiences incorrect. And it explains this, you said, because by insisting on the links of memory, we preserve in personal identity more psychological characteristics which are the most important features of a person. But Gretchen-A and Gretchen-B are psychologically indistinguishable. Though they will go their separate ways, at the moment of awakening they could well be exactly similar in every psychological respect. In terms of character and belief and the contents of their minds, Gretchen-A is no more like me than Gretchen-B. So there is nothing in your theory after all, to explain why anticipation is appropriate when we have identity, and not otherwise. You said, Sam, that I had an irrational attachment for this unworthy material object, my body. But you too are as irrationally attached to your brain. I have never seen my brain. I should have easily given it up, for a rejuvenated version, had that been the choice with which I was faced. I have never seen it, never felt it, and have no attachment to it. But my body? That seems to me all that I am. I see no point in trying to evade its fate. Perhaps I miss the merit of your arguments. I am tired, and perhaps my poor brain, feeling slighted, has begun to desert me…

Cohen: Oh don't worry Gretchen, you are still clever. Again you have left me befuddled. I don't know what to say. But answer me this. Suppose you are right and we are wrong. But suppose these arguments had not occurred to you, and, sharing in our error, you had agreed to the operation. You anticipate the operation until it happens, thinking you will survive. You are happy. The survivor takes herself to be you, and thinks she made a decision before the operation which has now turned out to be right. She is happy. Your friends are happy. Who would be worse off, either before or after the operation? Suppose even that you realize identity would not be preserved by such an operation but have it done anyway, and as the time for the operation approaches, you go ahead and anticipate the experiences of the survivor. Where exactly is the mistake? Do you really have any less reason to care for the survivor than for yourself? Can mere identity of body, the lack of which alone keeps you from being her, mean that much? Perhaps we were wrong, after all, in focusing on identity as the necessary condition of anticipation...

Miller: It's too late, Dave.

Notes

The First Night: The arguments against the position that personal identity consists in identity of an immaterial soul are similar to those found in John Locke, "Of Identity and Diversity," Chapter 1 of Book II of *Essay Concerning Human Understanding.* This chapter first appeared in the second edition of 1694.

The Second Night: The arguments against the view that personal identity consists in bodily identity are also suggested by Locke, as is the theory that memory is what is crucial. The argument that the memory theory is circular was made by Joseph Butler in "Of Personal Identity," an Appendix to his *Analogy of Religion,* first published in 1736. Locke's memory theory has been developed by a number of modern authors, including Sydney Shoemaker. The possibility of circumventing Butler's charge of circularity by an appeal to causation is noted by David

Wiggins in *Identity and Spatial Temporal Continuity.* The "duplication argument" was apparently first used by the eighteenth-century free thinker, Antony Collins. Collins assumed that something like Locke's theory of personal identity was correct, and used the duplication argument to raise problems for the doctrine of immortality.

The Third Night: Who Is Julia?, by Barbara Harris, is an engaging novel published in 1972. (Dr. Matthews had not yet thought of brain rejuvenations.) Locke considers the possibility of the "consciousness" of a prince being transferred to the body of a cobbler. The idea of using the removal of a brain to suggest how this might happen comes from Sydney Shoemaker's seminal book, *Self-Knowledge and Self-Identity* (1963). Bernard Williams has cleverly and articulately resisted the memory theory and the view that such a brain removal would amount to a body transplant in a number of important articles which are collected in his book *Problems of the Self* (1973). In particular, Williams has stressed the relevance of the duplication argument even in questions of terrestrial personal identity. Weirob's position in this essay is more inspired by Williams than anyone else. I have discussed Williams' arguments and related topics in "Can the Self Divide?" (*Journal of Philosophy,* 1972) and a review of his book (*Journal of Philosophy,* 1976).

An important article on the themes which emerge toward the end of the dialogue is Derek Parfit's "Personal Identity" (*Philosophical Review,* 1971). This article, along with Locke's chapter and a number of other important chapters and articles by Hume, Shoemaker, Williams, and others are collected in my anthology *Personal Identity* (1975). A number of new articles on personal identity appear in Amelie Rorty (ed.), *The Identities of Persons* (1976).

Determinism, Free Will, and Responsibility

WHAT ARE WE ASKING WHEN we ask *why* something happened? Will an adequate explanation show us that in some sense or other the event to be explained *had* to happen in the way it did? In principle, are voluntary actions subject to the same kinds of explanations as physical events? If, in principle, everything that happens can be explained by science, is there then no such thing in the universe as random chance, genuine contingency, and uncertainty? These questions have great interest to the philosopher in their own right, but they also are of strategic importance to the continuing arguments over the ancient riddle of determinism versus free will.

Determinism is the theory that all events, including human actions and choices, are, without exception, totally determined. What does it mean to say that an event (a past event, E, for instance) is "totally determined"? This question has produced various answers, which for our present purposes we can take to be roughly equivalent.[1]

1. E was completely caused.
2. There were antecedent sufficient conditions for E; that is, conditions such that given their occurrence E *had* to occur.
3. It was causally necessary that E occur.
4. Given what preceded it, it was inevitable that E take place.
5. E is subsumable under a universal law of nature; that is, the occurrence of E was deducible from a description of the conditions that obtained before its occurrence and certain universal laws.
6. The occurrence of E is subject in principle to scientific explanation.
7. The occurrence of E was in principle predictable.
8. There are circumstances and laws which, had they been known, would have made it possible to predict the occurrence and exact nature of E.

Indeterminism, the logical contradictory of determinism, is the theory that some events are not determined. Many defenders of indeterminism hold that the events that are not determined are human actions.

---

[1]Speaking more strictly, definitions 1–6 are "roughly equivalent" to one another, and definitions 7 and 8 are "roughly equivalent" to one another, although one should be aware of subtle differences even within these classes. Basically, there are two types of definitions: those in terms of prior sufficient conditions and those in terms of predictability.

There are a number of commonsense considerations that should at least incline a reflective person toward determinism. Whenever we plant seeds, or plug in a machine, or prepare for a storm, we act in the expectation that physical events will occur in accordance with known laws of nature. Hardly anyone would deny, moreover, that physical characteristics of human beings—the color of their eyes, the cellular structure of their brains, glands, and other organs—are determined exactly by their genetic inheritance. And pediatricians and parents of large broods have often observed that temperament is determined, at least to a large degree, right from birth. To a large extent our characters, personalities, and intellects are a consequence of our inherited temperaments and physical capacities, and our choices in turn reflect our personality and character. Similarly, our early childhood training, family environment, and education have formative influences on character. We do what we do because we are what we are, and we are what we are—at least to a large extent—because our genes and the influencing conduct of others have formed us that way.

At the same time, common sense recognizes that human beings do some things "of their own free will"—that is, act in circumstances in which they might very well have done something else instead. This commonsense observation is hard to reconcile with determinism, which seems to imply that every event that occurs is the only one that could have occurred in the circumstances. This in turn seems to imply that no matter what I did a moment ago, I *could not* have done otherwise—which, in turn, seems to say that I *had* to do what I did, that I was not a free agent. But, most of us would agree, my ability to do otherwise is a necessary condition of praise or blame, reward or punishment—in short, for my *being responsible*. Therefore, if determinism cannot be reconciled with the ability to do otherwise, it cannot be reconciled with moral responsibility either. But we *do* hold people responsible for what they do (indeed, some say we *must* hold people responsible); therefore (some have argued), so much the worse for determinism. Such is the commonsense case against determinism.

Common sense, however, is no more pleased with indeterminism, which seems to give no satisfactory answer at all to any query of the form "Why did *this* happen rather than some other thing?" The reply "It just happened, that's all" inevitably leaves us unsatisfied. If we drop a stone and, to our astonishment, it rises straight up in the air instead of falling, we won't rest content with the "explanation" that "it was just one of those things—a totally random chance occurrence without rhyme or reason." We are even less likely to accept "chance" as an "explanation" for human actions. Such an explanation, we feel, makes all human actions arbitrary and unintelligible; it also seems to destroy the intimate bond between a person and his actions that is required by judgments of moral responsibility. Yet insofar as a person's action was uncaused, it does seem to have occurred "without rhyme or reason," as a "matter of pure chance." In the words of one determinist, "in proportion as an act of volition starts of itself without cause it is exactly, so far as the freedom of the individual is concerned, as if it had been thrown into his mind from without—'suggested to him by a freakish demon.'"[2]

---

[2]R. E. Hobart, "Free-Will as Involving Determinism and Inconceivable Without It," *Mind* 43 (1934).

Common sense is thus tied up in knots. It looks with little favor either on determinism or indeterminism in respect to human actions. Yet because these two theories are defined as logical contradictories, one of them *must* be true. The plight of common sense thus takes the form of a **dilemma**—that is, an argument of the form

1. If P is true, then Q is true.
2. If not-P is true, then Q is true.
3. Either P is true or not-P is true.
4. Therefore, Q is true (where Q is something repugnant).

The dilemma of determinism can be stated thus:

1. If determinism is true, we can never do other than we do; hence, we are never responsible for what we do.
2. If indeterminism is true, then some events—namely, human actions—are random, hence not free; hence, we are never responsible for what we do.
3. Either determinism is true or else indeterminism is true.
4. Therefore, we are never responsible for what we do.

There are several ways we might try to escape being gored by the "horns of the dilemma," but one way is *not* open to us. We may not deny the third premise; for, given our definitions of *determinism* and *indeterminism*, it amounts simply to the statement that either determinism is true or else it is not—surely an innocuous claim! We are, in short, not able in this case to get "between the horns of the dilemma" by denying the third premise.

We are thus left with three possibilities. We can deny the first premise and hold that determinism is, after all, perfectly compatible with free will and responsibility. Or we can deny the second premise and hold that we can act freely, and are responsible for our actions, even though they are uncaused. Or, finally, we can accept the entire argument just as it stands and argue on independent grounds that its conclusion is not so "repugnant" as it seems at first appearance.

Those who deny the dilemma's first premise are nowadays called **compatibilists** (sometimes also **soft determinists**). Their central claim is that we can have free will, and be morally responsible for our choices and actions, even if determinism is true. Most compatibilists have believed that determinism is, in fact, true. Both David Hume and Helen Beebee, two of the compatibilists represented here, take this position.

The key issue that divides compatibilists from their opponents is usually the problem of how we should interpret "free to do otherwise," "could have done otherwise," "his act was avoidable," and similar phrases used in support of our ascriptions of blame and punishment, credit or reward. Most parties to the discussion agree that a person can be held morally responsible for his past action *only if* he was able to do other than he did. Put more tersely: Avoidability is a necessary condition of responsibility.

There are two importantly different senses of *avoidability* in play in these discussions, and we must be careful to distinguish them. In the *categorical sense*, to say that an act is avoidable is to say that there were no prior conditions (causes) sufficient for its occurrence. In the *hypothetical sense*, to say that an act is avoidable is to say that *if* the actor had chosen (or, perhaps, intended) to do otherwise, he would have done otherwise—nothing would have stopped him. Avoidability in the hypothetical sense is perfectly compatible with determinism. Avoidability in the categorical sense, by definition, is not. Now the question arises: In which of the senses of *avoidable*—the categorical sense, the hypothetical sense, or both—is it true that a person can be held responsible for his action only if it was avoidable?

David Hume (1711–1776), the author of the first compatibilist selection here, analyzes the long-standing debates surrounding free will and determinism as based on misunderstandings. Once we really get clear about the nature of human action, we must see that it follows its own laws of necessity, just as strictly as do those actions of inanimate objects. According to Hume, many have mistakenly thought that determinism is incompatible with human freedom because they have failed to understand that any free choice must be caused. For the absence of cause is pure chance, says Hume, and freedom cannot be based on chance. Free actions and decisions must therefore be caused, and if that is so, then there is no conflict between freedom and determinism.

Helen Beebee, a contemporary compatibilist, has written a new paper especially for this volume. In her piece, she focuses on a classic argument: If determinism is true, then we can't do anything other than what we in fact do. And that inability shows that we are not free to do otherwise. And if we aren't free to do otherwise, then we aren't morally responsible for what we do. Beebee agrees with this last claim—no freedom, no moral responsibility. And she agrees with the one before that—an inability to do otherwise shows that one isn't free to do otherwise. But since she rejects the conclusion of this classic argument, she has to reject its initial assumption. After laying out the problem carefully in the first half of her article, she devotes its second half to arguing that determinism is compatible with our ability to do something different from what we actually do.

Another approach to the dilemma of determinism—one that rejects its second premise—is found in the writings of Thomas Reid and Immanuel Kant, among others, and is represented here by the essays of Roderick Chisholm and Robert Kane. This is the **libertarian**[3] position, which argues that freedom is incompatible with determinism, that determinism is false, and that we do in fact often possess the sort of freedom necessary for moral responsibility. Libertarians remind us that human actions, unlike other events in nature, are subject to a special kind of explanation: the actor's own *reasons* for acting. An uncaused action, done deliberately for some reason, would therefore be a perfectly intelligible one, and adequately explained by an account of its reasons.

Roderick Chisholm's article tackles head-on perhaps the most troubling worry that besets libertarianism: the nature of the person whose choices can determine conduct but which are not themselves determined. Nothing else we know of has this sort of power. Physical things act in predictable ways and are governed by laws of cause and effect. Free human choices aren't like this. But they aren't random or purely matters of chance, either. Persons are controlling the choices they make, without in turn being necessitated to make them. Chisholm forthrightly sees the difficulty of such a position,

---

[3]Not to be confused with the political theory of the same name, which advocates a minimal state and argues that all laws, except those necessary to vindicate citizens' moral rights, are unjustified.

and fans of libertarianism would do well to attend carefully to his analysis, one of whose primary virtues is to sketch just how exceptional free choices and persons are in the grand scheme of things. Philosophers and scientists are by nature skeptical of exceptions, constantly on the alert to prevent ad hoc hypotheses from being introduced to save a familiar or comforting idea. Chisholm sets the debate about libertarianism right where it should be, and forces us to ask whether the libertarian is giving us what we want (a robust sense of free will) at the expense of an occult view of the person.

Robert Kane's paper picks up directly on this theme and outlines a new version of libertarianism that takes its indeterminist element very seriously. Kane struggles to preserve a full-blooded conception of freedom compatibly with the latest scientific views of the world. Taking his cue from findings that some events (especially at the microphysical level) are not wholly determined, Kane seeks to locate opportunities for free will and moral responsibility within the indeterministic openings whose existence is ratified by contemporary physics.

Libertarians deny the possibility that we can have free will if determinism is true. The incompatibility of free will and determinism is also asserted by those who respond to the dilemma of determinism in the third way (that is, by embracing the conclusion of the dilemma, instead of trying to avoid it). This is the approach of the **hard determinists**; instead of abandoning determinism as the libertarians do, they abandon free will and moral responsibility. Hard determinism was the view of Baruch Spinoza and Paul Holbach, among other philosophers; of Mark Twain and Thomas Hardy, among other literary figures; and of Clarence Darrow, the famous American criminal lawyer. It is represented here by the selections from James Rachels and Derk Pereboom.

Rachels offers, in his characteristically clear and engaging way, a variety of considerations that favor the truth of determinism. He does not argue decisively against the possibility of free will. But he claims that the best evidence tells us that the origins of our behavior lie in influences over which we have no control—primarily our genetic inheritance and our upbringing. Given the extent of these factors in determining our character and outlook, which in turn determine our choices, it is difficult to see how they can leave room for freedom of the will. He illustrates his views with a number of important historical episodes and references to work in psychology.

Derk Pereboom prefers to think of himself as a hard incompatibilist, rather than a hard determinist, since he is unsure whether determinism is true, but convinced nonetheless that determinism is not compatible with genuine freedom, and convinced as well that the sort of freedom worth having does not exist. Pereboom presents clear and accessible arguments against both compatibilism and libertarianism, and then offers an extended discussion of the many ways in which determinism is said to threaten our moral practices and our ability to find meaning in life. Pereboom argues that the common perceptions of determinism's threatening nature are largely unfounded, and that, in some surprising cases, we can vindicate (and even better justify) certain of our moral attitudes and practices by subscribing to hard incompatibilism.

The concluding chapter of Part V, "Freedom and Moral Responsibility," pursues several of the issues in the free will debate. The chapter opens with a brief piece by Galen Strawson, who presents, in truncated form, an argument that he has long pressed against the possibility of moral responsibility. Such responsibility, he claims, requires that we be ultimately responsible for "the way we are"—that is, for our nature, personality, and character. But we can't be responsible for this, since the causes of our nature, personality, and character are outside of our control. Therefore, we cannot be morally responsible for our actions.

Strawson's selection is followed by Harry Frankfurt's "Alternate Possibilities and Moral Responsibility," which challenges the widely held view that avoidability is a necessary condition of responsibility. He offers cases in which a person cannot avoid doing or choosing as he does, yet is properly held morally responsible for his choices or actions. The piece has become a contemporary classic in the free will discussion and continues to spark vigorous debate among philosophers as to the proper role (if any) of control and avoidability in determinations of freedom and responsibility.

The next selection is Thomas Nagel's "Moral Luck," in which Nagel sets out explicitly to challenge the Kantian view of moral responsibility. As Kant saw it, even in a world as dangerous and unpredictable as our own, there is at least one thing that is fully within our control: our moral integrity. Our moral integrity is a matter of intending to do what we believe to be our duty. We may fail to achieve the results we intend —that much may be out of our control. But we do control our intentions, and this control is enough to earn us moral credit or blame. Praise is properly merited for good intentions, and blame deserved for bad, precisely because such intentions are within our control.

Nagel challenges this widely held view in two ways. First, he argues that even if our intentions are fully within our control, our moral responsibility is based on other factors that are matters of luck. Suppose two drivers are speeding recklessly along a narrow road, and one driver hits and kills a pedestrian, while the other driver injures no one. Nagel argues that in such a case, we rightly charge the first driver with a graver wrong than the second, even though this disparity is based on something entirely outside of either driver's control (namely, the presence or absence of a pedestrian along the road). Nagel also argues that even when we attribute praise and blame on the basis of intentions alone, the intentions one forms and acts on are themselves matters of luck. What we intend to do is partly a function of how we are raised, what circumstances we find ourselves in, and what genetic inheritance we find ourselves with. All of these are in the relevant sense "matters of luck," since we cannot be said to have controlled or determined their presence. Nagel's article seems to expose a deep problem for our ordinary notions of how responsibility and control are related. It forces our attention right back to the initial concern that defines the classic debate: how (or whether) it is possible to be a free, morally responsible person while at the same time recognizing the role that genetics, upbringing, circumstance, and socialization have played in making you the person you are.

Our final offering is by Susan Wolf, who, in a highly original paper, methodically presents a theory with two basic parts. First of all, responsibility for one's actions and their consequences requires that those actions are within the control of one's will. Second, one's will must be within the control of one's "deeper self." But these two requirements are not sufficient to produce moral responsibility. One further condition must be met: one must also be *sane*, where insanity, in turn, is analyzed as having *unavoidably mistaken* moral beliefs and values. Wolf's full theory, then, has a "deep self" condition supplemented by a "sanity condition," and the latter incorporates a conception of moral beliefs and their acquisition. The result is a theory that fits more comfortably with determinism, should that theory just happen to be true, and which does not require what is impossible, according to Wolf—namely, that a person, to be responsible for anything, must have created her own "deeper self" from nothing.

CHAPTER 1

LIBERTARIANISM: THE CASE FOR FREE WILL AND ITS INCOMPATIBILITY WITH DETERMINISM

1.1 Human Freedom and the Self

RODERICK M. CHISHOLM

Roderick Chisholm (1916–1999) was one of the preeminent metaphysicians and epistemologists of the twentieth century. He spent nearly his entire career at Brown University.

'A staff moves a stone, and is moved by a hand, which is moved by a man.'

—ARISTOTLE, *Physics*, 256a

1. The Metaphysical Problem of human freedom might be summarized in the following way: Human beings are responsible agents; but this fact appears to conflict with a deterministic view of human action (the view that every event that is involved in an act is caused by some other event); and it *also* appears to conflict with an indeterministic view of human action (the view

that the act, or some event that is essential to the act, is not caused at all.) To solve the problem, I believe, we must make somewhat far-reaching assumptions about the self or the agent—about the man who performs the act.

Perhaps it is needless to remark that, in all likelihood, it is impossible to say anything significant about this ancient problem that has not been said before.[1]

2. Let us consider some deed, or misdeed, that may be attributed to a responsible agent: one man, say, shot another. If the man *was*

The Lindley Lecture, 1964, pp. 3–15. © Copyright 1964 by the Department of Philosophy, University of Kansas. Reprinted by permission of the author and of the Department of Philosophy of the University of Kansas, Lawrence, Kansas, USA.

responsible for what he did, then, I would urge, what was to happen at the time of the shooting was something that was entirely up to the man himself. There was a moment at which it was true, both that he could have fired the shot and also that he could have refrained from firing it. And if this is so, then, even though he did fire it, he could have done something else instead. (He didn't find himself firing the shot 'against his will,' as we say.) I think we can say, more generally, then, that if a man is responsible for a certain event or a certain state of affairs (in our example, the shooting of another man), then that event or state of affairs was brought about by some act of his, and the act was something that was in his power either to perform or not to perform.

But now if the act which he *did* perform was an act that was also in his power *not* to perform, then it could not have been caused or determined by any event that was not itself within his power either to bring about or not to bring about. For example, if what we say he did was really something that was brought about by a second man, one who forced his hand upon the trigger, say, or who, by means of hypnosis, compelled him to perform the act, then since the act was caused by the *second* man it was nothing that was within the power of the *first* man to prevent. And precisely the same thing is true, I think, if instead of referring to a second man who compelled the first one, we speak instead of the *desires* and *beliefs* which the first man happens to have had. For if what we say he did was really something that was brought about by his own beliefs and desires, if these beliefs and desires in the particular situation in which he happened to have found himself caused him to do just what it was that we say he did do, then, since *they* caused it, *he* was unable to do anything other than just what it was that he did do. It makes no difference whether the cause of the deed was internal or external; if the cause was some state or event for which the man himself was not responsible, then he was not responsible for what we have been mistakenly calling his act. If a flood caused the poorly constructed dam to

break, then, given the flood and the constitution of the dam, the break, we may say, *had* to occur and nothing could have happened in its place. And if the flood of desire caused the weak-willed man to give in, then he, too, had to do just what it was that he did do and he was no more responsible than was the dam for the results that followed. (It is true, of course, that if the man is responsible for the beliefs and desires that he happens to have, then he may also be responsible for the things they lead him to do. But the question now becomes: *is* he responsible for the beliefs and desires he happens to have? If he is, then there was a time when they were within his power either to acquire or not to acquire, and we are left, therefore, with our general point.)

One may object: But surely if there were such a thing as a man who is really *good*, then he would be responsible for things that he would do; yet, he would be unable to do anything other than just what it is that he does do, since, being good, he will always choose to do what is best. The answer, I think, is suggested by a comment that Thomas Reid makes upon an ancient author. The author had said of Cato, 'He was good because he could not be otherwise', and Reid observes: 'This saying, if understood literally and strictly, is not the praise of Cato, but of his constitution, which was no more the work of Cato than his existence.'[2] If Cato was himself responsible for the good things that he did, then Cato, as Reid suggests, was such that, although he had the power to do what was not good, he exercised his power only for that which was good.

All of this, if it is true, may give a certain amount of comfort to those who are tender-minded. But we should remind them that it also conflicts with a familiar view about the nature of God—with the view that St. Thomas Aquinas expresses by saying that 'every movement both of the will and of nature proceeds from God as the Prime Mover.'[3] If the act of the sinner *did* proceed from God as the Prime Mover, then God was in the position of the second agent we just discussed, the man who forced the trigger finger, or the hypnotist, and the sinner, so-called, was *not* responsible for what he did. (This may be a bold assertion, in view of the history of western theology, but I must say that I have never encountered a single good reason for denying it.)

There is one standard objection to all of this and we should consider it briefly.

3. The objection takes the form of a stratagem—one designed to show that determinism (and divine providence) is consistent with human responsibility. The stratagem is one that was used by Jonathan Edwards and by many philosophers in the present century, most notably, G. E. Moore.[4]

One proceeds as follows: The expression

(a) He could have done otherwise, it is argued, means no more nor less than

(b) If he had chosen to do otherwise, then he would have done otherwise.

(In place of 'chosen,' one might say 'tried,' 'set out,' 'decided,' 'undertaken,' or 'willed.') The truth of statement (b), it is then pointed out, is consistent with determinism (and with divine providence); for even if all of the man's actions were causally determined, the man could still be such that, *if* he had chosen otherwise, then he would have done otherwise. What the murderer saw, let us suppose, along with his beliefs and desires, *caused* him to fire the shot; yet he was such that *if,* just then, he had chosen or decided *not* to fire the shot, then he would not have fired it. All of this is certainly possible. Similarly, we could say, of the dam, that the flood caused it to break and also that the dam was such that, *if* there had been no flood or any similar pressure, then the dam would have remained intact. And therefore, the argument proceeds, if (b) is consistent with determinism, and if (a) and (b) say the same thing, then (a) is also consistent with determinism; hence we can say that the agent *could* have done otherwise even though he was caused to do what he did do;

and therefore determinism and moral responsibility are compatible.

Is the argument sound? The conclusion follows from the premises, but the catch, I think, lies in the first premise—the one saying that statement (a) tells us no more nor less than what statement (b) tells us. For (b), it would seem, could be true while (a) is false. That is to say, our man might be such that, if he had chosen to do otherwise, then he would have done otherwise, and yet *also* such that he could not have done otherwise. Suppose, after all, that our murderer could not have *chosen,* or could not have *decided,* to do otherwise. Then the fact that he happens also to be a man such that, if he had chosen not to shoot he would not have shot, would make no difference. For if he could *not* have chosen *not* to shoot, then he could not have done anything other than just what it was that he did do. In a word: from our statement (b) above ('If he had chosen to do otherwise, then he would have done otherwise'), we cannot make an inference to (a) above ('He could have done otherwise') unless we can *also* assert:

(c) He could have chosen to do otherwise.

And therefore, if we must reject this third statement (c), then, even though we may be justified in asserting (b), we are not justified in asserting (a). If the man could not have chosen to do otherwise, then he would not have done otherwise —*even if* he was such that, if he *had* chosen to do otherwise, then he would have done otherwise.

The stratagem in question, then, seems to me not to work, and I would say, therefore, that the ascription of responsibility conflicts with a deterministic view of action.

4. Perhaps there is less need to argue that the ascription of responsibility also conflicts with an indeterministic view of action—with the view that the act, or some event that is essential to the act, is not caused at all. If the act— the firing of the shot—was not caused at all, if it was fortuitous or capricious, happening so to speak out of the blue, then, presumably, no

one—and nothing was responsible for the act. Our conception of action, therefore, should be neither deterministic nor indeterministic. Is there any other possibility?

5. We must not say that every event involved in the act is caused by some other event; and we must not say that the act is something that is not caused at all. The possibility that remains, therefore, is this: We should say that at least one of the events that are involved in the act is caused, not by any other events, but by something else instead. And this something else can only be the agent—the man. If there is an event that is caused, not by other events, but by the man, then there are some events involved in the act that are not caused by other events. But if the event in question is caused by the man then it *is* caused and we are not committed to saying that there is something involved in the act that is not caused at all.

But this, of course, is a large consequence, implying something of considerable importance about the nature of the agent or the man.

6. If we consider only inanimate natural objects, we may say that causation, if it occurs, is a relation between *events* or *states of affairs*. The dam's breaking was an event that was caused by a set of other events—the dam being weak, the flood being strong, and so on. But if a man is responsible for a particular deed, then, if what I have said is true, there is some event, or set of events, that is caused, *not* by other events or states of affairs, but by the agent, whatever he may be.

I shall borrow a pair of medieval terms, using them, perhaps, in a way that is slightly different from that for which they were originally intended. I shall say that when one event or state of affairs (or set of events or states of affairs) causes some other event or state of affairs, then we have an instance of *transeunt* causation. And I shall say that when an *agent,* as distinguished from an event, causes an event or state of affairs, then we have an instance of *immanent* causation.

The nature of what is intended by the expression 'immanent causation' may be illustrated by this sentence from Aristotle's *Physics:* 'Thus, a staff moves a stone, and is moved by a hand, which is moved by a man.' (VII, 5, 256a, 6–8) If the man was responsible, then we have in this illustration a number of instances of causation—most of them transeunt but at least one of them immanent. What the staff did to the stone was an instance of transeunt causation, and thus we may describe it as a relation between events: 'the motion of the staff caused the motion of the stone.' And similarly for what the hand did to the staff: 'the motion of the hand caused the motion of the staff.' And, as we know from physiology, there are still other events which caused the motion of the hand. Hence we need not introduce the agent at this particular point, as Aristotle does—we *need* not, though we *may.* We *may* say that the hand was moved by the man, but we may *also* say that the motion of the hand was caused by the motion of certain muscles; and we may say that the motion of the muscles was caused by certain events that took place within the brain. But some event, and presumably one of those that took place within the brain, was caused by the agent and not by any other events.

There are, of course, objections to this way of putting the matter; I shall consider the two that seem to me to be most important.

7. One may object, firstly: 'If the *man* does anything, then, as Aristotle's remark suggests, what he does is to move the *hand.* But he certainly does not *do* anything to his brain—he may not even know that he *has* a brain. And if he doesn't do anything to the brain, and if the motion of the hand was caused by something that happened within the brain, then there is no point in appealing to "immanent causation" as being something incompatible with "transeunt causation"—for the whole thing, after all, is a matter of causal relations among events or states of affairs.'

The answer to this objection, I think, is this: It is true that the agent does not *do* anything with his brain, or to his brain, in the sense in which he *does* something with his hand and does something to the staff. But from this it does not follow that the agent was not the immanent cause of something that happened within his brain.

We should note a useful distinction that has been proposed by Professor A. I. Melden—namely, the distinction between 'making something A happen' and 'doing A.'[5] If I reach for the staff and pick it up, then one of the things that I *do* is just that—reach for the staff and pick it up. And if it is something that I do, then there is a very clear sense in which it may be said to be something that I know that I do. If you ask me, 'Are you doing something, or trying to do something, with the staff?' I will have no difficulty in finding an answer. But in doing something with the staff, I also make various things happen which are not in this same sense things that I do: I will make various air-particles move; I will free a number of blades of grass from the pressure that had been upon them; and I may cause a shadow to move from one place to another. If these are merely things that I make happen, as distinguished from things that I do, then I may know nothing whatever about them; I may not have the slightest idea that, in moving the staff, I am bringing about any such thing as the motion of air-particles, shadows, and blades of grass.

We may say, in answer to the first objection, therefore, that it is true that our agent does nothing to his brain or with his brain; but from this it does not follow that the agent is not the immanent cause of some event within his brain; for the brain event may be something which, like the motion of the air-particles, he made happen in picking up the staff. The only difference between the two cases is this: in each case, he made something happen when he picked up the staff; but in the one case—the motion of the air-particles or of the shadows—it was the motion of the staff that caused the event to happen; and in the other case—the event that took place in the brain—it was this event that caused the motion of the staff.

The point is, in a word, that whenever a man does something A, then (by 'immanent causation') he makes a certain cerebral event happen, and this cerebral event (by 'transeunt causation') makes A happen.

8. The second objection is more difficult and concerns the very concept of 'immanent causation,' or causation by an agent, as this concept is to be interpreted here. The concept is subject to a difficulty which has long been associated with that of the prime mover unmoved. We have said that there must be some event A, presumably some cerebral event, which is caused not by any other event, but by the agent. Since A was not caused by any other event, then the agent himself cannot be said to have undergone any change or produced any other event (such as 'an act of will' or the like) which brought A about. But if, when the agent made A happen, there was no event involved other than A itself, no event which could be described as *making* A happen, what did the agent's causation consist of? What, for example, is the difference between A's just happening, and the agents' *causing* A to happen? We cannot attribute the difference to any event that took place within the agent. And so far as the event A itself is concerned, there would seem to be no discernible difference. Thus Aristotle said that the activity of the prime mover is nothing in addition to the motion that it produces, and Suarez said that 'the action is in reality nothing but the effect as it flows from the agent.'[6] Must we conclude, then, that there is no more to the man's action in causing event A than there is to the event A's happening by itself? Here we would seem to have a distinction without a difference—in which case we have failed to find a *via media* between a deterministic and an indeterministic view of action.

The only answer, I think, can be this: that the difference between the man's causing A, on the one hand, and the event A just happening, on the other, lies in the fact that, in the first case but not the second, the event A *was* caused and was caused by the man. There was a brain event A; the agent did, in fact, cause the brain event; but there was nothing that he did to cause it.

This answer may not entirely satisfy and it will be likely to provoke the following question: 'But what are you really *adding* to the assertion that A happened when you utter the words "The agent *caused* A to happen"?' As soon as we have put the question this way, we see, I think, that whatever difficulty we may have encountered is one that may be traced to the concept of causation generally—whether 'immanent' or 'transeunt.' The problem, in other words, is not a problem that is peculiar to our conception of human action. It is a problem that must be faced by anyone who makes use of the concept of causation at all; and therefore, I would say, it is a problem for everyone but the complete indeterminist.

For the problem, as we put it, referring just to 'immanent causation,' or causation by an agent, was this: 'What is the difference between saying, of an event A, that A just happened and saying that someone caused A to happen?' The analogous problem, which holds for 'transeunt causation,' or causation by an event, is this: 'What is the difference between saying, of two events A and B, that B happened and then A happened, and saying that B's happening was the *cause* of A's happening?' And the only answer that one can give is this—that in the one case the agent was the cause of A's happening and in the other case event B was the cause of A's happening. The nature of transeunt causation is no more clear than is that of immanent causation.

9. But we may plausibly say—and there is a respectable philosophical tradition to which we may appeal—that the notion of immanent causation, or causation by an agent, is in fact more clear than that of transeunt causation, or causation by an event, and that it is only by understanding our own causal efficacy, as agents, that we can grasp the concept of *cause* at all. Hume may be said to have shown that we do not derive the concept of *cause* from what we perceive of external things. How, then, do we derive it? The most plausible suggestion, it seems to me, is that of Reid, once again: namely that 'the conception

of an efficient cause may very probably be derived from the experience we have had...of our own power to produce certain effects.'[7] If we did not understand the concept of immanent causation, we would not understand that of transeunt causation.

10. It may have been noted that I have avoided the term 'free will' in all of this. For even if there is such a faculty as 'the will,' which somehow sets our acts agoing, the question of freedom, as John Locke said, is not the question '*whether the will be free;*' it is the question '*whether a man be free.*'[8] For if there is a 'will,' as a moving faculty, the question is whether the man is free to will to do these things that he does will to do— and also whether he is free *not* to will any of those things that he does will to do, and, again, whether he is free to will any of those things that he does not will to do. Jonathan Edwards tried to restrict himself to the question—'Is the man free to do what it is that he wills?' but the answer to this question will not tell us whether the man is responsible for what it is that he *does* will to do. Using still another pair of medieval terms, we may say that the metaphysical problem of freedom does not concern the *actus imperatus;* it does not concern the question whether we are free to accomplish whatever it is that we will or set out to do; it concerns the *actus elicitus,* the question whether we are free to will or to set out to do those things that we do will or set out to do.

11. If we are responsible, and if what I have been trying to say is true, then we have a prerogative which some would attribute only to God: each of us, when we act, is a prime mover unmoved. In doing what we do, we cause certain events to happen, and nothing—or no one— causes us to cause those events to happen.

12. If we are thus prime movers unmoved and if our actions, or those for which we are responsible, are not causally determined, then they are not causally determined by our *desires.* And this means that the relation between what we want or what we desire, on the one hand, and

what it is that we do, on the other, is not as simple as most philosophers would have it.

We may distinguish between what we might call the 'Hobbist approach' and what we might call the 'Kantian approach' to this question. The Hobbist approach is the one that is generally accepted at the present time, but the Kantian approach, I believe, is the one that is true. According to Hobbism, if we *know*, of some man, what his beliefs and desires happen to be and how strong they are, if we know what he feels certain of, what he desires more than anything else, and if we know the state of his body and what stimuli he is being subjected to, then we may *deduce*, logically, just what it is that he will do—or, more accurately, just what it is that he will try, set out, or undertake to do. Thus Professor Melden has said that 'the connection between wanting and doing is logical.'[9] But according to the Kantian approach to our problem, and this is the one that I would take, there is no such logical connection between wanting and doing, nor need there even be a causal connection. No set of statements about a man's desires, beliefs, and stimulus situation at any time implies any statement telling us what the man will try, set out, or undertake to do at that time. As Reid put it, though we may 'reason from men's motives to their actions and, in many cases, with great probability,' we can never do so 'with absolute certainty.'[10]

This means that, in one very strict sense of the terms, there can be no science of man. If we think of science as a matter of finding out what laws happen to hold, and if the statement of a law tells us what kinds of events are caused by what other kinds of events, then there will be human actions which we cannot explain by subsuming them under any laws. We cannot say, 'It is causally necessary that, given such and such desires and beliefs, and being subject to such and such stimuli, the agent will do so and so.' For at times the agent, if he chooses, may rise above his desires and do something else instead.

But all of this is consistent with saying that, perhaps more often than not, our desires do exist under conditions such that those conditions

necessitate us to act. And we may also say, with Leibniz, that at other times our desires may 'incline without necessitating.'

13. Leibniz's phrase presents us with our final philosophical problem. What does it mean to say that a desire, or a motive, might 'incline without necessitating?' There is a temptation, certainly, to say that 'to incline' means to cause and that 'not to necessitate' means not to cause, but obviously we cannot have it both ways.

Nor will Leibniz's own solution do. In his letter to Coste, he puts the problem as follows: 'When a choice is proposed, for example to go out or not to go out, it is a question whether, with all the circumstances, internal and external, motives, perceptions, dispositions, impressions, passions, inclinations taken together, I am still in a contingent state, or whether I am necessitated to make the choice, for example, to go out; that is to say, whether this proposition true and determined in fact, *In all these circumstances taken together I shall choose to go out*, is contingent or necessary.'[11] Leibniz's answer might be put as follows: in one sense of the terms 'necessary' and 'contingent,' the proposition 'In all these circumstances taken together I shall choose to go out,' may be said to be contingent and not necessary, and in another sense of these terms, it may be said to be necessary and not contingent. But the sense in which the proposition may be said to be contingent, according to Leibniz, is only this: there is no logical contradiction involved in denying the proposition. And the sense in which it may be said to be necessary is this: since 'nothing ever occurs without cause or determining reason,' the proposition is causally necessary. 'Whenever all the circumstances taken together are such that the balance of deliberation is heavier on one side than on the other, it is certain and infallible that that is the side that is going to win out.' But if what we have been saying is true, the proposition 'In all these circumstances taken together I shall choose to go out,' may be causally as well as logically contingent. Hence we must find another interpretation for Leibniz's statement that our motives and desires may incline us, or influence us, to choose without thereby necessitating us to choose.

Let us consider a public official who has some moral scruples but who also, as one says, could be had. Because of the scruples that he does have, he would never take any positive steps to receive a bribe—he would not actively solicit one. But his morality has its limits and he is also such that, if we were to confront him with a *fait accompli* or to let him see what is about to happen ($10,000 in cash is being deposited behind the garage), then he would succumb and be unable to resist. The general situation is a familiar one and this is one reason that people pray to be delivered from temptation. (It also justifies Kant's remark: 'And how many there are who may have led a long blameless life, who are only *fortunate* in having escaped so many temptations.')[12] Our relation to the misdeed that we contemplate may not be a matter simply of being able to bring it about or not to bring it about. As St. Anselm noted, there are at least four possibilities. We may illustrate them by reference to our public official and the event which is his receiving the bribe, in the following way: (i) he may be able to bring the event about himself (*facere esse*), in which case he would actively cause himself to receive the bribe; (ii) he may be able to refrain from bringing it about himself (*non facere esse*), in which case he would not himself do anything to insure that he receive the bribe; (iii) he may be able to do something to prevent the event from occurring (*facere non esse*), in which case he would make sure that the $10,000 was *not* left behind the garage; or (iv) he may be unable to do anything to prevent the event from occurring (*non facere non esse*), in which case, though he may not solicit the bribe, he would allow himself to keep it.[13] We have envisaged our official as a man who can resist the temptation to (i) but cannot resist the temptation to (iv): he can refrain from bringing the event about himself, but he cannot bring himself to do anything to prevent it.

Let us think of 'inclination without necessitation,' then, in such terms as these. First we may contrast the two propositions:

(1) He can resist the temptation to do something in order to make A happen;

(2) He can resist the temptation to allow A to happen (i.e., to do nothing to prevent A from happening).

We may suppose that the man has some desire to have A happen and thus has a motive for making A happen. His motive for making A happen, I suggest, is one that *necessitates* provided that, because of the motive, (1) is false; he cannot resist the temptation to do something in order to make A happen. His motive for making A happen is one that *inclines* provided that, because of the motive, (2) is false; like our public official, he cannot bring himself to do anything to prevent A from happening. And therefore we can say that this motive for making A happen is one that *inclines but does not necessitate* provided that, because of the motive, (1) is true and (2) is false; he can resist the temptation to make it happen but he cannot resist the temptation to allow it to happen.

NOTES

1. The general position to be presented here is suggested in the following writings, among others: Aristotle, I *Eudemian Ethics*, bk. ii ch. 6; *Nicomachean Ethics*, bk. iii, ch. 1–5; Thomas Reid, *Essays on the Active Powers of Man*; C. A. Campbell, 'Is "Free Will" a Pseudo-Problem?' *Mind*, 1951, pp. 441–65; Roderick M. Chisholm, 'Responsibility and Avoidability', and Richard Taylor, 'Determination and the Theory of Agency', in *Determinism and Freedom in the Age of Modern Science*, ed. Sidney Hook (New York, 1958).

2. Thomas Reid, *Essays on the Active Powers of Man*, essay iv. ch. 4, *Works*, 600.

3. *Summa Theologica*, First Part of the Second Part, qu. vi ('On the Voluntary and Involuntary').

4. Jonathan Edwards, *Freedom of the Will* (New Haven, 1957); G. E. Moore, *Ethics* (Home University Library, 1912). ch. 6.

5. A. I. Melden, *Free Action* (London, 1961), especially ch. 3. Mr. Melden's own views, however, are quite the contrary of those that are proposed here.

6. Aristotle, *Physics*, bk. iii. ch. 3; Suarez, *Disputations Metaphysicae*, Disputation 18, s. 10.

7. Reid, *Works*, 524.
8. John Locke, *Essay Concerning Human Understanding*, bk. ii, ch. 21.
9. Melden, 166.
10. Reid, *Works*, 608, 612.
11. 'Lettre à Mr. Coste de la Nécessité et de la Contingence' (1707) in *Opera Philosophica*, ed. Erdmann, pp. 447–9.
12. In the Preface to the "Metaphysical Elements of Ethics," in *Kant's Critique of Practical Reason and Other Works on the Theory of Ethics*, ed. T. K. Abbott (London, 1959), 303.
13. Cf. D. P. Henry, 'Saint Anselm's De *"Grammatico"*,' *Philosophical Quarterly*, x (1960), 115–26. St. Anselm noted that (i) and (iii), respectively, may be thought of as forming the upper left and the upper right corners of a square of opposition, and (ii) and (iv) the lower left and the lower right.

1.2 Free Will: Ancient Dispute, New Themes

ROBERT KANE

Robert Kane teaches philosophy at the University of Texas.

I

"There is a disputation that will continue till mankind are raised from the dead, between the necessitarians and the partisans of free will." These are the words of twelfth-century Persian poet, Jalalu'ddin Rumi. The problem of free will and necessity (or determinism), of which Rumi speaks, has puzzled the greatest minds for centuries—including famous philosophers, literary figures, theologians, scientists, legal theorists, and psychologists—as well as many ordinary people. It has affected and been affected by both religion and science.

In his classic poem, *Paradise Lost*, John Milton describes the angels debating how some of them could have sinned of their own free wills given that God had made them intelligent and happy.[1] Why would they have done it? And why were they responsible for it rather than God, since God had made them the way they were and had complete foreknowledge of what they would do? While puzzling over such questions, even the angels, Milton tells us, were "in Endless Mazes lost" (not a comforting thought for us humans). On the scientific front, issues about free will lead us to ask about the nature of the physical universe and our place in it (are we determined by physical laws and movements of the atoms?), about human psychology and the springs of action (can our actions be predicted by those who know our psychology?), about social conditioning, moral responsibility, crime and punishment, right and wrong, good and evil, and much more.

To dive into these questions, the best way to begin is with the idea of *freedom* itself. Nothing could be more important than freedom to the modern world. All over the globe, the trend (often against resistance) is toward societies that are more free. But why do we want freedom? The simple, and not totally adequate, answer is that to be more free is to have the capacity and opportunity to satisfy more of our desires. In a free society we can walk into a store and buy almost anything we want. We can choose what movies to see, what music to listen to, whom to vote for.

But these are what you might call *surface* freedoms. What is meant by *free will* runs deeper than these everyday freedoms. To see how, suppose we had maximal freedom to make such choices to satisfy our desires and yet the choices we actually made were manipulated by others, by the powers-that-be. In such a world we would have a great deal of everyday freedom to do whatever we wanted, yet our free *will* would be severely limited. We would be free to *act* or choose *as* we will, but would not have the ultimate say about what it is that we will. Someone else would be pulling the strings, not by coercing us against our wishes, but by manipulating us into having the wishes they wanted us to have.

You may be thinking that, to some extent, we do live in such a world, where we are free to make numerous choices, but are manipulated into making many of our choices by advertising, television, public relations, spin doctors, salespersons, marketers, and sometimes even by friends, parents, relatives, rivals, or enemies. One indication of how important free will is to us is that people generally feel revulsion at such manipulation. When people find out that what they thought were their own wishes were actually manipulated by others who wanted them to choose in just the way they did, they feel demeaned. Such situations are demeaning because we realize we were not our own persons; and having free will is about being your own person.

The problem is brought out in a striking way by twentieth-century utopian novels, such as Aldous Huxley's *Brave New World* and B. F. Skinner's *Walden Two*.[2] In the fictional societies described in these famous works, people can have and do what they will or choose, but only to the extent that they have been conditioned by behavioral engineers or neuro-chemists to will or choose what they can have and do. In *Brave New World,* the lower-echelon workers are under the influence of powerful drugs so that they do not dream of things they cannot have. They are quite content to play miniature golf all weekend. They can do what they want, though their wants are meager and controlled by drugs.

The citizens of Skinner's *Walden Two* have a richer existence than the workers of *Brave New World.* Yet their desires and purposes are also covertly controlled, in this case by behavioral en-

gineers. Walden Two-ers live collectively in a kind of rural commune; and because they share duties of farming and raising children, they have plenty of leisure. They pursue arts, sciences, crafts, engage in musical performances, and enjoy what appears to be a pleasant existence. The fictional founder of Walden Two, a fellow named Frazier, forthrightly says that their pleasant existence is brought about by the fact that, in his community, persons can do whatever they want or choose because they have been behaviorally conditioned since childhood to want and choose only what they can have and do. In other words, they have maximal *surface freedom* of action and choice (they can choose or do anything they want), but they lack a *deeper freedom* of the will because their desires and purposes are created by their behavioral conditioners or controllers. Their wills are not of "their own" making. Indeed, what happens in Walden Two is that their surface freedom to act and choose as they will is maximized by minimizing the deeper freedom to have the ultimate say about what they will.

Thus Frazier can say that Walden Two "is the freest place on earth" (p. 297), because he has surface freedoms in mind. For there is no *coercion* in Walden Two and no *punishment* because no one has to be forced to do anything against his or her will. The citizens can have anything they want because they have been conditioned not to want anything they cannot have. As for the deeper freedom, or free will, it does not exist in Walden Two, as Frazier himself admits (p. 257). But this is no loss, according to Frazier. Echoing *Walden Two*'s author, B. F. Skinner (a foremost defender of behaviorism in psychology), Frazier thinks the deeper freedom of the will is an illusion in the first place. We do not have it anyway, inside or outside Walden Two. In our ordinary lives, he argues, we are just as much the products of upbringing and social conditioning as the citizens of Walden Two, though we may delude ourselves into thinking otherwise. The difference is that, unlike Walden Two, our everyday conditioning is often haphazard, incompetent, and harmful.

Why then, Skinner asks, reject the maximal surface freedom and happiness of Walden Two for a deeper freedom of the will that is something we do not and cannot have anyway? Along with many other scientists, he thinks the idea that we could be *ultimate* determiners of our own ends or purposes (which is what the deeper freedom of the will would require) is an impossible ideal that cannot fit into the modern scientific picture of the world. To have such freedom, we would have to have been the original creators of our own wills—causes of ourselves. But if we trace the psychological springs of action back further and further to childhood, we find that we were less free back then, not more, and more subject to conditioning. We thus delude ourselves into thinking that we have sacrificed some real (deeper) freedom for the happiness of Walden Two. Rather we have gained a maximum amount of the only kind of freedom we really can have (surface freedom), while giving up an illusion (free will).

Seductive as these arguments may be, there are many people (myself included) who continue to believe that something important is missing in Walden Two and that the deeper freedom is not a mere illusion. Such persons want to be the ultimate designers of their own lives as Frazier was for the lives of Walden Two. They want to be the creators, as he was, not the pawns—at least for their own lives. What they long for is what was traditionally meant by "free will."

Here is yet another way of looking at it. Free will in this deeper sense is also intimately related to notions of moral responsibility, blameworthiness, and praiseworthiness. Suppose a young man is on trial for an assault and robbery in which his victim was beaten to death. Let us say we attend his trial on a daily basis. At first, our thoughts of the young man are filled with anger and resentment. But as we listen daily to how he came to have such a mean character and perverse motives—a sordid story of parental neglect, child abuse, sexual abuse, bad role models—some of our resentment against the young man is shifted over to the parents and others who abused and influenced him. We begin to feel angry with them as well as him. Yet we aren't quite ready to shift all of the blame away from the young man himself. We wonder whether some residual responsibility may not belong to him. Our questions become: To what extent is *he* responsible for becoming the sort of person he now is? Was it *all* a question of bad parenting, societal neglect, social conditioning, and the like, or did he have any role to play in it?

These are crucial questions about free will, and about what may be called *ultimate responsibility*. We know that parenting and society, genetic makeup and upbringing, have an influence on what we become and what we are. But were these influences entirely *determining* or did they "leave anything over" for us to be responsible for? That's what we wanted to know about the young man. The question of whether he is merely a victim of his bad circumstances or has some residual responsibility for being what he is depends on whether these other factors were or were not *entirely* determining.[3]

Turning this around, if there were factors or circumstances that entirely determined what he did, then to be ultimately responsible, he would have had to be responsible to some degree for some of those factors by virtue of earlier acts through which he formed his present character. As the philosopher Aristotle put it centuries ago, if a man is responsible for the wicked acts that flow from his character, then he must at one time in the past have been responsible for forming the character from which these acts flow. But, of course, if *all* of our choices and actions were entirely determined by prior circumstances, we would have had to be responsible to some degree for some of these earlier circumstances by still earlier acts of ours, and so on indefinitely backward in time—an impossibility for finite creatures like ourselves. At some point, if we are to be ultimately responsible for being what we are, there must be acts in our life histories in which parenting and society, genetic make-up, and other factors did not completely determine how we acted, but left something over for us to be responsible for then and there. This is why many people have thought that the deeper freedom of the will is not compatible with being completely determined by the past. Surface freedoms (to do or choose what we will) may be compatible with determinism, but free will does not seem to be (as Skinner himself realized).

II

Yet such thoughts only lead to a further problem that has haunted free will debates for centuries: If this deeper freedom of the will is not compatible with determinism, it does not seem to be compatible with *indeterminism* either. An event that is undetermined might occur or might not occur, given the entire past. (A determined event *must* occur, given the entire past.) Thus, whether or not an undetermined event actually occurs, given its past, is a matter of chance. But chance events occur spontaneously and are not under the control of anything, hence not under the control of agents. How then could they be free and responsible actions? If, for example, a choice occurred by virtue of a quantum jump or other undetermined event in your brain, it would seem a fluke or accident rather than a responsible choice. Undetermined events in the brain or body, it seems, would inhibit or interfere with freedom, occurring spontaneously and not under our control. They would turn out to be a nuisance—or perhaps a curse, like epilepsy—rather than an enhancement of our freedom.

Or look at the problem in another way that goes a little deeper. If my choice is really undetermined, that means I could have made a different choice *given exactly the same past* right up to the moment when I did choose. This is what indeterminism and the denial of determinism mean: exactly the same past, different outcomes. Imagine, for example, that I had been deliberating about where to spend my vacation, in Hawaii or Colorado, and after much thought and deliberation had decided I preferred Hawaii, and chose it. If the choice was undetermined, then exactly the same deliberation, the same thought processes, the same beliefs, desires, and other motives—not a sliver of difference—that led to

my favoring and choosing Hawaii over Colorado, might by chance have resulted in my choosing Colorado instead. That is very strange. If such a thing happened it would seem a fluke or accident, like that quantum jump in the brain just mentioned, not a rational choice. Because I had come to favor Hawaii and was about to choose it, when by chance I chose Colorado, I would wonder what went wrong in my brain and perhaps consult a neurologist.

For reasons such as these, people have argued that undetermined free choices would be "arbitrary," "capricious," "random," "irrational," "uncontrolled," "inexplicable," or merely "matters of luck or chance," not really free and responsible choices at all. If free will is not compatible with determinism, it does not seem to be compatible with indeterminism either.

These charges are powerful ones and defenders of free will over the centuries have made extraordinary claims attempting to respond to them. Free will does require indeterminism, these defenders have said. But it cannot *merely* be indeterminism or chance. Some "extra factors" must be involved in free will that go beyond ordinary scientific or causal understanding. Immanuel Kant, for example, insisted that we can't explain free will in scientific and psychological terms. To account for it we have to appeal to the agency of what he called a "noumenal self" outside space and time that could not be studied in scientific terms.[4] Others have appealed to what Nobel physiologist John Eccles calls a "transempirical power center," which would intervene in the brain, filling the causal gaps left by indeterminism or chance.[5] Still others have appealed to a special kind of agent-causation—or, as Roderick Chisholm has called it, "immanent causation"—that cannot be explained in terms of the ordinary scientific modes of causation in terms of events or occurrences. Where all prior events, both physical and mental, leave a choice or action undetermined, the agent- or immanent cause determines it, but cannot be determined in turn because it is not an event. The agent-cause is, in Chisholm's words, a "prime mover unmoved."[6]

Such unusual strategems are common among defenders of an indeterminist free will (who often nowadays are called "incompatibilists" because they believe that free will is not compatible with determinism and "libertarians" because they believe in addition that free will is not an illusion). But these unusual strategems, such as noumenal selves, transempirical power centers, and agent- or immanent causes, have unfortunately reinforced the view, now widespread among philosophers and scientists, that traditional notions of free will requiring indeterminism are mysterious and have no place in the modern scientific picture of the world. Such libertarian strategems, to their critics, are reminiscent of the old debates about vital forces in the biology of the nineteenth century, where obscure forces were postulated to explain what otherwise could not be explained about living things. They remind us of the Arkansas farmer when he first saw an automobile. He listened intently to the explanation of how the internal combustion engine worked, and nodded in agreement, but insisted on looking under the hood anyway because, as he said, "there must be a horse in there somewhere."

Thus, defenders of a nondeterminist free will are faced with a dilemma that was expressed by philosopher Thomas Hobbes at the beginning of the modern era. When trying to explain free will, these incompatibilist or libertarian defenders tend to fall either into "confusion" or "emptiness"—the confusion of identifying free will with indeterminism or the emptiness of mysterious accounts of agency in terms of noumenal selves, transempirical power centers, nonoccurrent or agent-causes, or other strategems whose operations remain obscure and unexplained. What is needed to escape this dilemma is some new thinking about how free will can be reconciled with indeterminism and how it might fit into the modern scientific picture of the world, without appealing to extra factors that have made it seem so mysterious. In the remainder of this essay, I want to suggest some new ways of thinking about this problem and about free will generally, which may stir you to do likewise.[7]

III

The first thing to note is that indeterminism does not have to be a factor in all acts done "of our own free wills." Not all of them have to be undetermined. Frequently in everyday life we act from existing motives without having to think or deliberate about what to do. At such times, we may very well be determined by our existing characters and motives. Yet we may also at such times be acting "of our own free wills" to the extent that we formed our present characters and motives (our own wills) by earlier choices or actions that were not themselves determined. Recall again Aristotle's claim that if a man is responsible for the wicked acts that flow from his character, he must at one time in the past have been responsible for forming the character from which these acts flow. Not all choices or acts done "of our own free wills" have to be undetermined, but only those choices or acts in our lifetimes by which we made ourselves into the kinds of persons we are. Let us call these "self-forming choices or actions" or SFAs.

I believe that such undetermined self-forming choices and actions (SFAs) occur at those difficult times of life when we are torn between competing visions of what we should do or become, and that they are more frequent than we think. Perhaps we are torn between doing the moral thing or acting from ambition, or between powerful present desires and long-term goals, or we are faced with difficult tasks for which we have aversions. In all such cases, we are faced with competing motivations and have to make an effort to overcome temptation to do something else we also strongly want. At such times, there is tension and uncertainty in our minds about what to do. I suggest that this is reflected in appropriate regions of our brains by movement away from thermodynamic equilibrium— in short, a kind of stirring up of chaos in the brain that makes it sensitive to microindeterminacies at the neuronal level. The uncertainty and inner tension we feel at such soul-searching moments of self-formation would thus be reflected in the indeterminacy of our neural processes themselves. What is experienced personally as uncertainty corresponds physically to the opening of a window of opportunity that temporarily screens off complete determination by influences of the past. (By contrast, when we act from predominant motives or settled dispositions, the uncertainty or indeterminacy is muted. If it did play a role in such cases, it would be a mere nuisance or fluke, as critics suggest, like the choice of Colorado when we favored Hawaii.)

When we do decide under such conditions of uncertainty, the outcome is not determined because of the preceding indeterminacy—and yet it can be willed (and hence rational and voluntary) either way owing to the fact that, in such self-formation, the agents' prior wills are divided by conflicting motives. Consider a businesswoman who faces a conflict of this kind. She is on the way to a business meeting important to her career when she observes an assault taking place in an alley. An inner struggle ensues between her moral conscience telling her to stop and call for help, and her career ambitions telling her she cannot miss this meeting. She has to make an effort of will to overcome the temptation to go on to her meeting. If she overcomes this temptation, it will be the result of her effort, but if she fails, it will be because she did not *allow* her effort to succeed. And this is because, while she wanted to overcome temptation, she also wanted to fail, for quite different and incommensurable reasons. When we, like the businesswoman, decide in such circumstances, and the indeterminate efforts we are making become determinate choices, we *make* one set of competing reasons or motives prevail over the others then and there *by deciding*.

Now let us add a further piece to the puzzle. Just as indeterminism does not necessarily undermine rationality and voluntariness, so indeterminism, in and of itself, does not necessarily undermine control and responsibility. Suppose you are trying to think through a difficult problem, say a mathematical problem, and there is some indeterminacy in your neural processes complicating the task—a kind of chaotic background. It would be like trying to concentrate and solve a problem with background noise or distraction. Whether you are going to succeed in solving the mathematical problem is uncertain and undetermined because of the distracting indeterministic neural noise. Yet, if you concentrate and solve the problem nonetheless, we have reason to say you did it and are responsible for it even though it was undetermined whether you would succeed. The distracting neural noise would have been an obstacle that you overcame by your effort.

There are numerous other examples supporting this point, where indeterminism functions as an obstacle to success without precluding responsibility. Consider an assassin who is trying to shoot the prime minister, but might miss because of some undetermined events in his nervous system that may lead to a jerking or wavering of his arm. If the assassin does succeed in hitting his target, despite the indeterminism, can he be held responsible? The answer is obviously yes because he intentionally and voluntarily succeeded in doing what he was *trying* to do—kill the prime minister. Yet his action, killing the prime minister, was undetermined. One might even say "he got lucky" in killing the prime minister, because there was a chance he might have missed. Yet, for all that, he *did* kill the prime minister and *was* responsible for it.

Here is another example: A husband, while arguing with his wife, in a fit of rage swings his arm down on her favorite glass-top table, intending to break it. Again, we suppose that some indeterminism in the nerves of his arm makes the momentum of his swing indeterminate so that it is literally not determined whether the table will break right up to the moment when it is struck. Whether the husband breaks the table or not is undetermined and yet he is clearly responsible if he does break it. (It would be a poor excuse for him to say to his wife "chance did it, not me" or "it wasn't my doing; it happened by chance." She would not be impressed.)

To be sure, such examples—of the mathematical problem, the assassin, and the husband —do not amount to genuine exercises of free will in "self-forming actions" or SFAs, such as the businesswoman's, where the wills of the agents are divided between conflicting motives. The businesswoman wants to do the right thing and help the victim, but she also wants to go on to her meeting. By contrast, the will of the assassin is not equally divided. He wants to kill the prime minister, but does not also want to fail. (If his conscience bothered him and he was undecided about what to do up to the last minute, that would be another matter. *Then* his choice would be a self-forming action or SFA, like the businesswoman's. But such was not the case.) Thus, if the assassin fails to hit his target, it will be merely by chance or as a fluke, not voluntarily (and so also for the husband and mathematical problem-solver). Cases such as the assassin, husband, and mathematical problem-solver are therefore not all that we want. Yet they are a step in the right direction because they show that indeterminism does not necessarily rule out action and responsibility, any more than it necessarily rules out rationality and voluntariness. To go further, we have to dig more deeply and add some further ideas.

IV

Let us imagine in cases of self-forming choices, like the businesswoman's, where there *is* conflict in the will, that the indeterministic noise that is providing an obstacle to her overcoming temptation (and stopping to help the victim) is not coming from an external source, but is coming from her own will, because she also deeply desires to do the opposite (go on to her meeting). Imagine that in such conflicting circumstances, two competing (recurrent) neural networks are involved. (These are complex networks of interconnected neurons in the brain circulating impulses in feedback loops that are generally involved in high-level human cognitive processing.[8]) The input of one of these networks is coming from the woman's desires and motives for stopping to help the victim. If the network reaches a certain activation threshold (the simultaneous firing of a complex set of "output" neurons), that would represent her choice to help. For the competing network, the inputs are her ambitious motives for going on to her meeting, and its reaching an activation threshold would represent the choice to go on. (If one network activates, the other will be inhibited and the contrary choice will not be made.)

Now imagine further that these two competing networks are connected so that the indeterministic noise that is an obstacle to her making one of the choices is coming from her desire to make the other. Thus, as suggested for self-forming choices or SFAs, the indeterminism arises from a *tension-creating conflict in the will*. In such circumstances, when either of the pathways "wins" (i.e., reaches an activation threshold, which amounts to choice), it will be like the agent's solving the mathematical problem by overcoming the indeterministic background noise generated by the other. And just as we could say, when you solved the mathematical problem by overcoming the distracting noise through your effort, that you did it and are responsible for it, so one can say this as well, I would argue, in the present case, *whichever one is chosen*. The neural pathway through which she succeeds in reaching a choice threshold will have overcome the obstacle in the form of indeterministic noise coming from the other pathway.

Note that, in these circumstances, the choices either way will not be "inadvertent," "accidental," "capricious," or "merely random," because they will be *willed* by the woman either way, when they are made, and done for *reasons* either way (moral convictions if she turns back, ambitious motives if she goes on) which she then and there endorses. And these are the conditions usually required to say something is done "on purpose," rather than accidentally, capriciously, or merely by chance. Moreover, these conditions taken together (that she wills it, and does it for reasons, and could have done otherwise willingly and for reasons) rule out each of the normal motives we have for saying agents act, but do not have control over their actions (coercion, constraint, inadvertence, mistake, and control by others). None of these obtain in the business-woman's case. She is not coerced (no one is holding a gun to her head), not physically constrained or disabled, not forced or controlled by others; nor does she act inadvertently or by mistake, but on purpose either way, as just noted.

Of course, with "self-forming" choices of these kinds, agents cannot control or determine which choice outcome will occur *before* it occurs or the outcomes would be *pre*determined after all. (That would be like deciding beforehand what you are going to decide.) But it does not follow that, because one does not control or determine which of a set of outcomes is going to occur before it occurs, one does not control which of them occurs, *when* it occurs. When the above conditions for self-forming choices are satisfied, agents exercise control over their future lives *then and there* by deciding. Indeed, they have what may be called "plural voluntary control" in the following sense: Agents have plural voluntary control over a set of options (stopping to help or going on to a meeting) when they are able to bring about *whichever* of the options they will, *when* they will to do so, for the *reasons* they will to do so, *on purpose* rather than by mistake or accident, without being coerced or compelled in doing so, or otherwise controlled by other agents or mechanisms. We have seen that each of these conditions can be satisfied in cases of SFAs, like the business-woman's, despite the indeterminism involved.[9] These conditions of plural voluntary control may be summed by saying, as people often do, that the agents can choose either way "at will." ("Plural" in "plural voluntary control" means "more-than-one-way" and "voluntary" means "in accordance with one's will.")

Note also that this account of self-forming choices amounts to a kind of "doubling" of the mathematical problem. It is as if an agent faced with such a choice is *trying* or making an effort to solve *two* cognitive problems at once, or to complete two competing (deliberative) tasks at once—in our example, to make a moral choice

and to make a conflicting self-interested choice (corresponding to the two competing neural networks involved). Each task is being thwarted by the indeterminism coming from the other, so it might fail. But if it succeeds, then the agents can be held responsible because, as in the case of solving the mathematical problem, they will have succeeded in doing what they were knowingly and willingly trying to do. Recall again the cases of the assassin and the husband. Owing to indeterminacies in their neural pathways, the assassin might miss his target or the husband fail to break the table. But if they *succeed*, despite the probability of failure, they are responsible, because they will have succeeded in doing what they were trying to do.

And so it is, I suggest, with self-forming choices, except that in the case of self-forming choices, *whichever way the agents choose,* they will have succeeded in doing what they were trying to do because they were simultaneously trying to make both choices, and one is going to succeed. Their failure to do one thing is not a *mere* failure, but a voluntary succeeding in doing the other. Does it make sense to talk about the agent's trying to do two competing things at once in this way, or to solve two cognitive problems at once? Well, we know that the brain is a parallel processor; it can simultaneously process different kinds of information relevant to tasks such as perception or recognition through different neural pathways. Such a capacity, I believe, is essential to the exercise of free will.

In cases of self-formation (SFAs), agents are simultaneously trying to resolve plural and competing cognitive tasks. They are, as we say, of two minds. Yet they are not two separate persons. They are not dissociated from either task. The businesswoman who wants to go back to help the victim is the same ambitious woman who wants to go to her meeting and make a sale. She is a complex creature, torn inside by different visions of who she is and what she wants to be, as we all are from time to time. But this is the kind of complexity needed for genuine self-formation and free will. And when she succeeds in doing one of the things she is trying to do, she will endorse that as *her* resolution of the conflict in her will, voluntarily and intentionally, not by accident or mistake.

V

Yet it is still hard to shake the intuition that if choices are undetermined, they *must* happen merely by chance—and so must be "random," "capricious," "uncontrolled," "irrational," "inexplicable," and all the other things charged. I do not deny the powerful hold such intuitions have upon us. They are among the reasons why free will continues to be such a deep problem, even for those who want to believe in it. But the very fact that it has been such a problem for so long should also suggest that we cannot take ordinary intuitions about free will at face value without questioning them. If we are ever going to understand it, we will likely have to break old habits of thought and learn to think in new ways.

The first step in doing this is to question the intuitive connection in most people's minds between "indeterminism's being involved in something" and "its happening merely as a matter of chance or luck." "Chance" and "luck" are terms of ordinary language that carry the connotation of "it's out of my control." So using them already begs certain questions, whereas "indeterminism" is a technical term that merely precludes *deterministic* causation, though not causation altogether. Indeterminism is consistent with non-deterministic or probabilistic causation, where the outcome is not inevitable. It is therefore a mistake (alas, one of the most common in debates about free will) to assume that "undetermined" means "uncaused."

Another source of misunderstanding is this: Because the outcome of the businesswoman's effort (the choice) is undetermined up to the last minute, we may have the image of her first making an effort to overcome temptation (to go on to her meeting) and then at the last instant "chance taking over" and deciding the issue for her. But this image is misleading. On the view just described, one cannot separate the indeterminism and the effort of will, so that *first* the

effort occurs *followed* by chance or luck (or vice versa). One must think of the effort and the indeterminism as fused; the effort *is* indeterminate and the indeterminism is a *property* of the effort, not something separate that occurs after or before the effort. The fact that the effort has this property of being indeterminate does not make it any less the woman's *effort*. The complex recurrent neural network that realizes the effort in the brain is circulating impulses in feedback loops and there is some indeterminacy in these circulating impulses. But the whole process is her effort of will and it persists right up to the moment when the choice is made. There is no point at which the effort stops and chance "takes over." She chooses as a result of the effort, even though she might have failed. Similarly, the husband breaks the table as a result of his effort, even though he might have failed because of the indeterminacy. (That is why his excuse —"chance broke the table, not me"—is so lame.)

And just as expressions such as "she chose *by* chance" can mislead us in such contexts, so can expressions like "she got lucky." Recall that in the cases of the assassin and the husband, one might say "they got lucky" in killing the prime minister and breaking the table because their actions were undetermined. Yet, as we noted, it does not follow that they were not responsible. So ask yourself this question: Why does the inference "he got lucky, *so he was not responsible?*" fail when it does fail, in the cases of the husband and the assassin? The first part of an answer has to do with the point made earlier that "luck," like "chance," has question-begging implications in ordinary language that are not necessarily implications of "indeterminism" (which implies only the absence of deterministic causation). The core meaning of "he got lucky" in the assassin and husband cases, which *is* implied by indeterminism, I suggest, is that "he succeeded *despite the probability or chance of failure;*" and this core meaning does not imply lack of responsibility, if he succeeds.

If "he got lucky" had further meanings in the husband and assassin cases that are often associated with "luck" and "chance" in ordinary usage (for example, the outcome was not his doing, or occurred by *mere* chance, or he was not responsible for it), the inference would not fail for the husband and assassin, as it clearly does. But the point is that these further meanings of "luck" and "chance" do not follow *from the mere presence of indeterminism*. The second reason why the inference "he got lucky, so he was not responsible" fails for the assassin and the husband is that *what* they succeeded in doing was what they were trying and wanting to do all along (kill the minister and break the table respectively). The third reason is that *when* they succeeded, their reaction was not "oh dear, that was a mistake, an accident—something that *happened* to me, not something I *did*." Rather they *endorsed* the outcomes as something they were trying and wanting to do all along, that is to say, knowingly and purposefully, not by mistake or accident.

But these conditions are satisfied in the businesswoman's case as well, *either way* she chooses. If she succeeds in choosing to return to help the victim (or in choosing to go on to her meeting), first, she will have succeeded *despite the probability or chance of failure;* second, she will have succeeded in doing what she was trying and wanting to do all along (she wanted both outcomes very much, but for different reasons, and was trying to make those reasons prevail in both cases); and third, when she succeeded (in choosing to return to help) her reaction was not "oh dear, that was a mistake, an accident—something that happened to me, not something I did." Rather she endorsed the outcome as something she was trying and wanting to do all along; she recognized it as her resolution of the conflict in her will. And if she had chosen to go on to her meeting, she would have endorsed that outcome, recognizing it as her resolution of the conflict in her will.

Let us try another tack. Perhaps we are begging the question by assuming at the outset that the outcomes of the woman's efforts are her *choices*. If they are not choices to begin with,

they cannot be voluntary choices. One might argue this on the grounds that (A) "if an event is undetermined, it must be something that merely *happens* and cannot be somebody's choice;" or (B) "if an event is undetermined, it must be something that merely happens, it cannot be something an agent *does* (it cannot be an action)." But to see how question-begging these assumptions are, one has only to note that A and B imply respectively (A′) "if an event is a choice, it must be determined" ("all choices are determined") and (B′) "if an event is an action, it must be determined" ("all actions are determined"). Are these claims supposed to be true necessarily or by definition? If so, the free will issue would be solved by fiat; it would follow merely from the meanings of the words that all choices and actions are determined.

But why should we believe this? Was the husband's breaking the table not something he did because it was not determined? Recall that "undetermined" does not mean "uncaused." The breaking of the table was caused by the swing of his arm, and though the outcome was not inevitable, that was good enough for saying he did it and was responsible. As for choices, a choice is the formation of an intention or a purpose to do something. It resolves uncertainty and indecision in the mind about what to do, "setting the mind" on one alternative rather than another. Nothing in such a description implies that there could not be some indeterminism in the deliberation and neural processes of an agent's preceding choice corresponding to the agent's uncertainty about what to do. Recall from preceding arguments that the presence of indeterminism does not mean the outcome happened merely by chance and not by the agent's effort.

But it is one thing to choose, in the sense of forming an intention; it is another thing to have *control* over one's choosing. Perhaps this is where the real problem lies. Would not the presence of indeterminism at least *diminish* the control persons have over their choices and other actions? Is it not the case that the assassin's control over whether the prime minister is killed (his ability to realize his purposes or what he is trying to do) is lessened by the undetermined impulses in his arm—and so also for the husband and his breaking the table? Moreover, this limitation is connected with another often noted by critics— that indeterminism, wherever it occurs, seems to be a *hindrance* or *obstacle* to our realizing our purposes and hence an obstacle to our freedom.

These concerns are closer to the mark, and there is something to them. But rather than being devastating objections to an incompatibilist account of free will, I think they reveal something important about such a free will. I think we should concede that indeterminism, wherever it occurs, *does* diminish control over what we are trying to do and *is* a hindrance or obstacle to the realization of our purposes. But recall that in the case of the businesswoman (and for SFAs generally), the indeterminism that is admittedly diminishing her control over one thing she is trying to do (the moral act of helping the victim) *is coming from her own will*—from her desire and effort to do the opposite (go to her business meeting). And the indeterminism that is diminishing her control over the other thing she is trying to do (act selfishly and go to her meeting) is coming from her desire and effort to do the opposite (to be a moral person and act on moral reasons).

So, in each case, the indeterminism *is* functioning as a hindrance or obstacle to her realizing one of her purposes—a hindrance or obstacle in the form of resistance within her will. As a consequence, whichever choice she makes, whichever effort wins out, she will have to overcome the hindrance or obstacle provided by the indeterminism coming from the other. If there were no such hindrance—if there were no resistance in her will—she would indeed in a sense have "complete control" over one of her options. There would be no competing motives that would stand in the way of her choosing it. But then also she would not be free to rationally and voluntarily choose the other purpose because she would have no

good competing reasons to do so. Thus, by *being* a hindrance to the realization of some of our purposes, indeterminism paradoxically opens up the genuine possibility of pursuing other purposes— of choosing or doing *otherwise* in accordance with, rather than against, our wills (voluntarily) and reasons (rationally).

To be genuinely self-forming agents (creators of ourselves)—to have free will—there must at times in life be obstacles and hindrances in our wills of this sort that we must overcome. We can concede then that indeterminism is a hindrance and a nuisance, but a necessary one if we are to have ultimate responsibility for our own wills. Being "your own self" is a struggle. We can appreciate why existentialist philosopher Jean-Paul Sartre said that true freedom (free will) is a burden many people want to "escape"—preferring instead that others tell them what to do and how to live, or perhaps preferring that their choices always be easy.[10] In an earlier time, St. Augustine asked why God would have given us free will, since it is such a pain to us and to others; and the answer was that without it we would lack the greater good of being ultimately responsible for what we are and what we do.[11]

Perhaps we should look in another direction that has also led to doubts about whether free will can be reconciled with indeterminism or chance. What might be going on in the brain, we might ask, when free choices take place? If neuroscientists were to inspect the woman's brain when she was struggling with her moral decision, wouldn't it be the case that they would find nothing more than interconnected sets of neuron firings in which micro-indeterminacies were not negligible? These interconnected neuron firings would in turn terminate in some definite configuration of nerve firings that corresponded to the "choice" to stop and help the victim or in another set of firings corresponding to the "choice" to go on to her meeting. But why one of these outcomes occurred rather than the other would be inexplicable in terms of the preceding processes. Probabilities could be assigned for one outcome rather than the other, but that is all. And this looks like chance.

I agree that if the physical descriptions of these events were the only legitimate ones, then free will would look like nothing more than chance or probability. When neuroscientists described it in physico-chemical terms, all they would get are indeterministic chaotic processes with probabilistic outcomes. In short, if described from a physical perspective alone, free will looks like chance. But the physical description is not the only one to be considered. The indeterministic chaotic process is also, experientially considered, the agent's effort of will—something the agent is doing. And the undetermined outcome of the process, one way or the other, is experientially the agent's choice—something the agent does, not something that merely happens to the agent. So viewed from another perspective, the neural output that represents the choice is the result of the agent's effort even though the outcome is not determined.

If we did not add these mental descriptions of what is going on to the physical descriptions, something important would be left out of our picture of the world. To make sense of free will, we do not have to be complete (substance) dualists about mind and body, as Descartes was. But we cannot be extreme "eliminative" materialists either. We can't expect to lop off from the top of our world-view all psychological descriptions of human beings in terms of beliefs, desires, intentions, efforts, choices, and consciousness (leaving only descriptions in neurophysiological terms), *and expect free will to survive*. The fact is that a lot of other things important to us would not survive either if we were to lop off these psychological descriptions from our descriptions of the world, such as personhood, rationality, subjectivity, morality, and so on.

But notice that *this* problem is not a special one for theories of free will that presuppose indeterminism. Suppose you believed that all choices and actions were determined and that human free agency was compatible with determinism. You still could not adequately describe human agency, if you confined yourself to describing the brain in chemical and neurophysiological terms alone, leaving out all ordinary psychological descriptions in terms of beliefs, desires, intentions, efforts, choices, and consciousness. Determinists and compatibilists about free will cannot eliminate supervenient mental or psychological descriptions either, if they are going to describe human agency. It is no less a mystery how neural firings in the brain could be, or give rise to, conscious beliefs, efforts, or choices if these neural firings are *determined* than if they are undetermined. This problem (the problem of consciousness, or more generally, the "mind/body problem") is no special problem for indeterminist theories of free will like the one given here. It is a problem for anyone who wishes to talk about free agency, whatever position they take on free will, compatibilist or incompatibilist, determinist or indeterminist.

These reflections naturally raise the further question of whether the indeterminism that is required by an incompatibilist theory of free will is actually there in the brain. This is an empirical question that can only be decided by scientific research and not by a philosophical theory or armchair speculation (much as philosophers would like to decide all questions *a priori*, or before all experience). While we cannot resolve this question, we can at least keep our minds open about it. There is so much more to be learned about the brain and living things. One caution, however: If you are inclined to believe that free will is incompatible with determinism (if you are an incompatibilist or libertarian), don't think you can escape such scientific and empirical questions altogether unless you want to leave free will a complete mystery. Even if you appealed to "transempirical power centers" or "non-event" agent causes to make sense of free will (as libertarians often do), there would still have to be some indeterminacy in the natural world—and presumably in the brain where it counts—to make room in nature (to provide the "causal gaps") for the intervention of these additional causes or agencies. As the ancient Epicurean philosophers said centuries ago, if the atoms do not sometimes "swerve" in undetermined ways, there will be no room in nature for free will.

Addressing this problem earlier, I suggested that conflicts in the wills of agents associated with self-forming choices might "stir up chaos" in the brain, sensitizing it to quantum indeterminacies at the neuronal level, which would then be magnified to affect the neural networks as a whole. This is speculative to be sure, and other writers have suggested different ways in which indeterminacy might be involved in the brain.[12] But such speculations are not merely idle. There is some evidence that unpredictable chaotic activity plays a role in the brain and human cognition, providing some of the flexibility that the nervous system needs to react creatively to an ever-changing environment. A recent article in the journal *Behavior and Brain Sciences,* entitled "How Brains Make Chaos in Order to Make Sense of the World," defends this role, as do other recent writings.[13] Now it is true that chaos (or chaotic behavior) in physical systems, though unpredictable, is nonetheless usually deterministic. Chaos does not of itself imply indeterminism. But chaotic behavior in physical systems does involve "sensitivity to initial conditions." Minute differences in the initial conditions of chaotic physical systems, including living things, may be magnified, giving rise to large-scale, undetermined effects. If the brain does "make chaos to understand the world," its sensitivity to initial conditions may magnify quantum indeterminacies in neural networks whose outputs can depend on minute differences in the timings of individual neuron firings. So while quantum physics and the new sciences of chaos and complexity may not give us the indeterminism needed for free will alone (because the uncertainty of the former is usually negligible in larger physical systems and the latter need not be indeterministic by itself), they might do so together.

In any case, I have not tried to settle such empirical questions, nor could I. What I have been addressing is another set of questions that incline people to write off incompatibilist views of free will from the start, believing they could not possibly make sense and could not be reconciled with the modern scientific picture of human beings, *even if* indeterminism were somehow available in the physical world. I have argued to the contrary that if the indeterminism is there in nature, then something could be done to make sense of free will.

Let me conclude with one final objection that is perhaps the most telling and has not yet been discussed. Even if one granted that persons, such as the businesswoman, could make genuine self-forming choices that were undetermined, isn't there something to the charge that such choices would be "arbitrary?" A residual arbitrariness seems to remain in all self-forming choices because the agents cannot in principle have sufficient or overriding *prior* reasons for making one option and one set of reasons prevail over the other. The agents *make* one set of reasons prevail *by* choosing, to be sure, but they could as well have made the other set of reasons prevail by choosing differently.

I agree that there is some truth to this charge as well. But I would argue that such arbitrariness relative to prior reasons also tells us something important about free will. It tells us that every undetermined self-forming free choice is the initiation of what might be called a "value experiment" whose justification lies in the future and is not fully explained by past reasons. In making such a choice we say, in effect, "Let's try this. It is not required by my past, but is consistent with my past and is one branching pathway my life can now meaningfully take. Whether it is the right choice, only time will tell. Meanwhile, I am willing to take responsibility for it one way or the other."

It is worth noting that the term "arbitrary" comes from the Latin *arbitrium,* which means "judgment"—as in *liberum arbitrium voluntatis,* "free judgment of the will" (the medieval philosophers' designation for free will). Imagine a writer in the middle of a novel. The novel's heroine faces a crisis and the writer has not yet developed her character in sufficient detail to say exactly how she will act. The author makes a "judgment" about this that is not determined by the heroine's already formed past, which does not give unique direction. In this sense, the judgment (*arbitrium*) of how she will react is "arbitrary," but not entirely so. It had input from the heroine's fictional past and in turn gave input to her projected future. In a similar way, agents who exercise free will are both authors of and characters in their own stories all at once. By virtue of "self-forming" judgments of the will (*arbitria voluntatis*), they are "arbiters" of their own lives, "making themselves" out of a past that, if they are truly free, does not limit their future pathways to one.

Suppose we were to say to them, "But look, you didn't have sufficient or *conclusive* prior reasons for choosing as you did since you also had viable reasons for choosing the other way." They might reply, "True enough. But I did have *good* reasons for choosing as I did, which I'm willing to stand by and take responsibility for. If they were not sufficient or conclusive reasons, that's because, like the heroine of the novel, I was not a fully formed person before I chose (and still am not, for that matter). Like the author of the novel described above, I am in the process of writing an unfinished story and forming an unfinished character who, in my case, is myself."

NOTES

1. John Milton, *Paradise Lost* (London: Methuen, 1955), prologue.
2. Aldous Huxley, *Brave New World* (San Francisco: Harper-Collins, 1989). B. F. Skinner, *Walden Two* (New York: Macmillan, 1962). Page references in the paper to *Walden Two* are to this edition.
3. This is why we are naturally inclined to ask in cases like this whether someone else in exactly the same circumstances might have acted differently.
4. Kant, *The Critique of Practical Reason*. Trans. by L. W. Beck (Indianapolis: Bobbs-Merrill, 1956), part III.
5. Eccles, *Facing Reality* (New York: Springer-Verlag, 1970).

6. For defenses of this agent-causal position by various authors, see the essays in T. O'Connor (ed.), *Agents, Causes and Events: Essays on Indeterminism and Free Will* (Oxford: Oxford University Press, 1995).
7. These ideas are developed at greater length in my book, *The Significance of Free Will* (Oxford and New York: Oxford University Press, 1996; paperback edition, 1998).
8. A readable and accessible introduction to the role of neural networks (including recurrent networks) in cognitive processing is P. M. Churchland, *The Engine of Reason, the Seat of the Soul* (Cambridge, MA: MIT Press, 1996).
9. I show in greater detail that each of these conditions can be satisfied by self-forming choices or SFAs in *The Significance of Free Will* (op. cit.), chapter 8.
10. Sartre, "Selections from *Being and Nothingness*." In S. Morgenbesser et al. (eds.), *Free Will* (Englewood Cliffs, NJ: Prentice-Hall, 1962), pp. 95–113.
11. Augustine, *On the Free Choice of the Will* (Indianapolis: Bobbs-Merrill, 1964), Part I.
12. For example, H. Stapp, *Mind, Matter and Quantum Mechanics* (New York: Springer-Verlag, 1993); D. Hodgson, *The Mind Matters* (Oxford: Clarendon Press, 1991); R. Penrose, *The Emperor's New Mind* (Oxford: Oxford University Press, 1989); J. Eccles (op. cit.).
13. The article is C. Skarda and W. Freeman, *Behavioral and Brain Sciences* 10 (1987): 161–195; other writings on the subject include A. Babloyantz and A. Destexhe, "Strange Attractors in the Human Cortex." In L. Rensing (ed.), *Temporal Disorder in Human Oscillatory Systems* (New York: Springer-Verlag, 1985); G. Scott and M. McMillen (eds.), *Dissipative Structures and Spatiotemporal Organization Studies in Biomedical Research* (Ames: Iowa State University Press, 1980); H. Walter, *Neurophilosophy and Free Will*. Trans. by Cynthia Stohr (Cambridge, MA: MIT Press, 2001), Part III.

CHAPTER 2

HARD DETERMINISM: THE CASE FOR DETERMINISM AND ITS INCOMPATIBILITY WITH ANY IMPORTANT SENSE OF FREE WILL

2.1 The Case against Free Will

JAMES RACHELS

James Rachels (1941–2003) wrote many important works in moral philosophy.

A small part of the universe is contained within the skin of each of us. There is no reason why it should have any special physical status because it lies within this boundary.

—B. F. SKINNER, *About Behaviorism* (1974)

1. ARE PEOPLE RESPONSIBLE FOR WHAT THEY DO?

In 1924, two Chicago teenagers, Richard Loeb and Nathan Leopold, kidnapped and murdered a boy named Bobby Franks just to prove they could do it. The crime caused a sensation. Despite the brutality of what they had done, Leopold and Loeb did not appear to be especially wicked. They came from rich families and were both outstanding students. At 18 Leopold was the youngest graduate in the history of the University of Chicago, and at 19 Loeb was the youngest ever to have graduated from the University of Michigan. Leopold was about to enroll at the Harvard Law School. How could they have committed a senseless murder? Their trial would receive the same kind of attention as the O. J. Simpson trial 70 years later.

The parents hired Clarence Darrow, the most famous lawyer of the day, to defend them. Darrow was known as a champion of unpopular causes—he had defended labor organizers, communists, and a black man accused of killing a member of a racist mob. Three years later, in his most celebrated case, he would defend John Scopes of Tennessee from charges that he had taught evolution in a high school classroom. Darrow was also the country's best-known opponent of the death penalty. In 1902, he had been invited by the warden to give a talk to the inmates of the Cook County Jail, and he told the prisoners:

> I really do not in the least believe in crime. There is no such thing as a crime as the word is generally understood. I do not believe there is any sort of distinction between the real moral conditions of the people in and out of jail. One is just as good as the other. The people here can no more help being here than the people outside can avoid being outside. I do not believe that people are in jail because they deserve to be. They are in jail simply because they cannot avoid it on account of circumstances which are entirely beyond their control and for which they are in no way responsible.

James Rachels, *Problems from Philosophy* (McGraw-Hill, 2005), pp. 99–116. Reprinted with permission of McGraw-Hill Education.

These ideas would figure prominently in Darrow's defense of Leopold and Loeb.

The public wanted blood. As the trial began, the *Chicago Evening Standard* carried this headline:

DARROW PLEADS FOR MERCY: MOBS RIOT

BAILIFF'S ARM BROKEN AND WOMAN FAINTS

AS FRENZIED MOB STORMS PAST GUARDS;

JUDGE CALLS FOR 20 POLICE;

FEARS SOME WILL BE KILLED

Leopold and Loeb had already admitted their guilt, and so Darrow's job was just to keep them from the gallows. There would be no jury. The judge would listen to the lawyers' arguments and then decide whether the defendants would hang.

Darrow spoke for more than 12 hours. He did not argue that the boys were insane; nevertheless, he said, they were not responsible for what they had done. Darrow appealed to a new idea that psychologists had proposed, namely, that human character is shaped by an individual's genes and environment. He told the judge, "Intelligent people now know that every human being is the product of the endless heredity back of him and the infinite environment around him."

> I do not know what it was that made these boys do this mad act, but I do know there is a reason for it. I know they did not beget themselves. I know that any one of an infinite number of causes reaching back to the beginning might be working out in these boys' minds, whom you are asked to hang in malice and in hatred and injustice, because someone in the past sinned against them.

Psychiatrists had testified that the boys lacked normal feelings, because they showed no emotional reaction to what they had done. Darrow seized upon this:

> Is Dickie Loeb to blame because out of the infinite forces that conspired to form him, the infinite forces that were at work producing him ages before he was born, that because out of these infinite combinations he was born without [the right kind of emotions]? If he is, then there should be a new definition for justice. Is he to blame for what he did not have and never had?

Darrow portrays Loeb as having had a childhood bereft of the affection that boys need, spending his days studying and his evenings secretly reading crime stories, fantasizing about committing the perfect crime and fooling the cops. Leopold, meanwhile, was weak and without friends. He grew up to become obsessed with Nietzsche's philosophy of the "superman," disdaining other people and desperately wanting to prove his own superiority. Then the two boys found one another, and together they committed a crime that neither could have done alone. But they were just playing out the hand nature dealt them. "Nature is strong and she is pitiless," Darrow concluded. "She works in her own mysterious way, and we are her victims. We have not much to do with it ourselves."

The judge deliberated for a month and then sentenced Leopold and Loeb to life in prison. Twelve years later, Richard Loeb, who had been the instigator of the crime, was killed in a dispute with another prisoner. Nathan Leopold spent 34 years in prison, during which time he taught other prisoners, volunteered for malaria testing, ran the prison library, and worked in the prison hospital. After his release on parole, he moved to Puerto Rico, where he continued his lifelong effort to "become a human being again," largely through jobs that involved helping others. He died in 1971.

2. DETERMINISM

Clarence Darrow's defense of Leopold and Loeb was the first major criminal trial in which the modern idea that our personalities are the products of "heredity-plus-environment" was used to argue that the defendants were not responsible for their actions. But Darrow was not the first to doubt that we are in charge of our own destinies.

Aristotle worried that the laws of logic might imply that we have no control over what we do. Every proposition, he reasoned, must be true or false. So at this moment it is either true that you will wear a blue shirt tomorrow or false that you will wear a blue shirt tomorrow. If it is true, there is nothing you can do to prevent it—after all, *it will happen*. If it is false, there is nothing you can do to make it happen, for *it will not happen*. Either way, the future is fixed and you have no power to change it. This became known as the problem of Fatalism. Theologians from St. Augustine onward realized that the assumption of God's omniscience creates a similar difficulty. If God knows everything, he knows what you will do tomorrow. But if God already knows what you will do, then you cannot do otherwise.

As serious as the problem of Fatalism is, it is not the most worrisome challenge to human freedom. A greater threat is posed by Determinism, which was known in the ancient world but came into its own with the rise of modern science. To say that a system is deterministic means that everything that happens within it is the result of prior causes, and that once the causes occur the effects must inevitably follow, given the surrounding circumstances and the Laws of Nature. You probably regard the building you live in as a deterministic system. If the lights go out, you will think there must have been a cause; you will assume that, once the cause occurred, the effect was bound to follow. If the electrician told you "it just happened," for no reason, that would violate your conception of how things work.

With the rise of modern science, it became common to think of the whole universe as one great deterministic system. Nature consists of particles that obey the laws of physics, and everything that happens is governed by the invariable laws of cause and effect.

The most vivid expression of this idea was provided by the French mathematician Pierre-Simon Laplace (1749–1827), who said in 1819 that if a supremely intelligent observer knew the exact location and velocity of every particle in the universe and all the laws of physics, he could predict with certainty every future state of the universe. Nothing would surprise him; he would know everything before it happened. Of course, we cannot make such predictions, but that is only because we lack the necessary information and intelligence.

The universe includes us. We are part of nature, and what happens inside our skins is subject to the same physical laws as everything else. The movements of our arms, legs, and tongues are triggered by events in our brains, which in turn are caused by other physical occurrences. Thus, Laplace's perfect observer could predict our actions in the same way that he predicts everything else. In fact, by tracing the causes far enough back, he could have predicted whether you will wear a blue shirt tomorrow even before you were born. It may seem to us that we make our choices freely and spontaneously. But Laplace argued that our "freedom" is only an illusion created by our ignorance. Because we aren't aware of the underlying causes of our behavior, we assume it doesn't have any.

What, exactly, are "the underlying causes of our behavior?" As Clarence Darrow observed, the "ultimate" causes may stretch far back into time. But the immediate causes are events in our brains. Neurological events cause both our mental states and the motions of our bodies.

The idea that our conscious states are caused by neurological events is not mere speculation. Brain surgery sometimes takes place under only a local anesthetic, so that the patient can tell the surgeon what he or she is experiencing as various parts of the brain are probed. This technique was pioneered more than a half-century ago by Dr. Wilder Penfield, who described it vividly in his book *The Excitable Cortex in Conscious Man* (1958). Neurosurgeons have been using Wilder's technique ever since. They know that if you probe in one place, the patient will feel a tingle in her hand; probe in another place, and the patient will smell garlic; and if you probe in still another place, she may hear a song by Guns N' Roses.

Actions can also be induced by electrical stimulation of the brain. Jose Delgado, who did his research at Yale University four decades ago, discovered that by stimulating various regions of the brain he could cause all sorts of bodily motions, including frowning, the opening and closing of the eyes, and movements of the head, arms, legs, and fingers. When he first tried this using cats and monkeys, he noticed that the animals showed no surprise or fear when their bodies moved. Apparently the animals experienced the movements as if they were voluntary. In one instance, stimulating a monkey's brain caused the monkey to get up and walk around. The effect was repeated several times, and each time the animal strolled around, without surprise or discomfort, as if it had just decided to take a walk.

Some philosophers would say that Delgado's procedure did not cause actions, but only bodily movements. Actions involve reasons and decisions, not just motions. But there is more. When Delgado tried his experiment on humans, they were even more compliant than the animals —not only did they act out the movements without surprise or fear, but they also produced reasons for them. In one subject, electrical stimulation of the brain produced "head turning and slow displacement of the body to either side with a well-oriented and apparently normal sequence, as if the patient were looking for something." This was repeated six times over two days, confirming that the stimulation was actually producing the behavior. But the subject, who did not know about the electrical stimulation, considered the activity spontaneous and offered reasons for it. When asked "What are you doing?" he would reply "I am looking for my slippers," "I heard a noise," "I am restless," or "I was looking under the bed."

Are our *decisions* also produced by neural firings? There arc some experimental results about this, too, due to the German scientist H. H. Kornhuber. Suppose you sit quietly, and some time during the next minute you spontaneously move your finger. Subjectively, you may feel quite certain that the decision to move your finger was entirely within your control. But now suppose we attach some electrodes to your scalp and ask you to repeat the action. A technician watching an electroencephalograph would be able to observe a characteristic pattern of brain activity when you move your finger. The brain activity begins up to one-and-a-half seconds before the movement, and *it begins before you make your decision*. So the technician, watching his monitor, knows that you are going to move your finger before you do. He is, in a small way, like Laplace's perfect observer. Kornhuber first performed this experiment in the 1970s.

3. PSYCHOLOGY

It may seem odd that the primary argument against free will appeals to the principles of physics. After all, psychology, not physics, studies human behavior. So we might wonder what psychology has to say. Do psychological theories about human behavior have room for the notion of free will, or do they support Determinism?

Before turning to psychology, however, let me mention some of the ways in which our commonsense understanding of human beings already contains elements favorable to Determinism. Each of us was born to particular parents at a particular time and place, and only a little thought is needed to realize that if those circumstances were changed, we might have turned out different. A young man "chooses" to become a stockbroker—is it a coincidence that his father was a stockbroker? What would he choose if his parents had been missionaries?

We also know that social conditions influence our decisions in ways that we are not aware of but that show up in statistics. Social conditions influence the rates at which people decide to become engineers, move to the West Coast, take up golf, and commit suicide. (In the early 1980s, for example, it was found that the suicide rate in the United States varied directly with the rate of unemployment. Also, a 1986 study showed that teenagers are more likely to commit suicide in the days following nationally televised stories of suicide.) In each case, the individual may seem to be making a free, independent choice. Nonetheless, if the social circumstances are altered, the rate at which people make such decisions changes.

Take a related example: In the United States there are 2 million people currently in prison, and 12 million more are likely to spend time behind bars at some point in their lives. (America has the highest rate of imprisonment in the world.) A disproportionate number of those incarcerated are young Black and Hispanic men. Perhaps some of these men would be in prison no matter what, but clearly some of them would not be there if their social circumstances had been different. Considered as individuals, it may seem that each man "freely decided" to break the law. Perhaps that is right. Still, it is sobering to realize that there are all sorts of people who have never been in jail and think themselves morally superior, but who are merely lucky that social conditions never arose in which they would have acted differently.

When we set aside statistics and try to understand in more detail why specific people behave as they do, we always seem to end up with explanations in which "free choice" plays little part. Darrow's explanation of how Leopold and Loeb came to kill Bobby Franks is one example. For another, consider Eric Rudolph, accused by the FBI of a series of bombings, including an abortion-clinic bombing in Birmingham, Alabama, in January 1998 in which a policeman was killed and a nurse was terribly wounded. Rudolph disappeared into the woods of western North Carolina, where he eluded capture until 2003.

Why would he have done such a thing? Without knowing anything else about him, we might picture Rudolph as a man who hated abortion so much that he was willing to use any means to stop it. That may be correct as far as it goes, but a lot of people oppose abortion without planting bombs. Why would this particular man turn deadly?

According to *Newsweek*, "He is perhaps best understood as the product of a paranoid fringe of white supremacists, religious zealots and government haters. Rudolph's mind and motives are hard to fathom, but extremism seems to run in the family." When he was 13, Eric's father died and his family moved from Miami to rural North Carolina. They lived on a gravel road near a sawmill owner named Tom Branham. Branham, a survivalist who had been arrested on federal weapons charges and who claimed that the government had no authority over him, took an interest in Eric and his brother Daniel and became a substitute father to the boys. His mother, meanwhile, moved to the Missouri Ozarks to join a community of White separatists. By the time he was in the ninth grade, Eric was writing in a class paper that the Holocaust never happened, using as his "research" pamphlets issued by hate groups. As much as we might detest what he became, it is hard to resist the conclusion that the little boy never had a chance.

Whenever we try to understand extraordinary behavior, some such explanation always seems to come to mind. Indeed, such explanations seem necessary. "He just decided to do it" is no explanation at all.

Classical Psychology Although it is not the purpose of psychology to advance any such thesis, Determinism is a hard-to-avoid by-product of the search for a scientific explanation of behavior. As B. F. Skinner put it:

> If we are to use the methods of science in the field of human affairs, we must assume that behavior is lawful and determined. We must expect to discover that what a man does is the result of specifiable conditions and that once these conditions have been discovered, we can anticipate and to some extent determine his actions.

Thus, as the science of psychology has developed, one theory after another has competed for acceptance. But none of them has had much use for "free will."

During the first two-thirds of the twentieth century, Behaviorism vied with Freudian ideas for dominance among psychologists. Freud sought to understand human conduct by identifying the unconscious motives of action. Conscious processes of thought and deliberation are, on his view, only rationalizations for deeper forces hidden within the psyche. Long-forgotten events of infancy and early childhood created in each of us unconscious desires and impulses that control us even as adults. For example, a woman has a series of relationships with abusive men. Each time she rids herself of one, she swears never to make that mistake again; but she does, over and over. How can she keep making the same mistake? She appears to choose freely each time she begins a new relationship, but she does not. She has a masochistic personality, formed as a child when she was battered by an abusive father; now, as an adult, she helplessly reenacts her relationship with her father again and again. She will not be able to break the pattern until she confronts her repressed memories and feelings about her father, possibly after years of psychoanalysis.

The behaviorists would have none of this. On their view, unconscious thoughts play no part in explaining behavior. In fact, no thoughts of any kind enter the picture. Instead, a person's behavior is explained by reference to the process of conditioning that produced it. We tend to repeat behavior for which we are rewarded, and we tend not to repeat behavior when rewards are withheld or when we are punished. Suppose you get an electric shock every time you touch a fence; you will soon stop touching it. Or suppose a child is fed when he says "please" and not fed when he does not say "please." He will soon be saying "please" whenever he is hungry. These are simple examples. The real world is complex, but the principle is the same for all behavior.

B. F. Skinner, a leading behaviorist who taught at Harvard for many years, once explained how the process of conditioning can be demonstrated in the laboratory. First we place a pigeon in a cage for a few days, always feeding it from a small tray that is opened electrically. Then, after the pigeon has become accustomed to eating from the tray, "We select a relatively simple bit of behavior which may be freely and rapidly repeated, and which is easily observed and recorded.... [T]he behavior of raising the head above a given height is convenient." Whenever the pigeon raises its head above the given height, the food tray is opened. "If the experiment is conducted according to specifications,

the result is invariable: we observe an immediate change in the frequency with which the head crosses the line. ... In a minute or two, the bird's posture has changed so that the top of the head seldom falls below the line which we first chose." Of course the pigeon is not aware of why its posture has changed. The alteration in its behavior is just a mechanistic reaction to a stimulus.

The behaviorists argued that all our conduct is like this. In theory, everything we do can be explained as a response to prior conditioning, including our proudest and noblest actions as well as our most shameful ones. (If we cannot actually produce all the explanations, it is only because we do not know enough about the relevant causal chains.) In the same year that Clarence Darrow was defending Leopold and Loeb, John B. Watson, often called the father of Behaviorism, wrote:

> Give me a dozen healthy infants, well-formed, and my own specified world to bring them up in and I'll guarantee to take any one at random and train him to become any type of specialist I might select—doctor, lawyer, artist, merchant, chief, and, yes, even beggar-man and thief, regardless of his talents, penchants, tendencies, abilities, vocations, and race of his ancestors.

Many readers complained that such ideas violate our sense of freedom and dignity. In response, Skinner titled one of his books *Beyond Freedom and Dignity*.

Is "Character" a Matter of Luck? When we reflect on other people's foibles, we sometimes think "There but for the grace of God go I." It is worth pausing over the idea that the moral differences between human beings may be mainly a matter of luck. Some of the most famous experiments in social psychology suggest that any of us might behave badly if we were unlucky enough to be in the wrong circumstances at the wrong time.

In one experiment, Philip Zimbardo and his colleagues set up a simulated prison in the basement of a Stanford University building. Twenty-four volunteers were arbitrarily assigned to be guards or prisoners. The experiment was supposed to last two weeks, but it had to be called off after five days because the "guards," who were given great latitude in how to deal with the "prisoners," behaved so brutally.

In another study, Stanley Milgram asked volunteers to operate a device that administered increasingly severe electric shocks to someone in an adjoining room. The person in the other room was supposed to be "learning" by being punished for giving wrong answers to questions. (He was, in reality, an actor who was only pretending to be shocked.) Milgram was surprised to discover that every single volunteer was willing to continue shocking the other person even when the levels were labeled as extremely dangerous and the other person could be heard crying and begging the volunteer to stop.

When people hear about these experiments, they invariably feel that *they* would not have acted so badly. This feeling is hard to avoid, yet the participants in the experiments were ordinary people like you and me. Zimbardo comments that, after the guards-and-prisoners experiment was over, the "prisoners" insisted that they would not have been so abusive if they had been guards. But, Zimbardo emphasizes, there was no difference between those who were made guards and those who were made prisoners—the assignment was random. The natural conclusion is that the only difference between them was in their circumstances. Apparently, all of us—or at least the great majority of us—have the inner capacity to behave badly if we are in the relevant position.

I will mention one other study that makes a similar point: the "Good Samaritan" experiment of J. M. Darley and C. D. Batson. In Luke's gospel, the Good Samaritan is presented as a model of decent behavior:

"And who is my neighbor?"

Jesus replied, "A man was going down from Jerusalem to Jericho, and he fell among robbers, who stripped him and beat him, and departed, leaving him half dead. Now by chance a priest was going down the road; and when he saw

him he passed by on the other side. So likewise a Levite, when he came to the place and saw him, passed by on the other side.

"But a Samaritan, as he journeyed, came to where he was; and when he saw him, he had compassion and went to him and bound his wounds, pouring on oil and wine; then he set him on his own beast and brought him to an inn, and took care of him. And the next day he took out two dennarii and gave them to the innkeeper, saying, 'Take care of him; and whatever more you spend, I will repay you when I come back.' Which of these three, do you think, proved neighbor to him who fell among the robbers?"

He said, "The one who showed mercy on him."

And Jesus said to him, "Go and do likewise."

The traditional interpretation of this story is that the Samaritan was a man of better moral character—he "had compassion," while the priest and the Levite did not. (Samaritans, incidentally, were people of low standing, while priests and Levites played important roles in the Temple.) Is this right? Darley and Batson decided to investigate the circumstances in which we would be Good Samaritans, using Princeton theology students as their subjects.

In the study, the theology students first filled out forms giving pertinent information about themselves, including their ethical and religious beliefs. Then they were told, one at a time, that they must prepare a short talk on either ethics or job opportunities and deliver it in another building. Some students were told they needed to hurry, while others were told they had plenty of time. It had been arranged that on their way to the other building they would pass by someone slumped in a doorway, obviously in distress. Would they stop to help?

Some stopped and some did not. But it turned out that their ethical and religious views had nothing to do with it, nor did it matter whether they had ethics or job opportunities on their minds. All that mattered was whether they thought they had time to stop. This small change in circumstances made all the difference between exemplary moral conduct and heartlessness.

4. GENES AND BEHAVIOR

Neither Freudianism nor Behaviorism has much influence among psychologists today; both doctrines are now part of the history of psychology. Behaviorism went out of fashion partly because it greatly overrated the part played by the environment in shaping behavior—as it turns out, the human personality is not so malleable as Watson and Skinner thought. Researchers now believe that our genes are equally important in shaping our personalities, and our genes cannot be changed by conditioning—no matter how vigorous.

To what extent do our genes determine the kind of people we are? There is no uncontroversial way of measuring this, nor is there any uncontroversial way of understanding how genes exert their influence. Educated people commonly assume that organisms are products of genes-plus-environment, but that is too simple. One complication is that the picture must also accommodate what Richard Lewontin calls "*developmental noise*, a consequence of random events within cells at the level of molecular interactions." For example, there is considerable variation from cell to cell in the rate and number of molecules synthesized, and this changes the times at which cells divide or migrate. This can affect the development of the organism in unexpected ways. (From the point of view of "free will," of course, it makes little difference whether an aspect of one's personality is influenced by genes or by "developmental noise," since neither is controlled by the individual.) There may be still other factors at work. How do all these elements interact to produce the organism? We have some preliminary ideas but no definite knowledge. This area of science is in its infancy.

Twin Studies Nonetheless, some researchers have tried to devise ways to estimate the influence of genetic factors on human personality. One strategy is to study identical twins, especially those raised in different environments. The idea is that to the extent that such twins are alike their genes are responsible, and to the extent that they are different other factors, such as the environment, are responsible. Such studies may provide at least a rough idea of the extent to which various characteristics are genetically influenced.

At the University of Minnesota there is an ongoing research project, started in 1979, called the Minnesota Study of Twins Reared Apart. When such twins are located, they are invited to the university for a week of tests. The researchers have found that identical twins reared apart nevertheless resemble each other very closely. In some cases, the resemblances are so specific that they look like something out of science fiction.

Among those tested were the "Giggle Sisters," both of whom laughed all the time. Both had the habit of pushing at their noses, which they both called "squidging"; both claimed to have weak ankles as a result of falling when they were 15; both had met their husbands at dances when they were 16; and, although both shunned controversy, both had worked as polling clerks.

There were also brothers named Jim, who drove the same model car and smoked the same brand of cigarettes. Both had elaborate workshops at home where they made miniature furniture as a hobby. Both liked to leave little love notes for their wives lying around the house. They had named their sons James Alan and James Allan.

But perhaps the most remarkable were Jack Yufe and Oskar Stöhr, whose home environments had been as different as could be imagined. One twin was raised in Trinidad by his Jewish father, the other in Germany by his Nazi grandmother. Oskar was in the Hitler youth; Jack served in the Israeli navy. When reunited, both were wearing rectangular wireframe glasses and blue two-pocket shirts with epaulets. Both had small mustaches. Both liked to read magazines from back to front, and both flushed toilets before using them. And both liked the same odd practical joke, startling people by sneezing in elevators.

These are arresting anecdotes, but they are only anecdotes, and we can draw no firm conclusions from them. In the first place, an enormous amount of data would have to be gathered and analyzed before we could know what, if anything, to conclude. Take the blue-shirt-with-epaulets story, for example. How many such shirts were owned by men in the areas where Jack and Oskar lived? What are the chances of two men wearing that shirt on the same day? Or, more generally, in any group of males drawn from the same population, what are the chances that any two selected at random will be dressed similarly? Most important of all, what are the chances that there will be *some* striking similarity between two such men, even if it is not how they are dressed? (Try it: Pick two people at random, and see if you can't come up with some similarities between them.) In any case, critics also object that the anecdotes themselves should be taken with a grain of salt because the stories are likely exaggerated. Also, some of the twins, it turns out, had met one another before they were studied by the Minnesota researchers.

The researchers do not, however, base their conclusions on such anecdotes. Instead, the reared-apart twins are given standard psychological tests for such traits as flexibility, tolerance, conformity, self-control, conscientiousness, openness, toughmindedness, social dominance, alienation, authoritarianism, and aggressiveness. They are found to be remarkably alike in all these ways. They have similar senses of humor and levels of optimism or fearfulness. They share (or lack) similar talents, and they have similar mental illnesses and disabilities. On the basis of such studies, researchers have concluded that the major components of our personalities are about 50 percent due to our genes.

Are Some People Born Bad? The idea that traits like aggressiveness are linked to our genes will come as no surprise to neurologists and clinical psychologists, who have long known about the connection between biology and violence. Experiments with cats have shown that if a small section of the hypothalamus is removed, the animals will turn savage. Humans with head injuries sometimes experience fits of uncontrollable rage. Meanwhile, for people who are

"naturally" prone to violent behavior, effective treatments include lithium and beta-blockers. The genes-neurology-violence connection was further confirmed in 1995 when geneticists discovered that turning off the gene responsible for producing nitric oxide causes normally sociable mice to become vicious. (Nitric oxide is a neurotransmitter in both mice and humans.) So the fact that there is *some* sort of connection between genes, neurology, and violence is well established.

Some researchers believe this tells us something important about crime, although this thought is extremely controversial. The general notion of "crime" is too socially variable to be of much use—fornication, gambling, and heresy, for example, are sometimes counted as "crimes" and sometimes not. But suppose we focus on violence as an element in particular types of criminal behavior, for example, murder, assault, and rape. Is it "in the genes" for some people, but not others, to do violence? The evidence for this is, if not compelling, at least highly suggestive.

Various dispositions, including a propensity to violence, contribute to socially unacceptable behavior. Darrow believed that Leopold and Loeb were "born bad" because they were born without such feelings as pity and sympathy. There is no way for us to know the precise truth about Leopold and Loeb as individuals, but on the more general issue Darrow may have been right. Psychologist Judith Rich Harris puts it like this:

> Though we no longer say that some children are born bad, the facts are such, unfortunately, that a euphemism is needed. Now psychologists say that some children are born with "difficult" temperaments—difficult for their parents to rear, difficult to socialize. I can list for you some of the things that make a child difficult to rear and difficult to socialize: a tendency to be active, impulsive, aggressive, and quick to anger; a tendency to get bored with routine activities and to seek excitement; a tendency to be unafraid of getting hurt; an insensitivity to the feelings of others; and, more often than not, a

muscular build and an IQ a little lower than average. All of these characteristics have a significant genetic component.

It is easy to understand why such thoughts arouse controversy. It sounds like we are being told that some children are beyond help—they are born bad, and bad they'll stay. Moreover, in the context of discussions about crime, such remarks disregard completely the part played by environmental factors such as poverty and racism. Behaviorism, with its upbeat message "Improve the environment, and improve the child," seems more in line with a progressive social outlook.

But the idea that such traits as aggressiveness and insensitivity "have a significant genetic component" does not imply that some children are hopeless or that education and social conditions don't matter. No social scientist believes that genes determine everything. Your genes might incline you, in certain environments, to act in certain ways, but whether you actually behave in those ways will depend on other things. Thus education and the elimination of poverty and racism are still important. The research about genes only helps explain why virtue comes easier to some people than to others.

To avoid such misunderstandings, social scientists often take pains to point out that they are not endorsing Determinism. Anthropologist John Townsend writes:

> Many misinterpret biosocial explanations. They assume that such explanations are deterministic: that we are saying human beings are like animals, that we are "wired" for certain behaviors, and that these instinctive behaviors will emerge whether we want them to or not.... All of these assumptions are false. As human beings we have inherited certain predispositions from our evolutionary past, but that does not mean we have to act on them.

Despite such reassurances, however, there remain at least two reasons to worry about what this means for our freedom.

First, even if we are not "wired for certain behaviors," we are being told something deeply disturbing. It is being said that we come equipped by nature with deep-seated desires that we can resist only with difficulty. If, in some people, these desires prove irresistible, it is hard to see this as their fault. Moreover, these desires will be with us forever, or as close to forever as to make no difference, and they play a significant role in explaining our behavior. This may not be Determinism in the strict sense, but it looks like something suspiciously close to it.

Second, we need an explanation for why some people, but not others, are able to resist the impulses that nature has given them. Why do some people end up murderers, while others do not? Is it a matter of choice? Or is there some further aspect of their situations that makes the difference? Perhaps where biology leaves off, the environment takes over. One man, who was brought up in a certain way, is violent; another man, who was brought up differently, is not. Thus, even though genetic explanations are not deterministic by themselves, when we combine them with other plausible ideas, we end up with an overall picture in which "free will" plays a vanishingly small part. To say that biology does not determine us, because the environment also plays a part, is little consolation.

Conclusion In sum, our situation seems to be this. Psychologists and other investigators have developed a number of ideas that help explain human behavior. Each is supported by impressive evidence, and each seems to be at least part of the truth. We don't yet know how to combine these ideas into a comprehensive account. Nonetheless, as far as free will is concerned, the overall trend is not encouraging. Each new discovery chips away a bit more of our confidence. The more we learn about the sources of human conduct, the less room there seems to be for the idea of free choice.

2.2 Why We Have No Free Will and Can Live Without It

DEREK PEREBOOM

Derk Pereboom teaches philosophy at Cornell University.

1. OUTLINE OF HARD INCOMPATIBILISM

Baruch Spinoza (1677/1985: 440–4, 483–4, 496–7) maintained that due to certain general facts about the nature of the universe, we human beings do not have the sort of free will required for being morally responsible, that is, for being blameworthy just because we intentionally do wrong and praiseworthy just because we intentionally act rightly. I agree. More exactly, he argues that it is because causal determinism is true that we lack this sort of free will; he is thus a *hard determinist*. By contrast, the position I defend is agnostic about causal determinism. I contend, like Spinoza, that we would not have the sort of free will required for moral responsibility if causal determinism were true, but also that indeterministic theories do not significantly improve its prospects. Consequently, we need to take seriously the verdict that we lack the sort of free will required for moral responsibility. I call the resulting skeptical view *hard incompatibilism*. In addition, I argue that a conception of life without this kind of free will need not exclude morality or our sense of meaning in life, and in some respects it could even be beneficial.

2. AGAINST COMPATIBILISM

The case for hard incompatibilism involves arguing against two competing positions. The first of these is *compatibilism*, which claims that free will of the type required for moral responsibility is compatible with determinism. Compatibilists typically maintain, in addition, that we do in fact have this sort of free will. The second is *libertarianism*, which contends that although the sort of free will required for moral responsibility is not compatible with determinism, it turns out that determinism is false, and we do have this kind of free will.

Compatibilists typically attempt to formulate conditions on agency intended to provide an account of what it is to be morally responsible for an action. These conditions are compatibilist in that they allow for an agent to be morally responsible for an action even when she is causally determined to act as she does. For instance, David Hume and his followers specify that morally responsible action be caused by desires that flow from the agent's "durable and constant" character, and that the agent not be constrained to act, at least in the sense that the action not result from an irresistible desire (Hume 1739/1978: 319–412). Harry Frankfurt proposes that moral responsibility requires that the agent have endorsed and produced her will to perform the action in the right way. More specifically, she must have a second-order desire—that is, a desire to have a particular desire—to will to perform it, and her will must be her will because she has this second-order desire (Frankfurt 1971). John Fischer argues that morally responsible action must result from a rational consideration of the reasons at issue; among other things, the agent must be receptive to the reasons present in a situation, and she must be responsive to them to the degree that in at least some situations in which the reasons are different, she would have done otherwise (Fischer 1994). Finally, Jay Wallace proposes that moral responsibility requires that the agent have the general ability to grasp, apply, and regulate her behavior by moral reasons (Wallace 1994). Each of these compatibilists intends for his conditions to be sufficient for an agent's moral responsibility when they are supplemented by some fairly uncontroversial additional necessary conditions, such as the provision that the agent understands that killing is morally wrong.

In my view, the best type of challenge to the compatibilist begins with the intuition that if someone is causally determined to act by other agents, for example, by scientists who manipulate her brain, then she is not morally responsible for that action. This intuition remains strong even if she meets the compatibilist conditions on moral responsibility just canvassed. The following "four-case argument" first of all develops examples of actions that involve such manipulation, in which these compatibilist conditions on moral responsibility are satisfied. Manipulation cases, taken individually, indicate that it is possible for an agent not to be morally responsible even if the compatibilist conditions are satisfied, and that as a result these conditions are inadequate. But the argument has additional force, by way of setting out three such cases, each progressively more like a fourth scenario which the compatibilist would regard as realistic, in which the action is causally determined in a natural way. An additional challenge for the compatibilist is to point out a relevant difference between any two adjacent cases that would show why the agent might be morally responsible in the later example but not in the earlier one. I argue that this can't be done. So I contend that the agent's non-responsibility generalizes from the first two manipulation examples to the ordinary case.

In each of the four cases, Professor Plum decides to kill Ms. White for the sake of some personal advantage, and succeeds in doing so. We design the cases so that his act of murder conforms to the prominent compatibilist conditions. Plum's action meets the Humean conditions, since for him purely selfish reasons typically weigh heavily—much too heavily as judged from the moral point of view, while in addition the desire that motivates him to act is nevertheless not irresistible for him, and in this sense he is not constrained to act. It fits the condition proposed by Frankfurt: Plum's effective desire (i.e., his will) to murder White conforms appropriately to his second-order desires for which effective desires he will have. That is, he not only wills to murder her, but he also wants to will to do so. The action also satisfies the reasons-responsiveness condition advocated by Fischer: Plum's desires are modified by, and some of them arise from, his rational consideration of the reasons he has, and if he knew that the bad consequences for himself that would result from killing White would be much more severe than they are actually likely to be, he would have refrained from killing her for this reason. In addition, this action meets the condition advanced by Wallace: Plum retains general ability to grasp, apply, and regulate his behavior by moral reasons. When egoistic reasons that count against acting morally are relatively weak, he will usually regulate his behavior by moral reasons instead. This ability provides him with the capacity to revise and develop his moral character over time, as Alfred Mele (1995, 2006) requires. Now, supposing that causal determinism is true, is it plausible that Plum is morally responsible for his action?

Each of the four cases features different ways in which Plum's murder of White might be causally determined by factors beyond his control.

Case 1: A team of neuroscientists is able to manipulate Professor Plum's mental state at any moment through the use of radio-like technology. In this case, they do so by pressing a button just before he begins to reason about his situation. This causes Plum's reasoning process to be egoistic, which the neuroscientists know will deterministically result in his decision to kill White. Plum does not think and act contrary to character since his reasoning processes are not infrequently egoistic. His effective first-order desire to kill White conforms to his second-order desires. The process of deliberation from which his action results is reasons-responsive; in particular, this type of process would have resulted in his refraining from killing White in some situations in which the reasons were different. Still, his reasoning is not in general exclusively egoistic, since he often regulates his behavior by moral reasons, especially when the egoistic reasons are relatively weak. He is also not constrained, in the sense that he does not act because of an irresistible desire—the neuroscientists do not induce a desire of this kind.

In Case 1, Plum's action satisfies all the compatibilist conditions we just examined. But intuitively, he is not morally responsible for the murder, because his action is causally determined by what the neuroscientists do, which is beyond his control. Consequently, it would seem that these compatibilist conditions are not sufficient for moral responsibility—even if all taken together.

A compatibilist might resist this conclusion by arguing that although in Case 1 the process resulting in the action satisfies all of the prominent compatibilist conditions, yet Plum's relevant states are directly produced by the manipulators at the time of the action—he is locally manipulated—and this is the aspect of the story that undermines his moral responsibility. In reply, if the neuroscientists did all of their manipulating during one time interval and, after some length of time, the relevant states were produced in him, would he only then be morally responsible? It is my sense that such a time lag, all by itself, would make no difference to whether an agent is responsible.

So let us now consider a scenario in which the manipulation takes place long before the action:

> Case 2: Plum is like an ordinary human being, except that neuroscientists have programmed him at the beginning of his life so that his reasoning is frequently but not always egoistic (as in Case 1), with the consequence that in the particular circumstances in which he now finds himself, he is causally determined to engage in the egoistic reasons-responsive process of deliberation and to have the set of first- and second-order desires that result in his decision to kill White. Plum has the general ability to regulate his behavior by moral reasons, but in his

circumstances, due to the egoistic character of his reasoning, he is causally determined to make his decision. At the same time, he does not act because of an irresistible desire.

Here again, although Plum meets each of the compatibilist conditions, it is intuitive that he is not morally responsible. Thus Case 2 also shows that the prominent compatibilist conditions, either separately or in conjunction, are not sufficient for moral responsibility. Again, it would seem unprincipled to claim that here, by contrast with Case 1, Plum is morally responsible because the length of time between the programming and the action is now great enough. Here also it would seem that he is not morally responsible because he is causally determined to decide and act by forces beyond his control.

Imagine next a scenario more similar yet to an ordinary situation:

> Case 3: Plum is an ordinary human being, except that he was causally determined by the rigorous training practices of his household and community in such a way that his reasoning processes are often but not exclusively rationally egoistic (as in Cases 1 and 2). This training took place when he was too young to have the ability to prevent or alter the practices that determined this aspect of his character. This training, together with his particular current circumstances, causally determines him to engage in the egoistic reasons-responsive process of deliberation and to have the first- and second-order desires that result in his decision to kill White. Plum has the general ability to regulate his behavior by moral reasons, but in his circumstances, due to the egoistic nature of his reasoning processing, he is causally determined make his decision. Here again his action is not due to an irresistible desire.

If a compatibilist wishes to contend that Plum is morally responsible in Case 3, he needs to point to a feature of these circumstances that would explain why he is morally responsible here but not in Case 2. But it seems that there is no such feature. In each of these examples, Plum meets all the prominent compatibilist conditions for morally responsible action, so a divergence in judgment about moral responsibility between these examples will not be supported by a difference in whether these conditions are satisfied. Causal determination by factors beyond his control most plausibly explains the absence of moral responsibility in Case 2, and we are constrained to conclude that Plum is not morally responsible in Case 3 for the same reason.

Thus it appears that Plum's exemption from responsibility in Cases 1 and 2 generalizes to the nearer-to-normal Case 3. Does it generalize all the way to the ordinary case?

> Case 4: Physicalist determinism is true—everything in the universe is physical, and everything that happens is causally determined by virtue of the past states of the universe in conjunction with the laws of nature. Plum is an ordinary human being, raised in normal circumstances, and again his reasoning processes are frequently but not exclusively egoistic (as in Cases 1–3). His decision to kill White results from his reasons-responsive process of deliberation, and he has the specified first- and second-order desires. Again, he has the general ability to grasp, apply, and regulate his behavior by moral reasons, and his action is not due to an irresistible desire.

Given that we need to deny moral responsibility in Case 3, could Plum be responsible in this more ordinary case? There would seem to be no differences between Case 3 and Case 4 that could serve to justify the claim that Plum is not responsible in Case 3 but is in Case 4. One distinguishing feature of Case 4 is that the causal determination of Plum's crime is not brought about by other agents (Lycan 1997: 117–8). However, the claim that this is a relevant difference is implausible. Imagine a further example that is exactly the same as, say, Case 1 or Case 2, except that Plum's states are induced by a spontaneously generated machine—a machine that has no intelligent designer. Here also Plum would not be morally responsible.

The best explanation for the intuition that Plum is not morally responsible in the first three cases is that his action is produced by a deterministic causal process that traces back to factors beyond his control. Because his action is also causally determined in this way in Case 4, we should conclude that here again he is not morally responsible. So by this argument, Plum's non-responsibility in Case 1 generalizes to non-responsibility in Case 4. We should conclude that if an action results from any deterministic causal process that traces back to factors beyond the agent's control, then she will lack the control required to be morally responsible for it.

3. EVENT-CAUSAL LIBERTARIANISM AND THE LUCK OBJECTION

Let us now consider libertarianism, the variety of incompatibilism that claims that we do have the sort of free will required for moral responsibility. There are two major types of libertarianism, the event-causal and the agent-causal versions. In event-causal libertarianism, actions are caused solely by events—events such as *Joe's desiring at noon to have lunch*, or *Mary's believing today that if she sells her stock tomorrow she will maximize her gains*. Now it is often supposed that all causation in the physical world is by events, and not by things, such as stars, machines, and agents, which we call *substances*. Although one might say, for example, that a bomb—a substance—caused damage to the building, when we want to speak more accurately, we say instead that *the bomb's exploding at a certain time*—an event—caused the damage. So if we think carefully about what it is in the physical world that causes effects, it turns out to be events, not substances. In solidarity with this position, event-causal libertarianism maintains that all actions are caused solely by events, and further, that some type of indeterminacy in the production of actions by appropriate events is the decisive requirement for moral responsibility (Kane 1996; Ekstrom 2000).

Critics of libertarianism have contended that if actions are not causally determined, agents cannot be morally responsible for them. Its classical presentation of this objection is found in Hume's *Treatise of Human Nature*, and it has become known as the "luck objection" (Hume 1739/1978: 411–2). The key idea is that if, holding fixed all of the conditions that precede an action, the action could either occur or not, then whether it does occur is a matter of chance or luck, and the agent cannot be morally responsible for it (Hume 1739/1978: 411–2).

I contend that event-causal libertarianism is undermined by the luck objection. Intuitively, for an agent to be morally responsible for a decision, she must exercise a certain type and degree of control in making that decision. In an event-causal libertarian picture, the relevant causal conditions prior to a decision—events that involve the agent—leave it open whether this decision will occur, and the agent has no further causal role in determining whether it in fact does. Accordingly, whether the decision occurs or not is in this sense a matter of luck, and the agent lacks the control required for being morally responsible for it.

To illustrate, consider Robert Kane's example of a businesswoman—let's call her Anne—who has a choice between stopping to help out an assault victim, as a result of which she would be late for an important meeting, or not stopping, which would allow her to make it to a meeting on time (Kane 1996). For simplicity, suppose the causally relevant events that immediately precede the action are, against stopping, *Anne's desiring not make her boss angry*, and *Anne's believing that if she is late for the meeting her boss will be angry with her*; and for stopping, *Anne's desiring to help people in trouble*, and *Anne's belief that she can help the assault victim*. Imagine that the motivational force of each of these pairs of prior events is for her about the same. On an event-causal libertarian view, with the causal influence of these events already in place, both Anne's deciding to stop and her not deciding to stop remain significantly probable outcomes. Suppose that she in fact decides to stop. There is nothing else about Anne that can settle whether the decision to stop occurs, because in this theory her role in producing a decision is exhausted by these prior events. If nothing about Anne can settle whether the decision occurs, then she will not have the control required for moral responsibility for it. This

might be called *the problem of the disappearing agent*. On an event-causal libertarian theory, no provision allows the agent to have the right sort of control over whether the decision occurs, and for this reason she lacks the control required for moral responsibility for it.

4. AGENT-CAUSAL LIBERTARIANISM AND AN OBJECTION FROM OUR BEST PHYSICAL THEORIES

The agent-causal libertarian's solution to the problem of the disappearing agent is to reintroduce the agent as a cause, this time not merely as involved in events, but rather fundamentally as a substance (Chisholm 1976; O'Connor 2000; Clarke 2003). More exactly, agent-causal libertarians claim that we possess a special causal power—a power for an agent, fundamentally as a substance, to cause a decision without being causally determined to do so. The proposal is that if Anne had this power, by exercising it she would be able to settle which of the two competing decisions occurs—both of which remain as open possibilities given only the causal role of the events. In this way she could be morally responsible for her decision.

But can agent-causal libertarianism be reconciled with what we would expect given our best physical theories? If the agent-causal position is true, then when an agent makes a free decision, she causes the decision without being causally determined to do so. On the path to action that results from this undetermined decision, changes in the physical world, for example in the agent's brain or some other part of her body, are produced. But if the physical world were generally governed by deterministic laws, it seems that here we would encounter divergences from these laws. For the changes in the physical world that result from the undetermined decision would themselves not be causally determined, and they would thus not be governed by the deterministic laws. One might object that it is possible that the physical changes that result from every free decision just happen to dovetail with what could in principle be predicted on the basis of the deterministic laws, so nothing actually happens that diverges from these laws (Kant 1781/1997: 532–46). But this proposal would seem to involve coincidences too wild to be believed. For this reason, agent-causal libertarianism is not plausibly reconciled with the physical world's being governed by deterministic laws.

On the standard interpretation of quantum mechanics, however, the physical world is not in fact deterministic, but is rather governed by probabilistic statistical laws. Some philosophers have defended the claim that agent-causal libertarianism can be reconciled with physical laws of this sort (Clarke 2003: 181). However, wild coincidences would also arise on this suggestion. Consider the class of possible actions each of which has a physical component whose antecedent probability of occurring is approximately 0.32. It would not violate the statistical laws in the sense of being logically incompatible with them if, for a large number of instances, the physical components in this class were not actually realized close to 32% of the time. Rather, the force of the statistical law is that for a large number of instances it is correct to *expect* physical components in this class to be realized close to 32% of the time. Are free choices on the agent-causal libertarian model compatible with what the statistical law leads us to expect about them? If they were, then for a large enough number of instances the possible actions in our class would almost certainly be freely chosen close to 32% of the time. But if the occurrence of these physical components were settled by the choices of agent-causes, then their actually being chosen close to 32% of the time would amount to a wild coincidence. The proposal that agent-caused free choices do not diverge from what the statistical laws predict for the physical components of our actions would run so sharply counter to what we would expect as to make it incredible.

At this point, the libertarian might propose that there actually do exist divergences from the probabilities that we would expect without the presence of agent-causes, and that these divergences are to

be found at the interface between the agent-cause and that which it directly affects—an interface which is likely to be found in the brain. The problem for this proposal, however, is that we have no evidence that such divergences occur. This difficulty, all by itself, provides a strong reason to reject this approach.

It is sometimes claimed that our experience of deliberating and choosing provides us with good evidence for the broader thesis that we have libertarian free will. Perhaps, then, if we could have libertarian free will only if we were agent causes, then this evidence from our experience would count in favor of the existence of divergences from what our best physical theories predict. But Spinoza remarks, "experience itself, no less than reason, teaches that men believe themselves free because they are conscious of their own actions, and ignorant of the causes by which they are determined ..." (Spinoza 1677/1985: 496). Spinoza maintains that we believe our decisions are free only because we are ignorant of their causes. The lesson to draw from Spinoza here is that the evidence from experience that is apt to generate a belief that we have libertarian free will would be just the same if decisions were instead causally determined and we were ignorant of enough of their causes. For this reason, this evidence that experience provides for our having libertarian free will is not especially impressive. This consideration counts strongly against the proposal that such evidence gives us reason to believe that the divergences in question exist.

On the other hand, nothing we've said conclusively rules out the claim that because we are agent causes, there exist such divergences. We do not have a complete understanding of the human neural system, and it may turn out that some human neural structures are significantly different from anything else in nature we understand, and that they serve to ground agent causation. This approach may be the best one for libertarians to pursue. But at this point we have no evidence that it will turn out to be correct.

Thus each of the two versions of libertarianism faces serious difficulties. Earlier, we saw that compatibilism is vulnerable to an argument from manipulation cases. The position that remains is hard incompatibilism, which denies that we have the sort of free will required for moral responsibility. The concern for this skeptical view is not, I think, that there is significant empirical evidence that it is false, or that there is a good argument that it is somehow incoherent, and false for that reason. Rather, the questions it faces are practical: What would life be like if we believed it was true? Is this a sort of life that we can tolerate?

5. HARD INCOMPATIBILISM AND WRONGDOING

Accepting this skeptical view about the sort of free will required for moral responsibility demands giving up our ordinary view of ourselves as blameworthy for immoral actions and praiseworthy for actions that are morally exemplary. At this point one might object that this would have very harmful consequences, perhaps so harmful that thinking and acting as if hard incompatibilism is true is not a feasible option. Thus even if the claim that we are morally responsible turns out to be false, there may yet be weighty practical reasons to believe that we are, or at least to treat people as if they were.

For instance, one might think that if we gave up the belief that people are blameworthy, we could no longer legitimately judge any actions as wrong or even bad, or as right or good. But this seems mistaken. Even if we came to believe that some perpetrator of genocide was not morally responsible because of some degenerative brain disease he had, we would still maintain that his actions were morally wrong, and that it was extremely bad that he acted as he did. So, in general, denying blameworthiness would not at the same time threaten judgments of wrongness or badness, and, likewise, denying praiseworthiness would not undermine assessments of rightness or goodness.

Perhaps treating wrongdoers as blameworthy is often required for effective moral education and improvement. If we resolved never to treat people as blameworthy, one might fear that

we would be left with insufficient leverage to reform immoral behavior. Still, this option would have us treat people as blameworthy—by, for example, expressing anger toward them because of what they have done—when they do not deserve it, which would seem prima facie morally wrong. If people are not morally responsible for immoral behavior, treating them as if they were would seem to be unfair. However, it is possible to achieve moral reform by methods that would not be threatened by this sort of unfairness, and in ordinary situations such practices could arguably be as successful as those that presuppose moral responsibility. Instead of treating people as if they deserve blame, the hard incompatibilist can turn to moral admonition and encouragement, which presuppose only that the offender has done wrong. These methods can effectively communicate a sense of right and wrong and they can issue in salutary reform.

But does this position have resources adequate for contending with criminal behavior? Here it would appear to be at a disadvantage, and if so, practical considerations might yield strong reasons to treat criminals as if they were morally responsible. First of all, if the free will skeptic is right, a retributivist justification for criminal punishment would be unavailable, for it asserts that the criminal deserves pain or deprivation just for committing the crime, while hard incompatibilism denies this claim. And retributivism is one of the most naturally compelling ways to justify criminal punishment.

By contrast, a theory that justifies criminal punishment on the ground that punishment educates criminals morally is not threatened by hard incompatibilism specifically. However, we lack significant empirical evidence that punishing criminals brings about moral education, and without such evidence, it would be wrong to punish them in order to achieve this goal. In general, it is wrong to harm a person for the sake of realizing some good in the absence of impressive evidence that the harm will produce the good. Moreover, even if we had impressive evidence that punishment was effective in morally educating criminals, we should prefer non-punitive ways of achieving this result, if they are available—whether or not criminals are morally responsible.

Deterrence theories have it that punishing criminals is justified for the reason that it deters future crime. The two most-discussed deterrence theories, the utilitarian version and the one that grounds the right to punish on the right to self-defense, are not undermined by hard incompatibilism per se. Still, they are questionable on other grounds. The utilitarian theory, which claims that punishment is justified because it maximizes utility (i.e., the quantity of happiness or pleasure minus the quantity of unhappiness or pain), faces well-known challenges. It would seem at times to require punishing the innocent when doing so would maximize utility; in certain situations it would appear to prescribe punishment that is unduly severe; and it would authorize harming people merely as means to the well-being, in this case the safety, of others. The sort of deterrence theory that grounds the right to punish in the right of individuals to defend themselves against immediate threats (Farrell 1985: 38–60) is also objectionable. For when a criminal is sentenced to punishment he is most often not an immediate threat to anyone, since he is then in the custody of the law, and this fact about his circumstances distinguishes him from those who can legitimately be harmed on the basis the right of self-defense.

There is, however, a resilient theory of crime prevention that is consistent with hard incompatibilism. This view draws an analogy between the treatment of criminals and the treatment of carriers of dangerous diseases. Ferdinand Schoeman (1979) argues that if we have the right to quarantine carriers of serious communicable diseases to protect people, then for the same reason we also have the right to isolate the criminally dangerous. Notice that quarantining a person can be justified when she is not morally responsible for being dangerous to others. If a child is infected with a deadly contagious virus that was transmitted to her before she was born, quarantine can still be legitimate. Now imagine that a serial killer poses a grave danger to a community.

Even if he is not morally responsible for his crimes (say because no one is ever morally responsible), it would be as legitimate to isolate him as it is to quarantine a non-responsible carrier of a serious communicable disease.

Clearly, it would be morally wrong to treat carriers of communicable diseases more severely than is required to protect people from the resulting threat. Similarly, it would be wrong to treat criminals more harshly than is required to protect society against the danger posed by them. Furthermore, just as it would be wrong to quarantine someone whose disease was less than severe, so it would be wrong to lock someone up whose crime was less than severe. In addition, I suspect that a theory modeled on quarantine would not justify measures of the sort whose legitimacy is most in doubt, such as the death penalty or confinement in the worst prisons we have. Moreover, it would demand a degree of concern for the rehabilitation and well-being of the criminal that would alter much of current practice. Just as society must seek to cure the diseased it quarantines, so it would be required to try to rehabilitate the criminals it detains. In addition, if a criminal cannot be rehabilitated, and if protection of society demands his indefinite confinement, there would be no justification for making his life more miserable than needed to guard against the danger he poses.

6. MEANING IN LIFE

If hard incompatibilism is true, could we legitimately retain a sense of achievement for what makes our lives fulfilled, happy, satisfactory, or worthwhile, and hold on to our hopes for making these sorts of achievements in our lives (Honderich 1988)? It might be argued that if hard incompatibilism is true, there can be no genuine achievements, for an agent cannot have an achievement for which she is not also praiseworthy. However, achievement is not as closely connected to praiseworthiness as this objection supposes. If an agent hopes to achieve success in some project, and if she accomplishes what she hoped for, intuitively this outcome would be an achievement of hers even if she is not praiseworthy for it—although at the same time the sense in which it is her achievement may be diminished. For example, if someone hopes that her efforts as a teacher will result in well-educated children, and they do, there remains a clear sense in which she has achieved what she hoped for—even if it turns out she is not praiseworthy for anything she does.

One might think that hard incompatibilism would instill an attitude of resignation to whatever the future holds in store, and would thereby undermine any hope or motivation for achievement. But this isn't clearly right. Even if what we know about our behavioral dispositions and our environment gives us reason to believe that our futures will turn out in a particular way, it can often be reasonable to hope that they will turn out differently. For this to be so, it may sometimes be important that we lack complete knowledge of our dispositions and environmental conditions. For instance, imagine that someone aspires to become a successful politician, but he is concerned that his fear of public speaking will get in the way. He does not know whether this fear will in fact frustrate his ambition, since it is open for him that he will overcome this problem, perhaps due to a disposition for resolute self-discipline in transcending obstacles of this sort. As a result, he might reasonably hope that he will get over his fear and succeed in his ambition. Given hard incompatibilism, if he in fact does overcome his problem and succeeds in political life, this will not be an achievement of his in as robust a sense as we might naturally suppose, but it will be his achievement in a substantial sense nonetheless.

Still, with Saul Smilansky one might contend that although determinism leaves room for a limited foundation of the sense of self-worth that derives from achievement or virtue, the hard incompatibilist's perspective can nevertheless be "extremely damaging to our view of ourselves, to our sense of achievement, worth, and self-respect," especially when it comes to achievement in the formation of one's own moral

character. Because of this Smilansky thinks that it would be best for us to foster the illusion that we have free will (Smilansky 2000). Now I agree that there is a kind of self-respect that presupposes an incompatibilist foundation, and that it would be undercut if free will skepticism is true. I question, however, whether Smilanksy is right about how damaging it would be for us to give up this sort of self-respect, and whether his appeal to illusion is required.

First, note that our sense of self-worth—our sense that we have value and that our lives are worth living—is to a non-trivial extent due to features not produced by our will, let alone by free will. People place great value on natural beauty, native athletic ability, and intelligence, none of which have their source in our volition. To be sure, we also value efforts that are voluntary in the sense that they are willed by us—in productive work and altruistic behavior, and indeed, in the formation of moral character. However, does it matter very much to us that these voluntary efforts are also *freely* willed? Perhaps we should not overestimate how much we care.

Consider how someone comes to have a good moral character. It is not implausible that it is formed to a significant degree as a result of upbringing, and moreover, the belief that this is so is widespread. Parents typically regard themselves as having failed in raising their children if they turn out with immoral dispositions, and parents often take great care to bring their children up to prevent such a result. Accordingly, people often come to believe that they have the good moral character they do largely because they were raised with love and skill. But those who come to believe this about themselves seldom experience dismay because of it. People tend not to become dispirited upon coming to understand that their good moral character is not their own doing, and that they do not deserve a great deal of praise or respect for it. By contrast, they often come to feel more fortunate and thankful. Suppose, however, that there are some who would be overcome with dismay. Would it be justified or even desirable for them to foster the illusion that they nevertheless deserve praise and respect for producing their moral character? I suspect that most would eventually be able to accept the truth without incurring much loss. All of this, I think, would also hold for those who come to believe that they do not deserve praise and respect for producing their moral character because they are not, in general, morally responsible.

7. EMOTIONS, REACTIVE ATTITUDES, AND PERSONAL RELATIONSHIPS

Peter Strawson (1962) argues that the justification for judgments of blameworthiness and praiseworthiness has its foundation in what he calls the *reactive attitudes*, reactions to how people voluntarily behave—attitudes such as moral resentment, guilt, gratitude, forgiveness, and love. Moreover, because moral responsibility has this kind of foundation, the truth or falsity of determinism is irrelevant to whether we are justified in regarding agents as morally responsible. This is because these reactive attitudes are required for the kinds of interpersonal relationships that make our lives meaningful, and so even if we could give up the reactive attitudes we would never have sufficient practical reason to do so. Strawson believes that it is in fact psychologically impossible for us to give up the reactive attitudes altogether, but in a limited range of cases we can adopt what he calls the "objective attitude," a cold and calculating stance towards others, which he describes as follows:

> To adopt the objective attitude to another human being is to see him, perhaps, as an object of social policy; as a subject for what, in a wide range of sense, might be called treatment; as something certainly to be taken account, perhaps precautionary account, of; to be managed or handled or cured or trained; perhaps simply to be avoided.... The objective attitude may be emotionally toned in many ways: it may include repulsion or fear, it may include pity or love, though not all kinds of love. But it cannot include the range of reactive feelings and attitudes which belong to involvement or participation with others in interpersonal human relationships; it cannot include resentment, gratitude, forgiveness, anger, or the sort of love which two adults can sometimes be said to feel reciprocally, for each other.

If determinism did imperil the reactive attitudes, and we were able to relinquish them, Strawson suggests that we would face the prospect of adopting this objective attitude toward everyone, as a result of which our interpersonal relationships would be damaged. Since we have extremely good practical reasons for maintaining these relationships, we would never have sufficient practical reason to adopt the objective attitude in most cases, and hence we would never have sufficient reason to give up our reactive attitudes, and thus to stop regarding people as morally responsible.

If we persistently maintained an objective attitude toward others, I agree that our relationships would be threatened. However, I deny that it would be appropriate to adopt this stance if we came to believe the skeptical view about free will. Certain reactive attitudes would be undercut, because some of them, such as moral resentment and indignation, would have the false presupposition that the person who is the object of the attitude is morally responsible. But I claim that the reactive attitudes that we would want to retain either are not threatened by hard incompatibilism in this way, or else have analogues or aspects that would not have false presuppositions. The attitudes that would survive do not amount to the objective attitude, and they would be sufficient to sustain good human relationships.

It is plausible that to a certain degree moral resentment and indignation are beyond our power to affect. Even supposing that a free will skeptic is thoroughly committed to morality and rationality, and that she is admirably in control of her emotions, she might still be unable to eliminate these attitudes. Instead we might expect people to be morally resentful in certain circumstances, and we would not regard them as morally responsible for it. But we also have the ability to prevent, temper, and sometimes to dispel moral resentment, and given a belief in hard incompatibilism, we might attempt such measures for the sake of morality and rationality. Modifications of this sort, assisted by the skeptical conviction, might well be good for interpersonal relationships.

Forgiveness might appear to presuppose that the person being forgiven is blameworthy, and if this is so, this attitude would also be undercut. But certain key features of forgiveness would not be endangered, and they are sufficient to sustain the role forgiveness has in relationships. Suppose a friend repeatedly mistreats you, and because of this you decide to end your relationship with him. However, he then apologizes to you, indicating his recognition that his actions were wrong, his wish that he had not mistreated you, and his commitment to refrain from the immoral behavior. Because of this you decide not to end the friendship. In this case, the feature of forgiveness that is consistent with the skeptical view is the willingness to cease to regard past immoral behavior as a reason to weaken or end a relationship. The aspect of forgiveness that would be undermined is the willingness to disregard the friend's blameworthiness. But since she has given up the belief that we are morally responsible, the hard incompatibilist no longer needs a willingness to disregard blameworthiness to sustain good relationships.

One might object that hard incompatibilism threatens the self-directed attitudes of guilt and repentance, and that this would be especially bad for relationships. In the absence of guilt and repentance, we would not only be incapable of restoring relationships damaged because we have done wrong, but we would also be kept from restoring our moral integrity. For without the attitudes of guilt and repentance, we would lack the psychological mechanisms that can play these roles. But note first that it is because guilt essentially involves a belief that one is blameworthy that this attitude would be threatened by hard incompatibilism. It is for this reason that repentance would also seem to be (indirectly) threatened, for feeling guilty would appear to

be required to motivate repentance. Imagine, however, that you have acted immorally; still because you endorse the skeptical view, you deny that you are blameworthy. Instead, you acknowledge that you were the agent of wrongdoing, you feel sorrow on account of having done wrong, and you deeply regret having acted as you did. In addition, because you are committed to doing what is right and to your own moral improvement, you resolve not to act in this way again. None of these measures are jeopardized by hard incompatibilism.

Gratitude would appear to presuppose that the person to whom one is grateful is morally responsible for a beneficial act, as a result of which this attitude would also be endangered. But as in the case of forgiveness, certain aspects of this attitude would be unaffected, and these aspects can provide what is needed for good relationships. Gratitude involves, first of all, being thankful toward a person who has acted beneficially. It is true that being thankful toward someone usually involves the belief that she is praiseworthy for some action. Still, one can also be thankful to a small child for some kindness, without believing that she is morally responsible for it. This aspect of thankfulness could be retained even without the presupposition of praiseworthiness. Typically gratitude also involves joy as a response to what someone has done. But no feature of hard incompatibilism undermines being joyful and expressing joy when others are, for example, considerate or generous in one's behalf. Expressing joy can bring about the sense of harmony and goodwill often produced by gratitude, and thus here the skeptical position is not at a disadvantage.

Would the kind of love that mature adults have for each other in good relationships be imperiled, as Strawson's line of argument suggests? Consider first whether for loving someone it is important that the person who is loved has and exercises free will in the sense required for moral responsibility. Parents love their children rarely, if ever, for the reason that they possess this sort of free will, or decide to do what is right by free will, or deserve to be loved due to freely-willed choices.

Moreover, when adults love each other, it is also very seldom, if at all, for these sorts of reasons. Besides moral character and behavior, features such as intelligence, appearance, style, and resemblance to others in one's personal history all might play a part. Suppose morally admirable qualities are particularly important in occasioning, enriching, and maintaining love. Even if there is an aspect of love that we conceive as a deserved response to morally admirable qualities, it is unlikely that love would even be diminished if we came to believe that these qualities are not produced or sustained by freely-willed decisions. Such admirable qualities are loveable whether or not we deserve praise for having them.

One might contend that we want to be freely loved by others—to be loved by them as a result of their free will. Against this, the love parents have for their children typically comes about independently of the parents' will altogether, and we don't think that love of this sort is deficient. Robert Kane recognizes this fact about parents' love, and he acknowledges that romantic love is similar in this respect. However, he maintains that there is a kind of love we very much want that would not exist if all love were causally determined by factors beyond our control (Kane 1996: 88). The plausibility of Kane's claim might be enhanced by reflecting on how you would react upon discovering that someone you love was causally determined to love you by, say, a benevolent manipulator.

Setting aside *free* will for a moment, when does the will play any role at all in engendering love? When a relationship is disintegrating, people will at times decide to try to restore the love they once had for one another. When a student finds herself in conflict with a roommate from the outset, she might choose to take steps to improve the relationship. When a marriage is arranged, the partners may decide to do what they can to love each other. In these kinds of circumstances we might want others to make a decision that might produce or maintain love. But this is not to say that we would want that decision to be freely willed in the sense required for moral responsibility. For it is not clear that value would

be added by the decision's being free in this sense. Moreover, although in some circumstances we might want others to make decisions of this sort, we would typically prefer love that did not require such decisions. This is so not only for intimate romantic relationships—where it is quite obvious—but also for friendships and relationships between parents and children.

Suppose Kane's view could be defended, and we did want love that is freely willed in the sense required for moral responsibility. If we in fact desired love of this kind, then we would want a kind of love that is impossible if we lack the sort of free will required for moral responsibility. Still, the sorts of love not threatened by the skeptical view are sufficient for good relationships. If we can aspire to the kind of love parents typically have for their children, or the type romantic lovers share, or the sort had by friends who are deeply devoted to each other, and whose friendship became close through their interactions, then the possibility of fulfillment through interpersonal relationships remains intact.

Accepting hard incompatibilism, therefore, would not undermine interpersonal relationships. It might challenge certain attitudes that typically have a role in such relationships. Moral resentment, indignation and guilt would likely be irrational, since these attitudes would have presuppositions believed to be false. But these attitudes are either not required for good relationships, or they have analogues that could play their typical role. Moreover, love—the reactive attitude most essential to good interpersonal relationships—does not seem threatened at all. Love of another involves, fundamentally, wishing for the other's good, taking on her aims and desires, and a desire to be together with her, and none of this is endangered by the skeptical position.

8. THE GOOD IN HARD INCOMPATIBILISM

Hard incompatibilism also promises substantial benefits for human life. Of all the attitudes associated with the assumption that we are morally responsible, anger seems most closely connected with it. Discussions about moral responsibility most often focus not on how we judge morally exemplary agents, but rather on how we regard those who are morally deficient. Examples designed to elicit a strong intuition that an agent is morally responsible most often feature an especially heinous action, and the intuition usually involves sympathetic anger. It may be, then, that our attachment to the assumption that we are morally responsible derives to a significant degree from the role anger plays in our emotional lives. Perhaps we feel that giving up the assumption of responsibility is threatening because the rationality of anger would be undercut as a result.

The kind of anger at issue is the sort that is directed toward a person who is believed to have behaved immorally—it comprises both moral resentment and indignation. Let us call this attitude *moral anger*. Not all anger is moral anger. One type of non-moral anger is directed toward someone because his abilities are lacking in some respect or because he has performed poorly in some situation. We are sometimes angry with machines for malfunctioning. At times our anger has no object. Still, most human anger is moral anger.

Moral anger comprises a significant part of our moral lives as we ordinarily conceive them. It motivates us to resist abuse, discrimination, and oppression. At the same time, expression of moral anger often has harmful effects, failing to contribute to the well-being either of those toward whom it is directed or of those expressing the anger. Often its expression is intended to cause little else than emotional or physical pain. Consequently, it has a tendency to damage relationships, impair the functioning of organizations, and unsettle societies. In extreme cases, it can motivate people to torture and kill.

The realization that expression of moral anger can be damaging gives rise to a strong demand that it be morally justified when it occurs. The demand to morally justify behavior that is harmful is generally a very strong one, and

expressions of moral anger are often harmful. This demand is made more urgent by the fact that we are often attached to moral anger, and that we frequently enjoy expressing it. Most commonly we justify expression of moral anger by arguing that wrongdoers deserve it, and we believe that they deserve it because they are morally responsible for what they do. If hard incompatibilism is true, however, justification of this sort is undermined. Yet given the concerns to which expression of moral anger give rise, this may be a good thing.

Accepting hard incompatibilism is not likely to modify our attitudes to the extent that expression of moral anger ceases to be a problem for us. However, moral anger is often sustained and magnified by the belief that its object is morally responsible for immoral behavior. Destructive moral anger in relationships is nurtured in this way by the assumption that the other is blameworthy. The anger that fuels ethnic conflicts, for example, is almost always fostered by the conviction that a group of people deserves blame for past wrongs. Hard incompatibilism advocates giving up such beliefs because they are false. As a result, moral anger might decrease, and its expressions subside.

Would the benefits that would result if moral anger were modified in this way compensate for the losses that would ensue? Moral anger motivates us to oppose wrongful behavior. Would we lose the motivation to oppose immorality? If for hard incompatibilist reasons the assumption that wrongdoers are blameworthy is withdrawn, the belief that they have in fact behaved immorally would not be threatened. Even if those who commit genocide are not morally responsible, their actions are nonetheless clearly horribly immoral, and a conviction that this is so would remain untouched. This, together with a commitment to oppose wrongdoing, would permit a resolve to resist abuse, discrimination, and oppression. Accepting hard incompatibilism would thus allow us to retain the benefits moral anger can also provide, while at the same time challenging its destructive effects.

REFERENCES

Chisholm, Roderick. (1976). *Person and Object* (La Salle: Open Court).

Clarke, Randolph. (2003). *Libertarian Theories of Free Will* (Oxford: Oxford University Press).

Ekstrom, Laura W. (2000). *Free Will: A Philosophical Study* (Boulder: Westview).

Farrell, Daniel M. (1985). "The Justification of General Deterrence," *The Philosophical Review* 104.

Fischer, John Martin. (1994). *The Metaphysics of Free Will* (Oxford: Blackwell).

Frankfurt, Harry G. (1971). "Freedom of the Will and the Concept of a Person," *Journal of Philosophy* 68, pp. 5–20.

Honderich, Ted. (1988). *A Theory of Determinism* (Oxford: Oxford University Press).

Hume, David. (1739/1978). *A Treatise of Human Nature,* L. A. Selby-Bigge, ed. (Oxford: Oxford University Press).

Kane, Robert. (1996). *The Significance of Free Will* (New York: Oxford University Press).

Kant, Immanuel. (1781/1997). *Critique of Pure Reason,* tr. Paul Guyer and Allen Wood (Cambridge: Cambridge University Press, 1997).

Lycan, William G. (1997). *Consciousness* (Cambridge: MIT Press).

Mele, Alfred. (1995). *Autonomous Agents* (New York: Oxford University Press).

Mele, Alfred. (2006). *Free Will and Luck* (Oxford: Oxford University Press).

O'Connor, Timothy. (2000). *Persons and Causes* (Oxford: Oxford University Press).

Pereboom, Derk. (2001). *Living Without Free Will* (Cambridge: Cambridge University Press).

Schoeman, Ferdinand D. (1979). "On Incapacitating the Dangerous," *American Philosophical Quarterly* 16.

Smilansky, Saul. (2000). *Free Will and Illusion* (Oxford: Oxford University Press).

Spinoza, Baruch. (1677/1985). *Ethics,* in *The Collected Works of Spinoza,* ed. and tr. Edwin Curley, Volume 1 (Princeton: Princeton University Press).

Strawson, Peter F. (1962). "Freedom and Resentment," *Proceedings of the British Academy* 48 (1962), pp. 1–25.

van Inwagen, Peter. (1983). *An Essay On Free Will* (Oxford: Oxford University Press).

Wallace, R. Jay. (1994). *Responsibility and the Moral Sentiments* (Cambridge, Harvard University Press).

CHAPTER 3

COMPATIBILISM: THE CASE FOR DETERMINISM AND ITS COMPATIBILITY WITH THE MOST IMPORTANT SENSE OF FREE WILL

3.1 Of Liberty and Necessity

DAVID HUME

David Hume (1711–1176) was a leading philosopher of the Enlightenment, the author of a famous history of England, and the tutor of Adam Smith in political economy. He spent most of his life in Edinburgh.

From *An Inquiry Concerning Human Understanding,* 1748.

PART I

It might reasonably be expected in questions which have been canvassed and disputed with great eagerness, since the first origin of science, and philosophy, that the meaning of all the terms, at least, should have been agreed upon among the disputants; and our enquiries, in the course of two thousand years, been able to pass from words to the true and real subject of the controversy. For how easy may it seem to give exact definitions of the terms employed in reasoning, and make these definitions, not the mere sound of words, the object of future scrutiny and examination? But if we consider the matter more narrowly, we shall be apt to draw a quite opposite conclusion. From this circumstance alone, that a controversy has been long kept on foot, and remains still undecided, we may presume that there is some ambiguity in the expression, and that the disputants affix different ideas to the terms employed in the controversy. For as the faculties of the mind are supposed to be naturally alike in every individual; otherwise nothing could be more fruitless than to reason or dispute together; it were impossible, if men affix the same ideas to their terms, that they could so long form different opinions of the same subject; especially when they communicate their views, and each party turn themselves on all sides, in search of arguments which may give them the victory over their antagonists. It is true, if men attempt the discussion of questions which lie entirely beyond the reach of human capacity, such as those concerning the origin of worlds, or the economy of the intellectual system or region of spirits, they may long beat the air in their fruitless contests, and never arrive at any determinate conclusion. But if the question regard any subject of common life and experience, nothing, one would think, could preserve the dispute so long undecided but some ambiguous expressions, which keep the antagonists still at a distance, and hinder them from grappling with each other.

This has been the case in the long-disputed question concerning liberty and necessity; and to so remarkable a degree that, if I be not much mistaken, we shall find, that all mankind, both learned and ignorant, have always been of the same opinion with regard to this subject, and that a few intelligible definitions would immediately have put an end to the whole controversy. I own that this dispute has been so much canvassed on all hands, and has led philosophers into such a labyrinth of obscure sophistry, that it is no wonder, if a sensible reader indulge his ease so far as to turn a deaf ear to the proposal of such a question, from which he can expect neither instruction nor entertainment. But the state of the argument here proposed may, perhaps, serve to renew his attention; as it has more novelty, promises at least some decision of the controversy, and will not much disturb his ease by any intricate or obscure reasoning.

I hope, therefore, to make it appear that all men have ever agreed in the doctrine both of necessity and of liberty, according to any reasonable sense, which can be put on these terms; and that the whole controversy, has hitherto turned merely upon words. We shall begin with examining the doctrine of necessity.

It is universally allowed that matter, in all its operations, is actuated by a necessary force, and that every natural effect is so precisely determined by the energy of its cause that no other effect, in such particular circumstances, could possibly have resulted from it. The degree and direction of every motion is, by the laws of nature, prescribed with such exactness that a living creature may as soon arise from the shock of two bodies as motion in any other degree or direction than what is actually produced by it. Would we, therefore, form a just and precise idea of necessity, we must consider whence that idea arises when we apply it to the operation of bodies.

It seems evident that, if all the scenes of nature were continually shifted in such a manner that no two events bore any resemblance to each other, but every object was entirely new, without any similitude to whatever had been seen before, we should never, in that case, have attained the least idea of necessity, or of a connexion among these objects. We might say, upon such a supposition, that one object or event has followed another; not that one was produced by the other. The relation of cause and effect must be utterly unknown to mankind. Inference and reasoning concerning the operations of nature would, from that moment, be at an end; and the memory and senses remain the only canals, by which the knowledge of any real existence could possibly have access to the mind. Our idea, therefore, of necessity and causation arises entirely from the uniformity observable in the operations of nature, where similar objects are constantly conjoined together, and the mind is determined by custom to infer the one from the appearance of the other. These two circumstances form the whole of that necessity, which we ascribe to matter. Beyond the constant conjunction of similar objects, and the consequent inference from one to the other, we have no notion of any necessity or connexion.

If it appear, therefore, that all mankind have ever allowed, without any doubt or hesitation, that these two circumstances take place in the voluntary actions of men, and in the operations of mind; it must follow, that all mankind have ever agreed in the doctrine of necessity, and that they have hitherto disputed, merely for not understanding each other.

As to the first circumstance, the constant and regular conjunction of similar events, we may possibly satisfy ourselves by the following considerations: It is universally acknowledged that there is a great uniformity among the actions of men, in all nations and ages, and that human nature remains still the same, in its principles and operations. The same motives always produce the same actions: the same events follow from the same causes. Ambition, avarice, self-love, vanity, friendship, generosity, public spirit: these passions, mixed in various degrees, and distributed through society, have been, from the beginning of the world, and still are, the source of all the actions and enterprises, which have ever been observed among mankind. Would you know the sentiments, inclinations, and course

of life of the Greeks and Romans? Study well the temper and actions of the French and English: You cannot be much mistaken in transferring to the former most of the observations which you have made with regard to the latter. Mankind are so much the same, in all times and places, that history informs us of nothing new or strange in this particular. Its chief use is only to discover the constant and universal principles of human nature, by showing men in all varieties of circumstances and situations, and furnishing us with materials from which we may form our observations and become acquainted with the regular springs of human action and behaviour. These records of wars, intrigues, factions, and revolutions, are so many collections of experiments, by which the politician or moral philosopher fixes the principles of his science, in the same manner as the physician or natural philosopher becomes acquainted with the nature of plants, minerals, and other external objects, by the experiments which he forms concerning them. Nor are the earth, water, and other elements, examined by Aristotle, and Hippocrates, more like to those which at present lie under our observation than the men described by Polybius and Tacitus are to those who now govern the world.

Should a traveller, returning from a far country, bring us an account of men, wholly different from any with whom we were ever acquainted; men, who were entirely divested of avarice, ambition, or revenge; who knew no pleasure but friendship, generosity, and public spirit; we should immediately, from these circumstances, detect the falsehood, and prove him a liar, with the same certainty as if he had stuffed his narration with stories of centaurs and dragons, miracles and prodigies. And if we would explode any forgery in history, we cannot make use of a more convincing argument, than to prove, that the actions ascribed to any person are directly contrary to the course of nature, and that no human motives, in such circumstances, could ever induce him to such a conduct....

[W]ere there no uniformity in human actions, and were every experiment which we could form of this kind irregular and anomalous, it were impossible to collect any general observations concerning mankind; and no experience, however accurately digested by reflection, would ever serve to any purpose. Why is the aged husbandman more skilful in his calling than the young beginner but because there is a certain uniformity in the operation of the sun, rain, and earth towards the production of vegetables; and experience teaches the old practitioner the rules by which this operation is governed and directed.

We must not, however, expect that this uniformity of human actions should be carried to such a length as that all men, in the same circumstances, will always act precisely in the same manner, without making any allowance for the diversity of characters, prejudices, and opinions. Such a uniformity in every particular, is found in no part of nature. On the contrary, from observing the variety of conduct in different men, we are enabled to form a greater variety of maxims, which still suppose a degree of uniformity and regularity....

I grant it possible to find some actions, which seem to have no regular connexion with any known motives, and are exceptions to all the measures of conduct which have ever been established for the government of men. But if we would willingly know what judgment should be formed of such irregular and extraordinary actions, we may consider the sentiments commonly entertained with regard to those irregular events which appear in the course of nature, and the operations of external objects. All causes are not conjoined to their usual effects with like uniformity. An artificer, who handles only dead matter, may be disappointed of his aim, as well as the politician, who directs the conduct of sensible and intelligent agents.

The vulgar, who take things according to their first appearance, attribute the uncertainty of events to such an uncertainty in the causes as makes the latter often fail of their usual influence; though they meet with no impediment in their operation. But philosophers, observing that, almost in every part of nature, there is

contained a vast variety of springs and principles, which are hid, by reason of their minuteness or remoteness, find, that it is at least possible the contrariety of events may not proceed from any contingency in the cause, but from the secret operation of contrary causes. This possibility is converted into certainty by farther observation, when they remark that, upon an exact scrutiny, a contrariety of effects always betrays a contrariety of causes, and proceeds from their mutual opposition. A peasant can give no better reason for the stopping of any clock or watch than to say that it does not commonly go right: But an artist easily perceives that the same force in the spring or pendulum has always the same influence on the wheels; but fails of its usual effects, perhaps by reason of a grain of dust, which puts a stop to the whole movement. From the observation of several parallel instances, philosophers form a maxim that the connexion between all causes and effects is equally necessary, and that its seeming uncertainty in some instances proceeds from the secret opposition of contrary causes.

Thus, for instance, in the human body, when the usual symptoms of health or sickness disappoint our expectation; when medicines operate not with their wonted powers; when irregular events follow from any particular cause; the philosopher and physician are not surprised at the matter, nor are ever tempted to deny, in general, the necessity and uniformity of those principles by which the animal economy is conducted. They know that a human body is a mighty complicated machine: That many secret powers lurk in it, which are altogether beyond our comprehension: That to us it must often appear very uncertain in its operations: And that therefore the irregular events, which outwardly discover themselves, can be no proof that the laws of nature are not observed with the greatest regularity in its internal operations and government.

The philosopher, if he be consistent, must apply the same reasoning to the actions and volitions of intelligent agents. The most irregular and unexpected resolutions of men may frequently be accounted for by those who know every particular circumstance of their character and situation. A person of an obliging disposition gives a peevish answer: But he has the toothache, or has not dined. A stupid fellow discovers an uncommon alacrity in his carriage: But he has met with a sudden piece of good fortune. Or even when an action, as sometimes happens, cannot be particularly accounted for, either by the person himself or by others; we know, in general, that the characters of men are, to a certain degree, inconstant and irregular. This is, in a manner, the constant character of human nature; though it be applicable, in a more particular manner, to some persons who have no fixed rule for their conduct, but proceed in a continued course of caprice and inconstancy. The internal principles and motives may operate in a uniform manner, notwithstanding these seeming irregularities; in the same manner as the winds, rain, cloud, and other variations of the weather are supposed to be governed by steady principles; though not easily discoverable by human sagacity and enquiry.

Thus it appears, not only that the conjunction between motives and voluntary actions is as regular and uniform as that between the cause and effect in any part of nature; but also that this regular conjunction has been universally acknowledged among mankind, and has never been the subject of dispute, either in philosophy or common life....

Nor have philosophers even entertained a different opinion from the people in this particular. For, not to mention that almost every action of their life supposes that opinion, there are even few of the speculative parts of learning to which it is not essential. What would become of history, had we not a dependence on the veracity of the historian according to the experience which we have had of mankind? How could politics be a science, if laws and forms of government had not a uniform influence upon society? Where would be the foundation of morals, if particular characters had no certain or determinate power to produce particular sentiments, and if these sentiments had no constant operation on actions? And with what pretence could we employ our criticism upon any poet

or polite author, if we could not pronounce the conduct and sentiments of his actors either natural or unnatural to such characters, and in such circumstances? It seems almost impossible, therefore, to engage either in science or action of any kind without acknowledging the doctrine of necessity, and this inference from motive to voluntary actions, from characters to conduct....

I have frequently considered, what could possibly be the reason why all mankind, though they have ever, without hesitation, acknowledged the doctrine of necessity in their whole practice and reasoning, have yet discovered such a reluctance to acknowledge it in words, and have rather shown a propensity, in all ages, to profess the contrary opinion. The matter, I think, may be accounted for after the following manner. If we examine the operations of body, and the production of effects from their causes, we shall find that all our faculties can never carry us farther in our knowledge of this relation than barely to observe that particular objects are constantly conjoined together, and that the mind is carried, by a customary transition, from the appearance of one to the belief of the other. But though this conclusion concerning human ignorance be the result of the strictest scrutiny of this subject, men still entertain a strong propensity to believe that they penetrate farther into the powers of nature, and perceive something like a necessary connexion between the cause and the effect. When again they turn their reflections towards the operations of their own minds, and feel no such connexion of the motive and the action; they are thence apt to suppose, that there is a difference between the effects which result from material force, and those which arise from thought and intelligence. But being once convinced that we know nothing farther of causation of any kind than merely the constant conjunction of objects, and the consequent inference of the mind from one to another, and finding that these two circumstances are universally allowed to have place in voluntary actions; we may be more easily led to own the same necessity common to all causes. And though this reasoning may contradict the systems of many philosophers, in ascribing necessity to the determinations of the will, we shall find, upon reflection, that they dissent from it in words only, not in their real sentiment. Necessity, according to the sense in which it is here taken, has never yet been rejected, nor can ever, I think, be rejected by any philosopher. It may only, perhaps, be pretended that the mind can perceive, in the operations of matter, some farther connexion between the cause and effect; and connexion that has no place in voluntary actions of intelligent beings. Now whether it be so or not, can only appear upon examination; and it is incumbent on these philosophers to make good their assertion, by defining or describing that necessity, and pointing it out to us in the operations of material causes.

It would seem, indeed, that men begin at the wrong end of this question concerning liberty and necessity, when they enter upon it by examining the faculties of the soul, the influence of the understanding, and the operations of the will. Let them first discuss a more simple question, namely, the operations of body and of brute unintelligent matter; and try whether they can there form any idea of causation and necessity, except that of a constant conjunction of objects, and subsequent inference of the mind from one to another. If these circumstances form, in reality, the whole of that necessity, which we conceive in matter, and if these circumstances be also universally acknowledged to take place in the operations of the mind, the dispute is at an end; at least, must be owned to be thenceforth merely verbal. But as long as we will rashly suppose, that we have some farther idea of necessity and causation in the operations of external objects; at the same time, that we can find nothing farther in the voluntary actions of the mind; there is no possibility of bringing the question to any determinate issue, while we proceed upon so erroneous a supposition. The only method of undeceiving us is to mount up higher; to examine the narrow extent of science when applied to material causes; and to convince ourselves that all we know of them is the constant conjunction and inference above mentioned. We

may, perhaps, find that it is with difficulty we are induced to fix such narrow limits to human understanding: but we can afterwards find no difficulty when we come to apply this doctrine to the actions of the will. For as it is evident that these have a regular conjunction with motives and circumstances and characters, and as we always draw inferences from one to the other, we must be obliged to acknowledge in words that necessity, which we have already avowed, in every deliberation of our lives, and in every step of our conduct and behaviour.

But to proceed in this reconciling project with regard to the question of liberty and necessity; the most contentious question of metaphysics, the most contentious science; it will not require many words to prove, that all mankind have ever agreed in the doctrine of liberty as well as in that of necessity, and that the whole dispute, in this respect also, has been hitherto merely verbal. For what is meant by liberty, when applied to voluntary actions? We cannot surely mean that actions have so little connexion with motives, inclinations, and circumstances, that one does not follow with a certain degree of uniformity from the other, and that one affords no inference by which we can conclude the existence of the other. For these are plain and acknowledged matters of fact. By liberty, then, we can only mean a power of acting or not acting, according to the determinations of the will; this is, if we choose to remain at rest, we may; if we choose to move, we also may. Now this hypothetical liberty is universally allowed to belong to every one who is not a prisoner and in chains. Here, then, is no subject of dispute.

Whatever definition we may give of liberty, we should be careful to observe two requisite circumstances. First, that it be consistent with plain matter of fact; secondly, that it be consistent with itself. If we observe these circumstances, and render our definition intelligible, I am persuaded that all mankind will be found of one opinion with regard to it.

It is universally allowed that nothing exists without a cause of its existence, and that chance, when strictly examined, is a mere negative word, and means not any real power which has anywhere a being in nature. But it is pretended that some causes are necessary, some not necessary. Here then is the advantage of definitions. Let any one define a cause, without comprehending, as a part of the definition, a necessary connexion with its effect; and let him show distinctly the origin of the idea, expressed by the definition; and I shall readily give up the whole controversy. But if the foregoing explication of the matter be received, this must be absolutely impracticable. Had not objects a regular conjunction with each other, we should never have entertained any notion of cause and effect; and this regular conjunction produces that inference of the understanding, which is the only connexion, that we can have any comprehension of. Whoever attempts a definition of cause, exclusive of these circumstances, will be obliged either to employ unintelligible terms or such as are synonymous to the term which he endeavours to define. And if the definition above mentioned be admitted; liberty, when opposed to necessity, not to constraint, is the same thing with chance; which is universally allowed to have no existence.

3.2 Compatibilism and the Ability to Do Otherwise

HELEN BEEBEE

Helen Beebee is Samuel Hall Professor of Philosophy at the University of Manchester. She has written important works in metaphysics, philosophy of science, and the history of philosophy.

Keith is cooking dinner for his friend, Keisha. He knows Keisha really doesn't like chili very much at all, but Keith *loves* chili. Obviously he's not going to put *loads* of chili in—that would be mean. But maybe if he just puts a tiny bit in, she won't notice. So he does add a bit of chili. Unsurprisingly, Keisha notices. 'I can't believe you put chili in when you know I don't like it!', she says. 'Did you *have* to do that? Couldn't you have resisted, just this once, for my sake?'.

Keith feels chastened, contrite, a little guilty even. He was supposed to be doing something nice for Keisha, and he messed up. He was taking a risk in adding the chili; after all, if *he* was going to notice it, chances are Keisha would too. 'I'm sorry', he says. 'I should have resisted. I was being selfish. Please forgive me.'

Next door, by complete coincidence, James is cooking dinner for Jasmine, and the same scenario is playing out, culminating in Jasmine posing the very same question to James. But James is a convinced determinist. He thinks his decision was wholly determined by the prior state of his brain ten minutes ago—indeed, wholly determined by things that happened before he was even born—together with the laws of nature. After all (or so he believes) the laws govern the behaviour of everything whatsoever, and for any given state of the Universe at any given time, the laws specify *exactly* what state it will be in at the next moment. The Universe is (according to James) a big, deterministic machine: at any given time, given the state it's in at that time, there is only one possible state it can be in at the next moment, and so at the moment after that, and so on. And so the laws, plus facts about the distant past, determine what went on in James's brain ten minutes ago and hence they determined, in turn, that he would decide, just now, to add the chili— and then to actually go ahead and add it.

James thinks it follows that the answer to Jasmine's question is no. If determinism is true —and James thinks it is—then he *couldn't*, in fact, have resisted; that was something he was not *able* to do. And if he *couldn't*, or *wasn't able, to have done otherwise*—and, again, James thinks he wasn't able to do otherwise—then he didn't act freely. Finally, he reasons, if he didn't act freely (which he has established to his own satisfaction) then he really wasn't *morally responsible* for adding the chili: it really *wasn't his fault*. Of course, it's true that he was acting out of self-interest rather than paying more attention to what Jasmine wanted. But hey, that's just the way he is, he thinks. It's not *his* fault he was made that way. (It's not his parents' or anyone else's fault either; after all, everything *they* did was determined by the distant past plus the laws of nature. And we can go back in time, running the same line of argument, until we're back with the dinosaurs and there's *nobody* to blame.)

James says sorry just to keep the peace—he really doesn't want to fall out with Jasmine over a bit of chili—but he doesn't mean it. He doesn't *really* think he is to blame. If Jasmine insists on blaming him—which she apparently does—that's a mistake. But hey, her blaming him is just as much a product of factors outside *her* control as James's decision to add the chili was (he thinks) a product of factors outside *his* control. So, James thinks, he can't really blame her for that.

Who's right? Is it Keith, who accepts that he is blameworthy for adding the chili, or James, who did exactly the same thing as Keith but who thinks he *isn't* blameworthy? Correspondingly, are Keisha and Jasmine right to blame their friends? Well, first of all, we shouldn't take James's word for it that determinism is true; James is (I hereby stipulate) no expert on these matters. In fact, I think none of us knows whether or not determinism is true. That's important because a lot of philosophy students do seem to think it's pretty obvious that determinism is true. (Some professional philosophers seem to think that too, I should add.) I am really not at all sure what they think their evidence for that claim is. To put it more strongly, I don't think they have

any. So if your immediate reaction to James was 'yes, that's right! Determinism is true!', you really should reconsider. (A lot of *other* philosophy students seem to think it's obvious that determinism *isn't* true, and, in particular, that when we go around making decisions or forming intentions to do things—shall I add the chili? Shall I go to the party or stay home and write my essay?—the laws of nature plus facts about the past *don't* determine which choice they'll make. Quite a few professional philosophers also seem to think that. Again, I'm not sure what they think the evidence for that claim is.)

Let's just assume for now that James is right about determinism, however. Does that mean he's right that he isn't morally responsible, and therefore that he isn't blameworthy, for adding the chili? In other words, is the argument James gave a good argument? Does the fact (and we're assuming it is a fact) that James was determined by the past plus the laws of nature imply that was unable to do otherwise? And, if so, does *that* imply that he didn't act freely? And does *that* in turn imply that he lacked moral responsibility for what he did?

A lot of philosophers have spent *a lot* of time thinking about that question, and—you probably won't be surprised to learn if you've studied any philosophy—opinion remains resolutely divided on what the right answer to it is. But before I have a go at answering it, let's think about Keith again for a moment. You'll notice that Keith didn't actually answer Keisha's question. Keisha asked Keith whether he could have resisted putting in the chili, and Keith didn't say; he simply accepted that he was blameworthy and apologised. Now, one thing you might think at this point is that, while he didn't *directly* answer Keisha's question, he answered it implicitly. Why? Because he admitted that he *should* have done otherwise: he *should* have resisted. And you might think that this *does* commit him to thinking that he *could* have done otherwise. Why? Because, generally speaking, we don't go around saying that people *should* have done such-and-such when we don't think they *could* have done it.

Imagine Jasmine finds out from a mutual friend that Keisha plans to go round to Keith's tonight and break off their friendship. She is absolutely furious about the whole chili incident and hasn't forgiven Keith for it at all. Jasmine (rightly, let's assume) thinks this would be a terrible mistake. Keisha is seriously overreacting to what was really a fairly trivial incident. (After all, Jasmine has forgiven James, despite the fact that his apology seemed, frankly, a little half-hearted.) What's more, Keisha and Keith get on really well and she would really regret not seeing him any more. Jasmine thinks to herself that she should talk to Keisha and dissuade her from going round to Keith's. But she can't. She's out of town, Keisha's phone is turned off, and there's no other way for Jasmine to contact her. She's completely stuck: there's no way she *can* talk to Keisha. So Jasmine concludes that it's not true, as it turns out, that she *should* talk to Keisha—and that's because it's just not something she *can* do. If you're persuaded by Jasmine's line of thought, you might (admittedly generalising from a single example) think that we should subscribe to what's sometimes called the 'ought implies can' principle: if you *ought to*, or *should*, do something, then it must be the case that you *can* (or you are *able to*) do it. Hence if you *can't* do something (e.g. Jasmine can't talk to Keisha), then it's not the case that you *should* do it: it's not true that Jasmine *should* talk to Keisha. (Note: this doesn't imply that she *shouldn't* do it. It's not true that I *should* scratch my nose right now. That doesn't imply that I *shouldn't* scratch it. Morality has nothing to say one way or another on the nose-scratching issue.)

Let's get back to my point about Keith. Keith told Keisha that he *should* have resisted. If you subscribe to the 'ought implies can' principle, then, you'll think that it's true that Keith *should* have resisted only if he *could* have resisted—in which case, even though Keith doesn't directly answer Keisha's question ('couldn't you have resisted?'), Keith ought to think that the answer is yes: after all, he thinks that he *should* have resisted, so if ought implies can, he ought also to think that he *could* have. But in that case, Keith is committed to thinking that he *could have done* (or again, *was able to do*) *otherwise*

than adding the chili. And in *that* case—assuming determinism, which we are currently doing, and also assuming that James's argument works—Keith really shouldn't think that he is blameworthy for adding the chili. Keith is mistaken: he has no more reason to feel guilty than James has.

The moral seems to be that we really do need to think about whether or not James's argument is a good argument. Look again at the argument. It has four key premises. First, James is assuming that determinism is true. As I've said, I don't think James is entitled to that assumption, but let's assume it for now and see where it takes us. Second, *if* determinism is true, *then*—by the little argument James gives in the third paragraph—James was unable to do otherwise than add the chili. (So, since James thinks determinism *is* true, he infers that he was not, in fact, able to do otherwise.) Third, if James was unable to do otherwise, then he didn't act freely. (So, since James thinks he was, in fact, unable to do otherwise, he infers that he didn't act freely.) And, finally, if James didn't act freely, then he wasn't morally responsible for adding the chili. So, since James thinks he didn't act freely, he infers that he wasn't morally responsible for adding the chili.

Just to help us keep track, let's lay the argument out a little more formally, where (P1)–(P4) are the *premises* of James's argument and (C) is the *conclusion*:

(P1) Determinism is true: everything that happens, including James's adding the chili, is implied (or guaranteed, or necessitated) by facts about the distant past together with facts about the laws of nature.

(P2) If determinism is true, then James wasn't able to do otherwise than add the chili (since his doing so was guaranteed by facts about the distant past and the laws of nature).

Interim conclusion: James wasn't able to do otherwise than add the chili.

(P3) If James wasn't able to do otherwise than add the chili, then he didn't add it freely.

Interim conclusion: James didn't add the chili freely.

(P4) If James didn't add the chili freely, then he wasn't morally responsible for adding the chili.

Therefore

(C) James wasn't morally responsible for adding the chili.

Now, James (we may assume) is a perfectly normal agent. He is not suffering from any odd psychological compulsion that somehow makes him add chili to the dinner no matter how much he knows his dinner companion hates it. (There's a difference between someone who decides on a whim to steal from a shop and a kleptomaniac.) Also, nobody else is forcing him to add the chili; nobody's standing with a gun to his head, saying 'add the chili, or else!'. This being so, if determinism really is true, then—if James's argument is correct—what goes for James goes for all of us, all of the time. When you keep a promise, or buy your sister a nice present, or break a promise, or forget your sister's birthday, or scratch your nose or buy a coffee, you are no more able to do otherwise than James was; so you no more act freely than he did, and (in those cases where moral responsibility is in play) you are no more morally responsible than he was. And the same goes for me, and Keith, Keisha, Jasmine, and everyone else, all of the time.

That's a worrying thought. If you don't think it's worrying, reflect on this: in a 2009 study, social psychologists found that people who had been 'primed' not to believe in free will were more likely to behave in antisocial ways. In particular, when asked to prepare tortilla chips and hot salsa for fellow participants, having been told that the other participants did not like spicy food, they put more salsa on the chips compared to the subjects who *hadn't* been primed not to believe in free will. If only Jasmine had known about that, maybe she would have hidden the chili.

Even more worrying, however, is this: if we have no free will, and hence (given (P4)) we

aren't morally responsible for anything, then nobody is blameworthy for anything, ever. Not perpetrators of genocide, not serial killers, not that guy on the bus who refused to give up his seat for the pregnant woman—not even James. Nor is anyone ever praiseworthy for anything: not people who make huge personal sacrifices to devote themselves to unquestionably worthy causes, not the person who found the wallet you'd dropped in the street and went to great lengths to track you down and return it, and not Jasmine for at least *trying* to stop her friend doing something she'd come to regret. Not only would praising and blaming people be wholly inappropriate; it would also be inappropriate to engage in a whole host of commonplace human emotions and attitudes: guilt, resentment, gratitude and respect, to name just a few (see Strawson 1962; Strawson calls such attitudes 'reactive attitudes'). Reactive attitudes legitimately apply only to moral agents: agents capable of acting freely and responsibly. It's inappropriate to feel grateful to a newborn baby, or to genuinely respect a rock. (You might be glad that the baby has stopped crying. But that's different from being grateful. I'm glad I just narrowly avoided hitting my head on a cupboard door. I'm not grateful to the cupboard. That would be inappropriate.)

At this point, you might be thinking: OK, not having free will would be really bad. But all of this is premised on determinism—premise (P1)—and didn't you say earlier that we just don't know whether determinism is true? So, if we don't have any good reasons to believe in determinism, James's argument doesn't give us any good reasons to abandon our belief in free will. So what's the problem? The answer to that question is: *we just don't know*. Maybe determinism *is* true. And even if it *isn't* true, maybe at least *some* of the time when we act, our action was determined by facts about the past plus the laws of nature. (Just because not *everything* is determined by the past plus the laws, it doesn't follow that *nothing* is.) *Not knowing*, on any given occasion, whether or not someone is blameworthy or praiseworthy, or whether or not it would be appropriate to be grateful to them or whatever, would, itself, be a pretty bad result. (You want to blame that guy who didn't give up his seat, or be grateful to the person who returned your wallet? Well, go ahead—if you have *some* reason to think that their doing so wasn't determined by the past plus the laws of nature. But of course you don't have any particular reason to think that. So, now, how should you behave? How should you even *feel?* You just don't know.)

Here's a second thing to notice about James's argument. If we remove the first assumption—the assumption that determinism is true—we still end up with an argument for an interesting conclusion, namely that acting freely, and hence morally responsibly, is *incompatible with* determinism. That is to say, *if* determinism is true, then (generalising from the case of James) nobody ever acts freely or morally responsibly. Again, putting it a little more formally, we end up with the following argument:

(P2) If determinism is true, then James wasn't able to do otherwise than add the chili.

(P3) If James wasn't able to do otherwise than add the chili, then he didn't add it freely.

Therefore

(C1) If determinism is true, then James didn't add the chili freely.

Let's just stop there for a moment. The above is a version of what's known as the *Consequence Argument* (see van Inwagen 1975). If the reasoning is sound (which it certainly seems to be) and if the premises (P2) and (P3) are true, then determinism is *incompatible* with acting freely. People who do indeed believe that acting freely is incompatible with determinism are known, you will be astonished to learn, as *incompatibilists*. The Consequence Argument, then, is an argument for incompatibilism. Equally astonishingly, people who reject incompatibilism and claim instead that acting freely is compatible with determinism are known as *compatibilists*.

Notice, however, that the above argument doesn't, just by itself, imply anything about

moral responsibility. We get to a conclusion concerning moral responsibility by adding back in the fourth premise of James's argument:

(P4) If James didn't add the chili freely, then he wasn't morally responsible for adding the chili.

Putting (P4) together with (C1), we get to:

(C2) If determinism is true, then James wasn't morally responsible for adding the chili.

I think (P4) is true. Or, to put the point more generally, I think acting freely is a requirement for moral responsibility: if you don't act freely, then you aren't morally responsible for what you do. (Some philosophers disagree with me about this.) I also think moral responsibility is really important. Reactive attitudes aren't merely incidental add-ons to our lives; they are absolutely central to the meaningfulness of our relationships with other people and to our conception of our lives as genuinely worth living. So, given what I said earlier about not knowing whether or not determinism is true, I think it would be a *really good idea* to be a compatibilist. But *wanting* compatibilism to be true isn't good enough, unfortunately. We need to find a way to wriggle out of the Consequence Argument, since—given that I'm accepting (P4)—that's the only way to avoid the conclusion that we never really have any good reasons to think that someone is morally responsible for what they have done.

Compatibilists have thought of loads of different possible ways of wriggle out of the Consequence Argument, but I'll focus on just one kind of response, which appeals to what we might mean when we say that someone *was able to do otherwise*. According to (P2) of the Consequence Argument, if determinism is true then nobody is ever able to do otherwise than what they actually do—because what they do is determined by the past plus the laws of nature, and (whether or not determinism is true) we can't do anything about *those*. You can't now make it the case that your parents bought you that puppy you really wanted when you were eight, or that the American War of Independence never happened; nor can you make it the case that $e=mc^2$ isn't true. And, by (P3) (and assuming that James and his adding the chili are representative of normal people and their actions more generally), if you aren't able to do otherwise, then you don't act freely. But here's a question. Should we *really* think that determinism is incompatible with the ability to do otherwise? That is, should we *really* think that (P2) is true? I'm going to try and argue that we shouldn't.

So, let's have a go. (Warning: this is going to take up the rest of this article.) Let's start by thinking about abilities more generally. Here are some abilities I have: the ability to play the violin, the ability to make lasagne, the ability to write philosophy papers. Many people are able to verify that I am able to do these things because they've heard me play the violin, eaten one of my delicious lasagnes, or read one of my philosophy papers. Similarly, we may suppose, both Keith and James are perfectly capable of resisting temptation. They have managed to resist temptation on many occasions in the past. (If they didn't have this ability, it would have been rather unwise of Keisha and Jasmine to let their friends cook their dinner, given how much they dislike chili and how much they know their friends like it.) The fact that people have abilities like these is in no way undermined by determinism. If determinism is true, that doesn't at all undermine the claim that I am able to play the violin or make a lasagne. (Imagine that someone proves conclusively that determinism is true. We'd still perfectly well be able to divide people up into those who are able to play the violin and those who aren't.)

Note that, as we ordinarily talk about abilities—that is, *given what we mean* when we say that someone is or is not able to do something—abilities generally don't come and go from one time to another, or at least not unless some radical change happens in the person we're talking about. Here's a task for you. What abilities do you currently have? Check the ones that apply: play the violin, make a lasagne, drive a car, fly a plane, speak Urdu. That was easy, right? (Well,

you might conceivably be unsure. Maybe you had violin lessons for a short while when you were a kid, but that was ages ago and you're really not sure whether you can still do it. But in most cases, it was easy.) And—unless anything has changed, like you've been taking driving lessons recently—you would have ticked off the same items ten minutes ago, or last week, or a year ago. Right now, I am able to play the violin. I've been able to play it since I was a kid. Trust me.

So it looks as though the truth of determinism makes no difference to whether or not someone has a given ability *at a given time*. Remember the ability list. You filled that in really easily, right? Did it occur to you, even for a moment, to think: 'hang on, maybe I'm *not* able, *right now*, to play the violin or drive a car or make a lasagne, because if determinism is true, then I was determined *not* to do any of those things'? I'm guessing not. And rightly so: nobody thinks we're only able to drive a car when we are actually driving one. That's just not what we mean when we say that someone is able to drive a car. (I don't even own a car, but I am still very confident that, right now, I have the ability to drive. After all, I drove one a few weeks ago, and I know from experience that I don't lose the ability to drive over a period of a few weeks.) Similarly, then, the fact that Keith did not resist temptation on this particular occasion does not at all undermine the claim that he had the *ability* to do so. He *did* have that ability, just as I, right now, am able to play the violin and drive a car (though not at the same time). So: even if determinism is true, Keith was able to do otherwise. He was able to resist temptation and refrain from adding the chili. (P2) is false.

But—you might object—it's not just that Keith *merely happened not to* resist temptation; circumstances before Keith was born, together with the laws of nature, *guaranteed* that he didn't resist temptation. And he has, and never has had, the ability to do anything about *those*. So how *could* he have had the ability to do otherwise than add the chili? My reply is that one can retain the ability to do something even when circumstances make it impossible to *exercise* that ability. Imagine that my friend Amy just locked me in my bedroom—perhaps because she wanted to make sure that I don't play the violin in the next ten minutes. (I said I could play. I didn't say I was any good.) That's something, we may imagine, I had no control over: I had no *idea* Amy so badly wanted me not to play, or that she would go to such lengths to stop me. So I really wasn't in a position to do anything about *that*. So circumstances beyond my control have conspired to guarantee that I will not, in fact, play the violin in the next ten minutes. Nonetheless, it's still true that, right now—locked, as I am, in my bedroom—I have the ability to play the violin.

My point, then—and I admit that this is *way* too quick and really needs *a lot* more defence—is this. Just because you can't do anything about various circumstances that prevent you from doing something, it just doesn't follow that you lack the ability to do that thing. Just as I, currently, am able to play the violin despite being locked in my bedroom (not something I had any control over), Keith was able, when making the dinner, to resist temptation—even though he had no control over the circumstances—that is, facts about the past and the laws of nature—that prevented him from doing just that.

Are we done? Can we now conclude that since, even assuming determinism, Keith had the ability to otherwise, (P2) is false and hence the Consequence Argument fails? If only things were that simple! Unfortunately, there's a big problem with the above argument. As it happens, I *really want* to play the violin right now, and Amy, who, as I say, has locked me in my bedroom, has prevented me from doing that. Grant that I am nonetheless able to play the violin. However, it seems obvious that I am not, now, *freely* refraining from playing the violin. So if my and Keith's cases are analogous, we should conclude that Keith didn't freely add the chili. Oops!

Things are getting a bit complicated here. As philosophers tend to do, let's start clearing things up by making a distinction. Locked in

my bedroom, as I am, I *really want* to play the violin. As I said, I am still, right now, *able* to play the violin. But actually, that was a bit too quick, for there is surely *a* sense—again, a perfectly ordinary, commonsense sense—in which I am *not* able, right now, to play the violin. Imagine two things happen when I'm locked in my bedroom. First, someone calls me. 'Are you able to play the violin? We need someone for our concert next week.' 'Oh yes', I reply. 'I am certainly able to play'. (And I don't mean I *will* be able to play next week, having temporarily lost that ability while locked in my bedroom. I mean I really am, right now, able to play.) Second, Amy shouts at me somewhat sarcastically from outside my bedroom door: 'Go on, give us a tune!'. 'I'm afraid I'm unable to do that, Amy', I reply, 'because the door is locked and my violin is downstairs'.

I think both of my responses were correct. But they appear to contradict each other. How is that possible? Answer: there are *two* senses of 'ability' in play here. So when in response to Amy I said that I am *not* able to play, I was not contradicting my earlier response to the caller, when I said I *am* able to play. In *one* sense of 'ability'—the sense at work in my response to the phone call—my ability to play the violin does not come and go; it does not vary from circumstance to circumstance. It's an ability I retain when I am asleep and when I am making lasagne, and while locked in my bedroom. Following Kadri Vihvelin (2013)—whose work I am heavily drawing on in this article—let's call this kind of ability a 'narrow ability'.

What *does* vary from one circumstance to another, when it comes to my ability to play the violin, is whether I have the *opportunity* to *exercise* that narrow ability. Locked in my bedroom, for example, there are no violins at my disposal. So the *other* sense of 'ability', the sense at work in my reply to Amy, is one that requires not just a narrow ability, but, in addition, the opportunity to exercise it. Let's call this kind of ability a 'wide ability': wide ability = narrow ability + opportunity. So: I retain the *narrow* ability to play the violin even when Amy has locked me in my bedroom. But I lose the *wide* ability, since I do not have the opportunity to exercise that narrow ability.

Now we're in a position to return to the problem with my attempt to undermine premise (P2): locked in the bedroom, with no violin in sight, I am surely not refraining-from-playing-the-violin *freely* (supposing that I really want to play it and am being prevented from doing so by circumstances beyond my control). So, if this case and Keith's case are analogous, we should conclude that Keith isn't acting freely either. And that's the conclusion I want to avoid.

With the distinction between narrow and wide abilities in play, we can put the worry a little differently. Locked in my bedroom but wanting to play the violin, I have the narrow ability to play but I lack the wide ability: I lack the opportunity to exercise my narrow ability. Given we've agreed that I am not *freely* refraining from playing the violin, then, it looks as though it is not the *narrow* ability to do otherwise that is required for acting freely, but the *wide* ability. Right now, I lack the wide ability to play the violin, because I lack the opportunity to exercise my narrow ability to play. And, *for that very reason* (assuming I really want to play, which I do) I do not freely refrain from playing. And now the worry is this: it looks as though acting freely requires having the *wide* ability to do otherwise—and that's an ability that Keith lacks.

Keith, we have in effect agreed, had the narrow ability to resist adding the chili. But surely, like me, he lacks the *wide* ability to do this. After all, facts about the distant past and facts about the laws of nature—facts he can't do anything about—together conspired to ensure that he would not, at the relevant time, have the opportunity to exercise his ability to resist adding the chili, just as facts *I* can't do anything about, namely, Amy's locking me in the room, have conspired to ensure that I lack the opportunity to exercise *my* ability to play the violin. But if Keith lacked the wide ability to do otherwise, and having the *wide* ability to do otherwise is what's required for acting freely, then what

goes for me in the bedroom goes for him too: he did not *freely* add the chili. Hence the Consequence Argument stands: if we understand 'Keith wasn't able to do otherwise' to mean 'Keith lacked the wide ability to do otherwise', then (P2) and (P3) both come out true. And hence, given (P4)—the claim that if Keith didn't act freely then he wasn't morally responsible for adding the chili—it turns out that Keith wasn't morally responsible for doing so after all. Keisha was wrong to blame him for spoiling her dinner.

I'm going to argue that this objection fails, and I'm going to do that by *denying* that Keith lacked the wide ability to do otherwise. Unlike me, locked in my bedroom, he *did* have the wide ability to do otherwise, and hence freely added the chili. Let's get back to me and Amy. I lack the wide ability to play the violin because Amy has locked me in my bedroom. My being locked in is an *external* impediment to my exercising my narrow ability to play the violin—external, that is, to me. But now consider a case where the 'impediment' is *internal* to me; for example, suppose I'm in the vicinity of a violin, but I really, really don't want to play it. (It's a Stradivarius, worth an absolute fortune—or so I believe—and it would be *terrible* if I damaged it. It's just not worth the risk.) In this case, do I lack the opportunity to exercise my narrow ability? I say not. The opportunity is right there, in front of me—I just don't want to take it up. I have not only the narrow but the wide ability to play. Similarly, there is no *external* impediment to Keith's resisting temptation. So Keith, similarly, has the wide, and not just the narrow, ability to resist. Hence we have every reason to think that he acts freely in adding the chili.

Well, that was rather quick. Here's a slower story. First of all, notice that abilities look a lot like *dispositions*: saying that someone is *able* to do something is a lot like saying that someone or something is *disposed* to do something. In fact, I'll go further than that: I think abilities *are* dispositions. Dispositions are features like *being fragile* (roughly, something is fragile just if it's disposed to break when dropped), *being a carcinogen* (something is a carcinogen just if it's disposed to cause cancer in certain circumstances), and *being boring* (something—a film or a book, say—is boring just if it's disposed to bore people in certain circumstances).

To put things a bit formally, when some object O has disposition D, it will M in circumstances C. So for example when an object (O) is fragile (D), it will break (M) when dropped (C). We can think of circumstances C as the 'triggering' conditions for the disposition, and M as the 'manifestation' of the disposition. Notice that we *shouldn't* say the following about dispositions: O has disposition D *only when it is in circumstances C*. My wineglasses are fragile—even though they are currently sitting in a cupboard and, thankfully, not being dropped. (That's why they're in the cupboard, after all—to ensure that they're not in circumstances under which they would manifest their disposition to break.)

What about abilities? Well, as I said, I think abilities are just dispositions. When we say that someone is *able* to do something (and here I mean *narrowly* able), we mean that they are *disposed* to do that thing in certain kinds of (perhaps rather loosely specified) circumstances. For example, when I say that I am (narrowly) able to play the violin, I mean that I am disposed to play the violin in certain circumstances C. Those circumstances are things like: I want to play the violin, there's a violin lying around for me to play, and I don't have any good reasons *not* to play it, e.g. I don't believe that the violin is *hideously* expensive. Some of those circumstances, you'll notice, are external to me—in this case, the availability of a violin—and others are internal, e.g. I *want* to play.

Now, consider the wide/narrow ability distinction again. Clearly I retain the *narrow* ability to play the violin even if I'm not, in fact, in circumstances C. For example, I retain the narrow ability to play even though Amy has locked me in the bedroom (and even if I really don't want to play right now). Do I also have the *wide* ability to play the violin when circumstances C don't obtain? That, I think, depends on *which* of the circumstances don't obtain. In particular, I *lack* the wide ability when the *external* circumstances

don't obtain, e.g. when I'm locked in the bedroom. Remember, wide ability = narrow ability + opportunity. The lack of appropriate external circumstances is what deprives me of the opportunity to exercise my narrow ability. On the other hand, if the external circumstances required for me to have the opportunity *do* obtain, then it looks as though I *do* have the wide ability— *even if* not all of the *internal* circumstances obtain. For example, I retain the wide ability to play even though I am currently occupied making a lasagne (and my violin is just in the next room), or even though I believe that the violin I'm being asked to play is hideously expensive and hence don't want to play. (Actually this is all a little too crude, but it will have to do. If you can find fault with the above, good for you —you're doing some serious philosophical thinking.)

It follows that my having the *wide* ability to play the violin does *not* depend on *all* the required circumstances obtaining. Having the wide ability is more demanding than having the narrow ability—the external circumstances must be right, so that I have the opportunity to exercise my narrow ability—but it is not *so* demanding that *all* the circumstances, internal *and* external, must be right. After all, if having a wide ability required *that*, then I would only *ever* have the wide ability to play the violin on those occasions when I'm actually playing it. And that is clearly not the case. (Remember, I can have that wide ability even when I'm making a lasagne.)

So having the *wide ability* to do something does *not* amount to being in the very circumstances, C, that are the 'triggering' conditions for the ability, any more than having the disposition to do something amounts to being in the very circumstances that are the triggering conditions of a disposition: remember, it's clearly *not* the case that a glass is fragile only when it's actually dropped.

Now we can get back to Keith. The question we're interested in is this: does Keith have the *wide* ability to resist adding the chili? The answer to that question is important because, while Keith has the *narrow* ability to resist, acting freely seems to require having the *wide* ability to do otherwise. That's why I don't freely refrain from playing the violin when Amy has locked me in my bedroom (assuming that I want to play it). Even though in such a case I have the narrow ability to play, I lack the wide ability to do so.

Keith's having the *narrow* ability to *not* put any chili in Keisha's dinner is, like other abilities, a disposition—a disposition not to add any chili (M) in certain circumstances, C. (Things are getting a little convoluted here because in this case the ability to 'do' otherwise is the ability to *refrain* from doing something.) It's a bit hard to specify what those conditions might be, but, again, some of them will be internal (perhaps: he really wants to cook a nice dinner for someone, he knows they don't like chili, he knows full well they'll notice if he adds some) and some will be external (perhaps: there aren't a lot of other dinner guests who all threaten to go home if Keith doesn't add chili to their dishes).

But does Keith also have the *wide* ability to resist? Well, we know that Keith is not, in fact, in circumstances C: the circumstances that would trigger his disposition to resist. Assuming determinism (as we still are), he is in circumstances that guarantee that he *will* add the chili. (What are those circumstances? Well, they include the fact that, by an amazing feat of self-deception, Keith has managed to convince himself that Keisha won't notice. Had Keith not been in *that* situation—had he really thought about it and realised that Keisha would *obviously* notice —then he would have resisted.) But that, as we've seen, *just doesn't entail* that he lacks the wide ability to do otherwise, any more than my thinking that the violin is really expensive, or my being occupied in making a lasagne, robs me of the wide ability to play the violin. I claimed above that what's required for having a wide ability is that the *external* circumstances (such as the availability of a violin) are right. But, in Keith's case, the *external* circumstances *are* right. Keith's problem is not, for example, that of there being dinner guests demanding chili; it's that he's managed to convince himself that

Keisha won't notice the chili. And that's an *internal* feature of Keith—just like my desire to get the lasagne in the oven or not to damage the expensive violin. Thus Keith *does* have the wide ability to resist: he has the narrow ability, and he has the opportunity. So we have no reason to say that he doesn't act freely, and hence no reason to say that he isn't blameworthy for spoiling Keisha's dinner.

So, let's sum up where we've got to. What I've tried to argue is that James's argument fails: he has no grounds for thinking that *if* determinism is true, he didn't act freely and responsibly when he added the chili. He made that claim because he thought that if determinism is true, then we are unable to do anything other than what we in fact do. We freely do something only if we are able to do something else. I've argued instead that what's required for acting freely is the *wide* ability to do otherwise, and both Keith and James *had* that ability.

Now, you might, possibly, have become increasingly exasperated while reading this article. In particular, you might think that in focussing on what we ordinarily mean when we say that someone is or is not able to do something, I have missed the basic point of James's argument. If you're nodding at this point, you might be thinking something like this. Look, it was *completely guaranteed* by factors way outside of Keith's control that he would add the chili. He didn't have any control over the laws of nature (nobody has control over them), and he didn't have control over the facts about the distant past (nobody has control over them, either). And those two things together make it *impossible* for Keith to do anything other than add the chili. So *surely* he didn't have any control over that either.

Or you might be thinking this: the laws of nature aren't *up to Keith*. The facts about the distant past aren't up to Keith either. So—since those two things imply that he will add the chili —it wasn't up to Keith whether or not he added the chili. Or …

Spotted a pattern? It's this. In each case, my imagined objector (maybe it's you) has said: Keith fails to bear some really important relation to the laws of nature (call them L). The possible relations might include: being in control of them, their being up to him, etc. And he fails to bear the same relation to facts about the distant past (call those facts P): they aren't under his control, they aren't up to him, etc. And, since L and P together entail that Keith will add the chili (call this K), he fails to bear that same relation to K as well.

In effect, we can think of the argument of this article as addressing another instance of this general pattern: Keith was unable to do anything about L, and he was unable to do anything about P. But, since L and P together entail that Keith will add the chili, he was unable to do anything about that, too; in other words, he was unable to do otherwise. And my response to that argument, in effect, is just to deny that the inference holds: just because Keith lacked (as he surely did) the wide ability to do anything about L, and he lacked (again, as he surely did) the wide ability to do anything about P, it just doesn't follow that he lacked the wide ability to add or to not add chili. He *did* have the wide ability to do something about *that*.

So, you might want to respond to the argument of this article like this: "OK, suppose we run the Consequence Argument by using the phrase 'Keith lacked the (wide) ability to do otherwise', roughly as per (P2) and (P3). Then the argument doesn't work. But if, instead, we used some other phrase in our premises, such as 'it wasn't up to Keith whether or not he added the chili', or 'it wasn't under Keith's control', then the argument *would* work—because determinism is *not* compatible with its being *up to Keith* what he does, or with what Keith does being *under his control*. So the revised version of (P2) is true. Moreover, an action's being up to an agent, or its being under their control, is required for them to act freely. So (P3) is true too. So, suitably amended, the Consequence Argument works just fine."

Well, that's a move that might work; and nothing I've said undermines that possibility, since I've been focussing on the 'able to do otherwise' version of the Consequence Argument. But you'd have to have a convincing reason to think that the relevant phrase ('it isn't up to

Keith whether or not he adds the chili', or whatever) really does mean something different to 'Keith is unable to do otherwise'. And I'm inclined to think that your prospects aren't good. (You flunk your job interview. I wanted to give you the job, but I wasn't on the selection committee. You blame me. 'It's not my fault', I say. 'It wasn't up to me'. Or 'it wasn't under my control', or 'I couldn't do anything about it'. They all sound a quite lot like 'I wasn't able to give you the job'.)

Of course, the above isn't a knock-down objection to the strategy for saving the Consequence Argument that I've been considering—just an expression of scepticism about its prospects. I'm not saying that it can't be done; that would be rash. It would also be highly rash of me to claim that the overall argument of this article is entirely compelling and watertight in all other respects too. I'm certain that it's not, in fact—I already know that there are various gaps in the argument and problems that I've glossed over. I only had so many words at my disposal.

Even if I haven't managed to persuade you that the Consequence Argument—and hence James's argument—is flawed, I hope I've persuaded you of *something*. Here's the next episode in the story I started with. The next day, James comes clean about what he *really* thinks about the whole chili incident: he explains to Jasmine his philosophical reasons for thinking that he wasn't to blame, and admits that his 'apology' wasn't really sincere. In response, Jasmine—who has studied philosophy, as it turns out—runs the line of argument of this paper to James. Here are two ways to end the story. One: James thumps the table. He's annoyed. Has Jasmine not been listening? *'But I wasn't able to do otherwise!'*, he insists. 'So I didn't act freely, and I wasn't responsible, and so it was a mistake to blame me'. Two: James goes away and thinks *really hard* about where, exactly, Jasmine has gone wrong. If you, like James, are not inclined to accept the conclusion of my and Jasmine's argument, I hope you are at least persuaded that the second reaction is the reasonable one.

BIBLIOGRAPHY

van Inwagen, P. 1975. 'The Incompatibility of Free Will and Determinism', *Philosophical Studies*, 27: 185–99.

Strawson, P. F. 1962. 'Freedom and Resentment', *Proceedings of the British Academy*, 48: 1–25.

Vihvelin, K. 2013. *Causes, Laws, and Free Will: Why Determinism Doesn't Matter*. New York: Oxford University Press.

CHAPTER 4

FREEDOM AND MORAL RESPONSIBILITY

4.1 Luck Swallows Everything

GALEN STRAWSON

Galen Strawson teaches philosophy at the University of Reading. He writes on a variety of issues in metaphysics and is also a well-known literary critic.

Are we free agents? Can we be morally responsible for what we do? Philosophers distinguish these questions and have all the answers. Some say YES and YES (we are fully free, and wholly morally responsible for what we do). Others say YES and NO (certainly we are free agents—but we cannot be ultimately responsible for what we do). A third group says NO and NO (we are not free agents at all; a fortiori we cannot be morally responsible). A strange minority says NO and YES (we can be morally responsible for what we do even though we are not free agents). This view is rare, but it has a kind of existentialist panache, and appears to be embraced by Wintergreen in Joseph Heller's novel *Closing Time* (1994), as well as by some Protestants.

Who is right? Suppose that tomorrow is a holiday, and that you are wondering what to do. You can climb a mountain or read Lao Tzu. You can restring your mandolin or go to the zoo. At the moment you are reading about free will.

You are free to go on reading or stop now. You have started on this sentence, but you don't have to ... finish it. Right now, as so often in life, you have a number of options. Nothing forces your hand. Surely you are entirely free to choose what to do, and responsible for what you do?

This is what the Compatibilists think. They say YES and YES, and are very influential in the present day. Their name derives from their claim that free will is entirely compatible with *determinism*—the view that everything that happens in the universe is necessitated by what has already gone before, in such a way that nothing can happen otherwise than it does. Free will, they think, is just a matter of not being *constrained* or *compelled* in certain ways that have nothing to do with whether determinism is true or false. "Consider yourself at this moment", they say. "No one is holding a gun to your head. You are not being threatened or manhandled. You are not (surely) drugged, or in chains, or subject to a psychological compulsion like kleptomania, or a post-hypnotic command. So you are wholly free. This is what being a free agent is. It's wholly irrelevant that your character is determined, if indeed it is."

"And although things like guns and chains, threats to the life of your children, psychological obsessions, and so on, are standardly counted as constraints that can limit freedom and responsibility, there is another and more fundamental sense in which you are fully free in any situation in which you can choose or act in any way at all—in any situation in which you are not panicked, or literally compelled to do what you do, in such a way that it is not clear that you can still be said to choose or act at all (as when you press a button because your finger is forced down onto it). Consider pilots of hijacked aeroplanes. They usually stay calm. They *choose* to comply with the hijackers' demands. They act responsibly, as we naturally say. They are able to do other than they do, but they choose not to. They do what they most want to do, all things considered, in the circumstances in which they find themselves; and *all* circumstances limit one's options in some way. Some circumstances limit one's options much more drastically than others, but it doesn't follow that one isn't free to choose in those circumstances. Only literal compulsion, panic, or uncontrollable impulse really removes one's freedom to choose, and to (try to) do what one most wants to do given one's character or personality. Even when one's finger is being forced down on the button, one can still act freely in resisting the pressure or cursing one's oppressor, and in many other ways."

So most of us are wholly free to choose and act throughout our waking lives, according to the Compatibilists. We are free to choose between the options we perceive to be open to us. (Sometimes we would rather not face options, but are unable to avoid awareness of the fact that we do face them.) One has options even when one is in chains, or falling through space. Even if one is completely paralysed, one is still free in so far as one is free to choose to think about one thing rather than another. There is, as Sartre observed, a sense in which we are condemned to freedom, not free not to be free.

One may well not be able to do everything one wants—one may want to fly unassisted, vapourize every gun in the United States by an act of thought, or house all those who sleep on the streets of Calcutta by the end of the month—but few have supposed that free will is a matter of being able to do everything one wants. It is, doubtless, a possible view. But according to the Compatibilists, free will is simply a matter of being unconstrained in such a way that one has genuine options and opportunities for action, and is able to choose between them according to what one wants or thinks best. It doesn't matter if one's character, personality, preferences, and general motivational set are entirely determined by things for which one is in no way responsible—by one's genetic inheritance, upbringing, historical situation, chance encounters, and so on.

Even dogs count as free agents, on this view. So Compatibilists have to explain what distinguishes us from dogs—since we don't think that dogs are free in the way we are. Many of them say that it is our capacity for explicitly self-conscious thought. Not because self-consciousness liberates anyone from determinism: if determinism is true, one is determined to have whatever self-conscious thoughts one has, whatever their complexity. The idea is that self-consciousness makes it possible for one to be explicitly aware of oneself as facing choices and engaging in processes of reasoning about what to do, and thereby constitutes one as a radically free agent in a way unavailable to any unselfconscious agent. One's self-conscious deliberative presence in the situation of choice simply trumps the fact—if it is a fact—that one is, in the final analysis, wholly constituted as the sort of person one is by factors for which one is not in any way ultimately responsible.

Some Compatibilists add that human beings are sharply marked off from dogs by their capacity to act for reasons that they explicitly take to be moral reasons. Compatibilism has many variants. According to Harry Frankfurt's version, for example, one has free will if one wants to be moved to action by the motives that do in fact move one to action. On this view, freedom is just a matter of having a personality that is harmonious in a certain way.

The compatibilists, then, say YES and YES, and those who want to say YES and YES are well advised to follow them, for determinism is unfalsifiable, and may be true. (In the end, contemporary physics gives us no more reason to suppose that determinism is false than to suppose that it is true.) Many, however, think that the Compatibilist account of things does not even touch the real problem of free will. For what is it, they say, to define freedom in such a way that it is compatible with determinism? It is to define it in such a way that an agent can be a free agent even if all its actions throughout its life are determined to happen as they do by events that have taken place before it is born: so that there is a clear sense in which it could not at any point in its life have done otherwise than it did. This, they say, is certainly not free will or moral responsibility. How can one be truly or ultimately morally responsible for what one does if everything one does is ultimately a deterministic outcome of events for whose occurrence one is in no way responsible?

*   *   *

These are the Incompatibilists, and they divide into two groups: the Libertarians, on the one hand, and the No-Freedom theorists or Pessimists, on the other. The Libertarians are upbeat. They say YES and YES, and think the Compatibilists' account of freedom can be improved on. They hold (1) that we do have free will, (2) that free will is not compatible with determinism, and (3) that determinism is therefore false. But they face an extremely difficult task: they have to show how *indeterminism* (the falsity of determinism) can help with free will, and in particular with moral responsibility.

The Pessimists do not think this can be shown. They agree that free will is not compatible with determinism, but deny that indeterminism can help. They think that free will, of the sort that is necessary for genuine moral responsibility, is provably impossible. They say NO and NO.

They begin by granting what everyone must. They grant that there is a clear, important, compatibilist sense in which we can be free agents (we can be free, when unconstrained, to choose and to do what we want or think best, given how we are). But they insist that this isn't enough: it doesn't give us what we want, in the way of free will. Nor does it give us what we believe we have. But (they continue) it is not as if the Compatibilists have missed something. The truth is that nothing can give us what we think we want, and ordinarily think we have. We cannot be morally responsible, in the absolute, buck-stopping way in which we often unreflectively think we are. We cannot have "strong" free will of the kind that we would need to have, in order to be morally responsible in this way.

One way of setting out the Pessimists' argument is as follows:

(1) When you act, you do what you do, in the situation in which you find yourself, because of the way you are.

But then

(2) To be truly or ultimately morally responsible for what you do, you must be truly or ultimately responsible for the way you are, at least in certain crucial mental respects. (Obviously you don't have to be responsible for your height, age, sex, and so on.)

But

(3) You can't be ultimately responsible for the way you are in any respect at all, so you can't be ultimately responsible for what you do.

For

(4) To be ultimately responsible for the way you are, you must have somehow intentionally brought it about that you are the way you are.

And the problem is then this. Suppose

(5) You have somehow intentionally brought it about that you are the way you now are, in

certain mental respects: suppose you have brought it about that you have a certain mental nature Z, in such a way that you can be said to be ultimately responsible for Z.

For this to be true

(6) You must already have had a certain mental nature Y, in the light of which you brought it about that you now have Z. If you didn't already have a mental nature then you didn't have any intentions or preferences, and can't be responsible for the way you now are, even if you have changed.

But then

(7) For it to be true that you are ultimately responsible for how you now are, you must be ultimately responsible for having had that nature, Y, in the light of which you brought it about that you now have Z.

So

(8) You must have brought it about that you had Y.

But then

(9) You must have existed already with a prior nature, X, in the light of which you brought it about that you had Y, in the light of which you brought it about that you now have Z.

And so on. Here one is setting off on a potentially infinite regress. In order for one to be truly or ultimately responsible for *how one is* in such a way that one can be truly responsible for *what one does*, something impossible has to be true: there has to be, and cannot be, a starting point in the series of acts of bringing it about that one has a certain nature; a starting point that constitutes an act of ultimate self-origination.

There is a more concise way of putting the point: in order to be ultimately responsible, one would have to be *causa sui*—the ultimate cause or origin of oneself, or at least of some crucial part of one's mental nature. But nothing can be ultimately *causa sui* in any respect at all. Even if the property of being *causa sui* is allowed to

belong unintelligibly to God, it cannot plausibly be supposed to be possessed by ordinary finite human beings. "The *causa sui* is the best self-contradiction that has been conceived so far", as Nietzsche remarked in 1886:

> "it is a sort of rape and perversion of logic. But the extravagant pride of man has managed to entangle itself profoundly and frightfully with just this nonsense. The desire for "freedom of the will" in the superlative metaphysical sense, which still holds sway, unfortunately, in the minds of the half-educated; the desire to bear the entire and ultimate responsibility for one's actions oneself, and to absolve God, the world, ancestors, chance, and society involves nothing less than to be precisely this causa sui and, with more than Baron Munchhausen's audacity, to pull oneself up into existence by the hair, out of the swamps of nothingness...."

In fact, nearly all of those who believe in strong free will do so without any conscious thought that it requires ultimate self-origination. But self origination is the only thing that could actually ground the kind of strong free will that is regularly believed in.

The Pessimists' argument may seem contrived, but essentially the same argument can be given in a more natural form as follows. (A) One is the way one is, initially, as a result of heredity and early experience. (B) These are clearly things for which one cannot be held to be in any way responsible (this might not be true if there were reincarnation, but this would just shift the problem backwards). (C) One cannot at any later stage of one's life hope to accede to ultimate responsibility for the way one is by trying to change the way one already is as a result of heredity and experience. For one may well try to change oneself, but (D) both the particular way in which one is moved to try to change oneself, and the degree of one's success in one's attempt at change, will be determined by how one already is as a result of heredity and experience. And (E) any further changes that one can bring about only after one has brought about certain initial changes will in turn be determined, via the initial changes, by heredity and previous experience. (F) This may not be the whole story, for it may be that some changes in the way one is are traceable to the influence of indeterministic or random factors. But (G) it is absurd to suppose that indeterministic or random factors, for which one is ex hypothesi in no way responsible, can in themselves contribute to one's being truly or ultimately responsible for how one is.

*   *   *

The claim, then, is not that people cannot change the way they are. They can, in certain respects (which tend to be exaggerated by North Americans and underestimated, perhaps, by members of other cultures). The claim is only that people cannot be supposed to change themselves in such a way as to be or become ultimately responsible for the way they are, and hence for their actions. One can put the point by saying that in the final analysis the way you are is, in every last detail, a matter of luck—good or bad.

Philosophers will ask what exactly this "ultimate" responsibility is supposed to be. They will suggest that it doesn't really make sense, and try to move from there to the claim that it can't really be what we have in mind when we talk about moral responsibility. It is very clear to most people, however, and one dramatic way to characterize it is by reference to the story of heaven and hell: it is responsibility of such a kind that, if we have it, it *makes sense* to propose that it could be just to punish some of us with torment in hell and reward others with bliss in heaven. It makes sense because what we do is absolutely up to us. The words "makes sense" are stressed because one doesn't have to believe in the story of heaven and hell in order to understand the notion of ultimate responsibility that it is used to illustrate. Nor does one have to believe in it in order to believe in ultimate responsibility (many atheists have done so).

The story is useful because it illustrates the *kind* of absolute or ultimate responsibility that many have supposed—and do suppose—themselves to have. (Another way to characterize it is to say that it exists if punishment and reward can be fair without having any pragmatic—or indeed aesthetic—justification.) But one doesn't have to appeal to it when describing the sorts of everyday situation that are primarily influential in giving rise to our belief in ultimate responsibility. Suppose you set off for a shop on the evening of a national holiday, intending to buy a cake with your last ten pound note. Everything is closing down. There is one cake left; it costs ten pounds. On the steps of the shop someone is shaking an Oxfam tin. You stop, and it seems completely clear to you that it is entirely up to you what you do next: you are truly, radically free to choose, in such a way that you will be ultimately responsible for whatever you do choose. You can put the money in the tin, or go in and buy the cake, or just walk away. You are not only completely free to choose. You are not free not to choose.

Standing there, you may believe determinism is true: you may believe that in five minutes time you will be able to look back on the situation you are now in and say, of what you will by then have done, "It was determined that I should do that". But even if you do wholeheartedly believe this, it does not seem to touch your current sense of the absoluteness of your freedom and moral responsibility.

One diagnosis of this phenomenon is that one can't really believe that determinism is true, in such situations, and also can't help thinking that its falsity might make freedom possible. But the feeling of ultimate responsibility seems to remain inescapable even if this is not so. Suppose one fully accepts the Pessimists' argument that no one can be causa sui, and that one has to be *causa sui* (in certain crucial mental respects) in order to be ultimately responsible for one's actions. This does not seem to have any impact on one's sense of one's radical freedom and responsibility, as one stands there, wondering what to do. One's radical responsibility seems to stem simply from the fact that one is fully conscious of one's situation, and knows that one can choose, and believes that one action is morally better than the other. This seems to be immediately enough to confer full and ultimate responsibility. And yet it cannot really do so, according to the Pessimists. For whatever one actually does, one will do what one does because of the way one is, and the way one is is something for which one neither is nor can be responsible, however self-consciously aware of one's situation one is.

The Pessimists' argument is hard to stomach (even Hitler is let off the hook), and one challenge to it runs as follows. "Look, the reason why one can be ultimately responsible for what one does is that one's *self* is, in some crucial sense, independent of one's general *mental nature* (character or motivational structure). Suppose one faces a difficult choice between A, doing one's moral duty, and B, following one's desires. You Pessimists describe this situation as follows: Given one's mental nature, you say, one responds in a certain way. One is swayed by reasons for and against both A and B. One tends towards A or B, and in the end one does one or the other, given one's mental nature, which is something for which one cannot be ultimately responsible. But this description of yours forgets the *self*—it forgets what one might call 'the agent-self'. As an agent-self, one is in some way independent of one's mental nature. One's mental nature *inclines* one to do one thing rather than another, but it does not thereby *necessitate* one to do one thing rather than the other (to use Leibniz's terms). As an agent-self, one incorporates a power of free decision that is independent of all the particularities of one's mental nature in such a way that one can after all count as ultimately morally responsible in one's decisions and actions even though one is not ultimately responsible for any aspect of one's mental nature."

The Pessimists are unimpressed: "Even if one grants the validity of this conception of the agent-self for the sake of argument", they say, "it cannot help. For if the agent-self decides in the light of the agent's mental nature but is not determined by the agent's mental nature, the following question immediately arises: *Why* does the dear old agent-self decide as it does? The general answer is clear. Whatever it decides, it

decides as it does because of the overall way it is, and this necessary truth returns us to where we started: somehow, the agent-self is going to have to get to be responsible for being the way it is, in order for its decisions to be a source of ultimate responsibility. But this is impossible: nothing can be *causa sui* in the required way. Whatever the nature of the agent-self, it is ultimately a matter of luck. Maybe the agent-self decides as it does partly or wholly because of the presence of indeterministic occurrences in the decision process. Maybe, maybe not. It makes no difference, for indeterministic occurrences can never contribute to ultimate moral responsibility."

*   *   *

Some think they can avoid this debate by asserting that free will and moral responsibility are just a matter of being governed by reason—or by Reason with a dignifying capital "R". But being governed by Reason can't be the source of ultimate responsibility. It can't be a property that makes punishment ultimately just or fair for those who possess it, and unfair for those who don't. For to be morally responsible, on this view, is simply to possess one sort of motivational set among others. But if you do possess this motivational set then you are simply lucky —if it is indeed a good thing—while those who lack it are unlucky.

This will be denied. It will be said, truly, that some people struggle to become more morally responsible, and make an enormous effort. Their moral responsibility is then not a matter of luck: it is their own hard won achievement. The Pessimists' reply is immediate. "Suppose you are someone who struggles to be morally responsible, and make an enormous effort. Well, that too is a matter of luck. You are lucky to be someone who has a character of a sort that disposes you to make that sort of effort. Someone who lacks a character of that sort is merely unlucky."

In the end, luck swallows everything: This is one (admittedly contentious) way of putting the point that there can be no ultimate responsibility, given the natural, strong conception of responsibility that was characterized by reference to the story of heaven and hell. Relative to that conception, no punishment or reward is ever ultimately just or fair, however natural or useful or otherwise humanly appropriate it may be or seem.

The free will problem is like a carousel. One starts with the Compatibilist position ... But it cannot satisfy our intuitions about moral responsibility ... So it seems that an Incompatibilist and indeed Libertarian account of free will is needed, according to which free will requires the falsity of determinism ... But any such account immediately triggers the Pessimists' objection that indeterministic occurrences cannot possibly contribute to moral responsibility ... For one can hardly be supposed to be more truly morally responsible for one's choices and actions or character if indeterministic or random occurrences have played a part in their causation than if they have not played such a part ... But what this shows is that the Incompatibilists' "ultimate" moral responsibility is *obviously* impossible ... But that means that we should return to Compatibilism, since it is the best we can do ... But Compatibilism cannot possibly satisfy our intuitions about moral responsibility ....

What should we do? Get off the metaphysical merry-go-round, and take up psychology. The principal positions in the traditional debate are clear. No radically new options are likely to emerge after millennia of debate, and the interesting questions that remain are primarily psychological: *Why* exactly do we believe we have ultimate responsibility of the kind that can be characterized by reference to the story of heaven and hell? What is it like to live with this belief? What are its varieties? How might we be changed by dwelling intensely on the view that ultimate responsibility is impossible?

One reason for the belief has already been given: it has to do with the way we experience choice, as self-conscious agents confronting the Oxfam box and the cake. And this raises the interesting question whether *all* self-conscious agents who face choices and are fully self-consciously aware of the fact that they do so must experience themselves as having strong

free will, or as being radically self-determining? We human beings cannot experience our choices as determined, even if determinism is true, but perhaps this is a human peculiarity, not an inescapable feature of any possible self-conscious agent. And perhaps it is not even universal among human beings: Krishnamurti claims that "a truly intelligent [spiritually advanced] mind simply cannot have choice" because it "can ... only choose the path of truth.... Only the unintelligent mind has free will," and a related thought is expressed by Saul Bellow in *Humboldt's Gift*: "In the next realm, where things are clearer, clarity eats into freedom. We are free on earth because of cloudiness, because of error, because of marvellous limitation." Spinoza extends the point to God, who cannot, he says, "be said ... to act from freedom of the will".

Other causes of our belief in strong free will have been suggested, apart from the cake and the Oxfam box. Hume stresses our experience of indecision. Kant holds that our experience of moral obligation makes belief in strong free will inevitable. P. F. Strawson argues that our belief in freedom is grounded in certain fundamental natural reactions to other people—such as gratitude and resentment—that we cannot hope to give up. Those who think hard about free will are likely to conclude that the complex moral psychology of the experience of freedom is the most fruitful area of research. New generations, however, will continue to launch themselves onto the old carousel, and the debate is likely to continue for as long as human beings can think, as the Pessimists' argument that we can't possibly have strong free will keeps bumping into the fact that we can't help believing that we do.

The facts are clear, and they have been known for a long time. When it comes to the metaphysics of free will, Andre Gide's remark is apt: "Everything has been said before, but since nobody listens we have to keep going back and beginning all over again." It seems the only freedom that we can have is Compatibilist freedom. Since that is not enough for ultimate responsibility, we cannot have ultimate responsibility.

The debate continues, and some have thought that philosophy ought to move on. There is little reason to expect that it will, as new minds are seduced by the problem. And yet the facts are clear. One cannot be ultimately responsible for one's character or mental nature in any way at all. Heracleitus, Novalis, George Eliot, Nietzsche, Henry James and others are not quite right in so far as they say (in their various ways) that character is destiny; for external circumstances are also part of destiny. But the point seems good, and final, when it comes to the question of ultimate moral responsibility.

4.2 Alternate Possibilities and Moral Responsibility

HARRY FRANKFURT

Harry Frankfurt is Professor Emeritus at Princeton University. He has published several important papers on the issues of free will.

A dominant role in nearly all recent inquiries into the free-will problem has been played by a principle which I shall call "the principle of alternate possibilities." This principle states that a person is morally responsible for what he has done only if he could have done otherwise. Its exact meaning is a subject of controversy, particularly concerning whether someone who accepts it is thereby committed to believing that moral responsibility and determinism are incompatible. Practically no one, however, seems inclined to deny or even to question that the principle of alternate possibilities (construed in some way or other) is true. It has generally seemed so overwhelmingly plausible that some philosophers have even characterized it as an *a priori* truth. People whose accounts of free will or of moral responsibility are radically at odds evidently find in it a firm and convenient common ground upon which they can profitably take their opposing stands.

But the principle of alternate possibilities is false. A person may well be morally responsible for what he has done even though he could not have done otherwise. The principle's plausibility is an illusion, which can be made to vanish by bringing the relevant moral phenomena into sharper focus.

I

In seeking illustrations of the principle of alternate possibilities, it is most natural to think of situations in which the same circumstances both bring it about that a person does something and make it impossible for him to avoid doing it. These include, for example, situations in which a person is coerced into doing something, or in which he is impelled to act by a hypnotic suggestion, or in which some inner compulsion drives him to do what he does. In situations of these kinds there are circumstances that make it impossible for the person to do otherwise, and these very circumstances also serve to bring it about that he does whatever it is that he does.

However, there may be circumstances that constitute sufficient conditions for a certain action to be performed by someone and that therefore make it impossible for the person to do otherwise, but that do not actually impel the person to act or in any way produce his action. A person may do something in circumstances that

This paper first appeared in *Journal of Philosophy* vol. 66 (1969), pp. 829–839. Reprinted by permission of the publisher and author.

leave him no alternative to doing it, without these circumstances actually moving him or leading him to do it—without them playing any role, indeed, in bringing it about that he does what he does.

An examination of situations characterized by circumstances of this sort casts doubt, I believe, on the relevance to questions of moral responsibility of the fact that a person who has done something could not have done otherwise. I propose to develop some examples of this kind in the context of a discussion of coercion and to suggest that our moral intuitions concerning these examples tend to disconfirm the principle of alternate possibilities. Then I will discuss the principle in more general terms, explain what I think is wrong with it, and describe briefly and without argument how it might appropriately be revised.

II

It is generally agreed that a person who has been coerced to do something did not do it freely and is not morally responsible for having done it. Now the doctrine that coercion and moral responsibility are mutually exclusive may appear to be no more than a somewhat particularized version of the principle of alternate possibilities. It is natural enough to say of a person who has been coerced to do something that he could not have done otherwise. And it may easily seem that being coerced deprives a person of freedom and of moral responsibility simply because it is a special case of being unable to do otherwise. The principle of alternate possibilities may in this way derive some credibility from its association with the very plausible proposition that moral responsibility is excluded by coercion.

It is not right, however, that it should do so. The fact that a person was coerced to act as he did may entail both that he could not have done otherwise and that he bears no moral responsibility for his action. But his lack of moral responsibility is not entailed by his having been unable to do otherwise. The doctrine that coercion excludes moral responsibility is not correctly

understood, in other words, as a particularized version of the principle of alternate possibilities.

Let us suppose that someone is threatened convincingly with a penalty he finds unacceptable and that he then does what is required of him by the issuer of the threat. We can imagine details that would make it reasonable for us to think that the person was coerced to perform the action in question, that he could not have done otherwise, and that he bears no moral responsibility for having done what he did. But just what is it about situations of this kind that warrants the judgment that the threatened person is not morally responsible for his act?

This question may be approached by considering situations of the following kind. Jones decides for reasons of his own to do something, then someone threatens him with a very harsh penalty (so harsh that any reasonable person would submit to the threat) unless he does precisely that, and Jones does it. Will we hold Jones morally responsible for what he has done? I think this will depend on the roles we think were played, in leading him to act, by his original decision and by the threat.

One possibility is that $Jones_1$ is not a reasonable man: he is, rather, a man who does what he has once decided to do no matter what happens next and no matter what the cost. In that case, the threat actually exerted no effective force upon him. He acted without any regard to it, very much as if he were not aware that it had been made. If this is indeed the way it was, the situation did not involve coercion at all. The threat did not lead $Jones_1$ to do what he did. Nor was it in fact sufficient to have prevented him from doing otherwise: if his earlier decision had been to do something else, the threat would not have deterred him in the slightest. It seems evident that in these circumstances the fact that $Jones_1$ was threatened in no way reduces the moral responsibility he would otherwise bear for his act. This example, however, is not a counterexample either to the doctrine that coercion excuses or to the principle of alternate possibilities. For we have supposed that $Jones_1$ is a man upon whom the threat had no coercive effect and, hence, that it did not actually deprive him of alternatives to doing what he did.

Another possibility is that Jones$_2$ was stampeded by the threat. Given that threat, he would have performed that action regardless of what decision he had already made. The threat upset him so profoundly, moreover, that he completely forgot his own earlier decision and did what was demanded of him entirely because he was terrified of the penalty with which he was threatened. In this case, it is not relevant to his having performed the action that he had already decided on his own to perform it. When the chips were down he thought of nothing but the threat, and fear alone led him to act. The fact that at an earlier time Jones$_2$ had decided for his own reasons to act in just that way may be relevant to an evaluation of his character; he may bear full moral responsibility for having made *that* decision. But he can hardly be said to be morally responsible for his action. For he performed the action simply as a result of the coercion to which he was subjected. His earlier decision played no role in bringing it about that he did what he did, and it would therefore be gratuitous to assign it a role in the moral evaluation of his action.

Now consider a third possibility. Jones$_3$ was neither stampeded by the threat nor indifferent to it. The threat impressed him, as it would impress any reasonable man, and he would have submitted to it wholeheartedly if he had not already made a decision that coincided with the one demanded of him. In fact, however, he performed the action in question on the basis of the decision he had made before the threat was issued. When he acted, he was not actually motivated by the threat but solely by the considerations that had originally commended the action to him. It was not the threat that led him to act, though it would have done so if he had not already provided himself with a sufficient motive for performing the action in question.

No doubt it will be very difficult for anyone to know, in a case like this one, exactly what happened. Did Jones$_3$ perform the action because of the threat, or were his reasons for acting simply those which had already persuaded him to do so? Or did he act on the basis of two motives, each of which was sufficient for his action? It is not impossible, however, that the situation should be clearer than situations of this kind usually are. And suppose it is apparent to us that Jones$_3$ acted on the basis of his own decision and not because of the threat. Then I think we would be justified in regarding his moral responsibility for what he did as unaffected by the threat even though, since he would in any case have submitted to the threat, he could not have avoided doing what he did. It would be entirely reasonable for us to make the same judgment concerning his moral responsibility that we would have made if we had not known of the threat. For the threat did not in fact influence his performance of the action. He did what he did just as if the threat had not been made at all.

III

The case of Jones$_3$ may appear at first glance to combine coercion and moral responsibility, and thus to provide a counterexample to the doctrine that coercion excuses. It is not really so certain that it does so, however, because it is unclear whether the example constitutes a genuine instance of coercion. Can we say of Jones$_3$ that he was coerced to do something, when he had already decided on his own to do it and when he did it entirely on the basis of that decision? Or would it be more correct to say that Jones$_3$ was not coerced to do what he did, even though he himself recognized that there was an irresistible force at work in virtue of which he had to do it? My own linguistic intuitions lead me toward the second alternative, but they are somewhat equivocal. Perhaps we can say either of these things, or perhaps we must add a qualifying explanation to whichever of them we say.

This murkiness, however, does not interfere with our drawing an important moral from an examination of the example. Suppose we decide to say that Jones$_3$ was *not* coerced. Our basis for saying this will clearly be that it is incorrect to regard a man as being coerced to do something unless he does it *because of* the coercive force exerted against him The fact that an irresistible threat is made will not, then, entail that the person who receives it is coerced to do what he does. It will also be necessary that the threat is what actually accounts for his doing it. On the other hand, suppose we decide to say that Jones₃ *was* coerced. Then we will be bound to admit that being coerced does not exclude being morally responsible. And we will also surely be led to the view that coercion affects the judgment of a person's moral responsibility only when the person acts as he does because he is coerced to do so—i.e., when the fact that he is coerced is what accounts for his action.

Whichever we decide to say, then, we will recognize that the doctrine that coercion excludes moral responsibility is not a particularized version of the principle of alternate possibilities. Situations in which a person who does something cannot do otherwise because he is subject to coercive power are either not instances of coercion at all, or they are situations in which the person may still be morally responsible for what he does if it is not because of the coercion that he does it. When we excuse a person who has been coerced, we do not excuse him because he was unable to do otherwise. Even though a person is subject to a coercive force that precludes his performing any action but one, he may nonetheless bear full moral responsibility for performing that action.

IV

To the extent that the principle of alternate possibilities derives its plausibility from association with the doctrine that coercion excludes moral responsibility, a clear understanding of the latter diminishes the appeal of the former. Indeed the case of Jones₃ may appear to do more than illuminate the relationship between the two doctrines. It may well seem to provide a decisive counterexample to the principle of alternate possibilities and thus to show that this principle is false. For the irresistibility of the threat to which Jones₃ is subjected might well be taken to mean that he cannot but perform the action he performs. And yet the threat, since Jones₃ performs the action without regard to it, does not reduce his moral responsibility for what he does.

The following objection will doubtless be raised against the suggestion that the case of Jones₃ is a counterexample to the principle of alternate possibilities. There is perhaps a sense in which Jones₃ cannot do otherwise than perform the action he performs, since he is a reasonable man and the threat he encounters is sufficient to move any reasonable man. But it is not this sense that is germane to the principle of alternate possibilities. His knowledge that he stands to suffer an intolerably harsh penalty does not mean that Jones₃, strictly speaking, *cannot* perform any action but the one he does perform. After all it is still open to him, and this is crucial, to defy the threat if he wishes to do so and to accept the penalty his action would bring down upon him. In the sense in which the principle of alternate possibilities employs the concept of "could have done otherwise," Jones₃'s inability to resist the threat does not mean that he cannot do otherwise than perform the action he performs. Hence the case of Jones₃ does not constitute an instance contrary to the principle.

I do not propose to consider in what sense the concept of "could have done otherwise" figures in the principle of alternate possibilities, nor will I attempt to measure the force of the objection I have just described.[1] For I believe that whatever force this objection may be thought to have can be deflected by altering the example in the following way.[2] Suppose someone—Black, let us say—wants Jones₄ to perform a certain action. Black is prepared to go to considerable lengths to get his way, but he prefers to avoid showing his hand unnecessarily. So he waits until Jones₄ is about to make up his mind what to do, and he does nothing unless it is clear to him (Black is an excellent judge of such things) that Jones₄ is going to decide to do something *other* than what he wants him to do. If it does become clear that Jones₄ is going to decide to do something else, Black takes effective steps to ensure that Jones₄ decides to do, and that he does do, what he wants him to do.[3] Whatever Jones₄'s initial preferences and inclinations, then, Black will have his way.

What steps will Black take, if he believes he must take steps, in order to ensure that Jones₄ decides and acts as he wishes? Anyone with a theory concerning what "could have done otherwise" means may answer this question for himself by describing whatever measures he would regard as sufficient to guarantee that, in the relevant sense, Jones₄ cannot do otherwise. Let Black pronounce a terrible threat, and in this way both force Jones₄ to perform the desired action and prevent him from performing a forbidden one. Let Black give Jones₄ a potion, or put him under hypnosis, and in some such way as these generate in Jones₄ an irresistible inner compulsion to perform the act Black wants performed and to avoid others. Or let Black manipulate the minute processes of Jones₄'s brain and nervous system in some more direct way, so that causal forces running in and out of his synapses and along the poor man's nerves determine that he chooses to act and that he does act in the one way and not in any other. Given any conditions under which it will be maintained that Jones₄ cannot do otherwise, in other words, let Black bring it about that those conditions prevail. The structure of the example is flexible enough, I think, to find a way around any charge of irrelevance by accommodating the doctrine on which the charge is based.[4]

Now suppose that Black never has to show his hand because Jones₄, for reasons of his own, decides to perform and does perform the very action Black wants him to perform. In that case, it seems clear, Jones₄ will bear precisely the same moral responsibility for what he does as he would have borne if Black had not been ready to take steps to ensure that he do it. It would be quite unreasonable to excuse Jones₄ for his action, or to withhold the praise to which it would normally entitle him, on the basis of the fact that he could not have done otherwise. This fact played no role at all in leading him to act as he did. He would have acted the same even if it

had not been a fact. Indeed, everything happened just as it would have happened without Black's presence in the situation and without his readiness to intrude into it.

In this example there are sufficient conditions for Jones₄'s performing the action in question. What action he performs is not up to him. Of course it is in a way up to him whether he acts on his own or as a result of Black's intervention. That depends upon what action he himself is inclined to perform. But whether he finally acts on his own or as a result of Black's intervention, he performs the same action. He has no alternative but to do what Black wants him to do. If he does it on his own, however, his moral responsibility for doing it is not affected by the fact that Black was lurking in the background with sinister intent, since this intent never comes into play.

V

The fact that a person could not have avoided doing something is a sufficient condition of his having done it. But, as some of my examples show, this fact may play no role whatever in the explanation of why he did it. It may not figure at all among the circumstances that actually brought it about that he did what he did, so that his action is to be accounted for on another basis entirely. Even though the person was unable to do otherwise, that is to say, it may not be the case that he acted as he did *because* he could not have done otherwise. Now if someone had no alternative to performing a certain action but did not perform it because he was unable to do otherwise, then he would have performed exactly the same action even if he *could* have done otherwise. The circumstances that made it impossible for him to do otherwise could have been subtracted from the situation without affecting what happened or why it happened in any way. Whatever it was that actually led the person to do what he did, or that made him do it, would have led him to do it or made him do it even if it had been possible for him to do something else instead.

Thus it would have made no difference, so far as concerns his action or how he came to perform it, if the circumstances that made it impossible for him to avoid performing it had not prevailed. The fact that he could not have done otherwise clearly provides no basis for supposing that he *might* have done otherwise if he had been able to do so. When a fact is in this way irrelevant to the problem of accounting for a person's action it seems quite gratuitous to assign it any weight in the assessment of his moral responsibility. Why should the fact be considered in reaching a moral judgment concerning the person when it does not help in any way to understand either what made him act as he did or what, in other circumstances, he might have done?

This, then, is why the principle of alternate possibilities is mistaken. It asserts that a person bears no moral responsibility—that is, he is to be excused—for having performed an action if there were circumstances that made it impossible for him to avoid performing it. But there may be circumstances that make it impossible for a person to avoid performing some action without those circumstances in any way bringing it about that he performs that action. It would surely be no good for the person to refer to circumstances of this sort in an effort to absolve himself of moral responsibility for performing the action in question. For those circumstances, by hypothesis, actually had nothing to do with his having done what he did. He would have done precisely the same thing, and he would have been led or made in precisely the same way to do it, even if they had not prevailed.

We often do, to be sure, excuse people for what they have done when they tell us (and we believe them) that they could not have done otherwise. But this is because we assume that what they tell us serves to explain why they did what they did. We take it for granted that they are not being disingenuous, as a person would be who cited as an excuse the fact that he could not have avoided doing what he did but who knew full well that it was not at all because of this that he did it.

What I have said may suggest that the principle of alternate possibilities should be revised

so as to assert that a person is not morally responsible for what he has done if he did it because he could not have done otherwise. It may be noted that this revision of the principle does not seriously affect the arguments of those who have relied on the original principle in their efforts to maintain that moral responsibility and determinism are incompatible. For if it was causally determined that a person perform a certain action, then it will be true that the person performed it because of those causal determinants. And if the fact that it was causally determined that a person perform a certain action means that the person could not have done otherwise, as philosophers who argue for the incompatibility thesis characteristically suppose, then the fact that it was causally determined that a person perform a certain action will mean that the person performed it because he could not have done otherwise. The revised principle of alternate possibilities will entail, on this assumption concerning the meaning of 'could have done otherwise,' that a person is not morally responsible for what he has done if it was causally determined that he do it. I do not believe, however, that this revision of the principle is acceptable.

Suppose a person tells us that he did what he did because he was unable to do otherwise; or suppose he makes the similar statement that he did what he did because he had to do it. We do often accept statements like these (if we believe them) as valid excuses, and such statements may well seem at first glance to invoke the revised principle of alternate possibilities. But I think that when we accept such statements as valid excuses it is because we assume that we are being told more than the statements strictly and literally convey. We understand the person who offers the excuse to mean that he did what he did *only because* he was unable to do otherwise, or *only because* he had to do it. And we understand him to mean, more particularly, that when he did what he did it was not because that was what he really wanted to do. The principle of alternate possibilities should thus be replaced, in my opinion, by the following principle: a person is not morally responsible for what he has done if he did it only because he could not have done otherwise. This principle does not appear to conflict with the view that moral responsibility is compatible with determinism.

The following may all be true: there were circumstances that made it impossible for a person to avoid doing something; these circumstances actually played a role in bringing it about that he did it, so that it is correct to say that he did it because he could not have done otherwise; the person really wanted to do what he did; he did it because it was what he really wanted to do, so that it is not correct to say that he did what he did only because he could not have done otherwise. Under these conditions, the person may well be morally responsible for what he has done. On the other hand, he will not be morally responsible for what he has done if he did it only because he could not have done otherwise, even if what he did was something he really wanted to do.

NOTES

1. The two main concepts employed in the principle of alternate possibilities are "morally responsible" and "could have done otherwise." To discuss the principle without analyzing either of these concepts may well seem like an attempt at piracy. The reader should take notice that my Jolly Roger is now unfurled.
2. After thinking up the example that I am about to develop I learned that Robert Nozick, in lectures given several years ago, had formulated an example of the same general type and had proposed it as a counterexample to the principle of alternate possibilities.
3. The assumption that Black can predict what Jones$_4$ will decide to do does not beg the question of determinism. We can imagine that Jones$_4$ has often confronted the alternatives—A and B—that he now confronts, and that his face has invariably twitched when he was about to decide to do A and never when he was about to decide to do B. Knowing this, and observing the twitch, Black would have a basis for prediction. This does, to be sure, suppose that there is some sort of causal relation between Jones$_4$'s state at the time of the twitch and his subsequent states. But any plausible view of decision or of action will allow that reaching a decision and performing an action both involve earlier and later phases, with causal relations between them, and such that the earlier phases are not themselves part of the decision or of the action. The example does not require that these earlier phases be deterministically related to still earlier events.
4. The example is also flexible enough to allow for the elimination of Black altogether. Anyone who thinks that the effectiveness of the example is undermined by its reliance on a human manipulator, who imposes his will on Jones$_4$, can substitute for Black a machine programmed to do what Black does. If this is still not good enough, forget both Black and the machine and suppose that their role is played by natural forces involving no will or design at all.

4.3 Moral Luck

THOMAS NAGEL

Thomas Nagel teaches philosophy at New York University. He is the author of *Mortal Questions*, *The View from Nowhere*, and *The Last Word*, among many other titles. His work has been especially influential in the philosophy of mind and moral philosophy.

Kant believed that good or bad luck should influence neither our moral judgment of a person and his actions, nor his moral assessment of himself.

> The good will is not good because of what it effects or accomplishes or because of its adequacy to achieve some proposed end; it is good only because of its willing, i.e., it is good of itself. And, regarded for itself, it is to be esteemed incomparably higher than anything which could be brought about by it in favor of any inclination or even of the sum total of all inclinations. Even if it should happen that, by a particularly unfortunate fate or by the niggardly provision of a stepmotherly nature, this will should be wholly lacking in power to accomplish its purpose, and if even the greatest effort should not avail it to achieve anything of its end, and if there remained only the good will (not as a mere wish but as the summoning of all the means in our power), it would sparkle like a jewel in its own right, as something that had its full worth in itself. Usefulness or fruitlessness can neither diminish nor augment this worth.[1]

He would presumably have said the same about a bad will: whether it accomplishes its evil purposes is morally irrelevant. And a course of action that would be condemned if it had a bad outcome cannot be vindicated if by luck it turns out well. There cannot be moral risk. This view seems to be wrong, but it arises in response to a fundamental problem about moral responsibility to which we possess no satisfactory solution.

The problem develops out of the ordinary conditions of moral judgment. Prior to reflection it is intuitively plausible that people cannot be morally assessed for what is not their fault, or for what is due to factors beyond their control. Such judgment is different from the evaluation of something as a good or bad thing, or state of affairs. The latter may be present in addition to moral judgment, but when we blame someone for his actions we are not merely saying it is bad that they happened, or bad that he exists: we are judging *him*, saying he is bad, which is different from his being a bad thing. This kind of judgment takes only a certain kind of object. Without

being able to explain exactly why, we feel that the appropriateness of moral assessment is easily undermined by the discovery that the act or attribute, no matter how good or bad, is not under the person's control. While other evaluations remain, this one seems to lose its footing. So a clear absence of control, produced by involuntary movement, physical force, or ignorance of the circumstances, excuses what is done from moral judgment. But what we do depends in many more ways than these on what is not under our control—what is not produced by a good or a bad will, in Kant's phrase. And external influences in this broader range are not usually thought to excuse what is done from moral judgment, positive or negative.

Let me give a few examples, beginning with the type of case Kant has in mind. Whether we succeed or fail in what we try to do nearly always depends to some extent on factors beyond our control. This is true of murder, altruism, revolution, the sacrifice of certain interests for the sake of others—almost any morally important act. What has been done, and what is morally judged, is partly determined by external factors. However jewel-like the good will may be in its own right, there is a morally significant difference between rescuing someone from a burning building and dropping him from a twelfth-story window while trying to rescue him. Similarly, there is a morally significant difference between reckless driving and manslaughter. But whether a reckless driver hits a pedestrian depends on the presence of the pedestrian at the point where he recklessly passes a red light. What we do is also limited by the opportunities and choices with which we are faced, and these are largely determined by factors beyond our control. Someone who was an officer in a concentration camp might have led a quiet and harmless life if the Nazis had never come to power in Germany. And someone who led a quiet and harmless life in Argentina might have become an officer in a concentration camp if he had not left Germany for business reasons in 1930.

I shall say more later about these and other examples. I introduce them here to illustrate a general point. Where a significant aspect of what someone does depends on factors beyond his control, yet we continue to treat him in that respect as an object of moral judgment, it can be called moral luck. Such luck can be good or bad. And the problem posed by this phenomenon, which led Kant to deny its possibility, is that the broad range of external influences here identified seems on close examination to undermine moral assessment as surely as does the narrower range of familiar excusing conditions. If the condition of control is consistently applied, it threatens to erode most of the moral assessments we find it natural to make. The things for which people are morally judged are determined in more ways than we at first realize by what is beyond their control. And when the seemingly natural requirement of fault or responsibility is applied in light of these facts, it leaves few pre-reflective moral judgments intact. Ultimately, nothing or almost nothing about what a person does seems to be under his control.

Why not conclude, then, that the condition of control is false—that it is an initially plausible hypothesis refuted by clear counter-examples? One could in that case look instead for a more refined condition which picked out the *kinds* of lack of control that really undermine certain moral judgments, without yielding the unacceptable conclusion derived from the broader condition, that most or all ordinary moral judgments are illegitimate.

What rules out this escape is that we are dealing not with a theoretical conjecture but with a philosophical problem. The condition of control does not suggest itself merely as a generalization from certain clear cases. It seems *correct* in the further cases to which it is extended beyond the original set. When we undermine moral assessment by considering new ways in which control is absent, we are not just discovering what *would* follow given the general hypothesis, but are actually being persuaded that in itself the absence of control is relevant in these cases too. The erosion of moral judgment emerges not as the absurd consequence of an over-simple theory, but as a natural consequence of the ordinary idea of moral assessment, when it is applied in view of a more complete and precise account of the facts. It would therefore be a mistake to argue from the unacceptability of the conclusions to the need for a different account of the conditions of moral responsibility. The view that moral luck is paradoxical is not a *mistake,* ethical or logical, but a perception of one of the ways in which the intuitively acceptable conditions of moral judgment threaten to undermine it all.

There are roughly four ways in which the natural objects of moral assessment are disturbingly subject to luck. One is the phenomenon of constitutive luck—the kind of person you are, where this is not just a question of what you deliberately do, but of your inclinations, capacities, and temperament. Another category is luck in one's circumstances—the kind of problems and situations one faces. The other two have to do with the causes and effects of action: luck in how one is determined by antecedent circumstances, and luck in the way one's actions and projects turn out. All of them present a common problem. They are all opposed by the idea that one cannot be more culpable or estimable for anything than one is for that fraction of it which is under one's control. It seems irrational to take or dispense credit or blame for matters over which a person has no control, or for their influence on results over which he has partial control. Such things may create the conditions for action, but action can be judged only to the extent that it goes beyond these conditions and does not just result from them.

Let us first consider luck, good and bad, in the way things turn out. Kant, in the above-quoted passage, has one example of this in mind, but the category covers a wide range. It includes the truck driver who accidentally runs over a child, the artist who abandons his wife and five children to devote himself to painting, and other cases in which the possibilities of success and failure are even greater. The driver, if he is entirely without fault, will feel terrible about his role in the event, but will not have to reproach himself. Therefore this example of agent-regret is not yet a case of *moral* bad luck. However, if the driver was guilty of even a minor degree of negligence—failing to have his brakes checked recently, for example—then if that negligence contributes to the death of the child, he will not merely feel terrible. He will blame himself for the death. And what makes this an example of moral luck is that he would have to blame himself only slightly for the negligence itself if no situation arose which required him to brake suddenly and violently to avoid hitting a child. Yet the *negligence* is the same in both cases, and the driver has no control over whether a child will run into his path.

The same is true at higher levels of negligence. If someone has had too much to drink and his car swerves onto the sidewalk, he can count himself morally lucky if there are no pedestrians in its path. If there were, he would be to blame for their deaths, and would probably be prosecuted for manslaughter. But if he hurts no one, although his recklessness is exactly the same, he is guilty of a far less serious legal offense and will certainly reproach himself and be reproached by others much less severely. To take another legal example, the penalty for attempted murder is less than that for successful murder—however similar the intentions and motives of the assailant may be in the two cases. His degree of culpability can depend, it would seem, on whether the victim happened to be wearing a bullet-proof vest, or whether a bird flew into the path of the bullet—matters beyond his control.

Finally, there are cases of decision under uncertainty—common in public and in private life. Anna Karenina goes off with Vronsky, Gauguin leaves his family, Chamberlain signs the Munich agreement, the Decembrists persuade the troops under their command to revolt against the czar, the American colonies declare their independence from Britain, you introduce two people in an attempt at match-making. It is tempting in all such cases to feel that some decision must be possible, in the light of what is known at the time, which will make reproach unsuitable no matter how things turn out. But this is not

true; when someone acts in such ways he takes his life, or his moral position, into his hands, because how things turn out determines what he has done. It is possible *also* to assess the decision from the point of view of what could be known at the time, but this is not the end of the story. If the Decembrists had succeeded in overthrowing Nicholas I in 1825 and establishing a constitutional regime, they would be heroes. As it is, not only did they fail and pay for it, but they bore some responsibility for the terrible punishments meted out to the troops who had been persuaded to follow them. If the American Revolution had been a bloody failure resulting in greater repression, then Jefferson, Franklin and Washington would still have made a noble attempt, and might not even have regretted it on their way to the scaffold, but they would also have had to blame themselves for what they had helped to bring on their compatriots. (Perhaps peaceful efforts at reform would eventually have succeeded.) If Hitler had not overrun Europe and exterminated millions, but instead had died of a heart attack after occupying the Sudetenland, Chamberlain's action at Munich would still have utterly betrayed the Czechs, but it would not be the great moral disaster that has made his name a household word.

In many cases of difficult choice the outcome cannot be foreseen with certainty. One kind of assessment of the choice is possible in advance, but another kind must await the outcome, because the outcome determines what has been done. The same degree of culpability or estimability in intention, motive, or concern is compatible with a wide range of judgments, positive or negative, depending on what happened beyond the point of decision. The *mens rea* which could have existed in the absence of any consequences does not exhaust the grounds of moral judgment. Actual results influence culpability or esteem in a large class of unquestionably ethical cases ranging from negligence through political choice.

That these are genuine moral judgments rather than expressions of temporary attitude is evident from the fact that one can say *in advance* how the moral verdict will depend on the results. If one negligently leaves the bath running with the baby in it, one will realize, as one bounds up the stairs toward the bathroom, that if the baby has drowned one has done something awful, whereas if it has not one has merely been careless. Someone who launches a violent revolution against an authoritarian regime knows that if he fails he will be responsible for much suffering that is in vain, but if he succeeds he will be justified by the outcome. I do not mean that *any* action can be retroactively justified by history. Certain things are so bad in themselves, or so risky, that no results can make them all right. Nevertheless, when moral judgment does depend on the outcome, it is objective and timeless and not dependent on a change of standpoint produced by success or failure. The judgment after the fact follows from an hypothetical judgment that can be made beforehand, and it can be made as easily by someone else as by the agent.

From the point of view which makes responsibility dependent on control, all this seems absurd. How is it possible to be more or less culpable depending on whether a child gets into the path of one's car, or a bird into the path of one's bullet? Perhaps it is true that what is done depends on more than the agent's state of mind or intention. The problem then is, why is it not irrational to base moral assessment on what people do, in this broad sense? It amounts to holding them responsible for the contributions of fate as well as for their own—provided they have made some contribution to begin with. If we look at cases of negligence or attempt, the pattern seems to be that overall culpability corresponds to the product of mental or intentional fault and the seriousness of the outcome. Cases of decision under uncertainty are less easily explained in this way, for it seems that the overall judgment can even shift from positive to negative depending on the outcome. But here too it seems rational to subtract the effects of occurrences subsequent to the choice, that were merely possible at the time, and concentrate moral assessment on the actual decision in light of the probabilities. If the object of moral judgment is the *person,* then to hold him accountable for what he has done in the broader sense is akin to strict liability, which may have its legal uses but seems irrational as a moral position.

The result of such a line of thought is to pare down each act to its morally essential core, an inner act of pure will assessed by motive and intention. Adam Smith advocates such a position in *The Theory of Moral Sentiments,* but notes that it runs contrary to our actual judgments.

> But how well soever we may seem to be persuaded of the truth of this equitable maxim, when we consider it after this manner, in abstract, yet when we come to particular cases, the actual consequences which happen to proceed from any action, have a very great effect upon our sentiments concerning its merit or demerit, and almost always either enhance or diminish our sense of both. Scarce, in any one instance, perhaps, will our sentiments be found, after examination, to be entirely regulated by this rule, which we all acknowledge ought entirely to regulate them.[2]

Joel Feinberg points out further that restricting the domain of moral responsibility to the inner world will not immunize it to luck. Factors beyond the agent's control, like a coughing fit, can interfere with his decisions as surely as they can with the path of a bullet from his gun.[3] Nevertheless the tendency to cut down the scope of moral assessment is pervasive, and does not limit itself to the influence of effects. It attempts to isolate the will from the other direction, so to speak, by separating out constitutive luck. Let us consider that next.

Kant was particularly insistent on the moral irrelevance of qualities of temperament and personality that are not under the control of the will. Such qualities as sympathy or coldness might provide the background against which obedience to moral requirements is more or less difficult, but they could not be objects of moral assessment themselves, and might well interfere with confident assessment of its proper object—the determination of the will by the motive of duty. This rules out moral judgment of many of the virtues and vices, which are states of character that influence choice but are certainly not exhausted by dispositions to act deliberately in certain ways. A person may be greedy, envious, cowardly, cold, ungenerous, unkind, vain, or conceited, but *behave* perfectly by a monumental effort of will. To possess these vices is to be unable to help having certain feelings under certain circumstances, and to have strong spontaneous impulses to act badly. Even if one controls the impulses, one still has the vice. An envious person hates the greater success of others. He can be morally condemned as envious even if he congratulates them cordially and does nothing to denigrate or spoil their success. Conceit, likewise, need not be displayed. It is fully present in someone who cannot help dwelling with secret satisfaction on the superiority of his own achievements, talents, beauty, intelligence, or virtue. To some extent such a quality may be the product of earlier choices; to some extent it may be amenable to change by current actions. But it is largely a matter of constitutive bad fortune. Yet people are morally condemned for such qualities, and esteemed for others equally beyond control of the will: they are assessed for what they are *like*.

To Kant this seems incoherent because virtue is enjoined on everyone and therefore must in principle be possible for everyone. It may be easier for some than for others, but it must be possible to achieve it by making the right choices, against whatever temperamental background. One may want to have a generous spirit, or regret not having one, but it makes no sense to condemn oneself or anyone else for a quality which is not within the control of the will. Condemnation implies that you should not be like that, not that it is unfortunate that you are.

Nevertheless, Kant's conclusion remains intuitively unacceptable. We may be persuaded that these moral judgments are irrational, but they reappear involuntarily as soon as the argument is over. This is the pattern throughout the subject.

The third category to consider is luck in one's circumstances, and I shall mention it briefly. The things we are called upon to do, the moral tests we face, are importantly determined by factors beyond our control. It may be true of someone that in a dangerous situation he would behave in a cowardly or heroic fashion, but if the situation never arises, he will never have the chance to distinguish or disgrace himself in this way, and his moral record will be different.

A conspicuous example of this is political. Ordinary citizens of Nazi Germany had an opportunity to behave heroically by opposing the regime. They also had an opportunity to behave badly, and most of them are culpable for having failed this test. But it is a test to which the citizens of other countries were not subjected, with the result that even if they, or some of them, would have behaved as badly as the Germans in like circumstances, they simply did not and therefore are not similarly culpable. Here again one is morally at the mercy of fate, and it may seem irrational upon reflection, but our ordinary moral attitudes would be unrecognizable without it. We judge people for what they actually do or fail to do, not just for what they would have done if circumstances had been different.[4]

This form of moral determination by the actual is also paradoxical, but we can begin to see how deep in the concept of responsibility the paradox is embedded. A person can be morally responsible only for what he does; but what he does results from a great deal that he does not do; therefore he is not morally responsible for what he is and is not responsible for. (This is not a contradiction, but it is a paradox.)

It should be obvious that there is a connection between these problems about responsibility and control and an even more familiar problem, that of freedom of the will. That is the last type of moral luck I want to take up, though I can do no more within the scope of this essay than indicate its connection with the other types.

If one cannot be responsible for consequences of one's acts due to factors beyond one's control, or for antecedents of one's acts that are properties of temperament not subject to one's will, or for the circumstances that pose one's moral choices, then how can one be responsible even for the stripped-down acts of the will itself, if *they* are the product of antecedent circumstances outside of the will's control?

The area of genuine agency, and therefore of legitimate moral judgment, seems to shrink under this scrutiny to an extensionless point. Everything seems to result from the combined influence of factors, antecedent and posterior to action, that are not within the agent's control. Since he cannot be responsible for them, he cannot be responsible for their results—though it may remain possible to take up the aesthetic or other evaluative analogues of the moral attitudes that are thus displaced.

It is also possible, of course, to brazen it out and refuse to accept the results, which indeed seem unacceptable as soon as we stop thinking about the arguments. Admittedly, if certain surrounding circumstances had been different, then no unfortunate consequences would have followed from a wicked intention, and no seriously culpable act would have been performed; but since the circumstances were *not* different, and the agent *in fact* succeeded in perpetrating a particularly cruel murder, *that* is what he did, and that is what he is responsible for. Similarly, we may admit that if certain antecedent circumstances had been different, the agent would never have developed into the sort of person who would do such a thing; but since he *did* develop (as the inevitable result of those antecedent circumstances) into the sort of swine he is, and into the person who committed such a murder, *that* is what he is blameable for. In both cases one is responsible for what one actually does—even if what one actually does depends in important ways on what is not within one's control. This compatibilist account of our moral judgments would leave room for the ordinary conditions of responsibility—the absence of coercion, ignorance, or involuntary movement—as part of the determination of what someone has done—but it is understood not to exclude the influence of a great deal that he has not done.

The only thing wrong with this solution is its failure to explain how skeptical problems arise. For they arise not from the imposition of an arbitrary external requirement, but from the nature of moral judgment itself. Something in the ordinary idea of what someone does must explain how it can seem necessary to subtract from it anything that merely happens—even though the ultimate consequence of such subtraction is that nothing remains.

The problem arises, I believe, because the self which acts and is the object of moral judgment is threatened with dissolution by the absorption of its acts and impulses into the class of events. Moral judgment of a person is judgment not of what happens to him, but of him. It does not say merely that a certain event or state of affairs is fortunate or unfortunate or even terrible. It is not an evaluation of a state of the world, or of an individual as part of the world. We are not thinking just that it would be better if he were different, or did not exist, or had not done some of the things he has done. We are judging *him*, rather than his existence or characteristics. The effect of concentrating on the influence of what is not under his control is to make this responsible self seem to disappear, swallowed up by the order of mere events.

What, however, do we have in mind that a person must *be* to be the object of these moral attitudes? While the concept of agency is easily undermined, it is very difficult to give it a positive characterization. That is familiar from the literature on Free Will.

I believe that in a sense the problem has no solution, because something in the idea of agency is incompatible with actions being events, or people being things. But as the external determinants of what someone has done are gradually exposed, in their effect on consequences, character, and choice itself, it becomes gradually clear that actions are events and people things. Eventually nothing remains which can be ascribed to the responsible self, and we are left with nothing but a portion of the larger sequence of events, which can be deplored or celebrated, but not blamed or praised.

Though I cannot define the idea of the active self that is thus undermined, it is possible to say something about its sources. There is a close connection between our feelings about ourselves and our feelings about others. Guilt and indignation, shame and contempt, pride and admiration are internal and external sides of the same moral attitudes. We are unable to view ourselves simply as portions of the world, and from inside we have a rough idea of the boundary between what is us and what is not, what we do and what happens to us, what is our personality and what is an accidental handicap. We apply the same essentially internal conception of the self to others. About ourselves we feel pride, shame, guilt, remorse— and agent-regret. We do not regard our actions and our characters merely as fortunate or unfortunate episodes—though they may also be that. We cannot *simply* take an external evaluative view of ourselves—of what we most essentially are and what we do. And this remains true even when we have seen that we are not responsible for our own existence, or our nature, or the choices we have to make, or the circumstances that give our acts the consequences they have. Those acts remain ours and we remain ourselves, despite the persuasiveness of the reasons that seem to argue us out of existence.

The inclusion of consequences in the conception of what we have done is an acknowledgment that we are parts of the world, but the paradoxical character of moral luck which emerges from this acknowledgment shows that we are unable to operate with such a view, for it leaves us with no one to be. The same thing is revealed in the appearance that determinism obliterates responsibility. Once we see an aspect of what we or someone else does as something that happens, we lose our grip on the idea that it has been done and that we can judge the doer and not just the happening. This explains why the absence of determinism is no more hospitable to the concept of agency than is its presence—a point that has been noticed often. Either way the act is viewed externally, as part of the course of events.

The problem of moral luck cannot be understood without an account of the internal conception of agency and its special connection with the moral attitudes as opposed to other types of value. I do not have such an account. The degree to which the problem has a solution can be determined only by seeing whether in some degree the incompatibility between this conception and the various ways in which we do not control what we do is only apparent. I have nothing to offer on that topic either. But it is not enough to say merely that our basic moral attitudes toward ourselves and others are determined by what is actual; for they are also threatened by the sources of that actuality, and by the external view of action which forces itself on us when we see how everything we do belongs to a world that we have not created.

NOTES

1. Immanuel Kant, *Foundations of the Metaphysics of Morals,* first section, third paragraph.
2. Adam Smith, *The Theory of Moral Sentiments,* Pt II, sect. 3, Introduction, para. 5.
3. "Problematic Responsibility in Law and Morals," in Joel Feinberg, *Doing and Deserving* (Princeton: Princeton University Press, 1970).
4. Circumstantial luck can extend to aspects of the situation other than individual behavior. For example, during the Vietnam War even U.S. citizens who had opposed their country's actions vigorously from the start often felt compromised by its crimes. Here they were not even responsible; there was probably nothing they could do to stop what was happening, so the feeling of being implicated may seem unintelligible. But it is nearly impossible to view the crimes of one's own country in the same way that one views the crimes of another country, no matter how equal one's lack of power to stop them in the two cases. One *is* a citizen of one of them, and has a connection with its actions (even if only through taxes that cannot be withheld)—that one does not have with the other's. This makes it possible to be ashamed of one's country, and to feel a victim of moral bad luck that one was an American in the 1960s.

4.4 Sanity and the Metaphysics of Responsibility

SUSAN WOLF

Susan Wolf teaches philosophy at the University of North Carolina, Chapel Hill.

Philosophers who study the problems of free will and responsibility have an easier time than most in meeting challenges about the relevance of their work to ordinary, practical concerns. Indeed, philosophers who study these problems are rarely faced with such challenges at all, since questions concerning the conditions of responsibility come up so obviously and so frequently in everyday life. Under scrutiny, however, one might question whether the connections between philosophical and nonphilosophical concerns in this area are real.

In everyday contexts, when lawyers, judges, parents, and others are concerned with issues of responsibility, they know, or think they know, what in general the conditions of responsibility are. Their questions are questions of application: Does this or that particular person meet this or that particular condition? Is this person mature enough, or informed enough, or sane enough to be responsible? Was he or she acting under post-hypnotic suggestion or under the influence of a mind-impairing drug? It is assumed, in these contexts, that normal, fully developed adult human beings are responsible beings. The questions have to do with whether a given individual falls within the normal range.

By contrast, philosophers tend to be uncertain about the general conditions of responsibility, and they care less about dividing the responsible from the nonresponsible agents than about determining whether, and if so why, any of us are ever responsible for anything at all.

In the classroom, we might argue that the philosophical concerns grow out of the non-philosophical ones, that they take off where the nonphilosophical questions stop. In this way, we might convince our students that even if they are not plagued by the philosophical worries, they ought to be. If they worry about whether a person is mature enough, informed enough, and sane enough to be responsible, then they should worry about whether that person is metaphysically free enough, too.

The argument I make here, however, goes in the opposite direction. My aim is not to convince people who are interested in the apparently nonphilosophical conditions of responsibility that they should go on to worry about the philosophical conditions as well, but rather to urge those who already worry about the philosophical problems not to leave the more mundane, pre-philosophical problems behind. In particular, I suggest that the mundane recognition that *sanity* is a condition of responsibility has more to do with the murky and apparently metaphysical problems which surround the issue of responsibility than at first meets the eye. Once the significance of the condition of sanity is fully appreciated, at least some of the apparently insuperable metaphysical aspects of the problem of responsibility will dissolve.

My strategy is to examine a recent trend in philosophical discussions of responsibility, a trend that tries, but I think ultimately fails, to give an acceptable analysis of the conditions of responsibility. It fails due to what at first appear to be deep and irresolvable metaphysical problems. It is here that I suggest that the condition of sanity comes to the rescue. What at first appears to be an impossible requirement for responsibility—the requirement that the responsible agent have created her- or himself—turns out to be the vastly more mundane and noncontroversial requirement that the responsible agent must, in a fairly standard sense, be sane.

FRANKFURT, WATSON, AND TAYLOR

The trend I have in mind is exemplified by the writings of Harry Frankfurt, Gary Watson, and Charles Taylor. I will briefly discuss each of their separate proposals, and then offer a composite view that, while lacking the subtlety of any of the separate accounts, will highlight some important insights and some important blind spots they share.

In his seminal article "Freedom of the Will and the Concept of a Person,"[1] Harry Frankfurt notes a distinction between freedom of action and freedom of the will. A person has freedom of action, he points out, if she (or he) has the freedom to do whatever she wills to do—the freedom to walk or sit, to vote liberal or conservative, to publish a book or open a store, in accordance with her strongest desires. Even a person who has freedom of action may fail to be responsible for her actions, however, if the wants or desires she has the freedom to convert into action are themselves not subject to her control. Thus, the person who acts under post-hypnotic suggestion, the victim of brainwashing, and the kleptomaniac might all possess freedom of action. In the standard contexts in which these examples are raised, it is assumed that none of the individuals is locked up or bound. Rather, these individuals are understood to act on what, at one level at least, must be called *their own desires*. Their exemption from responsibility stems from the fact that their own desires (or at least the ones governing their actions) are not up to them. These cases may be described in

Frankfurt's terms as cases of people who possess freedom of action, but who fail to be responsible agents because they lack freedom of the will.

Philosophical problems about the conditions of responsibility naturally focus on an analysis of this latter kind of freedom: What *is* freedom of the will, and under what conditions can we reasonably be thought to possess it? Frankfurt's proposal is to understand freedom of the will by analogy to freedom of action. As freedom of action is the freedom to do whatever one wills to do, freedom of the will is the freedom to will whatever one wants to will. To make this point clearer, Frankfurt introduces a distinction between first-order and second-order desires. First-order desires are desires to do or to have various things; second-order desires are desires about what desires to have or what desires to make effective in action. In order for an agent to have both freedom of action and freedom of the will, that agent must be capable of governing his or her actions by first-order desires *and* capable of governing his or her first-order desires by second-order desires.

Gary Watson's view of free agency[2]—free and responsible agency, that is—is similar to Frankfurt's in holding that an agent is responsible for an action only if the desires expressed by that action are of a particular kind. While Frankfurt identifies the right kind of desires as desires that are supported by second-order desires, however, Watson draws a distinction between "mere" desires, so to speak, and desires that are *values*. According to Watson, the difference between free action and unfree action cannot be analyzed by reference to the logical form of the desires from which these various actions arise, but rather must relate to a difference in the quality of their source. Whereas some of my desires are just appetites or conditioned responses I find myself "stuck with," others are expressions of judgments on my part that the objects I desire are good. Insofar as my actions can be governed by the latter type of desire—governed, that is, by my values or valuational system—they are actions that I perform freely and for which I am responsible.

Frankfurt's and Watson's accounts may be understood as alternate developments of the intuition that in order to be responsible for one's actions, one must be responsible for the self that performs these actions. Charles Taylor, in an article entitled "Responsibility for Self,"[3] is concerned with the same intuition. Although Taylor does not describe his view in terms of different levels or types of desire, his view is related, for he claims that our freedom and responsibility depend on our ability to reflect on, criticize, and revise our selves. Like Frankfurt and Watson, Taylor seems to believe that if the characters from which our actions flowed were simply and permanently *given* to us, implanted by heredity, environment, or God, then we would be mere vehicles through which the causal forces of the world traveled, no more responsible than dumb animals or young children or machines. But like the others, he points out that, for most of us, our characters and desires are not so brutely implanted—or, at any rate, if they are, they are subject to revision by our own reflecting, valuing, or second-order desiring selves. We human beings—and as far as we know, only we human beings—have the ability to step back from ourselves and decide whether we are the selves we want to be. Because of this, these philosophers think, we are responsible for our selves and for the actions that we produce.

Although there are subtle and interesting differences among the accounts of Frankfurt, Watson, and Taylor, my concern is with features of their views that are common to them all. All share the idea that responsible agency involves something more than intentional agency. All agree that if we are responsible agents, it is not just because our actions are within the control of our wills, but because, in addition, our wills are not just psychological states *in* us, but expressions of characters that come *from* us, or that at any rate are acknowledged and affirmed *by* us. For Frankfurt, this means that our wills must be ruled by our second-order desires; for Watson, that our wills must be governable by our system of values; for Taylor, that our wills must issue from selves that are subject to self-

assessment and redefinition in terms of a vocabulary of worth. In one way or another, all these philosophers seem to be saying that the key to responsibility lies in the fact that responsible agents are those for whom it is not just the case that their actions are within the control of their wills, but also the case that their wills are within the control of their *selves* in some deeper sense. Because, at one level, the differences among Frankfurt, Watson, and Taylor may be understood as differences in the analysis or interpretation of what it is for an action to be under the control of this deeper self, we may speak of their separate positions as variations of one basic view about responsibility: the *deep-self view*.

THE DEEP-SELF VIEW

Much more must be said about the notion of a deep self before a fully satisfactory account of this view can be given. Providing a careful, detailed analysis of that notion poses an interesting, important, and difficult task in its own right. The degree of understanding achieved by abstraction from the views of Frankfurt, Watson, and Taylor, however, should be sufficient to allow us to recognize some important virtues as well as some important drawbacks of the deep-self view.

One virtue is that this view explains a good portion of our pretheoretical intuitions about responsibility. It explains why kleptomaniacs, victims of brainwashing, and people acting under posthypnotic suggestion may not be responsible for their actions, although most of us typically are. In the cases of people in these special categories, the connection between the agents' deep selves and their wills is dramatically severed—their wills are governed not by their deep selves, but by forces external to and independent from them. A different intuition is that we adult human beings can be responsible for our actions in a way that dumb animals, infants, and machines cannot. Here the explanation is not in terms of a split between these beings' deep selves and their wills; rather, the point is that these beings *lack* deep selves altogether. Kleptomaniacs and victims of hypnosis exemplify individuals whose selves are *alienated* from their actions; lower animals and machines, on the other hand, do not have the sorts of selves from which actions *can* be alienated, and so they do not have the sort of selves from which, in the happier cases, actions can responsibly flow

At a more theoretical level, the deep-self view has another virtue: It responds to at least one way in which the fear of determinism presents itself.

A naive reaction to the idea that everything we do is completely determined by a causal chain that extends backward beyond the times of our births involves thinking that in that case we would have no control over our behavior whatsoever. If everything is determined, it is thought, then what happens happens, whether we want it to or not. A common, and proper, response to this concern points out that determinism does not deny the causal efficacy an agent's desires might have on his or her behavior. On the contrary, determinism in its more plausible forms tends to affirm this connection, merely adding that as one's behavior is determined by one's desires, so one's desires are determined by something else.[4]

Those who were initially worried that determinism implied fatalism, however, are apt to find their fears merely transformed rather than erased. If our desires are governed by something else, they might say, they are not *really* ours after all—or, at any rate, they are ours in only a superficial sense.

The deep-self view offers an answer to this transformed fear of determinism, for it allows us to distinguish cases in which desires are determined by forces foreign to oneself from desires which are determined *by* one's self—by one's "real," or second-order desiring, or valuing, or deep self, that is. Admittedly, there are cases, like that of the kleptomaniac or the victim of hypnosis, in which the agent acts on desires that "belong to" him or her in only a superficial sense. But the proponent of the deep-self view will point out that even if determinism is true, ordinary adult human action can be distinguished from this. Determinism implies that the desires

which govern our actions are in turn governed by something else, but that something else will, in the fortunate cases, be our own deeper selves.

This account of responsibility thus offers a response to our fear of determinism; but it is a response with which many will remain unsatisfied. Even if my actions are governed by my desires and my desires are governed by my own deeper self, there remains the question: Who, or what, is responsible for this deeper self? The response above seems only to have pushed the problem further back.

Admittedly, some versions of the deep-self view, including Frankfurt's and Taylor's seem to anticipate this question by providing a place for the ideal that an agent's deep self may be governed by a still deeper self. Thus, for Frankfurt, second-order desires may themselves be governed by third-order desires, third-order desires by fourth-order desires, and so on. Also, Taylor points out that, as we can reflect on and evaluate our prereflective selves, so we can reflect on and evaluate the selves who are doing the first reflecting and evaluating, and so on. However, this capacity to recursively create endless levels of depth ultimately misses the criticism's point.

First of all, even if there is no *logical* limit to the number of levels of reflection or depth a person may have, there is certainly a psychological limit—it is virtually impossible imaginatively to conceive a fourth-, much less an eighth-order, desire. More important, no matter how many levels of self we posit, there will still, in any individual case, be a last level—a deepest self about whom the question "What governs it?" will arise, as problematic as ever. If determinism is true, it implies that even if my actions are governed by my desires, and my desires are governed by my deepest self, my deepest self will still be governed by something that must, logically, be external to myself altogether. Though I can step back from the values my parents and teachers have given me and ask whether these are the values I really want, the "I" that steps back will itself be a product of the parents and teachers I am questioning.

The problem seems even worse when one sees that one fares no better if determinism is false. For if my deepest self is not determined by something external to myself, it will still not be determined by *me*. Whether I am a product of carefully controlled forces or a result of random mutations, whether there is a complete explanation of my origin or no explanation at all, *I* am not, in any case, responsible for my existence; I am not in control of my deepest self.

Thus, though the claim that an agent is responsible for only those actions that are within the control of his or her deep self correctly identifies a necessary condition for responsibility—a condition that separates the hypnotized and the brainwashed, the immature and the lower animals from ourselves, for example—it fails to provide a sufficient condition of responsibility that puts all fears of determinism to rest. For one of the fears invoked by the thought of determinism seems to be connected to its implication that we are but intermediate links in a causal chain, rather than ultimate, self-initiating sources of movement and change. From the point of view of one who has this fear, the deep-self view seems merely to add loops to the chain, complicating the picture but not really improving it. From the point of view of one who has this fear, responsibility seems to require being a prime mover unmoved, whose deepest self is itself neither random *nor* externally determined, but is rather determined *by* itself—who is, in other words, self-created.

At this point, however, proponents of the deep-self view may wonder whether this fear is legitimate. For although people evidently can be brought to the point where they feel that responsible agency requires them to be ultimate sources of power, to the point where it seems that nothing short of self-creation will do, a return to the internal standpoint of the agent whose responsibility is in question makes it hard to see what good this metaphysical status is supposed to provide or what evil its absence is supposed to impose.

From the external standpoint, which discussions of determinism and indeterminism encourage us to take up, it may appear that a special metaphysical status is required to distinguish us

significantly from other members of the natural world. But proponents of the deep-self view will suggest this is an illusion that a return to the internal standpoint should dispel. The possession of a deep self that is effective in governing one's actions is a sufficient distinction, they will say. For while other members of the natural world are not in control of the selves that they are, we, possessors of effective deep selves, are in control. We can reflect on what sorts of beings we are, and on what sorts of marks we make on the world. We can change what we don't like about ourselves, and keep what we do. Admittedly, we do not create ourselves from nothing. But as long as we can revise ourselves, they will suggest, it is hard to find reason to complain. Harry Frankfurt writes that a person who is free to do what he wants to do and also free to want what he wants to want has "all the freedom it is possible to desire or to conceive."[5] This suggests a rhetorical question: If you are free to control your actions by your desires, and free to control your desires by your deeper desires, and free to control those desires by still deeper desires, what further kind of freedom can you want?

THE CONDITION OF SANITY

Unfortunately, there is a further kind of freedom we can want, which it is reasonable to think necessary for responsible agency. The deep-self view fails to be convincing when it is offered as a complete account of the conditions of responsibility. To see why, it will be helpful to consider another example of an agent whose responsibility is in question.

JoJo is the favorite son of Jo the First, an evil and sadistic dictator of a small, undeveloped country. Because of his father's special feelings for the boy, JoJo is given a special education and is allowed to accompany his father and observe his daily routine. In light of this treatment, it is not surprising that little JoJo takes his father as a role model and develops values very much like Dad's. As an adult, he does many of the same sorts of things his father did, including sending people to prison or to death or to torture chambers on the basis of whim. He is not *coerced* to do these things, he acts according to his own desires. Moreover, these are desires he wholly *wants* to have. When he steps back and asks, "Do I really want to be this sort of person?" his answer is resoundingly "Yes," for this way of life expresses a crazy sort of power that forms part of his deepest ideal.

In light of JoJo's heritage and upbringing—both of which he was powerless to control—it is dubious at best that he should be regarded as responsible for what he does. It is unclear whether anyone with a childhood such as his could have developed into anything but the twisted and perverse sort of person that he has become. However, note that JoJo is someone whose actions are controlled by his desires and whose desires are the desires he wants to have: That is, his actions are governed by desires that are governed by and expressive of his deepest self.

The Frankfurt–Watson–Taylor strategy that allowed us to differentiate our normal selves from the victims of hypnosis and brainwashing will not allow us to differentiate ourselves from the son of Jo the First. In the case of these earlier victims, we were able to say that although the actions of these individuals were, at one level, in control of the individuals themselves, these individuals themselves, qua agents, were not the selves they more deeply wanted to be. In this respect, these people were unlike our happily more integrated selves. However, we cannot say of JoJo that his self, qua agent, is not the self he wants it to be. It *is* the self he wants it to be. From the inside, he feels as integrated, free, and responsible as we do.

Our judgment that JoJo is not a responsible agent is one that we can make only from the outside—from reflecting on the fact, it seems, that his deepest self is not up to him. Looked at from the outside, however, our situation seems no different from his—for in the last analysis, it is not up to any of us to have the deepest selves we do. Once more, the problem seems metaphysical—and not just metaphysical, but

insuperable. For, as I mentioned before, the problem is independent of the truth of determinism. Whether we are determined or undetermined, we cannot have created our deepest selves. Literal self-creation is not just empirically, but logically impossible.

If JoJo is not responsible because his deepest self is not up to him, then we are not responsible either. Indeed, in that case responsibility would be impossible for anyone to achieve. But I believe the appearance that literal self-creation is required for freedom and responsibility is itself mistaken.

The deep-self view was right in pointing out that freedom and responsibility require us to have certain distinctive types of control over our behavior and our selves. Specifically, our actions need to be under the control of our selves, and our (superficial) selves need to be under the control of our deep selves. Having seen that these types of control are not enough to guarantee us the status of responsible agents, we are tempted to go on to suppose that we must have yet another kind of control to assure us that even our deepest selves are somehow up to us. But not all the things necessary for freedom and responsibility must be types of power and control. We may need simply to *be* a certain way, even though it is not within our power to determine whether we are that way or not.

Indeed, it becomes obvious that at least one condition of responsibility is of this form as soon as we remember what, in everyday contexts, we have known all along—namely, that in order to be responsible, an agent must be *sane*. It is not ordinarily in our power to determine whether we are or are not sane. Most of us, it would seem, are lucky, but some of us are not. Moreover, being sane does not necessarily mean that one has any type of power or control an insane person lacks. Some insane people, like JoJo and some actual political leaders who resemble him, may have complete control of their actions, and even complete control of their acting selves. The desire to be sane is thus not a desire for another form of control; it is rather a desire that one's self be connected to the world in a certain way—we could even say it is a desire that one's self be *controlled by* the world in certain ways and not in others.

This becomes clear if we attend to the criteria for sanity that have historically been dominant in legal questions about responsibility. According to the M'Naughten Rule, a person is sane if (1) he knows what he is doing and (2) he knows that what he is doing is, as the case may be, right or wrong. Insofar as one's desire to be sane involves a desire to know what one is doing—or more generally, a desire to live in the real world—it is a desire to be controlled (to have, in this case, one's *beliefs* controlled) by perceptions and sound reasoning that produce an accurate conception of the world, rather than by blind or distorted forms of response. The same goes for the second constituent of sanity—only, in this case, one's hope is that one's *values* be controlled by processes that afford an accurate conception of the world.[6] Putting these two conditions together, we may understand sanity, then, as the minimally sufficient ability cognitively and normatively to recognize and appreciate the world for what it is.

There are problems with this definition of sanity, at least some of which will become obvious in what follows, that make it ultimately unacceptable either as a gloss on or an improvement of the meaning of the term in many of the contexts in which it is used. The definition offered does seem to bring out the interest sanity has for us in connection with issues of responsibility, however, and some pedagogical as well as stylistic purposes will be served if we use sanity hereafter in this admittedly specialized sense.

THE SANE DEEP-SELF VIEW

So far I have argued that the conditions of responsible agency offered by the deep-self view are necessary but not sufficient. Moreover, the gap left open by the deep-self view seems to be one that can be filled only by a metaphysical, and, as it happens, metaphysically impossible addition. I now wish to argue, however, that the condition of sanity, as characterized above, is sufficient to fill the gap. In other words, the deep-self view, supplemented by the condition of sanity, provides a satisfying conception of responsibility. The conception of responsibility I am proposing, then, agrees with the deep-self view in requiring that a responsible agent be able to govern her (or his) actions by her desires and to govern her desires by her deep self. In addition, my conception insists that the agent's deep self be sane, and claims that this is *all* that is needed for responsible agency. By contrast to the plain deep-self view, let us call this new proposal the *sane deep-self view*.

It is worth noting, to begin with, that this new proposal deals with the case of JoJo and related cases of deprived childhood victims in ways that better match our pretheoretical intuitions. Unlike the plain deep-self view, the sane deep-self view offers a way of explaining why JoJo is not responsible for his actions without throwing our own responsibility into doubt. For, although like us, JoJo's actions flow from desires that flow from his deep self, unlike us, JoJo's deep self is itself insane. Sanity, remember, involves the ability to know the difference between right and wrong, and a person who, even on reflection, cannot see that having someone tortured because he failed to salute you is wrong plainly lacks the requisite ability.

Less obviously, but quite analogously, this new proposal explains why we give less than full responsibility to persons who, though acting badly, act in ways that are strongly encouraged by their societies—the slaveowners of the 1850s, the Nazis of the 1930s, and many male chauvinists of our fathers' generation, for example. These are people, we imagine, who falsely believe that the ways in which they are acting are morally acceptable, and so, we may assume, their behavior is expressive of or at least in accordance with these agents' deep selves. But their false beliefs in the moral permissibility of their actions and the false values from which these beliefs derived may have been inevitable, given the social circumstances in which they developed. If we think that the agents could not help but be mistaken about their values, we do not blame them for the actions those values inspired?[7]

It would unduly distort ordinary linguistic practice to call the slaveowner, the Nazi, or the male chauvinist even partially or locally insane. Nonetheless, the reason for withholding blame from them is at bottom the same as the reason for withholding it from JoJo. Like JoJo, they are, at the deepest level, unable cognitively and normatively to recognize and appreciate the world for what it is. In our sense of the term, their deepest selves are not fully *sane*.

The sane deep-self view thus offers an account of why victims of deprived childhoods as well as victims of misguided societies may not be responsible for their actions, without implying that we are not responsible for ours. The actions of these others are governed by mistaken conceptions of value that the agents in question cannot help but have. Since, as far as we know, our values are not, like theirs, unavoidably mistaken, the fact that these others are not responsible for their actions need not force us to conclude that we are not responsible for ours.

But it may not yet be clear why sanity, in this special sense, should make such a difference—why, in particular, the question of whether someone's values are unavoidably *mistaken* should have any bearing on their status as responsible agents. The fact that the sane deep-self view implies judgments that match our intuitions about the difference in status between characters like JoJo and ourselves provides little support for it if it cannot also defend these intuitions. So we must consider an objection that comes from the point of view we considered earlier which rejects the intuition that a relevant difference can be found.

Earlier, it seemed that the reason JoJo was not responsible for his actions was that although his actions were governed by his deep self, his deep self was not up to him. But this had nothing to do with his deep self's being mistaken or not mistaken, evil or good, insane or sane. If JoJo's values are unavoidably mistaken, our values, even if not mistaken, appear to be just as unavoidable. When it comes to freedom and

responsibility, isn't it the unavoidability, rather than the mistakenness, that matters?

Before answering this question, it is useful to point out a way in which it is ambiguous: The concepts of avoidability and mistakenness are not unequivocally distinct. One may, to be sure, construe the notion of avoidability in a purely metaphysical way. Whether an event or state of affairs is unavoidable under this construal depends, as it were, on the tightness of the causal connections that bear on the event's or state of affairs' coming about. In this sense, our deep selves do seem as unavoidable for us as JoJo's and the others' are for them. For presumably we are just as influenced by our parents, our cultures, and our schooling as they are influenced by theirs. In another sense, however, our characters are not similarly unavoidable.

In particular, in the cases of JoJo and the others, there are certain features of their characters that they cannot avoid *even though these features are seriously mistaken, misguided, or bad*. This is so because, in our special sense of the term, these characters are less than fully sane. Since these characters lack the ability to know right from wrong, they are unable to revise their characters on the basis of right and wrong, and so their deep selves lack the resources and the reasons that might have served as a basis for self-correction. Since the deep selves *we* unavoidably have, however, are sane deep selves—deep selves, that is, that unavoidably *contain* the ability to know right from wrong—we unavoidably do have the resources and reasons on which to base self-correction. What this means is that though in one sense we are no more in control of our deepest selves than JoJo et al., it does not follow in our case, as it does in theirs, that we would be the way we are, even if it is a bad or wrong way to be. However, if this does not follow, it seems to me, our absence of control at the deepest level should not upset us.

Consider what the absence of control at the deepest level amounts to for us: Whereas JoJo is unable to control the fact that, at the deepest level, he is not fully sane, we are not responsible for the fact that, at the deepest level, we are. It is not up to us to *have* minimally sufficient abilities cognitively and normatively to recognize and appreciate the world for what it is. Also, presumably, it is not up to us to have lots of other properties, at least to begin with—a fondness for purple, perhaps, or an antipathy for beets. As the proponents of the plain deep-self view have been at pains to point out, however, we do, if we are lucky, have the ability to revise our selves in terms of the values that are held by or constitutive of our deep selves. If we are lucky enough both to have this ability and to have our deep selves be sane, it follows that although there is much in our characters that we did not choose to have, there is nothing irrational or objectionable in our characters that we are compelled to keep.

Being sane, we are able to understand and evaluate our characters in a reasonable way, to notice what there is reason to hold on to, what there is reason to eliminate, and what, from a rational and reasonable standpoint, we may retain or get rid of as we please. Being able as well to govern our superficial selves by our deep selves, then, we are able to change the things we find there is reason to change. This being so, it seems that although we may not be *metaphysically* responsible for ourselves—for, after all, we did not create ourselves from nothing—we are *morally* responsible for ourselves, for we are able to understand and appreciate right and wrong, and to change our characters and our actions accordingly.

SELF-CREATION, SELF-REVISION, AND SELF-CORRECTION

At the beginning of this chapter, I claimed that recalling that sanity was a condition of responsibility would dissolve at least some of the appearance that responsibility was metaphysically impossible. To see how this is so, and to get a fuller sense of the sane deep-self view, it may be helpful to put that view into perspective by comparing it to the other views we have discussed along the way.

As Frankfurt, Watson, and Taylor showed us, in order to be free and responsible we need

not only to be able to control our actions in accordance with our desires, we need to be able to control our desires in accordance with our deepest selves. We need, in other words, to be able to *revise* ourselves—to get rid of some desires and traits, and perhaps replace them with others on the basis of our deeper desires or values or reflections. However, consideration of the fact that the selves who are doing the revising might themselves be either brute products of external forces or arbitrary outputs of random generation made us wonder whether the capacity for self-revision was enough to assure us of responsibility—and the example of JoJo added force to the suspicion that it was not. Still, if the ability to revise ourselves is not enough, the ability to create ourselves does not seem necessary either. Indeed, when you think of it, it is unclear why anyone should want self-creation. Why should anyone be disappointed at having to accept the idea that one has to get one's start somewhere? It is an idea that most of us have lived with quite contentedly all along. What we do have reason to want, then, is something more than the ability to revise ourselves, but less than the ability to create ourselves. Implicit in the sane deep-self view is the idea that what is needed is the ability to *correct* (or improve) ourselves.

Recognizing that in order to be responsible for our actions, we have to be responsible for our selves, the sane deep-self view analyzes what is necessary in order to be responsible for our selves as (1) the ability to evaluate ourselves sensibly and accurately, and (2) the ability to transform ourselves insofar as our evaluation tells us to do so. We may understand the exercise of these abilities as a process whereby we *take* responsibility for the selves that we are but did not ultimately create. The condition of sanity is intrinsically connected to the first ability; the condition that we are able to control our superficial selves by our deep selves is intrinsically connected to the second.

The difference between the plain deep-self view and the sane deep-self view, then, is the difference between the requirement of the capacity for self-revision and the requirement of the capacity for self-correction. Anyone with the first capacity can *try* to take responsibility for himself or herself. However, only someone with a sane deep self—a deep self that can see and appreciate the world for what it is—can self-evaluate sensibly and accurately. Therefore, although insane selves can try to take responsibility for themselves, only sane selves will properly be accorded responsibility.

TWO OBJECTIONS CONSIDERED

At least two problems with the sane deep-self view are so glaring as to have certainly struck many readers. In closing, I shall briefly address them. First, some will be wondering how, in light of my specialized use of the term "sanity," I can be so sure that "we" are any saner than the nonresponsible individuals I have discussed. What justifies my confidence that, unlike the slaveowners, Nazis, and male chauvinists, not to mention JoJo himself, we are able to understand and appreciate the world for what it is? The answer to this is that nothing justifies this except widespread intersubjective agreement and the considerable success we have in getting around in the world and satisfying our needs. These are not sufficient grounds for the smug assumption that we are in a position to see the truth about *all* aspects of ethical and social life. Indeed, it seems more reasonable to expect that time will reveal blind spots in our cognitive and normative outlook, just as it has revealed errors in the outlooks of those who have lived before. But our judgments of responsibility can only be made from here, on the basis of the understandings and values that we can develop by exercising the abilities we do possess as well and as fully as possible.

If some have been worried that my view implicitly expresses an overconfidence in the assumption that we are sane and therefore right about the world, others will be worried that my view too closely connects sanity with being right about the world, and fear that my view implies that anyone who acts wrongly or has false beliefs about the world is therefore insane and so not responsible for his or her actions. This seems to me to be a more serious worry, which I am sure I cannot answer to everyone's satisfaction.

First, it must be admitted that the sane deep-self view embraces a conception of sanity that is explicitly normative. But this seems to me a strength of that view, rather than a defect. Sanity *is* a normative concept, in its ordinary as well as in its specialized sense, and severely deviant behavior, such as that of a serial murderer of a sadistic dictator, does constitute evidence of a psychological defect in the agent. The suggestion that the most horrendous, stomach-turning crimes could be committed only by an insane person—an inverse of Catch-22, as it were—must be regarded as a serious possibility, despite the practical problems that would accompany general acceptance of that conclusion.

But, it will be objected, there is no justification, in the sane deep-self view, for regarding only horrendous and stomach-turning crimes as evidence of insanity in its specialized sense. If sanity is the ability cognitively and normatively to understand and appreciate the world for what it is, then *any* wrong action or false belief will count as evidence of the absence of that ability. This point may also be granted, but we must be careful about what conclusion to draw. To be sure, when someone acts in a way that is not in accordance with acceptable standards of rationality and reasonableness, it is always appropriate to look for an explanation of why he or she acted that way. The hypothesis that the person was unable to understand and appreciate that an action fell outside acceptable bound will always be a possible explanation. Bad performance on a math test always suggests the possibility that the testee is stupid. Typically, however, other explanations will be possible, too—for example, that the agent was too lazy to consider whether his or her action was acceptable, or too greedy to care, or, in the case of the math testee, that he or she was too occupied with other interests to attend class or study. Other facts about the agent's history will help us decide among these hypotheses.

This brings out the need to emphasize that sanity, in the specialized sense, is defined as the *ability* cognitively and normatively to understand and appreciate the world for what it is. According to our commonsense understandings, having this ability is one thing and exercising it is another—at least some wrong-acting, responsible agents presumably fall within the gap. The notion of "ability" is notoriously problematic, however, and there is a long history of controversy about whether the truth of determinism would show our ordinary ways of thinking to be simply confused on this matter. At this point, then, metaphysical concerns may voice themselves again—but at least they will have been pushed into a narrower, and perhaps a more manageable, corner.

The sane deep-self view does not, then, solve all the philosophical problems connected to the topics of free will and responsibility. If anything, it highlights some of the practical and empirical problems, rather than solves them. It may, however, resolve some of the philosophical, and particularly, some of the metaphysical problems, and reveal how intimate are the connections between the remaining philosophical problems and the practical ones.

NOTES

1. Harry Frankfurt, "Freedom of the Will and the Concept of a Person," *Journal of Philosophy* LXVIII (1971), pp. 5–20.
2. Gary Watson, "Free Agency," *Journal of Philosophy* LXXII (1975), pp. 205–20.
3. Charles Taylor, "Responsibility for Self," in A. E. Rorty, ed., *The Identities of Persons* (Berkeley: University of California Press, 1976), pp. 381–99.
4. See, e.g., David Hume. *A Treatise of Human Nature* (Oxford: Oxford University Press, 1967), pp. 399–406, and R. E. Hobart, "Free Will as Involving Determination and Inconceivable Without It," *Mind* 43 (1934).
5. Frankfurt, 16.
6. Strictly speaking, perception and sound reasoning may not be enough to ensure the ability to achieve an accurate conception of what one is doing and especially to achieve a reasonable normative assessment of one's situation. Sensitivity and exposure to certain realms of experience may also be necessary for these goals. For the purpose of this essay, I understand 'sanity' to include whatever it takes to enable one to develop an adequate conception of one's world. In other contexts, however, this would be an implausibly broad construction of the term.
7. Admittedly, it is open to question whether these individuals were in fact unable to help having mistaken values, and indeed, whether recognizing the errors of their society would even have required exceptional independence or strength of mind. This is presumably an empirical question, the answer to which is extraordinarily hard to determine. My point here is simply that *if* we believe they are unable to recognize that their values are mistaken, we do not hold them responsible for the actions that flow from these values, and *if* we believe their ability to recognize their normative errors is impaired, we hold them less than fully responsible for relevant actions.

Morality and Its Critics

T HESE DAYS THERE IS A good deal of skepticism about morality, skepticism that may take many forms. One challenge to morality comes from a famous theory of human motivation. The theory that human beings are so constituted by nature that they are incapable of desiring or pursuing anything but their own well-being as an end in itself is called **psychological egoism**. If "true morality" requires selfless devotion to others even at the cost of one's own interests, and if all persons are inherently selfish, as this theory claims, there may be no way to motivate persons to behave morally. Genuinely disinterested acts of benevolence, on this view, do not exist, although persons sometimes appear to be acting unselfishly when they take the interests of other people to be the means for promoting their own good.

This theory of motivation should be distinguished from the doctrine called **ethical egoism**, which, as its name indicates, is not a theory about how human beings in fact act, but rather a moral doctrine stating how they ought to act. According to this doctrine, one ought to pursue one's own well-being, and only one's own well-being, as an end in itself. A *psychological* egoist, insofar as he or she bothered with ethics at all, might be expected to be an *ethical* egoist; for if there is only one thing that we *can* pursue, there cannot be some other thing that we *ought* to pursue. Most psychological egoists, however, have sought some way to reconcile necessarily selfish motivation with the unselfish and even self-sacrificing conduct required by morality. Many argue, for example, that generally the best means to promote one's own happiness is to work for the public good or the happiness of others.

Joel Feinberg's essay on psychological egoism contains elementary distinctions and standard arguments reorganized and written in a clear and accessible manner. Because of its pedagogical intent, it might very well be used as the student's introduction to this section, or even perhaps to the whole volume. Many students, after much resistance, seem to be persuaded by its arguments; but some of the best students remain unconvinced to the end. Some of the students who resist the arguments against psychological egoism would admit that the a priori arguments for psychological egoism are fallacious, but insist that the biological sciences and particularly evolutionary theory may yet provide empirical evidence for the theory.

One may take a deeply skeptical attitude toward morality even if one allows that persons can be altruistically motivated, and allows as well that ethical standards require us to behave in ways that sometimes necessitate deep personal sacrifice. This form of moral skepticism assumes that we know what morality requires of us—occasional self-sacrifice—and proceeds to ask why it is rational, in such cases, to do what morality requires of us. If we can do better for ourselves by disregarding our moral duties, why shouldn't we do so? Suppose you find a wallet containing $5,000 in cash. Surely the morally right thing to do (at least according to the prevailing moral code) would be to return the wallet with the money to its owner. But would this truly be the most reasonable course of action? Think of what you have to gain: an expression of gratitude, some small satisfaction at having done your duty (mixed with nagging doubts that you are a fool), and *maybe* a small reward. Now compare these benefits with what you have to lose—namely, the $5,000. It would seem that the losses involved in doing your duty far outweigh the gains. (Perhaps the example might be still more convincing if the money belonged not to a single person but to a great corporation or the federal government.) Looking at the matter in this way, wouldn't you be a fool to return the money? Isn't it *unreasonable*, indeed profoundly contrary to reason, voluntarily to choose a loss in preference to a gain for oneself? And yet this is what morality often seems to require of us: that we put the interests of other people ahead of our own. How, then, can it be reasonable to be moral?

One line of reply to this challenge immediately suggests itself. Not to return the property of others is tantamount to stealing it. If other people were ever to find out that you are, in effect, a thief, their opinion of you would drop drastically and your reputation might never fully recover. If the authorities were to make this discovery about you, the consequences might be still worse. Even if no one ever found you out, you would have to live in continual anxiety and fear; and even if you got over that, you might become just a bit bolder in the face of subsequent temptations, until your very success finally betrayed you, and you were found out. The idea that it can *pay* to do what is morally wrong, in short, is usually a miscalculation.

Glaucon and Adeimantus, two characters in Plato's *Republic*, are not satisfied with this kind of answer. They grant that there are advantages in having the reputation of being moral and upright (or "just" as they put it). What they wish to learn from Socrates is whether there are corresponding advantages in really being, as opposed to merely seeming, morally upright. If it is reasonable to be honest only *because* dishonesty doesn't pay, then, it would seem, it is reasonable to be honest *only when* dishonesty doesn't pay. The ideally wise person would then be the one who is able to have the "best of both worlds" by seeming, but not really being, moral.

Friedrich Nietzsche (1844–1900), a brilliant classicist and philosopher, takes up where Plato's characters left off. Nietzsche seeks to turn morality on its head. He is deeply skeptical about the claims of moralists, and thinks that the Judeo-Christian conception of the virtues has things upside down. In an excerpt from his work *Beyond Good and Evil*, Nietzsche makes the case that morality has nothing to do with such virtues as humility, forgiveness, and charity. These, he claims, originated in a cult of people who were oppressed, resented it, could do nothing about it, and so elevated the effects of their humiliations into virtues. Nietzsche's even deeper claim is that morality has no external, universal, authoritative source. Nietzsche, who famously announced the death of God in an earlier work, seeks to undermine views that anchor morality in God's commands or any other objective source.

A new version of moral skepticism has recently appeared, under the guise of an evolutionary critique. Richard Joyce, a contemporary philosopher who has done much to advance this critique, presents his views in a paper that was specially commissioned for this book. According to Joyce, once we know how evolutionary pressures work—namely, to get us to adopt beliefs and practices that increase the chances of our survival and reproductive success—we have excellent reason to doubt that our moral beliefs are largely on target. As Joyce sees it, we think in moral terms primarily or exclusively because the pressures of natural selection have inclined us in that direction. If it weren't adaptive to hold moral beliefs, then we wouldn't do so. But the practical benefits of holding beliefs are one thing—their truth, another. If he is right, then it would be a miracle if our moral beliefs were accurate. As a result, we should suspend judgment about all of our moral beliefs, because we have excellent reason to doubt whether they are reliable.

There are still other grounds for doubts about morality. One further form of moral skepticism begins by noting the existence of deep disagreements that divide people on many ethical issues. The chances that we will all one day agree on issues of abortion, or capital punishment, or famine relief seem quite slim, even if those doing the talking are well-intentioned, open-minded, and knowledgeable about the topic under discussion. Many have inferred from this that ethics cannot be objective in the way that science or mathematics is. Subjects that admit of objective truth appear capable of progress and broad consensus, both on methods for discovering the truth and on the truths themselves. **Ethical subjectivists** claim that we do not see such progress or consensus in ethics, and that therefore ethics is simply not an objective area of inquiry. According to one version of subjectivism (**meta-ethical subjectivism**), ethical judgments are neither true nor false; they are simply expressions of commands, preferences, or emotions, and as such are not even eligible candidates for truth. A different version (**normative subjectivism**) claims that ethical judgments can be true (or false), but that their truth depends entirely on whether they accurately report the sentiments of those who issue the judgments. As Russ Shafer-Landau points out, in the article that leads off Chapter 2, "Proposed Standards of Right Conduct," normative subjectivism is less attractive than its meta-ethical cousin. And while most of us act as if meta-ethical subjectivism were false—we assess moral judgments as true or false, and deliberate and pursue investigations into ethical issues as if there were truth that awaited discovery—meta-ethical subjectivism is supported by a number of appealing arguments. Whether in the end it is entirely convincing is left to the reader to decide.

Shifting the focus from interpersonal ethical disagreements to intersocietal ones, Mary Midgley presents a consideration of **ethical relativism**—the view that actions are right if and only if they comport with the ultimate ethical standards of the society in which they are performed. This is a natural move to make for those who are convinced that ethics cannot be objective but have doubts about the plausibility of ethical subjectivism. Rather than view each person as an equally good moral judge, as subjectivists do, relativists make cultural mores the ultimate ethical standards. Midgley offers us a very interesting test case with which to examine assumptions about our abilities to make valid cross-cultural moral assessments. In the end, she thinks the relativists have overstated the difficulties in this area and that, in many cases, we can rightly say of one social code that it is morally superior (or inferior) to another.

In our selection from *Nicomachean Ethics*, Aristotle offers us a view of ethics that has inspired contemporary philosophers to reexplore the merits of virtue ethics. Aristotle thinks that the central notion in ethics is virtue (as opposed, say, to duty, or happiness, or contract), and that virtue is a matter of knowing and being disposed to behave in accordance with the mean between vicious extremes. As Aristotle frankly states, being virtuous and gaining ethical know-how are not a matter of simply following hard-and-fast rules, but rather of exercising one's judgment. Only the wise person, whose capacity for practical wisdom has been developed through experience and learning, will truly be in a position to exercise judgment properly and so to determine, in hard cases, what is noble, fine, or just.

Thomas Hobbes, the brilliant English philosopher (1588–1679), is often classed as an ethical egoist. But his is a sophisticated position, as readers will see for themselves, and he is just as often considered the founder of modern **social contract theory**. In our selection from *Leviathan*, Hobbes outlines a view according to which morality develops in response to the horrors of life without government (what he called the **state of nature**). Such a life he famously described as "solitary, poor, nasty, brutish and short," and he thought that any government, even despotism, was to be preferred to the state of nature. Hobbes claimed that there was no right or wrong, justice or injustice, in the state of nature, and that the standards of morality are properly given by the terms of the social compact to which parties in the state of nature agree. Hobbes thought that each person's well-being would be enhanced by agreeing to limit his liberty in exchange for the security offered by life under law. His view has had a wide-ranging impact not only on ethics, but also on theories of justice, where social contract views have recently experienced renewed popularity.

Though not very popular these days among professional philosophers, the **divine command theory** enjoys broad allegiance among nonphilosophers. This theory tells us that actions are right in virtue of being commanded by God. While this may seem the natural view for theists to take, there is an ages-old difficulty for the divine command theory. The difficulty was first aired in Plato's *Euthyphro*, reprinted here. In this dialogue, Plato has Socrates ask Euthyphro whether actions are pious because the gods command them, or whether they command such actions because they are [already] pious. The central difficulty for the divine command theory can be expressed as a dilemma: God either does or does not have excellent reasons for the commands that God issues to human beings. If God lacks such reasons, then divine commands are arbitrary, and this undermines divine perfection. But if God has excellent reasons, then these reasons can, all by themselves, explain why certain actions are required or forbidden.

Next follows an excerpt from one of the greatest systematic philosophers of Western civilization, Immanuel Kant. You have here a substantial portion of Books I and II of his *Groundwork of the Metaphysics of Morals*. In Book I Kant develops the notion of a **good will** and defends his claim that nothing else can be unconditionally good—that is, good in every instance, regardless of accompanying circumstances. The good will is simply the commitment to do one's duty for its own sake (rather than, say, because it will promote one's self-interest). But where does one's duty lie? In Book II Kant introduces his **categorical imperative**—a command of reason that is authoritative for moral agents regardless of their desires. Kant claims that the rightness or wrongness of an action lies not in the results it brings about, but in the principle that guides a person's conduct. Kant calls such a principle a **maxim**. The categorical imperative states that actions are right if and only if their maxim is such that the agent can will that everyone abide by it. In effect, the centerpiece of Kantian ethics is the directive not to make an exception of oneself, but to act only on those principles that one is willing to see everyone act on.

Kant's view is directly opposed to the **utilitarian** view of John Stuart Mill. Mill believes that pleasure is the sole intrinsic value, and that our fundamental moral obligation is to produce as much pleasure as we can. But here the focus is not just on one's own pleasure; rather, in the famous utilitarian phrase, "everybody is to count for one and nobody as more than one." Because of its dual emphasis on impartiality and on pleasure, utilitarianism is sometimes denominated **universalistic** (as opposed to egoistic) **hedonism**. This view places priority on achieving the greatest happiness for the greatest number, another utilitarian catchphrase, and thus locates the virtue of beneficence at the heart of ethics. Utilitarians sometimes seek to display the attractions of their view by asking a couple of apparently innocent questions: How could an action that produces the most happiness possibly fail to be right? And how could an action be right if another available action could have made people better off—that is, produced more pleasure?

Despite the apparently rhetorical nature of such questions, Kantians (and others) will find much to disagree with regarding the utilitarian theory. In fact, the contrast between Kant and Mill could not be sharper (though Mill insisted that Kant's theory is best understood as a version of utilitarianism, a claim whose merits have been debated for a century and a half). Kant and Mill disagree about what has value for its own sake (the good will or pleasure), about what makes actions right or wrong (proper intentions or results), and about which virtue stands at the center of ethics (fairness or beneficence).

Next we offer the most famous effort to strike a compromise between the Kantian and utilitarian theories. Sir David Ross, in his day the greatest translator of Aristotle's works, also found time to invent one of the few genuinely novel ethical theories of the twentieth century. He sees merit in the Kantian idea that there are sources of duty other than that of promoting greatest happiness, though he also agrees with utilitarians in saying that, nevertheless, it often is our duty to do what will maximize happiness. He can say such things because he believes that all moral principles specify duties that have only **prima facie** importance. Prima facie principles are those that may permissibly be broken in certain circumstances. Ross believes in **ethical pluralism**: rather than one single, absolute principle that lies at the foundation of ethics, there is a plurality of principles, each of which is independent, in the sense that it cannot be derived from the others. Such rules as those requiring truth-telling, the repayment of debts, and promise-keeping are valid principles, though they may, in certain cases, take a back seat to other principles. These further principles (such as those requiring beneficence, or the avoidance of harming others) are also prima facie, and so may themselves be outweighed in some cases by competing moral principles.

The final entry in this field of moral theories is by Hilde Lindemann, who provides us with some of the basics of feminist ethics. Unlike the other theories in this section, feminist ethics is a more general approach to morality, rather than a specific moral theory that tries to dictate the conditions under which actions are (perhaps only generally) right or wrong. As Lindemann sees it, the central role of feminist ethicists is to "*understand, criticize,* and *correct* how gender operates within our moral beliefs and practices." The feminist approach to ethics is marked by a focus on issues of gender equality, a concern with the lived experiences of women, and a suspicion of traditional efforts to separate moral theorizing from actual conditions of power.

As a way, in part, to test the implications of the proposed standards of right conduct, we turn now to Chapter 3, "Ethical Problems." The chapter starts off with an ingenious short piece by Princeton philosopher Kwame Anthony Appiah. Appiah invites us to reflect on the merits of conventional moral wisdom by asking us to imagine what future generations might condemn us for. His list includes such things as our treatment of convicted prisoners, non-human animals, the elderly and the environment. Appiah asks readers not only to consider the ethical standing of our behavior on these fronts but, more deeply, challenges us to utilize his test to discover other ways in which our currently accepted conduct might fall short of being truly moral.

We continue our survey of some ethical problems with a provocative article by Peter Singer, who argues for a solution to world poverty. He does this by recommending that those of us who are relatively well-off (by global standards) give a great deal to the less fortunate. That we don't know our beneficiaries is neither here nor there. What is most important is that we can relieve great suffering at relatively little cost to ourselves. When anyone is in such a position, it is morally incumbent on him or her to sacrifice self-interest for the sake of others. As a practical matter, this means that most of us in more developed countries have a moral duty to give a substantial amount to those who are less fortunate. Indeed, if Singer is right, then we are morally obligated to give as much as we have, just shy of making ourselves as badly off as those we are intending to help.

Following Singer's piece is another striking paper, written with an implicit utilitarian challenge. John Harris invites us to ponder the morality of what he calls a *survival lottery*. In societies that lack a sufficient number of donor organs to transplant to those in need, every citizen must participate in a lottery. If a citizen's number is drawn, then he or she will be killed in order to distribute the vital organs. Although one person will surely die as a result, each organ will be distributed to a different person in need, thereby saving many more lives. Though this strikes us as repugnant, Harris claims that there is no morally relevant difference between such a lottery and the present state of affairs. If we had (say) five vital organs, and one person needed a transplant of all five to survive, while five others each needed just one organ to survive, we'd have no qualms about allowing the one to die so that the five may live. If the results are the same in the survival lottery and in real life—we can save five at the cost of one life—why is it OK to save five in the latter case but not the former? The answer, presumably, has to do with the claim that it is morally worse to kill people than to allow them to die. Utilitarians deny this, since the consequences of killing may be just as bad or good as those of letting die, and for utilitarians it is consequences that count. For those with different convictions, it is incumbent on them to identify a morally relevant difference that can explain the intuitions surrounding the acceptability of the survival lottery.

James Rachels, though not a utilitarian, takes up this very issue in an article presented here on the topic of euthanasia, or mercy killing. Rachels' short paper, published in a preeminent medical journal, criticized the prevailing view among doctors that **active euthanasia** is immoral, though **passive euthanasia** need not be. Active euthanasia involves the intention, usually on the part of a medical professional, to terminate the life of a patient for the patient's own good. In the present context, the discussion is carried on with the understanding that the proposed euthanasia is voluntary—that is, that the patient's decision is made on the basis of adequate information and in the absence of coercion. Whereas active euthanasia seeks to intervene in an ongoing sequence to hasten the patient's death, passive euthanasia (also assumed here to be voluntary) involves a medical decision, in conjunction with the patient, to allow the patient to die. Rachels argues that there is a morally relevant difference between active and passive euthanasia only if there is a morally relevant difference between killing and letting die. But, he argues, there is no such difference. Therefore if, as most people assume, passive euthanasia is morally acceptable (when voluntarily undertaken), then so too is active euthanasia.

This chapter concludes with a pair of articles on the morality of abortion. In a very influential article, Mary Anne Warren offers several important arguments on behalf of a pro-choice position. First, she reconstructs and then criticizes a hugely influential argument by Judith Thomson, who sought to show that abortion is usually morally permissible even if we grant that the fetus is a person—i.e., a moral being possessed of the full battery of basic moral rights that you and I possess. Warren believes that pro-choice advocates must show two things: first, that fetuses are not persons in the sense just given, and second, that in any conflict between actual persons and nonpersons, the rights and interests of actual persons win out. She offers challenging arguments for both of these claims in the paper reprinted here. Warren believes that even third-trimester abortions are morally permissible. This opens her up to the following criticism: if these abortions are morally acceptable, then infanticide is also morally acceptable. But it isn't. So these abortions are immoral, too. Her article concludes with a rebuttal of this argument.

Don Marquis agrees that we can avoid the difficult matter of specifying the conditions of personhood (i.e., the conditions necessary and sufficient to qualify for a moral right to life) in the abortion debate. But he comes to just the opposite conclusion about the morality of abortion. On Marquis's account, it is just as wrong to kill a two-week-old fetus as it is to kill you or me. The basic argument is simple, and employs no religious assumptions. Marquis asks why it would be wrong to kill you or me. The answer: because doing so would deprive us of a valuable future. The fetus (except in rare cases of very severe trauma or disease) has a future of value, too. Therefore, it is just as wrong to kill a fetus as it is to kill you or me. Marquis anticipates a number of challenges to this view and offers his replies, before concluding that abortion is as grave a moral wrong as most murders. Much of the appeal of Marquis's argument depends on his claim to have identified the central wrong-making feature of killing people like us. Whether he has done so is, of course, left for the reader to decide.

The book concludes, fittingly, with a chapter on "The Meaning of Life." We begin with an ancient letter from the philosopher Epicurus, founder of the hedonistic school of philosophy. Epicurus summarizes the main tenets of his philosophy, which might come as a surprise to many who nowadays associate hedonism with the lustful pursuit of carnal pleasure. Epicurus does indeed advise us to pursue as pleasurable a life as possible, but he thinks that a life of *tranquility* best meets this description. Furthermore, Epicurus believes that philosophy is the best means of gaining pleasure, because it is perfectly suited to ridding us of the sorts of false beliefs that cause unhappiness. The beliefs he has in mind are as current today as they were two millennia ago: that sex, money, and physical appearance are the most important things in life; that we are right to greatly fear death; that the gods (or God) will punish those who stray from a certain prescribed path. Epicurus packs a great deal of unconventional wisdom into his brief letter.

Richard Taylor next recounts the Greek myth of Sisyphus, who angered the gods and was punished with an eternity of rolling a boulder up a hill. As soon as the summit was reached, the boulder would roll down again, and Sisyphus would then be forced to repeat his labors—forever. Sisyphus achieves nothing of permanence, and Taylor thinks that such a life is indeed meaningless. But he does not believe in God and does not think that meaning lies in religious pursuits. There can be no objective meaning in our lives, says Taylor, because, in the greater scheme of things, our pursuits have no more importance than those of the unfortunate Sisyphus. But there is nevertheless the possibility of what Taylor calls *subjective meaning*, which comes from a feeling of fulfilment in activities that one values. If the gods had injected Sisyphus with a serum that made him an enthusiastic boulder-roller, then his life would have an important sort of meaning that it lacks in the standard version of the tale. The sort of meaning that is available to us, then, is one that requires our commitment and pleasure in the activities that we pursue—even if, from an "objective" perspective, these activities are wholly without value.

This sort of view comes in for criticism by Richard Kraut, who targets the desire theory: the view that the good life is a matter of having one's desires satisfied, regardless of what one's desires are *for*. If Taylor is right, then it doesn't matter whether your desires are for something as absurd as rolling heavy rocks up hills; if that's what you want, and you get what you want, then your life is meaningful. Kraut will have none of this and develops a number of important criticisms of the desire view. He then offers (but does not argue in any detail for) an objective, pluralistic account, according to which a variety of things are objectively intrinsically good. Such things are good not because they are desired, but rather because of their objective nature; there is something about them that makes them intrinsically worthy of being desired or admired. If Kraut is correct, there is no single overarching value by virtue of which all valuable things are good.

Perhaps meaning in life does not derive from happiness or pleasure, or even fine achievements, a rich home life, and an exalted reputation. Leo Tolstoy had all of these things—and then he had a mental breakdown. He came to question the value of his fame, his brilliant novels, his wealth, and his contented family life. The thought that our time on earth is so short, and our achievements so short-lived, caused him the greatest anguish. He beautifully contrasts his lifestyle—the envy of almost all he knew —with that of the Russian peasants who worked on his estates, and found that their lives were filled with the meaning that he was searching for. The key to that meaning lay in religious devotion; without it, writes Tolstoy, even a life filled with worldly goods and pleasure is ultimately meaningless.

Susan Wolf next provides her vision of what a meaningful life consists in. She is intent on avoiding the perils of popular but (as she sees them) extreme views. These include hedonism—the idea that a meaningful or a good life is determined entirely by how much pleasure (and absence of pain) a life contains. Another extreme view is a radically "subjectivist" one, according to which your life is meaningful or personally beneficial just to the extent that you get what you want—no matter what you want. (See Taylor's view above.) At the other end of the spectrum, certain "objectivist" views argue that a meaningful life requires you to follow certain rules or attain certain goals, even if you have no interest in them and even if doing so would not bring you any enjoyment. Wolf develops a compromise view that, she believes, incorporates the insights of each of these views while striking a plausible balance. As she sees it, meaning in life is found "when subjective attraction meets objective attractiveness," or, as she otherwise puts it, when a person displays "active engagement in projects of worth." Crucially, on her view, there are objective standards of what is worth pursuing in a life. Not every pursuit is as worthwhile as every other. One must not only have the right pursuits but also derive fulfillment from them in order to live a meaningful life.

Thomas Nagel concludes this chapter, and the book, with his paper on the absurdity of human life. Nagel writes that absurdity arises when one is "full of doubts that he is unable to answer, but also full of purposes that he [is] unable to abandon." The human condition contains a central tension between an external perspective on one's life—according to which our life is of no permanent value, and the activities we are consumed by inherently worthless—and an internal point of view that guides our activities from moment to moment. We are thinking beings, and once we have taken a step back from our day-to-day existence and looked at it in a broader context, we are bound to question the value of our lives and attachments. But we are also active beings who must make our way in the world, faced with daily choices about what to do and which long-term projects and commitments to pursue. The means of escape from this central tension—death, on the one hand, or, on the other, a wholly passive existence, with no efforts made and no commitments at all—are both less appealing than toughing it out and recognizing our plight for what it is. There is no attractive way of escaping from absurdity, but there is, says Nagel, a certain nobility in facing the absurdity directly and getting on with our lives as best we can.

CHAPTER 1

CHALLENGES TO MORALITY

1.1 Psychological Egoism

JOEL FEINBERG

A. THE THEORY

1. "Psychological egoism" is the name given to a theory widely held by ordinary people, and at one time almost universally accepted by political economists, philosophers, and psychologists, according to which all human actions when properly understood can be seen to be motivated by selfish desires. More precisely, psychological egoism is the doctrine that the only thing anyone is capable of desiring or pursuing ultimately

---

From materials composed for philosophy students at Brown University, 1958.

(as an end in itself) is his *own* self-interest. No psychological egoist denies that people sometimes do desire things other than their own welfare—the happiness of other people, for example; but all psychological egoists insist that people are capable of desiring the happiness of others only when they take it to be a *means* to their own happiness. In short, purely altruistic and benevolent actions and desires do not exist; but people sometimes appear to be acting unselfishly and disinterestedly when they take the interests of others to be means to the promotion of their own self-interest.

2. This theory is called *psychological* egoism to indicate that it is not a theory about what *ought* to be the case, but rather about what, as a matter of fact, *is* the case. That is, the theory claims to be a description of psychological facts, not a prescription of ethical ideals. It asserts, however, not merely that all men do as a contingent matter of fact "put their own interests first," but also that they are capable of nothing else, human nature being what it is. Universal selfishness is not just an accident or a coincidence on this view; rather, it is an unavoidable consequence of psychological laws.

The theory is to be distinguished from another doctrine, so-called "ethical egoism," according to which all people *ought* to pursue their own well-being. This doctrine, being a prescription of what *ought* to be the case, makes no claim to be a psychological theory of human motives; hence the word "ethical" appears in its name to distinguish it from *psychological* egoism.

3. There are a number of types of motives and desires which might reasonably be called "egoistic" or "selfish," and corresponding to each of them is a possible version of psychological egoism. Perhaps the most common version of the theory is that apparently held by Jeremy Bentham.[1] According to this version, all persons have only one ultimate motive in all their voluntary behavior and that motive is a selfish one; more specifically, it is one particular kind of selfish motive—namely, a desire for one's own *pleasure*. According to this version of the theory,

"the only kind of ultimate desire is the desire to get or to prolong pleasant experiences, and to avoid or to cut short unpleasant experiences for oneself."[2] This form of psychological egoism is often given the cumbersome name—*psychological egoistic hedonism*.

B. PRIMA FACIE REASONS IN SUPPORT OF THE THEORY

4. Psychological egoism has seemed plausible to many people for a variety of reasons, of which the following are typical:

a. "Every action of mine is prompted by motives or desires or impulses which are *my* motives and not somebody else's. This fact might be expressed by saying that whenever I act I am always pursuing my own ends or trying to satisfy my own desires. And from this we might pass on to—'I am always pursuing something for myself or seeking my own satisfaction.' Here is what seems like a proper description of a man acting selfishly, and if the description applies to all actions of all men, then it follows that all men in all their actions are selfish."[3]

b. It is a truism that when a person gets what he wants he characteristically feels pleasure. This has suggested to many people that what we really want in every case is our own pleasure, and that we pursue other things only as a means.

c. *Self-Deception.* Often we deceive ourselves into thinking that we desire something fine or noble when what we really want is to be thought well of by others or to be able to congratulate ourselves, or to be able to enjoy the pleasures of a good conscience. It is a well-known fact that people tend to conceal their true motives from themselves by camouflaging them with words like "virtue," "duty," etc. Since we are so often misled concerning both our own real motives and the real motives of others, is it not reasonable to suspect that we might *always* be deceived when we think motives disinterested and altruistic? Indeed, it is a simple matter to explain away all allegedly unselfish motives: "Once the conviction that selfishness is universal finds root in a person's mind, it is very likely to burgeon out in a thousand corroborating generalizations. It will be discovered that a friendly smile is really only an attempt to win an approving nod from a more or less gullible recording angel; that a charitable deed is, for its performer, only an opportunity to congratulate himself on the good fortune or the cleverness that enables him to be charitable; that a public benefaction is just plain good business advertising. It will emerge that gods are worshiped only because they indulge men's selfish fears, or tastes, or hopes; that the 'golden rule' is no more than an eminently sound success formula; that social and political codes are created and subscribed to only because they serve to restrain other men's egoism as much as one's own, morality being only a special sort of 'racket' or intrigue using weapons of persuasion in place of bombs and machine guns. Under this interpretation of human nature, the categories of commercialism replace those of disinterested service and the spirit of the horse trader broods over the face of the earth."[4]

d. *Moral Education.* Morality, good manners, decency, and other virtues must be teachable. Psychological egoists often notice that moral education and the inculcation of manners usually utilize what Bentham calls the "sanctions of pleasure and pain."[5] Children are made to acquire the civilizing virtues only by the method of enticing rewards and painful punishments. Much the same is true of the history of the race. People in general have been inclined to behave well only when it is made plain to them that there is "something in it for them." Is it not then highly probable that just such a mechanism of human motivation as Bentham describes must be presupposed by our methods of moral education?

C. CRITIQUE OF PSYCHOLOGICAL EGOISM: CONFUSIONS IN THE ARGUMENTS

5. *Non-Empirical Character of the Arguments.* If the arguments of the psychological egoist consisted for the most part of carefully acquired empirical evidence (well-documented reports of controlled experiments, surveys, interviews, laboratory data, and so on), then the critical philosopher would have no business carping at them. After all, since psychological egoism purports to be a scientific theory of human motives, it is the concern of the experimental psychologist, not the philosopher, to accept or reject it. But as a matter of fact, empirical evidence of the required sort is seldom presented in support of psychological egoism. Psychologists, on the whole, shy away from generalizations about human motives which are so sweeping and so vaguely formulated that they are virtually incapable of scientific testing. It is usually the "armchair scientist" who holds the theory of universal selfishness, and his usual arguments are either based simply on his "impressions" or else are largely of a non-empirical sort. The latter are often shot full of a very subtle kind of logical confusion, and this makes their criticism a matter of special interest to the analytic philosopher.

6. The psychological egoist's first argument (4a, above) is a good example of logical confusion. It begins with a truism—namely, that all of my motives and desires are *my* motives and desires and not someone else's. (Who would deny this?) But from this simple tautology nothing whatever concerning the nature of my motives or the objective of my desires can possibly follow. The fallacy of this argument consists in its violation of the general logical rule that analytic statements (tautologies) cannot entail synthetic (factual) ones.[6] That every voluntary act is prompted by the agent's own motives is a tautology; hence, it cannot be equivalent to "A person is always seeking something for himself" or "All of a person's motives are selfish," which

are synthetic. What the egoist must prove is not merely:

(i) Every voluntary action is prompted by a motive of the agent's own.

but rather:

(ii) Every voluntary action is prompted by a motive of a quite particular kind, viz. a selfish one.

Statement (i) is obviously true, but it cannot all by itself give any logical support to statement (ii).

The source of the confusion in this argument is readily apparent. It is not the genesis of an action or the *origin* of its motives which makes it a "selfish" one, but rather the "purpose" of the act or the *objective* of its motives; *not where the motive comes from* (in voluntary actions it always comes from the agent) but *what it aims at* determines whether or not it is selfish. There is surely a valid distinction between voluntary behavior, in which the agent's action is motivated by purposes of his own, and *selfish* behavior in which the agent's motives are of one exclusive sort. The egoist's argument assimilates all voluntary action into the class of selfish action, by requiring, in effect, that an unselfish action be one which is not really motivated at all. In the words of Lucius Garvin, "to say that an act proceeds from our own...desire is only to say that the act is our own. To demand that we should act on motives that are not our own is to ask us to make ourselves living contradictions in terms."[7]

7. But if argument 4a fails to prove its point, argument 4b does no better. From the fact that all our successful actions (those in which we get what we were after) are accompanied or followed by pleasure it does not follow, as the egoist claims, that the *objective* of every action is to get pleasure for oneself. To begin with, the premise of the argument is not, strictly speaking, even true. Fulfillment of desire (simply getting what one was after) is no guarantee of satisfaction (pleasant feelings of gratification in the mind of the agent). Sometimes when we get what we want we *also* get, as a kind of extra dividend, a warm, glowing feeling of contentment;

but often, far too often, we get no dividend at all, or, even worse, the bitter taste of ashes. Indeed, it has been said that the characteristic psychological problem of our time is the *dissatisfaction* that attends the fulfillment of our very most powerful desires.

Even if we grant, however, for the sake of argument, that getting what one wants *usually* yields satisfaction, the egoist's conclusion does not follow. We can concede that we normally get pleasure (in the sense of satisfaction) when our desires are satisfied, *no matter what our desires are for;* but it does not follow from this roughly accurate generalization that the only thing we ever desire is our own satisfaction. Pleasure may well be the usual accompaniment of all actions in which the agent gets what he wants; but to infer from this that what the agent always wants is his own pleasure is like arguing, in William James's example,[8] that because an ocean liner constantly consumes coal on its trans-Atlantic passage that therefore the *purpose* of its voyage is to consume coal. The immediate inference from even constant accompaniment to purpose (or motive) is always a *non sequitur.*

Perhaps there is a sense of "satisfaction" (desire fulfillment) such that it is certainly and universally true that we get satisfaction whenever we get what we want. But satisfaction in this sense is simply the "coming into existence of that which is desired." Hence, to say that desire fulfillment always yields "satisfaction" in this sense is to say no more than that we always get what we want when we get what we want, which is to utter a tautology like "a rose is a rose." It can no more entail a synthetic truth in psychology (like the egoistic thesis) than "a rose is a rose" can entail significant information in botany.

8. *Disinterested Benevolence.* The fallacy in argument 4b then consists, as Garvin puts it, "in the supposition that the apparently unselfish desire to benefit others is transformed into a selfish one by the fact that we derive pleasure from carrying it out."[9] Not only is this argument fallacious; it also provides us with a suggestion of a counterargument to show that its conclusion (psychological egoistic hedonism) is false. Not

only is the presence of pleasure (satisfaction) as a by-product of an action no proof that the action was selfish; in some special cases it provides rather conclusive proof that the action was *unselfish*. For in those special cases the fact that we get pleasure from a particular action *presupposes that we desired something else*—something other than our own pleasure—as an end in itself and not merely as a means to our own pleasant state of mind.

This way of turning the egoistic hedonist's argument back on him can be illustrated by taking a typical egoist argument, one attributed (perhaps apocryphally) to Abraham Lincoln, and then examining it closely:

> Mr. Lincoln once remarked to a fellow-passenger on an old-time mud-coach that all men were prompted by selfishness in doing good. His fellow-passenger was antagonizing this position when they were passing over a corduroy bridge that spanned a slough. As they crossed this bridge they espied an old razor-backed sow on the bank making a terrible noise because her pigs had got into the slough and were in danger of drowning. As the old coach began to climb the hill, Mr. Lincoln called out, "Driver, can't you stop just a moment?" Then Mr. Lincoln jumped out, ran back and lifted the little pigs out of the mud and water and placed them on the bank. When he returned, his companion remarked: "Now Abe, where does selfishness come in on this little episode?" "Why, bless your soul Ed, that was the very essence of selfishness. I should have had no peace of mind all day had I gone on and left that suffering old sow worrying over those pigs. I did it to get peace of mind, don't you see?"[10]

If Lincoln had cared not a whit for the welfare of the little pigs and their "suffering" mother, but only for his own "peace of mind," it would be difficult to explain how he could have derived pleasure from helping them. The very fact that he did feel satisfaction as a result of helping the pigs presupposes that he had a preexisting desire for something other than his own happiness. Then when *that* desire was satisfied, Lincoln of course derived pleasure. The *object* of Lincoln's desire was not pleasure; rather pleasure was the *consequence* of his preexisting desire for something else. If Lincoln had been wholly indifferent to the plight of the little pigs as he claimed, how could he possibly have derived any pleasure from helping them? He could not have achieved peace of mind from rescuing the pigs, had he not a prior concern—on which his peace of mind depended—for the welfare of the pigs for its own sake.

In general, the psychological hedonist analyzes apparent benevolence into a desire for "benevolent pleasure." No doubt the benevolent person does get pleasure from his benevolence, but in most cases, this is only because he has previously desired the good of some person, or animal, or mankind at large. Where there is no such desire, benevolent conduct is not generally found to give pleasure to the agent.

9. *Malevolence.* Difficult cases for the psychological egoist include not only instances of disinterested benevolence, but also cases of "disinterested malevolence." Indeed, malice and hatred are generally no more "selfish" than benevolence. Both are motives likely to cause an agent to sacrifice his own interests—in the case of benevolence, in order to help someone else, in the case of malevolence in order to harm someone else. The selfish person is concerned ultimately only with his own pleasure, happiness, or power; the benevolent person is often equally concerned with the happiness of others; to the malevolent person, the *injury* of another is often an end in itself—an end to be pursued sometimes with no thought for his own interests. There is reason to think that people have as often sacrificed themselves to injure or kill others as to help or to save others, and with as much "heroism" in the one case as in the other. The unselfish nature of malevolence was first noticed by the Anglican Bishop and moral philosopher Joseph Butler (1692–1752), who regretted that people are no more selfish than they are.[11]

10. *Lack of Evidence for Universal Self-Deception.* The more cynical sort of psychological egoist who is impressed by the widespread phenomenon of self-deception (see 4c above) cannot be so quickly disposed of, for he has

committed no *logical* mistakes. We can only argue that the acknowledged frequency of self-deception is insufficient evidence for his universal generalization. His argument is not fallacious, but inconclusive.

No one but the agent himself can ever be certain what conscious motives really prompted his action, and where motives are disreputable, even the agent may not admit to himself the true nature of his desires. Thus, for every apparent case of altruistic behavior, the psychological egoist can argue, with some plausibility, that the true motivation *might* be selfish, appearance to the contrary. Philanthropic acts are really motivated by the desire to receive gratitude; acts of self-sacrifice, when truly understood, are seen to be motivated by the desire to feel self-esteem; and so on. We must concede to the egoist that all apparent altruism might be deceptive in this way; but such a sweeping generalization requires considerable empirical evidence, and such evidence is not presently available.

11. *The "Paradox of Hedonism" and Its Consequences for Education.* The psychological egoistic Hedonist (e.g., Jeremy Bentham) has the simplest possible theory of human motivation. According to this variety of egoistic theory, all human motives without exception can be reduced to one—namely, the desire for one's own pleasure. But this theory, despite its attractive simplicity, or perhaps because of it, involves one immediately in a paradox. Astute observers of human affairs from the time of the ancient Greeks have often noticed that pleasure, happiness, and satisfaction are states of mind which stand in a very peculiar relation to desire. An exclusive desire for happiness is the surest way to prevent happiness from coming into being. Happiness has a way of "sneaking up" on persons when they are preoccupied with other things; but when persons deliberately and single-mindedly set off in pursuit of happiness, it vanishes utterly from sight and cannot be captured. This is the famous "paradox of hedonism:" the single-minded pursuit of happiness is necessarily self-defeating, for *the way to get happiness is to forget it;* then perhaps it will come to you. If you aim exclusively at pleasure itself, with no concern for the things that bring pleasure, then pleasure will never come. To derive satisfaction, one must ordinarily first desire something other than satisfaction, and then find the means to get what one desires.

To feel the full force of the paradox of hedonism the reader should conduct an experiment in his imagination. Imagine a person (let's call him "Jones") who is, first of all, devoid of intellectual curiosity. He has no desire to acquire any kind of knowledge for its own sake, and thus is utterly indifferent to questions of science, mathematics, and philosophy. Imagine further that the beauties of nature leave Jones cold: he is unimpressed by the autumn foliage, the snow-capped mountains, and the rolling oceans. Long walks in the country on spring mornings and skiing forays in the winter are to him equally a bore. Moreover, let us suppose that Jones can find no appeal in art. Novels are dull, poetry a pain, paintings nonsense and music just noise. Suppose further that Jones has neither the participant's nor the spectator's passion for baseball, football, tennis, or any other sport. Swimming to him is a cruel aquatic form of calisthenics, the sun only a cause of sunburn. Dancing is coeducational idiocy, conversation a waste of time, the other sex an unappealing mystery. Politics is a fraud, religion mere superstition; and the misery of millions of underprivileged human beings is nothing to be concerned with or excited about. Suppose finally that Jones has no talent for any kind of handicraft, industry, or commerce, and that he does not regret that fact.

What then is Jones interested in? He must desire something. To be sure, he does. Jones has an overwhelming passion for, a complete preoccupation with, his own happiness. The one exclusive desire of his life is *to be happy.* It takes little imagination at this point to see that Jones's one desire is bound to be frustrated. People who—like Jones—most hotly pursue their own happiness are the least likely to find it. Happy people are those who successfully pursue such things as aesthetic or religious experience, self-expression, service to others, victory in competitions, knowledge, power, and so on. If none of these things in themselves and for their own sakes mean anything to a person, if they are valued at all then only as a means to one's own pleasant states of mind—then that pleasure can never come. The way to achieve happiness is to pursue something else.

Almost all people at one time or another in their lives feel pleasure. Some people (though perhaps not many) really do live lives which are on the whole happy. But if pleasure and happiness presuppose desires for something other than pleasure and happiness, then the existence of pleasure and happiness in the experience of some people proves that those people have strong desires for something other than their own happiness—egoistic hedonism to the contrary.

The implications of the "paradox of hedonism" for educational theory should be obvious. The parents least likely to raise a happy child are those who, even with the best intentions, train their child to seek happiness directly. How often have we heard parents say:

> I don't care if my child does not become an intellectual, or a sports star, or a great artist. I just want her to be a plain average sort of person. Happiness does not require great ambitions and great frustrations; it's not worth it to suffer and become neurotic for the sake of science, art, or do-goodism. I just want my child to be happy.

This can be a dangerous mistake, for it is the child (and the adult for that matter) without "outerdirected" interests who is the most likely to be unhappy. The pure egoist would be the most wretched of persons.

The educator might well beware of "life adjustment" as the conscious goal of the educational process for similar reasons. "Life adjustment" can be achieved only as a by-product of other pursuits. A whole curriculum of "life adjustment courses" unsupplemented by courses designed to incite an interest in things other than life adjustment would be tragically self-defeating.

As for moral education, it is probably true that punishment and reward are indispensable means of inculcation. But if the child comes to

believe that the *sole* reasons for being moral are that he will escape the pain of punishment thereby and/or that he will gain the pleasure of a good reputation, then what is to prevent him from doing the immoral thing whenever he is sure that he will not be found out? While punishment and reward then are important tools for the moral educator, they obviously have their limitations. Beware of the man who does the moral thing only out of fear of pain or love of pleasure. He is not likely to be wholly trustworthy. Moral education is truly successful when it produces persons who are willing to do the right thing *simply because it is right,* and not merely because it is popular or safe.

12. *Pleasure as Sensation.* One final argument against psychological hedonism should suffice to put that form of the egoistic psychology to rest once and for all. The egoistic hedonist claims that all desires can be reduced to the single desire for one's own *pleasure.* Now the word "pleasure" is ambiguous. On the one hand, it can stand for a certain indefinable, but very familiar and specific kind of sensation, or more accurately, a property of sensations; and it is generally, if not exclusively, associated with the senses. For example, certain taste sensations such as sweetness, thermal sensations of the sort derived from a hot bath or the feel of the August sun while one lies on a sandy beach, erotic sensations, olfactory sensations (say) of the fragrance of flowers or perfume, and tactual and kinesthetic sensations from a good massage, are all pleasant in this sense. Let us call this sense of "pleasure," which is the converse of "physical pain," pleasure$_1$.

On the other hand, the word "pleasure" is often used simply as a synonym for "satisfaction" (in the sense of gratification, not mere desire fulfillment.) In this sense, the existence of pleasure presupposes the prior existence of desire. Knowledge, religious experience, aesthetic expression, and other so-called "spiritual activities" often give pleasure in this sense. In fact, as we have seen, we tend to get pleasure in this sense whenever we get what we desire, no matter what we desire. The masochist even derives pleasure (in the sense of "satisfaction") from his own physically painful sensations. Let us call the sense of "pleasure" which means "satisfaction"—pleasure$_2$.

Now we can evaluate the psychological hedonist's claim that the sole human motive is a desire for one's own pleasure, bearing in mind (as he often does not) the ambiguity of the word "pleasure." First, let us take the hedonist to be saying that it is the desire for pleasure$_1$ (pleasant sensation) which is the sole ultimate desire of all people and the sole desire capable of providing a motive for action. Now I have little doubt that all (or most) people desire their own pleasure, *sometimes*. But even this familiar kind of desire occurs, I think, rather rarely. When I am very hungry, I often desire to eat, or, more specifically, to eat this piece of steak and these potatoes. Much less often do I desire to eat certain morsels simply for the sake of the pleasant gustatory sensations they might cause. I have, on the other hand, been motivated in the latter way when I have gone to especially exotic (and expensive) French or Chinese restaurants; but normally, pleasant gastronomic sensations are simply a happy consequence or by-product of my eating, not the antecedently desired objective of my eating. There are, of course, others who take gustatory sensations far more seriously: the *gourmet* who eats only to savor the textures and flavors of fine foods, and the wine fancier who "collects" the exquisitely subtle and very pleasant tastes of rare old wines. Such people are truly absorbed in their taste sensations when they eat and drink, and there may even be some (rich) persons whose desire for such sensations is the sole motive for eating and drinking. It should take little argument, however, to convince the reader that such persons are extremely rare.

Similarly, I usually derive pleasure from taking a hot bath, and on occasion (though not very often) I even decide to bathe simply for the sake of such sensations. Even if this is equally true of everyone, however, it hardly provides grounds for inferring that *no one ever* bathes from *any* other motive. It should be empirically obvious that we sometimes bathe simply in order to get clean, or to please others, or simply from habit.

The view then that we are never after anything in our actions but our own pleasure—that all people are complete "gourmets" of one sort or another—is not only morally cynical; it is also contrary to common sense and everyday experience. In fact, the view that pleasant sensations play such an enormous role in human affairs is so patently false, on the available evidence, that we must conclude that the psychological hedonist has the other sense of "pleasure"—satisfaction—in mind when he states his thesis. If, on the other hand, he really does try to reduce the apparent multitude of human motives to the one desire for pleasant sensations, then the abundance of historical counterexamples justifies our rejection out of hand of his thesis. It surely seems incredible that the Christian martyrs were ardently pursuing their own pleasure when they marched off to face the lions, or that what the Russian soldiers at Stalingrad "really" wanted when they doused themselves with gasoline, ignited themselves, and then threw the flaming torches of their own bodies on German tanks, was simply the experience of pleasant physical sensations.

13. *Pleasure as Satisfaction.* Let us consider now the other interpretation of the hedonist's thesis, that according to which it is one's own pleasure$_2$ (satisfaction) and not merely pleasure$_1$ (pleasant sensation) which is the sole ultimate objective of all voluntary behavior. In one respect, the "satisfaction thesis" is even less plausible than the "physical sensation thesis"; for the latter at least is a genuine empirical hypothesis, testable in experience, though contrary to the facts which experience discloses. The former, however, is so confused that it cannot even be completely stated without paradox. It is, so to speak, defeated in its own formulation. Any attempted explication of the theory that all men at all times desire only their own satisfaction leads to an *infinite regress* in the following way:

"All men desire only satisfaction."
　"Satisfaction of what?"
　　"Satisfaction of their desires."
　　"Their desires for what?"
　　　"Their desires for satisfaction."

"Satisfaction of what?"
"Their desires."
"For what?"
"For satisfaction?"—etc., *ad infinitum.*

In short, psychological hedonism interpreted in this way attributes to all people as their sole motive a wholly vacuous and infinitely self-defeating desire. The source of this absurdity is in the notion that satisfaction can, so to speak, feed on itself, and perform the miracle of perpetual self-regeneration in the absence of desires for anything other than itself.

To summarize the argument of sections 12 and 13: The word "pleasure" is ambiguous. Pleasure₁ means a certain indefinable characteristic of physical sensation. Pleasure₂ refers to the feeling of satisfaction that often comes when one gets what one desires whatever be the nature of that which one desires. Now, if the hedonist means pleasure₁ when he says that one's own pleasure is the ultimate objective of all of one's behavior, then his view is not supported by the facts. On the other hand, if he means pleasure₂, then his theory cannot even be clearly formulated, since it leads to the following infinite regress: "I desire only satisfaction of my desire for satisfaction of my desire for satisfaction…etc., *ad infinitum.*" I conclude then that psychological hedonism (the most common form of psychological egoism), however interpreted, is untenable.

D. CRITIQUE OF PSYCHOLOGICAL EGOISM: UNCLEAR LOGICAL STATUS OF THE THEORY

14. There remain, however, other possible forms of the egoistic psychology. The egoist might admit that not all human motives can be reduced to the one ultimate desire for one's own pleasure, or happiness, and yet still maintain that our ultimate motives, whether they be desire for happiness (J. S. Mill), self-fulfillment (Aristotle), power (Hobbes), or whatever, are always *self-regarding* motives. He might still maintain that, given our common human nature, wholly disinterested action impelled by exclusively other-regarding motives is psychologically impossible, and that therefore there is a profoundly important sense in which it is true that, whether they be hedonists or not, *all people are selfish.*

Now it seems to me that this highly paradoxical claim cannot be finally evaluated until it is properly understood, and that it cannot be properly understood until one knows what the psychological egoist is willing to accept as evidence either for or against it. In short, there are two things that must be decided: (a) whether the theory is true or false and (b) whether its truth or falsity (its truth value) depends entirely on the *meanings* of the words in which it is expressed or whether it is made true or false by certain *facts,* in this case the facts of psychology.

15. *Analytic Statements.* Statements whose truth is determined solely by the meanings of the words in which they are expressed, and thus can be held immune from empirical evidence, are often called analytic statements or tautologies. The following are examples of tautologies:

(1) All bachelors are unmarried.
(2) All effects have causes.
(3) Either Providence is the capital of Rhode Island or it is not.

The truth of (1) is derived solely from the meaning of the word "bachelor," which is defined (in part) as "unmarried man." To find out whether (1) is true or false we need not conduct interviews, compile statistics, or perform experiments. All empirical evidence is superfluous and irrelevant; for if we know the meanings of "bachelor" and "unmarried," then we know not only that (1) is true, but that it is *necessarily* true—i.e., that it cannot possibly be false, that no future experiences or observations could possibly upset it, that to deny it would be to assert a logical contradiction. But notice that what a tautology gains in certainty ("necessary truth") it loses in descriptive content. Statement (1) imparts no information whatever about any matter of fact; it simply records our determination to use certain words in a certain way. As we say, "It is true by definition."

Similarly, (2) is (necessarily) true solely in virtue of the meanings of the words "cause" and "effect" and thus requires no further observations to confirm it. And of course, no possible observations could falsify it, since it asserts no matter of fact. And finally, statement (3) is (necessarily) true solely in virtue of the meaning of the English expression "either...or." Such terms as "either...or," "If...then," "and," and "not" are called by logicians "logical constants." The *definitions* of logical constants are made explicit in the so-called "laws of thought"—the law of contradiction, the law of the excluded middle, and the law of identity. These "laws" are not laws in the same sense as are (say) the laws of physics. Rather, they are merely consequences of the *definitions* of logical constants, and as such, though they are necessarily true, they impart no information about the world. "Either Providence is the capital of Rhode Island or it is not" tells us nothing about geography; and "Either it is now raining or else it is not" tells us nothing about the weather. You don't have to look at a map or look out the window to know that they are true. Rather, they are known to be true *a priori* (independently of experience); and, like all (or many)[12] *a priori* statements, they are *vacuous,* i.e., devoid of informative content.

The denial of an analytic statement is called a contradiction. The following are typical examples of contradictions: "Some bachelors are married," "Some causes have no effects," "Providence both is and is not the capital of Rhode Island." As in the case of tautologies, the truth value of contradictions (their falsehood) is logically necessary, not contingent on any facts of experience, and uninformative. Their falsity is derived from the meanings (definitions) of the words in which they are expressed.

16. *Synthetic Statements.* On the other hand, statements whose truth or falsity is derived not from the meanings of words but rather from the facts of experience (observations) are called *synthetic.*[13] Prior to experience, there can be no

good reason to think either that they are true or that they are false. That is to say, their truth value is *contingent;* and they can be confirmed or disconfirmed only by *empirical* evidence,[14] i.e., controlled observations of the world. Unlike analytic statements, they do impart information about matters of fact. Obviously, "It is raining in Newport now," if true, is more informative than "Either it is raining in Newport now or it is not," even though the former *could* be false, while the latter is necessarily true. I take the following to be examples of synthetic (contingent) statements:

(1′) All bachelors are neurotic.
(2′) All events have causes.
(3′) Providence is the capital of Rhode Island.
(3″) Newport is the capital of Rhode Island.

Statement (3′) is true; (3″) is false; and (1′) is a matter for a psychologist (not for a philosopher) to decide; and the psychologist himself can only decide *empirically,* i.e., by making many observations. The status of (2′) is very difficult and its truth value is a matter of great controversy. That is because its truth or falsity depends on *all* the facts ("all events"); and, needless to say, not all of the evidence is in.

17. *Empirical Hypotheses.* Perhaps the most interesting subclass of synthetic statements are those generalizations of experience of the sort characteristically made by scientists; e.g., "All released objects heavier than air fall," "All swans are white," "All men have Oedipus complexes." I shall call such statements "empirical hypotheses" to indicate that their function is to sum up past experience and enable us successfully to predict or anticipate future experience.[15] They are never logically certain, since it is always at least conceivable that future experience will disconfirm them. For example, zoologists once believed that all swans are white, until black swans were discovered in Australia. The most important characteristic of empirical hypotheses for our present purposes is their relation to evidence. A person can be said to understand an empirical hypothesis only if he knows how to recognize evidence against it. *If a person asserts*

or believes a general statement in such a way that he cannot conceive of any possible experience which he would count as evidence against it, then he cannot be said to be asserting or believing an empirical hypothesis. We can refer to this important characteristic of empirical hypotheses as *falsifiability in principle*.

Some statements only appear to be empirical hypotheses but are in fact disguised tautologies reflecting the speaker's determination to use words in certain (often eccentric) ways. For example, a zoologist might refuse to allow the existence of "Australian swans" to count as evidence against the generalization that all swans are white, on the grounds that the black Australian swans are not "really" swans at all. This would indicate that he is holding *whiteness* to be part of the definition of "swan," and that therefore, the statement "All swans are white" is, for him, "true by definition"—and thus just as immune from counterevidence as the statement "All spinsters are unmarried." Similarly, most of us would refuse to allow any possible experience to count as evidence against "2 + 2 = 4" or "Either unicorns exist or they do not," indicating that the propositions of arithmetic and logic are not empirical hypotheses.

18. *Ordinary Language and Equivocation.* Philosophers, even more than ordinary people, are prone to make startling and paradoxical claims that take the form of universal generalizations and hence resemble empirical hypotheses. For example, "All things are mental (there are no physical objects)," "All things are good (there is no evil)," "All voluntary behavior is selfish," etc. Let us confine our attention for the moment to the latter which is a rough statement of psychological egoism. At first sight, the statement "All voluntary behavior is selfish" seems obviously false. One might reply to the psychological egoist in some such manner as this:

> I *know* some behavior, at least, is unselfish, because I saw my Aunt Emma yesterday give her last cent to a beggar. Now she will have to go a whole week with nothing to eat. Surely, *that* was not selfish of her.

Nevertheless, the psychological egoist is likely not to be convinced, and insist that, in this case, if we knew enough about Aunt Emma, we would learn that her primary motive in helping the beggar was to promote her own happiness or assuage her own conscience, or increase her own self-esteem, etc. We might then present the egoist with even more difficult cases for his theory—saints, martyrs, military heroes, patriots, and others who have sacrificed themselves for a cause. If psychological egoists nevertheless refuse to accept any of these as examples of unselfish behavior, then we have a right to be puzzled about what they are saying. Until we know what they would count as *unselfish* behavior, we can't very well know what they mean when they say that all voluntary behavior is *selfish*. And at this point we may suspect that they are holding their theory in a "privileged position"—that of immunity to evidence, that they would allow no *conceivable* behavior to count as evidence against it. What they say then, if true, must be true in virtue of the way they define—or redefine—the word "selfish." And in that case, it cannot be an empirical hypothesis.

If what the psychological egoist says is "true by redefinition," then I can "agree" with him and say "It is true that in *your* sense of the word 'selfish' my Aunt Emma's behavior was selfish; but in the ordinary sense of 'selfish,' which implies blameworthiness, she surely was not selfish." There is no point of course in arguing about a mere word. The important thing is not what particular words a person uses, but rather whether what he wishes to say in those words is true. Departures from ordinary language can often be justified by their utility for certain purposes; but they are dangerous when they invite equivocation. The psychological egoist may be saying something which is true when he says that Emma is selfish in *his* sense, but if he doesn't realize that his sense of "selfish" differs from the ordinary one, he may be tempted to infer that Emma is selfish in the ordinary sense which implies blameworthiness; and this of course would be unfair and illegitimate. It is indeed an extraordinary extension of the meaning of the word "self-indulgent" (as C. G. Chesterton remarks somewhere) which allows a philosopher to say that a man is self-indulgent when he wants to be burned at the stake.

19. *The Fallacy of the Suppressed Correlative.* Certain words in the English language operate in pairs—e.g., "selfish–unselfish," "good–bad," "large–small," "mental–physical." To assert that a thing has one of the above characteristics is to *contrast* it with the opposite in the pair. To know the meaning of one term in the pair, we must know the meaning of the correlative term with which it is contrasted. If we could not conceive of what it would be like for a thing to be bad, for example, then we could not possibly understand what is being said of a thing when it is called "good." Similarly, unless we had a notion of what it would be like for action to be *unselfish,* we could hardly understand the sentence "So-and-so acted selfishly;" for we would have nothing to contrast "selfishly" with. The so-called "fallacy of the suppressed correlative"[16] is committed by a person who consciously or unconsciously redefines one of the terms in a contrasting pair in such a way that its new meaning incorporates the sense of its correlative.

Webster's Collegiate Dictionary defines "selfish" (in part) as "regarding one's own comfort, advantage, etc. in disregard of, or at the expense of that of others." In this ordinary and proper sense of "selfish," Aunt Emma's action in giving her last cent to the beggar certainly was *not* selfish. Emma *disregarded* her *own* comfort (it is not "comfortable" to go a week without eating) and advantage (there is no "advantage" in malnutrition) *for the sake of* (not "at the expense of") another. Similarly, the martyr marching off to the stake is foregoing (not indulging) his "comfort" and indeed his very life for the sake of (not at the expense of) a cause. If Emma and the martyr then are "selfish," they must be so in a strange new sense of the word.

A careful examination of the egoist's arguments (see especially 4a above) reveals what new sense he gives to the word "selfish." He redefines the word so that it means (roughly) "motivated," or perhaps "intentional." "After all," says the egoist, "Aunt Emma had some *purpose* in giving the beggar all her money, and this purpose (desire, intention, motive, aim) was *her* purpose and no one else's. She was out to further some aim of her own, wasn't she? Therefore, she was pursuing her own ends (acting from her own motives); she was after something *for herself* in so acting, and that's what I mean by calling her action selfish. Moreover, all intentional action —action done 'on purpose,' deliberately from the agent's own motives—is selfish in the same sense." We can see now, from this reply, that since the egoist apparently means by "selfish" simply "motivated," when he says that all motivated action is selfish *he is not asserting a synthetic empirical hypothesis about human motives; rather, his statement is a tautology roughly equivalent to "all motivated actions are motivated."* And if that is the case, then what he says is true enough; but, like all tautologies, it is empty, uninteresting, and trivial.

Moreover, in redefining "selfish" in this way, the psychological egoist has committed the fallacy of the suppressed correlative. For what can we now contrast "selfish voluntary action" with? Not only are there no *actual* cases of unselfish voluntary actions on the new definition; there are not even any *theoretically possible* or *conceivable* cases of unselfish voluntary actions. And if we cannot even conceive of what an unselfish voluntary action would be like, how can we give any sense to the expression "selfish voluntary action"? The egoist, so to speak, has so blown up the sense of "selfish" that, like inflated currency, it will no longer buy anything.

20. *Psychological Egoism as a Linguistic Proposal.* There is still one way out for the egoist. He might admit that his theory is not really a psychological hypothesis about human nature designed to account for the facts and enable us to predict or anticipate future events. He may even willingly concede that his theory is really a disguised redefinition of a word. Still, he might argue, he has made no claim to be giving an accurate description of actual linguistic usage. Rather, he is making a proposal to *revise* our usage in the interest of economy and convenience,

just as the biologists once proposed that we change the ordinary meaning of "insect" in such a way that spiders are no longer called insects, and the ordinary meaning of "fish" so that whales and seals are no longer called fish.

What are we to say to this suggestion? First of all, stipulative definitions (proposals to revise usage) are never true or false. They are simply useful or not useful. Would it be useful to redefine "selfish" in the way the egoist recommends? It is difficult to see what would be gained thereby. The egoist has noticed some respects in which actions normally called "selfish" and actions normally called "unselfish" are alike, namely they are both motivated and they both can give satisfaction—either in prospect or in retrospect—to the agent. Because of these likenesses, the egoist feels justified in attaching the label "selfish" to *all* actions. Thus one word —"selfish"—must for him do the work of two words ("selfish" and "unselfish" in their old meanings); and, as a result, a very real distinction, that between actions for the sake of others and actions at the expense of others, can no longer be expressed in the language. Because the egoist has noticed some respects in which two types of actions are alike, he wishes to make it impossible to describe the respects in which they differ. It is difficult to see any utility in this state of affairs.

But suppose we adopt the egoist's "proposal" nevertheless. Now we would have to say that all actions are selfish; but, in addition, we would want to say that there are two different kinds of selfish actions, those which regard the interests of others and those which disregard the interests of others, and, furthermore, that only the latter are blameworthy. After a time our ear would adjust to the new uses of the word "selfish," and we would find nothing at all strange in such statements as ' Some selfish actions are morally praiseworthy.' After a while, we might even invent two new words, perhaps "selfitic" and "unselfitic," to distinguish the two important classes of "selfish" actions. Then we would be right back where we started, with new linguistic tools ("selfish" for "motivated," "selfitic" for "selfish," and "unselfitic" for "unselfish") to do

the same old necessary jobs. That is, until some new egoistic philosopher arose to announce with an air of discovery that "All selfish behavior is really selfitic—there are no truly unselfitic selfish actions." Then, God help us!

NOTES

1. See his *Introduction to the Principles of Morals and Legislation* (1789), Chap. I, first paragraph: "Nature has placed mankind under the governance of two sovereign masters, *pain* and *pleasure*. It is for them alone to point out what we ought to do, as well as to determine what we shall do.... They govern us in all we do, in all we say, in all we think: every effort we can make to throw off our subjection will serve but to demonstrate and confirm it."

2. C. D. Broad, *Ethics and the History of Philosophy* (New York: The Humanities Press, 1952), Essay 10—"Egoism as a Theory of Human Motives," p. 218. This essay is highly recommended.

3. Austin Duncan-Jones, *Butler's Moral Philosophy* (London; Penguin Books, 1952), p. 96. Duncan-Jones goes on to reject this argument. See p. 512f.

4. Lucius Garvin, *A Modern Introduction to Ethics* (Boston: Houghton Mifflin, 1953), p. 37. Quoted here by permission of the author and publisher.

5. *Op. cit.*, Chap. III.

6. See Part D, 15 and 16, below.

7. *Op. cit.*, p. 39.

8. William James, *The Principles of Psychology* (New York: Henry Holt, 1890), Vol. II, p. 558.

9. *Op. cit.*, p. 39.

10. Quoted from the *Springfield* (Illinois) *Monitor*, by F. C. Sharp in his *Ethics* (New York: Appleton-Century, 1928), p. 75.

11. See his *Fifteen Sermons on Human Nature Preached at the Rolls Chapel* (1726), especially the first and eleventh.

12. Whether or not there are some *a priori* statements that are not merely analytic, and hence *not* vacuous, is still a highly controversial question among philosophers.

13. Some philosophers (those called "rationalists") believe that there are some synthetic statements whose truth can be known *a priori* (see note 12). If they are right, then the statement above is not entirely accurate.

14. Again, subject to the qualification in notes 12 and 13.
15. The three examples given above all have the generic character there indicated, but they also differ from one another in various other ways, some of which are quite important. For our present purposes however, we can ignore the ways in which they differ from one another and concentrate on their common character as generalizations of experience ("inductive generalizations"). As such they are sharply contrasted with such a generalization as "All puppies are young dogs," which is analytic.
16. The phrase was coined by J. Lowenberg. See his article "What Is Empirical?" in the *Journal of Philosophy*, May 1940.

1.2 The Immoralist's Challenge

PLATO

Plato (427?–347 BCE) lived and taught in Athens. Most of his surviving works have the form of fictitious dialogues between Socrates (who had been his teacher) and other Greek contemporaries.

When I said this, I thought I had done with the discussion, but it turned out to have been only a prelude. Glaucon showed his characteristic courage on this occasion too and refused to accept Thrasymachus' abandonment of the argument. Socrates, he said, do you want to seem to have persuaded us that it is better in every way to be just than unjust, or do you want truly to convince us of this?

I want truly to convince you, I said, if I can.

Well, then, you certainly aren't doing what you want. Tell me, do you think there is a kind of good we welcome, not because we desire what comes from it, but because we welcome it for its own sake—joy, for example, and all the harmless pleasures that have no results beyond the joy of having them?

Certainly, I think there are such things.

And is there a kind of good we like for its own sake and also for the sake of what comes from it—knowing, for example, and seeing and being healthy? We welcome such things, I suppose, on both counts.

Yes.

And do you also see a third kind of good, such as physical training,[1] medical treatment when sick, medicine itself, and the other ways of making money? We'd say that these are onerous but beneficial to us, and we wouldn't choose them for their own sakes, but for the sake of the rewards and other things that come from them.

There is also this third kind. But what of it?

Where do you put justice?

I myself put it among the finest goods, as something to be valued by anyone who is going to be blessed with happiness, both because of itself and because of what comes from it.

That isn't most people's opinion. They'd say that justice belongs to the onerous kind, and is to be practiced for the sake of the rewards and popularity that come from a reputation for justice, but is to be avoided because of itself as something burdensome.

I know that's the general opinion. Thrasymachus faulted justice on these grounds a moment ago and praised injustice, but it seems that I'm a slow learner.

Come, then, and listen to me as well, and see whether you still have that problem, for I think that Thrasymachus gave up before he had to, charmed by you as if he were a snake. But

From Plato, *The Republic, Bk. II*, 357A–367E, trans. G. M. A. Grube, revised by C. D. C. Reeve (Hackett Publishing Company, 1992). Reprinted by permission of Hackett Publishing Company, Inc. All rights reserved.

I'm not yet satisfied by the argument on either side. I want to know what justice and injustice are and what power each itself has when it's by itself in the soul. I want to leave out of account their rewards and what comes from each of them. So, if you agree, I'll renew the argument of Thrasymachus. First, I'll state what kind of thing people consider justice to be and what its origins are. Second, I'll argue that all who practice it do so unwillingly, as something necessary, not as something good. Third, I'll argue that they have good reason to act as they do, for the life of an unjust person is, they say, much better than that of a just one.

It isn't, Socrates, that I believe any of that myself. I'm perplexed, indeed, and my ears are deafened listening to Thrasymachus and countless others. But I've yet to hear anyone defend justice in the way I want, proving that it is better than injustice. I want to hear it praised *by itself,* and I think that I'm most likely to hear this from you. Therefore, I'm going to speak at length in praise of the unjust life, and in doing so I'll show you the way I want to hear you praising justice and denouncing injustice. But see whether you want me to do that or not.

I want that most of all. Indeed, what subject could someone with any understanding enjoy discussing more often?

Excellent. Then let's discuss the first subject I mentioned—what justice is and what its origins are.

They say that to do injustice is naturally good and to suffer injustice bad, but that the badness of suffering it so far exceeds the goodness of doing it that those who have done and suffered injustice and tasted both, but who lack the power to do it and avoid suffering it, decide that it is profitable to come to an agreement with each other neither to do injustice nor to suffer it. As a result, they begin to make laws and covenants, and what the law commands they call lawful and just. This, they say, is the origin and essence of justice. It is intermediate between the best and the worst. The best is to do injustice without paying the penalty; the worst is to suffer it without being able to take revenge. Justice is a mean between these two extremes. People value

it not as a good but because they are too weak to do injustice with impunity. Someone who has the power to do this, however, and is a true man wouldn't make an agreement with anyone not to do injustice in order not to suffer it. For him that would be madness. This is the nature of justice, according to the argument, Socrates, and these are its natural origins.

We can see most clearly that those who practice justice do it unwillingly and because they lack the power to do injustice, if in our thoughts we grant to a just and an unjust person the freedom to do whatever they like. We can then follow both of them and see where their desires would lead. And we'll catch the just person red-handed travelling the same road as the unjust. The reason for this is the desire to outdo others and get more and more. This is what anyone's nature naturally pursues as good, but nature is forced by law into the perversion of treating fairness with respect.

The freedom I mentioned would be most easily realized if both people had the power they say the ancestor of Gyges of Lydia possessed. The story goes that he was a shepherd in the service of the ruler of Lydia. There was a violent thunderstorm, and an earthquake broke open the ground and created a chasm at the place where he was tending his sheep. Seeing this, he was filled with amazement and went down into it. And there, in addition to many other wonders of which we're told, he saw a hollow bronze horse. There were windowlike openings in it, and, peeping in, he saw a corpse, which seemed to be of more than human size, wearing nothing but a gold ring on its finger. He took the ring and came out of the chasm. He wore the ring at the usual monthly meeting that reported to the king on the state of the flocks. And as he was sitting among the others, he happened to turn the setting of the ring towards himself to the inside of his hand. When he did this, he became invisible to those sitting near him, and they went on talking as if he had gone. He wondered at this, and, fingering the ring, he turned the setting outwards again and became visible. So he experimented with the ring to test whether it indeed had this power—and it did. If he turned the setting inward, he became invisible; if he turned it outward, he became visible again. When he realized this, he at once arranged to become one of the messengers sent to report to the king. And when he arrived there, he seduced the king's wife, attacked the king with her help, killed him, and took over the kingdom.

Let's suppose, then, that there were two such rings, one worn by a just and the other by an unjust person. Now, no one, it seems, would be so incorruptible that he would stay on the path of justice or stay away from other people's property, when he could take whatever he wanted from the marketplace with impunity, go into people's houses and have sex with anyone he wished, kill or release from prison anyone he wished, and do all the other things that would make him like a god among humans. Rather his actions would be in no way different from those of an unjust person, and both would follow the same path. This, some would say, is a great proof that one is never just willingly but only when compelled to be. No one believes justice to be a good when it is kept private, since, wherever either person thinks he can do injustice with impunity, he does it. Indeed, every man believes that injustice is far more profitable to himself than justice. And any exponent of this argument will say he's right, for someone who didn't want to do injustice, given this sort of opportunity, and who didn't touch other people's property would be thought wretched and stupid by everyone aware of the situation, though, of course, they'd praise him in public, deceiving each other for fear of suffering injustice. So much for my second topic.

As for the choice between the lives we're discussing, we'll be able to make a correct judgment about that only if we separate the most just and the most unjust. Otherwise we won't be able to do it. Here's the separation I have in mind. We'll subtract nothing from the injustice of an unjust person and nothing from the justice of a just one, but we'll take each to be complete in his own way of life. First, therefore, we must suppose that an unjust person will act as clever craftsmen do: A first-rate captain or doctor, for

example, knows the difference between what his craft can and can't do. He attempts the first but lets the second go by, and if he happens to slip, he can put things right. In the same way, an unjust person's successful attempts at injustice must remain undetected, if he is to be fully unjust. Anyone who is caught should be thought inept, for the extreme of injustice is to be believed to be just without being just. And our completely unjust person must be given complete injustice; nothing may be subtracted from it. We must allow that, while doing the greatest injustice, he has nonetheless provided himself with the greatest reputation for justice. If he happens to make a slip, he must be able to put it right. If any of his unjust activities should be discovered, he must be able to speak persuasively or to use force. And if force is needed, he must have the help of courage and strength and of the substantial wealth and friends with which he has provided himself.

Having hypothesized such a person, let's now in our argument put beside him a just man, who is simple and noble and who, as Aeschylus says, doesn't want to be believed to be good but to be so. We must take away his reputation, for a reputation for justice would bring him honor and rewards, so that it wouldn't be clear whether he is just for the sake of justice itself or for the sake of those honors and rewards. We must strip him of everything except justice and make his situation the opposite of an unjust person's. Though he does no injustice, he must have the greatest reputation for it, so that his justice may be tested full strength and not diluted by wrong-doing and what comes from it. Let him stay like that unchanged until he dies—just, but all his life believed to be unjust. In this way, both will reach the extremes, the one of justice and the other of injustice, and we'll be able to judge which of them is happier.

Whew! Glaucon, I said, how vigorously you've scoured each of the men for our competition, just as you would a pair of statues for an art competition.

I do the best I can, he replied. Since the two are as I've described, in any case, it shouldn't be difficult to complete the account of the kind of life that awaits each of them, but it must be done. And if what I say sounds crude, Socrates, remember that it isn't I who speak but those who praise injustice at the expense of justice. They'll say that a just person in such circumstances will be whipped, stretched on a rack, chained, blinded with fire, and, at the end, when he has suffered every kind of evil, he'll be impaled, and will realize then that one shouldn't want to be just but to be believed to be just. Indeed, Aeschylus' words are far more correctly applied to unjust people than to just ones, for the supporters of injustice will say that a really unjust person, having a way of life based on the truth about things and not living in accordance with opinion, doesn't want simply to be believed to be unjust but actually to be so—

> *Harvesting a deep furrow in his mind,*
> *Where wise counsels propagate.*

He rules his city because of his reputation for justice; he marries into any family he wishes; he gives his children in marriage to anyone he wishes; he has contracts and partnerships with anyone he wants; and besides benefiting himself in all these ways, he profits because he has no scruples about doing injustice. In any contest, public or private, he's the winner and outdoes his enemies. And by outdoing them, he becomes wealthy, benefiting his friends and harming his enemies. He makes adequate sacrifices to the gods and sets up magnificent offerings to them. He takes better care of the gods, therefore, (and, indeed, of the human beings he's fond of) than a just person does. Hence it's likely that the gods, in turn, will take better care of him than of a just person. That's what they say, Socrates, that gods and humans provide a better life for unjust people than for just ones.

When Glaucon had said this, I had it in mind to respond, but his brother Adeimantus intervened: You surely don't think that the position has been adequately stated?

Why not? I said.

The most important thing to say hasn't been said yet.

Well, then, I replied, a man's brother must stand by him, as the saying goes.[2] If Glaucon has omitted something, you must help him. Yet what he has said is enough to throw me to the canvas and make me unable to come to the aid of justice.

Nonsense, he said. Hear what more I have to say, for we should also fully explore the arguments that are opposed to the ones Glaucon gave, the ones that praise justice and find fault with injustice, so that what I take to be his intention may be clearer.

When fathers speak to their sons, they say that one must be just, as do all the others who have charge of anyone. But they don't praise justice itself, only the high reputations it leads to and the consequences of being thought to be just, such as the public offices, marriages, and other things Glaucon listed. But they elaborate even further on the consequences of reputation. By bringing in the esteem of the gods, they are able to talk about the abundant good things that they themselves and the noble Hesiod and Homer say that the gods give to the pious,[3] for Hesiod says that the gods make the oak trees

> *Bear acorns at the top and bees in the middle*
> *And make fleecy sheep heavy laden with wool*

for the just, and tells of many other good things akin to these. And Homer is similar:

> *When a good king, in his piety,*
> *Upholds justice, the black earth bears*
> *Wheat and barley for him, and his trees are*
> *heavy with fruit.*
> *His sheep bear lambs unfailingly, and the sea*
> *yields up its fish.*

Musaeus and his son make the gods give the just more headstrong goods than these.[4] In their stories, they lead the just to Hades, seat them on couches, provide them with a symposium of pious people, crown them with wreaths, and make them spend all their time drinking—as if they thought drunkenness was the finest wage of virtue. Others stretch even further the wages that virtue receives from the gods, for they say that someone who is pious and keeps his promises leaves his children's children and a whole race behind him. In these and other similar ways, they praise justice. They bury the impious and unjust in mud in Hades; force them to carry water in a sieve; bring them into bad repute while they're still alive, and all those penalties that Glaucon gave to the just person they give to the unjust. But they have nothing else to say. This, then, is the way people praise justice and find fault with injustice.

Besides this, Socrates, consider another form of argument about justice and injustice employed both by private individuals and by poets. All go on repeating with one voice that justice and moderation are fine things, but hard and onerous, while licentiousness and injustice are sweet and easy to acquire and are shameful only in opinion and law. They add that unjust deeds are for the most part more profitable than just ones, and, whether in public or private, they willingly honor vicious people who have wealth and other types of power and declare them to be happy. But they dishonor and disregard the weak and the poor, even though they agree that they are better than the others.

But the most wonderful of all these arguments concerns what they have to say about the gods and virtue. They say that the gods, too, assign misfortune and a bad life to many good people, and the opposite fate to their opposites. Begging priests and prophets frequent the doors of the rich and persuade them that they possess a god-given power founded on sacrifices and incantations. If the rich person or any of his ancestors has committed an injustice, they can fix it with pleasant rituals. Moreover, if he wishes to injure some enemy, then, at little expense, he'll be able to harm just and unjust alike, for by means of spells and enchantments they can persuade the gods to serve them. And the poets are brought forward as witnesses to all these accounts. Some harp on the ease of vice, as follows:

Vice in abundance is easy to get;
The road is smooth and begins beside you,
But the gods have put sweat between us and
*   virtue,*

and a road that is long, rough, and steep.[5] Others quote Homer to bear witness that the gods can be influenced by humans, since he said:

The gods themselves can be swayed by prayer,
And with sacrifices and soothing promises,
Incense and libations, human beings turn
*   them from their purpose*
When someone has transgressed and
*   sinned.*[6]

And they present a noisy throng of books by Musaeus and Orpheus, offspring as they say of Selene and the Muses, in accordance with which they perform their rituals.[7] And they persuade not only individuals but whole cities that the unjust deeds of the living or the dead can be absolved or purified through sacrifices and pleasant games. These initiations, as they call them, free people from punishment hereafter, while a terrible fate awaits the uninitiated.

When all such sayings about the attitudes of gods and humans to virtue and vice are so often repeated, Socrates, what effect do you suppose they have on the souls of young people? I mean those who are clever and are able to flit from one of these sayings to another, so to speak, and gather from them an impression of what sort of person he should be and of how best to travel the road of life. He would surely ask himself Pindar's question, "Should I by justice or by crooked deceit scale this high wall and live my life guarded and secure?" And he'll answer: "The various sayings suggest that there is no advantage in my being just if I'm not also thought just, while the troubles and penalties of being just are apparent. But they tell me that an unjust person, who has secured for himself a reputation for justice, lives the life of a god. Since, then, 'opinion forcibly overcomes truth' and 'controls happiness,' as the wise men say, I must surely turn entirely to it.[8] I should create a façade of illusory virtue around me to deceive those who come near, but keep behind it the greedy and crafty fox of the wise Archilochus."[9]

"But surely," someone will object, "it isn't easy for vice to remain always hidden." We'll reply that nothing great is easy. And, in any case, if we're to be happy, we must follow the path indicated in these accounts. To remain undiscovered we'll form secret societies and political clubs. And there are teachers of persuasion to make us clever in dealing with assemblies and law courts. Therefore, using persuasion in one place and force in another, we'll outdo others without paying a penalty.

"What about the gods? Surely, we can't hide from them or use violent force against them!" Well, if the gods don't exist or don't concern themselves with human affairs, why should we worry at all about hiding from them? If they do exist and do concern themselves with us, we've learned all we know about them from the laws and the poets who give their genealogies—nowhere else. But these are the very people who tell us that the gods can be persuaded and influenced by sacrifices, gentle prayers, and offerings. Hence, we should believe them on both matters or neither. If we believe them, we should be unjust and offer sacrifices from the fruits of our injustice. If we are just, our only gain is not to be punished by the gods, since we lose the profits of injustice. But if we are unjust, we get the profits of our crimes and transgressions and afterwards persuade the gods by prayer and escape without punishment.

"But in Hades won't we pay the penalty for crimes committed here, either ourselves or our children's children?" "My friend," the young man will say as he does his calculation, "mystery rites have great power and the gods have great power of absolution. The greatest cities tell us this, as do those children of the gods who have become poets and prophets."

Why, then, should we still choose justice over the greatest injustice? Many eminent authorities agree that, if we practice such injustice with a false façade, we'll do well at the hands of gods and humans, living and dying as we've a mind to. So, given all that has been said, Socrates, how is it possible for anyone of any power—whether of mind, wealth, body, or birth—to be willing to honor justice and not laugh aloud when he hears it praised? Indeed,

if anyone can show that what we've said is false and has adequate knowledge that justice is best, he'll surely be full not of anger but of forgiveness for the unjust. He knows that, apart from someone of godlike character who is disgusted by injustice or one who has gained knowledge and avoids injustice for that reason, no one is just willingly. Through cowardice or old age or some other weakness, people do indeed object to injustice. But it's obvious that they do so only because they lack the power to do injustice, for the first of them to acquire it is the first to do as much injustice as he can.

And all of this has no other cause than the one that led Glaucon and me to say to you: "Socrates, of all of you who claim to praise justice, from the original heroes of old whose words survive, to the men of the present day, not one has ever blamed injustice or praised justice except by mentioning the reputations, honors, and rewards that are their consequences. No one has ever adequately described what each itself does of its own power by its presence in the soul of the person who possesses it, even if it remains hidden from gods and humans. No one, whether in poetry or in private conversations, has adequately argued that injustice is the worst thing a soul can have in it and that justice is the greatest good. If you had treated the subject in this way and persuaded us from youth, we wouldn't now be guarding against one another's injustices, but each would be his own best guardian, afraid that by doing injustice he'd be living with the worst thing possible."

Thrasymachus or anyone else might say what we've said, Socrates, or maybe even more, in discussing justice and injustice—crudely inverting their powers, in my opinion. And, frankly, it's because I want to hear the opposite from you that I speak with all the force I can muster. So don't merely give us a theoretical argument that justice is stronger than injustice, but tell us what each itself does, because of its own powers, to someone who possesses it, that makes injustice bad and justice good. Follow Glaucon's advice, and don't take reputations into account, for if you don't deprive justice and injustice of their true reputations and attach false ones to them, we'll say that you are not praising them but their reputations and that you're encouraging us to be unjust in secret. In that case, we'll say that you agree with Thrasymachus that justice is the good of another, the advantage of the stronger, while injustice is one's own advantage and profit, though not the advantage of the weaker.

You agree that justice is one of the greatest goods, the ones that are worth getting for the sake of what comes from them, but much more so for their own sake, such as seeing, hearing, knowing, being healthy, and all other goods that are fruitful by their own nature and not simply because of reputation. Therefore, praise justice as a good of that kind, explaining how—because of its very self—it benefits its possessors and how injustice harms them. Leave wages and reputations for others to praise.

Others would satisfy me if they praised justice and blamed injustice in that way, extolling the wages of one and denigrating those of the other. But you, unless you order me to be satisfied, wouldn't, for you've spent your whole life investigating this and nothing else. Don't, then, give us only a theoretical argument that justice is stronger than injustice, but show what effect each has because of itself on the person who has it—the one for good and the other for bad—whether it remains hidden from gods and human beings or not.

NOTES

1. "Music" or "music and poetry" and "physical training" are more transliterations than translations of *mousikē* and *gymnastikē*, which have no English equivalents. It is clear from Plato's discussion, for example, that *mousikē* includes poetry and stories, as well as music proper, and that *gymnastikē* includes dance and training in warfare, as well as what we call physical training.
2. See Homer, *Odyssey* 16.97–98.
3. The two quotations which follow are from Hesiod, *Works and Days* 332–33, and Homer, *Odyssey* 19.109.
4. Musaeus was a legendary poet closely associated with the mystery religion of Orphism.
5. *Works and Days* 287–89, with minor alterations.
6. *Iliad* 9.497–501, with minor alterations.
7. It is not clear whether Orpheus was a real person or a mythical figure. His fame in Greek myth rests on the poems in which the doctrines of the Orphic religion are set forth. These are discussed in W. Burkert, *Greek Religion* (Cambridge: Harvard University Press, 1985). Musaeus was a mythical singer closely related to Orpheus. Selene is the Moon.
8. The quotation is attributed to Simonides, whom Polemarchus cites in Book I.
9. Archilochus of Paros (c. 756–16 B.C.), was an iambic and elegiac poet who composed a famous fable about the fox and the hedgehog.

1.3 Master and Slave Morality

FRIEDRICH NIETZSCHE

Friedrich Nietzsche (1844–1900) was a brilliant classicist and philosopher whose criticisms of conventional morality have played an important role in the development of twentieth-century thought.

201

As long as herd utility is the only utility governing moral value judgments, as long as the preservation of the community is the only thing in view and questions concerning immorality are limited to those things that seem to threaten the survival of the community; as long as this is the case, there cannot yet be a "morality of neighbor love." Suppose that even here, consideration, pity, propriety, gentleness, and reciprocity of aid are already practiced in a small but steady way; suppose that even in this state of society, all the drives that would later come to be called by the honorable name of "virtues" (and, in the end, basically coincide with the concept of "morality")—suppose that they are already active: at this point they still do not belong to the realm of moral valuations at all—they are still *extra-moral*. During the best days of Rome, for instance, an act done out of pity was not called either good or evil, moral or immoral; and if it were praised on its own, the praise would be perfectly compatible with a type of reluctant disdain as soon as it was held up against any action that served to promote the common good, the *res publica*.[1] Ultimately, the "love of the neighbor" is always somewhat conventional, willfully feigned and beside the point compared to *fear of the neighbor*. After the structure of society seems on the whole to be established and secured against external dangers, it is this fear of the neighbor that again creates new perspectives of moral valuation. Until now, in the spirit of common utility, certain strong and dangerous drives such as enterprise, daring, vindictiveness, cunning, rapacity, and a domineering spirit must have been not only honored (under different names than these of course), but nurtured and cultivated (since, given the threats to the group, they were constantly needed against the common enemies). Now, however, since there are no more escape valves for these drives, they are seen as twice as dangerous and, one by one, they are denounced as immoral and abandoned to slander. Now the opposite drives and inclinations come into moral favor; step by step, the herd instinct draws its conclusion. How much or how little danger there is to the community or to equality in an opinion, in a condition or affect, in a will, in a talent, this is now the moral perspective: and fear is once again the mother of morality. When the highest and strongest drives erupt in passion, driving the individual up and out and far above the average, over the depths of the herd conscience, the self-esteem of the community is destroyed—its faith in itself, its backbone, as it were, is broken: as a result, these are the very drives that will be denounced and slandered the most. A high, independent spiritedness, a will to stand alone, even an excellent faculty of reason, will be perceived as a threat. Everything that raises the individual over the herd and frightens the neighbor will henceforth be called *evil;* the proper, modest, unobtrusive, equalizing attitude and the *mediocrity* of desires acquire moral names and honors. Finally, in very peaceable circumstances there are fewer and fewer opportunities and less and less need to nurture an instinct for severity or hardness; and now every severity starts disturbing the conscience, even where justice is concerned. A high and hard nobility and self-reliance is almost offensive, and provokes suspicion; "the lamb," and "the sheep" even more, gains respect.—There is a point in the history of a society when it becomes pathologically enervated and tenderized and it takes sides, quite honestly and earnestly, with those who do it harm, with *criminals.* Punishment: that seems somehow unjust to this society,—it certainly finds the thoughts of "punishment" and "needing to punish" both painful and frightening. "Isn't it enough to render him *unthreatening*? Why punish him as well? Punishment is itself fearful!"—with these questions, the herd morality, the morality of timidity, draws its final consequences. If the threat, the reason for the fear, could be totally abolished, this morality would be abolished as well: it would not be necessary any more, it would not *consider itself* necessary any more! Anyone who probes the conscience of today's European will have to extract the very same imperative from a thousand moral folds and hiding places, the imperative of herd timidity: "we want the day to come when there is *nothing more to fear!*" The day to come—the will and way *to that day* is now called "progress" everywhere in Europe.

202

Let us immediately repeat what we have already said a hundred times before, since there are no ready ears for such truths—for *our* truths—these days. We know all too well how offensive it sounds when someone classifies human beings as animals, without disguises or allegory; and we are considered almost *sinful* for constantly using expressions like "herd," and "herd instinct" with direct reference to people of "modern ideas." So what? We cannot help ourselves, since this is where our new insights happen to lie. Europe, we have found, has become unanimous in all major moral judgments; and this includes the countries under Europe's influence. People in Europe clearly *know* what Socrates claimed not to know, and what that famous old snake once promised to teach,—people these days "know" what is good and evil. Now it must sound harsh and strike the ear quite badly when we keep insisting on the following point: what it is that claims to know here, what glorifies itself with its praise and reproach and calls itself good is the instinct of the herd animal man, which has come to the fore, gaining and continuing to gain predominance and supremacy over the other instincts, in accordance with the growing physiological approach and approximation whose symptom it is. *Morality in Europe these days is the morality of herd animals:*—and therefore, as we understand things, it is only one type of human morality beside which, before which, and after which many other (and especially *higher*) moralities are or should be possible. But this morality fights tooth and nail against such a "possibility" and such a "should": it stubbornly and ruthlessly declares "I am morality itself and nothing else is moral!" And in fact, with the aid of a religion that indulged and flattered the loftiest herd desires, things have reached the point where this morality is increasingly apparent in even political and social institutions: the *democratic* movement is the heir to Christianity. But there are indications that the tempo of this morality is still much too slow and lethargic for those who have less patience, those who are sick or addicted to the above-mentioned instinct. This is attested to by the increasingly frantic howling, the increasingly undisguised snarling of the anarchist dogs that now wander the alleyways of European culture, in apparent opposition to the peaceable and industrious democrats and ideologists of revolution, and still more to the silly philosophasters and brotherhood enthusiasts who call themselves socialists and want a "free society." But, in fact, they are one and all united in thorough and instinctive hostility towards all forms of society besides that of the *autonomous* herd (even to the point of rejecting the concepts of "master" and "slave"—*ni dieu ni maître*[2] reads a socialist formula—); they are united in their dogged opposition to any special claims, special rights, or privileges (which means, in the last analysis, that they are opposed to *any* rights: since when everyone is equal, no one will need "rights" anymore—); they are united in their mistrust of punitive justice (as if it were a violation of those who are weaker, a wrong against the *necessary* result of all earlier societies—); but they are likewise united in the religion of pity, in sympathy for whatever feels, lives, suffers (down to the animal and up to "God":—the excessive notion of "pity for God" belongs in a democratic age—); they are all united in the cries and the impatience of pity, in deadly hatred against suffering in general, in the almost feminine inability to sit watching, to *let* suffering happen; they are united in the way they involuntarily raise the general level of sensitivity and gloom under whose spell Europe seems threatened with a new Buddhism; they are united in their faith in the morality of *communal* pity, as if it were morality in itself, the height, the *achieved* height of humanity, the sole hope for the future, the solace of the present, the great redemption of all guilt from the past:—they are all united in their faith in the community as *Redeemer,* which is to say: in the herd, in "themselves"...

203

We who have a different faith—, we who consider the democratic movement to be not merely an abased form of political organization, but rather an abased (more specifically a diminished) form of humanity, a mediocritization and depreciation of humanity in value: where do *we* need to reach with our hopes?—Towards *new philosophers,* there is no alternative; towards spirits who are strong and original enough to give impetus to opposed valuations and initiate a revaluation and reversal of "eternal values;" towards those sent out ahead; towards the men of the future who in the present tie the knots and gather the force that compels the will of millennia into *new* channels. To teach humanity its future as its *will,* as dependent on a human will, to prepare for the great risk and wholesale attempt at breeding and cultivation and so to put an end to the gruesome rule of chance and nonsense that has passed for "history" so far (the nonsense of the "greatest number" is only its latest form): a new type of philosopher and commander will be needed for this some day, and whatever hidden, dreadful, or benevolent spirits have existed on earth will pale into insignificance beside the image of this type. The image of such leaders hovers before *our* eyes:—may I say this out loud, you free spirits? The conditions that would have to be partly created and partly exploited for them to come into being; the probable paths and trials that would enable a soul to grow tall and strong enough to feel the *compulsion* for these tasks; a revaluation of values whose new pressure and hammer will steel a conscience and transform a heart into bronze to bear the weight of a responsibility like this; and, on the other hand, the necessity of such leaders, the terrible danger that they could fail to appear or simply fail and degenerate—these are *our* real worries and dark clouds, do you know this, you free spirits? These are the heavy, distant thoughts and storms that traverse the sky of *our* lives. There are few pains as intense as ever having seen, guessed, or sympathized while an extraordinary person ran off course and degenerated: but someone with an uncommon eye for the overall danger that "humanity" itself will *degenerate,* someone like us, who has recognized the outrageous contingency that has been playing games with the future of humanity so far—games in which no hand and not even a "finger of God" has taken part— someone who has sensed the disaster that lies hidden in the idiotic guilelessness and credulity of "modern ideas," and still more in the whole of Christian-European morality: someone like this will suffer from an unparalleled sense of alarm. In a single glance he will comprehend everything that *could be bred from humanity,* given a favorable accumulation and intensification of forces and tasks; he will know with all the prescience of his conscience how humanity has still not exhausted its greatest possibilities, and how often the type man has already faced mysterious decisions and new paths:—he will know even better, from his most painful memories, the sorts of miserable things that generally shatter, crush, sink, and turn a development of the highest rank into a miserable affair. The *total degeneration of humanity* down to what today's socialist fools and nitwits see as their "man of the future"—as their ideal!—this degeneration and diminution of humanity into the perfect herd animal (or, as they say, into man in a "free society"), this brutalizing process of turning humanity into stunted little animals with equal rights and equal claims is no doubt *possible!* Anyone who has ever thought this possibility through to the end knows one more disgust than other men,—and perhaps a new *task* as well!...

259

Mutually refraining from injury, violence, and exploitation, placing your will on par with the other's: in a certain, crude sense, these practices can become good manners between individuals when the right conditions are present (namely, that the individuals have genuinely similar quantities of force and measures of value, and belong together within a single body). But as soon as this principle is taken any further, and maybe even held to be the *fundamental principle of society*, it immediately shows itself for what it is: the will to *negate* life, the principle of disintegration and decay. Here we must think things through thoroughly, and ward off any sentimental weakness: life itself is *essentially* a process of appropriating, injuring, overpowering the alien and the weaker, oppressing, being harsh, imposing your own form, incorporating, and at least, the very least, exploiting,—but what is the point of always using words that have been stamped with slanderous intentions from time immemorial? Even a body within which (as we presupposed earlier) particular individuals treat each other as equal (which happens in every healthy aristocracy): if this body is living and not dying, it will have to treat other bodies in just those ways that the individuals it contains *refrain* from treating each other. It will have to be the embodiment of will to power, it will want to grow, spread, grab, win dominance,—not out of any morality or immorality, but because it is *alive,* and because life *is* precisely will to power. But there is no issue on which the base European consciousness is less willing to be instructed than this; these days, people everywhere are lost in rapturous enthusiasms, even in scientific disguise, about a future state of society where "the exploitative character" will fall away:—to my ears, that sounds as if someone is promising to invent a life that dispenses with all organic functions. "Exploitation" does not belong to a corrupted or imperfect, primitive society: it belongs to the *essence* of being alive as a fundamental organic function; it is a result of genuine will to power, which is just the will of life.—Although this is an innovation at the level of theory,—at the level of reality, it is the *primal fact* of all history. Let us be honest with ourselves to this extent at least!—

260

As I was wandering through the many subtle and crude moralities that have been dominant or that still dominate over the face of the earth, I found certain traits regularly recurring together and linked to each other. In the end, two basic types became apparent to me and a fundamental distinction leapt out. There is a *master morality* and a *slave morality*;—I will immediately add that in all higher and more mixed cultures, attempts to negotiate between these moralities also appear, although more frequently the two are confused and there are mutual misunderstandings. In fact, you sometimes find them sharply juxtaposed— inside the same person even, within a single soul. Moral value distinctions have arisen within either a dominating type that, with a feeling of well-being, was conscious of the difference between itself and those who were dominated— or alternatively, these distinctions arose among the dominated people themselves, the slaves and dependants of every rank. In the first case, when dominating people determine the concept of "good," it is the elevated, proud states of soul that are perceived as distinctive and as determining rank order. The noble person separates himself off from creatures in which the opposite of such elevated, proud states is expressed: he despises them. It is immediately apparent that, in this first type of morality, the contrast between "good" and "bad" amounts to one between "noble" and "despicable" (the contrast between "good" and *"evil"* has a different lineage). People who were cowardly, apprehensive, and petty, people who thought narrowly in terms of utility—these were the ones despised. But the same can be said about distrustful people with their uneasy glances, about grovelers, about dog-like types of people who let themselves be mistreated, about begging flatterers and, above all, about liars:—it is a basic belief of aristocrats that base peoples are liars. "We who are truthful"—that is what the nobility of ancient Greece called themselves. It is obvious that moral expressions everywhere were first applied to *people* and then, only later and derivatively, to *actions* (which is why it is a tremendous mistake when historians of morality take their point of departure from questions such as "Why do acts of pity get praised?"). The noble type of person feels that *he* determines value, he does not need anyone's approval, he judges that "what is harmful to me is harmful in itself," he knows that he is the one who gives honor to things in the first place, he *creates values*. He honors everything he sees in himself: this sort of morality is self-glorifying. In the foreground, there is the feeling of fullness, of power that wants to overflow, the happiness associated with a high state of tension, the consciousness of a wealth that wants to make gifts and give away. The noble person helps the unfortunate too, although not (or hardly ever) out of pity, but rather more out of an impulse generated by the over-abundance of power. In honoring himself, the noble man honors the powerful as well as those who have power over themselves, who know how to speak and be silent, who joyfully exercise severity and harshness over themselves, and have respect for all forms of severity and harshness. "Wotan has put a hard heart in my breast," reads a line from an old Scandinavian saga: this rightly comes from the soul of a proud Viking. This sort of a man is even proud of *not* being made for pity: which is why the hero of the saga adds, by way of warning, "If your heart is not hard when you are young, it will never be hard." The noble and brave types of people who think this way are the furthest removed from a morality that sees precisely pity, actions for others, and *désintéressement*[3] as emblematic of morality. A faith in yourself, pride in yourself, and a fundamental hostility and irony with respect to "selflessness" belong to a noble morality just as certainly as does a slight disdain and caution towards sympathetic feelings and "warm hearts."—The powerful are the ones who *know* how to honor; it is their art, their realm of invention. A profound reverence for age and origins—the whole notion of justice is based on this double reverence—, a faith and a prejudice in favor of forefathers and against future generations is typical of the morality of the powerful. And when, conversely, people with "modern ideas" believe almost instinctively in "progress" and "the future," and show a decreasing respect for age, this gives sufficient evidence of the ignoble origin of these "ideas." But, most of all, the morality of dominating types is

foreign and painful to contemporary taste due to its stern axiom that people have duties only towards their own kind; that when it comes to creatures of a lower rank, to everything alien, people are allowed to act as they see fit or "from the heart," and in any event, "beyond good and evil"—: things like pity might have a place here. The capacity and duty to experience extended gratitude and vengefulness—both only among your own kind—, subtlety in retaliation, refinement in concepts of friendship, a certain need to have enemies (as flue holes, as it were for the affects of jealousy, irascibility, arrogance, —basically, in order to be a good *friend*): all these are characteristic features of noble morality which, as I have suggested, is not the morality of "modern ideas," and this makes it difficult for us to relate to, and also difficult for us to dig it up and lay it open.—It is different with the second type of morality, *slave morality*. What if people who were violated, oppressed, suffering, unfree, exhausted, and unsure of themselves were to moralize: what type of moral valuations would they have? A pessimistic suspicion of the whole condition of humanity would probably find expression, perhaps a condemnation of humanity along with its condition. The slave's gaze resents the virtues of the powerful. It is skeptical and distrustful, it has a *subtle* mistrust of all the "good" that is honored there—, it wants to convince itself that even happiness is not genuine there. Conversely, qualities that serve to alleviate existence for suffering people are pulled out and flooded with light: pity, the obliging, helpful hand, the warm heart, patience, industriousness, humility, and friendliness receive full honors here—, since these are the most useful qualities and practically the only way of holding up under the pressure of existence. Slave morality is essentially a morality of utility. Here we have the point of origin for that famous opposition between "good" and *"evil."* Evil is perceived as something powerful and dangerous; it is felt to contain a certain awesome quality, a subtlety and strength that block any incipient contempt. According to the slave morality then, "evil" inspires fear; but according to the master morality, it is *"good"* that inspires and wants to inspire fear, while the "bad" man is seen as contemptible. The opposition comes to a head when, following the logic of slave morality, a hint of contempt (however slight and well disposed) finally comes to be associated with even its idea of "good," because within the terms of slave morality, the good man must always be *unthreatening:* he is good-natured, easy to deceive, maybe a bit stupid, *un bonhomme.*[4] Wherever slave morality holds sway, language shows a tendency for the words "good" and "stupid" to come closer together.—A final fundamental distinction: the desire for *freedom,* the instinct for happiness, and subtleties in the feeling of freedom necessarily belong to slave morals and morality, just as an artistry and enthusiasm in respect and devotion are invariant symptoms of an aristocratic mode of thinking and valuing.—This clearly shows why love *as passion* (our European specialty) must have had a purely noble descent: it is known to have been invented in the knightly poetry of Provence, by those magnificent, inventive men of the *"gai saber."*[5] Europe is indebted to these men for so many things, almost for itself.

261

Vanity is perhaps one of the most difficult things for a noble person to comprehend: he will be tempted to keep denying it when a different type of man will almost be able to feel it in his hands. He has difficulty imagining creatures who would try to inspire good opinions about themselves that they themselves do not hold—and consequently do not "deserve" either—, and who would then end up *believing* these good opinions. For one thing, this strikes the noble as being so tasteless and showing such a lack of self-respect, and, for another thing, it seems so baroque and unreasonable to him, that he would gladly see vanity as an exception and stay skeptical in most of the cases where it is brought up. For example, he will say: "I can be wrong about my own worth and still insist that other people acknowledge it to be what I say it is,—but that is not vanity (instead, it is arrogance or, more

frequently, it is what they call 'humility' or 'modesty')." Or alternatively: "There are many reasons why I can enjoy other people's good opinions, perhaps because I love and honor them and rejoice in each of their joys, and perhaps also because their good opinions confirm and reinforce my faith in my own good opinion of myself, perhaps because other people's good opinions are useful or look as though they could be useful to me, even when I don't agree with them,—but none of that is vanity." It is only when forced (namely with the help of history) that the noble person realizes that from time immemorial, in all strata of people who are in some way dependent, base people *were* only what they were *considered to be:*—not being at all accustomed to positing values, the only value the base person attributes to himself is the one his masters have attributed to him (creating values is the true *right of masters*). We can see it as the result of a tremendous atavism that, to this day, ordinary people still *wait* for an opinion to be pronounced about themselves before instinctively deferring to it. And this is by no means only the case with "good" opinions—they defer to bad and unfair ones as well (for instance, just think about most of the self-estimations and self-underestimations that devout women accept from their father confessors and, in general, that devout Christians accept from their church). As a matter of fact, in keeping with the slow approach of a democratic order of things (and its cause, the mixing of blood between masters and slaves), the originally rare and noble urge to ascribed to yourself a value that comes *from* yourself, and to "think well" of yourself is now increasingly widespread and encouraged. But in every age it is opposed by an older, broader, and more thoroughly ingrained tendency,—and in the phenomenon of "vanity," this older tendency gains mastery over the younger. The vain take pleasure in *every* good opinion they hear about themselves (abstracted entirely from the point of view of utility, and just as much removed from truth or falsity), just as they suffer from every bad opinion. This is because they submit—they *feel* submissive—to both good and bad opinions out of that oldest instinct of submissiveness which erupts within them.— This is "the slave" in the blood of the vain, a remnant of the mischief of the slave—and how much "slave" is still left over in women, for instance!—, they try to *seduce* people into having good opinions of them. By the same token, it is the slave who submits to these opinions immediately afterwards, as if he were not the one who had just called for them.—And to say it again: vanity is an atavism.

262

A *species*[6] originates, a type grows sturdy and strong, in the long struggle with essentially constant *unfavorable* conditions. Conversely, people know from the experience of breeders that species with overabundant diets and, in general, more than their share of protection and care, will immediately show a striking tendency towards variations of the type, and will be rich in wonders and monstrosities (including monstrous vices). You only need to see an aristocratic community (such as Venice or an ancient Greek *polis*[7]) as an organization that has been established, whether voluntarily or involuntarily, for the sake of *breeding*: the people living there together are self-reliant and want to see their species succeed, mainly because if they *do not* succeed they run a horrible risk of being eradicated. Here there are none of the advantages, excesses, and protections that are favorable to variation. The species needs itself to be a species, to be something that, by virtue of its very hardness, uniformity, and simplicity of form, can succeed and make itself persevere in constant struggle with its neighbors or with the oppressed who are or threaten to become rebellious. A tremendous range of experiences teaches it which qualities are primarily responsible for the fact that, despite all gods and men, it still exists, it keeps prevailing. It calls these qualities virtues, and these are the only virtues it fosters. It does so with harshness; in fact, it desires harshness. Every aristocratic morality is intolerant about the education of the young, disposal over women, marriage customs, relations

between old and young and penal laws (which only concern deviants):—it considers intolerance itself to be a virtue, under the rubric of "justice." A type whose traits are few in number but very strong, a species of people who are strict, warlike, clever, and silent, close to each other and closed up (which gives them the most subtle feeling for the charms and nuances of association) will, in this way, establish itself (as a species) over and above the change of generations. The continuous struggle with constant *unfavorable* conditions is, as I have said, what causes a type to become sturdy and hard. But, eventually, a fortunate state will arise and the enormous tension will relax; perhaps none of the neighbors are enemies anymore, and the means of life, even of enjoying life, exist in abundance. With a single stroke, the bonds and constrains of the old discipline are torn: it does not seem to be necessary any more, to be a condition of existence,—if it wanted to continue, it could do so only as a form of *luxury,* as an archaic *taste.* Variation, whether as deviation (into something higher, finer, rarer) or as degeneration and monstrosity, suddenly comes onto the scene in the greatest abundance and splendor; the individual dares to be individual and different. At these turning points of history, a magnificent, diverse, jungle-like growth and upward striving, a kind of *tropical* tempo in the competition to grow will appear alongside (and often mixed up and tangled together with) an immense destruction and self-destruction. This is due to the wild egoisms that are turned explosively against each other, that wrestle each other "for sun and light," and can no longer derive any limitation, restraint, or refuge from morality as it has existed so far. It was this very morality that accumulated the tremendous amount of force to put such a threatening tension into the bow:—and now it is, now it is being "outlived." The dangerous and uncanny point has been reached when the greatest, most diverse, most comprehensive life *lives past* the old morality. The "individual" is left standing there, forced to give himself laws, forced to rely on his own arts and wiles of self-preservation, self-enhancement, self-redemption. There is nothing but new whys and hows; there are no longer any shared formulas; misunderstanding is allied with disregard; decay, ruin, and the highest desires are horribly entwined; the genius of the race overflows from every cornucopia of good and bad; there is a disastrous simultaneity of spring and autumn, filled with new charms and veils that are well suited to the young, still unexhausted, still indefatigable corruption. Danger has returned, the mother of morals, great danger, displaced onto the individual this time, onto the neighbor or friend, onto the street, onto your own child, onto your own heart, onto all of your own-most, secret-most wishes and wills: and the moral philosophers emerging at this time —what will they have to preach? These sharp observers and layabouts discover that everything is rapidly coming to an end, that everything around them is ruined and creates ruin, that nothing lasts as long as the day after tomorrow except one species of person, the hopelessly *mediocre*. Only the mediocre have prospects for continuing on, for propagating—they are the people of the future, the only survivors: "Be like them! Be mediocre!" is the only morality that still makes sense, that still finds ears. But this morality of mediocrity is difficult to preach! It can never admit what it is and what it wants! It has to talk about moderation and dignity and duty and loving your neighbors,—it will have a hard time *hiding its irony!*—

263

There is an *instinct for rank* that, more than anything else, is itself the sign of a *high* rank; there is a *pleasure* in nuances of respect that indicates a noble origin and noble habits. The subtlety, quality, and stature of a soul is put dangerously to the test when something of the first rank passes by before the shudders of authority are there to protect it from intrusive clutches and crudeness: something that goes on its way like a living touchstone, undiscovered, unmarked, and experimenting, perhaps voluntarily covered and disguised. Anyone whose task and exercise is the investigation of souls will use this very art, in a variety of forms, to establish the ultimate value of a soul, the unalterable, inborn order of rank it belongs to: this sort of investigator will test out the soul's *instinct for respect. Différence engendre haine.*[8] Many natures have a baseness that suddenly bursts out, like dirty water, when any sort of holy vessel, any sort of treasure from a closed shrine, any sort of book that bears the mark of a great destiny is carried past. On the other hand, there is an involuntary hush, a hesitation of the eye and a quieting of every gesture, all of which indicate that the soul *feels* the presence of something deserving the highest honors. The way in which respect for the *Bible* has, on the whole, been maintained in Europe might be the best piece of discipline and refinement in manners that Europe owes to Christianity. Books with this sort of profundity and ultimate meaning need the protection of an externally imposed tyranny of authority; this way, they can *last* through the millennia that are needed to use them up and figure them out. It is a great achievement when the masses (people of all kinds who lack depth or have speedy bowels) have finally had the feeling bred into them that they cannot touch everything, that there are holy experiences which require them to take off their shoes and keep their dirty hands away,—and this is pretty much as high a level of humanity as they will ever reach. Conversely, what is perhaps the most disgusting thing about so-called scholars, the devout believers in "modern ideas," is their lack of shame, the careless impudence of their eyes and hands that touch, taste, and feel everything. And there might still be a greater *relative* nobility of taste and tactfulness of respect within a people these days, within a lower sort of people, namely within the peasantry, than among the newspaper-reading *demimonde* of the spirit, the educated.

NOTES

1. Commonwealth.
2. Neither God nor master.
3. Disinterestedness.
4. A good simple fellow.

5. Gay science.
6. In German: *Art*. In this section, *Art* is translated as "species" and *Typus* as "type."

7. City-state.
8. "Difference engenders hatred."

1.4 The Evolutionary Debunking of Morality

RICHARD JOYCE

Richard Joyce teaches philosophy at Victoria University in New Zealand.

In *The Descent of Man* (1871) Darwin provides a detailed account of the origins of the human "moral sense"—a trait that he classes as the "most important" difference between humans and other animals. Readers were quick to worry that this evolutionary treatment of human morality in some manner undermined it. One fierce critic wrote that if Darwin's view became widely adopted "the consequences would be disastrous indeed! We should be logically compelled to acquiesce in the vociferations of [those] who would banish altogether the senseless words 'duty' and 'merit'" (Mivart 1871/2008: 204).[1] Another called Darwin's position "dangerous" and expressed concern that his views on the origins of morality "aims ... a deadly blow at ethics" (Cobbe 1872: 10). Darwin himself remained unfazed; his general attitude to academic philosophy seems to have matched that of many contemporary scientists: slightly suspicious bafflement. But might these worries nevertheless be well-founded? Might a Darwinian account of moral genealogy somehow debunk morality? In order to answer this, we must first say something about what "a Darwinian account of moral genealogy" might involve, and also delineate different kinds of "debunking."

MORAL NATIVISM

Sometimes "nativism" is used to denote a claim about individual development: that a trait is "inborn" rather than acquired. In evolutionary contexts, however, it denotes the claim that a trait is an adaptation: the trait exists and was transmitted from our ancestors because it improved their reproductive fitness relative to competitors. The two uses are clearly not equivalent. Genetic diseases (such as Down syndrome) are inborn but not adaptations, and adaptations (such as language use) may require environmental input to become manifest. *Moral* nativism in the Darwinian context is the thesis that the capacity to make moral judgments is a human adaptation: The reason we classify the world in moral terms (good, bad, right, wrong, etc.) is that doing so helped our ancestors make more babies than those competitors lacking the moralizing trait.[2]

Moral nativism is compatible with moral variation. The nativist may claim only that a moral *faculty* is innate, allowing that the socialization process leads people in different cultures and eras to hold different moral principles and judgments. If, for example, a Naga warrior judges that beheading a foreigner is a noble act, while a Nebraskan teenager judges such an action to be a heinous crime, both are manifesting the same trait: that of exercising a moral faculty. (Analogy: A linguistic faculty may be a human adaptation, but which language one ends up speaking depends on which language one is exposed to as a child.) Moral nativism does not imply that the capacity to make moral judgments will develop irrespective of environmental

---

This essay was commissioned expressly for the fifteenth edition of *Reason and Responsibility*.

conditions, nor that this capacity will be universally present, nor that it is essential for being human, nor that there is a "gene for moral judgment." Nor should moral nativism be confused with the claim that humans are by nature *good*. To put the point provocatively: It is entirely possible that Hitler's decisions were as much guided by the workings of an innate moral faculty as were Mother Teresa's.

Whether moral nativism is true is much debated. It is an empirical hypothesis and must be tested as such: Predictions of the hypothesis must be identified, data must be gathered, and alternative hypotheses must be examined. Here our task is not to delve into that debate, but rather to examine what might follow if the nativist hypothesis is true. But there is one aspect of the nativist hypothesis that makes a big difference to that question, and so a little more must be said. The question is whether the most plausible version of moral nativism implies that moral judgment is a *truth-tracking* adaptation.

Most biological traits have nothing to do with truth. It makes no sense to say that one's gall bladder, or any of its activities, is true or false. (Of course, *that one has* a gall bladder is true or false, but that's a different matter entirely.) But *judgments* can be true or false, and thus an evolved faculty designed to produce some kind of judgment does have something to do with truth. It might be argued that the moral faculty governs only feelings and emotions, and that the "judgments" it produces are not really the right kind of thing to be assessed as true or false. But this extreme view is fairly implausible upon examination. It may be granted that the moral faculty has a great deal to do with emotions (like anger and guilt), but that is no reason to jump to the conclusion that truth-evaluable judgments (i.e., those that can be true or false) have no place in its operations. It is very hard to see, for example, how a mere *feeling*, absent any truth-evaluable judgments, could count literally as the emotion of guilt; guilt necessarily involves thoughts along the lines of "I have transgressed."[3] Let us assume then, that the moral faculty produces truth-evaluable judgments.

However, this is not to say that the evolutionary function of the moral faculty is to *track the truth*. The evolutionary function of a trait is the reason that it was selected for; it reflects why it was reproductively useful to our ancestors. In many cases truth is useful. Having a true belief about whether there are lions around was more useful to our ancestors than having a false belief on the matter. Were humans to have evolved a faculty specifically for producing beliefs about the location of lions, then it is highly likely that the faculty would have generally favored the production of *true* beliefs. In other words, the faculty would have had the function of tracking the truth.

But it doesn't always work out this way. Sometimes falsehood is useful. A fanciful example: Suppose that believing in the tooth fairy were an effective means of encouraging tooth-brushing. We can imagine that having clean teeth is such a benefit that those ancestors who believed in the tooth fairy out-competed their rivals, and that a faculty encouraging this belief gradually emerged as a prewired human adaptation. In this case, while the faculty's outputs remain truth-evaluable entities (i.e., beliefs), it is not a truth-tracking faculty. The reason it evolved is not because beliefs about the tooth fairy gave anyone information about her whereabouts, but rather because they encouraged dental hygiene. In this case, someone's belief that the tooth fairy exists can be assessed as true or false (hint: it's false), but it would be a mistake to say that the evolutionary function of this belief is to correspond (even roughly) to reality.

Returning to moral nativism: Of course, we don't know whether the moral faculty is an adaptation at all, but it is interesting to note that on all of the live versions of the nativist hypothesis, mention of *truth-tracking* is noticeably absent. Most nativist hypotheses suggest that morality plays a vital role in enhancing social cohesion. An individual who thinks that it is morally repugnant to cheat her comrades is less likely to do so—perhaps even less likely than a person who sees that cheating will harm her own long-term interests—and thus on the assumption that cheating is frequently maladaptive, the moral belief may be selected for. The plausibility of this claim seems independent of whether cheating one's comrades (or anything else) actually *is* morally repugnant. Other moral nativists emphasize the role that morality can play in signaling one's commitment to social projects. Perhaps by loudly proclaiming that cheating is repugnant (and acting accordingly) one advertises oneself to others as a worthy partner for mutually beneficial enterprises like hunting or rearing a family. Here the function of morality is its signaling role; again, whether one's assertion that cheating is repugnant is actually true is irrelevant to its fulfilling this function well.

DEBUNKING

The term "debunking" is intentionally vague, covering several distinct possibilities which I will here divide into three. The most extreme kind of debunking would show that all moral assertions are untrue. This view is known as the moral "error theory" (see Mackie 1977). The error theorist thinks that while moral concepts (*goodness, evil, virtue,* etc.) have the linguistic function of picking out real features of the world, the universe just doesn't contain any such features. Thus any statement that something possesses one of these features (e.g., "Keeping promises is morally good") is simply untrue. (Analogously, the atheist holds that religious terms like *God, sin, afterlife,* etc., function to pick out entities and features but that the universe simply doesn't contain such stuff. Thus, the atheist holds that most or all religious claims are untrue.) A weaker view would be that a certain substantial subset of moral assertions are false. Perhaps, for example, all talk of moral *rights* is flawed, but talk of moral values and virtues is fine. We can call both the strong and weak versions examples of *truth debunking*.

To establish a moral error theory would automatically debunk various rival moral theories (i.e., any theory according to which moral judgments are sometimes true). Yet it would be a slightly different enterprise to set out with the objective in mind of refuting particular moral theories. This can be classed as a second kind of debunking: *theory debunking*—aimed not at upsetting any accepted view concerning which moral judgments are true and which false, but rather aimed at showing that certain *interpretations* of moral judgments are false. For example, while it is widely accepted that "Keeping promises is morally good" is true, there is much disagreement concerning what makes it true. One might say that it's true because God commands promise-keeping, or because it maximizes happiness, or because it follows from the optimally coherent equilibrium of our intuitions, etc. To debunk one these theories (but not all of them) would probably leave the truth value of the claim "Keeping promises is morally good" intact.[4]

A very different, third kind of debunking—*justification debunking*—would show that all moral judgments are *unjustified*. Precisely what it takes for a judgment to be justified or unjustified is something over which philosophers wrangle, but on all accounts it is different from truth and falsity. If I form beliefs about whether someone is coming to dinner on the basis of rolling dice, then my beliefs are not justified, even if I happen to get lucky and have a true belief. If I form beliefs about when Napoleon died on the basis of books, websites, teachers, etc., then my belief is justified; but it is possible that I have fallen victim to a grand hoax (involving fake websites, etc.), such that my justified belief is actually false.

Justification is a relative affair. One may be justified in believing something while someone else is unjustified in believing that very same thing. One may be unjustified in believing something but later become justified (if one gains evidence); or one may be justified but later become unjustified (if some new countervailing evidence comes to light which one chooses to ignore). Thus this kind of debunking can come in various strengths. A strong view is that *everyone* is unjustified in holding their moral beliefs; an even stronger view is that this situation is permanent.

So some arguments employ moral nativism to undermine moral *truth*, some use it to undermine specific moral *theories*, and some use it to undermine moral *justification*. How might such arguments run?

EVOLUTIONARY DEBUNKING OF MORAL TRUTH

It has sometimes been claimed that one cannot show a belief to be false on the basis of discoveries about its origin; the putative error committed in trying to do so has been dubbed "the genetic fallacy." For a lot of cases this seems reasonable. For example, however ill-advised we may think it to form scientific ideas on the basis of dreams, it seems wrong to conclude that a scientific idea formed in this way must be false. (Friedrich Kekulé famously envisaged the ring-shaped structure of the benzene molecule after dreaming of a snake biting its own tail.) But for certain cases it doesn't seem reasonable. If Fred believes "My dreams never influence me in any way," then the discovery that he formed this belief on the basis of his dreams would allow us to infer that the belief is false. This, however, is clearly a carefully constructed example, since the belief in question implies something about its own origins, and on the face of it nothing like that goes on with moral beliefs. What then are the prospects of using moral nativism to show that moral judgments are untrue?

On one interpretation, Michael Ruse advocates such an argument (1986, 2006, 2009). In order to discuss Ruse's case, we must first introduce the concept of moral *objectivity*—a notion that gets used differently by different philosophers, and one so slippery that some have recommended its elimination. The basic idea is that some facts depend on us and some do not; but only certain kinds of *dependence* count. Chihuahuas depend on us (we bred them into existence, we keep them alive, etc.), but are clearly objective entities. The value of money, on the other hand, seems to depend on us in a different way. If we all ceased to believe in the value of money, it would lose all value (whereas if we all ceased to believe in chihuahuas, they wouldn't pop out of existence).

Some philosophers believe that moral facts depend on us (our beliefs, practices, institutions) in a similar way to the value of money. Such a position allows that moral facts exist but denies that they are *objective* facts. We can call this position "constructivism." Other moral philosophers think that it would be desirable to vindicate moral objectivity, if possible; they worry that a constructed morality lacks the kind of binding authority which we would like morality to have. If a criminal sees that the wrongness of his crimes is merely a matter of collective opinion, then what reason does he have to refrain (if he can evade punishment)? Some go so far as to think that objectivity is written into our very moral concepts, such that the idea of a "subjective morality" is not even coherent; for them, anything deserving the name "morality" *is* an objective morality. (Analogy: anything deserving the name "square" *is* a four-sided square.) Those who think that moral facts exist and are objective may be called "moral realists," while those that think that moral facts do not exist at all, or exist only subjectively, can be called "anti-realists."[5]

Ruse endorses moral nativism, arguing that having a faculty that issued moral judgments was adaptive because those judgments strengthened our ancestors' motivation to cooperate, and did so by seeming to be objectively binding. "The Darwinian argues that morality simply does not work (from a biological perspective) unless we believe that it is objective" (1986: 253). Of course, this doesn't mean that there *are* any objective moral facts, only that it was beneficial to our ancestors to believe that there are. Ruse goes on: "[M]orality is a collective illusion foisted upon us by our genes. Note, however, that the illusion lies not in the morality itself, but in its sense of objectivity" (ibid.). At this point it seems that Ruse thinks that only a certain aspect of morality is in error, not morality per se. But why is there any error at all?

Ruse's answer is that once armed with (his version of) moral nativism there is simply no need to posit objective moral facts in the world. Nativism fully explains why we believe in moral objectivity, and there is no need to appeal to actual objective moral facts to explain any other phenomena. Ruse thus relies on a principle of parsimony, according to which one should not endorse unnecessarily complicated theories. An analogy he often uses concerns the popularity of spiritualism after World War I: In order to explain why a grieving mother believes that her son spoke to her at a séance, all we need appeal to are psychological facts about her wishful thinking and vulnerable state of mind; there is no need to imagine that she was really in contact with a supernatural being.

One might, however, take issue with the analogy. In the case of the grieving mother, it is clear that in order to imagine her beliefs to be true we would have to posit a whole weird realm of facts that doesn't fit with our best current science. But this is not obviously so in the moral case. It is easy enough to make "moral objectivity" sound spooky, but it need not be. A utilitarian, for example, identifies moral facts with whatever produces the most happiness; and the question of which action available to a person produces the most happiness is an objective matter (it's something we could all be wrong about). Therefore it is not clear that accepting the existence of moral objectivity requires believing in categories of things above and beyond those we already accept. Thus it is not obvious that using a principle of parsimony to eliminate moral objectivity from the world is quite as straightforward as Ruse seems to think.

If Ruse aspired to nothing more than showing that moral objectivity is flawed, then we should classify him as a *theory debunker* (for he would be undermining any theory according to which morality is objective, leaving constructivist theories intact). But sometimes he seems to go further, accepting resources that allow him to go for a stronger conclusion: *truth debunking*. He writes: "Ethics is subjective, but its meaning is objective" (2006: 22; see also Ruse 2009: 507). If we take this claim seriously—that objectivity is an essential aspect of moral concepts—

then showing that there is no such thing as moral objectivity would amount to showing that there are no such things as moral properties at all. (To recycle an earlier analogy: To show that there are no four-sided square shapes in a box is to show that there are no square shapes in the box.) This claim that morality is essentially objective (conceptually speaking) is by no means implausible, though it is certainly contentious. In any case, it is not something that Ruse can just help himself to; if the debunking argument is to get all the way to the error theory then this crucial connecting premise will need a lot of support.

EVOLUTIONARY DEBUNKING OF ETHICAL THEORY

Sharon Street (2006) develops a debunking argument but explicitly *doesn't* endorse the aforementioned connecting premise. Her target is unambiguously moral realism, but since she doesn't hold that morality is essentially objective, she thinks that versions of moral constructivism survive the argument intact. Thus she is no error theorist; she doesn't think that morality itself is erroneous, but that a certain interpretation of morality (the realist's) is false. However, if one agreed with the debunking part of Street's argument, but disagreed with her tolerance of constructivism (because one thought morality essentially objective, say), then a moral error theory would beckon.

Street argues that moral nativism presents the moral realist with a dilemma. Either (i) there is no causal connection between the putative realm of moral facts and the moral judgments that we have evolved to make, or (ii) there is a connection—namely, that our moral judgments are in some manner responses to the features of that realm. Either horn of the dilemma, Street thinks, is unacceptable. The first horn seems to imply the unpalatable result that either our moral beliefs spectacularly fail to match the moral facts or their matching is a massive coincidence. The problem with the second horn is that, as we saw earlier, all serious versions of the nativist hypothesis appear to endorse a non-truth-tracking account of the evolutionary function of the moral faculty.

But even if moral judgments do not have the evolutionary function to track anything, they might nevertheless be reliably linked with the presence of some relevant feature of the world. For example, suppose that the adaptational function of the human blushing response is not to track the presence of anything, but rather to signal to others one's embarrassment over a social faux pas (thus advertising one's allegiance to social norms). Nevertheless, the blushing response presumably will correlate reliably with cases in which people violate social norms. Something similar could be happening in morality. Moral judgments may not have the evolutionary function to track anything, but nevertheless negative moral judgments (e.g., about what is bad) might correlate with actions that cause harm (say). It could then be argued (as indeed a certain kind of utilitarian does argue) that harm just *is* moral badness; thus negative moral judgments tend to occur in the presence of badness, after all.

An important part of Street's response to this is to invoke a principle of parsimony: "The tracking account obviously posits something extra…, namely independent evaluative truths" (2006: 129). Presumably she will say the same thing regarding any account that allows that moral judgments correlate reliably with independent evaluative facts (even though their evolutionary function is not to track them). But we have already seen in the discussion of Ruse that such a principle of parsimony is not to be used hastily. The "independent evaluative truths" that Street speaks of may very well be comprised of kinds of things (such as facts about whether a given action causes harm) that all parties to these debates already accept.[6]

EVOLUTIONARY DEBUNKING OF MORAL JUSTIFICATION

A third kind of genealogical debunking, which I have advocated myself (Joyce 2006), is weaker than the other forms in that it doesn't purport to show anything false but rather aims to undermine the justification of moral claims.[7] The argument is best approached via an imaginary thought experiment.

Suppose there were such things as different kinds of *belief pill*, each of which (somehow) caused one to start believing something (presumably also causing amnesia about having taken the pill). Pick one of your beliefs at random; say, your belief that Napoleon lost the battle of Waterloo. Imagine being unexpectedly given indubitable evidence that the only reason you believe this is that someone slipped you a Napoleon-lost-Waterloo belief pill last week. We'll suppose that this knowledge breaks the spell of the pill, so you now have control over what choices lie before you: You are free to carry on believing that Napoleon was defeated, or you can disbelieve it, or take some other kind of attitude. What should you do?

It would seem wrong to just carry on believing it without concern; but it would also seem wrong to assume that the belief is false. I suspect you'd be rather confused about what to believe, and should probably suspend judgment about whether Napoleon lost Waterloo (just as you currently suspend judgment about whether there is an odd or even number of footprints on the moon). Of course, you're not necessarily stuck in that position; you could do some research which could provide concrete grounds for reinstating your belief that Napoleon lost Waterloo. Or maybe you're happy to live with the indecision. (Even if the data about the footprints on the moon were available, you might just not care.)

Things would stand differently if you were warranted in thinking that the person who slipped you the pill was benign, in that he or she tended to deliberately give people pills that would produce *true* beliefs. That would be grounds for thinking that appropriate causal links are intact between the facts (Napoleon's defeat at Waterloo) and your beliefs on the matter. But absent evidence for any such thought, the discovery that you've taken a belief pill appears to remove justification from your belief, because it's the discovery that the belief was formed by a process that has no sensitivity to the relevant facts. (Whether it *removes* justification or reveals that the belief was unjustified all along depends on which general theory of justification is true—a matter we cannot discuss here.)

Might moral nativism be analogous to belief pills? One disanalogy is that (as we saw earlier) on many versions of moral nativism evolution doesn't hardwire whole beliefs, but rather provides a moral faculty of concepts, such as *right* and *wrong*. But this is more of a distraction than a disanalogy, because the belief-pill example can be modified accordingly. Suppose instead of belief pills we had *concept* pills, such that the only reasons you have the concept C is that you were slipped a pill. Your concept C now figures in whole beliefs, such as "X is C" and "Y is not C," and so forth. By what process this comes about is something we can leave unspecified; the point is that had you never been given the pill you'd have no beliefs involving C at all. It seems that, as before, the discovery of the pill origins of C undermines the justification of all beliefs essentially involving it. Might the discovery that moral nativism is true similarly undermine the justification of our moral judgments?

One thing that's clear is that if the best versions of nativism show the moral faculty to be *truth-tracking* then this result won't follow. That would be analogous to having grounds for thinking that the person who slipped you the belief pill was benign. This shows why this debunking argument isn't going to generalize to *any* evolved psychological faculty designed to produce certain kinds of judgment. Perhaps humans have an evolved faculty for doing simple arithmetic; yet the only plausible account of why it might have been beneficial to our ancestors to have these beliefs (like $3 + 1 = 4$) is that they are *true*. When fleeing four lions and seeing three quit the chase, having a false belief about whether there are any lions left is likely to be harmful. As we have seen, however, the corresponding supposition is doubtful in the moral case: Moral judgments might fulfill their adaptational function (e.g., motivating cooperation) even if such judgments are false.

But might the moral faculty, while not designed for truth-tracking, nevertheless produce judgments that reliably correlate with the moral facts? Here, I think, there is nothing to exclude a positive answer out of hand, but the burden really lies on the opponent of debunking to confirm the existence of this putative correlation. It's a bit like discovering that your beliefs about Napoleon are the product of a pill but choosing to maintain them on the grounds that the pill-pusher *might* be benign. That's not good enough to provide your belief with justification; you really need some positive reason for thinking that he or she is benign. In the moral case, the mere fact that moral judgments *might* correlate reliably with moral facts doesn't provide one iota of justification for those judgments; it's up to the opponent of debunking to provide a plausible concrete theory.

One possible reply to this argument is to adopt a theory of justification known as *reliabilism*, according to which a belief is justified if it is the product of a reliable process of formation—even if the believer is unaware of that process. A reliabilist might object to the preceding argument by saying that so long as our moral judgments reliably correlate with the moral facts (regardless of whether it is their evolutionary function to track them; regardless of whether we have access to a plausible concrete explanation of the relation), then our moral judgments *are* justified.

However, it seems to me that this just pushes the real problem back a level. The kind of debunker under consideration started out arguing that although our moral judgments *might* be true, they lack justification. The reliabilist responds by providing grounds for thinking that they might be justified after all. But in the absence of solid evidence that the relevant belief-forming process *is* reliable, the debunker can retort that although moral judgments *might* be justified, we have no grounds for thinking that they are justified. (And never mind that there are serious objections to reliabilism.) In the context of an argument about moral epistemology, that seems a significant skeptical conclusion.

CONCLUSION

No evolutionary discovery lands a knock-out blow to morality; all such findings require supplementation with substantive philosophical argument. In the case of Ruse and Street, the crucial use of a principle of parsimony raises delicate metaphysical issues concerning the nature of moral properties. In the case of the evolutionary debunking of moral justification, things are complicated in different ways. First, whether the conclusion of the argument is (A) that moral judgments are unjustified or (B) that we have no evidence that moral judgments are justified, depends on what kind of theory of justification is preferred. Either way, the argument doesn't purport to show that no justification can be provided; it represents a *challenge* for the moralist to do so. The debunker about justification argues that confirmation of a hypothesis about the origins of moral judgment—one that doesn't imply or presuppose that any such judgments are true—would shift a burden of proof onto the moralist's shoulders. It is open for the moralist to meet the challenge by retorting that while the moral faculty may not be evolutionarily designed for truth-tracking, it nevertheless produces judgments that reliably correlate with the moral facts. At this point, the moralist must advocate an account of the moral facts and the debunker may criticize the adequacy of this account. Although this may seem like a disappointing (though all too familiar) kind of philosophical impasse, the debunker may continue to insist that the presence of non-truth-tracking moral nativism places the burden of proof on the moralist to win the argument.

REFERENCES

Cobbe, F. P. 1872. *Darwinism in Morals and Other Essays*. London: Williams and Norgate.

Greene, J. 2003. "From neural 'is' to moral 'ought': What are the moral implications of neuroscientific moral psychology?" *Nature Reviews Neuroscience* 4: 847–850.

Joyce, R. 2001. *The Myth of Morality*. Cambridge: Cambridge University Press.

Joyce, R. 2006. *The Evolution of Morality*. Cambridge, MA.: MIT Press.

Mackie, J. L. 1977. *Ethics: Inventing Right and Wrong*. New York: Penguin Books.

Mivart, G. J. (1871) 2008. *On the Genesis of Species*. BiblioLife.

Ruse, M. 1986. *Taking Darwin Seriously*. Oxford: Basil Blackwell.

Ruse, M. 2006. "Is Darwinian metaethics possible (and if it is, is it well-taken)?" In G. Boniolo & G. de Anna (eds.), *Evolutionary Ethics and Contemporary Biology*. Cambridge: Cambridge University Press. 13–26.

Ruse, M. 2009. "Evolution and ethics: The sociobiological approach." In M. Ruse (ed.), *Philosophy After Darwin*. Princeton, NJ: Princeton University Press. 489–511.

Singer, P. 2005. "Ethics and intuitions." *Journal of Ethics* 9: 331–352.

Street, S. 2006. "A Darwinian dilemma for realist theories of value." *Philosophical Studies* 127: 109–166.

NOTES

1. Mivart in fact wrote these words prior to the publication of *Descent*; but he knew in advance the content of Darwin's forthcoming book, and when the latter was published wrote a scathing anonymous critique in the *Quarterly Review*.

2. While it is perfectly legitimate to speak of Darwinian *cultural* evolution (and thus *cultural* adaptations), in this context, as a matter of fact, the process is generally limited to traits that are genetically transmitted.

3. In cases of so-called *survivor guilt*, the person still has thoughts concerning "transgression," though perhaps doesn't really endorse them. The proposal that the survivor's guilt is literally nothing more than *a feeling* without any accompanying cognitive content (like a headache) doesn't withstand scrutiny.

4. The "theories" that can be attacked in *theory debunking* include both normative and metaethical theories. Normative ethics is the enterprise of building a general theory of moral action that is applicable across all or a large range of cases. An example of a normative theory is hedonic utilitarianism, which holds that one must always act so as to maximize overall happiness. Metaethics is concerned with a number of interrelated theoretical matters, such as the nature of moral properties, the nature of moral language, and the

justification of moral judgments. An example of a metaethical theory is moral constructivism, which holds that moral facts exist but are in some manner constituted by our attitudes or practices.

5. A word of warning: How the terms "moral realism" and "moral objectivity" should be used is itself disputed ground.

6. Other evolutionary theory debunkers include Joshua Greene (2003) and Peter Singer (2005), both of whom argue that nativism debunks certain non-consequentialist normative theories. (See footnote 4.)

7. It may cause some confusion that in other contexts I have argued for a full-blown moral error theory (Joyce, 2001), but not on evolutionary grounds.

CHAPTER 2

PROPOSED STANDARDS OF RIGHT CONDUCT

2.1 Ethical Subjectivism

RUSS SHAFER-LANDAU

Imagine two people debating the morality of giving to famine relief. Smith thinks that we are bound to give a great deal more than people typically do. Jones denies this. Suppose that these two, after talking a good while longer, have found themselves in agreement about all of the relevant facts, and have also sharpened their own positions so that the views they emerge with are each internally consistent. But suppose that the fundamental disagreement between them remains. Can this disagreement be rationally resolved?

Not likely, according to ethical subjectivists. Subjectivism claims that there is no ideal or uniquely correct resolution to ethical disagreements, because there are no ethical standards that are objectively correct, no standards to which all rational or fully informed people must agree. There is no overarching, universal yardstick that can be applied to determine the truth of one's ultimate moral principles. Once we have identified our deepest moral commitments, we can go no further. It makes no sense, according to subjectivism, to suppose that such commitments could be false or irrational.

To better understand ethical subjectivism, we need to appreciate the key notions of subjectivity and objectivity. A proposition or judgment is objectively true just in case it is true independently of anyone's thinking it is. So, for instance, the claim that the earth orbits around the sun is an objective truth, because the claim is true regardless of whether anyone believes it. A judgment is subjectively true just in case its truth depends on whether the speaker endorses it. To insist that chocolate is tastier than vanilla, or that beer is better than wine, is to make a subjective claim, because in this case truth is in the eye of the beholder.

This essay was written expressly for the eleventh edition of Reason and Responsibility.

TWO KINDS OF SUBJECTIVISM

Philosophers distinguish between two kinds of ethical theory. The first sort—**normative** theory—attempts to specify conditions under which an action is morally right or wrong. John Stuart Mill, for instance, held that an act is right insofar as it tends to produce happiness. Immanuel Kant thought that one acts rightly only if one is willing to see everyone act in accordance with one's own principles. Thomas Hobbes claimed that an act is right if it is permitted by rules that would be agreed to by self-interested parties seeking to band together to escape from anarchy.

Viewed as a normative theory, ethical subjectivism claims that an act is morally right if, and only if, the person judging the action approves of it. Similarly, personal disapproval is both necessary and sufficient for an action to qualify as wrong.

Normative subjectivism allows that moral judgments can be true or false. There is truth in ethics, but no objective truth. A moral judgment is true, according to normative subjectivism, just in case it accurately reports the sentiments of the speaker. Thus sincerity is the mark of ethical truth. If normative subjectivism is true, then one's sincere moral judgments cannot be mistaken.

The debate among Mill, Kant, Hobbes, and normative subjectivists is an intramural one. Each theory asserts its superiority as an answer to the question: Under what conditions are actions morally right? This is a very important debate within ethics. But we can step back from this debate and ask instead about the status of these competing theories. Specifically, we can ask of all of these theories how they might be justified, whether they are or can be true, and how, if at all, we might know that one or another is true. These are **meta-ethical** questions. Here we are not asking what makes actions right. Instead, we are focusing on whether normative theories can be justified in the first place.

Meta-ethical subjectivism is the particular claim that normative ethical theories, and moral judgments quite generally, cannot be true.

Contrast this with normative subjectivism, which claims that moral judgments can be true, provided they accurately report the speaker's feelings. Because of their different views about the possibility of ethical truth, meta-ethical subjectivism implies the falsity of normative subjectivism, and vice versa.

Let us consider the motivations and the plausibility of normative subjectivism first.

MOTIVATIONS FOR NORMATIVE SUBJECTIVISM

A. The Argument from Democracy

One of normative subjectivism's appeals is that it is so democratic. Subjectivism is a levelling doctrine—everyone issues true moral judgments, so long as they sincerely give voice to their feelings. Everyone's views are on a par with everyone else's. This democratic element is a genuine feature of subjectivism. But many take this democratic element a step further, expressing their allegiance to normative subjectivism by means of the following argument:

1. If everyone has an equal right to have and voice moral opinions, then everyone's moral opinions are equally plausible.
2. Everyone does have an equal right to have and voice moral opinions.
3. Therefore everyone's moral opinions are equally plausible.

This argument is *valid*—its premises entail its conclusion. *If* one were to accept premises (1) and (2), then logic requires one to accept the conclusion (3) as well. But should we accept these premises? The second premise seems generally plausible. But the first premise is false. Having a right to an opinion does not entail the plausibility of that opinion. Though everyone has an equal right to express views about mathematics or quantum physics, no one supposes that everyone's opinions here are equally plausible. I have lots of opinions about botany, about the content of the tax code, about the location of various buildings and landmarks.

Further, I have a right to each of these opinions. But many of them (I'm not sure which) are mistaken. I misidentify plants, misconstrue tax law, and my sense of direction is awful. These humdrum examples show that the plausibility of an opinion really has nothing to do with one's right to hold it: Having a right to an opinion is one thing, the truth of that opinion quite another. This directly undermines the first premise of the argument. Because we must reject one of its crucial premises, the argument from democracy is unsound. It does not supply a good basis for endorsing normative subjectivism.

B. The Argument from Disagreement

One thing that impresses many people about work in the sciences is the degree of consensus about which propositions are true, and about which methods are appropriate for discovering new truths. Things in ethics seem to be much different; there seems to be a great deal of disagreement about fundamental issues, and a lack of consensus about appropriate methods for resolving moral questions. The diversity of ethical opinion has struck many as an important indicator of morality's fundamentally subjective character.

Here is a representative sketch of an argument for subjectivism that takes the breadth of ethical disagreement as its focus:

1. If there is persistent disagreement among informed, good-willed, open-minded people about some subject matter, then that subject matter does not admit of objective truth.
2. There is persistent disagreement about ethical issues among informed, good-willed, open-minded people.
3. Therefore there are no objective ethical truths.

We can know that an argument's conclusion is true if we know that the argument is logically valid and that all of its premises are true. This argument is valid. The second premise seems to be true, though the breadth of moral *agreement* is often underappreciated. The divisive moral issues tend to get the most press, but this publicity can mask the significant degree of moral consensus that must form the core of any society. Further, though there clearly is disagreement about ethical issues, it is sensible to suppose that much of this is owing to mistaken beliefs—more information would lead to greater ethical agreement. Public debates about welfare reform in the United States, or about the morality of capital punishment, are chock full of misinformation. Getting the facts straight would get us a good distance toward resolving issues on these (and other) topics.

Still, we may suppose that even after gathering the facts, people of good will may disagree in their ethical views. So let us grant premise (2). Premise (1), however, is not plausible. There is persistent disagreement among informed, good-willed, open-minded physicists and mathematicians. We, and they, assume that their efforts are nevertheless aimed at discovering objective truths. We do not believe that taste is the arbiter of truth in math or physics. Indeed, we can make this quite general point about investigations of all sorts. When historians debate the causes of the Civil War, they are not *merely* entering their personal views, with nothing other than parochial preference to back them up. Historians are trying to discover what *really* caused the Civil War. They continue to disagree about this. But this is not evidence that their discipline is subjective, that the truths they arrive at are mere expressions of taste. It isn't the case that historical (or physical or mathematical) judgments are true just because someone believes in them. What this shows is that a discipline may deal in objective truths even if its open-minded, informed practitioners deeply disagree with one another. Because that is so, the argument from disagreement fails to provide adequate support for normative subjectivism.

C. The Argument from Tolerance

Many people find subjectivism attractive because of the support it seems to provide for tolerance. We nowadays reject the once-prevalent feelings of superiority that were used to justify the oppression of Asians, Africans, and indigenous

Americans during the past three centuries. We would encourage a respectful, tolerant attitude toward different cultures, rather than a dismissive outlook that brands other cultures as "primitive." This dismissive attitude always begins with an (implicit) endorsement of ethical objectivism—there is an objectively correct way to do things. And we all know how things go from here: "We have it right, they don't, thus we have to show them the true path. If this means exploiting them (for their own good), and possibly destroying their way of life, no great loss, since we will supply them with a far better one."

If you are like most people, you'll have bristled at the arrogance expressed in these last lines. This may lead you to endorse the following argument from tolerance:

1. If normative subjectivism is true, then no one's deepest opinions are more plausible than anyone else's.
2. If no one's deepest opinions are more plausible than anyone else's, then we have to respect and tolerate the opinions of all others.
3. Thus if normative subjectivism is true, then we have to respect and tolerate the opinions of all others.

There are two important points to note about this argument. The first is that even if it is sound—even if it is logically valid (it is), and all of its premises (and thus its conclusion) are true—this does not entail that ethical objectivists need to embrace an arrogant or disrespectful attitude toward different cultures. Objectivists believe that there are ethical truths that exist independently of whether anyone thinks so. An objectivist need not believe that *he himself* is in possession of such truth. Indeed, objectivists who are appropriately humble will recognize their own fallibility and the limits to their understanding, in much the same way as physicists or chemists might appreciate the depth of their own ignorance against the backdrop of objective truth. Arrogance and intolerance are poor character traits. They are not mandated by the intellectual position of ethical objectivism.

Let us return to the argument. Its first premise is true. But the second premise is suspect if normative subjectivism is true. Suppose that it is. This means that an action is morally right just in case someone approves of it. If one approves of tolerant behavior, then such behavior is morally correct. The problem, however, is that *if* one approves of intolerance, then intolerant behavior is morally appropriate. Subjectivism morally sanctions the intolerance of prejudiced and bigoted individuals, so long as such intolerance is sincerely felt. Regrettably, it often is. Those who think that even (and especially) racists and bigots are morally required to display respect for others will find no ground for their view in ethical subjectivism. To think that even a deeply prejudiced person should be tolerant is to embrace the universal or objective value of toleration. A concern for tolerance thus sits very uncomfortably with normative subjectivism.

D. The Argument from Atheism

A common thought that moves many to normative subjectivism is that objectivity in ethics can be purchased only through divine commands. If ethics is objective, then it must be God who validates the moral rules. The problem, according to subjectivists, is that God does not exist.

Here is the argument in somewhat tighter form:

1. If ethics is objective, then God must exist.
2. God does not exist.
3. Therefore ethics is not objective.

We could undermine the argument from atheism if we could show that God exists. We can't, at least not here (and perhaps not anywhere; this is one philosophical issue that may never be settled). But even if we could resolve this matter, and do so in favor of the atheist, this would not be enough to prove subjectivism. We can see that from the argument itself. The argument requires a further claim (premise 1), namely, that ethics is objective only if God exists.

There is an intuitive, widely shared view that underlies the first premise. The thought is that laws require lawgivers. There are laws against assault, forgery, and perjury only because lawmakers have enacted them. No legislators, no laws. By analogy, if there are moral laws, these require some lawmaker to validate them. If moral laws are objective, this lawmaker cannot be any one of us. (Remember: Objective moral rules are those whose truth does not depend on human endorsement) If not one of us, then who? Enter God.

There are two reasons to doubt premise (1). This premise seems to derive its strongest support from the common thought mentioned earlier (*viz.*, that rules require rulegivers). But this principle is suspect. Many think that the rules of logic and the axioms of mathematics are true quite independently of whether anyone has ordained them. *If* that is so (an issue too complex to tackle here), then moral rules too might be true or justified even in the absence of a moral lawgiver.

Further, there is reason to think that even if God exists, God cannot be the ultimate source of ethical principles, and so cannot be the missing link that supplies objectivity in ethics.

Suppose God exists. Suppose God issues commands to us. And further suppose that our moral law comprises these commands. Ethics is objective because the law comes from God, not from us. If it didn't come from God, it couldn't be objective.

This familiar line of thought, often used to support premise (1), is beset by a troubling dilemma: God either does or does not have reasons to support his (or her or its) commands. If God lacks justifying reasons, then God's commands are arbitrary, and so supply no authoritative basis for ethics. Alternatively, if God's commands *are* backed up by reasons, then divine commands are no longer arbitrary. They may be authoritative. We can envision a God who is omniscient, and so knows all facts, including moral facts. This God may also be omnibenevolent, and in his goodness may want to impart the moral facts (or rules) to us, in the form of divine commands. This traditional picture preserves the goodness and omniscience of God, precisely by envisioning divine commands as being well-supported by reasons.

The problem, however, is that these reasons, whatever they are, are what really justify the divine commands. If God commands us not to kill, extort, or perjure, he does so *because such actions are wrong;* they are not wrong because God forbids them. But this means that even theists, if they are to retain a picture of an all-good and all-knowing God, must acknowledge a source of ethical truth that exists independently of God's commands. This means that the objectivity of ethics does not hinge on God's commands. And that directly challenges premise (1)....

A final complication emerges when we consider the argument's conclusion—the claim that ethics is not objective. Even if premises (1) and (2) are true, the conclusion does not show that normative subjectivism is true. Put simply, the conclusion, (3) may be true *even if normative subjectivism is false*. There are at least two theories, in addition to normative subjectivism, that are compatible with the claim that ethics is not objective. One of these theories is meta-ethical subjectivism. The other is ethical relativism, the view that an action is morally right if, and only if, it is permitted by the ultimate mores of the society in which it is performed. Ethical relativism allows for moral truth—moral judgments are true just in case they accurately report a certain kind of social consensus. Because moral truth is a function of what people believe it to be, ethical relativism is a non-objective theory. Thus relativists, as well as normative and meta-ethical subjectivists, will embrace conclusion (3). This shows that the argument from atheism, if it is to support normative subjectivism, must be supplemented by additional arguments that rule out its two antiobjectivist competitors.

For our purposes, then, we must suspend judgment on the argument from atheism. The argument is sound only if both of its premises are true. They may be. But we could know this only after a very great deal of further philosophical investigation. And we would have an argument for normative subjectivism only if we also had in hand a battery of arguments that undermined both metaethical subjectivism and ethical relativism. All the more reason to wait and see before pronouncing a judgment on the argument from atheism.

Implications of Normative Subjectivism

As we have seen, many of the arguments that are advanced for ethical subjectivism are not very compelling. This is not a fatal flaw. Most philosophical positions are supported by a large battery of arguments, many of which, after serious attention, turn out to be unsound. Thus ethical subjectivism may be true even if the preceding arguments turn out to be less than convincing. But to gain plausibility, its supporters need to discharge two debts. First, they must advance a positive argument that survives scrutiny. Second, they must show that the essential implications of subjectivism are implications we can live with. Let us see whether this is so.

First, as we have seen, subjectivism is a doctrine of **moral equivalence**—everyone's ultimate moral views are as plausible as everyone else's. This is a handy weapon when dealing with arrogant or haughty individuals. But moral equivalence is a double-edged sword. If all moral views are on a par with one another, then we lose our basis for issuing substantive moral criticism of unsavory characters such as Nazis and terrorists. If subjectivism is true, then those who approve of antisemitism and terrorism are correct in calling such behavior morally right. The moral views of a Hitler or an IRA gunman are *true,* so long as these views are sincerely held.

Of course, subjectivism does not render us mute at this stage—we can criticize the views of Nazis and terrorists, but only from our own perspective. Importantly, our perspective is not superior to theirs. Moral equivalence entails that conflicting moral views are just different; neither one is better or worse than another. This may appeal when comparing the prayer or dietary rituals of Belgians and Polynesians. But it is likely to leave us cold in the face of serious evil.

Normative subjectivism also comes very close to rendering each person **morally infallible.** An infallible person is one who cannot make mistakes. Thus such a person has no false beliefs and all true ones. If subjectivism is true, then it is possible that all, or almost all, of our moral beliefs are correct. We can be morally mistaken in only one of two ways. We might base our moral views on false beliefs (e.g., a racist whose antipathy to blacks is based on a false belief about their intelligence). Or we might possess moral beliefs that conflict with other, deeper moral beliefs we already hold. We might, for instance, approve of the death penalty for a specially awful murderer, even though in a cooler moment we reject the principles that could justify the execution.

According to subjectivism, moral views that are free of either sort of error cannot be mistaken. Apart from exceptions of these two kinds, subjectivism entails that our moral feelings are self-certifying. Moral outlooks that seem to us vicious, ruthless, callous, selfish, or even maniacal cannot be wrong, so long as the views imply no factual errors and are consistent with other things a person holds. Literature and history offer a good supply of well-informed, consistent fanatics. Subjectivism implies that their views are true.

If we are ordinarily morally infallible, and if we disagree with others in our ethical views, then it follows that subjectivism **generates contradictions.** A contradiction occurs when a proposition is alleged to be both true and false. Theories that generate contradictions cannot be true. We would rightly dismiss a mathematical theory that entailed that two and two did, and at the same time did not, equal four. Suppose ethical subjectivism is correct. If Smith thinks that giving famine aid is mandatory, and Jones disagrees, then giving to famine relief is and is not morally required. It is both true and false that giving to famine relief is obligatory. That is a contradiction.

We can resolve this worrying implication in a fairly straightforward way. Rather than saying that Smith's approval of an action makes it morally right, period, we say that her approval makes it right *for her*. Thus, in the previous example, giving famine aid is not right and wrong in the same respect—it is right for Smith, and wrong for Jones. This is the strategy of relativizing moral judgments to their speakers.

This move really can solve the problem of contradiction. But the strategy has its costs. It renders subjectivism **incapable of explaining the point or existence of moral disagreement**. Think again of the debate about famine relief. If all Smith is saying is that she herself approves of it, and if all Jones is saying is that he doesn't, then Smith and Jones don't really disagree with one another. Further, we lose incentive to continue moral conversation, because moral truth just consists in reports of personal feelings.

It may appear that Smith and Jones, in their debate about famine relief, are trying to get at the truth, trying to discover what is *really* right. But if we relativize judgments to their speakers, this appearance is misleading. There can be no genuine disagreement about where truth lies, since it lies in the eyes of the beholder. If subjectivism is right, everyone's views are true, so long as they are sincerely expressed. Thus ethical disagreement could focus only on whether the interlocutors actually believe what they say they do. Disagreement cannot focus on whether famine relief is *really* right—right in a non-relative, objective sense—because (according to subjectivism) famine relief *cannot be* really right (or wrong). Subjectivism leaves us with an entirely unrecognizable picture of moral disagreement.

A final concern. If subjectivism is true, then **our moral views are arbitrary.** There is no better reason to adopt one ethical view over another. Subjectivism claims that moral views are true because one believes them; one does not believe them because they are true. Moral views are justified to the extent that they are believed, so any basis whatever (other than false belief) will confer plausibility. This allows us to see two ways in which subjectivism entails the arbitrariness of ethical views. First, one's moral outlook may be justified even if one has no reason at all that supports it—that one believes it is sufficient to make it true. In a second kind of case, one does possess

reasons that support one's moral views. But the reasons that support a moral belief may fail entirely to move other informed, rational, good-willed people. In this sense, one's views are arbitrary, because they are supported by reasons that could, with complete propriety, be rejected by any and all other rational people.

MOTIVATIONS FOR META-ETHICAL SUBJECTIVISM

Most people will find at least some of these implications troubling. For those who do, yet still balk at the idea of objectivity in ethics, meta-ethical subjectivism is a natural path to pursue. This brand of subjectivism denies that moral judgments can be true or false. They are neither true nor false because they are not attempting to describe anything. There are no facts that they might accurately capture—not even facts about our own feelings, or society's agreements. According to meta-ethical subjectivism, the purpose of moral judgment is not to *report* personal or social attitudes, but rather to *express* one's feelings or *voice* one's commitments.

On this view, moral judgments are closely analogous to commands and emotional responses. Though moral judgments look like factual judgments—"infanticide is wrong" has the same grammatical structure as straightforward descriptive judgments ("space is curved," "grass is green")—this appearance is misleading. To say that infanticide is wrong, for instance, is either to give vent to a visceral dislike of infanticide, or to issue a command that prohibits infanticide. On the first line, the moral judgment is equivalent to "Infanticide? Boo! Yuck!" On the second view, the moral judgment reduces to something like "Don't commit infanticide!" On either view, moral judgments cannot be true or false, since they don't purport to describe anything. Emotive ventings ("Spinach? Blech!") aren't true or false. Commands ("Rise and shine!") aren't true or false. According to meta-ethical subjectivists, because moral judgments are effectively utterances of either sort, they aren't true or false, either. Unlike normative subjectivism, which sees moral judgments as reports of personal feelings, and so usually true, metaethical subjectivism denies that such judgments are ever true (or false).

The distinction between normative and metaethical subjectivism may seem a minor one, a picayune footnote introduced by philosophers to impress one another and oppress their students. But the distinction is actually quite important. As we'll see, we can solve many of the problems that beset normative subjectivism if we deny that moral judgments can be true or false. Whether all of the problems disappear remains to be seen.

Let us begin our assessment of meta-ethical subjectivism by considering some of the most important arguments that have been advanced on its behalf.

A. The Argument from Moral Motivation

The great Scottish philosopher David Hume was no fan of ethical objectivism. One of the many arguments he offered against it began with what he took to be a striking difference between moral judgments and factual ones. Hume thought that one mark of moral judgment was its capacity to motivate people. A person who sincerely thinks that something is good will be really moved to pursue it; someone who thinks an action genuinely obligatory is thereby motivated to perform it. Nothing like this could be claimed of factual judgments.

Here is the argument put more succinctly:

1. Every moral judgment motivates all by itself.
2. Factual judgments cannot motivate all by themselves.
3. Therefore moral judgments are not factual judgments.

Premise (1) tells us that moral judgments are intrinsically motivational—to judge an action right is to be motivated to perform it. To avoid misunderstanding, note that one can be motivated to perform an action and still fail to do it. Motivations can be overridden; people can be weakwilled, for instance. Still, Hume claims that we cannot genuinely make a moral judgment unless we are motivated *to some extent* to comply with it.

This is what distinguishes moral judgments from factual judgments. We may believe all sorts of mathematical, chemical, or geographical propositions without being moved in the slightest. And when we are moved by factual judgments, it is only because of some accompanying desire that we happen to have. The factual judgments do not motivate all by themselves. Even a very likely candidate—"stepping out in front of that bus will surely kill you"—does not motivate all by itself. We cannot know how or whether a factual judgment will move us unless we also know which desires are associated with the judgment; whether, in this case, we want to commit suicide or to remain alive. Moral judgments intrinsically motivate. Factual judgments do not. Therefore moral judgments are not factual ones.

This is a classic of ethical argumentation. The second premise is widely, if not universally, accepted. The first premise, though, has attracted significant opposition, primarily from those who think that moral claims are a species of factual claims. On this line, moral judgments, like factual judgments, need to be supplemented by a desire before people will be motivated to act on them. Moral judgments do not motivate all by themselves. In order to generate motivation, some associated moral desire (e.g., to be beneficent or just) must be present. Those who reject premise (1) believe that it is possible for some people, known as amoralists, to lack moral desires. Amoralists are those who sincerely make moral judgments but entirely fail to be moved by them. These might be people who are depressed, rebellious, alienated, or just plain evil. If amoralists can exist, then premise (1) of the argument from moral motivation is false.

It might seem that this is an easy question to resolve. We can see that amoralists may exist just by imagining their possibility. We can readily imagine someone saying that some particular action is right, all the while remaining perfectly indifferent. The difficulty here is that our imagination is not a reliable indicator of genuine possibilities. People (claim to) imagine the possibility of a square circle, or a number that is both odd and even, but these things cannot exist. Likewise, even if we can imagine the amoralist, this isn't sufficient to show that such persons can exist. Premise (1) may be true after all.

Meta-ethical subjectivists will analyze moral judgments as expressions of emotion; since emotions are intrinsically motivating, moral judgments are intrinsically motivating, too. This is why subjectivists endorse premise (1) of the argument from moral motivation. If amoralists really can exist, then moral judgments are not intrinsically motivating, and hence not necessarily expressions of emotion. If they are not intrinsically motivating, then moral judgments might be factual judgments after all. The plausibility of meta-ethical subjectivism thus depends on whether the amoralist is a genuine possibility. That, unfortunately, is an issue that can't be briefly resolved. Hume's classic argument may be sound. But one would need to undertake a great deal of further investigation before having any warranted confidence one way or the other.

B. The Argument from Economy

Most philosophers believe that when one is comparing the plausibility of competing theories, we should, if all other things are equal, give the nod to the simpler, more economical theory. Theory A is more economical than theory B if A can explain all that B can, but with fewer assumptions. Copernicus' theory of elliptical orbit was simpler than Ptolemy's, and for this reason ultimately came to be viewed as more plausible. The reason scientists don't refer to hexes, spells, ghosts, or demons in their theories is because they can explain everything they need to explain without invoking such things. Supernatural phenomena are *superfluous;* they're added baggage, unnecessary extras that simpler theories can do without.

In a similar vein, meta-ethical subjectivists claim superiority for their view because their assumptions about what there is in the world are sparer than objectivism's. Subjectivists have an essentially scientific view of what the world consists of. The world contains physical things, and

physical forces that work on them. Morality is a complex human creation; when we ask what is in the world, *really,* no mention of moral facts need be made. We can explain all of the goings-on of this world, including all human activities—why people act as they do, say the things they do, think as they do—without invoking anything like a "moral fact."

This method of doing away with moral facts bears a striking resemblance to accounts that seek to undermine traditional religion. The Judaeo-Christian god is thought by many to be superfluous—we can explain all of the goings-on of our world without supposing that there is something further, something more (God) who must be put in the picture. As science progresses, we discover that the natural events we once attributed to God (or to the gods) can be explained solely in terms of the natural workings of the natural world. In the same way, many philosophers and neuroscientists have expressed doubt about the existence of a soul, claiming that it is more economical simply to posit the existence of the brain and the nervous system to explain all of our behavior. Without the brain and nervous system, we can't explain any conscious behavior. With it, we can explain all we need to explain. The notion of a soul does no explanatory work (or so it is alleged). A simpler, better theory would thus do without it.

Subjectivists take this strategy and apply it to ethics. What would moral facts be needed to explain? Subjectivists usually take this to be a rhetorical question. We can explain everything in the world by referring to scientific facts, including facts about human psychology. But objectivists have supplied answers. They claim that we can explain lots of things that need explaining by citing moral facts. We explain why Hitler did what he did by citing his *evil nature.* We explain why people opposed apartheid by citing its *injustice.* We explain the success of a con man by reference to his *duplicitous character.* These all seem to be moral facts. The question, of course, is whether we can explain the beliefs and actions mentioned in these examples without citing the moral facts themselves.

For instance, subjectivists will claim that we don't have to suppose that there really is some moral fact of injustice existing out there, somewhere, in order to explain why so many people protested against the apartheid regime. Instead, we simply need to mention the nonmoral facts about differential treatment that obtained in South Africa, and combine these facts with further non-moral, psychological facts, facts about what people believed. Citizens believed that there was grave injustice, they felt disgusted by the regime, and these beliefs and feelings, combined with various social, cultural, and economic facts, generated the protests that contributed to undermining apartheid society. This explanation makes no mention of any moral facts—just moral judgments and feelings, plus the social scientific facts just alluded to.

This subjectivist strategy is precisely the same sort of strategy we use to debunk metaphysical commitments in other areas. We can cite facts about the Salem society of 300 years ago, combined with people's beliefs and feelings about witches, to explain why so many people were hanged. We don't need to suppose that there really were witches in order to explain everything that needs explaining. Likewise, it is claimed, we don't need to assume the existence of moral facts in order to explain everything in the world that requires explanation.

If we compare the world that scientists depict with that same world, plus a further realm of moral facts, it is easy to see which view is simpler. But simplicity is not everything. The simpler theory must also be sufficiently explanatory. The question in ethics, as in theology and in the philosophy of mind, is whether we really can explain all that needs explaining with the sparer, more economical theories. As with matters of moral motivation, the issue of economy remains extremely controversial, with objectivists arguing that we do need moral facts to explain our practices, and subjectivists charging that moral facts are superfluous. Unsurprisingly, then, we must satisfy ourselves with only a sketch of the competing positions. Getting beyond the preliminaries requires a deeper dip into the philosophical waters than we can undertake here.

C. The Argument from Oddness

Meta-ethical subjectivists urge another reason for abandoning belief in objective moral facts. Suppose, with objectivism, that moral judgments are true, and true quite independently of what we happen to think of them. They are true, when they are, because they accurately report objective moral facts. But what could such things be? We readily grant that geologists and chemists, physicists and astronomers deal in objective truth, because we believe that their findings are constrained by the physical world whose features exist independently of whether anyone recognizes them. Botanical facts are facts about plants; geological facts are facts about rocks. In botany and geology, evidence is supplied by three-dimensional, tangible, physical stuff. We can taste it, smell it, touch it, and see it. We can't taste wrongness or hear rightness. Moral facts, if they were to exist, would have to be quite odd sorts of things, certainly nothing at all like the kinds of phenomena studied by recognized factual disciplines.

Objectivists typically reply, with some force, that they need not be committed to any ghostly realm of moral facts. Everyone agrees that there are moral rules. Moral facts are simply applications of those rules. If a moral rule prohibits infanticide, and Smith commits infanticide, then it is a moral fact that what he did was wrong. Nothing mysterious so far. But subjectivists will claim that the relevant question has simply been pushed back a step. Now we must ask what *justifies* or *validates the moral rule* against adultery (or promise-breaking, lying, killing, etc.). What is it that makes a moral rule (objectively) true?

As a first step in exploring possibilities, we should consider rules in nonmoral contexts and ask what makes them true. Rules of sports or etiquette are true, if they are, only because certain people believe they are. If no one endorsed the three strikes rule in baseball, or the ban on public nosepicking, then there simply would not be any such rules. Such rules are therefore subjective in the relevant sense.

On the other hand, most people believe that the laws of chemistry, geology, astronomy, and physics are true because of the way the world is. Our best thoughts in these disciplines track reality, as opposed to creating it. If moral rules are like scientific laws, however, then presumably they would have to be true in virtue of the operations of the physical world. This sounds very strange. The movement of protons makes certain physical laws true; the behavior of molecules validates certain chemical laws; the interactions of cells makes true particular laws of biology. But which operations of which physical things make moral rules true? The moral prohibition on torture does not seem to be vindicated by citing the workings of the physical world.

There are two standard moves for ethical objectivists to make at this point. The first strategy—**ethical naturalism**—claims that, despite appearances, moral facts really are natural, scientific facts. Whether something is right or wrong can be verified in just the same way that scientific hypotheses can be. Prominent examples of naturalism include the claims that actions are morally right if and only if they maximize pleasure, that things are good just because they are desired, and that exchanges are just if and only if all parties to the transfer have agreed to abide by its terms.

I don't want to take a stand on the success of these views. What is important for our purposes is that if these claims (or others like them) are true, then all it takes is ordinary empirical investigation to determine whether actions are right, good, or just. There doesn't seem to be anything especially weird or mysterious about pleasure, desire, or agreements. If moral facts consist of just these sorts of humdrum things, then moral facts are not at all strange.

Subjectivists acknowledge this. But they remain skeptical. Naturalists need to supply *plausible* connections that link moral and naturalistic (i.e., nonmoral) features. But does rightness really consist in maximizing happiness? Is something good just because it is desired? Do all mutual agreements really yield justice? After

thorough scrutiny, most philosophers have rejected these views. Now, objectivists needn't abandon hope—they may try to defend these theories in the face of criticisms, or they make seek better, improved naturalistic theories. There is no way to entirely discount the possibility that with greater application and ingenuity, objectivists may arrive at satisfactory naturalistic accounts of moral features. But the history of such efforts does not inspire confidence.

Try it yourself: an act is morally right if and only if_____. What fills in the blank is called an *analysis*. Naturalists disagree among themselves about which analyses are best. Naturalists are unified, however, in believing that the blank can ultimately be filled in naturalistically, that is, without the use of any moral terms. A classic case is that of the standard utilitarian doctrine cited above, which claims that an action is morally right if and only if it maximizes pleasure. The main benefit of such a theory is that it makes determining the rightness of actions a straightforward affair. Of course it won't, as a practical matter, always be easy to determine whether pleasure is maximized. But in principle, at least, we can see a clear path to justifying our moral claims and providing guidance for action.

Ethical nonnaturalists believe that there are no true naturalistic analyses of moral terms. For nonnaturalists, moral judgments cannot be empirically verified, and so there is a sharp disanalogy between ethics and science. Some nonnaturalists claim that we cannot give any analysis at all of moral terms—the above blank simply can't be filled in. The notion of goodness, for instance, may simply be basic, a fundamental term used to define other terms but not itself capable of definition. Alternatively, some nonnaturalists believe that we can define moral terms, but only if we employ other moral terms to do so. So, for instance, we might define morally right action as that which is reasonable and proper.

The basic worry for nonnaturalism is that if we abandon empirical verification in ethics, it is not easy to see how we could verify or justify moral claims at all. If goodness is indefinable, or definable only by use of other moral terms which themselves are indefinable, how are we to know what is good and bad, right and wrong? If I am puzzled about whether an action is morally right, I'm likely to be equally puzzled about whether it is reasonable and proper. And things are still worse if we claim that goodness or rightness are basic and indefinable. For then we've no criteria at all to assist us in discovering truth in ethics.

In facing this problem, nonnaturalists have usually fallen back on the idea that we somehow intuit what is right and wrong. Intuition involves an immediate grasp or apprehension of the truth of some proposition. In ethics, the claim would be that we just intuit the truth that pain is bad, that keeping promises is good, that disloyalty is wrong, etc. The problem, of course, is that different people will have different intuitions about what is right and good and just, and intuitionism doesn't seem to have the resources for rationally adjudicating these disputes. If we deny that there are any definitions of moral terms, then there will be no criteria at all for arbitrating ethical disagreement. If we allow that there are such definitions, but insist that they contain moral terms, then the disagreements will simply be replicated in disputes about whether the defining moral terms (e.g., "reasonable," "proper") apply.

So the objectivist is faced with a dilemma: Either (i) opt for ethical naturalism, in which case we must come up with some plausible naturalistic analyses, or (ii) opt for ethical nonnaturalism, in which case we need to explain how it is possible to acquire knowledge of objective ethical facts. The subjectivist claims that options (i) and (ii) are so fraught with difficulties that it is best to abandon the commitment to ethical objectivity that motivated their development.

IMPLICATIONS OF META-ETHICAL SUBJECTIVISM

In addition to the powerful motivating arguments we have just discussed, meta-ethical subjectivism appeals because of its ability to handle several of the problems that beset normative subjectivism. Specifically, the worry about moral infallibility is bypassed, because this brand of subjectivism denies that anyone can ever possess moral truth, much less possess it in all instances. The problem of contradiction is likewise avoided. Contradictions arise when a proposition is alleged to be both true and false. If meta-ethical subjectivism is true, moral judgments are *neither* true *nor* false. Thus contradictions never arise. Finally, the existence and point of moral disagreement is preserved. According to meta-ethical subjectivism, ethical disagreements are disagreements in attitude. People on opposite sides of the abortion debate, for instance, have clashing attitudes toward abortion. There is real disagreement—emotional disagreement. Because they each may feel very strongly about the issue, the point of such debate is to convince others to share their view, and so act in ways they favor. This seems to account for a great deal of what goes on in ethical disagreement.

Still, meta-ethical subjectivism cannot avoid the remaining two implications of its normative cousin. Both brands of subjectivism generate a widespread moral equivalence, though for different reasons. Normative subjectivism makes each person an equally good arbiter of moral truth. Meta-ethical subjectivism denies that there is any moral truth. This denial implies that no one is superior to another at identifying what is right, or fine, or good. And no one is inferior, either. Moral judgments are expressions of taste, and a taste for cruelty or sadism is not worse (or better) than one for compassion and honesty. *De gustibus non est disputandum.*

Meta-ethical subjectivism also suffers from the problem of arbitrariness. If our ethical attachments are ultimately entirely up to us, with no supporting reasons needed, and no rationally compelling ones available, then our moral views are arbitrary. We have no better reason to support the ideology of Gandhi than of Pol Pot. Of course, each person actually will take a side. But our preferences in this regard are not rationally or ethically mandated. There is nothing necessarily irrational, wrong, or inappropriate about those whose fundamental aims differ from ours, even if those aims require for their satisfaction a policy of intimidation and torture.

Meta-ethical subjectivism also has to explain why all of us do employ non-subjectivist language in expressing our ethical outlooks. We frequently take our moral views to be *true,* and say as much in discussions with others. Our ethical conversations seem to be governed by a background assumption that, at least sometimes, those who disagree with us are *in error* and have *false beliefs.* Those with specially bad or confused impulses often come in for criticism as *irrational.* At the extreme, we may say of some such people that they or their views are *illogical.* Being illogical seems to involve contradiction, which (as we've seen) requires the notions of truth and falsity. Because meta-ethical subjectivism abandons these notions, it has difficulty explaining what illogical ethical views could amount to. The flip side is that these subjectivists also have difficulty explaining what logical ethical views amount to. A logical position is one in which one's views, if true, logically entail a true conclusion. But if we abandon the notion of truth in ethics, we seem to take the notion of logic with it.

Finally, if meta-ethical subjectivism is true, we must abandon our aspirations for moral knowledge. Knowledge presupposes truth. Though we often make claims to moral knowledge, such as knowing that genocide or racism is wrong, such claims must be merely metaphorical or false. There is no moral wisdom, at least none that comes from having the sort of ethical sensibility that issues in true moral judgments. Subjectivists usually counter that ethical knowledge is a matter of *knowing how* to live, rather than *knowing that* something or other is morally right. But what would it be to know how to live, if any consistent way of life was just as good as another? If we could not know *that* certain things were valuable, good, or virtuous, how could we be successful at knowing *how* to live? This is a challenge that subjectivists have yet to fully meet.

Conclusion

In many ways, the paces we've been put through here are entirely typical of philosophical discussion. Perhaps most typical is the state of play at the end of the day. Rarely do philosophers have knockdown arguments that can eliminate a philosophical position from contention. Philosophical evaluation is ordinarily a matter of weighing the pros and cons of competing theories, and tentatively opting for one view over another. Justifying a philosophical view requires advancing positive arguments on its behalf, and deflecting criticisms that detractors have identified. One needn't worry about getting bored. There will always be detractors. Criticisms are never in short supply.

Thus when we come to assess the merits of ethical subjectivism, in either of its major forms, we are engaged in a process of judgment. We examine the arguments in support of the theory, develop them as best we can, and then scrutinize the implications of adoption. Whether we can live with the implications depends on one's assessment of the theory's attractions, and those of its competitors. There is no neat, simple method for discharging this task. Whether we can live with moral equivalence, arbitrariness, and the impossibility of moral knowledge depends on whether we can do better elsewhere. And *that* depends on how well ethical objectivists can respond to the motivating arguments of previous sections. Subjectivism's prospects may be bright (or dim). But we can measure its incandescence only after a very great deal of further philosophical labor.[1]

NOTE

1. I undertake some of this labor in *Whatever Happened to Good and Evil?* (Oxford University Press, 2003), an introductory book devoted to assessing the plausibility of ethical subjectivism and objectivism.

2.2 Trying Out One's New Sword

MARY MIDGLEY

Mary Midgley, now retired from the University of Newcastle-upon-Tyne, has written widely on a variety of issues regarding ethical theory, environmental ethics, and the relation between science and religion.

All of us are, more or less, in trouble today about trying to understand cultures strange to us. We hear constantly of alien customs. We see changes in our lifetime which would have astonished our parents. I want to discuss here one very short way of dealing with this difficulty, a drastic way which many people now theoretically favour. It consists in simply denying that we can ever understand any culture except our own well enough to make judgements about it. Those who recommend this hold that the world is sharply divided into separate societies, sealed units, each with its own system of thought. They feel that the respect and tolerance due from one system to another forbids us ever to take up a critical position to any other culture. Moral judgement, they suggest, is a kind of coinage valid only in its country of origin.

I shall call this position "moral isolationism". I shall suggest that it is certainly not forced upon us, and indeed that it makes no sense at all. People usually take it up because they think it is a respectful attitude to other cultures. In fact, however, it is not respectful. Nobody can respect what is entirely unintelligible to them. To respect someone, we have to know enough about him to make a *favourable* judgement, however general and tentative. And we do understand people in other cultures to this extent. Otherwise a great mass of our most valuable thinking would be paralysed.

To show this, I shall take a remote example, because we shall probably find it easier to think calmly about it than we should with a contemporary one, such as female circumcision in Africa or the Chinese Cultural Revolution. The principles involved will still be the same. My example is this. There is, it seems, a verb in classical Japanese which means "to try out one's new sword on a chance wayfarer". (The word is *tsujigiri*, literally "crossroads-cut".) A samurai sword had to be tried out because, if it was to work properly, it had to slice through someone at a single blow, from the shoulder to the opposite flank. Otherwise, the warrior bungled his stroke. This could injure his honour, offend his ancestors, and even let down his emperor. So tests were needed, and wayfarers had to be expended. Any wayfarer would do—provided, of course, that he was not another Samurai. Scientists will recognize a familiar problem about the rights of experimental subjects.

Now when we hear of a custom like this, we may well reflect that we simply do not understand it; and therefore are not qualified to criticize it at all, because we are not members of that culture. But we are not members of any other culture either, except our own. So we extend the principle to cover all extraneous cultures, and we seem therefore to be moral isolationists. But this is, as we shall see, an impossible position. Let us ask what it would involve.

We must ask first: Does the isolating barrier work both ways? Are people in other cultures equally unable to criticize *us*? This question struck me sharply when I read a remark in *The*

Guardian by an anthropologist about a South American Indian who had been taken into a Brazilian town for an operation, which saved his life. When he came back to his village, he made several highly critical remarks about the white Brazilians' way of life. They may very well have been justified. But the interesting point was that the anthropologist called these remarks "a damning indictment of Western civilization." Now the Indian had been in that town about two weeks. Was he in a position to deliver a damning indictment? Would we ourselves be qualified to deliver such an indictment on the Samurai, provided we could spend two weeks in ancient Japan? What do we really think about this?

My own impression is that we believe that outsiders can, in principle, deliver perfectly good indictments—only, it usually takes more than two weeks to make them damning. Understanding has degrees. It is not a slapdash yes-or-no matter. Intelligent outsiders can progress in it, and in some ways will be at an advantage over the locals. But if this is so, it must clearly apply to ourselves as much as anybody else.

Our next question is this: Does the isolating barrier between cultures block praise as well as blame? If I want to say that the Samurai culture has many virtues, or to praise the South American Indians, am I prevented from doing *that* by my outside status? Now, we certainly do need to praise other societies in this way. But it is hardly possible that we could praise them effectively if we could not, in principle, criticize them. Our praise would be worthless if it rested on no definite grounds, if it did not flow from some understanding. Certainly we may need to praise things which we do not *fully* understand. We say "there's something very good here, but I can't quite make out what it is yet". This happens when we want to learn from strangers. And we can learn from strangers. But to do this we have to distinguish between those strangers who are worth learning from and those who are not. Can we then judge which is which?

This brings us to our third question: What is involved in judging? Now plainly there is no

question here of sitting on a bench in a red robe and sentencing people. Judging simply means forming an opinion, and expressing it if it is called for. Is there anything wrong about this? Naturally, we ought to avoid forming—and expressing—*crude* opinions, like that of a simple-minded missionary, who might dismiss the whole Samurai culture as entirely bad, because non-Christian. But this is a different objection. The trouble with crude opinions is that they are crude, whoever forms them, not that they are formed by the wrong people. Anthropologists, after all, are outsiders quite as much as missionaries. Moral isolationism forbids us to form *any* opinions on these matters. Its ground for doing so is that we don't understand them. But there is much that we don't understand in our own culture too. This brings us to our last question: If we can't judge other cultures, can we really judge our own? Our efforts to do so will be much damaged if we are really deprived of our opinions about other societies, because these provide the range of comparison, the spectrum of alternatives against which we set what we want to understand. We would have to stop using the mirror which anthropology so helpfully holds up to us.

In short, moral isolationism would lay down a general ban on moral reasoning. Essentially, this is the programme of immoralism, and it carries a distressing logical difficulty. Immoralists like Nietzsche are actually just a rather specialized sect of moralists. They can no more afford to put moralizing out of business than smugglers can afford to abolish customs regulations. The power of moral judgement is, in fact, not a luxury, not a perverse indulgence of the self-righteous. It is a necessity. When we judge something to be bad or good, better or worse than something else, we are taking it as an example to aim at or avoid. Without opinions of this sort, we would have no framework of comparison for our own policy, no chance of profiting by other people's insights or mistakes. In this vacuum, we could form no judgements on our own actions.

Now it would be odd if Homo sapiens had really got himself into a position as bad as this—a position where his main evolutionary asset, his brain, was so little use to him. None of us is going to accept this sceptical diagnosis. We cannot do so because our inolvement in moral iso-lationism does not flow from apathy, but from a rather acute concern about human hypocrisy and other forms of wickedness. But we polarize that concern around a few selected moral truths. We are rightly angry with those who despise, oppress or steamroll other cultures. We think that doing these things is actually *wrong*. But this is itself a moral judgement. We could not condemn op-pression and insolence if we thought that all our condemnation were just a trivial local quirk of our own culture. We could still less do it if we tried to stop judging altogether.

Real moral scepticism, in fact, could lead only to inaction, to our losing all interest in moral questions, most of all in those which con-cern other societies. When we discuss these things, it becomes instantly clear how far we are from doing this. Suppose, for instance, that I criticize the bisecting Samurai, that I say his behaviour is brutal. What will usually happen next is that someone will protest, will say that I have no right to make criticisms like that of an-other culture. But it is most unlikely that he will use this move to end the discussion of the sub-ject. Instead, he will justify the Samurai. He will try to fill in the background, to make me under-stand the custom, by explaining the exalted ideals of discipline and devotion which produced it. He will probably talk of the lower value which the ancient Japanese placed on individual life generally. He may well suggest that this is a healthier attitude than our own obsession with security. He may add, too, that the wayfarers did not seriously mind being bisected, that in princi-ple they accepted the whole arrangement.

Now an objector who talks like this is imply-ing that it *is* possible to understand alien cus-toms. That is just what he is trying to make me do. And he implies, too, that if I do succeed in understanding them, I shall do something better than giving up judging them. He expects me to change my present judgement to a truer one—namely, one that is favourable. And the stan-dards I must use to do this cannot just be Samu-rai standards. They have to be ones current in my own culture. Ideals like discipline and devo-tion will not move anybody unless he himself accepts them. As it happens, neither discipline nor devotion is very popular in the West at pres-ent. Anyone who appeals to them may well have to do some more arguing to make *them* accept-able, before he can use them to explain the Samurai. But if he does succeed here, he will have persuaded us, not just that there was some-thing to be said for them in ancient Japan, but that there would be here as well.

Isolating barriers simply cannot arise here. If we accept something as a serious moral truth about one culture, we can't refuse to apply it—in however different an outward form—to other cultures as well, wherever circumstances admit it. If we refuse to do this, we just are not taking the other culture seriously. This becomes clear if we look at the last argument used by my objector—that of justification by consent of the victim. It is suggested that sudden bisection is quite in order, *provided* that it takes place between consenting adults. I cannot now discuss how conclusive this justification is. What I am pointing out is simply that it can only work if we believe that *consent* can make such a transaction respectable—and this is a thoroughly modern and Western idea. It would probably never occur to a Samurai; if it did, it would surprise him very much. It is *our* standard. In applying it, too, we are likely to make another typically Western demand. We shall ask for good factual evidence that the way-farers actually do have this rather surprising taste —that they are really willing to be bisected. In applying Western standards in this way, we are not being confused or irrelevant. We are ask-ing the questions which arise *from where we stand*, questions which we can see the sense of. We do this because asking questions which you can't see the sense of is humbug. Certainly we can extend our questioning by imaginative effort. We can come to understand other socie-ties better. By doing so, we may make their questions our own, or we may see that they are really forms of the questions which we are asking already. This is not impossible. It is just very hard work. The obstacles which often prevent it are simply those of ordinary ignorance, laziness, and prejudice.

If there were really an isolating barrier, of course, our own culture could never have been formed. It is no sealed box, but a fertile jungle of different influences—Greek, Jewish, Roman, Norse, Celtic and so forth, into which further influences are still pouring—American, Indian, Japanese, Jamaican, you name it. The moral isolationist's picture of separate unmixable cultures is quite unreal. People who talk about British history usually stress the value of this fertilizing mix, no doubt rightly. But this is not just an odd fact about Britain. Except for the very smallest and most remote, all cultures are formed out of many streams. All have the problem of digesting and assimilating things which, at the start, they do not understand. All have the choice of learning something from this challenge, or, alternatively, of refusing to learn, and fighting it mindlessly instead.

This universal predicament has been obscured by the fact that anthropologists used to concentrate largely on very small and remote cultures, which did not seem to have this problem. These tiny societies, which had often forgotten their own history, made neat, self-contained subjects for study. No doubt it was valuable to emphasize their remoteness, their extreme strangeness, their independence of our cultural tradition. This emphasis was, I think, the root of moral isolationism. But, as the tribal studies themselves showed, even there the anthropologists were able to interpret what they saw and make judgements—often favourable—about the tribesmen. And the tribesmen, too, were quite equal to making judgements about the anthropologists—and about the tourists and Coca-Cola salesmen who followed them. Both sets of judgements, no doubt, were somewhat hasty, both have been refined in the light of further experience. A similar transaction between us and the Samurai might take even longer. But that is no reason at all for deeming it impossible. Morally as well as physically, there is only one world, and we all have to live in it.

2.3 Virtue and the Good Life

ARISTOTLE

Aristotle (382–322 BCE) is, in the minds of many, the greatest philosopher who ever lived. He was a student of Plato, and in turn was tutor to Alexander the Great. In addition to his pathbreaking contributions to metaphysics, logic, ethics, rhetoric, and the philosophy of mind, he was also the preeminent scientist of his day.

[An Account of the Human Good]

§1 But let us return once again to the good we are looking for, and consider just what it could be. For it is apparently one thing in one action or craft, and another thing in another; for it is one thing in medicine, another in generalship, and so on for the rest. What, then, is the good of each action or craft? Surely it is that for the sake of

From Aristotle, *Nicomachean Ethics*, translated by Terence Irwin, 2nd ed. (Indianapolis: Hackett Publishing Company, 2000), pp. 7–12, 16–25. Reprinted by permission of Hackett Publishing Company, Inc. All rights reserved.

which the other things are done; in medicine this is health, in generalship victory, in house-building a house, in another case something else, but in every action and decision it is the end, since it is for the sake of the end that everyone does the other actions. And so, if there is some end of everything achievable in action, the good achievable in action will be this end; if there are more ends than one, [the good achievable in action] will be these ends.

§2 Our argument, then, has followed a different route to reach the same conclusion. But we must try to make this still more perspicuous. §3 Since there are apparently many ends, and we choose some of them (for instance, wealth, flutes, and, in general, instruments) because of something else, it is clear that not all ends are complete. But the best good is apparently something complete. And so, if only one end is complete, the good we are looking for will be this end; if more ends than one are complete, it will be the most complete end of these.

§4 We say that an end pursued in its own right is more complete than an end pursued because of something else, and that an end that is never choiceworthy because of something else is more complete than ends that are choiceworthy both in their own right and because of this end. Hence an end that is always choiceworthy in its own right, never because of something else, is complete without qualification.

§5 Now happiness, more than anything else, seems complete without qualification. For we always choose it because of itself, never because of something else. Honor, pleasure, understanding, and every virtue we certainly choose because of themselves, since we would choose each of them even if it had no further result; but we also choose them for the sake of happiness, supposing that through them we shall be happy. Happiness, by contrast, no one ever chooses for their sake, or for the sake of anything else at all.

§6 The same conclusion [that happiness is complete] also appears to follow from self-sufficiency. For the complete good seems to be self-sufficient. What we count as self-sufficient is not what suffices for a solitary person by himself, living an isolated life, but what suffices also for parents, children, wife, and, in general, for friends and fellow citizens, since a human being is a naturally political [animal]. §7 Here, however, we must impose some limit; for if we extend the good to parents' parents and children's children and to friends of friends, we shall go on without limit; but we must examine this another time. Anyhow, we regard something as self-sufficient when all by itself it makes a life choiceworthy and lacking nothing; and that is what we think happiness does.

§8 Moreover, we think happiness is most choiceworthy of all goods, [since] it is not counted as one good among many. [If it were] counted as one among many, then, clearly, we think it would be more choiceworthy if the smallest of goods were added; for the good that is added becomes an extra quantity of goods, and the larger of two goods is always more choiceworthy. Happiness, then, is apparently something complete and self-sufficient, since it is the end of the things achievable in action.

§9 But presumably the remark that the best good is happiness is apparently something [generally] agreed, and we still need a clearer statement of what the best good is. §10 Perhaps, then, we shall find this if we first grasp the function of a human being. For just as the good, i.e., [doing] well, for a flautist, a sculptor, and every craftsman, and, in general, for whatever has a function and [characteristic] action, seems to depend on its function, the same seems to be true for a human being, if a human being has some function.

§11 Then do the carpenter and the leather worker have their functions and actions, but has a human being no function? Is he by nature idle, without any function? Or, just as eye, hand, foot, and, in general, every [bodily] part apparently has its function, may we likewise ascribe to a human being some function apart from all of these?

§12 What, then, could this be? For living is apparently shared with plants, but what we are looking for is the special function of a human being; hence we should set aside the life of nutrition and growth. The life next in order is some sort of life of sense perception; but this too is apparently shared with horse, ox, and every animal.

§13 The remaining possibility, then, is some sort of life of action of the [part of the soul] that has reason. One [part] of it has reason as obeying reason; the other has it as itself having reason and thinking. Moreover, life is also spoken of in two ways [as capacity and as activity], and we must take [a human being's special function to be] life as activity, since this seems to be called life more fully. We have found, then, that the human function is activity of the soul in accord with reason or requiring reason.

§14 Now we say that the function of a [kind of thing]—of a harpist, for instance—is the same in kind as the function of an excellent individual of the kind—of an excellent harpist, for instance. And the same is true without qualification in every case, if we add to the function the superior achievement in accord with the virtue; for the function of a harpist is to play the harp, and the function of a good harpist is to play it well. Moreover, we take the human function to be a certain kind of life, and take this life to be activity and actions of the soul that involve reason; hence the function of the excellent man is to do this well and finely.

§15 Now each function is completed well by being completed in accord with the virtue proper [to that kind of thing]. And so the human good proves to be activity of the soul in accord with virtue, and indeed with the best and most complete virtue, if there are more virtues than one. §16 Moreover, it must be in a complete life. For one swallow does not make a spring, nor does one day; nor, similarly, does one day or a short time make us blessed and happy.

§17 This, then, is a sketch of the good; for, presumably, we must draw the outline first, and fill it in later. If the sketch is good, anyone, it seems, can advance and articulate it, and in such cases time discovers more, or is a good partner in discovery. That is also how the crafts have improved, since anyone can add what is lacking [in the outline].

§18 We must also remember our previous remarks, so that we do not look for the same degree of exactness in all areas, but the degree that accords with a given subject matter and is proper to a given line of inquiry. §19 For the carpenter's and the geometer's inquiries about the right angle are different also; the carpenter restricts himself to what helps his work, but the geometer inquires into what, or what sort of thing, the right angle is, since he studies the truth. We must do the same, then, in other areas too, [seeking the proper degree of exactness], so that digressions do not overwhelm our main task.

§20 Nor should we make the same demand for an explanation in all cases. On the contrary, in some cases it is enough to prove rightly that [something is true, without also explaining why it is true]. This is so, for instance, with principles, where the fact that [something is true] is the first thing, that is to say, the principle.

§21 Some principles are studied by means of induction, some by means of perception, some by means of some sort of habituation, and others by other means. §22 In each case we should try to find them out by means suited to their nature, and work hard to define them rightly. §23 For they carry great weight for what follows; for the principle seems to be more than half the whole, and makes evident the answer to many of our questions.

[Defense of the Account of the Good]

§1 We should examine the principle, however, not only from the conclusion and premises [of a deduction], but also from what is said about it; for all the facts harmonize with a true account, whereas the truth soon clashes with a false one.

§2 Goods are divided, then, into three types, some called external, some goods of the soul, others goods of the body. We say that the goods of the soul are goods most fully, and more than the others, and we take actions and activities of the soul to be [goods] of the soul. And so our account [of the good] is right, to judge by this belief anyhow—and it is an ancient belief, and accepted by philosophers.

§3 Our account is also correct in saying that some sort of actions and activities are the end; for in that way the end turns out to be a good of the soul, not an external good.

§4 The belief that the happy person lives well and does well also agrees with our account, since we have virtually said that the end is a sort of living well and doing well.

§5 Further, all the features that people look for in happiness appear to be true of the end described in our account. §6 For to some people happiness seems to be virtue; to others prudence; to others some sort of wisdom; to others again it seems to be these, or one of these, involving pleasure or requiring it to be added; others add in external prosperity as well. §7 Some of these views are traditional, held by many, while others are held by a few men who are widely esteemed. It is reasonable for each group not to be completely wrong, but to be correct on one point at least, or even on most points.

§8 First, our account agrees with those who say happiness is virtue [in general] or some [particular] virtue; for activity in accord with virtue is proper to virtue. §9 Presumably, though, it matters quite a bit whether we suppose that the best good consists in possessing or in using—that is to say, in a state or in an activity [that actualizes the state]. For someone may be in a state that achieves no good—if, for instance, he is asleep or inactive in some other way—but this cannot be true of the activity; for it will necessarily act and act well. And just as Olympic prizes are not for the finest and strongest, but for the contestants —since it is only these who win—the same is true in life; among the fine and good people, only those who act correctly win the prize.

§10 Moreover, the life of these active people is also pleasant in itself. For being pleased is a condition of the soul, [and hence is included in the activity of the soul]. Further, each type of person finds pleasure in whatever he is called a lover of; a horse, for instance, pleases the horse-lover, a spectacle the lover of spectacles. Similarly, what is just pleases the lover of justice, and in general what accords with virtue pleases the lover of virtue.

§11 Now the things that please most people conflict, because they are not pleasant by nature, whereas the things that please lovers of the fine are things pleasant by nature. Actions in accord with virtue are pleasant by nature, so that they both please lovers of the fine and are pleasant in their own right.

§12 Hence these people's life does not need pleasure to be added [to virtuous activity] as some sort of extra decoration; rather, it has its pleasure within itself. For besides the reasons already given, someone who does not enjoy fine actions is not good; for no one would call a person just, for instance, if he did not enjoy doing just actions, or generous if he did not enjoy generous actions, and similarly for the other virtues.

§13 If this is so, actions in accord with the virtues are pleasant in their own right. Moreover, these actions are good and fine as well as pleasant; indeed, they are good, fine, and pleasant more than anything else is, since on this question the excellent person judges rightly, and his judgment agrees with what we have said.

§14 Happiness, then, is best, finest, and most pleasant, and the Delian inscription is wrong to distinguish these things: 'What is most just is finest; being healthy is most beneficial; but it is most pleasant to win our heart's desire.' For all three features are found in the best activities, and we say happiness is these activities, or [rather] one of them, the best one.

§15 Nonetheless, happiness evidently also needs external goods to be added, as we said, since we cannot, or cannot easily, do fine actions if we lack the resources. For, first of all, in many actions we use friends, wealth, and political power just as we use instruments. §16 Further, deprivation of certain [externals]—for instance, good birth, good children, beauty—mars our blessedness. For we do not altogether have the character of happiness if we look utterly repulsive or are ill-born, solitary, or childless; and we have it even less, presumably, if our children or friends are totally bad, or were good but have died.

§17 And so, as we have said, happiness would seem to need this sort of prosperity added also. That is why some people identify happiness with good fortune, and others identify it with virtue.

[How Is Happiness Achieved?]

§1 This also leads to a puzzle: Is happiness acquired by learning, or habituation, or by some other form of cultivation? Or is it the result of some divine fate, or even of fortune?

§2 First, then, if the gods give any gift at all to human beings, it is reasonable for them to give us happiness more than any other human good, insofar as it is the best of human goods. §3 Presumably, however, this question is more suitable for a different inquiry.

But even if it is not sent by the gods, but instead results from virtue and some sort of learning or cultivation, happiness appears to be one of the most divine things, since the prize and goal of virtue appears to be the best good, something divine and blessed. §4 Moreover [if happiness comes in this way] it will be widely shared; for anyone who is not deformed [in his capacity] for virtue will be able to achieve happiness through some sort of learning and attention.

§5 And since it is better to be happy in this way than because of fortune, it is reasonable for this to be the way [we become] happy. For whatever is natural is naturally in the finest state possible. §6 The same is true of the products of crafts and of every other cause, especially the best cause; and it would be seriously inappropriate to entrust what is greatest and finest to fortune.

§7 The answer to our question is also evident from our account. For we have said that happiness is a certain sort of activity of the soul in accord with virtue, [and hence not a result of fortune]. Of the other goods, some are necessary conditions of happiness, while others are naturally useful and cooperative as instruments [but are not parts of it].

§8 Further, this conclusion agrees with our opening remarks. For we took the goal of political science to be the best good; and most of its attention is devoted to the character of the citizens, to make them good people who do fine actions.

§9 It is not surprising, then, that we regard neither ox, nor horse, nor any other kind of animal as happy; for none of them can share in this sort of activity. §10 For the same reason a child is not happy either, since his age prevents him from doing these sorts of actions. If he is called happy, he is being congratulated [simply] because of anticipated blessedness; for, as we have said, happiness requires both complete virtue and a complete life.

§11 It needs a complete life because life includes many reversals of fortune, good and bad, and the most prosperous person may fall into a terrible disaster in old age, as the Trojan stories tell us about Priam. If someone has suffered these sorts of misfortunes and comes to a miserable end, no one counts him happy.

[Introduction to the Virtues]

§1 Since happiness is a certain sort of activity of the soul in accord with complete virtue, we must examine virtue; for that will perhaps also be a way to study happiness better. §2 Moreover, the true politician seems to have put more effort into virtue than into anything else, since he wants to make the citizens good and law-abiding. §3 We find an example of this in the Spartan and Cretan legislators and in any others who share their concerns. §4 Since, then, the examination of virtue is proper for political science, the inquiry clearly suits our decision at the beginning.

§5 It is clear that the virtue we must examine is human virtue, since we are also seeking the human good and human happiness. §6 By human virtue we mean virtue of the soul, not of the body, since we also say that happiness is an activity of the soul. §7 If this is so, it is clear that the politician must in some way know about the soul, just as someone setting out to heal the eyes must know about the whole body as well. This is all the more true to the extent that political science is better and more honorable than medicine; even among doctors, the cultivated ones devote a lot of effort to finding out about the body. Hence the politician as well [as the student of nature] must study the soul. §8 But he must study it for his specific purpose, far enough for his inquiry [into virtue]; for a more exact treatment would presumably take more effort than his purpose requires.

§9 [We] have discussed the soul sufficiently [for our purposes] in [our] popular works as well [as our less popular], and we should use this discussion. We have said, for instance, that one [part] of the soul is nonrational, while one has reason. §10 Are these distinguished as parts of a body and everything divisible into parts are? Or are they two [only] in definition, and inseparable by nature, as the convex and the concave are in a surface? It does not matter for present purposes.

§11 Consider the nonrational [part]. One [part] of it, i.e., the cause of nutrition and growth, would seem to be plantlike and shared [with all living things]; for we can ascribe this capacity of the soul to everything that is nourished, including embryos, and the same capacity to full-grown living things, since this is more reasonable than to ascribe another capacity to them.

§12 Hence the virtue of this capacity is apparently shared, not [specifically] human. For this part and this capacity more than others seem to be active in sleep, and here the good and the bad person are least distinct; hence happy people are said to be no better off than miserable people for half their lives. §13 This lack of distinction is not surprising, since sleep is inactivity of the soul insofar as it is called excellent or base, unless to some small extent some movements penetrate [to our awareness], and in this way the decent person comes to have better images [in dreams] than just any random person has. §14 Enough about this, however, and let us leave aside the nutritive part, since by nature it has no share in human virtue.

§15 Another nature in the soul would also seem to be nonrational, though in a way it shares in reason. For in the continent and the incontinent person we praise their reason, that is to say, the [part] of the soul that has reason, because it exhorts them correctly and toward what is best; but they evidently also have in them some other [part] that is by nature something apart from reason, clashing and struggling with reason.

For just as paralyzed parts of a body, when we decide to move them to the right, do the contrary and move off to the left, the same is true of the soul; for incontinent people have impulses in contrary directions. §16 In bodies, admittedly, we see the part go astray, whereas we do not see it in the soul; nonetheless, presumably, we should suppose that the soul also has something apart from reason, countering and opposing reason. The [precise] way it is different does not matter.

§17 However, this [part] as well [as the rational part] appears, as we said, to share in reason. At any rate, in the continent person it obeys reason; and in the temperate and the brave person it presumably listens still better to reason, since there it agrees with reason in everything.

§18 The nonrational [part], then, as well [as the whole soul] apparently has two parts. For while the plantlike [part] shares in reason not at all, the [part] with appetites and in general desires shares in reason in a way, insofar as it both listens to reason and obeys it. This is the way in which we are said to 'listen to reason' from father or friends, as opposed to the way in which [we 'give the reason'] in mathematics. The nonrational part also [obeys and] is persuaded in some way by reason, as is shown by correction, and by every sort of reproof and exhortation.

§19 If, then, we ought to say that this [part] also has reason, then the [part] that has reason, as well [as the nonrational part], will have two parts. One will have reason fully, by having it within itself; the other will have reason by listening to reason as to a father.

The division between virtues accords with this difference. For some virtues are called virtues of thought, others virtues of character; wisdom, comprehension, and prudence are called virtues of thought, generosity and temperance virtues of character. For when we speak of someone's character we do not say that he is wise or has good comprehension, but that he is gentle or temperate. And yet, we also praise the wise person for his state, and the states that are praiseworthy are the ones we call virtues.

BOOK II [VIRTUE OF CHARACTER]

[How a Virtue of Character Is Acquired]

§1 Virtue, then, is of two sorts, virtue of thought and virtue of character. Virtue of thought arises and grows mostly from teaching; that is why it needs experience and time. Virtue of character [i.e., of *ethos*] results from habit [*ethos*]; hence its name 'ethical,' slightly varied from 'ethos.'

§2 Hence it is also clear that none of the virtues of character arises in us naturally. For if something is by nature in one condition, habituation cannot bring it into another condition. A stone, for instance, by nature moves downwards, and habituation could not make it move upwards, not even if you threw it up ten thousand times to habituate it; nor could habituation make fire move downwards, or bring anything that is by nature in one condition into another condition. §3 And so the virtues arise in us neither by nature nor against nature. Rather, we are by nature able to acquire them, and we are completed through habit.

§4 Further, if something arises in us by nature, we first have the capacity for it, and later perform the activity. This is clear in the case of the senses; for we did not acquire them by frequent seeing or hearing, but we already had them when we exercised them, and did not get them by exercising them. Virtues, by contrast, we acquire, just as we acquire crafts, by having first activated them. For we learn a craft by producing the same product that we must produce when we have learned it; we become builders, for instance, by building, and we become harpists by playing the harp. Similarly, then, we become just by doing just actions, temperate by doing temperate actions, brave by doing brave actions....

[Habituation]

§1 Our present discussion does not aim, as our others do, at study; for the purpose of our examination is not to know what virtue is, but to become good, since otherwise the inquiry would be of no benefit to us. And so we must examine the right ways of acting; for, as we have said, the actions also control the sorts of states we acquire.

§2 First, then, actions should accord with the correct reason. That is a common [belief], and let us assume it. We shall discuss it later, and say what the correct reason is and how it is related to the other virtues.

§3 But let us take it as agreed in advance that every account of the actions we must do has to be stated in outline, not exactly. As we also said at the beginning, the type of accounts we demand should accord with the subject matter; and questions about actions and expediency, like questions about health, have no fixed answers.

§4 While this is the character of our general account, the account of particular cases is still more inexact. For these fall under no craft or profession; the agents themselves must consider in each case what the opportune action is, as doctors and navigators do. §5 The account we offer, then, in our present inquiry is of this inexact sort; still, we must try to offer help.

§6 First, then, we should observe that these sorts of states naturally tend to be ruined by excess and deficiency. We see this happen with strength and health—for we must use evident cases [such as these] as witnesses to things that are not evident. For both excessive and deficient exercise ruin bodily strength, and, similarly, too much or too little eating or drinking ruins health, whereas the proportionate amount produces, increases, and preserves it.

§7 The same is true, then, of temperance, bravery, and the other virtues. For if, for instance, someone avoids and is afraid of everything, standing firm against nothing, he becomes cowardly; if he is afraid of nothing at all and goes to face everything, he becomes rash. Similarly, if he gratifies himself with every pleasure and abstains from none, he becomes intemperate; if he avoids them all, as boors do, he becomes some sort of insensible person. Temperance and bravery, then, are ruined by excess and deficiency, but preserved by the mean.

§8 But these actions are not only the sources and causes both of the emergence and growth of virtues and of their ruin; the activities of the virtues [once we have acquired them] also consist in these same actions. For this is also true of more evident cases; strength, for instance, arises from eating a lot and from withstanding much hard labor, and it is the strong person who is most capable of these very actions. §9 It is the same with the virtues. For abstaining from pleasures makes us become temperate, and once we have become temperate we are most capable of abstaining from pleasures. It is similar with bravery; habituation in disdain for frightening situations and in standing firm against them makes us become brave, and once we have become brave we shall be most capable of standing firm.

[The Importance of Pleasure and Pain]

§1 But we must take someone's pleasure or pain following on his actions to be a sign of his state. For if someone who abstains from bodily pleasures enjoys the abstinence itself, he is temperate; if he is grieved by it, he is intemperate. Again, if he stands firm against terrifying situations and enjoys it, or at least does not find it painful, he is brave; if he finds it painful, he is cowardly. For virtue of character is about pleasures and pains.

For pleasure causes us to do base actions, and pain causes us to abstain from fine ones. §2 That is why we need to have had the appropriate upbringing—right from early youth, as Plato says—to make us find enjoyment or pain in the right things; for this is the correct education.... §6 We assume, then, that virtue is the sort of state that does the best actions concerning pleasures and pains, and that vice is the contrary state.... §11 To sum up: Virtue is about pleasures and pains; the actions that are its sources also increase it or, if they are done badly, ruin it; and its activity is about the same actions as those that are its sources.

[Virtuous Actions versus Virtuous Character]

§1 Someone might be puzzled, however, about what we mean by saying that we become just by doing just actions and become temperate by doing temperate actions. For [one might suppose that] if we do grammatical or musical actions, we are grammarians or musicians, and, similarly, if we do just or temperate actions, we are thereby just or temperate.

§2 But surely actions are not enough, even in the case of crafts; for it is possible to produce a grammatical result by chance, or by following someone else's instructions. To be grammarians, then, we must both produce a grammatical result and produce it grammatically—that is to say, produce it in accord with the grammatical knowledge in us.

§3 Moreover, in any case, what is true of crafts is not true of virtues. For the products of a craft determine by their own qualities whether they have been produced well; and so it suffices that they have the right qualities when they have been produced. But for actions in accord with the virtues to be done temperately or justly it does not suffice that they themselves have the right qualities. Rather, the agent must also be in the right state when he does them. First, he must know [that he is doing virtuous actions]; second, he must decide on them, and decide on them for themselves; and, third, he must also do them from a firm and unchanging state....

§4 Hence actions are called just or temperate when they are the sort that a just or temperate person would do. But the just and temperate person is not the one who [merely] does these actions, but the one who also does them in the way in which just or temperate people do them.

§5 It is right, then, to say that a person comes to be just from doing just actions and temperate from doing temperate actions; for no one has the least prospect of becoming good from failing to do them....

[Virtue of Character: Its Genus]

§1 Next we must examine what virtue is. Since there are three conditions arising in the soul— feelings, capacities, and states—virtue must be one of these....

§3 First, then, neither virtues nor vices are feelings. For we are called excellent or base insofar as we have virtues or vices, not insofar as we have feelings. Further, we are neither praised nor blamed insofar as we have feelings; for we do not praise the angry or the frightened person, and do not blame the person who is simply angry, but only the person who is angry in a particular way. We are praised or blamed, however, insofar as we have virtues or vices....

§5 For these reasons the virtues are not capacities either; for we are neither called good nor called bad, nor are we praised or blamed, insofar as we are simply capable of feelings....

§6 If, then, the virtues are neither feelings nor capacities, the remaining possibility is that they are states. And so we have said what the genus of virtue is.

[Virtue of Character: Its Differentia]

§1 But we must say not only, as we already have, that it is a state, but also what sort of state it is.

§2 It should be said, then, that every virtue causes its possessors to be in a good state and to perform their functions well. The virtue of eyes, for instance, makes the eyes and their functioning excellent, because it makes us see well; and similarly, the virtue of a horse makes the horse excellent, and thereby good at galloping, at carrying its rider, and at standing steady in the face of the enemy. §3 If this is true in every case, the virtue of a human being will likewise be the state that makes a human being good and makes him perform his function well.

§4 We have already said how this will be true, and it will also be evident from our next remarks, if we consider the sort of nature that virtue has.

In everything continuous and divisible we can take more, less, and equal, and each of them either in the object itself or relative to us; and the equal is some intermediate between excess and deficiency. §5 By the intermediate in the object I mean what is equidistant from each extremity; this is one and the same for all. But relative to us the intermediate is what is neither superfluous nor deficient; this is not one, and is not the same for all.

§6 If, for instance, ten are many and two are few, we take six as intermediate in the object,

since it exceeds [two] and is exceeded [by ten] by an equal amount, [four]. §7 This is what is intermediate by numerical proportion. But that is not how we must take the intermediate that is relative to us. For if ten pounds [of food], for instance, are a lot for someone to eat, and two pounds a little, it does not follow that the trainer will prescribe six, since this might also be either a little or a lot for the person who is to take it—for Milo [the athlete] a little, but for the beginner in gymnastics a lot; and the same is true for running and wrestling. §8 In this way every scientific expert avoids excess and deficiency and seeks and chooses what is intermediate—but intermediate relative to us, not in the object....

§10 By virtue I mean virtue of character; for this is about feelings and actions, and these admit of excess, deficiency, and an intermediate condition. We can be afraid, for instance, or be confident, or have appetites, or get angry, or feel pity, and in general have pleasure or pain, both too much and too little, and in both ways not well. §11 But having these feelings at the right times, about the right things, toward the right people, for the right end, and in the right way, is the intermediate and best condition, and this is proper to virtue. §12 Similarly, actions also admit of excess, deficiency, and an intermediate condition.

Now virtue is about feelings and actions, in which excess and deficiency are in error and incur blame, whereas the intermediate condition is correct and wins praise, which are both proper to virtue. §13 Virtue, then, is a mean, insofar as it aims at what is intermediate....

§15 Virtue, then, is a state that decides, consisting in a mean, the mean relative to us, which is defined by reference to reason, that is to say, to the reason by reference to which the prudent person would define it. It is a mean between two vices, one of excess and one of deficiency.

§16 It is a mean for this reason also: Some vices miss what is right because they are deficient, others because they are excessive, in feelings or in actions, whereas virtue finds and chooses what is intermediate.

§17 That is why virtue, as far as its essence and the account stating what it is are concerned, is a mean, but, as far as the best [condition] and the good [result] are concerned, it is an extremity.

§18 Now not every action or feeling admits of the mean. For the names of some automatically include baseness—for instance, spite, shamelessness, envy [among feelings], and adultery, theft, murder, among actions. For all of these and similar things are called by these names because they themselves, not their excesses or deficiencies, are base. Hence in doing these things we can never be correct, but must invariably be in error. We cannot do them well or not well—by committing adultery, for instance, with the right woman at the right time in the right way. On the contrary, it is true without qualification that to do any of them is to be in error.

§19 [To think these admit of a mean], therefore, is like thinking that unjust or cowardly or intemperate action also admits of a mean, an excess and a deficiency. If it did, there would be a mean of excess, a mean of deficiency, an excess of excess and a deficiency of deficiency. §20 On the contrary, just as there is no excess or deficiency of temperance or of bravery (since the intermediate is a sort of extreme), so also there is no mean of these vicious actions either, but whatever way anyone does them, he is in error. For in general there is no mean of excess or of deficiency, and no excess or deficiency of a mean.

2.4 *Leviathan*

THOMAS HOBBES

Thomas Hobbes (1588–1679) was a brilliant English philosopher. His *Leviathan* (excerpted here) is a classic of the social contract tradition in ethics and political philosophy.

OF THE NATURAL CONDITION OF MANKIND AS CONCERNING THEIR FELICITY AND MISERY

Nature hath made men so equal in the faculties of body and mind as that, though there be found one man sometimes manifestly stronger in body or of quicker mind than another, yet when all is reckoned together the difference between man and man is not so considerable as that one man can thereupon claim to himself any benefit to which another may not pretend as well as he. For as to the strength of body, the weakest has strength enough to kill the strongest, either by secret machination or by confederacy with others that are in the same danger with himself.

And as to the faculties of the mind, setting aside the arts grounded upon words, and especially that skill of proceeding upon general and infallible rules, called science, which very few have and but in few things, as being not a native faculty born with us, nor attained, as prudence, while we look after somewhat else, I find yet a greater equality amongst men than that of strength. For prudence is but experience, which equal time equally bestows on all men in those things they equally apply themselves unto. That which may perhaps make such equality incredible is but a vain conceit of one's own wisdom, which almost all men think they have in a greater degree than the vulgar; that is, than all men but themselves, and a few others, whom by fame, or

From *Leviathan* (1651), chaps. 13–15.

for concurring with themselves, they approve. For such is the nature of men that howsoever they may acknowledge many others to be more witty, or more eloquent or more learned, yet they will hardly believe there be many so wise as themselves; for they see their own wit at hand, and other men's at a distance. But this proveth rather that men are in that point equal, than unequal. For there is not ordinarily a greater sign of the equal distribution of anything than that every man is contented with his share.

From this equality of ability ariseth equality of hope in the attaining of our ends. And therefore if any two men desire the same thing, which nevertheless they cannot both enjoy, they become enemies; and in the way to their end (which is principally their own conservation, and sometimes their delectation only) endeavour to destroy or subdue one another. And from hence it comes to pass that where an invader hath no more to fear than another man's single power, if one plant, sow, build, or possess a convenient seat, others may probably be expected to come prepared with forces united to dispossess and deprive him, not only of the fruit of his labour, but also of his life or liberty. And the invader again is in the like danger of another.

And from this diffidence of one another, there is no way for any man to secure himself so reasonable as anticipation; that is, by force, or wiles, to master the persons of all men he can so long till he see no other power great enough to endanger him: and this is no more than his own conservation requireth, and is generally allowed. Also, because there be some that, taking pleasure in contemplating their own power in the acts of conquest, which they pursue farther than their security requires, if others, that otherwise would be glad to be at ease within modest bounds, should not by invasion increase their power, they would not be able, long time, by standing only on their defence, to subsist. And by consequence, such augmentation of dominion over men being necessary to a man's conservation, it ought to be allowed him.

Again, men have no pleasure (but on the contrary a great deal of grief) in keeping company where there is no power able to overawe them all. For every man looketh that his companion should value him at the same rate he sets upon himself, and upon all signs of contempt or undervaluing naturally endeavours, as far as he dares (which amongst them that have no common power to keep them in quiet is far enough to make them destroy each other), to extort a greater value from his contemners, by damage; and from others, by the example.

So that in the nature of man, we find three principal causes of quarrel. First, competition; secondly, diffidence; thirdly, glory.

The first maketh men invade for gain; the second, for safety; and the third, for reputation. The first use violence, to make themselves masters of other men's persons, wives, children, and cattle; the second, to defend them; the third, for trifles, as a word, a smile, a different opinion, and any other sign of undervalue, either direct in their persons or by reflection in their kindred, their friends, their nation, their profession, or their name.

Hereby it is manifest that during the time men live without a common power to keep them all in awe, they are in that condition which is called war; and such a war as is of every man against every man. For war consisteth not in battle only, or the act of fighting, but in a tract of time, wherein the will to contend by battle is sufficiently known: and therefore the notion of time is to be considered in the nature of war, as it is in the nature of weather. For as the nature of foul weather lieth not in a shower or two of rain, but in an inclination thereto of many days together: so the nature of war consisteth not in actual fighting, but in the known disposition thereto during all the time there is no assurance to the contrary. All other time is peace.

Whatsoever therefore is consequent to a time of war, where every man is enemy to every man, the same consequent to the time wherein men live without other security than what their own strength and their own invention shall furnish them withal. In such condition there is no place for industry, because the fruit thereof is uncertain: and consequently no culture of the earth; no navigation, nor use of the commodities that may be imported by sea; no commodious building; no instruments of moving and removing such things as require much force; no knowledge of the face of the earth; no account of time; no arts; no letters; no society; and which is worst of all, continual fear, and danger of violent death; and the life of man, solitary, poor, nasty, brutish, and short.

It may seem strange to some man that has not well weighed these things that Nature should thus dissociate and render men apt to invade and destroy one another: and he may therefore, not trusting to this inference, made from the passions, desire perhaps to have the same confirmed by experience. Let him therefore consider with himself: when taking a journey, he arms himself and seeks to go well accompanied; when going to sleep, he locks his doors; when even in his house he locks his chests; and this when he knows there be laws and public officers, armed, to revenge all injuries shall be done him; what opinion he has of his fellow subjects, when he rides armed; of his fellow citizens, when he locks his doors; and of his children, and servants, when he locks his chests. Does he not there as much accuse mankind by his actions as I do by my words? But neither of us accuse man's nature in it. The desires, and other passions of man, are in themselves no sin. No more are the actions that proceed from those passions till they know a law that forbids them; which till laws be made they cannot know, nor can any law be made till they have agreed upon the person that shall make it.

It may peradventure be thought there was never such a time nor condition of war as this; and I believe it was never generally so, over all the world: but there are many places where they live so now. For the savage people in many places of America, except the government of small families, the concord whereof dependeth on natural lust, have no government at all, and live at this day in that brutish manner, as I said before. Howsoever, it may be perceived what manner of life there would be, where there were no common power to fear, by the manner of life which men that have formerly lived under a peaceful government use to degenerate into a civil war.

But though there had never been any time wherein particular men were in a condition of war one against another, yet in all times kings and persons of sovereign authority, because of their independency, are in continual jealousies, and in the state and posture of gladiators, having their weapons pointing, and their eyes fixed on one another; that is, their forts, garrisons, and guns upon the frontiers of their kingdoms, and continual spies upon their neighbours, which is a posture of war. But because they uphold thereby the industry of their subjects, there does not follow from it that misery which accompanies the liberty of particular men.

To this war of every man against every man, this also is consequent; that nothing can be unjust. The notions of right and wrong, justice and injustice, have there no place. Where there is no common power, there is no law; where no law, no injustice. Force and fraud are in war the two cardinal virtues. Justice and injustice are none of the faculties neither of the body nor mind. If they were, they might be in a man that were alone in the world, as well as his senses and passions. They are qualities that relate to men in society, not in solitude. It is consequent also to the same condition that there be no propriety, no dominion, no mine and thine distinct; but only that to be every man's that he can get, and for so long as he can keep it. And thus much for the ill condition which man by mere nature is actually placed in; though with a possibility to come out of it, consisting partly in the passions, partly in his reason.

The passions that incline men to peace are: fear of death; desire of such things as are necessary to commodious living; and a hope by their industry to obtain them. And reason suggesteth convenient articles of peace upon which men may be drawn to agreement. These articles are they which otherwise are called the laws of nature, whereof I shall speak more particularly in the two following chapters.

OF THE FIRST AND SECOND NATURAL LAWS, AND OF CONTRACTS

The right of nature, which writers commonly call *jus naturale*, is the liberty each man hath to use his own power as he will himself for the preservation of his own nature; that is to say, of his own life; and consequently, of doing anything which, in his own judgement and reason, he shall conceive to be the aptest means thereunto.

By liberty is understood, according to the proper signification of the word, the absence of external impediments; which impediments may oft take away part of a man's power to do what he would, but cannot hinder him from using the power left him according as his judgement and reason shall dictate to him.

A law of nature, *lex naturalis,* is a precept, or general rule, found out by reason, by which a man is forbidden to do that which is destructive of his life, or taketh away the means of preserving the same, and to omit that by which he thinketh it may be best preserved.

And because the condition of man (as hath been declared in the precedent chapter) is a condition of war of every one against every one, in which case every one is governed by his own reason, and there is nothing he can make use of that may not be a help unto him in preserving his life against his enemies; it followeth that in such a condition every man has a right to every thing, even to one another's body. And therefore, as long as this natural right of every man to every thing endureth, there can be no security to any man, how strong or wise soever he be, of living out the time which nature ordinarily alloweth men to live. And consequently it is a precept, or general rule of reason: that every man ought to endeavour peace, as far as he has hope of obtaining it; and when he cannot obtain it, that he may seek and use all helps and advantages of war. The first branch of which rule containeth the first and fundamental law of nature, which is: to seek peace and follow it. The second, the sum of the right of nature, which is: by all means we can to defend ourselves.

From this fundamental law of nature, by which men are commanded to endeavour peace, is derived this second law: that a man be willing, when others are so too, as far forth as for peace and defence of himself he shall think it necessary, to lay down this right to all things; and be contented with so much liberty against other men as he would allow other men against himself. For as long as every man holdeth this right, of doing anything he liketh; so long are all men in the condition of war. But if other men will not lay down their right, as well as he, then there is no reason for anyone to divest himself of his: for that were to expose himself to prey, which no man is bound to, rather than to dispose himself to peace. This is that law of the gospel: Whatsoever you require that others should do to you, that do ye to them.

Whensoever a man transferreth his right, or renounceth it, it is either in consideration of some right reciprocally transferred to himself, or for some other good he hopeth for thereby. For it is a voluntary act: and of the voluntary acts of every man, the object is some good to himself. And therefore there be some rights which no man can be understood by any words, or other signs, to have abandoned or transferred. As first a man cannot lay down the right of resisting them that assault him by force to take away his life, because he cannot be understood to aim thereby at any good to himself. The same may be said of wounds, and chains, and imprisonment, both because there is no benefit consequent to such patience, as there is to the patience of suffering another to be wounded or imprisoned, as also because a man cannot tell when he seeth men proceed against him by violence whether they intend his death or not. And lastly the motive and end for which this renouncing and transferring of right is introduced is nothing else but the security of a man's person, in his life, and in the means of so preserving life as not to be weary of it. And therefore if a man by words, or other signs, seems to despoil himself of the end for which those signs were intended, he is not to be understood as if he meant it, or that it was his will, but that he was ignorant of how such words and actions were to be interpreted.

The mutual transferring of right is that which men call contract.

Signs of contract are either express or by inference. Express are words spoken with understanding of what they signify: and such words are either of the time present or past; as, I give, I grant, I have given, I have granted, I will that this be yours: or of the future; as, I will give, I will grant, which words of the future are called promise.

Signs by inference are sometimes the consequence of words; sometimes the consequence of silence; sometimes the consequence of actions; sometimes the consequence of forbearing an action: and generally a sign by inference, of any contract, is whatsoever sufficiently argues the will of the contractor.

Words alone, if they be of the time to come, and contain a bare promise, are an insufficient sign of a free gift and therefore not obligatory. For if they be of the time to come, as, tomorrow I will give, they are a sign I have not given yet, and consequently that my right is not transferred, but remaineth till I transfer it by some other act.

If a covenant be made wherein neither of the parties perform presently, but trust one another, in the condition of mere nature (which is a condition of war of every man against every man) upon any reasonable suspicion, it is void: but if there be a common power set over them both, with right and force sufficient to compel performance, it is not void. For he that performeth first has no assurance the other will perform after, because the bonds of words are too weak to bridle men's ambition, avarice, anger, and other passions, without the fear of some coercive power; which in the condition of mere nature, where all men are equal, and judges of the justness of their own fears, cannot possibly be supposed. And therefore he which performeth first does but betray himself to his enemy, contrary to the right he can never abandon of defending his life and means of living.

But in a civil estate, where there is a power set up to constrain those that would otherwise violate their faith, that fear is no more reasonable; and for that cause, he which by the covenant is to perform first is obliged so to do.

OF OTHER LAWS OF NATURE

From that law of nature by which we are obliged to transfer to another such rights as, being retained, hinder the peace of mankind, there followeth a third; which is this: that men perform their covenants made; without which covenants are in vain, and but empty words; and the right of all men to all things remaining, we are still in the condition of war.

And in this law of nature consisteth the fountain and original of justice. For where no covenant hath preceded, there hath no right been transferred, and every man has right to everything and consequently, no action can be unjust. But when a covenant is made, then to break it is unjust and the definition of injustice is no other than the not performance of covenant. And whatsoever is not unjust is just.

But because covenants of mutual trust, where there is a fear of not performance on either part (as hath been said in the former chapter), are invalid, though the original of justice be the making of covenants, yet injustice actually there can be none till the cause of such fear be taken away; which, while men are in the natural condition of war, cannot be done. Therefore before the names of just and unjust can have place, there must be some coercive power to compel men equally to the performance of their covenants, by the terror of some punishment greater than the benefit they expect by the breach of their covenant, and to make good that propriety which by mutual contract men acquire in recompense of the universal right they abandon: and such power there is none before the erection of a Commonwealth. And this is also to be gathered out of the ordinary definition of justice in the Schools, for they say that justice is the constant will of giving to every man his own. And therefore where there is no own, that is, no propriety, there is no injustice; and where there is no coercive power erected, that is, where there is no Commonwealth, there is no propriety, all men having right to all things: therefore where there is no Commonwealth, there nothing is unjust. So that the nature of justice consisteth in keeping of valid covenants, but the validity of covenants begins not but with the constitution of a civil power sufficient to compel men to keep them: and then it is also that propriety begins.

The fool hath said in his heart, there is no such thing as justice, and sometimes also with his tongue, seriously alleging that every man's conservation and contentment being committed to his own care, there could be no reason why every man might not do what he thought conduced thereunto: and therefore also to make, or not make; keep, or not keep, covenants was not against reason when it conduced to one's benefit. He does not therein deny that there be covenants; and that they are sometimes broken, sometimes kept; and that such breach of them may be called injustice, and the observance of them justice: but he questioneth whether injustice, taking away the fear of God (for the same fool hath said in his heart there is no God), not sometimes stand with that reason which dictateth to every man his own good; and particularly then, when it conduceth to such a benefit as shall put a man in a condition to neglect not only the dispraise and revilings, but also the power of other men. The kingdom of God is gotten by violence: but what if it could be gotten by unjust violence? Were it against reason so to get it, when it is impossible to receive hurt by it? And if it be not against reason, it is not against justice: or else justice is not to be approved for good. From such reasoning as this, successful wickedness hath obtained the name of virtue: and some that in all other things have disallowed the violation of faith, yet have allowed it when it is for the getting of a kingdom. And the heathen that believed that Saturn was deposed by his son Jupiter believed nevertheless the same Jupiter to be the avenger of injustice, somewhat like to a piece of law in Coke's Commentaries on Littleton; where he says if the right heir of the crown be attainted

of treason, yet the crown shall descend to him, and *eo instante* the attainder be void: from which instances a man will be very prone to infer that when the heir apparent of a kingdom shall kill him that is in possession, though his father, you may call it injustice, or by what other name you will; yet it can never be against reason, seeing all the voluntary actions of men tend to the benefit of themselves; and those actions are most reasonable that conduce most to their ends. This specious reasoning is nevertheless false.

For the question is not of promises mutual, where there is no security of performance on either side, as when there is no civil power erected over the parties promising; for such promises are not covenants: but either where one of the parties has performed already, or where there is a power to make him perform, there is the question whether it be against reason; that is, against the benefit of the other to perform, or not. And I say it is not against reason. For the manifestation whereof we are to consider; first, that when a man doth a thing, which notwithstanding anything can be foreseen and reckoned on tendeth to his own destruction, howsoever some accident, which he could not expect, arriving may turn it to his benefit; yet such events do not make it reasonably or wisely done. Secondly, that in a condition of war, wherein every man to every man, for want of a common power to keep them all in awe, is an enemy, there is no man can hope by his own strength, or wit, to keep himself from destruction without the help of confederates; where every one expects the same defence by the confederation that any one else does: and therefore he which declares he thinks it reason to deceive those that help him can in reason expect no other means of safety than what can be had from his own single power. He, therefore, that breaketh his covenant, and consequently declareth that he thinks he may with reason do so, cannot be received into any society that unite themselves for peace and defence but by the error of them that receive him; nor when he is received be retained in it without seeing the danger of their error; which errors a man cannot reasonably reckon upon as the means of his security: and therefore if he be left, or cast out of society, he perisheth; and if he live in society, it is by the errors of other men, which he could not foresee nor reckon upon, and consequently against the reason of his preservation; and so, as all men that contribute not to his destruction forbear him only out of ignorance of what is good for themselves.

As for the instance of gaining the secure and perpetual felicity of heaven by any way, it is frivolous; there being but one way imaginable, and that is not breaking, but keeping of covenant.

And for the other instance of attaining sovereignty by rebellion; it is manifest that, though the event follow, yet because it cannot reasonably be expected, but rather the contrary, and because by gaining it so, others are taught to gain the same in like manner, the attempt thereof is against reason. Justice therefore, that is to say, keeping of covenant, is a rule of reason by which we are forbidden to do anything destructive to our life, and consequently a law of nature.

2.5 Euthyphro

PLATO

Euthyphro:[1] What's new, Socrates, to make you leave your usual haunts in the Lyceum and spend your time here by the king-archon's court?[2] Surely you are not prosecuting anyone before the king-archon as I am?

Socrates: The Athenians do not call this a prosecution but an indictment, Euthyphro.

Euthyphro: What is this you say? Someone must have indicted you, for you are not going to tell me that you have indicted someone else.

Socrates: No indeed.

Euthyphro: But someone else has indicted you?

Socrates: Quite so.

Euthyphro: Who is he?

Socrates: I do not really know him myself, Euthyphro. He is apparently young and unknown. They call him Meletus, I believe. He belongs to the Pitthean deme,[3] if you know anyone from that deme called Meletus, with long hair, not much of a beard, and a rather aquiline nose.

Euthyphro: I don't know him, Socrates. What charge does he bring against you?

Socrates: What charge? A not ignoble one I think, for it is no small thing for a young man to

have knowledge of such an important subject. He says he knows how our young men are corrupted and who corrupts them. He is likely to be wise, and when he sees my ignorance corrupting his contemporaries, he proceeds to accuse me to the city as to their mother. I think he is the only one of our public men to start out the right way, for it is right to care first that the young should be as good as possible, just as a good farmer is likely to take care of the young plants first, and of the others later. So, too, Meletus first gets rid of us who corrupt the young shoots, as he says, and then afterwards he will obviously take care of the older ones and become a source of great blessings for the city, as seems likely to happen to one who started out this way.

Euthyphro: I could wish this were true, Socrates, but I fear the opposite may happen. He seems to me to start out by harming the very heart of the city by attempting to wrong you. Tell me, what does he say you do to corrupt the young?

Socrates: Strange things, to hear him tell it, for he says that I am a maker of gods, and on the ground that I create new gods while not

From Plato, *Five Dialogues,* trans. G.M.A. Grube (Hackett 2002), pp. 2–18, 46–57. Reprinted by permission of Hackett Publishing Company, Inc. All rights reserved.

believing in the old gods, he has indicted me for their sake, as he puts it.

Euthyphro: I understand, Socrates. This is because you say that the divine sign keeps coming to you.[4] So he has written this indictment against you as one who makes innovations in religious matters, and he comes to court to slander you, knowing that such things are easily misrepresented to the crowd. The same is true in my case. Whenever I speak of divine matters in the assembly[5] and foretell the future, they laugh me down as if I were crazy; and yet I have foretold nothing that did not happen. Nevertheless, they envy all of us who do this. One need not worry about them, but meet them head-on.

Socrates: My dear Euthyphro, to be laughed at does not matter perhaps, for the Athenians do not mind anyone they think clever, as long as he does not teach his own wisdom, but if they think that he makes others to be like himself they get angry, whether through envy, as you say, or for some other reason.

Euthyphro: I have certainly no desire to test their feelings towards me in this matter.

Socrates: Perhaps you seem to make yourself but rarely available, and not be willing to teach your own wisdom, but I'm afraid that my liking for people makes them think that I pour out to anybody anything I have to say, not only without charging a fee but even glad to reward anyone who is willing to listen. If then they were intending to laugh at me, as you say they laugh at you, there would be nothing unpleasant in their spending their time in court laughing and jesting, but if they are going to be serious, the outcome is not clear except to you prophets.

Euthyphro: Perhaps it will come to nothing, Socrates, and you will fight your case as you think best, as I think I will mine.

Socrates: What is your case, Euthyphro? Are you the defendant or the prosecutor?

Euthyphro: The prosecutor.

Socrates: Whom do you prosecute?

Euthyphro: One whom I am thought crazy to prosecute.

Socrates: Are you pursuing someone who will easily escape you?

Euthyphro: Far from it, for he is quite old.

Socrates: Who is it?

Euthyphro: My father.

Socrates: My dear sir! Your own father?

Euthyphro: Certainly.

Socrates: What is the charge? What is the case about?

Euthyphro: Murder, Socrates.

Socrates: Good heavens! Certainly, Euthyphro, most men would not know how they could do this and be right. It is not the part of anyone to do this, but of one who is far advanced in wisdom.

Euthyphro: Yes, by Zeus, Socrates, that is so.

Socrates: Is then the man your father killed one of your relatives? Or is that obvious, for you would not prosecute your father for the murder of a stranger.

Euthyphro: It is ridiculous, Socrates, for you to think that it makes any difference whether the victim is a stranger or a relative. One should only watch whether the killer acted justly or not; if he acted justly, let him go, but if not, one should prosecute, if, that is to say, the killer shares your hearth and table. The pollution is the same if you knowingly keep company with such a man and do not cleanse yourself and him by bringing him to justice. The victim was a dependent of mine, and when we were farming in Naxos he was a servant of ours.[6] He killed one of our household slaves in drunken anger, so my father bound him hand and foot and threw him in a ditch, then sent a man here to inquire from the priest what should be done. During that time he gave no thought or care to the bound man, as being a killer, and it was no matter if he died, which he did. Hunger and cold and his bonds caused his death before the messenger came back from the seer. Both my father and my other relatives are angry that I am prosecuting my father for murder on behalf of a murderer when he hadn't even killed him, they say, and even if he had, the dead man does not deserve a thought, since he was a killer. For, they say, it is impious for a son to prosecute his father for murder. But their ideas of the divine attitude to piety and impiety are wrong, Socrates.

Socrates: Whereas, by Zeus, Euthyphro, you think that your knowledge of the divine, and of piety and impiety, is so accurate that, when those things happened as you say, you have no fear of having acted impiously in bringing your father to trial?

Euthyphro: I should be of no use, Socrates, and Euthyphro would not be superior to the majority of men, if I did not have accurate knowledge of all such things.

Socrates: It is indeed most important, my admirable Euthyphro, that I should become your pupil, and as regards this indictment, challenge Meletus about these very things and say to him: that in the past too I considered knowledge about the divine to be most important, and that now that he says that I am guilty of improvising and innovating about the gods I have become your pupil. I would say to him: "If, Meletus, you agree that Euthyphro is wise in these matters, consider me, too, to have the right beliefs and do not bring me to trial. If you do not think so, then prosecute that teacher of mine, not me, for corrupting the older men, me and his own father, by teaching me and by exhorting and punishing him." If he is not convinced, and does not discharge me or indict you instead of me, I shall repeat the same challenge in court.

Euthyphro: Yes, by Zeus, Socrates, and, if he should try to indict me, I think I would find his weak spots and the talk in court would be about him rather than about me.

Socrates: It is because I realize this that I am eager to become your pupil, my dear friend. I know that other people as well as this Meletus do not even seem to notice you, whereas he sees me so sharply and clearly that he indicts me for ungodliness. So tell me now, by Zeus, what you just now maintained you clearly knew: what kind of thing do you say that godliness and ungodliness are, both as regards murder and other things; or is the pious not the same and alike in every action, and the impious the opposite of all that is pious and like itself, and everything that is to be impious presents us with one form[7] or appearance insofar as it is impious?

Euthyphro: Most certainly, Socrates.

Socrates: Tell me then, what is the pious, and what the impious, do you say?

Euthyphro: I say that the pious is to do what I am doing now, to prosecute the wrongdoer, be it about murder or temple robbery or anything else, whether the wrongdoer is your father or your mother or anyone else; not to prosecute is impious. And observe, Socrates, that I can cite powerful evidence that the law is so. I have already said to others that such actions are right, not to favor the ungodly, whoever they are. These people themselves believe that Zeus is the best and most just of the gods, yet they agree that he bound his father because he unjustly swallowed his sons, and that he in turn castrated his father for similar reasons. But they are angry with me because I am prosecuting my father for his wrongdoing. They contradict themselves in what they say about the gods and about me.

Socrates: Indeed, Euthyphro, this is the reason why I am a defendant in the case, because I find it hard to accept things like that being said about the gods, and it is likely to be the reason why I shall be told I do wrong. Now, however, if you, who have full knowledge of such things, share their opinions, then we must agree with them, too, it would seem. For what are we to say, we who agree that we ourselves have no knowledge of them? Tell me, by the god of friendship, do you really believe these things are true?

Euthyphro: Yes, Socrates, and so are even more surprising things, of which the majority has no knowledge.

Socrates: And do you believe that there really is war among the gods, and terrible enmities and battles, and other such things as are told by the poets, and other sacred stories such as are embroidered by good writers and by representations of which the robe of the goddess is adorned when it is carried up to the Acropolis?[8] Are we to say these things are true, Euthyphro?

Euthyphro: Not only these, Socrates, but, as I was saying just now, I will, if you wish, relate many other things about the gods which I know will amaze you.

Socrates: I should not be surprised, but you will tell me these at leisure some other time. For now, try to tell me more clearly what I was asking just now, for, my friend, you did not teach me adequately when I asked you what the pious was, but you told me that what you are doing now, in prosecuting your father for murder, is pious.

Euthyphro: And I told the truth, Socrates.

Socrates: Perhaps. You agree, however, that there are many other pious actions.

Euthyphro: There are.

Socrates: Bear in mind then that I did not bid you tell me one or two of the many pious actions but that form itself that makes all pious actions pious, for you agreed that all impious actions are impious and all pious actions pious through one form, or don't you remember?

Euthyphro: I do.

Socrates: Tell me then what this form itself is, so that I may look upon it and, using it as a model, say that any action of yours or another's that is of that kind is pious, and if it is not that it is not.

Euthyphro: If that is how you want it, Socrates, that is how I will tell you.

Socrates: That is what I want.

Euthyphro: Well then, what is dear to the gods is pious, what is not is impious.

Socrates: Splendid, Euthyphro! You have now answered in the way I wanted. Whether your answer is true I do not know yet, but you will obviously show me that what you say is true.

Euthyphro: Certainly.

Socrates: Come then, let us examine what we mean. An action or a man dear to the gods is pious, but an action or a man hated by the gods is impious. They are not the same, but quite opposite, the pious and the impious. Is that not so?

Euthyphro: It is indeed.

Socrates: And that seems to be a good statement?

Euthyphro: I think so, Socrates.

Socrates: We have also stated that the gods are in a state of discord, that they are at odds with each other, Euthyphro, and that they are at enmity with each other. Has that, too, been said?

Euthyphro: It has.

Socrates: What are the subjects of difference that cause hatred and anger? Let us look at it this way. If you and I were to differ about numbers as to which is the greater, would this difference make us enemies and angry with each other, or would we proceed to count and soon resolve our difference about this?

Euthyphro: We would certainly do so.

Socrates: Again, if we differed about the larger and the smaller, we would turn to measurement and soon cease to differ.

Euthyphro: That is so.

Socrates: And about the heavier and the lighter, we would resort to weighing and be reconciled.

Euthyphro: Of course.

Socrates: What subject of difference would make us angry and hostile to each other if we were unable to come to a decision? Perhaps you do not have an answer ready, but examine as I tell you whether these subjects are the just and the unjust, the beautiful and the ugly, the good and the bad. Are these not the subjects of difference about which, when we are unable to come to a satisfactory decision, you and I and other men become hostile to each other whenever we do?

Euthyphro: That is the difference, Socrates, about those subjects.

Socrates: What about the gods, Euthyphro? If indeed they have differences, will it not be about these same subjects?

Euthyphro: It certainly must be so.

Socrates: Then according to your argument, my good Euthyphro, different gods consider different things to be just, beautiful, ugly, good, and bad, for they would not be at odds with one another unless they differed about these subjects, would they?

Euthyphro: You are right.

Socrates: And they like what each of them considers beautiful, good, and just, and hate the opposites of these?

Euthyphro: Certainly.

Socrates: But you say that the same things are considered just by some gods and unjust by others, and as they dispute about these things they are at odds and at war with each other. Is that not so?

Euthyphro: It is.

Socrates: The same things then are loved by the gods and hated by the gods, and would be both god-loved and god-hated.

Euthyphro: It seems likely.

Socrates: And the same things would be both pious and impious, according to this argument?

Euthyphro: I'm afraid so.

Socrates: So you did not answer my question, you surprising man. I did not ask you what same thing is both pious and impious, and it appears that what is loved by the gods is also hated by them. So it is in no way surprising if your present action, namely punishing your father, may be pleasing to Zeus but displeasing to Cronus and Uranus,[9] pleasing to Hephaestus but displeasing to Hera, and so with any other gods who differ from each other on this subject.

Euthyphro: I think, Socrates, that on this subject no gods would differ from one another, that whoever has killed anyone unjustly should pay the penalty.

Socrates: Well now, Euthyphro, have you ever heard any man maintaining that one who has killed or done anything else unjustly should not pay the penalty?

Euthyphro: They never cease to dispute on this subject, both elsewhere and in the courts, for when they have committed many wrongs they do and say anything to avoid the penalty.

Socrates: Do they agree they have done wrong, Euthyphro, and in spite of so agreeing do they nevertheless say they should not be punished?

Euthyphro: No, they do not agree on that point.

Socrates: So they do not say or do just anything. For they do not venture to say this, or dispute that they must not pay the penalty if they have done wrong, but I think they deny doing wrong. Is that not so?

Euthyphro: That is true.

Socrates: Then they do not dispute that the wrongdoer must be punished, but they may disagree as to who the wrongdoer is, what he did, and when.

Euthyphro: You are right.

Socrates: Do not the gods have the same experience, if indeed they are at odds with each other about the just and the unjust, as your argument maintains? Some assert that they wrong one another, while others deny it, but no one among gods or men ventures to say that the wrongdoer must not be punished.

Euthyphro: Yes, that is true, Socrates, as to the main point.

Socrates: And those who disagree, whether men or gods, dispute about each action, if indeed the gods disagree. Some say it is done justly, others unjustly. Is that not so?

Euthyphro: Yes, indeed.

Socrates: Come now, my dear Euthyphro, tell me, too, that I may become wiser, what proof you have that all the gods consider that man to have been killed unjustly who became a murderer while in your service, was bound by the master of his victim, and died in his bonds before the one who bound him found out from the seers what was to be done with him, and that it is right for a son to denounce and to prosecute his father on behalf of such a man. Come, try to show me a clear sign that all the gods definitely believe this action to be right. If you can give me adequate proof of this, I shall never cease to extol your wisdom.

Euthyphro: This is perhaps no light task, Socrates, though I could show you very clearly.

Socrates: I understand that you think me more dull-witted than the jury, as you will obviously show them that these actions were unjust and that all the gods hate such actions.

Euthyphro: I will show it to them clearly, Socrates, if only they will listen to me.

Socrates: They will listen if they think you show them well. But this thought came to me as you were speaking, and I am examining it, saying to myself: "If Euthyphro shows me conclusively that all the gods consider such a death unjust, to what greater extent have I learned from him the nature of piety and impiety? This action would then, it seems, be hated by the gods, but the pious and the impious were not thereby now defined, for what is hated by the gods has also been shown to be loved by them." So I will not insist on this point; let us assume, if you wish, that all the gods consider this unjust and that they all hate it. However, is this the correction we are making in our discussion, that what all the gods hate is impious, and what they all love is pious, and that what some gods love and others hate is neither or both? Is that how you now wish us to define piety and impiety?

Euthyphro: What prevents us from doing so, Socrates?

Socrates: For my part nothing, Euthyphro, but you look whether on your part this proposal will enable you to teach me most easily what you promised.

Euthyphro: I would certainly say that the pious is what all the gods love, and the opposite, what all the gods hate, is the impious.

Socrates: Then let us again examine whether that is a sound statement, or do we let it pass, and if one of us, or someone else, merely says that something is so, do we accept that it is so? Or should we examine what the speaker means?

Euthyphro: We must examine it, but I certainly think that this is now a fine statement.

Socrates: We shall soon know better whether it is. Consider this: Is the pious being loved by the gods because it is pious, or is it pious because it is being loved by the gods?

Euthyphro: I don't know what you mean, Socrates.

Socrates: I shall try to explain more clearly: we speak of something carried and something carrying, of something led and something leading, of something seen and something seeing, and you understand that these things are all different from one another and how they differ?

Euthyphro: I think I do.

Socrates: So there is also something loved and—a different thing—something loving.

Euthyphro: Of course.

Socrates: Tell me then whether the thing carried is a carried thing because it is being carried, or for some other reason?

Euthyphro: No, that is the reason.

Socrates: And the thing led is so because it is being led, and the thing seen because it is being seen?

Euthyphro: Certainly.

Socrates: It is not being seen because it is a thing seen but on the contrary it is a thing seen because it is being seen; nor is it because it is something led that it is being led but because it is being led that it is something led; nor is something being carried because it is something carried, but it is something carried because it is being carried. Is what I want to say clear, Euthyphro? I want to say this, namely, that if anything is being changed or is being affected in any way, it is not being changed because it is something changed, but rather it is something changed because it is being changed; nor is it being affected because it is something affected, but it is something affected because it is being affected.[10] Or do you not agree?

Euthyphro: I do.

Socrates: Is something loved either something changed or something affected by something?

Euthyphro: Certainly.

Socrates: So it is in the same case as the things just mentioned; it is not being loved by those who love it because it is something loved, but it is something loved because it is being loved by them?

Euthyphro: Necessarily.

Socrates: What then do we say about the pious, Euthyphro? Surely that it is being loved by all the gods, according to what you say?

Euthyphro: Yes.

Socrates: Is it being loved because it is pious, or for some other reason?

Euthyphro: For no other reason.

Socrates: It is being loved then because it is pious, but it is not pious because it is being loved?

Euthyphro: Apparently.

Socrates: And yet it is something loved and god-loved because it is being loved by the gods?

Euthyphro: Of course.

Socrates: Then the god-loved is not the same as the pious, Euthyphro, nor the pious the same as the god-loved, as you say it is, but one differs from the other.

Euthyphro: How so, Socrates?

Socrates: Because we agree that the pious is being loved for this reason, that it is pious, but it is not pious because it is being loved. Is that not so?

Euthyphro: Yes.

Socrates: And that the god-loved, on the other hand, is so because it is being loved by the gods, by the very fact of being loved, but it is not being loved because it is god-loved.

Euthyphro: True.

Socrates: But if the god-loved and the pious were the same, my dear Euthyphro, then if the pious was being loved because it was pious, the god-loved would also be being loved because it was god-loved; and if the god-loved was god-loved because it was being loved by the gods, then the pious would also be pious because it was being loved by the gods. But now you see that they are in opposite cases as being altogether different from each other: the one is such as to be loved because it is being loved, the other is being loved because it is such as to be loved. I'm afraid, Euthyphro, that when you were asked what piety is, you did not wish to make its nature clear to me, but you told me an affect or a quality of it, that the pious has the quality of being loved by all the gods, but you have not yet told me what the pious is. Now, if you will, do not hide things from me but tell me again from the beginning what piety is, whether being loved by the gods or having some other quality—we shall not quarrel about that—but be keen to tell me what the pious and the impious are.

Euthyphro: But Socrates, I have no way of telling you what I have in mind, for whatever proposition we put forward goes around and refuses to stay put where we establish it.

Socrates: Your statements, Euthyphro, seem to belong to my ancestor, Daedalus.[11] If I were stating them and putting them forward, you would perhaps be making fun of me and say that because of my kinship with him my conclusions in discussion run away and will not stay where one puts them. As these propositions are yours, however, we need some other jest, for they will not stay put for you, as you say yourself.

Euthyphro: I think the same jest will do for our discussion, Socrates, for I am not the one who makes them go around and not remain in the same place; it is you who are the Daedalus; for as far as I am concerned they would remain as they were.

Socrates: It looks as if I was cleverer than Daedalus in using my skill, my friend, insofar as he could only cause to move the things he made himself, but I can make other people's things move as well as my own. And the smartest part of my skill is that I am clever without wanting to be, for I would rather have your statements to me remain unmoved than possess the wealth of Tantalus as well as the cleverness of Daedalus. But enough of this. Since I think you are making unnecessary difficulties, I am as eager as you are to find a way to teach me about piety, and do not give up before you do. See whether you think all that is pious is of necessity just.

Euthyphro: I think so.

Socrates: And is then all that is just pious? Or is all that is pious just, but not all that is just pious, but some of it is and some is not?

Euthyphro: I do not follow what you are saying, Socrates.

Socrates: Yet you are younger than I by as much as you are wiser. As I say, you are making difficulties because of your wealth of wisdom. Pull yourself together, my dear sir, what I am saying is not difficult to grasp. I am saying the opposite of what the poet said who wrote: You do not wish to name Zeus, who had done it, and who made all things grow, for where there is fear there is also shame.[12] I disagree with the poet. Shall I tell you why?

Euthyphro: Please do.

Socrates: I do not think that "where there is fear there is also shame," for I think that many people who fear disease and poverty and many other such things feel fear, but are not ashamed of the things they fear. Do you not think so?

Euthyphro: I do indeed.

Socrates: But where there is shame there is also fear. For is there anyone who, in feeling shame and embarrassment at anything, does not also at the same time fear and dread a reputation for wickedness?

Euthyphro: He is certainly afraid.

Socrates: It is then not right to say "where there is fear there is also shame," but that where there is shame there is also fear, for fear covers a larger area than shame. Shame is a part of fear just as odd is a part of number, with the result that it is not true that where there is number there is also oddness, but that where there is oddness there is also number. Do you follow me now?

Euthyphro: Surely

Socrates: This is the kind of thing I was asking before, whether where there is piety there is also justice, but where there is justice there is not always piety, for the pious is a part of justice. Shall we say that, or do you think otherwise?

Euthyphro: No, but like that, for what you say appears to be right.

Socrates: See what comes next: if the pious is a part of the just, we must, it seems, find out what part of the just it is. Now if you asked me something of what we mentioned just now, such as what part of number is the even, and what number that is, I would say it is the number that is divisible into two equal, not unequal, parts. Or do you not think so?

Euthyphro: I do.

Socrates: Try in this way to tell me what part of the just the pious is, in order to tell Meletus not to wrong us any more and not to indict me for ungodliness, since I have learned from you sufficiently what is godly and pious and what is not.

Euthyphro: I think, Socrates, that the godly and pious is the part of the just that is concerned with the care of the gods, while that concerned with the care of men is the remaining part of justice.

Socrates: You seem to me to put that very well, but I still need a bit of information. I do not know yet what you mean by care, for you do not mean the care of the gods in the same sense as the care of other things, as, for example, we say, don't we, that not everyone knows how to care for horses, but the horse breeder does.

Euthyphro: Yes, I do mean it that way.

Socrates: So horse breeding is the care of horses.

Euthyphro: Yes.

Socrates: Nor does everyone know how to care for dogs, but the hunter does.

Euthyphro: That is so.

Socrates: So hunting is the care of dogs.

Euthyphro: Yes.

Socrates: And cattle raising is the care of cattle.

Euthyphro: Quite so.

Socrates: While piety and godliness is the care of the gods, Euthyphro. Is that what you mean?

Euthyphro: It is.

Socrates: Now care in each case has the same effect; it aims at the good and the benefit of the object cared for, as you can see that horses cared for by horse breeders are benefited and become better. Or do you not think so?

Euthyphro: I do.

Socrates: So dogs are benefited by dog breeding, cattle by cattle raising, and so with all the others. Or do you think that care aims to harm the object of its care?

Euthyphro: By Zeus, no.

Socrates: It aims to benefit the object of its care?

Euthyphro: Of course.

Socrates: Is piety then, which is the care of the gods, also to benefit the gods and make them better? Would you agree that when you do something pious you make some one of the gods better?

Euthyphro: By Zeus, no.

Socrates: Nor do I think that this is what you mean—far from it—but that is why I asked you what you meant by the care of gods, because I did not believe you meant this kind of care.

Euthyphro: Quite right, Socrates, that is not the kind of care I mean.

Socrates: Very well, but what kind of care of the gods would piety be?

Euthyphro: The kind of care, Socrates, that slaves take of their masters.

Socrates: I understand. It is likely to be a kind of service of the gods.

Euthyphro: Quite so.

Socrates: Could you tell me to the achievement of what goal service to doctors tends? Is it not, do you think, to achieving health?

Euthyphro: I think so.

Socrates: What about service to shipbuilders? To what achievement is it directed?

Euthyphro: Clearly, Socrates, to the building of a ship.

Socrates: And service to housebuilders to the building of a house?

Euthyphro: Yes.

Socrates: Tell me then, my good sir, to the achievement of what aim does service to the gods tend? You obviously know since you say that you, of all men, have the best knowledge of the divine.

Euthyphro: And I am telling the truth, Socrates.

Socrates: Tell me then, by Zeus, what is that excellent aim that the gods achieve, using us as their servants?

Euthyphro: Many fine things, Socrates.

Socrates: So do generals, my friend. Nevertheless you could easily tell me their main concern, which is to achieve victory in war, is it not?

Euthyphro: Of course.

Socrates: The farmers, too, I think, achieve many fine things, but the main point of their efforts is to produce food from the earth.

Euthyphro: Quite so.

Socrates: Well then, how would you sum up the many fine things that the gods achieve?

Euthyphro: I told you a short while ago, Socrates, that it is a considerable task to acquire any precise knowledge of these things, but, to put it simply, I say that if a man knows how to say and do what is pleasing to the gods at prayer and sacrifice, those are pious actions such as preserve both private houses and public affairs of state. The opposite of these pleasing actions are impious and overturn and destroy everything.

Socrates: You could tell me in far fewer words, if you were willing, the sum of what I asked, Euthyphro, but you are not keen to teach me, that is clear. You were on the point of doing so, but you turned away. If you had given that answer, I should now have acquired from you sufficient knowledge of the nature of piety. As it is, the lover of inquiry must follow his beloved wherever it may lead him. Once more then, what do you say that piety and the pious are? Are they a knowledge of how to sacrifice and pray?

Euthyphro: They are.

Socrates: To sacrifice is to make a gift to the gods, whereas to pray is to beg from the gods?

Euthyphro: Definitely, Socrates.

Socrates: It would follow from this statement that piety would be a knowledge of how to give to, and beg from, the gods.

Euthyphro: You understood what I said very well, Socrates.

Socrates: That is because I am so desirous of your wisdom, and I concentrate my mind on it, so that no word of yours may fall to the ground. But tell me, what is this service to the gods? You say it is to beg from them and to give to them?

Euthyphro: I do.

Socrates: And to beg correctly would be to ask from them things that we need?

Euthyphro: What else?

Socrates: And to give correctly is to give them what they need from us, for it would not be skillful to bring gifts to anyone that are in no way needed.

Euthyphro: True, Socrates.

Socrates: Piety would then be a sort of trading skill between gods and men?

Euthyphro: Trading yes, if you prefer to call it that.

Socrates: I prefer nothing, unless it is true. But tell me, what benefit do the gods derive from the gifts they receive from us? What they give us is obvious to all. There is for us no good that we do not receive from them, but how are they benefited by what they receive from us? Or do we have such an advantage over them in the trade that we receive all our blessings from them and they receive nothing from us?

Euthyphro: Do you suppose, Socrates, that the gods are benefited by what they receive from us?

Socrates: What could those gifts from us to the gods be, Euthyphro?

Euthyphro: What else, do you think, than honor, reverence, and what I mentioned just now, to please them?

Socrates: The pious is then, Euthyphro, pleasing to the gods, but not beneficial or dear to them?

Euthyphro: I think it is of all things most dear to them.

Socrates: So the pious is once again what is dear to the gods.

Euthyphro: Most certainly.

Socrates: When you say this, will you be surprised if your arguments seem to move about instead of staying put? And will you accuse me of being Daedalus who makes them move, though you are yourself much more skillful than Daedalus and make them go around in a circle? Or do you not realize that our argument has moved around and come again to the same place? You surely remember that earlier the pious and the god-loved were shown not to be the same but different from each other. Or do you not remember?

Euthyphro: I do.

Socrates: Do you then not realize now that you are saying that what is dear to the gods is the pious? Is this not the same as the god-loved? Or is it not?

Euthyphro: It certainly is.

Socrates: Either we were wrong when we agreed before, or, if we were right then, we are wrong now.

Euthyphro: That seems to be so.

Socrates: So we must investigate again from the beginning what piety is, as I shall not willingly give up before I learn this. Do not think me unworthy, but concentrate your attention and tell the truth. For you know it, if any man does, and I must not let you go, like Proteus,[13] before you tell me. If you had no clear knowledge of piety and impiety you would never have ventured to prosecute your old father for murder on behalf of a servant. For fear of the gods you would have been afraid to take the risk lest you should not be acting rightly, and would have been ashamed before men, but now I know well that you believe you have clear knowledge of piety and impiety. So tell me, my good Euthyphro, and do not hide what you think it is.

Euthyphro: Some other time, Socrates, for I am in a hurry now, and it is time for me to go.

Socrates: What a thing to do, my friend! By going you have cast me down from a great hope I had, that I would learn from you the nature of the pious and the impious and so escape Meletus' indictment by showing him that I had acquired wisdom in divine matters from Euthyphro, and my ignorance would no longer cause me to be careless and inventive about such things, and that I would be better for the rest of my life.

NOTES

1. We know nothing about Euthyphro except what we can gather from this dialogue. He is obviously a professional priest who considers himself an expert on ritual and on piety generally and, it seems, is generally so-considered. One Euthyphro is mentioned in Plato's *Cratylus* who is given to *enthousiasmos,* inspiration or possession, but we cannot be sure that it is the same person.

2. The Lyceum was an outdoor gymnasium, just outside the walls of Athens, where teenage young men engaged in exercises and athletic competitions. Socrates and other intellectuals carried on discussions with them there and exhibited their skills. See the beginnings of Plato's *Euthydemus* and *Lysis,* and the last paragraph of *Symposium.* The king-archon, one of the nine principal magistrates of Athens, had the responsibility to oversee religious rituals and purifications, and as such had oversight of legal cases involving alleged offenses against the Olympian gods, whose worship was a civic function—it was regarded as a serious offense to offend them.

3. A deme was, in effect, one of the constituent villages of Attica, the territory whose center was the city of Athens (though Athens itself was divided

into demes, too). Athenian citizens had first of all to be enrolled and recognized as citizens in their demes.

4. In Plato, Socrates always speaks of his divine sign or voice as intervening to prevent him from doing or saying something (…), but never positively. The popular view was that it enabled him to foretell the future, and Euthyphro here represents that view. Note, however, that Socrates dissociates himself from "you prophets."

5. The assembly was the final decision-making body of the Athenian democracy. All adult males could attend and vote.

6. Naxos is a large island in the Aegean Sea southeast of Athens, where Athens had appropriated land and settled many of its citizens under its imperial rule in the mid-fifth century BC.

7. This is the kind of passage that makes it easier for us to follow the transition from Socrates' universal definitions to the Platonic theory of separately existent eternal universal Forms. The words *eidos* and *idea,* the technical terms for the Platonic Forms, commonly mean physical stature or bodily appearance. As we apply a common epithet, in this case pious, to different actions or things, these must have a common characteristic, present a common appearance or form, to justify the use of the same term, but in the early dialogues, as here, it seems to be thought of as immanent in the particulars and without separate existence. The same is true of…where the word "form" is also used.

8. The Acropolis is the huge rocky outcropping in the center of Athens that served as the citadel for Attica, and also the center of its religious life.

Major temples to the gods were there, including the Parthenon, the temple of Athena, the city's protectress. Every four years in an elaborate festival in her honor maidens brought up the ceremonial robe referred to here, in which to clothe her statue.

9. Zeus' father, whom he fought and defeated, was Cronus; Cronus, in turn, had castrated his own father Uranus. The story of Hephaestus and his mother Hera, mentioned next, similarly involves a son punishing his parent.

10. Here Socrates gives the general principle under which, he says, the specific cases already examined—those of leading, carrying, and seeing—all fall. It is by being changed by something that changes *it* (e.g., by carrying it somewhere) that anything is a changed thing—not vice versa: it is not by something's being a changed thing that something *else* then changes it so that it comes to be being changed (e.g., by carrying it somewhere). Likewise for "affections" such as being seen by someone: it is by being "affected" by something that "affects" it that anything is an "affected" thing, not vice versa. It is not by being an "affected" thing (e.g., a thing seen) that something else then "affects" it.

11. Socrates may have been a stonemason, as his father was. In Greek mythology Daedalus' statues (made of wood) could move themselves.

12. Author unknown.

13. In Greek mythology Proteus was a sort of old man of the sea, who could keep on changing his form and so escape being questioned. See Homer, *Odyssey* iv.382 ff.

2.6 The Good Will and the Categorical Imperative

IMMANUEL KANT

Immanuel Kant (1724–1804) was the greatest of the German philosophers. He wrote in almost all of the major areas of philosophy, producing classics that continue to influence work in (among other areas) metaphysics, epistemology, aesthetics, the philosophy of religion, and ethics. He spent his entire academic career at the University of Königsberg.

THE GOOD WILL

It is impossible to think of anything at all in the world, or indeed even beyond it, that could be considered good without limitation except a **good will.** Understanding, wit, judgment and the like, whatever such *talents* of mind may be called, or courage, resolution, and perseverance in one's plans, as qualities of *temperament,* are undoubtedly good and desirable for many purposes, but they can also be extremely evil and harmful if the will which is to make use of these gifts of nature, and whose distinctive constitution is therefore called *character,* is not good. It is the same with *gifts of fortune.* Power, riches, honor, even health and that complete well-being and satisfaction with one's condition called *happiness,* produce boldness and thereby often arrogance as well unless a good will is present which corrects the influence of these on the mind and, in so doing, also corrects the whole principle of action and brings it into conformity with universal ends—not to mention that an impartial rational spectator can take no delight in seeing the uninterrupted prosperity of a being graced with no feature of a pure and good will, so that a good will seems to constitute the indispensable condition even of worthiness to be happy.

Some qualities are even conducive to this good will itself and can make its work much easier; despite this, however, they have no inner unconditional worth but always presuppose a good will, which limits the esteem one otherwise rightly has for them and does not permit their being taken as absolutely good. Moderation in affects and passions, self-control, and calm reflection are not only good for all sorts of purposes but even seem to constitute a part of the *inner* worth of a person; but they lack much that would be required to declare them good without limitation (however unconditionally they were praised by the ancients); for, without the basic principles of a good will they can become extremely evil, and the coolness of a scoundrel makes him not only far more dangerous but also immediately more abominable in our eyes than we would have taken him to be without it.

A good will is not good because of what it effects or accomplishes, because of its fitness to attain some proposed end, but only because of its volition, that is, it is good in itself and, regarded for itself, is to be valued incomparably higher than all that could merely be brought about by it in favor of some inclination and indeed, if you will, of the sum of all inclinations. Even if, by a special disfavor of fortune or by the niggardly provision of a stepmotherly nature, this will should wholly lack the capacity to carry out its purpose—if with its greatest efforts it should yet achieve nothing and only the good will were left (not, of course, as a mere wish but as the summoning of all means insofar as they are in our control)—then, like a jewel, it would still shine by itself, as something that has its full worth in itself. Usefulness or fruitlessness can neither add anything to this worth nor take anything away from it. Its usefulness would be, as it were, only the setting to enable us to handle it more conveniently in ordinary commerce or to attract to it the attention of those who are not yet expert enough, but not to recommend it to experts or to determine its worth.

We have, then, to explicate the concept of a will that is to be esteemed in itself and that is good apart from any further purpose, as it already dwells in natural sound understanding and needs not so much to be taught as only to be clarified—this concept that always takes first place in estimating the total worth of our actions and constitutes the condition of all the rest. In order to do so, we shall set before ourselves the concept of **duty,** which contains that of a good will though under certain subjective limitations and hindrances, which, however, far from concealing it and making it unrecognizable, rather bring it out by contrast and make it shine forth all the more brightly.

I here pass over all actions that are already recognized as contrary to duty, even though they may be useful for this or that purpose; for in their case the question whether they might have been done *from duty* never arises, since they even conflict with it. I also set aside actions that are really in conformity with duty but to which human beings have *no inclination* immediately and which they still perform because they are impelled to do so through another inclination. For in this case it is easy to distinguish whether an action in conformity with duty is done *from duty* or from a self-seeking purpose. It is much more difficult to note this distinction when an action conforms with duty and the subject has, besides, an *immediate* inclination to it. For example, it certainly conforms with duty that a shopkeeper not overcharge an inexperienced customer, and where there is a good deal of trade a prudent merchant does not overcharge but keeps a fixed general price for everyone, so that a child can buy from him as well as everyone else. People are thus served *honestly;* but this is not nearly enough for us to believe that the merchant acted in this way from duty and basic principles of honesty; his advantage required it; it cannot be assumed here that he had, besides, an immediate inclination toward his customers, so as from love, as it were, to give no one preference over another in the matter of price. Thus the action was done neither from duty nor from immediate inclination but merely for purposes of self-interest.

On the other hand, to preserve one's life is a duty, and besides everyone has an immediate inclination to do so. But on this account the often anxious care that most people take of it still has no inner worth and their maxim has no moral content. They look after their lives *in conformity with duty* but not *from duty.* On the other hand, if adversity and hopeless grief have quite taken away the taste for life; if an unfortunate man, strong of soul and more indignant about his fate than despondent or dejected, wishes for death and yet preserves his life without loving it, not from inclination or fear but from duty, then his maxim has moral content.

To be beneficent where one can is a duty, and besides there are many souls so sympathetically attuned that, without any other motive of vanity or self-interest they find an inner satisfaction in spreading joy around them and can take delight in the satisfaction of others so far as it is their own work. But I assert that in such a case an action of this kind, however it may conform with duty and however amiable it may be, has nevertheless no true moral worth but is on the same footing with other inclinations, for example, the inclination to honor, which, if it fortunately lights upon what is in fact in the common interest and in conformity with duty and hence honorable, deserves praise and encouragement but not esteem; for the maxim lacks moral content, namely that of doing such actions not from inclination but *from duty.* Suppose, then, that the mind of this philanthropist were overclouded by his own grief, which extinguished all sympathy with the fate of others, and that while he still had the means to benefit others in distress their troubles did not move him because he had enough to do with his own; and suppose that now, when no longer incited to it by any inclination, he nevertheless tears himself out of this deadly insensibility and does the action without any inclination, simply from duty; then the action first has its genuine moral worth. Still further: if nature had put little sympathy in the heart of this or that man; if (in other respects an honest man) he is by temperament cold and indifferent to the sufferings of others, perhaps because he himself is provided with the special gift of patience and endurance toward his own sufferings and presupposes the same in every other or even requires it; if nature had not properly fashioned such a man (who would in truth not be its worst product) for a philanthropist, would he not still find within himself a source from which to give himself a far higher worth than what a mere good-natured temperament might have? By all means! It is just then that the worth of character comes out, which is moral and incomparably the highest, namely that he is beneficent not from inclination but from duty.

Thus the moral worth of an action does not lie in the effect expected from it and so too does not lie in any principle of action that needs to borrow its motive from this expected effect. For, all these effects (agreeableness of one's condition, indeed even promotion of others' happiness) could have been also brought about by other causes, so that there would have been no need, for this, of the will of a rational being, in which, however, the highest and unconditional good alone can be found. Hence nothing other than the *representation of the law* in itself, *which can of course occur only in a rational being*, insofar as it and not the hoped-for effect is the determining ground of the will, can constitute the preeminent good we call moral, which is already present in the person himself who acts in accordance with this representation and need not wait upon the effect of his action.

But what kind of law can that be, the representation of which must determine the will, even without regard for the effect expected from it, in order for the will to be called good absolutely and without limitation? Since I have deprived the will of every impulse that could arise for it from obeying some law, nothing is left but the conformity of actions as such with universal law, which alone is to serve the will as its principle, that is, *I ought never to act except in such a way that I could also will that my maxim should become a universal law.* Here mere conformity to law as such, without having as its basis some law determined for certain actions, is what serves the will as its principle, and must so serve it, if duty is not to be everywhere an empty delusion and a chimerical concept. Common human reason also agrees completely with this in its practical appraisals and always has this principle before its eyes. Let the question be, for example: may I, when hard pressed, make a promise with the intention not to keep it? Here I easily distinguish two significations the question can have: whether it is prudent or whether it is in conformity with duty to make a false promise. The first can undoubtedly often be the case. I see very well that it is not enough to get out of a present difficulty by means of this subterfuge but that I must reflect carefully whether this lie may later give rise to much greater inconvenience for me than that from which I now extricate myself; and since, with all my supposed *cunning*, the results cannot be so easily foreseen but that once confidence in me is lost this could be far more prejudicial to me than all the troubles I now think to avoid, I must reflect whether the matter might be handled *more prudently* by proceeding on a general maxim and making it a habit to promise

nothing except with the intention of keeping it. But it is soon clear to me that such a maxim will still be based only on results feared. To be truthful from duty, however, is something entirely different from being truthful from anxiety about detrimental results, since in the first case the concept of the action in itself already contains a law for me while in the second I must first look about elsewhere to see what effects on me might be combined with it. For, if I deviate from the principle of duty this is quite certainly evil; but if I am unfaithful to my maxim of prudence this can sometimes be very advantageous to me, although it is certainly safer to abide by it. However, to inform myself in the shortest and yet infallible way about the answer to this problem, whether a lying promise is in conformity with duty, I ask myself: would I indeed be content that my maxim (to get myself out of difficulties by a false promise) should hold as a universal law (for myself as well as for others)? and could I indeed say to myself that every one may make a false promise when he finds himself in a difficulty he can get out of in no other way? Then I soon become aware that I could indeed will the lie, but by no means a universal law to lie; for in accordance with such a law there would properly be no promises at all, since it would be futile to avow my will with regard to my future actions to others who would not believe this avowal or, if they rashly did so, would pay me back in like coin; and thus my maxim, as soon as it were made a universal law, would have to destroy itself.

I do not, therefore, need any penetrating acuteness to see what I have to do in order that my volition be morally good. Inexperienced in the course of the world, incapable of being prepared for whatever might come to pass in it, I ask myself only: can you also will that your maxim become a universal law? If not, then it is to be repudiated, and that not because of a disadvantage to you or even to others forthcoming from it but because it cannot fit as a principle into a possible giving of universal law, for which lawgiving reason, however, forces from me immediate respect. Although I do not yet *see* what this respect is based upon (this the philosopher may investigate), I at least understand this much: that it is an estimation of a worth that far outweighs any worth of what is recommended by inclination, and that the necessity of my action from *pure* respect for the practical law is what constitutes duty, to which every other motive must give way because it is the condition of a will good *in itself*, the worth of which surpasses all else.

THE CATEGORICAL IMPERATIVE

Now, all imperatives command either *hypothetically* or *categorically*. The former represent the practical necessity of a possible action as a means to achieving something else that one wills (or that it is at least possible for one to will). The categorical imperative would be that which represented an action as objectively necessary of itself, without reference to another end.

Since every practical law represents a possible action as good and thus as necessary for a subject practically determinable by reason, all imperatives are formulae for the determination of action that is necessary in accordance with the principle of a will which is good in some way. Now, if the action would be good merely as a means *to something else* the imperative is *hypothetical;* if the action is represented as *in itself* good, hence as necessary in a will in itself conforming to reason, as its principle, *then it is categorical.*

There is one imperative that, without being based upon and having as its condition any other purpose to be attained by certain conduct, commands this conduct immediately. This imperative is **categorical.** It has to do not with the matter of the action and what is to result from it, but with the form and the principle from which the action itself follows; and the essentially good in the action consists in the disposition, let the result be what it may. This imperative may be called the **imperative of morality.**

When I think of a *hypothetical* imperative in general I do not know beforehand what it will contain; I do not know this until I am given the condition. But when I think of a *categorical* imperative I know at once what it contains. For, since the imperative contains, beyond the law,

only the necessity that the maxim* be in conformity with this law, while the law contains no condition to which it would be limited, nothing is left with which the maxim of action is to conform but the universality of a law as such; and this conformity alone is what the imperative properly represents as necessary.

There is, therefore, only a single categorical imperative and it is this: *act only in accordance with that maxim through which you can at the same time will that it become a universal law.*

Now, if all imperatives of duty can be derived from this single imperative as from their principle, then, even though we leave it undecided whether what is called duty is not as such an empty concept, we shall at least be able to show what we think by it and what the concept wants to say.

Since the universality of law in accordance with which effects take place constitutes what is properly called *nature* in the most general sense (as regards its form)—that is, the existence of things insofar as it is determined in accordance with universal laws—the universal imperative of duty can also go as follows: *act as if the maxim of your action were to become by your will a* **universal law of nature.**

We shall now enumerate a few duties in accordance with the usual division of them into duties to ourselves and to other human beings and into perfect and imperfect duties.†

---

*A *maxim* is the subjective principle of acting, and must be distinguished from the *objective* principle, namely the practical law. The former contains the practical rule determined by reason conformably with the conditions of the subject (often his ignorance or also his inclinations), and is therefore the principle in accordance with which the subject *acts;* but the law is the objective principle valid for every rational being, and the principle in accordance with which he *ought to act,* i.e., an imperative.

†It must be noted here that I reserve the division of duties entirely for a future *Metaphysics of Morals,* so that the division here stands only as one adopted at my discretion (for the sake of arranging my examples). For the rest, I understand here by a perfect duty one that admits no exception in favor of inclination, and then I have not merely external but also internal *perfect duties;* although this is contrary to the use of the word adopted in the schools, I do not intend to justify it here, since for my purpose it makes no difference whether or not it is granted me.

1) Someone feels sick of life because of a series of troubles that has grown to the point of despair, but is still so far in possession of his reason that he can ask himself whether it would not be contrary to his duty to himself to take his own life. Now he inquires whether the maxim of his action could indeed become a universal law of nature. His maxim, however, is: from self-love I make it my principle to shorten my life when its longer duration threatens more troubles than it promises agreeableness. The only further question is whether this principle of self-love could become a universal law of nature. It is then seen at once that a nature whose law it would be to destroy life itself by means of the same feeling whose destination is to impel toward the furtherance of life would contradict itself and would therefore not subsist as nature; thus that maxim could not possibly be a law of nature and, accordingly, altogether opposes the supreme principle of all duty.

2) Another finds himself urged by need to borrow money. He well knows that he will not be able to repay it but sees also that nothing will be lent him unless he promises firmly to repay it within a determinate time. He would like to make such a promise, but he still has enough conscience to ask himself: is it not forbidden and contrary to duty to help oneself out of need in such a way? Supposing that he still decided to do so, his maxim of action would go as follows: when I believe myself to be in need of money I shall borrow money and promise to repay it, even though I know that this will never happen. Now this principle of self-love or personal advantage is perhaps quite consistent with my whole future welfare, but the question now is whether it is right. I therefore turn the demand of self-love into a universal law and put the question as follows: how would it be if my maxim became a universal law? I then see at once that it could never hold as a universal law of nature and be consistent with itself, but must necessarily contradict itself. For, the universality of a law that everyone, when he believes himself to be in need, could promise whatever he pleases with the intention of not keeping it would

make the promise and the end one might have in it itself impossible, since no one would believe what was promised him but would laugh at all such expressions as vain pretenses.

3) A third finds in himself a talent that by means of some cultivation could make him a human being useful for all sorts of purposes. However, he finds himself in comfortable circumstances and prefers to give himself up to pleasure than to trouble himself with enlarging and improving his fortunate natural predispositions. But he still asks himself whether his maxim of neglecting his natural gifts, besides being consistent with his propensity to amusement, is also consistent with what one calls duty. He now sees that a nature could indeed always subsist with such a universal law, although (as with the South Sea Islanders) the human being should let his talents rust and be concerned with devoting his life merely to idleness, amusement, procreation —in a word, to enjoyment; only he cannot possibly **will** that this become a universal law or be put in us as such by means of natural instinct. For, as a rational being he necessarily wills that all the capacities in him be developed, since they serve him and are given to him for all sorts of possible purposes.

4) Yet a *fourth,* for whom things are going well while he sees that others (whom he could very well help) have to contend with great hardships, thinks: what is it to me? let each be as happy as heaven wills or as he can make himself; I shall take nothing from him nor even envy him; only I do not care to contribute anything to his welfare or to his assistance in need! Now, if such a way of thinking were to become a universal law the human race could admittedly very well subsist, no doubt even better than when everyone prates about sympathy and benevolence and even exerts himself to practice them occasionally, but on the other hand also cheats where he can, sells the right of human beings or otherwise infringes upon it. But although it is possible that a universal law of nature could very well subsist in accordance with such a maxim, it is still impossible to **will** that such a principle hold everywhere as a **law** of nature. For, a will that decided this

would conflict with itself, since many cases could occur in which one would need the love and sympathy of others and in which, by such a law of nature arisen from his own will, he would rob himself of all hope of the assistance he wishes for himself.

If we now attend to ourselves in any transgression of a duty, we find that we do not really will that our maxim should become a universal law, since that is impossible for us, but that the opposite of our maxim should instead remain a universal law, only we take the liberty of making an *exception* to it for ourselves (or just for this once) to the advantage of our inclination. Consequently, if we weighed all cases from one and the same point of view, namely that of reason, we would find a contradiction in our own will, namely that a certain principle be objectively necessary as a universal law and yet subjectively not hold universally but allow exceptions.

Suppose there were something the *existence of which in itself* has an absolute worth, something which as *an end in itself* could be a ground of determinate laws; then in it, and in it alone, would lie the ground of a possible categorical imperative, that is, of a practical law.

Now I say that the human being and in general every rational being *exists* as an end in itself, *not merely as a means* to be used by this or that will at its discretion; instead he must in all his actions, whether directed to himself or also to other rational beings, always be regarded *at the same time as an end*. All objects of the inclinations have only a conditional worth; for, if there were not inclinations and the needs based on them, their object would be without worth. But the inclinations themselves, as sources of needs, are so far from having an absolute worth, so as to make one wish to have them, that it must instead be the universal wish of every rational being to be altogether free from them. Thus the worth of any object *to be acquired* by our action is always conditional. Beings the existence of which rests not on our will but on nature, if they are beings without reason, still have only a relative worth, as means, and are therefore called *things*, whereas rational beings are called *persons*

because their nature already marks them out as an end in itself, that is, as something that may not be used merely as a means, and hence so far limits all choice (and is an object of respect). These, therefore, are not merely subjective ends, the existence of which as an effect of our action has a worth *for us,* but rather *objective ends,* that is, beings the existence of which is in itself an end, and indeed one such that no other end, to which they would serve *merely* as means, can be put in its place, since without it nothing of *absolute worth* would be found anywhere; but if all worth were conditional and therefore contingent, then no supreme practical principle for reason could be found anywhere.

If, then, there is to be a supreme practical principle and, with respect to the human will, a categorical imperative, it must be one such that, from the representation of what is necessarily an end for everyone because it is an *end in itself,* it constitutes an *objective* principle of the will and thus can serve as a universal practical law. The ground of this principle is: *rational nature exists as an end in itself.* The human being necessarily represents his own existence in this way; so far it is thus a *subjective* principle of human actions. But every other rational being also represents his existence in this way consequent on just the same rational ground that also holds for me; thus it is at the same time an *objective* principle from which, as a supreme practical ground, it must be possible to derive all laws of the will. The practical imperative will therefore be the following: *So act that you use humanity, whether in your own person or in the person of any other, always at the same time as an end, never merely as a means.* We shall see whether this can be carried out.

To keep to the preceding examples:

First, as regards the concept of necessary duty to oneself, someone who has suicide in mind will ask himself whether his action can be consistent with the idea of humanity *as an end in itself.* If he destroys himself in order to escape from a trying condition he makes use of a person *merely as a means* to maintain a tolerable condition up to the end of life. A human being, however, is not a thing and hence not something that can be used *merely* as a means, but must in all his actions always be regarded as an end in itself. I cannot, therefore, dispose of a human being in my own person by maiming, damaging or killing him. (I must here pass over a closer determination of this principle that would prevent any misinterpretation, e.g., as to having limbs amputated in order to preserve myself, or putting my life in danger in order to preserve my life, and so forth; that belongs to morals proper.)

Second, as regards necessary duty to others or duty owed them, he who has it in mind to make a false promise to others sees at once that he wants to make use of another human being *merely as a means,* without the other at the same time containing in himself the end. For, he whom I want to use for my purposes by such a promise cannot possibly agree to my way of behaving toward him, and so himself contain the end of this action. This conflict with the principle of other human beings is seen more distinctly if examples of assaults on the freedom and property of others are brought forward. For then it is obvious that he who transgresses the rights of human beings intends to make use of the person of others merely as means, without taking into consideration that, as rational beings, they are always to be valued at the same time as ends, that is, only as beings who must also be able to contain in themselves the end of the very same action.

Third, with respect to contingent (meritorious) duty to oneself, it is not enough that the action does not conflict with humanity in our person as an end in itself; it must also *harmonize with it.* Now there are in humanity predispositions to greater perfection, which belong to the end of nature with respect to humanity in our subject; to neglect these might admittedly be consistent with the *preservation* of humanity as an end in itself but not with the *furtherance* of this end.

Fourth, concerning meritorious duty to others, the natural end that all human beings have is their own happiness. Now, humanity might indeed subsist if no one contributed to the happiness of others but yet did not intentionally withdraw anything from it; but there is still only a negative and not a positive agreement with *humanity as an end in itself* unless everyone also tries, as far as he can, to further the ends of others. For, the ends of a subject who is an end in itself must as far as possible be also *my* ends, if that representation is to have its *full* effect in me.

2.7 *Utilitarianism*

JOHN STUART MILL

John Stuart Mill (1806–1873) was one of the leading British moral philosophers of the nineteenth century. He also wrote important works on logic, economics, education, and feminism, and served for a time as a member of Parliament.

WHAT UTILITARIANISM IS

The creed which accepts as the foundation of morals, Utility, or the Greatest Happiness Principle, holds that actions are right in proportion as they tend to promote happiness, wrong as they tend to produce the reverse of happiness. By happiness is intended pleasure, and the absence of pain; by unhappiness, pain, and the privation of pleasure. To give a clear view of the moral

From J. S. Mill, *Utilitarianism*, chaps. 1 and 2. First published in 1863.

standard set up by the theory, much more requires to be said; in particular, what things it includes in the ideas of pain and pleasure; and to what extent this is left an open question. But these supplementary explanations do not affect the theory of life on which this theory of morality is grounded—namely, that pleasure, and freedom from pain, are the only things desirable as ends; and that all desirable things (which are as numerous in the utilitarian as in any other scheme) are desirable either for the pleasure inherent in themselves, or as means to the promotion of pleasure and the prevention of pain.

Now, such a theory of life excites in many minds, and among them in some of the most estimable in feeling and purpose, inveterate dislike. To suppose that life has (as they express it) no higher end than pleasure—no better and nobler object of desire and pursuit—they designate as utterly mean and grovelling; as a doctrine worthy only of swine, to whom the followers of Epicurus were, at a very early period, contemptuously likened; and modern holders of the doctrine are occasionally made the subject of equally polite comparisons by its German, French, and English assailants.

When thus attacked, the Epicureans have always answered, that it is not they, but their accusers, who represent human nature in a degrading light; since the accusation supposes human beings to be capable of no pleasures except those of which swine are capable. If this supposition were true, the charge could not be gainsaid, but would then be no longer an imputation; for if the sources of pleasure were precisely the same to human beings and to swine, the rule of life which is good enough for the one would be good enough for the other. The comparison of the Epicurean life to that of beasts is felt as degrading, precisely because a beast's pleasures do not satisfy a human being's conceptions of happiness. Human beings have faculties more elevated than the animal appetites, and when once made conscious of them, do not regard anything as happiness which does not include their gratification. I do not, indeed, consider the Epicureans to have been by any means

faultless in drawing out their scheme of consequences from the utilitarian principle. To do this in any sufficient manner, many Stoic, as well as Christian elements require to be included. But there is no known Epicurean theory of life which does not assign to the pleasures of the intellect, of the feelings and imagination, and of the moral sentiments, a much higher value as pleasures than to those of mere sensation. It must be admitted, however, that utilitarian writers in general have placed the superiority of mental over bodily pleasures chiefly in the greater permanency, safety, uncostliness, etc., of the former—that is, in their circumstantial advantages rather than in their intrinsic nature. And on all these points utilitarians have fully proved their case; but they might have taken the other, and, as it may be called, higher ground, with entire consistency. It is quite compatible with the principle of utility to recognise the fact, that some kinds of pleasure are more desirable and more valuable than others. It would be absurd that while, in estimating all other things, quality is considered as well as quantity, the estimation of pleasures should be supposed to depend on quantity alone.

If I am asked, what I mean by difference of quality in pleasures, or what makes one pleasure more valuable than another, merely as a pleasure, except its being greater in amount, there is but one possible answer. Of two pleasures, if there be one to which all or almost all who have experience of both give a decided preference, irrespective of any feeling of moral obligation to prefer it, that is the more desirable pleasure. If one of the two is, by those who are competently acquainted with both, placed so far above the other that they prefer it, even though knowing it to be attended with a greater amount of discontent, and would not resign it for any quantity of the other pleasure which their nature is capable of, we are justified in ascribing to the preferred enjoyment a superiority in quality, so far outweighing quantity as to render it, in comparison, of small account.

Now it is an unquestionable fact that those who are equally acquainted with, and equally capable of appreciating and enjoying, both, do give a most marked preference to the manner of existence which employs their higher faculties. Few human creatures would consent to be changed into any of the lower animals, for a promise of the fullest allowance of a beast's pleasures; no intelligent human being would consent to be a fool, no instructed person would be an ignoramus, no person of feeling and conscience would be selfish and base, even though they should be persuaded that the fool, the dunce, or the rascal is better satisfied with his lot than they are with theirs. They would not resign what they possess more than he for the most complete satisfaction of all the desires which they have in common with him. If they ever fancy they would, it is only in cases of unhappiness so extreme, that to escape from it they would exchange their lot for almost any other, however undesirable in their own eyes. A being of higher faculties requires more to make him happy, is capable probably of more acute suffering, and certainly accessible to it at more points, than one of an inferior type; but in spite of these liabilities, he can never really wish to sink into what he feels to be a lower grade of existence. We may give what explanation we please of this unwillingness; we may attribute it to pride, a name which is given indiscriminately to some of the most and to some of the least estimable feelings of which mankind are capable: we may refer it to the love of liberty and personal independence, an appeal to which was with the Stoics one of the most effective means for the inculcation of it; to the love of power, or to the love of excitement, both of which do really enter into and contribute to it: but its most appropriate appellation is a sense of dignity, which all human beings possess in one form or other, and in some, though by no means in exact, proportion to their higher faculties, and which is so essential a part of the happiness of those in whom it is strong, that nothing which conflicts with it could be, otherwise than momentarily, an object of desire to them.

Whoever supposes that this preference takes place at a sacrifice of happiness—that the superior being, in anything like equal circumstances, is not happier than the inferior—confounds the two very different ideas, of happiness, and content. It is indisputable that the being whose capacities of enjoyment are low, has the greatest chance of having them fully satisfied; and a highly endowed being will always feel that any happiness which he can look for, as the world is constituted, is imperfect. But he can learn to bear its imperfections, if they are at all bearable; and they will not make him envy the being who is indeed unconscious of the imperfections, but only because he feels not at all the good which those imperfections qualify. It is better to be a human being dissatisfied than a pig satisfied; better to be Socrates dissatisfied than a fool satisfied. And if the fool, or the pig, are of a different opinion, it is because they only know their own side of the question. The other party to the comparison knows both sides.

It may be objected, that many who are capable of the higher pleasures, occasionally, under the influence of temptation, postpone them to the lower. But this is quite compatible with a full appreciation of the intrinsic superiority of the higher. Men often, from infirmity of character, make their election for the nearer good, though they know it to be the less valuable; and this no less when the choice is between two bodily pleasures, than when it is between bodily and mental. They pursue sensual indulgences to the injury of health, though perfectly aware that health is the greater good.

It may be further objected, that many who begin with youthful enthusiasm for everything noble, as they advance in years sink into indolence and selfishness. But I do not believe that those who undergo this very common change, voluntarily choose the lower description of pleasures in preference to the higher. I believe that before they devote themselves exclusively to the one, they have already become incapable of the other. Capacity for the nobler feelings is in most natures a very tender plant, easily killed, not only by hostile influences, but by mere want of sustenance; and in the majority of young persons it speedily dies away if the occupations to which their position in life has devoted them, and the society into which it has thrown them, are not favourable to keeping that higher capacity in exercise. Men lose their high aspirations as they lose their intellectual tastes, because they have not time or opportunity for indulging them; and they addict themselves to inferior pleasures, not because they deliberately prefer them, but because they are either the only ones to which they have access, or the only ones which they are any longer capable of enjoying. It may be questioned whether any one who has remained equally susceptible to both classes of pleasures, ever knowingly and calmly preferred the lower; though many, in all ages, have broken down in an ineffectual attempt to combine both.

From this verdict of the only competent judges, I apprehend there can be no appeal. On a question which is the best worth having of two pleasures, or which of two modes of existence is the most grateful to the feelings, apart from its moral attributes and from its consequences, the judgment of those who are qualified by knowledge of both, or, if they differ, that of the majority among them, must be admitted as final. And there needs be the less hesitation to accept this judgment respecting the quality of pleasures, since there is no other tribunal to be referred to even on the question of quantity. What means are there of determining which is the acutest of two pains, or the intensest of two pleasurable sensations, except the general suffrage of those who are familiar with both? Neither pains nor pleasures are homogeneous, and pain is always heterogeneous with pleasure. What is there to decide whether a particular pleasure is worth purchasing at the cost of a particular pain, except the feelings and judgment of the experienced? When, therefore, those feelings and judgment declare the pleasures derived from the higher faculties to be preferable in kind, apart from the question of intensity, to those of which the animal nature, disjoined from the higher faculties, is susceptible, they are entitled on this subject to the same regard.

I have dwelt on this point, as being a necessary part of a perfectly just conception of Utility or Happiness, considered as the directive rule of human conduct. But it is by no means an indispensable condition to the acceptance of the utilitarian standard; for that standard is not the agent's own greatest happiness, but the greatest amount of happiness altogether; and if it may possibly be doubted whether a noble character is always the happier for its nobleness, there can be no doubt that it makes other people happier, and that the world in general is immensely a gainer by it. Utilitarianism, therefore, could only attain its end by the general cultivation of nobleness of character, even if each individual were only benefited by the nobleness of others, and his own, so far as happiness is concerned, were a sheer deduction from the benefit. But the bare enunciation of such an absurdity as this last, renders refutation superfluous.

According to the Greatest Happiness Principle, as above explained, the ultimate end, with reference to and for the sake of which all other things are desirable (whether we are considering our own good or that of other people), is an existence exempt as far as possible from pain, and as rich as possible in enjoyments, both in point of quantity and quality; the test of quality, and the rule for measuring it against quantity, being the preference felt by those who in their opportunities of experience, to which must be added their habits of self-consciousness and self-observation, are best furnished with the means of comparison. This, being, according to the utilitarian opinion, the end of human action, is necessarily also the standard of morality; which may accordingly be defined, the rules and precepts for human conduct, by the observance of which an existence such as has been described might be, to the greatest extent possible, secured to all mankind; and not to them only, but, so far as the nature of things admits, to the whole sentient creation.

Against this doctrine, however, arises another class of objectors, who say that happiness, in any form, cannot be the rational purpose of human life and action; because, in the first place, it is unattainable: and they contemptuously ask, what right hast thou to be happy? a question which Mr. Carlyle clenches by the addition,

What right, a short time ago, hadst thou even to be? Next, they say, that men can do without happiness; that all noble human beings have felt this, and could not have become noble but by learning the lesson of Entsagen, or renunciation; which lesson, thoroughly learnt and submitted to, they affirm to be the beginning and necessary condition of all virtue.

The first of these objections would go to the root of the matter were it well founded; for if no happiness is to be had at all by human beings, the attainment of it cannot be the end of morality, or of any rational conduct. Though, even in that case, something might still be said for the utilitarian theory; since utility includes not solely the pursuit of happiness, but the prevention or mitigation of unhappiness; and if the former aim be chimerical, there will be all the greater scope and more imperative need for the latter, so long at least as mankind think fit to live, and do not take refuge in the simultaneous act of suicide recommended under certain conditions by Novalis. When, however, it is thus positively asserted to be impossible that human life should be happy, the assertion, if not something like a verbal quibble, is at least an exaggeration. If by happiness be meant a continuity of highly pleasurable excitement, it is evident enough that this is impossible. A state of exalted pleasure lasts only moments, or in some cases, and with some intermissions, hours or days, and is the occasional brilliant flash of enjoyment, not its permanent and steady flame. Of this the philosophers who have taught that happiness is the end of life were as fully aware as those who taunt them. The happiness which they meant was not a life of rapture; but moments of such, in an existence made up of few and transitory pains, many and various pleasures, with a decided predominance of the active over the passive, and having as the foundation of the whole, not to expect more from life than it is capable of bestowing. A life thus composed, to those who have been fortunate enough to obtain it, has always appeared worthy of the name of happiness. And such an existence is even now the lot of many, during some considerable portion of their lives. The present wretched education, and wretched social arrangements, are the only real hindrance to its being attainable by almost all.

The objectors perhaps may doubt whether human beings, if taught to consider happiness as the end of life, would be satisfied with such a moderate share of it. But great numbers of mankind have been satisfied with much less. The main constituents of a satisfied life appear to be two, either of which by itself is often found sufficient for the purpose: tranquillity, and excitement. With much tranquillity, many find that they can be content with very little pleasure: with much excitement, many can reconcile themselves to a considerable quantity of pain. There is assuredly no inherent impossibility in enabling even the mass of mankind to unite both; since the two are so far from being incompatible that they are in natural alliance, the prolongation of either being a preparation for, and exciting a wish for, the other. It is only those in whom indolence amounts to a vice, that do not desire excitement after an interval of repose: it is only those in whom the need of excitement is a disease, that feel the tranquillity which follows excitement dull and insipid, instead of pleasurable in direct proportion to the excitement which preceded it. When people who are tolerably fortunate in their outward lot do not find in life sufficient enjoyment to make it valuable to them, the cause generally is, caring for nobody but themselves. To those who have neither public nor private affections, the excitements of life are much curtailed, and in any case dwindle in value as the time approaches when all selfish interests must be terminated by death: while those who leave after them objects of personal affection, and especially those who have also cultivated a fellow-feeling with the collective interests of mankind, retain as lively an interest in life on the eve of death as in the vigour of youth and health. Next to selfishness, the principal cause which makes life unsatisfactory is want of mental cultivation. A cultivated mind—I do not mean that of a philosopher, but any mind to which the fountains of knowledge have been opened, and which has been taught, in any tolerable degree, to exercise its faculties—finds sources of inexhaustible interest in all that surrounds it; in the objects of nature, the achievements of art, the imaginations of poetry, the incidents of history, the ways of mankind, past and present, and their prospects in the future. It is possible, indeed, to become indifferent to all this, and that too without having exhausted a thousandth part of it; but only when one has had from the beginning no moral or human interest in these things, and has sought in them only the gratification of curiosity.

Now there is absolutely no reason in the nature of things why an amount of mental culture sufficient to give an intelligent interest in these objects of contemplation, should not be the inheritance of every one born in a civilised country. As little is there an inherent necessity that any human being should be a selfish egotist, devoid of every feeling or care but those which centre in his own miserable individuality. Something far superior to this is sufficiently common even now, to give ample earnest of what the human species may be made. Genuine private affections and a sincere interest in the public good, are possible, though in unequal degrees, to every rightly brought up human being. In a world in which there is so much to interest, so much to enjoy, and so much also to correct and improve, every one who has this moderate amount of moral and intellectual requisites is capable of an existence which may be called enviable; and unless such a person, through bad laws, or subjection to the will of others, is denied the liberty to use the sources of happiness within his reach, he will not fail to find this enviable existence, if he escape the positive evils of life, the great sources of physical and mental suffering—such as indigence, disease, and the unkindness, worthlessness, or premature loss of objects of affection. The main stress of the problem lies, therefore, in the contest with these calamities, from which it is a rare good fortune entirely to escape; which, as things now are, cannot be obviated, and often cannot be in any material degree mitigated. Yet no one whose opinion deserves a moment's consideration can doubt that most of the great positive evils of the world are in themselves removable, and will, if human affairs continue to improve, be in the end reduced within narrow limits. Poverty, in any sense implying suffering, may be completely extinguished by the wisdom of society, combined with the good sense and providence of individuals. Even that most intractable of enemies, disease, may be indefinitely reduced in dimensions by good physical and moral education, and proper control of noxious influences; while the progress of science holds out a promise for the future of still more direct conquests over this detestable foe. And every advance in that direction relieves us from some, not only of the chances which cut short our own lives, but, what concerns us still more, which deprive us of those in whom our happiness is wrapt up. As for vicissitudes of fortune, and other disappointments connected with worldly circumstances, these are principally the effect either of gross imprudence, of ill-regulated desires, or of bad or imperfect social institutions.

All the grand sources, in short, of human suffering are in a great degree, many of them almost entirely, conquerable by human care and effort; and though their removal is grievously slow—though a long succession of generations will perish in the breach before the conquest is completed, and this world becomes all that, if will and knowledge were not wanting, it might easily be made—yet every mind sufficiently intelligent and generous to bear a part, however small and unconspicuous, in the endeavour, will draw a noble enjoyment from the contest itself, which he would not for any bribe in the form of selfish indulgence consent to be without.

And this leads to the true estimation of what is said by the objectors concerning the possibility, and the obligation, of learning to do without happiness. Unquestionably it is possible to do without happiness; it is done involuntarily by nineteen-twentieths of mankind, even in those parts of our present world which are least deep in barbarism; and it often has to be done voluntarily by the hero or the martyr, for the sake of something which he prizes more than his individual happiness. But this something, what is it, unless the happiness of others or some of the requisites of happiness? It is noble to be capable of resigning entirely one's own portion of happiness, or chances of it: but, after all, this self-sacrifice must be for some end; it is not its own end; and if we are told that its end is not happiness, but virtue, which is better than happiness, I ask, would the sacrifice be made if the hero or martyr did not believe that it would earn for others immunity from similar sacrifices? Would it be made if he thought that his renunciation of happiness for himself would produce no fruit for any of his fellow creatures, but to make their lot like his, and place them also in the condition of persons who have renounced happiness? All honour to those who can abnegate for themselves the personal enjoyment of life, when by such renunciation they contribute worthily to increase the amount of happiness in the world; but he who does it, or professes to do it, for any other purpose, is no more deserving of admiration than the ascetic mounted on his pillar. He may be an inspiriting proof of what men can do, but assuredly not an example of what they should.

Though it is only in a very imperfect state of the world's arrangements that any one can best serve the happiness of others by the absolute sacrifice of his own, yet so long as the world is in that imperfect state, I fully acknowledge that the readiness to make such a sacrifice is the highest virtue which can be found in man. I will add, that in this condition the world, paradoxical as the assertion may be, the conscious ability to do without happiness gives the best prospect of realising, such happiness as is attainable. For nothing except that consciousness can raise a person above the chances of life, by making him feel that, let fate and fortune do their worst, they have not power to subdue him: which, once felt, frees him from excess of anxiety concerning the evils of life, and enables him, like many a Stoic in the worst times of the Roman Empire, to cultivate in tranquillity the sources of satisfaction accessible to him, without concerning himself about the uncertainty of their duration, any more than about their inevitable end.

Meanwhile, let utilitarians never cease to claim the morality of self devotion as a possession which belongs by as good a right to them, as either to the Stoic or to the Transcendentalist. The utilitarian morality does recognise in human beings the power of sacrificing their own greatest good for the good of others. It only refuses to admit that the sacrifice is itself a good. A sacrifice which does not increase, or tend to increase, the sum total of happiness, it considers as wasted. The only self-renunciation which it applauds, is devotion to the happiness, or to some of the means of happiness, of others; either of mankind collectively, or of individuals within the limits imposed by the collective interests of mankind.

I must again repeat, what the assailants of utilitarianism seldom have the justice to acknowledge, that the happiness which forms the utilitarian standard of what is right in conduct, is not the agent's own happiness, but that of all concerned. As between his own happiness and that of others, utilitarianism requires him to be as strictly impartial as a disinterested and benevolent spectator. In the golden rule of Jesus of Nazareth, we read the complete spirit of the ethics of utility. To do as you would be done by, and to love your neighbour as yourself, constitute the ideal perfection of utilitarian morality. As the means of making the nearest approach to this ideal, utility would enjoin, first, that laws and social arrangements should place the happiness, or (as speaking practically it may be called) the interest, of every individual, as nearly as possible in harmony with the interest of the whole; and secondly, that education and opinion, which have so vast a power over human character, should so use that power as to establish in the mind of every individual an indissoluble association between his own happiness and the good of the whole; especially between his own happiness and the practice of such modes of conduct, negative and positive, as regard for the universal happiness prescribes; so that not only he may be unable to conceive the possibility of happiness to himself, consistently with conduct opposed to the general good, but also that a direct impulse to promote the general good may be in every individual one of the habitual motives of action, and the sentiments connected therewith may fill a large and prominent place in every human being's sentient existence. If the impugners of the utilitarian morality represented it to their own minds in this, its true character, I know not what recommendation possessed by any other morality they could possibly affirm to be wanting to it; what more beautiful or more exalted developments of human nature any other ethical system can be supposed to foster, or what springs of action, not accessible to the utilitarian, such systems rely on for giving effect to their mandates.

The objectors to utilitarianism cannot always be charged with representing it in a discreditable light. On the contrary, those among them who entertain anything like a just idea of its disinterested character, sometimes find fault with its standard as being too high for humanity. They say it is exacting too much to require that people shall always act from the inducement of promoting the general interests of society. But this is to mistake the very meaning of a standard of morals, and confound the rule of action with the motive of it. It is the business of ethics to tell us what are our duties, or by what test we may know them; but no system of ethics requires that the sole motive of all we do shall be a feeling of duty; on the contrary, ninety-nine hundredths of all our actions are done from other motives, and rightly so done, if the rule of duty does not condemn them. It is the more unjust to utilitarianism that this particular misapprehension should be made a ground of objection to it, inasmuch as utilitarian moralists have gone beyond almost all others in affirming that the motive has nothing to do with the morality of the action, though much with the worth of the agent. He who saves a fellow creature from drowning does what is morally right, whether his motive be duty, or the hope of being paid for his trouble; he who betrays the friend that trusts him, is guilty of a crime, even if his object be to serve another friend to whom he is under greater obligations.

But to speak only of actions done from the motive of duty, and in direct obedience to principle: it is a misapprehension of the utilitarian mode of thought, to conceive it as implying that people should fix their minds upon so wide a generality as the world, or society at large. The great majority of good actions are intended not for the benefit of the world, but for that of individuals, of which the good of the world is made up; and the thoughts of the most virtuous man need not on these occasions travel beyond the particular persons concerned, except so far as is necessary to assure himself that in benefiting them he is not violating the rights, that is, the legitimate and authorised expectations, of any one else. The multiplication of happiness is, according to the utilitarian ethics, the object of virtue: the occasions on which any person (except one in a thousand) has it in his power to do this on an extended scale, in other words to be a public benefactor, are but exceptional; and on these occasions alone is he called on to consider public utility; in every other case, private utility, the interest or happiness of some few persons, is all he has to attend to. Those alone the influence of whose actions extends to society in general, need concern themselves habitually about so large an object. In the case of abstinences indeed—of things which people forbear to do from moral considerations, though the consequences in the particular case might be beneficial—it would be unworthy of an intelligent agent not to be consciously aware that the action is of a class which, if practised generally, would be generally injurious, and that this is the ground of the obligation to abstain from it. The amount of regard for the public interest implied in this recognition, is no greater than is demanded by every system of morals, for they all enjoin to abstain from whatever is manifestly pernicious to society.

The same considerations dispose of another reproach against the doctrine of utility, founded on a still grosser misconception of the purpose of a standard of morality, and of the very meaning of the words right and wrong. It is often affirmed that utilitarianism renders men cold and unsympathising; that it chills their moral feelings towards individuals; that it makes them regard only the dry and hard consideration of the consequences of actions, not taking into their moral estimate the qualities from which those actions emanate. If the assertion means that they do not allow their judgment respecting the rightness or wrongness of an action to be influenced by their opinion of the qualities of the person who does it, this is a complaint not against utilitarianism, but against having any standard of morality at all; for certainly no known ethical standard decides an action to be good or bad because it is done by a good or a bad man, still less because done by an amiable, a brave, or a benevolent man, or the contrary. These considerations are relevant, not to the estimation of actions, but of persons; and there is nothing in the utilitarian theory inconsistent with the fact that there are other things which interest us in persons besides the rightness and wrongness of their actions. The Stoics, indeed, with the paradoxical misuse of language which was part of their system, and by which they strove to raise themselves above all concern about anything but virtue, were fond of saying that he who has that has everything; that he, and only he, is rich, is beautiful, is a king. But no claim of this description is made for the virtuous man by the utilitarian doctrine. Utilitarians are quite aware that there are other desirable possessions and qualities besides virtue, and are perfectly willing to allow to all of them their full worth. They are also aware that a right action does not necessarily indicate a virtuous character, and that actions which are blamable, often proceed from qualities entitled to praise. When this is apparent in any particular case, it modifies their estimation, not certainly of the act, but of the agent. I grant that they are, notwithstanding, of opinion, that in the long run the best proof of a good character is good actions; and resolutely refuse to consider any mental disposition as good, of which the predominant tendency is to produce bad conduct. This makes them unpopular with many people; but it is an unpopularity which they must share with every one who regards the distinction between right and wrong

in a serious light; and the reproach is not one which a conscientious utilitarian need be anxious to repel.

If no more be meant by the objection than that many utilitarians look on the morality of actions, as measured by the utilitarian standard, with too exclusive a regard, and do not lay sufficient stress upon the other beauties of character which go towards making a human being lovable or admirable, this may be admitted. Utilitarians who have cultivated their moral feelings, but not their sympathies nor their artistic perceptions, do fall into this mistake; and so do all other moralists under the same conditions. What can be said in excuse for other moralists is equally available for them, namely, that, if there is to be any error, it is better that it should be on that side. As a matter of fact, we may affirm that among utilitarians as among adherents of other systems, there is every imaginable degree of rigidity and of laxity in the application of their standard: some are even puritanically rigorous, while others are as indulgent as can possibly be desired by sinner or by sentimentalist. But on the whole, a doctrine which brings prominently forward the interest that mankind have in the repression and prevention of conduct which violates the moral law, is likely to be inferior to no other in turning the sanctions of opinion again such violations. It is true, the question, What does violate the moral law? is one on which those who recognise different standards of morality are likely now and then to differ. But difference of opinion on moral questions was not first introduced into the world by utilitarianism, while that doctrine does supply, if not always an easy, at all events a tangible and intelligible mode of deciding such differences.

It may not be superfluous to notice a few more of the common misapprehensions of utilitarian ethics, even those which are so obvious and gross that it might appear impossible for any person of candour and intelligence to fall into them; since persons, even of considerable mental endowments, often give themselves so little trouble to understand the bearings of any opinion against which they entertain a prejudice, and men are in general so little conscious of this voluntary ignorance as a defect, that the vulgarest misunderstandings of ethical doctrines are continually met with in the deliberate writings of persons of the greatest pretensions both to high principle and to philosophy. We not uncommonly hear the doctrine of utility inveighed against as a godless doctrine. If it be necessary to say anything at all against so mere an assumption, we may say that the question depends upon what idea we have formed of the moral character of the Deity. If it be a true belief that God desires, above all things, the happiness of his creatures, and that this was his purpose in their creation, utility is not only not a godless doctrine, but more profoundly religious than any other. If it be meant that utilitarianism does not recognise the revealed will of God as the supreme law of morals, I answer, that a utilitarian who believes in the perfect goodness and wisdom of God, necessarily believes that whatever God has thought fit to reveal on the subject of morals, must fulfil the requirements of utility in a supreme degree. But others besides utilitarians have been of opinion that the Christian revelation was intended, and is fitted, to inform the hearts and minds of mankind with a spirit which should enable them to find for themselves what is right, and incline them to do it when found, rather than to tell them, except in a very general way, what it is; and that we need a doctrine of ethics, carefully followed out, to interpret to us the will of God. Whether this opinion is correct or not, it is superfluous here to discuss; since whatever aid religion, either natural or revealed, can afford to ethical investigation, is as open to the utilitarian moralist as to any other. He can use it as the testimony of God to the usefulness or hurtfulness of any given course of action, by as good a right as others can use it for the indication of a transcendental law, having no connection with usefulness or with happiness.

Again, Utility is often summarily stigmatised as an immoral doctrine by giving it the name of Expediency, and taking advantage of the popular use of that term to contrast it with Principle. But the Expedient, in the sense in which it is opposed to the Right, generally means that which is expedient for the particular interest of the agent himself; as when a minister sacrifices the interests of his country to keep himself in place. When it means anything better than this, it means that which is expedient for some immediate object, some temporary purpose, but which violates a rule whose observance is expedient in a much higher degree. The Expedient, in this sense, instead of being the same thing with the useful, is a branch of the hurtful. Thus, it would often be expedient, for the purpose of getting over some momentary embarrassment, or attaining some object immediately useful to ourselves or others, to tell a lie. But inasmuch as the cultivation in ourselves of a sensitive feeling on the subject of veracity, is one of the most useful, and the enfeeblement of that feeling one of the most hurtful, things to which our conduct can be instrumental; and inasmuch as any, even unintentional, deviation from truth, does that much towards weakening the trustworthiness of human assertion, which is not only the principal support of all present social well-being, but the insufficiency of which does more than any one thing that can be named to keep back civilisation, virtue, everything on which human happiness on the largest scale depends; we feel that the violation, for a present advantage, of a rule of such transcendant expediency, is not expedient, and that he who, for the sake of a convenience to himself or to some other individual, does what depends on him to deprive mankind of the good, and inflict upon them the evil, involved in the greater or less reliance which they can place in each other's word, acts the part of one of their worst enemies. Yet that even this rule, sacred as it is, admits of possible exceptions, is acknowledged by all moralists; the chief of which is when the withholding of some fact (as of information from a malefactor, or of bad news from a person dangerously ill) would save an individual (especially an individual other than oneself) from great and unmerited evil, and when the withholding can only be effected by denial. But in order that the exception may not extend itself beyond the need, and may have the least possible effect in weakening reliance on veracity, it ought to be recognised, and if possible, its limits defined; and if the principle of utility is good for anything, it must be good for weighing these conflicting utilities against one another, and marking out the region within which one or the other preponderates.

Again, defenders of utility often find themselves called upon to reply to such objections as this—that there is not time, previous to action, for calculating and weighing the effects of any line of conduct on the general happiness. This is exactly as if any one were to say that it is impossible to guide our conduct by Christianity, because there is not time, on every occasion on which anything has to be done, to read through the Old and New Testaments. The answer to the objection is, that there has been ample time, namely, the whole past duration of the human species. During all that time, mankind have been learning by experience the tendencies of actions; on which experience all the prudence, as well as all the morality of life, are dependent. People talk as if the commencement of this course of experience had hitherto been put off, and as if, at the moment when some man feels tempted to meddle with the property or life of another, he had to begin considering for the first time whether murder and theft are injurious to human happiness. Even then I do not think that he would find the question very puzzling; but, at all events, the matter is now done to his hand.

It is truly a whimsical supposition that, if mankind were agreed in considering utility to be the test of morality, they would remain without any agreement as to what is useful, and would take no measures for having their notions on the subject taught to the young, and enforced by law and opinion. There is no difficulty in proving any ethical standard whatever to work ill, if we suppose universal idiocy to be conjoined with it; but on any hypothesis short of that, mankind must by this time have acquired positive beliefs as to the effects of some actions on their happiness; and the beliefs which have thus come down are the rules of morality for the multitude, and for the philosopher until he has succeeded in

finding better. That philosophers might easily do this, even now, on many subjects; that the received code of ethics is by no means of divine right; and that mankind have still much to learn as to the effects of actions on the general happiness, I admit, or rather, earnestly maintain. The corollaries from the principle of utility, like the precepts of every practical art, admit of indefinite improvement, and, in a progressive state of the human mind, their improvement is perpetually going on.

But to consider the rules of morality as improvable, is one thing; to pass over the intermediate generalisations entirely, and endeavour to test each individual action directly by the first principle, is another. It is a strange notion that the acknowledgment of a first principle is inconsistent with the admission of secondary ones. To inform a traveller respecting the place of his ultimate destination, is not to forbid the use of landmarks and direction-posts on the way. The proposition that happiness is the end and aim of morality, does not mean that no road ought to be laid down to that goal, or that persons going thither should not be advised to take one direction rather than another. Men really ought to leave off talking a kind of nonsense on this subject, which they would neither talk nor listen to on other matters of practical concernment. Nobody argues that the art of navigation is not founded on astronomy, because sailors cannot wait to calculate the Nautical Almanack. Being rational creatures, they go to sea with it ready calculated; and all rational creatures go out upon the sea of life with their minds made up on the common questions of right and wrong, as well as on many of the far more difficult questions of wise and foolish. And this, as long as foresight is a human quality, it is to be presumed they will continue to do. Whatever we adopt as the fundamental principle of morality, we require subordinate principles to apply it by; the impossibility of doing without them, being common to all systems, can afford no argument against any one in particular; but gravely to argue as if no such secondary principles could be had, and as if mankind had remained till now, and always must remain, without drawing any general conclusions from the experience of human life, is as high a pitch, I think, as absurdity has ever reached in philosophical controversy.

The remainder of the stock arguments against utilitarianism mostly consist in laying to its charge the common infirmities of human nature, and the general difficulties which embarrass conscientious persons in shaping their course through life. We are told that a utilitarian will be apt to make his own particular case an exception to moral rules, and, when under temptation, will see a utility in the breach of a rule, greater than he will see in its observance. But is utility the only creed which is able to furnish us with excuses for evil doing, and means of cheating our own conscience? They are afforded in abundance by all doctrines which recognise as a fact in morals the existence of conflicting considerations; which all doctrines do, that have been believed by sane persons. It is not the fault of any creed, but of the complicated nature of human affairs, that rules of conduct cannot be so framed as to require no exceptions, and that hardly any kind of action can safely be laid down as either always obligatory or always condemnable. There is no ethical creed which does not temper the rigidity of its laws, by giving a certain latitude, under the moral responsibility of the agent, for accommodation to peculiarities of circumstances; and under every creed, at the opening thus made, self-deception and dishonest casuistry get in. There exists no moral system under which there do not arise unequivocal cases of conflicting obligation. These are the real difficulties, the knotty points both in the theory of ethics, and in the conscientious guidance of personal conduct. They are overcome practically, with greater or with less success, according to the intellect and virtue of the individual; but it can hardly be pretended that any one will be the less qualified for dealing with them, from possessing an ultimate standard to which conflicting rights and duties can be referred. If utility is the ultimate source of moral obligations, utility may be invoked to decide between them when their demands are incompatible. Though the application of the standard may

be difficult, it is better than none at all: while in other systems, the moral laws all claiming independent authority, there is no common umpire entitled to interfere between them; their claims to precedence one over another rest on little better than sophistry, and unless determined, as they generally are, by the unacknowledged influence of considerations of utility, afford a free scope for the action of personal desires and partialities. We must remember that only in these cases of conflict between secondary principles is it requisite that first principles should be appealed to. There is no case of moral obligation in which some secondary principle is not involved; and if only one, there can seldom be any real doubt which one it is, in the mind of any person by whom the principle itself is recognised.

OF WHAT SORT OF PROOF THE PRINCIPLE OF UTILITY IS SUSCEPTIBLE

It has already been remarked, that questions of ultimate ends do not admit of proof, in the ordinary acceptation of the term. To be incapable of proof by reasoning is common to all first principles; to the first premises of our knowledge, as well as to those of our conduct. But the former, being matters of fact, may be the subject of a direct appeal to the faculties which judge of fact—namely, our senses, and our internal consciousness. Can an appeal be made to the same faculties on questions of practical ends? Or by what other faculty is cognisance taken of them?

Questions about ends are, in other words, questions about what things are desirable. The utilitarian doctrine is, that happiness is desirable, and the only thing desirable, as an end; all other things being only desirable as means to that end. What ought to be required of this doctrine—what conditions is it requisite that the doctrine should fulfil—to make good its claim to be believed?

The only proof capable of being given that an object is visible, is that people actually see it. The only proof that a sound is audible, is that people hear it: and so of the other sources of our experience. In like manner, I apprehend, the sole evidence it is possible to produce that anything is desirable, is that people do actually desire it. If the end which the utilitarian doctrine proposes to itself were not, in theory and in practice, acknowledged to be an end, nothing could ever convince any person that it was so. No reason can be given why the general happiness is desirable, except that each person, so far as he believes it to be attainable, desires his own happiness. This, however, being a fact, we have not only all the proof which the case admits of, but all which it is possible to require, that happiness is a good: that each person's happiness is a good to that person, and the general happiness, therefore, a good to the aggregate of all persons. Happiness has made out its title as one of the ends of conduct, and consequently one of the criteria of morality.

But it has not, by this alone, proved itself to be the sole criterion. To do that, it would seem, by the same rule, necessary to show, not only that people desire happiness, but that they never desire anything else. Now it is palpable that they do desire things which, in common language, are decidedly distinguished from happiness. They desire, for example, virtue, and the absence of vice, no less really than pleasure and the absence of pain. The desire of virtue is not as universal, but it is as authentic a fact, as the desire of happiness. And hence the opponents of the utilitarian standard deem that they have a right to infer that there are other ends of human action besides happiness, and that happiness is not the standard of approbation and disapprobation.

But does the utilitarian doctrine deny that people desire virtue, or maintain that virtue is not a thing to be desired? The very reverse. It maintains not only that virtue is to be desired, but that it is to be desired disinterestedly, for itself. Whatever may be the opinion of utilitarian moralists as to the original conditions by which virtue is made virtue; however they may believe (as they do) that actions and dispositions are only virtuous because they promote another end than virtue; yet this being granted, and it

having been decided, from considerations of this description, what is virtuous, they not only place virtue at the very head of the things which are good as means to the ultimate end, but they also recognise as a psychological fact the possibility of its being, to the individual, a good in itself, without looking to any end beyond it; and hold, that the mind is not in a right state, not in a state conformable to Utility, not in the state most conducive to the general happiness, unless it does love virtue in this manner—as a thing desirable in itself, even although, in the individual instance, it should not produce those other desirable consequences which it tends to produce, and on account of which it is held to be virtue. This opinion is not, in the smallest degree, a departure from the Happiness principle. The ingredients of happiness are very various, and each of them is desirable in itself, and not merely when considered as swelling an aggregate. The principle of utility does not mean that any given pleasure, as music, for instance, or any given exemption from pain, as for example health, is to be looked upon as means to a collective something termed happiness, and to be desired on that account. They are desired and desirable in and for themselves; besides being means, they are a part of the end. Virtue, according to the utilitarian doctrine, is not naturally and originally part of the end, but it is capable of becoming so; and in those who love it disinterestedly it has become so, and is desired and cherished, not as a means to happiness, but as a part of their happiness.

To illustrate this farther, we may remember that virtue is not the only thing, originally a means, and which if it were not a means to anything else, would be and remain indifferent, but which by association with what it is a means to, comes to be desired for itself, and that too with the utmost intensity. What, for example, shall we say of the love of money? There is nothing originally more desirable about money than about any heap of glittering pebbles. Its worth is solely that of the things which it will buy; the desires for other things than itself, which it is a means of gratifying. Yet the love of money is not only one of the strongest moving forces of human life, but money is, in many cases, desired in and for itself; the desire to possess it is often stronger than the desire to use it, and goes on increasing when all the desires which point to ends beyond it, to be compassed by it, are falling off. It may, then, be said truly, that money is desired not for the sake of an end, but as part of the end. From being a means to happiness, it has come to be itself a principal ingredient of the individual's conception of happiness. The same may be said of the majority of the great objects of human life— power, for example, or fame; except that to each of these there is a certain amount of immediate pleasure annexed, which has at least the semblance of being naturally inherent in them; a thing which cannot be said of money. Still, however, the strongest natural attraction, both of power and of fame, is the immense aid they give to the attainment of our other wishes; and it is the strong association thus generated between them and all our objects of desire, which gives to the direct desire of them the intensity it often assumes, so as in some characters to surpass in strength all other desires. In these cases the means have become a part of the end, and a more important part of it than any of the things which they are means to. What was once desired as an instrument for the attainment of happiness, has come to be desired for its own sake. In being desired for its own sake it is, however, desired as part of happiness. The person is made, or thinks he would be made, happy by its mere possession; and is made unhappy by failure to obtain it. The desire of it is not a different thing from the desire of happiness, any more than the love of music, or the desire of health. They are included in happiness. They are some of the elements of which the desire of happiness is made up. Happiness is not an abstract idea, but a concrete whole; and these are some of its parts. And the utilitarian standard sanctions and approves their being so. Life would be a poor thing, very ill provided with sources of happiness, if there were not this provision of nature, by which things originally indifferent, but conducive to, or otherwise associated with, the satisfaction of our primitive desires,

become in themselves sources of pleasure more valuable than the primitive pleasures, both in permanency, in the space of human existence that they are capable of covering, and even in intensity.

Virtue, according to the utilitarian conception, is a good of this description. There was no original desire of it, or motive to it, save its conduciveness to pleasure, and especially to protection from pain. But through the association thus formed, it may be felt a good in itself, and desired as such with as great intensity as any other good; and with this difference between it and the love of money, of power, or of fame, that all of these may, and often do, render the individual noxious to the other members of the society to which he belongs, whereas there is nothing which makes him so much a blessing to them as the cultivation of the disinterested love of virtue. And consequently, the utilitarian standard, while it tolerates and approves those other acquired desires, up to the point beyond which they would be more injurious to the general happiness than promotive of it, enjoins and requires the cultivation of the love of virtue up to the greatest strength possible, as being above all things important to the general happiness.

It results from the preceding considerations, that there is in reality nothing desired except happiness. Whatever is desired otherwise than as a means to some end beyond itself, and ultimately to happiness, is desired as itself a part of happiness, and is not desired for itself until it has become so. Those who desire virtue for its own sake, desire it either because the consciousness of it is a pleasure, or because the consciousness of being without it is a pain, or for both reasons united; as in truth the pleasure and pain seldom exist separately, but almost always together, the same person feeling pleasure in the degree of virtue attained, and pain in not having attained more. If one of these gave him no pleasure, and the other no pain, he would not love or desire virtue, or would desire it only for the other benefits which it might produce to himself or to persons whom he cared for. We have now, then, an answer to the question, of what sort of proof the principle of utility is susceptible. If the opinion which I have now stated is psychologically true—if human nature is so constituted as to desire nothing which is not either a part of happiness or a means of happiness, we can have no other proof, and we require no other, that these are the only things desirable. If so, happiness is the sole end of human action, and the promotion of it the test by which to judge of all human conduct; from whence it necessarily follows that it must be the criterion of morality, since a part is included in the whole.

And now to decide whether this is really so; whether mankind do desire nothing for itself but that which is a pleasure to them, or of which the absence is a pain; we have evidently arrived at a question of fact and experience, dependent, like all similar questions, upon evidence. It can only be determined by practised self-consciousness and self-observation, assisted by observation of others. I believe that these sources of evidence, impartially consulted, will declare that desiring a thing and finding it pleasant, aversion to it and thinking of it as painful, are phenomena entirely inseparable, or rather two parts of the same phenomenon; in strictness of language, two different modes of naming the same psychological fact: that to think of an object as desirable (unless for the sake of its consequences), and to think of it as pleasant, are one and the same thing; and that to desire anything, except in proportion as the idea of it is pleasant, is a physical and metaphysical impossibility.

So obvious does this appear to me, that I expect it will hardly be disputed: and the objection made will be, not that desire can possibly be directed to anything ultimately except pleasure and exemption from pain, but that the will is a different thing from desire; that a person of confirmed virtue, or any other person whose purposes are fixed, carries out his purposes without any thought of the pleasure he has in contemplating them, or expects to derive from their fulfilment; and persists in acting on them, even though these pleasures are much diminished, by changes in his character or decay of his passive sensibilities, or are outweighed by the pains

which the pursuit of the purposes may bring upon him. All this I fully admit, and have stated it elsewhere, as positively and emphatically as any one. Will, the active phenomenon, is a different thing from desire, the state of passive sensibility, and though originally an offshoot from it, may in time take root and detach itself from the parent stock; so much so, that in the case of an habitual purpose, instead of willing the thing because we desire it, we often desire it only because we will it. This, however, is but an instance of that familiar fact, the power of habit, and is nowise confined to the case of virtuous actions. Many indifferent things, which men originally did from a motive of some sort, they continue to do from habit. Sometimes this is done unconsciously, the consciousness coming only after the action: at other times with conscious volition, but volition which has become habitual, and is put in operation by the force of habit, in opposition perhaps to the deliberate preference, as often happens with those who have contracted habits of vicious or hurtful indulgence.

Third and last comes the case in which the habitual act of will in the individual instance is not in contradiction to the general intention prevailing at other times, but in fulfilment of it; as in the case of the person of confirmed virtue, and of all who pursue deliberately and consistently any determinate end. The distinction between will and desire thus understood is an authentic and highly important psychological fact; but the fact consists solely in this—that will, like all other parts of our constitution, is amenable to habit, and that we may will from habit what we no longer desire for itself or desire only because we will it. It is not the less true that will, in the beginning, is entirely produced by desire; including in that term the repelling influence of pain as well as the attractive one of pleasure. Let us take into consideration, no longer the person who has a confirmed will to do right, but him in whom that virtuous will is still feeble, conquerable by temptation, and not to be fully relied on; by what means can it be strengthened? How can the will to be virtuous, where it does not exist in sufficient force, be implanted or awakened?

Only by making the person desire virtue—by making him think of it in a pleasurable light, or of its absence in a painful one. It is by associating the doing right with pleasure, or the doing wrong with pain, or by eliciting and impressing and bringing home to the person's experience the pleasure naturally involved in the one or the pain in the other, that it is possible to call forth that will to be virtuous, which, when confirmed, acts without any thought of either pleasure or pain. Will is the child of desire, and passes out of the dominion of its parent only to come under that of habit. That which is the result of habit affords no presumption of being intrinsically good; and there would be no reason for wishing that the purpose of virtue should become independent of pleasure and pain, were it not that the influence of the pleasurable and painful associations which prompt to virtue is not sufficiently to be depended on for unerring constancy of action until it has acquired the support of habit. Both in feeling and in conduct, habit is the only thing which imparts certainty; and it is because of the importance to others of being able to rely absolutely on one's feelings and conduct, and to oneself of being able to rely on one's own, that the will to do right ought to be cultivated into this habitual independence. In other words, this state of the will is a means to good, not intrinsically a good; and does not contradict the doctrine that nothing is a good to human beings but in so far as it is either itself pleasurable, or a means of attaining pleasure or averting pain.

But if this doctrine be true, the principle of utility is proved. Whether it is so or not, must now be left to the consideration of the thoughtful reader.

2.8 What Makes Right Acts Right?

W. D. ROSS

W. D. Ross (1877–1967) was a British classical scholar and influential moral philosopher who spent his career at Oxford.

The point at issue is that to which we now pass, viz. whether there is any general character which makes right acts right and, if so, what it is. Among the main historical attempts to state a single characteristic of all right actions which is the foundation of their rightness are those made by egoism and utilitarianism. But I do not propose to discuss these, not because the subject is unimportant, but because it has been dealt with so often and so well already, and because there has come to be so much agreement among moral philosophers that neither of these theories is satisfactory. A much more attractive theory has been put forward by Professor Moore: that what makes actions right is that they are productive of more *good* than could have been produced by any other action open to the agent....

In fact the theory of "ideal utilitarianism," if I may for brevity refer so to the theory of Professor Moore, seems to simplify unduly our relations to our fellows. It says, in effect, that the only morally significant relation in which my neighbours stand to me is that of being possible beneficiaries by my action. They do stand in this relation to me, and this relation is morally significant. But they may also stand to me in the relation of promisee to promiser, of creditor to debtor, of wife to husband, of child to parent, of friend to friend, of fellow countryman to fellow countryman, and the like; and each of these relations is the foundation of a *prima facie* duty, which is more or less incumbent on me according to the circumstances of the case. When I am in a situation, as perhaps I always am, in which more than one of these *prima facie* duties is incumbent on me, what I have to do is to study the situation as fully as I can until I form the considered opinion (it is never more) that in the circumstances one of them is more incumbent than any other; then I am bound to think that to do this *prima facie* duty is my duty *sans phrase* in the situation.

I suggest "*prima facie* duty" or "conditional duty" as a brief way of referring to the characteristic (quite distinct from that of being a duty proper) which an act has, in virtue of being of a certain kind (e.g., the keeping of a promise), of being an act which would be a duty proper if it were not at the same time of another kind which is morally significant. Whether an act is a duty proper or actual duty depends on *all* the morally significant kinds it is an instance of.

The phrase "*prima facie* duty" must be apologized for, since (1) it suggests that what we are speaking of is a certain kind of duty, whereas it is in fact not a duty, but something related in a special way to duty. Strictly speaking, we want not a phrase in which duty is qualified by an adjective, but a separate noun. (2) *"Prima"* facie suggests that one is speaking only of an appearance which a moral situation presents at first sight, and which may turn out to be illusory; whereas what I am speaking of is an objective fact involved in the nature of the situation, or more strictly in an element of its nature, though not, as duty proper does, arising from its whole nature.

There is nothing arbitrary about these *prima facie* duties. Each rests on a definite circumstance which cannot seriously be held to be without moral significance. Of *prima facie* duties I suggest, without claiming completeness or finality for it, the following division:

1. Some duties rest on previous acts of my own. These duties seem to include two kinds,

   A. Those resting on a promise or what may fairly be called an implicit promise, such as the implicit undertaking not to tell lies which seems to be implied in the act of entering into conversation (at any rate by civilized men), or of writing books that purport to be history and not fiction. These may be called the duties of fidelity.
   B. Those resting on a previous wrongful act. These may be called the duties of reparation.
2. Some rest on previous acts of other men, i.e., services done by them to me. These may be loosely described as the duties of gratitude.
3. Some rest on the fact or possibility of a distribution of pleasure or happiness (or of the means thereto) which is not in accordance with the merit of the persons concerned; in such cases there arises a duty to upset or prevent such a distribution. These are the duties of justice.
4. Some rest on the mere fact that there are beings in the world whose condition we can make better in respect of virtue, or of intelligence, or of pleasure. These are the duties of beneficence.
5. Some rest on the fact that we can improve our own condition in respect of virtue or of intelligence. These are the duties of self-improvement.
6. I think that we should distinguish from (4) the duties that may be summed up under the title of "not injuring others." No doubt to injure others is incidentally to fail to do them good; but it seems to me clear that non-maleficence is apprehended as a duty distinct from that of beneficence, and as a duty of a more stringent character.

The essential defect of the "ideal utilitarian" theory is that it ignores, or at least does not do full justice to, the highly personal character of duty. If the only duty is to produce the maximum of good, the question who is to have the good—whether it is myself, or my benefactor, or a person to whom I have made a promise to confer that good on him, or a mere fellow man to whom I stand in no such special relation—should make no difference to my having a duty to produce that good. But we are all in fact sure that it makes a vast difference.

If the objection be made, that this catalogue of the main types of duty is an unsystematic one resting on no logical principle, it may be replied, first, that it makes no claim to being ultimate. It is a *prima facie* classification of the duties which reflection on our moral convictions seems actually to reveal. And if these convictions are, as I would claim that they are, of the nature of knowledge, and if I have not misstated them, the list will be a list of authentic conditional duties, correct as far as it goes though not necessarily complete. The list of *goods* put forward by the rival theory is reached by exactly the same method—the only sound one in the circumstances—viz. that of direct reflection on what we really think. Loyalty to the facts is worth more than a symmetrical architectonic or a hastily reached simplicity. If further reflection discovers a perfect logical basis for this or for a better classification, so much the better.

It may, again, be objected that our theory that there are these various and often conflicting types of *prima facie* duty leaves us with no principle upon which to discern what is our actual duty in particular circumstances. But this objection is not one which the rival theory is in a position to bring forward. For when we have to choose between the production of two heterogeneous goods, say knowledge and pleasure, the "ideal utilitarian" theory can only fall back on an opinion, for which no logical basis can be offered, that one of the goods is the greater; and this is no better than a similar opinion that one of two duties is the more urgent. And again, when we consider the infinite variety of the effects of our actions in the way of pleasure, it must surely be admitted that the claim which *hedonism* sometimes makes, that it offers a readily applicable criterion of right conduct, is quite illusory.

I am unwilling, however, to content myself with an *argumentum ad hominem,* and I would contend that in principle there is no reason to anticipate that every act that is our duty is so for one and the same reason. Why should two

sets of circumstances, or one set of circumstances, not possess different characteristics, any one of which makes a certain act our *prima facie* duty? When I ask what it is that makes me in certain cases sure that I have a *prima facie* duty to do so and so, I find that it lies in the fact that I have made a promise; when I ask the same question in another case, I find the answer lies in the fact that I have done a wrong. And if on reflection I find (as I think I do) that neither of these reasons is reducible to the other, I must not on any *a priori* ground assume that such a reduction is possible.

It is necessary to say something by way of clearing up the relation between *prima facie* duties and the actual or absolute duty to do one particular act in particular circumstances. If, as almost all moralists except Kant are agreed, and as most plain men think, it is sometimes right to tell a lie or to break a promise, it must be maintained that there is a difference between *prima facie* duty and actual or absolute duty. When we think ourselves justified in breaking, and indeed morally obliged to break, a promise in order to relieve some one's distress, we do not for a moment cease to recognize a *prima facie* duty to keep our promise, and this leads us to feel, not indeed shame or repentance, but certainly compunction, for behaving as we do; we recognize, further, that it is our duty to make up somehow to the promisee for the breaking of the promise. We have to distinguish from the characteristic of being our duty that of tending to be our duty. Any act that we do contains various elements in virtue of which it falls under various categories. In virtue of being the breaking of a promise, for instance, it tends to be wrong; in virtue of being an instance of relieving distress it tends to be right.

Something should be said of the relation between our apprehension of the *prima facie* rightness of certain types of act and our mental attitude towards particular acts. It is proper to use the word "apprehension" in the former case and not in the latter. That an act, *qua* fulfilling a promise, or *qua* effecting a just distribution of good, or *qua* returning services rendered, or *qua* promoting the good of others, or *qua* promoting the virtue or insight of the agent, is *prima facie* right, is self-evident; not in the sense that it is evident from the beginning of our lives, or as soon as we attend to the proposition for the first time, but in the sense that when we have reached sufficient mental maturity and have given sufficient attention to the proposition it is evident without any need of proof, or of evidence beyond itself. It is self-evident just as a mathematical axiom, or the validity of a form of inference, is evident. The moral order expressed in these propositions is just as much part of the fundamental nature of the universe (and, we may add, of any possible universe in which there were moral agents at all) as is the spatial or numerical structure expressed in the axioms of geometry or arithmetic. In our confidence that these propositions are true there is involved the same trust in our reason that is involved in our confidence in mathematics; and we should have no justification for trusting it in the latter sphere and distrusting it in the former. In both cases we are dealing with propositions that cannot be proved, but that just as certainly need no proof....

We have no more direct way of access to the facts about rightness and goodness and about what things are right or good, than by thinking about them; the moral convictions of thoughtful and well-educated people are the data of ethics just as sense-perceptions are the data of a natural science. Just as some of the latter have to be rejected as illusory, so have some of the former; but as the latter are rejected only when they are in conflict with other more accurate sense-perceptions, the former are rejected only when they are in conflict with other convictions which stand better the test of reflection. The existing body of moral convictions of the best people is the cumulative product of the moral reflection of many generations, which has developed an extremely delicate power of appreciation of moral distinctions; and this the theorist cannot afford to treat with anything other than the greatest respect. The verdicts of the moral consciousness of the best people are the foundation on which he must build; though he must first compare them with one another and eliminate any contradictions they may contain.

2.9 What Is Feminist Ethics?

HILDE LINDEMANN

Hilde Lindemann teaches moral philosophy and bioethics at Michigan State University.

A few years ago, a dentist in Ohio was convicted of having sex with his female patients while they were under anesthesia. I haven't been able to discover whether he had to pay a fine or do jail time, but I do remember that the judge ordered him to take a course in ethics. And I recall thinking how odd that order was. Let's suppose, as the judge apparently did, that the dentist really and truly didn't know it was wrong to have sex

with anesthetized patients (this will tax your imagination, but try to suppose it anyway). Can we expect—again, as the judge apparently did—that on completing the ethics course, the dentist would be a better, finer man?

Hardly. If studying ethics could make you good, then the people who have advanced academic degrees in the subject would be paragons of moral uprightness. I can't speak for all of

Hilde Lindemann, *Invitation to Feminist Ethics,* pp. 2–3, 6–16. © 2006 The McGraw-Hill Companies. Reprinted with permission of McGraw-Hill Education.

them, of course, but though the ones I know are nice enough, they're no more moral than anyone else. Ethics doesn't improve your character. Its *subject* is morality, but its relationship to morality is that of a scholarly study to the thing being studied. In that respect, the relationship is a little like the relationship between grammar and language.

Let's explore that analogy. People who speak fluent English don't have to stop and think about the correctness of the sentence "He gave it to *her*." But here's a harder one. Should you say, "He gave it to *her* who must be obeyed"? or "He gave it to *she* who must be obeyed"? To sort this out, it helps to know a little grammar —the systematic, scholarly description of the structure of the language and the rules for speaking and writing in it. According to those rules, the object of the preposition "to" is the entire clause that comes after it, and the subject of that clause is "she." So, even though it sounds peculiar, the correct answer is "He gave it to she who must be obeyed."

In a roughly similar vein, morally competent adults don't have to stop and think about whether it's wrong to have sex with one's anesthetized patients. But if you want to understand whether it's wrong to have large signs in bars telling pregnant women not to drink, or to sort out the conditions under which it's all right to tell a lie, it helps to know a little ethics. The analogy between grammar and ethics isn't exact, of course. For one thing, there's considerably more agreement about what language is than about what morality is. For another, grammarians are concerned only with the structure of language, not with the meaning or usage of particular words. In both cases, however, the same point can be made: You already have to know quite a lot about how to behave—linguistically or morally—before there's much point in studying either grammar or ethics.

WHAT IS FEMINISM?

What, then, is feminism? As a social and political movement with a long, intermittent history, feminism has repeatedly come into public awareness, generated change, and then disappeared again. As an eclectic body of theory, feminism entered colleges and universities in the early 1970s as a part of the women's studies movement, contributing to scholarship in every academic discipline, though probably most heavily in the arts, social sciences, literature, and the humanities in general. Feminist ethics is a part of the body of theory that is being developed primarily in colleges and universities.

Many people in the United States think of feminism as a movement that aims to make women the social equals of men, and this impression has been reinforced by references to feminism and feminists in the newspapers, on television, and in the movies. But bell hooks has pointed out in *Feminist Theory from Margin to Center* (1984, 18–19) that this way of defining feminism raises some serious problems. Which men do women want to be equal to? Women who are socially well off wouldn't get much advantage from being the equals of the men who are poor and lower class, particularly if they aren't white. Hooks's point is that there are no women and men in the abstract. They are poor, black, young, Latino/a, old, gay, able-bodied, upper class, down on their luck, Native American, straight, and all the rest of it. When a woman doesn't think about this, it's probably because she doesn't have to. And that's usually a sign that her own social position is privileged. In fact, privilege often means that there's something uncomfortable going on that others have to pay attention to but you don't. So, when hooks asks which men women want to be equal to, she's reminding us that there's an unconscious presumption of privilege built right in to this sort of demand for equality.

There's a second problem with the equality definition. Even if we could figure out which men are the ones to whom women should be equal, that way of putting it suggests that the point of feminism is somehow to get women to measure up to what (at least some) men already are. Men remain the point of reference; theirs are the lives that women would naturally want. If the first problem with the equality definition is "Equal to *which* men?" the second problem could be put as "Why equal to *any* men?" Reforming a system in which men are the point of reference by allowing women to perform as their equals "forces women to focus on men and address men's conceptions of women rather than creating and developing women's values about themselves," as Sarah Lucia Hoagland puts it in *Lesbian Ethics* (1988, 57). For that reason, Hoagland and some other feminists believe that feminism is first and foremost about women.

But characterizing feminism as about women has its problems too. What, after all, is a woman? In her 1949 book, *The Second Sex,* the French feminist philosopher Simone de Beauvoir famously observed, "One is not born, but becomes a woman. No biological, psychological, or economic fate determines the figure that the human female presents in society: it is civilization as a whole that produces this creature, intermediate between male and eunuch, which is described as feminine" (Beauvoir 1949, 301). Her point is that while plenty of human beings are born female, "woman" is not a natural fact about them—it's a social invention. According to that invention, which is widespread in "civilization as a whole," man represents the positive, typical human being, while woman represents only the negative, the not-man. She is the Other against whom man defines himself—he is all the things that she is not. And she exists only in relation to him. In a later essay called "One Is Not Born a Woman," the lesbian author and theorist Monique Wittig (1981, 49) adds that because women belong to men sexually as well as in every other way, women are necessarily heterosexual. For that reason, she argued, lesbians aren't women.

But, you are probably thinking, everybody knows what a woman is, and lesbians certainly *are* women. And you're right. These French feminists aren't denying that there's a perfectly ordinary use of the word *woman* by which it means exactly what you think it means. But they're explaining what this comes down to, if you look at it from a particular point of view.

Their answer to the question "What is a woman?" is that women are different from men. But they don't mean this as a trite observation. They're saying that "woman" refers to *nothing but* difference from men, so that apart from men, women aren't anything. "Man" is the positive term, "woman" is the negative one, just like "light" is the positive term and "dark" is nothing but the absence of light.

A later generation of feminists have agreed with Beauvoir and Wittig that women are different from men, but rather than seeing that difference as simply negative, they put it in positive terms, affirming feminine qualities as a source of personal strength and pride. For example, the philosopher Virginia Held thinks that women's moral experience as mothers, attentively nurturing their children, may serve as a better model for social relations than the contract model that the free market provides. The poet Adrienne Rich celebrated women's passionate nature (as opposed, in stereotype, to the rational nature of men), regarding the emotions as morally valuable rather than as signs of weakness.

But defining feminism as about the positive differences between men and women creates yet another set of problems. In her 1987 *Feminism Unmodified,* the feminist legal theorist Catharine A. MacKinnon points out that this kind of difference, as such, is a symmetrical relationship: If I am different from you, then you are different from me in exactly the same respects and to exactly the same degree. "Men's differences from women are equal to women's differences from men," she writes. "There is an *equality* there. Yet the sexes are not socially equal" (MacKinnon 1987, 37). No amount of attention to the differences between men and women explains why men, as a group, are more socially powerful, valued, advantaged, or free than women. For that, you have to see differences as counting in certain ways, and certain differences being created precisely because they give men *power* over women.

Although feminists disagree about this, my own view is that feminism isn't—at least not directly—about equality, and it isn't about women, and it isn't about difference. It's about power. Specifically, it's about the social pattern, widespread across cultures and history, that distributes power asymmetrically to favor men over women. This asymmetry has been given many names, including the subjugation of women, sexism, male dominance, patriarchy, systemic misogyny, phallocracy, and the oppression of women. A number of feminist theorists simply call it gender, and... I will too.

WHAT IS GENDER?

Most people think their gender is a natural fact about them, like their hair and eye color: "Jones is 5 foot 8, has red hair, and is a man." But gender is a *norm*, not a fact. It's a prescription for how people are supposed to act; what they must or must not wear; how they're supposed to sit, walk, or stand; what kind of person they're supposed to marry; what sorts of things they're supposed to be interested in or good at; and what they're entitled to. And because it's an *effective* norm, it creates the differences between men and women in these areas.

Gender doesn't just tell women to behave one way and men another, though. It's a *power* relation, so it tells men that they're entitled to things that women aren't supposed to have, and it tells women that they are supposed to defer to men and serve them. It says, for example, that men are supposed to occupy positions of religious authority and women are supposed to run the church suppers. It says that mothers are supposed to take care of their children but fathers have more important things to do. And it says that the things associated with femininity are supposed to take a back seat to the things that are coded masculine. Think of the many tax dollars allocated to the military as compared with the few tax dollars allocated to the arts. Think about how kindergarten teachers are paid as compared to how stockbrokers are paid. And think about how many presidents of the United States have been women. Gender operates through social institutions (like marriage and the law) and practices (like education and medicine) by disproportionately conferring entitlements and the control of resources on men, while disproportionately assigning women to subordinate positions in the service of men's interests.

To make this power relation seem perfectly natural—like the fact that plants grow up instead of down, or that human beings grow old and die —gender constructs its norms for behavior around what is supposed to be the natural biological distinction between the sexes. According to this distinction, people who have penises and testicles, XY chromosomes, and beards as adults belong to the male sex, while people who have clitorises and ovaries, XX chromosomes, and breasts as adults belong to the female sex, and those are the only sexes there are. Gender, then, is the complicated set of cultural meanings that are constructed around the two sexes. Your sex is either male or female, and your gender—either masculine, or feminine—corresponds socially to your sex.

As a matter of fact, though, sex isn't quite so simple. Some people with XY chromosomes don't have penises and never develop beards, because they don't have the receptors that allow them to make use of the male hormones that their testicles produce. Are they male or female? Other people have ambiguous genitals or internal reproductive structures that don't correspond in the usual manner to their external genitalia. How should we classify them? People with Turner's syndrome have XO chromosomes instead of XX. People with Klinefelter's syndrome have three sex chromosomes: XXY. Nature is a good bit looser in its categories than the simple male/female distinction acknowledges. Most human beings can certainly be classified as one sex or the other, but a considerable number of them fall somewhere in between.

The powerful norm of gender doesn't acknowledge the existence of the in-betweens, though. When, for example, have you ever filled out an application for a job or a driver's license or a passport that gave you a choice other than M or F? Instead, by basing its distinction between masculine and feminine on the existence of two and only two sexes, gender makes the inequality of power between men and women appear natural and therefore legitimate.

Gender, then, is about power. But it's not about the power of just one group over another. Gender always interacts with other social markers—such as race, class, level of education, sexual orientation, age, religion, physical and mental health, and ethnicity—to distribute power unevenly among women positioned differently in the various social orders, and it does the same to men. A man's social status, for example, can have a great deal to do with the extent to which he's even perceived as a man. There's a wonderful passage in the English travel writer Frances Trollope's *Domestic Manners of the Americans* (1831), in which she describes the exaggerated delicacy of middle-class young ladies she met in Kentucky and Ohio. They wouldn't dream of sitting in a chair that was still warm from contact with a gentleman's bottom, but thought nothing of getting laced into their corsets in front of a male house slave. The slave, it's clear, didn't count as a man—not in the relevant sense, anyway. Gender is the force that makes it matter whether you are male or female, but it always works hand in glove with all the other things about you that matter at the same time. It's one power relation intertwined with others in a complex social system that distinguishes your betters from your inferiors in all kinds of ways and for all kinds of purposes.

POWER AND MORALITY

If feminism is about gender, and gender is the name for a social system that distributes power unequally between men and women, then you'd expect feminist ethicists to try to *understand, criticize,* and *correct* how gender operates within our moral beliefs and practices. And they do just that. In the first place, they challenge, on moral grounds, the powers men have over women, and they claim for women, again on moral grounds, the powers that gender denies them. As the moral reasons for opposing gender are similar to the moral reasons for opposing power systems based on social markers other than gender,

feminist ethicists also offer moral arguments against systems based on class, race, physical or mental ability, sexuality, and age. And because all these systems, including gender, are powerful enough to *conceal* many of the forces that keep them in place, it's often necessary to make the forces visible by explicitly identifying—and condemning—the various ugly ways they allow some people to treat others. This is a central task for feminist ethics.

Feminist ethicists also produce theory about the moral meaning of various kinds of *legitimate* relations of unequal power, including relationships of dependency and vulnerability, relationships of trust, and relationships based on something other than choice. Parent-child relationships, for example, are necessarily unequal and for the most part unchosen. Parents can't help having power over their children, and while they may have chosen to have children, most don't choose to have the particular children they do, nor do children choose their parents. This raises questions about the responsible use of parental power and the nature of involuntary obligations, and these are topics for feminist ethics. Similarly, when you trust someone, that person has power over you. Whom should you trust, for what purposes, and when is trust not warranted? What's involved in being trustworthy, and what must be done to repair breaches of trust? These too are questions for feminist ethics.

Third, feminist ethicists look at the various forms of power that are required for morality to operate properly at all. How do we learn right from wrong in the first place? We usually learn it from our parents, whose power to permit and forbid, praise and punish, is essential to our moral training. For whom or what are we ethically responsible? Often this depends on the kind of power we have over the person or thing in question. If, for instance, someone is particularly vulnerable to harm because of something I've done, I might well have special duties toward that person. Powerful social institutions—medicine, religion, government, and the market, to take just a few examples—typically dictate what is morally required of us and to whom we are morally answerable. Relations of power set the terms for who must answer to whom, who has authority over whom, and who gets excused from certain kinds of accountability to whom. But because so many of these power relations are illegitimate, in that they're instances of gender, racism, or other kinds of bigotry, figuring out which ones are morally justified is a task for feminist ethics.

DESCRIPTION AND PRESCRIPTION

So far it sounds as if feminist ethics devotes considerable attention to *description*—as if feminist ethicists were like poets or painters who want to show you something about reality that you might otherwise have missed. And indeed, many feminist ethicists emphasize the importance of understanding how social power actually works, rather than concentrating solely on how it ought to work. But why, you might ask, should ethicists worry about how power operates within societies? Isn't it up to sociologists and political scientists to describe how things *are,* while ethicists concentrate on how things *ought* to be?

As the philosopher Margaret Urban Walker has pointed out in *Moral Contexts,* there is a tradition in Western philosophy, going all the way back to Plato, to the effect that morality is something ideal and that ethics, being the study of morality, properly examines only that ideal. According to this tradition, notions of right and wrong as they are found in the world are unreliable and shadowy manifestations of something lying outside of human experience—something to which we ought to aspire but can't hope to reach. Plato's Idea of the Good, in fact, is precisely not of this earth, and only the gods could truly know it. Christian ethics incorporates Platonism into its insistence that earthly existence is fraught with sin and error and that heaven is our real home. Kant too insists that moral judgments transcend the histories and circumstances of people's actual lives, and most moral philosophers of the twentieth century have likewise shown little

interest in how people really live and what it's like for them to live that way. "They think," remarks Walker (2001), "that there is little to be learned from what is about what ought to be" (3).

...If you don't know how things are, your prescriptions for how things ought to be won't have much practical effect. Imagine trying to sail a ship without knowing anything about the tides or where the hidden rocks and shoals lie. You might have a very fine idea of where you are trying to go, but if you don't know the waters, at best you are likely to go off course, and at worst you'll end up going down with all your shipmates. If, as many feminists have noted, a crucial fact about human selves is that they are always embedded in a vast web of relationships, then the forces at play within those relationships must be understood. It's knowing how people are situated with respect to these forces, what they are going through as they are subjected to them, and what life is like in the face of them, that lets us decide which of the forces are morally justified. Careful description of how things are is a crucial part of feminist methodology, because the power that puts certain groups of people at risk of physical harm, denies them full access to the good things their society has to offer, or treats them as if they were useful only for other people's purposes is often hidden and hard to see. If this power isn't seen, it's likely to remain in place, doing untold amounts of damage to great numbers of people.

All the same, feminist ethics is *normative* as well as descriptive. It's fundamentally about how things ought to be, while description plays the crucial but secondary role of helping us to figure that out. Normative language is the language of "ought" instead of "is," the language of "worth" and "value," "right" and "wrong," "good" and "bad." Feminist ethicists differ on a number of normative issues, but as the philosopher Alison Jaggar (1991) has famously put it, they all share two moral commitments: "that the subordination of women is morally wrong and that the moral experience of women is worthy of respect" (95). The first commitment—that women's interests ought not systematically to be set in the service of men's—can be understood as a moral challenge to power under the guise of gender. The second commitment—that women's experience must be taken seriously—can be understood as a call to acknowledge how that power operates. These twin commitments are the two normative legs on which any feminist ethics stands.

MORALITY AND POLITICS

If the idealization of morality goes back over two thousand years in Western thought, a newer tradition, only a couple of centuries old, has split off morality from politics. According to this tradition, which can be traced to Kant and some other Enlightenment philosophers, morality concerns the relations between persons, whereas politics concerns the relations among nation-states, or between a state and its citizens. So, as Iris Marion Young (1990) puts it, ethicists have tended to focus on intentional actions by individual persons, conceiving of moral life as "conscious, deliberate, a rational weighing of alternatives," whereas political philosophers have focused on impersonal governmental systems, studying "laws, policies, the large-scale distribution of social goods, countable quantities like votes and taxes" (149).

For feminists, though, the line between ethics and political theory isn't quite so bright as this tradition makes out. It's not always easy to tell where feminist ethics leaves off and feminist political theory begins. There are two reasons for this. In the first place, while ethics certainly concerns personal behavior, there is a long-standing insistence on the part of feminists that the personal is political. In a 1970 essay called "The Personal Is Political," the political activist Carol Hanisch observed that "personal problems are political problems. There are no personal solutions at this time" (204–205). What Hanisch meant is that even the most private areas of everyday life, including such intensely personal areas as sex, can function to maintain abusive power systems like gender. If

a heterosexual woman believes, for example, that contraception is primarily her responsibility because she'll have to take care of the baby if she gets pregnant, she is propping up a system that lets men evade responsibility not only for pregnancy, but for their own offspring as well. Conversely, while unjust social arrangements such as gender and race invade every aspect of people's personal lives, "there are no personal solutions," either when Hanisch wrote those words or now, because to shift dominant understandings of how certain groups may be treated, and what other groups are entitled to expect of them, requires concerted political action, not just personal good intentions.

The second reason why it's hard to separate feminist ethics from feminist politics is that feminists typically subject the ethical theory they produce to critical political scrutiny, not only to keep untoward political biases out, but also to make sure that the work accurately reflects their feminist politics. Many nonfeminist ethicists, on the other hand, don't acknowledge that their work reflects their politics, because they don't think it should. Their aim, by and large, has been to develop ideal moral theory that applies to all people, regardless of their social position or experience of life, and to do that objectively, without favoritism, which requires them to leave their own personal politics behind. The trouble, though, is that they aren't really leaving their own personal politics behind. They're merely refusing to notice that their politics is inevitably built right in to their theories. (This is an instance of Lindemann's ad hoc rule Number 22: Just because you think you are doing something doesn't mean you're actually doing it.) Feminists, by contrast, are generally skeptical of the idealism nonfeminists favor, and they're equally doubtful that objectivity can be achieved by stripping away what's distinctive about people's experiences or commitments. Believing that it's no wiser to shed one's political allegiances in the service of ethics than it would be to shed one's moral allegiances, feminists prefer to be transparent about their politics as a way of keeping their ethics intellectually honest.

REFERENCES

Beauvoir, Simone de. 1949 [1974]. *The Second Sex.* Trans, and ed. H. M. Parshley. New York: Modern Library.

Hanisch, Carol. 1970. "The Personal Is Political." In *Notes from the Second Year.* New York: Radical Feminism.

Hoagland, Sarah Lucia. 1988. *Lesbian Ethics: Toward New Value.* Palo Alto, CA: Institute of Lesbian Studies.

Hooks, bell. 1984. *Feminist Theory from Margin to Center.* Boston: South End Press.

Jaggar, Alison. 1991. "Feminist Ethics: Projects, Problems, Prospects." In *Feminist Ethics,* ed. Claudia Card. Lawrence: University Press of Kansas.

MacKinnon, Catharine A. 1987. *Feminism Unmodified.* Cambridge, MA: Harvard University Press.

Walker, Margaret Urban. 2001. "Seeing Power in Morality: A Proposal for Feminist Naturalism in Ethics." In *Feminists Doing Ethics,* ed. Peggy Des- Autels and Joanne Waugh. Lanham, MD: Rowman & Littlefield.

_____. 2003. *Moral Contexts.* Lanham, MD: Rowman & Littlefield.

Wittig, Monique. 1981. "One Is Not Born a Woman." *Feminist Issues* 1, no. 2.

Young, Iris Marion. 1990. *Justice and the Politics of Difference.* Princeton, NJ: Princeton University Press.

CHAPTER 3

ETHICAL PROBLEMS

3.1 What Will Future Generations Condemn Us For?

KWAME ANTHONY APPIAH

Kwame Anthony Appiah, a philosophy professor at Princeton University, is the author of *The Honor Code: How Moral Revolutions Happen.*

Once, pretty much everywhere, beating your wife and children was regarded as a father's duty, homosexuality was a hanging offense, and waterboarding was approved—in fact, invented —by the Catholic Church.

Through the middle of the 19th century, the United States and other nations in the Americas condoned plantation slavery. Many of our grandparents were born in states where women were forbidden to vote. And well into the 20th century, lynch mobs in this country stripped, tortured, hanged and burned human beings at picnics.

Looking back at such horrors, it is easy to ask: What were people thinking?

Yet, the chances are that our own descendants will ask the same question, with the same incomprehension, about some of our practices today.

Is there a way to guess which ones? After all, not every disputed institution or practice is destined to be discredited. And it can be hard to distinguish in real time between movements, such as abolition, that will come to represent moral common sense and those, such as

Kwame Anthony Appiah, "What Will Future Generations Condemn us For?" Washington Post, September 26, 2010.

prohibition, that will come to seem quaint or misguided. Recall the book-burners of Boston's old Watch and Ward Society or the organizations for the suppression of vice, with their crusades against claret, contraceptives and sexually candid novels.

Still, a look at the past suggests three signs that a particular practice is destined for future condemnation.

First, people have already heard the arguments against the practice. The case against slavery didn't emerge in a blinding moment of moral clarity, for instance; it had been around for centuries.

Second, defenders of the custom tend not to offer moral counterarguments but instead invoke tradition, human nature or necessity. (As in, "We've always had slaves, and how could we grow cotton without them?")

And third, supporters engage in what one might call strategic ignorance, avoiding truths that might force them to face the evils in which they're complicit. Those who ate the sugar or wore the cotton that the slaves grew simply didn't think about what made those goods possible. That's why abolitionists sought to direct attention toward the conditions of the Middle Passage, through detailed illustrations of slave ships and horrifying stories of the suffering below decks.

With these signs in mind, here are four contenders for future moral condemnation.

OUR PRISON SYSTEM

We already know that the massive waste of life in our prisons is morally troubling; those who defend the conditions of incarceration usually do so in non-moral terms (citing costs or the administrative difficulty of reforms); and we're inclined to avert our eyes from the details. Check, check and check.

Roughly 1 percent of adults in this country are incarcerated. We have 4 percent of the world's population but 25 percent of its prisoners. No other nation has as large a proportion of its population in prison; even China's rate is less than half of ours. What's more, the majority of our prisoners are non-violent offenders, many of them detained on drug charges. (Whether a country that was truly free would criminalize recreational drug use is a related question worth pondering.)

And the full extent of the punishment prisoners face isn't detailed in any judge's sentence. More than 100,000 inmates suffer sexual abuse, including rape, each year; some contract HIV as a result. Our country holds at least 25,000 prisoners in isolation in so-called supermax facilities, under conditions that many psychologists say amount to torture.

INDUSTRIAL MEAT PRODUCTION

The arguments against the cruelty of factory farming have certainly been around a long time; it was Jeremy Bentham, in the 18th century, who observed that, when it comes to the treatment of animals, the key question is not whether animals can reason but whether they can suffer. People who eat factory-farmed bacon or chicken rarely offer a moral justification for what they're doing. Instead, they try not to think about it too much, shying away from stomach-turning stories about what goes on in our industrial abattoirs.

Of the more than 90 million cattle in our country, at least 10 million at any time are packed into feedlots, saved from the inevitable diseases of overcrowding only by regular doses of antibiotics, surrounded by piles of their own feces, their nostrils filled with the smell of their own urine. Picture it—and then imagine your grandchildren seeing that picture. In the European Union, many of the most inhumane conditions we allow are already illegal or—like the sow stalls into which pregnant pigs are often crammed in the United States—will be illegal soon.

THE INSTITUTIONALIZED AND ISOLATED ELDERLY

Nearly 2 million of America's elderly are warehoused in nursing homes, out of sight and, to some extent, out of mind. Some 10,000 for-profit facilities have arisen across the country in recent decades to hold them. Other elderly Americans may live independently, but often they are isolated and cut off from their families. (The United States is not alone among advanced democracies in this. Consider the heat wave that hit France in 2003: While many families were enjoying their summer vacations, some 14,000 elderly parents and grandparents were left to perish in the stifling temperatures.) Is this what Western modernity amounts to—societies that feel no filial obligations to their inconvenient elders?

Sometimes we can learn from societies much poorer than ours. My English mother spent the last 50 years of her life in Ghana, where I grew up. In her final years, it was her good fortune not only to have the resources to stay at home, but also to live in a country where doing so was customary. She had family next door who visited her every day, and she was cared for by doctors and nurses who were willing to come to her when she was too ill to come to them. In short, she had the advantages of a society in which older people are treated with respect and concern.

Keeping aging parents and their children closer is a challenge, particularly in a society where almost everybody has a job outside the home (if not across the country). Yet the three signs apply here as well: When we see old people who, despite many living relatives, suffer growing isolation, we know something is wrong. We scarcely try to defend the situation; when we can, we put it out of our minds. Self-interest, if

nothing else, should make us hope that our descendants will have worked out a better way.

THE ENVIRONMENT

Of course, most transgenerational obligations run the other way—from parents to children—and of these the most obvious candidate for opprobrium is our wasteful attitude toward the planet's natural resources and ecology. Look at a satellite picture of Russia, and you'll see a vast expanse of parched wasteland where decades earlier was a lush and verdant landscape. That's the Republic of Kalmykia, home to what was recognized in the 1990s as Europe's first man-made desert. Desertification, which is primarily the result of destructive land-management practices, threatens a third of the Earth's surface; tens of thousands of Chinese villages have been overrun by sand drifts in the past few decades.

It's not as though we're unaware of what we're doing to the planet: We know the harm done by deforestation, wetland destruction, pollution, overfishing, greenhouse gas emissions—the whole litany. Our descendants, who will inherit this devastated Earth, are unlikely to have the luxury of such recklessness. Chances are, they won't be able to avert their eyes, even if they want to.

* * *

Let's not stop there, though. We will all have our own suspicions about which practices will someday prompt people to ask, in dismay: What were they thinking?

Even when we don't have a good answer, we'll be better off for anticipating the question.

3.2 Famine, Affluence, and Morality

PETER SINGER

As I write this, in November 1971, people are dying in East Bengal from lack of food, shelter, and medical care. The suffering and death that are occurring there now are not inevitable, not unavoidable in any fatalistic sense of the term. Constant poverty, a cyclone, and a civil war have turned at least nine million people into destitute refugees; nevertheless, it is not beyond the capacity of the richer nations to give enough assistance to reduce any further suffering to very small proportions. The decisions and actions of human beings can prevent this kind of suffering.

What are the moral implications of a situation like this? In what follows, I shall argue that the way people in relatively affluent countries react to a situation like that in Bengal cannot be justified; indeed, the whole way we look at moral issues —our moral conceptual scheme—needs to be altered, and with it, the way of life that has come to be taken for granted in our society.

I begin with the assumption that suffering and death from lack of food, shelter, and medical care are bad. I think most people will agree about this, although one may reach the same view by different routes. I shall not argue for this view. People can hold all sorts of eccentric positions, and perhaps from some of them it would not follow that death by starvation is in itself bad. It is difficult, perhaps impossible, to refute such positions, and so for brevity I will henceforth take this assumption as accepted. Those who disagree need read no further.

My next point is this: if it is in our power to prevent something bad from happening, without thereby sacrificing anything of comparable moral importance, we ought, morally, to do it. By "without sacrificing anything of comparable moral importance" I mean without causing anything else comparably bad to happen, or doing something that is wrong in itself, or failing to promote some moral good, comparable in significance to the bad thing that we can prevent. This principle seems almost as uncontroversial as the last one. It requires us only to prevent what is bad, and not to promote what is good, and it requires this of us only when we can do it without sacrificing anything that is, from the moral point of view, comparably important. I could even, as far as the application of my argument to the Ben-

gal emergency is concerned, qualify the point so as to make it: if it is in our power to prevent something very bad from happening, without thereby sacrificing anything morally significant, we ought, morally, to do it. An application of this principle would be as follows: if I am walking past a shallow pond and see a child drowning in it, I ought to wade in and pull the child out. This will mean getting my clothes muddy, but this is insignificant, while the death of the child would presumably be a very bad thing.

The uncontroversial appearance of the principle just stated is deceptive. If it were acted upon, even in its qualified form, our lives, our society, and our world would be fundamentally changed. For the principle takes, firstly, no account of proximity or distance. It makes no moral difference whether the person I can help is a neighbor's child ten yards from me or a Bengali whose name I shall never know, ten thousand miles away. Secondly, the principle makes no distinction between cases in which I am the only person who could possibly do anything and cases in which I am just one among millions in the same position.

I do not think I need to say much in defense of the refusal to take proximity and distance into account. The fact that a person is physically near to us, so that we have personal contact with him, may make it more likely that we *shall* assist him, but this does not show that we *ought* to help him rather than another who happens to be further away. If we accept any principle of impartiality, universalizability, equality, or whatever, we cannot discriminate against someone merely because he is far away from us (or we are far away from him). Admittedly, it is possible that we are in a better position to judge what needs

Republished with permission of John Wiley & Sons, from Peter Singer, "Famine, Affluence and Morality," *Philosophy and Public Affairs*, vol. 1 (1972), pp. 229–243; permission conveyed through Copyright Clearance Center, Inc.

to be done to help a person near to us than one far away, and perhaps also to provide the assistance we judge to be necessary. If this were the case, it would be a reason for helping those near to us first. This may once have been a justification for being more concerned with the poor in one's own town than with famine victims in India. Unfortunately for those who like to keep their moral responsibilities limited, instant communication and swift transportation have changed the situation. From the moral point of view, the development of the world into a "global village" has made an important, though still unrecognized, difference to our moral situation. Expert observers and supervisors, sent out by famine relief organizations or permanently stationed in famine-prone areas, can direct our aid to a refugee in Bengal almost as effectively as we could get it to someone in our own block. There would seem, therefore, to be no possible justification for discriminating on geographical grounds.

There may be a greater need to defend the second implication of my principle—that the fact that there are millions of other people in the same position, in respect to the Bengali refugees, as I am, does not make the situation significantly different from a situation in which I am the only person who can prevent something very bad from occurring. Again, of course, I admit that there is a psychological difference between the cases; one feels less guilty about doing nothing if one can point to others, similarly placed, who have also done nothing. Yet this can make no real difference to our moral obligations.[1] Should I consider that I am less obliged to pull the drowning child out of the pond if on looking around I see other people, no further away than I am, who have also noticed the child but are doing nothing? One has only to ask this question to see the absurdity of the view that numbers lessen obligation. It is a view that is an ideal excuse for inactivity; unfortunately most of the major evils—poverty, overpopulation, pollution—are problems in which everyone is almost equally involved.

The view that numbers do make a difference can be made plausible if stated in this way: if everyone in circumstances like mine gave £5 to the Bengal Relief Fund, there would be enough to provide food, shelter, and medical care for the refugees; there is no reason why I should give more than anyone else in the same circumstances as I am; therefore I have no obligation to give more than £5. Each premise in this argument is true, and the argument looks sound. It may convince us, unless we notice that it is based on a hypothetical premise, although the conclusion is not stated hypothetically. The argument would be sound if the conclusion were: if everyone in circumstances like mine were to give £5, I would have no obligation to give more than £5. If the conclusion were so stated, however, it would be obvious that the argument has no bearing on a situation in which it is not the case that everyone else gives £5. This, of course, is the actual situation. It is more or less certain that not everyone in circumstances like mine will give £5. So there will not be enough to provide the needed food, shelter, and medical care. Therefore by giving more than £5 I will prevent more suffering than I would if I gave just £5.

It might be thought that this argument has an absurd consequence. Since the situation appears to be that very few people are likely to give substantial amounts, it follows that I and everyone else in similar circumstances ought to give as much as possible, that is, at least up to the point at which by giving more one would begin to cause serious suffering for oneself and one's dependents—perhaps even beyond this point to the point of marginal utility, at which by giving more one would cause oneself and one's dependents as much suffering as one would prevent in Bengal. If everyone does this, however, there will be more than can be used for the benefit of the refugees, and some of the sacrifice will have been unnecessary. Thus, if everyone does what he ought to do, the result will not be as good as it would be if everyone did a little less than he ought to do, or if only some do all that they ought to do.

The paradox here arises only if we assume that the actions in question—sending money to the relief funds—are performed more or less simultaneously, and are also unexpected. For if it is to be expected that everyone is going to contribute something, then clearly each is not obliged to give as much as he would have been obliged to had others not been giving too. And if everyone is not acting more or less simultaneously, then those giving later will know how much more is needed, and will have no obligation to give more than is necessary to reach this amount. To say this is not to deny the principle that people in the same circumstances have the same obligations, but to point out that the fact that others have given, or may be expected to give, is a relevant circumstance: those giving after it has become known that many others are giving and those giving before are not in the same circumstances. So the seemingly absurd consequence of the principle I have put forward can occur only if people are in error about the actual circumstances—that is, if they think they are giving when others are not, but in fact they are giving when others are. The result of everyone doing what he really ought to do cannot be worse than the result of everyone doing less than he ought to do, although the result of everyone doing what he reasonably believes he ought to do could be.

If my argument so far has been sound, neither our distance from a preventable evil nor the number of other people who, in respect to that evil, are in the same situation as we are, lessens our obligation to mitigate or prevent that evil. I shall therefore take as established the principle I asserted earlier. As I have already said, I need to assert it only in its qualified form: if it is in our power to prevent something very bad from happening, without thereby sacrificing anything else morally significant, we ought, morally, to do it.

The outcome of this argument is that our traditional moral categories are upset. The traditional distinction between duty and charity cannot be drawn, or at least, not in the place we normally draw it. Giving money to the Bengal Relief Fund is regarded as an act of charity in our society. The bodies which collect money are known as "charities." These organizations see themselves in this way—if you send them a check, you will be thanked for your "generosity." Because giving money is regarded as an act of

charity, it is not thought that there is anything wrong with not giving. The charitable man may be praised, but the man who is not charitable is not condemned. People do not feel in any way ashamed or guilty about spending money on new clothes or a new car instead of giving it to famine relief. (Indeed, the alternative does not occur to them.) This way of looking at the matter cannot be justified. When we buy new clothes not to keep ourselves warm but to look "well-dressed" we are not providing for any important need. We would not be sacrificing anything significant if we were to continue to wear our old clothes, and give the money to famine relief. By doing so, we would be preventing another person from starving. It follows from what I have said earlier that we ought to give money away, rather than spend it on clothes which we do not need to keep us warm. To do so is not charitable, or generous. Nor is it the kind of act which philosophers and theologians have called "supererogatory"—an act which it would be good to do, but not wrong not to do. On the contrary, we ought to give the money away, and it is wrong not to do so.

I am not maintaining that there are no acts which are charitable, or that there are no acts which it would be good to do but not wrong not to do. It may be possible to redraw the distinction between duty and charity in some other place. All I am arguing here is that the present way of drawing the distinction, which makes it an act of charity for a man living at the level of affluence which most people in the "developed nations" enjoy to give money to save someone else from starvation, cannot be supported. It is beyond the scope of my argument to consider whether the distinction should be redrawn or abolished altogether. There would be many other possible ways of drawing the distinction —for instance, one might decide that it is good to make other people as happy as possible, but not wrong not to do so.

Despite the limited nature of the revision in our moral conceptual scheme which I am proposing, the revision would, given the extent of both affluence and famine in the world today, have radical implications. These implications may lead to further objections, distinct from those I have already considered. I shall discuss two of these.

One objection to the position I have taken might be simply that it is too drastic a revision of our moral scheme. People do not ordinarily judge in the way I have suggested they should. Most people reserve their moral condemnation for those who violate some moral norm, such as the norm against taking another person's property. They do not condemn those who indulge in luxury instead of giving to famine relief. But given that I did not set out to present a morally neutral description of the way people make moral judgments, the way people do in fact judge has nothing to do with the validity of my conclusion. My conclusion follows from the principle which I advanced earlier, and unless that principle is rejected, or the arguments shown to be unsound, I think the conclusion must stand, however strange it appears.

It has been argued by some writers, that we need to have a basic moral code which is not too far beyond the capacities of the ordinary man, for otherwise there will be a general breakdown of compliance with the moral code. Crudely stated, this argument suggests that if we tell people that they ought to refrain from murder and give everything they do not really need to famine relief, they will do neither, whereas if we tell them that they ought to refrain from murder and that it is good to give to famine relief but not wrong not to do. so, they will at least refrain from murder. The issue here is: Where should we drawn the line between conduct that is required and conduct that is good although not required, so as to get the best possible result? This would seem to be an empirical question, although a very difficult one. One objection to this line of argument is that it takes insufficient account of the effect that moral standards can have on the decisions we make. Given a society in which a wealthy man who gives five percent of his income to famine relief is regarded as most generous, it is not surprising that a proposal that we all ought to give away half our incomes will be thought to be absurdly unrealistic. In a society which held that no man should have more than enough while others

have less than they need, such a proposal might seem narrow-minded. What it is possible for a man to do and what he is likely to do are both, I think, very greatly influenced by what people around him are doing and expecting him to do. In any case, the possibility that by spreading the idea that we ought to be doing very much more than we are to relieve famine we shall bring about a general breakdown of moral behavior seems remote. If the stakes are an end to widespread starvation, it is worth the risk. Finally, it should be emphasized that these considerations are relevant only to the issue of what we should require from others, and not to what we ourselves ought to do.

The second objection to my attack on the present distinction between duty and charity is one which has from time to time been made against utilitarianism. It follows from some forms of utilitarian theory that we all ought, morally, to be working full time to increase the balance of happiness over misery. The position I have taken here would not lead to this conclusion in all circumstances, for if there were no bad occurrences that we could prevent without sacrificing something of comparable moral importance, my argument would have no application. Given the present conditions in many parts of the world, however, it does follow from my argument that we ought, morally, to be working full time to relieve great suffering of the sort that occurs as a result of famine or other disasters. Of course, mitigating circumstances can be adduced—for instance, that if we wear ourselves out through overwork, we shall be less effective than we would otherwise have been. Nevertheless, when all considerations of this sort have been taken into account, the conclusion remains: we ought to be preventing as much suffering as we can without sacrificing something else of comparable moral importance. This conclusion is one which we may be reluctant to face. I cannot see, though, why it should be regarded as a criticism of the position for which I have argued, rather than a criticism of our ordinary standards of behavior. Since most people are self-interested to some degree, very few of us are likely to do everything that we ought to do. It would, however, hardly be honest to take this as evidence that it is not the case that we ought to do it.

I now want to consider a number of points, more practical than philosophical, which are relevant to the application of the moral conclusion we have reached. These points challenge not the idea that we ought to be doing all we can to prevent starvation, but the idea that giving away a great deal of money is the best means to this end.

It is sometimes said that overseas aid should be a government responsibility, and that therefore one ought not to give to privately run charities. Giving privately, it is said, allows the government and the noncontributing members of society to escape their responsibilities.

This argument seems to assume that the more people there are who give to privately organized famine relief funds, the less likely it is that the government will take over full responsibility for such aid. This assumption is unsupported, and does not strike me as at all plausible. The opposite view—that if no one gives voluntarily, a government will assume that its citizens are uninterested in famine relief and would not wish to be forced into giving aid—seems more plausible. In any case, unless there were a definite probability that by refusing to give one would be helping to bring about massive government assistance, people who do refuse to make voluntary contributions are refusing to prevent a certain amount of suffering without being able to point to any tangible beneficial consequence of their refusal. So the onus of showing how their refusal will bring about government action is on those who refuse to give.

Another, more serious reason for not giving to famine relief funds is that until there is effective population control, relieving famine merely postpones starvation. If we save the Bengal refugees now, others, perhaps the children of these refugees, will face starvation in a few years' time. In support of this, one may cite the now well-known facts about the population explosion and the relatively limited scope for expanded production.

This point, like the previous one, is an argument against relieving suffering that is happening now, because of a belief about what might happen in the future; it is unlike the previous point in that very good evidence can be adduced in support of this belief about the future. I will not go into the evidence here. I accept that the earth cannot support indefinitely a population rising at the present rate. This certainly poses a problem for anyone who thinks it important to prevent famine. Again, however, one could accept the argument without drawing the conclusion that it absolves one from any obligation to do anything to prevent famine. The conclusion that should be drawn is that the best means of preventing famine, in the long run, is population control. It would then follow from the position reached earlier that one ought to be doing all one can to promote population control (unless one held that all forms of population control were wrong in themselves, or would have significantly bad consequences). Since there are organizations working specifically for population control, one would then support them rather than more orthodox methods of preventing famine.

A third point raised by the conclusion reached earlier relates to the question of just how much we all ought to be giving away. One possibility, which has already been mentioned, is that we ought to give until we reach the level of marginal utility—that is, the level at which, by giving more, I would cause as much suffering to myself or my dependents as I would relieve by my gift. This would mean, of course, that one would reduce oneself to very near the material circumstances of a Bengali refugee. It will be recalled that earlier I put forward both a strong and a moderate version of the principle of preventing bad occurrences. The strong version, which required us to prevent bad things from happening unless in doing so we would be sacrificing something of comparable moral significance, does seem to require reducing ourselves to the level of marginal utility. I should also say that the strong version seems to me to be the correct one. I proposed the more moderate version—that we should prevent bad occurrences unless, to do so, we had to sacrifice something morally significant—only in order to show that even on this surely undeniable principle a great change in our way of life is required.

It is sometimes said, though less often now than it used to be, that philosophers have no special role to play in public affairs, since most public issues depend primarily on an assessment of facts. On questions of fact, it is said, philosophers as such have no special expertise, and so it has been possible to engage in philosophy without committing oneself to any position on major public issues. No doubt there are some issues of social policy and foreign policy about which it can truly be said that a really expert assessment of the facts is required before taking sides or acting, but the issue of famine is surely not one of these. The facts about the existence of suffering are beyond dispute. If philosophy is to deal with matters that are relevant to both teachers and students, this is an issue that philosophers should discuss.

Discussion, though, is not enough. What is the point of relating philosophy to public (and personal) affairs if we do not take our conclusions seriously? In this instance, taking our conclusion seriously means acting upon it. The

philosopher will not find it any easier than anyone else to alter his attitudes and way of life to the extent that, if I am right, is involved in doing everything that we ought to be doing.

At the very least, though, one can make a start. The philosopher who does so will have to sacrifice some of the benefits of the consumer society, but he can find compensation in the satisfaction of a way of life in which theory and practice, if not yet in harmony, are at least coming together.

NOTE

1. In view of the special sense philosophers often give to the term, I should say that I use "obligation" simply as the abstract noun derived from "ought," so that "I have an obligation to" means no more, and no less, than "I ought to." This usage is in accordance with the definition of "ought" given by the *Shorter Oxford English Dictionary*: "the general verb to express duty or obligation." I do not think any issue of substance hangs on the way the term is used; sentences in which I use "obligation" could all be rewritten, although somewhat clumsily, as sentences in which a clause containing "ought" replaces the term "obligation."

3.3 The Survival Lottery

JOHN HARRIS

John Harris works mainly in ethics and political philosophy. He teaches at the University of Manchester.

Let us suppose that organ transplant procedures have been perfected; in such circumstances if two dying patients could be saved by organ transplants then, if surgeons have the requisite organs in stock and no other needy patients, but nevertheless allow their patients to die, we would be

inclined to say, and be justified in saying, that the patients died because the doctors refused to save them. But if there are no spare organs in stock and none otherwise available, the doctors have no choice, they cannot save their patients and so must let them die. In this case we would be disinclined to say that the doctors are in any sense the cause of their patients' deaths. But let us further suppose that the two dying patients, Y and Z, are not happy about being left to die. They might argue that it is not strictly true that there are no organs which could be used to save them. Y needs a new heart and Z new lungs. They point out that if just one healthy person were to be killed his organs could be removed and both of them be saved. We and the doctors would probably be alike in thinking that such a step, while technically possible, would be out of the question. We would not say that the doctors were killing their patients if they refused to prey upon the healthy to save the sick. And because this sort of surgical Robin Hoodery is out of the question we can tell Y and Z that they cannot be saved, and that when they die they will have died of natural causes and not of the neglect of their doctors. Y and Z do not however agree, they insist that if the doctors fail to kill a healthy man and use his organs to save them, then the doctors will be responsible for their deaths.

Many philosophers have for various reasons believed that we must not kill even if by doing so we could save life. They believe that there is a moral difference between killing and letting die. On this view, to kill A so that Y and Z might live is ruled out because we have a strict obligation not to kill but a duty of some lesser kind to save life. A. H. Clough's dictum "Thou shalt not kill but need'st not strive officiously to keep alive" expresses bluntly this point of view. The dying Y and Z may be excused for not being much impressed by Clough's dictum. They agree that it is wrong to kill the innocent and are prepared to agree to an absolute prohibition against so doing. They do not agree, however, that A is more innocent than they are. Y and Z might go on to point out that the currently acknowledged right of the innocent not to be killed, even where their deaths might give life to others, is just a decision to prefer the lives of the fortunate to those of the unfortunate. A is innocent in the sense that he has done nothing to deserve death, but Y and Z are also innocent in this sense. Why should they be the ones to die simply because they are so unlucky

as to have diseased organs? Why, they might argue, should their living or dying be left to chance when in so many other areas of human life we believe that we have an obligation to ensure the survival of the maximum number of lives possible?

Y and Z argue that if a doctor refuses to treat a patient, with the result that the patient dies, he has killed that patient as sure as shooting, and that, in exactly the same way, if the doctors refuse Y and Z the transplants that they need, then their refusal will kill Y and Z, again as sure as shooting. The doctors, and indeed the society which supports their inaction, cannot defend themselves by arguing that they are neither expected, nor required by law or convention, to kill so that lives may be saved (indeed, quite the reverse) since this is just an appeal to custom or authority. A man who does his own moral thinking must decide whether, in these circumstances, he ought to save two lives at the cost of one, or one life at the cost of two. The fact that so called "third parties" have never before been brought into such calculations, have never before been thought of as being involved, is not an argument against their now becoming so. There are of course, good arguments against allowing doctors simply to haul passers-by off the streets whenever they have a couple of patients in need of new organs. And the harmful side-effects of such a practice in terms of terror and distress to the victims, the witnesses and society generally, would give us further reasons for dismissing the idea. Y and Z realize this and have a proposal, which they will shortly produce, which would largely meet objections to placing such power in the hands of doctors and eliminate at least some of the harmful side-effects.

In the unlikely event of their feeling obliged to reply to the reproaches of Y and Z, the doctors might offer the following argument: they might maintain that a man is only responsible for the death of someone whose life he might have saved, if, in all the circumstances of the case, he ought to have saved the man by the means available. This is why a doctor might be a murderer if he simply refused or neglected to treat a patient who would die without treatment, but not if he could only save the patient by doing something he ought in no circumstances to do— kill the innocent. Y and Z readily agree that a man ought not to do what he ought not to do, but they point out that if the doctors, and for that matter society at large, ought on balance to kill one man if two can thereby be saved, then failure to do so will involve responsibility for the consequent deaths. The fact that Y's and Z's proposal involves killing the innocent cannot be a reason for refusing to consider their proposal, for this would just be a refusal to face the question at issue and so avoid having to make a decision as to what ought to be done in circumstances like these. It is Y's and Z's claim that failure to adopt their plan will also involve killing the innocent, rather more of the innocent than the proposed alternative.

To back up this last point, to remove the arbitrariness of permitting doctors to select their donors from among the chance passers-by outside hospitals, and the tremendous power this would place in doctors' hands, to mitigate worries about side-effects and lastly to appease those who wonder why poor old A should be singled out for sacrifice, Y and Z put forward the following scheme: they propose that everyone be given a sort of lottery number. Whenever doctors have two or more dying patients who could be saved by transplants, and no suitable organs have come to hand through "natural" deaths, they can ask a central computer to supply a suitable donor. The computer will then pick the number of a suitable donor at random and he will be killed so that the lives of two or more others may be saved. No doubt if the scheme were ever to be implemented a suitable euphemism for "killed" would be employed. Perhaps we would begin to talk about citizens being called upon to "give life" to others. With the refinement of transplant procedures such a scheme could offer the chance of saving large numbers of lives that are now lost. Indeed, even taking into account the loss of the lives of donors, the numbers of untimely deaths each year might be dramatically reduced, so much so that everyone's chance of living to a ripe old age might be increased. If this were to be the consequence

of the adoption of such a scheme, and it might well be, it could not be dismissed lightly. It might of course be objected that it is likely that more old people will need transplants to prolong their lives than will the young, and so the scheme would inevitably lead to a society dominated by the old. But if such a society is thought objectionable, there is no reason to suppose that a program could not be designed for the computer that would ensure the maintenance of whatever is considered to be an optimum age distribution throughout the population.

Suppose that inter-planetary travel revealed a world of people like ourselves, but who organized their society according to this scheme. No one was considered to have an absolute right to life or freedom from interference, but everything was always done to ensure that as many people as possible would enjoy long and happy lives. In such a world a man who attempted to escape when his number was up or who resisted on the grounds that no one had a right to take his life, might well be regarded as a murderer. We might or might not prefer to live in such a world, but the morality of its inhabitants would surely be one that we could respect. It would not be obviously more barbaric or cruel or immoral than our own.

Y and Z are willing to concede one exception to the universal application of their scheme. They realize that it would be unfair to allow people who have brought their misfortune on themselves to benefit from the lottery. There would clearly be something unjust about killing the abstemious B so that W (whose heavy smoking has given him lung cancer) and X (whose drinking has destroyed his liver) should be preserved to over-indulge again.

What objections could be made to the lottery scheme? A first straw to clutch at would be the desire for security. Under such a scheme we would never know when we would hear *them* knocking at the door. Every post might bring a sentence of death, every sound in the night might be the sound of boots on the stairs. But, as we have seen, the chances of actually being called upon to make the ultimate sacrifice might be slimmer than is the present risk of being killed on the roads, and most of us do not lie trembling a-bed, appalled at the prospect of being dispatched on the morrow. The truth is that lives might well be more secure under such a scheme.

If we respect individuality and see every human being as unique in his own way, we might want to reject a society in which it appeared that individuals were seen merely as interchangeable units in a structure, the value of which lies in its having as many healthy units as possible. But of course Y and Z would want to know why A's individuality was more worthy of respect than theirs.

Another plausible objection is the natural reluctance to play God with men's lives, the feeling that it is wrong to make any attempt to reallot the life opportunities that fate has determined, that the deaths of Y and Z would be "natural," whereas the death of anyone killed to save them would have been perpetrated by men. But if we are able to change things, then to elect not to do so is also to determine what will happen in the world.

Neither does the alleged moral differences between killing and letting die afford a respectable way of rejecting the claims of Y and Z. For if we really want to counter proponents of the lottery, if we really want to answer Y and Z and not just put them off, we cannot do so by saying that the lottery involves killing and object to it for that reason, because to do so would, as we have seen, just beg the question as to whether the failure to save as many people as possible might not also amount to killing.

To opt for the society which Y and Z propose would be then to adopt a society in which saintliness would be mandatory. Each of us would have to recognize a binding obligation to give up his own life for others when called upon to do so. In such a society anyone who reneged upon this duty would be a murderer. The most promising objection to such a society, and indeed to any principle which required us to kill A in order to save Y and Z, is, I suspect, that we are committed to the right of self-defence. If I can kill A to save Y and Z then he can kill me to save P and Q, and it is only if I am prepared to agree to this that I will opt for the lottery or be prepared to agree to a man's being killed if doing so would save the lives of more than one other man. Of course there is something paradoxical about basing objections to the lottery scheme on the right of self-defence since, *ex hypothesi,* each person would have a better chance of living to a ripe old age if the lottery scheme were to be implemented. Nonetheless, the feeling that no man should be required to lay down his life for others makes many people shy away from such a scheme, even though it might be rational to accept it on prudential grounds, and perhaps even mandatory on utilitarian grounds. Again, Y and Z would reply that the right of self-defence must extend to them as much as to anyone else; and while it is true that they can only live if another man is killed, they would claim that it is also true that if they are left to die, then someone who lives on does so over their dead bodies.

It might be argued that the institution of the survival lottery has not gone far to mitigate the harmful side-effects in terms of terror and distress to victims, witnesses and society generally, that would be occasioned by doctors simply snatching passers-by off the streets and disorganizing them for the benefit of the unfortunate. Donors would after all still have to be procured, and this process, however it was carried out, would still be likely to prove distressing to all concerned. The lottery scheme would eliminate the arbitrariness of leaving the life and death decisions to the doctors, and remove the possibility of such terrible power falling into the hands of any individuals, but the terror and distress would remain. The effect of having to apprehend presumably unwilling victims would give us pause. Perhaps only a long period of education or propaganda could remove our abhorrence. What this abhorrence reveals about the rights and wrongs of the situation is however more difficult to assess. We might be inclined to say that only monsters could ignore the promptings of conscience so far as to operate the lottery scheme. But the promptings of conscience are not necessarily the most reliable guide. In the present case

Y and Z would argue that such promptings are mere squeamishness, an over-nice self-indulgence that costs lives. Death, Y and Z would remind us, is a distressing experience whenever and to whomever it occurs, so the less it occurs the better. Fewer victims and witnesses will be distressed as part of the side-effects of the lottery scheme than would suffer as part of the side-effects of not instituting it.

Lastly, a more limited objection might be made, not to the idea of killing to save lives, but to the involvement of "third parties." Why, so the objection goes, should we not give X's heart to Y or Y's lungs to X, the same number of lives being thereby preserved and no one else's life set at risk? Y's and Z's reply to this objection differs from their previous line of argument. To amend their plan so that the involvement of so called "third parties" is ruled out would, Y and Z claim, violate their right to equal concern and respect with the rest of society. They argue that such a proposal would amount to treating the unfortunate who need new organs as a class within society whose lives are considered to be of less value than those of its more fortunate members. What possible justification could there be for singling out one group of people whom we would be justified in using as donors but not another? The idea in the mind of those who would propose such a step must be something like the following: since Y and Z cannot survive, since they are going to die in any event, there is no harm in putting their names into the lottery, for the chances of their dying cannot thereby be increased and will in fact almost certainly be reduced. But this is just to ignore everything that Y and Z have been saying. For if their lottery scheme is adopted they are not going to die anyway—their chances of dying are no greater and no less than those of any other participant in the lottery whose number may come up. This ground for confining selection of donors to the unfortunate therefore disappears. Any other ground must discriminate against Y and Z as members of a class whose lives are less worthy of respect than those of the rest of society.

It might more plausibly be argued that the dying who cannot themselves be saved by transplants, or by any other means at all, should be the priority selection group for the computer programme. But how far off must death be for a man to be classified as "dying"? Those so classified might argue that their last few days or weeks of life are as valuable to them (if not more valuable) than the possibly longer span remaining to others. The problem of narrowing down the class of possible donors without discriminating unfairly against some sub-class of society is, I suspect, insoluble.

Such is the case for the survival lottery. Utilitarians ought to be in favour of it, and absolutists cannot object to it on the ground that it involves killing the innocent, for it is Y's and Z's case that any alternative must also involve killing the innocent. If the absolutist wishes to maintain his objection he must point to some morally relevant difference between positive and negative killing. This challenge opens the door to a large topic with a whole library of literature, but Y and Z are dying and do not have time to explore it exhaustively. In their own case the most likely candidate for some feature which might make this moral difference is the malevolent intent of Y and Z themselves. An absolutist might well argue that while no one intends the deaths of Y and Z, no one necessarily wishes them dead, or aims at their demise for any reason, they do mean to kill A (or have him killed). But Y and Z can reply that the death of A is no part of their plan, they merely wish to use acouple of his organs, and if he cannot live without them...*tant pis!* None would be more delighted than Y and Z if artificial organs would do as well, and so render the lottery scheme otiose.

One form of absolutist argument perhaps remains. This involves taking an Orwellian stand on some principle of common decency. The argument would then be that even to enter into the sort of "macabre" calculations that Y and Z propose displays a blunted sensibility, a corrupted and vitiated mind. Forms of this argument have recently been advanced by Noam Chomsky (*American Power and the New Mandarins*) and

Stuart Hampshire (*Morality and Pessimism*). The indefatigable Y and Z would of course deny that their calculations are in any sense "macabre," and would present them as the most humane course available in the circumstances. Moreover they would claim that the Orwellian stand on decency is the product of a closed mind, and not susceptible to rational argument. Any reasoned defence of such a principle must appeal to notions like respect for human life, as Hampshire's argument in fact does, and these Y and Z could make conformable to their own position.

Can Y and Z be answered? Perhaps only by relying on moral intuition, on the insistence that we do feel there is something wrong with the survival lottery and our confidence that this feeling is prompted by some morally relevant difference between our bringing about the death of A and our bringing about the deaths of Y and Z. Whether we could retain this confidence in our intuitions if we were to be confronted by a society in which the survival lottery operated, was accepted by all, and was seen to save many lives that would otherwise have been lost, it would be interesting to know.

There would of course be great practical difficulties in the way of implementing the lottery. In so many cases it would be agonizingly difficult to decide whether or not a person had brought his misfortune on himself. There are numerous ways in which a person may contribute to his predicament, and the task of deciding how far, or how decisively, a person is himself responsible for his fate would be formidable. And in those cases where we can be confident that a person is innocent of responsibility for his predicament, can we acquire this confidence in time to save him? The lottery scheme would be a powerful weapon in the hands of someone willing and able to misuse it. Could we ever feel certain the lottery was safe from unscrupulous computer programmers? Perhaps we should be thankful that such practical difficulties make the survival lottery an unlikely consequence of the perfection of transplants. Or perhaps we should be appalled.

It may be that we would want to tell Y and Z that the difficulties and dangers of their scheme would be too great a price to pay for its benefits. It is as well to be clear, however, that there is also a high, perhaps an even higher, price to be paid for the rejection of the scheme. That price is the lives of Y and Z and many like them, and we delude ourselves if we suppose that the reason why we reject their plan is that we accept the sixth commandment.

3.4 Active and Passive Euthanasia

JAMES RACHELS

The distinction between active and passive euthanasia is thought to be crucial for medical ethics. The idea is that it is permissible, at least in some cases, to withhold treatment and allow a patient to die, but it is never permissible to take any direct action designed to kill the patient. This doctrine seems to be accepted by most doctors, and it is endorsed in a statement adopted by the House of Delegates of the American Medical Association on December 4, 1973:

> The intentional termination of the life of one human being by another—mercy killing—is contrary to that for which the medical profession stands and is contrary to the policy of the American Medical Association.

From "Active and Passive Euthanasia" by James Rachels. In the *New England Journal of Medicine*, vol. 292 (Jan 9, 1975), pp. 78–80. Copyright © 1975 Massachusetts Medical Society. Reprinted with permission from Massachusetts Medical Society.

The cessation of the employment of extraordinary means to prolong the life of the body when there is irrefutable evidence that biological death is imminent is the decision of the patient and/or his immediate family. The advice and judgment of the physician should be freely available to the patient and/or his immediate family.

However, a strong case can be made against this doctrine. In what follows, I will set out some of the relevant arguments, and urge doctors to reconsider their views on this matter.

To begin with a familiar type of situation, a patient who is dying of incurable cancer of the throat is in terrible pain, which can no longer be satisfactorily alleviated. He is certain to die within a few days, even if present treatment is continued, but he does not want to go on living for those days since the pain is unbearable. So he asks the doctor for an end to it, and his family joins in the request.

Suppose the doctor agrees to withhold treatment, as the conventional doctrine says he may. The justification for his doing so is that the patient is in terrible agony, and since he is going to die anyway, it would be wrong to prolong his suffering needlessly. But now notice this. If one simply withholds treatment, it may take the patient longer to die, and so he may suffer more than he would if more direct action were taken and a lethal injection given. This fact provides strong reason for thinking that, once the initial decision not to prolong his agony has been made, active euthanasia is actually preferable to passive euthanasia, rather than the reverse. To say otherwise is to endorse the option that leads to more suffering rather than less, and is contrary to the humanitarian impulse that prompts the decision not to prolong his life in the first place.

Part of my point is that the process of being "allowed to die" can be relatively slow and painful, whereas being given a lethal injection is relatively quick and painless. Let me give a different sort of example. In the United States about one in 600 babies is born with Down's syndrome. Most of these babies are otherwise healthy—that is, with only the usual pediatric care, they will proceed to an otherwise normal infancy. Some, however, are born with congenital defects such as intestinal obstructions that require operations if they are to live. Sometimes, the parents and the doctor will decide not to operate, and let the infant die. Anthony Shaw describes what happens then:

> … When surgery is denied [the doctor] must try to keep the infant from suffering while natural forces sap the baby's life away. As a surgeon whose natural inclination is to use the scalpel to fight off death, standing by and watching a salvageable baby die is the most emotionally exhausting experience I know. It is easy at a conference, in a theoretical discussion, to decide that such infants should be allowed to die. It is altogether different to stand by in the nursery and watch as dehydration and infection wither a tiny being over hours and days. This is a terrible ordeal for me and the hospital staff—much more so than for the parents who never set foot in the nursery.[1]

I can understand why some people are opposed to all euthanasia, and insist that such infants must be allowed to live. I think I can also understand why other people favor destroying these babies quickly and painlessly. But why should anyone favor letting "dehydration and infection wither a tiny being over hours and days"? The doctrine that says that a baby may be allowed to dehydrate and wither, but may not be given an injection that would end its life without suffering, seems so patently cruel as to require no further refutation. The strong language is not intended to offend, but only to put the point in the clearest possible way.

My second argument is that the conventional doctrine leads to decisions concerning life and death made on irrelevant grounds.

Consider again the case of the infants with Down's syndrome who need operations for congenital defects unrelated to the syndrome to live. Sometimes, there is no operation, and the baby dies, but when there is no such defect, the baby lives on. Now, an operation such as that to remove an intestinal obstruction is not prohibitively difficult. The reason why such operations are not performed in these cases is, clearly, that the child has Down's syndrome and the parents and doctor judge that because of that fact it is better for the child to die.

But notice that this situation is absurd, no matter what view one takes of the lives and potentials of such babies. If the life of such an infant is worth preserving, what does it matter if it needs a simple operation? Or, if one thinks it better that such a baby should not live on, what difference does it make that it happens to have an unobstructed intestinal tract? In either case, the matter of life and death is being decided on irrelevant grounds. It is the Down's syndrome, and not the intestines, that is the issue. The matter should be decided, if at all, on that basis, and not be allowed to depend on the essentially irrelevant question of whether the intestinal tract is blocked.

What makes this situation possible, of course, is the idea that when there is an intestinal blockage, one can "let the baby die," but when there is no such defect there is nothing that can be done, for one must not "kill" it. The fact that this idea leads to such results as deciding life or death on irrelevant grounds is another good reason why the doctrine should be rejected.

One reason why so many people think that there is an important moral difference between active and passive euthanasia is that they think killing someone is morally worse than letting someone die. But is it? Is killing, in itself, worse than letting die? To investigate this issue, two cases may be considered that are exactly alike except that one involves killing whereas the other involves letting someone die. Then, it can be asked whether this difference makes any difference to the moral assessments. It is important that the cases be exactly alike, except for this one difference, since otherwise one cannot be confident that it is this difference and not some other that accounts for any variation in the assessments of the two cases. So, let us consider this pair of cases:

In the first, Smith stands to gain a large inheritance if anything should happen to his six-year-old cousin. One evening while the child is taking his bath, Smith sneaks into the bathroom and drowns the child, and then arranges things so that it will look like an accident.

In the second, Jones also stands to gain if anything should happen to his six-year-old cousin. Like Smith, Jones sneaks in planning to drown the child in his bath. However, just as he enters the bathroom Jones sees the child slip and hit his head, and fall face down in the water. Jones is delighted; he stands by, ready to push the child's head back under if it is necessary, but it is not necessary. With only a little thrashing about the child drowns all by himself, "accidentally," as Jones watches and does nothing.

Now Smith killed the child, whereas Jones "merely" let the child die. That is the only difference between them. Did either man behave better, from a moral point of view? If the difference between killing and letting die were in itself a morally important matter, one should say that Jones's behavior was less reprehensible than Smith's. But does one really want to say that? I think not. In the first place, both men acted from the same motive, personal gain, and both had exactly the same end in view when they acted. It may be inferred from Smith's conduct that he is a bad man, although that judgment may be withdrawn or modified if certain further facts are learned about him—for example, that he is mentally deranged. But would not the very same thing be inferred about Jones from his conduct? And would not the same further considerations also be relevant to any modification of this judgment? Moreover, suppose Jones pleaded, in his own defense, "After all, I didn't do anything except just stand there and watch the child drown. I didn't kill him; I only let him die." Again, if letting die were in itself less bad than killing, this defense should have at least some weight. But it does not. Such a "defense" can only be regarded as a grotesque perversion of moral reasoning. Morally speaking, it is no defense at all.

Now, it may be pointed out, quite properly, that the cases of euthanasia with which doctors are concerned are not like this at all. They do not involve personal gain or the destruction of normally healthy children. Doctors are concerned only with cases in which the patient's life is of no further use to him, or in which the patient's life has become or will soon become a terrible burden. However, the point is the same in these cases: the bare difference between killing and letting die does not, in itself, make a moral difference. If a doctor lets a patient die, for humane reasons, he is in the same moral position as if he had given the patient a lethal injection for humane reasons. If his decision was wrong—if, for example, the patient's illness was in fact curable—the decision would be equally regrettable no matter which method was used to carry it out. And if the doctor's decision was the right one, the method used is not in itself important.

The AMA policy statement isolates the crucial issue very well; the crucial issue is "the intentional termination of the life of one human being by another." But after identifying this issue, and forbidding "mercy killing," the statement goes on to deny that the cessation of treatment is the intentional termination of a life. This is where the mistake comes in, for what is the cessation of treatment, in these circumstances, if it is not "the intentional termination of the life of one human being by another"? Of course, it is exactly that, and if it were not, there would be no point to it.

Many people will find this judgment hard to accept. One reason, I think, is that it is very easy to conflate the question of whether killing is, in itself, worse than letting die, with the very different question of whether most actual cases of killing are more reprehensible than most actual cases of letting die. Most actual cases of killing are clearly terrible (think, for example, of all the murders reported in the newspapers), and one hears of such cases every day. On the other hand, one hardly ever hears of a case of letting die, except for the actions of doctors who are motivated by humanitarian reasons. So one learns to think of killing in a much worse light than of letting die. But this does not mean that there is something about killing that makes it in itself worse than letting die, for it is not the bare difference between killing and letting die that

makes the difference in these cases. Rather, the other factors—the murderer's motive of personal gain, for example, contrasted with the doctor's humanitarian motivation—account for different reactions to the different cases.

I have argued that killing is not in itself any worse than letting die; if my contention is right, it follows that active euthanasia is not any worse than passive euthanasia. What arguments can be given on the other side? The most common, I believe, is the following:

"The important difference between active and passive euthanasia is that, in passive euthanasia, the doctor does not do anything to bring about the patient's death. The doctor does nothing, and the patient dies of whatever ills already afflict him. In active euthanasia, however, the doctor does something to bring about the patient's death: he kills him. The doctor who gives the patient with cancer a lethal injection has himself caused his patient's death; whereas if he merely ceases treatment, the cancer is the cause of the death."

A number of points need to be made here. The first is that it is not exactly correct to say that in passive euthanasia the doctor does nothing, for he does do one thing that is very important: he lets the patient die. "Letting someone die" is certainly different, in some respects, from other types of action—mainly in that it is a kind of action that one may perform by way of not performing certain other actions. For example, one may let a patient die by way of not giving medication, just as one may insult someone by way of not shaking his hand. But for any purpose of moral assessment, it is a type of action nonetheless. The decision to let a patient die is subject to moral appraisal in the same way that a decision to kill him would be subject to moral appraisal: it may be assessed as wise or unwise, compassionate or sadistic, right or wrong. If a doctor deliberately let a patient die who was suffering from a routinely curable illness, the doctor would certainly be to blame for what he had done, just as he would be to blame if he had needlessly killed the patient. Charges against him would then be appropriate. If so, it would be no defense at all for him to insist that he didn't "do anything." He would have done something very serious indeed, for he let his patient die.

Fixing the cause of death may be very important from a legal point of view, for it may determine whether criminal charges are brought against the doctor. But I do not think that this notion can be used to show a moral difference between active and passive euthanasia. The reason why it is considered bad to be the cause of someone's death is that death is regarded as a great evil—and so it is. However, if it has been decided that euthanasia—even passive euthanasia—is desirable in a given case, it has also been decided that in this instance death is no greater an evil than the patient's continued existence. And if this is true, the usual reason for not wanting to be the cause of someone's death simply does not apply.

Finally, doctors may think that all of this is only of academic interest—the sort of thing that philosophers may worry about but that has no practical bearing on their own work. After all, doctors must be concerned about the legal consequences of what they do, and active euthanasia is clearly forbidden by the law. But even so, doctors should also be concerned with the fact that the law is forcing upon them a moral doctrine that may well be indefensible, and has a considerable effect on their practices. Of course, most doctors are not now in the position of being coerced in this matter, for they do not regard themselves as merely going along with what the law requires. Rather, in statements such as the AMA policy statement that I have quoted, they are endorsing this doctrine as a central point of medical ethics. In that statement, active euthanasia is condemned not merely as illegal but as "contrary to that for which the medical profession stands," whereas passive euthanasia is approved. However, the preceding considerations suggest that there is really no moral difference between the two, considered in themselves (there may be important moral differences in some cases in their *consequences,* but, as I pointed out, these differences may make active euthanasia, and not passive euthanasia, the morally preferable option). So, whereas doctors may have to discriminate between active and passive euthanasia to satisfy the law, they should not do any more than that. In particular, they should not give the distinction any added authority and weight by writing it into official statements of medical ethics.

NOTE

1. A. Shaw: "Doctor, Do We Have a Choice?" *The New York Times Magazine,* Jan. 30, 1972, 54.

3.5 On the Moral and Legal Status of Abortion

MARY ANNE WARREN

Mary Anne Warren (1946–2010) worked primarily in applied ethics and taught for many years at San Francisco State University.

We will be concerned with both the moral status of abortion, which for our purposes we may define as the act which a woman performs in voluntarily terminating, or allowing another person to terminate, her pregnancy, and the legal status which is appropriate for this act. I will argue that, while it is not possible to produce a satisfactory defense of a woman's right to obtain an abortion without showing that a fetus is not a human being, in the morally relevant sense of that term,

Mary Anne Warren, "On the Moral and Legal Status of Abortion." *The Monist,* Vol. 57, No. 4, 1973.

we ought not to conclude that the difficulties involved in determining whether or not a fetus is human make it impossible to produce any satisfactory solution to the problem of the moral status of abortion. For it is possible to show that, on the basis of intuitions which we may expect even the opponents of abortion to share, a fetus is not a person, and hence not the sort of entity to which it is proper to ascribe full moral rights.

Of course, wholesome philosophers would deny the possibility of any such proof, others will deny that there is any need for it, since the moral permissibility of abortion appears to them to be too obvious to require proof. But the inadequacy of this attitude should be evident from the fact that both the friends and the foes of abortion consider their position to be morally self-evident. Because proabortionists have never adequately come to grips with the conceptual issues surrounding abortion, most if not all, of the arguments which they advance in opposition to laws restricting access to abortion fail to refute or even weaken the traditional antiabortion argument, i.e., that a fetus is a human being, and therefore abortion is murder.

These arguments are typically of one of two sorts. Either they point to the terrible side effects of the restrictive laws, e.g., the deaths due to illegal abortions, and the fact that it is poor women who suffer the most as a result of these laws, or else they state that to deny a woman access to abortion is to deprive her of her right to control her own body. Unfortunately, however, the fact that restricting access to abortion has tragic side effects does not, in itself, show that the restrictions are unjustified, since murder is wrong regardless of the consequences of prohibiting it; and the appeal to the right to control one's body, which is generally construed as a property right, is at best a rather feeble argument for the permissibility of abortion. Mere ownership does not give me the right to kill innocent people whom I find on my property, and indeed I am apt to be held responsible if such people injure themselves while on my property. It is equally unclear that I have any moral right to expel an innocent person from my property when I know that doing so will result in his death.

Furthermore, it is probably inappropriate to describe a woman's body as her property, since it seems natural to hold that a person is something distinct from her property, but not from her body. Even those who would object to the identification of a person with his body, or with the conjunction of his body and his mind, must admit that it would be very odd to describe, say, breaking a leg, as damaging one's property, and much more appropriate to describe it as injuring *oneself*. Thus it is probably a mistake to argue that the right to obtain an abortion is in any way derived from the right to own and regulate property.

But however we wish to construe the right to abortion, we cannot hope to convince those who consider abortion a form of murder of the existence of any such right unless we are able to produce a clear and convincing refutation of the traditional antiabortion argument, and this has not, to my knowledge, been done. With respect to the two most vital issues which that argument involves, i.e., the humanity of the fetus and its implication for the moral status of abortion, confusion has prevailed on both sides of the dispute....

Our own inquiry will have two stages. In Section I, we will consider whether, or not it is possible to establish that abortion is morally permissible even on the assumption that a fetus is an entity with a full-fledged right to life. I will argue that in fact this cannot be established, at least not with the conclusiveness which is essential to our hopes of convincing those who are skeptical about the morality of abortion, and that we therefore cannot avoid dealing with the question of whether or not a fetus really does have the same right to life **as** a (more fully developed) human being.

In Section II, I will propose an answer to this question, namely, that a fetus cannot be considered a member of the moral community, the set of beings with full and equal moral rights, for the simple reason that it is not a person, and that it is personhood, and not genetic humanity, i.e., humanity as defined by Noonan, which is the basis for membership in this community. I will argue that a fetus, whatever its stage of development, satisfies none of the basic criteria of personhood, and is not even enough *like* a person to be accorded even some of the same rights on the basis of this resemblance. Nor, as we will see, is a fetus's *potential* personhood a threat to the morality of abortion, since, whatever the rights of potential people may be, they are invariably overridden in any conflict with the moral rights of actual people.

I

We turn now to Professor Judith Thomson's case[1] for the claim that even if a fetus has full moral rights, abortion is still morally permissible, at least sometimes, and for some reasons other than to save the woman's life. Her argument is based upon a clever, but I think faulty, analogy. She asks us to picture ourselves waking up one day, in bed with a famous violinist. Imagine that you have been kidnapped, and your bloodstream hooked up to that of the violinist, who happens to have an ailment which will certainly kill him unless he is permitted to share your kidneys for a period of nine months. No one else can save him, since you alone have the right type of blood. He will be unconscious all that time, and you will have to stay in bed with him, but after the nine months are over he may be unplugged, completely cured, that is provided that you have cooperated.

Now then, she continues, what are your obligations in this situation? The antiabortionist, if he is consistent, will have to say that you are obligated to stay in bed with the violinist: for all people have a right to life, and violinists are people, and therefore it would be murder for you to disconnect yourself from him and let him die (p. 49). But this is outrageous, and so there must be something wrong with the same argument when it is applied to abortion. It would certainly be commendable of you to agree to save the violinist, but it is absurd to suggest

that your refusal to do so would be murder. His right to life does not obligate you to do whatever is required to keep him alive; nor does it justify anyone else in forcing you to do so. A law which required you to stay in bed with the violinist would clearly be an unjust law, since it is no proper function of the law to force unwilling people to make huge sacrifices for the sake of other people toward whom they have no such prior obligation.

Thomson concludes that, if this analogy is an apt one, then we can grant the antiabortionist his claim that a fetus is a human being, and still hold that it is at least sometimes the case that a pregnant woman has the right to refuse to be a Good Samaritan towards the fetus, i.e., to obtain an abortion. For there is a great gap between the claim that x has a right to life, and the claim that y is obligated to do whatever is necessary to keep x alive, let alone that he ought to be forced to do so. It is y's duty to keep x alive only if he has somehow contracted a *special* obligation to do so; and a woman who is unwillingly pregnant, e.g., who was raped, has done nothing which obligates her to make the enormous sacrifice which is necessary to preserve the conceptus.

This argument is initially quite plausible, and in the extreme case of pregnancy due to rape it is probably conclusive. Difficulties arise, however, when we try to specify more exactly the range of cases in which abortion is clearly justifiable even on the assumption that the fetus is human. Professor Thomson considers it a virtue of her argument that it does not enable us to conclude that abortion is *always* permissible. It would, she says, be "indecent" for a woman in her seventh month to obtain an abortion just to avoid having to postpone a trip to Europe. On the other hand, her argument enables us to see that "a sick and desperately frightened schoolgirl pregnant due to rape may *of course* choose abortion, and that any law which rules this out is an insane law" (p. 65). So far, so good; but what are we to say about the woman who becomes pregnant not through rape but as a result of her own carelessness, or because of contraceptive failure, or who gets pregnant intentionally and then changes her mind about wanting a child? With respect to such cases, the violinist analogy is of much less use to the defender of the woman's right to obtain an abortion.

Indeed, the choice of a pregnancy due to rape, as an example of a case in which abortion is permissible even if a fetus is considered a human being, is extremely significant; for it is only in the case of pregnancy due to rape that the woman's situation is adequately analogous to the violinist case for our intuitions about the latter to transfer convincingly. The crucial difference between a pregnancy due to rape and the *normal* case of an unwanted pregnancy is that in the normal case we cannot claim that the woman is in no way responsible for her predicament; she could have remained chaste, or taken her pills more faithfully, or abstained on dangerous days, and so on. If, on the other hand, you are kidnapped by strangers, and hooked up to a strange violinist, then you are free of any shred of responsibility for the situation, on the basis of which it could be argued that you are obligated to keep the violinist alive. Only when her pregnancy is due to rape is a woman clearly just as nonresponsible.

Consequently, there is room for the anti-abortionist to argue that in the normal case of unwanted pregnancy a woman has, by her own actions, assumed responsibility for the fetus. For if x behaves in a way which he could have avoided, and which he knows involves, let us say, a 1 percent chance of bringing into existence a human being, with a right to life, and does so knowing that if this should happen then that human being will perish unless x does certain things to keep him alive, then it is by no means clear that when it does happen x is free of any obligation to what he knew in advance would be required to keep that human being alive.

The plausibility of such an argument is enough to show that the Thomson analogy can provide a clear and persuasive defense of a woman's right to obtain an abortion only with respect to those cases in which the woman is in no way responsible for her pregnancy, e.g., where it is due to rape. In all other cases, we would

almost certainly conclude that it was necessary to look carefully at the particular circumstances in order to determine the extent of the woman's responsibility, and hence the extent of her obligation. This is an extremely unsatisfactory outcome, from the viewpoint of the opponents of restrictive abortion laws, most of whom are convinced that a woman has a right to obtain an abortion regardless of how and why she got pregnant.

Of course a supporter of the violinist analogy might point out that it is absurd to suggest that forgetting her pill one day might be sufficient to obligate a woman to complete an unwanted pregnancy. And indeed it *is* absurd to suggest this. As we will see, the moral right to obtain an abortion is not in the least dependent upon the extent to which the woman is responsible for her pregnancy. But unfortunately, once we allow the assumption that a fetus has full moral rights, we cannot avoid taking this absurd suggestion seriously. Perhaps we can make this point more clear by altering the violinist story just enough to make it more analogous to a normal unwanted pregnancy and less to a pregnancy due to rape, and then seeing whether it is still obvious that you are not obligated to stay in bed with the fellow.

Suppose, then, that violinists are peculiarly prone to the sort of illness the only cure for which is the use of someone else's bloodstream for nine months, and that because of this there has been formed a society of music lovers who agree that whenever a violinist is stricken they will draw lots and the loser will, by some means, be made the one and only person capable of saving him. Now then, would you be obligated to cooperate in curing the violinist if you had voluntarily joined this society, knowing the possible consequences, and then your name had been drawn and you had been kidnapped? Admittedly, you did not promise ahead of time that you would, but you did deliberately place yourself in a position in which it might happen that a human life would be lost if you did not. Surely this is at least a prima facie reason for supposing that you have an obligation to stay in bed with the violinist. Suppose that you had gotten your name drawn deliberately; surely *that* would be quite a strong reason for thinking that you had such an obligation.

It might be suggested that there is one important disanalogy between the modified violinist case and the case of an unwanted pregnancy, which makes the woman's responsibility significantly less, namely, the fact that the fetus *comes into existence* as the result of the result of the woman's actions. This fact might give her a right to refuse to keep it alive, whereas she would not have had this right had it existed previously, independently, and then as a result of her actions become dependent upon her for its survival.

My own intuition, however, is that *x* has no more right to bring into existence, either deliberately or as a foreseeable result of actions he could have avoided, a being with full moral rights (*y*), and then refuse to do what he knew beforehand would be required to keep that being alive, than he has to enter into an agreement with an existing person, whereby he may be called upon to save that person's life, and then refuse to do so when so called upon. Thus, *x*'s responsibility for *y*'s existence does not seem to lessen his obligation to keep *y* alive, if he is also responsible for *y*'s being in a situation in which only he can save him.

Whether or not this intuition is entirely correct, it brings us back once again to the conclusion that once we allow the assumption that a fetus has full moral rights it becomes an extremely complex and difficult question whether and when abortion is justifiable. Thus the Thomson analogy cannot help us produce a clear and persuasive proof of the moral permissibility of abortion. Nor will the opponents of the restrictive laws thank us for anything less; for their conviction (for the most part) is that abortion is obviously *not* a morally serious and extremely unfortunate, even though sometimes justified act, comparable to killing in self-defense or to letting the violinist die, but rather is closer to being a morally neutral act, like cutting one's hair.

The basis of this conviction, I believe, is the realization that a fetus is not a person, and thus does not have a full-fledged right to life. Perhaps the reason why this claim has been so inadequately defended is that it seems self-evident to those who accept it. And so it is, insofar as it follows from what I take to be perfectly obvious claims about the nature of personhood, and about the proper grounds for ascribing moral rights, claims which ought, indeed, to be obvious to both the friends and foes of abortion. Nevertheless, it is worth examining these claims, and showing how they demonstrate the moral innocuousness of abortion, since this apparently has not been adequately done before.

II

The question which we must answer in order to produce a satisfactory solution to the problem of the moral status of abortion is this: How are we to define the moral community, the set of beings with full and equal moral rights, such that we can decide whether a human fetus is a member of this community or not? What sort of entity, exactly, has the inalienable rights to life, liberty, and the pursuit of happiness? Jefferson attributed these rights to all *men*, and it may or may not be fair to suggest that he intended to attribute them *only* to men. Perhaps he ought to have attributed them to all human beings. If so, then we arrive, first, at Noonan's problem of defining what makes a being human, and, second, at the equally vital question which Noonan does not consider, namely, What reason is there for identifying the moral community with the set of all human beings, in whatever way we have chosen to define that term?

1. On the Definition of 'Human'

One reason why this vital second question is so frequently overlooked in the debate over the moral status of abortion is that the term 'human' has two distinct, but not often distinguished, senses. This fact results in a slide of meaning, which serves to conceal the fallaciousness of the traditional argument that since (1) it is wrong to kill innocent human beings, and (2) fetuses are innocent human beings, then (3) it is wrong to kill fetuses. For if 'human' is used in the same sense in both (1) and (2) then, whichever of the two senses is meant, one of these premises is question-begging. And if it is used in two different senses then of course the conclusion doesn't follow.

Thus, (1) is a self-evident moral truth[2] and avoids begging the question about abortion, only if 'human being' is used to mean something like "a full-fledged member of the moral community." (It may or may not also be meant to refer exclusively to members of the species *Homo sapiens.*) We may call this the *moral* sense of 'human'. It is not to be confused with what we will call the *genetic* sense, i.e., the sense in which *any* member of the species is a human being, and no member of any other species could be. If (1) is acceptable only if the moral sense is intended, (2) is non-question-begging only if what is intended is the genetic sense.

In "Deciding Who is Human"[3] Noonan argues for the classification of fetuses with human beings by pointing to the presence of the full genetic code, and the potential capacity for rational thought (p. 135). It is clear that what he needs to show, for his version of the traditional argument to be valid, is that fetuses are human in the moral sense, the sense in which it is analytically true that all human beings have full moral rights. But, in the absence of any argument showing that whatever is genetically human is also morally human, and he gives none, nothing more than genetic humanity can be demonstrated by the presence of the human genetic code. And, as we will see, the *potential* capacity for rational thought can at most show that an entity has the potential for *becoming* human in the moral sense.

2. Defining the Moral Community

Can it be established that genetic humanity is sufficient for moral humanity? I think that there are very good reasons for not defining the moral community in this way. I would like to suggest an alternative way of defining the moral community, which I will argue for only to the extent of explaining why it is, or should be, self-evident.

The suggestion is simply that the moral community consists of all and only *people*, rather than all and only human beings;[4] and probably the best way of demonstrating its self-evidence is by considering the concept of personhood, to see what sorts of entity are and are not persons, and what the decision that a being is or is not a person implies about its moral rights.

What characteristics entitle an entity to be considered a person? This is obviously not the place to attempt a complete analysis of the concept of personhood, but we do not need such a fully adequate analysis just to determine whether and why a fetus is or isn't a person. All we need is a rough and approximate list of the most basic criteria of personhood, and some idea of which, or how many, of these an entity must satisfy in order to properly be considered a person.

In searching for such criteria, it is useful to look beyond the set of people with whom we are acquainted, and ask how we would decide whether a totally alien being was a person or not. (For we have no right to assume that genetic humanity is necessary for personhood.) Imagine a space traveler who lands on an unknown planet and encounters a race of beings utterly unlike any he has ever seen, or heard of. If he wants to be sure of behaving morally toward these beings, he has to somehow decide whether they are people, and hence have full moral rights, or whether they are the sort of thing which he need not feel guilty about treating as, for example, a source of food.

How should he go about making this decision? If he has some anthropological background, he might look for such things as religion, art, and the manufacturing of tools, weapons, or shelters, since these factors have been used to distinguish our human from our prehuman ancestors, in what seems to be closer to the moral than the genetic sense of 'human'. And no doubt he would be right to consider the presence of such factors as good evidence that the alien beings were people, and morally human. It would, however, be overly anthropocentric of him to take the absence of these things as adequate evidence that they were not, since we can imagine people who have progressed beyond, or evolved without ever developing, these cultural characteristics.

I suggest that the traits which are most central to the concept of personhood, or humanity in the moral sense, are, very roughly, the following:

(1) consciousness (of objects and events external and/or internal to the being), and in particular the capacity to feel pain;
(2) reasoning (the *developed* capacity to solve new and relatively complex problems);
(3) self-motivated activity (activity which is relatively independent of either genetic or direct external control)
(4) the capacity to communicate, by whatever means, messages of an indefinite variety of types, that is, not just with an indefinite number of possible contents, but on indefinitely many possible topics;
(5) the presence of self-concepts, and self-awareness, either individual or racial, or both.

Admittedly, there are apt to be a great many problems involved in formulating precise definitions of these criteria, let alone in developing universally valid behavioral criteria for deciding when they apply. But I will assume that both we and our explorer know approximately what (1)–(5) mean, and that he is also able to determine whether or not they apply. How, then, should he use his findings to decide whether or not the alien beings are people? We needn't suppose that an entity must have *all* of these attributes to be properly considered a person; (1) and (2) alone may well be sufficient for personhood, and quite probably (1)–(3) are sufficient. Neither do we need to insist that any one of these criteria is *necessary* for personhood, although once again (1) and (2) look like fairly good candidates for necessary conditions, as does (3), if 'activity' is construed so as to include the activity of reasoning.

All we need to claim, to demonstrate that a fetus is not a person, is that any being which satisfies *none* of (1)–(5) is certainly not a person. I

consider this claim to be so obvious that I think anyone who denied it, and claimed that a being which satisfied none of (1)–(5) was a person all the same, would thereby demonstrate that he had no notion at all of what a person is—perhaps because he had confused the concept of a person with that of genetic humanity. If the opponents of abortion were to deny the appropriateness of these five criteria, I do not know what further arguments would convince them. We would probably have to admit that our conceptual schemes were indeed irreconcilably different, and that our dispute could not be settled objectively.

I do not expect this to happen, however, since I think that the concept of a person is one which is very nearly universal (to people), and that it is common to both proabortionists and antiabortionists, even though neither group has fully realized the relevance of this concept to the resolution of their dispute. Furthermore, I think that on reflection even the antiabortionists ought to agree not only that (1)–(5) are central to the concept of personhood, but also that it is a part of this concept that all and only people have full moral rights. The concept of a person is in part a moral concept; once we have admitted that *x* is a person we have recognized, even if we have not agreed to respect, *x's* right to be treated as a member of the moral community. It is true that the claim that *x* is a *human being* is more commonly voiced as part of an appeal to treat *x* decently than is the claim that *x* is a person, but this is either because 'human being' is here used in the sense which implies personhood, or because the genetic and moral senses of 'human' have been confused.

Now if (1)–(5) are indeed the primary criteria of personhood, then it is clear that genetic humanity is neither necessary nor sufficient for establishing that an entity is a person. Some human beings are not people, and there may well be people who are not human beings. A man or woman whose consciousness has been permanently obliterated but who remains alive is a human being which is no longer a person; defective human beings, with no appreciable mental capacity, are not and presumably never will be people; and a fetus is a human being which is not yet a person, and which therefore cannot coherently be said to have full moral rights. Citizens of the next century should be prepared to recognize highly advanced, self-aware robots or computers, should such be developed, and intelligent inhabitants of other worlds, should such be found, as people in the fullest sense, and to respect their moral rights. But to ascribe full moral rights to an entity which is not a person is as absurd as to ascribe moral obligations and responsibilities to such an entity.

3. *Fetal Development and the Right to Life*

Two problems arise in the application of these suggestions for the definition of the moral community to the determination of the precise moral status of a human fetus. Given that the paradigm example of a person is a normal adult human being, then (1) How like this paradigm, in particular how far advanced since conception, does a human being need to be before it begins to have a right to life by virtue, not of being fully a person as of yet, but of being *like* a person? and (2) To what extent, if any, does the fact that a fetus has the *potential* for becoming a person endow it with some of the same rights? Each of these questions requires some comment.

In answering the first question, we need not attempt a detailed consideration of the moral rights of organisms which are not developed enough, aware enough, intelligent enough, etc., to be considered people, but which resemble people in some respects. It does seem reasonable to suggest that the more like a person, in the relevant respects, a being is, the stronger is the case for regarding it as having a right to life, and indeed the stronger its right to life is. Thus we ought to take seriously the suggestion that, insofar as "the human individual develops biologically in a continuous fashion the rights of a human person might develop in the same way." But we must keep in mind that the attributes which are relevant in determining whether or not an entity is enough like a person to be

regarded as having some of the same moral rights are no different from those which are relevant to determining whether or not it is fully a person—i.e., are no different from (1)–(5)—and that being genetically human, or having recognizably human facial and other physical features, or detectable brain activity, or the capacity to survive outside the uterus, are simply not among these relevant attributes.

Thus it is clear that even though a seven- or eight-month fetus has features which make it apt to arouse in us almost the same powerful protective instinct as is commonly aroused by a small infant, nevertheless it is not significantly more personlike than is a very small embryo. It is *somewhat* more personlike; it can apparently feel and respond to pain, and it may even have a rudimentary form of consciousness, insofar as its brain is quite active. Nevertheless, it seems safe to say that it is not fully conscious, in the way that an infant of a few months is, and that it cannot reason, or communicate messages of indefinitely many sorts, does not engage in self-motivated activity, and has no self-awareness. Thus, in the *relevant* respects, a fetus, even a fully developed one, is considerably less personlike than is the average mature mammal, indeed the average fish. And I think that a rational person must conclude that if the right to life of a fetus is to be based upon its resemblance to a person, then it cannot be said to have any more right to life than, let us say, a newborn guppy (which also seems to be capable of feeling pain), and that a right of that magnitude could never override a woman's right to obtain an abortion, at any stage of her pregnancy.

There may, of course, be other arguments in favor of placing legal limits upon the stage of pregnancy in which an abortion may be performed. Given the relative safety of the new techniques of artifically inducing labor during the third trimester, the danger to the woman's life or health is no longer such an argument. Neither is the fact that people tend to respond to the thought of abortion in the later stages of pregnancy with emotional repulsion, since mere emotional responses cannot take the place of moral reasoning in determining what ought to be permitted. Nor, finally, is the frequently heard argument that legalizing abortion, especially late in the pregnancy, may erode the level of respect for human life, leading, perhaps, to an increase in unjustified euthanasia and other crimes. For this threat, if it is a threat, can be better met by educating people to the kinds of moral distinctions which we are making here than by limiting access to abortion (which limitation may, in its disregard for the rights of women, be just as damaging to the level of respect for human rights).

Thus, since the fact that even a fully developed fetus is not personlike enough to have any significant right to life on the basis of its personlikeness shows that no legal restrictions upon the stage of pregnancy in which an abortion may be performed can be justified on the grounds that we should protect the rights of the older fetus; and since there is no other apparent justification for such restrictions, we may conclude that they are entirely unjustified. Whether or not it would be *indecent* (whatever that means) for a woman in her seventh month to obtain an abortion just to avoid having to postpone a trip to Europe, it would not, in itself, be *immoral*, and therefore it ought to be permitted.

4. *Potential Personhood and the Right to Life*

We have seen that a fetus does not resemble a person in any way which can support the claim that it has even some of the same rights. But what about its *potential*, the fact that if nurtured and allowed to develop naturally it will very probably become a person? Doesn't that alone give it at least some right to life? It is hard to deny that the fact that an entity is a potential person is a strong prima facie reason for not destroying it; but we need not conclude from this that a potential person has a right to life, by virtue of that potential. It may be that our feeling that it is better, other things being equal, not to destroy a potential person is better explained by the fact that potential people are still (felt to be) an invaluable resource, not to be lightly squandered. Surely, if every speck of dust were a potential person, we would be much less apt to conclude that every potential person has a right to become actual.

Still, we do not need to insist that a potential person has no right to life whatever. There may well be something immoral, and riot just imprudent, about wantonly destroying potential people, when doing so isn't necessary to protect anyone's rights. But even if a potential person does have some prima facie right to life, such a right could not possibly outweigh the right of a woman to obtain an abortion, since the rights of any actual person invariably outweigh those of any potential person, whenever the two conflict. Since this may not be immediately obvious in the case of a human fetus, let us look at another case.

Suppose that our space explorer falls into the hands of an alien culture, whose scientists decide to create a few hundred thousand or more human beings, by breaking his body into its component cells, and using these to create fully developed human beings, with, of course, his genetic code. We may imagine that each of these newly created men will have all of the original man's abilities, skills, knowledge, and so on, and also have an individual self-concept, in short that each of them will be a bona fide (though hardly unique) person. Imagine that the whole project will take only seconds, and that its chances of success are extremely high, and that our explorer knows all of this, and also knows that these people will be treated fairly. I maintain that in such a situation he would have every right to escape if he could, and thus to deprive all of these potential people of their potential lives; for his right to life outweighs all of theirs together, in spite of the fact that they are all genetically human, all innocent, and all have a very high probability of becoming people very soon, if only he refrains from acting.

Indeed, I think he would have a right to escape even if it were not his life which the alien scientists planned to take, but only a year of his freedom, or, indeed, only a day. Nor would he be obligated to stay if he had gotten captured (thus bringing all these people-potentials into existence) because of his own carelessness, or even if he had done so deliberately, knowing the consequences. Regardless of how he got captured, he is not morally obligated to remain in captivity for *any* period of time for the sake of permitting any number of potential people to come into actuality, so great is the margin by which one actual person's right to liberty outweighs whatever right to life even a hundred thousand potential people have. And it seems reasonable to conclude that the rights of a woman will outweigh by a similar margin whatever right to life a fetus may have by virtue of its potential personhood.

Thus, neither a fetus's resemblance to a person, nor its potential for becoming a person provides any basis whatever for the claim that it has any significant right to life. Consequently, a woman's right to protect her health, happiness, freedom, and even her life by terminating an unwanted pregnancy, will always override whatever right to life it may be appropriate to ascribe to a fetus, even a fully developed one. And thus, in the absence of any overwhelming social need for every possible child, the laws which restrict the right to obtain an abortion, or limit the period of pregnancy during which an abortion may be performed, are a wholly unjustified violation of a woman's most basic moral and constitutional rights.

NOTES

1. Judith Thomson, "A Defense of Abortion," *Philosophy and Public Affairs* 1 (1971): 47–66.
2. Of course, the principle that it is (always) wrong to kill innocent human beings is in need of many other modifications, e.g., that it may be permissible to do so to save a greater number of other innocent human beings, but we may safely ignore these complications here.
3. John Noonan, "Deciding who Is Human," *National Law Review* 13 (1968): 134–140.
4. From here on, we will use 'human' to mean genetically human, since the moral sense seems closely connected to, and perhaps derived from, the assumption that genetic humanity is sufficient for membership in the moral community.

3.6 Why Abortion Is Immoral

DON MARQUIS

> Don Marquis has written many articles in medical ethics. He is professor emeritus at the University of Kansas.

The view that abortion is, with rare exceptions, seriously immoral has received little support in the recent philosophical literature. No doubt most philosophers affiliated with secular institutions of higher education believe that the anti-abortion position is either a symptom of irrational religious dogma or a conclusion generated by seriously confused philosophical argument. The purpose of this essay is to undermine this general belief. This essay sets out an argument that purports to show, as well as any argument in ethics can show, that abortion is, except possibly in rare cases, seriously immoral, that it is in the same moral category as killing an innocent adult human being....

I.

A sketch of standard anti-abortion and pro-choice arguments exhibits how those arguments possess certain symmetries that explain why partisans of those positions are so convinced of the

From Don Marquis, "Why Abortion is Immoral," *The Journal of Philosophy,* 86, no. 4 (April 1989): 183–85, 189–92, 194, 198–99, 201.

correctness of their own positions, why they are not successful in convincing their opponents, and why, to others, this issue seems to be unresolvable. An analysis of the nature of this stand-off suggests a strategy for surmounting it.

Consider the way a typical anti-abortionist argues. She will argue or assert that life is present from the moment of conception or that fetuses look like babies or that fetuses possess a characteristic such as a genetic code that is both necessary and sufficient for being human. Anti-abortionists seem to believe that (1) the truth of all of these claims is quite obvious, and (2) establishing any of these claims is sufficient to show that abortion is morally akin to murder.

A standard pro-choice strategy exhibits similarities. The pro-choicer will argue or assert that fetuses are not persons or that fetuses are not rational agents or that fetuses are not social beings. Pro-choicers seem to believe that (1) the truth of any of these claims is quite obvious, and (2) establishing any of these claims is sufficient to show that an abortion is not a wrongful killing.

In fact, both the pro-choice and the anti-abortion claims do seem to be true, although the "it looks like a baby" claim is more difficult to establish the earlier the pregnancy. We seem to have a standoff. How can it be resolved?

As everyone who has taken a bit of logic knows, if any of these arguments concerning abortion is a good argument, it requires not only some claim characterizing fetuses, but also some general moral principle that ties a characteristic of fetuses to having or not having the right to life or to some other moral characteristic that will generate the obligation or the lack of obligation not to end the life of a fetus. Accordingly, the arguments of the anti-abortionist and the pro-choicer need a bit of filling in to be regarded as adequate.

Note what each partisan will say. The anti-abortionist will claim that her position is supported by such generally accepted moral principles as "It is always prima facie seriously wrong to take a human life" or "It is always prima facie seriously wrong to end the life of a baby." Since

these are generally accepted moral principles, her position is certainly not obviously wrong. The pro-choicer will claim that her position is supported by such plausible moral principles as "Being a person is what gives an individual intrinsic moral worth" or "It is only seriously prima facie wrong to take the life of a member of the human community." Since these are generally accepted moral principles, the pro-choice position is certainly not obviously wrong. Unfortunately, we have again arrived at a standoff.

Now, how might one deal with this standoff? The standard approach is to try to show how the moral principles of one's opponent lose their plausibility under analysis. It is easy to see how this is possible. On the one hand, the anti-abortionist will defend a moral principle concerning the wrongness of killing which tends to be broad in scope in order that even fetuses at an early stage of pregnancy will fall under it. The problem with broad principles is that they often embrace too much. In this particular instance, the principle "It is always prima facie wrong to take a human life" seems to entail that it is wrong to end the existence of a living human cancer-cell culture, on the grounds that the culture is both living and human. Therefore, it seems that the anti-abortionist's favored principle is too broad.

On the other hand, the pro-choicer wants to find a moral principle concerning the wrongness of killing which tends to be narrow in scope in order that fetuses will *not* fall under it. The problem with narrow principles is that they often do not embrace enough. Hence, the needed principles such as "It is prima facie seriously wrong to kill only persons" or "It is prima facie wrong to kill only rational agents" do not explain why it is wrong to kill infants or young children or the severely retarded or even perhaps the severely mentally ill. Therefore, we seem again to have a standoff. The anti-abortionist charges, not unreasonably, that pro-choice principles concerning killing are too narrow to be acceptable; the pro-choicer charges, not unreasonably, that anti-abortionist principles concerning killing are too broad to be acceptable....

All this suggests that a necessary condition of resolving the abortion controversy is a more theoretical account of the wrongness of killing. After all, if we merely believe, but do not understand, why killing adult human beings such as ourselves is wrong, how could we conceivably show that abortion is either immoral or permissible?

II.

In order to develop such an account, we can start from the following unproblematic assumption concerning our own case: it is wrong to kill *us*. Why is it wrong? Some answers can be easily eliminated. It might be said that what makes killing us wrong is that a killing brutalizes the one who kills. But the brutalization consists of being inured to the performance of an act that is hideously immoral; hence, the brutalization does not explain the immorality. It might be said that what makes killing us wrong is the great loss others would experience due to our absence. Although such hubris is understandable, such an explanation does not account for the wrongness of killing hermits, or those whose lives are relatively independent and whose friends find it easy to make new friends.

A more obvious answer is better. What primarily makes killing wrong is neither its effect on the murderer nor its effect on the victim's friends and relatives, but its effect on the victim. The loss of one's life is one of the greatest losses one can suffer. The loss of one's life deprives one of all the experiences, activities, projects, and enjoyments that would otherwise have constituted one's future. Therefore, killing someone is wrong, primarily because the killing inflicts (one of) the greatest possible losses on the victim. To describe this as the loss of life can be misleading, however. The change in my biological state does not by itself make killing me wrong. The effect of the loss of my biological life is the loss to me of all those activities, projects, experiences, and enjoyments which would otherwise have constituted my future personal life. These activities, projects, experiences, and enjoyments are either valuable for their own sakes or are means to something else that is valuable for its own sake. Some parts of my future are not valued by me now, but will come to be valued by me as I grow older and as my values and capacities change. When I am killed, I am deprived both of what I now value which would have been part of my future personal life, but also what I would come to value. Therefore, when I die, I am deprived of all of the value of my future. Inflicting this loss on me is ultimately what makes killing me wrong. This being the case, it would seem that what makes killing *any* adult human being prima facie seriously wrong is the loss of his or her future.[1]

How should this rudimentary theory of the wrongness of killing be evaluated? It cannot be faulted for deriving an "ought" from an "is," for it does not. The analysis assumes that killing me (or you, reader) is prima facie seriously wrong. The point of the analysis is to establish which natural property ultimately explains the wrongness of the killing, given that it is wrong. A natural property will ultimately explain the wrongness of killing, only if (1) the explanation fits with our intuitions about the matter and (2) there is no other natural property that provides the basis for a better explanation of the wrongness of killing. This analysis rests on the intuition that what makes killing a particular human or animal wrong is what it does to that particular human or animal. What makes killing wrong is some natural effect or other of the killing. Some would deny this. For instance, a divine-command theorist in ethics would deny it. Surely this denial is, however, one of those features of divine-command theory which renders it so implausible.

The claim that what makes killing wrong is the loss of the victim's future is directly supported by two considerations. In the first place, this theory explains why we regard killing as one of the worst of crimes. Killing is especially wrong, because it deprives the victim of more than perhaps any other crime. In the second place, people with AIDS or cancer who know they are dying believe, of course, that dying is a very bad thing for them. They believe that the loss of a future to them that they would otherwise have experienced is what makes their premature death a very bad thing for them. A better theory of the wrongness of killing would require a different natural property associated with killing which better fits with the attitudes of the dying. What could it be?

The view that what makes killing wrong is the loss to the victim of the value of the victim's future gains additional support when some of its implications are examined. In the first place, it is incompatible with the view that it is wrong to kill only beings who are biologically human. It is possible that there exists a different species from another planet whose members have a future like ours. Since having a future like that is what makes killing someone wrong, this theory entails that it would be wrong to kill members of such a species. Hence, this theory is opposed to the claim that only life that is biologically human has great moral worth, a claim which many anti-abortionists have seemed to adopt. This opposition, which this theory has in common with personhood theories, seems to be a merit of the theory.

In the second place, the claim that the loss of one's future is the wrong-making feature of one's being killed entails the possibility that the futures of some actual nonhuman mammals on our own planet are sufficiently like ours that it is seriously wrong to kill them also. Whether some animals do have the same right to life as human beings depends on adding to the account of the wrongness of killing some additional account of just what it is about my future or the futures of other adult human beings which makes it wrong to kill us. No such additional account will be offered in this essay. Undoubtedly, the provision of such an account would be a very difficult matter. Undoubtedly, any such account would be quite controversial. Hence, it surely should not reflect badly on this sketch of an elementary theory of the wrongness of killing that it is indeterminate with respect to some very difficult issues regarding animal rights.

In the third place, the claim that the loss of one's future is the wrong-making feature of one's being killed does not entail, as sanctity of human life theories do, that active euthanasia is wrong. Persons who are severely and incurably ill, who face a future of pain and despair, and who wish to die will not have suffered a loss if they are killed. It is, strictly speaking, the value of a human's future which makes killing wrong in this theory. This being so, killing does not necessarily wrong some persons who are sick and dying. Of course, there may be other reasons for a prohibition of active euthanasia, but that is another matter. Sanctity-of-human-life theories seem to hold that active euthanasia is seriously wrong even in an individual case where there seems to be good reason for it independently of public policy considerations. This consequence is most implausible, and it is a plus for the claim that the loss of a future of value is what makes killing wrong that it does not share this consequence.

In the fourth place, the account of the wrongness of killing defended in this essay does straightforwardly entail that it is prima facie seriously wrong to kill children and infants, for we do presume that they have futures of value. Since we do believe that it is wrong to kill defenseless little babies, it is important that a theory of the wrongness of killing easily account for this. Personhood theories of the wrongness of killing, on the other hand, cannot straightforwardly account for the wrongness of killing infants and young children. Hence, such theories must add special ad hoc accounts of the wrongness of killing the young. The plausibility of such ad hoc theories seems to be a function of how desperately one wants such theories to work. The claim that the primary wrong-making feature of a killing is the loss to the victim of the value of its future accounts for the wrongness of killing young children and infants directly; it makes the wrongness of such acts as obvious as we actually think it is. This is a further merit of this theory. Accordingly, it seems that this value of a future-like-ours theory of the wrongness of killing shares strengths of both sanctity-of-life and personhood accounts while avoiding weaknesses of both. In addition, it meshes with a central intuition concerning what makes killing wrong.

The claim that the primary wrong-making feature of a killing is the loss to the victim of the value of its future has obvious consequences for the ethics of abortion. The future of a standard fetus includes a set of experiences, projects, activities, and such which are identical with the futures of adult human beings and are identical with the futures of young children. Since the reason that is sufficient to explain why it is wrong to kill human beings after the time of birth is a reason that also applies to fetuses, it follows that abortion is prima facie seriously morally wrong.

This argument does not rely on the invalid inference that, since it is wrong to kill persons, it is wrong to kill potential persons also. The category that is morally central to this analysis is the category of having a valuable future like ours; it is not the category of personhood. The argument to the conclusion that abortion is prima facie seriously morally wrong proceeded independently of the notion of person or potential person or any equivalent. Someone may wish to start with this analysis in terms of the value of a human future, conclude that abortion is, except perhaps in rare circumstances, seriously morally wrong, infer that fetuses have the right to life, and then call fetuses "persons" as a result of their having the right to life. Clearly, in this case, the category of person is being used to state the *conclusion* of the analysis rather than to generate the *argument* of the analysis....

Of course, this value of a future-like-ours argument, if sound, shows only that abortion is prima facie wrong, not that it is wrong in any and all circumstances. Since the loss of the future to a standard fetus, if killed, is, however, at least as great a loss as the loss of the future to a standard adult human being who is killed, abortion, like ordinary killing, could be justified only by the most compelling reasons. The loss of one's life is almost the greatest misfortune that can happen to one. Presumably abortion could be justified in some circumstances, only if the loss

consequent on failing to abort would be at least as great. Accordingly, morally permissible abortions will be rare indeed unless, perhaps, they occur so early in pregnancy that a fetus is not yet definitely an individual. Hence, this argument should be taken as showing that abortion is presumptively very seriously wrong, where the presumption is very strong—as strong as the presumption that killing another adult human being is wrong.

III.

How complete an account of the wrongness of killing does the value of a future-like-ours account have to be in order that the wrongness of abortion is a consequence? This account does not have to be an account of the necessary conditions for the wrongness of killing. Some persons in nursing homes may lack valuable human futures, yet it may be wrong to kill them for other reasons. Furthermore, this account does not obviously have to be the sole reason killing is wrong where the victim did have a valuable future. This analysis claims only that, for any killing where the victim did have a valuable future like ours, having that future by itself is sufficient to create the strong presumption that the killing is seriously wrong.

One way to overturn the value of a future-like-ours argument would be to find some account of the wrongness of killing which is at least as intelligible and which has different implications for the ethics of abortion....

One move of this sort is based upon the claim that a necessary condition of one's future being valuable is that one values it. Value implies a valuer. Given this one might argue that, since fetuses cannot value their futures, their futures are not valuable to them. Hence, it does not seriously wrong them deliberately to end their lives.

This move fails, however, because of some ambiguities. Let us assume that something cannot be of value unless it is valued by someone. This does not entail that my life is of no value unless it is valued by me. I may think, in a period of despair, that my future is of no worth whatsoever, but I may be wrong because others rightly see value—even great value—in it. Furthermore, my future can be valuable to me even if I do not value it. This is the case when a young person attempts suicide, but is rescued and goes on to significant human achievements. Such young people's futures are ultimately valuable to them, even though such futures do not seem to be valuable to them at the moment of attempted suicide. A fetus's future can be valuable to it in the same way. Accordingly, this attempt to limit the anti-abortion argument fails.

Another similar attempt to reject the anti-abortion position is based on Tooley's claim that an entity cannot possess the right to life unless it has the capacity to desire its continued existence. It follows that, since fetuses lack the conceptual capacity to desire to continue to live, they lack the right to life. Accordingly, Tooley concludes that abortion cannot be seriously prima facie wrong.[2] ..

One might attempt to defend Tooley's basic claim on the grounds that, because a fetus cannot apprehend continued life as a benefit, its continued life cannot be a benefit or cannot be something it has a right to or cannot be something that is in its interest. This might be defended in terms of the general proposition that, if an individual is literally incapable of caring about or taking an interest in some X, then one does not have a right to X or X is not a benefit or X is not something that is in one's interest.

Each member of this family of claims seems to be open to objections. As John C. Stevens[3] has pointed out, one may have a right to be treated with a certain medical procedure (because of a health insurance policy one has purchased), even though one cannot conceive of the nature of the procedure. And, as Tooley himself has pointed out, persons who have been indoctrinated, or drugged, or rendered temporarily unconscious may be literally incapable of caring about or taking an interest in something that is in their interest or is something to which they have a right, or is something that benefits them. Hence, the Tooley claim that would restrict the

scope of the value of a future-like-ours argument is undermined by counterexamples.[4]...

IV.

In this essay, it has been argued that the correct ethic of the wrongness of killing can be extended to fetal life and used to show that there is a strong presumption that any abortion is morally impermissible. If the ethic of killing adopted here entails, however, that contraception is also seriously immoral, then there would appear to be a difficulty with the analysis of this essay.

But this analysis does not entail that contraception is wrong. Of course, contraception prevents the actualization of a possible future of value. Hence, it follows from the claim that futures of value should be maximized that contraception is prima facie immoral. This obligation to maximize does not exist, however; furthermore, nothing in the ethics of killing in this paper entails that it does. The ethics of killing in this essay would entail that contraception is wrong only if something were denied a human future of value by contraception. Nothing at all is denied such a future by contraception, however.

Candidates for a subject of harm by contraception fall into four categories: (1) some sperm or other, (2) some ovum or other, (3) a sperm and an ovum separately, and (4) a sperm and an ovum together. Assigning the harm to some sperm is utterly arbitrary, for no reason can be given for making a sperm the subject of harm rather than an ovum. Assigning the harm to some ovum is utterly arbitrary, for no reason can be given for making an ovum the subject of harm rather than a sperm. One might attempt to avoid these problems by insisting that contraception deprives both the sperm and the ovum separately of a valuable future like ours. On this alternative, too many futures are lost. Contraception was supposed to be wrong, because it deprived us of one future of value, not two. One might attempt to avoid this problem by holding that contraception deprives the combination of sperm and ovum of a valuable future like ours.

But here the definite article misleads. At the time of contraception, there are hundreds of millions of sperm, one (released) ovum and millions of possible combinations of all of these. There is no actual combination at all. Is the subject of the loss to be a merely possible combination? Which one? This alternative does not yield an actual subject of harm either. Accordingly, the immorality of contraception is not entailed by the loss of a future-like-ours argument simply because there is no nonarbitrarily identifiable subject of the loss in the case of contraception....

NOTES

1. I have been most influenced on this matter by Jonathan Glover, *Causing Death and Saving Lives* (New York: Penguin, 1977), ch. 3; and Robert Young, "What Is So Wrong with Killing People?" *Philosophy*, LIV, 210 (1979): 515–528.
2. Michael Tooley, *Abortion and Infanticide*. (New York: Oxford, 1984), pp. 46–47.
3. John C. Stevens, "Must the Bearer of a Right Have the Concept of That to Which He Has a Right?" *Ethics*, xcv, 1 (1984): 68–74.
4. See Tooley again in *Abortion and Infanticide*, pp. 47–49.

CHAPTER 4

THE MEANING OF LIFE

4.1 Letter to Menoeceus

EPICURUS

Epicurus (341–270 BCE), from the Greek island of Samos, was the first of the great hedonistic philosophers. Only a small number of his many writings survive. This *Letter* summarizes some of the main tenets of his influential philosophy.

Epicurus to Menoeceus, greetings:

Let no one be slow to seek wisdom when he is young nor weary in the search of it when he has grown old. For no age is too early or too late for the health of the soul. And to say that the season for studying philosophy has not yet come, or that it is past and gone, is like saying that the season for happiness is not yet or that it is now no more. Therefore, both old and young alike ought to seek wisdom, the former in order that, as age comes over him, he may be young in good things because of the grace of what has been, and the latter in order that, while he is young, he may at the same time be old, because

he has no fear of the things which are to come. So we must exercise ourselves in the things which bring happiness, since, if that be present, we have everything, and, if that be absent, all our actions are directed towards attaining it.

Those things which without ceasing I have declared unto you, do them, and exercise yourself in them, holding them to be the elements of right life. First believe that God is a living being immortal and blessed, according to the notion of a god indicated by the common sense of mankind; and so believing, you shall not affirm of him anything that is foreign to his immortality or that is repugnant to his blessedness. Believe

Epicurus, *Letter to Menoeceus*, trans. Robert Drew Hicks.

about him whatever may uphold both his blessedness and his immortality. For there are gods, and the knowledge of them is manifest; but they are not such as the multitude believe, seeing that men do not steadfastly maintain the notions they form respecting them. Not the man who denies the gods worshipped by the multitude, but he who affirms of the gods what the multitude believes about them is truly impious. For the utterances of the multitude about the gods are not true preconceptions but false assumptions; hence it is that the greatest evils happen to the wicked and the greatest blessings happen to the good from the hand of the gods, seeing that they are always favorable to their own good qualities and take pleasure in men like themselves, but reject as alien whatever is not of their kind.

Accustom yourself to believing that death is nothing to us, for good and evil imply the capacity for sensation, and death is the privation of all sentience; therefore a correct understanding that death is nothing to us makes the mortality of life enjoyable, not by adding to life a limitless time, but by taking away the yearning after immortality. For life has no terrors for him who has thoroughly understood that there are no terrors for him in ceasing to live. Foolish, therefore, is the man who says that he fears death, not because it will pain when it comes, but because it pains in the prospect. Whatever causes no annoyance when it is present causes only a groundless pain in the expectation. Death, therefore, the most awful of evils, is nothing to us, seeing that, when we are, death is not come, and, when death is come, we are not. It is nothing, then, either to the living or to the dead, for with the living it is not and the dead exist no longer.

But in the world, at one time men shun death as the greatest of all evils, and at another time choose it as a respite from the evils in life. The wise man does not deprecate life nor does he fear the cessation of life. The thought of life is no offense to him, nor is the cessation of life regarded as an evil. And even as men choose of food not merely and simply the larger portion, but the more pleasant, so the wise seek to enjoy the time which is most pleasant and not merely that which is longest. And he who admonishes the young to live well and the old to make a good end speaks foolishly, not merely because of the desirability of life, but because the same exercise at once teaches to live well and to die well. Much worse is he who says that it were good not to be born, but when once one is born to pass quickly through the gates of Hades. For if he truly believes this, why does he not depart from life? It would be easy for him to do so once he were firmly convinced. If he speaks only in jest, his words are foolishness as those who hear him do not believe.

We must remember that the future is neither wholly ours nor wholly not ours, so that neither must we count upon it as quite certain to come nor despair of it as quite certain not to come.

We must also reflect that of desires some are natural, others are groundless; and that of the natural some are necessary as well as natural, and some natural only. And of the necessary desires some are necessary if we are to be happy, some if the body is to be rid of uneasiness, some if we are even to live. He who has a clear and certain understanding of these things will direct every preference and aversion toward securing health of body and tranquility of mind, seeing that this is the sum and end of a blessed life. For the end of all our actions is to be free from pain and fear, and, when once we have attained all this, the tempest of the soul is laid; seeing that the living creature has no need to go in search of something that is lacking, nor to look for anything else by which the good of the soul and of the body will be fulfilled. When we are pained because of the absence of pleasure, then, and then only, do we feel the need of pleasure. Wherefore we call pleasure the alpha and omega of a blessed life. Pleasure is our first and kindred good. It is the starting-point of every choice and of every aversion, and to it we come back, inasmuch as we make feeling the rule by which to judge of every good thing.

And since pleasure is our first and native good, for that reason we do not choose every pleasure whatsoever, but will often pass over many pleasures when a greater annoyance ensues from them. And often we consider pains superior to pleasures when submission to the pains for a long time brings us as a consequence a greater pleasure. While therefore all pleasure because it is naturally akin to us is good, not all pleasure should be chosen, just as all pain is an evil and yet not all pain is to be shunned. It is, however, by measuring one against another, and by looking at the conveniences and inconveniences, that all these matters must be judged. Sometimes we treat the good as an evil, and the evil, on the contrary, as a good.

Again, we regard independence of outward things as a great good, not so as in all cases to use little, but so as to be contented with little if we have not much, being honestly persuaded that they have the sweetest enjoyment of luxury who stand least in need of it, and that whatever is natural is easily procured and only the vain and worthless hard to win. Plain fare gives as much pleasure as a costly diet, when once the pain of want has been removed, while bread and water confer the highest possible pleasure when they are brought to hungry lips. To habituate one's self, therefore, to simple and inexpensive diet supplies all that is needful for health, and enables a man to meet the necessary requirements of life without shrinking, and it places us in a better condition when we approach at intervals a costly fare and renders us fearless of fortune.

When we say, then, that pleasure is the end and aim, we do not mean the pleasures of the prodigal or the pleasures of sensuality, as we are understood to do by some through ignorance, prejudice, or willful misrepresentation. By pleasure we mean the absence of pain in the body and of trouble in the soul. It is not an unbroken succession of drinking-bouts and of revelry, not sexual lust, not the enjoyment of the fish and other delicacies of a luxurious table, which produce a pleasant life; it is sober reasoning, searching out the grounds of every choice and avoidance, and banishing those beliefs through which the greatest tumults take possession of the soul. Of all this the beginning and the greatest good is wisdom. Therefore wisdom is a

more precious thing even than philosophy; from it spring all the other virtues, for it teaches that we cannot live pleasantly without living wisely, honorably, and justly; nor live wisely, honorably, and justly without living pleasantly. For the virtues have grown into one with a pleasant life, and a pleasant life is inseparable from them.

Who, then, is superior in your judgment to such a man? He holds a holy belief concerning the gods, and is altogether free from the fear of death. He has diligently considered the end fixed by nature, and understands how easily the limit of good things can be reached and attained, and how either the duration or the intensity of evils is but slight. Fate, which some introduce as sovereign over all things, he scorns, affirming rather that some things happen of necessity, others by chance, others through our own agency. For he sees that necessity destroys responsibility and that chance is inconstant; whereas our own actions are autonomous, and it is to them that praise and blame naturally attach. It were better, indeed, to accept the legends of the gods than to bow beneath that yoke of destiny which the natural philosophers have imposed. The one holds out some faint hope that we may escape if we honor the gods, while the necessity of the naturalists is deaf to all entreaties. Nor does he hold chance to be a god, as the world in general does, for in the acts of a god there is no disorder; nor to be a cause, though an uncertain one, for he believes that no good or evil is dispensed by chance to men so as to make life blessed, though it supplies the starting point of great good and great evil. He believes that the misfortune of the wise is better than the prosperity of the fool. It is better, in short, that what is well judged in action should not owe its successful issue to the aid of chance.

Exercise yourself in these and related precepts day and night, both by yourself and with one who is like-minded; then never, either in waking or in dream, will you be disturbed, but will live as a god among men. For man loses all semblance of mortality by living in the midst of immortal blessings.

4.2 The Meaning of Life

RICHARD TAYLOR

Richard Taylor (1919–2003) wrote on a wide variety of philosophical issues. He taught at Brown University and Columbia University, and then for many years at the University of Rochester. He also was an internationally recognized authority on beekeeping.

The question whether life has any meaning is difficult to interpret, and the more one concentrates his critical faculty on it the more it seems to elude him, or to evaporate as any intelligible question. One wants to turn it aside, as a source of embarrassment, as something that, if it cannot be abolished, should at least be decently covered. And yet I think any reflective person recognizes that the question it raises is important, and that it ought to have a significant answer.

If the idea of meaningfulness is difficult to grasp in this context so that we are unsure what sort of thing would amount to answering the question, the idea of meaninglessness is perhaps less so. If, then, we can bring before our minds a clear image of meaningless existence, then perhaps we can take a step toward coping with our original question by seeing to what extent our lives, as we actually find them, resemble that image, and draw such lessons as we are able to from the comparison.

MEANINGLESS EXISTENCE

A perfect image of meaninglessness, of the kind we are seeking, is found in the ancient myth of Sisyphus. Sisyphus, it will be remembered, betrayed divine secrets to mortals, and for this he was condemned by the gods to roll a stone to the top of a hill, the stone then immediately to roll back down, again to be pushed to the top by Sisyphus, to roll down once more, and so on again and again, *forever*. Now in this we have the picture of meaningless, pointless toil, of a meaningless existence that is absolutely *never* redeemed. It is not even redeemed by a death that, if it were to accomplish nothing more, would at least bring this idiotic cycle to a close. If we were invited to imagine Sisyphus struggling for awhile and accomplishing nothing, perhaps eventually falling from exhaustion, so that we might suppose him then eventually turning to something having some sort of promise, then the meaninglessness of that chapter of his life would not be so stark. It would be a dark and dreadful dream, from which he eventually awakens to sunlight and reality. But he does not awaken, for there is nothing for him to awaken to. His repetitive toil is his life and reality, and it goes on forever, and it is without any meaning whatever. Nothing ever comes of what he is doing, except simply, more of the same. Not by one step, nor by a thousand, nor by ten thousand does he even expiate by the smallest token the sin against the gods that led him into this fate. Nothing comes of it, nothing at all.

This ancient myth has always enchanted men, for countless meanings can be read into it. Some of the ancients apparently thought it symbolized the perpetual rising and setting of the sun, and others the repetitious crashing of the waves upon the shore. Probably the commonest interpretation is that it symbolizes man's eternal struggle and unquenchable spirit, his determination always to try once more in the face of overwhelming discouragement. This interpretation is further supported by that version of the myth according to which Sisyphus was commanded to roll the stone *over* the hill, so that it would finally roll down the other side, but was never quite able to make it.

I am not concerned with rendering or defending any interpretation of this myth, however. I have cited it only for the one element it does unmistakably contain, namely, that of a repetitious, cyclic activity that never comes to anything. We could contrive other images of this that would serve just as well, and no myth-makers are needed to supply the materials of it. Thus, we can imagine two persons transporting a stone—or even a precious gem, it does not matter—back and forth, relay style. One carries it to a near or distant point where it is received by the other; it is returned to its starting point, there to be recovered by the first, and the process is repeated over and over. Except in this relay nothing counts as winning, and nothing brings the contest to any close, each step only leads to a repetition of itself. Or we can imagine two groups of prisoners, one of them engaged in digging a prodigious hole in the ground that is no sooner finished than it is filled in again by the other group, the latter then digging a new hole that is at once filled in by the first group, and so on and on endlessly.

Now what stands out in all such pictures as oppressive and dejecting is not that the beings who enact these roles suffer any torture or pain, for it need not be assumed that they do. Nor is it that their labors are great, for they are no greater than the labors commonly undertaken by most men most of the time. According to the original myth, the stone is so large that Sisyphus never quite gets it to the top and must groan under every step, so that his enormous labor is all for nought. But this is not what appalls. It is not that his great struggle comes to nothing, but that his existence itself is without meaning. Even if we suppose, for example, that the stone is but a pebble that can be carried effortlessly, or that the holes dug by the prisoners are but small ones, not the slightest meaning is introduced into their lives. The stone that Sisyphus moves to the top of the hill, whether we think of it as large or small, still rolls back every

time, and the process is repeated forever. Nothing comes of it, and the work is simply pointless. That is the element of the myth that I wish to capture.

Again, it is not the fact that the labors of Sisyphus continue forever that deprives them of meaning. It is, rather, the implication of this: that they come to nothing. The image would not be changed by our supposing him to push a different stone up every time, each to roll down again. But if we supposed that these stones, instead of rolling back to their places as if they had never been moved, were assembled at the top of the hill and there incorporated, say, in a beautiful and enduring temple, then the aspect of meaninglessness would disappear. His labors would then have a point, something would come of them all, and although one could perhaps still say it was not worth it, one could not say that the life of Sisyphus was devoid of meaning altogether. Meaningfulness would at least have made an appearance, and we could see what it was.

That point will need remembering. But in the meantime, let us note another way in which the image of meaninglessness can be altered by making only a very slight change. Let us suppose that the gods, while condemning Sisyphus to the fate just described, at the same time, as an afterthought, waxed perversely merciful by implanting in him a strange and irrational impulse; namely, a compulsive impulse to roll stones. We may if we like, to make this more graphic, suppose they accomplish this by implanting in him some substance that has this effect on his character and drives. I call this perverse, because from our point of view there is clearly no reason why anyone should have a persistent and insatiable desire to do something so pointless as that. Nevertheless, suppose that is Sisyphus' condition. He has but one obsession, which is to roll stones, and it is an obsession that is only for the moment appeased by his rolling them—he no sooner gets a stone rolled to the top of the hill than he is restless to roll up another.

Now it can be seen why this little afterthought of the gods, which I called perverse, was also in fact merciful. For they have by this device managed to give Sisyphus precisely what he wants—by making him want precisely what they inflict on him. However it may appear to us, Sisyphus' fate now does not appear to him as a condemnation, but the very reverse. His one desire in life is to roll stones, and he is absolutely guaranteed its endless fulfillment. Where otherwise he might profoundly have wished surcease, and even welcomed the quiet of death to release him from endless boredom and meaninglessness, his life is now filled with mission and meaning, and he seems to himself to have been given an entry to heaven. Nor need he even fear death, for the gods have promised him an endless opportunity to indulge his single purpose, without concern or frustration. He will be able to roll stones *forever*.

What we need to mark most carefully at this point is that the picture with which we began has not really been changed in the least by adding this supposition. Exactly the same things happen as before. The only change is in Sisyphus' view of them. The picture before was the image of meaningless activity and existence. It was created precisely to be an image of that. It has not lost that meaninglessness, it has now gained not the least shred of meaningfulness. The stones still roll back as before, each phase of Sisyphus' life still exactly resembles all the others, the task is never completed, nothing comes of it, no temple ever begins to rise, and all this cycle of the same pointless thing over and over goes on forever in this picture as in the other. The *only* thing that has happened is this: Sisyphus has been reconciled to it, and indeed more, he has been led to embrace it. Not, however, by reason or persuasion, but by nothing more rational than the potency of a new substance in his veins.

THE MEANINGLESSNESS OF LIFE

I believe the foregoing provides a fairly clear content to the idea of meaninglessness and, through it, some hint of what meaningfulness, in this sense, might be. Meaninglessness is essentially endless pointlessness, and meaningfulness is therefore the opposite. Activity, and even long,

drawn out and repetitive activity, has a meaning if it has some significant culmination, some more or less lasting end that can be considered to have been the direction and purpose of the activity. But the descriptions so far also provide something else; namely, the suggestion of how an existence that is objectively meaningless, in this sense, can nevertheless acquire a meaning for him whose existence it is.

Now let us ask: Which of these pictures does life in fact resemble? And let us not begin with our own lives, for here both our prejudices and wishes are great, but with the life in general that we share with the rest of creation. We shall find, I think, that it all has a certain pattern, and that this pattern is by now easily recognized.

We can begin anywhere, only saving human existence for our last consideration. We can, for example, begin with any animal. It does not matter where we begin, because the result is going to be exactly the same.

Thus, for example, there are caves in New Zealand, deep and dark, whose floors are quiet pools and whose walls and ceilings are covered with soft light. As one gazes in wonder in the stillness of these caves it seems that the Creator has reproduced there in microcosm the heavens themselves, until one scarcely remembers the enclosing presence of the walls. As one looks more closely, however, the scene is explained. Each dot of light identifies an ugly worm, whose luminous tail is meant to attract insects from the surrounding darkness. As from time to time one of these insects draws near it becomes entangled in a sticky thread lowered by the worm, and is eaten. This goes on month after month, the blind worm lying there in the barren stillness waiting to entrap an occasional bit of nourishment that will only sustain it to another bit of nourishment until.... Until what? What great thing awaits all this long and repetitious effort and makes it worthwhile? Really nothing. The larva just transforms itself finally to a tiny winged adult that lacks even mouth parts to feed and lives only a day or two. These adults, as soon as they have mated and laid eggs, are themselves caught in the threads and are devoured by the cannibalist worms, often without having ventured into the day, the only point to their existence having now been fulfilled. This has been going on for millions of years, and to no end other than that the same meaningless cycle may continue for another millions of years.

All living things present essentially the same spectacle. The larva of a certain cicada burrows in the darkness of the earth for seventeen years, through season after season, to emerge finally into the daylight for a brief flight, lay its eggs, and die—this all to repeat itself during the next seventeen years, and so on to eternity. We have already noted, in another connection, the struggles of fish, made only that others may do the same after them and that this cycle, having no other point than itself, may never cease. Some birds span an entire side of the globe each year and then return, only to insure that others may follow the same incredibly long path again and again. One is led to wonder what the point of it all is, with what great triumph this ceaseless effort, repeating itself through millions of years, might finally culminate, and why it should go on and on for so long, accomplishing nothing, getting nowhere. But then one realizes that there is no point to it at all, that it really culminates in nothing, that each of these cycles, so filled with toil, is to be followed only by more of the same. The point of any living thing's life is, evidently, nothing but life itself.

This life of the world thus presents itself to our eyes as a vast machine, feeding on itself, running on and on forever to nothing. And we are part of that life. To be sure, we are not just the same, but the differences are not so great as we like to think; many are merely invented, and none really cancels the kind of meaninglessness that we found in Sisyphus and that we find all around, wherever anything lives. We are conscious of our activity. Our goals, whether in any significant sense we choose them or not, are things of which we are at least partly aware and can therefore in some sense appraise. More significantly, perhaps, men have a history, as other animals do not, such that each generation does not precisely resemble all those before. Still,

if we can in imagination disengage our wills from our lives and disregard the deep interest each man has in his own existence, we shall find that they do not so little resemble the existence of Sisyphus. We toil after goals, most of them—indeed every single one of them—of transitory significance and, having gained one of them, we immediately set forth for the next, as if that one had never been, with this next one being essentially more of the same. Look at a busy street any day, and observe the throng going hither and thither. To what? Some office or shop, where the same things will be done today as were done yesterday, and are done now so they may be repeated tomorrow. And if we think that, unlike Sisyphus, these labors do have a point, that they culminate in something lasting and, independently of our own deep interests in them, very worthwhile, then we simply have not considered the thing closely enough. Most such effort is directed only to the establishment and perpetuation of home and family; that is, to the begetting of others who will follow in our steps to do more of the same. Each man's life thus resembles one of Sisyphus' climbs to the summit of his hill, and each day of it one of his steps; the difference is that whereas Sisyphus himself returns to push the stone up again, we leave this to our children. We at one point imagined that the labors of Sisyphus finally culminated in the creation of a temple, but for this to make any difference it had to be a temple that would at least endure, adding beauty to the world for the remainder of time. Our achievements, even though they are often beautiful, are mostly bubbles; and those that do last, like the sand-swept pyramids, soon become mere curiosities while around them the rest of mankind continues its perpetual toting of rocks, only to see them roll down. Nations are built upon the bones of their founders and pioneers, but only to decay and crumble before long, their rubble then becoming the foundation for others directed to exactly the same fate. The picture of Sisyphus is the picture of existence of the individual man, great or unknown, of nations, of the race of men, and of the very life of the world.

On a country road one sometimes comes upon the ruined hulks of a house and once extensive buildings, all in collapse and spread over with weeds. A curious eye can in imagination reconstruct from what is left a once warm and thriving life, filled with purpose. There was the hearth, where a family once talked, sang, and made plans; there were the rooms, where people loved, and babes were born to a rejoicing mother; there are the musty remains of a sofa, infested with bugs, once bought at a dear price to enhance an ever-growing comfort, beauty, and warmth. Every small piece of junk fills the mind with what once, not long ago, was utterly real, with children's voices, plans made, and enterprises embarked upon. That is how these stones of Sisyphus were rolled up, and that is how they became incorporated into a beautiful temple, and that temple is what now lies before you. Meanwhile other buildings, institutions, nations, and civilizations spring up all around, only to share the same fate before long. And if the question "What for?" is now asked, the answer is clear: so that just this may go on forever.

The two pictures—of Sisyphus and of our own lives, if we look at them from a distance—are in outline the same and convey to the mind the same image. It is not surprising, then, that men invent ways of denying it, their religions proclaiming a heaven that does not crumble, their hymnals and prayer books declaring a significance to life of which our eyes provide no hint whatever.[1] Even our philosophies portray some permanent and lasting good at which all may aim, from the changeless forms invented by Plato to the beatific vision of St. Thomas and the ideals of permanence contrived by the moderns. When these fail to convince, then earthly ideals such as universal justice and brotherhood are conjured up to take their places and give meaning to man's seemingly endless pilgrimage, some final state that will be ushered in when the last obstacle is removed and the last stone pushed to the hilltop. No one believes, of course, that any such state will be final, or even wants it to be in case it means that human existence would then cease to be a struggle; but

in the meantime such ideas serve a very real need.

THE MEANING OF LIFE

We noted that Sisyphus' existence would have meaning if there were some point to his labors, if his efforts ever culminated in something that was not just an occasion for fresh labors of the same kind. But that is precisely the meaning it lacks. And human existence resembles his in that respect. Men do achieve things—they scale their towers and raise their stones to their hilltops—but every such accomplishment fades, providing only an occasion for renewed labors of the same kind.

But here we need to note something else that has been mentioned, but its significance not explored, and that is the state of mind and feeling with which such labors are undertaken. We noted that if Sisyphus had a keen and unappeasable desire to be doing just what he found himself doing, then, although his life would in no way be changed, it would nevertheless have a meaning for him. It would be an irrational one, no doubt, because the desire itself would be only the product of the substance in his veins, and not any that reason could discover, but a meaning nevertheless.

And would it not, in fact, be a meaning incomparably better than the other? For let us examine again the first kind of meaning it could have. Let us suppose that, without having any interest in rolling stones, as such, and finding this, in fact, a galling toil, Sisyphus did nevertheless have a deep interest in raising a temple, one that would be beautiful and lasting. And let us suppose he succeeded in this, that after ages of dreadful toil, all directed at this final result, he did at last complete his temple, such that now he could say his work was done, and he could rest and forever enjoy the result. Now what? What picture now presents itself to our minds? It is precisely the picture of infinite boredom! Of Sisyphus doing nothing ever again, but contemplating what he has already wrought and can no longer add anything to, and contemplating it for an eternity! Now in this picture we have a meaning for Sisyphus' existence, a point for his prodigious labor, because we have put it there; yet, at the same time, that which is really worthwhile seems to have slipped away entirely. Where before we were presented with the nightmare of eternal and pointless activity, we are now confronted with the hell of its eternal absence.

Our second picture, then, wherein we imagined Sisyphus to have had inflicted on him the irrational desire to be doing just what he found himself doing, should not have been dismissed so abruptly. The meaning that picture lacked was no meaning that he or anyone could crave, and the strange meaning it had was perhaps just what we were seeking.

At this point, then, we can reintroduce what has been until now, it is hoped, resolutely pushed aside in an effort to view our lives and human existence with objectivity; namely, our own wills, our deep interest in what we find ourselves doing. If we do this we find that our lives do indeed still resemble that of Sisyphus, but that the meaningfulness they thus lack is precisely the meaningfulness of infinite boredom. At the same time, the strange meaningfulness they possess is that of the inner compulsion to be doing just what we were put here to do, and to go on doing it forever. This is the nearest we may hope to get to heaven, but the redeeming side of that fact is that we do thereby avoid a genuine hell.

If the builders of a great and flourishing ancient civilization could somehow return now to see archaeologists unearthing the trivial remnants of what they had once accomplished with such effort—see the fragments of pots and vases, a few broken statues, and such tokens of another age and greatness—they could indeed ask themselves what the point of it all was, if this is all it finally came to. Yet, it did not seem so to them then, for it was just the building, and not what was finally built, that gave their life meaning. Similarly, if the builders of the ruined home and farm that I described a short while ago could be brought back to see what is left, they would have the same feelings. What we construct in our

imaginations as we look over these decayed and rusting pieces would reconstruct itself in their very memories, and certainly with unspeakable sadness. The piece of a sled at our feet would revive in them a warm Christmas. And what rich memories would there be in the broken crib? And the weed-covered remains of a fence would reproduce the scene of a great herd of livestock, so laboriously built up over so many years. What was it all worth, if this is the final result? Yet, again, it did not seem so to them through those many years of struggle and toil, and they did not imagine they were building a Gibraltar. The things to which they bent their backs day after day, realizing one by one their ephemeral plans, were precisely the things in which their wills were deeply involved, precisely the things in which their interests lay, and there was no need then to ask questions. There is no more need of them now—the day was sufficient to itself, and so was the life.

This is surely the way to look at all of life—at one's own life, and each day and moment it contains; of the life of a nation; of the species; of the life of the world; and of everything that breathes. Even the glow worms I described, whose cycles of existence over the millions of years seem so pointless when looked at by us, will seem entirely different to us if we can somehow try to view their existence from within. Their endless activity, which gets nowhere, is just what it is their will to pursue. This is its whole justification and meaning. Nor would it be any salvation to the birds who span the globe every year, back and forth, to have a home made for them in a cage with plenty of food and protection, so that they would not have to migrate any more. It would be their condemnation, for it is the doing that counts for them, and not what they hope to win by it. Flying these prodigious distances, never ending, is what it is in their veins to do, exactly as it was in Sisyphus' veins to roll stones, without end, after the gods had waxed merciful and implanted this in him.

A human being no sooner draws his first breath than he responds to the will that is in him to live. He no more asks whether it will be worthwhile, or whether anything of significance will come of it, than the worms and the birds. The point of his living is simply to be living, in the manner that it is his nature to be living. He goes through his life building his castles, each of these beginning to fade into time as the next is begun; yet, it would be no salvation to rest from all this. It would be a condemnation, and one that would in no way be redeemed were he able to gaze upon the things he has done, even if these were beautiful and absolutely permanent, as they never are. What counts is that one should be able to begin a new task, a new castle, a new bubble. It counts only because it is there to be done and he has the will to do it. The same will be the life of his children, and of theirs; and if the philosopher is apt to see in this a pattern similar to the unending cycles of the existence of Sisyphus, and to despair, then it is indeed because the meaning and point he is seeking is not there —but mercifully so. The meaning of life is from within us, it is not bestowed from without, and it far exceeds in both its beauty and permanence any heaven of which men have ever dreamed or yearned for.

NOTE

1. A popular Christian hymn, sung often at funerals and typical of many hymns, expresses this thought:
   Swift to its close ebbs out life's little day;
   Earth's joys grow dim, its glories pass away;
   Change and decay in all around I see:
   O thou who changest not, abide with me.

4.3 Desire and the Human Good

RICHARD KRAUT

Richard Kraut is Charles and Emma Morrison Professor in the Humanities of Northwestern University. He has written many important works in ancient philosophy and in value theory.

I

When we compare contemporary moral philosophy with the well-known moral systems of earlier centuries, we should be struck by the fact that a certain assumption about human well being that is now widely taken for granted was universally rejected in the past. The contemporary moral climate predisposes us to be pluralistic about the human good, whereas earlier systems of ethics embraced a conception of well being that we would now call narrow and restrictive. One way to convey the sort of contrast I have in mind is to note that according to Plato and Aristotle, there is one kind of life, that of the philosopher, that represents the summit of human flourishing,

and all other lives are worth leading to the extent that they approximate this ideal. Certain other ethical theories of the past were in a way more narrow than this, for whereas Plato and Aristotle maintained that many things are in themselves worthwhile, others argued that there is only one intrinsic good—pleasure according to the Epicureans, virtue according to the Stoics. By contrast, it is now widely assumed that all such approaches are too exclusive, that not only are there many types of intrinsic goods but there is no one specific kind of life—whether it is that of a philosopher or a poet or anyone else—that is the single human ideal. Even hedonism, a conception of the good that had a powerful

Richard Kraut, "Desire and the Human Good," *Proceedings of the American Philosophical Association*, vol. 68 (1994), pp. 39–45.

influence in the modern period, has few contemporary proponents. A consensus has arisen in our time that there is no single ultimate end that provides the measure by which the worth of all other goods must be assessed.

But if we want not merely to take note of our departure from the past, but also to show why we are justified in being pluralists about the good, then we must have something, to say about what human well being is. We should not simply assert that there are many goods and many kinds of good lives, but must offer some general account of what well being is that explains why it is so multiform. In response to this demand, many philosophers would, as a first approximation, equate the human good with the satisfaction of desire, and would explain the multiplicity of the good by pointing out that because of the enormous variety of our interests and tastes, our desires exhibit a similar heterogeneity. Roughly speaking, what makes a state of affairs good for someone is its satisfaction of one of that person's desires; accordingly our lives go well to the extent that our desires, or the ones to which we give the greatest weight, are satisfied.

A complication is created by the fact that sometimes we have desires—those created by addictions, for example—that we wish we were without. But this can easily be handled in familiar ways by giving special weight to second-order desires. The general idea is that so long as one wants something wholeheartedly and with open eyes, then it is good for one's desire to be satisfied, regardless of the content of the desire. The objects we now want or will want are made good for us by our wanting them; they are not already good for us, apart from our having a present or future desire for them. There are no facts about what is ultimately good for me that are independent of my aims, facts that I need to discover in order to know what to aim at. No wonder, then, that well being is multiform. Our good is invented and constructed rather than discovered; and because of the great variation in our personalities and abilities, we invent different plans of life and our desires are directed at many different kinds of objects.

Although the "desire theory," as it might be called, is widely accepted, in part because it gives some backing to the assumption that the good is multiform, I will argue that it nonetheless has weaknesses serious enough to justify its rejection. At bottom, its main deficiency is that it is too accepting of desires as they stand, and cannot account for some of the ways in which they are subject to evaluation. What we need is a theory that is more objective and in this respect closer to the eudai-monistic theories of ancient and medieval philosophy. I would like to show now we can abandon the desire theory and still hold onto our sense that many different kinds of life are worth living—more than earlier systems realized, but not so many as the desire theory endorses.

II

I begin with a point that, despite its familiarity, cannot easily be accommodated by the desire theory. It is conceptually and psychologically possible for people to decide, voluntarily and with due deliberation, to renounce their good in favor of an alternative goal. They can clearheadedly design a long-range plan and fulfill it, thereby satisfying their deepest desires, in spite of the fact that they realize all the while that what they are doing is bad for them. In fact, they can carry out certain plans precisely *because* they think that it is bad for them to do so. For example, suppose a man has committed a serious crime at an earlier point in his life, and although he now regrets having done so, he realms that no one will believe him if he confesses. So he decides to inflict a punishment upon himself for a period of several years. He abandons his current line of work, which he loves, and takes a job that he considers boring, arduous, and insignificant. He does not regard this as a way of serving others, because he realizes that what he will be doing is useless. His aim is simply to balance the evil he has done to others with a comparable evil for himself. Taking a pill to relieve his pangs of guilt would be of no use, since his aim is to do himself harm, not to make himself feel good. He punishes himself because he regards this as a moral necessity, and when he carries out his punishment, he does so from a sense of duty rather than a joy fid love of justice and certainly with no relish for the particular job he is doing. In an ordinary sense of "want," he doesn't want to punish himself, but the desire theory cannot take refuge in this point, since it uses a much broader notion of desire, according to which what we voluntarily seek is what we desire. And in this sense, our self-punisher does want above all to punish himself.

Spending ones days performing a task that one rightly regards as boring, arduous and useless is not something we would ordinarily consider advantageous, and so we can plausibly assume that when the self-punisher carries out his plan, he is not only trying to act against his good, but he succeeds in harming himself, despite the fact that he gets precisely what he wants. It would be dogmatic and counterintuitive to insist that he must benefit from his punishment simply because he desires it. The more reasonable response is to concede that sometimes carrying out one's plans and getting what one above all wants conflicts with one's good.

Furthermore, *I* see no plausible way for the desire theory to make adjustments that convincingly accommodate this sort of counterexample. Bringing in the notions of rationality and full information will not help. The self-punisher is not violating any obvious principle of rationality and he has all the empirical information he needs. The moral that is most naturally drawn from this case is that there are circumstances in which people voluntarily renounce their good. When they do so, they are still getting what they want, and so we cannot equate well being with the satisfaction of desires, even when these desires are rational and exposed to full information. Other sorts of cases in which this happens, which are more common than self-punishment, are those in which we willingly make sacrifices in our well-being in order to promote the good of others. But rather than pursue this idea, I will turn to another type of objection to the desire

theory. The weakness of the theory is best appreciated when we see the variety of difficulties it encounters.

III

Imagine a boy who, while walking through the park, sees a duck, and at the same time spots a rock on the ground. Impulsively, he picks up the rock and throws it at the duck. Is it good for him, to some extent, if his desire to hit the duck is satisfied? I find that implausible. Surely he would be no worse off if he had never felt an impulse to hit the duck; and once this impulse does arise, he would be no worse off if it evaporated before he acted on it. We might even say, with some plausibility, that it is *bad* for him to satisfy this desire, that for his own good he should be free of such destructive impulses. Someone who wants to defend the desire theory may suggest that we should salvage it by making a slight modification. The boy's desire to hit the duck is a mere passing whim, and so what we should say is that satisfying desires is good for us only when they are more enduring than fleeting urges. The desires that are good to satisfy are those that organize our lives and lead to projects that absorb considerable time and energy. The problem with this idea is that we can easily imagine desires that are unobjectionable as whims but become perverse when given more significance than that. Consider for example the impulse one might feel on a winter walk to reach out and knock an icicle to the ground. And imagine someone who has more than a fleeting urge to do this. Rather, he has the project of knocking down as many icicles as he can before they melt. He hires a crew of workers and a fleet of trucks, so that he can reach icicles hanging from tall buildings; and this is how he spends his winters. It is implausible to suppose that now that this desire is no mere whim but a grand project, its satisfaction has become good. Rather, our reaction to the example is that the subject has become the victim of a senseless passion. The amount of time and effort he devotes to his plan does not make us confident that this is where his good lies; on the contrary, this feature of the example is precisely what inclines us to think that he is wasting his time.

Some philosophers will react to this case by saying that if the icicle fanatic really has carefully considered all of the alternatives available to him, and decides after due deliberation that this is the plan he wishes to pursue, then, peculiar as it may seem, the satisfaction of this desire *is* where his good lies. Who are we, it might be asked rhetorically, to stand in judgment of his conception of the good? To this it can be replied that we cannot responsibly avoid considering the specific content of people's projects when we make decisions about whether we should assist them. If the icicle fanatic appealed to us for financial support, we would not and should not set aside doubts about whether he is doing himself any good, and these doubts arise precisely because we focus on the object of his desire and fail to see why it is worth his while to undertake this project.

IV

There is one other aspect of the desire theory that should be considered, before I propose an alternative approach. The theory holds that it is the satisfaction of *my* desires that constitutes my good. We can gain a better perspective on the theory if we construe it as one among a family of closely related views. For example, what we might call the parental desire theory would hold that what makes something good for a person is the fact that it is something *his parents* want for him. The sibling desire theory and the grandparent desire theory would have the same structure: each could identify the good of X with the satisfaction of the desires some Y has regarding X, alternative versions of the theory picking out a different Y. The desire theory is the special case in which Y is identical to X. This leads us to ask why we should take the desire theory to be more plausible than the parental desire theory or any other member of this family of theories. We cannot reply: because each person knows where his best interest lies. For we recognize that as a

hazardous generalization. If the parental desire theory must be rejected because there are times when parents fail to have the necessary love and knowledge to guide the lives of their children, then we will be faced with the question why these failures cannot also occur in the relation one has to oneself.

Perhaps the parental desire theory (and all other variations in which X is not identical to Y) should be rejected because its general acceptance would lead to passivity and submissiveness. Children would continually make their most important decisions by looking to the blueprint for their lives drawn up by others, and they would fail to develop such qualities as self-reliance, creativity, autonomy and the like. But why should we think that these are qualities that children should develop? An appealing answer is that it is part of a person's good to be a designer of one's life and a molder of one's desires. But that is not a suggestion the desire theorist can accept because, according to that theory, if my good consists partly in exercising initiative and expressing autonomy, then that is true only on condition that these are qualities I want to have. If I don't want them because I haven't been educated to value them, then, according to the desire theory, my lacking them is in itself no loss.

Although no one thinks that the parental desire theory is correct, there is nonetheless a modest and obvious truth that lies in its vicinity, namely that in the first stages of human life, it is best for children to be looked after by adults who take responsibility for their present and future good. And one reason why this is so is because there are many things that are or will be good for children that they are in no position to know about and cannot be said to want. A baby wants food, warmth, stimulation, and contact; but we cannot attribute to it a desire to develop its capacities or to be nurtured in the customs of its society. Education about these matters is beneficial for children, but the desire-theory cannot easily explain why, because children are for a time too young to have any desire for such learning. The desire-theory says that one's well-being is constituted by the satisfaction of one's desires, but the example of small children forces us to recognize a gap in the theory: it cannot be one's present desires alone that constitute one's well-being.

The gap could be filled if we say that the satisfaction of one's future desires is also a component of well-being. Even though a child may not now want an education she will want this at some future time, and so it is in her interests if we prepare her for the satisfaction of this future desire. But this way of expanding the desire theory does not fully capture our reasons for educating children: the child isn't going to have a desire to be educated independently of the way we bring her up; rather we train her so that she develops this desire and can satisfy it, and we do so because we think that having and satisfying this desire will be good for her. We encourage the interest children show in music, or their curiosity about the natural world, because we think it is and will be good for them to have a love of music or of nature. But there is nothing inevitable about their developing these desires. When we promote the future good of young children, we do not merely aim at desire satisfaction in general, but we try to instill certain desires rather than others on the grounds that some things are worth developing a desire for, and others are not.

V

I conclude from what I have said so far that wanting something does not by itself confer desirability on what we want or getting it. It is intelligible and at times appropriate to act on the thought, "I want to do this, even though I don't think that it's good for me or will make my life better." That expresses the attitude many of us normally have towards our whims and impulses. Although we act on them, and need not be subject to criticism for doing so, we don't puff up the importance of these desires by supposing that it will be good even to the slightest degree if they are satisfied.

But if wanting something does not make it good for the want to be satisfied, then we have

to ask what does. My response is that what makes a desire good to satisfy is its being a desire for something that has features that make it worth wanting. Notice the difference between this approach and the one that lies behind the desire theory. It says that we confer goodness on objects by wanting them; by contrast, my idea is that the objects we desire must prove themselves worthy of being wanted by having certain characteristics. If they lack features that make them worth wanting, then the fact that we want them does not make up for that deficiency.

The sort of view I have in mind can also be expressed if I switch for the moment from talking about what people want to talking about what they love. It is widely accepted that someone who is living a good life should love something or someone. If one has no interests or attachments at all, how can one's life be going well? Or if one is only slightly interested in things, if one has no strong emotional attachments, then that too is a deficiency, because there are objects to which a more enthusiastic response is appropriate. But, according to the conception of the good that I am presenting, some things are worthy of our interest and love, whereas others are not. So what makes one's life a good one is one's caring about something worth caring about. But of course that cannot be the whole story, because we can care a great deal about what is worthy of love and yet be cut off from it in some way. Imagine someone who loves painting but is imprisoned and unable to carry out her work; or someone who loves his children but is prevented from having any relationship with them. These people may love what is worth loving, but they don't have a satisfactory relationship with what they love, and as a result their lives are not going well. So, there are at least three conditions that make a life a good one: one must love something, what one loves must be worth loving, and one must be related in the right way to what one loves. Perhaps other conditions must be specified, but I will not explore that possibility here.

It might be objected that the thesis I am proposing is empty unless it is backed by a systematic theory that enables us to decide which among alternative ways of life is most worth living and which objects are most worth loving. It would of course be nice to have such a theory, but it is possible to do without one and still make defensible judgments about what is worth wanting and what is not. Recall the examples used earlier: we can judge, without having a systematic conception of the good, that the self-punisher is harming himself by doing boring, arduous, and insignificant work; or that the icicle fanatic is wasting his time. To take other cases: We believe that in normal circumstances only a certain amount of attention deserves to be paid to such things as neatness, appearance, or health, and we consider an interest that goes beyond this to be obsessive, because it undermine's a person's good. We think that certain intellectual or artistic projects would be a waste of time because they would produce uninteresting results or none at all. To take another sort of case: if someone devotes considerable time to friendships with people who are contemptible and undeserving of affection, then we think that his life is to some degree misspent.

What these examples suggest is that when we choose the objects of our interests successfully we can justify our choice of a way of life by pointing to the qualities of those objects. We have more to say in these cases than "this is what I want to do," we can explain why we want to do these things by describing the admirable qualities of the objects we love. And by educating others to recognize and care about those qualities, we can rationally persuade them that it was worth their while for them to develop an interest in objects to which they were initially indifferent.

If this approach is correct, then certain widespread and powerful human desires may be such that their satisfaction does us no good. Consider, for example, the desire to have positions of power over other people, simply tor its own sake. Those who love power in this way are not making any obvious error of fact or reasoning. Yet, if one asks what it is about power that makes it worth loving, it is hard to know how to answer

or even to see that the question admits of an answer. Someone who develops a desire for power does not do so by being trained to focus on its properties; we don't become sensitized or educated so that we can respond to or articulate the admirable qualities that power has. So it's no wonder that we draw a blank when we ask what it is about power that makes it desirable.

Notice how different the situation is when it comes to certain other things we care about. If we are experienced and articulate, we can say a great deal about why we love our favorite novel or piece of music or friend. This is because we become attached to these objects through a process of training that makes us adept at recognizing and articulating certain properties that we respond to. Power, by contrast, is typically sought for no reason at all. And if we reject the desire theory, then we have no reason to think that satisfying the desire for power is in itself good for people. The same holds true of other deep-seated worldly motives, such as the desires for fame, recognition, and wealth.

It is here that we find one of the greatest contrasts between certain traditional conceptions of the good and the desire theory. The older conceptions took the desires for power, reputation, wealth, and the like to be, at best, of limited value; in fact, despite many disagreements among Platonists, Aristotelians, Stoics, Epicureans, and Christians about what the good is, there was until recent times a striking consensus among philosophers in these traditions that strong desires for power, status, material goods, and the like are contrary to self-interest properly understood. By contrast, the desire theory must hold that, so long as we pursue these goals without psychological division and with open eyes, making no mistake of fact or logic, then they are no less worth pursuing as ends than any other possible goals. That is why I said earlier that the chief weakness of the desire theory is that it is too accepting of desires as they stand and that it underestimates the ways in which we can subject desires to criticism. The desire theory does not demand that the objects in which we take an interest have in themselves desirable features, since its basic idea is that we invest those objects with desirability by being attracted to them. Traditional conceptions are more able to criticize desires as they stand because they insist that the objects we love prove themselves worthy of our interest by their possession of desirable characteristics.

VI

The controversial nature of the proposal I am making can be brought out still further if we notice what it says about pain. It is often taken to be obvious that physical pain is in itself bad; but my doubts about the intrinsic goodness of power lead me also to question the intrinsic badness of pain. When I said that power is not good in itself, my reason was that I saw no feature of it that makes it worth wanting. Similarly, even though we all want to avoid pain, I see no feature of it that makes it worthy of avoidance. We don't notice any characteristic of pain that grounds our aversion to it; we just hate the way it feels. But according to my proposal that is not enough to show that it really is bad in itself. Just as our going for something does not show it to be good, so our avoiding it does not show it to be bad. And the fact that we *all* avoid it, and instinctively so, does not show it to be bad either. Our instincts are subject to evaluation, and so something more must be said about our aversion to pain besides its instinctual character, if we are to conclude that it is bad in itself.

To avoid misunderstanding, let me add that of course I think that pain is almost always bad to some extent. But my reason for thinking this has to do with the things that physical pain normally accompanies, namely some injury or the interruption of healthy processes. Almost every pain distracts us from devoting full attention to the things we care about, and over time pain depresses the level of energy we have. Pain is an animal's generally reliable mechanism for keeping it out of harm's way, and this applies no less to human animals than others. When we take into account the other events that accompany pain, we can see why it is generally

bad for us to some degree. What I am questioning is whether, when we leave aside these other features of pain and just concentrate on the way it feels, we have any reason to think it is bad, and not merely something we dislike.

Perhaps I can create some doubt about whether pain is intrinsically bad by calling attention to a number of other sensations that are disliked even though they are not physically painful: for example, foul odors and grating noises. Should we say that these are in themselves bad to experience, apart from the harm they typically bring about by distracting or annoying us? Suppose I am the only person who is repelled by a certain sound, and everyone else is indifferent to it: if we say that it is intrinsically bad for me but not for others to hear the sound, then we are presupposing that it is a person's likes and dislikes that create what is good and bad for him. And we will then have to say that satisfying our whims and urges is good, and in particular that it is good for the boy in our earlier example to hit the duck. On the other hand, if we say that a grating sound is bad for me to hear only if everyone else has the same response then we have to explain why the reaction of others should be so important to my good. The most plausible way of disposing of this whole problem is to say that we should not infer from our aversion to something that it is contrary to our good, just as we should not infer from the presence of an urge that it does one good to satisfy it. If we accept this proposal, then we should become doubtful abut the intrinsic badness of pain.

VII

There is one further matter that should be addressed before we return to the theme of pluralism with which we began. I have been focusing exclusively on the *human* good and have said nothing about the good of other sorts of animals. But it might be objected that this is the wrong way to go about things, because we need to locate the human good within a framework that has broader application. And it should be obvious that much of what I have said about the human good does not apply to other animals. I claim that for a human life to go well one must love something worth loving. But it would be absurd to hold that the life of a non-human animal goes well only on this condition. What in the life of a salmon or a snake or a mole is worth loving? Can these animals be said to love anything at all?

The inapplicability of these conditions of human well being to non-human life might suggest that we have been on the wrong track all along. Perhaps we should have begun by looking for an account of well being that covers all cases, not just the human condition. Such a thought may partially account for the attraction of hedonism to earlier thinkers. Pleasure and pain guide the behavior of all animals; and hedonists, ancient and modern, have always appealed to the universality of these forces to support their doctrine. Hedonism has an apparent advantage in that it determines the good of all animals with one fell swoop. But we should not be impressed, for the implausibility of hedonism as applied to human life still stands. What we must do therefore is find some substitute for it. We need a general account of the well being of all animals, and then we must ask how the more specific conception of human well being is related to this broader framework.

The general formula that we should apply across the board is one that we find in Aristotle and the Stoics, namely that the good for each animal consists in leading the kind of life that is appropriate to its nature, And since each animal species has a different nature, we must consider the peculiar physical characteristics of each species to determine more specifically where its good lies. The nature of non-human animals is fixed by their bodies and physical capacities, and so for them living well consists in the maintenance of physical health and the full use of the capacities of their bodies. That is why the confinement of a bird to a small space would be contrary to its good, even if it were attached during its confinement to a machine that constantly stimulated the pleasure center of its brain.

But what should we say about the peculiar nature of human beings? Because of our possession of the kind of brain we have, the lives we can lead are far less restricted than are those of other animals. Our intellectual capacity allows far greater plasticity in our development, and it makes the kind of life we lead far more a matter of choice than it is for other animals. The good of a non-human animal is, as it were, built into its body, whereas for human beings the good is an object of rational choice and its achievement requires the training of desires and emotions so that they take appropriate objects as determined by reason. This is not to deny that we have a nature. Rather, it is to say that it is our nature to be choosers, to be capable of using reason to make choices and to mold our desires and emotions. And so the nature of human beings is reflected in our theory of the good when we say that in order for our lives to go well our desires and emotions must be directed at objects whose features make them appropriate choices for us. It is implicit in the notion of choiceworthiness that the objects of our desires are open to evaluation by means of reflection. By insisting that desire satisfaction is not in itself good, that the object of the desire must be worth wanting, we bring in the need for evaluation and reflection, and we thus ground our good in our capacity for rational choice. We explain the human good not as hedonism does, by means of a single comprehensive theory applicable to all animals, but by a two-stage process in which a broad account that applies universally is then made more specific by being tied to the peculiarities of the human situation.

Since I have accepted the traditional view that our nature as human beings consists in the exercise of our capacity for rational choice, it might be asked why I do not go further and accept a more determinate conception of the good, one that holds that human lives are worthwhile to the extent that they are devoted to reasoning. My reply is that the extent to which it is intrinsically worthwhile to engage in reasoning, or good reasoning, is itself a matter that is subject to rational evaluation; there is no self-contradiction in the idea that one might *reason* to the conclusion that there are activities that are better than *reasoning*, or that one's life goes best if reason plays a secondary or minor role. So the fact that reasoning is distinctive of human beings does not itself determine the proper place of reasoning in a human life. The best way of establishing the importance of reason in a good life is to take note of the various kinds of worthwhile activities there are, and recognize how many of them we would be incapable of undertaking, if our capacity for reasoning were seriously impaired.

VIII

We can now return to the ideas with which we started: that the good for human beings is highly varied, that there is no single master good that measures the worth of all others; that there is no specific kind of life that is best for everyone. Pluralism, so construed, is a newcomer to the philosophical scene, and it is worth asking whether any arguments can be found for it. One of the apparent attractions of the desire theory is that it offers an explanation for this variety, but in light of that theory's deficiencies we have reason to seek an alternative account of why pluralism about the good might be true.

A better way to defend pluralistic intuitions, I suggest, is to accept the general thesis that some objects of human pursuit have qualities that make them objectively worth wanting and that others are without merit, but to reject any of the more specific theses that have been proposed in the past about how to achieve a more determinate ranking of human lives. The modern philosophers sense that many different kinds of lives are worth living, but that we cannot arrange them in a hierarchy ranging from best to worst,

is best supported by concrete illustration rather than a highly general argument: the favored strategy should be to take note of all of the different objects that are worth pursuing and the diversity of worthwhile lives devoted to these pursuits, and then to show that none of the objective conceptions of the good with which we are familiar from the history of philosophy does justice to this rich variety. But this pluralistic project cannot succeed simply by pointing to the great variety of lives people in fact lead; what must be shown is considerably more difficult, namely that these different kinds of lives are worth living, and none more so than any others.

If this is correct, then the hierarchical conceptions of the good that are now out of favor cannot be undermined with a single blow; if there is no supremely desirable object or life, in comparison with which all other objects or lives must be evaluated, then this must be established on a case-by-case basis by showing why each proposed candidate fails to provide a plausible standard. The defender of the multiplicity of the human good must support this thesis by persuading us that many different types of thing are worth wanting and by showing why we should reject attempts to assign each of them a discrete place on a single hierarchical scale. Although I am sympathetic to such a project, I have not undertaken it here. My main point has been that the multiplicity of the good cannot be directly inferred from the variability of human desire. So my conclusion is a conditional one: if we wish to be pluralists, then we should accept the point, once widely taken for granted, that in deciding which sorts of lives it is good to live, we cannot bypass the task of evaluating our desires by asking whether their objects possess the qualities that make them worth wanting.

4.4 My Confession

LEO TOLSTOY

Count Leo Tolstoy (1828–1910) was one of the great Russian novelists. His works include Anna Karenina *and* War and Peace.

Although I regarded authorship as a waste of time, I continued to write during those fifteen years. I had tasted of the seduction of authorship, of the seduction of enormous monetary remunerations and applauses for my insignificant labour, and so I submitted to it, as being a means for improving my material condition and for stifling in my soul all questions about the meaning of my life and life in general.

In my writing I advocated, what to me was the only truth, that it was necessary to live in such a way as to derive the greatest comfort for oneself and one's family.

Thus I proceeded to live, but five years ago something very strange began to happen with me: I was overcome by minutes at first of perplexity and then of an arrest of life, as though I did not know how to live or what to do, and I lost myself and was dejected. But that passed, and I continued to live as before. Then those minutes of perplexity were repeated oftener and oftener, and always in one and the same form. These arrests of life found their expression in ever the same questions: "Why? Well, and then?"

At first I thought that those were simply aimless, inappropriate questions. It seemed to me that that was all well known and that if I ever wanted to busy myself with their solution, it would not cost me much labour,—that now I had no time to attend to them, but that if I wanted to I should find the proper answers. But the questions began to repeat themselves oftener and oftener, answers were demanded more and more persistently, and, like dots that fall on the same spot, these questions, without any answers, thickened into one black blotch.

There happened what happens with any person who falls ill with a mortal internal disease. At first there appear insignificant symptoms of indisposition, to which the patient pays no attention; then these symptoms are repeated more and more frequently and blend into one temporally indivisible suffering. The suffering keeps growing, and before the patient has had time to look around, he becomes conscious that what he took for an indisposition is the most significant thing in the world to him,—is death.

The same happened with me. I understood that it was not a passing indisposition, but something very important, and that, if the questions were going to repeat themselves, it would be necessary to find an answer for them. And I tried to answer them. The questions seemed to be so foolish, simple, and childish. But the moment I touched them and tried to solve them, I became convinced, in the first place, that they were not childish and foolish, but very important and profound questions in life, and, in the second, that, no matter how much I might try, I should not be able to answer them. Before attending to my Samára estate, to my son's education, or to the writing of a book, I ought to know why I should do that. So long as I did not know why, I could not do anything. I could not live. Amidst my thoughts of farming, which interested me very much during that time, there would suddenly pass through my head a question like this: "All right, you are going to have six thousand desyatínas of land in the Government of Samára, and

From Leo Tolstoy, *My Confession* (Dent, 1905), trans. Leo Weiner.

three hundred horses,—and then?" And I completely lost my senses and did not know what to think farther Or, when I thought of the education of my children, I said to myself: "Why?" Or, reflecting on the manner in which the masses might obtain their welfare, I suddenly said to myself: "What is that to me?" Or, thinking of the fame which my works would get me, I said to myself: "All right, you will be more famous than Gógol, Púshkin, Shakespeare, Molière, and all the writers in the world,—what of it?" And I was absolutely unable to make any reply. The questions were not waiting, and I had to answer them at once; if I did not answer them, I could not live....

All that happened with me when I was on every side surrounded by what is considered to be complete happiness. I had a good, loving, and beloved wife, good children, and a large estate, which grew and increased without any labour on my part. I was respected by my neighbours and friends, more than ever before, was praised by strangers, and, without any self-deception, could consider my name famous. With all that, I was not deranged or mentally unsound,—on the contrary, I was in full command of my mental and physical powers, such as I had rarely met with in people of my age: physically I could work in a field, mowing, without falling behind a peasant; mentally I could work from eight to ten hours in succession, without experiencing any consequences from the strain. And while in such condition I arrived at the conclusion that I could not live, and, fearing death, I had to use cunning against myself, in order that I might not take my life.

This mental condition expressed itself to me in this form: my life is a stupid, mean trick played on me by somebody. Although I did not recognize that "somebody" as having created me, the form of the conception that someone had played a mean, stupid trick on me by bringing me into the world was the most natural one that presented itself to me.

Involuntarily I imagined that there, somewhere, there was somebody who was now having fun as he looked down upon me and saw me, who had lived for thirty or forty years, learning, developing, growing in body and mind, now that I had become strengthened in mind and had reached that summit of life from which it lay all before me, standing as a complete fool on that summit and seeing clearly that there was nothing in life and never would be. And that was fun to him—

But whether there was or was not that somebody who made fun of me, did not make it easier for me. I could not ascribe any sensible meaning to a single act, or to my whole life. I was only surprised that I had not understood that from the start. All that had long ago been known to everybody. Sooner or later there would come diseases and death (they had come already) to my dear ones and to me, and there would be nothing left but stench and worms. All my affairs, no matter what they might be, would sooner or later be forgotten, and I myself should not exist. So why should I worry about all these things? How could a man fail to see that and live, —that was surprising! A person could live only so long as he was drunk; but the moment he sobered up, he could not help seeing that all that was only a deception, and a stupid deception at that! Really, there was nothing funny and ingenious about it, but only something cruel and stupid.

Long ago has been told the Eastern story about the traveller who in the steppe is overtaken by an infuriated beast. Trying to save himself from the animal, the traveller jumps into a waterless well, but at its bottom he sees a dragon who opens his jaws in order to swallow him. And the unfortunate man does not dare climb out, lest he perish from the infuriated beast, and does not dare jump down to the bottom of the well, lest he be devoured by the dragon, and so clutches the twig of a wild bush growing in the cleft of the well and holds on to it. His hands grow weak and he feels that soon he shall have to surrender to the peril which awaits him at either side; but he still holds on and sees two mice, one white, the other black, in even measure making a circle around the main trunk of the bush to which he is clinging, and nibbling at it on all sides. Now, at any moment, the bush will break and tear off, and he will fall into the dragon's jaws. The traveller sees that and knows that he will inevitably perish; but while he is still clinging, he sees some drops of honey hanging on the leaves of the bush, and so reaches out for them with his tongue and licks the leaves. Just so I hold on to the branch of life, knowing that the dragon of death is waiting inevitably for me, ready to tear me to pieces, and I cannot understand why I have fallen on such suffering. And I try to lick that honey which used to give me pleasure; but now it no longer gives me joy, and the white and the black mouse day and night nibble at the branch to which I am holding on. I clearly see the dragon, and the honey is no longer sweet to me. I see only the inevitable dragon and the mice, and am unable to turn my glance away from them. That is not a fable, but a veritable, indisputable, comprehensible truth.

The former deception of the pleasures of life, which stifled the terror of the dragon, no longer deceives me. No matter how much one should say to me, "You cannot understand the meaning of life, do not think, live!" I am unable to do so, because I have been doing it too long before. Now I cannot help seeing day and night, which run and lead me up to death. I see that alone, because that alone is the truth. Everything else is a lie.

The two drops of honey that have longest turned my eyes away from the cruel truth, the love of family and of authorship, which I have called an art, are no longer sweet to me.

"My family—" I said to myself, "but my family, my wife and children, they are also human beings. They are in precisely the same condition that I am in: they must either live in the lie or see the terrible truth. Why should they live? Why should I love them, why guard, raise, and watch them? Is it for the same despair which is in me, or for dullness of perception? Since I love them, I cannot conceal the truth from them,—every step in cognition leads them up to this truth. And the truth is death."

"Art, poetry?" For a long time, under the influence of the success of human praise, I tried to persuade myself that that was a thing which could be done, even though death should come and destroy everything, my deeds, as well as my memory of them; but soon I came to see that that, too, was a deception. It was clear to me that art was an adornment of life, a decoy of life. But life lost all its attractiveness for me. How, then, could I entrap others? So long as I did not live my own life, and a strange life bore me on its waves; so long as I believed that life had some sense, although I was not able to express it,—the reflections of life of every description in poetry and in the arts afforded me pleasure, and I was delighted to look at life through this little mirror of art; but when I began to look for the meaning of life, when I experienced the necessity of living myself, that little mirror became either useless, superfluous, and ridiculous, or painful to me. I could no longer console myself with what I was in the mirror, namely, that my situation was stupid and desperate....

By abandoning myself to the bright side of knowledge I saw that I only turned my eyes away from the question. No matter how enticing and clear the horizons were that were disclosed to me, no matter how enticing it was to bury myself in the infinitude of this knowledge, I comprehended that these sciences were the more clear, the less I needed them, the less they answered my question.

"Well, I know," I said to myself, "all which science wants so persistently to know, but there is no answer to the question about the meaning of my life." But in the speculative sphere I saw that, in spite of the fact that the aim of the knowledge was directed straight to the answer of my question, or because of that fact, there could be no other answer than what I was giving to myself: "What is the meaning of my life?"—"None." Or, "What will come of my life?"—"Nothing." Or, "Why does everything which exists exist, and why do I exist?"—"Because it exists."

Putting the question to the one side of human knowledge, I received an endless quantity of exact answers about what I did not ask: about the chemical composition of the stars, about the movement of the sun toward the constellation of Hercules, about the origin of species and of man, about the forms of infinitely small, imponderable particles of ether; but the answer in this sphere of knowledge to my question what the meaning of my life was, was always: "You are what you call your life; you are a temporal, accidental conglomeration of particles. The interrelation, the change of these particles, produces in you that which you call life. This congeries will last for some time; then the interaction of these particles will cease, and that which you call life and all your questions will come to an end. You are an accidentally cohering globule of something. The globule is fermenting. This fermentation the globule calls its life. The globule falls to pieces, and all fermentation and all questions will come to an end." Thus the clear side of knowledge answers, and it cannot say anything else, if only it strictly follows its principles.

With such an answer it appears that the answer is not a reply to the question. I want to know the meaning of my life, but the fact that it is a particle of the infinite not only gives it no meaning, but even destroys every possible meaning....

I lived for a long time in this madness, which, not in words, but in deeds, is particularly characteristic of us, the most liberal and learned of men. But, thanks either to my strange, physical love for the real working class, which made me understand it and see that it is not so stupid as we suppose, or to the sincerity of my conviction, which was that I could know nothing and that the best that I could do was to hang myself, —I felt that if I wanted to live and understand the meaning of life, I ought naturally to look for it, not among those who had lost the meaning of life and wanted to kill themselves, but among those billions of departed and living men who had been carrying their own lives and ours upon their shoulders. And I looked around at the enormous masses of deceased and living men, not learned and wealthy, but simple men, —and I saw something quite different. I saw that all these billions of men that lived or had lived,

all, with rare exceptions, did not fit into my subdivisions, and that I could not recognize them as not understanding the question, because they themselves put it and answered it with surprising clearness. Nor could I recognize them as Epicureans, because their lives were composed rather of privations and suffering than of enjoyment. Still less could I recognize them as senselessly living out their meaningless lives, because every act of theirs and death itself was explained by them. They regarded it as the greatest evil to kill themselves. It appeared, then, that all humanity was in possession of a knowledge of the meaning of life, which I did not recognize and which I condemned. It turned out that rational knowledge did not give any meaning to life, excluded life, while the meaning which by billions of people, by all humanity, was ascribed to life was based on some despised, false knowledge.

The rational knowledge in the person of the learned and the wise denied the meaning of life, but the enormous masses of men, all humanity, recognized this meaning in an irrational knowledge. This irrational knowledge was faith, the same that I could not help but reject. That was God as one and three, the creation in six days, devils and angels, and all that which I could not accept so long as I had not lost my senses.

My situation was a terrible one. I knew that I should not find anything on the path of rational knowledge but the negation of life, and there, in faith, nothing but the negation of reason, which was still more impossible than the negation of life. From the rational knowledge it followed that life was an evil and men knew it,— it depended on men whether they should cease living, and yet they lived and continued to live, and I myself lived, though I had known long ago that life was meaningless and an evil. From faith it followed that, in order to understand life, I must renounce reason, for which alone a meaning was needed.

There resulted a contradiction, from which there were two ways out: either what I called rational was not so rational as I had thought; or that which to me appeared irrational was not so irrational as I had thought. And I began to verify the train of thoughts of my rational knowledge.

In verifying the train of thoughts of my rational knowledge, I found that it was quite correct. The deduction that life was nothing was inevitable; but I saw a mistake. The mistake was that I had not reasoned in conformity with the question put by me. The question was, "Why should I live?" that is, "What real, indestructible essence will come from my phantasmal, destructible life? What meaning has my finite existence in this infinite world?" And in order to answer this question, I studied life.

The solutions of all possible questions of life apparently could not satisfy me, because my question, no matter how simple it appeared in the beginning, included the necessity of explaining the finite through the infinite, and vice versa.

I asked, "What is the extra-temporal, extra-causal, extra-spatial meaning of life?" But I gave an answer to the question, "What is the temporal, causal, spatial meaning of my life?" The result was that after a long labour of mind I answered, "None."...

When I saw that [...for philosophy the solution remains insoluble,] I understood that it was not right for me to look for an answer to my question in rational knowledge, and that the answer given by rational knowledge was only an indication that the answer might be got if the question were differently put, but only when into the discussion of the question should be introduced the question of the relation of the finite to the infinite. I also understood that, no matter how irrational and monstrous the answers might be that faith gave, they had this advantage that they introduced into each answer the relation of the finite to the infinite, without which there could be no answer.

No matter how I may put the question, "How must I live?" the answer is, "According to God's law." "What real result will there be from my life?"—"Eternal torment or eternal bliss." "What is the meaning which is not destroyed by death?"—"The union with infinite God, paradise."

Thus, outside the rational knowledge, which had to me appeared as the only one, I was inevitably led to recognize that all living humanity had a certain other irrational knowledge, faith, which made it possible to live.

All the irrationality of faith remained the same for me, but I could not help recognizing that it alone gave to humanity answers to the questions of life, and, in consequence of them, the possibility of living.

The rational knowledge brought me to the recognition that life was meaningless,—my life stopped, and I wanted to destroy myself. When I looked around at people, at all humanity, I saw that people lived and asserted that they knew the meaning of life. I looked back at myself: I lived so long as I knew the meaning of life. As to other people, so even to me, did faith give the meaning of life and the possibility of living.

Looking again at the people of other countries, contemporaries of mine and those passed away, I saw again the same. Where life had been, there faith, ever since humanity had existed, had given the possibility of living, and the chief features of faith were everywhere one and the same.

No matter what answers faith may give, its every answer gives to the finite existence of man the sense of the infinite,—a sense which is not destroyed by suffering, privation, and death. Consequently in faith alone could we find the meaning and possibility of life. What, then, was faith? I understood that faith was not merely an evidence of things not seen, and so forth, not revelation (that is only the description of one of the symptoms of faith), not the relation of man to man (faith has to be defined, and then God, and not first God, and faith through him), not merely an agreement with what a man was told, as faith was generally understood,—that faith was the knowledge of the meaning of human life, in consequence of which man did not destroy himself, but lived. Faith is the power of life. If a man lives he believes in something. If he did not believe that he ought to live for some purpose, he would not live. If he does not see and understand the phantasm of the finite, he believes in that finite, if he understands the phantasm of the finite, he must believe in the infinite. Without faith one cannot live....

In order that all humanity may be able to live, in order that they may continue living, giving a meaning to life, they, those billions, must have another, a real knowledge of faith, for not the fact that I, with Solomon and Schopenhauer, did not kill myself convinced me of the existence of faith, but that these billions had lived and had borne us, me and Solomon, on the waves of life.

Then I began to cultivate the acquaintance of the believers from among the poor, the simple and unlettered folk, of pilgrims, monks, dissenters, peasants. The doctrine of these people from among the masses was also the Christian doctrine that the quasi-believers of our circle professed. With the Christian truths were also mixed in very many superstitions, but there was this difference: the superstitions of our circle were quite unnecessary to them, had no connection with their lives, were only a kind of an Epicurean amusement, while the superstitions of the believers from among the labouring classes were to such an extent blended with their life that it would have been impossible to imagine it without these superstitions,—it was a necessary condition of that life. I began to examine closely the lives and beliefs of these people, and the more I examined them, the more did I become convinced that they had the real faith, that their faith was necessary for them, and that it alone gave them a meaning and possibility of life. In contradistinction to what I saw in our circle, where life without faith was possible, and where hardly one in a thousand professed to be a believer, among them there was hardly one in a thousand who was not a believer. In contradistinction to what I saw in our circle, where all life passed in idleness, amusements, and tedium of life, I saw that the whole life of these people was passed in hard work, and that they were satisfied with life. In contradistinction to the people of our circle, who struggled and murmured against fate because of their privations and their suffering, these people accepted diseases and sorrows without any perplexity or opposition, but with the calm and firm conviction that it was all for good. In contradistinction to the fact that the more intelligent we are, the less do we understand the meaning of life and the more do we see a kind of a bad joke in our suffering and death, these people live, suffer, and approach death, and suffer in peace and more often in joy. In contradistinction to the fact that a calm death, a death without terror or despair, is the greatest exception in our circle, a restless, insubmissive, joyless death is one of the greatest exceptions among the masses. And of such people, who are deprived of everything which for Solomon and for me constitutes the only good of life, and who withal experience the greatest happiness, there is an enormous number. I cast a broader glance about me. I examined the life of past and present vast masses of men, and I saw people who in like manner had understood the meaning of life, who had known how to live and die, not two, not three, not ten, but hundreds, thousands, millions. All of them, infinitely diversified as to habits, intellect, culture, situation, all equally and quite contrary to my ignorance knew the meaning of life and of death, worked calmly, bore privations and suffering, lived and died, seeing in that not vanity, but good.

I began to love those people. The more I penetrated into their life, the life of the men now living, and the life of men departed, of whom I had read and heard, the more did I love them, and the easier it became for me to live. Thus I lived for about two years, and within me took place a transformation, which had long been working within me, and the germ of which had always been in me. What happened with me was that the life of our circle,—of the rich and the learned,—not only disgusted me, but even lost all its meaning. All our acts, reflections, sciences, arts,—all that appeared to me in a new light. I saw that all that was mere pampering of the appetites, and that no meaning could be found in it; but the life of all the working masses, of all humanity, which created life, presented itself to me in its real significance. I saw that that was life itself and that the meaning given to this life was truth, and I accepted it.

4.5 Happiness and Meaning: Two Aspects of the Good Life

SUSAN WOLF

The topic of self-interest raises large and intractable philosophical questions—most obviously, the question "In what does self-interest consist?" The concept, as opposed to the content of self-interest, however, seems clear enough. Self-interest is interest in one's own good. To act self-interestedly is to act on the motive of advancing one's own good. Whether what one does actually is in one's self-interest depends on whether it actually does advance, or at least, minimize the decline of, one's own good. Though it may be difficult to tell whether a person is motivated by self-interest in a particular instance, and difficult also to determine whether a given act or decision really is in one's self-interest, the meaning of the claims in question seems unproblematic.

My main concern in this essay is to make a point about the content of self-interest.[1] Specifically I shall put forward the view that meaningfulness, in a sense I shall elaborate, is an important element of a good life. It follows, then, that it is part of an enlightened self-interest that one wants to secure meaning in one's life, or, at any rate, to allow and promote meaningful activity within it. Accepting this substantial conception of self-interest, however, carries with it a curious consequence: the concept of self-interest which formerly seemed so clear begins to grow fuzzy. Fortunately, it comes to seem less important as well.

1. THEORIES OF SELF-INTEREST

In *Reasons and Persons*,[2] Derek Parfit distinguishes three sorts of theories about self-interest—hedonistic theories, preference theories, and what he calls "objective-list theories." *Hedonistic theories* hold that one's good is a matter of the felt quality of one's experiences. The most popular theory of self-interest, which identifies self-interest with happiness, and happiness with pleasure and the absence of pain, is a prime

example of a hedonistic theory. Noting that some people do not care that much about their own happiness, however—and, importantly, that they do not even regard their own happiness as the exclusive element of their own good—has led some to propose a *preference theory of self-interest*, which would identify a person's good with what the person most wants for herself. Thus, for example, if a person cares more about being famous, even posthumously famous, than about being happy, then a preference theory would accord fame a proportionate weight in the identification of her self-interest. If a person cares more about knowing the truth than about believing what it is pleasant or comfortable to believe, then it is in her self-interest to have the truth, unpleasant as it may be.

A person's preferences regarding herself, however, may be self-destructive or otherwise bizarre, and it may be that some things (including pleasure) are good for a person whether the person prefers them or not. It is not absurd to think that being deceived is bad for a person (and thus that not being deceived is good for a person) whether or not the person in question

---

Susan Wolf, "Happiness and Meaning: Two Aspects of the Good Life," *Social Philosophy and Policy* (1997) pp. 207–225. Copyright © 1997 Social Philosophy and Policy Foundation. Reprinted with the permission of Cambridge University Press.

consciously values this state. Friendship and love may also seem to be things whose goodness explains, rather than results from, people's preferences for them. The plausibility of these last thoughts explains the appeal of *objective-list theories*, according to which a person's good includes at least some elements that are independent of or prior to her preferences and to their effect on the felt quality of her experience. On this view, there are some items, ideally specifiable on an "objective list," whose relevance to a fully successful life are not conditional on the subject's choice.

The view that I shall be advancing, that meaningfulness is an ingredient of the good life, commits one to a version of this last kind of theory, for my claim is that meaningfulness is a non-derivative aspect of a good life—its goodness does not result from its making us happy or its satisfying the preferences of the person whose life it is. Thus, it follows that any theory that takes self-interest to be a wholly subjective matter, either in a sense that identifies self-interest with the subjective quality of a person's experiences or in a sense that allows the standards of self-interest to be set by a person's subjective preferences, must be inadequate. At the same time, it would be a mistake to think that the objective good of a meaningful life is one that is wholly independent of the subject's experience or preferences, as if it could be good for a person to live a meaningful life whether or not it makes her happy or satisfies her preferences. Indeed, as we will see, the very idea that activities can make a life meaningful without the subject's endorsement is a dubious one.

II. MEANING IN LIFE

What is a meaningful life? Spelling it out will constitute the bulk of my essay, for my hope is that once the idea is *spelled out, it will be readily* agreed that it is an element of a fully successful life.

A meaningful life is, first of all, one that has within it the basis for an affirmative answer to the needs or longings that are characteristically described as needs for meaning. I have in mind, for example, the sort of questions people ask on their deathbeds, or simply in contemplation of their eventual deaths, about whether their lives have been (or are) worth living, whether they have had any point, and the sort of questions one asks when considering suicide and wondering whether one has any reason to go on. These questions are familiar from Russian novels and existentialist philosophy, if not from personal experience. Though they arise most poignantly in times of crisis and intense emotion, they also have their place in moments of calm reflection, when considering important life choices. Moreover, paradigms of what are taken to be meaningful and meaningless lives in our culture are readily available. Lives of great moral or intellectual accomplishment—Gandhi, Mother Teresa, Albert Einstein—come to mind as unquestionably meaningful lives (if any are); lives of waste and isolation—Thoreau's "lives of quiet desperation," typically anonymous to the rest of us, and the mythical figure of Sisyphus—represent meaninglessness.

To what general characteristics of meaningfulness do these images lead us and how do they provide an answer to the longings mentioned above? Roughly, I would say that meaningful lives are lives of active engagement in projects of worth. Of course, a good deal needs to be said in elaboration of this statement. Let me begin by discussing the two key phrases, "active engagement" and "projects of worth."

A person is actively engaged by something if she is gripped, excited, involved by it. Most obviously, we are actively engaged by the things and people about which and whom we are passionate. Opposites of active engagement are boredom and alienation. To be actively engaged in something is not always pleasant in the ordinary sense of the word. Activities in which people are actively engaged frequently involve stress, danger, exertion, or sorrow (consider, for example; writing a book, climbing a mountain, training for a marathon, caring for an ailing friend). However, there is something good about the feeling of engagement: one feels (typically without thinking about it) especially alive.

That a meaningful life must involve "projects of worth" will, I expect, be more controversial, for the phrase hints of a commitment to some sort of objective value. This is not accidental, for I believe that the idea of meaningfulness, and the concern that our lives possess it, are conceptually linked to such a commitment.[3] Indeed, it is this linkage that I want to defend, for I have neither a philosophical theory of what objective value is nor a substantive theory about what has this sort of value. What is clear to me is that there can be no sense to the idea of meaningfulness without a distinction between more and less worthwhile ways to spend one's time, where the test of worth is at least partly independent of a subject's ungrounded preferences or enjoyment.

Consider first the longings or concerns about meaning that people have, their wondering whether their lives are meaningful, their vows to add more meaning to their lives. The sense of these concerns and resolves cannot fully be captured by an account in which what one does with one's life doesn't matter, as long as one enjoys or prefers it. Sometimes people have concerns about meaning despite their knowledge that their lives to date have been satisfying. Indeed, their enjoyment and "active engagement" with activities and values they now see as shallow seems only to heighten the sense of meaninglessness that comes to afflict them. Their sense that their lives so far have been meaningless cannot be a sense that their activities have not been chosen or fun. When they look for sources of meaning or ways to add meaning to their lives, they are searching for projects whose justifications lie elsewhere.

Second, we need an explanation for why certain sorts of activities and involvements come to mind as contributors to meaningfulness while others seem intuitively inappropriate. Think about what gives meaning to your own life and the lives of your friends and acquaintances. Among the things that tend to come up on such lists, I have already mentioned moral and intellectual accomplishments and the ongoing activities that lead to them. Relationships with friends and relatives are perhaps even more important for most of us. Aesthetic enterprises (both creative and appreciative), the cultivation of personal virtues, and religious practices frequently loom large. By contrast, it would be odd, if not bizarre, to think of crossword puzzles, sitcoms, or the kind of computer games to which I am fighting off addiction as providing meaning in our lives, though there is no question that they afford a sort of satisfaction and that they are the objects of choice. Some things, such as chocolate and aerobics class, I choose even at considerable cost to myself (it is irrelevant that these particular choices may be related), so I must find them worthwhile in a sense. But they are not the sorts of things that make life worth living.[4]

"Active engagement in projects of worth," I suggest, answers to the needs an account of meaningfulness in life must meet. If a person is or has been thus actively engaged, then she does have an answer to the question of whether her life is or has been worthwhile, whether it has or has had a point. When someone looks for ways to add meaning to her life, she is looking (though perhaps not under this description) for worthwhile projects about which she can get enthused. The account also explains why some activities and projects but not others come to mind as contributors to meaning in life. Some projects, or at any rate, particular acts, are worthwhile but too boring or mechanical to be sources of meaning. People do not get meaning from recycling or from writing checks to Oxfam and the ACLU. Other acts and activities, though highly pleasurable and deeply involving, like riding a roller coaster or meeting a movie star, do not seem to have the right kind of value to contribute to meaning.

Bernard Williams once distinguished categorical desires from the rest. Categorical desires give us reasons for living—they are not premised on the assumption that we will live. The sorts of things that give meaning to life tend to be objects of categorical desire. We desire them, at least so I would suggest, because we think them worthwhile. They are not worthwhile simply because we desire them or simply because they make our lives more pleasant.

Roughly, then, according to my proposal, a meaningful life must satisfy two criteria, suitably linked. First, there must be active engagement, and second, it must be engagement in (or with) projects of worth. A life is meaningless if it lacks active engagement with anything. A person who is bored or alienated from most of what she spends her life doing is one whose life can be said to lack meaning. Note that she may in fact be performing functions of worth. A housewife and mother, a doctor, or a busdriver may be competently doing a socially valuable job, but because she is not engaged by her work (or, as we are assuming, by anything else in her life), she has no categorical desires that give her a reason to live. At the same time, someone who *is* actively engaged may also live a meaningless life, if the objects of her involvement are utterly worthless. It is difficult to come up with examples of such lives that will be uncontroversial without being bizarre. But both bizarre and controversial examples have their place. In the bizarre category, we might consider pathological cases: someone whose sole passion in life is collecting rubber bands, or memorizing the dictionary, or making handwritten copies of *War and Peace*. Controversial cases will include the corporate lawyer who sacrifices her private life and health for success along the professional ladder, the devotee of a religious cult, or—an example offered by Wiggins[5]—the pig farmer who buys more land to grow more corn to feed more pigs to buy more land to grow more corn to feed more pigs.

We may summarize my proposal in terms of a slogan: "Meaning arises when subjective attraction meets objective attractiveness." The idea is that in a world in which some things are more worthwhile than others, meaning arises when a subject discovers or develops an affinity for one or typically several of the more worthwhile things and has and makes use of the opportunity to engage with it or them in a positive way.

An advantage of the slogan is that it avoids the somewhat misleading reference to "projects." That term is less than ideal in its suggestion of well-defined and goal-oriented tasks. To be sure, many projects do add meaning to life—mastering a field of study, building a house, turning a swamp into a garden, curing cancer—but much of what gives meaning to life consists in ongoing relationships and involvements—with friends, family, the scientific community, with church or ballet or chess. These ongoing strands of life give rise to and are partly constituted by projects — you plan a surprise party for your spouse, coach a little league team, review an article for a journal—but the meaning comes less from the individuated projects than from the larger involvements of which they are parts. The slogan, moreover, is intentionally vague, for if pretheoretical judgments about meaning even approximate the truth, then not only the objects of worth but also the sorts of interaction with them that are capable of contributing to meaning are immensely variable. One can get meaning from creating, promoting, protecting (worthwhile) things, from helping people one loves and people in need, from achieving levels of skill and excellence, from overcoming obstacles, from gaining understanding, and even from just communing with or actively appreciating what is there to be appreciated.

It is part of our job, if not our natural bent, as philosophers to be skeptical—about the correctness of these pretheoretical judgments, about our ability reliably to distinguish meaningful from meaningless activities, and about the very coherence of the distinction. About the first two worries I am not very concerned. Assuming that the distinctions are coherent and that some activities are more worthwhile than others, our culture-bound, contemporary judgments of which activities are worthwhile are bound to be partly erroneous. History is full of unappreciated geniuses, of artists, inventors, explorers whose activities at their time were scorned, as it is full of models of behavior and accomplishment that later seem to have been overrated. Though we may improve our judgments, both particular and general, by an open-minded, concentrated, and communal effort to examine and articulate the basis for them (a project that strikes me as both worthwhile and intrinsically interesting), the hope or expectation that such scrutiny will yield a reliable method for generally distinguishing worthwhile from worthless activities seems overly optimistic. Why do we respect people who devote themselves to chess more than those who become champions at pinball? Why do we admire basketball stars more than jump-rope champions? What is more worthwhile about writing a book on the philosophy of language than writing one on Nicole Brown Simpson's sex life? It is useful to ask and to answer such questions, so far as we can, both to widen and correct our horizons and to increase our understanding. But our inability to give complete and adequate answers, or to be confident in the details of our assessments, need not be a serious problem. The point of recognizing the distinction, after all, is not to give rankings of meaningful lives. There is no need, in general, to pass judgment on individuals or even on activities in which people want to engage. The point is rather at a more general level to understand the ingredients of our own and others' good, and to get a better idea of the sorts of considerations that provide reasons for living our lives one way rather than another.

The point, which I am in the midst of developing, is that meaningfulness is a nonderivative part of an individual's good, and that meaningfulness consists in active engagement in projects or activities of worth. Though it seems to me that the point and most of its usefulness can stand despite acknowledged difficulties with identifying precisely which projects or activities these are, it would be utterly destroyed if it turned out that there were no such things as projects or activities of worth at all—if it turned out, in other words, as Bentham thought, that pushpin were as good as poetry,[6] not because of some heretofore undiscovered excellences in the game of pushpin, but because the very idea of distinctions in worth is bankrupt or incoherent. If there are no projects of worth (in contrast to other projects), then there are no such things as what I have in mind by more and less meaningful

lives, and so it cannot be a part *of one's* good to live a more meaningful rather than a less meaningful life. If the idea of a worthwhile project is just a fraud or a hoax, then my account of self-interest is undone by it.

Since I have no *theory* of worth by which to prove the coherence of the concept or refute all skeptical challenges, I can only acknowledge the vulnerability of my account of self-interest in this regard. That we do, most of us, believe that some activities and projects are more worthwhile than others, that we regard certain activities as wastes of time (or near wastes of time) and others as inherently valuable, seems undeniable. These beliefs lie behind dispositions to feel proud or disgusted with ourselves for time spent well or badly, and they account for at least some of our efforts to steer our children and our friends toward some activities and away from others. Wlien I try to take up a point of view that denies the distinction between worthwhile and worthless activity, I cannot find it convincing. Still, it is an article of faith that these untheoretical judgments, or some core of them, are philosophically defensible. It is on the assumption that they are defensible that my views about meaningfulness and self-interest are built.

III. TWO CHALLENGES

My proposal so far has been that meaningfulness in life arises from engagement in worthwhile activity. I have argued for the plausibility of this account on the grounds that it fits well both with the needs that are typically referred to as needs for meaning and with the concrete judgments of meaningful and meaningless activity that are most commonly made. Before proceeding with an examination of the relation between meaning and self-interest, two challenges to this account of meaning should be answered.

The first objects that, contrary to my claims, my account of meaning fails to meet the requirements I have set up for it. It fails, more particularly, to answer to the needs of at least one type of longing for meaning that members of our species tend to have. Traditional worries about the meaning of life, often set off by reflections on our own mortality and on the indifference of the cosmos in which we occupy so tiny a place, are rarely appeased by the reflection that one can actively engage in projects of worth. At least, they are not appeased by reflection on the availability of the kind of projects I have been talking about, like taking up the cello, writing a novel, volunteering at a child's day-care center or a nursing home. Tolstoy, the publicly acclaimed author of some of the greatest works of literature ever written, the father and spouse of what he described (perhaps inaccurately) as a loving and successful family, could have had no doubt that, relatively speaking, his life was spent in projects as worthwhile as any. Yet he was plagued by the thought that it was all for naught.[7] Nothing he did seemed to save his life from meaninglessness. Like Tolstoy, such philosophers as Albert Camus[8] and Thomas Nagel[9] see the meaning or meaninglessness of life as an issue relating to the human condition. The difference between a person who wastes her time in frivolous or shallow pursuits and one who makes something of herself and serves humanity cannot, on their views, make the difference between a meaningful and a meaningless life.

To try to give a wholly adequate answer to this challenge would take us too far afield from the purposes of this essay. The issue of The Meaning of Life is too obscure and complex, and the differences among the philosophers whose views seem to pose a challenge to the one I am offering call for different responses. Some brief remarks, however, will at least indicate what a more detailed answer might look like and will give some reason for thinking that the challenge can be met.

Among those who think that meaning in life, or the lack of it, is primarily concerned with facts about the human condition, some disagree not with my general account of meaning but with, if you will, its application. Their position, in other words, shares my view that meaning comes from engagement in projects of worth, but assigns certain facts about the human condition a crucial role in settling whether there

are any such projects. If God does not exist, they think, then nothing is any more worthwhile than anything else. Within this group, some believe that God is the only possible standard for judgments of nonsubjective value. If God does not exist, they think, then neither does moral or aesthetic value or any other sort of value that could distinguish some projects as better than others. Others believe that though there may be a difference between great literature and junk, and between virtue and vice, there is no point in bothering about which you occupy yourself with. Nothing lasts forever; the human race will be destroyed; the earth will crash into the sun. Only God, and the promise of an eternal life either for ourselves or for the universe in which our accomplishments have a place, can give a point to our living lives one way rather than another. Only God can make meaningful life so much as a possibility.

My own view about this position is that it expresses an irrational obsession with permanence; but it is enough for the purposes of this essay to note that it does not really challenge the account of meaning I have offered. I have already acknowledged that the usefulness of my account rests on the assumption that the distinction between worthwhile and worthless projects is defensible, and on *the* assumption that at least a core of our beliefs about what is worthwhile and what is worthless is roughly correct. Those who think that God is a necessary grounding for these assumptions and who believe in Him may still find my account of meaning acceptable. Those who think that God is a necessary grounding that unfortunately does not exist will reject my substantive claims about meaning for reasons we have already admitted.

Others, including Nagel and arguably Camus, think that there are differences between better and worse ways to live our lives. Evidently, they think that projects and activities can be more and less worthwhile, and that we have some sort of reason to favor the more worthwhile. They do not, however, see these facts as supplying a basis for meaning. Like the group just discussed, they link meaning inextricably to facts about our place in space-time and in the order of the cosmos. In an indifferent universe, they think, our lives are unavoidably meaningless no matter what we do with them. On the other hand, there may be some other point to choosing to do something good or worthwhile. This view disagrees explicitly with my own proposal—indeed, it appears to be in outright contradiction to it. However, it seems to me to be largely a disagreement in the use of words. *The* issue of meaning, which these philosophers tie essentially to issues about our significance (or lack of it) in the universe, seems to me to be really a tangle of issues with overlapping strands. Though talk about meaning sometimes expresses a concern about our relation to the cosmos, the use of the term and its cognates to refer to differences among human lives and activities is no less common. I believe that there are relations between these different uses that have not been fully appreciated, and that philosophers like Nagel and Camus have insufficiently recognized the degree to which anthropocentric values can serve as a basis for addressing worries about our place in the universe.[10] However, this issue is not relevant to my present purpose. My purpose here is to advance the view that it is in our interest to live lives of a certain sort, and to explore some of that view's implications. Whether we should describe these lives as more meaningful than others, or describe the desire to live them as a desire for meaning, is relatively superficial and may in any case be left to another day. I shall continue to use my terminology, however, and hope that no one will be confused by it.

The second challenge to my account of meaningfulness is more directly relevant to the issue of the nature of self-interest. It consists of an alternative subjective account of meaning that is forcefully suggested, although not in quite the terms I shall use, by Richard Taylor's discussion of the meaning of life in his book *Good and Evil*.[11] According to this position, meaning is not a matter of one's projects in life being worthwhile from some objective point of view. (Taylor himself seems to think that no projects could

meet this standard.) Rather, a person's life is meaningful, one might say, if it is meaningful *to her*, and it is meaningful to her if she thinks or feels it is.

The suggestion that something is meaningful to someone as long as she thinks it is can be of no help to us in developing an account of meaningfulness, for we cannot understand what it would be for someone to think her life meaningful until we have an account of what meaningfulness is. The view I want to discuss, however, is, strictly speaking, more concerned with a feeling or, better, a sense or qualitative character that some of our experiences have. We may use the term "fulfillment" to refer to it. It is pleasant to be or to feel fulfilled or to find an activity or a relationship fulfilling, but it is a pleasure of a specific sort, one that seems closely associated with the thought that our lives or certain activities within them are meaningful. Recognizing this, it may be suggested, gives us all the basis we need for an account of meaning that meets my requirements. We may understand people's longing for meaning as a longing for this particular feeling, a longing which other sorts of pleasure cannot satisfy. We can also explain why some activities characteristically answer the call of meaning better than others. Some yield the feeling of fulfillment while others do not. Chocolate is filling but not fulfilling; it gives pleasure but not of this particular kind. When a person steps back, wondering whether her life has had meaning, or searching for a way to give it more meaning, she may simply be surveying her life for its quotient of fulfillment or looking for ways to increase it.

The very close ties between meaningfulness and fulfillment on which this account of meaning relies are important for understanding both the concept of meaning and its value. That meaningful activity or a meaningful life is at least partly fulfilling is, as this account suggests, a conceptual truth. To *identify* meaningfulness with fulfillment, however, neglects aspects of our use of the terms, and aspects of the experiences that are described by them, that my more objective account of meaningfulness better accommodates.

For one thing, fulfillment is not a brute feeling but one with some cognitive content or concomitant. That certain activities tend to be fulfilling and others not seems connected to features of the relevant activities that make this fact intelligible. There is a fittingness between certain kinds of activities and the potential for fulfillment. When a relationship or a job is fulfilling, there is something about it that makes it so. One feels appreciated or loved, or has the sense of doing good, or finds the challenge of the work rewarding. It is not just that the activities in question meet our expectations, though that is a part of it. Some things are fine but not fulfilling—my relationship with my hairdresser, for example, or my weekly trips to the supermarket.

These considerations suggest that we find things fulfilling only if we can think about them in a certain way. It is difficult precisely to identify a single belief that is always associated with the experience of fulfillment. Still, I propose that there is some association between finding an activity fulfilling and believing, or at least dimly, inarticulately perceiving, there to be something independently worthwhile or good about it.

In his discussion of the meaning of life, Richard Taylor considers the case of Sisyphus and imagines that the gods, by inserting some substance in Sisyphus's veins, give Sisyphus a love for stone-rolling. Sisyphus's life is thereby transformed from one of miserable bondage to one of ecstatic fulfillment. Taylor himself recognizes that the thought experiment is an odd one, and that the passion for stone-rolling will strike his readers as bizarre. Taylor, however, seems to think that the strangeness of the example comes simply from its being unusual. People do not characteristically get passionate about mindless, futile, never-ending tasks; nor is this the sort of disposition that drugs typically induce. To many, however, the example is not just surprising but somewhat horrifying. The state of being fulfilled by perpetual stone-rolling is not unreservedly enviable. Of course, for Sisyphus, who is condemned to roll stones in any case, there is a great benefit in being able to be happy with his lot. In general, however, I suspect that most people would think that stone-rolling (mere stone-rolling, that is, without any purpose or development of skill) is not the sort of thing by which one ought to be fulfilled.[12] That Sisyphus is fulfilled by stone-rolling suggests an understanding of Sisyphus as a victim (albeit a happy one) of a kind of drug-induced illusion. He finds something in stone-rolling that isn't really there.

If we accept the idea that the feeling of fulfillment is necessarily connected with beliefs about its objects—if we accept that an activity or relationship can be fulfilling only if one believes it to be somehow independently good—then we can distinguish two hypotheses about the relationship between meaning and fulfillment. Does meaning come from the experience of fulfillment, no matter what its cause, or is a meaningful life one in which a subject is fulfilled by activities suitable to the experience? The subjective account suggested by Taylor opts for the former; but the latter seems to square better with our ordinary use of the concept.[13]

One test case is Taylor's version of Sisyphus itself. That Sisyphus finds his life fulfilling is built in by assumption. But should we describe his life as meaningful? This seems to me a misuse of the word. "It is meaningful to him," someone will say, and we understand what this means. It means that he finds his life fulfilling, and, perhaps, that he thinks it is meaningful (or would think it, if asked). But, for those who find the example horrifying, that is part of the problem: he thinks his life gets meaning from mindless, futile stone-rolling, but it does not.

We can construct a second test case by considering someone whose judgment of an aspect of her life has changed. A woman previously blissfully in love discovers that the man she loved has been using her. She had found the relationship fulfilling before she learned of his deceits. She would have said, had you asked her earlier, that the relationship contributed to the meaningfulness of her life. What would she say now, however, and what should we say about her? No one can take away the feelings of fulfillment she experienced during the period she was deceived; but it seems unlikely that she would say, after the fact, that the relationship truly had given meaning to her life. Indeed, part of what makes this sort of event so sad is that, in addition to the pain that is caused when the deception is discovered, it undermines the value of all the pleasure that came before.

Less fanciful than Sisyphus are cases of addicts or inductees of religious cults whose feelings of contentment are caused, but not justified, by the things that bring them about. Though we should be cautious about passing judgment on the activities that others take to be worthwhile, this is no reason to rule out the possibility that people are sometimes mistaken, that their finding something fulfilling can be wrongly induced, either through the establishment of false factual beliefs (such as belief in a loved one's fidelity or in the divine status of a charismatic leader) or by drugs or electrodes. If, moreover, they are led by such mind-altering means to spend their lives occupied by some equivalent of stone-rolling—watching endless reruns of *Leave It to Beaver* or counting and recounting the number of tiles on the bathroom floor—then it seems to me most in line with ordinary language to describe them as leading meaningless lives, however fulfilled they may feel themselves to be. If, further, such people wake up or snap out of it—if they come to occupy a point of view that devalues their former lives—then their later descriptions would not, I think, grant meaning to the things in which they had found contentment before.

IV. MEANINGFULNESS AND SELF-INTEREST

So far I have been occupied with spelling out a conception of what meaningfulness in life is. My point in doing so, in the present context, is to bring it to bear on the idea of self-interest. Meaningfulness seems to me an important ingredient of a good life, and one that is too often either neglected or distorted by contemporary accounts of individual wellbeing.

I do not know what an argument for this claim would look like. My hope, as I mentioned

before, is that the mere spelling out of the claim will be enough to incline most people to assent to it. Still, I think that without attending explicitly to our interest in meaning, we tend to misunderstand and misdescribe it, with the eventual result that the shapes our lives take have less meaning than may be good for us.

Most people—at least most people within a certain group, bounded perhaps by class or education as well as by culture and history—behave in ways that suggest that they are looking for worthwhile things to do with their lives. They actively seek projects or, more typically, happily seize upon activities, from among those to which they are attracted, that they believe to be worthwhile. Explicit thoughts about worth and meaning often occur in connection with major life decisions, in addition to those moments of crisis to which I referred before. Some people decide to have children because they think it will give meaning to their lives. Others decide not to have children because they fear that the attendant responsibilities will deprive them of the time and resources and peace of mind that they need for other things in which they do find meaning. Deliberations about whether to pursue a particular career, or any career, may similarly involve concerns about whether the job is worthwhile, or whether it would demand time and energy that would distract one from what is worthwhile. Even many who do not talk explicitly in terms of meaning or worth make choices that are best explained by reference to them. In other words, our behavior, including some of our speech, seems to reveal a preference for a meaningful life.

We are, however, more apt to explain our choices in terms of fulfillment than meaning. A man opts for the more challenging of two possible careers, even at the cost of stress and insecurity. A woman chooses to work for less pay at a job she believes is morally valuable. People arrange their lives so as to give a few hours a week to Meals on Wheels, or to practicing piano, or to keeping up with their book group, even though it means going with a little less sleep, less flexibility, less straightforward fun. Why?

Because, they will say, they find these things fulfilling. They choose to live this way because they regard it as, in some sense, best for them.

To defend these choices in terms of fulfillment establishes them as choices made out of self-interest. Talk of fulfillment may, however, suggest a more hedonistic interpretation of what is going on than the one I have offered. To choose something because it is fulfilling is, after all, to choose it because of a qualitative character of one's experience—and though fulfilling activities are not always as much fun or as intensely pleasurable as some of the alternatives, it may be that in the long run, or the wide run (taking into account Mill's differences in the quality as well as the quantity of pleasure, as it were), a fulfilling life is qualitatively better, and thus happier in the truest sense, than a life with as many or more pleasures but no fulfillment. So at least must the people described in the paragraph above believe, and so must we believe if we think their choices are rational, and are rational for the reason they give.

It is no part of my aim to deny this suggestion. On the contrary, that fulfillment is a great qualitative good, and that it deserves an important place in an adequate theory of happiness, are important contributing factors to my claim that meaning is a component of our good. We have already seen that the links between meaningfulness and fulfillment are very tight. Since a meaningful life is necessarily at least partly fulfilling, and since fulfillment is a major component of happiness, a very important reason for taking meaningfulness to be in our interest is that it brings fulfillment with it. It would be misleading, however, to draw from this the conclusion that meaningfulness is an instrumental good for us. To think of meaning as good because it is a means to an independent good of fulfillment would be a mistake.

It is doubtful that fulfillment is an independent good, although feeling fulfilled is pleasant and feeling unfulfilled unpleasant. If fulfillment were an independent good, it would follow that the feeling of fulfillment would be desirable no matter what its cause. It would have to be better

to be Sisyphus happy (or, more precisely, Sisyphus fulfilled) than Sisyphus unhappy (unfulfilled), even if this required that Sisyphus was perpetually stoned out of his normal mind. Opinion, however, divides on this matter. Many value fulfillment only on the condition that it be based on appropriate thoughts or perceptions. Moreover, even among those who believe that feeling fulfilled is unconditionally better than the alternative, many would still prefer that these feelings were suitably caused. Better to be Sisyphus happy than Sisyphus unhappy, they may say, but better still not to be Sisyphus at all.

A proponent of a purely hedonistic theory of self-interest may point out that reports of such intuitions prove nothing. People's thinking that justified or appropriate fulfillment is better than unjustified inappropriate fulfillment doesn't make it so. To those who have these intuitions, however, the burden of proof seems to lie with the hedonist. Unless one is committed to a purely hedonistic account of value ahead of time, there seems no reason to doubt that what is principally desirable is getting fulfillment from genuinely fulfilling activities, from activities, that is, whose accompanying feeling of fulfillment comes from the correct perception of their value. There seems no reason to doubt, in other words, that what is principally desirable is living a meaningful life and not living a life that seems or feels meaningful. Insofar as we prefer a truly meaningful life to one that merely seems or feels meaningful, a purely hedonistic theory of self-interest will not account for it.

A preference theory of self-interest, however, would not have to account for it—preference theorists simply accept our preferences and go on to compute our self-interest from there. This suggests an alternative account of the relation between meaning and self-interest. According to preference theories, meaning is important to our well-being if and only if meaning matters to us. Since many of us do want to live meaningful lives—since we think it is better for us if we do—preference theorists will agree that it is in our interest that our lives are meaningful.

From their point of view, there is no need to make any more objective claims than that.

From a practical perspective, it matters little whether we accept this theory or a more objective one, particularly if you think, as I do, that the preference for a meaningful life is widespread and deep. If it is accepted as a fact of human nature (even a statistical fact, and even of a culturally created human nature) that people just do care about meaning in their lives, then this gives us reason enough to shape our lives in ways that will encourage not just fulfillment but meaningfulness, and it gives us reason enough to shape our social and political institutions in ways that will increase the opportunities for everyone to live not just happily and comfortably but meaningfully as well.

A preference theory does not, however, seem accurately to reflect the status a meaningful life has for most of us. Most of us, it seems, do not regard our preference for a meaningful life as an ungrounded preference we just happen to have. If we did think so, then we would judge it a matter of indifference whether anyone else had or lacked this preference, and indeed, we would have no reason to want to keep this preference ourselves if we were convinced that we would be better off without it. For most people, however, at least so it seems to me, having a meaningful life is a value and not just a preference. We do not just want our lives to be meaningful, we think it good that we want it. Indeed, our interest and concern for meaning is sometimes mentioned as a mark of our humanity, as an aspect of what raises us above brutes. We think that we would be diminished as a species if we lost the aspiration, or the interest, in living meaningful lives and not just happy ones. Individuals who lack the desire that their lives be meaningful we regard with regret or even pity.

Again it may be noted that our believing something is no proof of its being true, and again I must acknowledge that I have no proof of the value or objective desirability of meaningfulness. At the same time, the claim that a meaningful life is preferable (and not just brutely preferred) to a meaningless one may seem so nearly self-evident as to require no proof. Once one is willing to apply the terms of meaningfulness and meaninglessness at all, it may seem unstable to believe that a life that lacks meaning is no worse than one that possesses it. Even if we can logically distinguish the position that some lives are more meaningful than others from the position which adds that (some) meaningfulness is a good, this latter position seems more natural than one which denies it. Though we may be unable to argue for caring about meaning in a way that would convince someone who doesn't care to begin with, the concern or the desire for meaningful activity is, for those who have it, more rationally coherent with other values and dispositions than its absence would be.

In response to the question "Why care about living a meaningful life rather than a meaningless one?" the answer that I believe best expresses reflective common sense will begin with the connection between meaning and happiness: Nine times out of ten, perhaps ninety-nine times out of a hundred, a meaningful life will be happier than a meaningless one. The feelings of fulfillment one gets from interacting positively and supportively with things or creatures (or "realms") whose love seems deserved are wonderful feelings, worth more, on qualitative grounds alone, than many other sorts of pleasure, and worth the cost of putting up with considerable quantities of pain. Moreover, the awareness, even dim and inarticulate, of a lack of anything that can constitute a source of pride or a source of connection to anything valuable outside of oneself can be awful, making one irritable, restless, and contemptuous of oneself.

Except in an academic philosophical context such as this, it is perhaps unnatural to press further. If we do press further, however, it seems to me that the strength and character of these feelings of pleasure and pain are not best explained as mere quirks of our natural or culturally conditioned psyches. Rather, that we feel so good or so bad in accordance with our sense of connection to value outside ourselves seems to me best explained in terms of an underlying belief that a life is better when it possesses such connections.

What precisely is better about it is difficult to say. But perhaps it has to do with our place in the universe: since we are, each of us, occupants in a world full of value independent of our individual selves, living in such a way as to connect positively and supportively with some nonsubjective value harmonizes better with our objective situation than would a life whose chief occupations can be only subjectively defended.[14]

V. THE DECONSTRUCTION OF SELF-INTEREST

I have in this essay been concerned to defend, or rather to elaborate, what I take to be a deeply and widely held view about individual human good, namely, that a fully successful life is, among other things, a meaningful one. Further, I have urged that this claim is distorted if it is understood as an element of either a hedonistic or a preference theory of self-interest. Properly understood, it requires a rejection of both of these sorts of theories.

As a substantive claim, I do not expect that the point that a good life must be meaningful will be surprising. We are not used to thinking very explicitly or very analytically about it, however; and in popular unreflective consciousness, a substantive interest in a meaningful life often sits side by side with assumptions that are incompatible with it. How often have you heard someone say, "What's the point of doing something if it isn't fun, or if you don't enjoy it?" I hear this sentiment expressed quite frequently, despite living on the East Coast. To be fair, such expressions tend to be limited to contexts of self-interest. They are not intended as rejections of the rational authority of moral or legal obligation. Moreover, there is often a point behind such remarks that I would strongly endorse. Against a kind of workaholism and related neurotic obsessions with some forms of success and achievement, it can be useful to step back and reflect in the way these remarks would invoke. Still, the suggestion that there can be no point to things if they are neither duties nor fun is, strictly speaking, both false and dangerous.

Much of what we do would be inexplicable, or at least indefensible, if its justification depended either on its being a duty or, even in the long run, on its maximally contributing to our net fun. Relationships with friends and family, nonobligatory aspects of professional roles, and longterm commitments to artistic, scholarly, or athletic endeavors typically lead us to devote time and energy to things that are difficult and unpleasant, and to forgo opportunities for relaxation and enjoyment. It is arguable that many of these choices advance our happiness (in the broadest sense, our fun) in the long run, but such arguments are at best uncertain, and the thought that they are necessary for the defense of these choices puts a regrettable kind of pressure on the commitments that give rise to them. There is, however, a point—even a self-interested point—to doing things that fall outside the categories both of duty and of fun. One can find a reason, or at least a justifying explanation, for doing something in the fact that the act or activity in question contributes to the meaningfulness of one's life.

Once we have ceased to identify self-interest with happiness, however, other assumptions are also undermined. The concept of self-interest becomes more difficult to work with. Specifically, a conception of self-interest that recognizes the importance of meaning to a good life admits of much greater indeterminacy than the more traditional conceptions. This is partly a function of indeterminacy within the category of meaningfulness itself. Though meaningfulness is not an all-or-nothing concept—some lives are more meaningful than others, a person's life may not have *enough* meaning in it to be satisfactory—there is no well-formed system for making comparative judgments. The meaningfulness of a life may vary depending on how much of it is spent in meaningful activity, on how worthwhile the activities in question are,[15] or on how fully engaged (or attracted) the individual is. In many instances, however, it seems absurd to think there is a correct comparison to be made. Is the life of a great but lonely philosopher more or less meaningful than that of a beloved housekeeper? There seems to be no reason to assume that there is a fact of the matter about this. Moreover, from a self-interested point of view, it is unclear whether, beyond a certain point, it matters whether one's life is more meaningful. A meaningful life is better than a meaningless one, but once it is meaningful enough, there may be no self-interested reason to want, as it were, to squeeze more meaning into it. Finally, the mix between meaning and felt happiness may have no determinate ideal. A person often has to choose between taking a path that would strengthen or expand a part of his or her life that contributes to its meaningfulness (going to graduate school, adopting a child, getting politically involved) and taking an easier or more pleasant road. Once one has accepted a conception of self-interest that recognizes meaningfulness as an independent aspect of one's personal good, one may have to admit that in such cases there may be no answer to the question of what is most in one's self-interest.

Fortunately, as the concept of self-interest becomes more difficult to apply, it becomes less important to be able to apply it. In accepting the value of meaningfulness as an ingredient of our own interest, we necessarily also accept that meaningful activity has a value that is partly independent of our interest. We accept, in other words, the availability of a kind of reason for doing things that can compete with self-interest, a kind that will, at any rate, draw us away from a concern for our self-interest. What I have in mind is the sort of reason given by the worthiness of the meaningful activity (or its object) itself.

Meaningful activity, remember, involves engagement in projects of worth. It occurs where subjective attraction meets objective attractiveness. To acknowledge that an activity or a project is worthwhile, however, is to acknowledge, among other things, that there is a reason for doing it—a reason, at least, for doing it if you are attracted to doing it. A reason for writing a book on free will is to stimulate thought in a fruitful direction. A reason to plant bulbs and weed the garden is to maintain a place of natural beauty. A reason to sew a groundhog costume for an eight-year-old girl is to make her happy.

To those who get meaning from the activities just mentioned, these sorts of reasons will dominate. Being suitably engaged in these activities in the way in which people who get meaning from them *are* engaged involves being drawn by their specific good or value. One so engaged is not likely to step back from the activity and ask, "Is this the best thing I can be doing *for me?*"

The point here is not just the one with which we are familiar from the paradox of hedonism. It is not just that, by not caring too much about whether her activities will be best for her, the agent is more likely to be living a life that is best for her. Rather, it is that she has a reason for her activities that is not conditional on their being best for her. Accepting a conception of self-interest that incorporates meaningfulness, then, involves rejecting too dominant a place for self-interest. Yet meaningful activity and self-interest cannot psychologically stretch too far apart. Activity is meaningful only if one can engage with it, be attracted to it, be in love with it or with the object around which it revolves. Such activity will always be somewhat fulfilling, and therefore will always make one somewhat happy. And as the fulfillment and happiness will be appropriate or deserved, that is all to one's good.

NOTES

1. The view described and defended here shows the influence of and my sympathy with the views of Aristotle and John Stuart Mill throughout. I cannot individuate my debts to them; they are pervasive.
2. Derek Parfit, *Reasons and Persons* (Oxford: Oxford University Press, 1984).
3. This point is made by David Wiggins in his brilliant but difficult essay "Truth, Invention, and the Meaning of Life," *Proceedings of the British Academy*, vol. 62 (1976).
4. Woody Allen appears to have a different view. His list of the things that make life worth living at the end of *Manhattan* includes, for example "the crabs at Sam Woo's," which would seem to be on the level of chocolates. On the other hand, the crabs' appearance on the list may be

taken to show that he regards the dish as an accomplishment meriting aesthetic appreciation, where such appreciation is a worthy activity in itself; in this respect, the crabs might be akin to other items on his list such as the second movement of the *Jupiter Symphony*, Louis Armstrong's recording of "Potatohead Blues," and "those apples and pears of Cézanne." Strictly speaking, the appreciation of great chocolate might also qualify as such an activity.

5. See Wiggins, "Truth, Invention, and the Meaning of life," p. 342.
6. This remark was made famous by John Stuart Mill, who quoted it in his essay on Bentham. See J. M. Robson, ed. *Collected Works of John Stuart Mill*, vol. 10 (Toronto: University of Toronto Press, 1969), p. 113.
7. See Leo Tolstoy, "My Confession," in E. D. Klemke, ed., *The Meaning of Life* (New York: Oxford University Press, 1981).
8. Albert Camus, *The Myth of Sisyphus and Other Essays* (New York: Vintage Books, 1955).

9. Thomas Nagel, "The Absurd," in Nagel, *Mortal Questions* (Cambridge: Cambridge University Press, 1979).
10. I discuss this in my "Meaningful Lives in a Meaningless World," unpublished manuscript.
11. Richard Taylor, *Good and Evil* (New York: Macmillan, 1970).
12. See Joel Feinberg, *Freedom and Fulfillment* (Princeton: Princeton University Press, 1992), ch. 13.
13. Robert Nozick makes a similar suggestion in *The Examined Life* (New York: Simon and Schuster, 1989). In addition to wanting happiness, Nozick writes, "[w]e also want this emotion of happiness to be *fitting*" (p. 112).
14. I explore this in "Meaningful Lives in a Meaningless World."
15. The relevant scale of worth, however, will itself be a matter of contention. As my examples have probably made clear, there is no reason to identify the relevant kind of worth here with moral worth.

4.6 The Absurd

THOMAS NAGEL

Thomas Nagel teaches philosophy at New York University. He is the author of *Mortal Questions, The View from Nowhere,* and *The Last Word,* among many other titles. His work has been especially influential in the philosophy of mind and moral philosophy.

Most people feel on occasion that life is absurd, and some feel it vividly and continually. Yet the reasons usually offered in defense of this conviction are patently inadequate: they *could* not really explain why life is absurd. Why then do they provide a natural expression for the sense that it is?

I

Consider some examples. It is often remarked that nothing we do now will matter in a million years. But if that is true, then by the same token, nothing that will be the case in a million years matters now. In particular, it does not matter now that in a million years nothing we do now will matter. Moreover, even if what we did now *were* going to matter in a million years, how could that keep our present concerns from being absurd? If their mattering now is not enough to accomplish that, how would it help if they mattered a million years from now?

Thomas Nagel, "The Absurd," *The Journal of Philosophy*, LXVII, 20 (October 1971): 716–727. Reprinted by permission of the Journal of Philosophy and the author.

Whether what we do now will matter in a million years could make the crucial difference only if its mattering in a million years depended on its mattering, period. But then to deny that whatever happens now will matter in a million years is to beg the question against its mattering, period; for in that sense one cannot know that it will not matter in a million years whether (for example) someone now is happy or miserable, without knowing that it does not matter, period.

What we say to convey the absurdity of our lives often has to do with space or time: we are tiny specks in the infinite vastness of the universe; our lives are mere instants even on a geological time scale, let alone a cosmic one; we will all be dead any minute. But of course none of these evident facts can be what *makes* life absurd, if it is absurd. For suppose we lived forever; would not a life that is absurd if it lasts seventy years be infinitely absurd if it lasted through eternity? And if our lives are absurd given our present size, why would they be any less absurd if we filled the universe (either because we were larger or because the universe was smaller)? Reflection on our minuteness and brevity appears to be intimately connected with the sense that life is meaningless; but it is not clear what the connection is.

Another inadequate argument is that because we are going to die, all chains of justification must leave off in mid-air: one studies and works to earn money to pay for clothing, housing, entertainment, food, to sustain oneself from year to year, perhaps to support a family and pursue a career—but to what final end? All of it is an elaborate journey leading nowhere. (One will also have some effect on other people's lives, but that simply reproduces the problem, for they will die too.)

There are several replies to this argument. First, life does not consist of a sequence of activities each of which has as its purpose some later member of the sequence. Chains of justification come repeatedly to an end within life, and whether the process as a whole can be justified has no bearing on the finality of these end-points. No further justification is needed to make it reasonable to take aspirin for a headache, attend an exhibition of the work of a painter one admires, or stop a child from putting his hand on a hot stove. No larger context or further purpose is needed to prevent these acts from being pointless.

Even if someone wished to supply a further justification for pursuing all the things in life that are commonly regarded as self-justifying, that justification would have to end somewhere too. If *nothing* can justify unless it is justified in terms of something outside itself, which is also justified, then an infinite regress results, and no chain of justification can be complete. Moreover, if a finite chain of reasons cannot justify anything, what could be accomplished by an infinite chain, each link of which must be justified by something outside itself?

Since justifications must come to an end somewhere, nothing is gained by denying that they end where they appear to, within life—or by trying to subsume the multiple, often trivial ordinary justifications of action under a single, controlling life scheme. We can be satisfied more easily than that. In fact, through its misrepresentation of the process of justification, the argument makes a vacuous demand. It insists that the reasons available within life are incomplete, but suggests thereby that all reasons that come to an end are incomplete. This makes it impossible to supply any reasons at all.

The standard arguments for absurdity appear therefore to fail as arguments. Yet I believe they attempt to express something that is difficult to state, but fundamentally correct.

II

In ordinary life a situation is absurd when it includes a conspicuous discrepancy between pretension or aspiration and reality: someone gives a complicated speech in support of a motion that has already been passed; a notorious criminal is made president of a major philanthropic foundation; you declare your love over the telephone to a recorded announcement; as you are being knighted, your pants fall down.

When a person finds himself in an absurd situation, he will usually attempt to change it, by modifying his aspirations, or by trying to bring reality into better accord with them, or by removing himself from the situation entirely. We are not always willing or able to extricate ourselves from a position whose absurdity has become clear to us. Nevertheless, it is usually possible to imagine some change that would remove the absurdity—whether or not we can or will implement it. The sense that life as a whole is absurd arises when we perceive, perhaps dimly, an inflated pretension or aspiration which is inseparable from the continuation of human life and which makes its absurdity inescapable, short of escape from life itself.

Many people's lives are absurd, temporarily or permanently, for conventional reasons having to do with their particular ambitions, circumstances, and personal relations. If there is a philosophical sense of absurdity, however, it must arise from the perception of something universal—some respect in which pretension and reality inevitably clash for us all. This condition is supplied, I shall argue, by the collision between the seriousness with which we take our lives and the perpetual possibility of regarding everything about which we are serious as arbitrary, or open to doubt.

We cannot live human lives without energy and attention, nor without making choices which show that we take some things more seriously than others. Yet we have always available a point of view outside the particular form of our lives, from which the seriousness appears gratuitous. These two inescapable viewpoints collide in us, and that is what makes life absurd. It is absurd because we ignore the doubts that we know cannot be settled, continuing to live with nearly undiminished seriousness in spite of them.

This analysis requires defense in two respects: first as regards the unavoidability of seriousness; second as regards the inescapability of doubt.

We take ourselves seriously whether we lead serious lives or not and whether we are concerned primarily with fame, pleasure, virtues, luxury, triumph, beauty, justice, knowledge, salvation, or mere survival. If we take other people seriously and devote ourselves to them, that only multiplies the problem. Human life is full of effort, plans, calculation, success and failure: we *pursue* our lives, with varying degrees of sloth and energy.

It would be different if we could not step back and reflect on the process, but were merely led from impulse to impulse without self-consciousness. But human beings do not act solely on impulse. They are prudent, they reflect, they weigh consequences, they ask whether what they are doing is worthwhile. Not only are their lives full of particular choices that hang together in larger activities with temporal structure: they also decide in the broadest terms what to pursue and what to avoid, what the priorities among their various aims should be, and what kind of people they want to be or become. Some men are faced with such choices by the large decisions they make from time to time; some merely by reflection on the course their lives are taking as the product of countless small decisions. They decide whom to marry, what profession to follow, whether to join the Country Club, or the Resistance; or they may just wonder why they go on being salesmen or academics or taxi drivers, and then stop thinking about it after a certain period of inconclusive reflection.

Although they may be motivated from act to act by those immediate needs with which life presents them, they allow the process to continue by adhering to the general system of habits and the form of life in which such motives have their place—or perhaps only by clinging to life itself. They spend enormous quantities of energy, risk, and calculation on the details. Think of how an ordinary individual sweats over his appearance, his health, his sex life, his emotional honesty, his social utility, his self-knowledge, the quality of his ties with family, colleagues, and friends, how well he does his job, whether he understands the world and what is going on in it. Leading a human life is a full-time occupation, to which everyone devotes decades of intense concern.

This fact is so obvious that it is hard to find it extraordinary and important. Each of us lives his own life—lives with himself twenty-four hours a day. What else is he supposed to do—live someone else's life? Yet humans have the special capacity to step back and survey themselves, and the lives to which they are committed, with that detached amazement which comes from watching an ant struggle up a heap of sand. Without developing the illusion that they are able to escape from their highly specific and idiosyncratic position, they can view it *sub specie aeternitatis*—and the view is at once sobering and comical.

The crucial backward step is not taken by asking for still another justification in the chain, and failing to get it. The objections to that line of attack have already been stated; justifications come to an end. But this is precisely what provides universal doubt with its object. We step back to find that the whole system of justification and criticism, which controls our choices and supports our claims to rationality, rests on responses and habits that we never question, that we should not know how to defend without circularity, and to which we shall continue to adhere even after they are called into question.

The things we do or want without reasons, and without requiring reasons—the things that define what is a reason for us and what is not—are the starting points of our skepticism. We see ourselves from outside, and all the contingency and specificity of our aims and pursuits become clear. Yet when we take this view and recognize what we do as arbitrary, it does not disengage us from life, and there lies our absurdity: not in the fact that such an external view can be taken of us, but in the fact that we ourselves can take it, without ceasing to be the persons whose ultimate concerns are so coolly regarded.

III

One may try to escape the position by seeking broader ultimate concerns, from which it is impossible to step back—the idea being that absurdity results because what we take seriously is something small and insignificant and individual. Those seeking to supply their lives with meaning usually envision a role or function in something larger than themselves. They therefore seek fulfillment in service to society, the state, the revolution, the progress of history, the advance of science, or religion and the glory of God.

But a role in some larger enterprise cannot confer significance unless that enterprise is itself significant. And its significance must come back to what we can understand, or it will not even appear to give us what we are seeking. If we learned that we were being raised to provide food for other creatures fond of human flesh, who planned to turn us into cutlets before we got too stringy—even if we learned that the human race had been developed by animal breeders precisely for this purpose—that would still not give our lives meaning, for two reasons. First, we would still be in the dark as to the significance of the lives of those other beings; second, although we might acknowledge that this culinary role would make our lives meaningful to them, it is not clear how it would make them meaningful to us.

Admittedly, the usual form of service to a higher being is different from this. One is supposed to behold and partake of the glory of God, for example, in a way in which chickens do not share in the glory of coq au vin. The same is true of service to a state, a movement, or a revolution. People can come to feel, when they are part of something bigger, that it is part of them too. They worry less about what is peculiar to themselves, but identify enough with the larger enterprise to find their role in it fulfilling.

However, any such larger purpose can be put in doubt in the same way that the aims of an individual life can be, and for the same reasons. It is as legitimate to find ultimate justification there as to find it earlier, among the details of individual life. But this does not alter the fact that justifications come to an end when we are content to have them end—when we do not find it necessary to look any further. If we can step back from the purposes of individual life and doubt their point, we can step back also from the progress of human history, or of science, or the success of a society, or the kingdom, power, and glory of God, and put all these things into question in the same way. What seems to us to confer meaning, justification, significance, does so in virtue of the fact that we need no more reasons after a certain point.

What makes doubt inescapable with regard to the limited aims of individual life also makes it inescapable with regard to any larger purpose that encourages the sense that life is meaningful. Once the fundamental doubt has begun, it cannot be laid to rest.

Camus maintains in *The Myth of Sisyphus* that the absurd arises because the world fails to meet our demands for meaning. This suggests that the world might satisfy those demands if it were different. But now we can see that this is not the case. There does not appear to be any conceivable world (containing us) about which unsettlable doubts could not arise. Consequently the absurdity of our situation derives not from a collision between our expectations and the world, but from a collision within ourselves.

IV

It may be objected that the standpoint from which these doubts are supposed to be felt does not exist—that if we take the recommended backward step we will land on thin air, without any basis for judgment about the natural responses we are supposed to be surveying. If we retain our usual standards of what is important, then questions about the significance of what we are doing with our lives will be answerable in the usual way. But if we do not, then those questions can mean nothing to us, since there is no longer any content to the idea of what matters, and hence no content to the idea that nothing does.

But this objection misconceives the nature of the backward step. It is not supposed to give us an understanding of what is *really* important, so that we see by contrast that our lives are insignificant. We never, in the course of these reflections, abandon the ordinary standards that guide our lives. We merely observe them in

operation, and recognize that if they are called into question we can justify them only by reference to themselves, uselessly. We adhere to them because of the way we are put together; what seems to us important or serious or valuable would not seem so if we were differently constituted.

In ordinary life, to be sure, we do not judge a situation absurd unless we have in mind some standards of seriousness, significance, or harmony with which the absurd can be contrasted. This contrast is not implied by the philosophical judgment of absurdity, and that might be thought to make the concept unsuitable for the expression of such judgments. This is not so, however, for the philosophical judgment depends on another contrast which makes it a natural extension from more ordinary cases. It departs from them only in contrasting the pretensions of life with a larger context in which *no* standards can be discovered, rather than with a context from which alternative, overriding standards may be applied.

V

In this respect, as in others, philosophical perception of the absurd resembles epistemological skepticism. In both cases the final, philosophical doubt is not contrasted with any unchallenged certainties, though it is arrived at by extrapolation from examples of doubt within the system of evidence or justification, where a contrast with other certainties *is* implied. In both cases our limitedness joins with a capacity to transcend those limitations in thought (thus seeing them as limitations, and as inescapable).

Skepticism begins when we include ourselves in the world about which we claim knowledge. We notice that certain types of evidence convince us, that we are content to allow justifications of belief to come to an end at certain points, that we feel we know many things even without knowing or having grounds for believing the denial of others which, if true, would make what we claim to know false.

For example, I know that I am looking at a piece of paper, although I have no adequate grounds for claiming I know that I am not dreaming; and if I am dreaming then I am not looking at a piece of paper. Here an ordinary conception of how appearance may diverge from reality is employed to show that we take our world largely for granted; the certainty that we are not dreaming cannot be justified except circularly, in terms of those very appearances which are being put in doubt. It is somewhat far-fetched to suggest I may be dreaming; but the possibility is only illustrative. It reveals that our claims to knowledge depend on our not feeling it necessary to exclude certain incompatible alternatives, and the dreaming possibility or the total-hallucination possibility are just representatives for limitless possibilities most of which we cannot even conceive.[1]

Once we have taken the backward step to an abstract view of our whole system of beliefs, evidence, and justification, and seen that it works only, despite its pretensions, by taking the world largely for granted, we are *not* in a position to contrast all these appearances with an alternative reality. We cannot shed our ordinary responses, and if we could it would leave us with no means of conceiving a reality of any kind.

It is the same in the practical domain. We do not step outside our lives to a new vantage point from which we see what is really, objectively significant. We continue to take life largely for granted while seeing that all our decisions and certainties are possible only because there is a great deal we do not bother to rule out.

Both epistemological skepticism and a sense of the absurd can be reached via initial doubts posed within systems of evidence and justification that we accept, and can be stated without violence to our ordinary concepts. We can ask not only why we should believe there is a floor under us, but also why we should believe the evidence of our senses at all—and at some point the framable questions will have outlasted the answers. Similarly, we can ask not only why we should take aspirin, but why we should take trouble over our own comfort at all. The fact that we shall take the aspirin without waiting for an answer to this last question does not

show that it is an unreal question. We shall also continue to believe there is a floor under us without waiting for an answer to the other question. In both cases it is this unsupported natural confidence that generates skeptical doubts; so it cannot be used to settle them.

Philosophical skepticism does not cause us to abandon our ordinary beliefs, but it lends them a peculiar flavor. After acknowledging that their truth is incompatible with possibilities that we have no grounds for believing do not obtain—apart from grounds in those very beliefs which we have called into question—we return to our familiar convictions with a certain irony and resignation. Unable to abandon the natural responses on which they depend, we take them back, like a spouse who has run off with someone else and then decided to return; but we regard them differently (not that the new attitude is necessarily inferior to the old, in either case).

The same situation obtains after we have put in question the seriousness with which we take our lives and human life in general and have looked at ourselves without presuppositions. We then return to our lives, as we must, but our seriousness is laced with irony. Not that irony enables us to escape the absurd. It is useless to mutter: "Life is meaningless; life is meaningless…" as an accompaniment to everything we do. In continuing to live and work and strive, we take ourselves seriously in action no matter what we say.

What sustains us, in belief as in action, is not reason or justification, but something more basic than these—for we go on in the same way even after we are convinced that the reasons have given out.[2] If we tried to rely entirely on reason, and pressed it hard, our lives and beliefs would collapse—a form of madness that may actually occur if the inertial force of taking the world and life for granted is somehow lost. If we lose our grip on that, reason will not give it back to us.

VI

In viewing ourselves from a perspective broader than we can occupy in the flesh, we become spectators of our own lives. We cannot do very much as pure spectators of our own lives, so we continue to lead them, and devote ourselves to what we are able at the same time to view as no more than a curiosity, like the ritual of an alien religion.

This explains why the sense of absurdity finds its natural expression in those bad arguments with which the discussion began. Reference to our small size and short lifespan and to the fact that all of mankind will eventually vanish without a trace are metaphors for the backward step which permits us to regard ourselves from without and to find the particular form of our lives curious and slightly surprising. By feigning a nebula's-eye view, we illustrate the capacity to see ourselves without presuppositions, as arbitrary, idiosyncratic, highly specific occupants of the world, one of countless possible forms of life.

Before turning to the question whether the absurdity of our lives is something to be regretted and if possible escaped, let me consider what would have to be given up in order to avoid it.

Why is the life of a mouse not absurd? The orbit of the moon is not absurd either, but that involves no strivings or aims at all. A mouse, however, has to work to stay alive. Yet he is not absurd, because he lacks the capacities for self-consciousness and self-transcendence that would enable him to see that he is only a mouse. If that *did* happen, his life would become absurd, since self-awareness would not make him cease to be a mouse and would not enable him to rise above his mousely strivings. Bringing his new-found self-consciousness with him, he would have to return to his meager yet frantic life, full of doubts that he was unable to answer, but also full of purposes that he was unable to abandon.

Given that the transcendental step is natural to us humans, can we avoid absurdity by refusing to take that step and remaining entirely within our sublunar lives? Well, we cannot refuse consciously, for to do that we would have to be aware of the viewpoint we were refusing to adopt. The only way to avoid the relevant self-consciousness would be either never to attain it or to forget it—neither of which can be achieved by the will.

On the other hand, it is possible to expend effort on an attempt to destroy the other component of the absurd—abandoning one's earthly, individual, human life in order to identify as completely as possible with that universal viewpoint from which human life seems arbitrary and trivial. (This appears to be the ideal of certain Oriental religions.) If one succeeds, then one will not have to drag the superior awareness through a strenuous mundane life, and absurdity will be diminished.

However, insofar as this self-etiolation is the result of effort, will-power, asceticism, and so forth, it requires that one take oneself seriously as an individual—that one be willing to take considerable trouble to avoid being creaturely and absurd. Thus one may undermine the aim of unworldliness by pursuing it too vigorously. Still, if someone simply allowed his individual, animal nature to drift and respond to impulse, without making the pursuit of its needs a central conscious aim, then he might, at considerable dissociative cost, achieve a life that was less absurd than most. It would not be a meaningful life either, of course; but it would not involve the engagement of a transcendent awareness in the assiduous pursuit of mundane goals. And that is the main condition of absurdity—the dragooning of an unconvinced transcendent consciousness into the service of an immanent, limited enterprise like a human life.

The final escape is suicide; but before adopting any hasty solutions, it would be wise to consider carefully whether the absurdity of our existence truly presents us with a *problem,* to which some solution must be found—a way of dealing with *prima facie* disaster. That is certainly the attitude with which Camus approaches the issue, and it gains support from the fact that we are all eager to escape from absurd situations on a smaller scale.

Camus—not on uniformly good grounds—rejects suicide and the other solutions he regards as escapist. What he recommends is defiance or scorn. We can salvage our dignity, he appears to believe, by shaking a fist at the world which is deaf to our pleas, and continuing to live in spite of it. This will not make our lives un-absurd, but it will lend them a certain nobility.[3]

This seems to me romantic and slightly self-pitying. Our absurdity warrants neither that much distress nor that much defiance. At the risk of falling into romanticism by a different route, I would argue that absurdity is one of the most human things about us: a manifestation of our most advanced and interesting characteristics. Like skepticism in epistemology, it is possible only because we possess a certain kind of insight—the capacity to transcend ourselves in thought.

If a sense of the absurd is a way of perceiving our true situation (even though the situation is not absurd until the perception arises), then what reason can we have to resent or escape it? Like the capacity for epistemological skepticism, it results from the ability to understand our human limitations. It need not be a matter for agony unless we make it so. Nor need it evoke a defiant contempt of fate that allows us to feel brave or proud. Such dramatics, even if carried on in private, betray a failure to appreciate the cosmic unimportance of the situation. If *sub specie aeternitatis* there is no reason to believe that anything matters, then that does not matter either, and we can approach our absurd lives with irony instead of heroism or despair.

NOTES

1. I am aware that skepticism about the external world is widely thought to have been refuted, but I have remained convinced of its irrefutability since being exposed at Berkeley to Thompson Clarke's largely unpublished ideas on the subject.

2. As Hume says in a famous passage of the *Treatise:* "Most fortunately it happens, that since reason is incapable of dispelling these clouds, nature herself suffices to that purpose, and cures me of this philosophical melancholy and delirium, either by relaxing this bent of mind, or by some avocation, and lively impression of my senses, which obliterate all these chimeras. I dine, I play a game of backgammon, I converse, and am merry with my friends; and when after three or four hours' amusement, I would return to these speculations, they appear so cold, and strain'd, and ridiculous, that I cannot find in my heart to enter into them any farther" (bk i, pt iv, sect. 7; Selby-Bigge, p. 269).

3. "Sisyphus, proletarian of the gods, powerless and rebellious, knows the whole extent of his wretched condition: it is what he thinks of during his descent. The lucidity that was to constitute his torture at the same time crowns his victory. There is no fate that cannot be surmounted by scorn" (*The Myth of Sisyphus,* trans. Justin O'Brien [New York: Vintage, 1959], p. 90; first published, Paris: Gallimard, 1942).

MindTap

MindTap is a fully online, highly personalized learning experience built upon Cengage Learning content. MindTap combines student learning tools—readings, multimedia, activities, and assessments—into a singular Learning Path that guides students through the course.

Italic terms within the definition are defined in the glossary.

Academics Members of Plato's school of philosophy.

***Active euthanasia** Mercy killing that involves the intention on the part of a doctor to terminate the life of a patient for the patient's own good.

Ad hoc (Latin, "for a specific purpose") An hypothesis is ad hoc if it is adopted purely to save a theory from a difficulty without an independent motivation of its own.

Ad infinitum Into infinity; endlessly.

Aesthetic Belonging to the appreciation of beauty.

Aesthetics Pertaining to the appreciation of beauty and other values of pictorial art, music, poetry, fiction, and drama.

A fortiori (Latin, "from the stronger") This means "and even more so" or "all the more." For example, John owns horses of all ages; a fortiori he owns young horses.

***Affirming the consequent** The logical fallacy of asserting the truth of the consequent of a conditional, and then supposing that the truth of the conditional's antecedent follows.

Agnoiology The theory of ignorance.

Agnosticism The view that something is not known, and perhaps cannot be known. In theology, the view that the existence or nonexistence of God is not known. Neither *theism* nor *atheism* can be justified.

Akrasia (Greek, "weakness of the will") Not being able to make yourself do what you think would be best for you to do.

Altruism Any act that seeks to advance the good of others for their own sake and not for the sake of advancing the self-interest of the agent. (See *ethical altruism*.)

Analytical behaviorism See *behaviorism, logical*.

Analytic statement Originally introduced by Kant, an analytic statement is one where the concept of the predicate is contained within the concept of the subject. For example, the statement that all bachelors are unmarried is analytic. The concept "unmarried" is contained within the concept "bachelor." Frege generalized the notion to cover more than just subject-predicate statements. For Frege, an analytic statement is true solely in virtue of the meanings of the words in which it is expressed. Also known as a "tautology." (See *synthetic statement*.)

Antecedent What comes before. In a statement of the form "If A then B," A is the antecedent, and B is the consequent.

Anthropomorphism Attributing human characteristics, such as human form or human thoughts and intentions, to something that is not human—for example, attributing intentions to rocks to explain why they move or attributing a human appearance to God.

***A posteriori** Knowledge that is not a priori. A posteriori knowledge, though it may involve the use of reason, depends upon evidence from experience.

***A priori** Knowledge that is based on reason, independently of experience. The *ontological argument* is an example of an a priori argument.

***Arbitrary** Providing no better reason to adopt one position rather than another.

Argument A series of one or more statements called *premises* that are meant to support another statement called *conclusion*. (See also *valid* and *sound*.)

Argument from design See *teleological argument*.

Argumentum ad hominem An argument that attacks the character of an opponent and not the content of the opponent's position or argument. For example, arguing that because John is a jerk or John is uneducated, he cannot be correct.

Artificial intelligence (AI), strong The view that an appropriately programmed computer can have "intelligence," or, more generally, that such a computer can have a whole range of cognitive states such as believing, wanting, intending, and understanding.

Artificial intelligence (AI), weak The view that computers provide a useful research tool for investigating the mind, but they do not have and cannot be programmed to have true cognitive states in the sense that humans have such states.

Atheism The view that God does not exist.

Automaton A self-moving mechanical being capable of simulating the behavior of a conscious agent, but itself not a conscious agent.

Autonomy The capacity, right, or actual condition of self-government, or the determination of one's own actions.

Bayes's theorem A statistical theorem describing how, given an observed outcome, the conditional probability of each of a set of possible causes can be computed from knowledge of the probability of each cause and the conditional probability of the outcome, given each cause.

Begging the question The logical fallacy of assuming in the premises of an argument the very conclusion which is to be proved. For example, to argue that God exists because the Bible says so, and the Bible is reliable because it is the word of God, is to assume the very proposition one set out to prove in the process of its own proof. Also called petitio principii. (See *circular reasoning*.)

Behaviorism, logical A view about the meaning of mental state terms. The view claims that mental terms such as "pain," "belief," or "desire" are equivalent in meaning to behavioral terms. This is supposed to show that mental states are dispositions to behave in certain ways. (Also called analytical behaviorism.)

Behaviorism, radical The methodological claim that psychology should study only regularities exhibited in behavior, such as principles connecting stimuli and responses. (Also called methodological behaviorism.)

Benevolence Desire or disposition to be good to others, to be kindly and charitable.

Bourgeois A member of the middle class in a market economy, with its characteristic tastes and ideas. Originally, the term referred to the class of capitalists in a market economy who owned the means of production.

Brute fact A fact for which there can be no explanation.

Capitalism An economic system in which trade and industry are controlled by private owners. The owners provide the capital with which to produce goods and employ workers.

Cartesian Of, pertaining to, or related to Descartes or his philosophy.

Catastrophism The geological doctrine, prevalent well into the eighteenth century, that the geological features of the surface of the Earth are the result of violent cataclysms. The doctrine assumed that the Earth is only a few thousand years old, and was congenial to theological accounts of the origin and history of the Earth.

***Categorical imperative** A moral directive from reason that is binding without condition; a command that applies to all rational beings, no matter what. Kant formulated the categorical imperative as: "Act only according to that maxim by which you can at the same time will that it should become a universal law."

Causally possible Consistent with the causal laws of nature. A statement is causally possible if it is true in at least one physically possible world.

***Causal theory of perception** The theory that material objects are the causes of the ideas, appearances, or sense data we have of them. The material substance itself is distinct from its own qualities (including its *primary qualities*) and, not being directly perceivable, must simply be posited as an unknowable *substratum* for its powers and properties.

Causa sui The cause of itself.

Causation The relationship between two events, one as cause, the other as effect. If the first event occurs, it produces or necessitates the second.

Ceteris paribus Other things being equal.

Christolatry The worship of Christ as divine.

Circular reasoning When the conclusion is concealed within the premises of an argument. (See *begging the question*.)

Civil disobedience A nonviolent, conscientious, public form of protest contrary to the law that is done with the aim of bringing about a change in the law or policies of a government.

Cogito ergo sum "I think, therefore I am." This inference played a central role in Descartes's argument for the distinction between the mental and the physical and in his response to *skepticism*.

Cognitive process Mental operations such as reasoning, inferring, deliberating, planning, and perceiving.

Cognitive science The interdisciplinary study of cognitive processes in human beings, animals, and machines. The core disciplines are psychology, computer science, linguistics, neuroscience, and philosophy.

***Compatibilism** See *determinism, soft*.

Computational theory of mind The view that mental states and processes are identical to computational states and processes. On this view, the mind is a (suitably programmed) computer.

Conclusion In an argument, the statement that is being argued for and that the premises are meant to jointly establish.

Consequentialism A type of moral theory stating that to act morally we must base our actions on their probable results or consequences, rather than acting out of duty,

in cases where duty and promoting good consequences come into conflict. It can be contrasted with *deontology*. Examples of consequentialism are *ethical egoism*, *utilitarianism*, and *ethical altruism*.

Contiguity Contact or proximity; the state of being close together.

Contingent being A being whose existence depends on something else and therefore might not have come to exist. For example, your existence was contingent on your mother's having conceived. (See also *necessary being*.)

Contractarianism The theory that the correct way to derive a principle of justice is to decide whether it would be chosen over any alternative principle of justice that could be proposed to a group of normally self-interested, rational persons.

***Contradiction** Occurs when a statement is alleged to be both true and false at the same time.

Conventionalism The doctrine that the truth of a proposition, or a class of propositions, is determined not by fact but by social agreement or usage. Conventionalism is opposed to versions of realism, which hold that the truth of a proposition, or a class of propositions, is determined by objective facts of nature.

Corollary A proposition that is incidentally proved in proving another proposition.

Corporeal Bodily.

***Corporeal substances** Bodily substances.

Cosmogony (From the Greek word "kosmogonia" for "creation of the world") Theory of the origin and development of the *cosmos*.

Cosmological argument Argument for the existence of God that holds (1) every being is either a *dependent being* or a *self-existent being*; (2) not every being can be a dependent being; (3) therefore, there exists a self-existent being, who is God.

Cosmos (From the Greek word for "order") The whole universe conceived as ordered and law-governed.

Counterfactuals Statements describing what would have been true if something else were true. The interesting property of such statements for philosophical purposes is that they can be true even when the conditions described are not actually met. For instance, the statement that this wine glass would shatter if thrown to the ground could be true of only an unshattered glass —one that has never met the conditional part of the counterfactual. Counterfactuals are thus a good way of expressing dispositions, tendencies, and other scientifically interesting regularities.

Creationism The theory in the philosophy of biology that God intervenes into the natural order to create new species and to create people.

Criterion A standard of judgment that is either a sufficient condition for something being the case, or a condition that provides good evidence for something being the case.

Culpable Deserving blame.

Cultural relativism The view that morality is relative to a given culture; what is right in one culture may be wrong in another. For example, cannibalism might be wrong for Greeks but right for Callations. Cultural relativism goes beyond merely stating the fact that different cultures have different beliefs; it asserts that for each society, its beliefs are really right (not just believed to be right by its members). (See *moral relativism*.)

Darwinism Acceptance of the theory of *evolution* by natural selection developed originally by Charles Darwin (1809–1882).

Decision theory The theory of rational choices aimed at achieving an optimal outcome where the amount of information available to the agent is limited. The agent has only incomplete information about the true state of affairs and the possible consequences of each possible action.

*Deductive argument An argument whose *conclusion* must be true if the *premises* are all true, as long as the argument is valid.

Deicide The killing of God.

De novo Anew.

*Denying the antecedent The logical fallacy of inferring the falsity of a conditional's consequent from having asserted the falsity of its antecedent.

Deontology A type of moral theory stating that morality consists in doing one's duty, rather than in considering the probable consequences of one's actions, in cases where duty and the promotion of good consequences come into conflict. Can be contrasted to *consequentialism*. An example of a deontological theory is Kantian ethics.

Dependent being A being whose existence is causally dependent on and explained by other things.

*Determinism The theory that all events, including human actions and choices, are, without exception, totally determined.

*Determinism, hard A kind of determinist view that rejects the compatibility of determinism and free will.

*Determinism, soft The view that holds that *determinism* is true and that determinism is compatible with free will and responsibility.

*Deus ex machina "God from a machine." An artificial or improbable device introduced to resolve an entanglement in a plot or argument. A person invokes a deus ex machina when introducing some contrivance to save a theory from some large problem.

Diallelus A vicious circle in a proof.

Diarchal Pertaining to a joint mode of government by two independent authorities.

*Dilemma An argument that presents a choice between two alternatives.

Divine command theory The view that actions are right in virtue of being commanded by God.

Doxastic (From the Greek word "doxa" for "belief") Theories of justification that are doxastic are those that hold that a belief can be justified only by another belief.

*Dualism Generally, the view that there are two kinds of stuff. More specifically, dualism is associated with the doctrine that mental states, events, or processes are distinct from physical or material states, events, or processes.

Dualistic interactionism The view that mental states, events, and processes can causally affect physical state events and process.

*Duty Moral obligation or requirement

Efficient cause The physical or mechanical cause of an effect or thing. The efficient cause is one of Aristotle's four types of causes. Consider a table. For Aristotle, the "material" cause of the table is the material or stuff that the table is made of. The "formal" cause is the blueprint or shape that determines the form of the table. The "final" cause is the reason or purpose for which the table was built. The "efficient" cause is the actual agency or mechanical production of the table by the builder out of material. Efficient causation is often contrasted with "teleological" causation, causation that is the result of purposes or ends (Aristotelian "final" cause).

Egalitarianism A theory asserting equality among all people, usually political or economic.

Egoistic hedonism The theory that, in deciding how to act, a person ought to choose (among those acts open) the act that is likely to cause the greatest net balance of pleasure over pain for oneself.

Elective freedom The freedom to do, or to forebear from doing, one's duty. (See also *rational freedom*.)

*Eliminative materialism The view that mental states and processes as we ordinarily conceive of them simply do not exist, in the same way as witches and phlogiston do not exist. [IV intro]

Empirical generalization A statement of the form: All *R* are *G*s. For example, "All the coins in my pockets are pennies." Such generalizations need not express a tendency, disposition, or natural law.

Empirical hypothesis A kind of synthetic statement whose function is to sum up past experience and enable us to successfully predict or anticipate future experience.

*Empiricism The theory that all our ideas come from experience and that no proposition about any matter of fact can be known independently of experience.

Epicureanism From the views of the Greek philosopher Epicurus, 341–270 BC. Epicureans advocated the pursuit of certain pleasures that bring tranquility and freedom from mental anxiety in order to achieve happiness. In metaphysics, Epicurus was an atomist who attempted to avoid *determinism* by allowing for chance events due to the unpredictable "swerving" of atoms.

*Epiphenomenalism The view that there is only one form of interaction between the mental and the physical, that in which the physical affects the mental. In this view, the mental can never affect the physical. The mind is not itself a material thing; rather, it is a distinct but causally impotent by-product (*epiphenomenon*) of the world of physics. This is a kind of *dualism*.

Epiphenomenon A mere by-product of a process that has no real effect on the process itself.

Epistemic Relating to knowledge.

Epistemology The theory of knowledge. The study of the origin, nature, and limits of knowledge, including especially the study of the nature of epistemic justification.

Equivocation A *fallacy* of *argument* whereby one uses an ambiguous word in more than one way.

Ergo Therefore.

Eros Sexual longing or desire; love.

Eschatology The development of theories relating to the end of life, as in Christian theology, or to the ultimate end of the *cosmos*.

Esoteric Intended only for people with special knowledge or interest. The opposite of "exoteric" (opinions or ideas suitable for the uninitiated).

Ethical altruism The theory that morality requires us to forget our own interests and selflessly devote ourselves to the interests of others.

*Ethical egoism The view that to act morally, individuals should act solely so as to promote their own best interests. Ethical egoism is a moral view; it states a thesis about how humans ought to act. In this it differs from *psychological egoism*, which states a thesis about how humans always do act. An ethical egoist holds that people do not always act to promote their own well-being, even though they should.

*Ethical naturalism The theory which claims that, despite appearances, moral facts really are natural, scientific facts.

*Ethical nonnaturalism The theory which claims that there are no true naturalistic analyses of moral terms.

*Ethical pluralism The view that a plurality of independent principles lie at the foundation of ethics.

*Ethical relativism The view that actions are right if and only if they comport with the ultimate ethical standards of the society in which they are performed.

Ethical skepticism The view that no moral knowledge is possible.

*Ethical subjectivism The claim that ethics is not an objective area of inquiry. See also *meta-ethical subjectivism* and *normative subjectivism*.

Evolution The process by which something develops gradually from a different form. In biology, evolution is the origin and transformations of biological populations over time through genetic variation and interaction with the environment, and not by special creation.

Ex hypothesi By hypothesis.

Existentialism A loose-knit philosophical viewpoint connecting a rejection of determinism with a focus on the responsibility of the agent for making one's own character out of one's freely chosen actions. Existentialists reject the rationalistic view of the universe as planned and comprehensible and consequently face life with a feeling of dread and a sense of the absurdity of life. Major existentialists are Kierkegaard and Sartre.

Ex nihilo Out of nothing.

Expected utility (EU) The utility of an uncertain outcome multiplied by its probability.

Fallacy A logical mistake in reasoning, especially one that often gives the appearance of being sound.

Falsifiable Refutable by experience. For example, if a theory predicts that an eclipse will occur on a certain day, then experience will refute the theory if the eclipse does not occur. *Freudianism* and *creationism* are often criticized as being unfalsifiable.

Fatalism The theory that all events are fated to happen; the event would have happened no matter what the person involved might have done to avoid it. This is a stronger view than *determinism*.

*Fideist A theist whose belief is based on faith rather than argument or reason.

Final cause The end, purpose, or goal toward which something is working or moving; one of Aristotle's four causes. (See *efficient cause*.)

*Free will defense The free will defense seeks to justify God's goodness in the face of so much suffering in the world by claiming that such suffering is caused primarily by the freely chosen actions of human beings.

Freudianism Relating to the views of Sigmund Freud, 1856–1939. Freud developed an elaborate psychological theory focusing on sexual desires and the subconscious. For Freud, the ego is the conscious self. The ego stands between the id, which demands that basic sexual and physical desires are satisfied, and the superego, which represses the desires of the id. Freud hypothesized that there exists a variety of repressive mechanisms responsible for neurotic behavior. Freud developed the therapeutic technique of psychoanalysis.

Functional equivalence Two systems are functionally equivalent when they do the same tasks or when they have the same capacities. (See *strong equivalence*.)

*Functionalism Generally, the view that concepts should be defined according to their function. In cognitive theory, the view that mental states, events, and processes are "functional" states of the brain (or other *hardware*). Functional states of a device are those that are defined in terms of their relations to the device's input, its internal transitions, and its output. According to the functionalist, these causal relations and dispositions are what constitute the mental.

Gestalt A conception of organization based on the idea that a perceived whole is not just the sum of its parts. The parts are organized into structures and derive their character from the structure of the whole. Gestalt psychology denies the atomistic theory of perception whereby perceptions of patterns or wholes arrive from constructing the whole out of its independently existing parts.

*Good will The stable disposition to do one's duty for its own sake.

Greatest happiness principle The utilitarian principle, put forth by John Stuart Mill, stating that actions are right in proportion as they promote happiness (pleasure) and wrong in proportion as they promote pain. (See *utilitarianism*.)

*Hard determinism See *determinism, hard*.

Hardware The physical apparatus that executes the software in programming a computer. The analog for an organism is its brain (often called its "wetware"). (See also *software*.)

Hedonism The view that pleasure is the ultimate good for humans.

Hedonism, universalistic The theory that in deciding how to act, I ought to choose (among those acts open to me) the act that is likely to cause the greatest net balance of pleasure over pain, counting my own interests as no less and no more important than everyone else's. The theory is universalistic because it considers everyone equally and hedonistic because it tells us to choose the act that will create the most pleasure.

Heuristics Rules of thumb that are useful generalizations for problem-solving tasks, such as "Get your queen out early" in chess.

Hierophany Pertaining to the official expounding of sacred mysteries or ceremonies or the interpretation of *esoteric* principles.

Humanism Generally, any view in which human interests and welfare play a central role. More specifically, the theory that emphasizes reason, scientific inquiry, and human welfare, often rejecting the importance of belief in God.

Humanitarian theory of punishment The theory that the goal of punishment should be to mend or "cure" the offender, rather than to punish because he or she deserves it.

Hypothetical imperative An action that you should do if you want to promote some goal or end you already have. For example, if you want a good grade, you have a hypothetical imperative to study; if you want some chocolate ice cream, you have a hypothetical imperative to go to the store and buy some. Can be contrasted to a *categorical imperative*, which says that you should perform an action regardless of your ends.

***Hypothetical syllogism** Any logically valid inference that takes the following form: (1) If P, then Q; (2) If Q, then R; Therefore, (3) If P, then R.

***Idealism** The theory that there are only immaterial minds and their mental "contents." The body itself is nothing but a collection of actual or possible sense data—sights, sounds, touches, and smells. By holding that there is only mind and no matter, idealism avoids the problems of causal interaction between radically different kinds of substances.

***Idealism, subjective** The theory that matter is merely the projection of a finite mind and has no external, independent existence.

Ideal morality Standards of moral excellence that a moral tradition or community sets up as models to aspire to and admire. Praise, honor, and respect are the rewards of those who live according to the standards of ideal morality. However, people are not in general blamed for failing to live up to the standards of ideal morality, or even for not aiming at them. (See *practice morality*.)

***Identity theory** A kind of *materialism* stating that mental events are simply identical to brain processes, the same way that lightning flashes are "identical" to electrical discharges. The mental event (a thought, desire, or sensation) *is* a brain process.

Ideology Any set of general ideas or system of beliefs that forms the basis of an economic or political theory. The term is used pejoratively to characterize a person's set of beliefs both as false and as adopted to disguise or ignore the economic or political realities of the status quo.

Ignoratio elenchi The *fallacy* of irrelevance—that is, of proving a *conclusion* that is not relevant to the matter at hand.

Immaterialist One who believes that reality is not material. (See *idealism*.)

Immoralist One who rejects conventional morality, arguing that it is in his or her, or even our, best interests, and therefore rational, to act against the dictates of conventional morality.

Immutable Unchangeable.

Imperative Command. (See also *categorical imperative*; *hypothetical imperative*.)

Imperfect duty A duty that is not owed to any particular person or persons. For example, I have an imperfect duty to help alleviate poverty, but I do not owe it to any particular poor person to feed her, nor to each individual poor person. (See *perfect duty*.)

Impersonal evil Evil that is natural and not caused by human action—for example, natural disasters and disease. Even if humans were morally perfect, there would still be impersonal evil. (Also called nonmoral evil.)

Incompatibilism See *determinism, hard*.

Indeterminate Not fixed in extent or character. The truth value of a statement is indeterminate when the relevant facts fail to determine whether the statement is true or false.

***Indeterminism** The view that some events are not determined.

Indeterminism, simple The theory that human action is not determined; rather, it is caused by inner *volition*.

Indubitable Incapable of being doubted; beyond all doubt. Descartes, for example, searched for indubitable truths to combat *skepticism*.

***Inductive argument** An argument whose *premises* establish a probability (rather than a certainty) that its conclusion is true; for example, if no one has ever seen a green flamingo, then there probably are no green flamingos. The argument from design is an example of an inductive argument.

Inductive inference An *inference* from evidence to hypothesis, where the evidence does not entail or necessitate that the hypothesis is true, but it is nevertheless reasonable to suppose that the hypothesis is true.

Inference The movement from premises to a *conclusion*. Inferences can be deductive or inductive.

In infinitum Into infinity; endlessly.

***Innate idea** An idea that we are born with inherited dispositions to have. *Rationalism* argues that human minds have the disposition to acquire concepts such as being, substance, duration, and even God, once a certain amount of experience is added.

Intentionality The property that some mental states have of being about something. Thus, one belief might be about Caesar's crossing the Rubicon, and another might be about the first person to orbit the Earth. By contrast, a mental state such as a free-floating anxiety need not be about anything in particular and thus not have intentionality.

Interactionism See *dualistic interactionism*.

***Intertheoretic reduction** See *reduction*.

Intrinsic good Something that is good in and of itself.

Intuition Direct knowledge or awareness of a truth or fact, independent of any reasoning process.

Intuitionism Any theory in which *intuition* is appealed to as the basis of knowledge.

Ipso facto By that very fact.

Justification In *epistemology*, knowledge is traditionally defined as justified true belief. To know p you must not only believe p, p must be true and your belief that p is true must be justified. Epistemologists disagree about the nature of justification. Some think that a belief is justified if it is caused in the right way or if it is based on another belief that counts as knowledge or if the agent can give reasons in defense of why she holds the belief, and so forth.

Kin altruism The disposition to favor the interests of one's near relatives (as distinct from one's own interests) over the interests of complete strangers. Such a disposition may have evolutionary advantages by increasing the probability that those who share many of the individual's genes will survive and reproduce.

Lamarckism In the philosophy of biology, the view that offspring may inherit the characteristics that their parents acquired during their adult lives. This view is no longer held to be credible.

Lexical order In John Rawls's theory of justice, the ordering of principles that requires us to satisfy the first principle before going on to consider the second principle; once the first principle is satisfied, we can go on to attempt to satisfy the second principle. (Also called serial order.)

***Libertarianism** In metaphysics, the theory that we possess free will and that our free will is neither determined nor the result of random chance, but is instead the result of rational agency. In politics and economics, the theory that emphasizes the importance of personal liberty as opposed to state interference. Political libertarians often oppose taxation for social welfare programs as unjust intrusions into personal freedom.

Liberum arbitrium indifferentiae The freedom of indifference; the ability of the will to choose independently of *antecedent* determination.

Liturgy A fixed form of public worship used in churches.

Logically impossible Not *logically possible*.

Logically possible Consistent with the laws of logic. A statement is logically possible if it is true in at least one logically *possible world*—for example, that the next president of the United States is a woman. A statement is logically impossible if it is inconsistent with the laws of logic. A logically impossible statement is, or entails, a contradiction—for example, that some squares are round. Since squares are, by definition, not round, it is a contradiction to say that some squares are round.

Manslaughter The act of killing a person unlawfully but not intentionally or by negligence.

Marxism From the views of the German philosopher Karl Marx (1818–1883), on which communism is putatively based. Marxism rejects *capitalism* and predicts the development of society beyond capitalism through a revolution by the working class. Inherent to all forms of Marxism is a rejection of the exploitation of labor due to the private control of the means of production.

*Materialism The view that everything—every object, state, event, and process—is a material object, state, event, or process and nothing else. According to materialists, there is no immaterial mind or soul and thus no problem of interaction between radically different kinds of substances. (Also called *physicalism*.)

*Maxim A principle or rule of conduct.

Maximin strategy A principle of decision theory for choice under uncertainty. The strategy ranks the best decision as one that is superior to the worst outcomes of other possible decisions. The strategy "maximizes" the "minimum" outcome.

Mediately perceivable Perceivable indirectly, by means of something else.

Mendelian genetics The theory developed by Gregor Mendel (1822–1884) that the inheritance of any particular characteristic is controlled by the inheritance of genes, which occur in pairs and separate independently of each other in meiosis, a stage of cell division.

Mens rea The accompanying intention to commit a crime or pursue a wrongful aim which makes the act a crime.

Mentalism Originally, the term referred to idealistic doctrines such as Berkeley's, which held that only minds and their subjective states exist. In contemporary philosophy of mind, mentalism is the view that *cognitive processes* can be explained only by postulating a set of internal mental representations and rules that operate on the representations. (See *artificial intelligence* and *computational theory of mind*.)

*Meta-ethical subjectivism The view that ethical judgments are neither true nor false; they are simply expressions of commands, preferences, or emotions, and as such are not eligible candidates for truth.

*Meta-ethical theory A theory that focuses on whether normative theories can be justified or true.

Metaphysics The study of the ultimate nature of reality. Common metaphysical views are *materialism*, *idealism*, and *dualism*.

Methodicide The death or killing of method or methodology.

Methodists Epistemologists who first answer the questions, How are we to decide whether we know? What are the *criteria* of knowledge? and then use their answers to go on to answer the questions, What do we know? What is the extent of our knowledge? A methodist is the opposite of a *particularist*.

Methodological behaviorism See *behaviorism, radical*.

*Modus ponens In logic, an argument of the following form: If P then Q. P. Therefore Q.

*Modus tollens In logic, an argument of the following form: If P then Q. Not-Q. Therefore Not-P.

Monism The view that reality is ultimately made up of only one kind of thing. *Idealism* and *materialism* are two different monistic theories. Can be contrasted to *dualism*, which holds that there are two kinds of things: mind and body.

Monotheism Belief in one, and only one, God.

*Moral equivalence The idea that everyone's ultimate moral views are as plausible as everyone else's.

*Moral evil Evil that is caused by human action, rather than by natural causes such as earthquakes. If humans were as morally perfect as God, there would be no moral evil.

*Morally infallible Unable to make mistakes in moral matters.

Moral relativism The view that the "truth" of moral judgments is always relative to a given system of beliefs that itself cannot be proven correct.

Mutation Change or alteration in form.

Myth of Gyges The story in Plato's *Republic* that is meant to show that injustice is in our self-interest. Gyges found a ring of invisibility that allowed him to act unjustly and reap the benefits. Plato argues against the *immoralist*'s challenge presented by the Myth of Gyges in the rest of the *Republic*.

*Naïve realism See *realism, naïve*.

Narcissism A tendency to self-worship. An excessive or erotic interest in one's own personal features.

Naturalism (1) The view that the universe is self-existent, self-explanatory, and self-operating, requiring no supernatural or spiritual cause or explanation. (2) The view that nature does not require a *teleological* explanation; scientific laws are adequate to cover all phenomena.

Necessary being A being whose existence depends on nothing else and who necessarily has to exist. Some people have argued that God is such a being. (See also *contingent being*.)

Necessary condition If *A* is a necessary condition for *B*, then *B* cannot be true unless *A* is true. For instance, being alive is a necessary condition for going golfing. If you are dead, you cannot golf. (See *sufficient condition*.)

Negligence Lack of proper care or attention; carelessness.

Nonmaleficence Not injuring others.

Nonmoral evil See *impersonal evil*.

*Normative Having to do with norms or standards; regulative. In ethics, norms are standards for right conduct.

*Normative subjectivism The view that ethical judgments can be true or false, but their truth depends entirely on whether they accurately report the sentiments of those who issue the judgments.

Normative theory A theory that attempts to specify conditions under which an action is morally right or wrong.

Objective Something that is objective has a particular nature that is not dependent on us or our judgments of it.

For example, those who hold that there are objective moral truths believe that such truths are there for us to discover and hold regardless of any of our beliefs or judgments.

*Occasionalism A kind of *dualism* stating that mind and body do not really interact. Being kicked does not cause my pain; rather, it is the occasion for God, whose infinite nature somehow encompasses both mind and matter, to cause me to feel pain. Similarly, my mental states are occasions for God to cause my body to act.

Omnipotent All-powerful; able to do anything.

Omniscient All-knowing.

Ontological argument An *a priori* argument for the existence of God stating that the very concept or definition of God automatically entails that God exists; because of the special nature of the concept, there is no way that God could fail to exist.

Ontology The theory of being, or of existence. From the Greek "ontos" (being) and "logos" (theory, account).

Ontophany The appearance of being; the manifestation of existence.

Original contract In *social contract theories*, the hypothetical contract that establishes the fundamental principles of justice and/or structure of society, to which all rational, normally self-interested persons would agree in entering society.

Original position In John Rawls's contractarian theory of justice (*contractarianism*), the original position is the hypothetical gathering of people in a condition of equal power and ignorance for the purpose of determining fair principles of justice for society. (See *veil of ignorance*.)

Orthodox Beliefs that are declared by a group to be true and normative. Heresy is a departure from and relative to a given orthodoxy. Of or holding correct or conventional or currently accepted beliefs, especially in religion.

Paradox of hedonism This paradox is that the single-minded pursuit of happiness is necessarily self-defeating, for the way to get happiness is to forget it; then it may come to you. If you aim exclusively at pleasure itself, with no concern for the things that bring pleasure, then pleasure will never come. One must first desire something other than satisfaction to achieve satisfaction.

Paradox of omnipotence Can an *omnipotent* being make things that he subsequently cannot control, or make rules that bind himself? For example, can God create a rock so heavy that even he cannot lift it? On one hand, it seems as though he should be able to, since he is, by definition, able to do anything. But if he did make a rule that bound him—which he could not violate—it seems as though he would not still be all-powerful.

*Parallelism A kind of *dualism* stating that mind and body only appear to interact because of a kind of "preestablished harmony" between them, like two clocks independently striking at the same moment. Thus, because of this harmony, when I kick the table, I also feel pain; the kicking does not cause the pain.

Particular A specific example of a class of things, rather than the class itself or what defines the class. An individual rather than a *universal*.

Particularists Epistemologists who first answer the questions, What do we know? and What is the extent of our knowledge? and then use their answers to go on to answer the questions, How are we to decide whether we know? What are the *criteria* of knowledge? A particularist is the opposite of a *methodist*.

Pascal's wager Blaise Pascal's argument that we should believe in (or "bet on") God because the stakes are infinitely high on the side of God. The rewards for believing correctly and the penalties for wrongly not believing are high, and the costs of believing mistakenly are low. (Also called a wager argument.)

*Passive euthanasia Mercy killing that involves a medical decision, in conjunction with the patient, to allow the patient to die.

Paternalism Governing as though a benevolent parent-figure.

Patriarchy The domination or government of a social structure or institution by the fathers or male elders.

Pedagogy The art of teaching.

Perceptron A device designed by Frank Rosenblatt in the 1950s to understand perceptual recognition tasks. A perceptron consists of three layers of connected units: an input layer, an associative layer, and an output layer. Additional layers of units can be added to further complicate the device.

Perfect duty A duty that is owed to a particular person or persons. For example, I have a perfect duty to my banker to repay my loan and to every person not to lie to them. (See *imperfect duty*.)

Personal identity The problem of explaining what constitutes both the identity of a person at a time and the identity of a person through time.

Petitio principii See *begging the question* and *circular reasoning*.

*Phenomenalism The theory that our only knowledge of reality is mind-dependent; the phenomena we experience are the only objects of knowledge. Phenomenalists may affirm or deny the existence of a reality of things-in-themselves behind the phenomena.

Phenomenology A descriptive study of subjective processes such as consciousness, feelings, and emotions. The study of "what it is like" to be in a certain mental state. (See *qualia*.)

Physicalism (1) *Materialism*. (2) The theory that every object, state, event, or process can be completely described and explained by the physical sciences, with the understanding that some things in the physical sciences are *not* material—for instance, gravitational fields and electromagnetic radiation. According to this use of the term, one could believe that physicalism is true but *materialism* is false.

Physicalism, token A version of *physicalism* that contends that being in a mental state (process, etc.) always involves being in a physical state (process, etc.). This allows for the possibility that there might be different physical states for different thinking beings. For instance, adding 2 + 2 for a human being might involve certain electrical activity in neurons located in certain areas of the brain, but adding 2 + 2 for a computer might involve electrical activity in silicon chips.

Physicalism, type A version of *physicalism* that denies that it is possible for different thinkers to have the same kind of mental state without being in the same kind of physical state. Thus, in this view, a person and a computer could both be said to be adding 2 + 2 only if there were some physical process that they were both in at the same time.

Platonism The philosophy of Plato stating that the *particular* individual things we see are merely imperfect "copies" of perfect, unchanging, universal forms.

Polytheism Belief in more than one God.

Posit To assume that something is true without argument, either because it is a self-evident truth or merely as an arbitrary assumption.

Possible world A complete state of affairs, and so the actual world is itself a possible world. Complete states of affairs distinct from the actual world are ways the actual world might have been. Complete states of affairs that are consistent with the laws of logic are logically possible worlds. Complete states of affairs that are consistent with both the laws of logic and the laws of nature are physically or causally possible worlds.

Postulate A self-evident truth or fundamental principle.

Practice morality The standards of conduct actually expected of, and generally practiced by, persons living within a given moral tradition or community. The part of morality concerned with requirements, those standards for which people are blamed, criticized, or punished for failing to live up to. See *ideal morality* and *supererogation*.

Pragmatic Of or pertaining to practical considerations.

Pragmatism The theory that the meaning or value of concepts should be understood in terms of their practical consequences.

Predicate That which is said of a subject.

Predominant egoism The claim that as a matter of fact the egoistic or self-interested motivations of human behavior tend to override their altruistic or other-regarding motivations until they have achieved a satisfactory level of security and well-being. (See *altruism* and *psychological egoism*.)

Premises In an *argument*, the reasons that are given to support the *conclusion*.

*Prima facie At first appearance.

Prima facie duty A self-evident duty, such as promise keeping, which we are required to act upon if no other, more weighty, duty intervenes.

*Primary qualities Intrinsic characteristics of a physical object itself, such as solidity, extension in space (size), figure (shape), motion or rest, and number. Primary qualities are ones that objects would continue to possess even if there were no perceiving beings in the world; they are inseparable from the material object and found in every part of it. (See also *secondary qualities*.)

Principle of sufficient reason (PSR) For everything that happens there must be a sufficient reason for its happening and not some other thing.

Privation The condition of a substance that lacks a certain quality that it is capable of possessing and normally does possess. Loss or lack of something.

*Problem of evil Problem posed for theists: If God is all-good, omnipotent, and omniscient, how can his existence be compatible with the existence of evil?

Program A sequence of instructions, in some computer language, that causes a physical apparatus (*hardware*) to perform some task or sequence of operations.

Projectable property When past instances of a property are a guide to predictions about future instances of a property. For example, if every raven I have seen is black, then it is reasonable to predict that future ravens will be black. But if every raven I have seen is alive in the twentieth century, it does not follow that it is reasonable to predict that future ravens will be alive in the twentieth century. Being black is a projectable property of ravens; being alive in the twentieth century is not.

Propositional calculus (logic) Systems of logic that concern themselves with how statements can be combined —using such connectives as "and," "or," "if then," and "not"—into more complex statements and with the logical properties possessed by such statements.

Prudential reasonableness When an act conforms to the norms of rationality that govern the selection and performance of actions.

*Psychological egoism A theory about the psychology of humans stating that the only thing anyone is capable of desiring or pursuing ultimately (as an end in itself) is one's own self-interest. According to psychological egoism, people always act selfishly. If someone appears to act altruistically, that person is only using the interests of other people as a means to promoting his or her own good; genuinely disinterested acts of benevolence do not exist. (See also *ethical egoism*.)

Psychological egoistic hedonism A common form of *psychological egoism* stating that our only kind of ultimate desire is to prolong our own pleasure and reduce our own pains.

Punitive Inflicting or intending to inflict punishment.

QED Which has been demonstrated.

Qua As; in the character or capacity of. For example, your duties qua student are different from your duties qua friend.

*Qualia The qualitative feel of mental experiences: the hurt of pain, the color of red, the taste of wine, the scent of a rose, the longing of love, the ecstasy of an orgasm. The qualitative character of an experience is "what it is like" to have that experience. (See *phenomenology*.)

Ratiocination The process of logical reasoning.

Rational freedom The freedom that a person has to the degree that her will is led by moral principles. (See also *elective freedom*.)

*Rationalism The theory that there are innate ideas and that certain general propositions (usually called necessary, or *a priori*, propositions) can be known to be true in advance of or in the absence of empirical verification.

Rawls, John American moral and political philosopher (1921–2002), author of *A Theory of Justice* (1971).

Realism The theory that the objects of our knowledge have an independent existence rather than being mind-dependent.

*Realism, naïve The theory that *primary* and *secondary qualities* are both strictly part of physical objects and that both can exist quite independently of perceiving minds.

*Realism, representative The theory that our ideas are faithful representations of the real, external world.

*Realism, sophisticated The theory that physical substances and their *primary qualities* can exist independently of perceiving beings and only the *secondary qualities* are mind-dependent.

Reciprocity A relation of mutual exchange.

Reductio ad absurdum A method of demonstrating that a proposition is false by showing that its truth, along with other accepted propositions, would entail a logical contradiction.

*Reduction One theory (T_1) reduces to another theory (T_2) when the propositions and principles of the first are entailed by the second, then applied to the same cases, but the second theory does not contain some items (such as "light" or "belief") from the first. These items in T_1 have been reduced to something else in T_2. (Also called *intertheoretic reduction.*)

Reify To treat a concept or idea as a thing. Reification is the philosophical mistake of treating a concept, abstraction, convention, or artificial construct as if it were a real, natural thing.

Relativism In general, the doctrine that truth is relative to the standpoint of the individual or of the community or culture.

Relativism, cultural Relativism about values stems from the fact that the values or ethical principles of individuals vary widely. Cultural relativism holds that most disagreements about values or ethical principles stem from enculturation in different ethical traditions. Cultural relativism need not entail *moral relativism.*

Relativism, moral The view that the truth of moral judgments is relative to the judging subject or community. We ought to do that, and only that, which we think we ought to do. The having of an opinion about what we ought to do, individually or collectively, makes it true that that is what we ought to do.

Repentance A feeling of regret about what one has done or failed to do.

*Representative realism See *realism, representative.*

Res cogitans (Latin, "thinking thing") Used by Descartes to refer to the mind.

Result theories of punishment See *utilitarian theories of punishment.*

Retributive theory A theory of punishment stating that the primary justification of punishment is the fact that a committed offense deserves punishment, rather than any advantage gained through punishment.

Rule utilitarianism The view that the standards of conduct should be those which, if widely adopted, would lead to the greatest overall utility.

*Secondary qualities Those qualities of an object (such as color, taste, smell, sound, warmth, and cold) that exist (according to some theories) only when actually sensed and then only "in the mind" of the one who senses them. (See also *primary qualities.*)

Self-existent being A being whose existence is not dependent on other things, but rather is accounted for by its own nature.

Self-presenting That which is directly evident to an agent. Thoughts are self-presenting if to have them is to think that you have them. So if I believe that Socrates is mortal, then if my belief is self-presenting it will be the case by that very fact that it is evident to me that I believe that Socrates is mortal.

Semantics The study of the meanings of words.

Serial order See *lexical order.*

*Skepticism The position that denies the possibility of knowledge. A skeptic might hold that no knowledge of any sort is possible or might confine skepticism to a particular field such as ethics.

*Social contract theory The theory that grounds political obligations in a hypothetical social contract to which all rational, normally self-interested persons would agree in forming a society.

Sociobiology The study of the social behavior of animals, especially the role of behavior in survival and reproduction.

*Soft determinism See *determinism, soft.*

Software Computer *program* (set of instructions) that can be loaded and executed on computer *hardware.*

Sophism A piece of deceptive reasoning characteristic of the ancient Greek Sophists.

*Sophisticated realism See *realism, sophisticated.*

Sophists Wandering teachers in ancient Greece who claimed to teach people (for a fee) how to achieve political success. Socrates objected to the way in which they argued; they would use tricks to win the argument and would argue for anything, regardless of its truth.

Sound An *argument* is sound if it is *valid* and its *premises* are true.

Species chauvinism The limitation of mentality and consciousness to animals physically similar to human beings, to the exclusion of machines and, perhaps, silicon-based life-forms.

Speciesism The view that species membership is in itself a morally relevant trait.

Spinoza Dutch Jewish rationalist (1632–1677). He held that God is immanent in the world, and individual things are modes or modifications of God.

*State of nature A phrase used to describe the situation (either historical or hypothetical) in which human beings live without government.

Stoicism To be stoic is to be calm and not excitable, bearing difficulties or discomfort without complaining. A school of philosophy founded by Zeno of Citium c. 300 BC.

Strong equivalence Two systems are strongly equivalent if they are not only weakly equivalent but also produce the same outputs (given the same inputs) in the same way—that is, their internal functionings are the same. (See *weak equivalence.*)

*Subjective idealism See *idealism, subjective.*

Subjectivism (1) The view that all knowledge is limited to the nature of objects as known through human experience, rather than objectively in themselves; it is impossible for us to transcend human subjectivity. (2) In ethics, the view that no objective moral truths exist; moral judgments are based on the subjective emotional or mental reactions of the individual or community.

*Substratum That which underlies all of an object's attributes or qualities and on which the attributes are predicated.

Sufficient condition If A is a sufficient condition for B, then given that A is true, B is true as well. For instance, it is a sufficient condition for being alive that you are golfing. If you are golfing, then it follows that you are alive.

Summum bonum (Latin, "supreme good") The summum bonum is the ultimate end of human action, the worth of which is intrinsically good (good in and of itself).

Supererogation An act that would be good to do, but not wrong not to do; it is "above and beyond the call of duty." An example might be throwing yourself on a live grenade to save your friends.

Syllogism A logically valid argument containing a conclusion entailed by a major premise and a minor premise. (See, e.g., *modus ponens* and *modus tollens.*)

Synthetic statement The opposite of an *analytic statement.* A synthetic statement is true partly in virtue of the meanings of the words used to express it, but also by the nature of things. A synthetic statement can be known *a priori*—for example, the statement that every event has a cause; or a synthetic statement can be known *a posteriori*—for example, snow is wet.

*Tabula rasa A blank tablet. Empiricists hold that the mind at birth is a tabula rasa; it awaits experience and has no *innate ideas.*

Tautology A statement of logic that is true under any assignment of truth values to the constituent parts of the statement. For example, either *p* or not *p*, as in it is either raining here now or it is not raining here now.

*Teleological argument *Inductive argument* for the existence of God that cites purported examples of design in nature as proof for the existence of a designer who is God. (Also called argument from design.)

Teleology The view that there is a purpose or goal to the universe. From the Greek "telos" (goal, end) and "logos" (theory, account).

Theism The view that God (or gods) exist.

Theodicy An attempted justification for the existence of God despite the existence of evil.

Theogony An account of the origin of the gods.

Theology The study of God—his nature and his relation to the world.

Theoretical entities Usually contrasted with observational entities. As the terminology suggests, observational entities can be observed by the senses, but theoretical entities are postulated to explain observable phenomena. The distinction between observation and postulation is difficult to draw.

Theoretical terms The opposite of observational terms. Observational terms are the terms of a scientific theory that refer to objects that can be observed by the senses. Theoretical terms refer to the objects putatively postulated by a theory to explain the existence and nature of observed entities. The distinction between theoretical and observational terms is notoriously difficult to draw.

Theory of agency The view that although human behavior is caused, not every chain of causes and effects is infinite; some causal chains begin with agents themselves.

Truth tables A method of tabulating how the truth of constituent propositions of a statement in a *propositional calculus* determines the truth of the complex proposition.

Turing machine Despite its name, it is not a machine but a kind of mathematical system that can be viewed as plans for a device for executing *programs* or other sequences of instructions. Turing machines are very restricted in that they can do only a limited number of basic things (such as read a 0 or a 1, write a 0 or a 1, move left one step, move right one step). However, they are very flexible and can be programmed to do anything any computer can do—at least, if given enough time and memory.

*Two-way interactionism The commonsense assumption that mind and body interact causally.

*Type physicalism See *identity theory.*

Type-token relations (for behavior) Relations that determine how to categorize a particular output in the vocabulary of behavior—for example, "In raising his arm, he was signaling that he knew the answer."

Ultimate cause The goal or purpose toward which a thing acts or moves.

Universal A general concept rather than a *particular* individual; that which is definitive of a class of individuals.

*Universalistic hedonism The view that places priority on achieving the greatest happiness for the greatest number.

Universalizable Capable of being applied universally, to everything or everyone.

*Universal law of nature a principle that applies at all times to all things.

*Utilitarianism The moral theory stating that individuals should choose the act, among those available to the agent, that is likely to create the greatest amount of happiness and the least amount of pain. Each person's (and perhaps each animal's) pleasures and pains are to count equally; you may not count your own pleasures and pains more (or less) than anyone else's.

Utilitarian theories of punishment These theories hold that punishment is at best a necessary evil, justifiable if and only if the good of its consequences (its social utility) outweigh its own immediate and intrinsic evil. Punishment is an evil inflicted upon a person for the sake of greater future goods, such as correction or reform of the offender, protection of society, and deterrence.

Valid An *argument* is valid if its *conclusion* follows logically from its *premises*. Arguments are either valid or invalid; premises and conclusions are either true or false.

Veil of ignorance In John Rawls's contractarian theory of justice, the veil of ignorance is what keeps the people in the (hypothetical) original position from knowing the facts about their own condition (such as their race, gender, talents, and social position) that could bias their decisions. (See *original position.*)

Vengeance theory of punishment, emotional version The view that the justification of punishment is to be found in the emotions of hate and anger, allegedly felt by all normal or right-thinking people, that it expresses.

Vengeance theory of punishment, escape-valve version The theory that legal punishment is an orderly outlet for aggressive feelings that would otherwise demand satisfaction in socially disruptive ways.

Vengeance theory of punishment, hedonistic version The view that the justification of punishment is the pleasure that it gives people to see the criminal suffer for his or her crime.

Volition The act or capacity of willing or choosing.

Voluntariness The quality of having been freely chosen by an agent without compulsion or any other sort of excuse (such as insanity or intoxication) that might make the choice less than free.

Wager argument See *Pascal's wager.*

Weak equivalence Two systems are weakly equivalent if they both produce the same output, given the same input.

Peter J. Graham
Evan Kreider
Michelle Svatos